Government and Inforn
the Law relating to Acce
and their Regulation

Government and Information: the Law relating to Access, Disclosure and their Regulation

Fourth Edition

Professor Patrick Birkinshaw
LLB Hons, Barrister at Law

Dr Mike Varney
LLB Hons, PhD

Bloomsbury Professional

Bloomsbury Professional Ltd, Maxwelton House, 41–43 Boltro Road, Haywards Heath, West Sussex RH16 1BJ

© Bloomsbury Professional Ltd 2011

Bloomsbury Professional is an imprint of Bloomsbury Publishing plc

A CIP Catalogue record for this book is available from the British Library.

ISBN 978 1 84766 708 3

Typeset by Phoenix Photosetting, Chatham, Kent
Printed and bound in Great Britain by Hobbs the Printers Ltd, Totton, Hampshire

Acknowledgement

The chart at para 7.14 is reproduced by kind permission of the Office of the Information Commissioner.

Dedication

To Oliver Patrick Birkinshaw and Olivia Jane Larney and all our future grandchildren.

To Eliza and Alexandra Varney.

Preface

The last edition of this book (authored by Patrick Birkinshaw alone) was published in 2005 shortly after the Freedom of Information Act and the Environmental Information Regulations became operational. Since that time there has been the development of a varied jurisprudence in the decisions of the Information Commissioner, the Information Tribunal (now First Tier Information Rights Tribunal) and the Administrative Appeals Tribunal. The latter replaced the High Court in England and Wales and Northern Ireland as the appeal body from first tier appeals. We also have case law from the Court of Appeal and Supreme Court (formerly House of Lords) on 'information rights'. This book examines in detail and analyses those newly established rights and their determination.

The context of information rights is always going to be suffused with sensationalism. The MPs expenses' saga, Prince Charles' communications with ministers and Cabinet minutes on the war in Iraq have all featured in information decisions. More recently, the lack of security for personal data, invasions of privacy whether by 'hacking' or other practices and the massive unauthorised leak of US diplomatic and intelligence files by WikiLeaks and Julian Assange have dramatically illustrated the porous nature of the digitalised globe. Information rights, together with their regulation and disclosure, and access to information assume greater and greater importance. The coalition government has also promised to make the UK government among the 'most transparent' in the world as Information Technology assumes ever greater prominence.

With this edition Patrick Birkinshaw welcomes as co-author his colleague at Hull University Law School, Dr Mike Varney. We are both specialist public lawyers and are intent on setting the world of information rights in its public law context. We have tried to cover materials up until July 2011. For the sake of completeness, Patrick Birkinshaw wrote chapters one, two, three, seven, the Environmental Information Regulations' section in chapter eight, chapter nine and chapter eleven. Mike Varney dealt with chapter four, five, six, the remaining content of chapter eight and chapter ten. We would both like to thank the staff at Bloomsbury Professional for their assistance and support.

Patrick Birkinshaw and Mike Varney
Hull, September 2011

Contents

List of abbreviations

ACA 1998	Audit Commission Act 1998
ACPO	Association of Chief Police Officers
ADC	Association of District Councils
ADR	alternative dispute resolution
AJTC	Administrative Justice and Tribunals Council
AP	adjudication panel
APO	Anton Piller order
APPSI	Advisory Panel on Public Sector Information
ATMRA 1988	Access to Medical Reports Act 1988
BID	business improvement district
BIOA	British and Irish Ombudsmen Association
BVA	best value authority
BVI	best value inspection
CAB	Citizens Advice Bureau
CAG	Comptroller and Auditor General
CCT	compulsory competitive tendering
CDC	Commonwealth Development Corporation
CEARA 2007	Consumers, Estate Agents and Redress Act 2007
CFI	Court of First Instance
CHIS	covert human intelligence sources
CIS	Customs Information System
CLA	Commission for Local Administration
CM	complaints manager
CMA 1990	Computer Misuse Act 1990
CO	Cabinet Office
COCA 1981	Contempt of Court Act 1981
CPR 1998	Civil Procedure Rules 1998
CPV	Common Procurement Vocabulary
CRB	Criminal Records Bureau
CRCA 2005	Commissioners of Revenue and Customs Act 2005
CRGA 2010	Constitutional Reform and Governance Act 2010
CSCI	Commission for Social Care Inspection
CSP	communication services provider
CS(U)A 1992	Competition and Service (Utilities) Act 1992
CYPA 1933	Children and Young Persons Act 1933
DBIS	Department for Business, Innovation and Skills
DC	data controller
DCA	Department for Constitutional Affairs
DCLG	Department for Communities and Local Government
DESO	Defence Export Services Organisation
DfT	Department for Transport
DHSSPS	Department of Health, Social Services and Public Safety

DLO	Direct Labour Organisation
DN	decision notice
DO	designated officer
DoH	Department of Health
DP	data processor
DPA 1998	Data Protection Act 1998
DPC	Data Protection Commissioner
DS	data subject
EA	Environment Agency
EA 1995	Environment Act 1995
EA 1996	Education Act 1996
ECA	European Court of Auditors
ECGD	Export Credit Guarantee Department
ECHR	European Convention on Human Rights
ECtHR	European Court of Human Rights
ED	enhanced disclosure
EDM	Early Day Motion
EEA	European Economic Area
EI	environmental information
EIA	environmental impact assessment
EIP	examination in public
EIR 2004	Environmental Information Regulations 2004
EN	enforcement notice
EP	European Parliament
EPA 1990	Environmental Protection Act 1990
ERA 1996	Employment Rights Act 1996
ERO	electoral registration officer
ESO	ethical standards officer
EU	European Union
EUC	European Union Constitution
FCO	Foreign and Commonwealth Office
FOI	freedom of information
FOIA 2000	Freedom of Information Act 2000
FSA	Financial Services Authority
FSA 1999	Food Standards Act 1999
FSMA 2000	Financial Services and Markets Act 2000
FTT	First Tier Tribunal
FWP	forward work programme
GEMA	Gas and Electricity Markets Authority
GMC	General Medical Council
GR	gateway review
GSS	Government Statistical Service
HA 1985, 1988, 1996	Housing Act 1985, 1988, 1996
HAT	housing action trust
HCA	Homes and Communities Agency
HEA 2004	Higher Education Act 2004
HEFCE	Higher Education Funding Council for England
HMIC	Her Majesty's Inspectorate of Constabulary
HMSO	Her Majesty's Stationery Office
HoPS	Heads of Profession for Statistics
HRA 1998	Human Rights Act 1998
HRA 2008	Housing and Regeneration Act 2008
HSWA 1974	Health and Safety at Work etc Act 1974
HSWC	Health and Safety at Work Commission
IAR	Information Asset Register
IBB	Independent Barring Board
IC	Information Commissioner

ICA 1985	Interception of Communications Act 1985
ICC	International Criminal Court
ICO	Information Commissioner's Office
IFTS	Information Fair Trader Scheme
IN	information notice
IPCC	Independent Police Complaints Commission
IPSA	Independent Parliamentary Standards Authority
ISA	intrusive surveillance (authorised)
ISA 1994	Intelligence Services Act 1994
IT	Information Tribunal
LGA 1985, 1986, 1988, 1999, 2000, 2003	Local Government Act 1985, 1986, 1988, 1999, 2000, 2003
LG(ATI)A 1985	Local Government (Access to Information) Act 1985
LGFA 1992	Local Government Finance Act 1992
LGHA 1989	Local Government and Housing Act 1989
LGO	Local Government Ombudsman's
LGPIHA 2007	Local Government and Public Involvement in Health Act 2007
LGPLA 1980	Local Government Planning and Land Act 1980
LPA	local planning authority
LPP	legal professional privilege
LSCB	Local Safeguarding Children Boards
MO	monitoring officer
MoJ	Ministry of Justice
MNO	mobile network operators
MPN	monetary penalty notice
NAA 1983	National Audit Act 1983
NAO	National Audit Office
NCA	National Crime Agency
NCND	neither confirm nor deny
NDA	Nuclear Decommissioning Agency
NDPB	non-departmental public body
NHSA 1977	National Health Service Act 1977
NHSA 2006	National Health Service Act 2006
NP	National Parliament
NRA	National Rivers Authority
OBR	Office of Budget Responsibility
ODA	Overseas Development Administration
OECD	Organisation for Economic Co-operation and Development
OGC	Office of Government Commerce
OGL	Open Government Licence
OJEC	Official Journal of the European Communities
OPSI	Office of Public Sector Information
OSA 1989	Official Secrets Act 1989
OSC	overview and scrutiny committee
OSC	Office of Surveillance Commissioners
OTSL	Office for Tenants and Social Landlords
PA	public authority
PA	police authority
PA 1996	Police Act 1996
PAC	Public Accounts Committee
PACE 1984	Police and Criminal Evidence Act 1984
PASC	Parliamentary Affairs Select Committee
PB(ATM)A 1960	Public Bodies (Admission to Meetings) Act 1960
PC	principal council
PCA	Parliamentary Commissioner for Administration
PCA 1967	Parliamentary Commissioner Act 1967

PCS	Parliamentary Commissioner for Standards
PFI	Private Finance Initiative
PHSO	Parliamentary and Health Service Ombudsman
PII	public interest immunity
PNC	Police National Computer
PNQ	Private notice question
PO	Parliamentary Ombudsman
PONI	Police Ombudsman for Northern Ireland
PPP	Public Private Partnership
PQ	Parliamentary Question
PR	Practice Recommendation
PRA 1967	Public Records Act 1967
PrO	Principal Officer
PS	publication scheme
PSO(W)A 2005	Public Services Ombudsman (Wales) Act 2005
QD	qualifying disclosure
QMV	qualified majority voting
Quango	quasi-autonomous international governmental organisation
RIPA 2000	Regulation of Investigatory Powers Act 2000
RPB	regional planning body
RSS	regional spatial strategy
SB	Standards Board
SC	Standards Committee
SCR	serious case review
SD	standard disclosure
SEN	special educational needs
SFOIA 2002	Freedom of Information (Scotland) Act 2002
SIAC	Special Immigration Appeals Commission
SIC	Scottish Information Commissioner
SIN	special information notice
SLC	Student Loans Company
SO	Standing Order
SOCA	Serious Organised Crime Agency
SPA	Scottish public authority
SSA 1989	Security Service Act 1989
SSFA 1998	School Standards and Framework Act 1998
SSFA 2001	Social Security Fraud Act 2001
STP	second transitional period
TA	transferred authority
TCEA 2007	Tribunals, Courts and Enforcement Act 2007
TCPA 1990	Town and Country Planning Act 1990
TCSC	Treasury and Civil Service Committee
TEU	Treaty of Lisbon on the European Union
TFEU	Treaty on the Functioning of the European Union
TPN	transfer prohibition notice
UA 2000	Utilities Act 2000
UCAS	Universities and Colleges Admissions Service
UDC	urban development corporation
UDP	unitary development plan
VFM	value for money
VO	valuation officer
WAQ	written answer question
WIA 1991	Water Industries Act 1991
WP	White Paper
WRA	waste regulation authority
WRA 1991	Water Resources Act 1991

Table of statutes

All references are to paragraph number.

Table of statutory instruments

Table of cases

References are to paragraph number. A chronological table of European Cases follows the alphabetical table.

B

T

CHRONOLOGICAL TABLE OF EUROPEAN CASES

Chapter 1

The freedom of information legislation

'Truth, like all other good things, may be loved unwisely – may be pursued too keenly – may cost too much' Knight Bruce V-C in *Pearse v Pearse* (1846) 1 De G & Sm 12 at 28–29

'... but at the length truth will out.' *Merchant of Venice* II.2 645

'The concepts of freedom of information and open government are the political equivalent of motherhood and apple pie' D. McLetchie, Stage 1 debate on the Scottish Freedom of Information Act

INTRODUCTION AND OVERVIEW

1.1 In December 1997, the new Labour government published its proposals for freedom of information (FOI) legislation.[1] These were widely acclaimed among the FOI community in the UK, and further afield, for being liberal and for making a bold statement about the future emphasis of openness in the conduct of British government. Prime Minister Blair had been a keen advocate for freedom of information when leader of the opposition although in his memoirs he described the Act as an act of stupidity 'undermining ... serious government'.[2] Some observers felt that the White Paper was too bold to become a reality. The White Paper (WP) was hotly contested in government and the Minister responsible for its drafting was subsequently dismissed from the Cabinet.[3] In May 1999, a draft Bill was published together with a Consultation Paper.[4] Like the White Paper, these were subject to scrutiny by the House of Commons Select Committee on Public Administration in the House of Commons[5] and also, and in this case unlike the WP, by a committee of the House of Lords.[6] The Commons Committee noted that 'legislation on the information rights of citizens is a historic moment for our history'. In November 1999, the Bill was published and presented to Parliament. The Bill received Royal Assent on 30 November 2000 after the government imposed a guillotine to force the Bill through the Commons following its return from the Lords, to avoid debate of 118 late amendments.

[1]   *Your Right to Know: Freedom of Information* Cm 3818, December 1997.
[2]   T Blair *A Journey* (2010) pp 516–517.
[3]   David Clark, Chancellor of the Duchy of Lancaster.
[4]   *Freedom of Information. Consultation on Draft Legislation* Cm 4355 (Home Office).
[5]   In the case of the Bill, pre-legislative scrutiny: see HC 398 I and II (1997/98) on the White Paper, HC 1020 (1997/98) for the Government Reply; HC 570 I and II (1998/99) for the Select Committee on Public Administration's report on the draft Bill.
[6]   HL 97 (1998/99).

1.2   The path to freedom of information in the United Kingdom had been a labyrinthine one and the Bill emerged well over thirty years after the Americans introduced the first of various laws on access rights to information and meetings[1] and long after various laws on FOI were introduced in the Commonwealth, on the Continent and in Ireland.[2] Sweden's laws on access to information go back to 1766 and were introduced under a Freedom of Press Act. There are over 70 states with FOI statutes and they are becoming features of international organisations such as the European Union (see ch 3).[3]

[1]   P Birkinshaw *Freedom of Information: the Law, the Practice and the Ideal* (4th edn, 2010) ch 12.
[2]   A useful account is contained in: A McDonald and G Terril (eds) *Open Government: Freedom of Information and Privacy* (1998). Two recent works on FOI are: McDonald and Jones (eds) *The Law of Freedom of Information* (2009, 2nd edn); and P Coppel *Information Rights* (2010, 3rd edn), both of which cover overseas regimes. See J Wadham et al *Blackstone's Guide to the Freedom of Information Act 2000* (2011, 4th edn). See J Plotnikoff and R Woolfson *Management of FOI Requests in Other Jurisdictions* (2003) at www.dca.gov.uk/foi/impgroup/07-07c.pdf, and M McDonagh *Freedom of Information Law in Ireland* (2006, 2nd edn) for some useful comparative aspects. The impact of the FOIA 2000 on central government has been examined in R Hazell, B Worthy and M Glover *The Impact of the FOI Act 2000 on Central Government in the UK. Does FOI Work?* (2010).
[3]   In 2011 FOIAs were passed in Nigeria, Mongolia and Jersey and plans were afoot in Egypt and Morocco. However, in South Africa a Protection of Official Information Bill sought to punish severely those who disclosed information without authorisation, undermining its very liberal access to information law.

1.3   There had been numerous Private Members' Bills which Labour when previously in power and while in opposition continually supported.[1] The excessive secrecy of British government and the hostility of Mrs Thatcher in particular to any interference to the British way of doing things under the banner of representative government and collective and individual responsibility of Ministers to Parliament ensured that no laws would be introduced under a Conservative government which imposed a legal duty on central government to disclose information. Laws relating to public records had been introduced in 1958 allowing publication of public records held in the Public Record Office (now National Archives) after originally 50 years, successively reduced to 30 and now 20 years (see para 2.62 below). Concessions were made by the Major government which produced a Code of Practice on Open Government[2] which was in operation until 31 December 2004 (see ch 2). This Code covered bodies within the jurisdiction of the Parliamentary Commissioner for Administration (PCA) – the Parliamentary ombudsman.[3] Local government produced their own guidance on access to information and guidance was provided by the Commission for Local Administration and health authorities and trusts had their own guidance and codes.[4] Virtually all UK public authorities are now subject to the Freedom of Information Act 2000 which came into effect, to allow individual access to records held by public authorities, on 1 January 2005. The provisions on publication schemes have been operational since November 2002 (see para 1.48 below).

1   See P Birkinshaw and A Parkin 'Freedom of Information' in *Constitutional Reform* eds R Blackburn and R Plant (1999).
2   *Code of Practice on Access to Government Information: Open Government* (2nd edn, 1997) and accompanying Guidance on Interpretation.
3   The Code was tagged on to his governing Act but was non-statutory. See paras 2.18 et seq below.
4   *Open Government: A Good Practice Note on Access to Information* ACC, AMA, AMA (1995); *LGO* Issue 6 March 1996, Commission for Local Administration; *Code of Practice on Openness in the NHS*, NHS Executive (1995).

1.4   The 1994 Code, which was revised in 1997, has been praised for helping to introduce greater openness into the operations of government and, in spite of some criticisms, for making officials less defensive about access to information requests. It remained, however, an *administrative code*, and had serious shortcomings in its design and contents. Many of these deficiencies were highlighted in the government's 1997 white paper on open government.[1] Many individual statutory provisions allowed for access to information in specific circumstances – this book is replete with such examples. One such is s 66 of the Land Registration Act 2002 which allows inspection of the register of title to real estate subject to exemptions.

1   *Your Right to Know* above.

1.5   The Freedom of Information Act 2000 (FOIA 2000), or more accurately its individual access provisions, was delayed from coming into force for over four years from the date of the completion of its passage through Parliament. Although the White Paper was very green at the edges, and did nothing to allay anxieties about the relationship between access to information and privacy protection,[1] it was generally very liberal in its content. There were fears that the longer the delay in producing legislation, the more cautious the government would become as it experienced the usual leaks and information disclosures which caused it maximum embarrassment. Particularly affected were the Foreign Secretary, the Trade and Industry Secretary, the Prime Minister and, conspicuously, the Home Secretary who suffered a series of difficulties over the premature disclosure and then wrongful publication of sensitive facts in the Stephen Lawrence inquiry.[2] Responsibility for the Bill had in fact been transferred to the Home Office and had been taken away from the Cabinet Office in the summer of 1998 when the Minister who had inspired the liberal contents of the White Paper was dismissed.

1   This was subject to a great deal of criticism in the Select Committee in the Commons.
2   Cm 4262 I and II (revised). Identities and addresses of witnesses had been revealed in the original report. Stephen Lawrence was the victim of a notorious racist gang attack in which he was murdered.

1.6   As at the time of writing, the FOIA is under the sponsorship of the Ministry of Justice (formerly Department for Constitutional Affairs – formerly Lord Chancellor's Department – and the Secretary of State for Justice/Lord Chancellor. The operations and administration of the Act fall within the remit of the Commons Select Committee on Justice and not the Select Committee on Public Administration.

1.7   Since the Act was passed in 2000 the world has become far more security conscious after the events of 11 September 2001. The war in Iraq promoted the Prime Minister into the glare of unremitting publicity in relation to the use of intelligence and information by the government in its case for armed intervention in Iraq. Three major inquiries have been conducted: one into the circumstances surrounding the death of the scientific adviser, David Kelly, whose comments on weapons of mass destruction in Iraq to a reporter for the BBC led to internationally sensational events concerning allegations of Prime Ministerial doctoring of intelligence; the second concerned the use of intelligence on weapons of mass destruction (WMD) by the government. The first was conducted by a Law Lord, Lord Hutton, the second by the former Cabinet Secretary, Lord Butler.[1] The third is chaired by Sir John Chilcot and was commissioned by the Prime Minister Gordon Brown in 2009 to consider the period from the summer of 2001 to the end of July 2009, embracing the run-up to the conflict in Iraq, the military action and its aftermath. The inquiry is considering the 'UK's involvement in Iraq, including the way decisions were made and actions taken, to establish, as accurately as possible, what happened and to identify the lessons that can be learned.'[2] The government's reply setting out key actions following the Butler inquiry into the use of intelligence is Cm 6492 (March 2005). These inquiries had unparalleled access to the most sensitive of information – much of it unobtainable under the FOIA. The Secretary to the Hutton Inquiry adopted a public interest test like the one under the FOIA to determine which materials should not be published (see para 1.98 below). In the event, he withheld two pages of documents on grounds of national security and personal information. He adopted a 'bold view' of the public interest although he embargoed some medical information for 70 years, the *Daily Mail* reported.[3] The Chilcot inquiry took evidence in public and private sessions after protest over the possibility of an exclusively private inquiry. The Inquiry committee intends to include in the report 'all but the most sensitive information essential to our national security'. The report will then be debated in Parliament. Witnesses included the former Prime Minister Tony Blair (who was called to give further evidence after the publication of a note from the Attorney General in his government indicating an opinion on the need for a further resolution of UN support for war in Iraq which differed from hitherto published opinions), the then Prime Minister Gordon Brown and a former head of the secret service. Shortly after coming to office in May 2010, the Prime Minister of the coalition government announced an inquiry into allegations of British security and intelligence services' involvement in torture of terrorist suspects. This followed litigation in which US intelligence information was handed to a litigant despite protests from the US and UK governments.[4] Sensitive intelligence information would not be made public and there were indications that the government would take measures aimed at preventing disclosure of intelligence information in future litigation.[5] We return to these points in chapters 9 and 10.

---

[1]   HC 247 (2003–04) for Hutton and HC 898 (2003–04) for Butler. See *Hutton and Butler: Lifting the Lid on the Workings of Power*, ed W Runciman (2004). The whole question of investigatory inquiries

has been examined by the Department for Constitutional Affairs in *Effective Inquiries* (2004) leading to an Inquiries Act 2005 (see para 9.104 below). The method of inquiry into ministerial irregularities – ad hoc, terms of reference from the Prime Minister and usually by a former civil servant – was heavily criticsed. The Committee on Standards in Public Life recommended a standing independent panel of two or three persons who would be independent and of 'senior standing' and from which one would be chosen to conduct inquiries into alleged breaches of the Ministerial Code. The panel would last for a Parliament, would be publicly known and reports would be published: Ninth Report Cm 5775 (2003) ch 5. See the Public Administration Committee HC 51 (2004–05) on *Government by Inquiry* (and see para 9.104 below). On inquiries generally, the chair of the Bichard inquiry (para 7.233 et seq below) was reportedly sceptical about the effects of inquiries in relation to reform: *Guardian* (2010) 16 September.

2   http://www.iraqinquiry.org.uk/about.aspx.

3   http://www.dailymail.co.uk/news/article-1245599/David-Kelly-post-mortem-kept-secret-70-years-doctors-accuse-Lord-Hutton-concealing-vital-information.html.

4   *R (Mohamed) v Secretary of State for Foreign Affairs* [2010] EWCA Civ 65 and 158. See Information Commissioner decision notice FS 50279042.

5   Hansard, HC cols 175–90 (6 July 2010).

1.8   The FOIA will rarely operate in such lofty circumstances. It will deal with the hum-drum of government and its daily progress – from the infrequent magnificent to the perpetual mundane. Mundanities may of course topple governments. As we will see, there have been sensational cases involving the Information Commissioner and Information Tribunal (now officially: First Tier Tribunal Information Rights). Those on MPs expenses, Cabinet minutes, reviews of the identity cards and other IT schemes, export credit guarantees, death rates in hospitals, and Prince Charles' correspondence with ministers readily spring to mind. Also in constant spotlight in the years following the passage of FOIA was the relationship of the Prime Minister to his press secretary and the use by the Government of publicity and communications. This led to a review of *Government Communications* and a report in January 2004. The report made recommendations for amendment of FOIA before it had come into effect (para 1.42 below) and other recommendations which can be examined in ch 2 together with a House of Lords committee report on government communications (para 2.114 below).

1.9   Reviews of the FOIA have been conducted by Parliamentary committees and a review of the operation of the Act was conducted by Frontier Economics for the Prime Minister in 2006.[1] A review by Paul Dacre into the 'Thirty Year Rule' under the Public Records Acts reported in 2009 and made some interesting observations on the operation of FOIA and public records legislation.[2] These can be examined below (see para 2.62). The reforms were brought into effect by the Constitutional Reform and Governance Act 2010.

1   Review of the Impact of the FOIA (2006).

2   Dacre Review of 30 Year Rule (2009): 14 http://www.30yearrulereview.org.uk/.

1.10   Generally the 1999 draft Bill was faithful to many of the government's statements on its legislative plans for freedom of information, but there were serious deviations. There will be access to information, a term which is broadly defined and includes records. A person is entitled to be informed in writing whether a 'public authority' (PA) holds information of the description specified in the request. If that is the case, the person is entitled to have that information communicated to him/her. The Act makes provision for the automatic disclosure of certain kinds of information by public authorities under publication schemes. A person requesting information has a right to be informed by a public authority whether it holds information of the description specified in the request. If so, the information must be communicated to the requester, subject to various conditions concerning fees, assistance in identifying information requested and other matters (see below). The duty will not cover exempt information under Part II of the Act. Section 11 deals with means of communicating information under the Act (see below).

1.11 Public authorities covered by the FOIA 2000 are scheduled in the Act,[1] and this comprises a very wide list along the lines set out by the White Paper but with some modifications. Bodies scheduled in a particular capacity are only subject to access requests in that capacity. The Secretary of State is given wide powers to designate 'public authorities' in order to add to the scheduled bodies and this clearly will include a power to bring private bodies within the definition, as stated in the WP, although the designation may be restricted to certain 'functions' of such bodies, ie those which fulfil a public as opposed to a private purpose. Those under contract with public bodies to provide a service which is a function of the public authority may also be designated. In such a case the FOIA 2000 provisions only apply to functions covering public service and not coincidental ones. In 2009, the then government published plans to designate bodies as public authorities for the FOIA and the incoming coalition government announced further proposed additions in 2010.[1] The coalition government also announced plans to extend FOIA.[2] The Act incorporates provisions on public records which, when the Bill was initially published, remained incomplete.[3] Provision is made to repeal or amend statutory prohibitions on disclosing information (see para 1.263). See Annex A below for the list of bodies covered by the Act.

[1]   http://www.homeoffice.gov.uk/publications/about-us/legislation/freedom-bill/extending-foi-ia?view=Binary.   A consultation has also been taking place in connection with the Scottish FOIA and extension.
[2]   Contained in the Protection of Freedoms Bill 2011 (see para 1.85). See SI 1041/2011 and SI 1042/2011 Order on adding and removing bodies.
[3]   Part VI of the FOIA 2000 refers to 'Historical Records' ie those in existence 30 years (reduced to 20 years) after their creation. Certain exemptions are removed after 30 years, 60 and 100 years. Some appear to have no time limit (see paras 2.53 et seq below). See also A McDonald 'Archives and Open Government' in *Open Government* eds A McDonald and G Terrill (1998). Under FOIA 2000, s 46 the Lord Chancellor has to make a code of practice for authorities in relation to the holding of public records: see Lord Chancellor's *Code of Practice on the Management of Records under s 46 FOIA*, July 2009, Ministry of Justice: http://www.justice.gov.uk/guidance/docs/foi-section-46-code-of-practice.pdf.

1.12 Crucially, the Bill dropped several of the *exclusions* outlined for categories of information in the White Paper and made them exemptions. Critically, this covers information relating to the criminal investigation process. Excluded information is totally outside the operation of the Act – the Act has no relevance to it whatsoever. Exempt information is in most cases subject to a public interest test: although notionally exempt the public interest in being disclosed must be considered by the public authority. Public bodies, including designated bodies, will have to consider the public interest in disclosing information even though the information is exempt. Such exemptions are known as 'qualified' exemptions. They are to be distinguished from 'absolute' exemptions under which public interest disclosures cannot be made. A good deal was made of the public interest test in the white paper – the balancing that will have to take place between the public interest in disclosure and the public interest in preventing a harm to an identified interest. Interestingly, the Major Code contained a clear public interest override where a harm test applied in considering whether to disclose information. The provisions under the FOI Bill 2000 were not as full-bloodied as the override test in the Code (1997 edn, p 5, para 2) and disclosures under the public interest provision were referred to as discretionary. However, the Bill as it progressed was amended to impose a duty on authorities to disclose unless 'in all the circumstances of the case' the public interest in maintaining the exemption outweighed the public interest in disclosure; the case for secrecy had to outweigh that for openness. It should also be recalled that the white paper criticised the Code for its lack of clarity in relation to the concepts of 'harm' and 'public interest' which were addressed in making the appropriate balance. Furthermore, the Bill published for consultation allowed a public authority to consider the motives of the applicant and the use to which an applicant intends to put the information. These provisions, which met with almost universal condemnation, were removed.

THE COMMONS PUBLIC ADMINISTRATION COMMITTEE'S INVESTIGATION

1.13 The Commons Select Committee reported that the Bill as drafted had 'significant deficiencies which, if not remedied, would undermine the potential' of the Bill. 'Key improvements' were recommended to rebalance the Bill 'and enable it to fulfil its potential.' Amendments accepted by the government included: a statement that the right to information was now at the beginning of the Bill in clause/section 1 and the long title had been amended. However, there was no overriding purpose clause emphasising that greater openness was to be an overarching consideration.[1] The public interest in discretionary disclosure was given greater emphasis in the later Bill so that the authority shall have regard 'to the desirability of' disclosing the information 'wherever the public interest in disclosure outweighs the public interest in maintaining the exemption in question.' A more explicit statement that the balance was in favour of disclosure absent a good reason not to disclose was not forthcoming at this stage but it was inserted as the Bill went to the Lords (see below).

[1]   Purpose clauses in statutes are not uncommon: see Crime and Disorder Act 1998, s 37(1), Children Act 1989, s 1(1) and, in regulations, the Civil Procedure Rules 1998, SI 1998/3132, r 1.1.

1.14 Under the original Bill, the Information Commissioner (IC) could only recommend disclosure; the final decision is with Ministers and public authorities. The Select Committee in the Commons (and Lords) wanted the

IC to have power to overrule a Minister's or authority's decision not to disclose discretionary information. The latter Bill gave the IC a specific power to recommend disclosure 'specifying information which ought, in his opinion, to be disclosed.' However, in the first Bill discretionary disclosures applied to all but two of the exempt categories. In the latter Bill, they did not apply to **eight** (subsequently increased to **nine**) categories. This was the position in the final Act. 'It appears that although the Commissioner has been given wider powers, the field on which they can be deployed has been significantly narrowed.'[1] On subsequent amendment, Bill No 2 did give the Commissioner power to insist on disclosure but this was subject to a Ministerial veto (see below). Under Bill No 1 the exemption for information relating to civil proceedings, statutory or other investigations including investigations into the causes of accidents or under the Companies Acts (not including criminal investigations for which there was and still is a separate and widely drawn provision) was a class-based exemption. In Bill No 2, information relating to regulatory law enforcement functions, including accident investigation is protected by a contents-based exemption. The very wide protection given to information relating to the formulation of government policy and information whose disclosure 'would prejudice the commercial interests of any person' remain in spite of widespread criticism. The government rejected the Select Committee's recommendation that the contents-based exemption should be whether 'substantial' or 'significant' prejudice would result making the test of prejudice or harm 'weaker than it should be.'[2] Some of the information exempted will remain closed long after it has become 'historical' under the FOIA 2000. Bill No 2 included a duty on public authorities to give reasons for refusal to disclose information whereas general provisions covering reasons for decisions would be placed in publication schemes. A Code of Practice will deal with other procedural matters.

[1]   HC 78 (1999–00), para 4, fourth indent.
[2]   HC 78 (1999–00), para 4, seventh indent.

THE EXEMPTIONS

1.15   The exemptions, as detailed below, have increased significantly under the Act from the White Paper. In the latter, exempting interests numbered seven (in John Major's Code on access it was 15). Those now in the Act number 25 (we include ss 12 and 4 below) and cover areas such as: where compliance cost exceeds 'appropriate limit' of expenditure for complying (ie, as defined in regulations but which will be £600 for central government and Parliament), and vexatious or repeated requests. These are not in the general body of exemptions under Part II of the Bill. Information which is available to the public by other means (see below) and information intended for future publication were brought within the Part II exemptions. Information supplied by or covering the work of the security and intelligence services, GCHQ or the 'special services', information required for national security, information prejudicing – or which would be likely to prejudice (a formula which is repeated where 'prejudice' (see below) is present) – inter-governmental relationships in the UK, information whose disclosure would prejudice or be likely to prejudice defence, and international relations are exempt.

This latter category would cover the EC and EU institutions where their own laws may be more restrictive than our access laws and so could take priority over information coming from or going to such bodies (see para 3.78 below). Further exemptions cover the economy – this is a completely new exemption from the White Paper – information held for criminal investigations and proceedings, and also information held for civil or administrative proceedings under a statutory or prerogative power. This includes investigations 'with a view to ascertaining the cause of an accident'[1] as well as a raft of other investigations concerning safety, breaches of law and other improper conduct. Information otherwise relating to law enforcement – which is drafted in very wide terms – is afforded separate exemption. Information relating to judicial functions and proceedings of courts and tribunals (though not administrative functions) is also exempt and, because it is not covered by the public interest test in what is now s 2, is arguably effectively excluded.[2] In fact the amount of information excluded from the public interest test increased as the Bill progressed.

[1] See paras 1.145 et seq below.
[2] On disclosure of documents by the 'court' from trial dockets and subject to appropriate safeguards: see CPR 1998, r 5.4 and the accompanying Practice Direction. In criminal cases, any disclosure would be subject to the Criminal Procedure Rules 2010, SI 2010/60 (L2) and Criminal Procedure (Amendment) Rules 2010, SI 2010/1921 (L12). See *R Guardian News and Media Ltd v City of Westminster Magistrates' Court etc* [2010] EWHC 3376 (Admin) (see para 1.155 below). Under Major's Code, courts, tribunals and inquiries were not included, but were subject to 'present practice': para 10.

1.16 Information concerned with decision-making and policy formulation in central government and for these purposes Northern Ireland Ministers are included, and information whose disclosure would prejudice the effective conduct of public affairs which is not restricted to central government, is exempt as is that information whose disclosure would endanger the health and safety of an individual or concerns deceased persons and would cause distress to living persons. Personal information is exempt, as well as information provided in confidence, that covered by legal professional privilege, trade secrets and commercial interests. Conferral of honours by the Crown is exempt and so is that information whose disclosure is prohibited by any enactment, or a court order. This refers to specific items of information rather than general classes of information as under the Official Secrets Act 1989. The latter legislation is concerned with *unauthorised* disclosures. The clause includes that which is 'incompatible with' any Community 'obligation'. A Community obligation could be extremely broad, however. As we note below, there was a power to add to the exemptions by retrospective ministerial order. In Bill No 2 this was amended so that only contents based exemptions may be created. Before making such an order – to be approved by positive resolution – the Secretary of State will consult with the IC. This was, however, removed in the Lords.

THE INFORMATION COMMISSIONER

1.17 The IC, as outlined in the White Paper, has promotional and investigatory powers in order to assist in the creation of a more open culture in government and to deal with complaints. The IC (currently Christopher Graham, succeeding Richard Thomas) may enforce 'any of the requirements of Part I' of the Act and not simply those relating to access complaints by individuals. The IC (who has in fact taken over the office of the Data Protection Commissioner (DPC) formerly Registrar) will approve publication schemes produced by public authorities which relate to the mandatory publication of information that they have to select. The IC may approve model schemes for classes of authority such as smaller bodies or schools, universities and not the typical governmental or regulatory bodies. The government, and they should be congratulated for this, responded positively to several of the recommendations of the Select Committee on Public Administration including, as we noted above, the removal of the protection of criminal investigations from the excluded category to an exemption.[1] In this latter case, however, there is a sting in the tail. The IC is, it should be noted, a public authority covered by the FOIA 2000 and he investigates complaints against his actions under the FOIA where, eg, he refuses to disclose information to a requester (see, eg, FS50271526 where the IC invoked FOIA 2000, s 31 to deny acces to the enforcement referral log).

[1]   HC 398 I (1997–98) pp xxv et seq.

1.18   There was some unease about the fact that the IC's headquarters were to be based in Wilmslow, Cheshire and not in London[1] and that the advertised salary was considerably below the very senior civil service remuneration levels. The Bichard inquiry into the Soham murders made some critical remarks about the relationship between ACPO and the IC over police practices in relation to data retention (see paras 7.194 et seq below). Furthermore, the most important judicial decision on the Data Protection Act 1998 (DPA 1998) made no reference to the role of the IC[2] although subsequent case law has overruled the IC's and tribunal's decisions on alleged police breaches of the DPA 1998 (see para 7.236 below).[3] The Protection of Freedoms Bill 2011 makes some changes to the appointment and tenure of the Commissioner amending both FOIA and the DPA 1998. The IC can only be removed by Her Majesty in pursuance of an addess from both houses of Parliament. Specified grounds are now stated, at least one of which has to be made out and reported on by the Minister. Appointment must be on merit and competition and not subject to re-appointment.

[1]   The website (www.ico.gov.uk) has details of regional offices and the press office.
[2]   *Durant v Financial Services Authority* [2003] EWCA Civ 1746.
[3]   *Humberside Chief Constable of Police v Information Commissioner* [2009] EWCA Civ 1079.

DATA PROTECTION AND ACCESS TO INFORMATION

1.19   The government also followed the Commons Select Committee's advice on the division of functions between the data protection and information acts. The White Paper revealed a great deal of confused thinking which, it has to be said, government members before the Select Committee did little to eradicate.[1] The White Paper envisaged a dual operation scheme involving both pieces of legislation and the cooperation of the separate Commissioners. The divisions in jurisdiction were far from clear and there was a pressing concern that the uncertainty might well promote privacy protection as a more important objective than access to information. Certainly in overseas jurisdictions there was evidence of a privacy regime dominating an access to information regime.[2] This conflict also featured in the Human Rights Act 1998 (HRA 1998) where special safeguards had to be written in to protect freedom of speech[3] and also in the data protection legislation to protect journalism, art and literature.[4] What the FOIA 2000 does is to provide for only one Commissioner thereby eliminating potential and damaging clashes between different Commissioners taking opposing lines on areas within their jurisdiction. Furthermore, claims by data subjects to information about themselves will be made under the DPA 1998 (it does this by making such data exempt under the FOIA 2000) whereas claims by others to information about someone else will be dealt with by the same Commissioner under the FOIA 2000. Such claims will, however, be subject to the principles and safeguards of the DPA 1998 (see ch 7). These latter points are now much clearer in principle although perhaps unavoidably technical and difficult in application as is evidenced for instance by the extension of 'data' covered by the Act to include 'unstructured personal data' and the consequential exemptions from the DPA 1998 of such data. In the White Paper, personnel files of employees of public bodies were to be excluded from the FOIA 2000. The Act reduces them to an exemption from the provisions of the DPA 1998. Making the DPC the IC does raise certain possible problems (see below).

[1]   See the evidence of the Lord Chancellor: HC 398 I (1997–98), pp 84 et seq.
[2]   See R Hazell in A McDonald and G Terrill, para 1.2, note 2 above.
[3]   HRA 1998, s 12. See para 2.349 et seq below.
[4]   DPA 1998, ss 3 and 32. See paras 7.31 and 7.85 below.

COVERAGE

1.20   The FOIA 2000 applies to Northern Ireland – although the Northern Ireland Assembly may make provisions for completely devolved items – as well as England and Wales and, although the accompanying *Consultation Document* stated that the Bill applies to Scotland, its application appears extremely limited. It appears to cover the Scottish Office and those scheduled bodies which have addresses in Scotland, eg the BBC, so that provision is made for an appeal to the Court of Session against the Tribunal's (below) decision involving such a body (FOIA 2000, s 59(b)). The FOIA 2000 does not apply to devolved public bodies including the Edinburgh Parliament and Scottish Executive and information held by them unless entrusted 'in confidence' by the UK government (Freedom of Information (Scotland) Act 2002 ('SFOIA 2002'), s 3(2)(a)(ii)). (Such information is not held under the FOIA (Scotland) Act.) The UK Act applies to 'cross-border' authorities even in relation to devolved matters.[1] In fact Scottish *plans* for legislation on FOI were more liberal than their UK counterparts and although SFOIA 2002 is modelled on the UK legislation, there are some important differences (see paras 1.240 et seq below). Disquiet was expressed during examination of the White Paper that if FOI was a devolved as opposed to a reserved matter for purely Scottish public authorities, unlike human rights which was a reserved matter, there was no guarantee that the new Scottish Parliament would actually legislate for access. This proved unfounded.

¹   Eg the Scotland Act 1998 (Cross-Border Public Authorities) (Specification) Order 1999, SI 1999/1319, designates 65 public bodies as cross-border public authorities, including the British Library, the National Heritage Memorial Fund, the Theatres Trust, the Meat and Livestock Commission and their responsibilities extend throughout the United Kingdom.

1.21   A Code of Practice (2007) on access to information has been produced by the Welsh Assembly Government¹ and replaces an earlier code. It outlines the provisions under which the Assembly will operate. The Code undertakes to operate under a presumption of openness and sets out information it will publish automatically (see www.wales.gov.uk). Originally the Code sets a response rate of 15 working days but it now states that it will be subject to 'legal limits' set out in the FOIA 2000 or Environmental Information Regulations. Where 'harm or prejudice' are referred to as a ground for not allowing disclosure, these may be outweighed by a greater public interest in disclosure. Now that FOIA is in force, its provisions apply to Welsh public authorities including the Assembly, although some more liberal features of the Code are retained (see para 1.248 below). There is an undertaking to reply in the language of request and, if other than English or Welsh, in the language of request 'where practicable'. The range of 'public authorities' covered by the UK legislation is dealt with below (para 1.85).

¹   http://wales.gov.uk/cisd/publications/codeaccessinfo2007/codee.pdf;jsessionid=vsT7MTFD6n KX2yNxzN2JCph4Zk28s7GTfQtttcZkMVS50n8p0LGn!-450763871?lang=en.

CODES

1.22   Many of the details of administrative practice for English public authorities will be contained in a code under s 45 of the FOIA 2000 (HC 33 2004–05), setting out what the Secretary of State deems 'desirable practice' for authorities to follow when discharging their functions under Part I. The Commissioner must be consulted on its contents. Codes have been published under s 45 (see eg para 1.273) and also s 46 (see para 2.73). The s 45 Code was revised (considerably) in 2004 before the access provisions came into effect. Where the code is not followed, the Commissioner may issue a Practice Recommendation. What happens if this is not followed is not clear: is it a matter for the Secretary of State and, if so, under political pressure, or can the Commissioner seek judicial review; or is it a matter for the IC or maladministration for the Parliamentary Ombudsman? A breach of a Part I requirement may attract an Enforcement Notice (see below). The code says that such failures may form part of an adverse comment in a report to Parliament. This code will cover crucial items such as advice to requesters, transfers of requests between authorities, consultation with parties whose interests are likely to be affected by a disclosure, contractual terms relating to the disclosure of information and complaints procedures within authorities for those who are unhappy about the way their complaint is dealt with (see below). Even though the code is not legislation itself, this does not mean the courts will take no cognisance of its terms.¹

¹   It could be the basis of a legitimate expectation or it may constitute a relevant factor to consider when exercising discretion.

1.23 Much of government and public service is today performed under contract with private parties, either under Private Finance Initiatives (PFI) and Public Private Partnerships (PPP) or other arrangements and the provisions of the code on contracts with private sector contractors should be highlighted. Terms which seek to restrict provision of information beyond those contained in the act should be refused, the original code advised but this was removed on revision. It did not say they were forbidden. Authorities should not agree to hold information in confidence which is not in fact confidential in nature; it does not say not covered by the law of confidence. The following from the original draft while exhorting good practice seems to bow to market reality:

> 'Public authorities when entering into contracts with non-public authority contractors may be under pressure to accept confidentiality clauses so that information relating to the terms of the contract, its value and performance will be exempt from disclosure. Public authorities should, wherever commercially viable, endeavour to obtain the agreement of the non-public authority contractor that no such confidentiality can be set up against a request for the disclosure of such information.' (para 25)

1.24 If it's a powerful contractor, forget it! Otherwise try and get their consent. What if they refuse?

1.25 Confidentiality clauses must be capable of being justified to the Commissioner. Except where designated as a public authority under the FOIA 2000, it is the authority that will disclose information in accordance with the Act. Where designation occurs, the cost of compliance with the Act should be costed in the terms of the contract. Authorities should not impose secrecy clauses in excess of the Act! – although this was also removed from the revised code. The question of contracts is of enormous practical importance and will be returned to later in this chapter (paras 1.281 et seq below) where it will be seen that the Code was considerably revised.

1.26 Fees may be charged and it was hoped that for 'most applications' these will not exceed a maximum of £60 plus copying costs and postage. The question of fees became highly contested and subject to significant revision and the £60 maximum fee did not find its way into the regulations (see below). Under the DPA 1998, the data user may charge £10 for supplying the information from one register entry. Fees may be waived in prescribed cases. Public authorities are given 20 days to comply with the request for information, a reduction from the 40 days originally drafted.

1.27 It was mentioned above that the longer the delay in introducing FOI in the government's term of office, the greater the risk that the more radical tinges of the White Paper would be diluted. This certainly appears to be the case. In what follows, the author attempts to highlight major differences between the White Paper on *Freedom of Information: Your Right to Know* and the Bill, as well as specific points which may be of interest.

POINTS OF SIGNIFICANT DEPARTURE FROM THE WHITE PAPER

Reduction in the 'harm' test for refusing disclosure

1.28 Some exemptions require no test of any damage whatsoever in order to be exempt. This means they are protected as a class because they belong to documents within that class. Out of 25 exemptions, including ss 12 and 14 of the FOIA 2000, 17 are on a class basis. So, information collected as a result of criminal investigations relating to law enforcement requires no test of damage to withhold it. Also, information relating to the formulation and development of governmental policy is subject to no test of damage although information whose disclosure would inhibit, or would be likely to inhibit, the free and frank provision of advice, etc, can be withheld on the 'reasonable opinion' of a qualified person that such inhibition would be likely to take place. Where the exemption is not on a class basis, it will be because disclosure of the contents will have, or could have, an undesirable effect causing damage.[1]

[1] For class and contents claims in Public Interest Immunity see paras 10.52 et seq below.

1.29 Where a damage test is required, the test in the Bill for exempting information is where its disclosure 'prejudices' or is likely to prejudice particular interests rather than where its disclosure would cause 'substantial harm' to interests as in the White Paper. This is a significant reduction from the White Paper in the test for refusing to disclose information, making withholding information much easier. The White Paper stated that the test would be substantial harm to a variety of interests although in the case of policy-making simple harm would be the test. 'Harm', 'damage' and 'prejudice' are basically the same it is submitted, and to remove the qualifying 'substantial' is deeply significant. The Home Secretary stated in the House of Commons that 'prejudice' must be 'real, actual or of substance' and references could be made to his statement under *Pepper v Hart* if necessary.[1] Home Office spokespersons correlated 'prejudices' with 'damages' in the Official Secrets Act 1989 (OSA 1989) and much of the wording in the OSA 1989 is borrowed or very close to that in the FOIA 2000 in several of the exemptions. The Select Committee had drawn attention to the undesirability of comparing access provisions with crimes relating to unauthorised disclosure[2] and it might appear unfortunate that the wording of the access provisions is so close to the laws punishing unauthorised disclosures. The fear was that too close an association with official secrecy would weaken the spirit and operation of the access laws. The Bill says nothing about liberalising the Official Secrets Act. The breadth of some of the provisions in the OSA 1989 could, arguably, be found to be in breach of the European Convention on Human Rights (ECHR) by the European Court of Human Rights (ECtHR) (see ch 2). The House of Lords has ruled that the absolute prohibitions on disclosure in ss 1 and 4 of the OSA 1989 do not breach the Human Rights Act 1998 – UK courts are, they have emphasised, bound to put a British gloss on the ECHR under domestic legislation although the ECtHR sets the framework for interpretation.[3]

[1] 332 HC Official Report (6th series), cols 22 and 26 (24 May 1999); *Pepper v Hart* [1993] 1 All ER 42, HL – the higher courts have been cautious in their use of *Pepper*. Other statutes to use these terms include: Local Government Act 1972, Sch 12A; Taxes Management Act 1970, s 20(8H);

Drug Trafficking Act 1994, s 53(2)(b); DPA 1998, ss 29, 30 and 31; Contempt of Court Act 1981, s 2. *Pepper v Hart* cannot be used to interpret the *extent* of a statutory power, only its meaning: *R v Secretary of State for the Environment, Transport and the Regions ex parte Spath Holme Ltd* [2001] 2 AC 349.

2   HC 398 I (1997–98), paras 77 et seq.

3   *R v Shayler* [2002] 2 All ER 477 (HL) and [2001] 1 WLR 2206 (CA). Former MI5 officer David Shayler's lawyers submitted this argument by when they sought to persuade a French court not to extradite Shayler to England for prosecution under the OSA 1989. Extradition was refused by the French court. Shayler eventually made his own way to England and was duly arrested. The ECHR sets the framework for the interpretation of Convention rights under the Human Rights Act 1998 to attempt to ensure consistent interpretation: *R (Ullah) v Special Adjudication Officer* [2004] UKHL 26 at 20. However, the usual rules of precedent apply and are not overridden by contradictory judgments of the ECtHR: *Kay and Others v LB of Lambeth* [2006] UKHL 10; see further *R (GC) v Commissioner of Police of the Metropolis* [2011] UKSC 21.

1.30   The tribunal has ruled on the meanings of the words 'would or would be likely' to cause damage or prejudice. The wording changes in exemptions and one has to be alive to that fact. The tribunal has ruled that the chance of prejudice should not be a 'hypothetical possibility' – there must have been a real and significant risk' of the prejudice.[1] It should be 'real, actual or of substance.' Various decisions have given their own nuanced interpretations to these words but the sense is that 'would be likely to occur' the risk should be real and significant – a 'very significant and weighty chance';[2] in 'prejudice would occur' the chance of prejudice should be greater meaning 'more likely than not (FS 501233488 at 48)[3] although one could argue that would denotes certainty. The tests are demanding ones.

1   *J Connor Press Associates* EA/2005/0005 at 15.

2   *Hogan v IC* EA/2005/0026.

3   'FS' denotes a decision notice of the Commissioner, FER denotes a decision notice under the Environmental Information Regulations.

A new tribunal

1.31   A tribunal has been added to hear appeals from the Commissioner. This is now the First Tier Tribunal Information Rights. No tribunal featured in the White Paper. And none features in the Scottish FOIA. The Commissioner – resort to whom will involve no 'additional cost' – is not the sole independent arbiter of disputes as in the White Paper and in the draft Bill the IC could not enforce disclosure of exempt information. In the White Paper the IC could make binding decisions which were enforceable via contempt proceedings where the authority refused to comply with the Commissioner's decision. Challenge to the Commissioner's decisions in the White Paper was via the High Court in a judicial review.

1.32   The new tribunal is empowered to allow an appeal where, inter alia, it would exercise its discretion differently to the Commissioner, ie on the merits. The tribunal can review findings of fact on which a Commissioner's notice is based as well as take appeal on points of law. These are copious grounds of appeal. These powers have been spelt out by the tribunal on numerous occasions. Two of the members of the tribunal are to be appointed by the Secretary of State, one each representing the interests of public authorities and access requesters respectively.[1] The chairs and deputy chairs will be appointed by the Lord Chancellor and will satisfy legal qualification requirements.[2]

[1]   Data Protection Act 1998, s 6(6) and FOIA 2000, Sch 2, para 16.
[2]   Data Protection Act 1998, s 6(5).

1.33   From the tribunal there is to be a right of appeal on a point of law (judicial review – a 'speedy process' was present in the White Paper as we saw) originally to the High Court but from 2010 appeal lies to the Upper Tribunal Administrative Appeals Chamber. Further appeal to the Court of Appeal and Supreme Court will be possible.

1.34   This could be a drawn-out process and diminishes the importance of speed and effectiveness outlined in the White Paper. An additional stage of appeal has been added and will inevitably assist the public authority whose legal costs are met from the public purse and which has time on its side. Can a private party be guaranteed such support? Legal aid does not apply before the tribunal and costs may be awarded where behaviour is 'unreasonable' (see para 1.253). Delay in disclosure can defeat the purpose of seeking information – this is certainly not going to be a 'hot news item' provision. Some cases have lasted several years and the IC's office (ICO) has been criticised for delay in dealing with requests as well as in other practices.[1] Could a Commissioner be empowered to take up a complainant's case on an appeal by an applicant for access if the Commissioner recommended in favour of disclosure but the authority refused to disclose? This is the situation in Canada, and could be of great assistance to the applicant who is indigent and who might not qualify for legal aid. The government did not think this was appropriate but its reasoning was not clear. It was felt this would compromise the IC's independence.

[1]   See eg *E.Barber v IC* EA/2005/0004.

Increase in exemptions

1.35   The White Paper identified seven or so exempting interests. The Bill had 25 exemptions. Part of this may be explained by the fact that unlike the White Paper which specified several exclusions, the exclusions in the Bill only cover the Security Service, Intelligence Service, GCHQ and the special forces – although other exemptions come close to an exclusion. The other exclusions in the White Paper (criminal investigation and public sector employee records as amended under the DPA 1998 which otherwise allows access to 'unstructured' personal files) are brought into the exemptions. However, information relating to the judicial functions or legal proceedings of courts and tribunals is not subject to the public interest test in s 2 and nor is that relating to security and intelligence service information as well as other exempted information. In the case of national security information which is properly certified by a Minister, it is hard to imagine the public interest being weighed against a 'conclusive' certificate. The 'gateways' identified in the White Paper, ie criteria on which access decisions are made, and other provisions which relate to repeated and vexatious requests etc, are now grounds for refusing information.

1.36   However, the exemptions themselves are further qualified in that the duty on public authorities under s 1(1)(a) of the FOIA 2000, to inform applicants of whether the authority holds information of the description specified in the request, is not operable for many of the exemptions where the information requested would itself constitute exempt information and its disclosure would therefore defeat the purpose of the exemption. This is because 'information' is given a broad interpretation under the Bill whereas in some FOI provisions elsewhere it only covers 'documents' broadly understood. Refusal to confirm or deny the existence of those documents or information is authorised where revealing their existence would undermine the exemption.

Adding to exemptions by ministerial order

1.37   Until the Committee stage of the House of Lords, a clause provided a power to make additional exemptions by order – these may have retrospective effect. This was a provision that was not present in the White Paper. It gave the Minister a considerable discretion which could be a *de lege* veto, again contrary to the White Paper which stated there would be no ministerial vetoes. The exemption was restricted to a contents-based exemption and does not cover class exemptions: the information is covered by the order and 'its disclosure under this Act would, or would be likely to, have such effects adverse to the public interest as may be specified in the order'. In the first version of the Bill, the power to add to exemptions covered class based claims to exemption. This introduced a general public interest override against information disclosure in relation to exempted information. Under cl 43(2), where 'at any time' it appears to the Secretary of State in relation to particular information already in existence at that time that the public interest in exemption outweighs disclosure, he may by order provide that the information is to be exempt information. Would this in any way bind a particular decision involving access to the exempted information? By cl 13(2)(h), cl 43(2) was included in those provisions where the public authority or its officials or the IC, cannot exercise a discretion to disclose or recommend disclosure respectively. Nothing in the original clause (cl 36) overrode the duties on an official to exercise a specific discretion on the facts under the discretionary disclosure provision. It might be added that s 38 of the DPA 1998 confers a similar ministerial power to add to exemptions under that legislation.

1.38   An order under the clause provided that the duty to confirm or deny did not apply to information exempt by the order. It may also apply any provision of s 63 or 64 which place limits on exemptions for historical records (see paras 2.48 et seq below).

1.39   Delegated orders are judicially reviewable on substantive and procedural grounds.[1] While an attack on abuse of power or misleading the House is possible, the courts would require evidence of wildly excessive abuse given Parliament's role in approving the order. Successful challenge on review is in practice a non-starter. In rare cases, courts have investigated orders *before* approval has been given.[2] This clause was, however, dropped by the government in the Lords Committee. One of the most criticised features of the Bill was thereby removed.

[1]   See Woolf, Jowell and Le Sueur *De Smith's Judicial Review* (6th edn, 2007) para 3–011 and cases cited.
[2]   *R v HM Treasury, ex p Smedley* [1985] QB 657.

Classes and contents of documents

1.40   The White Paper stated that it would only seek to protect the *contents* of documents and not *classes* of documents. This would align FOI policy with the change of position announced by the then Attorney General and Lord Chancellor following the Scott Report into the Iraqi supergun affair.[1] The White Paper was itself ambivalent on this point. However, classes of documents are protected in the following exemptions: information accessible through other means; where information is intended for future publication; information supplied by, or relating to, security and intelligence bodies; national security, although a ministerial certificate stating as much is subject to limited challenge in the Tribunal; investigations and proceedings conducted by public authorities; court records; Parliamentary privilege; formulation of government policy; communications with Her Majesty and conferral of honours; environmental information (though this will be available under other provisions; personal information (available under the DPA 1998 or exempted under FOIA); confidential information; that protected by legal professional privilege; trade secrets; information subject to other legal prohibitions on disclosure. (See para 1.42 below on the Phillis recommendations.)

[1]   287 HC Official Report (6th series), col 949 and 576 HL Official Report (5th series), col 1507 (18 Dec 1996) and 297 HC Official Report (6th series), col 616 (11 July 1997).

Ministerial vetoes

1.41   The White Paper stated that there would be no ministerial certificates defeating the thrust of openness as there had been in previous Private Member's Bills. There will be the possibility of certificates under ss 23(2) and 24(3) of the FOIA 2000, concerning security and intelligence services and national security, and ss 34(3) and 36(2). These certificates will be 'conclusive evidence' of relevant items. Those under ss 23(2) and 24(3) are subject, however, to an appeal to the tribunal – this is now the Upper Tribunal. Those issued under s 34(3) – Parliamentary privilege – are not challengeable elsewhere in line with Parliamentary privilege.[1] More crucially, there is a veto in relation to the IC's decision and enforcement notices which could cover those issued under s 36. See below (para 1.239) for detail and s 53.

1   See *R v Chaytor and Others* [2010] UKSC 52 for a recent illustration of the limits of such privilege into allegations of false accounting by MPs – this case followed on from the notorious FOI investigations into MPs expenses.

1.42   The Phillis *Review of Government Communications* (Cabinet Office January 2004) recommended that FOIA should be implemented with an 'overriding presumption of disclosure' (p 23). His view was that Government should announce that Ministers should not use the veto and that class exemptions should be replaced as far as possible by exemptions based on a harm test. This was especially important in relation to the exemption which restricts analyses on which policy is built. There should be use of the Scottish and Welsh tests of 'substantial harm or prejudice'. Replies should be met within 20 days under an 'all purpose limit' and, in complex cases involving significant issues of public interest, the limit of £600 as the cost of providing information should be removed. As opposed to the endorsement of Phillis' recommendations on government communications (para 2.114 below), these proposals were received with appreciable neutrality.

FURTHER REVIEWS

1.43   A review of the Act was conducted by a private research enterprise Frontier Economics with a view towards review of the Act by the Government in 2006.[1] Aspects of the FOIA were examined by Paul Dacre in his review of the Thirty Year Rule in 2009.[2]

[1]   http://webarchive.nationalarchives.gov.uk/+/http:/www.dca.gov.uk/foi/reference/
      foi-independent-review.pdf.
[2]   *Review of the 30 Year Rule* (2009) at www.30yearrulereview.org.uk.

PREPARING FOR THE ACT[1]

1.44   It has to be realised that the preparation for the FOIA has been undertaken with preparations for the introduction of the Environmental Information Regulations 2004 (EIR), SI 2004/3391. The implementation of the latter is an EU requirement in order to comply with a Directive (2003/4/EC, OJ L 41/26, 14.2.2003) and EU Treaty obligations under Art 175(1) EC. The regulations, which come into effect on the same day as the access provisions of FOIA (1 January 2005), are dealt with in ch 8 (paras 8.192 et seq). There has been an Advisory Group on Openness in the Public Sector advising the Lord Chancellor/ Secretary of State. An Access to Information Project Board has also advised the Department of Constitutional Affairs (DCA), now the Ministry of Justice (MoJ). The DCA established a monitoring system within the Information Rights Division of the DCA to advise on eg key performance targets and implementation of the access to information monitoring regime across government. A clearing house has been established within the MoJ to assist departments with difficult or sensitive requests or cross-departmental requests.[2] This sets out guidance on when requests should be referred to the central section. Detailed work has been carried out on how to establish specifications for IT systems to manage

FOI and EIR inquiries. Liaison has been exercised between the DCA (MoJ), IC Office and the National Audit Office on a guide for departmental preparations. The MoJ assumes central responsibility for information on FOIA guidance on records processing and management, exemptions (after consultation with the Attorney General). The MoJ has been at the centre of a Government Information Strategy for central government covering the public, the media and Parliament. As shall be seen the FOIA has profound implications for the Public Records Office, now renamed the National Archives. Central government communications and information responsibilities are now within the Office of Public Sector Information (now part of National Archives) having previously been within the Office of e-Envoy and successors (see para 2.34).

¹ See FOI Annual Report HC 6 (2002–03) on bringing into force provisions in FOIA not yet fully in force; and HC 5 (2004–05) and *Government Reply* Cm 6470 (2005).
² http://www.justice.gov.uk/guidance/foi-procedural-referring.htm.

1.45   There has been nothing less than a revolution in government use of IT resources in the last ten years. This point is examined in chapter 2 (para 2.34 et seq).

1.46   And yet, despite the flurry of activity, the Commons Select Committee on Constitutional Affairs criticised the state of ill-preparedness of many public authorities for FOI. Health, in particular, followed by local government caused concern although the committee was impressed by the police preparation, as evidenced by the Association of Chief Police Officers (ACPO).[1] ACPO have also agreed with members of the judiciary a protocol on disclosure of police information in family proceedings (see www.dca.gov.uk and para 10.22 below), which has been updated.[2] This gives guidance on how to apply, and how to challenge, refusals to disclose.

¹ *First Report* HC 79 I & II (2004–05).
² http://www.met.police.uk/scd/specialist_units/Police_Family_Disclosure_Protocol.pdf.

1.47   The ICO has prepared guidance on a very wide range of deatails under the FOIA 2000 and DPA 1998 covering: personal information; information received in confidence; the public interest; legal professional privilege; commercial interests; information accessible by other means; information intended for future publication; and frequently asked questions in records management as well as on exemptions.[1] The MoJ has provided detailed guidance on handling requests as well as on exemptions and other items (www.moj.gov.uk). The lists are growing. Much work had been done on other areas such as fees and refusal notices; how to communicate information; identification of vexatious and repetitious requests; development of policy around disability and other access issues; and records held by National Archives. A central 'clearing house' has been established in the MoJ to assist departments with difficult or sensitive requests or cross-departmental requests.[2]

¹ http://www.ico.gov.uk/.
² http://www.justice.gov.uk/guidance/foi-procedural-referring.htm.

HOW THE ACT WORKS

Publication schemes

1.48 Every public authority is under a duty to adopt and maintain a 'publication scheme' which relates to information published automatically by the authority and which will be approved by the Commissioner – approval may be for a specified period. As a result of the Publication Scheme Development and Maintenance Initiative the ICO introduced a model publication scheme that all public sector organisations should have adopted from 1 January 2009.[1] The authority has to publish its scheme but is given discretion to publish its scheme in 'such manner as it sees fit' though this may be subject to approval by the Commissioner.[1] The scheme in terms of both contents and operation, will be reviewable on ordinary principles of judicial review. The authority will state what it intends to publish and it will be under a duty to publish such information. Failure to publish could be a breach of a 'legitimate expectation'. Could the IC investigate a complaint concerning a failure to publish information in a scheme? Section 50 refers to a 'request for information' which is not dealt with in accordance with Part I, which includes s 19. However, a 'request for information' seems to be confined to s 1 requests (see s 8). The power to award an enforcement notice under s 52 is not so confined and may be awarded where an authority has failed to comply with any of the requirements of Part I. The authority will also be under a duty to review the scheme from time to time. The scheme will specify the classes of information which the authority publishes or intends to publish; the manner in which it is or is intended to be published and whether it will be publicly available free of charge. The ICO launched a consultation for revising publication schemes in September 2011.

[1] http://www.ico.gov.uk/what_we_cover/freedom_of_information/publication_schemes.aspx.
[2] If, for instance, publication was in a form which prevented effective access by the requester.

1.49 In adopting or reviewing a scheme, an authority must have regard to the public interest in allowing access to the public to information held by the authority and also in the publication of reasons for decisions made by the authority. This latter will refer to reasons generally for decisions as opposed to reasons for decisions under the FOIA 2000 for refusals etc. It is regrettable that a fully fledged duty to give reasons was not contained in primary legislation. In relation to publication in the public interest, the IC is given power to approve content but not to compel his view on the authority. Where an authority ignores the IC's opinion, the Home Office said this would be a breach of what is now s 19(1). The IC can issue an enforcement notice (EN) to indicate the steps required to be taken by the authority to comply with s 19(1), the Home Office believed. Ultimate sanction for non-compliance with an EN is punishment by the court as contempt. The Act seems to suggest that the 'remedy' is a refusal to approve a scheme or its revocation where in some sense it is inadequate.

1.50 Where an authority failed to publish information under the original Bill in accordance with its scheme, this could be remedied by the issue of a Practice Recommendation (PR) by the Commissioner under what is now s 48. This may have been correct under the original Bill, but not under the FOIA 2000 which restricts the matters on which a PR may be issued to those contained in the Code. The first Code did not deal with publication schemes. Arguments could be advanced, however, that a publication scheme could be enforceable through public law process on the basis of legitimate expectation as we saw above.

1.51 Publication schemes could be very beneficial from the point of view of greater openness. They could include departmental rules, manuals and guidance as well as the kinds of information that has to be published by agencies in the USA under the US FOIA 1966, as amended. The Department of Health, the Department of Work and Pensions and the Inland Revenue publish internal guidance and summaries of decisions as well as the redress manual in the latter case. Information about mission, objectives and functions and who is responsible for decisions, contacts and board meetings together with agendas and minutes should be published. Regulatory decisions by PAs should be published. It might further include information which has been requested on, say, three previous occasions or all information requested and previously released – through, for instance, a disclosure log which is a web-based list of FOI requests and links to documents linked to those requests. It could cover information on government contracts.[1]

[1]   See Evidence of the Select Committee HC 570 I, paras 45–47 (1998–99).

1.52 Approval for a scheme may be revoked six months after notice of revocation is given by the IC. Where there is a revocation, or where the IC refuses to approve a scheme, the authority must be given a statement of the reasons for such a decision. This will clearly support a challenge by the authority but it is not subject to appeal to the tribunal[1] by the authority. Presumably they may seek judicial review.

[1]   See FOIA 2000, s 57 which only allows appeals against Enforcement, Information and Decision Notices; see below.

1.53 The Commissioner may also approve model publication schemes for different classes of authorities prepared by the IC or others (eg 10,000 parish councils, parish meetings, schools, universities). Where so approved, authorities within a relevant class adopting a scheme without modification will require no further approval. Similar provisions apply to expiration of approval, revocation and refusal to approve as apply to schemes in s 19.

1.54 Publication schemes were introduced on a rolling programme starting with central government, Parliament, the Welsh National Assembly and non-departmental public bodies (NDPBs) subject to the 1997 Code on Access in November 2002. In February 2003 local government was to be included (excepting police authorities). These latter were to be finalised by June 2003 together with the Crown Prosecution Service, Serious Fraud Office and armed forces. By October 2003, NHS bodies were to be included and schools, universities and remaining NDPBs. By June 2004, all remaining public authorities were to be included. This has taken place.

1.55 There have been some important concerns in the process of producing publication schemes (PSs). The Freedom of Information Campaign believes that the IC and government encouraged PAs to publish only existing information that is already published and not new information.[1] This was denied. A class should represent a continuing commitment to publish all the information falling within a class. Many, the Campaign felt, were not classes at all but one-off single publications. The IC in the 2002–03 *Annual Report* stated that PSs tended to publish existing information rather than new information. It was felt that, despite provisions in numerous overseas statutes that internal guidance and advice should be published, not enough was being done to encourage this. The Department of Health had published three online collections of internal guidance covering business planning, finance and personnel matters. The Inland Revenue publishes internal guidance and guidance on customers aimed externally including the purchasing manual and redress manual. The IC's expectation was that future schemes will set out the intention to publish routinely information which 'was previously not available at all or only available on request.'[2] DEFRA and the Welsh Assembly were singled out for good practices. Interesting features included:

1.56 Facts and analysis of facts behind decisions – *Your Right to Know – Background Material* was published, as was *Preparation of Draft Legislation – Background Material* on the FOIA by the Home Office.

PURPOSES OF SCHEMES

1.57 The Lord Chancellor's Department (now MoJ) stated as follows: 'The purpose of the PS is to ensure that a large amount of information is readily available to members of the public ie without the need for specific consideration under FOIA, and to inform the public of the extent of material that is available. By "readily available" we mean that the information is available: on the LCD website; another website; may be purchased from the Stationery Office; may be obtained from a public library; may be supplied immediately on receipt of a telephone call or letter to the department'.

MINUTES

1.58 Should these be draft or revised? Many bodies initially opted for the latter. The ICO has stated that 'There are a number of considerations which might lead authorities to decide to publish unconfirmed minutes if they are aware that a lengthy time delay may ensue prior to the publication of confirmed minutes in the publication scheme. Perhaps the main factor would be the ability, in any event, for individuals to request copies of the unconfirmed minutes via their s 1 access rights, where they are aware that the minutes will not be available via the publication scheme for a period of time. On each such request the authority would need to decide whether s 21 would apply, (could the information be considered to be reasonably accessible to the applicant if it is not scheduled to be published for many months). Whilst in some cases s 22 may apply (see para 1.118), the exemption is qualified in so far as its use would only apply in cases where it is reasonable in all the circumstances to withhold the information until the intended date of publication. In each case disclosure was agreed then consideration would also need to be given as to including the information within the publication scheme in any event.' Excessive delays in the publication of minutes are therefore likely to generate individual requests which will require a full response from the authority within the 20-day limit. In considering the request the authority would need to give full consideration to the available exemptions and their application to the individual request. In many cases therefore, it may prove prudent for the authority to simply include unconfirmed minutes in the publication scheme, together with a warning that they are as yet unconfirmed and may be subject to change. Minutes and papers of all departmental advisory committees which contain non-governmental representatives should be published and this is done by the Inland Revenue, the Food Standards Agency and DEFRA.

DISCLOSURE LOG

1.59　The DCA has disclosed information made available under the 1997 Code on Access (www.dca.gov.uk/foi/publicationsscheme/htm). The Welsh Assembly publishes Cabinet Minutes. A pervasive feature in FOI practice has been the publication of disclosure logs identifying information released under FOIA by authorities sometimes on a selective basis.

INFORMATION ON CONTRACTS

1.60　Paragraph 42 of the Lord Chancellor's draft s 45 code states that there should be a considerable amount of information in schemes about contracts and the way they are awarded. This was not in the final version of the code but a commitment was given to revise the 'final version'. In fact, the CFOI found that information about contracts was generally small. The Treasury Solicitor's Department was one of the few to publish details of contract values, and then only on those valued at over £30,000. 'Commercial sensitivity' was frequently cited as a reason for not publishing information about values. The Department for International Development and DTI and DCA all developed helpful practices. The Campaign found little evidence of information on contract performance standards, performance reviews as well as results of contract performance although this was urged by government. There was no evidence of publication of the existence of 'confidentiality clauses' between contractors and PAs. The Office of Government Commerce (part of HM Treasury) publishes detailed guidance on contracting and FOI[3] and the subject of contracts has featured in many complaints and investigations and appeals as will be seen.[4] The ICO has also published guidance on contracting.[5]

[1]　See open letter to the IC from the Campaign, 13 September 2002.
[2]　Campaign for FOI *Publication Schemes Good Practice* (February 2004). A list of good practice web sites is contained on p 7.

³   http://www.ogc.gov.uk/documents/OGC_FOI_and_Civil_Procurement_guidance.pdf.
⁴   See para 1.281 below.
⁵   http://www.ico.gov.uk/upload/documents/library/freedom_of_information/detailed_specialist_
    guides/awareness_guidance_5_annexe_-_public_sector_contracts.pdf

INFORMATION ASSET REGISTER

1.61   This is published by HMSO.[1] It concerns the holdings by departments and bodies of unpublished information. This would be a useful addition to schemes and should include newly created files that are not published (see para 2.35).

¹   http://www.opsi.gov.uk/advice/crown-copyright/copyright-guidance/information-asset-
    register-and-freedom-of-information.

1.62   Shortly before the access provisions of FOIA came into effect, the Lord Chancellor announced that information requested by a journalist would, if not exempt, be placed on the web. This, the press argued, would mean the FOIA would not be used by investigative journalists because they would be denied a coup. In fact, the FOIA has been widely used by the press and media.

1.63   The idea behind schemes was proactive availability of information by those covered by the FOIA 2000. At the time of the passage of the legislation through Parliament, IT was still in its infancy. Ever increasingly sophisticated search engines and growing familairity with online information retrieval have caused some to question whether schemes have become anachronistic. In setting a positive duty on proactive publication they provide a valuable service and increasing development of IT by government should enhance schemes' capability and not diminish it. Information under schemes was also to be available in paper form. We look at the use of IT by government in chapter 2 (see para 2.34).

Applying for access[1]

1.64   Requests for information under FOIA 2000 may be so broad that any government or public activity will be included. The Act covers 'recorded information'. 'Any person' – it is not restricted to a British national or EU citizen – making a request for information to a public authority is entitled to be informed in writing by the authority whether it 'holds' information of the description specified in the request. If that is the case, the PA must communicate the information to the requester. The right is a right to 'information' but documents may be requested. MoJ guidance states that, 'It may often be the case that the easiest way to provide the information is to supply a copy of the relevant document, since a document may contain the information that has been requested. However, it may also contain a great deal of other information.'[2] The tribunal has ruled on several occasions that the accuracy of information held is not its concern – the point is has all the information held and disclosable been disclosed.[3]

¹   Helpful guidance to the FOIA is provided by the Ministry of Justice and the Information
    Commissioner's Office: http://www.justice.gov.uk/guidance/foi-procedural-information.htm#

information. The Campaign for Freedom of Information has also produced guides on the Act and the Environmental Information Regulations, eg http://foia.blogspot.com/2009/09/updated-ico-freedom-of-information.html.

2   Note 1 above.

3   *Simmons v IC EA/2005/0003; J Nisbet v IC EA/2007/0031.*

HOLDS INFORMATION

1.65   Guidance attempts to clarify what is meant by 'holds' and there is now a corpus of case law on this (see 1.65 below). The authority does not have to create new information to comply with a request. However, compiling a list or schedule of information from existing information is not creating 'new' information: FS50070854. Extracting information from existing files by manual manipulation or electronic searching is not creating new information: the information already exists. However, there may well be costs considerations under s 12 where compilation is necessary.[1] Information from existing databases is 'held'.[2] However, where access to online data sets is provided under contract the terms of the contract may indicate that data is not held by the authority.[3] See FS50318306 in relation to a request to King's College Cambridge for information about King's College School.

1   *Johnston v IC and MoJ* EA/2006/0085.
2   *Home Office v IC* EA/2008/0027.
3   *G Marlow v IC* EA/2005/0031.

1.66   The term 'holds' does not include information held solely on behalf of another. The expression does cover information held principally or partly for another and the authority exercises control over the information. It will not be held if it is trade union information about employment with the public authority; constituency or 'party political' information; or purely personal information from spouses or family. Diaries for official use by Ministers which are kept by officials are likely to be covered, for instance. The Act's headnote makes 'provision for the disclosure of information "held" by PAs or persons providing services for them'. This is a broad formulation. If the authority does 'hold' such information, requesters have a right to have the information communicated to them. The authority may request additional information which it reasonably requires to identify and locate the information requested. Where a requester is informed of this requirement, the authority does not have to comply with the request until the further information is supplied (FOIA 2000, s 1).

1.67   The right to have information 'held' communicated above has effect subject to what is known as the situation where the 'duty to confirm or deny' that the authority holds information as requested does not arise. This is known as the 'NCND' (neither confirm nor deny) provision. Confirmation or denial would itself undermine an exemption. The authority is excused from complying with the above duty of disclosure where the information requested is exempt under any relevant provisions of the FOIA 2000, Part II, although the public interest in disclosure will have to be considered. The duty does not cover bodies that are excluded from the Act. The information covered by the basic duty is information held at the time the request is received although 'account may be taken of any amendment or deletion made between that time and the time when the information is to be communicated' where this amendment or deletion would have been made regardless of the request. This could have both positive and negative aspects for the requester.

1.68 Case law shows that where the authority is merely providing storage for information and exercises no control in creating, adding to, removing or editing information it has no control and does not hold the information. In *Digby Cameron v IC* EA/2008/0010, a council provided funding and administrative support for a coroner held the coroner's case records solely on behalf of the coroner as the latter had sole statutory control over the information in the records. If the authority can allow access, or remove, add to or delete information and the budget for holding is part of the overall budget of the authority, and enquiries about the information are dealt with by the authority, the information will also be held by the authority.[1] In FS50266932 (05/08/10) the complainant made a request to the BBC for a series of statistics relating to annual payments made by its pension scheme and copies of all correspondence between the BBC's human resources department and BBC Pension Trust relating to the financial state of the pension fund. The BBC responded that the statistical information was held on behalf of the BBC Pension Trust and therefore fell outside the definition of information held by a public authority under FOIA 2000, s 3(2)(a). It also responded that it does not hold information falling within the scope of the request for correspondence. The Commissioner decided that the BBC handled the request in accordance with the Act. In FS50314236 (02/08/2010) the complainant requested full details of the income of the Chief Executive of the Isle of Anglesey County Council. The council stated that the individual referred to in the request was its Interim Managing Director and that he was employed by a third-party company to whom the council paid a fee for his services. The council stated that the individual concerned was employed directly by the council in a limited role for which he received a nominal fee. The latter was disclosed. The complainant did not accept that the council did not hold further information about the income of the Interim Managing Director and the council maintained that it had disclosed all the relevant information it held. The Commissioner was satisfied that, on the balance of probabilities, the council did not hold further information although procedural breaches in relation to the council's handling of the request were found.[2]

[1]   *McBride v IC* EA/2007/0105.
[2]   See *M Hood v IC* EA/2010/0167.

1.69 Searches may be requested and may involve FOIA 2000, s 3 where information is held by another body on behalf of the authority (FS50180545). Searches may be onerous but s 12 on costs is then likely to come into consideration.[1] An authority is not expected to conduct research or create new information to comply with a request.[2] However the House of Lords has ruled that 'barnardising' information, ie coding it so as not to reveal personal data, is not creating new information and was therefore held.[3] However, compiling a list of documents held has been ruled not to create new documents (FS50155552).

[1]   *Quinn v IC and Home Office* EA/2006/0010.
[2]   *Home Office v IC* EA/2008/0027.
[3]   Common Services Agency v Scottish IC [2008] UKHL 47 (see para 7.24 below).

1.70   A request for information must be in writing, state the name of the applicant and an address for correspondence, and must describe the information requested. A request is to be treated as being in writing where it is transmitted by electronic means, is received in legible form and is capable of being used for subsequent reference. An email address would seem adequate but the Act states that 'a request for information' is one 'which states the name of the applicant' (s 8). A non-electronic address would have to be provided for non-electronic documents. The government resisted calls for mandatory indexes of files for bodies covered by the Act. If publication schemes work effectively (above) they should go some way to remedying this. Information Asset Registers should also be consulted (see para 2.44).

FEES AND EXCESSIVE COST

1.71   The authority is not obliged to comply with a request under s 1 of the FOIA 2000 if the cost of so doing exceeds the 'appropriate limit'. This is by virtue of s 12. The authority is not exempted from its obligation under s 1(1) (a) which entitles the applicant to be informed of whether the authority holds information requested unless the cost of compliance with that obligation exceeds the appropriate limit. This limit, which may be variable 'in relation to different cases', will be set in regulations. The basic limit is £600 for central government, the armed forces and Parliament – £450 for non-central government PAs – according to regulations approved in November 2004 (SI 2004/3244). ICO guidance states that where an authority underestimates a fee it cannot claim an additional amount. Refunds should be made where it overcalculates. Estimates must be reasonable[1] and 'sensible, realistic and supported by cogent evidence'.[2] A fees estimate does not have to be served before a search commences.[3] Where two or more requests for information are made to a public authority by a single person, or by different persons who appear to the authority to be acting in concert or in pursuance of a campaign, the authority will calculate the estimated cost of compliance with any request as the estimated total cost of compliance with them all. The circumstances in which these criteria are to take effect will be prescribed. It is hoped that they operate in a way that does not defeat requests for information because the information happens to cover a popular issue. The costs and manner of their estimation are provided for by regulations.[4] Charges may be made for 'disbursements', ie photocopying and postage. Under reg 4(3) in a case in which this regulation has effect, a public authority may, for the purpose of its estimate, take account only of the costs it reasonably expects to incur in relation to the request in:
(a)   determining whether it holds the information;
(b)   locating the information, or a document which may contain the information;

(c) retrieving the information, or a document which may contain the information; and

(d) extracting the information from a document containing it.

Charges may not be made for considering or removing exempt information.[5] However, costs involved in use of, eg, equipment to extract such information may be charged as disbursements. Charges may not made for calculating the public interest in disclosure.[6] In costing time spent on a request a sum of £25 per hour is used regardless of the level of official. Section 12 is a safeguard against a large number of requests, not against repeat requests, which is covered by s 14.[7]

[1] *Urmenyi v IC and LB Sutton* EA/2006/0093.

[2] *Randall v IC and MHPRA* EA/2006/0004.

[3] *Quinn v IC and Home Office* EA/2006/0010.

[4] SI 2004/3244.

[5] *Jenkins v IC and DEFRA* EA/2006/0067; *DBERR v IC and FoE* EA/2007/0072; and *Chief Constable of S Yorks Police v IC* [2011] EWHC 44 (Admin) (cf however para 51).

[6] This would seem to follow from ICO Guidance that 'the actual or anticipated time spent in considering exemptions' cannot be included in a fees notice: http://www.ico. gov.uk/upload/documents/library/freedom_of_information/practical_application/ redactingandextractinginformation.pdf.

[7] *R Brown v IC and National Archives* EA/2006/0088; and see *W Urmeni v IC and LB of Sutton* EA/2006/0093.

FEES FOR DISCLOSURES WHERE COSTS EXCEEDS APPROPRIATE LIMIT

1.72 A clause added in the Lords Committee (and incorporated in the Act) allows a public authority to charge for the communication of any information whose communication is not required by FOIA 2000, s 1, because of the cost of compliance under s 12 and it is not otherwise required by law. The fee charged will be in accordance with regulations made by the Secretary of State (s 13(1)). Maximum fees and the manner of prescribing fees may be laid down in regulations. MoJ guidance states that 'where section 13 does apply, Regulation 7 states the maximum amount that can be charged, although there is nothing to prevent authorities from charging less than this or charging no fee at all. If the costs exceed the appropriate limit, the maximum charge is the sum of:

(a) the costs which the authority was entitled to take into account in calculating that the appropriate limit was exceeded (see explanation of Reg 4(3) above); and

(b) the costs of informing the requester whether the information is held, and of communicating the information to the requester. When the appropriate limit is exceeded, these costs can also include the cost of staff time in carrying out these activities (calculated at a flat £25 per hour).

For example, if it takes 30 hours of staff time to locate, sort and edit information in response to a request, costing £750 (based on the standard rate of £25 per hour), and the cost of photocopying and sending out the information is £100, the authority can charge up to a total of £850 for answering the request'[1] – surprisingly the £600 waiver does not seem to apply. Or the request may be refused, as explained above. The Regulations described in the following section set out the appropriate limit. This provision does not apply where fees for any disclosure are contained in any other enactment. VAT will not apply where information is provided under FOIA 2000 by a public authority. It will apply to provision of information under a publication scheme where provision for fees is contained in the scheme and fees are charged. Information provided by archives or trading funds which is covered by other legislation may charge fees in accordance with that legislation and are exempt from FOIA fees requirements.

[1] http://www.justice.gov.uk/guidance/foi-procedural-fees.htm#calculating_the_maximum_fee_section_13.

FEES NOTICES

1.73 An authority may give an applicant for information, and within the time set for compliance with s 1 of the FOIA 2000, a notice in writing (a 'fees notice') stating the fee to be charged for compliance with s 1(1).[1] Compliance with s 1(1) by the authority does not have to begin until the fee is paid within a period of three months from the day on which the fees notice is given. Unless special statutory fees for information are in effect, fees will be determined in accordance with regulations made by the Secretary of State (above).

[1] FOIA 2000, s 9.

1.74 The details of what may be charged under SI 2004/3244 and contained in a fees notice have been explained. PAs have a discretion to charge a fee if above the statutory levels, answer without charge, or refuse to answer (see para 1.72 above). All PAs will be able to charge the full cost of disbursements including copying or printing and sending out information. Special provision is made under s 12(4) for two or more requests for information either by one person, or persons who appear to the PA to be acting in concert or in pursuance of a campaign. Regulation 5 specifies the circumstances under which the regulation applies: it applies where two or more requests are for information by one person etc which is on the same or a similar subject matter and the requests are received by the PA within a 60-working-day[1] consecutive period. The estimated costs of complying with any of the requests is taken to be the total costs which may be taken into account by the PA in complying with all of them. Regulation 6 provides for the maximum fee a PA may specify in a fees notice under s 9 of the FOIA as a charge for complying with a s 1(1) request. Regulation 7 makes provision for s 13 and maximum fees where cost exceeds the appropriate limit. The regulations do not apply if other enactments lay down fees to be charged for disclosure. FOI fees do not apply to 'Publication Schemes' (PS) information (Code paras 19 and 20, but subsequently revised). Where bodies are entitled to levy a charge for information, such as Trading Funds, and which are asked to provide information relating to commercial interests, they should be able to charge the full market rate for their work (see para 2.40). If a fee is not to be paid, the PA should identify any information that may be of interest and which is free of charge. Fees for unstructured personal data (see paras 7.10 et seq below) under DPA 1998 (as amended by FOIA 2000) will be subject to FOIA 2000 upper 'appropriate' limits as above, ie £600 and £450 (SI 2004/3244, reg 3(1)).[2]

1   Regulation 5(3) defines working days
2   The usual subject access fee under DPA 1998 is £10 (see para 7.151 below).

COMPLIANCE TIME

1.75   An authority to which a request has been made must comply with s 1(1) of the FOIA 2000 promptly and not later than the 20th 'working day' (s 10(6)) following the date of receipt. It excludes Saturdays, Sundays, Christmas Day, Good Friday and bank holidays as defined. This is subject to s 10(2), which states that where a fees notice is given and payment duly made the period of working days from the day of notice and ending with the day of receipt of the fee is to be disregarded in calculating the 20 days. The period of 20 days may be extended by regulations to 60 working days. So far, four cases, the guidance states, have been identified for such treatment but these have been added to (and see SI 2004/3364 and SI 2010/2768 bringing academy schools into line with other schools re extensions to 30 days in school vacation):

'i)   to deal with school holidays, since the school will not be staffed at that time;

ii)   when frontline units of the armed forces are impossible to reach for operational reasons;

iii)   if a public authority needs to consult posts, governments or companies abroad to obtain information; and

iv)   when the National Archives need to determine whether requested information in a transferred public record that has not been designated as open information is exempt, or whether the duty to confirm or deny is excluded under Part II.'

And see now for Northern Ireland, SI 2009/1369.

1.76   Regulations may also prescribe different numbers of days in relation to different cases and confer a discretion on the commissioner.

1.77   In cases where a public interest disclosure is being considered, the public authority does not have to comply with s 1(1)(a) or (b) 'until such time as is reasonable in the circumstances'. This does not affect the time by which a notice under s 17(1) must be given. This means that a public authority that wishes to claim that any provision within Part II of FOIA on exemptions in relation to the duty to confirm or deny is relevant, or that the information is exempt, must give the applicant a notice stating three things: the notice must state that fact; it must specify the exemption in question; and it must state why the exemption applies (if that would not otherwise be apparent). This must be done within the 20-day period. Where the public interest is being considered, under s 17(2) the PA should provide an estimate of the date by which a decision is expected to be reached (see para 1.108 below). This should be realistic (eg taking into account third party consultation). If exceeded, there should be an apology. The applicant should be kept informed and a record of excess times should be maintained. The guidance for officials states:

'If the information being sought has to be considered under an exemption to which the public interest test applies ... then the timescale [twenty days] is extended by a "reasonable period". Although there is no statutory time limit on how long the "reasonable period" may be, if you are considering the public interest test you must, under section 17(2), give an estimate of the date by which you expect to reach such a decision.' (*Procedural Guidance* chapter 6)

The ICO guidance states that an authority should be prepared to justify to the IC time taken beyond 20 days (in addition to the initial 20 days) to consider the public interest.[1]

[1] http://www.ico.gov.uk/upload/documents/library/freedom_of_information/detailed_specialist_ guides/timeforcompliance.pdf.

METHOD OF COMMUNICATION

1.78   Under FOIA 2000, s 11, the authority must supply the information to the applicant in the applicant's preferred form of communication where this has been expressed by the applicant 'so far as reasonably practicable'. The means are in 'permanent form', ie paper or another form acceptable to the applicant; provision of a reasonable opportunity to inspect the record containing the information; the provision of a digest or summary of the information in permanent form or in another form acceptable to the applicant. Where it cannot reasonably comply with the applicant's request, the public authority shall notify the applicant of the reasons for its determination. Subject to the applicant's preference, the public authority may communicate information by any means which are reasonable in the circumstances. In assessing whether it is reasonably practicable to communicate information by a particular means, the public authority may have regard to all the circumstances including the cost.

1.79   The Protection of Freedoms Bill 2011 added new provisions to s 11. The amendment provides that where information requested is a data set, or which forms part of a data set, and the applicant requests that information held by a PA is communicated in electronic form, then the PA must, as far as reasonably practicable, provide the information to the requester in an electronic form that is capable of re-use, ie a re-usable format (on re-use of public sector information, see para 2.40). The duty is not absolute because there may be IT problems and questions of cost. A re-usable format is one where the information is available in machine-readable form using open standards enabling its re-use and manipulation. The new duty does not apply to hard-copy data sets but the existing duty to comply with the requester's preference (above) still applies 'so far as it is reasonably practicable to do so'. A new sub-s 5 provides a definition of data set: it is a collection of information held in electronic form obtained or recorded by a PA for the purpose of providing the PA with information in the provision of a service by that PA or the carrying out of any other function by the PA. The information should be factual in nature and 'raw' or source data, and not an official statistic under the Statistics and Registration Service Act 2007 – statistics are produced and published under the 2007 Act. It should not be the product of interpretation or analysis. The amendment requires that data sets have not been materially altered or have been 'value-added' since obtained or recorded. The amendment allows for the data set to be available for re-use on specified conditions (see para 2.40), including: the copyright is only owned by the PA; and the information is disclosed under FOIA 2000. A specified licence for re-use will be produced. Under FOIA 2000, s 19, PAs must include in their publication schemes any data sets they hold and updated versions of data sets unless the PA is satisfied that it is not appropriate for the datas et to be so published. There are further requirements regarding copyright and specified licences.

FOIA DISCLOSURES ARE TO THE 'WHOLE WORLD'

1.80 Disclosures under the Act cannot be selective. If the requester has a malicious motive in making a request, that is not sufficient under FOIA 2000 to refuse a request. An exemption must be relied upon. A variety of exemptions would be relevant if a risk to personal safety were involved. In *K McCluskey v IC & PPS NI*[1] EA/2007/0056 there was a was a request for information about police officers involved in legal proceedings in which the requester was acquitted. The tribunal noted that there was a 'fundamental difference between a right to information, as under FOIA, and the voluntary discretionary disclosure of information by a PA, pursuant to agreement, as took place here' (para 14). FOIA 2000, s 40(2)2 applied by IC. There are also dangers of agreements regarding voluntary disclosure where general access is not made – it could foster or lead to favouritism, abuse and a lack of transparency. In *Kennedy v IC* [2011] EWCA Civ 367 the court of appeal remitted a case concerning FOIA 2000, s 32(2) (below) to the tribunal in order to consider the impact of Strasbourg case law and the Human Rights Act 1998, art 10 on rights to freedom of information for a journalist who faced a refusal from a body with a monopoly of state information rights thereby interfering with the journalist's freedom of speech rights (para 1.155 below).[1]

[1]   See *Tarsasag v Hungary* [2009] ECHR 618 and *Kenedi v Hungary* [2009] ECHR 78 for the ECtHR rulings.

VEXATIOUS OR REPEATED REQUESTS

1.81 An authority is not obliged to deal with a request which is vexatious. No statutory definition is provided. Guidance indicates that a person cannot be a vexatious requester: it is the *request* that is vexatious. Authorities are allowed not to comply with a request from a person which is 'identical or substantially similar' to a previous request from that person unless a reasonable interval has elapsed between the two requests. This is left very open and could leave a great deal to judgement which might confound a genuine applicant. It aims to deal with repetitious requests but a slight variation in request could be crucial from an applicant's point of view but considered of no significance by the authority. Where there are repeated requests, PAs should consider use of their disclosure log or website and indicate this to applicants. Both the IC and MoJ websites provide guidance on 'vexatious requests'.[1] The basic tests are: would the request be regarded as obsessive, constitute harassment, cause distress, cause a significant burden, is it designed to be disruptive or annoying, or lack any serious purpose or objective (bearing in mind motive is not a factor in FOIA requests)? Advice and assistance (below) do not have to be given to a requester making a vexatious request.

[1]   http://www.ico.gov.uk/upload/documents/library/freedom_of_information/detailed_specialist_
        guides/22_06_09_foi_advice_and_assistance_v2.pdf.

1.82   The case law has shown that where a person adopted a haranguing tone and made 20 campaigning requests in 90 pieces of correspondence over two years the requester was vexatious.[1] Authorities should not be over-quick in making presumptions.[2] Guidance is provided in D Young v IC[3] and on repeated requests.[4] A vexatious request does not necessarily entail that an appeal is vexatious.[5]

[1]   *Coggins v IC* EA/2007/0130. See FS50290108 and FS50288182.
[2]   *V Ahilathirunayagam v IC* EA/2006/0070.
[3]   EA/2010/0004.
[4]   *M Jacobs v IC* EA/2010/0040.
[5]   *J Hossack v IC* EA/2007/0024.

DUTY TO PROVIDE ADVICE AND ASSISTANCE TO REQUESTERS

1.83   An amendment at Report stage in the Lords introduced a duty to provide advice and assistance to requesters 'so far as it would be reasonable to expect the authority to do so (FOIA 2000, s 16(1)).' Conforming with the code of practice issued under s 45 (below) is taken to be compliance with this duty. The objective of assistance is to assist the applicant to clarify the information sought: for example, providing access to detailed catalogues and indexes 'where available' (Code para 10) and a general response setting out options. It will be very important where requests are unclear. In the 'Foreword' the s 45 Code adds that other statutes may be relevant in how a PA discharges its duty. The Disability Discrimination Act 1995, the Race Relations Act 1976 as amended by the Race Relations (Amendment) Act 2000 (Equality Act 2010) are referred to. PAs should publish their procedures for dealing with requests for information. Where a request cannot be made in writing, an applicant should be advised to contact a Citizens Advice Bureau (CAB) or 'in exceptional circumstances' the PA might offer to take a note of the application over the phone and then send it to the applicant for confirmation and then to use the note as a request. PAs should be flexible in providing the advice most appropriate to the circumstances of the applicant. Advice and assistance may be applicant-specific and MPs could not expect authorities to act as their research assistant.[1] Advice may suggest setting out a request particularising the items required.[2]

[1]   *HM Treasury v IC* EA/2007/0001.
[2]   *C Lamb v IC* EA/2006/0046.

Clarifying the request

1.84   The Guidance advises on assistance in clarifying requests. The PA may ask for more detail to identify and locate the information requested. Assistance should, as far as reasonably practicable, be provided by the PA. The aim in seeking clarification is not to establish motive on the part of the requester but to clarify the nature of information required. Motive is irrelevant under FOIA 2000. Refusal to disclose has to be based on a FOIA exemption. Explanations should be given as to why further information is sought from a requester. Assistance on such points might include: providing an outline of the different kinds of information which might meet the terms of the request; providing access to detailed catalogues and indexes 'where these are available' (para 10); providing a general response setting out options for further information that could be provided on request. The list, it is advised, is not exhaustive and again flexibility is recommended. Requesters will not have access to identifiers or file numbers unless this is provided by the PA. Advice may cover fees (above).

PUBLIC AUTHORITIES

1.85 'Public authorities' covered by the Act are those contained in s 3 of and Sch 1 to the FOIA 2000 (see Annex A) or which are designated by order under s 5, or which is a publicly owned company as defined by s 6.[1] Section 6 has been amended by the Protection of Freedoms Bill to include companies owned jointly by PAs. The definition of 'owned' is amended to cover joint public ownership, eg bodies such as waste disposal companies and purchasing organisations will be covered. Companies listed only in relation to certain information are not PAs for FOIA purposes. The approach in FOIA 2000 is indicative and not conceptual. The term covers all government departments and includes any other body exercising statutory functions on behalf of the Crown. It would cover the Cabinet Office and by implication the Cabinet, Cabinet secretariat and Cabinet Committees. These bodies would be covered by numerous exemptions (see below). The term does not cover devolved Scottish bodies which are under the Scottish FOIA. Nor does it cover the security and intelligence services or GCHQ. The Queen and royal family are not covered. The Serious and Organised Crime Authority (SOCA) is excluded from the Act, but that body is to be brought into the National Crimes Agency (September 2010), which will deal with organised cybercrime and cover SOCA's remit. Banks nationalised after the 2007–08 financial crisis are excluded. The Act's coverage is truly comprehensive and readers are referred to Annex A (below) for the relevant bodies. There is none of the confused jurisprudence which we find under the Environment Information Regulations 2004, SI 2004/3391 (EIR 2004) (see para 8.204) judicial review and under the HRA 1998 to determine what is a public body or a public function for the purposes of review or duties under the legislation.[2] Information is held by a public authority if:

(a) it is held by the authority otherwise than on behalf of another person (eg it is entrusted for safe-keeping to a PA but is not given to the PA as part of its public or regulatory responsibilities; or

(b) it is held by another person on behalf of the authority (eg a contractor holds information provided by a PA).

[1] It is wholly owned by the Crown or it is wholly owned by a public authority listed in FOIA 2000, Sch 1 other than a government department or any authority listed only in relation to

particular information. FOIA 2000, s 6(2)(a) and (b) deal with membership of the companies. On
such companies see the ICO's: http://www.ico.gov.uk/upload/documents/library/freedom_of_
information/detailed_specialist_guides/fep105_publicly_owned_companies_v1.pdf.
² See eg *Aston Cantlow v Wallbank* [2004] 1 AC 546 displaying poor reasoning but probably correct
on its facts and *YL v Birmingham City Council and Others* [2007] UKHL 58; see Joint Committee
on Human Rights *Seventh Report* HL 39 and HC 382 (2003–04). The decision in *YL* was reversed
by legislation.

1.86   Under FOIA 2000, s 5, the Secretary of State may so designate as a public
authority for the purposes of the Act any person who is not listed in Sch 1, nor
capable of being added to that Schedule under s 4(1) but who appears to the
Secretary of State to exercise functions of a public nature – it does not provide
that the 'function' has to be statutory; or who is providing under a contract
made with a public authority any service whose provision is a function of that
authority. This latter formulation is very broad and will cover private bodies
providing services of a public authority to the public under contract eg, private
prisons. It was felt that simply referring to those bodies exercising statutory
functions was too broad because some functions would not be provided to the
public. The first part relies upon the Secretary of State's discretion and will
clearly cover bodies such as public utilities even though privately owned. Not
all their functions will be of a public nature.¹ It compares interestingly with the
approach adopted in the HRA 1998 to establish those bodies covered by the
HRA 1998,² as well as the general development of judicial review to cover bodies
acting in some sort of quasi-public regulatory or monopoly capacity.³ An order
may designate a specified person or office or persons or offices falling within a
specified description. Duties of consultation attend the making of orders.

¹   Utilities may perform many functions which may be non-statutory but public – or vice versa.
²   HRA 1998, s 6(3).
³   As developed from the decision in *R v Panel on Take-overs and Mergers, ex p Datafin plc* [1987] 1 All
ER 564, CA. See, Woolf, Jowell and LeSueur *de Smith's Judicial Review of Administrative Action*
(6th edn, 2007) paras 3.041 et seq. See *R (West) v Lloyd's of London* [2004] EWCA Civ 506 where
Lloyd's was not acting as a public authority under HRA 1998, s 6 or otherwise in its regulatory
functions.

1.87   After a consultation exercise in 2009, it was announced in 2010 that four
bodies were to be designated from October 2010. The bodies covered by the
designation are: the Association of Chief Police Officers (ACPO), the Financial
Ombudsman Service (FOS), the Universities and Colleges Admissions Service
(UCAS) and Academy Trusts – the bodies responsible for Academy Schools.¹
On coming to power, the coalition government announced possible subjects
for designation including nationalised banks and Network Rail – the latter has
caused some difficulties of interpretation under EIR 2004 (see para 8.215).
The Freedom of Information (Additional Public Authorities) Order 2011,
SI 2011/1041 contains a list of additional bodies.

¹   http://www.justice.gov.uk/news/newsrelease300310a.htm.

1.88   Section 4 of the FOIA 2000 allows the list of authorities in Sch 1 to be
amended by the Secretary of State by adding a reference to any body or the
holder of any office which (in either case) is not in the Schedule but for which

both of the following are satisfied. First, that the body is established by royal prerogative or primary or secondary legislation, or is established 'in any other way by a Minister of the Crown in his capacity as Minister or by a government department or the Welsh Ministers, the First Minister for Wales or the Counsel General to the Welsh Assembly Government.'[1] Secondly, that in the case of a body it is wholly or partly constituted by appointment made by the Crown, a Minister of the Crown (including a Northern Ireland Minister), a government department or by the the Welsh Ministers, the First Minister for Wales or the Counsel General to the Welsh Assembly Government and, in the case of an office, appointments to the office are made by the same parties.[2] Before making an order under sub-s (1), the Secretary of State must consult the Welsh Ministers where the bodies or office holders perform functions which are exercisable only or mainly in relation to Wales. Similar provisions apply to Northern Ireland bodies and office holders. Where either of these conditions fails to be satisfied in relation to any body in Parts VI or VII of Sch I, that body or office-holder shall cease to be a public authority by virtue of its entry in those parts. This covers non-departmental bodies or colloquially 'quangos'. Parts VI and VII may be amended where a body or office has ceased to exist or where either of the two conditions has ceased to be satisfied. The provisions do not apply to devolved Scottish institutions.[3]

[1]   FOIA 2000, s 4(2). The present Welsh provisions were as a consequence of the Government of Wales Act 2006.
[2]   FOIA 2000, s 4(3).
[3]   See FOIA 2000, s 79 which includes the Scottish Parliament, any part of the Scottish administration, the Scottish Parliamentary Corporate body or any Scottish public authority with mixed functions or no reserved functions within the meaning of the Scotland Act 1998.

1.89   Section 7 makes provision for public authorities for which the Act has limited application. Where an authority is listed only in relation to information of a specified description, nothing in Parts I to V of the Act applies to other information held by the authority. Limitations to information may be added or removed by order. Where an authority is listed in relation to functions under s 5(1)(a) the designating order must specify the functions with respect to which the designation is to have effect. Information not related to the exercise of those functions is not covered. Similar provisions apply to authorities designated by the Secretary of State because of services under s 5(1)(b). Special provisions on consultation apply in the case of Welsh and Northern Ireland bodies. The Secretary of State may also exclude by order information from the provisions of the Act – which means the Act will have no relevance to the information – in relation to publicly owned companies (s 7(7)). So, in relation to the Bank of England FOIA 2000 does not include information on monetary policy, financial support to maintain financial stability and provision of private banking services.

1.90   The exclusion of the BBC as a public authority in relation to information held for the purposes of 'journalism, art or literature' has generated a significant body of litigation. The Balen report concerned BBC coverage in the Middle East and a FOIA request was made for the report. The House of Lords ruled in *Sugar v BBC* [2009] UKHL 9 that a decision by the IC that the report was held for the purposes of journalism etc and was not thereby held in its capacity as a public authority and was therefore a matter over which he did not have jurisdiction was nonetheless a Decision Notice under FOIA 2000, s 50(3) and was consequentially appealable to the tribunal. The tribunal reversed the IC and maintained it had jurisdiction but it in turn was reversed by the High Court and Court of Appeal.[1] The Law Lords ruled by a 3–2 majority that the request could be processed under the appeal provisions of FOIA 2000 and did not have to be challenged under judicial review.

[1]   [2008] EWCA Civ 191.

1.91   FOIA 2000, s 7(1) provides:

'Where a public authority is listed in Schedule 1 only in relation to information of a specified description, nothing in Parts I to V of this Act applies to any other information held by the authority.'

Under FOIA 2000, s 50(3), a decision notice (DN) could only be issued in cases of a failure to comply with s 1 in relation to a public body. The BBC's argument was that for journalistic information it was not a public authority; thus s 1 did not apply to it in respect of such information and the IC could not therefore issue a DN. The question of whether the BBC is a public body or not was anterior to the powers of the IC and tribunal under the Act. It amounted to a question of jurisdiction and the IC and tribunal could not make a decision determining their own jurisdiction. Such a jurisdiction was provided by the Act and involved a public authority failing in its s 1 duties. Additionally, if correct, the IC could not exercise powers to obtain the information for his own examination because s 51 depended upon him having jurisdiction. Crucially, the IC agreed with the BBC as to the status of the information (he subsequently changed his mind!). In such a case the only recourse would appear to be a judicial review of the classification of the information in the High Court. This is what took place and both the High Court and Court of Appeal agreed with the IC's initial conclusion and overruled the tribunal, which had ruled that an application had been made to a public authority and the IC's decision letter was in effect a DN and so appealable. This would be a much more convenient and cheaper route for the requester than judicial review. However, had the IC disagreed with the BBC on the classification, he would have proceeded to make a decision under s 50(3) in relation to that information which would have been appealable. The problem arose where the IC agreed with the BBC.

1.92   Lord Philips believed that the BBC was a hybrid authority holding public and excluded information. The request was made to a public authority but involved excluded information. The IC's letter to this effect was a DN and appealable. What if excluded material were requested?

'Section 7 confines the hybrid authority's obligations to public information. Thus, its obligation under section 1 is to ascertain whether or not it holds information of the description requested as part of its public information, as specified in Schedule 1. If it does not, it is entitled to answer the inquirer "information of the description that you have requested does not form part of the information that I hold in respect of..." followed by the description of public information specified in Schedule 1.' (Para 33)

1.93 Lord Hoffmann believed that a power of determining the status of the authority was not conferred on the IC by the Act. He lacked jurisdiction, as did the tribunal. Furthermore, the terms 'hybrid' and 'excluded' were not contained in the Act. The question was, was it holding information as a public authority, although he believed that it would have been better had this power of determination been conferred on the IC. Baroness Hale agreed with Hoffman on outcome but they were in the minority. Neuberger agreed with Philips and used the terms 'hybrid' and 'excluded', and whereas Lord Hope agreed with the their outcome, he disapproved of these terms. Simply, the BBC was a public authority according to the schedule to which a request had been made and refused as illustrated in the decision of the IC which was appealable.

1.94 When the case was heard on appeal from the tribunal on the substantive question – ie was the report in question information concerned with journalism, art or literature? – the High Court adopted a different interpretation to the tribunal. In *BBC and IC v Sugar*[1] the court ruled that the tribunal's finding – that it was only where a predominant purpose in holding information was for journalism, etc (where there was more than one reason for holding it) that it was excluded material – was not statutorily endorsed and was an unlawful interpretation. The argument that the information originally related to journalism but then became managerial and resource-allocation information, the latter being the predominant purpose, did not stop the information relating to journalism, the court believed. The Court of Appeal held that the predominant test for holding information relied upon by the tribunal was not supported by the legislation.[2] That court also made some further points of importance. On an appeal from a specialist tribunal, such as the Information Tribunal, as Sir Richard Buxton pointed out when granting permission to appeal, a court (whether the High Court or this court) should always bear in mind the remarks of Baroness Hale of Richmond in *Secretary of State for the Home Department v AH (Sudan)*,[3] who stated:

'This is an expert Tribunal charged with administering a complex area of law in challenging circumstances. ... [T]he ordinary courts should approach appeals from them with an appropriate degree of caution; it is probable that in understanding and applying the law in their specialised field the Tribunal will have got it right ... .They and they alone are judges of the facts. ... Their decisions should be respected unless it is quite clear that they have misdirected themselves in law. Appellate courts should not rush to find misdirections simply because they may have reached a different conclusion on the facts or expressed themselves differently.' (para 24)

'In some cases, it may be difficult to decide whether the issue raised on an appeal is really one of law, as opposed to judgment or inference, and sometimes the point may be almost a mixture of law and judgment or inference. The clear message from Baroness Hale is that the court should not go out of its way to find an error of law, and I would respectfully endorse that approach. However, I would add that the court would be failing in its duty if it did not step in where an error of law had been made by the Tribunal, which, if corrected, produced a different outcome from that arrived at by the Tribunal.' (para 27)

'Further, if the dominant purpose test applies in relation to the BBC, it should, as a matter of logic, also apply to the Bank of England and the Competition Commission, in the provisions of part VI of schedule 1 to FOIA relating to them. If information is held in part by the Competition Commission as a tribunal and in part for other purposes, or by the Bank of England in part for monetary policy purposes and in part for other purposes, it seems to me unlikely that the legislature would have intended that the information would be subject to FOIA unless the tribunal or monetary purpose was the dominant purpose.' (para 42)

'So, one is faced with the stark choice between the two more extreme rival interpretations of the expression. On this issue, again I am in agreement with Irwin J. In my view, the BBC's interpretation is to be preferred: once it is established that the information sought is held by the BBC for the purposes of journalism, it is effectively exempt from production under FOIA, even if the information is also held by the BBC for other purposes.' (para 44)

'In my view, whatever meaning is given to "journalism" I would not be sympathetic to the notion that information about, for instance, advertising revenue, property ownership or outgoings, financial debt, and the like would normally be "held for purposes ... of journalism". No doubt there can be said to be a link between such information and journalism: the more that is spent on wages, rent or interest payments, the less there is for programmes. However, on that basis, literally every piece of information held by the BBC could be said to be held for the purposes of journalism. In my view, save on particular facts, such information, although it may well affect journalism-related issues and decisions, would not normally be "held for purposes ... of journalism". The question whether information is held for the purposes of journalism should thus be considered in a relatively narrow, rather than a relatively wide, way.' (para 55)

'As the Tribunal rightly observed, information held at one point for purposes of journalism may, at some later point, cease (either temporarily or permanently) to be held for that purpose. In the case of journalism, above all news journalism, information "held for purposes ... of journalism" may soon stop being held for that purpose and be held, instead, for historical or archival purposes. The BBC, and the Commissioner and the Tribunal, will no doubt carefully consider whether this applies to the information, which originated as purely journalistic-related material.' (para 58)

---

[1]   [2009] EWHC 2349.
[2]   [2010] EWCA Civ 715.
[3]   [2007] UKHL 49, [2008] 1 AC 678, at 30.

1.95   For a subsequent case where FOIA 2000, ss 21, 38 and 43 did not protect BBC contracts with commercial bodies, see FS50296349 (and FS50228493); where the expenditure of the BBC in coverage of the Pope's visit to the UK was protected by 'journalism etc', see FS50352659; and likewise correspondence with Prince Charles, see FS50318444 and further FS50265745.

TRANSFERRED RECORDS

1.96   Section 15 of the FOIA 2000 concerns requests for records transferred to, or if they existed would be contained in a transferred record to, the National Archives (formerly Public Record Office), another place of deposit approved by the Lord Chancellor/Secretary of State or the Public Record Office Northern Ireland. Copies of requests will be sent to the 'responsible authority' provided the information requested does not fall within an 'absolute exemption' set out in s 2(3) (see paras 1.105 and 1.106 below; and see further paras 2.48 et seq below). The responsible authority shall, on receiving a copy and within such time as is reasonable in all the circumstances, inform the appropriate records authority (s 15(5)) of its decisions under s 66(3) and (4) (see ch 2). It should be pointed out that records which are more than 30 years old are referred to as 'historical records', and special provision is made for these under ss 63–67 (see para 2.64 below). The period of 30 years has been reduced to 20 years.[1] The 20-year period is important because most exemptions end when they become 'historical records' at 20 years (see para 2.62 below).

[1]   Constitutional Reform and Governance Act 2010, Part 6 and Sch 7.

1.97   The s 45 Code (paras 16–24) provides details on transfers between PAs. This might involve contacting the other PA to confirm that it holds the information. This does not include holding a record under s 3(2)(a) of the Act (it is not held on behalf of another person (see above). The time for measuring a time limit for a request by a transferred authority (TA) runs from the date on which the TA received the request.

Public interest disclosures

1.98   In common with many overseas access to information regimes, the FOIA 2000 allows exempt information to be disclosed where disclosure is in the public interest. This provision was present in the 1997 White Paper.[1] The Parliamentary Ombudsman had ruled under the 1994 Code that the public interest may be served where publication might help public understanding of issues of current national debate or which has generated Parliamentary debate (see para 2.10 below). Since the draft Bill of 1999, the provision was more carefully drafted to reflect the central importance of the balancing of public interests. The provision is now s 2 of the Act. However, there were eight exemptions that cannot be the subject of a public interest disclosure (see below). These are called 'absolute exemptions'. To these has been added a ninth concerning correspondence with the monarch and the first and second in line to the throne following requests for correspondence to

Ministers from Prince Charles (below). Other 'qualified' or 'ordinary' exemptions are subject to the public interest test. So we have: exclusions (ie information or PAs not covered by FOIA), absolute exemptions and exemptions. In the case of exemptions there may be a public interest disclosure of whether the public authority holds the information requested instead of neither confirming nor denying (NCDC) that it holds the information. In the case of exemptions, there may be a public interest disclosure of the exempt information itself. The public interest is determined by the authority concluding that, in all the circumstances of the case, the public interest in maintaining the exemption outweighs the public interest in disclosure (of the fact of holding information or the information itself). This reversed the emphasis so that where the balance was even, the scales would tip down in favour of disclosure although some decisions of the tribunal seem to confuse this.[2] It was a late amendment in the Report stage of the Lords. It is an important reversal helping to create a presumption of disclosure. Public interest disclosures feature in other areas of law and information. A public interest may negative a duty of confidentiality and, in the case of information held by public bodies, the courts will require evidence that disclosure is not in the public interest before preventing publication (see paras 2.294 et seq below). The public interest applies in the law of copyright (para 2.314, note 1 below) as well as in the Public Interest Disclosure Act 1998 where the test is heavily regulated by statutory qualifications (paras 2.270 et seq below). The courts have for many years applied a public interest test to determine whether information in the possession of a public authority should be disclosed to a litigant, and where the courts weigh the public interests of disclosure in the interests of justice or secrecy in the interests of an overriding aspect of governance or security (see paras 10.52 et seq below for a fuller discussion).

[1]   See M Carter and A Bouris *Balancing the Public Interest: Applying the Public Interest Test to Exemptions in the FOIA* (2nd edn 2006). The IC has produced his own guidance on public interest disclosures. Several overseas laws have a public interest test, including: Ireland – see M McDonagh *Freedom of Information Law in Ireland* (2nd ed, 2006); Canada – see M Drapeau and M-A Racicot *Federal Access to Information 2002* (2001); Australia – see Bayne *The Laws of Australia* (1995) Part 2.3; and New Zealand – see Eagles, Taggart and Liddell *Freedom of Information in New Zealand* (1992). In none of these countries does a public interest test apply to all exemptions. See also in ch 3 the EU Regulation on access to documents which also has a public interest test for some exceptions.

[2]   See P Birkinshaw *Freedom of Information: the Law, the Practice and the Ideal* (4th edn, 2010) chs 5 and 6.

1.99   The DCA Guidance suggests the following areas where it would not favour the public interest to disclose information:[1]

- where disclosure would engender some risk to public or personal safety;
- where disclosure would be damaging to effective public administration;
- where there are contractual obligations in favour of maintaining confidence (in such cases legal advice is likely to be essential). It should be added that agreements cannot evade duties contained in FOIA 2000;
- where the duty of confidentiality arises out of a professional relationship;
- where disclosure would affect the continued supply of important information (for example, information provided by whistleblowers).

[1]   See for MoJ: http://www.justice.gov.uk/guidance/freedom-and-rights/freedom-of-information/foi-exemptions-public-interest.htm.

1.100 The ICO guidance states that in favour of disclosure may be:
- general arguments in favour of promoting transparency, accountability and participation;
- disclosure might enhance the quality of discussions and decision-making generally;
- financial issues – for instance, if the information requested involved a large amount of public money disclosure may be in the public interest;
- the specific circumstances of the case and the content of the information requested in relation to those circumstances;
- the age of the information might affect the interest in disclosure. Passage of time may well impact upon the strength of the interest in disclosure;
- timing of a request in relation to information about an investigation may be relevant. The stage of the investigation and information already released would be important;
- the impact, beneficial or otherwise, on individuals and/or the wider public.

1.101 Conversely the public interest may be advanced in disclosing:
- information revealing misconduct/mismanagement of public funds;
- information that shows that a particular public contract is bad value for money;
- information that would correct untrue statements or misleading acts on the part of public authorities or high-profile individuals;
- information where a substantial length of time has passed since the information was obtained, and the harm which would have been caused by disclosure at the time the information was obtained has depleted;
- specific circumstances of the case and the content of information in relation to those circumstances;
- the passage of time – by implication recent information or events may need protecting;
- likelihood of any harm and its severity caused by disclosure;
- is it 'live', ie sensitive or significant;
- safe space for government thinking, formulation and debate away from scrutiny;
- clear evidence that frankness and candour in debate and decision-making in government will be inhibited. The evidence will need to be clear on this effect;
- timing and impact above are repeated.

Irrelevant considerations are the identity of the requester; the possibility of misunderstanding information; the status of the information (classified or relating to senior individuals); the number of exemptions being claimed; the accuracy of the information; or that disclosure will lead to poorer record-keeping.

1.102 There is a general public interest in disclosure. Under FOIA 2000, the tribunal has ruled that in applying the test, the considerations in each exemption should be considered individually and not cumulatively[1] and that general considerations which might appear relevant should not apply. The focus is on each exemption individually. The sum cannot be greater than its parts. Under

EIR 2004, the Court of Appeal has ruled that exemptions may be considered as a whole to assess the overall weight of the public interest. The public interests may be aggregated: *Ofcom v IC*.[2] This was referred to the ECJ by the Supreme Court.[3] The ICO believed this approach only applied to the EIR.[4] Our view is that the better approach under FOIA 2000 is that adopted under the EIR. In *Home Office and MoJ v IC*[5] the tribunal's reasoning was upheld on a request for 'meta' requests and meta data – information generated by FOI requests themselves. The judgment seems to favour a cumulative test: paras 25 and 38.

[1] *Bellamy v IC* EA 2005/0023.
[2] [2009] EWCA Civ 90.
[3] [2010] UKSC 3. The CJEU confirmed that the grounds for non-disclosure may be cumulatively taken into account: Case C-71/10: *Ofcom v IC* Case C-71/10 [2011] EUECJ (28.07.11). See para 8.237.
[4] http://www.ico.gov.uk/upload/documents/library/freedom_of_information/detailed_specialist_guides/fep038_public_interest_test_v3.pdf.
[5] [2009] EWHC 1611 Admin.

1.103 Further guidance has been produced on: Cabinet Committees (the presumption is not to disclose information concerning such committees);[1] policy advice; requests for legal advice in relation to the formulation of policy (presumption not to disclose); legal advice (likewise); oral parliamentary questions (PQs); written PQs; press releases and handling strategies; and confidential information obtained from a foreign government or international organisation.

[1] http://www.justice.gov.uk/guidance/foi-assumptions-cabinet.htm.

The exemptions

1.104 It should be recalled that the IC and MoJ have produced guidance on the exemptions available from their websites. Where an authority confirms that it holds information requested and the information is not exempt, or excluded when a public body is not listed in a schedule, it will be available for public inspection subject to the requirements outlined above. Authorities will have to set out in Publication Schemes what information they are going to publish (see above). These are approved by the Commissioner. The exemptions are pivotal to the operation of the legislation as a code of openness and need the closest scrutiny. We have already observed that some exemptions, eg where the cost of compliance exceeds an appropriate financial limit to meet the request, including the duty to confirm or deny, or where there are vexatious or repeated requests are not within the exemptions contained in Part II of the Act. Official publications refer to 23 exemptions, but in fact there are more than this.

Absolute exemptions

1.105 Although exempt, the public authority may, as we have seen, make a discretionary disclosure under s 2 of the FOIA 2000 of exempt information which has been requested. However, this does not apply to information which is exempt[1] by virtue of ss 21 (accessible by other means); 23 (bodies dealing with security etc); 32 (court records); 34 (information covered by Parliamentary privilege);[2] 36 (prejudice to effective working of government) in so far as it applies to information held by either House of Parliament; 37, where the information concerns communications with the sovereign, heir to or second in line of succession to the throne, communications with a person who has subsequently acceded to the throne or become heir to or second in line of succession to the throne, and other communications with members of the royal family or household where they are made or received on behalf of a person falling within the previous descriptions; 40(i) and (ii), in relation to the first condition where it is satisfied by virtue of sub-s (3)(a)(i) or (b) of that section (this concerns personal information); 41 (information provided in confidence); and 44 (prohibited by enactment etc). These are absolute exemptions.

[1]   The April 2000 Bill omitted a reference to cl 11 information – the cost of compliance provision.
[2]   This would be determined by the Bill of Rights 1689, Art 9. See *R v D Chaylor etc* [2010] EWCA Crim 1910; [2010] UKSC 52.

1.106   These exemptions are described as 'absolute exemptions' because the authority has no authority to disclose this information. This discretion applies under the section and it does not state that it interferes with, detracts from or otherwise prejudices powers under common law, especially the public interest disclosure provisions under the law of confidentiality.[1] To this extent, it is not entirely clear whether the provisions in the statute operate to preclude the common law or whether they act as an alternative. Section 78 does in fact state 'Nothing in the Act is to be taken to limit the powers of a public authority to disclose information held by it'. This might include powers under common law and so the limitations under s 2 would not apply in such cases. On the contrary, as FOIA 2000 is a comprehensive code, it arguably overrides the common law but not specific provisions in other statutes. Section 2 also prevents the IC exercising a power of requiring disclosure of exempt information in these areas. The NCND public interest override does not apply where the exemption is absolute.

[1]   See paras 2.312 et seq below. The terms of the statutory powers of public interest disclosure will be wider than that under the common law. The latter will have regard to the mode of disclosure, the extent of disclosure, the recipient of disclosure, the motive and so on as limiting factors. Conversely, the common law will not be restricted by the eight 'absolute exemptions'. They only apply to disclosures under the statute.

1.107   Where the authority holds information of the description specified in the request and has informed or intends to inform the applicant that it does so, the authority must consider whether to communicate the information in their discretion unless the exemption that applies is absolute. In the case of a qualified exemption such decisions must be made within a time-scale that is reasonable within all the circumstances. They have to regard all the circumstances of the case[1] and unless it appears that the public interest in maintaining the exemption in question outweighs the public interest in disclosure, they shall communicate the information to the applicant. There must be a specific balancing and the manner in which they exercise their discretion is investigable by the IC. To what extent may a disclosure be specific to an individual? This is a measure providing for a general right of access and individual factors are not provided for. Disclosure under FOIA 2000 is disclosure to the world. To avoid revealing their identities in the USA, requesters frequently use commercial bodies to make their requests under US FOIA laws.

1   In the original Bill there was included the desirability of 'informing the applicant whether it holds information' and 'communicating information to him'. This was removed from the April 2000 Bill.

Refusal of request

1.108   Where the public authority is minded to refuse any request under s 1 of the FOIA 2000 on the basis that the duty to confirm or deny is excluded or that the information is exempt under s 2, it must give the applicant a notice stating that fact, which specifies the exemption in question and which states if not otherwise apparent why the exemption applies (s 17(1)). This has to be done within the 20-day period. This is nowhere near the detail of the famous Vaughn index in the USA where exemptions have to be justified line by line.[1] The Code of Practice under s 45 stated that good practice might involve preparation of a statement of policies about disclosure which can be provided to applicants 'without the risk of implying comment upon particular requests'. The notice must specify, where a decision under s 2 is to be taken on the public interest, that no decision has yet been taken. The notice under s 17(1), or a separate notice within such time as is reasonable in the circumstances, must state the reason for claiming why the public interest in maintaining the exclusion of the duty to confirm or deny or in not allowing disclosure outweighs the public interest in disclosing whether it holds the information or in disclosing the information (s 17(3)). Section 17(3) makes a deliberate reference to 'all the circumstances of the case' and this has helped to ensure that reasons are specific and detailed. The authority in making such statements or giving such reasons is not obliged to reveal exempt information. Where the authority claims that s 12 or 14 (cost of compliance and vexatious etc) is to be relied upon by the authority it must give the applicant a notice stating that fact and within the time-scale for compliance with s 1(1). This does not apply where a previous notice relating to s 14 has been given and a further notice would be unreasonable in all the circumstances.

1   *Vaughan v Rosen* 484 F 2d 820 (CA, DC) (1973).

1.109   A notice under sub-s (1), (2) or (5) must contain details of any complaints procedures provided by the authority for information complaints or a statement that no such procedure exists (see paras 1.235 and 1.233 below), as well as the applicant's right to apply to the IC for a decision notice (a formal decision).

1.110   The s 45 Code stated in a draft that when refusing information, an exemption that is used should not merely be a paraphrase of the wording in the Act (subject to s 17(4)). An authority should also specify any public interest features necessitating reliance upon an exemption. Authorities should keep a record of all applications for monitoring by line managers.

The specific exemptions

(I) INFORMATION ACCESSIBLE TO THE APPLICANT

1.111 Where information is reasonably accessible to the applicant otherwise than under s 1 of the FOIA 2000, it is exempt. Reasonably accessible includes that which is available only on payment of a fee (s 21(2)(a)). It is reasonably accessible if the authority or any other person is obliged under any enactment to communicate the information to members of the public on request whether on payment of a charge or otherwise but not by simply making information available for inspection (s 21(2)(b)).[1] The authority or other person must be under a duty to communicate the information. If it does not fall within s 21(2)(b) then it is not reasonably accessible merely because it *may* be available on request unless it is available with the authority's publication scheme and any payments are specified in that scheme. The use of 'applicant' suggests that the personal circumstances of the applicant eg financial, ability to travel etc, may be considered. The scheme, including payments, has to be approved by the Commissioner. The authority has to state why the exemption applies and thereby implies a duty to inform the applicant of its location. If information is not reasonably accessible to the applicant, that may be a ground of complaint to the IC. Section 21 was wrongly relied on where information was in databases and not accessible (FS50146907). Reforms will address this question (see para 1.79).

[1]   Eg, birth, marriage and death certificates.

1.112 FS 50073646 concerned a request for information from the Ministry of Justice (MoJ) about a complaint made by the requester concerning a judge who dealt with the requester's judicial review application and appeal proceedings. Different exemptions applied to protect different documents. The IC found that the MoJ were wrong in failing to identify information subject to the s 21 exemption and therefore were in breach of s 17(1)(c) and had to provide the requester with an 'accurate and comprehensive list of all documents it holds' to which s 21 is applicable. In FS 50086060 s 21 was correctly invoked as the information was available via web addresses.

1.113 *C Ames v IC et Cabinet Office* EA/2007/0110 was a request for the identity of the person who redrafted the executive summary of the Iraq Weapons of Mass Destruction dossier. The tribunal ruled ruled that s 21 was incorrectly invoked by stating the information was available in the Hutton report: it was not. The IC's DN was substituted. Where bodies are funded by a PA, the tribunal has not inferred that the PA holds information by relying on s 21. In *G Tuckley v IC & Birmingham City Council*[1] the case concerned a request for a list of all neighbourhood forums from 1992 and money paid to each by Birmingham City Council matters that were irrelevant in the case. *Rhondda Cynon Taff CBC v IC*[2] concerned a request for a copy of the Land Drainage Act 1991. The tribunal believed the Act was reasonably accessible and s 21 was rightly claimed by the PA. Information about the workplace email addresses of all university staff were rightly refused under s 21: FS50311065. Section 21 was correctly invoked by the

Home Office when a manual on the treatment of police informers was requested, which was publicly available in the British Library: FS50302058.

1   EA/2006/0077.
2   EA/2007/0065.

1.114   This is an absolute exemption.

(II) INFORMATION INTENDED FOR FUTURE PUBLICATION

1.115   Information is exempt under s 22 of the FOIA 2000 where it is held by the public authority with a view to its publication by the authority or another person at 'some future date' (whether determined or not); it was already held with a view to such publication at the time the request for information was made and it is reasonable in all the circumstances that it be withheld from disclosure until the date referred to above. 'Reasonable' connotes an objective standard which may be assessed by the IC. The duty to confirm or deny does not arise for information where compliance would involve the disclosure of any information falling in the above categories. This is a useful device to prevent access to information where a matter is under internal investigation and report, and eventual publication. However, the withholding has to be objectively justified as reasonable in all the circumstances. This will be facts specific. The exemption has been successfully claimed in relation to a thesis held by Liverpool University (FS50349323).

1.116   The UK Act and the Scottish FOIA differed in their approaches to this exemption. The Scottish FOIA limited the period of publication to twelve weeks. FS50081543 determined that under s 22 there has to be a settled intention to publish the information at the time of the request; in the absence of such anintention s.22 could not be relied upon (and likewise FS50323585). Sectin 22 has been wrongly resorted to where it was not responsible to withhold information from the complainant at the time of the request (FS50070741).

(III) BODIES DEALING WITH SECURITY MATTERS

1.117   These bodies are not included in the Schedule of public bodies covered by the Act and so they are excluded.[1] This exemption in s 23 of the FOIA 2000 deals with information from these bodies, whether supplied directly or indirectly, or about them and which is held by scheduled bodies. Where a certificate signed by a Minister of the Crown certifies that information falls within the above category, that will be conclusive evidence of that fact. The certificate signed under s 23(2) is subject to the provisions of s 60 (see below).

1.118   The bodies covered are:
- the Security Service;
- the Secret Intelligence Service;
- the Government Communications HQ (which includes any unit or part of a unit of the armed forces of the Crown which is for the time being required by the Secretary of State to assist GCHQ in carrying out its functions);

- the special forces;
- tribunals established under the Interception of Communications Act 1985, the Security Service Act 1989, the Intelligence Service Act 1994 (and now under the Regulation of Investigatory Powers Act 2000);
- the Security Vetting Appeals Panel;
- the Security Commission;
- the National Criminal Intelligence Service (NCIS which became a part of SOCA; below);
- the Service Authority for the NCIS (as above);
- the Serious Organised Crime Agency (SOCA, which is likely to become the National Crime Agency[2]).

[1]   The secret services have been subjected to increasing examination in recent years, most notably by the 'Coroner's Inquests into the London bombings of 7 July 2005' by Lady Justice Hallett: http://7julyinquests.independent.gov.uk/docs/orders/rule43-report.pdf. See Birkinshaw *Freedom of Information etc* (2010) ch 2.
[2]   Cm 8097 (2011).

1.119   The point has been made that the Security Service has extended its remit beyond the traditional territory of MI5 to cover more routine forms of policing as well as computer security in central government see eg Security Services Act 1996[1] NCIS was responsible, inter alia, for supervision of football hooligans.

[1]   P Birkinshaw *Freedom of Information: the Law, the Practice and ther Ideal* (4th edn, 2010) ch 2.

1.120   The duty to confirm or deny does not arise if, or to the extent that, compliance with s 1(1)(a) would involve the disclosure of any information, whether or not already recorded which was directly or indirectly supplied to the public authority by, or relates to, any of the bodies specified in sub-s (3).

1.121   Under s 23 a murder inquiry report was rightly refused by the Northern Ireland Office (FS50209828). *S M Gradwick v IC*[1] drew critical comments from the tribunal about the Cabinet Office (CO) when it noted that s 23 protects anodyne information. The request was for the CO's annual of Protective Security – detailed guidance on controls for government assets and information. Section 23 (and 24) protects information about money paid to police informers – information was provided force-wide but not on a borough basis. The request was rightly rejected reversing the IC's decision.[2] *Comr Met Police v IC*[3] saw the invocation of s 23(5) and a NCND to information about a statement by President Bush about terrorist attacks on London. The IC overruled the MPC and the tribunal overruled the IC, holding the section was correctly invoked. In *All Party Parliamentary Group on Extraordinary Rendition v IC and MoD*,[4] while disclosure of documents relating to the UK's involvement in extraordinary rendition of terrorist suspects to other countries where they faced torture was ordered, s 23 protected information coming from the special forces.

[1]   EA/2010/0030.
[2]   *Comr Met Police v IC* EA/2010/ 0006.
[3]   EA/2010/0008.
[4]   [2011] UKUT 153 (AAC).

1.122 The IC has shown a propensity to accept official claims that information is protected under s 23 (see FS 50090742 concerning 'the assessment by the Joint Intelligence Committee of Iraq's declaration of its weapons of mass destruction in December 2002'). In FS50134744 the IC stated he was satisfied to accept an assurance from the Director of Security and Intelligence in the CO on the protected status of the information. The IC would only accept such an assurance where the official occupies a position in relation to the security bodies which allows them genuinely to validate the origins of the information. In FS 50102023 the complainant requested all the documents held by the CO in relation to the bombing of the Rainbow Warrior by French intelligence services. Rainbow Warrior had been Greenpeace's flagship. The CO refused to confirm or deny if information is held under ss 23(5) and 24(2) of the Act. The IC investigated and upheld the application of ss 23(5) and 24(2) to neither confirm nor deny if information is held.

1.123   This is an absolute exemption.

(IV) NATIONAL SECURITY

1.124   Information not falling within the previous section is exempt information if exemption from s 1(1)(b) of the FOIA 2000 is required for the purpose of safeguarding national security.[1] In *Secretary of State for the Home Department v Rehman*, the House of Lords, in a case concerning deportation of a suspected terrorist, held that national security did not simply involve a direct threat to the UK nor action targeted at the UK, its system of government or its people: 'In contemporary world conditions, actions against a foreign state might be capable of affecting the security of the UK'. In determining whether a deportation was conducive to the public good on grounds of national security, the Secretary of State did not have to show that all the evidence was proved or that his conclusion was justified to a high civil degree of probability. In making such a decision, the Secretary of State was entitled 'to have regard to all the information in his possession about the actual and potential activities and the connections of the persons concerned. He was entitled to have regard to the precautionary and preventative principles rather than to wait until directly harmful activities had taken place ... he was not merely finding facts but forming an executive judgment or assessment.' Degrees of probability did not seem appropriate although there had to be material on which proportionately and reasonably there were activities harmful to national security.[2] The Secretary of State was 'undoubtedly in the best position to judge what national security required, and the assessment of what was needed in the light of changing circumstances was primarily for him.' This test (operative post 9/11) has clearly established a very wide margin of appreciation in favour of executive decisions on national security. The duty to confirm or deny, etc does not arise if, or to the extent that, exemption from s 1(1) (a) is required for the purposes of safeguarding national security. A Minister of the Crown may certify that information is, or at any time was, required for purposes of safeguarding national security and again, subject to appeals to the tribunal under s 60, such a certificate is *conclusive evidence* of that fact (s 24(3)).

This would in effect prevent the Commissioner determining the public interest or issuing notices under Part IV and would leave any redress to the tribunal. It is hard to see what room is left to the public authority or the Commissioner after the award of a certificate unless it is quashed by the tribunal. It should be noted that, under EIR 2004, the issue of a ministerial certificate on the grounds of national security excludes Part IV of FOIA 2000 (the enforcement provisions) presumably pending a successful appeal (paras 8.268 and 8.251 below). In the absence of such a certificate, the public interest must be considered by the public authority and the Commissioner may investigate a complaint. The certificate may identify information by means of a general description and 'may be expressed to have prospective effect'.

[1]   See *R v Ministry of Defence, ex p Smith* [1996] 1 All ER 257, CA; cf *R v Secretary of State for the Home Department, ex p Simms* [1999] 3 All ER 400, HL Lord Hoffmann.

[2]   *Secretary of State for the Home Department v Rehman* [2002] 1 All ER 122 (HL). See para 9.127 below and *A etc v Secretary of State for the Home Department* [2005] UKHL 71: the Home Secretary may not use intelligence obtained under torture before a judicial body to justify detention of foreign nationals under the Anti-terrorism, Crime and Security Act 2001, s 23. The person alleging torture has to prove the allegation to prevent the evidence being admitted which in security cases will be extremely difficult as acknowledged by Baroness Hale in *Secretary of State for the Home Department v MB* [2007] UKHL 46. In *A etc* the law lords reversed the court of appeal although there was a powerful dissent by Neuberger LJ. See also *A v Secretary of State for the Home Department* [2004] UKHL 56 and *Secretary of State for the Home Department v AF* [2009] UKHL 28.

1.125   Section 60 provides that, where a certificate is issued under s 23(2) or 24(3), the Commissioner or any applicant whose request is affected by the issue of a certificate may appeal to the Tribunal. In the case of security etc information, the Tribunal may quash the certificate if it finds it is not exempt information within s 23(1). The effect of quashing is that the exemption will not apply and other exemptions will have to be invoked. The Tribunal may also quash the certificate if the Minister did not have reasonable grounds for exempting it in relation to national security under s 24(3). In reaching its finding, the Tribunal will apply 'principles applied by a court on judicial review'. This is a well-worn formula which was devised at a time when courts had not developed the principles of judicial review into the sophisticated body of law that it represents today.[1] However, the judgments in *Rehman* above should be noted. The burden will be on the appellant. Any other party to the proceedings may appeal against a claim that a certificate applying to information of a general description applies to particular information. The Tribunal may determine whether it does so apply. Section 25 concerns various evidentiary points in relation to certificates.[2] Changes to procedures now require a mandatory reference to the Upper Tribunal of cases concerned with certificates under ss 23 and 24. Previously they were heard by a specially constituted Information Tribunal.

[1]   See eg de Smith, Woolf and Jowell (eds) *De Smith's Judicial Review* (6th edn, 2007). The courts have travelled far beyond the territory of *Wednesbury* unreasonableness. See on similar provisions under the Data Protection Act: *Norman Baker MP v Secretary of State for the Home Department* at para 7.79 below.

[2]   A document purporting to be a certificate under FOIA 2000, s 23(2) or 24(3) shall be received in evidence and deemed to be such a certificate unless the contrary is proved. A document which purports to be certified by or on behalf a Minister of the Crown as a true copy of a

certificate issued by that Minister under the sections shall be evidence of that certificate in any legal proceedings. The Minister must be a member of the Cabinet, the Attorney General, Lord Advocate or Attorney General (Northern Ireland).

1.126   Section 24 has been invoked in cases examined above under s 23 (see *S M Gradwick*; FS50209828; FS50090742 and FS50102023). The tribunal has given short shrift to appeals against refusals to disclose intelligence agreements concerning signals between the UK and USA – even from 1948[1]. A full discussion of the relationship between s 24 and s 23 took place in *N Baker MP v IC* and *Cabinet Office & NCCL*.[2] *Baker* concerned information about the tapping of MPs' phones and Prime Minister Wilson's statement of 17 November 1966 that MPs would not be subject to intercepts and any change of policy would be announced in the House 'at such moments as seemed compatible with the security of the country'. Prime Minister Blair announced on 30 March 2006 that that doctrine was being maintained. An additional request was made as to how many MPs had been subject to intrusive surveillance or tapping since that date. Had there been a change of policy since that time? Sections 24(2) and 23(5) were claimed together. The CO responded with a NCND. After 12 months of investigation, the IC agreed with the Secretary of State (CA) that a ministerial notice under s 23(2) or 24(3) would only be issued after a complaint had been made to the IC. The tribunal noted that it possessed wide powers to review the merits of the IC's decision and it further observed the wide definition of national security from the Law Lords' decision in *Rehman* (above). The case for invoking s 24 is dealt with in paras 30–33. This included evidence from the Director of Security and Intelligence in the Cabinet Office (who was named) who supplied reasons for the NCND response. In essence, a response might blow national security cover (para 34) and so both s 23(5) and s 24(2) were claimed together. Disclosure of the holding of information would negate the ability of the PM to judge at what point it was safe to make any public announcement of change in policy in relation to the tapping of MPs' phones (para 51(2)). Under s 24, the public interest favoured maintenance of the exemption.

[1]   *M McCarthy v IC* EA/2006/0053.
[2]   EA/2006/0045.

(V) DEFENCE

1.127   Information is exempt if its disclosure under the Act would, or would be likely to prejudice the defence of the British Islands or of any colony, or the capability, effectiveness or security of any relevant forces (FOIA 2000, s 26). 'Any relevant forces' means armed forces of the Crown and any forces co-operating with those forces or any part of those forces. Would this cover details of contracts relating to inadequate armaments which were tantamount to a fraud on the taxpayer, or which exposed the forces to unnecessary danger? The public interest in knowing such would be very high. The duty to confirm or deny does not arise if, or to the extent that, compliance with s 1(1)(a) would, or would be likely to, prejudice any of the matters referred to in sub-s (1).

1.128 FS50200146 involved a Ministry of Defence rejection of a request for information on detentions in Iraq, which the IC ruled had been rightly denied. This exemption has featured rarely in the case law and a helpful guidance note from the ICO has been published: http://www.ico.gov.uk/upload/documents/library/ freedom_of_information/detailed_specialist_guides/awareness_guidance_10_-_ the_defense_exemption.pdf.

(VI) INTERNATIONAL RELATIONS

1.129 Information is exempt information if its disclosure would, or would be likely to, prejudice:
(1) Relations between the United Kingdom and any other State: FOIA 2000, s 27(5) defines a 'State' as including the government of any state and any organ of its government.
(2) Relations between the United Kingdom and any international organisation or international court (s 27(5) defines 'international organisation' and 'international court').
(3) The interests of the United Kingdom abroad or the promotion or protection by the United Kingdom of those interests.
(4) Information is also exempt where if it is confidential information obtained from a state other than the UK or from an international organisation or international court.

1.130 Section 27(3) states that any such information is confidential at any time while the terms on which it was obtained require it to be held in confidence or the circumstances in which it was obtained make it reasonable for the state etc to expect that it will be so held. The duty to confirm or deny does not arise which would involve disclosure prejudicing any of the matters in sub-s (1) or disclosure of any information (whether or not already recorded) which is confidential information obtained from another state, international organisation or court.

1.131 This covers a very sensitive subject area and the IC has ruled that records of meetings involving King Hussein and British PM were rightly refused in most cases but some were disclosed (FS50205398; and see FS50260727 where information was correctly refused by the FCO and FS50278116 and FER0081530). In FS50199771 the complainant made a request to the Export Credit Guarantee Department (ECGD) for information relating to the sale of armoured vehicles to Indonesia and the payment of an agent's commission on the transaction. ECGD refused to disclose the information relying inter alia on s 27(1)(a). The IC found that ECGD was correct to withhold the information and required no further steps to be taken. FS50292976 concerns information held by the National Archives on arms sales to Saudi Arabia which in some cases, but not all, was rightly withheld on PI grounds. In FS50080115 s 27 was used to block information on recipients of Christmas cards from the Prime Minister in 2003 and 2004. The names of foreign leaders and heads of state should be released (ss 36, 38 and 40 also invoked). (See also FS 50178057).

1.132 In FS50134744 the complainant asked the CO for the contents of a file, 'PREM 8/928', listed in the National Archive catalogue. The IC decided that the s 27(1)(a) exemption did not apply because the information was historical and was highly unlikely to provoke a reaction from the foreign state involved. In FS50125539 Foreign and Commonwealth Office information was requested from the National Archives about arms sales to Saudi Arabia. Section 27 was properly engaged and the public interest favoured disclosure (much of the information had already been disclosed). FS 50070854 concerned information that was requested from the FCO on the UK/US Energy Dialogue. This dealt with a task force set up by Vice President Cheney. The IC believed that most items were properly withheld but some could be disclosed. Those withheld related to continuing confidential discussions. Para 24 states that some information related to corruption and political stability in foreign states, comments upon prominent individuals and the potential for countries to be long-term energy suppliers – information that was not shared with the foreign countries and whose disclosure could prejudice UK/US relationships which would not be in the public interest. This was the kind of information released by Wikileaks in 2010–2011 when 250,000 US intelligence and diplomatic reports were published without authorisation. Case FS 500110720 concerned a copy of the letter from the European Commission to the UK government (Department for Constitutional Affairs) regarding the implementation of the Data Protection Directive (95/46/EC) by the UK. Section 27 was invoked together with other exemptions. Because the case dealt with policy formulation and the early stages of infraction proceedings by the Commission under then Art 226 EC, s 27(1)(c) was correctly invoked and the public interest was in favour of retention (see pp 11–12). FS50290504 concerned the MoJ and similar requests. Here, s 27(1)(c) and 27(2) were either wrongly invoked or the public interest favoured disclosure in some but not all cases. The IC 'considers the public interest in disclosure of the specific information in question here to be of particularly significant weight' (para 54). *Campaign against the Arms Trade v IC and MoD*[1] concerns a request for information relating to a Memorandum of Understanding with the Saudi Arabian government about sale of defence weapons. The use by the tribunal of special counsel to assist the claimants who were excluded from closed sessions was examined and criticism was made of the documentation served by the Ministry of Defence on the tribunal: 'the documentation provided to us was provided without explanation, piecemeal and in an incoherent manner that made it effectively impossible to understand' (para 21(d)). The complexity of the documentation required the 'exceptional' resort to a special counsel from the Attorney General's approved list in accordance with CPR Pt 76. The IT found s 27(1) engaged and the balance of public interest favoured non-disclosure. Shortly before this decision the House of Lords ruled that the SFO's cessation of a prosecution for fraud involving Saudi Arabian arms contracts was not unlawful.[2] Subsequently, employees of the company involved, BAE Systems, were prosecuted and a plea bargaining arrangement was criticised in the High Court.[3]

---

[1] EA/2006/0040.

[2] *R (Corner House Research) v Director of the SFO* [2008] UKHL 60.

[3] *Financial Times* 22 December 2010 'Plea deal is sorry end to BAE affair'.

1.133   This provision is inspired by a provision in OSA 1989, s 3

1.134   This exemption was felt necessary in the light of devolution. Where disclosure would, or would be likely to, prejudice relations between any administration in the United Kingdom and any other such administration the information is exempt under s 28(1) of the FOIA 2000. This refers to the government of the United Kingdom, the Scottish Administration, the Executive Committee of the Northern Ireland Assembly or the Welsh Assembly Government. The duty to confirm or deny does not arise where compliance would, or would be likely to, prejudice information in sub-s (1).

1.135   The relationship between central government and devolved government is heavily reliant upon non-legally binding 'Concordats' covering a wide range of topics, eg EU policy, international relations, government statistics, and financial aid to industry. A Joint Ministerial Committee is established. The arrangements work by sharing of 'confidential' information supplementing more formal legal provisions such as s 123 of the Government of Wales Act 1998. These concordats continue the Whitehall tradition of secrecy it is maintained.[1] It should be noted that information given in confidence by the UK government is not disclosable under the Scottish FOIA 2002 (para 1.240 below).

[1]   R Rawlings (2000) LQR 257.

1.136   See FS50121252 involving the Scotland Office. The Ministry of Justice guidance on s 28 is at http://www.justice.gov.uk/docs/foi-exemption-s28.pdf.

1.137   Information is exempt where its disclosure would, or would be likely to, prejudice the economic interests of the United Kingdom or any part of the United Kingdom or the financial interests of any administration in the United Kingdom as described above (FOIA 2000, s 29). The duty to confirm or deny has a slight variation from the usual formula.

1.138   This exemption is rarely invoked. See FS50105898, where a request was made for information to the Treasury that had been introduced into the macroeconomic model forecasting the performance of the UK economy. The IC was satisfied that s 29 was correctly claimed. In *Derry City Council v IC*[1] (ss 41 and 43 below: see paras 1.207 and 1.215 below) the tribunal ruled that s 29 would have been unsuccessful in that case and would not have allowed exemption.

[1]   EA/2006/0014.

1.139   Clauses 25 and 26 of the No 1 Bill published in May 1999 had extremely, if not excessively, broad exemptions, indeed wildly so. Clause 25 protected information which has at any time been held for the purpose of criminal investigations for charges, or if charged, for ascertaining guilt. The second part of the section exempts information concerning investigations of a civil or administrative nature concerning, eg, professional misconduct, breaches of hygiene or environmental regulations such as noise and so on as well as information produced for the purpose of ascertaining the cause of an accident which is a lot more restricted than case law covering privileged documents relating to accidents.[1] The second part included investigations relating to wrongdoing in charities, and health and safety investigations. Overall, the breadth of this exemption was breath-taking and fulfilled the Home Secretary's warning to the Select Committee that if this information were removed from the excluded category, the necessary exemption would be almost as impenetrable. It was much wider than the American equivalent and it has to be questioned why information about major mistakes in criminal investigations cannot be revealed as in the Stephen Lawrence inquiry or why we should not know the facts relating to an accident or a nuisance or a public health danger. The Home Secretary has not accepted the Macpherson Inquiry report's recommendation that there should be no class exemptions for police information and operational and administrative police information should only be withheld on grounds of 'substantial harm'.[2] Clause 26 related to law enforcement and caught specific items of information not caught by cl 25[3] as well as any 'functions' of a public authority concerned with the civil side of its investigations under cl 25(2).

[1]   See eg, *Re Barings plc* [1998] 1 All ER 673.
[2]   See Cm 4262, vol I, para 46.32 and Recommendation 9 and Campaign for FOI Press Release 22 May 1999, p 5. See also: *R v Chief Constable of the West Midlands Police, ex p Wiley* [1994] 3 All ER 420, HL.
[3]   Eg, prevention or detection of crime, the administration of justice, assessment etc of tax, immigration controls, maintenance of security and good order in prisons or other institution where persons are lawfully detained and 'the exercise by any public authority of its functions for any of the purposes specified in [now] section 31(1)(a) to (i)'.

1.140   Section 30 of the FOIA 2000 now covers investigations and proceedings conducted by public authorities and confers a class exemption for such information. It exempts information which has (a) 'at any time been held by the authority' for the purposes of any investigation which the public authority (and not another) has a duty to conduct with a view to it being ascertained whether a person should be charged with an offence or whether a person charged is guilty of the offence. This will cover information where it has been decided *not* to prosecute and where there is no prejudice to any future prosecution. Additionally, it covers (b) any investigation which is conducted by the authority which may lead to the authority instituting criminal proceedings which it has power to conduct or (c) any criminal proceedings which the authority has power to conduct. By s 63, the above information could not be kept exempt for longer than 30 years (see now on the effect of the Constitutional Reform and Governance Act 2010, para 2.62).[1] Information held by an authority is exempt if relates to the obtaining of information from confidential sources and was obtained by the authority for the purposes of its functions relating to (a) or (b) above, criminal proceedings which the authority has power to conduct, investigations conducted for purposes under s 31(2) (see below) either under prerogative or statutory powers, or civil proceedings which are brought by or on behalf of the authority.[2] The duty to confirm or deny does not apply to information exempt by virtue of the above provisions. This is a broader formulation than the usual proviso.

[1] On the public records aspects of the FOIA 2000, see paras 2.48 et seq below.
[2] This obviously protects informers on a class basis and maintains the class protection under Public Interest Immunity for this group: see ch 10 below. The statements made by the government (see para 10.66 below) that it would no longer make claims for public interest immunity on a class basis do not cover the police but will cover prosecuting authorities. On police complaints and removal of class immunity from public interest immunity, see *R v Chief Constable West Midlands Police ex p Wiley* [1994] 3 All ER 420 (HL) and para 10.72 below.

1.141 Section 30(4) spells out what a public authority means in terms of authorised officers, Ministers of the Crown or Northern Ireland (sic) Ministers. Subsection (5) explains 'criminal proceedings' as including courts-martial and naval disciplinary courts and 'offence' to include military offences.

1.142 In FS50132101 the complaint concerned information about current investigations conducted by the Civil Aviation Authority concerning air carriers and non-compliance with Council Regulation (EC) No 261/2004 (compensation and assistance to air passengers denied boarding rights). The CAA withheld the information on the basis, inter alia, of the s 30(1)(b) exemption. The IC decided that the information was covered by s 30 and then considered the public interest test. The CAA argued that disclosure could lead to the carriers refusing to engage in informal dispute resolution and consumers' interests would be prejudiced. The IC decided that there was a significant public interest in disclosing the information so as to hold the CAA to account for its conduct of the investigations. The IC ruled that the information in relation to investigations before the request should be disclosed. However he thought that investigations which were current at the time of the request would not be suitable for disclosure under the public interest test. FS50106800 concerned the Metropolitan police and a request for files on Special Branch investigations from over 100 years previously. Section 30(2) on informers was engaged but the public interest in disclosure was stronger than in retention – on appeal the tribunal ordered the names to be redacted (EA/2008/0078).

1.143 The exemption has been properly claimed for papers concering an investigation into former leader of the Liberal Party, Jeremy Thorpe, for conspiracy to murder almost 30 years previously.[1] Even after almost 30 years the public interest favoured maintenance of the exemption under s 30(1). The overriding public interest in protecting informers' identities under s 30(2)(b) has been emphasised.[2] The tribunal, overruling the IC, has given very strong protection to Companies Act investigations into serious company irregularities including director disqualifications and fraud.[3] The IC had required 'a generalised explanation' into the investigations but which would not reveal the identities of witnesses. The standard practice of the PA was not to provide any reasons for a Companies Act investigation. The IC showed himself to be an advocate of open government in this case but the tribunal clearly thought it was misplaced in ruling that the PI favoured maintenance of the exemption. In *Bellamy v IC*[4] the IT sought to confine PI considerations to the specific ones inherent in a particular exemption. Balancing the PI factors is not a discretion – by which presumably it means that it is not an open free choice – it is a mixed question of fact and law for the IT!

1   *Guardian Newspapers v IC & Chief Constable of Avon & Somerset Police* EA/2006/0017.
2   *E Alcock v IC* EA/2006/0022; *D v NSPCC* [1978] AC 171.
3   *DTI v IC* EA/2006/0007.
4   EA/2005/0023.

(X) LAW ENFORCEMENT

1.144 Section 31 of the FOIA 2000 concerns information covering law enforcement. It should be noted that by virtue of s 63(4) exemption under this section lasts for 100 years (see para 2.70)) following the year in which the record was created. Compliance with s 1(1)(a) in relation to any record after a similar period will not be taken to be capable of having any of the effects in s 31(1); it may be judged to have those effects up to 100 years (see para 2.70).[1] Section 30 covers information which although not exempt under s 30, is exempt under this section if its disclosure would, or would be likely to, prejudice:

(a)   the prevention or detection of crime;
(b)   the apprehension or prosecution of offenders;
(c)   the administration of justice, which in case law has been given both wide and narrower meanings. An interference with the system of justice is preferred here because other exemptions exempt more specific information;[2]
(d)   the assessment of any tax or duty or similar imposition;
(e)   the operation of the immigration controls;
(f)   the maintenance of good order and security in prisons or in other places where persons are lawfully detained;
(g)   the exercise by any authority of its functions for any of the purposes specified in sub-s (2);
(h)   civil proceedings brought for or arising out of an inquiry for any of the purposes listed below or under prerogative or statutory powers;
(i)   any inquiry under the Fatal Accidents and Sudden Deaths Act (Scotland) 1976 to the extent that the inquiry arises from an investigation conducted for any of the purposes below by or on behalf of the authority under prerogative or statutory powers.

1   In evidence to the Select Committee the Home Secretary stated that some records relating to the secret police in Ireland had been closed since 1874: HC 398 I (1997–98), para 101.
2   See eg Lord Diplock in *Secretary of State for Defence v Guardian Newspapers Ltd* [1984] 3 All ER 601, HL and Lord Bridge in *X Ltd v Morgan Grampian* [1990] 2 All ER 1, HL etc and ch 10 (paras 10.37 et seq) below for developing case-law.

1.145 The purposes are:
(1)   Ascertaining whether any person has failed to comply with the law.
(2)   Ascertaining whether any person is responsible for any conduct which is improper.
(3)   Ascertaining whether circumstances which would justify regulatory action in pursuance of any enactment exist or may arise.

(4) Ascertaining a person's fitness or competence in relation to the management of bodies corporate or in relation to any profession or other activity which he is or seeks to become authorised to carry on.

(5) Ascertaining the cause of an accident. This caused a good deal of controversy in the first version of the published Bill. It is a contents claim and is subject to the public interest test. The IC may make recommendations. It gives far greater protection, however, than would legal professional privilege and is more restrictive than comparable laws elsewhere.

(6) Protecting charities against misconduct or mismanagement in their administration and whether by trustees or others.

(7) Protecting the property of charities from loss or misapplication.

(8) Recovering the property of charities; obviously there was a good deal of special pleading on behalf of charities.

(9) The purpose of securing the health, safety and welfare of persons at work.

(10) Protecting persons other than persons at work against risk to health or safety arising out of or in connection with the actions of persons at work.

1.146 Relevant here would be the secrecy surrounding events such as those leading to the Paddington or Hatfield rail disasters to give appropriate protection to civil litigation brought for such purposes and, on the other hand, giving the public sufficient warning about risk and danger and under-investment (this might also cover commercial exemptions). It is important to see the connection between (g) and (h) above and these purposes, especially (5), (9) and (10). While it is fair and proper that civil proceedings arising from these investigations should not be prejudiced, there is an acute public interest in having responsible reporting about serious accidents and near-accidents of dangerous activities. Retention of personal data under these provisions (ss 30 and 31) would have to comply with the DPA 1998 if applicable and this has been a subject of great complexity (see ch 7).

1.147 The duty to confirm or deny applies in the normal manner to this information.

1.148 Under s 31(1)(a) and (g) information on bringing prosecutions for speeding in the band 70–75 mph was rightly refused (EA/2010/0071) as was information on the BBC's requests for search warrants for evasion of licence fee investigations. In FS50197056 concerning the Police Ombudsman for Northern Ireland (PONI), the complainant requested information held by PONI relating to an inspection undertaken by the Office of Surveillance Commissioners (the OSC). PONI refused to provide this, citing the exemptions at ss 31(1)(a) and 31(1)(g) (law enforcement). Following the IC's intervention PONI disclosed some of the requested information to the complainant. The IC found that the remaining withheld information was exempt under the provisions claimed, and that the public interest in maintaining the exemptions outweighed the public interest in disclosing the information. Therefore the IC did not require any steps to be taken. In FS50209828 (see above under s 23) a request for a murder inquiry report was rightly refused. The complainant in FS50137475 requested from the BBC information relating to the use and effectiveness of television detector vans.

The BBC refused to disclose the majority of the information, relying on ss 31 and 42. The BBC pursued several arguments to the effect that the disclosure would reduce the deterrent effect of vans, enable evaders to find weaknesses in their use and otherwise encourage evasion. On application of the 'would or would be likely to prejudice' test the IC decided that disclosure would have adverse consequences. In considering the public interest test, the arguments for disclosure were increased legitimacy and scrutiny of the application of public funds. However, in deciding that the public interest lay with non-disclosure, he believed that the use of the equipment is strictly and independently regulated and that disclosure would have a negative effect on the public interest for legitimate licence feepayers. In FS50138964 similar considerations came to play in upholding the refusal by HM Revenue and Customs of internal guidance on processing self assessed tax returns.

1.149   Case FS 50069091 was a request to the Sussex Police for numbers of people (generic not identifiable individuals) subject to Sex Offences Act orders; a geographical breakdown of where they resided was requested. The IC emphasised that the request was for generic information not specific and s 31 was not engaged. The IC reported that the information was already published. He stated that courts do not usually impose restrictions on the reporting of an adult defendant's name and address in cases regarding sexual offences in spite of the fact that such information could lead to a violent reaction against the defendant or his family. In FS50309111 information was rightly refused under s 31(1)(a) in relation to individuals who were at risk of recruitment to terrorist activities in the West Midlands. There were numerous similar requests to other police forces.

1.150   *C England v LB Bexley and IC*[1] was a request for the addresses and ownership details of empty properties that came to the council's notice. Section 31(1)(a) was cited as an exemption although the information had not been collected for prevention of crime. It was decided that addresses are personal data for s 40 exemption (para 98). The decision contains a detailed and instructive analysis of the strength of evidence linking s 31 and preventing the commission of crime. The IT found on the evidence that disclosure would be likely to have a 'significant negative impact on the prevention of crime'. In *Bucks Free Press v IC*,[2] (referred to above), the tribunal allowed the appeal. The request concerned information of the number of times a notice of intended prosecution has been issued by the Thames Valley Police as a result of alleged speeding offences at two speed cameras. The IC held that ss 31 and 38 were correctly applied and non-dislosure was justified. The tribunal noted that the information sought constituted general information and 'the connection between disclosure and drivers' behaviour' was so 'tenuous' that 'site specific safety factors did not come into effect and the exemptions were not engaged.' (See FS50357713 for requests to the Big Lottery Fund, which were correctly denied under this section.)

[1]   EA/2006/0060 and EA/2006/000066.
[2]   EA/2006/0071.

1.151   Information on speed cameras has been a popular subject of request. *P Hemsley v IC and Chief Constable of Northants (AP)*[1] was a request for information about speed cameras which are active intermittently at sites. In sunny weather in the early morning a driver in one direction would be looking into the sun, which would impair his vision of speed restriction signs. Section 31(1)(a) and (b) were invoked. The tribunal identified the information that should be available to the general public about speed cameras (para 23). It was concerned about the difficulty in distinguishing between 'a public spirited request' and one which was more self-rewarding eg 'the creation of a commercial website selling forecasts on the operation of safety cameras'. Disclosure was rightly denied on the facts (and see *C Martin and Oxford City Council v IC* EA/2005/0026 and EA/2005/0030).

¹   EA/2005/0026.

(XI) COURT RECORDS

1.152   Section 32 of the FOIA 2000 deals with court records. Information is exempt information if held by a public authority and if 'held only by virtue of being contained in': any document filed with, or otherwise placed in the custody of, a court for the purposes of proceedings in a particular cause or matter; any documents served upon or by a public authority for legal proceedings; any document created by a court or member of the administrative staff of a court for legal proceedings.

1.153   It is also exempt information if similarly held and contained in any document placed in the custody of a person conducting an inquiry or arbitration for the purposes of such inquiry or arbitration, or if created by such a person for such purposes. The duty to confirm or deny does not arise to information covered by this section. Furthermore, the discretionary disclosure provisions do not apply to this exempt information under s 32 (though see para 1.155 below) and the IC's recommendatory powers do not apply.

1.154   'Court' includes any tribunal or body exercising the judicial power of the State;¹ 'proceedings in any cause or matter' includes any inquest or post-mortem examination; 'inquiry' means any inquiry or hearing of a statutory nature, but not one conducted under prerogative powers; 'arbitration' means, except for Scotland, any arbitration to which Part I of the Arbitration Act 1996 applies (sub-s (4)). Where an authority has powers of holding an inquiry, information transferred by it to the inquiry receive the protection of s 32(2) and the inquiry maintains that exemption after the conclusion of the inquiry. This was the case even though inquiries have no comparable mechanisms to courts allowing disclosure of documents. Furthermore 'document' means an electronic document and not simply one in 'hard' form.² The case was remitted on appeal by the court of appeal to the First Tier Tribunal (FTT) to determine whether ECHR, art 10 rights enshrined in the HRA 1998 gave s 32(2) a different interpretation in the light of case law from the ECtHR at Strasbourg.³ Of especial importance were the facts that the requester was a journalist who may need access to the documents to realise art 10 freedom of speech rights. The court was otherwise minded to reject the appeal.

1   *A-G v BBC* [1980] 3 All ER 161.
2   *D.Kennedy v IC and Charity Commission* [2010] EWHC 475 Admin.
3   *D Kennedy v IC etc* [2011] EWCA Civ 367 and *Tarsasag* (para 1.155 note 1, below).

1.155 Courts do exercise powers to allow access to documents filed with the court subject to protection for confidential information.[1] **This is an absolute exemption.**[2]

1   Rule 39.2 of the Civil Procedure Rules 1998 states that as a general rule, hearings are in public, but no special provision has to be made to accommodate members of the public (r 39.2). Under r 39.3, provision is made for hearings in private. See *A Health Authority v X* [2002] 2 All ER 780 (CA). See *The Guardian* 9 December 2004 for it s headline report on a successful application to obtain case records from an arms bribery case *Chan v Alvis Vehicles Ltd* [2003] EWHC 1238: *In re Guardian Newspapers (Court Record: Disclosure)* (2004) *Times*, 18 December and CPR 5.4(5)(b). Rule 5(4) deals with the supply of documents from court records to parties or other persons. Under r 5.4(2)(c) a court's permission was required before a search could be made of any document other than a claim form, judgment or order: see *Dian AO v Davis, Frankel & Mead (a firm)* [2005] 1 All ER 1074 on the requirement for permission, the exercise of the court's discretion and searching classes of documents. Where documents had not been read by the court as part of the decision-making process, such as affidavits or statements, access should only be given where there were 'strong grounds for thinking that it was necessary in the interests of justice'. See *Chan U Seek v Alvis Vehicles Ltd* [2005] 1 WLR 2965 on access by non parties to the court file. On witness statements see CPR 32.13. There is no comparable provision to CPR 5.4(5)(b) or Part 32.13 in the Criminal Procedure Rules 2010. The Criminal Procedure Rules 2010 (see now SI 2011/1709) govern access in criminal proceedings and the Administrative Court has ruled that there is no right of access to skeleton arguments, statements etc under ECHR, Art 10: *R (Guardian News and Media Ltd) v City of Westminster Magistrates' Court* [2010] EWHC 3376 (Admin). All the submissions in a high profile extradition case that were in the requested documents were fully set out in open judgment after argument in open court. It was not a case where denial of access prevented knowledge of the case or there had been a denial of access to open proceedings: *Tarsasag v Hungary* Application no 37374/05 14 July 2009 and *Independent News and Media Ltd v A* [2010] 1 WLR 262 (CA). The court noted that FOIA 2000, s 32(1) would not have allowed access in the *City of Westminster* case to such information held by the Court Service or MoJ. The impact of increasing use of skeleton arguments on open justice was seen by Lord Scarman in *Harman v Home Office* [1983] AC 280 at 316. See *R v Howell* [2003] EWCA Crim 486. See *D Kennedy v Information Commissioner etc* [2011] EWCA Civ 367 and reading down s 32(2) by virtue of the HRA 1998 and the influence of *Tarsasag* above.

2   See Inquiries Act 2005, s 18 which disapplies s 32(2) in relation to concluded inquiries.

1.156 The case law has decided that written transcripts of court proceedings held in public are not documents created by the court or an administrative member of the court and are not protected by s 32. The documents had been produced by a commercial body. The IC had decided otherwise but was overruled by the tribunal.[1] Audio recordings of court hearings and where the proceedings were in public were similarly not covered by s 32. Nor were they protected by s 21 because application to the court does not make them 'reasonably accessible' (FS50150314).

1   *Mitchell v IC* EA/2005/0002.

1.157 EA/2005/0002 (above) also ruled that s 32 will protect internal notes from the judge to jury or vice versa but not orders under the Contempt of Court Act 1981.[1]

1   See *A Szuchs v IC UK Intellectual Property Office* EA/2007/0075.

(XII) AUDIT FUNCTIONS

1.158 Where a public authority has audit functions in relation to another authority's accounts or in relation to the economy, efficiency or effectiveness (the three 'Es')[1] with which the latter carries out its functions then information held for those purposes is exempt where its disclosure would, or would be likely to, prejudice any of the above audit or three 'Es' functions (FOIA 2000, s 33: para 11.08 below). The duty to confirm or deny does not arise under the usual formula but in an amended form.

[1] See ch 11.

1.159 There have been several cases involving the 'gateways reviews' (GRs) of large-scale government procurement concerning information technology contracts. Many large, complex, and novel civil programmes had missed delivery dates. The Office of Government Commerce (OGC) had produced a Gateway Process Review Pack. The 'Gateway' process was now mandatory across central government including the Ministry of Defence and executive agencies, and local government adopted the reviews on a voluntary basis. They were carried out at five key stages of a programme and were treated as confidential. Reviewers are mainly senior civil servants or outside consultants. GRs saved the Exchequer £1.5b between 2003 and 2005. Under the reviews, projects are colour-coded periodically at critical stages. These are known as RAG reviews (red, amber, green). Red signifies the necessity of immediate action; amber suggests recommendations and green is an 'all clear'. A request was made to the OGC for 'double red warnings reports'. The OGC invoked s 33 on the ground of prejudice in relation to the economy, efficiency, and effectiveness achieved by other PAs in their use of resources. Publication, it was argued, would also discourage cooperation by those who supplied information to OGC. The IC was not convinced by such arguments: 'Information was not given purely voluntarily by those persons' (para 23). IC decided that s 33 was not engaged (FS 50095679). FS 50070196 also related to a request for GRs of iIdentity cards programmes and contracts run by the Home Office. Sections 33 and 35 were invoked. The information in question was examined by the IC and his officers in the premises of the OGC. The OGC repeated the argument about disclosure reducing cooperation, but it was similarly rejected by the IC. ('Those persons operate in a professional capacity and cooperation is a part of their professional responsibilities'). Section 33 was not engaged. In FS50180545 the IC did not consider that auditing documents were of a sufficiently 'free and frank' nature to merit protection under s 33.

1.160 EA/2006/0068 and 0080 continue the case law on gateways. 'Misinterpretation' of messages was not a good reason for non-disclosure, the tribunal ruled. The Select Committee on Works and Pensions and the Committee of Public Accounts had both recommended publication of GRs and the tribunal had allowed itself to be influenced by this. The government did not agree with the routine publication of GRs but did not invoke a 'blanket exemption' for them. Each FOIA request is considered on its merits by the OGC. The point was that Parliamentary reports are often after the event, whereas the tribunal believed major projects should be scrutinised during their actual operation as ongoing concerns. The OGC's case, also argued under s 35, was rejected. OGC appealed to the High Court. That court allowed the appeal because the tribunal was too influenced in its judgment by a select committee report and this was not something upon which judicial notice could be taken. The tribunal had not exercised its judicial functions correctly in so doing and had made an error of law. But the court did not rule on the merits as it made perfectly clear.[1] The case was remitted to the tribunal for a rehearing on the merits.[2] The tribunal upheld the publication of two GR reports. The tribunal emphasised that its ruling did not set a precedent for all GRs; each would have to be determined on its particular facts. Names of those involved in reviews should be redacted, but not the grades of functions of parties.

1   [2008] EWHC 737 (Admin) and 774 (Admin).
2   *Office of Government Commerce v IC* EA/2006/0068 and 0080) (original cases FS50070196 and FS50132936).

1.161   In *Office of Government Commerce v and Anor*,[1] a request was made for information about the RAG system for overseeing government procurement contracts involving IT. Sections 33(1)(b) and 35 were invoked. Of relevance here was that the tribunal could not examine Parliamentary Questions (PQs) to assess the adequacy of a Minister's answers to such questions. Ministers should not answer PQs by reference to the exemptions in the FOIA! Parliamentary privilege had been interfered with by judicial reliance on a select committee's findings and opinions. It denied the full separation of powers. In FS50318502, the NAO rightly refused under ss 33(1)(b) and 33(2) to disclose information needed to audit preparations for the 2012 Olympic games.

1   [2008] EWHC 737 (Admin).

(XIII) PARLIAMENTARY PRIVILEGE

1.162   The original Bill did not include Parliament within the FOIA 2000's coverage. It was a recommendation from the Select Committee on Public Administration in its review of the draft Bill which contained no such provision although the White Paper of 1997 referred to 'continuing discussions' about Parliament's inclusion.[1] Where disclosure would cause a breach of privilege of either House of Parliament it is exempt information under s 34 of the FOIA 2000. The duty to confirm or deny does not apply if, or to the extent that, exemption from s 1(1)(a) is required for the purpose of avoiding an infringement of the privileges of either House. A certificate signed by the Speaker of the House of Commons or Clerk of the Parliaments stating that exemption from s 1(1)(b) or (a) and (b) is, or at any time was, required to avoid an infringement of Parliamentary privilege shall be conclusive evidence of that fact. It is unlikely that the IC would have any grounds or capability to question such a certificate.[2] There has been extensive discussion in the higher courts of the extent of the ancient privilege necessitated by the prosecution of those MPs and peers who had allegedly entered false accounts in making claims for expenses.[3] **This is an absolute exemption.**

1   See HC 570 I (1998–99), para 24, and HC 398 I (1997–98), para 37.
2   See eg *Hamilton v Al Fayed* [2000] 2 All ER 224, HL.
3   *R v Chaytor and Others* [2010] EWCA 1910 Crim and [2010] UKSC 52.

1.163   This has not been a frequently employed exemption. Contrary to some reports, the Speaker did not claim the privilege in relation to MPs' expenses.[1] The exemption prayed in aid in that case was s 40 (see para 7.107). The information requested about additional expenses allowances for MPs including addresses did not interfere with their privacy, was not unwarranted, and had to be disclosed in full. The system of expenses (now reformed; see para 7.111) was 'deeply flawed'. The arguments that MPs had a reasonable expectation of privacy and the disclosure of addresses was neither proportionate nor necessary were rejected by the court as clear reasons had been given for these findings by the tribunal. The House of Commons could not operate on the basis that legislation did not apply to it or that MPs could dispense with or suspend such legislation. The expenses system was so bad that MPs could not expect anything less than – as necessity required – full disclosure. Only the most pressing of MPs' privacy requirements could prevent publication, eg security. The tribunal had 'carefully balanced' all factors. In FS50327178, the privilege under s 34(1) was claimed successfully in relation to a request for names and numbers of MPs under investigation by the Parliamentary Commissioner for Standards.

1   *Corporate Officer House of Commons v IC, Brooke etc* [2008] EWHC 1084 (Admin) at 2.

(XIV) FORMULATION OF GOVERNMENT POLICY ETC

1.164   The original cl 28(1)(a) exempted information relating to the formulation or development of government policy, and this is now s 35(1)(a). The totality of this made it truly an amazing exemption but the subsection then specified various aspects of central government decision-making which are specifically protected, including communications between Ministers of the Crown particularly in Cabinet and Cabinet committee proceedings.[1] For safe measure, information of central government (and devolved government) which is not caught by the above and information of other public authorities was protected under cl 28(3) if 'in the reasonable opinion of a qualified person' disclosure:

'(c)   would otherwise prejudice, or would be likely otherwise to prejudice, the effective conduct of public affairs.'

1   This is much stricter than the law relating to confidentiality in Crown or public service or Public Interest Immunity: *A-G v Jonathan Cape Ltd* [1976] QB 752; *A-G v Guardian Newspapers Ltd (No 2)* [1988] 3 All ER 545, HL; *Burmah Oil v Bank of England* [1980] AC 1090, HL; *Air Canada v Secretary of State for Trade (No 2)* [1983] 2 AC 394, HL. The Ministerial Code formerly stated at ch 2, para 16: 'The internal process through which a decision has been made, or the level of [Cabinet] Committee by which it was taken, should not be disclosed' On the current Code, see para 2.99.

1.165   The FOIA 2000 now creates two exemptions in ss 35 and 36. Section 35 covers the formulation of government policy. This includes the policy of the Executive Committee of Northern Ireland and the Welsh Assembly Government

– it covers UK central government and devolved government. It does not cover other PAs.

1.166 Information held by a government department (which includes the Welsh Assembly Government) is exempt where it relates to: the formulation of government policy; Ministerial communications including in particular proceedings of the Cabinet or Cabinet Committees, the Executive Committee of the Northern Ireland Assembly or the Cabinet or Cabinet Committees of the Welsh Assembly Government; the provision of advice by any of the Law Officers (sub-s (3)) or any request for the provision of such advice; or, the operation of any Ministerial private office. This last office means any part of a government department which provides personal administrative support to a Minister of the Crown, to a Northern Ireland Minister or a Northern Ireland junior Minister (see s 19 of the Northern Ireland Act 1998) and personal administrative support provided by any part of the administration of the Welsh Assembly Government to members of the Welsh Assembly Government. The duty to confirm or deny provision applies in the standard manner.

1.167 This will cover all advice on policy, from whatever sources, alternatives to policies adopted and any draft policies, draft statements and opinions. The totality of this exemption is breathtaking. The dangers in its absoluteness were brought home by the report of Lord Philips into the BSE inquiry where suppression of the truth of the BSE epidemic was as contagious as the epidemic itself.[1] The provision of advice by the Law officers was illustrated dramatically when the Attorney General refused to publish his advice on the legality of commencing armed hostilities against Iraq in 2003.[2] Following publication of leaked extracts of the advice by the press, the government published the Attorney General's advice to the Prime Minister a week before the general election of 2005. The publication of the advice raised more questions than it resolved and contradictory opinions of the Attorney General to the Prime Minister were subsequently published.

[1] See HC 887 I-XVI (1999–2000), 16 vols. It is available on: http://62.189.42.105/index.htm.
[2] See *Review of Intelligence on Weapons of Mass Destruction* HC 898 (2003–04), Annex D. See the Ministerial Code (2010) ch 2, on the Law Officers and note: 'By convention, written opinions of the Law Officers, unlike other Ministerial papers, are generally made available to succeeding Administrations' at para 2.10. The advice of Law Officers has been made public on a number of occasions.

1.168 What of factual, scientific or technical advice? Can this not be revealed even before the decision is finalised? An amendment to the Bill stated that when exercising discretion under cl 13, where information is exempt by virtue of relating to the formulation of policy, the public authority shall have regard **in particular** to the desirability of communicating to the applicant factual information which has been used, or is intended to be used, to provide an informed background to decision-taking. What if it was factual information that was not used? What is factual?[1] Does the reference to *applicant* personalise the decision in any way? What of the post-decisional stage and release of information? Can information which is not simply 'factual' not then be released? The National Assembly for

Wales publishes 'decision reports' which are summaries of facts and analyses of the facts relating to all formal decisions taken by Ministers under legal powers. These vary from brief statements to very detailed documents. A minute covering advice is not published and constitutes part A of a 'split report'.

[1]   See *Bushell v Secretary of State for the Environment* [1981] AC 75, HL, and cf *R (NASHA) v Secretary of State for Health* (2005) *Times*, 9 March – knowledge of civil servant not imputed to Minister.

1.169   The amendment was itself further amended so that the reference to factual information, either pre- or post-decision, became 'statistical' information used to provide any informed background to the taking of the decision. *Secretary of State for Work & Pensions v IC*[1] concerned a request for the feasibility of the government's ID cards programme and relevant instructions and their full impact, costs and benefits. Section 35 was invoked. Para 20 deals with 'statistical information' test under s 35(2) and also para 75. There is MoJ (formerly Department for Constitutional Affairs) guidance on 'statistical information'.[1] This is not to be treated as relating to the formulation or development of policy or as relating to ministerial communications. This was only to be released, it seemed, post-decision. This was an especially limiting provision.

[1]   http://www.justice.gov.uk/docs/foi-exemption-s35.pdf at p 9.
[2]   EA/2005/0040.

1.170   On Report in the Lords, the original provision concerning factual information was restored and it emerged in the Act as s 35(4) – 'regard shall be had to the particular public interest in the disclosure of factual information which has been used, or is intended to be used, to provide an informed background to decision-taking'. So that when making a decision on a public interest override of the exclusion of the duty to confirm or deny or a disclosure under s 2(1)(b) or (2)(b) of information which is exempt because it relates to the formulation or development of government policy, regard shall be had to that particular public interest in the disclosure of factual information. EA/2005/0040 (above) discusses factual information and s 35(4) in paras 71 et seq. The onus will be on those justifying secrecy under s 2. The provision does not, however, refer to access to the *analysis* of facts as did the 1997 Code on Access. Access to such analysis underlying policy decisions and proposals was allowed under the Code after decisions are made. The Code also allowed policy-related material to be withheld only if disclosure would harm 'the frankness and candour of internal discussion'. A public interest disclosure of such information may be made. The reference to 'applicant' has been removed from the Act. The Parliamentary Ombudsman has not allowed factual information to be withheld under the Code.[1]

[1]   Case A 8/00 HC 494 (1999/00); Case A 31/99 HC 21 (1999/00).

1.171   This exemption is a class exemption and is much wider than say Public Interest Immunity certificates where a class basis of immunity was abandoned by the government in 1996.[1] This seems a very sweeping exemption only partially limited by the amendment introduced in the Bill explained above. Protection of timing of release of information is understandable when timing is crucial because of a legitimate sensitivity on eg presentation. The government said it would keep the situation under review.[2]

[1]   See ch 10 and para 1.28 above.
[2]   See my article in (1998) PL 176.

1.172   *DBERR v D O'Brien and IC* [2009] EWHC 164 (Admin) displayed a marked reluctance to interfere with a tribunal's assessment of PI factors under s 35 (but not under s 42 (below). FS50126011 contains a useful analysis and discussion of the PI under s 35(1)(a) and (b). The requester wanted information concerning Cabinet Office (CO) papers in relation to an Asylum and Immigration working group. The papers covered the approach to registration of workers from new EU accession states. The CO claimed s 35 was operative and the PI favoured non disclosure. The IC relied upon the IT's decision in *DfES v the Commissioner and the Evening Standard* (EA/2006/0006, at 75). The PI factors that were relevant involved a balancing of:

'In favour of disclosure:
(i)   Promoting public understanding behind decisions taken.
(ii)   Public participation and debate in policy issues, especially where the

subject matter is of a controversial nature.
(iii) Accountability for decisions taken.
(iv)   Transparency in decision making.
(v)   Information contained within the paper which is already in the public domain.

Against disclosure:
(i)   The short period of time that had elapsed between the meeting and the complainant's request, and that the policy in question continues to be kept under review.
(ii)   Effects on the principle of collective responsibility for decisions by revealing interdepartmental considerations which may reveal disagreements between Ministers and departments.
(iii) Revealing the policy options presented to Ministers for collective discussion and decision-making could undermine the process of collective government and inhibit Ministers' from having a frank and fully-informed discussion in order to reach informed decisions.
(iv)   Effects on the comprehensiveness of information provided for consideration in policy making.
(Para 19)

The IC set out his reasons for ordering disclosure: much of the information was already in the public domain; the decision was controversial and that much of the controversy had its origins in a 'lack of public engagement' in the process of reaching the decision. It was in the PI for the public to see the reasons behind the decision; release of information would not adversely affect any ongoing reviews of the policy and the information would assist public debate. It was difficult to see how collective responsibility of Ministers could be adversely affected. The IC did not believe there would be any adverse impact on civil service candour by disclosure: names of officials were not included, the discussion was objective and balanced and the IC relied on the tribunal's decision in *DfES v IC and Evening Standard* EA/2006/0006. In *DfES* which is examined directly below. Finally, timing of a request and its relationship to a decision is crucial. Where a decision is announced, as in this case, although aspects may still need to be protected, once a decision was announced less weight may be accorded to the need for protection. The PI favoured disclosure. In *Secretary of State for Work and Pensions IC* EA/2005/0040 the information was requested about feasibility studies, instructions and costs and benefits for the New Labour government's ID cards programme. The tribunal stated that application was at a late stage of policy implementation (an advanced stage of policy formulation) and this 'second stage' related to the 'detailed implementation of the scheme at departmental level'. The ID scheme was unprecedented in its complexity and scale 'incurring costs of several billion pounds'. It was likely to have a profound affect on access to public services (para 96). The disputed information was introduced at a 'late stage in the formulation and development of an ID scheme' after the decision by government to introduce such a scheme. Both the IC and tribunal believed the PI in these circumstances was in favour of disclosure.[1]

[1]   The identities of junior civil servants were correctly redacted.

1.173   In *DfES v IC and Evening Standard (AP)* EA/2006/0006 – in which, incidentally, it was stated that FOIA 2000, s 1 creates a 'new fundamental right to information' (para 61) – s 35(1)(a) was invoked. High-level witnesses on behalf of the PA included the Cabinet Secretary. The request involved information about setting of school budgets in England including the minutes of a policy committee. Arguments on the 'chilling effect' on advice and record-keeping were rejected. The tribunal ruled crucially that the formulation and development of policy had to be distinguished from implementation of policy and its analysis (para 13). The tribunal acknowledged the dangers of 'sofa government' by the use of specialist advisers. The words 'Relates to formulation and development of policy' in s 35 should be construed broadly. There was no need to prevent disclosure of officials' identities. The status of minutes does is not an automatic ground for exemption; this is the case even where they concern the 'most senior of officials'. 'To treat such status as automatically conferring exemption would be tantamount to intervening within s.35(1) a class of absolutely exempt information for which the subsection gives no warrant ...' (para 69).[1] In para 75 the guiding principles in cases such as the present are: the content of particular information. As we have seen, no status is automatically exempt. The protection is against compromise or unjust public opprobrium of civil servants not ministers. A paramount feature is the timing of a request. What is highly relevant in June 2007 may carry little weight by January 2011 (earlier years were actually useed). A Parliamentary statement announcing the policy 'will normally mark the end of the process of policy formulation'. But the tribunal emphasised that all specific facts must be viewed carefully, however, and PI in exemption may not necessarily disappear on announcement. One should expect fortitude, impartiality and independence of civil servants. But good reasons may exist to withhold the names of 'more junior civil servants'. The tribunal assumed that Ministers will 'behave fairly and responsibly to civil servants who may be associated with unpopular advice'. A blanket policy, however, of refusing to identify civil servants cannot be justified. There must be a specific reason justifying non-disclosure of civil servant's identity and junior status may qualify for such. There is 'a general PI in transparency and a better understanding of how the government tackles important policy problems' the tribunal believed. In the present case the 'funding crisis' in schools had caused and was of great public concern. Even though the information may not prove to be significant in any public debate the PI favoured disclosure.[2] In FS50153967 the complainant wrote to the CO to request records of exchanges between Tony Blair and Rupert Murdoch. The documents were more than seven years old and the PI favoured disclosure. *Cabinet Office v IC* EA/2008/0049 concerned Prime Minister's meetings. The complainant requested a full list of all those who met with the Prime Minister at 10 Downing Street in June 2005. Some information was disclosed, but information relating to internal meetings with ministerial colleagues under ss 35 and 36 was withheld. A list of appointments would not come within the definition of policy formulation. Further, it would not be possible to determine the content of any meetings which were held. Therefore the Commissioner decided that details as to the names of officials were not exempt. However, the exemption would apply in respect of references to Cabinet Committees under s 35(1)(a). The commissioner considered the public interest test. The CO argued that disclosure could:

(a) disenable ministers from discussing sensitive policy issues without inhibition;
(b) cause individuals with whom the Prime Minister met to be targeted by lobbyists;
(c) affect the perceived neutrality of particular civil servants;
(d) undermine the convention of collective responsibility;
(e) link civil servants to particular areas of policy.

The tribunal upheld the IC's decision favouring disclosure under the PI. In *Department for Culture, Media and Sport v IC* EA/2007/0090 the tribunal reversed the IC's decision on disclosure on PI grounds under s 35. It concerned advice from civil servants to the Minister on the list of sporting events that were protected under the Broadcasting Act 1996 from being exclusively pay per view. The IC said that encouraging good practice, promoting accountability and understanding, encouraging public debate, and broadening policy input in the age of information were all relevant factors. On examination of the material the tribunal did not consider the first four benefits were advanced by disclosure. The grounds for release have to be supported by good arguments – otherwise s 35 would be used in favour of indiscriminate disclosure. There is no fixed point beyond which a PI in non disclosure may not be argued. The material here was seven years old. But the tribunal did not consider that release would help public debate. On the facts, and unlike the DfS&S case above, there was no PI to match the PI in maintaining the 'private thinking space' of ministers and civil servants. In terms of the public interest this is a difficult case to understand. The facts constitute a very important public interest question in relation to broadcasting sporting events yet the tribunal felt the evidence for disclosure 'anodyne'.

1.174 In *Scotland Office v IC* EA/2007/0128 the tribunal noted that there was no evidence post-FOIA or the decision in *DfS&S* EA/2006/0006 of the 'chilling effect' of disclosure on civil servants.[1] Where outside advisers contributed to 'blue sky thinking' in policy development and where they would have expected confidentiality that has been a good reason not to order disclosure: *Cabinet Office v IC* EA 2008/0030 (concerning Lord Birt). In FS 50104994 there was a request to HM Treasury for information on 'all relevant documentation covering the decision in principle' about the reduction of income tax by 1p in the pound announced in 1999. Section 35(1)(a) was invoked. In January 2007, the Treasury released the greater part of the information but the DN itself was appealed in *HM Treasury v IC* EA/2007/0001. The tribunal was not impressed by the warnings from HM Treasury of 'dire consequences' of releasing information much of which had been subsequently released. The undisclosed information was considered sensitive by the Treasury because if disclosed it might confine the range of topics on which Ministers might seek advice from their civil servants. The appeal was allowed in relation to one item of information and a substituted DN was issued. It concerned Budget papers. Section 35(1)(a) was invoked. Section 35 is a class exemption but any 'damage' is considered in balancing PI factors. The central question in s 35(1) is 'the content of specific information in relation to the exemption'. The tribunal believed chilling effect is inherent in the Act (para 57(3)) and was not impressed by the usual arguments trotted out by the Treasury. The PI arguments in favour of disclosure included: 'the relevant date is 1999 and the effluxion of time; the benefit of participation in government decisions; publication of some information does not remove the desirability of disclosing more; possible contribution and utility so knowing about rejected options for proposals in the future; the general benefits of greater transparency, accountability and public debate. The PI was in favour of disclosure except in relation to one item of information which had to be assessed as at the time of the appraisal in 2005. Interestingly the tribunal believed that information generated before the FOIA had no effect on assessing the PI. An underlying assumption of FOIA 2000 is that 'disclosure of information held by PAs is in itself of value and in the PI' citing *Guardian Newspapers v IC* EA/2006/0011. In FS50196977 the complainant requested minutes of the meetings of the cross-party group on House of Lords reform from the Ministry of Justice. This request was refused under s 35(1)(a). The IC believed the exemption was properly claimed because the group was a 'part of government' containing government members and its recommendations would be in a white paper. But the public interest favoured non-disclosure. The information itself 'related to a matter of constitutional significance which indicates that there is a significant public interest in disclosure, but that very fact also means that it is desirable for the government to be given space to make decisions in order to ensure full and frank discussions'.

[1]   In *OGC v IC* [2008] EWHC 737 (Admin) Stanley Burnton J approved the formulation adopted in *DfES*.

1.175   Section 35 has been the section where decisions on the public interest involving Cabinet documents were overridden by the veto in s 53 on two occasions by the Labour government in 2009. In both cases, as will be seen, the information involved Cabinet discussions. Cabinet confidentiality and collective responsibility both demanded that the information remained undisclosed. However, in *Cabinet Office v IC* EA/2010/0031 a request was made in 2005 for information concerning the minutes of the Cabinet discussions of the *Westland* case in 1986. This decision involving the future of a British helicopter manufacturer with important consequences British and European manufacturers and caused a serious scandal in Mrs Thatcher's government. The IC had decided that disclosure should be made in the public interest. This was upheld by the tribunal noting that although disclosure of Cabinet minutes will rarely be ordered within 30 years (the 30-year rule then applicable) Mrs Thatcher had 'abandoned' the convention of collective responsibility in her statement in January 1986 about the affair. Crucially, the coalition government decided not to issue a veto. Disclosures involving Cabinet documents under s 35 are rare.[1] In FS50350458 the government appealed against a ruling of the IC that information presented to Mrs Thatcher as Prime Minister on the Hillsborough football stadium disaster in 1989 be disclosed by virtue of the public interest under ss 31 and 35, although some was rightfully withheld under s 40. This became the subject of an e-petition to the government (para 2.92) attracting over 100,000 supporters for disclosure. A panel appointed by the government is due to report on the disaster, in which 96 fans were killed, in the spring of 2012.

[1]   See *R Hazell and D Busfield-Birch* (2011) PL 260.

1.176   *Cabinet Office v IC and C.Lamb* EA/2008/0024 and 0029 (F550165372) was the first case that witnessed the application of the Secretary of State's veto in response to the majority decision of the tribunal upholding the IC's decision to disclose documents (the minutes subject to specified redactions) of two Cabinet meetings in March 2003. The veto was issued in February 2009, four weeks after the tribunal decision to disclose. In December 2009, the Justice Secretary issued a second veto in relation to the disclosure of minutes of a Cabinet sub-committee on devolution to Scotland, Wales and the English regions dating from 1997. In this case, the Cabinet Office did not even appeal to the tribunal but took action after the IC's DN.[1]

The Cabinet at the Iraq meetings discussed and decided to send UK troops to engage in war on Iraq. The request for the minutes was made in April 2007. The tribunal ruled that informal documents accompanying the minutes were protected under s 35(1)(a) and (b) – these were notes taken by civil servants of the meetings. The tribunal described the case as 'exceptional' creating very powerful public interest reasons for publication. An important feature of the Cabinet meetings in relation to hostilities were papers from the Attorney General outlining his opinion on the legality of using armed force in Iraq without the necessity of a further UN Security Council resolution authorising armed invasion. The reported view of the Attorney General was that a further resolution was not required. A memorandum of the Attorney General was subsequently disclosed showing a contrary view from the Attorney General to the Prime Minister from that that had previously been made public and which differed from the Attorney General's advice that was before the Cabinet. Iraq had been in breach of resolutions concerning inspection and information on its alleged weapons of mass destruction (WMD). No evidence of WMD were actually found and the circumstances leading to warfare and huge loss of life remain highly controversial. The tribunal recounted how the Butler review of the use of intelligence on the WMD had made critical findings on the nature of Cabinet proceedings and their management in the period in question leading to hostilities. Briefing papers prepared by officials had not been circulated to the Cabinet but had been replaced by 'unscripted briefings' by the Prime Minister and Foreign and Defence Secretaries. Discussion took place in detail only between 'a small circle of individuals' for which the Cabinet as a whole would bear responsibility. 'The scope for informed overall political judgement by the Cabinet had been reduced' (para 28). The Butler inquiry discussion of intelligence and its materials was in closed session. The conclusions alone were published. The IC had previously issued an EN ordering the publication of information supporting the Attorney General's legal opinion dated 17 March 2003. Confidentiality was maintained for information in 'uncirculated drafts' or which were 'preliminary, provisional or tentative' or which might 'reveal legal risks, reservations and counter-arguments' by those involved in giving advice to the Attorney General. The Government agreed on a Disclosure Statement of materials to be published. The arguments from the Cabinet Office in favour of non-disclosure of the Cabinet Minutes were formulated around collective responsibility of ministers and government – these were general arguments – in relation to the particular information in question, the arguments were more specific. To repeat, additional materials were not ordered to be disclosed. The arguments in favour of collective responsibility revolved around conficentiality and a united public facade. In chapter 2 we examine some legal limits to the role of confidentiality in Cabinet discussions (para 2.329) as well as the whole context of ministerial confdences and frequent breaches of the convention by ministers themselves in their publications. The tribunal noted several publications where ministers had publicised events at the meetings in question including their differences of opinion and there had been ministerial leaks to the press and media. The IC stated the minutes revealed no dissent in the Cabinet beyond that contained in other published materials; no member of the Cabinet would face a compromise of their public agreement and private dissent.

1.177 The Cabinet position was that publishing these official minutes would undermine a central feature of the British constitution thereby damaging the public interest. The CO argued that if a pattern emerged of publishing minutes where there was no dissent, but not otherwise, that would lead to the obvious presumption that dissent had occurred at those meetings with a weakening of the convention.

While the IC accepted the convention of collective responsibility was deserving of 'great respect' being a 'strong factor' (para 51), these documents had to be decided upon 'in their specific context' and bearing in mind that over four years had passed since the Cabinet meeting. The IC's case for public interest disclosure included: the gravity and controversial nature of the subject; accountability for government decisions; transparency of decision-making; and public participation in government decisions (paras 58–59). Some suggested that the probing and testing of the material before the Cabinet was not sufficiently robust to assess the reliability of information used for life and death decisions, quite literally for thousands of individuals. The majority of the IT were persuaded by the 'compelling' arguments for disclosure in the PI. The decision was 'momentous' and the public had to see and understand the context of that decision 'and on the effectiveness of the decision-making context' (para 82). The majority ruled that publication, subject to agreed redactions for reasons of diplomatic sensitivity, was in the public interest. The dissenting member of the tribunal, a former senior civil servant, was that publication of the minutes would drive Cabinet governance towards informality and 'sofa government' thereby weakening the public record and undermining good and accountable government. As we have described, on 24 February 2009, four weeks after the tribunal's decision, the Justice Secretary issued his veto under FOIA 2000, s 53 blocking release of the minutes. His decision was one in which he reported that he had taken the view of the Cabinet. Lord Falconer as Lord Chancellor had variously stated there would be a Cabinet decision and Cabinet consultation. Collective responsibility and Cabinet confidentiality are crucial to the accountability of the executive to Parliament and the people. Free debate in Cabinet would be jeopardised by disclosure and that 'that damage to the public interest far outweighs any public interest in disclosure'. The 'integrity of our system of government' cannot be prejudiced by 'openness and accountability'. Suggestions for reform may also mean a reduction in the 30-year rule.

1.178 One may surmise that the coalition government in the *Westland* decision where an appeal against the IC's decision to disclose Cabinet minutes was appealed but where a s 53 veto was not issued reflects a different possible approach to use of s 35 and disclosure of Cabinet minutes on the facts of that case.

1.179 In FS50215878 involving the CO, the complainant requested any documentation emanating from, or sent to, the Office of the Prime Minister between 1997 and 2001 that made reference to the Michael Stone case, in any context. The CO confirmed it held some information falling within the request but refused to disclose the information under the exemption at s 35(1)(b) (ministerial communications). In submissions to the Commissioner, the CO also placed reliance upon s 35(1)(a) (formulation or development of government policy). The Commissioner found that s 35(1)(a) (and to a limited extent, s 35(1)(b)) were engaged and that the public interest in maintaining the exemption outweighed the public interest in disclosure of the information. Documents relating to the generation of legislative provisions are also according sensitive treatment. In FS50269514 HM Treasury was asked to disclose all documentation generated by its consideration and formulation of Finance Act 2008, s 58 (retrospective legislation that sought to end a scheme that the government considered to be a 'highly artificial and aggressive tax avoidance scheme'). The Commissioner concluded that all the withheld information was exempt either under the provisions of s 35(1)(a) or under the provisions of s 36(2)(b)(i) and that the public interest favoured the maintenance of the exemptions.

1.180 Section 35(1)(a) was involved in *Crown Prosecution Service v IC* EA/2009/ 0077. Wells made a request to the CPS asking for information on the CPS's change of position towards the reasonable punishment defence as amended by the Children Act 2004, s 58; this limited the defence to battery only. He wanted to know why the CPS changed its position from 'wrong to change the law' in 2000 to 'comfortable with the change' in 2004 and requested copies of any related correspondence and minutes. The CPS refused on the basis of s 35(1)(a). The IC decided that the exemption was engaged, but that the public interest favoured disclosure. The parties agreed various redactions on this basis and the only issue remaining for the tribunal was that of the application of s 35(1)(a). On that issue the tribunal found that the exemption was clearly engaged during the legislative process and therefore up until 2004. The outstanding disputed information related to this period and therefore the exemption remained engaged. However, the fact that the Minister for Children continued to take an interest in the development of policy in the area until 2007 was neither here nor there. There was no sunset clause in the statute and there was no ability to produce secondary legislation. No ongoing review was announced, or conducted, until two years had passed and at the time of the request (2005) there was no 'policy development' in any significant sense; the CPS could not rely on this argument. The tribunal found that the public interest favoured disclosure because, whilst all the usual reasons for non-disclosure existed, there was a lack of understanding about the law, the information would inform the wider debate, the public needed to know about the involvement of lobbyists and their influence on the government and it was important for the public to understand how the government negotiates with the opposition. This case also has a discussion on late claims for exemptions which is dealt with below (paras 1.23 et seq). For disclosures under s 35(1)(a) involving other departments where disclosure was allowed, see *Department for Culture, Media and Sport v IC* EA/2009/0038. In FS50275939 involving the MoJ the complainant requested background information relating to Lord Carter's report 'Securing the Future: Proposals for the efficient and sustainable use of custody in England and Wales'. The MoJ indicated some information was in the public domain. Other information falling within s 35(1)(a) was exempt, MoJ argued. The IC decided that this exemption was engaged, but that the public interest in the maintenance of this exemption did not outweigh the public interest in disclosure and that, in failing to disclose this information within 20 working days of receipt of the request, the public authority failed in its duties under ss 1(1)(b) and 10(1) of the Act. In FS50313758 information on filling Supreme Court vacances was wrongly refused to some extent under s 35 and a complaint was partly upheld.

1.181 Although the courts and Upper Tribunal on appeal from the tribunal are confined to appeals on questions of law, the high court has been vigilant in reminding the tribunal giving in sufficient weight to relevant factors is an error of law. Section 35(1)(c) was involved in *HM Treasury v IC and Owen* [2009] EWHC 1811 (Admin): insufficient weight had been given by the IC and tribunal to the convention of non-disclosure of law officers' advice to departments (on the compatibility of the Financial Services and Markets Act 2000 (FSMA 2000) with the Human Rights Act 1998).

'In my judgment, although mere deficiencies in the reasoning process or even isolated errors of law will not suffice to set aside a determination by the Information Tribunal, I am satisfied that this Tribunal has erred in considering how to approach the strength of the public interest in maintaining the exemption from disclosure of the information whether the Law Officers have advised or not. I am satisfied that the Tribunal misdirected itself:

(i) By failing to conclude that Parliament intended real weight should continue to be afforded to this aspect of the Law Officers' Convention.

(ii) By failing to conclude that the general considerations of good government underlining the history and nature of the convention were capable of affording weight to the interest in maintaining an exemption even in the absence of evidence of particular damage.

(iii) By failing to conclude that the evidence of the two witnesses before it, supported with detailed arguments the reasons why the general principles applied in this case, deserved some weight as emanating from senior civil servants with experience of the requirements of government in this field. This does not mean that the Tribunal were bound by these decisions or prevented from reaching their own conclusion upon the issue. Since preparing a draft of this judgment I have became aware of the decision of Keith J in *Home Office v Information Commissioner QBD* [2009] EWHC 1611 (Admin) where he rejected any suggestion of deference being required on the facts in that case at [65]. I see no inconsistency with the conclusion I have reached on the facts of the present case.

(iv) The Tribunal were unduly and wrongly influenced by a misdirection that the FOIA had tended to modify the Law Officer's Convention, as opposed to preserve it but render it amenable to being out-weighed by greater considerations of the public interest requiring disclosure of information in either limb of the Convention.

(v) The Tribunal misdirected itself that the way the Convention worked operated as a trump card in the hands of the Ministerial department concerned as to whether or not to disclose but could be deployed for its advantage. If this were the case I would agree with the Tribunal's comments that this is inconsistent with the principled reasoning and the interests of transparency required by the FOIA. The history of the convention and the evidence of Mr Jones precisely in point demonstrated that it was not. Where Ministers had disclosed without the prior consent of the Law Officers this was considered to be a breach rather than an application of the convention and a matter for reprimand.'[1]

---

[1] *Ministry of Justice v IC* EA/2007/0016 was a refusal to confirm or deny under s 35(3) whether information is held in relation to the s 35(1) exemption. Disclosure was sought on the Attorney General's advice in relation to the public interest test. Section 35(1)(c) was relied upon. An information notice was served under s 51(a) and (b) by the IC, which provides that no information is required to be given to the IC in relation to advice to a PA by a professional legal adviser, covers general and specific advice from a law officer on advice in response to an FOIA claim. The tribunal accepted the MoJ's argument that s 51 operated to protect a PA's legal advice on a FOIA claim. It is wider than s 42 (below) and does not carry a public interest test allowing disclosure. There is a strong convention on not confirming or denying law officers' advice (paras 15 and 42).

(XV) PREJUDICE TO CONDUCT OF PUBLIC AFFAIRS

1.182 Information held by a government department as defined in s 35 and not caught by FOIA 2000, s 35, and information held by public authorities apart from government departments is exempt under s 36 if 'in the reasonable opinion of a qualified person'[1] disclosure of information would, or would be likely to, prejudice the maintenance of the convention of the collective responsibility of Ministers of the Crown, the work of the executive committee of the Northern Ireland Assembly or the Cabinet Committee of the Welsh Assembly Government (sub-s (2)(a)). It is also exempt where its disclosure would, or would be likely to, inhibit the 'free and frank provision of advice' or the 'free and frank exchange of views for the purposes of deliberation (sub-s (2)(b)) or 'would otherwise prejudice, or would be likely to prejudice, *the effective conduct of public affairs* (sub-s (2)(c)). The focus is on the effects of disclosure.

[1] See FOIA 2000, s 36(5). The 'Qualified Person' (QP) is likely to be the most senior person in a PA. Power of appointment will be delegated to PAs and the Ministry of Justice will take responsibility for those bodies not falling within s 36(5)(a)–(n) where a sponsoring department cannot be identified. Advice will be given on QPs. See http://www.justice.gov.uk/guidance/docs/foi-exemption-s36.pdf at pp 11 and 12 and *Guardian Newspapers and H Brooke v IC and BBC* EA/2006/0011 and 0013 and FS 50269514, and see below.

1.183 The duty to confirm or deny does not apply to information within this section if, or to the extent that, in the reasonable opinion of a qualified person, compliance with s 1(1)(a) would or would be likely to have any of the effects above (ie in sub-s (2)).

1.184 The disclosure of statistical information under this section is not subject to the 'reasonable opinion of an authorised person' to prevent disclosure. It may be withheld where its disclosure would etc have the prejudicial effects under sub-ss (2) and (3). The authority would make the claim. If the information was releasable under s 35(2) it may be withheld under s 36(4).

1.185 Sub-s (5) spells out who are 'qualified persons' for the taking of decisions on non disclosure (see 1.182, note 1 above).

1.186 Is collective responsibility so important, or indeed so religiously observed, that revealing differences after the decision is made would undermine good government? In the gestation period of the present Act for instance, talk of a rift between the Lord Chancellor and the Home Secretary on the scope of the Bill, and between the Lord Chancellor and the Chancellor of the Duchy of Lancaster at the time of the White Paper was commonplace and seemingly well informed. Were ministerial relations or collective responsibility in any way undermined? If not then what is so important about such communications or conventions that they are, absent discretionary disclosures, only appropriate for the Public Records office (National Archives)?

1.187 Under s 36(2)(c) of the FOIA 2000, the exemption seems excessively broad. Under s 36(2) the government seems influenced by the New Zealand legislation but without any of the overriding public interest qualifications in that legislation. And furthermore, the exemption in New Zealand only applied to advice etc in the course of performance of a duty – and not where a duty was not being performed – or to protect advisers from *improper harassment* or *pressure*. The Select Committee had a good deal to say on these points in its enquiry into the White Paper. In its reply to the Committee's report, the government stated that factual and background material may be made available under the general disclosure provisions in the publication schemes as well as under the specific access provisions. 'Wherever possible, however, the aim will be to publish information and analysis before final decisions are taken so that it can inform public discussion and debate of the policy options that are available.'[1] The contents of the publication schemes and code on this, and so many other items, will be crucial but the position does not look promising.

[1] HC 1020 (1997–98), para 28.

1.188 Insofar as information is held by either House of Parliament, then by virtue of s 36(7) **this is an absolute exemption.**

(XVI) THE POLICY-MAKING EXEMPTION AND CENTRAL GOVERNMENT

1.189 In the White Paper, the government appeared to indicate that the good and effective policy-making exemption would be likely to apply 'particularly' to central government: 'high level government records' of Cabinet or Ministerial level and policy advice to ministers was the context in which it was envisaged this exemption operating. The section in the WP is given the heading, 'Formulation of government policy, etc'. The government did subsequently develop its thinking to include all public bodies within this exemption which has become s 36 of the FOIA 2000.[1] The Minister may authorise public authorities or officials etc in public authorities to take the appropriate decisions (s 36(5)(o)(i) and (ii)). Authorisations may be related to a specified person(s) or persons falling within a specified class, may be general or limited to particular classes of cases and may be granted subject to conditions. Certificates signed by the Speaker of the House of Commons or the Clerk of the Parliaments shall be conclusive evidence of the fact of the effects of disclosure of information referred to in sub-s (2).

[1] HC 1020 (1997–98), para 29.

1.190 Section 36 exempts disclosure which would, etc, inhibit the free and frank exchange of advice, or exchange of views for deliberation or would otherwise prejudice, etc, the effective conduct of public affairs. Under the White Paper, this information was protected by a more retentive test than all other exempt information – the test was a 'harm' test not a substantial harm test. Sections 35 and 36 aim to protect the policy-making and deliberative processes of government so that advisers will not feel inhibited either by being identified with a particular piece of advice or by being seen to disagree with the views of a Minister. It also seeks to prevent disclosures which could threaten policy initiative. One can appreciate the difficulties of government in a gold-fish bowl but several points will be made about the undesirable breadth of this exemption below. It will be recalled that provision is made for the release of 'statistical information' for an informed background in relation to information under s 35(1)(a) and (b) – the formulation of government policy and Ministerial communications. The concession applies also to information which would otherwise be exempt under s 36 and which is purely statistical information. In s 36, it may still be exempt if its disclosure would, or would be likely to, prejudice or inhibit those areas covered by s 36(2) and (3). The coalition government proposals in 2011 stated that s 36 would be subject to a 20-year exemption period. How effectively publication schemes address such matters relating to s 36 will be a true barometer of how productive the publication schemes will be of greater openness in our public life. Attention should also be drawn to the revised code of practice and register on public consultation between government departments and those affected by decisions of government (see para 1.238 below).

1.191   FS 50093255: para 37 has a website for list of qualified persons for s 36:[1] *Chief Constable of Surrey Police v IC* EA/2010/0081 ruled that a PA must keep a good record of the 'opinion' of a QP. *R Salmon v IC and King's College Cambridge* EA/2007/0135 deals with the situation where there is no 'qualified person' for s 36 exemption – s 36 is not thereby engaged. However, the fact that a PA (King's College Cambridge) is largely dependent on private funding does not diminish the nature of its obligations under FOIA. FS 50096973 was a request to DfES for the list of schools suitable for City Academy status. Section 36 was properly invoked to avoid damage to a 'flagship education programme'. Sponsors would be reluctant to come forward of the information was released. The PI favoured non-disclosure. In relation to a QP's opinion the IC ruled that 'If the opinion is reasonable, the IC should not under s 36 substitute his own view for that of the qualified person. Nor should the Tribunal' (para 13). *Hogan v IC* EA/2005/0026 saw the IT disagree with the IC's test for 'reasonable decision' of QP under s 36. The tribunal was unhappy that the IC seemed to repeat the test of unreasonableness in judicial review (the *Wednesbury* test) rather than objective reasonableness which is required by the section. In *University of Central Lancashire v IC and David Colquhoun* EA/2009/0034, Professor Colquhoun made a request for copies of the course materials for the University's BSc in homeopathy. The issue of homeopathy training was the subject of significant academic and public debate; Colquhoun thought that the materials might inform that debate. During the course of the IC's investigations the University's Vice-Chancellor issued a certificate under FOIA 2000, s 36(2)(c), claiming that disclosure would or would be likely to prejudice the effective conduct of public affairs, namely the administration of the University. The IC found that this exemption did not apply. As regards the public interest on this point, the University's main argument was that disclosure of course materials in general would hinder innovation in their creation; this was rejected by the tribunal. The tribunal then moved on to consider s 36. The exemption was not made out because there was no evidence that it was a reasonable opinion reasonably arrived at. The University claimed that there would be disruption and consequent expense resulting from a flood of similar claims prompted by disclosure of the information; the tribunal thought that this conclusion was tenuous. The evidence put forward to support a reasonable procedure for gathering the opinion was also inadequate; it consisted of a short email which tacitly acknowledged that the claim was speculative. Disclosure was ordered. FS 50108125 concerned a request about animal experiments in which it was alleged mice had been deprived of water for two days. If correct, this would constitute an infringement of experiment licensing conditions. Various exemptions were invoked as well as s 36. Names and addresses were not supplied and this was not challenged. The IC discussed s 36 and inspectors' inhibitions. Under s 36, the PI favoured an anonymous disclosure. Para 62 et seq discusses 'reasonable opinion' of 'qualified persons' under s 36 – it must be an objective decision objectively arrived at. Section 36 did not favour non-disclosure but some information was protected under other sections. Some important general points are contained in FS 50072316 which concerned Iraq and concerned the unpublished early draft of Iraq's WMD dossier published on 24 September 2002 which was requested from the Foreign and Commonwealth Office (FCO). Section 36(2) (b) was invoked. The document had been sent to the Hutton inquiry but had not been subject to discussion or placed in the inquiry report's annex. The FCO took three months to conduct an internal review of a FOI appeal (IC's good practice guide states it should take 20 working days, extendable to 40). Because of oversight in the IC's office there was a delay of four months before investigation commenced. The FCO wanted the IC (or his official) with 'suitable vetting' to examine the dossier in the FCO. This had been a point of contention within government where sensitive documents were concerned: they should not leave the department. Eventually the document was sent to the IC at his office. The IC ruled that s 36 was wrongly invoked and material ordered to be disclosed. This DN was appealed in EA 2007/0047 and the judgment delivered in January 2008 ordering disclosure subject to a minor redaction. The tribunal ruled that there was no presumption in favour of maintaining the exemption under s 36(2) as counsel for FCO had argued. The qualified person's opinion was not presented to the tribunal and opinions should be so presented, the tribunal believed so their reasonableness may be assessed. Civil servants must expect increased openness post-FOIA and have to come to terms with the so-called 'chilling effect' generated by that Act. Factors in favour of maintaining exemption did not, at the date when disclosure was refused, outweigh the PI in disclosure. The information possessed no great intrinsic value but disclosure would enhance the 'transparency process' of the drafting process in what was a very sensitive matter (and, one may add, on which a war was based – and see FS50098388 and FS50098388). Section 36(2) and (7) are absolute in relation to requests for the names and salaries of MPs staff and salaries (but s 40 could be considered (chapter 7) (FS50073128)). Information on an inquiry into leaks at the Home Office was correctly rejected under s 36(3) (FS50226603). *Home Office and Ministry of Justice v IC* EA/2008/0062 contains a full discussion on the public interest factors in s 36 exemptions. The High Court refused to interfere with the balancing exercise of the tribunal which ruled that the PI favoured disclosure of 'meta data' information (that is information generated by a request).[2] Whilst the Tribunal found that the s 36 exemption was engaged, they criticised the IC's approach to this issue; the IC had not seen the submissions to ministers or the ministers' responses. In *McIntyre v ICO and MOD* EA/2007/0068, the tribunal made clear that it was 'unsafe' for the IC to conclude that s 36 was engaged without seeing those submissions; any other approach would make it difficult to consider whether that 'opinion was reasonable in substance and reasonably arrived at'.

In addition, as there was no evidence as to which limb of prejudice the opinion had related (inhibit/prejudice), the lower threshold of prejudice would be adopted. This is significant because the higher threshold requires greater weight to the inherent public interest in the exemption being claimed.

1 www.foi.gov.uk/guidance/exguide/sec36/annex-d.htm.
2 *Home Office and MoJ v IC* [2009] 164 1611 (Admin).

1.192 Section 36(2)(b) was considered in *Export Credit Guarantees Department v IC and Campaign Against Arms Trade* EA/2009/0021. The Export Credit Guarantees Department (ECGD) is a department which reports to the Secretary of State for Business, Innovation and Skills. It provides guarantees and insurance for UK exporters and banks. The request for information related to an export agreement between Saudi Arabia and the UK government for the export of arms supplied by BAE; the Campaign Against Arms Trade (CAAT) wanted a copy of the ECGD risk committee's assessment of the Saudi deal. The ECGD refused on the basis of *inter alia* s 36(2)(b). The information covered under that section was to be disclosed because, whilst s 36(2)(b) was engaged, the public interest favoured disclosure. The central issue before the tribunal was whether the public interest test in respect of the latter exemption had been properly considered. The tribunal was encouraged by the ECGD to accept the evidence of the civil servants without reservation; that they were best placed to determine the likely effect of disclosure. The tribunal rejected this argument outright, particularly considering the case of *Home Office and Ministry of Justice v IC* [2009] EWHC 1611. The ECGD submitted that the tribunal should take into account the Court of Appeal's ruling in *The Office of Communications v IC* [2009] EWCA Civ 90, that there should be an aggregation of public interest factors. The ECGD submitted that this principle required the tribunal to consider all relevant public interest factors even where another potentially relevant exemption has not been asserted. The tribunal did not read the case as requiring this; the exemption claimed was s 36(2)(b) and the public interest factors to be considered were only those which were relevant for that specific exemption. The ECGD submitted that the IC had not given sufficient weight to the opinion of the qualified person when balancing the public interest; in fact the IC had not even seen the opinion. The tribunal agreed and found that the IC had failed to acknowledge the relevance of that opinion in balancing the public interest and that in future cases involving the exemption, it would be crucial for the IC to have a copy of the opinion. The public interest factors submitted in favour of maintaining the exemption were as follows: (a) free and frank exchange of views for the purpose of deliberation; (b) free and frank provision of advice to Ministers by public officials so as to fully inform; (c) accurate and efficient recording of meetings about sensitive and significant matters; (d) proper assessment of risk in order to prevent unacceptable financial loss to the taxpayer. The tribunal found that these public interest factors were overstated, particularly the one as to the 'chilling effect', which one witness had described in this case as the 'freezing effect'. In fact, it was thought that disclosure might improve reasoning and recording of meetings; the tribunal appeared to think that the 'chilling effect' argument had been overused and overstated since the introduction of FOIA. The factors in favour of disclosure were: (a) the information concerned the sale of military equipment to a county located in an area of conflict and to a regime accused of human rights violation – this was a cause for significant public concern; (b) a substantial sum of public money was at risk – transparency was needed; (c) it is beneficial if the public has a clear understanding of the decision-making process when a policy decision is being promoted or defended; (d) increased transparency may improve future decision-making; (e) there was a continuing public interest in the Saudi–UK agreement. The tribunal decided that the public interest favoured disclosure. In FS50111678 the complainant requested the disclosure of correspondence between the Prime Minister and Lord Birt (his former strategy advisor). The CO refused disclosure initially under s 35 (1)(a), but subsequently under s 36 (2) (b). The Minister for the Cabinet Office as qualified person gave his opinion, which was accepted as reasonable by the Commissioner. The public interest favoured maintenance of the exemption. The Commissioner recognised that there was a public interest in transparency of governmental affairs, especially considering the debate on the role of special advisors, particularly Lord Birt, but the information withheld was not of such significance that it would contribute to the debate. However the IC considered it appropriate to clarify that Lord Birt did play an informal role in relation to the appointment of senior staff – that fact should have been disclosed. In FS 50150598 the IC believed that as far as the advice to a minister was concerned, it was thought that the exemption would apply, because the release of such information would be likely to inhibit such candid and all encompassing advice being supplied to ministers in the future and would make officials less likely to engage in written discussions of such controversial issues. However, the Commissioner in this case considered that the exemption did not outweigh the public interest in disclosure. FS 50086128 was a request to the CO for information on various dates on which Prime Minister Blair met or had formal conversations with Rupert Murdoch. Sections 36(2)(b) (i) and (2)(c) were invoked. The IC believed that dates of official meetings should be disclosed. Disclosure will not put, be further believed, too much pressure on the PM's diary. The PI favoured disclosure. In this case as in many breaches of FOIA 2000, s 17 were recorded.

1.193   The request in FS50234513 concerned invocation of FOIA 2000, s 36(2) (b)ii and involved the London Borough of Haringey. The complainant requested a copy of the first serious case review ('SCR') dated October 2008 into the death of Peter Connelly (formerly known as 'Baby P') – a notorious case. The London Borough of Haringey applied the exemptions under s 36(2)(b)(ii) and (2) (c); its conclusions were that the public interest in maintaining both exemptions outweighed the public interest in disclosing the information. The Commissioner investigated and decided that the exemption under s 36(2)(b)(ii) was engaged and that the public interest in maintaining the exemption outweighed the public interest in disclosing the information in all the circumstances of the case. *Alasdair Roberts v IC and the Department for Business, Innovation and Skills* EA/2009/0035 concerned the s 36(2)(c) exemption. Professor Roberts made a request for information to the then Department of Trade and Industry. He sought certain data held on a computer database/document management system called Matrix. He restricted his request to documents and folders created within one specified week in December 2004; he asked for the document reference number and the name of the person who appeared to have written it. He wanted the information in order to carry out some analytical research into the workflows within the department. The Department for Business, Innovation and Skills (DBIS) refused disclosure, citing s 40, and the internal review confirmed that disclosure would breach the first data protection principle. The appellant complained to the IC, who was criticised by the tribunal for the inordinate delay in dealing with the complaint. During the IC's investigation, DBIS sought to rely on s 36 and obtained the relevant statement from the qualified person. The IC decided that s 36(2)(c) applied and that the information was exempt from disclosure. The main ground for appeal was that DBIS had failed to establish that the prejudice to public affairs was more than a hypothetical possibility, or that it was real, actual and of substance. However, the tribunal noticed a discrepancy between the facts of the case and the claiming of the exemption. Due to the wording of s 36, a public authority cannot rely on the relevant statement if it is not made at the time of initial refusal; an opinion formed later cannot justify refusal because the information was not exempt at the time when the challenged decision not to release it was made. 'An opinion formed by a qualified person after the public authority had concluded the process of dealing with the request cannot form part of the Information Commissioner's investigation, or decision'; it was not an issue of late claiming, but of inappropriate claiming. In coming to this conclusion the IT relied on *The Department for Business Enterprise and Regulatory Reform v ICO and Friends of the Earth* EA/2007/0072; *McIntyre v ICO and MOD* EA/2007/0068; and *MOD v ICO and R Evans* EA/2006/0027. The tribunal nevertheless considered the application of the exemption and found that the evidence for the reasonableness of the opinion was inadequate, but that the IC had rightly decided that the public interest would have favoured maintenance of the exemption. As a general rule the PI in maintaining an exemption diminishes over time (*R Evans v IC and MoD* EA/2006/0064 concerning ministerial/arms lobbyists meetings). Section 36(2)(b)(i) was invoked with other exemptions. The case examines the question of hearing of fresh evidence by the tribunal in respect of determining the PI under s 36. The timing of grounds for claiming an exemption is that at the time of refusal, not the tribunal hearing (paras 22–23). The PI is that as assessed at the time of request. The tribunal controversially ruled that it cannot hear fresh evidence but this must be seen in the light of subsequent rulings (para 1.231 below). The witnesses were not able to show evidence of inhibitory effects of disclosure. 'Where the information is in a raw unconsidered form the PI in maintaining the exemption is likely to diminish more slowly than where the information is in a finished considered form' (para 41). The tribunal found that fear of inhibition on lobbyists from disclosure was overstated. In relation to notes of meetings and telephone conversations the exemptions were maintained on PI grounds because these were unfinished and incomplete. In relation to 'finished' background notes, there was no such inhibition and the PI favoured disclosure. However, another exemption (s 40) favoured non-disclosure (decided subsequently) (and see *MoD v IC & R Evans* EA/2006/0027 concerning disclosure of a complete copy of the 2004 edition of the Directory of the Defence Export Services Organisation (DESO). DESO assists in the export of UK military equipment. Information about DESO was limited to the MoD and security-cleared members of the UK defence industry. The IC emphasised the need for transparency in the defence industry/ MoD relations. MoD claimed that transparency was satisfied by publication of redacted copy and names of senior MoD officials. This involved disclosure of senior officials' identities and those who appear in the Diplomatic Service List. It would not cover junior rankings unless their names were published in, eg, the Civil Service Yearbook. The tribunal, which substituted the DN but otherwise upheld disclosure, emphasised that this is a 'one-off decision and does not set a precedent'. The 'anonymity of civil servants' is not an 'immutable principle' and civil servants have to be made accountable. The requirements of the DPA 1998 were satisfied (chapter 7). 'The tribunal is not minded, however, to sanction the disclosure of all telephone and email details, save for those in the Civil Service Yearbook' and otherwise kept details of officials below level B2 anonymous (para 88).

In FS50315973, a request to Kingston University for all staff workplace email addresses was rightly refused under s 36(2)(c) (and likewise Manchester University: FS50318502). Disclosure of information about discussions between the Conservatives and Liberal Democrats in May 2010 were rightlly refused by the CO under s 36(2): FS50350899.

(XVII) COMMUNICATIONS WITH HER MAJESTY, ETC

1.194   Information is exempt information if it relates to communications with Her Majesty, other members of the royal family or royal household or the conferring by the Crown of any honour (FOIA 2000, s 37). The duty to confirm or deny does not arise on the usual basis. Para 1.105 above describes how the communications with her majesty and first and second heirs to the throne are covered by an **absolute exemption** under the Constitutional Reform and Governance Act 2010, s 46 and Sch 7. The coalition government has announced that the life span of the exemption will be reduced from 30 to 20 years, or five years after the death of the relevant member of the royal family, whichever is later. Additional protection for the royal family was announced in January 2011 to protect 'long-standing conventions surrounding the Monarchy and its records' including the Monarch's right to counsel, encourage and warn her government and the heir to the throne's right to be instructed in the business of government in preparation for their future role as monarch. The extension of the exemption does not refer to their spouses. Under the Protection of Freedoms Bill 2011, the exemptions as reformed will apply to Northern Ireland bodies. The Public Administration Committee of the House of Commons has reported on the honours system.[1]

[1]   HC 212 (2003–04) *A Matter of Honour*. See: http://www.direct.gov.uk/en/Governmentcitizens andrights/UKgovernment/Honoursawardsandmedals/TheUKHonourssystem/index.htm.

1.195   There has been a large number of requests for information about Prince Charles' correspondence with ministers. These have been refused although disclosures have been made of Prince's Trust correspondence and also disclosures of the Prince's correspondence have been ordered in the course of litigation. The refusal to disclose information from correspondence has been the subject of an appeal to the tribunal: FS50119029 House of Lords Appointments Commission;

FS50088853 HM Treasury.[1] The *Guardian* ran a series on the hitherto secret *de facto* veto of the Prince of Wales on legislation affecting his interests; see the *Guardian*, 31 October 2011. See para 8.215 on the application of the EIRs to the Duchy of Cornwall's estates, ie the Prince of Wales.

[1]   http://www.justice.gov.uk/docs/foi-exemption-s38.pdf. See FS 50088853 under s 40 below and FS50142320 involving the CO and requests about the Princess of Wales.

(XVIII)   HEALTH AND SAFETY

1.196   Under s 38(1) of the FOIA 2000, information is exempt information if its disclosure would, or would be likely to, endanger the physical or mental health of any individual or endanger the safety of any individual. The duty to confirm or deny does not arise if, or to the extent that, compliance with s 1(1)(a) would etc have either of the effects mentioned above.

1.197   In *People for the Ethical Treatment of Animals Europe v IC and University of Oxford* EA/2009/0076, PETA requested information from Oxford in August 2007 about scientific experiments carried out on a macaque named Felix which had appeared in a BBC television documentary. The requests related to the licence held by Professor Aziz of Oxford. The information sought was: (a) the intended duration of the Felix project; (b) the scientific background of the work, including references; (c) the anticipated benefits; (d) detailed work plan; (e) how the number of animals would be kept to a minimum; (f) a list of each protocol to be applied to Felix under the licence. Other information was requested as to which of the procedures specified in the licence had been used and when. Further, PETA wanted information as to Felix's health status throughout and details of veterinary care. Oxford responded by disclosing some information, particularly in relation to (b)–(f) above, but claimed that the remaining information was exempt under s 38. The IC, in the course of his investigation, identified some further information which could be disclosed, but otherwise found that s 38 was engaged and that the public interest lay in withholding the information. PETA appealed on the grounds that: (a) s 38 was not engaged; and (b) if it was engaged, the public interest lay with disclosure. As regards the scope of the request, the tribunal found that Oxford and the IC were entitled to confine the scope of the request to procedures which had actually been performed on Felix, as opposed to procedures which were permitted under the terms of the licence. When interpreting s 38, the FTT followed the approach in *Hogan and Oxford City Council v IC* EA/2005/0026 and EA/2005/0030; it looked at: (a) the applicable interest; (b) the nature of the endangerment; (c) the causal relationship; (d) the *de minimus* threshold of endangerment which is 'real, actual or of substance'. Oxford relied only upon the 'would be likely to endanger' limb of s 38 and PETA argued that for it to be engaged, Oxford would have to provide evidence of any possible mental health problems from a psychiatrist. The tribunal rejected this contention; the test was whether the physical threat was sufficient that on the balance of probabilities the effect upon mental health would be more than mere stress or worry. The danger to Professor Aziz and his colleagues was very serious. Many attacks had already been carried out by activists, including death threats and in one instance a letter bomb. The risk of endangerment would be increased by disclosure and therefore s 38 was engaged. The public interest factors in favour of disclosure were: (a) transparency in the way research is conducted; (b) transparency in the way the public were kept informed; (c) transparency in open public debate; (d) transparency in the regulatory system. However, the tribunal found that the public interest in disclosure was limited by the fact that: (a) there was a mismatch between the scope of the request and the contents of the other protocols on the licence; (b) the request related only to a single project licence; (c) information had already been given in the television programme and substantial other information was in the public domain. The risk of escalation of the campaign of the activists from distortion and an increased pool of identifiable targets tipped the balance in favour of non-disclosure (see FS50082472 where s 38 was successfully invoked to protect the names of individuals, companies and academic institutions holding licences to conduct scientific research on animals was refused under s 38. The PI under s 38 favoured non-disclosure. In addition, s 40 also engaged and allowed exemption (chapter 7). Section 38 has also been successfully used where information was sought about an anti-fascist organisation held by a local authority (FS50077877).

(XIX) ENVIRONMENTAL INFORMATION

1.198   In ch 8 there is a detailed examination of the Environmental Information Regulations 2004 (EIR 2004) together with other access to information provisions relating to the environment (see below). Information is exempt if it has to be disclosed to the public under regulations made under s 74 of the FOIA 2000, or it would be so obliged but for any exemption within the regulations (s 39). S 74 concerns the 'Aarhus' Convention on Access to Information, Public Participation in Decision-making and Access to Justice in Environmental Matters which has now been the subject of an EC Directive which has to be implemented into domestic law of member states by 14 February 2005.[1] The information provisions are in Art 4 of the Convention together with arts 3 and 9 which concern access to justice. Articles 6, 7 and 8 deal with public participation. The Secretary of State may implement the information provisions by regulations made under s 74(4) and this has been done. Regulations provide for charges to be made to make information available; provide that the obligation to make information available is to apply notwithstanding any contrary rule of law; and may make provision for the publication by the Secretary of State of a code of guidance. The EIR 2004 are examined in detail in paras 8.192 et seq below. The Regulations use the framework of the FOIA 2000 in relation to the IC, tribunal and so on, although it constitutes a separate regime.

[1]   *Convention on Access to Information, Public Participation in Decision Making and Access to Justice in Environmental Matters* Cm 4736 June 2000. See EP and Council Directive 2003/4/EC OJ L 41/26 (14/2/2003).

1.199   It should be noted at this stage that, although a requester for information may specify that information is requested under the EIR 2004, the PA is under an obligation to establish which information regime is relevant: FOIA 2000, DPA 1998 or the EIR 2004. The latter covers any 'environmental information' – a term which is very broadly defined (para 8.212). The relevant case law is examined in chapter 8.

(XX) PERSONAL INFORMATION

1.200 Section 40 of the FOIA 2000 concerns personal information. The provisions relating to personal data are treated in greater detail in ch 7. Basically, the FOIA 2000 makes all personal information on data subjects exempt under the FOIA 2000 where they are applying to see the information about themselves. Applications in such cases are to be made under the DPA 1998 the provisions of which will dictate the outcome. Information is also exempt where it constitutes personal data on another person and the applicant is not the data subject of that information and it satisfies either of two conditions. The first condition is that disclosure is of information which falls within paragraphs (a) to (d) of the definition of personal data in s 1(1) of the DPA 1998 and disclosure of the information to a member of the public 'otherwise than under this Act' would contravene any of the data protection principles which govern the holding and processing of personal data or s 10 of the DPA 1998 which concerns a right to prevent processing likely to cause damage or distress. In cases not falling within paras (a) to (d) ie manual and unstructured information (see paras 7.9 et seq below) its disclosure to a member of the public 'otherwise than under this Act' would contravene any of the data protection principles which but for s 33A(1) of the DPA 1998[1] would usually apply. In other words, the effect of s 33A(1) – which exempts publicly held unstructured data from virtually all the data protection principles – is disregarded for these purposes. Information is also exempt (the second condition) if the person to whom it relates would not have a right of access to, or a right to know about it under the DPA 1998 because of the exemptions under that Act.

[1]   Section 33A(1) of the DPA 1998 was added by the FOIA 2000 and basically brings a wider range of non-automated personal information into the DPA 1998 but exempts it from most of the 1998 Act's data protection principles (see ch 7 below). The effect is that breaches of the data protection principles are relevant for such disclosures by virtue of the FOIA 2000 but under the DPA 1998 they would not apply to such information. No-one can pretend these provisions are easy!

1.201 The point has been made that an official's name is 'personal data' under the DPA 1998 which may well result in a reluctance to name officials as the authors of official documents or who were in attendance at meetings if this could breach the DPA 1998. The policy making exemption would also be likely to be applicable in this case and many cases involve a combination of s 40 and other exemptions. The data protection aspects could be of wide application. A similar problem might attend the revelation eg the identity of individuals acting on behalf of representative bodies or that of sole traders where safety concerns have been in issue and they are identified from documents. A way around this problem will not be possible where the public authority was not willing to act accordingly under the DPA 1998, Sch 2, para 5(d).[1] The balance between Data protection and access to information has also caused difficulties in relation to the EU provisions (see para 1.272 below).

[1]   That disclosure was 'necessary for the exercise of any functions of the Crown ...'. FOI Campaign *Briefing* 5, 25 October 2000. This point is fully dealt with in chapter 7.

1.202 The duty to confirm or deny does not arise in relation to exempt information under s 40(1) or disclosures having the effect specified above in relation to breaches of data protection principles etc but for the effect of s 33A(1). In other words although the data protection principles do not apply to the data in a general sense, they are relevant if disclosure would involve their breach as expressed in the section. The authority is also free from the duty to confirm or deny where it would breach any provision of Part IV of the DPA 1998.[1] **Section 40 provides an absolute exemption when it is covered by s 40(1), or s 40(3) (a)(i) or (b).** Other information under s 40(3)(a)(ii) or s 40(4) is only protected by a qualified exemption. The case law on this exemption is more conveniently dealt with in chapter 7.

[1]   This concerns the data subject's right to be informed of whether personal data about them are being processed.

(XXI) INFORMATION PROTECTED BY A LEGAL OBLIGATION OF CONFIDENCE

1.203 Information is exempt information if it was obtained by a public authority from any other person (including another public authority) (FOIA 2000, s 81 excludes this exemption between government departments) and the disclosure of the information to the public (otherwise than under this Act) by the public authority holding it would constitute a breach of confidence actionable by that other person (s 41). This only covers information protected by the law of confidentiality, not that simply stamped 'confidential' which may not be confidential as a matter of law (see paras 2.300 et seq below). The information must possess the necessary quality of 'confidentiality' and the belief of the donor must be reasonably based, ie its release would be damaging to his or her interests and not trivial – the law of confidentiality does not protect trivia. When a donor or supplier of information simply stamps 'confidential' on the information supplied, or indicates in some other fashion that it is confidential, that may be persuasive and advisable, but it is not conclusive.[1] If a contract specifies that information is to be treated as confidential this is a matter to be determined under the law of contract as a breach of contract if it is disclosed without authorisation. Where, however, the information apart from the contract would not be treated by the courts as 'confidential' then arguably s 41 would not exempt the information which lacks a necessary component of confidentiality. Otherwise parties would be free to label all forms of information as confidential and could by-pass these statutory provisions on access. The first version of the s 45 code spelt out that confidentiality clauses should only be used 'exceptionally' (see the s 45 Code advice: paras 1.281 et seq below). The code now advises parties to be mindful of duties within the Act. If 'confidential' under the law of confidentiality, there may still be a public interest defence in disclosure under common law, not under the statute. This removes any action that the party providing the information may have. It also removes the 'confidentiality' of the material and therefore this exemption will not apply in such circumstances. The case law shows that the onus of establishing the public interest under the law of confidentiality lies on the person who asserts that interest, ie the person who has disclosed or wishes to disclose the information if they were sued or, under FOIA 2000, the person applying to see the information. FS 50105717 was a request to the Commission for Professional and Public Involvement in Health for an internal report about an investigation into the relationship between some NHS Patient Forum members and support organisations. The IC ordered disclosure. Much of the information including names was publicly available the IC found. The IC made the important point that in the PI of confidentiality at common law, the burden of establishing the PI, unlike the PI test under FOIA, is on the applicant for the information seeking to overcome a claim of confidence properly raised. The IC and tribunal case law also emphasise that the information has to come from another party which sometimes produces complications. For instance, FS 50088977 involved a request for a copy of an ACAS agreement leading to reinstatement of a senior police officer, Ali Dizaei. Section 41 was not breached because the information was not provided to the PA by a third party – it was not 'obtained from a third party'. This follows the wording of the section and is narrower than the common law which will protect information generated by employees of the PA which is confidential – disclosure would be detrimental and there is a reasonable expectation in the confidor that information will be treated as confidential. In similar vein, FS 50065053 featured a request for information about a grievance procedure and settlement of legal claims against employees. The amounts received in settlement were not received from a third party and so s 41 did not cover these. (See also *Department of Health v IC Mr Stimson* EA/2008/0018 and *Zacharides v Information Commissioner* EA/2010/0162).

The provision does not protect information which has come to a government department from another government department by virtue of s 81(2)(a), and (2)(b) in relation to NI departments. There is no similar provision in relation to other PAs. Guidance is available on this exemption from the MoJ.[2]

1   R G Toulson and C M Phipps *Confidentiality*, 2nd ed (2006).
2   http://www.justice.gov.uk/docs/foi-exemption-s41.pdf, p 2.

1.204 The duty to confirm or deny does not arise if, or to the extent that, the confirmation or denial that would have to be given to comply with s 1(1)(a) would (apart from this Act) constitute an actionable breach of confidence.

1.205 FS50111328 involved a request for information about ministerial declarations of interest under the ministerial code. Some information was disclosed but some was protected under s 41.This had been a contentious issue under the 1994 code on access. In *Higher Education Funding Council for England v IC and Guardian News and Media Ltd* EA/2009/0036 the request was for information relating to the state of buildings at the Higher Education Institutions (HEIs) that contributed to a database of information about the management of land and buildings under their control. The information would be important for potential students and their choice of HEI. The Higher Education Funding Council for England (HEFCE) refused disclosure on the basis that the third parties expected information would be treated with confidence and therefore it was exempt under FOIA 2000, s 41. The IC decided that the exemption was not engaged because he did not believe that the HEIs would suffer any detriment if the information were to be disclosed; there would be no cause of action for breach of confidence as required by s 41. On appeal the IC argued that 'actionable' meant that a claim for breach of confidence would succeed on the balance of probabilities. HEFCE argued that the threshold was 'properly arguable'. The tribunal reasoned that: (a) the point was novel and that a consideration of previous tribunal decisions was not helpful; (b) the parliamentary intention, with reference to Hansard, clearly favoured the IC's position; (c) departmental guidance, issue by the MoJ, stated that a 'breach of confidence will only be actionable if a person could bring a legal action and be successful'. The tribunal found that it was for HEFCE to demonstrate that disclosure would expose it to the risk of a breach of confidence, which, on the balance of probabilities, would succeed. The tribunal therefore had to determine whether any breach of confidence might be actionable. The information was thought to have the necessary quality of confidence, because there would be a detriment in disclosure. There was potential detriment: (a) disclosure could damage the reputation of the HEIs which had confided the information, with a subsequent effect on their ability to recruit staff and students; (b) HEIs would not submit data, or would submit less extensive data, with the consequence that all HEIs would suffer from a reduction in the value of an important benchmarking tool. However, the tribunal, using the test in *HRH Prince of Wales v Associated Newspapers Ltd* [2006] EWCA Civ 1776, found that HEFCE would clearly be able to rely on the public interest defence against any HEI minded to bring an action for breach of confidence. It was sceptical as to whether HEIs would withdraw themselves from the data collection system; they had not done so as a result of FOIA coming into force, the alteration of the Code of Conduct or the disclosure of environmental information. Further, HEFCE has powers compulsorily to acquire information. The public interest factors in favour of disclosure were as follows: (a) the need to give information to those choosing a university; (b) disclosure of the proportion of HEIs which are in relatively poor repair; (c) disclosure of the proportion of HEIs not suitable for intended function; (d) the need to inform public debate on the adequacy of HEI funding; (e) concerns about the challenge of maintaining adequate investment in HEI estates. The tribunal ruled that the information should be disclosed (see also FS50123005). Section 41 has protected the identity of informants to Companies House (FS50152888). In *Anderson v Parades Commission* EA/2007/0103 letters from those complaining about the conduct of marchers in a parade in Northern Ireland were protetced by s 41.[1] However, the tribunal supported the IC's service of information notices to obtain information possessed by a professional body (Health Professions Council) dealing with complaints against medical practitioners. The Council kept a register of practitioners and argued information from practitioners was received in confidence. The PA's arguments that a new complaints procedure aimed at informal resolution did not carry much weight. FOIA 2000, s 59 also imposes criminal offence on the IC and his office for wrongful disclosure of information (without authorisation) the tribunal reminded the PA in its concerns about breaches through wrongful disclosure.[2]

[1]   See *Tweed v NI Parades Commission* [2006] UKHL 53.
[2]   *Health Professions Council (HPC) v IC* EA/2007/0116.

1.206   FS50155387 (one of 36 such reports into various authorities) was a request for information on the commission payments made by investment managers on behalf of East Riding of Yorkshire Council ('the Council'). The

Council supplied the name of its investment manager. However, it claimed that the remainder of the information was exempt on the basis that the exemptions *inter alia* in s 41 applied. The IC decided that the exemption in s 41 was partially applicable; however, the confidentiality was overridden by a public interest defence inherent in the common law of confidence. A disclosure of a majority of the information would not be actionable in law. The exemption was not therefore engaged by this information. The IC's decision was that the information should be disclosed to the complainant, with minor redactions. In FS 50146982 the IC ruled that a duty of confidence owed to a patient survived the patient's death (and see *P Bluck v IC & Epsom etc NHS Trust* EA/2006/0090). FS 50101391 dealt with a request to the National Archives for information from the 1911 census. The IC ruled that a government undertaking that the information would be held in confidence for 100 years was not conclusive in itself. The undertaking would be relevant where information was 'medical, concerned family relationships that would usually be kept secret, or was about very young children who were born in prison and whose birthplace is not recorded, or which is otherwise sensitive'. The IC did not believe that the information breached the criteria set out by the Law Lords in *Campbell v MCN Ltd* [2004] 2 All ER 995 (HL); that there should be a reasonable expectation of privacy and a breach of that expectation. It was not all confidential, although some was. To be 'actionable' a PA did not have to identify a plaintiff. Each 1911 census case must be treated on its merits. The duty of confidence in much of the information had evaporated with the effluxion of time and even though it was protected by the Official Secrets Act 1889. The point here is that the information was imparted in circumstances of confidence (a promise of confidentiality was not enough (para 41)) and was protected by Official Secrets Act 1889, which does reinforce confidentiality, but in most cases the confidence will now have evaporated, the IC believed. The IC arguably made a very brave decision in this case.

1.207 The position on information having to come from a third party to be confidential under s 41 was also analysed in EA/2006/0014 (see also s 43 below). The tribunal maintained the position relating to information having to come from a third party. At issue in the case was a request for the written agreement between Ryanair and Derry City Council for Ryanair to use Derry airport. As the 'concluded' contract was not information received from a third party, it could not be protected by s 41(1)(a). Commercial agreements often contain information received from the other party which they regard as confidential, either in the terms of a schedule specifying the information or information otherwise identified. The same principle applied to a fax between the parties which set out the main points of agreement (para 32(e)). The tribunal accepted that some information on technical details in a schedule may be confidential. Commercial terms would usually be regarded as confidential and confidentiality attached to Ryanair's negotiations and contracts with airports (para 34(c)). Confidentiality did cover the commercially sensitive information under s 41. The common law test of public interest in confidentiality has already been explained. The PI supported disclosure of 'key financial information in a contract, a redacted version of which had already been produced' (para 35(i)). The public interest was also advanced by allowing the public to be informed of 'serious criticism from a reliable source of a VFM evaluation'. The tribunal indicated further information which may be disclosed in an unpublished schedule if there was no appeal or an unsuccessful appeal. *P Buck v IC and Epsom etc NHS Trust* EA/2006/0090 information was requested by the parents about their daughter's death in hospital five years previously. The daughter's spouse refused consent as he was entitled to do. Confidentiality regarding deceased patients is still protected by s 41. Personal representatives can bring breach-of-confidence actions making a claim 'actionable'.

1.208   This information is also an absolute exemption.

(XXII) LEGAL PROFESSIONAL PRIVILEGE

1.209   Information in respect of which a claim to legal professional privilege or, in Scotland, to confidentiality of communications could be maintained in legal proceedings is exempt information (FOIA 2000, s 42).[1] Judgments of the courts have supported the view that this privilege has assumed the status of a human right and has to be accorded resolute protection. It is not, however, an absolute exemption. In *DBERR v D O'Brien and IC* [2009] EWHC 164 QB the High Court ruled that while the reasoning on PI under ss 35 and 36 was adequate and not challengeable on grounds of legality, insufficient weight had nonetheless been given to the importance of the privilege LPP in assessing the PI – 'significant weight' has to be given to this interest which the tribunal had failed in making the balance. In *D O'Brien v IC and DBERR* EA/2008/0011(second hearing) a differently constituted tribunal upheld the original ruling that the public interest under s 42 was in favour of disclosure and so ordered. While the decisions show that information may be incorrectly withheld under s 42 (FS50273866 concerning Ofwat) the decisions are well aware of the importance of maintaining this privilege (*A Fisher v IC* EA/2010/0044: s 42 rightly claimed for advice on compliance with ECHR; and see *C Bellamy v IC and DTI (AP)* EA/2005/0023). An important statement of principle was made in *HM Treasury v IC* EA/2007/0054. This concerned the convention that opinions of law officers of the Crown are not to be disclosed, and nor is the fact that their advice was sought, without their consent. HM Treasury claimed this convention was an inbuilt immunity against disclosure. The IC disagreed. The information requested concerned an opinion on compatibility of the FSMA 2000 with the ECHR. Section 42(1) *inter alia* was invoked. There were numerous examples of breach of the convention by governments in the past including the Westland episode, the Scott report, the advice on the decision in *Factortame*[2] and the war on Iraq (see above). The convention involving law officers' advice is subject to FOIA. Neither the convention nor s 42 provided an absolute immunity although s 42 is a powerful exemption nonetheless. Once again, in *Dr J Pugh MP v IC & MoD* EA/2007/0055 the request concerned information on the response to two judgments of the ECJ on the Transfer of Undertakings Protection of Employment Regulations 2006, SI 2006/246 and the Acquired Rights Directive. Section 42 was properly engaged and the tribunal undertook an animated discussion of the nature of the public interest in that section. The PI in preserving the privilege is very strong and is fully supported in the case law.[3] However, it is not correct to say that there is an 'inbuilt weight' automatically attaching to qualified exemptions. 'In the legal professional privilege exemption the weight of judicial opinion referred to in [the] cases gives the exemption itself greater weight and to that extent may be described as having an 'inbuilt weight' requiring equally weighty PIs in favour of disclosure' (para 40). This evolves from the jurisprudence on the privilege not the words of the statute. But the exemption is not 'exceptional' as IC suggested. It is not thereby converted into an absolute exemption. The PI here was in favour of maintaining the exemption. Again in *Martin George v IC and the House of Lords Appointments Commission (HOLAC)* EA/2008/0035 there is a strong element of public interest inbuilt into the privilege itself. The tribunal was 'satisfied that LPP has an inbuilt weight derived from its historical importance, it is a greater weight than that inherent in other exemptions to which the balancing test applies, but it can be countered by equally weighty arguments in favour of disclosure. If the scales are equal disclosure must take place.' In *Mersey Tunnel Users Assoc v IT & Merseytravel* EA/2007/0052 the tribunal raised a query of whether legal privilege is the same for all areas of law or whether the privilege may be nuanced. Would a criminal, child care or other context colour its application?

[1] For legal professional privilege, see para 10.89 below.
[2] *R v Secretary of State for Transport ex p Factortame* [1990] 2 AC 85 concerning breaches of EC law by the UK leading eventually to legal liability to pay damages to injured victims of the breach.
[3] See *R v Derby Magistrates Court ex p B* [1995] 4 All ER 526 (HL).

1.210 In a House of Lords judgment on this subject area, Lord Scott believed that communications between Parliamentary draftsmen of legislation and Government lawyers in relation to draft legislation would be protected by 'legal advice privilege'.[1] It might appear a little strange that in relation to the law of the land, as opposed to a government interest under a law, that such a privilege might obtain. It is not absolute and would be subject to the public interest test. This privilege was claimed on behalf of the Attorney General's advice on the legality of the Iraq war (see HL Debs Vol 646 col WA2, 17 March 2003; HC Debs Vol 402 col 236W, 26 March 2003 and the Butler report HC 898 (2003–04), paras 366 et seq and Annex D).[2] Before FOIA took effect a request was made under the Code on Access for the date on which the Attorney General's advice on legality was first sought. This request was upheld by the parliamentary ombudsman but refused by the government on the grounds that it might inhibit free and frank discussion. Under FOIA many requests for details behind the advice were sought basically to establish whether published statements were consistent with 'fuller advice that had been given'.[3] The IC found that the PA's reliance on s 27 and a PI in non-disclosure was made out, but under ss 35(1)(c) and 42 some further information did have to be disclosed. An agreed statement on what would be disclosed was settled by the PAs and the IC. Further disclosures revealed that in private advice to the Prime Minister.

[1] *Three Rivers DC v Bank of England* [2004] UKHL 48.
[2] See P Sands *Lawless World* (2005).
[3] http://www.ico.gov.uk/upload/documents/library/freedom_of_information/notices/full_transcript_of_enforcement_notice_220506.pdf.

1.211   The duty to confirm or deny does not arise if, or to the extent that compliance with s 1(1)(a) would involve the disclosure of any information (whether or not already recorded) in respect of which such a claim could be maintained in legal proceedings.

1.212   *J Kessler QC v IC & HMR&C* EA/2007/0043 is a leading discussion of the PI factors involved in s 42 and also on the doctrine of collateral or partial waiver of the privilege. The information requested was for the legal advice concerning removal of the 'professional trustee residence rule' given by the DTI to HM Revenue and Customs. PI favoured maintenance of exemption. The requester claimed privilege had been waived. In *Kessler*, the legal advice was given by an 'in-house' lawyer and not an outside 'independent' practitioner. An early ruling of the tribunal in *Kirkaldie* v *IC and Thanet DC* EA/2006/0001 was distinguished. The tribunal in *Kirkaldie* had improperly interpreted the waiver rule – partial disclosure of the privileged information removes the privilege – to extend the rule to disclosures outside litigation. 'We are satisfied that the rule [namely] that by relying upon part of a privileged document before a court the party doing so waives privilege in the whole document does not apply to partial disclosure of privileged information outside the context of litigation.' The tribunal continued: 'There is an assumption built into FOIA that disclosure of information by PAs on request is in the PI in order to promote transparency and accountability in relation to the activities of PAs. The strength of that interest and the strength of competing interests must be assessed on a case by case basis' (para 57(d)). The tribunal repeated a point made in relation to other exemptions: 'The passage of time since the creation of information may have an important bearing on the balancing exercise. As a general rule, the PI in maintaining an exemption diminishes over time' (para 57(e)). 'In considering the PI factors in favour of maintaining the exemption, the focus should be upon the public interest expressed explicitly or implicitly in the particular exemption provision at issue' (para 57(f)). 'The PI factors in favour of disclosure are not so restricted and can take into account the general PIs in promotion of transparency, accountability, public understanding and involvement in the democratic process' (para 57(g)). The factors to be balanced are set out at pp 23–24 of the judgment. According to the judgment, the arguments in favour of disclosure were:

(a)   furthering the understanding of and participation in the public debate of issues of the day, specifically an informed debate into the necessity of the measures;

(b)   promoting accountability and transparency, obliging public authorities to explain the reasons for decisions taken and allowing the public to understand decisions made by public authorities;

(c)   allowing individuals and companies to understand how decisions are reached by public authorities;

(d)   as the decision has now been taken, disclosure would not impair any current decision-making process;

(e)   obtaining the advice did not involve the provision of confidential information;

(f)   considerable damage has been and will continue to be caused to the UK professional trustee business;

(g) it is impossible to lobby for change to the legislation without being provided with the advice;

(h) there is no suggestion that disclosure would disadvantage the government in any legal proceedings;

(i) the advice and legislation do not relate to tax avoidance;

(j) the advice was not required with any urgency;

(k) the Government had made a specific promise to 'share its findings on the viability of tax simplifications with business' in the Pre-Budget Report 2007;

(l) HMRC relied on the existence and conclusion of the advice as the sole justification of their decision to abolish the residence rule.

In favour of maintaining the exemption:

(a) there is a strong public interest in maintaining legal professional privilege. That is, to an individual or body seeking access to legal advice being able to communicate freely with legal advisors in confidence and being able to receive advice in confidence;

(b) if legal advice were routinely disclosed, there would be disincentive to such advice being sought and/or as a disincentive to seeking advice on the basis of full and frank instructions;

(c) if legal advice were routinely disclosed, caveats, qualifications or professional expressions of opinion might be given in advice which would therefore prevent free and frank correspondence between government and its legal advisers;

(d) legal advice in relation to policy matters should be obtained without the risk of that advice being prematurely disclosed;

(e) it is important that legal advice includes a full assessment of all aspects of an issue, which may include arguments both for and against a conclusion, publication of this information may undermine public confidence in decision-making and without comprehensive advice the quality of decision-making would be reduced because it would not be fully informed and balanced;

(f) there is a significant risk that the value placed on legal advice would be diminished if there is a lack of confidence that it had been provided without fear that it might be disclosed.

This was not a straightforward process of aggregation and addition. The process requires balancing and judgment: 'great weight must be attached to the PI in the accountability and transparency of PAs and the decision-making process. 'A substantial PI would be served by disclosure of fuller reasoning on why the Government reached the conclusions it reached on the State aid' (in relation to abolition of the rule) (para 69). However, despite all these ruminations, the tribunal ruled that the PI under s 42 was in favour of non-disclosure in this case because the issue was still 'live'.

1.213 In *Martin George v IC and the House of Lords Appointments Commission (HOLAC)* EA/2008/0035 the tribunal came to a different conclusion on what the PI required. An executive producer at the BBC, requested information from the HOLAC for the minutes, agendas and papers of meetings. HOLAC provided the information in a redacted form but relied on various exemptions protecting the redactions. The IC subsequently considered that the information was exempt because s 42 was engaged in respect of the information for which legal professional privilege was claimed. The IC found that the public interest favoured non-disclosure. The appellant appealed to the tribunal arguing that: (a) the information contained nothing to which privilege attaches; (b) that the public interest was in favour of disclosure. The tribunal took the following points as determinants. Firstly on the basis of case law (*Three Rivers DC v Bank of England* above); a broad interpretation has to be afforded to what is coverd by the privilege (see chapter 10). The 'general effect' or 'broad thrust' of legal advice is covered by the privilege. Applying that test, and considering the information involved, privilege was correctly claimed. Secondly, the tribunal considered that the amount of information already in the public domain was of relevance (this information was sufficient to inform the public debate). However the tribunal decided that some of the redacted information must be disclosed because the decisions of the House of Lords have an important impact upon the lives of the population and the members of the Commission through the Commission's work have 'a significant influence on the composition of parliament and thus its decisions'. In ruling on this point the tribunal accepted the requester's submissions.

1.214 There have been several cases involving the Mersey Tunnel Users Association which have raised important points in relation to s 42 (although the second case decided that the Environmental Information Regulations 2004, SI 2004/3391 were in fact the relevant code. The cases are *Mersey Tunnel Users Assoc v IT & Merseytravel* EA/2007/0052 and *Mersey Tunnel Users Association v IT & Halton BC* EA/2009/0001 (two hearings were involved). The first of these involved an appeal about a dispute over access to counsel's opinion concerning the operating costs and financing of the Mersey Tunnel. A complex arrangement had been made to finance loans basically on the collateral of income from users. Users had faced significant increases in charges. The PA argued that the advice was protected under s 42 and the PI was not in favour of disclosure. The disputed information had in fact been seen by the requester. It had been shown to him by the district auditor who had extracted an undertaking that it could not be further divulged to others. The requester wished to use the counsel's opinion to assist in marshalling his own arguments and this was why the present proceedings were brought. Both the IC and PA opposed the ruling in *Kirkaldie* and the application of the doctrine of partial disclosure of a privileged document. Such waiver only applies to litigation – not to legal advice more generally as in *Kirkaldie* where a councillor made a public statement about advice from a lawyer but not in the context of litigation. This point distinguished a ruling of the tribunal in *Kirkaldie* and followed *Kessler* above. The tribunal continued with the nature of the exemption under s 42. The often repeated points about the 'strong in-built PI in s 42' as a result of case law in the higher courts was examined and accepted. But importantly, the tribunal reported that s 42 is not consequentially promoted into an absolute exemption. When the advice was requested it was ten and a half years old and the request was made over three and a half years earlier. The PA pointed out that any legal action by the appellant was now statute barred, and in fact there had been no litigation (para 46). It has to be said that the tribunal placed a great emphasis on transparency. The tribunal did not doubt the 'in-built PI in non-disclosure in s 42' and this carried considerable weight, but in this case and on these facts the PI in disclosure was paramount. A significant allocation of money had been invested into one form of financing a public service instead of alleviating the burden on the fee-paying public users. The countervailing PI arguments in favour of publication were stronger in this case than non-disclosure. In the second case, the governing provision was the EIR 2004 and this is addressed in chapter 8 (para 8.204).

(XXIII) COMMERCIAL INTERESTS AND TRADE SECRETS[1]

1.215   Departments, agencies and other PAs hold a great deal of commercial information: some as regulators eg the DBERR, regulatory commissions, the Export Credit and Guarantee Department: some hold such information to help them formulate policy; through PAs being commercial contracting entities themselves and as support services to businesses under industrial development legislation. Information is exempt if it constitutes a trade secret (FOIA 2000, s 43(1)). It is also exempt if its disclosure under this Act would, or would be likely to, prejudice the commercial interests of any person (including the public authority holding it: s 43(2)). Where compliance with s 1(1)(a) would or would be likely to prejudice the commercial interests as described, the duty to confirm or deny does not apply. Further comment is made about this heading below (see para 1.299). The Parliamentary Commissioner for Administration (PCA) has made several reports on investigation complaints arising under the 1994 and 1997 code on access to information which is claimed by authorities to be commercially confidential.[2] A frequent point of some sensitivity concerns tenders and contracts. As discussed below, 'commercial interests' potentially has far greater scope to be used as a barrier to openness in the process of government by contract. The local government ombudsman has been very critical of the arrangements made by some authorities to contract out housing benefit administration to private companies. There is no doubt that this information could damage the 'commercial interests' of the companies involved. Could they claim the benefit of this exemption? Or would it not apply to such a situation? The Office of Government Commerce literature on contracting *OGC (Civil Procurement) Policy and Guidance* version 1.1. Section 1 of the Guidance says that: 'Generally speaking, there is a public interest in disclosing information about public procurement to ensure:

●   that there is transparency in the spending of public money;

●   that public money is being used effectively, and that public authorities are getting value for money when purchasing goods and services;

●   that authorities' procurement processes are conducted in an open and honest way.'

Section 2 discusses what should not be disclosed. FS 50085775 contains a powerful statement in relation to s 43 and the new context of transparency. 'PAs must expect a robust approach to the issue of commercial sensitivity, and be prepared for a greater degree of openness than prior to the advent of the Act' (para 65).

1   See *Commercial Confidentiality* NCC (1998). App 1 has a list of statutes prohibiting disclosure of trade secrets. See R Baxter (1997) JBL 97. See *Re Smith Kline & French Laboratories Ltd* [1990] 1 AC 64, HL, and commercial confidentiality under EC Directives. See EC Directive 2002/02 and the requirement to publish percentage declarations of ingredients in animal foodstuffs following the BSE and Dioxin episodes. Domestic regulations implementing the Directive were suspended by interim injunction pending a reference to the ECJ on the legality of the Directive because of the 'serious and irreparable damage' that would be caused by the disclosure of commercially confidential information and trade secrets, the High Court ruled: *R (ABNA) v Secretary of State for Health* [2004] 2 CMLR 39. For Scotland, see: *ABNA Ltd v Scottish Ministers* [2004] 2 CMLR 40.
2   NCC (1998), pp 14 et seq.

1.216   'Trade secret' is a legal term of art and has been stated by the Law Commission to cover information which is not generally known, which derives its value from that fact, whose owner has indicated expressly or by implication the wish to maintain it as secret and probably it is information used in trade or business.[1] A common point of reference is *Lansing Linde Ltd v Kerr*[2] 'Trade secrets are not restricted to secret formulae ... but can include highly confidential information of a non-technical or non scientific nature, such as customers' names, which if disclosed to a competitor would cause real or significant harm to the owner and which the owner is entitled to have protected.' An amendment in the Lords sought to define a trade secret as: 'confidential trade information which if disclosed to a competitor would cause harm to its owner'. This was unsuccessful. In the USA, 'trade secret' has been defined as 'a secret, commercially valuable plan, formula, process, or device that is used for the making, preparing, compounding, or processing of trade commodities and that can be said to be the end product of either innovation or substantial effort': *Public Citizen Health Research Group v FDA* 704 F 2d 1280 (DC Circuit 1983). This 'common law' definition was adopted because the definition in the US Restatement of Torts Sec. 757, comment b (1939) was rejected as too broad for FOI purposes.[3]

1   Law Commission *Misuse of Trade Secrets* (1997) No 150, para 1.29.
2   [1991] 1 WLR 251, [1991] 1 All ER 418 (CA) per Staughton LJ and Butler-Sloss LJ.
3   *Freedom of Information Act Guide and Privacy Act Overview* (2004) ed US Department of Justice, pp 269 et seq.

1.217   Disclosures which would, or would be likely to, prejudice the commercial interests of any person is an extremely elastic formulation. It would apply to information such as research and development, product testing, performance assessments, strategic business plans. Under EC procurement directives information has to be made public in relation to contract bids that fall within the directives (see paras 8.265 et seq below) The basic test in relation to contractual information is: will its release endanger the commercial interests of *any* person. Is information still sensitive to further competition or are negotiations relating to which the information is relevant still continuing? The Guidance accompanying the Code on Access stated that the following should be disclosed after a tendering process identity of successful tenderers, nature of the job, service or goods to be supplied, performance standards, award criteria, winning tender price or range of prices. Costings that have gone into prices have been regarded as confidential.[1] Could commercial interests cover numbers of disconnections by utilities? A further amendment in the Lords sought to exempt information whose disclosure 'would prejudice to an unreasonable degree the commercial interests of any person.[2] The MoJ has guidance on this exemption.[3]

[1]   The Parliamentary Ombudsman has received and reported on many cases concerning contracts and exemption 13 of the 1997 Code. He has recommended disclosure in complaints about sale and export of weapons for possible use in torture (A.30/95), disclosure of information about defects in a vehicle (A.25/97) and see (A.16/99) re Committee on Safety of Medicines, (A.2/01) on the early release of information that might be used for further bids re data used in public sector comparator for a London Transport contract, and (A.28/02) where there was no evidence that contract prices would cause prejudice to the commercial position of the contractor or department.

[2]   See for similar tests which are more demanding than under the FOIA 2000: Control of Atmospheric Pollution (Appeals) Regulations 1977, SI 1977/17; Food and Environmental Protection Act 1985, s 14(2)(b); Water Resources Act 1991, s 191B; Clean Air Act 1993, s 37; Control of Major Accident Hazards Regulations 1999, Sch 8, para 18; Competition Act 1998 (Directors' Rules) Order 2000, r 30(1)(c)(i); Food Industry Development Scheme 1997, SI 1997/2673, para 10(2); see note 1 above for reference.

[3]   http://www.justice.gov.uk/guidance/docs/foi-exemption-s43.pdf.

1.218   Virtually all the case law concerns s 43(2) and not trade secrets. In one of the few cases involving s 43(1) the Student Loans Company's (SLC) 'Class Training Manual' used to train staff was requested. The information was widely disseminated within the organisation and the SLC was in a monopoly position in providing student loans (FS50156040). The IC ordered disclosure but the tribunal subsequently amended another decision of the IC allowing some of the information to be withheld in relation to how to deal with defaulting debtors (*Student Loands Company v IC* EA/2008/0092). In *Department of Health v IC* EA/2008/0018 exemptions in ss 41, 43(1) and 43(2) were in question. The case concerned a request for a copy of a contract between the Department of Health (DoH) and Methods Consulting Ltd for the provision of an electronic recruitment service for the NHS. The DoH refused, citing *inter alia* s 43(1), and the DoH argued that the information requested was exempt under that section. Methods Consulting Ltd had provided the final version of the contract although DoH had negotiated its details and specific terms. The DoH claimed that the information was exempt from disclosure under s 43(1). Whilst the tribunal accepted that the information was clearly used for the purposes of a trade and the release of the information would cause harm to MC Ltd, it did not have the highest level of secrecy which a trade secret would appear to merit. Competitors would have found it difficult to reproduce the information and use it although this in itself raises important questions. The tribunal considered that any of the information which could constitute a trade secret would more easily be exempt under s 43(2) and it proceeded to discuss that section (below).

1.219   In EA/2008/0018 the DoH argued that disclosure would prejudice its commercial interests in several ways because its future negotiating position would be weakened; disclosure would remove any incentive for tenderers to be innovative and create products different to those specified in the contract; the negotiating position of other departments may be adversely affected; the quality of service provided by Methods Consulting Ltd could have been a reduced; and disclosure could lead to a reduction in the number of qualified tenderers for DoH's future contracts thereby prejudicing its commercial position and competitors would have an unfair advantage. Addressing itself to the argument of commercial sensitivity, the tribunal found that although some of the information remained secret, a recruitment website and other loci had published some of the information. Although s 43(2) was engaged the tribunal found after a very useful analysis that some information should be disclosed in the public interest and certain other information should not. The tribunal tabulated reasons for disclosure/non-disclosure for each piece of information. There is also discussion on the impact of the *Office of Government Commerce Guidance on Civil Procurement* (para 1.215 above). The Guidance sets out what should be disclosed in procurement practice and the DoH had apparently failed to consult the guidance. Section 2 of the Guidance covers information that should not usually be disclosed (see para 88 et seq*). Dept for Work and Pensions v IC* EA/2010/0073 also has an interesting discussion on s 43(2) and its successful and unsuccessful invocation in relation to government contracts. In *University of Central Lancashire v IC and David Colquhoun* EA/2009/0034 the tribunal ruled that an interest in course materials could be commercial but no prejudice was found under s 43(2).

1.220 In the light of the extensive discussion in the courts in the Sugar case (para 1.90) and the wide coverage of the exclusion of information relating to journalism, art or literature and its repetitive incantation by the BBC in FS50259955, it is interesting to witness a case in which a requester was successful. The complainant requested information relating to the BBC's total taxi spend over the previous financial year and to the BBC's contract and taxi spend with a particular ground transportation booking and management company. The BBC provided answers to some of the requested information but withheld part of the information under s 43(2). The IC decided that s 43(2) was not engaged. Many decisions of the IC concerning the BBC found that the exemption in s 43(2) was not engaged but these would now have to take into account the ruling of the Court of Appeal in the *Sugar* case (see FS50086077, FS 50102474 and *BBC v IC* EA 2008/0019, 0034, 0051, 0058 and EA/2009/0015).

1.221 Section 43(2) does not protect information about a private contractor engaging in vehicle recovery work for a police force (FS50124423) nor tendering documents concerning quoted prices (FS50131138). Section 43(2) was engaged in relation to a drug used to prevent dietary-induced laminitis in horses but the PI favoured disclosure (FS50066054). Arguments on prejudice must be carefully presented and 'well reasoned' even to engage s 43(2) (FS50168782). In FS50131138 the complainant requested the council to release a copy of the tendering document submitted by the contractor awarded the contract to carry out maintenance work at the council leisure centre. The council responded, informing the complainant that it was willing to disclose a redacted version of the document, with the financial details edited out; it claimed exemption under s 43(2). The IC rejected the arguments that disclosure would be prejudicial to the commercial interests of the contractor and/or the council. He concluded that third parties entering into business with a public authority should be aware of the freedom of information decisions; accountability in the spending of public funds is important. Further, the concerns *vis-à-vis* disclosure did not appear to be raised by the contractor. The council claimed that disclosure could affect the achievement of best prices for future tenders and that disclosure would likely deter other contractors from working with the council. As the tendering process had been finalised 18 months prior to the request and because no two tenders for work are the same the IC rejected these points.

1.222 FS 50101105 reminds us that refusal notices must be properly reasoned to comply with s 17. DEFRA was asked for information about a tendering process for a research contract. DEFRA claimed s 43 was engaged but its reasoning on this and the PI were inadequate and breached s 17. The information requested was not commercially sensitive and s 43 was not engaged, the IC believed. The requested information included a summary of costs and overall cost, a breakdown of those costs giving details of individual tasks, who would conduct those tasks, the number of days involved and daily rates. DEFRA argued that such information would allow competitors to assess how 'the tenderer scoped and costed projects'. The IC believed that such information would not reveal the profit margins of the company, however, which was the crucial aspect in assessing the commercial interest. The IC has sought evidence of a 'real and substantial risk of commercial prejudice' for the s 43(2) exemption to operate (FS50163364). *J Connor Press Associates Ltd v IC* EA/2005/0005 also illustrates that this prejudice must be established: the tribunal overruled the IC in holding that it was not established on the facts of the case. *Derry City Council v IC* EA/2006/0014 has already been encountered under s 41 where it was ruled that s 41 did not exempt the information comprising a copy of the agreement between Ryanair and Derry City Council for the use of Derry airport. Section 43(2) was additionally invoked by the PA. The agreement was made in 1999 and constituted a 'special arrangement'. There had been inter-governmental involvement in discussions from the UK and Irish governments. The subject of the arrangement was an agreement between Derry Council and Ryanair concerning charges and fees, building extensions and other commercial spin-offs if Ryanair provided a flight service to Derry. The PA argued that even in 2005 disclosure of the requested information would still have the effect of giving any counterparty in negotiations an indication of the PA's final negotiating position. The issue was still to that extent 'live'. On the facts s 43 was properly engaged. However, five years after the agreement in question at the time the request was made the PI test was in favour of disclosure. An audit would not have provided 'for inspection of the contracts under which particular invoices may have been raised' and there was a PI in this information being made available.

1.223 FS50094891 concerned the Commonwealth Development Corporation (CDC), a government-owned company and PA, which invests in private equity funds focused on emerging markets in developing parts of the world. The complainant requested the contract between CDC and Actis, one of its fund managers. CDC refused to disclose the contract on the basis that it was exempt under s 43 of the Act (s 41 was also cited). In relation to the s 43 exemption the IC considered CDC's five arguments that disclosure would harm Actis' negotiating position when attracting new investors who could use the information to enhance their own bargaining position – s 43(2) applied in this context; disclosure would harm CDC's negotiating position when looking for new fund managers and the IC accepted this as a reason for s 43(2) applying; disclosure would harm Actis' negotiating position when acquiring/disposing of investments. Counterparties may have been able to seek a lower price for disposal and would also have a bidding advantage at investment auctions – again s 43(2) applied; public disclosure would prevent CDC from being able to invest in certain funds because disclosure of its dealings would cause it to be treated a a 'second rate investor'. The IC decided that the CDC's ability to invest in a number of investment funds would be damaged and its commercial interests would thus be harmed; disclosure would enable rivals to use proprietary information at no cost. The IC considered that there was insufficient evidence to demonstrate that the redacted sections constituted proprietary information which could be used by Actis' rivals to the detriment of Actis' commercial interests. The majority of the information was covered by s 43(2). In relation to the PI in disclosure, the arguments for disclosure were: transparency in government commercial arrangements (particularly as it was controversial and had the potential to create environmental, social and economic impacts) and scrutiny of checks and balances and the application of public funds. The arguments against disclosure were: that the industry was already regulated and subject to suitable disclosure, that the investment of public funds would be undermined, that CDC should be in a position to negotiate best price and that confidentiality would enhance CDC's operating performance. The public interest was deemed to weigh in favour of non-disclosure of the exempted information (and see FS50114967). Section 43(2) protected some information about wine stocks held by the Foreign and Commonwealth Office: FS50347157.

(XXIV) PROHIBITIONS ON DISCLOSURE

1.224 Under FOIA 2000, s 44(1), information is exempt information if its disclosure, otherwise than under this Act, is prohibited by or under any enactment; is incompatible with any European Union (Community) obligations;[1] or would constitute or be punishable as a contempt of court.[2] Annex B of this book contains a list of statutory prohibitions on disclosure. The most notorious will be the Official Secrets Acts of 1911 (s 1) and 1989 (see paras 2.131 et seq below). The Official Secrets Acts are concerned with *unauthorised* disclosure. A formal decision to make a disclosure under FOIA 2000 will provide the necessary authority making the disclosure authorised. The two Acts do not approach the subject of disclosure from the same direction. Official secrets are about discipline; FOIA is about transparency.

[1] See ch 3 for a discussion of the regulation on access and proposed amendments in the EU.
[2] Under the Contempt of Court Act 1981 and common law: *A–G v Newspaper Publishing plc* [1987] 3 All ER 276, CA.

1.225 The duty to confirm or deny is excluded if confirmation or denial in compliance with s 1(1)(a) would (apart from this Act) fall within any of the above three provisions under s 44(1).

1.226   This is an absolute exemption.

1.227   Section 44 is widely resorted to. *Financial Services Authority v IC* [2009] EWHC 1548 (Admin) contains an important legal point in relation to this section. Section 44 has often been used by regulators, law enforcers, ombudsmen and so on who receive information 'in confidence' and who are statutorily prohibited from disclosing this information unless it is to an authorised recipient for an authorised purpose – these are often referred to as 'gateways'. In this case, although s 43 did not protect the information in question because it was not commercially sensitive or a trade secret as we have seen. However, when that information was pieced together with 'other information' held by the FSA together it included information given in confidence and therefore caught by prohibition against disclosure in FSMA 2000, s 348. When the information was combined with other accessible information it would include that from person 'given in confidence'. *Secretary of State for the Home Department v Br Union for Abolition of Vivisection & IC* [2008] EWHC 892 (Admin, [2008] EWCA Civ 870 concerned the breeding and supply of animals for scientific procedures which was governed by Animals (Scientific Procedures) Act 1986. Information 'given in confidence' in the licensing process was prohibited from disclosure. The tribunal ruled that these words had to satisfy the three-stage test of achieving protection under the law of confidentiality in *Coco v AN Clark Ltd* (1968) FSR 415 Ch (nature of the information qualifies it as confidential; the information was imparted in circumstances in which confidentiality applies; and there was unauthorised use). The tribunal ruled that the information did not satisfy that test under the law of confidentiality and so the information was not given 'in confidence' for the purposes of the statutory prohibition. This was wrong in law ruled the high court and court of appeal and failed to acknowledge the development of the law protecting personal data and information. The words meant given on the understanding that the information was given in confidence and would not be disclosed and did not import the *Coco* test of the law of confidentiality. The information was therefore protected under the 1986 Act and consequently prohibited from disclosure under s 44 (See *Br Union for Abolition of Vivisection v IC and Newcastle University* EA/2010/0064 concerning the same provisions where information was 'held' by the University and not the researchers and s 44 did not apply. The tribunal's decision was upheld by the Upper Tribunal: *University of Newcastle upon Tyne v Information Commissioner and BUAV* [2011] UKUT 185 (AAC) (11 May 2011).

1.228   In *C Lamb v IC* EA/2009/0108 the tribunal ruled that information in the possession of the IC's office which had been produced in its examination of a previous request in relation to Cabinet minutes on the decision to invade Iraq were exempt under s 44 by virtue of the prohibition in DPA 1998, s 59(1). *Pricewaterhouse Coopers v IC and HMRC* EA/2009/0049 concerned an appeal involving the construction of the Commissioners of Revenue and Customs Act 2005 (CRCA 2005), ss 18 and 23 and their relationship with FOIA 2000, s 44. CRCA 2005, s 18(1) imposes a duty of confidentiality which is limited by s 18(2), which allows various gateways to access (above). This includes s 18(2) (h): 'disclosure which is made with the consent of each person to whom the information relates'. Under CRCA 2005, s 23 information is exempt under FOIA 2000, s 44 where disclosure would either specify the identity, or allow the identity to be deduced, of a person to whom the information relates. The request was made by an agent acting for the taxpayer about information provided by the taxpayer, ie the taxpayer wanted access to his records; in effect he was using FOIA 2000 as a DPA 1998 vehicle. Did his consent to disclosure justify a FOIA disclosure removing s 44? In such a disclosure under FOIA disclosure would potentially be to the whole world. The tribunal ruled that it did justify disclosure. It also noted that such an issue of complicated statutory interpretation was really better suited for the high court or now the Upper Tribunal to where an appeal was made. On a number of occasions PAs have attempted to argue that the general provisions on private and family life under ECHR, Art 8 constitute a prohibition under s 44. This has not been accepted (FS 50099223). Information has been refused on abortion statistics where it would constitute a breach of abortion regulations, but the IC did not accept on the facts that it would breach s. 44 because it had been anonymised (FS50122432). FS 50074331 was a request to HMRC for correspondence with three tobacco firms which led to a memorandum of understanding between the PA and companies to reduce tobacco smuggling. Section 44 was invoked (Finance Act 1989, s 182 – which prohibits release of information about an identifiable individual by tax authorities, and CCRA 2005, ss 18 and 23 as above). Section 182(5) is a gateway provision. The FOIA was a general duty of diclosure and was not an authorised function under the customs and revenue code. FOIA did not amount to a gateway; disclosure had to take place within the terms of the parent statute.

1.229 Many of the cases have involved FMSA 2000, s 348 (see eg FS 50082955). In this case the IC accepted that an unauthorised leak of the information in question did not place it in the public domain. Section 349 allows 'gateways' for disclosure for various public official functions. Section 348 places restrictions on the disclosure by a primary recipient (here the FSA) of 'confidential information' as defined which 'relates to the business or other affairs of any person' and which was received by the 'primary recipient' for the purposes of the FSA. This would protect information given by one regulator to another if 'confidential information'. Section 349 allows gateways for disclosure for various public official functions. The request was for copy of a draft report prepared by the FSA's predecessor and covered events in the 1980s and 1990s involving mis-marketing of products by building societies. The IC believed that s 44 would cover background information but not 'opinion' information. The opinion of one regulator passed to another represented 'self generated information' he believed. However, s 43(2) would protect the information. The Commissioner investigated the application of these exemptions and found that FSA was correct to apply both of them and that opinion information was protected by s 43 and by the PI in non-disclosure. This decision notice was appealed to the Information Tribunal (see also *R Rowland and FSA v IC* EA/2008/0075 and 0077). In FS 50150138 the IC ruled that disclosure of information to carry out a public function of FSA related to functions under the FSMA 2000 and not general duties such as FOIA 2000 (see above). This point of law was upheld in *J Calland v IC* EA/2007/0136. (For a difficult FSA case see FS50075781 upheld on appeal:

EA/2007/0093 and 0100; see also *Financial Services Authority v IC* EA/2008/0061 and *N Slann v IC and FSA (JP)* EA/2005/0019). *M Dey v IC & OFT* EA/2006/0057 made similar points in relation to 'functions' under the Enterprise Act 2002, s 237. The requester argued that gateways for access under that Act (ss 239–243) overcame the absolute exemption in s 4. Sections 239–243 referred to disclosures in accordance with the Enterprise Act 2002 Act not under FOIA, repeating the point of other cases.

1.230 On a variety of occasions the IC has ruled that the Local Government Act 1974, s 32(2) prevented disclosure by the s 44 exemption although the ombudsman has sometimes been at fault under FOIA 2000, s 1 and the Parliamentary Ombudsman under s 17 (*C Parker v IC and Parliamentary Ombudsman* EA/2007/0046). In FS50200163 concerning the Parliamentary and Health Service Ombudsman, a request for information was rightly refused. FS 50112347 concerned an unsuccessful request for a complaints file of the Local Government Ombudsman; and see FS 50094124 where most of the information was protected. *Commission for Local Administration v IC* EA/2007/0087 also involved the local ombudsman and LGA 1974, s 32(2) and FOIA 2000, s 44. Information obtained in the course of investigating a complaint by the ombudsman was properly exempt under s 44. The tribunal ruled that information which does not refer to the complaint itself can be disclosed. This might include: the name of the authority, the name of the investigator, and the method and process ('mechanics') of an investigation. Such information may be accessible under FOIA providing it does not refer to the 'substance of the complaint', questions of fact or any evidence collected. is information about processes adopted protected or about ways of proceeding. These matters did not cover the subject of the complaint and did not in effect cover matters of substance. The decision can create problems in definition. For instance in drawing a distinction between information received from a third party (which is protected) and information that has been passed between an ombudsman and an officer employed by the ombudsman (which is not) the tribunal's decision can present some very difficult questions of distinction. Surely that passing between officials must not have come from a third party and must not be in any otherwise exempt? The tribunal did not believe that this, ie separating protected and unprotected information in the future, would unduly burden the local ombudsman. FS 50073646 was a request for information from the MoJ concerning a complaint the requester had made about a judge in dealing with his judicial review application and appeal proceedings. In relation to FOIA 2000, s 44, the Constitutional Reform Act 2005, s 139 provides for confidentiality of information in relation to judicial appointments. Other exemptions applied to protect other information. The IC has a relevant s 44 exemption by virtue of DPA 1998, s 59 (see FS 50126668). The case also highlights a problem of procedural justice – the ICO investigates the IC under the FOIA. In J *Allison v IC and HMRC* EA/2007/0089 the tribunal recorded in the strongest of terms that FOIA was not to be utilised to obtain 'reasons behind a decision'. The Act's function was to provide access to information. The appellant was seeking interpretations of law under FOIA. Such interpretations are not accessible if not recorded. The case involved CCRA 2005, ss 18–20, which is discussed above. The IC ruled against disclosure and the DN was upheld by the tribunal. On s 44 and Civil Aviation Authority Act 1982, s 23 see *J Hoyte v IC and CAA* EA/2007/0101 where s 44 was correctly invoked to protect a Closure Report (CR) after a Mandatory Occurrence Reporting Scheme (MOR) to the Civil Aviation Authority concerning a hazardous or potentially hazardous flight incident or defect. MOR was regulated under EC Directive (EC 2003/42/ EC) and a statutory instrument (Air Navigation (General) Regulations 2006, SI 2006/601) and Air Navigation Order. In *B Higginson v IC* EA/2005/0008 there was a request to the Independent Police Complaints Commission for information, denied by s 44 (prohibition by the Police Act 1996, s 80).

Late reliance on an exemption

1.231 The question of whether an additional exemption can be raised after an initial refusal has been raised on numerous occasions. The IC and tribunal (subject to the next paragraph) have dealt with the situation as a matter of discretion (see the early case Bowrick v IC and Nottingham City Council EA/2005/0006). If there were an element of bad faith in delaying an invocation of an exemption this might have costs implications. There is no duty on the IC to raise an exemption for a PA *(P Bowrick v IC and Nottingham City Council* EA/2005/0006 at 46) although he may invoke an appropriate exemption not claimed by the PA. In that case, costs were awarded against the authority. In *Home Office and Ministry of Justice v IC* [2009] EWHC 1611 (Admin) – the point was raised in the High Court but not dealt with in judgment because the IC and tribunal agreed on remission of the case on additional exemptions. *Crown Prosecution Service v IC* EA/2009/0077 involved a request to the CPS asking for information on the CPS's change of position towards the reasonable punishment defence as amended by the Children Act 2004, s 58; this limited the defence to battery only. He wanted to know why the CPS changed its position from 'wrong to change the law' in 2000 to 'comfortable with the change' in 2004 and requested copies of any related correspondence and minutes. The CPS refused on the basis of FOIA 2000, s 35(1)(a). The IC decided that the exemption was engaged, but that the public interest favoured disclosure. The CPS appealed to the FTT out of time, but the appeal was nevertheless accepted. The CPS sought to raise further exemptions at the appeal stage: ss 35(1)(b), s 42 and s 40(2). The FTT followed the decision of the IT in *Home Office and Ministry of Justice v IC* (EA/2008/0062) that FOIA 2000, ss 10 and 17 do not prohibit the late claiming of exemptions, but the decision as to whether to permit the claim depends on the particular circumstances of the case. Further, the appellant must provide reasonable justification. Whilst there was a public interest in permitting a late claim, there was also a public interest in being required to identify all of the relevant exemptions in the first instance. The tribunal did not accept that the IC was under a duty to identify additional possible exemptions; it applied *Bowbrick v Nottingham City Council* EA/2005/0006.

1.232 In Home Office v IC EA/2010/0011 the tribunal broke with a consistent pattern and ruled that PAs have a right to make a late claim for exemptions, ie they can raise an exemption at a later stage to any initial exemptions that were raised in response to a request. This was subject to appeal to the Upper Tribunal which upheld the decision of the FTT noting that the right was subject to the tribunal's case management powers under the Tribunal Procedure (First-tier Tribunal) (General Regulatory Chamber) Rules 2009, SI 2009/1976) ([2011] UKUT 17 AAC). The case concerned the Asylum and Immigration (Treatment of Claimants) Act 2004, s 12 and the evidence used by the UK Border Authority when the provision was placed before Parliament. The request was rejected under s 35(1)(a) on which the IC ruled against the PA which introduced late invocation of ss 40 and 42. The reasoning of the tribunal did not altogether appear convincing and centered on the appeal provisions in FOIA, specifically s 58(1). The tribunal believed that this was subject to a narrow interpretation namely that in relation to a DN of the IC being 'not in accordance with the law' meant the tribunal had a discretion to allow a late invocation of an exemption. A broad interpretation of the words meant looking at the totality of relevant evidence including late and relevant exemptions. We prefer the discretionary approach arguing that it should be allowed where justice demands it. This is fair and consistent with principle but was not the approach of the Upper Tribunal (see also a similar ruling under the EIR 2004: *Defra v IC and Simon Birkett* [2011] UKUT 39 AAC).

1.233 In *All Party Parliamentary Group Extraordinary Rendition v IC and MoD* [2011] UKUT 153 (AAC) the Upper Tribunal ruled that such a flexible approach will not be accorded to late claims under FOIA 2000, s 12 for excessive cost of compliance. 'It would be disproportionate and contrary to the UTs overriding objective to allow this point to be taken now' (para 95).

Enforcement

1.234 To state the position in concise terms, the authority may claim an exemption applies. Originally, the IC could, and still can, challenge this finding on the ground that if it existed, it would not cause 'prejudice' if disclosed or the grounds of exemption were simply not established. Now, the authority must consider s 2 and the public interest and although the IC may overrule their decision, the authority may have a veto under s 53 (see below). In the case of an absolute discretion, there is no reference to the public interest, and the IC may have limited grounds to challenge whether a claim for exemption is correctly made, ie there is no factual basis supporting the claim although the IC could not displace other procedures, such as those under s 23.

1.235 Part IV of the FOIA 2000 is concerned with enforcement. These provisions lean heavily on those under the DPA 1998. Any person viz, the 'complainant' may apply to the Commissioner for a decision whether, in any specified respect, a request for information has not been dealt with according to the requirements of Part I. This includes, inter alia, the general duty under s 1 and discretionary disclosures in the public interest under s 2. Having received the application the Commissioner has to make a decision unless the applicant has not exhausted any internal complaints procedure in accordance with the code of practice under s 45 (see para 1.233 below). Guidance states that these complaints procedures should seek to resolve simple cases within 20 days of receiving the complaint. More complex cases concerning the public interest should be dealt with within six weeks of receiving the complaint (http://www.justice.gov.uk/guidance/foi-procedural-unhappy.htm). Further grounds for not making a decision include undue delay in making the application, that it is frivolous or vexatious or that it has been withdrawn or abandoned. The Commissioner has either to inform the complainant that he is not making a decision under this section and the grounds for not doing so or serve a 'decision notice' (literally a notice of his decision) on both the public authority and complainant.

1.236 Where the Commissioner decides that an authority has failed to communicate information or make a confirmation or denial where required by s 1(1) or has failed to comply with any of the requirements of s 11 (form of communication of information), or s 17 (steps that have to be taken on refusing a request) her decision notice must specify the steps that have to be taken for compliance and the period within which they must be taken. The decision notice must contain particulars of the right of appeal under s 57 (see para 1.246). Where a notice requires steps to be taken by the authority, no time can be specified for the taking of such steps until the time for making an appeal has expired. Section 50 is subject to s 53.[1]

---

[1] In the Bill, where a decision notice stated that there has been a failure to comply with cl 13(3) or (4) it may not require the public authority to inform the applicant whether it holds particular information or to disclose particular information. It may require the authority to make a decision in accordance with that section and specify matters to which the authority must have regard in making that decision. Elided on third reading. See below on the government's refusals to accept adverse decisions etc on what was cl 13 (now FOIA 2000, s 2) – the discretionary disclosure.

1.237 Under s 52 the IC may issue the authority with an enforcement notice (EN) where the IC is satisfied that the authority has failed to comply with 'any of the requirements of Part I of the Act'. The authority will be required to take specified steps in order to comply. An EN must contain a statement of the requirement(s) in Part I which are not complied with and the IC's reasons for his conclusion as well as particulars of the right of appeal under s 57. The EN must not contain any provisions requiring compliance with the notice before appeal rights, including determination or withdrawal of the appeal, have expired. An EN may be cancelled by service of a written notice on the authority.

1.238 In February 2005, the Secretary of State and the IC signed a memorandum of understanding on the operation of the Act in relation to enforcement and FOIA 2000, ss 50 and 51 and EIR 2004, reg 18 (www.dca.gov.uk). This cannot override any legal requirements or duties. Nevertheless, it raises some very interesting points. The understanding only applies to government departments (see Annex 1 of the memorandum). Where the IC receives an application under s 50 for a decision, the IC will contact the relevant department involved, requesting 'all information relevant to the application' including redacted information. Response times are set out – 20 days initially. Advance notice 'wherever possible' should be served before issuing an information notice (para 1.243 below). Information should not be disclosed by the IC to any third party unless consent has been given or all appeal processes have been finalised, and then a case 'summary' only will be published. The memorandum seeks to limit access to information by the IC where this is not necessary (para 12). Information supplied to the IC will be kept according to the conditions of security set out in the *Manual of Protective Security* where it is so protected, and papers which are 'particularly sensitive' will only be inspected *in situ* in the department. The memorandum provides that a 'preliminary decision notice' may be considered before serving a decision notice (para 1.236). The criteria for making this non-statutory notice are set out in Annex 3 of the memorandum. If not accepted by a department, there will be discussion to explore alternatives. A formal decision notice will be 'served' on the department and complainant simultaneously and, where 'market-sensitive' information is involved, the IC must first be 'satisfied as to the relevant regulatory requirements' (para 25). Annex 2 provides guidance on requests involving FOIA 2000, s 23 or 24 (and EIR 2004, reg 12(5)(a) (see para 8.234 below)) – those involving the security and intelligence services and national security (paras 1.117 to 1.125 above). Settlement is urged wherever practicable. Where information is withheld as a consequence of invoking either section, 'the department does not commit itself to providing the withheld information to the Commissioner, but will consider any request to [do] so on a case by case basis' (para 4). The department will only seek a s 23 or 24 certificate where the IC receives a complaint and indicates that he is minded to embark on the enforcement process.

THE VETO OVERRIDING THE IC'S DECISION ON THE PUBLIC INTEREST (S 53)

1.239   The above section is subject to a provision inserted at Committee Stage in the Commons. It was further amended in the Lords. This provides that a decision notice or an enforcement notice, which relates to a failure to comply with s 1(1)(a) or (b) of the FOIA 2000, and concerns request(s) for information where the authority believes that the duty to confirm or deny is excluded, or which is exempt (s 53(1)(b)), shall cease to have effect where an 'accountable person' in relation to that authority gives the Commissioner a certificate signed by that person. The certificate must be given not later than the twentieth working day following the day on which the notice was given to the public authority. The memorandum referred to above states that advance notice of a s 53 certificate will be given to the IC 'wherever possible'. The certificate will state that that person has on reasonable grounds formed the opinion that the authority did not fail to comply with any duty within sub-s 1(b) so far as the request(s) are concerned. Where such a certificate is given then crucially, under s 53(6), the accountable person has to provide the complainant (ie requester) with reasons for the decision as soon as it is practicable to do so. But, this *only applies in relation to decision notices*. It does not cover enforcement notices. In complying with this duty to provide reasons nothing is required which would disclose exempt information.

1.240   It should be noted that this opinion must be supported by 'reasonable grounds' implying a degree of objectivity in the decision which although beyond the IC's bailiwick and not appealable to the Tribunal may be challengeable by judicial review. The reasonable grounds are a jurisdictional fact and on whose existence the proper exercise of the power turns.[1] Whether there are reasonable grounds is something that will have to be supportable by evidence – in the case of decisions, this will be facilitated by the duty to supply reasons. In the case of an EN, the absence of reasons will make challenge more difficult and may only be successful where the decision appears perverse on its face. Could the court infer a duty to give reasons in the case of ENs? If the courts do review a certificate under s 53, a quashing order (formerly certiorari) could be accompanied by a mandatory order (mandamus) to exercise discretion properly.

[1] *Secretary of State for Education and Science v Tameside Metropolitan Borough Council* [1977] AC 1014, HL.

1.241 The accountable person who makes a decision under s 53 is set out in sub-s (7). Originally, s 53 applied to all public authorities. They all had the veto. However, the clause was amended so that the veto only applied to government departments, the National Assembly for Wales and 'designated authorities' – the designation was made by the Secretary of State and can apply to all authorities. The veto covers notices relating to a failure to comply with either s 1(1)(a) in relation to a duty to confirm or deny the holding of information, or s 1(1)(b) in respect of disclosing exempt information. A veto may only be issued by a Minister of the Crown who is a member of the Cabinet or the Attorney General, Advocate General for Scotland or the Attorney General (Northern Ireland). Special provisions apply to Welsh and Northern Irish bodies. In relation to these bodies consultation has to take place between the Secretary of State and relevant Welsh and Northern Irish bodies before he may make an order. Designated bodies will not be able to issue their own veto; but what is to stop special pleading between designated bodies and the Minister? The Lord Chancellor has stated that a veto will have to be agreed by the Cabinet and would be 'very, very exceptional' (*The Guardian* (2005) 1 January).

1.242 To date two vetoes have been issued. Both concerned access to the minutes of Cabinet meetings, in the first case involving discussion of the invasion of Iraq (see HC 622 (2008–09) and HC 218 (2009–10)). It should be noted that when the coalition government came to power, a case had been decided by the IC concerning the minutes from the Cabinet meeting discussing the Westland helicopter saga in the 1980s. A refusal to disclose the minutes was overrueld by the IC and the case was appealed to the tribunal unsuccessfully: *Cabinet Office v IC* EA/2010/0031. It reveals that the coalition government was initially adopting a similar approach to protection of Cabinet minutes. However, although the CO lost its appeal no veto was issued in this case which showed a new approach by the new government.

INFORMATION NOTICES

1.243 Under s 51 of the FOIA 2000, the IC may serve on an authority an information notice. Information includes 'unrecorded information' (s 51(8)).

This may be served (i) after an application for a decision under s 50, or (ii) where the IC reasonably requires any information in order to establish compliance with the requirements of Part I, or (iii) to determine whether an authority's practice complies with that laid down in the codes under ss 45 and 46. The former code has been examined in a variety of contexts (and see eg paras 1.272 et seq and 1.284 et seq below). The Code under s 46 is concerned with records management (see para 2.73). The notice requires the authority to furnish the IC within a specified time and in any specified form with information relating to the above three matters. Notices must contain statements relating to an application under s 51 or in relation to (i) or (ii) above a statement of the relevance of the information and the reasons why the IC regards it as relevant. Particulars of rights of appeal and setting time limits which will not undermine appeal rights are also provided for.[1]

[1]   See FOIA 2000, ss 50(5) and (6), 51(3) and (4), 52(3)(b) and (3) and cf s 52(4).

1.244   By s 51(5), legal professional privilege is protected from an information notice in so far as it covers communications between a professional legal adviser and his client in connection with giving of legal advice 'with respect to his obligations, liabilities or rights under this Act' and with respect to any communications between those parties and any other person 'made in connection with or in contemplation of proceedings under or arising out of this Act' and for the purposes of such proceedings. This includes proceedings before the Tribunal. The question of Information Notices and unsuccessful appeals against them is examined in *Governing Body Aberdare Girls School v IC* EA/2010/0102 and *Swanage TC v IC* EA/2009/0058. The tribunal has ruled that a PA does not have to comply with a DN served under s 51 where the request was for legal advice from the Attorney General on dealing with the PI factor.[1]

[1]   *Ministry of Justice v IC* EA/2007/0016.

FAILURE TO COMPLY WITH A NOTICE AND APPEALS

1.245   Where an authority has failed to comply with any of the above notices, the IC may certify such failure for the court[1] which may after due procedures, punish the failure as a contempt. An authority which in purported compliance with an information notice makes a false statement, either intentionally or recklessly, will be taken to have failed to comply with the notice. Under FOIA 2000, Sch 3 the IC is given considerable powers of entry and inspection under warrant issued by a circuit judge. Decision notices end with a reference to these powers and they have only rarely been invoked.

[1]   This is the High Court or Court of Session: s 53(4).

1.246   Both complainants and public authorities on whom a decision notice has been served may appeal to the Tribunal against the notice. A public authority may appeal against service upon it of an information or enforcement notice. The Tribunal has extensive powers to allow an appeal on the ground that a notice is not in accordance with the law or where the notice involved an exercise of discretion by the Commissioner, 'that he ought to have exercised his discretion differently'. This allows the Tribunal to reverse a finding on its merits. It may also on appeal review any finding of fact on which the notice was based. Schedules 2 and 4 contain further provisions relating to the Tribunal.[1] From the Tribunal's decision there is an appeal on a point of law to the Upper Tribunal. Notice of appeal must contain a postal and not just an email address: *W Thackeray v IC* EA/2010/0088 – Tribunal Procedure (First-tier Tribunal) (General Regulatory Chamber) Rules 2009, r 22(a) and (b).

[1] One of the lay members of the Tribunal will represent the interests of requesters of information under the FOIA 2000. This amends DPA 1998, s 6(6). Schedule 4 contains details inter alia on the constitution of the Tribunal in national security cases. See SI 2000/189, amended by SI 2002/2722, and SI 2005/13 which, inter alia, revokes SI 2000/206 on national security appeals relating to data protection. SI 2005/13, r 24 states that hearings are to be in private, unless the Tribunal otherwise directs, with the consent of the minister and parties. SI 2005/14 concerns enforcement appeals: proceedings are in public unless the Tribunal otherwise directs under the terms of r 22. Appeals under ss 23 and 24 are made now to the Upper Tribunal.

1.247   *The Cabinet Office v IC* EA/2010/0028 was an appeal that concerned the transition of the IT into the FTT and, more particularly, the Practice Note dealing with Confidentiality and Redaction. A new Practice Note was issued for the new regime entitled 'Protection of Confidential Information in Information Rights Appeals before the First-tier Tribunal in the General Regulatory Tribunal on or after 18 January 2010'. The public authority initially sought to oppose the revelation of a confidential annex appended to its Notice of Appeal. The Practice Note stated that the 'old system would continue, namely, that there would probably be in most cases an open bundle and a closed bundle'. The primary principal is that the tribunal should have all the relevant information necessary for it to make a just and fair decision. The appellant withdrew its objection to confidential disclosure before the conclusion of the appeal. However the FTT thought it necessary to confirm that the old system would continue.

1.248   The addition of the Tribunal has complicated the question of enforcement. Under the White Paper some of the operations of the Act establishing the PCA were borrowed so that while the IC could make a decision instructing the public body to disclose information, enforcement would be via the courts by way of contempt where there was a refusal to comply with the Commissioner's decision. The analogy with the PCA was not quite appropriate because the latter only recommends and the contempt powers were there to protect the PCA from deliberate interference or obstruction in the course of his investigation.

1.249   The Commissioner can make a decision notice in relation to disclosure under s 1(1) and s 2 and in relation to provisions under ss 11 and 17. Such notices may be issued in relation to other failures to comply with the requirements of Part I of the Act. Decisions are binding subject to appeal or veto. Where information is covered by s 2 – the clause dealing with discretionary decisions by the authority on disclosure of exempt information – the Commissioner can make a decision requiring disclosure – the IC can even enforce such a decision unless a certificate is served under s 53(1). This differs from the situation in the Consultation Bill and the Bills published in November 1999 and February 2000. The IC is not restricted to the correction of the process of decision-making by the authority. The Campaign for FOI believed that the Commissioner's role under these earlier versions of the Bill was basically that of checking that relevant factors had been considered. There is, in other words, no role for appraisal, balancing or judgement on the merits by the Commissioner. It may be that this original power was not so restricted because the Commissioner will have wide access to the relevant information and records and will be able more easily to fathom how the decision was made and therefore will have ammunition to criticise it. Under s 51 the Commissioner may serve the authority with an information notice. The IC should, in other words, have access to the relevant information as well as the decision record and the reasons for the decision – unlike the applicant under the draft Bill. Will the IC have access to the records generated by the complaint – the internal correspondence? Although the Commissioner acts like a reviewing court in the above enquiry, the IC will have far more material to dig beneath the surface than a reviewing court usually possess. The Act has made it clearer that the onus is on the authority to justify its decision to withhold information in all cases, especially to the 'discretionary' information. Authorities are required to give reasons for their decisions; this was added in the second Bill. In looking at the considerations on the public interest, and armed with the information itself, the authorities will of necessity have to explain their decisions. If explained satisfactorily, fine. But if the explanation is not justified by the evidence, or appears disproportionate and suggests a failure not only to consider relevant factors but a failure to give them proper weight, then this could reveal a fault in the decision-making process under s 2 and the Commissioner may, by virtue of s 52(1) and (2) which concerns enforcement notices, require the authority to take, within a specified time, specified steps in order to comply, and the EN must contain a statement of the requirements of Part I which the IC is satisfied that the public authority has failed to comply with and her reasons for so concluding. The Commissioner, to repeat, will have access to all relevant information and reasoning. Reviewing courts are rarely given this amount of ammunition. This is reinforced by the fact that on an appeal to the Tribunal the Commissioner's exercise of discretion may be overturned where the IC 'ought to have exercised his discretion differently' (s 58(1)(b)). This suggests considerable power in the Commissioner but of course much depends on how the Tribunal exercises its appellate powers. Furthermore, where there is a failure to act upon an EN by the authority, the Commissioner may certify the failure to the court which it can punish as a contempt (s 54(3)).

1.250 Under the later Bill, a power to recommend disclosure of discretionary information was given to the IC. This expresses what would probably have occurred de facto. Under a later version of the Bill, this recommendation was removed because the Commissioner may enforce his decision including disclosure of exempt information subject to a certificate from the accountable person vetoing the IC's decision. This is yet another example of a veto power in the Minister or other specified person. The Home Secretary expressed his intention that the IC's decision would prevail over bodies such as local authorities and quangos etc. Details were to be provided. The only method by which a veto may be challenged is via a judicial review. The IC will possess a great deal of evidence if he is permitted to seek review as a person with a 'sufficient interest' under Part 54 of the Civil Procedure Rules 1998 (CPR).

1.251 It seems that contempt proceedings are unlikely to have any, or any significant, role in enforcement unless there is no appeal and the authority does not comply with a decision or other notice of the Commissioner. DNs contain notice of the contempt provisions and the IC has had to remind PAs of this power. In a difficult case it might be asked whether it would not have been better to give the Commissioner a power similar to the Northern Ireland Commissioner to seek an injunction to force a recalcitrant authority to comply in particular with decisions relating to ss 1 and 2? More generally, injunctions may be issued against Ministers in their official capacity under judicial review proceedings. Contempt seems to be confined in practice to those cases where, as with the PCA, there is obstruction or wilful interference with the Commissioner's powers and duties of investigation or, possibly, persistent refusal. Would these not be more appropriately dealt with by an injunction?[1] In 1967, it was the case that injunctions would not issue against officers of the Crown in their official capacity. Case law has changed this position. If an injunction is not complied with, *then* it becomes a matter of contempt. In *M v Home Office*,[2] the Law Lords said that the courts would not enforce a finding of contempt against a Minister – for failing to comply with an injunction – but would leave enforcement to the political arena.

[1]   Under FOIA 2000, s 77, a criminal offence is created of altering documents etc to prevent disclosure. This is broader than the proposal in the WP.
[2]   [1993] 3 All ER 537, HL.

1.252 It is interesting that the Scottish FOIA does not provide for a tribunal, thereby reviving the importance of the above discussion vis-à-vis the Scottish IC.

Awarding costs

1.253 A discussion on the principles involved in awarding costs is in *Royal Mail Group Ltd v IC* EA/2010/0005 where an appeal was withdrawn. Should costs be awarded? The governing provisions used to be in the Information Tribunal (Enforcement Appeals) Rules 2005, SI 2005/14, r 29. They are now in the Tribunals, Courts and Enforcement Act 2007, s 29 and the Tribunal Procedure (First-tier Tribunal) (General Regulatory Chamber) Rules 2009, r 10 – and may be awarded against a party 'acting unreasonably' in bringing, defending or conducting proceedings or where the IC acted unreasonably in making a decision, order or direction. The previous provision in r 29 stated that costs could be awarded where appealing or decisions were 'manifestly unreasonable' or where action was frivolous, vexatious, improper or unreasonable.

What matters are within the jurisdiction of the commissioner and tribunal?

1.254 This question became a matter of contention very early in the operational life of FOIA 2000 and led to a decision of the House of Lords which has been examined in detail above (1.90).

General functions of Secretary of State, Lord Chancellor and Information Commissioner

1.255 Part III of the FOIA 2000 concerns the general functions of the above Ministers and the IC. Under s 45, the Secretary of State is to issue a code of practice giving guidance to authorities about the practice which it would be desirable, in his opinion, for them to follow in connection with the discharge of their duties under Part I of the Act. This may be revised. The Commissioner has to be consulted before the issuing or revising of a code and any codes or revisions have to be placed before both Houses of Parliament. The codes will in particular advise on: advice by authorities to those who are making requests for access – compliance with the code is taken as evidence of performing the duty under s 16 (see para 1.83 above); transfer of requests between authorities; consultation with persons to whom the information requested relates or 'persons who are likely to be affected by the disclosure of information'; the inclusion of contracts entered into between public authorities of terms relating to the disclosure of information; and procedures provided by public authorities for dealing with complaints about requests for information. The code may make different provision for different public authorities. Two codes have been published and approved (see below). The Protection of Freedoms Bill makes provision for the s 45 code to cover disclosure of data sets and re-se of information (1.79 above).

1.256 A code is also to be issued by the Lord Chancellor under s 46 on the public records aspects of the legislation. A code was updated in 2009 (see para 2.73 below).[1]

[1] http://www.justice.gov.uk/guidance/foi-procedural-unhappy.htm.

1.257 Under s 47, the IC is given a wide range of promotional powers to encourage the pursuit of good practice by authorities and to promote the observance by authorities of the Act's requirements and the provisions of the codes referred to above. The IC may publicise in such manner as she deems appropriate such information for the public as the IC deems expedient about the operation of the Act, good practice – which is not limited to compliance with the Act or the codes – other matters within the scope of the Act and the IC may advise on those matters. The IC may assess whether the authority is following good practice, but, and this is important, only with the consent of the authority and the Commissioner may charge for this service and any others under s 47. The Protection of Freedoms Bill 2011 removes the requirement under s 47(4) of the IC having to obtain the Secretary of State's consent before charging for services. Those services for which a charge may be made are listed and may be amended by order. Similar amendments are made to the DPA 1998, s 51(8).

Under the Bill, the Secretary of State's approval for the number of staff has been removed but appointments must have regard to the principle of selection on merit on the basis of fair and open competition.

1.258   Where an authority does not appear to be complying with a code of practice, the IC may give the authority a Practice Recommendation in writing (see para 1.22 above) specifying the steps which in the IC's opinion ought to be taken for promoting such conformity. We have seen how nothing in the Act makes this enforceable under the Act unless it breaches a requirement under Part I. Interestingly, a power to issue recommendations as to outcome in relation to s 2 information was removed in Committee in the Commons (see above). The IC lays an annual report before both Houses of Parliament on the IC's work and has power to lay other reports as he thinks fit – see below under conclusion where a 'veto' is exercised and the IC has undertaken to issue a report.

Public records aspects of the FOIA 2000

1.259   The FOIA 2000 has made some significant amendments to the Public Records Acts 1958 as amended and the Public Records (Northern Ireland) Act 1923. These are examined in ch 2 (paras 2.62 et seq below).

Disclosure of information between Commissioner and Ombudsmen

1.260   Under s 76 of the FOIA 2000, the Commissioner is given a specific power to disclose information obtained by or furnished to the Commissioner to the Ombudsmen. These include: the Parliamentary Ombudsman (PO); the Health Service Ombudsman; and local Commissioners. Details of the Scottish and Welsh Ombudsmen have moved on (see para 4.137 below). The Northern Ireland Commissioner for Complaints and the Assembly Ombudsman for Northern Ireland are included. The information which may be supplied is that obtained or furnished under the FOIA 2000 or the DPA 1998. It may be disclosed if it appears to the IC that the information relates to a matter which could be the subject of an investigation by that person under their governing enactments. Schedule 7 to the FOIA 2000 amends the governing statutes or Orders of Ombudsmen to allow them to disclose information to the IC where the Ombudsmen believe that the information relates to a matter in which the IC could exercise power by virtue of Part V of the DPA 1998 (enforcement); s 48 of the FOIA 2000 (practice recommendations); Part IV of the FOIA 2000 (enforcement); or commission of an offence under the DPA 1998 except under Sch 9, para 12; or under s 77 of the FOIA 2000 (altering etc records). The Commissioner may disclose to the Scottish Information Commissioner any information obtained or furnished as mentioned in FOIA 2000, s 76(1) if it appears to the Commissioner that the information is of the same type that could be obtained by, or furnished to, the Scottish Information Commissioner under or for the purposes of the Freedom of Information (Scotland) Act 2002. Finally, there will be occasions when a complaint received by the PO will be wholly or partly about a breach of the FOIA 2000; or, conversely, a complaint received by the Information Commissioner might include matters of alleged maladministration. The Parliamentary Ombudsman's website the British and Irish Ombudsman Association prepared a protocol to establish broad principles for the 'referral and handling of such 'hybrid' complaints, which can then be used by all ombudsman and complaint-handling schemes' (and see SI 2007/1889 which covers ombudsmen only).

1.261 This suggests a very close working relationship between the IC and Ombudsmen.

Some general points

NO STATUTORY RIGHTS OF ACTION

1.262 The FOIA 2000 confers no right of action in civil proceedings for any failure to comply with any duty imposed by or under this act. This will not prevent actions for negligent exercise of duties or breaches of confidence because these are not imposed by or under the Act.

REPEAL OF EXISTING SECRECY PROVISIONS

1.263 If it appears that an existing enactment (which does not include a statutory instrument or order) prohibits the disclosure of information (including 'unrecorded information') under s 1 or 2 of the FOIA 2000, it may be repealed or amended by order. The list of such statutes as published in 1993 and updated is contained in Annex B. It now numbers in the region of 330–340 legal provisions. This did not include the OSA 1989. It nonetheless represents a considerable corpus of provisions preventing access to information including many which impose criminal penalties for unauthorised disclosures. The Select Committee recommended a procedure not unlike the one used for deregulation orders to review existing legislation with a view to its repeal by order. A publication from the Lord Chancellor's Department *Interim Report on Statutory Provisions concerning Disclosure of Information* (May 2002) did include the OSA 1989. (See http://www.dca.gov.uk/foi/foidoirpt.htm#part1tp for the list of those chosen as candidates for repeal). Orders under FOIA, s 75 repealing, or amending, some statutes were laid before Parliament in November 2004 and included: Factories Act 1961, s 154; Offices, Shops and Railway Premises Act 1963, s 59; Medicines Act 1968, s 118; National Health Service Act 1977, Sch 11, para 5; Health and Safety at Work Act 1974, s 28; Audit Commission Act 1998, s 49; Access to Justice Act 1999, s 20 and Biological Standards Act 1975, s 5 (SI 2004/3364). In 2005, the Department for Constitutional Affairs reported that there were in existence over 330 provisions prohibiting the publication of information in addition to the Official Secrecy Acts, but only just over 200 were relevant to FOIA.[1] Candidates for repeal, modification, sunset clauses etc were identified.

---

[1] DCA *Review of Statutory Prohibitions on Disclosure* (2005) http://webarchive.nationalarchives.gov. uk/+/http://www.dca.gov.uk/StatutoryBarsReport2005.pdf.

OFFENCES UNDER THE ACT

1.264 Section 77 creates an offence of altering, defacing, blocking, erasing, destroying or concealing any record which has been requested under the FOIA 2000 or to which an applicant would have been entitled under s 1 or 2 of the FOIA 2000, or under s 7 of the DPA 1998. The offence is committed by any person who does any of the above with the intention of preventing its disclosure by the authority of all, or any part of, the information to a person entitled to receive it. Proceedings may only be instituted by the Commissioner or Director of Public Prosecutions.[1]

[1]   Or NI analogues and level 5 on the standard scale.

EXISTING POWERS OF DISCLOSURE

1.265 Section 78 states that nothing in the FOIA 2000 is to be taken to limit the powers of a public authority to disclose information held by it. This would include both statutory and common law powers. Authorities are free to disclose whatever is not prohibited from disclosure, especially in relation to central government and police under the Official Secrets Acts, which carry a significant degree of self-authorisation, however vague this is in practice (see ch 2). If statutory powers are more extensive than the FOIA 2000, then the statutory powers prevail. Could common law powers be more extensive than the FOIA 2000? Could the FOIA 2000 be by-passed by resort to a more relaxed common law power? It would appear strange if the code represented by the FOIA 2000 could be by-passed in such a manner, or indeed what advantage there may be in seeking to do this. However, in the Select Committee's scrutiny of the Consultation Paper and Bill, the Home Office legal adviser pointed out that refusals to disclose under discretionary powers contained in the Act could be challenged by judicial review. This was because the clause merely dealt with an existing discretion.[1] This in spite of the comprehensive provisions contained in the Act via the IC and tribunal. This seems questionable in relation to any common law powers. A specific provision allowing disclosure would have to be invoked. Information holders must be free to disclose information as they wish in the absence of statutory restrictions or where a disclosure would be otherwise unlawful. The existing administrative provisions in the Code on Access ceased to apply on 31 December 2004.

[1]   HC 570-xii (1998–99) q 1068. It raises some very difficult points on the relationship between statutory remedies and judicial review: see *R v Falmouth etc Health Authority, ex p South West Water Services* [2000] 3 All ER 306, CA.

Some problems with the FOIA 2000

(I) DELAY IN THE FOIA 2000 BECOMING EFFECTIVE

1.266 The long wait for the right to know is nearly over' declared the WP in its closing sentence. It could be as long as five years after enactment before the Act became effective: (FOIA 2000, s 85(3)). In fact, access rights took just over four years to emerge. What Neil Kinnock declared as the first Bill a Labour Government would introduce and what Tony Blair said would be a central plank in a new constitution for the new millennium seemed to have slipped in prominence. Even the HRA 1998 was fully implemented within just over two years and in spite of the fact that thousands of judges, magistrates and tribunal members would have to be educated and trained in human rights' provisions. In many cases bodies not covered by the 1994 Code of John Major on access will not be used to FOI regimes and may need training and preparation. Nonetheless, this seems an extraordinarily long implementation period.

1.267   In March 2001, it was reported that, because of serious problems in locating and retrieving missing files, the date of introduction for central government was likely to be July 2002.[1] This would refer to publication schemes; access rights would come later. As already observed, the date for individual access rights was to be 1 January 2005. But, it should be recalled that the Act is retrospective in its application, is extremely wide in its scope and involved almost unprecedented detailed preparation. The Government also decided not to stagger the introduction of FOIA by starting with central government but to introduce the Act in a 'big bang' for all public authorities at the same time.

[1]   *The Guardian* (2001) 7 March.

(II)   RECORDED INFORMATION

1.268   The first clause of the Draft Bill stated that the duty to disclose will only cover *recorded* information. This will not apply to *unrecorded* information. This provision has now been moved to FOIA 2000, s 84, the interpretation clause which states that information means information recorded in any form. Arguably, the WP went further than this in that it covered *information* even in non-recorded form as did the code, ie opinion and advice may be disclosed (paras 57 and 58 of the *Guidance* (1997 edn)). Section 84 is now subject to ss 51(8) and 75(2) which both include a reference to unrecorded information, ie for information notices and in relation to existing prohibitions on disclosure.

(III)   UNION OF DATA PROTECTION AND INFORMATION COMMISSIONERS AND TRIBUNALS

1.269   The IC and the Data Protection Commissioner (DPC) (the former Data Protection Registrar) became one and the same, as indeed did the Data Protection Tribunal and the Information Tribunal. The apprehension was that privacy would predominate over access rights reinforced by the fact that the DPC has concentrated on privacy protection as provided within the terms of the data protection legislation. A similar point may be made about the tribunal, although it deals with very few DPA cases. Most of the DPC's work involved regulation, promotion and supervision rather than taking up individuals' rights of access. The IC's remit comes from a different angle – access for individuals and openness although the IC has promotional features also. A fear that privacy may predominate over access to information featured in other constitutional reforms such as human rights and the balance between freedom of speech and privacy protection. Where separate access and privacy regimes exist in other jurisdictions, privacy regimes have taken the dominant role, though not always, and much seems to depend upon force of personality.[1]

[1]   See Hazell, para 1.19, note 2 above. Note also *R v Minister of Agriculture, Fisheries and Food, ex p Fisher*: C-369/98 (2000) *Times*, 10 October, ECJ. In *ex p Fisher*, the MAFF refused to provide a farmer with data which concerned the set-aside scheme under the EC agricultural policy. The data was supplied by the applicant's predecessor in title and concerned 'set aside' fields. MAFF claimed it was protected by the DPA 1984. The farmer, without the information, was fined when he used fields that were set aside. The ECJ held that the data contained no privacy interests that overrode a legitimate claim for access. Nothing interfered with the data provider's interests, or fundamental rights or freedoms. The question of the relationship between the Data Protection Directive and the Regulation on access to information in the EU (see ch 3) has been contentious; this has been an issue between the Commission and the EU Ombudsman: see Ian Harden Queen's Papers on Europeanisation No 9/02 – *Openness and Data Protection in The European Union* (2002); see Art 8 ECHR and *Amann v Switzerland* (Application no.27798/95). Stories of unnecessary secrecy on officials' names are legion. See chapter 7 (para 7.114).

1.270   On the other side, no-one can accuse the Commissioner of *actually* coming with pre-inclined views against access although, in her evidence to the Select Committee on Public Administration, the previous Commissioner saw herself very much as the champion of privacy in relation to personal information.[1] Now her statutory remit will be broadened. And new Commissioners were appointed in 2002 and 2009. The union of Commissioners has the benefit of addressing and removing the lack of clarity on this point revealed by the White Paper and highlighted by the Committee. Furthermore, the Act has taken up the suggestion made by the Committee on Public Administration[2] that access by data subjects to information about themselves is made under the DPA 1998 and access by applicants to personal information concerning others is made under the FOIA 2000 amending the DPA 1998 and subject to data protection principles and exemptions. The new bodies are also given the title of IC and Tribunal, perhaps emphasising a point. The decisions of the IC and tribunal on the FOI/DP interface have not given precedence to one regime over the other. However, under s 72 disclosures under FOIA do not override DPA obligations unlike the case with other statutory regimes on disclosure.[3]

[1]   HC 398–I (1997–98), pp 56 et seq.
[2]   HC 398–I (1997–98), para 19.
[3]   Under DPA 1998, s 3, which makes data available under statutes apart from FOIA and regulations exempt from DPA provisions. The fullest judicial explanation of the relationship between FOIA and DPA is from Lord Hope in *Common Services Agency v Scottish Information Commissioner* [2008] UKHL: 'It is obvious that not all government can be completely open, and special consideration also had to be given to the release of personal information relating to individuals.'

(IV) DEFAMATION

1.271   Communication of information under s 1 of the FOIA 2000 to a person and which has been supplied by a third party will attract qualified privilege unless the publication is shown to have been made with malice (s 79).

(V) THIRD PARTY RIGHTS

1.272 The White Paper stated that further thought would have to be given to the question of third party rights, ie those affected by another's request for information, very often commercial information but it often includes personal information. This allows a procedure whereby third parties who 'own' or are the subjects of the information are notified and may challenge applications or decisions to disclose information. Clearly, in relation to personal data, the DPA 1998 will have to be complied with (see DPA 1998, s 40). Section 41 of the FOIA 2000, on information covered by legal rights of confidentiality, may be engaged. Under s 45(2)(c) of the FOIA 2000 such persons are to be consulted under the terms of the code of practice made by the Secretary of State. 'Any party' may be joined on appeal to the Tribunal. This all appears a little jejune. A third party is unlikely to be a complainant to the Commissioner under the terms of the Act – they have not requested information (s 50(1)). Presumably they may, however, be a complainant re maladministration to the PCA via an MP but only apropos of those authorities covered by the PCA's legislation. After the access provisions had been in force for a matter of weeks, there was a considerable generation of interest in the disclosure of papers from the previous Conservative government on the 'Black Wednesday' episode concerning the UK's departure from the Exchange Rate Mechanism in 1992. A protocol was drafted allowing former Ministers to seek the support of the Attorney-General to block disclosure of ministerial papers from their period in office. If this involved consultation, this was understandable. If it went further, it would seem to breach the Act. Requests would be handled by civil servants.

1.273 The Code under s 45 offers advice on 'Consultation with Third Parties'. An earlier version of the Code stated that where the consent of a third party would enable disclosure to be made the third party should be consulted before reaching a decision unless it is clear that their consent would not be forthcoming. Where a third party's legal rights are not involved, consultation may still be appropriate to establish whether disclosure would not be allowed on some other ground, whether other laws prohibit disclosure or whether the cost would be disproportionate. Where the views of a third party may help in establishing whether an exemption exists or whether discretion should be exercised on public interest grounds under s 2, they should be consulted. The version laid before Parliament is more general. It is 'highly recommended' that PAs take appropriate steps to ensure third parties and those who supply information are aware of the PAs duties under the Act and the extent of the exemptions. Consultation may be necessary to establish whether advice on copyright or intellectual property needs to be given to the requester. Where information is supplied by one government department to another, the latter should not disclose the information without first consulting the supplying department. Representative bodies may be consulted and authorities are reminded that consultation cannot deny applicants' rights under the Act. Consultation is not necessary where the PA does not intend to disclose information (para 37) or where the third party's views can have no effect, where no exemption applies so that information should be disclosed. However, it seems some points of complication have been overlooked. These provisions are weak compared with those which exist elsewhere such as the USA or Canada.

1.274 What if there is a wrongful disclosure that causes damage to the provider of the information – the company? Imagine that the department did not notify the third party about an access request when it should have done. If the failure is an oversight then this would appear to be a pretty straightforward case of negligence and could also justify an action for breach of confidence if the information is confidential in law, especially where provided voluntarily by the company. Even when provided compulsorily, that would not automatically mean that there is no duty of confidentiality (though see para 1.276 below). But negligence would suffice if the necessary elements were established:[1] in *Swinney* a police force negligently allowed confidential information to be entered on documents from which an informer's identity could be established and then failed to keep the information secure with the result that it was stolen with serious consequences for the plaintiff. The Court of Appeal, upholding Laws J, accepted that a special relationship arguably arose from these confidential circumstances and the plaintiff's claim was not precluded by any general principle of immunity. An application to strike out the claim was rejected.

[1]   *Swinney v Chief Constable of the Northumbria Police* [1996] 3 All ER 449, CA.

1.275 What if the authority did not think there was any need to refer the matter to the third party? Basically, the situation here covers that where the authority has made an allegedly wrong judgment about the exempt nature of the information and wrongly allows access without warning the third party provider. Or the department considered it was notionally exempt but there was a public interest override in disclosure. Negligence is going to be difficult to establish because of the question of judgement or discretion that is involved. It would, arguably, at least have to be *Wednesbury unreasonable* or irrational to mount a private law action in negligence on an analogy with *Anns v London Borough of Merton*[1] and that difficult line of cases. Unreasonableness or irrationality are not actionable per se; the only relief may be under Part 54 of the Civil Procedure Rules 1998 for a declaration after the event or possibly, but extremely unlikely, a quashing order (*certiorari*). Damages may be awarded under actions for breach of confidentiality. In the latter case especially, the real damage brought about by disclosure may already have been perpetrated and the money remedy will offer little solace.

[1]   [1978] AC 728, HL, and *Barrett v Enfield London Borough Council* [1999] 3 All ER 193, HL.

1.276 If the information were protected by the law of confidentiality, might there be a remedy for breach of confidentiality? Would there be any difference between information provided under enforcement and that provided voluntarily by the company – it has been seen how distinctions have been drawn by FOI regimes between information supplied voluntarily and otherwise. Case law has not precisely addressed this point but the courts have been reluctant to circumscribe official use of information for causes which are in the public interest:[1]

'In my view, where information has been obtained under statutory powers the duty of confidence owed on the *Marcel* principle cannot operate so as to prevent the person obtaining the information from disclosing it to those persons to whom the statutory provisions either require or authorise him to make disclosure.'[2]

[1] See eg *Smith Kline & French Laboratories Ltd v Licensing Authority* [1989] 1 All ER 578, HL; *Hellewell v Chief Constable of Derbyshire* [1995] 4 All ER 473; *Marcel v Metropolitan Police Comr* [1992] Ch 225 esp at 262, CA, and *Hamilton v Naviede* [1995] 2 AC 75. And note the cases on the Monopolies and Mergers Commission: *R v MMC, ex p Elders IXL Ltd* [1987] 1 All ER 451 and *R v MMC, ex p Matthew Brown plc* [1987] 1 All ER 463. And note *Melton Medes Ltd v SIB* [1995] 3 All ER 880, CA. Also, *R v Chief Constable of North Wales Police, ex p AB* [1998] 3 All ER 310, CA; *Re Joseph Hargreaves Ltd* [1900] 1 Ch 347, CA; Lord Reid in *Conway v Rimmer* [1968] AC 910, HL; *Lonrho v Fayed (No 4)* [1994] QB 775, CA; *Preston Borough Council v McGrath* (2000) *Times*, 19 May, CA; *Woolgar v Chief Constable of the Sussex Police* [1999] 3 All ER 604, CA; *R v Chief Constables of C and D, ex p A* (2000) *Times*, 7 November; *R (X) v Chief Constable of West Midlands Police* [2005] 1 All ER 610 (CA) and para 7.239.

[2] *Hamilton v Naviede* above at 102 per Lord Browne-Wilkinson.

1.277 Furthermore, increased sensitivity to privacy will doubtless be an important factor.[1]

[1] See paras 7.164 et seq below, and *R (Ellis) v Chief Constable of Essex Police* [2003] EWHC 1321 (Admin): from the headnote: 'E applied for a declaration from the court as to the lawfulness of a proposed police initiative whereby posters showing offenders' names and faces would be displayed in public places. The purpose of the scheme was to reduce the incidence of burglaries and car crimes in the Brentwood area. E, who had a number of previous convictions for dishonesty and car related crime, had been sentenced to three years and six months' imprisonment and the police considered that he might be a suitable candidate for the scheme. It was thought that, given his record, there was little risk of the scheme affecting E's future conduct and although his former partner and daughter lived in the Brentwood area, they had taken new names so would not suffer as a result of the publicity. E contended that the notoriety resulting from the poster campaign could reduce his chances of obtaining accommodation or employment in the future, and that his family might suffer adverse consequences. **Held**, making no order on the application, that the question of whether the scheme was lawful or unlawful would depend on the individual circumstances of the offenders selected for inclusion in the scheme, and on how the scheme would operate in practice. Further information was required before it could be determined whether the possible benefits of the scheme were proportionate to the intrusion into the offender's rights under the Human Rights Act 1998 Sch 1, Part I, Art. 8. The offender's family also had rights under Art 8, and the need to safeguard children was particularly important'. See *R(H) v A City Council* [2011] EWCA Civ 403, where restrictions were placed on blanket notification of sex assault convictions.

1.278 Almost all these cases deal with the situation where there has been a proper disclosure – the putative argument from the provider of information in our case will be that the disclosure was unlawful because the discretion was not exercised lawfully. An unlawful decision cannot defeat the confidentiality in the information even if it causes the 'secrecy' to evaporate. The Law Commission in its 1981 paper on *Breach of Confidence* (Cmnd 8388 (1981)) did not wish to commit itself to so robust a statement on the position of information given for reward or under compulsion, ie that it would remain confidential. Furthermore, the courts have noted that confidentiality may exist between authorities and information providers even when provided under compulsion.[1] There seems no good reason why the recipient of information should not maintain confidentiality even where the information is acquired under compulsory power unless there is a *clear* statutory authorisation for disclosure. Where information is given to another Crown body by a department it may well be there is no question of breach of confidence because the information is owned by the 'Crown'.[2] Particular attention must be paid to the facts of each case and there may be a judicial willingness to confine such practice.[3]

1   *IRC v National Federation etc* [1981] 2 All ER 93, HL.
2   *R v Blackledge* (1996) 1 Cr App Rep 326, CA. And see FOIA 2000, s 81.
3   And note recent legislation allowing disclosure of information between government bodies of personal information: Finance Act 1997, s 110. See *Secretary of State for Trade and Industry v Baker* [1998] Ch 356 – no privilege (lawyer/client/litigation) for a statutory report.

1.279   There might of course be maladministration in such a decision which would attract the PCA, although to what extent would there be an overlap between a legal remedy and a remedy provided by the PCA would be a point to consider (see paras 2.134 et seq below).

1.280   There may well be occasions when although the public interest will not justify disclosure of a trade secret, 'commercial interests' is not a sufficient justification not to disclose and although the provider of information should usually be consulted, this may not be practicable where a public health notice or warning 'must be issued as a matter of urgency'.[1]

1   See the 1997 *Guidance* on the Code of Access, p 76.

(VI)   GOVERNMENT CONTRACTORS

1.281   Will duties exist on such contractors ie, companies, to provide information? Under the 1994 Code as revised they were under such a duty when providing services because they were within the terms of the PCA 1967 which governed the operation of the Code. This would be especially important where information had to be provided under the Citizen's Charter, the *Service First* initiative – and presumably any successor. Arrangements will have to be made as between the department and contractor as to who should disclose the information and how. Section 75 of, and Sch 15 to, the Deregulation and Contracting Out Act 1994 (as amended) allow restricted or confidential information to be handed to contractors on terms that they give it the protection owed by Ministers and civil servants. This would in any event be implied by the contract as a matter of law. Nothing should require the disclosure of commercially confidential information.

1.282   Where services are provided to government, there may well be considerations of intellectual property, commercial confidentiality or management and negotiating positions requiring confidentiality. The Guidance on the 1994 Code stated that disclosure under the Code will have to be decided on a case by case basis. This is a situation which ought to be covered clearly by contractual provisions relating to property rights in information or reports and confidentiality.

1.283   While the tendency in the law and practice has been to introduce greater openness and transparency into the tendering process, some of these

tendencies have been driven by EC requirements implemented into our law, the general position relating to genuine commercial confidences of tenderers and contractors will be maintained. It was noted above how the Guidance on the Code on Access stated that the following should be disclosed:
(a) the identity of the successful tenderer;
(b) the nature of the job, service or goods to be supplied;
(c) the performance standards set (which should be output based);
(d) the criteria for award of contract; and
(e) the winning tender price or range of prices (maximum/minimum) paid.

1.284 The s 45 code on the FOIA 2000 in the first version stated that public authorities should not agree to hold information 'in confidence' which is not confidential in nature (ie protected by the law of confidentiality: see para 1.203 above and para 2.299 below). Improper pressure to incorporate confidentiality claims in contracts should be resisted, and acceptance will have to be justified. The Code reminded PAs that duties under FOIA are not, to use a phrase, 'biddable'. If 'exceptionally' non disclosure provisions need to be incorporated in a contract, the schedule to the contract should identify what information should not be disclosed. However, this is subject to duties to disclose under the Act if the information is not exempt. If a PA wishes to prevent a contractor disclosing information, this should be done in accordance with the Act by contractual terms drafted as 'narrowly as possible'. The public authority will have to disclose any information in compliance with the Act unless the contractor is 'designated' under s 5. If a contractor is designated as a PA, cost of compliance will then have to be incorporated within the contractual terms. Needless to say, prohibitions contained in the Official Secrets Acts will have to be maintained. The second version of the Code approved by Parliament provided that 'Public Authorities should bear clearly in mind their obligations under the FOIA when preparing to enter into contracts which may contain terms relating to the disclosure of information by them' (para 31). Confidentiality must be consistent with the Act's exemptions. It has been seen how a duty of confidence can only arise where the law of confidentiality imposes such an obligation. It is not open to parties to reinvent, by contract or otherwise, the law of confidentiality. The later version of the Code also stipulates that reasons for claiming confidentiality should be provided. The Private Finance Initiative (PFI) adviser Partnership UK, which is part publicly owned, posted an online database providing details (but not shares), capital values and, in some cases, advisers on PFI arrangements. Much depends on what departments are willing to release, prompted in some cases by FOIA (www.partnershipsuk.org.uk).

1.285 One should not overlook the public interest in disclosure where items of fraud, waste or mismanagement occur. One should also note the legislation to protect employee whistleblowers who disclose evidence of serious wrongdoing in the genuine public interest (see paras 2.299 et seq below).

1.286 The Office of Government Commerce has produced guidance on government contracts and FOIA[1] and the MoJ has produced guidance on 'gateways reviews' involving IT contracts.[2]

(VII) RESPONSE TIMES

1.287 The response time was 40 days in the Bill. The White Paper did not commit itself to any length so there is no obvious inconsistency but 40 days is longer than any period identified in any comparable FOI regime that is set out in the White Paper. The Code response time is 20 days for 'simple requests' and can be extended. The Act states that responses must be made promptly to requests for access 'and in any event not later than the twentieth working day following the date of receipt'. The response period has been halved. This does not include any period taken to pay for a fee following a fees notice. The period may be modified by regulations which may specify a different period of days in relation to different cases and which confer a discretion on the Commissioner. By December 2004, four circumstances justifying extension had been identified (see para 1.75 above).

(VIII) REASONS FOR DECISIONS

1.288 The White Paper's promise to create a duty to provide reasons for decisions by bodies covered by the Act appears in s 19(3)(b) of the FOIA 2000, in the section that deals with publication schemes and seems a little diminished. This is a general provision relating to the giving of reasons for decisions by public bodies when adopting or reviewing a publication scheme. The PA has to have regard to the public interest in allowing access to the PA's information and in publication of reasons for decisions made by the authority. There may be reasons of commercial confidentiality or of a personal nature why access to information may be restricted. The IC's office has stated that the section requires: evidence of inclusion of information related to processes used to determine decisions and evidence of inclusion of information relating to decision-making processes.

1.289 This is not a universal requirement of reasons for administrative decisions generally: indeed, advice was circulated to PAs by representative bodies that it only applied to reasons for decisions published under schemes. The view of the IC's Office was that in all cases therefore the response from the office is the same; where decision-making information is not included within schemes the IC will question its absence if the reasons for omitting such information are not clear from the questionnaire, or if the IC feels that the consideration given towards disclosure has been in some way inadequate. It should perhaps be noted that the Commissioner's office has openly stated that in the first round of approvals it will not be prescriptive of content within schemes. It is the IC's belief that in this first round the priority should be to obtain as much sign up to schemes as possible, and that in the second cycle, in light of the four-year running experience plus the introduction of rights, both the IC's office and the authorities concerned will have a better knowledge and understanding of the sorts of information which are appropriate to include within schemes. The office is in the process of carrying out a review of the effectiveness of schemes as they now stand, with a view to introducing further criteria for approval for the second round (which starts in 2006). This may include, for instance, making comparisons between schemes from organisations which are similar in nature with a view to understanding the differences between the amounts or types of information being made available through the schemes. As an example, if a particular police authority makes much more information available than another, on what grounds does the second police authority feel it is correct or able to withhold similar information from publication.

1.290 Duties to give reasons in relation to unsuccessful FOI applications were actually strengthened in the Bill as it went through Parliament. This requirement of reasons for decisions is a central feature of an administrative regime operating under legal order[1] and many would argue that it requires greater positive emphasis as a primary duty in statute rather than a presence in a publication scheme. It is an increasingly important feature of EC law.[2] The duty should be one set out in statute although publication schemes would indicate why reasons were being given for different kinds of decision and could perhaps identify what the purpose of giving reasons was.[3] There was no provision in the Bill originally to give reasons to an unsuccessful applicant for information, beyond naming the exemption claimed. Presumably, however, had matters remained unaltered, the Commissioner would expect reasoned and coherent answers to his enquiries when investigating complaints. The Guidance accompanying the 1997 Code certainly felt 'that an explanation will normally be given' (para 65).[4]

[1] English law has seen a significant development of a duty to give reasons for decisions: see note 4 below and *Baker v Canada* (1999) 2 SCR 817 and a duty to give reasons in Canadian administrative law.
[2] Under Art 253 [190] EC and *UNECTEF v Heylens*: 222/86 [1987] ECR 4097, ECJ. Such a right is contained in the EU Charter of Fundamental Rights, Article 41(2) which is given the full legal force of the TEU, art 6(1).
[3] See the useful article by A Le Sueur 'Legal Duties to Give Reasons' (1999) 52 *Current Legal Problems* 150.
[4] On giving reasons and legal requirements, see paras 9.125 et seq below.

1.291 Duties are now to be contained in ss 17 and 53(5) to provide reasons where there is to be no confirmation or denial or where a discretionary disclosure is not to be made under s 2; in the latter case it covers those situations where the 'accountable officer' issues a certificate overriding the Commissioner's decision re exempt information and discretionary disclosures; reasons for the certificate must be given to the complainant. The s 45 Code in its first version specified that this must not simply involve a regurgitation of the words of the exemption (see para 1.110 above). The case law examined above has insisted on good reasons being given under relevant provisions of FOIA.

(IX) REQUESTS HAVE TO BE IN WRITING

1.292 As experience with ombudsmen shows this can be a prohibiting factor for the poorly educated etc, but it is difficult to see how this requirement can be avoided in FOI requests although the Environmental Information Regulations 2004 do not impose this requirement (paras 8.192 et seq below). The problem will be exacerbated if there are inadequate provisions to provide advice and assistance to requesters. The provisions on advice by authorities to applicants are contained in a code of practice drawn up by the Secretary of State 'which it will be desirable for them to follow' and the observance of which the Commissioner will be under a duty to promote. The Commissioner has power to make a practice recommendation but it is not clear how, if at all, it can be enforced (see below). It is all a bit anaemic. The Code advises that where a person is unable to frame their request in writing, appropriate assistance should be given. This could include advising them of a body to assist such as the CAB (sic) or offering to take a note over the telephone and sending that to the applicant for confirmation. When confirmed this would constitute the written confirmation and time would run from receipt of the confirmation (see paras 1.83 et seq above).

1.293 Where a requester provides insufficient information to enable the authority to identify and locate the information requested, or the request is ambiguous, the authority should provide assistance to assist in clarifying the information sought 'as far as practicable'. The aim of such assistance, the Guidance states, is to clarify the nature of the information sought, not to determine the aims or motivation of the applicant. Appropriate assistance could include provision of an outline of different kinds of information that could meet the request; the provision of detailed catalogues and indexes, where these are available, to help the applicant ascertain the nature and extent of the information held by the authority. The government refused to make provision of indexes a statutory duty. As seen above, however, public authorities are under a duty in FOIA 2000, s 16 to provide assistance which duty is complied with when they follow the code. The code advises on the provision of a general response to the request setting out options for further information which could be provided on request; where cost is a ground for refusal an idea of what can be provided within cost should be given. Even though the information requested has not been identified any relevant information identified and found must be disclosed if within the Act. An explanation should be forthcoming why the authority can proceed no further (see para 1.83 above). Information should not be unreasonably requested and assistance, the code advises, should not be provided to vexatious requesters. Guidance is given by the DCA on what is 'vexatious'. Being branded such may be a subject of complaint to the IC. The later version of the Code makes some adjustments to the guidance.

(X) REPEATED REQUESTS

1.294 Section 14(2) of the FOIA 2000 deals with requests made by any persons – perhaps as part of a campaign but it is not confined to such requests – which have been complied with and which are repeated. These do not have to be processed where they are the same or substantially similar. What happens if the first request was only partially complied with or indeed not complied with?

(XI) CHANNELLING FOI INFORMATION REQUESTS TO MORE EXPENSIVE INFORMATION ACCESS REGIMES

1.295   Section 21 of the FOIA 2000 allows for the practice criticised by the Canadian Commissioner[1] of channelling FOI requests to far more expensive statutory access or charging schemes thereby avoiding FOI provisions which will be reasonably cheap. There appears to be no safeguard to prevent abuse. 'Reasonably accessible' includes that which is 'accessible on payment'. In the discussion on this provision above (para 1.111) it was observed that it had to be reasonably accessible to the applicant which could allow for personal items such as excessive cost to *this* applicant to be borne in mind. 'Reasonable accessibility' also includes information available through Publication Schemes.

[1]   AR of the Canadian Information Commissioner 1993–4, p 6.

(XII) PURPOSE OF SEEKING INFORMATION AND RESTRICTING USE OF INFORMATION

1.296   A clause in the original Bill forced the applicant to state the purpose for which access is claimed and why information is requested. It was not known how, or to what extent, this would have been checked to prevent abuse. The authority could also consider *whether disclosure to the applicant* would be in the public interest. Also cl 14(6) of the draft Bill empowered the authority to impose restrictions on the use of information provided. Why should information disclosed in the public interest be so restricted? How will this be affected by Art 10 ECHR and the HRA 1998 (see eg s 12 of the latter)? If a newspaper wishes to publish information then surely the provisions of the HRA 1998 come into effect? HRA 1998, s 12 makes court interim injunctions more difficult to obtain than under previous law where freedom of publication is involved and the court must specifically address various points.[1] However, use of superinjunctions has not been thwarted (para 7.203). In the USA, motive on the part of an applicant is irrelevant although different charging scales are present for different classes of user. However, the English courts have taken motive into consideration in deciding whether to allow access to information under other statutory provisions.[2]

[1]   See paras 2.320 et seq below for discussion of HRA 1998, s 12.
[2]   *R v Registrar General, ex p Smith* [1990] 2 All ER 170; *Re Application pursuant to r 7.28 of the Insolvency Rules 1986* [1994] BCC 369.

1.297   These provisions and restrictions were removed in the face of widespread criticism of the Bill that was presented to Parliament. Motive for a request is irrelevant. Denial would have to fit within an existing exemption and a public interest refusal where applicable.

(XIII) APPEALS AGAINST MINISTERIAL CERTIFICATES UNDER SS 23(2) AND 24(3)

1.298   Section 60 of the FOIA 2000 allows appeals to the Tribunal against Ministerial certificates issued under s 23(2) or 24(3) which, in the first case, certify that information covered by the certificate was supplied by or relates to the work of the Security and Intelligence services.[1] In the second situation the certificate certifies that exemptions are required for the purpose of safeguarding national security. Subject to appeal, these certificates are 'conclusive evidence of that fact'. In the first case, the Tribunal may rule that the information was not exempt because it was not supplied etc, as stated. In the second case, if the Tribunal finds that, 'applying the principles applied by the court on an application for judicial review, the Minister did not have reasonable grounds for issuing the certificate' it may allow the appeal and quash the certificate. This repeats earlier provisions in statutes[2] but is not as full a legal challenge as is allowed under the ECHR or EU law to national security or allied grounds[3] where relevant rights are being denied. The Upper Tribunal now receives these appeals on a mandatory reference.

[1]   See 1.117 et seq above.
[2]   Eg Security Service Act 1989, Sch 1, para 4(1) and cognate statutes.
[3]   *Tinnelly & Sons v UK* (1999) 4 BHRC 393 (ECtHR) and Northern Ireland Act 1998, ss 90 and 91; *Johnstone v Chief Constable RUC*: 222/84 [1986] 3 All ER 135, ECJ; *Svenska Journalistförbundet v EU Council*: T-174/95 [1998] All ER (EC) 545, CFI and see Employment Tribunals (Constitution and Rules of Procedure) Regulations 2004, SI 2004/1861 and procedures where national security is involved and *Home Office v Tariq* [2010] EWCA Civ 462 and on appeal [2011] UKSC 35, and see para 10.87.

(XIV) 'COMMERCIAL INTERESTS'

1.299   Such interests are given a very wide protection under s 43 of the FOIA 2000, wider even than the phrase commercial confidentiality. Will information need to possess the quality of commercial 'confidentiality' to be protected? If that is the test then if the onus is on the withholder to establish the ground it might not too easily lead to abuse. But 'commercial interests' is a far vaguer phrase and one that could lead to unnecessary over-protection. No attempt is made to define 'trade secret' as we have seen although there is considerable discussion of the subject in case law (para 1.215 above). Much government business will now be conducted commercially. In its reply to the committee's report the government stated that public authorities will be required to justify their claim for this exemption; the onus is on them.[1] The Act leaves this unclear (see below) although the public interest must be considered under this exemption. See para 1.215 above.

[1]   HC 1020 1997–98, para 27.

(XV) EXCLUDING RIGHTS OF ACTION

1.300   Section 56 of the FOIA 2000 provides that no right of action is conferred by failure to comply with any duty under this Act. Would this protect negligence or malice on the authority's part? We would suggest not – the immunity is only for breaches of statutory duties directly involved under the Act, ie wrongfully refusing information. It will not provide an immunity for breaches of common law duties. Actionable breaches of confidence brought about by disclosure would exempt information from disclosure but s 41(1)(b) then adds 'otherwise than under this Act'. What does this mean? That if information is disclosed under the Act, then even though confidential its release is not actionable? The section is seeking rather to preserve rights to confidentiality in private law. It should also be recalled that s 41 creates an absolute exemption, reinforcing such a right. Negligent disclosures were dealt with above (para 1.275).

(XVI) RECOMMENDATIONS AS TO GOOD PRACTICE

1.301 Should the Commissioner not be empowered to carry out an audit of a public authority's practices in relation to FOI rather than have to seek its consent as under s 47(3) of the FOIA 2000? The Commissioner may issue practice recommendations where there are breaches of the codes of practice under the Act. Where recommendations are not complied with, no means of enforcement are mentioned. Could the Commissioner seek a mandatory order (mandamus)? Is this not an appropriate matter to refer to the Select Committee on Justice as recommended by the Committee on Public Administration in its report? More generally, what is to be the role of the Committee in relation to the Commissioner? The Committee made recommendations in its report on the White Paper on this point believing it should become the 'Parliamentary focus' for the work of the Commissioner.[1] Events moved on. The power of the Commissioner to issue a special report should not be overlooked in the face of serious defiance. Reports were issued where the veto was resorted to.

[1]   HC 398 I (1997–98), para 90; HC 570 I (1998–99), para 140.

(XVII) THE ONUS OF PROOF

1.302 On one vital and practical point, the position under the Act is not entirely clear. Where does the onus of justification or proof fall under the Act – on the public authority in refusing information; on the applicant; on the Commissioner? Where reasons have to be given for decisions then to that extent it places an onus on the party who has to provide reasons. The burden does seem to shift at various stages of the decision. There will be an initial decision that information is or is not covered by an exemption. If an exemption applies, there will be a public interest determination under s 2. What is required is a clear commitment to a right to information subject to exemptions which the authority has to justify. This could perhaps have been best achieved in a purpose clause which set out clearly the duty of public authorities to advance open government. No such clause presently exists.[1] The government was opposed to such a clause as unnecessary. In terms of disclosures under the public interest provisions in s 2, the onus appears was shifted as was seen above (para 1.98) so that in a fine balance between secrecy and disclosure, secrecy has to be justified by the authority. The onus here seems squarely on the authority. On numerous occasions, the IC and tribunal have stated that the Act creates a presumption in favour of disclosure.

[1]   The inclusion of such a clause was strongly supported by Lord Woolf and Sir Richard Scott HC 570 I (1998–99), paras 56 and 59.

(XVIII) COMPLAINTS PROCEDURES

1.303 The Code of Practice emphasises the need for procedures for dealing with complaints from people who consider that their request has not been properly handled or are otherwise dissatisfied with the outcome of their request. Such procedures should encourage a *prompt* determination of the complaint (see para 1.235 above on recommended time-limits). Authorities should publicise their existence including information on how to make a complaint and this should accompany all decisions taken under the Act. The complaints procedure, although it constitutes internal review, should be fair and impartial and should be capable of reviewing all decisions under the Act including those under s 2 of the FOIA 2000. The procedures should come into effect when the publication schemes' provisions come into effect for the PA. It will therefore also deal with complaints about PSs as well as access complaints post 1 January 2005. They should be easy to understand, prompt and capable or reversing or amending decisions. A earlier draft of the Code stated: 'Where practicable, complaints procedures should be handled by a person who was not a party to the original decision'. In small organisations this may not be practicable. If a decision is irreversible, eg made by a Minister, the PA should consider waiving internal review and the complainant should then be free to go to the IC although MoJ guidance states that a review should be made to the Minister 'in the light of the complaint'. The guidance now states (para 40) that where a request involves a general access request, a review should be undertaken by someone more senior than the person who took the initial decision 'where reasonably practicable'. 'The public authority should in any event undertake a full re-evaluation of the case, taking into account the matters raised by the investigation of the complaint.' The procedure should be triggered whenever an applicant indicates that he believes the authority has failed to fulfil its obligations under Part I of the Act and the matter cannot be resolved by discussion with the official dealing with the request. Or it may be prompted by a complaint by the requester or another (presumably a third party). As well as setting target times and success rates, records should be kept for all complaints and their outcome. Procedures should be monitored and should be reviewed and amended where regular reversals of initial decisions indicate this as appropriate. If the outcome states that information should be disclosed and not withheld it should be disclosed as soon as practicable and the applicant should be informed how soon this will be. Apologies should be given if procedures were not followed and steps taken to prevent any repetition. Where a decision upholds the authority, the requester should be informed of his right to complain to the Commissioner. In principle it is right that PAs should be given the opportunity to correct their decisions. But this provision must not be read to allow PAs to cause unnecessary delay and anxiety.

(XIX) COMPANIES AND THE FREEDOM OF INFORMATION ACT 2000

1.304 The FOIA 2000 was notable amongst such statutes for imposing a duty of disclosure on private bodies ie companies, that were designated as public authorities. The Act imposes no duties on companies that are not so designated. FOI is correctly associated with accountability of power wielded on behalf of the public interest and provision of opportunities for greater involvement by citizens in the process of rule that governs their lives. It is inevitably an obligation that falls on government and public authorities. As well as government, economic organisation is also a form of power that invariably purports to operate on behalf of the public interest. No company would openly declare that it operates against the public interest although serving a public interest is not a primary reason for its existence – it is an indirect consequence of its existence. Fifty of the world's largest economies are companies. The 500 biggest corporations control 25 per cent of the world's economic output.[1] The FOI movement is bound to affect companies both indirectly in so far as the regulatory state collects and stores information gathered under statutory, or other provisions, as well as directly in that companies are under an increasing range of duties to supply information to the public.

[1] D C Korten *When Corporations Rule the World* (1995), pp 220–1. See *A Guide for Business to the FOIA 2000* J.Amos and J. McDermott The Constitution Unit and Lovells.

1.305 Companies have learned to live with FOI regimes elsewhere, where for instance regulators hold information from or about them which is frequently requested. On one point company secretaries can rest assured; no FOI regime routinely imposes incursions into corporate or personal privacy that would be sanctioned by disclosure processes under English or US litigation, let alone anything like Anton Piller or disclosure orders. Under the former, confidentiality may not be a bar to access where justice demands their disclosure, although safeguards may have to be applied.[1] Under the latter, where there is a danger that relevant documents will be destroyed by one party, the court will allow the other party who is usually asserting intellectual property rights to enter relevant premises to copy them. Various safeguards have been built into this process to prevent abuse but it constitutes a remarkable invasion of privacy.[2] Furthermore, British companies are used to an ever increasing range of duties to make information publicly available through Companies' House or whatever about financial disclosure covering accounts, audit and share-holding. Numerous statutory provisions alongside the Companies Acts allow various bodies to obtain information, even in circumstances which may appear self-incriminating and which may lead to a clash between English law and the ECHR. Regulators are engaging in ever more open practices of consultation. The Companies Act 1985 had some limited 'social disclosure' requirements concerning the company's policy on employment of disabled persons, arrangements for securing the health and safety of company employees, action taken to inform and consult the workforce on matters relevant to them as employees and promotion of employee share schemes[3] and charitable and political donations and these were developed under the Companies Act 2006.[4] Additional information is published voluntarily including that on companies' environmental performance and 79 of the FTSE 100 companies produced an environmental report in 1996 although there are problems concerning reliability where much of the information was not independently audited. There are growing demands for Eco Product labelling (see eg Council Regulation 880/92 23 March 1992 on a Community Eco Label and Award Scheme). Nor should it be overlooked that many major UK companies operate in countries where FOIA regimes exist and will be used to their operation. However, unless designated under FOIA, companies will remain outside FOIA. The question of access to environmental information held by private companies has become a vexed question under the EIR 2004 (para 8.204).

[1] See *Science Research Council v Nassé* [1979] 3 All ER 673, HL.
[2] See *Practice Direction* at [1994] 4 All ER 52 and [1997] 1 All ER 288 and Civil Jurisdiction Act 1997 and ch 10.

³ CA 1985, s 234 and Sch 7, Part III. See Parkinson in D Campbell and D Lewis eds *Promoting Participation* (1999).
⁴ CA 1985, s 234 and Sch 7, Part I. Parkinson, ibid.

(XX) USE OF FOIA

1.306 The MoJ publishes quarterly statistics on FOI requests and an annual report. These contain detailed figures but only cover central government (departments and monitored authorities – 42 in all). Most of the 100,000–115,000 or so bodies are not covered. The MoJ reported in 2010[1] that monitored bodies received 40,548 FOI requests. 82 per cent were met within the 20-day period; five per cent were subject to a public interest extension; 58 per cent of resolvable requests were met in full; 23 per cent resulted in information being withheld. Fees were levied in three per cent of cases and 99 per cent of these were in the National Archives. 1,502 internal reviews were conducted across all monitored bodies. 206 appeals were made to the Commissioner. The report has details on exemptions claimed and other matters.

[1] *Freedom of Information Act 2000* Fifth Annual Report (MoJ April 2010).

1.307 The Commissioner[1] received 3,734 complaints in 2009–10 (3,100 complaints in 2008–09). 49 per cent were closed in 30 days or less (47 per cent). 66 per cent were closed in 90 days or less (62 per cent). 24 per cent took longer than a year to close, ie come to a conclusion (33 per cent). Eleven cases were still ongoing after two years (118). Of closed cases in 2009–10, 52 per cent were informally resolved (49 per cent); 15 per cent were ineligible (24 per cent); in 17 per cent a decision notice was issued (ten per cent); in five per cent no internal review was carried out by the authority (nine per cent); nine per cent were reopened (six per cent); in two per cent, cases were withdrawn or the Commissioner required no action (two per cent). 628 decision notices were served in that year (296). The outcome was complaint upheld in 142 cases (23 per cent) (105: 35 per cent); complaint partially upheld in 198 cases (31 per cent) (153: 52 per cent); complaint not upheld 288 (46 per cent) (38: 13 per cent). On appeals to the Tribunal between 2005–2009 (322), the Commissioner's decision was upheld in 54 per cent of cases; the decision was overturned or varied in 30 per cent; and 15 per cent were withdrawn. There is no systematic collection of all requests and figures concerning requests covering all authorities. An estimate from the Commissioner was that in the first four and a half years of operation (May 2009) there had been a half million FOI requests, 11,500 complaints to the Commissioner, 1,225 DNs, and 415 appeals to the Information Tribunal. The IC's annual report for 2010–11 is HC 1124 (2010–12).

[1] ICO *Annual Report (2009–10)* HC 220 (2010–11). Figures in square brackets are from ICO *Annual Report 2008–09* HC619 (2008–09).

(xxi) code of practice on consultation

1.308 Although not part of the FOIA 2000, a new Code of Practice on Consultation was announced by the Cabinet Office in November 2000 and this was revised in January 2004 and in 2008. A new code now operates. The stated aims of the 2004 code were to increase the involvement of people and groups in public consultations, minimising the burden such consultation places on them while ensuring a proper time to respond – a minimum of 12 weeks. A new register of current consultations will also be launched on www.UKOnline.gov.uk bringing together all the main written public consultations taking place across government. It will be updated to take account of decisions the government takes following consultation. Parties will be able to get e-mail notice of consultations in subject areas in which they are interested. The announcement of these developments followed a meeting between 'entrepreneurs' and the Prime Minister in Downing Street. The Code will require proper feed-back from government after a consultation including an explanation of why particular options were, or were not, favoured. Departments will have to set up machinery to police compliance. The Register will maintain a listing of all the main consultations in progress or completed. Each department will maintain on its website all its public national consultations. Departments must consider email responses as well as traditional responses. The revised code of 2004 set out six consultation criteria: consult widely allowing a minimum of twelve weeks for written consultations at least once during the development of the policy; be clear in proposals and who may be affected, what questions are being asked and any timescale for responses; ensure consultation is clear, concise and widely accessible; give feed-back regarding the responses received and how consultation process influenced policy; monitor departments' effectiveness at consultation, including the use of designated consultation coordinator; ensure any consultation follows 'Better regulation Best Practice', including the carrying out of a Regional Impact Assessment if necessary. The Code is available on www.cabinet-office.gov.uk/regulation/consultation/Code.htm. (See also HC 316 I and II (2004–05) on local government.) See also Cabinet Office *Effective Consultation* and Response (http://www.bis.gov.uk/files/file44374.pdf) for the most recent developments.

1.309 In the next chapter, we will examine coalition plans for provision of information and transparency on a non statutory basis (para 2.28).

THE SCOTTISH FREEDOM OF INFORMATION ACT 2002

1.310 In the spring of 2001 the Scottish Executive published a draft consultation paper and FOI Scotland Bill. In much of its design it revealed the influence of the UK model. The resulting Freedom of Information (Scotland) Act 2002 (SFOIA) came into effect on 1 January 2005. FOI is a reserved matter except in so far as FOI applies to purely Scottish public authorities (SPAs). The Act applies to SPAs listed in Schedule 1, those designated under s 5(1), or a publicly owned company under s 6 (see paras 1.85 et seq above). Cross-border public authorities, such as the Forestry Commission, are covered by the UK regime; this is the case even for purely devolved matters. Information covered is that 'held' by a SPA other than information held on behalf of another person (s 3(2)(a)(i)). It is not held by a SPA if it is held 'in confidence having been supplied by a Minister of the Crown or by a department of the Government of the UK' (s 3(2)(a)(ii)). By this means it is clear that UK Ministers and departments are not within the SFOIA. Special provision is made for records transferred by UK public authorities to the Keeper of the Records of Scotland. These are not held by the Keeper unless it is information to which s 22(2)–(5) of the SFOIA apply by virtue of subsection (6),[1] or it is designated as 'open information' for the purposes of s 3(4) of the SFOIA. The Scottish Ministers may designate information as 'open' which was transferred to the Keeper before 1 July 1999 by the Secretary of State for Scotland.

[1]   This section contains special provisions relating to records transferred to the Keeper.

1.311   The structure of the Act and much of its wording is taken from the UK legislation. There are publication schemes (paras 1.48 et seq above). The initial time limit is 20 working days. But there are some crucial differences. There are absolute exemptions covering information otherwise accessible (s 25); legal prohibitions on disclosure (s 26); that protected by a duty of confidentiality (s 36(2)); court records (s 37); and most of the personal information in s 38. The Scottish Act has fewer exemptions so that information from the security and intelligence services is not specifically provided for as in UK FOIA, s 23. Such information held by the Scottish Executive will presumably be held in confidence. There is no equivalent of parliamentary privilege for the Scottish Parliament. Some exemptions are coupled in SFOIA such as 'commercial interests and the economy' (s 33) and 'confidentiality' and equivalent of legal professional privilege although its scope may be wider. The test for withholding information on a contents basis – there were also class exemptions – is 'substantial prejudice' in the case of contents exemptions. It is not the simple 'prejudice' test as in the UK.

1.312   There is no reference to the duty to confirm or deny as in UK FOIA, s 1 so there is no reference to the exclusion of that duty in virtually all of the exemptions as in the UK FOIA. SFOIA, s 18 makes provision for non-disclosure of the existence of information in the situation where if information existed and was held by a SPA and the SPA could give a refusal of access notice under SFOIA, s 16 because it is exempt information. Where, in such a case, the SPA considers that to reveal whether the information exists or is held would be contrary to the public interest, it may (whether or not the information does exist and is held by it) give the applicant a refusal notice under s 18. This means the SPA does not have to reveal whether the information exists or is held by it and it does not have to give reasons why the public interest in maintaining the exemptions outweighs the public interest in disclosure. It applies to the following exemptions:

- disclosure would prejudice substantially relations within the United Kingdom (s 28);
- disclosure would relate to the formulation of Scottish administration policy, Ministerial communications, advice by the Law Officers, or the operation of a Ministerial private office (s 29);
- disclosure would prejudice substantially the effect of conduct of public affairs (s 30);
- exemption is required to maintain national security or disclosure would prejudice substantially defence (s 31);

- disclosure would prejudice substantially international relations or is confidential information from another state or international organisation or court (s 32);
- disclosure would prejudice substantially commercial interests or the economy (s 33);
- disclosure would relate to investigations by a SPA or proceedings arising from such investigations (s 34);
- disclosure would prejudice substantially law enforcement (s 35);
- disclosure would be likely to endanger the physical or mental health or safety of an individual (s 39(1));
- disclosure would relate to communications with the Royal Family or the granting of honours (s 41).

1.313   A limit of not later than 12 weeks after the date on which the information is required is set for the exemption concerning information intended for future publication in the Scottish Act (SFOIA, s 27) and is not left open as in the UK legislation (para 1.115 above). The exemption for personal information (s 38), and most of the information is an absolute exemption, adds personal census information and a deceased person's health record. In the case of the latter two, the exemption goes after 100 years (s 58(2)(b)). The wording differs in minor ways which may have a significant difference. So in relation to information relating to the formulation of Scottish Administration policy, the Scottish Administration must have regard to the *particular* public interest in the disclosure of factual information used, or intended to be used, in order to provide an informed background (s 29(3)). There is an exemption where disclosure would, or would be likely to, *inhibit substantially* the free and frank provision of advice etc and not 'inhibit' or 'prejudice' as in the UK FOIA (see para 1.182 above).

1.314   Provision is made for internal review by the SPA of its decision (ss 20 and 21). There was to be no tribunal as in the UK model. The SIC may issue decision, enforcement and information notices and has powers of entry and inspection (s 54 and Sch 3). The SIC's reports are laid before the Scottish Parliament and s 46(2) makes provision for specific facts to be published. The Commissioner's decision was binding except in the case of five absolute exemptions[1] and in six exemptions[2] where the First Minister, after consulting other Ministers of the Executive, may issue a veto. The Commissioner's decision could be enforced through the courts on grounds set out in the 1997 White Paper (see para 1.249 above). Both the complainant and public authority could apply to the courts after a Commissioner's decision. SFOIA, s 63 allows for the disclosure of information by the SIC to Scottish Public Service Ombudsman and the UK IC.

[1]   Information otherwise accessible (SFOIA, s 25); prohibitions on disclosure (s 26); information protected by the law of confidentiality (s 36(2)); court records (s 37); and personal information including personal census information and health records (for 100 years) but otherwise in terms similar to the exemption for personal information under s 40 of the UK Act (para 1.200 above).

[2]   Under SFOIA, s 52 these are: formulation of Scottish Administration policy (SFOIA, s 29); safeguarding national security (s 31(1)); confidential information obtained from a state other than the UK or an international organisation or international court (s 32(1)(b)); investigations by Scottish PAs and proceedings arising out of such investigations (s 34); confidentiality of communications in legal proceedings controversially described as the equivalent of legal

professional privilege (s 36(1), and see paras 10.73 et seq below); the exercise by Her Majesty of Her prerogative of honour (s 41(b)).

1.315 Regulations set out fees for information (SSI 2004/467). These use the concept of 'projected costs' which means the total costs which a SPA reasonably estimates in accordance with the regulations is likely to be incurred in locating, retrieving and providing such information under the Act. It does not include costs incurred in determining whether the SPA holds the specified information, the entitlement of the requester to receive the information and estimates of staff time involved in locating, retrieving or providing information must not exceed £15 per hour per member of staff. Where projected costs do not exceed £100, no fee is payable. Up to £600, the maximum fee is £50. Over that amount, provision is made in SSI 2004/376 for fees.

1.316 More generally, the Scottish IC established under SFOIA has no responsibility for data protection under the DPA 1998 (a reserved matter). Appointment of the Scottish IC is by the Scottish Parliament on a recommendation to the Queen – not to the Executive and because the Scottish system has no tribunal it has been claimed that the Scottish IC's decisions constitute precedents. They are subject to judicial challenge. It is estimated there are about 10,000 PAs in Scotland covered by the SFOIA.[1] The s 45 Code covers consultation with devolved administration.

[1]   K Dunion (2003) *Government Computing* 10.

1.317 The Scottish IC has shown a greater degree of imagination than UK counterparts in, for insatnce, exploring the range of private bodies that should be designated under SFOIA.[1] The web site for the SIC is http://www.itspublicknowledge.info/home/ScottishInformationCommissioner.asp.

The DNs may be viewed at: http://www.itspublicknowledge.info/Applicationsand Decisions/Decisions/Decisions.php.

Guidance is available at: http://www.itspublicknowledge.info/ScottishPublic Authorities/ScottishPublicAuthorities.asp.

The latest annual report is available at:

http://www.itspublicknowledge.info/home/SICReports/AnnualReports.asp

[1]   See K Dunion in R Chapman and M Hunt (eds) *Freedom of Information: Local Government and Accountability* (2010) ch 6 and http://www.itspublicknowledge.info/ScottishPublicAuthorities/ ScottishPublicAuthorities.asp.

THE WELSH ASSEMBLY CODE

1.318 The Code of Practice on Access (2007) applies to information held by the Welsh Assembly Government. This sets out standards it will apply based on the FOIA, and other information statutes. It does not create legal rights. The code seeks to maximise openness, promises use of clear language, publish on the internet, respect privacy and confidentiality. It states that it will only make charges in 'exceptional circumstances' but it may refuse requests where fees limits under FOIA are reached. The response rate is that under FOIA.

1.319 A disclosure log is available online. http://wales.gov.uk/publications/accessinfo/disclosurelogs/?lang=en.

CONCLUSION

1.320 With specific regard to the FOIA 2000, it was subject to an enormous degree of criticism from the government back-benches, the libertarian right, the consumer lobby and the press and media. This criticism was fomented by the enormous width of the exemptions, and by many provisions which were removed. The IC was, however, left powerless under a s 53 veto or an absolute exemption. By not being able to enforce decisions in relation to absolute exemptions, or by being subject to a veto power in relation to discretionary disclosures in the public interest, the FOI regime is among the weaker of those in existence, certainly weaker than the American, New Zealand or Irish models. However, the IC can report to Parliament where a veto has been exercised and has undertaken to do this whenever a Ministerial veto is used. He will, to that extent, enter the political arena. By setting the test of damage at the level of 'prejudice' or its equivalents and not serious prejudice, the threshold for withholding information has been set at too low a level. However, by enshrining this regime in law the government has built a stronger model than the Code that it will replace and one which will be more easily subject to judicial interpretation. An exacting test may be set for 'prejudice' for instance in the courts, making its application in effect little different from 'substantial prejudice'. The FOIA 2000 will also stand behind every aspect of access that we are about to encounter in the rest of this book. From a weak and highly dubious Bill, a better statute emerged. The coalition government has given strong support to FOIA. Its future seems secure. The next chapter undertakes an analysis of access provisions apart from the FOIA 2000 affecting central government.

1.321 The final point to note is that in the summer of 2011, the Cabinet Office launched a consultation involving reforms to the FOIA. These involved lifting time limits for considering FOIA requests to extend permissible time for consideration of a request; increasing the fees limit from their present levels to allow more requests; exploring whether the IC has sufficient enforcement powers; and changing the law to provide statutory time limits for internal reviews.[1]

[1] http://data.gov.uk/opendataconsultation.

Chapter 2

Central government

INTRODUCTION

2.1   Until the reforms covered in the previous chapter, Britain was virtually alone in the Western liberal-democratic world in not possessing a freedom of information (FOI) statute for central government. A FOI Act of sorts did and does exist for local government as we shall see.[1] In 1994, an administrative code on access was published (see below). In Commonwealth countries heavily influenced by the Westminster style of government, FOI legislation has also been adopted.[2] A FOI Act operates in the Republic of Ireland and in numerous member states of the European Union and in the Union itself.[3] Today, over 70 states have freedom of information laws.[4] The most notable feature of central government administration in the United Kingdom and information involved the use of the Official Secrets Acts 1911–1989 to punish by the criminal law the unauthorised dissemination of official information. Section 2 of the 1911 Act was 'reformed' in 1989, restricting its ambit but making it less troublesome, the government hoped, to punish and gain convictions for 'damaging' disclosures of official secrets (see below).

[1]   See ch 6.
[2]   See chs 5 and 6.
[3]   See ch 3.
[4]   https://www.privacyinternational.org/article/freedom-information-around-world-2006-report (the position in 2006). In July 2011, there had been several recruits to the FOI fold within the previous twelve months.

2.2   The position in law is that unpublished information in the possession of central government,[1] however stored, and which has been created, received or used for official business is the 'property' of the Crown[2] unless property rights are retained by a third party. That being the case, no one has a right of access to Crown property in the absence of a legal right or a statutory entitlement such as exists under the Freedom of Information Act 2000 (FOIA 2000), Public Records Acts 1958 and 1967 (as amended by the Constitutional Reform and Governance Act 2010 (CRGA 2010) (para 2.62)) or the Data Protection Act 1998 (DPA 1998). The latter legislation confers rights of access to personal information on individuals, data subjects, held by data users or data controllers as they are now called and which can be stored and retrieved automatically although rights have been extended to a much wider range of data under the DPA 1998 to include certain groups of paper files: 'structured', accessible and those added to by the FOIA 2000 amendments to the DPA 1998. These terms will be explained in ch 7.

1   Basically in the possession of Crown bodies, official information in the possession of Crown servants, officers or government contractors.
2   See *R v Blackledge* [1996] 1 Cr App Rep 326, CA.

2.3   The Crown may invoke the law of confidence,[1] copyright[2] or other aspects of intellectual property law to protect the information in its possession. The House of Lords has afforded a remedy by way of an account of profits where a former member of the security and intelligence services wrote memoirs about his service without permission and in breach of contract.[3] Where physical property is concerned, eg documents on which information is recorded, it may invoke the law of theft if there is an intention permanently to deprive the owner of that property, but information itself cannot be the object of theft.[4] The Crown may, of course, employ the Official Secrets Acts to punish unauthorised leaks.[5] The US, as graphically illustrated by the WikiLeaks episode in 2010 and 2011, has no Official Secrets Act but has to rely upon the limited Espionage Act, or military offences under the US Uniform Code of Military Justice, to punish wrongful disclosures. The Internet, Twitter, etc have made the world of intelligence and secrets increasingly porous and confidentiality and privacy have suffered in a similar manner (paras 2.154 and 7.3). Conversely, greater protection is afforded to intellectual property rights.[6]

1   See paras 2.312 et seq below.
2   See para 2.312 below. See Copyright, Designs and Patents Act 1988.
3   *A-G v Blake* [2000] 4 All ER 385, HL.
4   *Oxford v Moss* (1978) 68 Cr App Rep 183; *R v Absolon* (1983) *Times*, 14 September.
5   See paras 2.154 et seq below.
6   See Digital Economy Act 2010.

2.4   In the UK government, dissemination of information *within* government is a matter of ministerial prerogative and convention.[1] Access by Ministers to the papers of a previous administration is governed by conventions and it was noted in ch 1 how the Lord Chancellor had attempted to make special provision for requests for access to former Ministerial papers (para 1.272).[2] Previous ministers should be consulted and any decision involving FOI requests should be dealt with by the Attorney General.[3] The Ministerial Code provides guidance on publications and speeches by Ministers, on Cabinet circulation, Prime Minister's clearance and consultation between Ministers where business involves another department[4] Government possesses powers to publish information under common law powers although the courts have sometimes referred to these as prerogative powers. Claiming a prerogative for what any individual is entitled to do as a servant of the Crown seems a little overblown.[5] It will be recalled from chapter 1 (at para 1.265) that in addition to the FOIA powers and duties, central government possesses statutory and common law powers to disseminate information although disclosure through FOIA will usually be required where information is requested to achieve consistency. Whatever the relationship between these regimes, the government must always act in the public interest and any disclosure, as well as complying with any applicable statutory requirements must not endanger the collective interests or welfare of the nation or individual security or confidence.[6] Case law is increasingly imposing duties or limitations on government's use of information in its dealings with citizens so that it has been held by the House of Lords to be wrong to require an applicant for funeral expenses to prove justification when the department was in possession of all relevant information.[7] In *R (Salih) v Secretary of State for the Home Department* the policy of the Secretary of State not to inform asylum seekers of discretionary schemes for accommodation was unlawful.[8] The House of Lords has also ruled that an adverse administrative decision had to be communicated to an applicant before it could have legal effect.[9]

[1]   For Northern Ireland see *Re Morrow's Application* [2001] NI 261.
[2]   Lord Hunt (1982) *Public Law* 514.
[3]   *Freedom of Information: Working with the Central Clearing House Toolkit for Practitioners* (2008) http://www.justice.gov.uk/guidance/docs/foi-clearing-house.pdf.
[4]   *Ministerial Code* (Cabinet Office 2010) http://www.civilservant.org.uk/ministerialcode2010.pdf.
[5]   *Jenkins v Att-Gen* (1971) *Times*, 14 August; R *v Secretary of State for the Environment ex p Greenwich LBC* [1989] COD 530.
[6]   By analogy with public interest immunity (para 10.64 below), the public interest may be raised by the court and not only by government: see Lord Reid in *Rogers v Secretary of State for the Home Department* [1972] 2 All ER 1057 at 1060 (HL) and on judicial deference to [bona fide] publications Lord Woolf in *R v Chief Constable of the West Midlands Police ex p Wiley* [1994] 3 All ER 420 at 438c-h (HL).
[7]   *Kerr v Department for Social Security (NI)* [2004] UKHL 23.
[8]   [2003] EWHC 2273, (2003) *Times*, 13 October, QBD.
[9]   *R (Anufrijeva) v Secretary of State* [2003] 3 All ER 827 (HL). On the reverse duty to inform a department of change of facts: *Hinchy v Secretary of State for Work and Pensions* [2005] UKHL 16 and incidentally *R (CPAG) v Secretary of State W&P* [2010] UKSC 54.

2.5   Judicial law-making has opened up the possibility of a duty in public law to disclose information by way of reasons and explanations for decisions or actions where in the circumstances such an explanation is demanded in the interests of fairness.[1] Numerous statutes provide that reasons shall be given for decisions and under the FOIA 2000, general duties will be set out in publication schemes (see para 1.48 above). Where a discretion to publish is involved, then failures to publish may involve abuses of a discretion which can be the subject of a suitable judicial order possibly even to publish.[2] The courts have gradually encroached on the area of discretion involved in withholding information so that the power to refuse disclosure of personal documents or confidential reports is not absolute and may be outweighed by duties of fairness or what is in the best interests of the individual.[3] These discretionary powers exist in addition to those under the FOIA 2000. There is evidence of an increasing awareness of the benefits of openness among the judiciary and the Secretary of State was held to be acting irrationally when he ordered the inquiry into the questions raised by the murders of 15 patients by Dr Harold Shipman to be conducted privately. The decision contravened Art 10 of the ECHR guaranteeing freedom of speech and the right to communicate information.[4] However, the treatment of such situations by the courts turns on the specific facts of each case. There has been a notable reluctance to spread the ambit of Art 10 too widely in other inquiries, notably that into the foot and mouth disease (see para 9.175 below) although Art 2 of the ECHR has been successfully invoked in other subject areas. The reluctance of the courts to step into the shoes, or the mind, of the Minister should not be overlooked, nor should the readiness of the courts to give full weight and deference to such factors as the element of prematurity of publication which may be present where inquiries, especially of a criminal nature, are continuing and where publication might hinder such inquiries.[5] Where government seeks to restrain publication of information on behalf of the public interest the courts have insisted that the public interest must be at risk of being damaged and not simply the reputation of the government.[6] Section 12 of HRA 1998 will make the award of interim injunctions to prevent publication more difficult to obtain although this has not prevented the award of so called 'superinjunctions'.[7]

[1]   *Padfield v Minister of Agriculture, Fisheries and Food* [1968] AC 997, HL; *R v Lancashire County Council ex p Huddleston* [1986] 2 All ER 941, CA; *Lonrho plc v Secretary of State for Trade and Industry* [1989] 2 All ER 609, HL.

[2]   By mandatory order (mandamus): *R v Secretary of State for Trade and Industry, ex p Lonrho* (1989) 5 BCC 284, CA, overruled on the merits by *Lonrho plc* above and see in particular Lord Keith at 615–616j.

[3]   *R v Mid Glamorgan Family Health Services Authority, ex p Martin* [1995] 1 All ER 356, CA. *R (Anufrijeva) v Secretary of State* [2003] 3 All ER 827 (HL). In proceedings before Simon Brown LJ involving General Pinochet and his notorious extradition the judge ruled that fairness demanded that medical reports on the General should be disclosed to those requesting his extradition under conditions of strict confidentiality: *The Guardian*, 16 February 2000: 'If ever a case required the highest standards of transparency and fairness, this was it'. The reports were subsequently leaked to the press: *The Guardian*, 22 February 2000; note the influence of Art 8 ECHR and *Gaskin v UK* (1990) 12 EHRR 36 and cases at para 8.85 below). However, complete openness may not be encouraged where life could be endangered: *R v Lord Saville of Newdigate, ex p A* [1999] 4 All ER 860, CA – maintaining anonymity of military witnesses giving evidence at the 'Bloody Sunday' inquiry. In *R (A) v Lord Saville of Newdigate* [2001] EWHC Admin 888 compelling former British soldiers to give evidence to the Bloody Sunday Inquiry in Derry breached Art 2 ECHR – the right to life. The decision maker was obliged to ask whether there was a 'real and serious risk of interference with life. If so, it was incumbent upon Lord Saville to prove compelling evidence for such an interference. The wrong test had been applied: not whether there was a real and immediate risk to life but whether the tribunal was in breach of its obligation not to make a decision which would expose another to the real possibility of a risk to life in the future. See *R v Bedfordshire Coroner ex p Local Sunday Newspapers Ltd* (2000) 164 JP QBD and *R (A and Another) v Inner South London Coroner* (2005) *Times*, 17 January. On the Bloody Sunday inquiry see: http://report.bloody-sunday-inquiry.org/.

[4]   *R v Secretary of State for Health, ex p Wagstaff* [2001] 1 WLR 292: Art 10 does not confer a right of access to information but a freedom to impart information (see paras 2.290 et seq and 2.329 et seq below). The House of Lords has also held that a 'public meeting' for the purposes of s 7 and para 9 of Part II of the Schedule to the Defamation Act (NI) 1955 was not restricted to a meeting open to all the public, but would cover a press conference with a meeting of invited members of the public who were sympathetic to a particular cause in order to attract qualified privilege for press reports. Lord Steyn believed that 'freedom of expression is a basic norm of our constitution' and quoted Justice Brandeis in *Whitney v California* 274 US 357 at 375–376 (1927): 'the path of safety lies in the opportunity to discuss freely supposed grievances and proposed remedies.' *McCartan Turkington Breen (a firm) v Times Newspapers Ltd* [2000] 4 All ER 913, HL.

[5]   As in *Lonrho plc*, note 2 above.

[6]   See paras 2.257 et seq below.

[7]   See para 2.349 below.

THE 1994 CODE ON ACCESS (REVISED IN 1997)

2.6   This Code was replaced by the FOIA 2000 (described in ch 1) on 1 January 2005 in relation to individual rights of access.

2.7   The Code followed the 1993 White Paper on *Open Government*.[1] The Code was policed by the Parliamentary Ombudsman and applied to bodies within his jurisdiction. A code also applied to requests for NHS information (see *Code of Practice on Openness in the NHS*, NHS Executive 1995). A code was not produced for local government by their representative association, but authorities were expected to have suitable arrangements and the Commission for Local Administration produced a code of practice for itself in 1995 on access to information.

[1]   Cm 2290 (1993). See HC 41(ii) (2003–04) for critical evidence on the operation of the code to the Public Administration Committee.

2.8   Having resisted a FOI statute from 1979, the government in 1993 published the White Paper as part of the Prime Minister's – John Major – Citizen's Charter (CC) initiative (see below).[1] The paper proposed, and this was the eventual outcome, to give access to 'information' and not to documents. In other words, information would be gleaned from officially held documents and sifted before being handed over to requesters. I do not know of a similar restriction in any other access to information provisions, although Scotland developed its own Code on Access in June 2000 pending the introduction of its legislation on access.

[1]   See Birkinshaw (1993) *Public Law* 557.

2.9   Of crucial importance were two points. First of all, the government opted for a code on openness not laws. By adopting a code, the government had hoped to keep questions of 'openness' away from the courts. Courts have been noticeably critical of high-handed governmental action in the UK in recent years. Such an attitude on the government's part might reveal an over sanguine comprehension of the state of development of judicial review in England but it was anxious to avoid judicial interference and so the provisions were expressions of administrative practice rather than primary, or even secondary, legislation.

THE USE OF THE OMBUDSMAN

2.10   This desire to evade judicial control was reinforced by the second factor which really constituted a 'brainwave' from the government's perspective. In order to encourage courts not to intervene the government decided to use the Parliamentary Commissioner for Administration (PCA) (hereafter Ombudsman) to supervise and deal with complaints under the Code where those requesting information were refused access. This was crucial for a variety of reasons none of which reflect badly on ombudsmen themselves but rather on the terms in which the access scheme was couched. The legal provisions under which the ombudsman operates are still relevant to the later discussion of the ombudsman.

2.11   The Ombudsman does not have power to enforce his decisions against reluctant departments. He is not a court in that respect. Rather he has to negotiate a settlement where there is a reluctance to accept his conclusions. He is backed up by the House of Commons Select Committee on Public Administration (formerly on the Parliamentary Commissioner) who will summon reluctant Ministers and their advisers before them to explain their position. The success rate of the Ombudsman is very high indeed but on several occasions departments have opposed his findings. An example of this happened in the 1990s and concerned a complaint relating to the Channel Tunnel and government delay in deciding upon an approach route from the Tunnel to London thereby causing blight to numerous properties on affected sections of the route.[1] The indication is that the government will do what it inevitably has in the past, and that is give in after a lengthy protest and as discreetly as possible.[2] This, however, has not been the case in some access complaints where the government had refused to accept an Ombudsman's recommendations to disclose documents in two cases.[3] In one case, the Lord Chancellor's Department and the Cabinet Office issued notices under the Parliamentary Commissioner Act 1967 (PCA 1967), s 11(3) (see below). These were withdrawn when the complainant sought judicial review of the issue of the certificates and the investigation continued. The Ombudsman has reported on difficulties in obtaining information necessary for Code investigations and a Memorandum of Understanding was published by the Cabinet Office in July 2003 on the Ombudsman's requirements when investigating Code complaints. Nonetheless difficulties persisted in two areas: responding to statements of complaint and draft reports issued by the Office for comment. Secondly, in providing the Ombudsman's Office with information sought by the complainant . This made it 'impossible for us to carry out our responsibilities under the Code'.[4]

[1]   HC 193 (1994–95).
[2]   HC 819 (1994–95). See the Public Accounts Committee *Work of the Ombudsmen* HC 781 (2010–11).
[3]   *The Parliamentary Ombudsman Annual Report 2003–04* p 28 A7/03 and HC 353 (2001–02) *Declarations under the Ministerial Code* and A16/03. For investigations see: HC 115 (2002–03), HC 951 (2002–03) and HC 701 (2003–04) and generally HC 41 (2003–04) etc. There has been increasing reluctance to accept recommendations in several high-profile cases since the last edition of this book. See para 9.52.
[4]   *Annual Report* 2003–04, p 28.

2.12   The Ombudsman already operates within a statutory framework dating from 1967 when the office was introduced. This represented a particular philosophy which in several respects is now looking very dated. The Ombudsman (as of writing Ann Abrahams but soon to retire) is an Officer of the House of Commons and so complainants may only reach her through the intervention of an elected Member of the House of Commons. She may not question the 'merits' of a decision taken without 'maladministration' and she is then confined to questioning the 'maladministration' not the merits. This seemed to pose particular problems from the point of view of access to information complaints because many disputes would potentially lie within the area of the merits and so therefore be outside the Ombudsman's jurisdiction – and the High Court has ruled that the Ombudsman is judicially reviewable.[1] She has to be careful not to exceed or abuse her powers or otherwise act unlawfully or unfairly and indeed, in October 1996, the Parliamentary Ombudsman was successfully judicially reviewed in the High Court in a non-information complaint.[2] That said, the courts have in more recent years approached the office of ombudsmen in a more cooperative manner (paras 2.134 and 9.47 et seq).

[1]   *R v Parliamentary Comr for Administration, ex p Dyer* [1994] 1 All ER 375. See *In Re a Subpoena Issued by the Comr for Local Administration* [1996] 3 FCR 190, holding that a local ombudsman was entitled to obtain privileged confidential information from a local authority's adoption files.
[2]   *R v Parliamentary Comr for Administration, ex p Balchin* [1997] JPL 917; and *ex p Balchin (No 2)* (2000) 2 LGLR 87.

2.13 Section 11(3) of the Parliamentary Commissioner Act 1967 gave the Minister a veto power to prevent the Ombudsman handing information to anyone, other than his officers, which had been gathered from an investigation where its disclosure would be prejudicial to the safety of the state or contrary to the public interest – and it must be emphasised that the Ombudsman has enormous powers to gather information and interview officials as well as powers to hand over to the High Court to punish for contempt in cases where he is obstructed in his investigations. Section 11(3) was a particularly fortuitous provision from the government's perspective, and one hardly ever used before the Code came into effect. In the event of a disagreement between a department and the Ombudsman over what should be disclosed, the Minister was given the final word and not an independent decision-making body.[1] The Ombudsmen, as we have seen in ch 1 (para 1.260), may disclose information to the Information Commissioner (IC) for the assistance of certain of the IC's functions under the DPA 1998 and FOI Acts and the IC may disclose information to them likewise. There has been close liaison between the IC's office and the Ombudsman's office and a Memorandum of Understanding was introduced to set out relationships up until and after the Code ceases to exist and the Ombudsman has been a member of the Advisory group advising the Lord Chancellor/Secretary of State.

[1]   The National Audit Office which is headed by the Comptroller and Auditor General is supposed to have the widest of access to government documents in carrying out his audit responsibilities, but he operates under a 'Not for the Eyes of the NAO' convention: see White, Harden and Donnelly (1994) *Public Law* 526 and see ch 11 below.

2.14 Another limitation is that the legislation does not allow the Ombudsman to investigate all complaints. The PCA is limited in that she can only investigate named departments in the Schedule to the PCA 1967 (or agencies or bodies). Many departments are not included although all of those dealing regularly with the public, as do the new executive agencies, are included. These agencies, introduced in the premiership of Mrs Thatcher, have been in existence since 1988 and the government intends to transfer all functions of government that do not require a ministerial departmental status to these in due course to be run on more commercial and managerial lines. Originally seen as a staging post to privatisation or contracting out of government functions, their future within the public sector appears secure for the mid-term future. A large number of non-departmental bodies has also been added to the Ombudsman's jurisdiction. The Code does not cover information held by courts, tribunals or 'inquiries'.

2.15 As well as bodies excluded from his jurisdiction there are functions which are excluded. These are considerable indeed. They include for instance contractual and commercial matters – excepting compulsory purchase of land – and personnel matters – the former at the insistence of the Ministry of Defence which did not want armaments contracts to be the subject of complaint and investigation. Matters affecting international relations, commencement of civil or criminal legal proceedings, military disciplinary or international legal proceedings, exercise of mercy, criminal investigation, or action taken to protect the security of the state, or the grant of honours, privileges or gifts 'within the gift of the Crown' are all excluded.

2.16 This represents a considerable corpus of exclusions. More importantly perhaps is the fact that the Ombudsman is not very well known in the UK. He can only be approached by an MP and his decisions are not enforceable as judgments of courts of law.[1] He may only make recommendations. To superimpose a statutory scheme from over 40 years ago when the Ombudsman was first introduced into the UK and when his powers were deliberately confined so as not to interfere too rudely into governing conventions like parliamentary supremacy and ministerial responsibility seems excessively cautious. It is a scheme which all but a few in government, as well as the staff of the Ombudsman's Office, understand. Even a large number of MPs are not as well acquainted with the Ombudsman as desirable.[2] On to this scheme was placed the operation of the access to information Code.

[1] The scheme is modified for local government ombudsmen, the health service commissioner and the Northern Ireland Commissioner for Complaints.
[2] HC 33 I (1993–94). See *Review of the Public Sector Ombudsman in England* Cabinet Office 2000, P Colcutt and M Hourihan, and the Public Administration Committee HC 612 (1999–2000).

2.17 On one point, however, the 1993 White Paper outlining the policy on access reported how the Ombudsman was to broaden the opportunity to take complaints from pressure groups and those who had not actually suffered injury as a consequence of maladministration. It was sufficient that they alleged non-compliance with the Code. This was practically of considerable significance. Furthermore, in the face of more privatisation and contracting out, it is worth emphasising that the Ombudsman has access to bodies operating under contract with Ministers to provide public services or with local authorities – the local ombudsman in the case of the latter. Information complaints concerning such bodies are within his jurisdiction as are the regulators of privatised bodies and information complaints concerning the regulators. The industries themselves are not within the Ombudsman's jurisdiction.

THE CODE

2.18 The Code was outlined in the White Paper on *Open Government*[1] which also provided plans for reforms of practice under Public Records legislation. These would shorten the period of 'closure' of many public records to 30 years or less and allow access to those public records. The White Paper further announced the introduction of legislation for access to personal files by the subjects of those files and also access to health and safety information. Provision was made for personal access in the DPA 1998; specific provision for health and safety concerns had to wait until the FOIA 2000.[2]

[1]   Cm 2290 (1993). Annual reports are made on the operation of the Code.
[2]   EC Council Directive 95/46/EC on Data Protection was implemented into UK legal systems by DPA 1998: see ch 7. This will apply to both paper and electronically stored data. There were indications that the government would exclude subject areas from implementing legislation which it believes are not covered by EC law, eg police and national security, immigration and taxation. This did not occur.

2.19   The Code on access to information was published only days before it came into effect. It was revised in 1997. It sets out on one page the information it will allow access to and on four and a half pages the information which will be exempt from disclosure. These exemptions in other words operate *in addition* to the statutory exclusions which were outlined above. The Code has now gone and need not be examined further. However, the ombudsman published a report on the operation of the Code in *Access to Official Information: Monitoring of the Codes of Practice 1994–2005* (HC 59 2005–06).

Balancing the public interest in disclosure and confidentiality

2.20   Although the Code has gone, assessing the public interest under the Code may still hold some interesting lessons. Basically, under the Code access is to be allowed except in the case where harm or prejudice, actual or reasonably apprehended, may be caused to the public interest or to individuals. However, there were some very important provisions which have been seized by the Ombudsman to give him a discretion to disclose where 'any harm or prejudice arising from disclosure is outweighed by the public interest in making information available'. The Ombudsman has stated that this gives him a discretion to disclose where a greater public interest is served by disclosure than by secrecy in those cases where a reason for holding back information is the harm, damage, prejudice etc that may be caused by disclosure:

'As I see it, the issue of when the public interest in disclosure will override any harm or prejudice which might arise from disclosure is a matter of judgement in the light of the facts of each individual case' (Case A 12/95, para 8).

2.21   In giving evidence to the Select Committee on Public Administration in July 1999, the Ombudsman indicated that he can disagree with the decision on disclosure on the merits, and that has been accepted. Where harm or prejudice is not referred to, there would seem to be no scope for such a balancing of public interests eg information received in confidence from foreign governments, foreign courts or international organisations, communications with the Royal Household or proceedings of the Privy Council, information relating to legal proceedings including tribunals and public inquiries and that covered by legal professional privilege and information relating to public employment, appointments and honours, voluminous or vexatious requests, information to be published, information relating to research, statistics and analysis, information supplied in confidence or subject to legal restriction. Some exemptions refer to 'unwarranted' or other qualifying epithets and these leave scope for judgment on the part of the Ombudsman. Is the case for 'unwarranted' established? The factors that the Ombudsman has relied upon to weigh in favour of disclosure are: the age of documents; the interest of the public as well as the 'public interest' (on taxation policy (A 31/02)).

2.22 It was the ombudsman's decision and in that respect it is not unlike the discretion exercised by the courts where a claim for Public Interest Immunity has been correctly entered by a government Minister or civil servant (see paras 10.64 et seq below). The government have not challenged this interpretation but commentators have been quick to point out that the Minister retains the right to veto publication of information in the Ombudsman's possession under s 11(3) (para 2.13 above). Both the Prime Minister and Minister for the Duchy of Lancaster have stated that the Ombudsman 'has it in his hands' to publish information in such circumstances. This is a significant achievement and the government has not acted contrary to this interpretation. However, in April 2005, the government refused to disclose documents under the Code which related to meetings between the Prime Minister and business donors to the Labour Party. This was despite the Ombudsman finding that public interest weighed in favour of disclosure. Disclosure, it was claimed, would damage 'free and frank disclosure of views' between the government and outside stakeholders (*The Guardian* (2005) 19 April). This was not the first time that the government had refused to disclose documents in defiance of the Ombudsman's recommendations (see para 1.209 above).

2.23 The exemptions – which technically are discretionary and may be waived by departments unless a legal obstacle prevents this – cover many of the areas already found in FOI legislation: viz disclosures which would harm defence, security and international relations, law enforcement and legal proceedings, effective management of the economy and collection of tax, effective management and operations of the public service, communications with the Royal Household and information related to public appointments, public employment and conferral of honours. The code writes in safeguards to refuse vexatious or numerous requests requiring 'unreasonable diversion of resources' and premature publication of information. Privacy and commercially confidential information are protected. So too is information 'relating to incomplete analysis, research or statistics, where disclosure could be misleading': it does not say why it is misleading, eg, because of fault or insufficient research on the part of government.

2.24 Information given in confidence is protected in wide terms especially where the future supply of such information would be threatened by disclosure and so is information where there is a statutory or other national or international provision preventing release or where information cannot be released except by breaching parliamentary privilege.

2.25   Two kinds of information call for particular comment. Information relating to immigration, nationality, consular and entry clearance was given a total exemption – an exemption the ombudsman has described as 'slightly surprising'. Subsequently, information would be provided 'though not through access to personal records, where there is no risk that disclosure would prejudice the effective administration of immigration controls or other statutory provisions'.[1]

[1]   Access by the data subjects will be allowed under DPA 1998, as amended by FOIA 2000, to immigration files, subject to exemptions.

2.26   Secondly, information concerning the policy making process where disclosure would harm internal discussion and advice. This is a very controversial exemption. What it seeks to prevent is 'government in a gold-fish bowl' and the privacy/inviolability of the policy making process and to protect the anonymity of civil servants' advice. My own belief is that the exemption is too broad.

2.27   The Code became operational on 4 April 1994. Also published are a *Code of Guidance on Interpretation* and an *Annual Report* which contains a good deal of otherwise unpublished material. The Annual Report of 1999 was particularly instructive and contains contact points in public authorities for access requests and departmental websites. The Ombudsman had let it be known that the *Code of Guidance* is not binding on him, only the *Code on Open Government* (see below).

THE COALITION GOVERNMENT PLANS FOR TRANSPARENCY

2.28   The Conservative Government's 1994 Code was a last-ditch effort to avoid duties to give the public information they requested in law. Traditionally, the Conservative Party had been hostile to a FOIA in the UK. In the 2010 election, the Conservatives pledged that 'within weeks of the general election' they would extend the FOIA to a wider range of bodies. These would include Network Rail, Northern Rock, the Carbon Trust, the Energy Saving Trust, the NHS Confederation, the Local Government Association and Traffic Penalty Tribunals. The Liberal Democrat manifesto also mentioned Network Rail's inclusion under FOIA, together with other 'private companies delivering monopoly public services'. However, the coalition programme[1] said nothing on how the Act would be extended. This silence contrasts dramatically with their detailed proposals to effect an increase in state transparency. In the summer of 2011, the Cabinet Office launched a consultation on *Making Open Data Real: a Public Consultation* in a drive to increase openness and transparency in government.[2]

[1]   http://programmeforgovernment.hmg.gov.uk/files/2010/05/coalition-programme.pdf.
[2]   http://data.gov.uk/opendataconsultation.

2.29   The proposals, based on the Conservative manifesto, include enforcing much greater online disclosure of salaries and expenses of senior officials, job descriptions of all public sector employees, everyone in the centrally funded public sector paid more than the Prime Minister will have to have their salary signed off by the Treasury, a statutory register of lobbyists would be introduced, parliamentary select committees would be given greater powers of scrutiny of public appointments, greater protection for whistleblowers, a level playing field for open source software, ICT contracts, council spending over £500 and central government spending over £25,000; and also creating a 'right to data' so that the public can request and use government data sets. Reforms were to be introduced to data sets under the Protection of Freedoms Bill 2010–11 (para 1.79). All data will be published in an easily usable format which is cheap to use. Council minutes would be published – this already occurs under the local government legislation (para 6.3 et seq). A Public Sector Transparency Board was established in June 2010 and set about establishing public data principles which included free re-use and commercial re-use. Data released under FOIA or the 'new right to data' will be automatically released under an open licence. Public bodies should actively encourage reuse of their data and should maintain and publish inventories of their data holdings.

2.30 The Treasury published 'millions of items' of spending data from its combined online information system and these were published shortly after the coalition came to power. It was accepted that this was raw data rather than easily usable comparative data. An Independent Office of Budget Responsibility would report of financial forecasting forming the basis of the budget although its independence was questioned as it comprised many Treasury officials. This was initially set up on a non-statutory basis but its legal basis was established in the Budget Responsibility and National Audit Bill 2010–11, now enacted (para 11.5). In health care, information was to be published on outcomes and results of treatment and not on waiting lists.[1]

[1]   Equity and Excellence: Liberating the NHS Cm 7881 (July 2010). See para 9.106.

2.31 There was no initial sign of hostility to FOIA. However, many of the developments to date are non-statutory – a favourite means in the past of introducing open government in the UK. As it is non-statutory it is to a considerable extent discretionary. Amendments to the FOIA in the Protection of Liberties Bill were dealt with in chapter 1. Further amendments reducing the extent of government retention of personal data are covered in chapter 7.

GOVERNMENT AND THE INTERNET[1]

2.32 Like governments everywhere, the UK government and devolved government have made full use of IT. Tony Blair was a devotee of IT in government and for public service. An E Government Unit (2007) existed in the Cabinet Office although its webpage ceased in 2007 and the site now is a new Cabinet Office site[2] and Directgov.[3] Further focal points include govtalk[4] and policy documents.[5]

The White Paper *Putting the Frontline First: Smarter Government* (Cm 7753 December 2009) and the launch of www.data.gov.uk in beta in early 2010 following the developer site testing were the last contributions under the Brown government. This is an ambitious programme aiming to put government information on the Internet to enhance public service and service delivery and to enhance government performance. The Prime Minister of the coalition government utilises his own website.[6]

The Central Office of Information (COI)[7] is the focal point for usability of web sites and COI works with the Power of Information Taskforce established in 2008 to advise on social and economic gains to be achieved through better use of government information. Open source and accessibility are key themes.[8]

[1]   See Council of Europe *edemocracy* Rec CM/Rec (2009) 1.
[2]   http://www.cabinetoffice.gov.uk/government_it.aspx.
[3]   http://www.direct.gov.uk/en/index.htm.
[4]   http://www.cabinetoffice.gov.uk/govtalk.aspx.
[5]   http://www.cabinetoffice.gov.uk/govtalk/policydocuments.aspx.
[6]   http://transparency.number10.gov.uk.
[7]   http://usability.coi.gov.uk.
[8]   http://powerofinformation.wordpress.com.

2.33   The Cabinet Office has established a transparency initiative and a Transparency Board. A DirectGov Strategic Review was published in 2010.[1] The Chancellor announced proposals for use of the internet by government in a speech at Google Zeitgeist in May 2011[2] and a Public Data Corporation was established 'to open up opportunities for innovative developers, businesses and members of the public to generate social and economic growth through the use of data.'[3] In the same month the Government's new Executive Director of Digital was appointed and is responsible for overseeing and improving all of the Government's online presence and extending the number of public services available online. He is based in the Cabinet Office.[4]

1   http://www.cabinetoffice.gov.uk/sites/default/files/Directgov%20Executive%20Sum%20 FINAL.pdf.
2   www.hm-treasury.gov.uk/press_48_11.htm.
3   http://www.cabinetoffice.gov.uk/news/public-data-corporation-free-public-data-and-drive- innovation.
4   http://www.cabinetoffice.gov.uk/news/new-executive-director-digital-appointed.

2.34   A particularly important initiative came with the EU laws on Re-use of Public Sector information. This has now been implemented in the UK by the Re-use of Public Sector Information Regulations 2005, SI 2005/1515. These aim to allow public sector information to be re-used for commercial purposes. The scheme is quite complicated and detailed. In the UK Crown and Parliament publications are protected by copyright. The Office of Public Sector Information (OPSI) in the National Archives is responsible for overseeing the operation of re-use.

2.35   A further development is the Information Asset Register (IAR) which is accessed via inforoute.[1] The following leans on official literature. The IAR lists information resources held by the UK Government, concentrating on unpublished resources. IAR enables users to identify, from one single source, the information held in a wide variety of government departments, agencies and other organisations. 'inforoute' is a key part of the Government's agenda for freeing up access to official information. The UK government cites analogues existing in the US and in Canada. As departments identify information to be published through their FOI Publication Schemes (above), so unpublished information can also be identified for inclusion in the IAR. IAR will include: central government databases, old sets of files, recent electronic files, collections of statistics, research, etc. The IAR concentrates on information resources that have not yet been, or will not be formally published. Responsibility for IARs is placed on individual departments. OPSI has overall responsibility for IAR formats and standards and for maintaining the inforoute website. It complements but does not duplicate existing lists of published materials. It has links to other sources of official information and lists of official publications (eg Directgov, UKOP and The Stationery Office). The Government does not wish IAR to become 'resource-intensive or over centralised'. OPSI is establishing agreed indexing practices across all IAR web sites to build an evolving central service. Contact names are given.

¹   http://www.opsi.gov.uk/iar/index.

2.36   An increasingly crucial question concerns computer security. This affects governments, commercial and financial institutions and individuals. Methods of interfering through unauthorised access to computers ('hacking') have become ever more complex and sophisticated through the use of 'worms', viruses and so on. The detail would take us into the realm of specialised IT, but the capabilities involved concern massive government and commercial investment because of the potential threat to security, public services and intellectual property. The Cabinet Office in the UK has traditionally taken the lead on this subject – currently through the Cyber Security and Information Assurance Operations Centre in conjunction with the Cyber Security Operations Centre based at General Communications HQ. MI5 and special police units work alongside the Home Office.

2.37   As long ago as 2002, the National Audit Office published a trilogy on *Better Public Services through e-government* (HC 704 I-III (2001–02). There are publications reviewing, describing and evaluating each major government department's website together with appropriate addresses and profiles.¹ One specific problem originally related to the use of Crown and Parliamentary copyright in the UK to prevent the placing of statutes and official publications and Hansard – the official reports of Parliamentary proceedings – on the Internet. These reports, together with other Parliamentary publications are available on www.parliament.uk.

¹   http://www.publicservice.co.uk/news_story.asp?id=15329 and Directgov: http://www.direct.gov. uk/en/index.htm. D Jellinek '*Official UK*' (1st edn, 2000) Stationery Office Books; United Nations. *E-Government Survey* (2010). C Reed *Internet Law: Text and Materials* (2nd edn, 2004). See also I Lloyd *Information Technology Law* (6th edn, 2011). On facilitating electronic commerce, see the Electronic Communications Act 2000 and on online infringement of copyright, powers in relation to Internet domain registries etc see the Digital Economy Act 2010.

2.38   The government has informally expressed the view that it will not enforce copyright laws where statutory provisions allowing access to information are placed on a website for access on the Internet. This concession was given to the FOI Campaign which has championed the cause of Open Government in the UK. Since then, there has been a significant relaxation of Crown copyright law.[1]

[1]   Cm 4300 (1999).

2.39 Before turning to the area of official secrecy, there are several areas covering the provision of information by central government which call for specific attention.

RE-USE OF PUBLIC SECTOR INFORMATION

2.40 The following leans heavily on official guidance produced by OPSI. It deals with how public sector bodies covered by the Regulations should best meet the obligations contained in the European Directive on the Re-use of Public Sector Information (2003/98/EC) to be implemented across the UK under SI 2005/1515 ('the Regulations'). The impetus behind the Directive was the recognition that public sector information is a valuable information resource that could be utilised by the private sector to develop value-added products and services. The removal of barriers to re-use would act as a stimulus to the information and publishing industry in Europe so providing significant economic opportunities and enhancing job creation across Europe. An additional benefit would be to improve the flow of information from the public sector to the citizen. The Regulations define terms such as 'public sector body', 're-use' and 'document'. In September 2010, the National Archives introduced a new *Open Government Licence* for re-use of public sector information.[1]

[1]   http://www.nationalarchives.gov.uk/news/498.htm.

Key principles and objectives

2.41 The main objective of the Regulations is to establish methods facilitating:[1]
(a) the ready identification of public sector documents that are available for re-use;
(b) documents are generally available for re-use at marginal cost;
(c) public sector bodies to deal with applications to re-use in a timely, open and transparent manner;
(s) the process should be fair, consistent and non-discriminatory;
(e) encouraging the sharing of best practice across the public sector.

[1]   See OPSI *UK Report on RE-use of Public Sector Information* (2009).

Scope

2.42 The Regulations apply to all documents held by public sector bodies unless specifically excluded. The definition is wide and includes corporations or groups appointed 'for the specific purposes of meeting needs in the general interest not having an industrial or commercial character' (reg 3(1)(w)). The provisions of data protection legislation are not affected by the Regulations. The exclusions fall under the following headings:

(a) documents that are exempt from disclosure under Freedom of Information (FOI) legislation. This includes those cases where a particular interest needs to be demonstrated eg commercial interests;

(b) documents in which the copyright and/or other intellectual property rights are owned or controlled by a person or organisation other than the public sector body;

(c) documents that fall outside the scope of the public task of the public sector body. This covers those situations where a public sector body produces documents that are not directly related to the core responsibilities of the public sector body. This may cover documents that are of a value-added or commercial nature;

(d) documents that are held by public service broadcasters and other bodies or their subsidiaries for the fulfilment of a public service broadcasting remit;

(e) documents held by educational and research establishments such as schools, universities, archives, libraries and research facilities;

(f) documents held by cultural establishments, including museums, libraries, archives, orchestras, theatre and performing arts establishments.

Partnerships

2.43 Public sector bodies often develop information products and services with partners in the public and private sectors. The Guidance emphasises the importance of clarifying when any copyright or any other intellectual property rights in such products and services are owned by a private sector partner. The public sector body should also make it clear whom the re-user should contact about re-use. In the case of information that is jointly owned by private and public sector partners and where it is impossible to identify the copyright elements owned by each partner, re-users would need the permission of both parties unless the private sector partner agreed that the public sector should have the responsibility for authorising re-use. Public sector bodies should not authorise private sector partners to authorise re-use of public sector documents. One of the parties in joint enterprise partnerships should be nominated to process requests for re-use to avoid unnecessary bureaucracy. The presumption is that the public sector bodies have the necessary authority to license re-use. Licensing of most copyright material produced at central government level is managed centrally by OPSI, incorporating Her Majesty's Stationery Office (HMSO).

Asset lists

2.44 An asset is any information that a public sector body produces that is of interest or value to the organisation itself, and potentially to others. An asset list is simply a register of these information assets, usually categorised using a standard classification method. The asset list register has been outlined above.

The first step to re-using public sector information is to know what documents are available for re-use. Public sector bodies should produce asset lists that provide details of what is available, how the information can be obtained and the terms and conditions of re-use.

2.45 Some public sector bodies already publish clear and transparent information to help re-users find documents to re-use. Often in practice these information sources have been developed to meet their obligations under FOI legislation. While the obligations under FOI and the production of asset lists under these Regulations are not synonymous, there are, nevertheless, synergies between the two. Public sector bodies should consider ways in which they can meet these obligations in a way that avoids unnecessary duplication of effort and also provides potential re-users with a one-stop shop in terms of finding out what information is available.

2.46 OPSI, incorporating HMSO has the policy lead for the Information Asset Register (IAR) which is used widely across central government as a way of identifying and accessing asset lists. OPSI has been developing a model for the next generation IAR with advanced search capabilities in a way that will enable public sector bodies to easily identify information assets that are available for re-use in a joined-up and effective way. The key message for redeveloping IAR is the need to join up the similarities in existing and emerging information initiatives, polices and legislation to ensure that public sector information assets are easy to manage and easy to find, use and share. To facilitate the transition to the next generation IAR, there is a requirement to rationalise existing documentation relating to IAR and links with other information policy, particularly Freedom of Information Publication Schemes. Further information on how the IAR model can be developed and adapted across the wider public sector is available from http://tna.europarchive.org/20100402134329/http://www.opsi.gov.uk/iar/index.htm and http://www.bis.gov.uk/site/foi/information-asset-register.

Charging

2.47 The Regulations state that where charges are made the charges should not exceed the cost of collection, production, reproduction and dissemination. The Guidance acknowledges that 'much material held by public sector bodies is available in digital format, often by being published on the web, the costs of allowing re-use does not involve any additional cost to the public sector.' Quite often 'the cost of raising a charge will in many cases be uneconomic.'

2.48 A commercial rate for the re-use of documents may be charged where appropriate. 'This will be particularly applicable to public sector bodies that are required to operate in a commercial manner in order to cover their costs. This includes government trading funds. Where this applies, the charges should cover the costs of collection, production, reproduction and dissemination, together with a reasonable return on investment, based on normal accounting cycles.' Neither the Regulations nor the Directive actually define what is meant by a reasonable return on investment. Such a return is dependent on the particular facts and the costs incurred of developing specific products and services. Challenges by applicants for re-use may be made to justify the charges that they apply and the grievance procedure set out below may be used. It is stipulated that fees charged under Freedom of Information legislation should be offset against any for re-use. Guidance is available from the Treasury on Fees and Charges,[1] and charges and conditions for re-use should be published. These may well have to be justified.

[1] http://www.hm-treasury.gov.uk/about/open_government/opengov_charging.cfm; http://www. opsi.gov.uk/advice/crown-copyright/crown-copyright-licensing-consultation-outcome.pdf and www.partnershipsuk.org.uk/.

Licensing[1]

2.49 It is not compulsory to use licences to permit the re-use of documents. Where licences are used the Guidance spells out essential features such as fairness and openness and equality; terms should not be anti-competitive and should be online digital. Licence terms should be standardised. Where the Crown retains copyright a recipient of that information has an automatic right to copy, publish distribute and adapt the information under the Open Government Licence (OGL) for public sector information. They may exploit the information commercially. This is free but subject to conditions. Public authorities that have adopted the OGL are likewise covered. If not covered, copyright retained by them will protect the information. Re-use is subject to the re-use regulations.

[1] http://www.hmso.gov.uk/psi/standard-licence.htm.

Exclusive arrangements

2.50 Exclusive arrangements with one re-user will restrict competition and should generally be avoided. Such arrangements cut against the objectives of the Directive and Regulations. Where the provision of a service is in the public interest and the service would not otherwise be capable of being made available then an exception may be made. All such arrangements (pre- and post-the Regulations) have to be reviewed regularly and must be transparent and published subject to genuine requirements of commercial confidentiality (post-Regulations). The Guidance states that: 'Existing exclusive arrangements entered into for any other reason than being in the public interest, should be terminated by the end of the contract and in any event no later than 31 December 2008.' Exclusive arrangements should be reviewed every three years. A list of exclusive arrangements is published at http://www.nationalarchives.gov.uk/information-management/policies/exclusive-agreements.htm.

Transparency, openness and non-discrimination

2.51 All information such as asset lists, standard licence terms and charging information should be published. Complaints procedures should be published.

Conditions for the re-use of public sector documents must be non-discriminatory between comparable categories of re-use. Exceptions may be made in the case of libraries, archives and educational establishments, which enjoy special privileges under the Copyright, Designs and Patents Act 1988, which also includes special provisions for the reproduction of material for visually impaired persons. Principles of non-discrimination apply to the public sector body itself in, eg, developing their own commercial products outside their core public tasks. 'This is aimed at ensuring a level playing field between the public sector and others when competing in the commercial market place. Private sector applicants may seek evidence that this has been properly applied.' OPSI has developed best practice in this area. The Information Fair Trader Scheme (IFTS) was introduced in 2000 to support various UK policy initiatives that sought to encourage the re-use of Crown copyright material and other public sector information. IFTS is 'highly visible' seeks to promote an open, fair and transparent system and to ensure fair grievance procedures and a robust audit. It verifies major information traders such as Ordnance Survey and the Met Office. It ranges from significant producers and traders of information to parish councils and doctors surgeries. Verification has involved site visits and detailed audits and verification models reflecting the diversity of bodies. For further information on IFTS see http://www.hmso.gov.uk/copyright/standards/ifts.htm.

2.52   The Guidance states that IFTS verifies:
(a)   Openness – that the organisation maximises the information available for re-use.
(b)   Transparency – that the organisation has clear and simple policies and procedures.
(c)   Fairness – that all customers are treated the same.
(d)   Compliance – that the organisation's procedure should comply with the first three principles.
(e)   Challenge – that the organisation has a robust complaints procedure.

IFTS accreditation is usually only given after interviews with key personnel, detailed case file and licence review and a website audit.

Processing applications

2.53   Applications must be in writing, state the applicant's name and address and state the purpose for which the information is to be re-used. Permission should be given within a reasonable period of time. The Regulations allow public sector bodies up to 20 working days (as for FOI legislation) following date of receipt of the request for re-use to finalise any licence offer. The same timelines apply to documents that are not readily available in a published form. Consideration of whether re-use is allowed does not affect the 20 working days time limit for access to the information under FOI legislation. If the information can be released under FOI then it must be made available within 20 working days or within a reasonable time if what is known as a public interest exemption applies. If there is a combined release and re-use request then it must be dealt with fully in terms of access to the information (unless exempt under FOI) within 20 working days irrespective of whether the final decision on re-use has been made.

Availability of documents

2.54 Documents available through electronic means if this is possible, and in any format in which they already exist. If a web document exists, this is the format the re-user will receive. Public sector bodies are not under any obligation to create or adapt documents in response to a request. Nor do public sector bodies have to provide extracts of documents if this would entail considerable work and cost. Public sector bodies are not required to 'continue the production of documents just because there is a demand for their re-use'. The National Archive's central policy responsibility for archiving and records management remains unchanged. Under the Protection of Freedoms Bill, datasets are to be available under the terms of the FOIA.

Right to refuse the re-use of documents

2.55 The Regulations provide that bodies have the right to refuse the re-use of documents where there are good reasons for doing so. This will usually be because the document falls outside the scope of the EC Directive because:
(a)   the copyright in the document is owned by a third party;
(b)   the supply of the document falls outside the scope of the public sector body's public task;
(c)   the document falls within the scope of the exempted classes of material under FOI and data protection legislation

Reason(s) for refusing to allow re-use must be explained to applicants within 20 working days. Where a refusal is made, the public sector body must provide details to the applicant on how they may complain or appeal against the decision.

Complaints, means of redress and dispute resolution

2.56 The Guidance emphasises that all public sector bodies should operate an effective, transparent complaints procedure. This will explain how complaints will be handled; where complaints should be sent to; how long it will take to respond to complaints; and what the means of redress are. Re-users should complain direct to the public sector body that is the subject of the complaint in the first instance. The Regulations establish a dispute resolution process.

The dispute resolution process

2.57 The following guidance on the dispute resolution process, which is described as 'independent', constitutes best practice:

(a)   the dispute process will be managed by OPSI. Complainants will be expected to specify the basis of their complaint and how a public sector body is failing to comply with the Regulations;

(b)   the complaint will be investigated by OPSI. A decision will be issued within 30 working days. 'Complex' cases may be subject to non-refundable payment of £500;

(c)   both parties can appeal to the specially constituted panel of the Advisory Panel on Public Sector Information (APPSI). The Chair or the Deputy Chair of APPSI will convene an appropriately independent and balanced panel of experts (the panel). The panel will investigate and reach a decision within 60 working days;

(d)   generally evidence will only be considered in written form. The Chair of the panel will have the discretion to co-opt individuals who are not existing members of APPSI;

(e)   complaints about OPSI will be referred to APPSI so as to maintain an equivalent level of independence;

(f)   a summary of each case and all decisions will be published;

(g)   compliance with decisions will be monitored by OPSI (or APPSI in the case of complaints made against OPSI);

(h)   non-compliance will be referred to the Minister to the Cabinet Office who will consider issuing a ministerial letter of direction.

2.58   Each party is free at any stage during this process to seek the assistance of the courts or to refer issues to regulatory bodies such as the Office of Fair Trading or the Office of the Information Commissioner. The courts or other regulatory bodies may take into account any decision or letter of direction in its deliberations.

The Role of the Advisory Panel on Public Sector Information (APPSI)

2.59   APPSI acts both as adviser and in an executive capacity determining disputes. Each of the two roles will be differently constituted to 'ensure impartiality'. Historically, APPSI has had three key responsibilities:

(a)   to advise ministers on how to encourage and create opportunities in the information industry for greater re-use of public sector information;

(b)   to advise OPSI about changes and opportunities in the information industry, so that the licensing of public sector information is aligned with current and emerging developments; and

(c)   to advise on the impact of the complaints procedures under the Information Fair Trader Scheme.

Freedom of information

2.60   In the UK access to public sector information rights are given by the FOIA 2000 and the Freedom of Information (Scotland) Act 2002 (SFOIA). FOI legislation specifies categories of exempt information that cannot be supplied.

Exemptions may be absolute or ordinary. The latter are subject to public interest disclosures. It follows that if access is denied, then re-use is not permitted either. The supply of information under FOI does not automatically give the recipient of the information the right to re-use it; for example, the right to publish it unless covered by open use. In most cases, separate permission, often in the form of a licence, needs to be obtained from the public sector body that owns the copyright. The Protection of Freedoms Bill 2011 makes some important amendments on access to data sets held by PAs and rights of re-use (para 1.79).

A protocol[1] has been drawn up between OPSI and the Information Commissioner on their cooperation and working relationship in their work on FOI, data protection, the EIR 2004 and the 2005 Regulations.

[1] www.opsi.gov.uk/advice/psi-regulations/disputes-resolution/opsi-ico-protocol-2005–08.pdf.

Useful sites
2.61

- http://www.nationalarchives.gov.uk/documents/uk-report-reuse-psi-2009. pdf ('The United Kingdom Report on the Re-use of Public Sector Information 2009')
- http://www.nationalarchives.gov.uk/information-management/uk-gov-licensing-framework.htm (the UK government's licensing framework arrangements)
- http://www.opsi.gov.uk/ (Office of Public Sector Information)
- http://www.appsi.gov.uk/ (Advisory Panel on Public Sector Information)
- www.opsi.gov.uk/si/em2005/uksiem_20051515_en.pdf (Cabinet Office Explanatory Memorandum to the Regulations)
- www.opsi.gov.uk/about/contact-us/complaints/complaints-procedure.htm
- www.info4local.gov.uk/relatedlinks.asp? (for local government)

PUBLIC RECORDS ACTS AS AMENDED BY THE FREEDOM OF INFORMATION ACT 2000[1]

2.62 Before 1959 there was no legal right of access to public records in the Public Record Office (PRO), now renamed National Archives, which also incorporates the Historical Manuscripts Commission. In what follows, for PRO read National Archives; the title of Lord Chancellor has been retained for the time being. Certain discretionary practices on disclosure existed but it was not until the Public Records Act was passed in 1958 that a legal right, subject to exceptions, conferred access to public records. The Act does not apply to Scottish[2] and Northern Ireland records. These are covered by other provisions. The Act required courts, government departments and specified non-departmental bodies to transfer records selected for permanent preservation to the PRO, or another approved place. This was to occur before they were 30 years old; they would be available for public inspection when 50 years old. The Public Records Act 1967 (PRA 1967) reduced the period of closure to 30 years in the '30 year rule'. Documents may be retained in departments for more than 30 years. The CRGA 2010 has reduced the period to 20 years.

[1]   See A McDonald 'Archives and Open Government' in A McDonald and G Terrill *Open Government: Freedom of Information and Privacy* (1998). On PRO fees, see SI 2005/471.
[2]   See Public Records (Scotland) Act 2011.

2.63   A statement of practice was made in 1993 when John Major's government published the White Paper on *Open Government* which stated that more information would be released following administrative changes to the criteria used for withholding information for longer than 30 years – noting that 30 years was becoming a norm adopted by EC member states. Its revised arrangements would apply to Scotland and Northern Ireland. All records which were not retained in departments (under s 3(4) of the Public Records Act 1958) should be released after 30 years (see above) unless it was possible to prove actual damage by release falling within criteria set out in the guidance.[1] Section 3(4) allows retention within departments for special reason which the Lord Chancellor has approved. Public records of other bodies not covered by the PRA 1967, eg local authorities, are covered by different practices and the FOIA 2000 has significantly amended the law for bodies covered by the FOIA 2000. The variations on the basic practice are as follows.

[1]   See HC 570 I (1998–99), Annex 5.

2.64   The FOIA 2000 has now sought to put this regime which was discretionary of both a statutory and non-statutory nature on a par with the FOIA 2000, an intention which was set out in the 1997 White Paper. Most of the provisions of s 5 of the PRA 1967 which set out the previous regime are repealed. Public records become 'historical records' after 30 (20 when the CRGA 2010 takes effect) years and are governed by the provisions of Part VI of the FOIA 2000. The provisions of the FOIA 2000 apply to these, presumably even those retained in departments for purposes of administrative convenience because they were in constant use or subject to review, though *quaere* where they related to civil servants or because they related to security or intelligence. So, while the security and intelligence services and records they hold are excluded from the Act, information within s 23 of the FOIA 2000, ie from such bodies or relating to them which is contained in a historical record in the PRO and PRO (NI) are exempt *and* in the case of such records the provisions of s 2 are not overridden by absolute exemption as they are with FOIA applications. In other words there is a discretion to disclose in the public interest once they are 30 (20) years old but only where they are in the PRO. Where a request is made for historical records in the public authority which are exempt, the Lord Chancellor/Secretary of State has to be consulted and, under s 15, the PRO is obliged to consult the originating department before releasing an exempt record.

2.65   Section 66 concerns transferred public records (see para 1.96 above on s 15 of the FOIA 2000). These relate to information which is, or if it existed would be, contained in records transferred from responsible authorities (public authorities basically) to the National Archives (NA), another place of deposit appointed by the Lord Chancellor or the PRO (NI). It does not apply to that designated as 'open information' for the purposes of s 66. The 'appropriate records' authorities' are the NA and PRO (NI) and the Lord Chancellor. Before making a decision on whether information covered by the section falls within any of the exemptions under Part II concerning confirmation and denial or exemptions from disclosure, the 'responsible authority' (s 15(5)) has to be consulted. These are basically, the Ministers of the Crown, 'other persons', Northern Ireland Ministers of the Crown and Ministers and other persons (in Northern Ireland) appearing to the Lord Chancellor or Northern Ireland Minister to be 'primarily concerned'. Decisions under s 2(1)(b) (confirmation or denial) are determined by the responsible authority, not the appropriate records authority. This is the same for decisions on exemption and disclosure under s 2(2)(b). This provision will not allow disclosure etc of absolute exemptions under s 2(3) (though see s 64(2) above in relation to s 23 information). The Lord Chancellor and the appropriate NI Minister must be consulted before the responsible authority makes any determination that s 2(1)(b) or (2)(b) do not apply. Special provisions apply to responsible authorities which are not, apart from s 15(6), public authorities.

2.66 The Lord Chancellor has to publish under s 46 a code of practice on records management. This was published in November 2002 and revised in 2009 (see below). The IC will deal with complaints relating to refusal of historical records as he does with ordinary requests.

2.67 Some of the exemptions disapply after 30 years (20 when CRGA 2010 applies) and so the historical records are not exempt, they are only exempt as records before that date. This covers: relations within the UK (s 28 – although this will be removed under CRGA 2010, Sch 7 in relation to 20 years and will therefore remain at 30); investigations which an authority has a duty to conduct in relation to criminal charges, ascertainment of guilt, institution of criminal proceedings and any criminal proceedings (s 30(1) (though see below on s 31); court records (s 32); audit functions (s 33); the formulation of government policy-making (s 35); prejudice to the effective conduct of public affairs (s 36 although this will be removed under CRGA 2010 in relation to 20 years and remain at 30 for cases involving Northern Ireland (see para 2.68 below but note the Protection of Freedoms Bill 2011); communications with Her Majesty, members of the Royal Family or Royal Household (s 37(1)(a) although this will be removed under CRGA 2010; see below); legal professional privilege (s 42); and commercial interests (s 43 although this will be removed under CRGA 2010 in relation to 20 years and remain at 30). The duty to inform in writing a requester for information whether it holds information of the description specified under s 1(1)(a) in relation to an historical record shall not be taken to be capable of having any of the effects referred to in s 28(3) (removed as above), 33(3), 36(3) (removed as above), 42(2) or 43(3) removed as above), ie it is not to be taken as revealing the interest which the exemption seeks to protect (see ch 1) (para 2.69 below).

2.68 The CGRA 2010 specifies that information in a historical record cannot be exempt information by virtue of s 36 except in a case falling within s 36(2) (a)(ii) (see para 1.182) or in a case falling within s 36(2)(c) where the prejudice or likely prejudice relates to the effective conduct of public affairs in Northern Ireland. The duty to inform in writing a requester for information whether it holds information of the description specified under s 1(1)(a) in relation to an historical record shall not be taken to be capable of having any of the effects referred to in s 36(3) unless it falls within the two previous provisions.

2.69   Information in CGRA 2010, ss 28, 43 and 36(2)(a)(ii) and (2)(c) will lose their exemption after 30 years under CRGA 2010 and provision is made for the 'neither confirm nor deny' provision in relation to ss 28(1) 43(2) and 36(3) for 30 years likewise. New sub-sections 63(2E) and (2F) create time limits after which the exemptions in the new ss 37(1)(a) to (ad) of the FOIA 2000 no longer apply (see para 1.194). The exemption ceases to apply 20 years after the creation of the record in which the information is contained, or five years after the death of the relevant member of the royal family, whichever is longer. In the case of communications with the royal household falling within the fifth category, the relevant member of the royal family for these purposes is the sovereign reigning when the record in question was created. The amendments made by Sch 7 will not apply to information held by the Northern Ireland Assembly, any Northern Ireland department and any Northern Ireland public authority. The FOIA 2000 will apply to these bodies as if the amendments had not been made. However, under the Protection of Freedoms Bill 2011, the relevant period for NI bodies is 20 years except in the case of s 36(2)(a)(ii) and (2)(c) where the period is 30 years. The period remains at 30 years for ss 28 and 43 and Northern Ireland historical records.

2.70   Historical records within s 37(1)(b) (the conferring of honours) lose their exemption after 60 years. Information within s 31 (law enforcement) is given a 100-year exemption. Information exempt under s 30(1) loses its exemption after 30 years (see above and CGRA 2010 and reduction to 20 years); it is therefore no longer exempt under that section but could be exempt under s 31. A similar provision as above covers compliance with s 1(1)(a) and s 31 although it refers to any record, not historical records. It means that authorities must inform requesters whether they hold information 100 years from the year after which it was created.

2.71   Information contained in a historical record in the PRO or PRO (NI) is not exempt by virtue of s 21 (information accessible by other means)[1] or s 22 (information intended for future publication).

[1]   Public Keeper under a duty to supply.

2.72   Historical records apart from the above are given indefinite exemption. In the case of parliamentary privilege, personal information within s 40(1) or (2) in relation to the first condition (see para 7.54 below), information given in confidence under s 41 or where there is a prohibition on disclosure under s 44, this is not information subject to FOI public interest disclosure or decisions as to disclosure by the IC.[1] Information given an indefinite period of exemption therefore covers: information supplied by or relating to bodies dealing with security matters (although the provisions of s 2(3) do not apply to this information so after 30 (above) years it may be subject to public interest disclosure where it is in the PRO. The following are given indefinite exemption but are subject to public interest disclosure: national security; defence; international relations; the economy; information falling within s 30(2) ie, information obtained or recorded for the purposes of its functions relating to investigations into criminal charges, ascertaining guilt, into criminal proceedings, or civil proceedings arising from any of the above investigations **and** the information relates to the obtaining of information from confidential sources. Health and safety and environmental information are given indefinite exemption. Information covered by Parliamentary privilege is given indefinite exemption and the public interest disclosure provisions do not apply. Personal information as identified in s 40 (s 2(3)(f)) is given an indefinite exemption and is not subject to public interest disclosure, so too is information provided in confidence; information whose disclosure is prohibited by statute, or is incompatible with Community law or would constitute etc a contempt is similarly treated. Historical information given an expansive protection is that which is given an indefinite period of closure and to which the absolute exemptions under s 2(3) apply.

¹ To recall, the IC had no authority over these 'absolute exemptions' and the public authorities may not make discretionary disclosures of such information.

2.73 The Lord Chancellor shall issue and may revise a code of practice for relevant authorities on the practice which it would, in his opinion, be desirable for them to follow in connection with the keeping, management and destruction of their records. Guidance may also be provided on transfer of documents. In exercising these functions the Lord Chancellor shall have regard to the public interest in allowing access to documents. A draft Code was published in June 2000 and a final version in November 2002 which was itself revised in 2009. This states that failure to comply with the Code may lead to breach of one of several statutory provisions under the Public Records Acts and local government legislation. 'Access rights are of limited value if information cannot be found when requested, or, when found, cannot be relied upon as authoritative' (Introduction (iv)) and how poor records create serious risks for an authority. It reminds PAs of the IC's powers under the FOIA. Part One of the Code deals with the practices which PAs subject to the Public Records Act 1958 and Public Records (NI) Act 1923 should follow in relation to the creation, keeping, management and destruction of these records. Part Two concerns arrangements to be followed in reviewing records and in transferring them to the NA, place of deposit or PRO (NI). A policy statement on records management should exist which should be reviewed every three to five years and which would cover electronic records. The 2002 Code also provided that: 'records created by the authority should be arranged in a record keeping system that will enable the authority to obtain the maximum benefit from the quick and easy retrieval of information' (para 8.3). The 2009 Code states that 'Authorities should keep their records in systems that enable records to be stored and retrieved as necessary' (para 9). Guidance is given on storage, security and disposal as well as 'collaborative working' and outsourcing, ie contracting out. Records may be transferred to the NA or to 'places of deposit appointed by the Lord Chancellor' (para 17.2). In reviewing records for public release, authorities should ensure that public records become available to the public at the earliest possible time in accordance with the FOIA and EIR. Guidance is given on exemptions for PAs, the NA and the Advisory Council. Electronic and paper records' keeping systems shall contain descriptive and technical documentation to enable the system and records to be understood and to be operated efficiently and to allow for effective management of records.

2.74   The Public Records Acts are concerned with the maintenance of records which are of historical importance and significance. Most of the records in the NA are open. Of those records in the NA closed for 30 (above) years or more, 'no more than about 1 per cent of its total holdings of 447,000 shelf feet (85 miles)' is unavailable for public inspection.[1] Papers within departments are examined twice to see whether they need to be kept for NA purposes or destroyed. An Advisory Council under the Master of the Rolls advises on public records (Advisory Council on National Records and Archives). This has representatives of historians, readers, IT experts and lawyers as well as representatives from the three major political parties. Most documents are delivered to readers within 30 minutes at the NA at Kew. The NA catalogue became available over the Internet in 1999 containing over eight million individual descriptions. In 2011 the figure was 11 million. The NA had taken the lead in records management within government departments.

[1]   *Roper*, in *Open Government* eds R Chapman and M Hunt (1987), p 88. See S Healy 'Freedom of Information and its Impact on Archives' in R Chapman and M Hunt (eds) *Open Government in a Theoretical and Practical Context eds* (2006).

2.75   The Statistics and Registration Service Act 2007 makes provision for the creation of a new body, the Statistics Board, with a statutory responsibility to promote and safeguard the production and publication of official statistics that serve the public good. The Act establishes the Board as a Non-Ministerial Department, acting at arm's length from Ministers, composed of a majority of non-executive members. The Board's responsibilities will cover the whole UK statistical system, including England, Scotland, Wales and Northern Ireland. The Board replaces the Office for National Statistics. The Government Statistical Service (GSS) was maintained and is a professional grouping of around 7,000 civil servants who collect, analyse and disseminate statistics, working in the Board, in government departments and agencies and in the Devolved Administrations in Scotland and Wales. There are also in existence departmental Heads of Profession for Statistics (HoPs) in government departments or agencies that produce National Statistics.

PROVISION OF INFORMATION TO PARLIAMENT[1]

2.76   One cannot overestimate the importance in our constitutional history and practice of the present topic. The Major government's failure to keep Parliament informed of changes in export licensing arrangements for dual use equipment was one of the central issues in the inquiry by Sir Richard Scott into *Matrix Churchill*. Parliament voted for an invasion of Iraq on the basis of incomplete and inadequate information leading ultimately to the Chilcot inquiry. On assuming the office of Speaker in October 2000, Michael Martin MP criticised the government for publishing policy statements on the Web and for leaking statements to the press before announcing them to Parliament.[2] Annual reports are made to Parliament on departmental performance. To do this whole subject anything like justice would take us far away from our current remit in describing access, or the lack of it, to government information. The legislative process is one that can provide, or ought to provide, detailed information behind government Bills. The committee stages, now before renamed legislative committees, in particular, can be the place for detailed probing and examination, and for Private Bills[3] and Hybrid Bills[4] there is opportunity after Second Reading for petitioners against the Bill to present their case in an oral hearing with legal representation. Earlier publication of Bills and pre-presentation scrutiny have increased opportunities for informed debate as has the special examination of Bills by select committees as in the case of the Constitutional Reform Bill (2003–04) by the Lords Select Committee on Constitutional Reform. The on-line possibilities of pre-legislative scrutiny were debated at HC Debs Vol 416 col 1 (6 January 2004). As early as 1979, the Electricity Bill was published in draft form. Explanatory information on both legislation and statutory instruments has improved enormously in recent years.[5]

[1] hcinfo@parliament.uk.
[2] (2000) *Guardian*, 31 October.
[3] Bills relating to a special, and not a public, matter.
[4] A Public Bill which affects a particular private interest in a manner differently from the private interests of other persons or bodies of the same category or class.
[5] See *Parliament, Politics and Law-Making: Issues and Developments in the Legislative Process* Hansard Society (2004).

Question Time

2.77 The system of Westminster government has developed the idea of ministerial responsibility to the House of Commons as the primary means for ensuring the accountability of government and its administration. Parliamentary Questions (PQs) are central to this process.[1] The abuse by MPs of the process of asking questions in return for cash payments led to the establishment of the Committee on Public Standards originally under Lord Nolan, a Law Lord. The present chair is Sir Christopher Kelly, a former civil servant.[2] The weaknesses of PQs as a means of extracting responsibility and accountability have been well noted elsewhere,[3] but it is a central feature of our constitutional practice. The High Court has ruled that the undesirability of answering a PQ with reference to a specific application and suggested answer to the application of the FOIA risks conflict between the judiciary and Parliament. The minister risks 'creat[ing] the potential for a judicial ruling to the contrary effect, as indeed happened in this case: implicitly, and obviously, the effect of the Tribunal's decision is that the Parliamentary answer given by Mr Boateng, that the gateway reviews were exempt from disclosure under the Act, was wrong. It is, I think, undesirable for the potentiality for such conflicts to be created.'[4]

[1] See the Public Administration Committee HC 622 (2001–02), HC 1086 (2001–02), HC 136 (2002–03) and HC Debs Vol 416 col 151 8 January 2004 on Parliamentary Questions. From

the same committee HC 355 (2003–04) *Taming the Prerogative: Ministerial Responsibility and Parliamentary Questions* and Government Reply HC 1262 (2003–04) and HC 449 I and II (2004–05); and *Strengthening Ministerial Accountability to Parliament* HC 422 (2003–04) and Government Reply Cm 6187. PQs cost in the region of £6 million per session. Also Government Response to Treasury Committee report *Accountability of Departments to Parliament* HC 149 (2002–03). See PAC HC 122 (2006–07) *Politics and Administration: Ministers and Civil Servants* and HC 1063 (2010–12) *Improving Effectiveness of Parliamentary Scrutiny* and Government Reply to HC 800 (2010–11).

2   In Scotland, the Scottish Commissions and Commissioners etc Act 2010 establishes the Commission for Ethical Standards in Public Life in Scotland.

3   Most dramatically in Scott's Report of the Inquiry into the Export of Defence Equipment and Dual-Use Goods to Iraq and Related Prosecutions HC 115 (1996–97), vols I–V.

4   *Office of Government Commerce v IC* [2008] EWHC 737 (Admin).

2.78 MPs can ask questions – lots of them. These PQs may require an oral answer in the House from the responsible minister, notice of which must be given to the clerks at the Table[1] or in the Table office. The details of the procedure are contained in *Erskine May*.[2] 1924 questions were made for oral answer and 25,467 tabled for written answer according to the Order papers in 2009–10. In the past the total for questions asked has been as high as 80,000 or so PQs asked and answered each year. The House of Commons *Factsheet* of 2010 states that over 57,000 questions were asked for written answer in 2007–08. Procedures were altered after reports from the Select Committee on Procedure and the Select Committee on Modernisation were debated and approved in the Commons on 29 October 2002. Further reforms have been made. Since 2003, 'cross-cutting' questions have been allowed involving several departments. Further reforms include a split question time with the second part, comprising about a quarter of the time, devoted to topical questions following a recommendation from the Modernisation Committee in 2007. The list specifying when ministers are to answer questions – the question rota – is decided by the government and prepared by the Table office. Questions are subject to a computer shuffle relating to the department to which questions are put and the successful questions are listed in order in the Notice of Questions section of the vote bundle – the blue pages. Notice of questions must be given no later than three days before questions for that department but they may be tabled at any time after the previous session involving that department – the precise timing depends upon the day it was given. Fridays and weekends are not included. Question Time lasts for an hour of business on Mondays (2.35 pm), Tuesdays (2.35 pm), Wednesdays (11.35 am) and Thursdays (10.35 am). Supplementary questions may be asked, first by the MP asking the original question, then, at the Speaker's invitation, by other MPs, usually alternating between government and opposition MPs. When the first question is concluded, the MP with the second question is called, and so on. Those left unanswered at the end of the Question Time proceed to a written answer printed in a subsequent issue of Hansard. The Speaker controls the process and about 15–20 questions are answered each session. The Prime Minister's Question Time now takes place on a Wednesday at 12.00 noon lasting for about 30 minutes. PQs should not involve matters that are devolved.

1   The Table of the House directly in front of the Speaker.

2   *Treatise on the Law, Privileges, Proceedings and Usage of Parliament* (23rd edn) (2004) McKay, Sir W. and Wilson, R. pp 339 et seq. See also House of Commons Factsheet *Parliamentary Questions*

Revised August 2010. See generally: J Griffith et al *Parliament: Functions, Practice and Procedure* (2nd edn, 2003) ch 6.

2.79 Ministers apart from the Prime Minister on average face questions about once every three to four weeks. A question should either seek information or press for action; it should not deal with opinion, 'though it may be based on facts for the accuracy of which the Member is himself responsible'. It must relate to a matter for which the minister to whom it is addressed is responsible as a minister. Legal opinions must not be sought. A list of questions or topics that will not be answered is available.[1] Matters within the responsibility of devolved bodies are not subject to PQs at Westminster.

[1] See the Report of the Select Committee on Public Administration: *Ministerial Accountability and Parliamentary Questions* HC 820 (1997–98) and Fourth Report (1998–99) and HC 61 (2000–01) and para 2.77, note 1 above.

2.80 A PQ which has already been asked and fully answered cannot normally be asked again. Where a Minister has refused to take some action or to provide information, the same question may be asked again after three months. There are a number of subjects such as the security services or matters of commercial confidence on which Ministers have consistently refused to answer. A refusal prevents a question being admitted on such a subject, though Ministers may be asked once each Session if they will now answer questions on a subject previously blocked.

2.81 The rules on blocking PQs were amended in 1993. Blocking still prevents a PQ being tabled if a Minister has previously refused to answer it but only if the refusal has been made in the current session. The practice of refusing to answer PQs 'of their nature secret' or where there was a persistent refusal was amended but Ministers still persisted in pre-1993 practice. The government also undertook to answer PQs on the same basis as requests for information under 1994 Code on Access to information as revised, ie where it would be provided under the Code, it would be provided in answer to PQs.[1] The judicial response to answering PQs in line with the FOIA anticipated responses was set out above (para 2.77). It is the duty of the Clerks to ensure that the questions comply with these and other rules of the House. Their method is to advise a Member, if his question appears to breach a rule, how by amendment he can bring it into order. If a Member is not satisfied with the advice given to him, he may have his question submitted to the Speaker, whose decision about admissibility is final. Only with very few questions in each Session is it necessary to go to this length.[2]

[1] Reversing original plan; see HC 820 1997–98 and Fourth Report above.
[2] House of Commons Factsheet above 2010, p 3.

2.82 The order of questions is dealt with by a ballot – the 'five o'clock [now 12.30 pm] shuffle'. Questions are put in a ballot and selected electronically. The number of PQs that may be put to a department was reduced to a new quota – and MPs are limited in the number of questions they may ask (eight in every ten sitting days, two in any one day, and only one question may be put to the same minister on any day).

2.83   The department concerned first receives warning of a question on the morning after the question has been tabled. The officials responsible for the department's parliamentary business extract their own questions from the Notice Paper and send them, in specially marked folders, to the officials within their departments who deal with the subject matter of the questions. Drafts of answers for the minister's consideration are then made. If approved, it goes forward for inclusion in the answer file to be used on the day the question is answered in the House. Oral questions are far more onerous than written answers as civil servants have to give full background briefing on which a minister can base his answers to supplementary questions, and every ramification must be anticipated from the factual to the highly political. Questions may well be inspired by a minister or put down by colleagues to give full publicity to successes and to announce popular decisions. If the question is directed to the wrong minister, it will be re-routed to the appropriate one. The content of the reply is a matter for the minister.

2.84   *Ministerial Accountability and PQs* has been the subject of several Select Committee reports.[1] These contain details of PQs that have been blocked in the respective sessions. 'Will write' answers – usually published in Hansard but longer replies are in the deposited papers collection (http://deposits. parliament.uk/). *The Ministerial Code on Conduct and Guidance* (below) spells out that Ministers have a duty to account to Parliament by giving accurate and truthful information correcting any error at the earliest opportunity. Ministers who knowingly mislead will be expected to offer their resignation to the Prime Minister. Ministers should be as open as possible with Parliament only refusing to disclose information when this would be against the public interest.And resolutions have been made in the House on the nature of a Minister's duty.[2] It was a matter of some consternation that before the summer recess in 2004, the government announced that from the end of the 2003–04 session, those PQs that were unanswered would not survive the session and would have to be asked again.

[1]   Select Committee on Public Administration HC 820 (1997–98), Fourth Report (1998–99) and HC 61 (2000–01) and see para 2.77, note 1 above and HC 449 I & II (2004–05) and GR HC 853 (2005–06).
[2]   Resolution of the House of Commons, Official Report (6th series) 292 Vol 292, cols 1046–7, 19 March 1997.

Urgent questions (private notice questions)

2.85   In the case of an emergency, a procedure allows an expedited form of questioning. An MP must apply to the Speaker before noon on the day on which an answer is required. The department concerned is informed immediately. The rules above apply to private notice questions (PNQs) with two additional criteria: it must be urgent, and it must be of public importance. One example would be an immediate threat to the liberty of the subject; another airport security. They are dealt with after Question Time and only about four or five PNQs a month have averaged in recent sessions.[1]

[1]   This does not include routine PQs from the Leader of the Opposition to the Prime Minister.

Written answer questions (WAQs)

2.86 There is no limit to the number of questions hich may be tabled for written answers. As many as 250 may be tabled in a single day. The questions, governed by the same rules as oral questions, amount to about 94 per cent of all questions (the total being around 35,000–52,000 in each session prior to 2000; now about 77,000). A WAQ is usually dated for two days after it is tabled; the question is usually answered within seven days of that date. Where an answer on a specified day is required, it must be signified as a 'Named Day' or 'Priority' question, with an 'N' in the Order Book. It receives priority, but to obtain this the MP has to give two days' notice – the answer may be that an answer will be given as soon as possible!

2.87 When Next Steps agencies were established ministers devolved to the appropriate Chief Executive responsibility for answering PQs. They can only supply written answers. Until 1992, these replies were placed in the Library and House of Commons Information Office, although after that date they are published in Hansard.

2.88 In 2003–04, it was estimated that the total annual cost for answering all questions was £6 million. 'Inordinate expense' is a frequent excuse for not providing a written answer to a question, eg over £750. This is the limit (disproportionate cost threshold) for dealing with a PQ. FOIA requests under the fees arrangements in relation to central departments and Parliament have a fees limit of £600. The average cost at December 2008 was £149 for a written answer £410 for an oral question.

Papers

2.89 Many research papers into PQs are Deposited Papers and together with other unpublished papers are placed in the House of Commons library. Papers deposited after 2007 may be available on http://deposits.parliament.uk/ All House of Commons Papers from 1980 onwards are indexed on the House of Commons Library Parliamentary Database (PIMS). Many papers are placed on www.parliament.uk under *Publications and Records*. Papers may be accessed through the House of Commons Library Service. They are available to all MPs and may be restricted to MPs. Ministers 'will write' replies to MPs after a question are available to MPs. The public has no access to the library but some of the work produced in papers by the research staff is publicly available. Older papers, over 30 years old, are available to the public via the Parliamentary Archives (formerly House of Lords Record Office). Requests to the House of Commons library for Deposited Papers from a member of the public are referred to the parliamentary clerk of the depositing department who may well arrange for the policy division concerned to send it to the requester or to allow access. Many such documents are published by HMSO as non-parliamentary or departmentally circulated papers.

2.90   Papers laid before the House which are not ordered to be printed and unprinted Command Papers are available to the public through Parliamentary Archives. After 1955, unpublished indexes exist direct from the subject and, after 1982, papers are retrievable on POLIS.[1] Readers are reminded that the FOIA 2000 now covers documents of both Houses of Parliament, subject to parliamentary privilege.

[1]   On the House of Commons Library, see Factsheet G (18 September 2010) http://www. parliament.uk/factsheets and note the Indexing and Data Management Service (IDMS). A variety of Factsheets deal with publication. POLIS is available on subscription www.polis.parliament.uk.

2.91   Since 2006, arrangements have been in place to answer written questions in the recess in September and three days are presently set aside to table questions and three to give replies.

Debates

2.92   Time for debates is arranged through the Whips of the government and opposition parties. Government controls most of this time. Opposition days allow for 20 days to be allotted for opposition business. A third block, for private members, is allocated by a ballot for private members' motions and not by Whips. At the end of each day, the government moves the adjournment of the House and an MP's particular subject may be debated. This is the Adjournment Debate and it lasts for up to 30 minutes. MPs are selected by a private ballot conducted by the Speaker except for the Thursday Adjournment Debate when a member is chosen by the Speaker. An Early Day Motion (EDM) may be put down by an MP although no date is fixed for debate. In the vast majority of cases there is no prospect of these motions being debated. Any number of MPs may sign the motion.[1] The full text of EDMs since 1997–98 is available at http:// edmi.parliament.uk?edmi/ Since 2000, adjournment debates may take place in Westminster Hall lasting between three and four and a half hours. Subjects are chosen by ballot through application to the Speaker's Office. The select committee on reform of the House of Commons reported it was time to give members in a committee of the House of Commons greater powers over debates.[2] In 2010, a Back-bench Business Committee was established with responsibility for arranging debates on 35 days. The chair is appointed after a secret ballot of MPs not by patronage. The other seven members are also elected by secret ballots but using a system to ensure overall party and gender balance. Elections take place every parliamentary year. Plans to move to a House Business Committee which would decide weekly agendas in the Commons including government business are moving slowly. The coalition government has committed itself to establish this by the end of the third year of Parliament (2013). A development supported by the Speaker was the use of e-petitions whereby if 100,000 petitions were received on a government e-petition web site this would trigger a debate in Parliament. It came to being just as riots caused huge disruption in English cities in August 2011.[3]

[1]   Factsheet P3 June 2010 *Early Day Motions*. See generally *Revitalising the Chamber: the Role of the Backbencher* Modernisation Committee HC 337 (2006–07).

2   HC 1117 (2008–09) and HC 372 (2009–10).
3   http://www.direct.gov.uk/en/Diol1/DoItOnline/DG_066327.

Publications

2.93 Government publishes Green Papers and White Papers on policy proposals or as the basis for an annual parliamentary debate. It publishes consultative documents on important issues, planned policy decisions, to stimulate debate or to test the water. It publishes statistical data[1] and background papers – an example was the Croham Directive exhorting greater publication of background information. Under the FOIA 2000 and under the Code on Access it published various background papers to policy making. Public bodies have to publish publication schemes under the FOIA 2000. The Government publishes its responses, memoranda and oral evidence of government departments to select committees of the Commons which examine the policy, administration and expenditure of government departments. Since 1991, departments have published annual reports as part of the annual expenditure process (see ch 10 below). These are published as Command Papers. Such papers have their provenance from ministers of the Crown and 'are laid before Parliament as conveying information or decisions which the government think should be drawn to the attention of one or both Houses'.[2] The main types of such papers are:

(a) treaties;

(b) White Papers (ie government proposals for legislation), policy statements, and some annual reviews (eg defence);

(c) most government replies to select committee reports (see below);

(d) reports of royal commissions (but not normally the evidence thereof);

(e) reports of some major committees of inquiry, and other commissions and non-parliamentary bodies;

(f) state papers (including communiques, etc);

(g) annual reports, statistics, etc of certain bodies; and

(h) some, but not the majority of consultative documents (sometimes called Green Papers).[3]

1   D Englefield *Whitehall and Westminster: Government Informs Parliament* (1985).
2   House of Commons Papers Factsheet revised August 2010 (www.parliament.uk/factsheets). On privilege, see para 2.95, note 1 below.
3   House of Commons Factsheet *Commons Papers* (August 2010).

2.94 House of Commons papers include, as a basic principle, papers arising out of the deliberation of the House and its committees or those required for its work. The actual corpus is wider than this, however, the main categories being:

(a) select committee papers–

    (i)   reports of select committees,

    (ii) evidence taken by select committees,

    (iii) minutes of proceedings of select committees (government replies to their reports may appear as special reports of the committee concerned);

(b) minutes of proceedings of standing committees;

(c) returns to addresses by the House;

(d) estimates and appropriation, etc, accounts;

(e)   certain annual and other reports;[1] and/or accounts; and

(f)   House returns.

[1]   Those that are not Command papers.

2.95 'Proceedings in Parliament' are covered by absolute privilege in defamation proceedings, or indeed any other legal proceedings.[1] Privilege for publication of Parliamentary papers published under the authority of Parliament is governed by the Parliamentary Papers Act 1840 which confers absolute privilege on Parliamentary papers and reports. Command papers may be brought within this protection if produced to Parliament. Fair and accurate extracts of such papers in press or media reports are protected by qualified privilege under s 3 and the Broadcasting Act 1990, s 203(1) and Sch 20(1). On the question of privilege concerning Parliamentary proceedings, s 13 of the Defamation Act 1996, allows an MP to waive privilege in order to enable the MP to bring proceedings in defamation. The Court of Appeal has ruled that the report of the Commissioner for Standards finding that an MP had received cash for asking questions and which had been adopted by the Committee on Standards and Privileges did not prevent the MP waiving his privilege by virtue of s 1, Art 9 of the Bill of Rights 1689 under s 13. The court added that the plaintiff's action did not seek to impugn the procedures in Parliament. The court was not challenging Parliament's authority and was not seeking to judge the procedural quality of an earlier decision of Parliament or one of its officers. The court therefore refused to strike out the plaintiff's action which the plaintiff – Neil Hamilton – subsequently lost. On appeal to the House of Lords, the reasoning of the Court of Appeal, and Lord Woolf's views in particular were criticised by the Law Lords. Section 13 was the determining factor and allowed an MP to waive his rights to privilege. The wider statements of Lord Woolf would have meant that the court would have questioned material which was placed before a Commons Committee which is precisely what the courts are jealous to prevent to avoid any conflict.[2]

[1]   These are not self-explanatory terms: On privilege, see A Bradley and K Ewing *Constitutional and Administrative Law* (15th edn, 2010) ch 11 and Leopold (1990) Public Law 183. The privilege could allow an MP to obtain an unfair advantage in litigation if the adversary was unable to rely upon crucial evidence for the case thereby causing the court to stay the action.

[2]   *Hamilton v Al Fayed* [2000] 2 All ER 224, HL. Section 13 was a response to the Privy Council decision in: *Prebble v Television New Zealand Ltd* [1994] 3 All ER 407; for criticism of s 13 see HL 43-I, HC 214-I (1998–99). Where the extent of a privilege is disputed is for judicial determination but infringements are determined by the House (*Pepper v Hart* [1993] AC 595, 645). There have been attempts by injunction to prevent the press reporting on what has been said in Parliament which is likely to be a breach of privilege. Statements by members which breach the *sub judice* rule are within the jurisdiction of the Standards and Privileges Committee.

2.96 Hansard is an independent record of the proceedings of the House of Commons in the Chamber and its standing committees. The report of one day's sitting (up to about 10.00 pm) is on MPs' breakfast tables the next day. It is also available on the Parliament website: www.parliament.uk.

2.97 The press were first allocated seats in the public gallery in 1803, although their presence in the Commons goes back to an earlier period. Prior to this in 1762, the House had resolved that publication in the press of members' speeches in the House was a breach of privilege. In December 1987, the House of Commons took the decision to broadcast its proceedings on television.[1] Broadcasting commenced in November 1989.

[1] First Report: Commons Select Committee on TV. Procedure, 17 May 1989. TV broadcasting on an experimental basis has taken place in the Lords since 1968. See the Modernisation Committee's *Connecting Parliament with the Public* HC 69 (2004–05) for a discussion on the eponymous theme. See also: *Hansard Commission on the Communication of Parliamentary Democracy – Members Only? Parliament in the Public Eye*. Hansard Society (2005).

House of Comons publication scheme

2.98   Under FOIA, both Houses are separate public authorities and each has its own publication scheme. The following classes of information are published under the Commons scheme:[1]
1.   Business papers of the House of Commons
 1.1 Official Report (Hansard) (Daily parts, weekly parts, bound volumes and indexes)
 1.2 Standing Committee Official Reports (Standing Committee Hansard)
 1.3 Special Standing Committees Memoranda of Evidence
 1.4 Standing Committee Minutes of Proceedings
 1.5 Daily Business Papers (Vote Bundle)
 1.6 House of Commons Journal and Indexes
 1.7 Parliamentary Papers: Sessional Indexes
 1.8 Public and Private Bills
 1.9 Sessional Returns
 1.10 Registers of Interests
 1.11 Standing Orders of the House of Commons
 1.12 Codes of Conduct for Members of Parliament
 1.13 Select and Joint Committee Reports
 1.14 Select and Joint Committee Minutes of Evidence, Report Appendices and Published Memoranda
 1.15 Select and Joint Committee Minutes of Proceedings
 1.16 Select and Joint Committee Press Notices
2.   Information and Services for the Public
 2.1 House of Commons Information Office Factsheets (removed in latest version)
 2.2 Weekly Information Bulletins and Sessional Information Digests
 2.3 Guides for Select Committee Witnesses
 2.4 Visitor Information
 2.5 Educational Material from the Parliamentary Education Unit
 2.6 Recordings of the House of Commons
3.   Research and Background Information
 3.1 Library Research Papers (removed from latest version)
 3.2 House of Commons Library Documents
 3.3 Parliamentary Office of Science and Technology Publications
4.   Administration of the House of Commons

4.1   Domestic Committee Reports (removed from latest version)
4.2   Administration Committee Minutes of Evidence, Report Appendices and Published Memoranda
4.3   Administration and Finance and Services Committee Minutes of Proceedings
4.4   House of Commons Commission Annual Reports and Corporate Business Plan
4.5   House of Commons Annual Resource Accounts
4.6   Occupational Health and Safety Policies
4.7   Staff Handbook
4.8   Members' Allowances and Travel Allowance Costs
4.9   Procurement.
4.10 Freedom of Information Request Logs
5.2   Catalogue and Finding Aids

[1]   http://www.parliament.uk/mps-lords-and-offices/offices/commons/commons-foi/classes.

Ministers

2.99   The *Ministerial Code*, which was revised in 2010, is a detailed statement of ministerial practice which Ministers are expected to follow in the letter as well as the spirit. It constitutes guidance on good practice and is not a legal code. Detailed guidance is contained in section 9 (formerly Part 3) of the Code on 'Ministers and Parliament'. Section 3 contains advice on use of special advisers – a subject which has generated reports from the Committee on Standards in Public Life (*Ninth Report* Cm 5775) and other bodies (see para 2.113). Ministers are reminded that it is Parliament where the 'most important' announcements are to be made. Section 8 is concerned with 'Ministers and the Presentation of Policy'. The No10 press office should where possible be consulted and clear in draft 'all major announcements, speeches, press releases and new policy initiatives 24 hours in advance. The reference to the Prime Minister has gone. Prime Minister Blair's Code was examined by the Commons Committee on Public Administration at the same time as Peter Mandelson was forced to resign over his alleged role in obtaining passports for the Hinduja brothers (HC 821 (1999–2000) and was subsequently revised. In ch 1 (para 1.7) reference was made to the recommendations of the Committee on Standards in Public Life concerning inquiries into allegations of breaches of the code by Ministers. The Committee also recommended an Independent Adviser on Ministerial Interests to advise on political conflicts of interests. The Adviser would be able to ask questions about the organisation of business within departments and would keep a record of Ministerial interests. Information on the facts of interests would be published as well as guidance for Ministers (Cm 5775, ch 5). Subsequently, the remit of the adviser was widened (HC 381 (2007–08) and GR HC 1056 (2007–08)). The following are set out as guiding principles for Ministers and the Code has to be set beside the coalition agreement of May 2010:

'i)   Collective responsibility applies to all government ministers;

ii)   Ministers have a duty to Parliament to account, and be held to account, for the policies, decisions and actions of their departments and "next steps" agencies;[1]

iii) it is of paramount importance that Ministers give accurate and truthful information to Parliament, correcting any inadvertent error at the earliest opportunity. Ministers who knowingly mislead Parliament will be expected to offer their resignation to the Prime Minister;[2]

iv) Ministers should be as open as possible with Parliament and the public, refusing to provide information only when disclosure would not be in the public interest which should be decided in accordance with the relevant statutes and the FOIA 2000;

v) Ministers should similarly require civil servants who give evidence before Parliamentary Committees on their behalf and under their direction to be as helpful as possible in providing accurate, truthful and full information in accordance with the duties and responsibilities of civil servants as set out in the Civil Service Code;

vi) Ministers must ensure that no conflict arises, or appears to arise, between their public duties and their private interests;

vii) Ministers should not accept any gift or hospitality which might, or might reasonably appear to, compromise their judgement or place them under an improper obligation;

viii) Ministers in the House of Commons must keep separate their roles as Minister and constituency Member;

ix) Ministers must not use government resources for Party political purposes. They must uphold the political impartiality of the Civil Service and not ask civil servants to act in any way which would conflict with the Civil Service Code as set out in the CRGA 2010.'

Allegations of a breach of the code will be referred to the 'independent adviser on ministers' interests' by the Prime Minister after consulting the Cabinet Secretary where further investigation is warranted. This procedure was not followed when the Defence Secretary, Liam Fox, was investigated in 2011 because of his relationship with an unofficial 'adviser', Adam Werritty, who had not been given security clearance. The Cabinet Secretary investigated the affair. Subsequently, permanent secretaries would have direct access to the Prime Minister and Cabinet Secretary to report misgivings about ministers' conduct. The posts of Cabinet Secretary and Head of the Home Civil Service were also to be split.

[1] The position of agencies can be a complicating factor in establishing who is responsible for what, as the Home Secretary's experience illustrated when the UK Borders Agency relaxed passport entry controls in 2011.

[2] See HC Deb (19 March 1997) col 1046 and HL Deb (20 March 1997) col 1055. According to PAC, Ministers are under a duty to give an account and to be held to account HC 313 (1995–96).

GOVERNMENT PUBLICITY AND THE MEDIA AND PRESS

2.100 The use by the government of the media, the operation of the press lobby and press and information officers takes us beyond our present brief, although it is a subject causing increasing concern. Like the former Conservative governments in the 1980s and 1990s the New Labour government was also accused of abusing the position of its use of press officers.[1] The relationship between government and the media has also caused numerous controversies including the use by the government in 1988 of its powers to ban the broadcasting of certain subjects and information[2] and the explosive relationship between the Director General of the BBC and the PM Press Secretary over the role of the BBC in the Gilligan Radio 4 report about 'sexing up' intelligence on Iraqi weapons of mass destruction (WMD). These events centred on the death of David Kelly, a specialist on WMD in notorious circumstances, events that were investigated by Lord Hutton at the PM's behest although the request was formally made by the Secretary of State for Constitutional Affairs, aka the Lord Chancellor.[3] 'Spin', it was claimed, had become a pre-occupation of government.[4] Central to the promotion of spin it was alleged was the Prime Minister's communications director, Alastair Campbell. Under the coalition government, the Prime Minister's communications director Andy Coulson had to resign because of his former position as editor of the *News of the World* during a period when there had been extensive use of private investigators by the newspaper to obtain personal information that had been illegally hacked. Coulson claimed to know nothing about such usage. He was subsequently arrested in relation to these events. Coulson's deputy editor at the paper had also taken up a position as a consultant for Scotland Yard at a time when the police vigorously refused to conduct inquiries into the hacking allegations. The Metropolitan Police Commissioner, Sir Paul Stephenson, subsequently resigned.

[1]   See HC 770 (1997–98) and *Government Reply* HC 162 (1998–99).
[2]   See *Brind v Secretary of State for the Home Department* [1991] 1 All ER 720, HL.
[3]   HC 247 (2003–04). See the Public Administration Committee HC 274 (2003–04).
[4]   T.Daintith 'Spin: a Constitutional and Legal Analysis' (2001) 7 *European Public Law* 593.

2.101   The BBC is not a spokesperson for the government. The BBC's independence is guaranteed by the Charter (Cm 6925, 2006). Hutton's report into the death of David Kelly was critical of editorial control at the BBC and led to the resignation of the Chair of the Board of Governors and the Chief Executive and to the reorganisation of the BBC. The BBC Trust is the body appointed under its Charter to oversee the work of the BBC and to promote the public interest. It has a Chair. The executive board under a Chairman delivers the BBC's services in accordance with priorities and strategic directions set by the Trust. The Trust makes protocols setting out in greater detail its responsibilities and on engaging with fee-payers and on openness and transparency. Its chief executive is the Director General who is also its editor in chief. The corporation may enter into framework agreements with the Secretary of State which are binding upon the BBC but which are subject to the terms of the charter. In the event of conflict, the charter prevails. The BBC exists to serve the public interest and to promote its six public purposes. Its licence fee is subject to periodical negotiation with the government and was set in October 2010 for six years.

2.102   Cabinet Office Guidance on communications – Propriety Guidance – has been issued on a regular basis since 1989 and the present guidance dates from 2006. The revisions have been made in the light of the growth in the volume of government publicity, and are concerned with the conventions governing publicity and that the mechanisms for ensuring propriety should be observed, as well as value for money. Specific guidance is published before national, local or EU elections. In all cases Ministers should follow the advice on publicity in the Ministerial Code. Civil servants should follow the Civil Service Code remaining impartial and objective. Political advertising is governed by the Communications Act 2003 regulated by Ofcom and this sets out limits on information campaigns – they should not be partial or promote a government policy or directed towards a political end. Guidance is provided on seeking sponsorship.

¹ Government Publicity Cabinet Office, May 1989. See the National Audit Office's Report: *Publicity Services for Government Departments* HC 46 (1989–90). The NAO found that departments and agencies spent about £200 million pa on publicity. Government departments 'are amongst the biggest spenders on publicity in the UK'. See *Central Government Conventions on Publicity and Advertising* (1997).

2.103 Under 'propriety', the main conventions require that government publicity:
(a) should be relevant to government responsibilities;
(b) should be objective and explanatory, not tendentious or polemical;
(c) should not be, or not be liable to, misrepresentation as being party political; and
(d) should be conducted in an economic and relevant way, having regard to the need to be able to justify the costs as expenditure of public funds.

Offficials should speak on the record wherever possible and act professionally, avoiding party political content. Impartial and objective presentation should be aimed for. Advice is given on dealing with Ministers, announcing new policies, The guidance covers both paid and unpaid publicity. The former includes: advertising, software and filmed presentations, leaflets, use of the internet, and exhibitions in particular.

2.104 The reviews have been undertaken during a period when government had become 'one of the largest purchasers of paid publicity, and, as well as providing general information for the public, uses publicity to influence the social behaviour of individuals and the economic behaviour of individuals and businessmen'. Government publicity should be aimed at 'informing the public' even when seeking to influence behaviour and should not 'image build' the government or ministers. There is nothing new in government 'spin'.

2.105 In cases of paid publicity those responsible for the proposal need to be able to respond persuasively to the following:
(i) make sure that the topic is relevant to the government's responsibilities;
(ii) make sure that the resources used are proportional to the objectives, affordable and represent good value for money;
(iii) make sure that the channels and media are targeted effectively to make best use of resources;
(iv) ensure there are precise goals and precise targets;
(v) set out clear success measures and ways in which they will be evaluated, especially where publicity aims to change the behaviour of individuals;
(vi) check whether the publicity required can be achieved through existing channels (eg Parliamentary announcement, ministerial speech, regular publication);
(vii) encourage creativity to make the most of limited budgets;
(viii)stick to facts and avoid political bias;

(ix) make sure the communication is not used for party political purposes;

(x) keep a record of the options considerd for the campaign and the rationale for a decision taken;

(xi) observe Parliamentray privilege, particularly when arranging publicity for White Papers or similar documents;

(xii) remember that not all legislative proposals obtain Parliamentary approval.

2.106 In departmental arrangements involving heads of department, heads of information and departmental finance divisions there should be little need to refer to central departments, ie Cabinet Office and the Treasury. This must occur where central reference is mandatory (paid publicity in advance of legislative approval); where it is novel or contentious; where a minister, head of department or head of information wants a second opinion.

2.107 In the future, responsibility for provision of central advice on the conventions will be provided through the Cabinet Secretary's Office for propriety questions, and in the relevant Treasury expenditure division for value for money issues. The division of subjects will be as follows:[1]

Cabinet Office:	relevance objectivity propriety non-polemical non-party political	Treasury:	production/distribution in an economic way and a value for money justified use of public funds

[1] The Chief Secretary of the Treasury acts as a point of reference at ministerial level and adjudicates on conflicting departmental approaches.

2.108 Public relations or similar consultancies should not be used 'if the relevant skills are available within government' and a list of criteria are to be considered before considering the appointment of such consultancies, including adequate supervision and 'demonstrably objective and thorough arrangements for appointment'.[1]

[1] Government Publicity, above, p 8.

2.109 The Guidance covers use of direct marketing, which was being used increasingly to communicate with particular businesses and audiences, including use by the former Data Protection Commissioner (DPC), to reach small firms and for the AIDS campaign. Unsolicited distribution of material requiring, but which has not obtained, parliamentary approval will be considered improper. It must be appropriate, not over-intrusive, there should be suitable address lists available within guidelines laid down by the Information Commissioner and it should not coincide with another department approaching the same audience over that period. The Guidance offers advice on public relations and consultancies and it should be asked whether the in-house expertise could suffice. Special care should be taken on subjects concerning commercial and legal sensitivity, market sensitivity, criminal matters, court reporting restrictions, contempt of court, civil litigation and judicial review proceedings. The legislative context including freedom of information, data protection, disability, copyright and the use of the Welsh language.

2.110 Government publicity over the former community charge was challenged as unlawful in May 1989 because of allegedly serious inaccuracies. The Divisional Court ruled that it only had limited powers of intervention, viz where publicity or guidance mistook the law or was manifestly inaccurate or misleading. Such an 'exceptional power' of review should not be exercised in a grey area between what was, and was not, acceptable.[1]

1   *R v Secretary of State for the Environment, ex p Greenwich London Borough Council* (1989) Times, 17 May. See also *Gillick v West Norfolk and Wisbech Area Health Authority* [1985] 3 All ER 402, HL. NB HL 105 (2010–11) Merits Committee On The Local Authority Code Of Practice On Publicity and HC 834 (2010–11) Proposed Code Of Recommended Practice On Local Authority Publicity, A Government Reply.

2.111 It should be noted that the use of publicity here is controlled by conventions and guidelines, whereas for the case of local government it has been regulated by legislation (see ch 4). The sixth Report from the Committee on Standards in Public Life, chaired originally by Lord Nolan and subsequently by Lord Neill QC, reported on the use by government of political advisers and the subject has featured extensively in more recent reports (para 2.113 below).[1]

1   Cm 4557, vols I and II (2000).

2.112 Although the methods of communication continually develop and change, including use of all forms of information communications, and government disseminates increasing amounts of information, the basic conventions remain. Civil Service Information Officers are at all times bound by the provisions of the Civil Service Code. Paragraph 1 requires civil servants 'with integrity, honesty, impartiality and objectivity, to assist the duly constituted government of whatever political complexion…'. The Code and servants' activities under the Code, are to be seen in the context of the duties and responsibilities of Ministers as set out in the Ministerial Code so they must not be asked to act contrary to the Code or in a way which would compromise their political objectivity. 'Heads of Information must be able to ensure Heads of Departments that working arrangements preserve proper professional distance between Information Officers and Ministers. Civil servants must conduct themselves with integrity, impartiality and honesty … they should not knowingly mislead Ministers, Parliament or the public and they must endeavour to ensure the proper, effective and efficient use of public money. They should conduct themselves to ensure that confidence in their work can be given by Ministers and future Ministers.' Particular advice is spelt out for Departmental Press Officers on avoidance of abuse of publicity for party political or 'image building' objectives.

2.113 The use of specialist advisers by government has been investigated by the Commons Public Administration Committee.[1] A code of conduct exists for special advisers and was revised in 2009.[2] The Ministerial Code at paragraph 3.2 lays down broad limits on the number of special advisers that a minister may appoint. There is advice on the 'Model Contract for Special Advisers'. The conventions basically state that such consultants should not be used where employees are able to do the work which it would not be improper for a civil servant to perform. The last annex covers 'Government Use of Direct Marketing'. Guidance is also provided to civil servants on 'Contacts with Lobbyists'. The Neill Committee on Standards in Public Life reported on lobbying in January 2000 (Cm 4557, vol 1, ch 7). The public administration has reported on lobbying PASC lobbying and influence in Whitehall (HC 36 I (2008–09)). The same committee was to launch an inquiry into vetting procedures for special advisers to avoid conflicts of interest after it was disclosed that David Cameron's press secretary, Andy Coulson (para 2.100) was paid by News International while employed by the Conservative Party. By November 2011, the Coalition Agreement plans of May 2010 for its government to introduce a register for lobbyists had not been introduced.

1 http://www.civilservant.org.uk/spadscode2009.pdf.
2 HC 727 (1999–00) and HC 610 (2010–11) on *Central Government Use of Advisers*.

2.114 Government communications formed the subject of an investigation by the Commons Public Administration Committee (HC 303 (2002–03); HC 274 (2003–04)) and the response of the government was the establishment of an enquiry into Government Communications by the Phillis Review (Cabinet Office, 2004); there was an interim review in August 2003. Phillis recommended a 'sustained commitment to a long-term programme of radical change in the conduct, process and style of government communications' (p 2). The review believed that government communications should be based on the following principles: openness not secrecy; more direct, unmediated communications to the public; genuine engagement with the public as part of policy formulation and delivery, not communication as an afterthought; positive presentation of government policies, not misleading spin; use of all relevant channels of communication, not excessive use of national press and broadcasters; co-ordinated communication of issues that cut across departments, not conflicting or duplicated departmental messages; reinforcement of the civil services political neutrality, rather than a blurring of government and party communications. The CRGA 2010 places the civil service on a statutory basis as well as establishing a statutory Civil Service Commission and Code.

2.115 Phillis recommended a new Permanent Secretary for Government Communications who would provide a strategic leadership for communications across government, building a 'new and authoritative communications service within government'. There has been a permanent secretary for government communication since 2004 and the position was reappointed in 2009. The Prime Minister's Official Spokesperson will report to and will work alongside the Prime Minister's Director of Communications. There should be a strong and integrated departmental communications structure. The Government Information and Communications Service should be disbanded, with greater emphasis on regional communications. There would be new rules on special advisers and new rules would also spell out the boundaries between civil servants and special advisers. There should be clearer rules on releasing statistical information. *All* major government briefings should be on the record, live on TV and radio with full transcripts available promptly online. Ministers should deliver departmental statements at the daily lobby. The existing lobby was no longer working effectively. There should be customer-driven online communications. The relationship between politicians and the media needed to be reappraised. The government gave fairly enthusiastic support to these recommendations.

2.116 Government information policy is led by OPSI. OPSI (now within the National Archives) is responsible for making public sector information available through print and online services. Directgov.uk is the government website (para 2.33 above) and the use of the Number 10 website was outlined above. The Government Communications Network is a network of communications specialists working across government in the UK and it provides best practice framework for communicators, entitled *engage*. The Government News Network supports central government and regional offices communications to the public through the press and publicity. The Government Knowledge and Information Management Network is the team that supports the delivery of the knowledge and information management strategy for government and is the Secretariat for the Knowledge Council which is a 'strategic body established to lead government in the better use and management of its knowledge and information'.[1]

[1]   http://gkimn.nationalarchives.gov.uk/default.htm.

2.117 The House of Lords Communications Committee reported on government communications in 2009 and recommended that special advisers should follow guidance set out on their practice in the Model Contract for Special Advisers and the Code of Conduct for Special Advisers, more open press conferences and tours of duty by 'high flying civil servants in government press and communications' offices. This report, Government Communications (HL 7 (2008–09)), sets out a number of recommendations HL 7 (2008–09):

- When there is sensitive information, the Government should commit to return to Parliament at the earliest opportunity to give an account of developments.
- The Prime Minister should draw all Ministers' attention to the guidance in the Ministerial Code that the most important announcements of Government policy should be made in the first instance to Parliament.
- Further, new information should always be provided on a fair and equal basis to all interested journalists.
- The morning briefing to journalists should appear live on the Number 10 website.
- The Leader of the House of Commons should reinstate a weekly briefing on parliamentary business.
- All major press conferences should be live on the internet.
- It is important that Ministers make clear that special advisers must follow the guidance available and stay within set limits.
- That where possible, high-flying civil servants should spend a period of service in the departmental press office.

- The Chief Executive of the Central Office of Information should take the lead in improving standards, with training and guidance to regional press officers, tailoring regional press releases, having greater contact with the regional media and making more senior officials and Ministers available for interview on the local impact of policies.
- The Committee states that Government information should always be available and accessible to as many people as possible and that the Cabinet Office should collate annual statistics on the costs of Government communications across departments.

The government response is at: http://webcache.googleusercontent.com/ search?q=cache:zjahyg2vhyoj:www.parliament.uk/documents/upload/ govtcommunications-govtresponse.doc+engage+-+strategic+communications+ framework&cd=2&hl=en&ct=clnk&gl=uk.

ELECTIONS AND REFERENDUMS

2.118 Although referendums are the direct voice of the people, that voice will be influenced by government as well as others. The Political Parties, Elections and Referendums Act 2000 as well as establishing the Electoral Commission to oversee wide-ranging regulation of the party political and electioneering process places restrictions on government, and local government, influence on referendums (see Part VII) and places limits on expenses. In addition, ss 139–140 provide for the disclosure of political donations by companies and for share-holder approval. These provisions amended the Companies Act 1985, Part XA and Sch 7, Part I (now Companies Act 2006). Further reforms were made under the Political Parties and Elections Act 2009. Free time is made available for political parties for party political broadcasts and election broadcasts covering both the BBC (under charter) and the independent sector (Communications Act 2003, s 333). 'Time' emerges after consultations between the parties and the broadcasters. Communications Act 2003, s 319 imposes a duty on OFCOM to ensure the accuracy and impartiality of news programmes and the impartiality of political programmes. The BBC is bound by its Charter in relation to fairness and impartiality. Political advertising is otherwise banned for commercial broadcasters (Communications Act 2003, ss 319–322). The OFCOM code deals with participation of candidates in Parliamentary or local elections and the BBC Trust agrees a new code before each election.

SELECT COMMITTEES

2.119 Once again, a comprehensive survey of this topic is not possible,[1] but the use and publication by parliamentary select committees of otherwise unpublished information, and their role as siphons in informing Parliament and the public, must be addressed. A report of the Liaison Committee in 2000 recommended changes in the manner of appointment to Select Committees (then chiefly by Whips) and a change to the title of the Committee to the Select Committee Panel. It also listed examples of best practice where Select Committees had engaged in innovative techniques.[2] Select Committees were advised to concentrate on a limited number of topics for inquiry or core tasks.[3] A Select Committee on Selection was established and it allocates chairs and members to committees based on the proprtion of party membership of the House. The Liaison Committee noted the patchy quality of many government responses to Select Committee reports. In addition to select committees there are committees for bills and grand committees. In the First Report of the House of Commons Select Committee on *Reform of the House of Commons* (HC 1117 (2008–09) the committee recommended that select committee chairs should be appointed by secret ballot among MPs and not by patronage. The committee also recommended that a failure by a committee member to attend 60 per cent or more of meetings would lead to their removal. The Commons agreed to accept these recommendations and to change its standing orders.

[1]   See Liaison Committee: *Select Committees and the Executive* HC 300 (1999/2000) and Government Response (Cm 4737) and HC 321 (2000–01). See *The Challenge for Parliament: Making Scrutiny Work* Hansard Society (2001) and Modernisation Committee *Select Committees* HC 224 (2001–02) and House of Commons Factsheet P2 *Departmental Select Committees* August 2010 www.parliament.uk.

[2]   See Liaison Committee: *Select Committees and the Executive* HC 300 (1999/2000), para 24.

[3]   HC 692 (2001–02).

2.120   The most visible of the select committees, apart from the Public Accounts Committee, are the departmentally-related committees, of which there are 19 and which were reformed in 1979, but all together there are over 30 select committees (including 'domestic' committees and various joint (with House of Lords) committees including the human rights committee and statutory instruments committee). It would be a serious mistake to overlook the importance of other committees such as the Commons Select Committee on Public Administration which emerged from the Select Committee on the Parliamentary Commissioner and then from the Select Committee on Public Service or the Select Committee on the European Union in the House of Lords which has six sub-committees. Other Lords committees include the Constitution Committee, the Economic Affairs Committee, the Delegated Powers and Regulatory Reform Committee, the Merits of Statutory Instruments Committee and the Science and Technology Committee. Special committees may be established to deal with specific bills in both Houses.

2.121   The Intelligence and Security Committee operates under specific statutory provisions and reports to the PM. Suggestions for changes to enhance the oversight role of the ISC are set out in *Justice and Security* CM 8194 (2010); see para 10.16 below. The departmental select committees investigate and overview the policy, administration and expenditure of government departments and their related or 'associated' bodies, ie for which a minister must ultimately answer. A resolution is usually passed under Standing Order to allow the public and press to attend their meetings and hear its evidence. When deliberating, however, the invariable practice is for the press and public ('strangers') to be excluded, but this does not cover appropriate officers of the House or specialist advisers who may assist committees. MPs who are not members of the committee can only be excluded from any stage of a committee's proceedings by resolution of the House. Such an MP cannot, however, take a part in the proceedings, eg address the committee or put questions to witnesses.[1] Secret committees have, however, existed in the past on the order of the House.[2]

[1]   An MP who is being examined has no right to be present during the deliberations upon his answers by the committee.

[2]   *Erskine May* 21st edn at 701. See now EM on 'Select Committees', 23rd edn (2004) at 738 et seq.

2.122   Select committees are given power by the House to send for persons, papers and records. However, there have been refusals to attend from several Ministers[1] and an MP[2] although the latter relented. The Joint Committee on Human Rights has reported on repeated refusals by Ministers to give oral evidence on British government complicity in torture of terrorist suspects.[3] Where an MP refuses to attend, only a motion of the House can ultimately compel his/her attendance. For a non-MP the committee can issue a summons: it has done so with a trade union member;[4] a permanent secretary of the former DES[5] before the Public Accounts Committee; and the Trade and Industry Committee has 'pressurised' heads of big oil companies to attend and give evidence. The Maxwell brothers famously stonewalled the committee in their questioning by the committee on the Mirror Group pension scandal and in 2011 Rupert Murdoch, Rebekah Brooks and others agreed to appear before the Culture, Media and Sports Committee to answer questions in relation to the 'phone hacking' scandal. The most difficult of cases in practical terms concerns civil servants. Ministers have insisted that they have the right to embargo such appearances.

[1]   Including Mrs Thatcher as Prime Minister.

[2]   Edwina Currie in the 'salmonella in eggs' saga.

[3]   HL 152 and HC 230 (2008–09).

4   Arthur Scargill, former NUM president. There has been some fairly contumacious treatment of Select Committees by 'lay' witnesses and even by civil servants. On a refusal by a witness (a journalist, Andrew Gilligan) to reveal a source, see HC 1044 (2002–03).

5   Sir David Andrew (1989) *Guardian*, 5 January. Former Ministers are making increasing appearances before committees.

2.123   A memorandum of guidance for officials appearing before select committees was produced by the Civil Service Department in 1980, and it was revised most recently in 2005 by the Cabinet Office.[1] It is described as a 'government document' without any formal parliamentary standing or approval. This provides guidance to officials giving evidence before, or preparing memoranda for submission to, select committees. This is 'generally applicable' to House of Lords select committees. Because the Public Accounts Committee has the power to question the Accounting Officer[2] of departments and bodies subject to its inquiries, and because of the investigatory powers of the Comptroller and Auditor-General, the guidelines are not 'literally applicable' to the Public Accounts Committee. Guidance for civil servants when dealing with the joint and select committees on statutory instruments is provided in Statutory Instrument Practice. The Cabinet Office has issued separate guidance for the appearance before the then Commons Select Committee on European Legislation (now European Scrutiny) and on the handling of EC documents.[3] The House of Lords also has select committees including, notably, that on the

European Union and its sub committees, Constitutional Affairs and Delegated Powers and Regulatory Reform.

1   http://interim.cabinetoffice.gov.uk/media/cabinetoffice/propriety_and_ethics/assets/
    osmotherly_rules.pdf (*Departmental Evidence and Response to Select Committees* Cabinet Office
    2005 and 2009).
2   Usually the Permanent Secretary. It rarely questions a minister (see ch 11 below).
3   See C Kerse (2000) *European Public Law* 81. See also: House of Lords Select Committee on the
    EU, Fourth Report (2000–01).

2.124 Of appreciable constitutional significance was the innovation of the Liaison Committee in 2002 to take evidence from the Prime Minister. This is done twice a year in January and July. This was the first appearance of the Prime Minister qua head of government to answer questions qua head of government although in 1927 a prime Minister had appeared before a select committee.[1]

1   See HC 1095 (2002–03) and Cm 5628 and HC 318 (2004–05).

Committees and civil servants

2.125 Committees should not usually enforce their rights for information from the executive at a level below that of ministerial head of the department concerned. Although earlier guidance on appearances of witnesses before select committee stated that 'Select Committees are free to seek evidence from whomsoever they please, and are entitled to require the production of papers by private bodies or individuals so long as they are relevant to the Committee's work' civil servants in fact operate under ministerial instructions.[1] They may be called upon to give a full account of government policies, but their purpose in doing so is to assist the process of ministerial accountability 'not to offer personal views or judgements on matters of political controversy'.[2]

1   Gen Notice 80/38.
2   *Departmental Evidence and Response to Select Committees* (2005, and 2009), paras 41 and 55–56.

2.126 For civil servants, ministers decide which officials should appear to give evidence. S/he may suggest an alternative official or her/himself,[1] but if a committee insists on the presence of a named official, s/he must attend, subject to the 'ministerial instructions' as to how s/he should answer questions. Select Committees should not act as disciplinary tribunals so a Minister is likely to consider 'carefully' a request to take evidence from a named official which is likely to expose the official to questioning about personal responsibility or allocation of blame between them and others. The questioning of David Kelly, the expert on weapons of mass destruction, by the Foreign Affairs Committee in July 2003 was widely criticised for appearing to act in contravention of this convention (para 1.19 above and HC 247 (2003–04), ch 4). Especially sensitive are situations where disciplinary proceedings or internal departmental inquiries have been pursued or may be pursued.

1   A Cabinet Secretary, Sir Robert Armstrong, has appeared instead of specific civil servants
    requested initially by a Select Committee: HC 519 (1985–86) lxv–lxviii.

2.127 Agency Chief Executives give evidence on behalf of the Minister on matters within their Framework Documents setting out their managerial authority. Members of non-departmental bodies that are free of ministerial control are unlikely to be under such constraint.[1] It is not usually appropriate to call retired officials who lack up to date information and who cannot be said to represent the Minister and 'hence cannot contribute directly to his accountability to the House'.[2] Sir Richard Scott was critical of the refusal to allow former officials to testify to the Treasury and Industry Committee in its inquiries related to the Iraqi supergun affair:

> '[The civil servants] were primary witnesses to the facts … Far from being unproductive, their evidence would have been highly pertinent and helpful. A Minister's duty to account to Parliament for what his department has done ought … to be recognised as extending … to an obligation to assist an investigating Select Committee to obtain the best first hand evidence available on the matters being investigated. The refusal to facilitate the giving of evidence … may be regarded as a failure to comply fully with the obligations of accountability owed to Parliament.'[3]

1   HC 210, 447 and 1055 (2003–04).
2   Gen Notice 80/38, para 44.
3   Scott (above), para F4.66.

2.128 Officials should be as helpful as possible to committees in providing information within the terms of the FOIA 2000 (para 9). Holding information back should only be on grounds that are necessary in the public interest as set out in law. They should ensure the accuracy of their evidence and not be drawn into the discussion of merits of alternative policies sticking to facts and explanations of policies. Specialist officials should be very cautious in discussing technical or professional matters underlying government policy. Memoranda or appearances should be adequate. Evidence may be given in confidence and is then protected by Parliamentary privilege. Agreement has been reached with the Liaison Committee on how to treat classified information. Special provision is made about Parliamentary Ombudsman and Comptroller and Auditor General investigations and evidence seen. Views of Ministers should be sought if there is a question of withholding information. Inter-departmental liaison may have to take place where more than one department is involved and a 'lead' department established to co-ordinate responses – usually the department which is 'shadowed' by the Committee in question. If necessary, the Cabinet Office may on rare occasions provide this role. If additional research is required, the department may wish to remind committees of their power to contract specialist advisers or researchers. Suitable advance notice of ministerial statements should be given to committees on matters within their remit.

2.129 Reasons for not providing information as well as those spelt out in the FOIA 2000 include matters sub judice, information covering the behaviour of individual officers 'with the implication of allocating individual criticism or blame' (para 73). The Minister should conduct an *internal* enquiry into such events and report to the Committee on the outcome, either personally or through a senior official, *not* the officials involved. Where committees need such information to discharge their duties they should take evidence in closed session. This will be on a clear understanding of confidentiality along with other safeguards, ie waiting until disciplinary proceedings are completed and in a manner which protects identity where not publicly known. After any proceedings, the Committee will be informed what has been done to correct any shortcomings. Well established conventions cover the use of policy papers of a previous administration of a different political complexion.[1] Officials cannot show documents to Committees that they could not show to their Ministers. Guidance is issued on the handling of evidence so that where oral evidence is given in closed session, departments should not disclose the evidence before it has been published, after appropriate 'sidelining' or redaction.[2] Special provisions apply for the receipt of 'confidential' information. Publication without authorisation before report to Parliament is a contempt of Parliament. In more recent years the Committee of Privileges has decided not to punish journalists for publishing leaked documents;[3] witnesses and departments are asked to identify which parts of evidence given in closed session should be sidelined and as this may face challenge before the committee. Officials should be prepared to defend requests by reference to statutory exemptions but not giving detailed citations or 'protective marking systems' (see below). Instructions also exist in relation to classified information. Guidance is also given in relation to non-departmental public bodies and evidence from commercial parties particularly government contractors. Steps should be taken to achieve transparency but also to protect commercial confidentiality and sensitive third party and private information handled by contractors. Government contracts very often specify the contractor's obligation to provide information to the public and to protect confidential and sensitive information. Contractors, like non-departmental public bodies may need advice on answering questions. In advice given to businesses some years ago, business was more or less told to treat all information as if it were classified.[4] Advice is also given on Government Responses to Select Committee Reports.

[1]   HC Official Report (6th series) 24 January 1980, cols 305–7.
[2]   A committee may only release 'top security' information on ministerial authorisation alone. On Official Secrets and Parliamentary Privilege, see paras 2.271 et seq below.
[3]   HC 476 (1989–90). See HC 1055 (2003–04) on protection of witnesses before select committees.
[4]   *Protecting Business Information: Keeping it Confidential and Understanding the Risks* (DTI, 1996).

2.130   In October 2004, the Liaison Committee of the House of Commons questioned the Minister about a proposed revised draft of the Guidance on Departmental Evidence and Response to Select Committees. In his evidence, the Minister stated:[1]

'In fact Select Committee activity has increased vastly since we came into office in 1997, with 350 substantive reports from the Departmental Select Committees alone last session. Ministerial appearances before Select Committees are running at over 200 a year and appearances by civil servants are many more than that. ... We have made a number of positive and very significant changes in response: namely, making clear the presumption that Committees' requests on attendance of civil servant witnesses, including Special Advisers, will be agreed to; making clear the presumption that the provision of information will be agreed to, including the presumption of cooperation on joined-up inquiries, including a new paragraph on parliamentary privilege in relation to evidence from civil servants and non-departmental public body staff, and encouraging departments to be proactive in providing relevant information and documents to Committees. So I see this as an opportunity for reform, but if you have any further issues or suggest amendments to the initial stab at this, then we would be very pleased to look at them in a constructive way.'

[1]   Liaison Committee HC 1180(i) (2003–04) and see Committee on Privileges Sixth Report (2003–04).

2.131   Reference has been made elsewhere to the reports on inquiries conducted by Lord Hutton and Lord Butler into events surrounding the use of intelligence on weapons of mass destruction in Iraq to persuade Parliament of the need for invasion, and the Chilcot inquiry into the war against Iraq. These inquiries were notable for the access to intelligence material and in the case of Hutton for the application of the public interest test under FOIA to determine what evidence should be made public (see para 1.7 above) although some medical and other evidence was embargoed (para 1.7).

PARLIAMENTARY COMMISSIONER FOR ADMINISTRATION – PARLIAMENTARY OMBUDSMAN

2.132   The above guidelines apply to the select committee on the Parliamentary Ombudsman (PO) and officials' appearances before that committee. However, the powers that the PO has to inquire and receive information must be explained.[1] A Cabinet Office report has made a series of outline recommendations to modernise the ombudsman regime by establishing an Ombudsmen Commission comprising public sector ombudsmen.[2] In Scotland, a Scottish Public Services Ombudsman has been established since 2002 (when the Parliamentary Ombudsman ceased acting as Scottish Parliamentary Commissioner). This is an integrated organisation examining complaints against Scottish government departments, local councils, housing associations, the NHS in Scotland and other public bodies. The Public Services Ombudsman (Wales) Act 2005 effected a similar development for public sector ombudsmen in Wales. The Public Administration Committee has conducted several investigations into the work of the Ombudsman.[3]

[1]   On the PCA and a 'right' to official advice/information, see Mowbray in *Public Law* 68 (1990).
[2]   P Collcutt and M Hourihan *Review of the Public Sector Ombudsman in England* Cabinet Office April 2000; Select Committee on Public Administration HC 612 (1999–00). T Buck, R Kirkham and B Thompson *The Ombudsman Enterprise and Administrative Justice* (2011).
[3]   HC 448 (2002–03), HC 506 (2002–03) Government Reply Cm 5890, and HC 41 (2003–04), and reports on Equitable Life *Justice Denied* HC 41 I & II (2008–09) and HC 219 *Parliament and the Ombudsmen* HC 107 (2009–10) and *Work of the Ombudsmen* HC 781 (2011–12).

2.133   The PO was appointed by the Parliamentary Commissioner Act 1967 (PCA 1967) as amended, especially by the Parliamentary and Health

Service Commissioners Act 1987 (PHSCA 1987). A full list of amendments is available at http://www.ombudsman.org.uk/about-us/our-role/history-and-legislation/legislation-for-the-po. The Regulatory Reform (Collaboration etc. between Ombudsmen) Order 2007, SI 2007/1889 facilitated collaboration in investigations by the Parliamentary, Health Services and local ombudsmen and the transfer of information between them. The PO investigates complaints handed to him by an MP, with the consent of the person who made it, requesting the PO to conduct an investigation thereon. The complaint has to be made in writing to an MP by a 'member of the public claiming to have sustained injustice in consequence of maladministration in connection with the actions so taken'.[1] The PO may investigate the action of any, or on behalf of any, body listed in Sch 2 to the PCA 1967, being action taken in the exercise of administrative functions of the body. The scheduled bodies were significantly extended in 1987 and the schedule is subject to continuing amendment so that in 1998/99, for instance, a further 150 bodies were added to his jurisdiction. Executive agencies have been included since their inception. A list of bodies subject to investigation is available at: http://www.ombudsman.org.uk/make-a-complaint/how-to-complain/government-departments-and-other-public-bodies-which-the-ombudsman-can-investigate.

[1] PCA 1967, s 5(1)(a) and (b). On 'maladministration' see M.Seneviratne *Ombudsmen: Public Services and Administrative Justice* (2002). The Parliamentary Ombudsman has added items to the list: HC 112 (1993–94), para 7.

2.134 PCA 1967, Sch 3 lists the items not subject to complaint[1] and s 5 also stipulates that the Commissioner shall not conduct an investigation where the person aggrieved has a right of appeal, reference or review to or before a tribunal constituted by or under any enactment or HM prerogative, or a remedy before a court of law. The PCA has a discretion to investigate notwithstanding such a right 'if satisfied that in the particular circumstances it is not reasonable to expect the complainant to resort to it'.[2] Nevertheless, the courts have ruled that a statutory ombudsman is subject to judicial review, and the PCA has himself been successfully reviewed in the courts.[3] The spectre of judicial review is taking an increasing profile in the work of the Ombudsmen generally (see para 9.47) and the courts have seen the benefits of ombudsmen investigations. They have also been very critical of government responses to PO reports. In relation to the Parliamentary Ombudsman the Equitable Life saga led to a re-investigation of the complaint by the Ombudsman after a judicial review of her initial decision not to investigate the case. The PCA is given complete discretion, subject to the above, to determine whether to initiate, continue or discontinue an investigation.[4]

[1] Foreign affairs, action taken outside the UK (except by consular officers), action relating to territory overseas, extradition and fugitive offenders, investigation of crime, state security (incl passports), legal proceedings, certain prerogative powers, personnel matters in the civil service, and contractual and commercial transactions.

[2] The local government ombudsman who operated under many similar features to the PO has been given strict guidance by the courts as to when he should not investigate when a court is more appropriate: *R v Comr for Local Administration, ex p Croydon London Borough Council* [1989] 1 All ER 1033. In *R v Local Comr for Administration, ex p Liverpool City Council* [1999] 3 All ER 85 the High Court interpreted the powers of the local ombudsman benevolently. The defendants claimed there was a remedy by judicial review but that process would not have uncovered the

information that the complainants to the Commissioner required to sustain a successful challenge. The Commissioner's decision to proceed and also her decision to apply a more relaxed test of 'bias' in a planning decision were lawful, a decision upheld by the Court of Appeal: [2001] 1 All ER 462. See also the discussion in chapter 9 para 9 but note *R (Bradley) v Secretary of State for Work and Pensions* [2008] EWCA Civ 36. See R Kirkham et al (2008) Public Law 510. *R (EMAG) v HM Treasury* [2009] EWHC 2495 (Admin).

3   *R v PCA, ex p Balchin* [1997] JPL 917 and *R v PCA ex p Balchin (No 2)* (2000) 2 LGLR 87.

4   *Re Fletcher's Application* [1970] 2 All ER 527, CA (refusal to investigate). His selection of matters to investigate is unlikely to be reviewed by the courts and he has no power to re-open an investigation once his report had been sent to the MP without a new referral: *R v PCA, ex p Dyer* [1994] 1 All ER 375. See *R (Murray) v PCA* [2002] EWCA Civ 1472 on an MP's refusal to refer a case – not challengeable by judicial review.

2.135   Any individual, natural or corporate, may make a complaint except local authorities or public authorities or nationalised industries and 'any other authority or body whose members are appointed by Her Majesty or any minister of the Crown or government department, or whose revenues consist wholly or mainly of moneys provided by Parliament'.[1] Other formalities include the fact that the complaint must be made to the MP (any MP)[2] not later than 12 months from the day on which the person aggrieved first had notice of the matters alleged in the complaint although the PO has a discretion to waive such a requirement as to time 'if he considers that there are special circumstances which make it proper to do so'.[3]

1   PCA 1967, s 6(1)(a) and (b).
2   Not a member of the House of Lords. The Committee on Public Administration has recommended for more than a decade that this 'filter' should be removed: HC 612 (1999–00), para 12.
3   Eg residence or death.

2.136   The PO will attempt resolution through intervention without the need for a full investigation. Under PCA 1967, s 7, where the PO proposes to conduct an investigation, s/he must provide an opportunity, to the Principal Officer of the department concerned and any other person alleged in the complaint to have taken or authorised the action complained of, to comment on any allegations contained in the complaint.[1] Investigations are conducted in private according to what the PCA thinks appropriate in the specific circumstances; s/he 'may obtain information from such persons and in such manner, and make such inquiries, as s/he thinks fit'. S/he may determine whether any person may be represented, by counsel or solicitor or otherwise, in the investigation.[2] Expenses and compensation for lost time may be made. The PO has sought to resolve an increasing number of disputes informally rather than conduct a formal investigation. In 2009, the total of cases accepted for investigation was 52 (the total number of complaints was 8543). Four departments dominate the number of complaints received: Work and Pensions, HMRC, Home Office and MoJ. In 1997–98 it was 376. 1208 complaints were made about the ombudsman – both the PO and Health ombudsman. The largest proportion of upheld complaints against investigated bodies related to delays. In 2009–10 65 per cent of complaints were dealt with within 12 months. The 2010–11 target is 90 per cent.

1   PCA 1967, s 7(1).
2   Ibid, s 7(2).

2.137 The PO may require, for the purposes of an investigation, any minister, officer or members of the department or authority concerned or any other person who in the PCA's opinion is able to furnish information or produce documents relevant to the investigation to furnish any such information or produce any such document.[1] The PO is given the same power as the High Court, Court of Session and High Court NI to demand attendance and examine witnesses and for production of documents.[2] Evidence may be taken on oath although this practice, if it happened at all, occurred with the Health Service Commissioner (HSC) rather than the PO. The Official Secrets Acts do not apply to prevent access to information by the PO and the Crown cannot rely upon public interest immunity (see ch 10 below) to prevent disclosure of documents.[3] The list of subject areas that the PO cannot investigate should be kept in mind. However, no person may be required or authorised to furnish any information or answer any question relating to proceedings of the Cabinet or of any committee of the Cabinet or to produce so much of any document as relates to such proceedings. A certificate issued by the Cabinet Secretary with the Prime Minister's approval certifying that any information, question, document or part of a document so related shall be conclusive.[4] In the past the drafts of papers to be submitted to a meeting of a Cabinet committee were not certified as excluded. The certificate was limited to documents covering the actual transactions of the Cabinet Committee.[5]

[1]   PCA 1967, s 8(1).
[2]   PCA 1967, s 8(2).
[3]   PCA 1967, s 8(3).
[4]   PCA 1967, s 8(4).
[5]   HC 498 (1974–75).

2.138 Whereas the Crown cannot rely upon public interest immunity, an individual shall not be compelled to give any evidence or produce any document which he could not be compelled to give or produce in proceedings before the Court, ie where documents in their possession are privileged, eg they contain legal advice, they remain immune.[1]

[1]   PCA 1967, s 8(5).

2.139 Obstruction of the PO or his officers in their functions without lawful excuse, or being guilty of any act or omission which before a court would constitute a contempt, may lead the PO to certify the offence for the court to deal with and punish as if committed before the court.[1] It would appear that the file generated by the PO investigation is not covered by these provisions.[2]

[1]   PCA 1967, s 9, although s 7(4) above concerning Cabinet documents is not overridden.
[2]   By analogy with the position of the Comptroller and Auditor General: see ch 11.

2.140 Section 10 concerns reports. The PO sends the report of an investigation, or the reasons for not investigating, to the sponsoring MP.[1] A copy is not sent to the complainant by the PO. The PO also sends a copy of the report of results of an investigation to the Principal Officer (PrO) of the department or authority concerned, and to any other person who is alleged in the relevant complaint to have taken or authorised the action complained of. In fact, reports are sent in draft to the PO for comments. There may be significant differences between the draft versions and the final version. The complainant has no right to see a copy of the draft report which is sent to the PrO.[2] Where the PO finds maladministration which remains unremedied, the PO may, if s/he thinks fit, lay before each House of Parliament a special report upon the case (s 10(3)).[3] The PO lays before Parliament, and publishes, an annual report by the PO, and four quarterly select investigations' reports are published. The PO has published several detailed investigation reports, a practice which has increased and he has also published detailed reports of investigations into the Child Support Agency (s 10(4)).[4] Reports from recent years include *A Breach of Confidence* concerning a variety of departments (HC 709 (2010–11)) and an *Assessment of the Loss of Personal Data by a Home Office Contractor* (HC 448 (2009–10)), *Equitable Life: A Decade of Regulatory Failure* (HC 815 (2007–08 Parts 1–5)), *Trusting in the Pensions Promise* (HC 984 (2005–06)) and a *Debt of Honour the ex gratia scheme for British Groups Interned by the Japanese in the Second World War* (HC 324 (2005–06)).[5] All reports are protected by absolute privilege by virtue of s 10(5).

[1] Or, if no longer an MP, to an appropriate one. When Parliament is dissolved no MPs are in existence to take a complaint.
[2] *R v PCA, ex p Dyer* [1994] 1 All ER 375.
[3] Eg HC 666 (1977–78); and, for the report into the failure by the Department of Transport to remedy findings of maladministration in relation to delays in choosing a route for the Channel tunnel, see: HC 193 (1994–95); PCA 1967, s 10(3). The department eventually accepted the recommendations.
[4] Eg into Barlow-Clowes: HC 76 (1988–89); HC 20 (1995–96) for the Child Support Agency; and HC 809 I & II (2002–03) on *The Prudential Regulation of Equitable Life*. The refusal by the Home Secretary to provide information on the *number* of times Ministers had made declarations of interest under the Code on Access was dealt with by a report under s 10(4) and not section 10(3): HC 353 (2001–02).
[5] On the latter see: *R (Elias) v Secretary of State for War* [2006] EWCA Civ 1293.

2.141 Information collected by officers of the PO and the PO might itself be covered by the Official Secrets Act 1989, although it may be disclosed in reports and for the purposes of investigation as above and in legal proceedings for offences under that Act or inquiries into possible proceedings, ie where the information is disseminated without authority, or for offences under s 9 of the 1967 Act.[1] Apart from such proceedings, the PO and the PO's officers will have an immunity from disclosing information in any other proceedings.[2]

[1] PCA 1967, s 11(2).
[2] PCA 1967, s 11(2)(c).

2.142 By s 11(3) a minister of the Crown may give notice in writing to the PO, the effect of which is that the disclosure of any document, information or class of documents or information as specified would be prejudicial to the interests of the state or otherwise contrary to the public interest. The result is that the PO and his or her officers must keep such information etc as specified secret to themselves.[1]

[1] Minister includes Commissioners of Customs and Excise and Inland Revenue.

2.143 There has been a Parliamentary Commissioner for Northern Ireland government departments. The PO, however, dealt with complaints against scheduled bodies in the PCA 1967, even though they came from Northern Ireland. Under the legislative schemes for devolution, in Northern Ireland the PO is responsible for reserved matters and an Assembly ombudsman deals with devolved matters. The Commissioner for Complaints deals with health and local government. Both offices are held by the one person known as the Northern Ireland Ombudsman. Scotland was addressed above. Reserved matters are the responsibility of the PO. The Welsh system was reformed by the Public Services Ombudsman (Wales) Act 2005 (see para 4.137 below).

2.144 The PHSCA 1987 allows greater delegation of responsibilities by the PCA to officials of the Health Service Commissioner (they work in the same office in fact)[1] and s 4 enables consultation and exchange of information between the Parliamentary and the Health Service Ombudsdmen. As of May 2010, the office of the ombudsmen is held by the same person. The section allows information received in one capacity to be used in another and it also allows such exchange where the posts are held by different people. If a complaint is received by an ombudsman, which appears to involve the bailiwick of another, s/he should consult that other and perhaps advise the complainant of the proper steps to recommence a complaint. The provisions in the FOIA 2000 allowing the public sector ombudsmen to exchange information with the IC were noted above (at para 1.260).

[1] PHSCA 1987, s 3.

2.145 In 2003 the Parliamentary Ombudsman together with the Commission for Local Administration (the body responsible for local ombudsmen) commissioned a MORI public awareness survey on the ombudsmen's offices. More than half of those questioned had never heard of ombudsmen – very often unskilled individuals, black and minority groups – and the level of unresolved grievance among those who had not contacted the ombudsmen was alarmingly high. A Customer Service Unit was fully operational in 2003 and is a first port of call for those making telephone, email or fax contacts.

CIVIL SERVANTS AND THEIR DUTIES AND RESPONSIBILITIES TO MINISTERS

2.146 Before we examine the Official Secrets Acts, it has to be established precisely what is the constitutional relationship between civil servants and their ministers. Is it one of undivided loyalty? Is it protected by the law of confidentiality?[1] Are duties owed purely to the Minister, or are there duties of a superior nature owed to the nation, the public, or the Crown as representative of the public weal, or the state? The reform of s 2 of the Official Secrets Act 1911 was partially due to certain ambiguities surrounding the nature of a civil servant's duty to his or her Minister which the government wished to be resolved (see below). Ambiguities have remained. The law has long recognised that the relationship between Ministers and civil servants is symbiotic with the widest of powers of delegation.[2]

[1]   See HC 92 I and II (1985–86), and paras 2.312 et seq below.

[2]   From the famous case of *Carltona v Commissioners of Works* [1943] 2 All ER 560 (CA) and and cf *R (NASHA) v Secretary of State for Health* [2005] EWCA Civ 154; *R v Secretary of State for the Home Department, ex p Oladehinde* [1990] 2 All ER 367, CA.

2.147   The orthodoxy was set out in guidelines by the Cabinet Secretary in 1985 and which were amended in 1987 and again to take account of changes to the Civil Service Code in 1996 and 1999.[1] The Code is now issued under CRGA 2010 which has placed the civil service on a statutory basis removing it from being an organisation under the royal prerogative. Although employed under the prerogative, civil servants were and are given legal and judicial protection in the enjoyment of their employment rights. The Code operating under CRGA 2001 – and which is supplemented by departmental or agency guidance – states that it forms part of the contractual relationship between the civil servant and their employer and creates an expectation of 'high standards of behaviour'. Under the same Act, the civil service is defined as 'the civil service of the State'. The 'State' is not legally defined in English or UK law although the term is widely used in governance and government and to some extent in legislation (see 2.156 below). Executive power is organised around the Crown which can mean both the sovereign and monarch, and the formal organised basis of central government. The Crown in the latter sense is represented by the government of the day: in general, the executive powers of the Crown (monarch) are exercised by and on the advice of HM Ministers, who are answerable to Parliament. The Civil Service has no constitutional personality or responsibility separate from the duly elected government of the day – it is there to advise and assist the government, or its administration, in policy-making putting decisions into effect, to manage and deliver services, and to present government policies and decisions. While civil servants serve the government of the day as a whole, a servant's primary duty is to the Minister in charge of the department in which he or she is serving and to junior Ministers. The Minister is answerable to Parliament and civil servants must serve their Minister with complete integrity, honesty, impartiality and objectivity and to the best of their ability. Under devolution, civil servants remain members of the Home Civil Service, but in Wales and Scotland and Northern Ireland, their primary loyalty is to the 'administration in which they serve.' There are appropriate modifications to take account of regional Parliaments/Assemblies, Assembly Secretaries etc. Those working in executive agencies are civil servants

[1]   HC Official Report (6th series) cols 130–132, 26 February 1985 subject to amendments as specified in the text. See also Treasury and Civil Service Committee HC 27-II (1993–94) p 188. The May 1999 revisions to the Code took account of certain items concerning devolution: see *Civil Service Code* (May, 1999) para 2 now updated. The Code is available with the Civil Service Management Code which from 1 April 2000 is only available through the website: http://www.civilservice.gov.uk/about/resources/csmc/index.aspx.

2.148   The Civil Service, unlike the government of the day, must be politically neutral[1] and ready to serve masters of differing political persuasions in a way which deserves and retains the confidence of Ministers, thereby building up a relationship of total confidence 'and that the Civil Service will at all times conscientiously fulfil its duties and obligations to, and impartially assist, advise and carry out the policies of, the duly constituted government of the day, Assembly Secretaries' etc. Under the Code, civil servants are expected to perform their role 'with dedication and a commitment to the Civil Service and its core values: integrity, honesty, objectivity and impartiality'. Integrity requires that public money is spent properly and efficiently and they must deal with the public fairly and promptly, upholding the law and administration of justice. They must set out facts and issues honestly and fairly and use resources only for specified purposes. They should refrain from deceiving Ministers, Parliament and the public. They should provide accurate and evidence based advice to Ministers, take proper account of expert and other advice and must not frustrate the implementation of policies. They must carry out their duties in a fair, just and equitable manner without discrimination or unjustifiable favour. The determination of policy is the minister's etc responsibility. The civil servant has no distinct role or constitutional responsibility separate from the Minister. It is a civil servant's duty 'to make available to a Minister all the information and experience at his or her disposal' which is relevant, and to provide 'honest and impartial advice' without fear or favour. Withholding information is a breach of duty, as is obstructing or delaying a decision 'because they do not agree with it'. Theirs is not to agree or disagree, but to perform a minister's lawful instructions:

'Civil servants are under an obligation to keep the confidences to which they become privy in the course of their official duties; not only the maintenance of trust between Ministers and civil servants but also the efficiency of government depend on their doing so. There is and must be a general duty upon every civil servant, serving or retired, not to make disclosures which breach that obligation. This duty applies to any document or information or knowledge of the course of business which has come to a civil servant in confidence in the course of duty. Any such unauthorised disclosures, whether for political or personal motives, or for pecuniary gain, and quite apart from liability to prosecution under the Official Secrets Act 1989 or other statutes restricting disclosure of government information, may result in the civil servant concerned forfeiting the trust that is put in him or her as an employee and making him or her liable to disciplinary action ... or to civil proceedings. He or she also undermines the confidence that ought to subsist between Ministers and civil servants and thus damages colleagues and the Service as well as him or herself.'[2]

1   For local government see ch 5 below and in Scotland: Ethical Standards in Public Life etc (Scotland) Act 2000 covering local and devolved government in Scotland.
2   For the most recent guidance on civil servants' confidentiality see *Civil Service Management Code* section 4.2: http://www.civilservice.gov.uk/about/resources/csmc/index.aspx.

2.149   The Civil Service Management Code sets out standards of behaviour in realtion to civil servants financial interests, political activities, business appointments after service and guidance is provided on lobbying and lobbyists. Advice sets out instructions for appearances before Select Committees (see above). Civil servants should not be requested to do anything unlawful, unethical, in breach of a constitutional convention or professional code, or which constitutes maladministration. Civil servants who are being asked to act in a way which would breach the Civil Service Management Code, or in a way which raises a fundamental issue of conscience for them, should proceed in accordance with procedures laid down in departmental guidance or rules of conduct. These provide for assistance after a suggestion by Lord Nolan's Committee on Standards in Public Life[1] and appeal to the Civil Service Commissioners instead of reporting to the Head of Department and through that person to the Head of the Home Civil Service and Prime Minister. Breaches should be reported to appropriate authorities. 'It is not acceptable for a serving or former civil servant to seek to frustrate policies or decisions of Ministers by the disclosure outside the government, in breach of confidence, of information to which he or she has had access as a civil servant.' Detailed provisions for appeals are included in the Civil Service Management Code.[2] Specific departments may possess their own supplements on disclosure by civil servants (eg Vol 7 MoD Personnel Manual). The public interest defence under the law of confidentiality and the provisions of the Public Interest Disclosure Act 1998 are dealt with below.

[1]   Cm 2850 I, pp 59 et seq.
[2]   http://www.civilservice.gov.uk/about/resources/csmc/index.aspx And see further, HC 94 (2000–01).

2.150 Ministers' duties include integrity; the duty to give Parliament and the public 'as full information as possible' about policies, decisions and actions of government 'and not to deceive or mislead Parliament or the public'. Civil servants' advice must be considered fairly and properly, they must not be asked to do what ministers should not do; nor should appointments be made by abusing partisan purposes.[1]

[1]   Cmnd 9841. The Civil Service Commissioners are responsible for maintaining the principle of recruitment after fair and open competition and producing a recruitment code and auditing recruitment practices. Since 1995, none of the Commissioners has been a civil servant.

2.151 However, for over 30 years governments have engaged in the process of 'hiving off' responsibilities to executive and independent agencies; devolving more responsibility to line managers and executives and also devolving far greater responsibility for reaching targets of performance under agreements – most recently public service agreements – which will make the traditional model of the civil servant and ministerial responsibility something of an anachronism if fully developed, or at least much more restricted to a core of senior civil servants. Even at this level, short-term contracts and dismissal are becoming more common. The size of the Civil Service has been reduced and non-civil servant 'special advisers' are more frequently resorted to which has caused increasing friction as we saw above. In 2001, the government produced a Code of Conduct for Special Advisers and more recent developments were outlined above (para 2.117). Changes in organisation have included contracting out public services to the private sector under the provisions of the Deregulation and Contracting Out Act 1994 (amended by the Regulatory Reform Act 2001), the movement towards the Private Finance Initiative and now Public Private Partnerships in the provision of public services and the creation of Task Forces to advise on special areas of policy and activity. These have been identified with tensions which have been addressed in the reports of the Committee on Public Standards.[1] The coalition government has pursued these arrangements with enthusiasm and has accelerated their utilisation.

[1]   See the Sixth Report Cm 4557 I and II (2000). The appointment of special advisers is not subject to the usual Civil Service rules for appointments: *Lord Chancellor v Coker* [2001] IRLR 116, EAT. See also the Public Administration Committee: HC 293 (2000–01) on Special Advisers the Committee on Standards in Public Life *Defining the Boundaries within the Executive: Ministers, Special Advisers and the permanent Civil Service* Cm 5775 and the Government Response Cm 5964. See the *Ministerial Code* (2010).

2.152   A Civil Service Bill 2003–04 contained provisions for a statutory Civil Service Commission, a renamed Civil Service of the State; provided a Ministerial power for the issue a code under the statute on civil service conduct. The Civil Service No 2 Bill 2003–04 provided for the impartial appointment of civil servants, makes provision for the duties of Ministers and special advisers to uphold impartiality and their respective duties and restrictions. Provision is made in relation to information relating to special advisers and codes of conduct for civil servants and special advisers and on procedure. Neither Bill survived the 2003–04 session although the Cabinet Office produced draft Civil Service Bill in November 2004 (Cm 6373). CRGA 2010 now provides the legal framework for the civil service.

2.153   Until the passage of the Public Interest Disclosure Act 1998 the UK afforded the civil servant who 'went public' without authority little if any legal protection against reprisal where he or she believes that they have acted in the public interest. This was in marked contrast to the position in overseas common law countries, particularly the USA and to a lesser extent Canada.[1] The general framework concerning disclosures was covered by the Official Secrets Acts. The breadth of the British official secrecy laws have been widely commented upon. The notorious events surrounding WikiLeaks in 2010 when the first group of 250,000 US diplomatic and intelligence reports were published without authorisation were not susceptible to prosecution under the OSA 1989 because the alleged perpetrators were not UK citizens and the information did not belong to the UK Crown. The episode brought home the impossibility of controlling the dissemination of official information in the digitalised and networked globe.[2]

[1]   Under s 10, Crown servants are brought within the Public Interest Disclosure Act 1998 but not members of the armed services or those working in 'national security'. See The US Civil Service Reform Act 1978 and paras 2.281 et seq below. In disciplinary proceedings, Canadian civil servants may invoke the 'public interest' defence only available in civil proceedings in the UK or under PIDA 1998.
[2]   D Leigh and L Harding *WikiLeaks* (2011); M L Sifry *WikiLeaks and the Age of Transparency* (2011).

OFFICIAL SECRETS ACTS 1911–1989 (OSAS 1911–1989)1

Section 1 of the Official Secrets Act 1911

2.154   Section 1 concerns, according to its marginal heading, 'penalties for spying'.[2] The section can be quoted:

'(1) If any person for any purpose prejudicial to the safety or interests of the State –

(a) approaches [inspects, passes over][3] or is in the neighbourhood of, or enters any prohibited place[4] within the meaning of this Act; or

(b) makes any sketch, plan, model, or note which is calculated to be or might be or is intended to be directly or indirectly useful to an enemy; or

(c) obtains, [collects, records, or publishes,] or communicates to any other person [any secret official code word, pass word, or] any sketch, plan, model, article, or note, or other document or information which is calculated to be or might be or is intended to be directly or indirectly useful to an enemy;

he shall be guilty of [an offence].

(2) On a prosecution under this section, it shall not be necessary to show that the accused person was guilty of any particular act tending to show a purpose prejudicial to the safety or interests of the State, and, notwithstanding that no such act is proved against him, he may be convicted if from the circumstances of the case, or his conduct, or his known character as proved, it appears that his purpose was a purpose prejudicial to the safety or interests of the State; and if any sketch, plan, model, article, note, document, or information relating to or used in any prohibited place within the meaning of this Act, or anything in such a place [or any secret official code word or pass word], is made, obtained, [collected, recorded, published], or communicated by any person other than a person acting under lawful authority, it shall be deemed to have been made, obtained [collected, recorded, published] or communicated for a purpose prejudicial to the safety or interests of the State unless the contrary is proved.'

[1] For the background, see Birkinshaw *Freedom of Information: The Law, The Practice and The Ideal* (4th edn, 2010) ch 3 and DGT Williams *Not In The Public Interest* (1965).
[2] See, however, *Chandler v DPP* [1964] AC 763, HL.
[3] The words in square brackets were added by the Official Secrets Act 1920 (OSA 1920, ss 10, 11(2) and Schs 1 and 2).
[4] See OSA 1911, s 3.

2.155 In *Chandler v DPP*[1] the House of Lords held that the section was not limited to spying but also extended to the saboteur, viz those who had entered a US air base – a prohibited place – to cause disruption by way of demonstration against nuclear weapons. 'Purpose' was to be distinguished from the motive for doing an act and 'any purpose' included direct or immediate purpose as distinguished from an 'ultimate aim'. Where there were several purposes, including an ultimate purpose of alerting the nation to the folly of nuclear weapons, an immediate purpose nonetheless remained one of them and was therefore within the words 'any purpose'.[2]

[1] [1964] AC 763, HL.
[2] It was held that the 'immediate purpose' was to obstruct the operational activity of the air base: this was prejudicial to the interests of the state, on incontrovertible Crown evidence, and contrary evidence was inadmissible; cf however, Lord Devlin. Section 1(2) allows guilt to be inferred in very wide circumstances and reverses the onus of proof.

2.156 The court will accept the government's evidence on what is prejudicial to the safety or interests of the state. The House of Lords also held, variably, that the word 'State' in the phrase 'interests of the State' meant the 'organised community' (Lords Reid and Hodson) or the organs of government of a national community (Lords Devlin and Pearce). In matters of national security which is what s 1 is concerned with, the interests of the state are the same as the interests of the government of the day because it falls to the government of the day to advise the Crown on national security and the disposition of the armed forces for the protection of the nation. On such matters, there cannot be two competing interpretations of the interests of the state. It is not settled law, however, that the interests of the state are always synonymous with the interests of the government of the day where national security is not involved, as the 'State' may signify an entity which is larger than the government of the day.[1] As we saw above, the government did not accept this possibility.

[1] What, for instance, is meant by the Crown?

2.157 'Enemy' in s 1 includes a potential enemy with whom there might be war.[1] 'Prohibited place' is defined in s 3 and is given an exhaustive definition which can be added to by order (SI 1975/182). Under s 12:

> 'Expressions referring to communicating or receiving include any communicating or receiving, whether in whole or in part, and whether the sketch, plan, model, article, note, document, or information itself or the substance, effect, or description thereof only be communicated or received; expressions referring to obtaining or retaining any sketch, plan, model, article, note, or document, include the copying or causing to be copied the whole or any part of any sketch, plan, model, article, note, or document; and expressions referring to the communication of any sketch, plan, model, article, note or document include the transfer or transmission of the sketch, plan, model, article, note or document;
>
> The expression "document" includes part of a document;
>
> The expression "model" includes design, pattern, and specimen;
>
> The expression "sketch" includes any photograph or other mode of representing any place or thing;
>
> [The expression "munitions of war" includes the whole or any part of any ship, submarine, aircraft, tank or similar engine, arms and ammunition, torpedo, or mine, intended or adapted for use in war, and any other article, material, or device, whether actual or proposed, intended for such use;]'

[1] *R v Parrott* (1913) 8 Cr App Rep 186, CCA.

2.158 Section 1 of the OSA 1920 prohibits the unauthorised use of uniforms; the falsification of reports, forgery, personation and the use of false documents to gain admission to a prohibited place or for any other purpose prejudicial to the safety or interests of the state within the Act.

2.159   Section 2 of the OSA 1920 allows communications with foreign agents to be used as evidence of the commission of certain offences under s 1 relating to the obtaining or attempting to obtain information.

2.160   Under OSA 1911, s 1 no prosecution may proceed except with the consent of the Attorney-General.[1]

1   And Scottish and Northern Ireland equivalents.

2.161   Section 7 of the OSA 1911 imposes penalties for harbouring spies. Section 7 of the OSA 1920 makes it an offence to attempt to commit any offence under the principal Act or the OSA 1920 or to solicit, incite or endeavour to persuade another person to commit an offence or to aid and abet or do any act preparatory to the commission of an offence under the principal Act or the OSA 1920 (para 2.163).

2.162   Section 2 of the 1911 Act has been repealed and replaced by the OSA 1989. This Act came into force on 1 March 1990.

Official Secrets Act 1989

'We are legislating for a generation; we are not legislating for the next five years.'[1]

1   N Bugden MP, HC Official Report (6th series) col 1005 22 February 1989.

2.163   The breadth of the British official secrecy laws have been widely commented upon. The headnote to the 1989 Act states that it replaces s 2 of the OSA 1911. One section is replaced by an Act of 16 sections and two schedules! The 1989 Act is not cited as being a part of the principal Act (1911); it therefore presumably stands as a substantive measure in its own right. Therefore, the provisions under s 7 of the OSA 1920 on attempting, inciting or aiding and abetting offences under the 1911 Act do not apply, if this is correct, to offences under the 1989 Act.[1]

1   Cf the common law of attempt, incitement and conspiracy. NB, OSA 1920, s 1(2)(b).

2.164   More has probably been written about OSA 1911, s 2 than any other legal provision in British, and British-inspired, legal system(s).[1] One could say very little with any certainty about s 2; however, this much is certain: it has been repealed and its much criticised replacement is still on the statute book.[2]

1   Birkinshaw, above, para 2.154, note 1.
2   It is a substantive Act in its own right and not simply a replacement of s 2.

2.165   In 1972, a committee under the chairmanship of Lord Franks reported that s 2 should be replaced. It was a wide catch-all provision, the very breadth of which had brought it into disrepute. However, Franks' recommendations were not acted upon and a series of events[1] led the government to publish its own reforms in 1988 after an abortive Bill in 1979. These came in the White Paper Reform of s 2 of the OSA 1911.[2]

1   The Franks Report on Reform of the OSA 1920, s 2; Cmnd 5104 (1972); the Ponting trial *R v Ponting* [1985] Crim LR 318; the Shepherd Bill reforming s 2, 1988 inter alia.
2   Cm 408 (1988).

White Paper of 1988

2.166   The White Paper followed Franks in believing that s 1 of the OSA 1911 left important areas of information unprotected. 'Effective protection requires that the law should cover leakage of information, as well as espionage', concluded Franks.

2.167   The government believed that unauthorised leaks of information causing 'damage to the public interest' should be punishable by the criminal law. Separate tests of likely harm for the different categories of information to be covered were proposed for the legislation and these would be 'concrete and specific', not general such as the Franks test of 'likely to cause serious injury to the interests of the nation or endanger the safety of a citizen of the UK and Colonies'. However, the government scrapped the idea of ministerial certificates conclusively establishing before a court that leaking of the specified information would cause serious injury. Such a certificate could not be challenged by a defendant. Instead, the government proposed 'where it is necessary for the courts to consider the harm likely to arise from the disclosure of particular information, the prosecution should be required to adduce evidence as to that harm and the defence should be free to produce its own evidence in rebuttal. The burden of proof would be on the prosecution ...'.[1]

1   Cm 408, para 18.

2.168   The legislation would confine the operation of criminal law to six areas of information. It would not be suitable to cover breaches causing 'local damage to individuals or groups, or result in political embarrassment' or which would 'obstruct sensible and equitable administration'.[1] The criminal law would not cover Cabinet documents as a class or advice to ministers as a class although specific items of such classes may be protected if they are within the six categories of protected information. Nor will economic or financial information[2] be protected as a class. Nor will blanket protection be given to information entrusted in confidence to government – it will have to fall within a protected category. In these cases the government and third parties would have to rely upon civil remedies, such as the law of confidentiality (see paras 2.312 et seq below) and the government could invoke disciplinary measures contained in Civil Service codes (see paras 2.281 et seq below). However, specific statutes protect the secrecy of information in the possession of civil servants. The government will keep under review whether the reform of s 2 will 'leave without a criminal safeguard any private information provided to the government in confidence which merits such protection' and 'separate specific offences of disclosure' may be created.3 The FOIA 2000 exempts information from disclosure on a class basis especially in the field of the formulation of government policy and the security services, it should be noted.

1   Cm 408, para 24.
2   On the budget, lending rate etc.
3   Cm 408, para 35.

2.169   The Home Secretary on behalf of the government affirmed, however, that 'there could not conceivably be a prosecution under the Bill on the ground of embarrassment to a British Minister'.[1]

1   HC Official Report (6th series) col 428, 15 February 1989. See further the Select Committee on Public Administration HC 94 (2000–01).

2.170   As the reform meant that only a 'very small proportion of the information in the hands of Crown servants would be protected by the criminal law' this does not mean that there will be freedom of information. 'Ministers will continue to determine what information should be disclosed and to account to Parliament for those decisions' (Cm 408, para 71). The government did not 'address such matters as the question of public access to official information not covered by the Government's proposals' (Cm 408, para 5). Further, the Civil Service Discipline Code will continue to operate against unauthorised disclosure of information and conduct rules for Crown servants on disclosure of official information will be amended, as will departmental rules and guidance to ensure that Crown servants are clear on 'what types of information they cannot disclose without authority without rendering themselves liable to criminal or ... disciplinary action' (Cm 408, para 73).

SECURITY CLASSIFICATIONS

2.171   Security classifications will remain and continue to play 'an essential administrative role in handling information' (Cm 408, para 76). These are:

TOP SECRET	Exceptionally grave damage to the nation (by unauthorised disclosure)
SECRET	Serious injury to the interests of the nation[1]
CONFIDENTIAL	Prejudicial to the interests of the nation
RESTRICTED	Undesirable in the interests of the nation

1   'Interests of the nation are interpreted broadly and are not confined to questions of national security in the military sense', Franks, above, para 62.

2.172   Privacy markings are used by departments to identify information not warranting a security classification, but which requires protection, eg entrusted in confidence:

COMMERCIAL – IN CONFIDENCE[1]	Confidential information of a commercial nature
STAFF – IN CONFIDENCE	Confidential information about staff appointments in government departments

1   'Confidence' here means a secret, not 'confidential' as in civil law.

2.173   Others cover 'contracts', 'medical', 'regulatory' and so on.

2.174 Classifications of documents will have no evidential relevance for a jury or for the degree of harm or injury caused by the leak; 'it is only evidence of the view of the persons who awarded the classification' and only evidence of the view at the time of classification. However, the:

> 'grade of classification may be relevant in a prosecution as evidence tending to show that the defendant had reason to believe that the disclosure of the information was likely to harm the public interest, but the prosecution will have to adduce separate evidence to prove that the disclosure was inde-ed likely to cause such harm'.[1]

[1] Cm 408, para 75.

2.175 In short the legislation will not 'apply criminal sanctions to disclosures which are not likely to harm the public interest, nor to anyone who could not reasonably have been expected to foresee the effect of his disclosure'.[1] The government also believed that 'responsible media reporting would not be affected by the government's proposals'.[2] The government was happy to entrust the safeguarding of the public interest in this area to the juries and the courts.

[1] Cm 408, para 77.
[2] Cm 408, para 78.

THE CATEGORIES OF PROTECTED INFORMATION

Security and intelligence[1]

2.176 Under s 1(1) of the Official Secrets Act 1989 (OSA 1989) a person who is or has been a member of the security and intelligence services[2] or a person 'notified' that s/he is subject to the provisions of this subsection is guilty of an offence if, without lawful authority,[3] s/he discloses[4] *any* information, document or other article relating to security or intelligence which is or has been in his or her possession by virtue of his or her position as a member of any of those services or in the course of his or her work while the notification is or was in force. The government refused to publish the list of such related officials or to define in regulations what kinds of service would be covered. Members of the Parliamentary Security and Intelligence Committee are notified under s 1(1). By s 1(2), the offence is committed when statements by the above which 'purport' to be such disclosures are made or where it is 'intended to be taken by those to whom it is addressed as being such a disclosure'. In other words empty rhetoric pretending to be such information will be covered. The offences in sub-ss (1) and (2) are, almost, absolute (see below). No damage has to be proved beyond the unauthorised disclosure[5] which, absent a perverse jury decision, would be sufficient to ground a conviction.

[1] OSA 1989, s 1(7) describes this as the work of, or in support of, the security and intelligence services or any part of them, and references to information relating to security and intelligence include references to information held or transmitted by those services or by persons in support of, or any part of, them.
[2] MI5, MI6, GCHQ being the more obvious – and now referred to as the Intelligence services – Regulation of Investigatory Powers Act 2000 (RIPA 2000). Notified persons, presumably, will be

civil servants on sensitive committees, and those whose work is related to security and intelligence. After equivocation, the government accepted that notification decisions are judicially reviewable.
3   See OSA 1989, s 7 for 'authorised disclosures', paras 2.248 et seq below.
4   This includes parting with possession of a document or other article, OSA 1989, s 13(1).
5   The Ponting, Tisdall, Massiter, etc leaks would be covered by the criminal law. The Wright episode would still be problematical because he was outside the jurisdiction a difficulty the government discovered in the Shayler episode until he voluntarily returned to England.

2.177   For persons who are or who have been Crown servants[1] or government contractors,[2] they will be guilty of an offence under sub-s (3) if, without lawful authority,[3] they make a *damaging* disclosure of any information, document or other article relating to security or intelligence which is or has been in their possession.[4] A disclosure for these purposes is damaging if:

(a)   it causes damage – this is not defined so presumably any 'damage' would suffice for a prosecution, ie ridicules botched amateurism or wastage of funds? – to the work of, or any part of, the security and intelligence services; or

(b)   it is information or a document or other article which is such that its unauthorised disclosure[5] would be likely to cause such damage or which falls within a class or description of information, documents or articles the unauthorised disclosure of which would be likely to have that effect.[6]

1   By OSA 1989, s 12 this includes Ministers, civil servants, members of the armed forces and police officers, as well as prescribed persons and office holders. The Secretary of State may prescribe as Crown servants office holders and some or all of their staff by statutory instrument (affirmative resolution). The Comptroller and Auditor General and the National Audit Office have been included: SI 1990/200.
2   OSA 1989, s 12(2). Section 12(3) excludes certain parties from being government contractors for the purposes of the Act.
3   OSA 1989, s 7. See paras 2.248 et seq below for 'lawful authority'.
4   OSA 1989, s 1(3).
5   See paras 2.248 et seq below.
6   OSA 1989, s 1(4).

2.178   It is up to the prosecution to prove the damage, but the 'class or description' provision seems to re-introduce to some extent the concept of ministerial certificate. How will documents be classed or described and by whom? This classification is evidence of its damaging quality, unlike the classification system described above which only reflects the opinion of the classifier.

2.179   A defence is available for a person charged with an offence under this section where s/he can prove that at the time of the alleged offence s/he did not know, and had no reasonable cause to believe[1] that the information, document or article in question related to security or intelligence or, in the case of an offence under sub-s (3), that the disclosure would be damaging as set out. In other words there is no presence of mens rea and they had not shut their eyes to the reality of the situation. The onus is on the defendant.

1   A virtual impossibility for security and intelligence personnel.

2.180   The persons under sub-s (1) who will be subject to 'notification' that they are bound by an absolute duty will be notified in writing of such by a

Minister. The Minister may serve such a notice if, in the Minister's opinion, the work undertaken by the person in question is or includes work connected with the security and intelligence services and its nature is such that the interests of national security require that s/he should be subject to the provisions of that subsection.[1] A notification may at any time be revoked and will be subject to a duration of five years, and renewable at five-year periods. The Minister is under a duty to serve a notice of revocation as soon as, in his/her opinion, the work undertaken by that person ceases to be such as mentioned in s 1(6).[2] Information obtained etc within period of notification will still be covered after the period has ended. The most obvious persons notified under this section are members of the Parliamentary Security and Intelligence Committee.

[1]   OSA 1989, s 1(6).
[2]   OSA 1989, s 1(7).

2.181   For several years at the end of the 1990s and early in 2000, a former MI5 officer, David Shayler, was the object of the attention of the Attorney-General and prosecuting authorities on this side of the Channel. Shayler, who lived in Paris, had sent a letter to *The Guardian* which the latter published in edited portions. *The Observer* also published an article about the allegations made by Shayler which included allegations and knowledge of the identities (these were not disclosed) of those British agents who had set about plotting the assassination of Colonel Gadafy of Libya. The attempt to gain access to the letter under Police and Criminal Evidence Act 1984, s 9 and Sch 1, para 2 failed in the case of *The Guardian* and orders of the Crown Court judge were quashed. The access conditions had not been established in relation to the letter to *The Guardian*. Furthermore, Judge LJ believed, the privilege against self-incrimination had to be given sufficient weight. The other two judges were not as protective of the privilege against self incrimination. In relation to *The Observer's* reporter his letter from Shayler had not been the subject of a wrongful order of access under the Act.[1] Shayler returned to the jurisdiction in August 2000, was arrested, charged with offences under s 1 and also s 4 (which covers information obtained by interception and by the security and intelligence services – below) and bailed. He was not charged in relation to the disclosure of any plot to kill Colonel Gadafy. In the spring of 2001, the trial judge in Shayler's case ordered a preparatory hearing under s 29(1) of the Criminal Procedure and Investigations Act 1996. The trial judge ruled that no public interest defence was available to Shayler under those sections and that ss 1 and 4 were compatible with Art 10 ECHR guaranteeing freedom of speech. If Shayler had been successful, the government was not duty bound to repeal s 1, but its future utility would be called seriously into question. If the government were successful, as it was, there would have to be careful judgment exercised in relation to bringing any future prosecution.

[1]   *R v Central Criminal Court, ex p Bright* [2001] 2 All ER 244, DC.

2.182   An appeal was made to the Court of Appeal which upheld the first instance judgment.[1] The further appeal to the House of Lords was unsuccessful.[2] The provisions in question gave the defendant no opportunity to show that the disclosure was in the public interest and imposed on the prosecution no obligation to prove that the disclosure was not in the public interest. Giving the sections their natural meaning and interpreting them in the context of the Act as a whole, it was clear that a defendant was not entitled to be acquitted if he showed it was, or believed it was, in the public or national interest to make the disclosure in question. Nor was he entitled to acquittal if the jury believed it was in the public interest to make the disclosure. The sections in question were furthermore not in breach of Article 10. The need to preserve the secrecy of the information in question had been recognised by the European Court and Commission on Human Rights.[3] The test to be applied was whether in all the circumstances the interference with the individual's right to freedom of expression prescribed by national law was greater than was required to meet the legitimate object that the state was seeking to achieve. In addition, the ban the Law Lords held was not absolute because disclosure could be made lawfully. A former or acting member of those services could make a disclosure *internally* under s 7(3)(a) to the staff counsellor, the Attorney-General, the DPP, the Commissioner of the Metropolitan Police or the Prime Minister or other Ministers if s/he had concerns about the lawfulness of conduct, or concerns about misbehaviour, irregularity, maladministration, waste of resources or incompetence. If no appropriate action followed, the officer could under s 7(3)(b) seek official authorisation to a 'wider audience'. Such a request would have to be dealt with in accordance with the importance attached to freedom of speech, and the need for any restriction to be necessary, responsive to a pressing social need and proportionate. A refusal could be subjected to a judicial review.[4] These procedures properly applied 'provided sufficient and effective safeguards' to ensure unlawfulness and wrongdoing were reported. It was not open to a defendant to argue that in effect these procedures would have provided no safeguard or would have been of no avail.

[1]   *R v Shayler* [2001] 1 WLR 2206 (CA).
[2]   [2002] 2 All ER 477 (HL).
[3]   See the case-law cited by Lord Bingham at para 26 commencing with *Engel v The Netherlands (No 1)* (1976) 1 EHRR 647 at 684–686 and ending with *Vereniging Weekblad Bluf! v The Netherlands* (1995) 20 EHRR 189 at 201–202.
[4]   *R (A) v B* [2009] UKSC 12 establishes that the only body to hear compalints if the tribunal now established under the Regulation of Investigatory Powers Act 2000 and not a judicial review.

2.183   One can only say that is a very sanguine view of the procedures and their efficacy. In early 2004, a civil servant at GCHQ and a former Minister both made disclosures which seemed prima facie a breach of ss 1 and 4. These related to interception of communications of Kofi Annan in the United Nations in New York by MI6 and GCHQ. The prospect of raising the illegality of the Iraq war in 2003 – the opinion on the legality of which the Attorney-General had refused to publish – as a defence and the calling of the Prime Minister and even Attorney-General as witnesses inevitably caused the trial against the civil servant to collapse and ensured that no prosecution was brought against the former Minister, Claire Short. There was some irony in the Law Lords' reminder that under OSA 1989, s 9 the Attorney-General must give his consent to a prosecution under the OSA (see para 2.259 below).

DEFENCE

2.184 Section 2 of the OSA 1989 covers defence information. Those who have been or who are Crown servants or government contractors are guilty of an offence if, without lawful authority, they make a damaging disclosure of any information, document or other article relating to defence which is or has been in their possession by virtue of their position.[1] 'Damaging' under this section means where:

(1) The disclosure damages[2] the capability of, or any part of, the armed forces of the Crown to carry out their tasks or leads to loss of life or injury to members of those forces or serious damage to the equipment or installations of those forces.

(2) Otherwise than as mentioned in para (1), it endangers the interests of the United Kingdom abroad, seriously obstructs the promotion or protection by the United Kingdom of those interests or endangers the safety of British citizens abroad. It is not clear from the first part whether this might include commercial interests relating to defence, although s 2(4)(b), below, might make such an interpretation untenable.

(3) It is of information or of a document or article which is such that its unauthorised disclosure would be likely to have any of those effects.

[1] OSA 1989, s 2(1).
[2] The original clause had 'prejudices' – note the discussion in ch 1 on the FOIA 2000.

2.185 It is a defence to charges under s 2 for a defendant to prove that at the time of the alleged offence s/he did not know, and had no reasonable cause to believe, that the information, document or article in question related to defence, or that a disclosure would be damaging within the meaning of s 2(1).1 'Damaging' means it damages the capability of, or any part of, the armed forces of the Crown to carry out their tasks or leads to loss of life or injury to members of those forces or serious damage to the equipment or installations of those forces. It covers endangering the interests of the UK abroad seriously obstructing the promotion or protection by the UK of those interests or endangers the safety of British citizens abroad. A disclosure is also damaging which is of information or a document or article which is such that its unauthorised disclosure would be likely to have any of the above effects.

2.186 'Defence' means for s 2:

'(a) the size, shape, organisation, logistics, order of battle, deployment, operations, state of readiness and training of the armed forces of the Crown;

(b) the weapons, stores or other equipment of those forces and the invention, development, production and operation of such equipment and research relating to it;

(c) defence policy and strategy and military planning and intelligence;

(d) plans and measures for the maintenance of essential supplies and services that are or would be needed in time of war.'[2]

¹   *R v Keogh* [2007] EWCA 528 Crim. OSA 1989, ss 2 and 3 (below) do not reverse the burden of proof placing it onto the defendant; there is, however, an evidentiary burden to make out the defence.
²   OSA 1989, s 2(4)(b).

INTERNATIONAL RELATIONS

2.187   By OSA 1989, s 3(5) these are defined as:

'the relations between States, between international organisations or between one or more States and one or more such organisations and includes any matter relating to a State other than the UK or to an international organisation which is capable of affecting the relations of the UK with another State or with an international organisation'.¹

¹   Note the discussion of the EU Regulation on access in ch 3 below.

2.188   Section 3 concerns offences relating to international relations and covers Crown servants and government contractors, present or past, and damaging disclosures without authority of any information, document or other article relating to international relations or 'any confidential information, document or other article which was obtained from a State¹ other than the United Kingdom or an international organisation'.² It applies to information etc which is or has been in a person's possession by virtue of that person's position as a Crown servant or government contractor. 'Confidential' for the purposes of this section covers situations where the terms on which information etc received from a State or organisation require it to be held in confidence, or 'while the circumstances in which it was obtained make it reasonable' for the latter to expect as much.³ In other words stamping it 'confidential', no matter how innocuous the contents, will make it confidential, as will those occasions where the custom and practice of diplomacy etc require confidentiality. It is not 'confidential' according to principles developed by the courts (see below).

¹   'State': s 13(1).
²   OSA 1989, s 3(1)(b). Eg the European Commission, and see s 13(1), (2) and (3).
³   OSA 1989, s 3(6).

2.189   A disclosure is damaging if: it endangers¹ the interests of the UK abroad (for example if commercial interests would be concerned, or if there would be a lowering of esteem because of revelations of environmental contamination); it seriously obstructs the promotion or protection by the UK of those interests;² or, it endangers the safety of British citizens abroad;³ or, it is of information or of a document or article which is such that its unauthorised disclosure would be likely to have any of those effects.⁴ Arguably, this could apply to information exempted under the 2001 EC Regulation on Access discussed in ch 3.

¹   Originally 'prejudices'.
²   Would this include commercial interests?
³   OSA 1989, s 3(2)(a).
⁴   OSA 1989, s 3(2)(b).

2.190 When information is 'confidential' under s 3(1)(b), and sub-s (6), it may[1] be regarded for the purposes of s 3(2)(b) as such that its unauthorised disclosure would be likely to have any of the effects there mentioned, ie those in s 3(2)(a) above, either by reason of the fact that it is confidential or by reason of its contents or nature.[2] In other words, damaging effects may be presumed to follow where it is confidential without actual proof. This provision[3] was highly criticised.

[1] Not 'must', but a discretionary test depending upon the seriousness of the damage.
[2] OSA 1989, s 3(3).
[3] Because it is simply stamped 'Confidential'. The government emphasised the discretionary nature of the test; see para 2.188.

2.191 Again, a defence can be made out by the defendant in terms almost identical to those in s 2: basically that at the time of the alleged offence the defendant did not know etc that the information was protected under s 3 and s/he had no knowledge etc that its disclosure would be damaging.

CRIME

2.192 A former, or present, Crown servant or government contractor is guilty of an offence if without lawful authority[1] s/he discloses any information etc which is or has been in his or her possession by virtue of his or her position as such[2] and the disclosure of which:
(a) results in the commission of an offence (any offence);[3]
(b) facilitates an escape from legal custody[4] or the doing of any other act prejudicial to the safekeeping of persons in legal custody;[5] or
(c) impedes the prevention or detection of offences or the apprehension or prosecution of suspected offenders,[6]

or which is such that its unauthorised disclosure would be likely to have any of these effects.[7]

[1] OSA 1989, s 7 and paras 2.248 et seq below.
[2] OSA 1989, s 4(1).
[3] OSA 1989, s 4(2)(a)(i), eg publicising a faulty burglar alarm, or security system. Cf disclosures by members of the armed services in Northern Ireland which led to attacks on putative Republicans: see *DPP v Channel Four Television Co Ltd* [1992] 2 All ER 517, DC, ch 10 below.
[4] OSA 1989, s 4(6).
[5] OSA 1989, s 4(2)(a)(ii).
[6] OSA 1989, s 4(2)(a)(iii).
[7] OSA 1989, s 4(2)(b).

2.193 A defence can be made out by the defendant to a charge under (a)–(c) that at the time of the alleged offence s/he did not know and had no reasonable cause to believe that the disclosure would have any of the effects listed above.[1]

[1] OSA 1989, s 4(4).

INFORMATION OBTAINED BY INTERCEPTION AND BY THE SECURITY SERVICES AND INTELLIGENCE SERVICES (S 4(3))

2.194 Although within OSA 1989, s 4, this category in fact constitutes a clearly separable class of information. No damage has to be proved for unauthorised disclosure of the information within this category, although the defence can prove (on a balance of probabilities) that the defendant did not know at the time of the alleged offence and had no reasonable cause to know that the information etc was that to which s 4(3) applies.

2.195 Section 4(3) applies to any information obtained by reason of the interception of any communication in obedience to a warrant issued under s 5 of the Regulation of Investigatory Powers Act 2000, any information relating to the obtaining of information by reason of any such interception and any document or other article which is or has been used or held for use in, or has been obtained by reason of, any such interception. The 2000 Act repealed the Interception of Communications Act 1985 and also implements Article 5 of the EC Council Directive 97/66 'Telecommunications Data Protection Directive'. The section also applies to information obtained under the issue of warrants to the security and intelligence services under the Security Service Act 1989, s 3, Intelligence Services Act 1994, s 5 and s 7 (para 2.220 below). Basically s 4(3) prohibits the unauthorised disclosure of intercept and security and intelligence services' special investigation powers information.

2.196 The ICA 1985 followed litigation in the European Court of Human Rights (ECtHR) in which the UK was ultimately found to be in breach of Art 8 of the Convention because interceptions did not take place under any appropriate legal framework.[1] The legislation sought to produce a legal framework that would comply with the provisions of the Convention. The Act was widely criticised for providing only an absolute minimum safeguard and for leaving the power to grant warrants within the executive and not handing it to the courts. Basically all interceptions of communications covered by the 1985 Act[2] (and now under s 5 of RIPA 2000) have to be authorised by warrant of the Secretary of State.[3] Those not so authorised are a criminal offence.[4] A warrant may only be issued for any one of four grounds: protection of national security, prevention of serious crime or disorder, for the protection of the economic well-being of the country, to give effect to an international mutual assistance agreement (s 5(3)). A Commissioner[5] is established to investigate allegations that the terms of a warrant have been abused, and a tribunal may adjudicate on the matter.[6] Unauthorised interceptions did not fall within the regulation of the 1985 Act , and nor did a host of other eavesdropping devices.[7] In other words, a victim of such practices had to rely upon breaches of the civil or criminal law, and criminal prosecutions may be stopped by a *nolle prosequi* instruction by the Attorney-General.

---

[1] *Malone v UK* (1984) 7 EHRR 14. See *Kruslin v France* (1990) 12 EHRR 547 and *Kopp v Switzerland* 4 BHRC 277.

[2] The Act was effective from 10 April 1986. The Act covered postal and telephone interceptions.

[3] Or those warranted by an authorised delegate.

[4] Outside the Act, civil redress is unlikely; see RIPA 2000, s 1(3) and, for the powers of the RIPA tribunal, s 67(7).

[5] A senior judge.

[6] See paras 2.200 et seq below on RIPA 2000.

[7] These were covered by Home Office Guidelines on the Use of Equipment in Police Surveillance Operations until regulated by Police Act 1997, Part III and RIPA 2000: see para 2.220, note 1 below.

2.197   The relevant provisions of the ICA 1985 have now been repealed by RIPA 2000 which as well as covering the interception of a wider range of communications which may be authorised – and thereby unlawful if not authorised – also creates a tort of 'unlawful interception' under s 1(3). The remit of the Commissioner has been extended by ss 57 and 58 of RIPA 2000.

2.198   Section 4(3)(a) of the OSA 1989 makes it an offence to disclose any information obtained under a warrant under s 5 of the RIPA 2000. It does not apply to the disclosure of unauthorised obtaining of such information, it should be noted, although it might fall within s 4(2)(a)(i) of the OSA 1989 above, ie it results in the commission of an offence. Nor does it apply to information obtained by other eavesdropping devices, although this may have been covered by s 4(3)(b) of the OSA 1920 until repealed by the 1985 Act. Covert operations by police were, however, placed on a statutory basis by the Police Act 1997, Part III and by the RIPA 2000.

2.199   It is necessary to say a little more about the Regulation of Investigatory Powers Act 2000.

THE REGULATION OF INVESTIGATORY POWERS ACT 2000

2.200   As already described, the Regulation of Investigatory Powers Act 2000 (RIPA 2000) established a new framework for the regulation of investigatory powers.[1] The ICA 1985 is therefore repealed to the extent necessary. RIPA 2000 sought to address various problems identified by statutory shortcomings, case law, especially in the *Halford* decision before the ECtHR which involved an unregulated intercept on a private network by an employer,[2] the impact of the Human Rights Act 1998 and the fact that the ICA 1985 was introduced when there were basically only two telecommunications companies offering fixed line services; there are now about 757 telecommunications providers (the telecoms ombudsman lists 300 members).[3] There is a mass ownership in mobile phones; totally new services have been introduced such as international simple resale; there has been a rapid evolution of the satellite telephone market; a dramatic increase in communications via the internet; use of radio pagers; there has also been a rapid development in the number and type of postal services.[4] The government saw the extension of the powers of interception to cover these communications as vital for the fight against crime. In 1996 and 1997, interception of communications led to 1200 arrests by police and HM customs; seizure of drugs with a street value of £600 million; and seizure of over 450 firearms.

[1]   See Regulation of Investigatory Powers (Monetary Penalty Notices and Consents for Interceptions) Order 2011, SI 2011/1340 which allows the Interception Commissioner to issue monetary penalty notices where there are unlawful intercepts and where an offence under s 1(1) has not been committed (see the schedule) and which amends s 3(1) to remove the words 'or which that person has reasonable grounds for believing'.

[2]   *Halford v UK* (1997) 24 EHRR 523; see also *Allen v UK* (2002) Times, 12 November (ECtHR). No 'tapping' is involved when tapping one's own phone calls: *R v Hardy*, B. 31/10/02 (CA CD).

Liberty v UK No 58243/00 Times 11/7/08 on art 8 breach and 1985 ICA 'virtually uncontrollable discretion and guidelines cy Commissioner but not in law or published.

3   http://www.freeindex.co.uk/categories/business_services/business_communications/ telecommunication. (21/03/11).

4   Cm 4368 Interception of Communications in the UK (1999).

2.201   The government therefore sought to update the legislation to take account of communications services introduced since 1985, to extend the law to cover interception on private telephone networks which were linked to public networks – the problem posed by the ECtHR decision in *Halford*'s case (though see s 1(6)(a) and (b)); to provide a 'clear, statutory framework for authorising the disclosure of data held by communications service providers'; as well as providing a legislative framework for the police and security services etc to obtain communications data (information about the use of a communications service but not the contents of those communications)[1] and such data may be obtained on grounds that are wider than obtaining an intercept;[2] retain existing safeguards ensuring that interception is only authorised by the Secretary of State (or officials where authorised under s 6(2)) when justified according to strict statutory criteria and that the power is subject to judicial scrutiny via the Tribunal. Power to intercept public postage is retained. Section 5(2)(b) introduces a proportionality test when issuing warrants for intercepts under s 5 – any breach of a Convention right must be proportionate with intended and legitimate objectives. In November 2010, the Home Office published results of a 'targeted' consultation on the Act, which was criticised for breaching government guidance on consultation: http://webarchive.nationalarchives.gov.uk/+/http://www.homeoffice.gov.uk/ documents/cons-2009-ripa/ripa-cons-response?view=Binary.

1   See RIPA 2000, s 21 and Regulation of Investigatory Powers (Communications Data) Order 2003 (SI 2003/3172 and SI 2003/3172, SI 2005/1083 and SI 2006/1878, now consolidated in Regulation of Investigatory Powers (Communications Data) Order 2010, SI 2010/480) which adds to the public authorities entitled to acquire communications data under s 25. The Order specifies which individuals within those public authorities, and the public authorities already listed in the 2000 Act, are entitled to acquire communications data. It also places restrictions on the grounds on which they may acquire communications data and the types of communications data they may acquire. See also Anti-terrorism, Crime and Security Act 2001, Part 11 (ss 102–106) and *Retention of Communications Data under Part 11 Antiterrorism, Crime and Security Act 2001 Voluntary Code of Practice* (2003, Home Office). This is addressed to service providers asking them to retain such data for 'extended periods of time'. It covers traffic data, the use made of the service and other information relating to the subscriber. The IC was consulted over the code and it states it complies with the Data Protection Act 1998. See SI 2003/3175 on the latter. The relevant provisions on data retention are now EC Directive 2006/241/EC and SI 2007/2199 and SI 2009/859 (para 2.206, note 2 below). Data must be retained for 12 months from the date of communication in question.

2   RIPA 2000, s 22(a)–(h).

2.202

1985 Act	2000 Act (in 2000)
EXISTING LEGISLATION	PROPOSED CHANGES
IOCA is restricted to interception of communications sent by post or by means of public telecommunications systems.	Interception legislation to encompass all communications in the course of their transmission by telecommunications operators or mail delivery systems.
Currently interception warrants specify the address to be intercepted.	Interception warrants to specify a person, and to include a schedule listing all the addresses which the Agency wishes to intercept in relation to that person.
Interception warrants may only be issued under the authority of the Secretary of State. Modifications may be made by senior civil servants with the express authorisation of the Secretary of State, or by a person holding office under the Crown, where they have been expressly authorised by the warrant to do so.	The issue of the warrant to continue to be authorised by the Secretary of State. Susequent modifications to the warrant adding new addresses to be authorised at senior civil servant level. Provision to be made allowing urgent modifications with limited lifespan to be made by Head of Agency or nominated deputy who are expressly authorised by the warrant.
Interception warrants are served on the PTO or Post Office, who are required to intercept such communications as are described in the warrant.	Interception warrants to be served on the agency making the application, who will then use it to achieve the interception with reasonable assistance from the Communications Service Provider.
All warrants are authorised for an initial period of two months. Thereafter, warrants issued on serious crime grounds are renewed on a monthly basis and those issued on national security or economic well-being grounds are renewed on a six-monthly basis.	All warrants to be authorised for an initial period of three months. Warrants to be renewed at three-monthly (serious crime warrants) and six-monthly (national security and economic well-being warrants) intervals, bringing them into line with intrusive surveillance provisions.
There is currently no legislative framework for authorising interception of private (non-public) networks.	Provision to be made allowing employers to continue recording communications in the course of lawful business practice to provide evidence of commercial transactions or any other business communication, in both the public and private sectors.

	1985 Act	2000 Act (in 2000)
	EXISTING LEGISLATION	PROPOSED CHANGES
	Communications data may be supplied voluntarily by holders for specified reasons (eg investigation of crime) under the DPA 1998 and the Telecommunications Act 1984. They may additionally be required to produce it in obedience to a Production Order authorised by a Crown Court judge.	The law regarding provision of communications data for law enforcement, security or intelligence purposes to be amended to require the holder of such data to provide it in response to a properly authorised request.

2.203　There will continue to be an offence of unlawful interception. There will be no change to the criteria which must be met before the interception of communications is authorised. These are contained in RIPA 2000, s 5(3).

2.204　There will be no change initially to procedures for warrants authorising interception of external communications although additional safeguards may be imposed (see SI 2004/158 on lawful interception of persons outside the UK).

2.205　There will continue to be 'strict controls' over the extent to which intercepted material is disclosed or copied restricting this to the minimum necessary. This is especially true in relation to use of intercept evidence and related communications data in court, although such restrictions of court use do not apply to information obtained under other Parts of the Act. Such use of intercepts in court is prohibited under s 17 of RIPA 2000.[1] RIPA 2000, s 18 allows for numerous exemptions to s 17, including use of intercept material in criminal proceedings for breaches of the Act. The Prevention of Terrorism Act 2005 adds 'control orders', so controversially introduced under that Act, to s 18 exceptions. The Special Immigration Appeals Commission is already within s 18. There is, it should be noted, increasing pressure on the government to introduce measures allowing use of intercept evidence in trials, especially those involving suspected terrorists, but their use in trials involving organised criminals is also supported. A Code of Practice on *Interception of Communications* (2002, now 2010) advises on the treatment of confidential and legally privileged information. It has been ruled by the House of Lords that s 17(1) does not prevent questions being asked, evidence adduced or disclosure made in a criminal trial to establish whether a telecommunications system is a public or private system and whether, if a private system whether it has been carried out with the consent of the person who controls the operation or use of that system.[2] Communication services providers (CSPs) will be required to give assistance to police and others in accordance with an interception warrant (s 12) and they must do everything reasonably required in order to effect the intercept. CSPs may be obliged by the Secretary of State to maintain a reasonable intercept capability (and see SI 2002/1931 on maintenance of interception capability). The Secretary of State may contribute towards the costs incurred by CSPs of providing an intercept capability. Regulations have been made authorising interception of communications for the purposes of monitoring or keeping a record of communications for a range of purposes.[3]

1 See RIPA 2000, s 18: *R v Preston* [1994] 2 AC 130, HL; *Morgans v DPP* [1999] 1 WLR 968. See *R v P* [2001] 2 All ER 58, HL which held that evidence under foreign intercepts was not subject to the s 9 (1985 Act) restrictions and was admissible and this was not a breach of Art 8 ECHR (see SI 2004/158 on lawful interception of persons outside UK). Also *R v Sargent* [2002] 1 All ER 161 (HL) – interception by employee for personal use. See *R v E* [2004] EWCA Crim 124.

2 *A-G's Reference No 5 of 2002* [2004] UKHL 40.

3 Telecommunications (Lawful Business Practice) (Interception of Communications) Regulations 2000, SI 2000/2699. See also the Code of Practice on *Interception of Communications* (2010).

2.206 A Tribunal and a body of Commissioners will continue to operate to deal with grievances.[1] The Tribunal's powers are fuller than under the 1985 legislation in terms of its ability to challenge the substantive merits of an authorisation. By RIPA 2000, s 67(8), decisions of RIPA are not challengeable by appeal or review except as the Secretary of State otherwise determines by order but such an order must exist for challenges against orders of the tribunal under s 65(2) (c) or (d) (s 67(9)). Part I, chapter two of RIPA 2000 also authorises the obtaining and disclosure of 'communications data' as opposed to interceptions.[2]

1 The current Interceptions' Commissioner is Sir Swinton Thomas, former Lord Justice of Appeal. Commissioners are senior judges. The annual report for 2010 from the Commissioner is at HC 1239 (2010–12).

2 The Data Retention (EC Directive) Regs 2009, SI 2009/859 – data as specified in the schedule must be retained for 12 months

2.207 The first part of OSA 1989, s 4(3) only applies to RIPA 2000, s 5 material in Part I, chapter one, ie interceptions.1 It does not cover communications data in chapter two of Part I. But, for completeness, it should be added that Part II of RIPA 2000 puts the use of covert surveillance which is not already covered by Part III of the Police Act 1997 and the Intelligence Services Act 1994 as well as covert human resources, ie informants, agents and undercover officers under statutory regulation.[1] Foreign surveillance concerning foreign police and customs officers in the UK is authorised under the Crime (International Cooperation) Act 2003, s 83; and cessation of authorisations by the Serious Organised Crime Agency is covered by regulations (SI 2004/1128). Evidence has been given to the Home Affairs Committee by a senior metropolitan police officer (Assistant Commissioner John Yates) that 'hacking' into mobile phones may not be an 'interception' for RIPA purposes where the voice box or email box message has been read. It may be an interception where the message in the box has not been read.[3] Can such a distinction remove 'hacking' from RIPA offences? RIPA 2000, s 1 refers to intentionally and without lawful authority 'to intercept .. any communication *in the course of its transmission* ..'. Arguably, as s 1 creates a criminal offence the words should be interpreted strictly. This is without prejudice to offences under the DPA or actions under civil law including the HRA. Arrests have also been brought under the Criminal Law Act 1977, s 1 for conspiracy to intercept communications.[4] It would be strange and regrettable if the offence under the Act did not cover hacking given that the Crown possessed a prerogative power to intercept (reinforced by its ownership historically of the Post Office) whereas to enter, search and seize it possessed no such prerogative and a warrant was necessary.[5] The statements to the committee were made as part of the allegations against the *News of the World* for its use of investigators to hack into individuals' phones. Originally, the victims were the powerful and famous but it transpired that such practices had involved child murder victims and bereaved parents and included deleting messages prompting hopes in relatives that the victim was not dead, soldiers killed in Afghanistan, victims of the London terrorist bombings in 2005 and widespread corruption of police officers by reporters and others including those on royal protection duties. In July 2011, News International (a subsidiary of News Corporation owned by Rupert Murdoch) closed the *News of the World* as a response to the outcry but this did not assuage anxieties. A judicial inquiry under Lord Justice Leveson was announced by the Prime Minister along with other measures.[6] But the affair brought into question the relationships and influence involving Rupert Murdoch and UK governments and the fitness of News Corporation to take over BSkyB. His bid was withdrawn in July 2011. The metropolitan police commissioner and the assistant commissioner John Yates both resigned spawning a welter of official inquiries into police conduct.

[1]   On 'interceptions', see: *R v E* [2004] EWCA Crim 1243.

[2]   The ECtHR ruled that the legally unregulated use of surreptitious devices to obtain information was a breach of ECHR Art 8: *Khan v UK* (2000) 8 BHRC 310, following the House of Lords decision that whether a breach or not it was not unlawful under English law and evidence was admissible in a trial under the provisions of the Police and Criminal Evidence Act 1984, s 78: *R v Khan* [1996] 3 All ER 289, HL and see *Schenk v Switzerland* (1988) 13 EHRR 242. For pre-RIPA: *Hewitson v UK* (2003) *Times*, 10 June (ECtHR); *PG and JH v UK* (2001) *Times*, 19 October (ECtHR). For the civil law position on the use of improperly obtained evidence and CPR 1998, r 32.1, see *Jones v University of Warwick* [2003] 3 All ER 760.

[3]   HAC *Specialist Operations* HC 441 (2010–11) Q 5. See http://www.parliament.uk/documents/commons-committees/home-affairs/Memoranda.pdf.
      See HC 907 (2010–12) and Government Reply Cm 8182 on unauthorised tapping or hacking. The police officer was asked to return to give further evidence. In a civil action for disclosure of hacking material, the high court ordered the police to disclose information held by them on hacking by private companies largely for the press, in particular the *News of the World, Financial Times* 19 March 2011. Select Committee on Media, Culture and Sport 24 March 2011. On private investigators and supply of personal data through illegal means, see IC *What Price Privacy?* HC 1056 (2005–06) and *What Price Privacy Now?* HC 36 (2006–07).

[4]   On declarations rejecting claims to the privilege of self incrimination and the loss of the privilege by virtue of Senior Courts Act 1981, s 72 in relation attempting to plead self incrimination in revealing by those involved in voicemail hacking, see: *Gray and Coogan v News Group Newspapers Ltd* [2011] EWHC 349. An appeal to the court of appeal was refused.

[5]   *Entick v Carrington* (1765) 19 St Trials 1029.

[6]   For the Leveson inquiry on the culture, practice, ethics of the press, see www.levesoninquiry.org.uk.

2.208 Section 26 concerns three types of activity covered by Part II of RIPA 2000. 'Directed surveillance' is covert surveillance that is undertaken in relation to a specific investigation in order to obtain information about, or identify of, a particular person or to determine who is involved in a matter under investigation.[1] It may also include an intercept without warrant where a necessary consent has been given (s 48(4)). The Regulation of Investigatory Powers (Directed Surveillance and Covert Human Intelligence Sources) Order 2010, SI 2010/521 lists the ranks of individuals who may give authorisations and limits on authorisations. A code of guidance covers such intelligence: http://www.homeoffice.gov.uk/publications/counter-terrorism/ripa-forms/code-practice-human-intel?view=Binary.

¹ The Information Commissioner has dealt with requests for information about surveillance. In FS50289146 a request was made to the MoJ for a list of prisoners who had been subject to covert surveillance in either Belgium, HMP Belmarsh or the Old Bailey during a specified period. The public authority refused to confirm or deny if it held information falling within the scope of this request, citing the exemptions provided by ss 23(5) (information relating to, or supplied by, security bodies), 24(2) (national security), 31(3) (prejudice to law enforcement), 40(5) (personal information) and 44(2) (statutory prohibitions to disclosure) of the Act in relation to HMP Belmarsh. In relation to Belgium and the Old Bailey, the complainant was advised to redirect his requests elsewhere. In relation to the HMP Belmarsh request, the Commissioner found that the public authority applied the exemptions provided by ss 23(5) and 24(2) correctly. However, in relation to the Belgium and Old Bailey requests, the Commissioner ruled that the public authority failed to confirm or deny whether it held information falling within the scope of these requests and, in so doing, did not comply with ss 1(1)(a) and 10(1). The Commissioner also found that the public authority breached FOIA 2000, ss 17(1), 17(1)(c) and 17(3)(a). See T Pitt-Payne and A Proops *Employee Surveillance* (2011). The report of the chief surveillance commissioner for 2010 is HC 1111 (2010–12).

2.209 'Intrusive surveillance' is covert surveillance carried out in relation to anything taking place on residential premises or in any private vehicle. This surveillance may be by a person or device inside such premises or a private vehicle or by means of a device placed outside 'which consistently provides a product of equivalent quality and detail as a product which would be obtained from a device located outside.' The use of a tracking device eg to locate a vehicle is not intrusive surveillance (s 25(4)) and nor is that obtained under s 48(4) above. Codes of practice cover covert surveillance and property interference: The Regulation of Investigatory Powers (Covert Surveillance and Property Interference: Code of Practice) Order 2010, SI 2010/463; The Regulation of Investigatory Powers (Covert Human Intelligence Sources: Code of Practice) Order 2010, SI 2010/462 and http://www.homeoffice.gov.uk/publications/counter-terrorism/ripa-forms/code-of-practice-covert?view=Binary.

Directed surveillance may be treated as intrusive by order of the Secretary of State such as, for instance where property is used for legal consultations (RIPA 2000, s 47(1)(b) and SI 2010/461).

2.210 A 'covert human intelligence source' is someone who establishes relationships with another to facilitate: covert use of the relationship to obtain information or to provide access to any information to another person or (b) covertly discloses information obtained by the use of such a relationship or as a consequence of its existence. These may be added to by order. The Secretary of State may prescribe by order who within public authorities may authorise directed surveillance and covert human intelligence sources – details are contained in a code. These authorities have been extended by order (see SI 2010/521 below). Authorisations will only be given where necessary and proportionate.

2.211 Section 32 allows intrusive surveillance to be authorised (ISA) by respective parties and ss 33–40 set out the procedure for obtaining ISAs for investigations carried out by the police, the Serious Organised Crime Agency and HMRC. ISA can only be given for one of three grounds: protection of national security; prevention of serious crime or disorder; or protection of the economic well-being of the country. Where surveillance is necessary and proportionate, an ISA will be given by the Chief Constable, or where necessary by the Secretary of State, except where this is not practicable because of urgency. Approval will be given by a Surveillance Commissioner (established under Part III of the Police Act 1997) before an ISA can take effect. Under the 1997 Act, approval was required for sensitive information covered eg by legal privilege or confidentiality. Even where authorisations take effect without approval because of urgency, the chief constable etc will have to notify the Commissioner as soon as reasonably practicable giving reasons for proceeding without approval. Approval has to satisfy the dual tests of proportionality and necessity. A Commissioner may quash an authorisation for the grounds stated in s 37 and an appeal lies to the Chief Surveillance Commissioner by a Chief Constable, etc where an authorisation is not approved or renewed. Special provisions apply to ISAs carried out by the intelligence services, the Ministry of Defence, HM forces or persons designated for the purposes of the section. These are authorised by the Secretary of State and do not involve the Commissioner. From the Secretary of State's decision there is no appeal. Codes of Practice exist for Covert Human Intelligence Sources and Covert Surveillance (see above). Guidance is provided on precautions necessary for confidential (including confidential journalistic) and legally privileged information. In *R v Robinson* the Court of Appeal Criminal Division examined the Code on Covert Human Intelligence Sources and held that use of solicitors or their clerks as informers would breach their duties to their clients and would also amount to breaches by police of duties owed to citizens.[1] In *McE v NI Prison Service*[2] the House of Lords ruled that intrusive surveillance may be used to eavesdrop on conversations between lawyers and their clients. Some forms of police surveillance such as keeping someone under observation, taking photographs, using informants or infiltration into organisations do not require prior approval of the surveillance commissioner. In *Wood v Commissioner of Metropolitan Police* the Court of Appeal ruled that on the facts taking and retaining photographs of Wood who was engaging in political protests at a meeting breached his ECHR, Art 8 rights.[3]

[1]   (2003) *Times*, 13 November.
[2]   [2009] UKHL 15
[3]   [2009] EWCA Civ 414.

2.212   Intelligence services authorisations under Part II are made by warrant in accordance with s 5 of the Intelligence Services Act 1994 (see below).

2.213   Schedule 1 to RIPA 2000 lists those who are entitled to authorise directed surveillance and the use and conduct of covert intelligence sources under RIPA 2000, ss 28 and 29. As explained above, these authorities have been extended by SI 2003/521, arts 2 and 3 amend Schedule 1 to RIPA 2000 by adding to it a number of new public authorities. Additional offices, ranks and persons for 'urgent cases' are listed in Art 4. Articles 5–8 list restrictions on authorisations. Designated individuals in the public authorities listed in Part I of Schedule 1 are entitled to authorise directed surveillance and the use and conduct of covert human intelligence sources under ss 28(3) and 29(3) of the 2000 Act, respectively. Designated individuals in the public authorities listed in Part II of Schedule 1 are only entitled to authorise directed surveillance under s 28(3) of the 2000 Act. Article 4 of this Order prescribes offices, ranks and positions for the purposes of s 30(1) of the 2000 Act for both the public authorities already in Schedule 1 and those added to it by this Order. Individuals holding these prescribed offices, ranks or positions are designated under ss 28 and 29 of the 2000 Act as being able to authorise directed surveillance and the use and conduct of covert human intelligence sources. Earlier Orders are revoked by Art 10 of this Order.

2.214 Column 1 of the Schedule to the Order lists the public authorities. Column 2 specifies the individuals within each public authority that can authorise directed surveillance and the use and conduct of covert human intelligence sources. An individual holding an office, rank or position listed in column 2 of Part I of the Schedule may grant an authorisation under either s 28(3) or s 29(3) of the 2000 Act, other than where the Schedule indicates to the contrary. An individual holding an office, rank or position listed in column 2 of Part II of the Schedule may only grant an authorisation under s 28(3) of the 2000 Act. Individuals holding more senior offices, ranks or positions to those listed in column 2 may also authorise in the same circumstances as those to whom they are senior. Column 3 sets out certain less senior officials who can authorise in urgent cases. Column 4 sets out the grounds on which an authorisation can be given by reference to the grounds set out in the different paragraphs of ss 28(3) and 29(3) of the 2000 Act. For example, ground (b) is for the purpose of preventing or detecting crime or of preventing disorder. These are baffling regimes and the chief surveillance commissioner has the duty of keeping the operation of RIPA part two under review.

2.215 The Protection of Liberties Bill 2011, Part 2, chapter 2 amends RIPA 2000 so as to require local authorities to obtain judicial approval for the use of any one of the three covert investigatory techniques available to them under the Act, namely the acquisition and disclosure of communications data, and the use of directed surveillance and covert human intelligence sources ('CHIS').

2.216 Finally, Part III of the RIPA 2000 deals with 'Encryption'.[1] In order to authenticate electronic messages and to help guarantee their integrity and confidentiality, two techniques are commonly employed: electronic signatures and encryption. Both of these may be achieved by the same technology: public key cryptography. 'Each user of public key cryptography has both a private key, which is kept secret, and a public key, which can be published. The "keys" are long numbers which cannot be derived from each other, but which are related through the application of mathematical functions.'[2] The public key may be used to scramble a text sent electronically and the text can only be decrypted with the private key.

[1] *Building Confidence in Electronic Commerce* HC 187 (1998–99) (Trade & Industry Committee); *Building Confidence in Electronic Commerce*, DTI 5 March 1999.
[2] HC 187, paras 9–12. See *R v S* [2009] 1 All ER 716.

2.217 The legislation allows a person who has come into possession of protected information – basically that lawfully obtained after seizure, interception etc and which is protected by keys – to serve a notice under s 49 on any person possessing a key to that information requiring the disclosure of the key. The requirement must be necessary and proportionate in the interests of national security, for the purpose of preventing or detecting crime or in the interests of the economic well-being of the UK. Disclosure of the information in an intelligible form instead of the key is permissible. Failure to comply with a notice is a criminal offence. A variety of statutory defences apply under s 53(4). A specific offence of 'tipping off' is created. This is where a person on whom a s 49 notice is served discloses anything required by the notice to be kept secret.[1] Section 55 provides for safeguards in the exercise of powers under this part of the Act which must be read together with Sch 2. Schedule 2 provides that only a person with the appropriate authorisation can issue a notice and in paragraph 1 this means an authorisation obtained by a judge. However, it then goes on to cover a warrant issued by the Secretary of State! In *R v S* the Court of Appeal ruled that although requesting a key leading to a criminal charge may be self-incriminatory, it was not unfair or a breach of proportionality.[2]

[1]   RIPA 2000, s 54.
[2]   [2009] 1 All ER 716. See also *Jalloh v Germany* (2006) 20 BHRC 575, ECHR.

2.218 This aspect of the Act was heavily criticised by software groups, technology groups and pressure groups as well as civil liberties groups. Central to their concerns was a desire for judicial authorisation via a court and a technical evaluation by a board of industry experts.

2.219 Unless any of the above information falls within s 4(3)(a) of the OSA 1989 (ie intercepts), it would have to fall within s 4(1) or (2) of the OSA 1989 to be punishable under that Act. Special provision is made for the security and intelligence services.

THE SECURITY SERVICE ACTS 1989 AND 1996, THE INTELLIGENCE SERVICES ACT 1994 AND DISCLOSURES UNDER OSA 1989, S 4(3)(B)

2.220 Section 4(3)(b) of OSA 1989 makes it a criminal offence to disclose without authority any information obtained by reason of action authorised by a warrant issued under s 3 of the Security Service Act 1989 (SSA 1989), any information relating to the obtaining of information by reason of any such action and any document or other article which is or has been used or held for use in, or has been obtained by reason of, any such action. Similar protection was afforded to information obtained by MI6 and General Communications Headquarters (the government's intelligence gathering centre: see above) and warrants issued under s 5 and authorisations for overseas activities under s 7 of the Intelligence Services Act 1994 (ISA 1994). Section 7 was amended by the Anti-terrorism, Crime and Security Act 2001, s 116 which added GCHQ to the list of agencies entitled to seek authorisation under s 7 for overseas activities. The 2001 amendment also allows GCHQ and SIS to engage in authorised acts within the UK but only where the intention is to affect apparatus which is located abroad. Section 116 also aligns the definitions of prevention and detection of crime under which the security and intelligence services operate to that in RIPA

2000, s 81(5). The ISA 1994 further provided for a Parliamentary Committee to oversee the services. The Security Service Act 1996 attempted to define what amounts to serious criminal conduct for the purposes of invoking powers to issue warrants to intercept communications or enter or interfere with property or with wireless telegraphy within the UK or British islands by the Security Service. Where activities are carried out by the security and intelligence services under Part II of the RIPA 2000, concerning the use of covert, directed and intrusive surveillance techniques, are these covered by OSA 1989, s 4(3)(b)? They have to fall within the terms of the security and intelligence legislation, ie they concern interference with private property, wireless telegraphy or unlawful acts (contrary to criminal or civil law) committed outside the UK. Those matters not so covered may well be offences under OSA 1989, s 1 and possibly s 3 and also s 5 below. The Police Act 1997 regulated the use by police of electronic surveillance devices or 'bugs' on private property. Initial authorisation is by a Chief police or HMRC officer subject to prior approval by a Surveillance Commissioner where the intrusion was into people's homes, offices or hotel bedrooms or on other grounds except in a case of urgency. A code was issued under s 101(3) of the Police Act 1997.[1] Codes have been drawn up by the Home Office on interception of communications, surveillance, use of informants, undercover operations and recording and dissemination of information.[2] As explained, RIPA 2000 provided additional safeguards for intrusive surveillance.[3] The activities of the police and others under Part II of the RIPA 2000 who are not members of the intelligence and security services are not covered by OSA 1989, s 4(3)(b).

[1]   *Intrusive Surveillance Code of Practice* (1999) and see Commons Research Paper 00/25.
[2]   Above para 2.208.
[3]   See para 2.201, note 1 above, and SI 2002/1298 under RIPA 2000, ss 28 and 29.

2.221   The Security Service Act 1989 placed the UK security services (MI5) on a statutory footing.[1] ISA 1994 does likewise with the Secret Intelligence Service (MI6) and General Communications HQ – now known as the 'Intelligence Services'. The Secretary of State shall appoint a Director-General (DG) who is responsible for the efficiency of the secret service and who is under a duty, under s 2(2), to ensure:

'(a)   that there are arrangements for securing that no information is obtained by the service except so far as necessary for the proper discharge of its functions, or disclosed by it except so far as necessary for that purpose or for the purpose of preventing or detecting serious crime or for the purpose of any criminal proceedings;[2] and also

(b)   that the service does not take any action to further the interests of any political party.'[3]

[1]   MI6 is secret intelligence. Until the 1989 Act MI5 operated under the Maxwell-Fyfe Directive of 24 September 1952 issued to its Director-General by the then Home Secretary. See Lord Denning's inquiry into the Profumo scandal, Cmnd 2152 (1963). See also Lord Donaldson MR in *A-G v Guardian Newspapers Ltd (No 2)* [1988] 3 All ER 545 at 605 on MI5 and breaches of the law. It is not clear what prerogative powers survive the Act: *R v Secretary of State for the Home Department, ex p Northumbria Police Authority* [1988] 1 All ER 556, CA – a chief officer of police's powers were not exhausted by the Police Act 1964. See generally, Birkinshaw *Freedom of Information: the Law, the Practice and the Ideal* (4th edn, 2010) ch 2.

2   Security Service Act 1989, s 2(2)(a) as amended.
3   ISA 1994, s 2(2)(b).

2.222   The DG is also under a duty in relation to arrangements to coordinate activities with police forces and law enforcement agencies under s 1(4) below.

2.223   By s 1(2) and (3) the functions of the service are:

'the protection of national security and, in particular, its protection against threats from espionage, terrorism and sabotage, from the activities of agents of foreign powers and from actions intended to overthrow or undermine parliamentary democracy by political, industrial or violent means; and to safeguard the economic well-being of the United Kingdom against threats posed by the actions or intentions of persons outside the British Islands.'[1]

1   The Australian and Canadian security services have a much narrower remit: Birkinshaw *Freedom of Information: The Law, The Practice and The Ideal* (2010) ch 2 and Leigh and Lustgarten (1989) Mod LR 801 and *In from the Cold* (1994 OUP). See the Hutton Inquiry HC 247 (2003–04) and the Butler Inquiry HC 898 (2003–04) and the Chilcot Inquiry web site: http://www.iraqinquiry. org.uk/.

2.224   A new s 1(4) was added by the Security Service Act 1996 and gives the service the function of supporting police forces and other law enforcement agencies in the prevention and detection of serious crime. The 1996 Act also amended the ISA 1994 by enabling the Home Secretary to issue warrants to the security service entitling it to enter upon or interfere with property or to interfere with wireless telegraphy in the UK in relation to their new powers in circumstances where such entry or interference would otherwise be unlawful.

2.225   Information obtained by the service shall not be disclosed for use in determining whether a person should be employed, or continue to be employed, by any person, or in any office or capacity, except in accordance with provisions on that behalf approved by the Secretary of State.[1]

1   ISA 1994, s 2(3).

2.226   Annual reports must be made by the Director on the work of the service to the Prime Minister and the Secretary of State, and the Director may make reports to either of them on any matter relating to its work.

2.227   Under s 3(1) of the SSA 1989, entry or interference with property shall not be unlawful (ie neither a crime nor a tort) if authorised by the Secretary of State's warrant. By s 3(2):

'The Secretary of State may on an application made by the Service issue a warrant under this section authorising the taking of such action as is specified in the warrant in respect of any property so specified if the Secretary of State:
(a)   thinks it necessary for the action to be taken in order to obtain information which:

(i)   it is likely to be of substantial value in assisting the Service to discharge any of its functions; and

(ii) cannot reasonably be obtained by other means; and

(b) is satisfied that satisfactory arrangements are in force under section 2(2)(a) above with respect to the disclosure of information obtained by virtue of this section and that the information obtained under the warrant will be subject to those arrangements.'

2.228   Under s 3(3) a warrant shall not be issued under this section except:

'(a) under the hand of the Secretary of State; or

(b) in an urgent case where the Secretary of State has expressly authorised its issue and a statement of that fact is endorsed on it, under the hand of an official of his department of or above Grade 3.'

2.229   By s 3(4), a warrant shall, unless renewed under sub-s (5), cease to have effect:

'(a) if the warrant was under the hand of the Secretary of State, at the end of the period of six months beginning with the day on which it was issued;

(b) in any other case, at the end of the period ending with the second working day following that day.

(5) If at any time before the day on which a warrant would cease to have effect the Secretary of State considers it necessary for the warrant to continue to have effect for the purpose for which it was issued, he may by an instrument under his hand renew it for a period of six months beginning with that day.

(6) The Secretary of State shall cancel a warrant if he is satisfied that the action authorised by it is no longer necessary.'

2.230   A Commissioner will be appointed[1] under s 4 to keep under review the exercise of s 3 powers by the Secretary of State although the position is now taken by the Intelligence Services (MI5, MI6 and GCHQ) Commissioner appointed under RIPA 2000, s 59. The provisions concerning the Commissioner and his investigation of complaints under the SSA 1989, and similar provisions relating to the Commissioner and complaints under the ISA 1994, are therefore repealed and taken over by RIPA 2000. The Commissioner, who is or was a senior judge, keeps under review the exercise of the powers by the Secretary of State, inter alia, to issue warrants under ss 5 and 7 of the ISA 1994 (which now covers the Security Service); powers and duties conferred or imposed upon the Secretary of State by Parts II and III of the RIPA 2000 in connection with the activities of the Intelligence services under Parts II and III as well as similar powers exercised in stated circumstances by Ministry of Defence officials and Her Majesty's forces. The Commissioner must also assist the Tribunal (which succeeds the Tribunal established under the earlier legislation) in, significantly, the investigation of complaints within the Tribunal's jurisdiction. The jurisdiction is spelt out in s 65 and crucially covers 'proceedings against the intelligence services' or others acting on their behalf. It involves a complaint by a 'person who is aggrieved by any conduct' falling within the section.[2] It would include a complaint by a member or former member of the Intelligence services. An Investigatory Powers Commissioner for Northern Ireland is established under s 61.

[1]   By the PM. The Commissioner is a person holding, or who has held, high judicial office. The present Commissioner is Sir Peter Gibson (until 2012) a former judge of the Court of Appeal. The report for 2010 is HC 1240 (2010–12).

[2]   RIPA 2000, s 65 states that the Tribunal shall be the only body dealing with alleged actions incompatible with the Convention rights which are actions of the intelligence services or persons acting on their behalf; proceedings under s 55(4) concerning loss or damage involving a key; and proceedings taking place in challengeable circumstances (see sub-s (7)) of conduct falling within sub-s (5). Such circumstances are established where there is no warrant or authority but 'the circumstances are such that (whether or not there is such authority) it would not have been appropriate for the conduct to take place without it, or at least without proper consideration having been given to whether such authority should be sought.' Where Intelligence services' action is not authorised by warrant or authorisation, the service is subject to the ordinary law of the land: cf Lord Donaldson MR in *A-G v Guardian Newspapers Ltd (No 2)* [1988] 3 All ER 545 at 605. However, the Tribunal will be the only, or the 'appropriate' Tribunal for matters within this section. See *R (A) v B* [2010] UKSC 12 at para 2.232 below.

2.231   The Commissioner has to inform the Tribunal of his or her opinion on any complaint referred if the Tribunal so requires. Every member of the services, and every official of the department of the Secretary of State, and every member of the armed forces shall disclose or give to the Commissioner such documents or information as s/he may require for the purpose of enabling the Commissioner to discharge his or her functions.[1] The Commissioner makes an annual report to the Prime Minister and may make additional reports.[2] Annual reports are laid before Parliament, but under s 60(5) the Prime Minister may exclude material from the parliamentary report, after consulting the Commissioner, the publication of which would be 'contrary to the public interest or prejudicial to: national security; the prevention or detection of serious crime; the economic well-being of the UK …'. Where this appears to the Prime Minister to be necessary, a statement signifying that material is excluded will also be presented under s 60(4).

[1]   RIPA 2000, s 60(1).
[2]   RIPA 2000, s 60(2) and (3).

2.232   Section 65 establishes a Tribunal to deal with complaints as specified in the section or in relation to any actions of the Intelligence services incompatible with Convention rights 'or people acting on their behalf';[1] complaints concerning the use of investigatory powers under the 2000 Act; 'or any other entry on or interference with property or any interference with wireless telegraphy' and various other matters including the disclosure of encryption keys (see below). The 'determinations, awards, orders and other decisions' of the Tribunal, including those on its jurisdiction, shall not be subject to appeal or liable to be questioned in any court except as provided otherwise by the Secretary of State.[2] This provision may prove difficult for the purposes of the ECHR, Art 6. It may pose problems also under domestic law.[3] Regulations have been made under s 69 in relation to s 7 complaints (SI 2000/2665). Additionally, the Supreme Court has ruled that complaints about breaches of ECHR, Art 10 when a former member of MI5 was refused authorisation to publish his memoirs had to be dealt with before the RIPA tribunal and not by judicial review. This would protect the secrecy and closed nature of the tribunal's procedures where necesary.[4] Furthermore, the ECtHR has found no breaches of arts 8 and 13 in the use of the tribunal and its use of secretive processes. The 2000 Act and relevant codes contained necessary safeguards and were proportionate.[5]

[1] This will cover employment vetting.
[2] RIPA 2000, s 67(8).
[3] In *R v Security Service Tribunal, ex p Harman and Hewitt* (14 February 1992, unreported) QB Kennedy J questioned the efficacy of s 5(4) of the Security Service Act 1989 which sought to prevent legal challenge of decisions of the forerunner to the present Tribunal; see also *R v Secretary of State for the Home Department, ex p Al Fayed* [1997] 1 All ER 228, CA, where Lord Woolf ruled that the British Nationality Act 1981, s 44(2) which stated that nothing in the Act required reasons for decisions on nationality did not prevent the giving of an outline explanation for a refusal and any decision made unfairly was made outside jurisdiction.
[4] *R (on the application of A) v B* [2010] UKSC 12.
[5] *Kennedy v UK* (2011) 52 EHRR 4 and see *Edwards v UK* [2005] 40 EHRR 24.

2.233 Sections 67–68 concern the jurisdiction and procedure of the Tribunal and s 69 makes extensive provision for rules regulating tribunal jurisdiction including its treatment of evidence. The Secretary of State may make codes for the exercise of powers under the Act and other matters, and failure to comply with the codes shall not of itself make any person liable to any criminal or civil proceedings (s 72(2)).

2.234 RIPA 2000 poses a variety of problems. Warrants must be necessary and proportionate and are subject in particular to Art 8 ECHR – hence the legislation. But no information is 'privileged' vis-à-vis warrants, unlike the Police and Criminal Evidence Act 1984 (PACE 1984). If otherwise privileged, it will of course be inadmissible in a court in the absence of consent although in relation to intercepts and related communications data, s 17 of RIPA 2000, places stringent restrictions on the use of material obtained from such intercepts in legal proceedings. The government has questioned whether such inadmissibility should continuc.[1] Because of a Court of Appeal decision[2], the relationship between prerogative powers exercisable by members of the security service and the powers under the SSA 1989 are unclear. Bearing in mind the absolute prohibition on disclosures by members of the security and intelligence services under s 1 of the OSA 1989, it is extremely unlikely – though not impossible of course in the case of disgruntled former members of the services – that information upon which to build a complaint will come from that source, and it is difficult to believe that the Tribunal will not require the identity of such an informant. The courts have accepted that under civil law, the members and former members of the intelligence services are under a life-long or an 'absolute' duty of confidentiality. Further, the 'staff counsellor' for security and intelligence officials' grievances, together with other existing channels for raising a grievance internally, will obviate, in the government's eyes, any need for an official to go public.

[1] See *Privy Council Review of Intercept as Evidence* Cm 7324 (2008).
[2] *R v Secretary of State for the Home Department ex p Northumbria Police Authority* [1989] 1 QB 26.

INFORMATION ENTRUSTED 'IN CONFIDENCE' TO OTHER STATES OR INTERNATIONAL ORGANISATIONS

2.235   This area is covered by s 6(1) of the OSA 1989. It applies where any information, document or other article, which relates to security or intelligence, defence or international relations – as defined in ss 1, 2 and 3 respectively – and which has been communicated in confidence by or on behalf of the UK to another state or to an international organisation, has come into a person's[1] possession as a result of having been disclosed (whether to that person or another) without the authority of the state or organisation or, in the case of an organisation, of a state which is a member of it. The offence relates to 'damaging' (infra) disclosures made without lawful authority which are not offences under ss 1–3 above (s 6(2)). In other words, the offence is aimed at persons who receive, and make a damaging disclosure of, such information without authority, even when leaked and published, without authority, overseas.[2]

[1]   'Person' is not defined; Crown servants' and government contractors' offences will be catered for by ss 1–3.
[2]   See note 1.

2.236   Information etc is communicated 'in confidence' if it is communicated on terms requiring it to be held in confidence or in circumstances in which the person communicating it could reasonably expect that it would be so held (s 6(5)). There is no requirement that the information is protected by the law of confidentiality.

2.237   'Damaging' vis-à-vis a disclosure shall be determined in the same way as it would for a Crown servant acting in contravention of s 1(3), 2(1) or 3(1) above.[1] It is an essential requirement that the defendant knows, or has reasonable cause to believe, that the information etc is of the kind mentioned in s 6(1), that it came into his or her possession as there mentioned and that its disclosure would be damaging. In other words, these are ingredients of the substantive offence under s 6 and indicate that the prosecution must prove to the criminal standard the presence of mens rea in relation to the category of information, the method of acquisition (without authority), and that its disclosure would be damaging.

[1]   OSA 1989, s 6(4). For the purposes of s 6 'security or intelligence', 'defence' and 'international relations' have the same meaning as in OSA 1989, ss 1, 2 and 3.

2.238   An offence is not committed if the information etc is disclosed by that person with the lawful authority, or it has previously been made publicly available with the authority, of the state or organisations concerned or, in the case of an organisation, of a member of it. Authority would have to be from an appropriate level.[1]

[1]   'Duly given' on behalf of: OSA 1989, s 7(6).

RECEIPT OF UNAUTHORISED INFORMATION OR THAT ENTRUSTED IN CONFIDENCE

2.239 Sections 1–4 of the OSA 1989 constitute the six categories of information to be protected by the OSA 1989: security and intelligence; defence; international relations; information obtained in confidence from other states or from international organisations; crime; and special investigation powers. Section 5 is concerned with the recipient of information etc protected by ss 1–4. The section applies when 'protected' information comes into a person's possession after:[1]

(a) disclosure (whether to that person or another) by a Crown servant or government contractor without lawful authority[2]; or

(b) it is entrusted by a Crown servant or government contractor on terms requiring it to be held in confidence or in circumstances in which the Crown servant or government contractor could reasonably expect that it would be so held (so disclosing is not authorised); or

(c) it was disclosed (whether to that person or another) without lawful authority by a person to whom it was entrusted as specified in (b), supra;

and the disclosure as above is not an offence under ss 1–4 by the recipient (he is not a Crown servant, notified person or government contractor).

---

[1] OSA 1989, s 5(1)(a)(i), (ii) and (iii).

[2] Much has been made of the fact that OSA 1989, s 5(1) appears to contain a serious (from the government's perspective) omission. It does not refer to former Crown servants or government contractors. As the situation was meant to deal with the 'Wright' situation, infra, where the press published information from a former security official, there appears to be substance in the observation. OSA 1989, s 5(1)(a)(iii) only deals with intermediaries who have received 'in confidence'. What are the possibilities of conspiracy charges under the Criminal Law Act 1977 involving members of the press and media and offences involving attempts, aiding and abetting or encouraging crime under the common law or other statutory provisions? See *Freedom of Information: The Law, The Practice and The Ideal* (4th edn, 2010) pp 103–105. The Police and Criminal Evidence Act 1984 was used by the police to attempt to obtain information from journalists about those police officers who had leaked information in breach of OSA 1989, s 4(1) and (2) in the hacking scandal in 2011. The application to the court was dropped after much public criticism.

2.240 The person into whose possession the information etc has come will be guilty of an offence if s/he discloses it without lawful authority, knowing or having reasonable cause to believe that it is protected against disclosure by the foregoing provisions, and that it came into that person's possession as above. No offence is committed by a person under this section (s 5) where the disclosure is an offence by that person (a Crown servant, government contractor or a 'notified person') under ss 1–4. The prosecution must prove these matters on the criminal standard of proof to gain a conviction and it must also prove that the disclosure of information protected by ss 1–3 above was damaging – as described in s 1(3), 2(1) or 3(1) – and that the defendant made it knowing, or having reasonable cause to believe, that it would be damaging. This requirement does not apply to disclosures under s 4(3) concerning intercept or special investigation powers and unauthorised disclosure of information about or from these. Damage is assumed in the disclosure itself of such information.

2.241 A limitation on the chain is effected by s 5(4) which stipulates that, where it was disclosed without lawful authority by a government contractor or it was disclosed without lawful authority to a person to whom it was entrusted in confidence by a Crown servant or government contractor, an offence is not committed unless the disclosure was by a British citizen or took place in the United Kingdom, in any of the Channel Islands, or in the Isle of Man or colony.

2.242   The further along a chain of recipients information goes, the more difficult it will be for the prosecution to establish the essential conditions for the offence. The provisions certainly contemplate and embrace a journalist receiving information in contravention of the provisions and an editor publishing that disclosure.

2.243

Crown servant				fourth party?
or		recipient		Caught by
government	→	'in confidence	→ third party →	'whether
contractor		etc'		to him or
				another'?

Figure 2.1 Who is caught by s 5(1)?

2.244   This interpretation seems to create a chain ad infinitum potentially (see above).

2.245   Under s 5(5) information is protected against disclosure by the foregoing provisions of this Act if:
(a)   it relates to security or intelligence, defence or international relations within the meaning of s 1, 2 or 3 or is confidential information etc obtained from a foreign state or international organisation; or
(b)   it is information etc to which s 4 applies (crime and special investigation powers).

2.246   A person is guilty of an offence if without lawful authority s/he discloses any information, document or other article which s/he knows or has reasonable cause to believe, to have come into his or her possession as a result of a contravention of s 1 of the OSA 1911 (see para 2.154 above on OSA 1911, s 1).

2.247   A defence of prior publication (above) was rejected by the government in relation to this section of the 1989 Act.

WHAT CONSTITUTES LAWFUL AUTHORITY?

2.248   Lawful authority is central to the scheme of the OSA 1989. The 1989 legislation avoids problematic phrases such as 'interest' or 'interests' of the state when describing those occasions when a person is justified in disclosing information, although s 2 of the OSA 1911 spoke of being 'authorised'.

2.249   For the purposes of the OSA 1989 a disclosure by a Crown servant or a person notified under OSA 1989, s 1(1) is made with lawful authority, 'if, and only if, it is made in accordance with his official duty' (and see SI 1990/200). There is judicial support for the view that official duty means within the ordinary chain of command, presumably going up to and including the Permanent Secretary and minister as adviser to the Crown.[1] Although a civil servant is a servant of the Crown in constitutional and legal doctrine, s/he is a servant to his or her minister who is head of the department or institution, and ultimately the government collectively in a *functional* sense. His or her terms and conditions of employment are laid out in great detail in codes, regulations and circulars. The view of the Head of the Home Civil Service on the relationship between, and duties owed by, civil servants to ministers have been described above, and in July 1989 a draft revision of the code insisted upon a lifelong duty of confidentiality by all existing and former civil servants to government and the duty covers all information not sanctioned to be made public, whether or not it is covered by the OSA 1989. The Civil Service Code and Management Code now set out the range of duties (para 2.147 above).[2] As we saw above, the present position is not as strict as this as it refers to 'civil servants', not former civil servants and does not speak of a lifelong duty. The strict approach is the judicially accepted version of official duty for security and intelligence staff and related civil servants,[3] though whether the courts will protect it by interim injunction will depend upon the circumstances (see para 2.347 below). A distinction has been drawn between members of the security and intelligence services and designated officials who work with them and other civil servants. Both the common law and the OSA 1989 impose stricter duties of confidentiality on the former.

[1] See: McGowan J in *R v Ponting* [1985] Crim LR 318. See, incidentally, *Carltona Ltd v Comrs of Works* [1943] 2 All ER 560, CA and cf *R (NASHA) v Secretary of State for Health* (2005) *Times*, 9 March; *R v Secretary of State for the Home Department, ex p Oladehinde* [1990] 2 All ER 367, CA.

[2] In 1989, it was reported that about ten civil servants a year were disciplined for breaches of confidentiality and 'political offences' Official Report (6th series), 30 October 1989 (R Luce MP). Civil Service unions have argued that duties are owed to, eg the Crown in Parliament, ie MPs. The 'Crown in Parliament' is a legislative device and might refer to the presence of Ministers in Parliament. It does not cover MPs individually. On leaks from the Home Office to MPs see HC 157 (2008–09) Home Affairs Committee and the Public Administration Committee's *Leaks and Whistleblowing in Whitehall* HC 83 (2008–09). See para 2.272 below.

[3] See paras 2.332 et seq and *R v Shayler* below.

2.250 A disclosure by a government contractor is made with lawful authority if, and only if, it is made in accordance with an official authorisation[1] or for the purposes of the functions by virtue of which s/he is a government contractor and without contravening an official restriction.[2]

[1] One which is duly given or imposed by a Crown servant or government contractor, or by or on behalf of a prescribed body or a body of a prescribed class.

[2] OSA 1989, s 7(2).

2.251 A disclosure made by 'any other person' is made with lawful authority if, and only if, it is made:

(a) to a Crown servant for the purposes of his or her functions as such (above); or

(b) in accordance with an official authorisation.

2.252 If authorisation 'by any other person' is sought and refused, the refusal must comply with the House of Lords decision in *R v Shayler*.[1] Shayler was a former Crown servant and not one still in service. A prohibition must be prescribed by law. There must be a pressing social need for which a prohibition is sought by the authorities and prohibition must be necessary in accordance with the discussion in Shayler and as exemplified in decisions such as *ex p Daly* which concerned rights under Article 8 and reading prisoners' privileged correspondence in their forcible absence from their cells in routine cell searches: by analogy with *Daly* the reasons for a prohibition on freedom of speech must be subjected to rigorous and intrusive review by the court to establish that the ban is 'proportionate'.[2] However, in other contexts courts have not insisted on such an invasive review and have been content to allow the body entrusted with the discretion to make an order on the merits banning a political broadcast on grounds of taste and decency with which the courts would be slow to interfere.[3]

[1]   See [2002] 2 All ER 477 (HL) and para 2.369, note 4.
[2]   *R (Daly) v Secretary of State for the Home Department* [2001] 2 AC 532 (HL).
[3]   *R (ProLife Alliance) v BBC* [2003] 2 All ER 977. See para 2.369 below.

2.253   Self-authorisation will presumably apply until such time as a disclosure by a Crown servant or minister is damaging and thereby outside official duties unless the latter is justified in making a damaging disclosure or permitting a servant to do likewise. Here, as ever, self-authorisation will be a mystery[1] and doubtless widely practised where 'damage' as set out in the Act will not follow.

[1]   See Franks, op cit, para 18.

2.254   A party[1] charged with an offence under ss 1–6 may prove, with the onus on that party, that at the time of the alleged offence s/he believed that s/he had lawful authority to make the disclosure in question and had no reasonable cause to believe otherwise. His or her simple belief is not enough, even if mistaken. S/he must not close his or her eyes to those things that would give that person reasonable cause to believe otherwise.[2] Section 7(5) and (6) give further circuitous explanation on 'official authorisation' and 'official restriction' including that duly given under s 6 in relation to foreign states or international organisations.

[1]   A Crown servant, government contractor, a person notified under s 1 or 'any other person'.
[2]   A jury should be told to consider whether prior publicity for information or acquiescence by the authorities may be taken as an implicit authorisation: *R v Galvin* [1987] 2 All ER 851, CA.

SAFEGUARDING INFORMATION

2.255   Unlawful retention by a Crown servant,[1] ie contrary to his or her official duty, of documents[2] etc which it would be an offence under the previous sections to disclose without lawful authority, is an offence (OSA 1989, s 8(1)(a)), as is failure to comply with an official direction (s 8(8)) to return or dispose of a document or article by a government contractor. For both parties it is an offence to fail to take such care to prevent the unauthorised disclosure of the document or article as a person in his or her position may reasonably be expected to take (s 8(1)).

[1]   OSA 1989, s 8(3) includes as such those notified under s 1(1) even though not servants or contractors.
[2]   Discs, tapes etc.

2.256 It is a defence under s 8(1)(a) for a defendant who is a Crown servant[1] to prove that at the time of the alleged offence s/he believed that s/he was acting in accordance with his or her official duty and had no reasonable cause to believe otherwise.

[1] This includes those under a 'notification' in OSA 1989, s 1(1): s 8(3).

2.257 Section 8(4) covers those who are not Crown servants and government contractors and makes it an offence for them not to comply with an official direction for the return or disposal of information etc, or, when entrusted in confidence under s 5, s/he fails to take such care to prevent its unauthorised disclosure as a person in their position may reasonably be expected to take (s 8(4)). Failure by a person to comply with an official direction to return documents or articles as described in s 6 is an offence (s 8(5)).

2.258 It is an offence to disclose any official information etc which a Crown servant or government contractor has had or has in their possession by their position as such, or which the discloser knows or has reasonable cause to believe was or is so possessed, and which can be used for the purpose of obtaining access to any information etc protected against disclosure by the foregoing provisions of this Act, and the circumstances of disclosure are such that it would be reasonable to expect that it might be used for that purpose without authority (s 8(6)).

ROLE OF THE ATTORNEY-GENERAL[1] AND PENALTIES

2.259 Prosecution may only be brought with the consent of the Attorney-General or A-G (Northern Ireland), except for offences under s 4(2) of the OSA 1989 (relating to crime) where the respective Directors of Public Prosecutions have to consent. In Scotland, the Lord Advocate is responsible for prosecutions.

[1] In the *Spycatcher* episode, a decision not to seek an injunction against publishers and other authors was wrongly attributed to Sir Michael Havers, the Attorney General, by Sir Robert Armstrong, the Cabinet Secretary. In fact, Havers had not been consulted on the decision! Very often the role of the Attorney-General has raised questions. He is a member of the government and Cabinet as well as the government's (Crown) legal officer. The suspicion is he is already a parti pris or, worse, a cover for decisions taken elsewhere. When plans were developing for the Constitutional Governance and Reform Bill it was envisaged that the Attorney General's consent for prosecution would be removed from many offences; the OSA 1989 was not included. See now *A Protocol between the Attorney General and Prosecuting Authorities* (July 2009) which retains the requirement for the Attorney General's consent for prosecution under the OSA 1989 or where national security is concerned.

2.260 Section 10 stipulates that for offences other than under s 8(1), (4) or (5) the penalty on conviction on indictment should be imprisonment for up to two years, or a fine, or both; on summary conviction, to imprisonment for a term not exceeding six months or a fine not exceeding the statutory maximum, or both.

POLICE POWERS

2.261 Offences under the OSA 1989 are made arrestable under PACE 1984, s 24(2) except those under OSA 1989, s 8(1), (4) or (5). Section 9(1) of the OSA

1911 concerning search warrants shall include references to offences under the OSA 1989 except for s 8(1), (4) or (5) offences. Section 9(2) and Sch 1, para 3(b) of PACE 1984 shall apply to s 9(1) of the OSA 1989 as extended by this subsection; the former provisions in the PACE 1984 contain restrictions on obtaining evidence.[1]

[1]   Section 9(2) of PACE 1984 excludes items subject to legal privilege and certain other material from powers of search conferred by previous enactments; Sch 1, para 3(b) prescribes the access provisions for the special procedure laid down in the schedule. See para 2.181 above. See also *R v Central Criminal Court, ex p Bright* [2001] 2 All ER 244, DC.

EXCLUSION OF PUBLIC FROM PROCEEDINGS

2.262   Section 8(4) of the OSA 1920 which allows the public to be excluded from committals or trials shall have effect as if references to offences under that Act included references under the OSA 1989 apart from those in s 8(1), (4) or (5).[1]

[1]   OSA 1989, s 11(4).

2.263   An act done abroad by British citizens or Crown servants, if an offence under the Act if performed in the UK, apart from s 8(1), (4) or (5), shall be an offence.

PUBLIC INTEREST DEFENCE

2.264   Previous attempts to reform s 2 of the OSA 1989 had included a public interest defence, viz that no offence was committed where an unauthorised disclosure was in the public interest. An amendment in the Commons allowed disclosure etc in the public interest 'in so far as the [discloser] has reasonable cause to believe that it indicated the existence of crime, fraud, abuse of authority, neglect in the performance of official duty or other serious misconduct ... or a serious threat to the health or safety of the public'.

2.265   The government rejected such a defence, arguing that the 'public interest' was present in deciding whether to prosecute and the prosecution assessing the degree of harm and public benefit. Further, a jury would have to be persuaded of damage and would be invited to consider the benefit in disclosure by the defence which would necessarily, in such a case, reject the allegation that the defendant's act caused 'harm'. 'The Bill does not allow the defendant to argue that although the disclosure has caused the specific harm, and he knew that it would, the court should weigh that against some other consideration.'[1] The government also believed that the presence of such a defence would not help to clarify the law.[2] We shall see how the public interest defence operates in the civil law of confidence in a later section (para 2.323 below).

[1]   D Hurd MP HC Official Report (6th series) col 469, 21 December 1988.
[2]   Cm 408 (1988) para 60. NB Financial Services Act 1986, s 180(2) and the original OSA 1889 had a public interest defence.

2.266 The extent to which there is a defence available under the law of 'necessity' has been adverted to but not authoritatively determined.[1] However, as was seen above, the prospect of damaging revelations of illegal or highly embarrassing high-handed actions by British officials and Ministers will doubtless have a constraining impact on decisions by the Attorney-General to prosecute.

[1] See *R v Shayler* in both the Court of Appeal and House of Lords (para 2.252, note 1 above).

2.267 The FOIA 2000 has, as we saw in ch 1, a pronounced public interest element in allowing disclosures. However, that Act, unlike previous unsuccessful FOI Bills, made no provision for reform of the OSA 1989.

DEFENCE OF PRIOR PUBLICATION

2.268 Such a defence was present for certain categories of information within the Protection of Information Bill 1979 which sought to reform OSA 1911, s 2. Basically, the defence would be available where the information had been published before. In the Lords an amendment was moved allowing a defence where 'before the time of the alleged offence the information in question had become widely disseminated to the public whether in the UK or elsewhere' adding 'there was no reasonable likelihood that its further disclosure would damage the work of, or any part of, the security and intelligence services'. This latter part was to meet the government's objection to such a defence, viz[1] additional or more serious damage would be perpetrated by a second or further disclosure.

[1] In the USA under the FOI, this is described partially as an aspect of the 'mosaic' principle ie superficially innocuous information can be pieced together to make a damaging disclosure. The mosaic or 'jigsaw' was introduced into the draft 1999 FOI Bill but was removed in Parliament.

2.269 Prior publication was the government's downfall in the *Spycatcher* litigation – the confidentiality of the information had evaporated by the time the final court order was sought. However, information can still be officially secret even though published,[1] it was previously decided under the former s 2.[2] Official secrecy and confidentiality may overlap but they are not the same thing, and the government insisted that no such defence would be available under the statute. If information is published prior to the disclosure, this will be an issue for the jury to consider in assessing the 'damage'. This will not be available to breaches by security, intelligence and 'notified' officials under s 1 as that section creates an absolute offence for unauthorised disclosures when disclosed by such persons, whether or not theirs is an initial or subsequent disclosure,[3] nor for offences under s 4(3). In case law concerning confidentiality, the courts have accepted a life-long or 'absolute' duty of confidentiality is owed by members of the intelligence services. Disclosures by them of information already in the public domain may cause additional damage; a disclosure of this information by such officials would certainly be a breach of contract the House of Lords has held.[4]

[1] *R v Crisp and Homewood* (1919) 83 JP 121, CCA; *R v Galvin* [1987] 2 All ER 851, CA. See also *Boyer v R* (1948) 94 CCC 195 and *R v Toronto Sun Publishing Ltd* (1979) 47 CCC (2d) 535.

2 Acquiescence in publication by the authorities might amount to authorisation.
3 Financial Services Act 1986, s 180(1)(r) allows a defence of prior publication.
4 *A-G v Blake* [2000] 4 All ER 385, HL.

2.270 A defence is available under s 6(3) for disclosure by a person where information has been published by the proper authorities in foreign states or by the authority of an international organisation or member of it.

MPS AND PRIVILEGE

2.271 Disclosures to MPs are not protected under the statute as such; they are not *ipso facto* authorised recipients. An amendment (defeated) would have allowed non-Crown servants and non-government contractors to have disclosed information to MPs (147 HC Official Report (6th series), cols 505–543).

2.272 OSA 1989 does not interfere with parliamentary privilege, and statements by MPs in the House or anything said in committee proceedings are protected by absolute privilege. But this does not protect a communicator.[1] The question of an MP's privilege remains unaffected by this Act, but the other party will not be protected unless, eg, information was given in a parliamentary proceeding. In 2008, an opposition front-bench spokesperson, Damian Green MP, was arrested after information was leaked to him by a civil servant. No charges were brought under OSA 1989, but the police were given permission, controversially, to search the MP's office in Parliament by the serjeant-at-arms. A special committee on privilege was established to investigate and report on the affair: *Police Searches on the Parliamentary Estate* HC 62 (2009–10). A Cabinet Office guidance document exists on dealing with leaks: *Official Information: Standards of Conduct and Procedures* (2009). Previous versions were not made public but the 2009 version is in the library of ther House of Commons. The leaker was dismissed but no prosecutions were brought under the OSA 1989 or a common law offence of misconduct in public office: *R v Bembridge* (1783) 3 Doug KB 32. Conviction carries a maximum sentence of life imprisonment and prosecutions under the common law offence have risen steadily in recent years to 21 in 2007 (para 49) mainly involving police officers and including offences of wrongful disclosure. Some of Green's papers were covered by Parliamentary privilege and were returned to him. The committee recommended that the common law offence should not be used to subvert the intention of Parliament in the OSA 1989 to use the criminal law for specific and serious disclosures (para 54).

1 The Committee on Privileges discussed the relationship between the OSA and an MP's privilege in the Duncan Sandys MP case: HC 173 (1937–38) and HC 101 (1938–39); official secrecy and privilege were raised again in the 'Zircon' episode in 1987: HC 365 (1986–87). See *Rost v Edwards* [1990] 2 All ER 641; *Prebble v NZTV Ltd* [1994] 3 All ER 407; *Hamilton v Al Fayed* [2000] 2 All ER 224, HL and *R v Chaytor* [2010] UKSC 52.

LEGAL PROFESSIONAL PRIVILEGE

2.273 Legal professional privilege (LPP) basically covers two situations:
(a) communications between a lawyer and his client; and

(b) communications with third parties concerning pending or contemplated litigation.

2.274   Legal professional privilege is examined in chapter 10. It has been a topic of considerable litigation in recent years.

2.275   The point was raised that a communication under the Act would not attract such privilege since the communication constituted the crime itself, an interpretation loosely supported by the Law Society.

2.276   The government believed that 'the common law relating to LPP communications between a client and his solicitor' was not affected by the Act:[1]

> 'LPP acts to prevent the production in evidence of [a communication between a client and a legal adviser] and hence to deprive of its foundation any prosecution that might ever be sought to be founded on such a communication ... But of course it is well established that anyone who, when communicating with his solicitor, seeks the latter's help in the furtherance of some criminal purpose, is disqualified in respect of that communication from the benefit of privilege.'

[1]   *Wheeler v Le Marchant* (1881) 17 Ch D 675; *R v Cox and Railton* (1884) 14 QBD 153; cf PACE 1984, s 10(2) and the Drug Trafficking Offences Act 1986 and *R v Central Criminal Court, ex p Francis & Francis (a firm)* [1989] AC 346, HL. See Part III of the Police Act 1997, s 98.

2.277   The function of LPP is to aid the administration of justice and not to aid crime. But a wrongdoer's position is 'quite different from that of someone who discloses information to his solicitor in the process of seeking advice in good faith about his own legal position in relation to it'.[1]

[1]   HC Official Report (6th series) (Committee) cols 503–504, 16 February 1989.

2.278   The distinction lies in the use of a solicitor by a person to advance a crime and the seeking of advice by a party without criminal design, to be guided on where s/he stands in relation to the law. A disclosure for the latter is privileged. However, a lawyer may need information from the opponents to advance his client's case or undermine the adversary's. This may necessitate abandoning a prosecution or it might involve use of 'special counsel' where information could not be entrusted to lawyers advising their clients (para 10.85 below).

D NOTICE SYSTEM

2.279   The D notice system (now DA notice) of the Defence Press and Broadcasting Advisory Committee[1] and its usefulness will, the government stated,[2] remain unaffected by the Act. This exists as a public/private body advising the press and media on the limits of responsible and permissible publication of sensitive defence and security information. Like the lobby system,[3] the benefits are that membership will keep one informed by official sources; exclusion or non-involvement in the system may mean a greater preparedness on the authorities' part to prosecute those who go outside the terms of a D notice. They advise editors and media personnel, usually in general terms, on what may not be published. D notices have no legal authority – it is a voluntary system.

1   Basically comprised of members of the armed services and relevant departments concerned with defence and national security and representatives of the press and media. D Notices, as of writing, are still regularly resorted to: see P Sadler *National Security and the D Notice System* (2001).
2   HC Official Report (6th series) col 1131, 25 January 1989.
3   An informal arrangement whereby members of the press and media are briefed by government officials and ministers on a 'no names' basis. The power and influence of the PM's Chief Press Officer and the PM's Press Office have been the subject of mounting criticism: see HC Official Report (6th series), 30 October 1989 (Richard Luce MP) and HC 770 (1997–98) and HC 162 (1998–99). On the Central Office of Information see: the National Audit Office Publicity Services for Government Departments HC 46 (1989–90); and HC 81 (1989–90). The lobby system was amended in 2000 when sources' identities were revealed; see also paras 2.114 et seq above on the Phillis Review of 2004. The PM makes monthly televised press briefings.

2.280   Staying within a D notice is no guarantee that a prosecution will not follow, although given the high quality of official representation on the committee, it is unlikely that a jury would be easily persuaded that where a D notice allowing certain publications was given, a disclosure was without lawful authority. However, in late 1987 and early 1988, the government sought an injunction (a civil remedy) to stop broadcasting, allegedly in breach of confidentiality, of a series of programmes about the views and activities of security personnel.[1] This was in spite of the fact that a D notice allowing publication had been issued by the Defence Press and Broadcasting Advisory Committee.[2] The D notice system was modified slightly in 1992 and from 1993 they have been called DA notices. DA notices were revised in 2000. They presently cover: military operations, plans and capabilities; nuclear and non-nuclear weapons and equipment; ciphers and security classifications; sensitive installations and home addresses; UK security and intelligence services and special forces.

1   *A-G v BBC* (1987) *Times*, 18 December.
2   See HC Official Report (6th series) vol 126 col 483.

FORMALITIES, DISCIPLINE, AUTHORS AND THE OSA 1989

2.281   Franks reported that every civil servant signs the 'Official Secrets Act Declaration' at least twice in his or her career, on entering and leaving the Civil Service; and it may be signed on other occasions. According to Franks in 1972:

'Declarations are also signed by numbers of non-civil servants, eg employees of Government contractors working on classified contracts, officers of public authorities involved in planning for war and emergency and members of official committees, consultants and research workers who are given access to official information in confidence.'[1]

1   Franks, above, paras 34–36. Appendix VI for copies.

2.282   These serve to draw their attention to the terms of the legislation and to point out that where a civil servant wishes to use and publish information for his personal use, eg as memoirs, s/he must obtain 'prior official sanction'. This is achieved, if at all, through an application to the Permanent Under-Secretary in the department in which s/he worked. Ministerial memoirs are cleared via the Secretary to the Cabinet and Prime Minister, and outsiders have to approach the Secretary to the D notice committee.[1] Civil servants who wish to report wrongdoing must follow internal procedures in accordance with the *Civil Service Code*. After exhausting such procedures they may appeal if necessary to the Civil Service Commissioners (*Appeal* OCSC). The procedures will now be based on the CRGA 2010 and codes thereunder (para 2.147 et seq above).

[1]   See *A-G v Jonathan Cape Ltd* [1976] QB 752.

2.283   For members of the security and intelligence services, the OSA 1989 prohibits, forever, their unauthorised disclosure of such information. OSA 1989, s 1(1) serves as legal notice of the absolute nature of offences under that provision for members and former members of the security and intelligence services and those notified under the terms of s 1 (para 2.176 above). However, a system of vetting has existed 'informally' to approve publication, although there was no contractual undertaking on either side that the procedure would be exercised,[1] let alone that works would be vetted and approved. Publication without approval will therefore be a breach of s 1 of the OSA 1989, and if the author and publisher are outside the jurisdiction, publication may be restrained in the UK by use of the law of confidentiality where the information is not already sufficiently in the public domain or if a public interest may still be served by prohibiting publication.[2] Any public interest defence is dealt with below.

[1]   Both *Spycatcher* and *Inside Intelligence* were refused examination for approval. See *Blake* below, however.
[2]   See paras 2.312 et seq below.

2.284   The government did not wish to introduce a formal vetting procedure in the OSA 1989 especially for security and intelligence as this might encourage applications.[1] It is in complete contrast to the USA, for instance, where vetting agreements cover the work of the CIA agents,[2] breach of which may lead to the employer seeking to seize all the proceeds of the sale of memoirs on the basis of breach of constructive trust[3] where they were published without vetting approval. This would not rule out the possibility of criminal proceedings under the US espionage laws, as well, for such breaches.

[1]   HL Official Report (5th series) col 754, 18 April 1989.
[2]   There is extensive resort to secrecy agreements in the USA among federal employees.
[3]   *Snepp v United States* 444 US 507 (1980); and see *United States v Marchetti* 466 F 2d 1309 (1972). In the *Spycatcher* litigation, Scott J believed that had Peter Wright sought permission to publish, and were this refused, that decision would have been amenable to judicial review: and see *R v Shayler* at para 2.252, note 1 above where this was confirmed by the Law Lords.

2.285   After prolonged legal proceedings involving the spy George Blake, who was seeking the profits from the sale of his book *No Other Choice* published in 1990, the House of Lords held, in July 2000, that the Attorney-General was entitled to receive on behalf of the Crown the profits payable by the publisher to Blake from agreed advances. Blake had been in breach of a contractual undertaking signed in 1944 'not to divulge any official information gained by me as a result of my employment, either in the press or in book form'.[1] The High Court had found that Blake was not a fiduciary in relation to the information because it was no longer confidential. The Court of Appeal held that the Attorney-General was possessed of public law powers entitling him to a court injunction freezing the royalties in question until a court determined who was entitled to the assets. In the House of Lords, this claim on behalf of the public interest in public law was found to be without support. There was no prospect of Blake's return to the jurisdiction and so no likelihood of confiscation orders under appropriate legislation.[2] The order looked to all intents and purposes as confiscatory and without any statutory underpinning. It appeared pro tanto contrary to all principles of common law. In the House of Lords it was established that the Attorney-General had a private law right to an account of profits representing the result of Blake's breach of promise not to do precisely what he had done and where no other remedy was available. This broke new ground in the law of contract and realising its adverse impact in more conventional commercial arrangements Lord Nicholls described it as 'exceptional' a remedy only available in 'exceptional circumstances' such as the present case which concerned secret intelligence information, 'the life-blood' of security and intelligence officers.

[1]   *A-G v Blake* [2001] 1 AC 268, HL. The Law Lords accepted this as a contractual claim in spite of the usually held view – a view subject now to significant qualification – that civil servants do not have contracts of employment. No reference was made in the contract to film or TV rights! SAS members also have to sign contracts of confidentiality introduced because of increasing publications of memoirs: *R v A-G for England and Wales* [2003] UKPC 22. Lord Scott dissented, believing such contracts were vitiated by undue influence.

[2]   Part VI of the Criminal Justice Act 1988 and the Proceeds of Crime Act 1995 following conviction under OSA 1989, s 1(1); see *Jennings v CPS* [2005] 4 All ER 391 (CA).

2.286   If individuals assign copyright for the Crown in published work based on information gleaned from official duties, this could lead to actions on behalf of the Crown for breach of copyright.[1] Civil Service Management codes of practice[2] set out the duties of secrecy, and details of disciplinary procedures and appeals. For security-sensitive posts, positive vetting procedures may be invoked. An appeal procedure, with procedural limitations,[3] exists for those who fail such tests. There are also less probing tests known as negative vetting tests.[4] A staff counsellor exists for members of the security and intelligence services who feel they cannot in conscience comply with their instructions and duties. The procedures available for civil servants in government departments who wish to publish information or who are disconcerted are examined above.[5]

[1]   See *A-G v Times Newspapers Ltd* [2001] 09 LS Gaz R 38, CA and the events surrounding former MI6 officer Richard Tomlinson's *The Big Breach: From Top Secret to Maximum Security*.

[2]   See paras 2.147 et seq above.

[3]   And note the terms of the Security Service Act 1989 (paras 2.220 et seq above).

[4]   On vetting, see: 563 HC Official Report (6th series) cols 152–156, 29 January 1957; HC 242 (1983–84) and Cmnd 8540; HC 59 (1982–83); Cmnd 8876. See I Linn *Application Refused: Employment Vetting By the State* (1990). On new tests under negative vetting, 177 HC Official Report (6th series), cols 159–61, 24 July 1990 Written Answers. See L Lustgarten and I Leigh *In from the Cold: National Security and Parliamentary Democracy* (1994) ch 6. A Defence Vetting Agency has been established. The DVA is 'the largest government organisation carrying out national security checks on people, and action around 140,000 checks and clearances each year.

This process is called "vetting".' The DVA's 'aim is to carry out security checks on people in the armed services, the MOD civil service, certain other government departments, and in Defence Industry. We check that these people are suitable to hold security clearances, to allow them access to government installations, valuable assets, and sensitive information': www.mod.uk/dva. For vetting appeals, see HC cols 764–766 (15 December 1994) and the RIPA 2000.
5   See para 2.282 above.

2.287   However, we had until comparatively recently no equivalent of the 'Whistleblower's Charter' as it exists in the United States, which seeks to protect from administrative reprisals officials who 'go public' on wrongdoing within their departments or agencies. For certain kinds of information[1] only a designated official may be informed and not the press. The whistleblower has to establish that there is a link between the disclosure of information and the alleged reprisals, and the investigation of the wrongdoing itself – not the reprisal – is conducted by agency heads and not by the Office of Inspector-General. However, this is not a public interest defence against criminal prosecution and the UK government successfully resisted attempts to introduce such a defence in the Official Secrets Bill 1989. Reference must now be made to PIDA 1998 (see paras 2.299 et seq below).

1   Intelligence and counter-intelligence. Following the Irangate episode, a version of the procedure was recommended for the CIA.

2.288   In the UK, a civil servant's pension rights can only be automatically forfeited where there is a conviction for treason, although the Treasury has the power to withhold pensions in whole or in part for conviction of offences under the OSA 1989 which attracted prison sentences of ten years, singly or consecutively. Forfeiture is not used to punish a disciplinary offence although a civil servant may face dismissal.

THE OFFICIAL SECRETS ACT 1989 AND THE EUROPEAN COURT OF HUMAN RIGHTS

2.289   Before we turn to the PIDA 1998, the question has to be put whether the OSA 1989 is in breach of the European Convention on Human Rights in seeking to prevent *any* disclosure by security and intelligence officers past and present. Particularly relevant will be Art 10, and also increasingly pertinent to access to information rights has been Art 8.

Articles 10 and 8 ECHR

2.290   **Article 10** gives everyone a right to freedom of expression. It includes a freedom to hold opinions and to receive and impart information and ideas without interference by public authority and regardless of frontiers. Nothing, however, in Art 10 prevents states licensing broadcasting, television and cinemas. This right which 'carries with it duties and responsibilities' may be subject to formalities, conditions, restrictions or penalties 'as are prescribed by law' and are *necessary* in a democratic society in the interests of national security, territorial integrity or public safety, for the prevention of disorder or crime, for the protection of health or morals, for the protection of the reputation or rights of others, for preventing the disclosure on information received in confidence, or for maintaining the authority and impartiality of the judiciary.'

1   Ie statute or delegated legislation or a published code regarded as binding.

2.291   Article 8 provides a right to respect for one's private and family life, one's home and correspondence. Public authorities are prohibited from interfering with the exercise of this right except where it is in accordance with the law and where again 'it is necessary in a democratic society in the interests of national security, public safety or the economic well-being of the country, for the prevention of disorder or crime, for the protection of health or morals, or for the protection of the rights and freedoms of others.'

2.292   The rights under Arts 8 and 10 are not absolute but they can only be subjected to limitation where necessary to safeguard the interests listed and in a manner which is proportionate. There can be no doubt that the Human Rights Act 1998 (HRA 1998) has introduced proportionality into domestic law whatever its status may have been before that Act was brought into effect. The courts may engage in 'anxious scrutiny' and a high level of intensity of review where Convention rights under the HRA are concerned. But this does not allow for a 'merits review'. Furthermore, even in Convention cases, the intensity of review may vary according to the subject matter.[1] How widely beyond the area of human rights 'proportionality' may be applied we shall have to wait and see.

1   *R (Daly) v Secretary of State for the Home Department* [2001] UKHL 26, [2001] 3 All ER 433 per Lord Steyn; see *Smith and Grady v UK* (1999) 29 EHRR 493 (ECtHR) criticising the high threshold required before English courts would allow judicial review, and *Hatton v UK* (2003) 37 EHRR 28.

2.293   In the extradition proceedings brought by the English prosecuting authorities in a Paris court, it was argued on behalf of David Shayler, a former MI5 officer, that the OSA 1989 was in breach of the Convention. In particular there was a breach of Art 10. The success of such an argument would depend on a court – and now an English court by virtue of the HRA 1998 – accepting that such restraints as the Act contains are not necessary in a democratic society to protect those 'pressing social needs' referred to in the Convention including national security. The absence in the Act of a public interest defence and the prohibition of all information being disclosed, even trivia, could prove embarrassing – no balance is allowed. The prohibition in s 1 is absolute whereas for other officials there must be damaging disclosures. However, the ECtHR has deferred to national security arguments advanced by states when seeking to defend various practices such as refusing access to security registers.[1] In *Segerstedt-Wiberg v Sweden* the ECtHR ruled that there had been a denial of art 8 rights on the facts by keeping certain security files on individuals (but not in relation to the named claimant). Retention was neither necessary nor in accordance with the law. However, not allowing disclosure of the full extent of grounds for maintaining national security files on a secret register did not breach art 8. It was within the margin of appreciation. There had in addition been breaches of art 10 and freedom of speech, and arts 11 (concerning political freedom and in so far as art 8 had been breached) and 13.[2]

1   *Leander v Sweden* (1987) 9 EHRR 433. See also: *Engel v The Netherlands (No 1)* (1979–80) 1 EHRR 647 and *Murray v UK* (1995) 19 EHRR 193. See *Kennedy v UK* [2010] ECHR 26839/05 where the ECtHR ruled that there had been no breach by the UK of ECHR, arts 6, 8 and 13 when the Investigatory Powers Tribunal examined his complaints (about MI5 and GCHQ processing hid persoanl data) in private and simply stated no findings had been made in his favour.
2   [2007] EHRR 2.

2.294   But there are many who believe the Act – like s 2 before it – is ready for pensioning off. In the Court of Appeal litigation involving publication of Shayler's letters by *The Guardian* and *The Observer* judicial dicta seemed vigilant to protect the rights of the press to freedom of speech and to defend the privilege against self-incrimination (see below). Could a new era encouraged by the 'common law of human rights' see judicial inroads into the Act? These judgments must be seen in the light of *Attorney-General v Punch Ltd*[1] (para 2.366 below). The decision in *R v Shayler* dealt with at length above (paras 2.18 et seq) held virtually unequivocally that s 1 was not incompatible with Art 10 providing the proper approach was adopted in balancing the respective rights and interests involved. In the *Blake* case, the leading judgment emphasised the special position of trust occupied by security and intelligence officers who commit a crime by divulging non-harmful information whereas civil servants must make a 'damaging' disclosure evidenced by some independent harm. Blake had agreed to secrecy and 'An absolute rule against disclosure, visible to all, makes good sense.'[2] See para 2.182 for the *Shayler* decision.

1   [2003] 1 All ER 289 (HL) reversing the Court of Appeal.
2   Per Lord Nicholls in *A-G v Blake* [2000] 4 All ER 385, HL.

2.295   Under OSA 1989, prosecutions are brought regularly.[1] As mentioned in the introduction to this chapter, the ECtHR has not been over anxious to create a right to freedom of information from Art 10 and indeed the erstwhile Commission on Human Rights had shown a greater propensity to create such a right. People kept in ignorance of the state of toxicity of a chemical plant had not been victims of a breach of Art 10, the court ruled; the government had not sought actively to suppress any information the court held. They were under no duty actively to provide it. By a slender majority the Commission ruled there was an active right to such information: 'the current state of European law … confirms that public information is now an essential tool for protecting public well-being and health in situations of danger to the environment'. The Commission cited a 1996 resolution of the Parliamentary Assembly of the Council of Europe which stated that where nuclear energy and related matters are concerned 'public access to clear and full information … must be viewed as a basic human right'. States were under a positive duty to publish it. The court did hold however, that Art 8 could provide a duty to publish information where in protecting family and private life knowledge of such information was essential for such enjoyment. The applicants were denied 'essential information that would have enabled them to assess the risk they and their families might run if they continued to live in Manfredonia, a town particularly exposed to danger in the event of an accident at the factory.'[2]

[1]   Figures supplied by Home Office: 18 July 2000. Shayler was charged under OSA 1989 in August 2000. More recent figures are available at HC Debs 22 January 2002 col 830W. There were no prosecutions in 2009 – information from MoJ under FOIA 2000.
[2]   *Guerra v Italy* (1998) 4 BHRC 63. See also *Oneryildiz v Turkey* (2004) 39 EHRR 12 and failure to inform of public danger by an authority leading to a breach of Art 2 ECHR and *Gaskin v UK* (para 8.85 below).

2.296   In *McGinley and Egan v UK* servicemen were exposed to nuclear testing by way of explosions. Although the claim failed on its facts the following was conceded:

'Where a government engages in hazardous activities such as those in issue in the present case, which might have hidden adverse consequences on the health of those involved in such activities, respect for family life under article 8 requires that an effective and accessible procedure be established which enables such persons to seek all relevant and appropriate information.'[1]

These cases have significant implications for the law relating to privacy protection (see paras 7.185 and 8.85 below).

[1]   (1998) 27 EHRR 1. See also *Roche v UK* Application No 32555/96.

2.297   Recent ECtHR judgments have journeyed even further so that while not asserting that art 10 creates a free-standing right of access to information, where access to state-held information, otherwise unavailable, was necessary in order for a journalist to exercise freedom-of-speech rights, a fundamental right of access to documents was thereby established.[1] The impact of these cases is influencing English judgments[2] and led the Court of Appeal to re-submit a case to the First Tier Tribunal for a reconsideration of FOIA 2000, s 32 under the duties of interpretation in the HRA 1998 and ECHR, Art 10.[3]

[1]   *Társaság a Szabadságjogokért v Hungary* (2009) Application No 37374/05 and *Jihoceske v Czech Republic* (2006) Application No 19101/03. For the successful use of a freedom of speech right to gain access to documents in the American Human Rights Court under the AHRC, art 13, see *Cheyes v Chile case 12.108 (2003).* See paras 1.54–1.55 above. See generally P Birkinshaw 'Freedom of Information and Openness: Fundamental Human Rights?' (2006) *58 Administrative LR* 177.
[2]   *A v Independent News Media Ltd* [2010] EWCA Civ 343 (paras 1.54–1.55).
[3]   *Kennedy v IC* [2011] EWCA Civ 367.

2.298   As will be seen (paras 2.343 et seq below), Art 10 has had some effect in English courts in allowing access to information by way of opening up inquiries into serious wrongdoing to the public but the position is mixed; and, more recently, Art 2 ECHR, a right to protecting life, has met with more appreciable success.

PUBLIC INTEREST DISCLOSURE ACT 1998

2.299   It is exhorted as good practice for employers to possess whistleblowing procedures. In relation to the law, the Public Interest Disclosure Act 1998

(PIDA 1998) 'creates a framework for whistleblowing across the private, public and voluntary sectors'.[1] The Act amends the Employment Rights Act 1996 (ERA 1996), adding a new Part IVA (ss 43A–43L). The Act applies to those in service of the Crown (PIDA 1998, s 10), and workers generally, but not to those involved in national security and intelligence work (s 11). To much criticism, including that from the Police Complaints Authority and ACPO, the Act did not protect police officers (s 13) but the provisions were extended to police officers by Police Reform Act 2002, s 37. Workers are protected against any detriment or failure to act by their employer where they have made a 'qualifying disclosure' (s 2). Where the reason for a dismissal or redundancy, or principal reason, was a qualifying disclosure, the dismissal is automatically unfair (see para 2.309). A protected disclosure is a qualifying disclosure (QD) where it is made by a worker in accordance with the Act's provisions. A QD is one where information[2] is disclosed in the reasonable belief of the worker making the disclosure that it tends to show one or more of the following:

(1) That a criminal offence has been committed, is being committed or is likely to be committed (the latter two – 'present and future' – denoted as 'etc' in what follows).
(2) That a person has failed etc to comply with any legal obligation to which he is subject.
(3) That a miscarriage of justice has occurred etc.
(4) That the health or safety of any individual has been endangered etc.
(5) That the environment has been damaged etc.
(6) That information tending to show any matter falling within any one of the preceding paragraphs has been deliberately concealed etc.

[1] G Dehn *Annotation CL Statutes* (1998) ch 23, p 1. See also Cm 6394 I, II, II *Shipman Inquiry Fifth Report* and *Tenth Report* Committee of Standards in Public Life, Cm 6407, ch 4.
[2] A QD covers information not an allegation: *Cavendish Munro Professional Risk Management Ltd v Geduld* [2010] IRLR 38.

2.300 It is immaterial where the failure/event occurred ctc and also what the governing law is. However, a disclosure of information is not a QD if the person making the disclosure commits an offence by making it – this would include the Official Secrets Acts although internal channels may properly be pursued under the 1989 Act. Information covered by legal professional privilege cannot be the subject of a QD. A QD is made in accordance with ERA 1996, s 43C if the worker makes the disclosure in good faith to his employer, or to another person where the worker reasonably believes that the relevant failure relates mainly or solely to the conduct of another person other than his employer or concerns any matter for which a person other than his employer has responsibility. It is then made to that other person. If the worker has made a disclosure to another under a procedure whose use is authorised by the employer, it is to be treated as making the QD to the employer.

2.301 A QD is made if made in the course of obtaining legal advice. There is no good faith requirement (ERA 1996, s 43D).

2.302   A QD is made if made in good faith to a Minister of the Crown where the worker's employer is appointed by a Minister of the Crown under any enactment or is a body any of whose members are so appointed. This covers government appointed bodies.

2.303   A QD is made if the worker makes the disclosure in good faith to a person prescribed by an order made by the Secretary of State for the purposes of this section and the worker reasonably believes that the relevant failure falls within any description of matters in respect of which the person is so prescribed. The 'prescribed person' is set out in the Schedule to the Public Interest Disclosure (Prescribed Persons) Order 1999, SI 1999/1549 (substituted by SI 2003/1993 and amended by SI 2010/7), to which the Independent Police Complaints Commission has been added by SI 2004/3265. The information disclosed and any allegation contained in it must be 'substantially true' (ERA 1996, s 43F).

2.304   In other cases (ERA 1996, s 43G), a QD is made otherwise than via an employer etc where the worker makes the disclosure in good faith; he reasonably believes that the information disclosed and any allegation contained in it are substantially true; the disclosure is not made for personal gain;[1] any of the conditions in sub-s (2) is met; and in all the circumstances of the case it is reasonable for him to make the disclosure. The conditions in sub-s (2) are that at the time he makes the disclosure the worker reasonably believes that he will be subjected to detriment by his employer if he makes a disclosure to his employer or as under s 43F; that where no person is prescribed for the purposes of s 43F, the worker reasonably believes that it is likely that evidence relating to the relevant failure will be concealed or destroyed if the disclosure is made to the employer; or, that the worker has previously made a disclosure of substantially the same information[2] either to the employer (s 43G(2)(c)(i)) or in accordance with s 43F.

[1]   See ERA 1996, s 43L(2) whereby any statutory reward is disregarded. See *Street v Derbyshire UWC* [2004] 4 All ER 839 (CA): a belief in the veracity of the material was not sufficient to meet the good faith requirement. It was possible to believe the truth of the material but to promote it for reasons of personal antagonism and such conduct did not equal good faith under ERA 1996, s 43G. The purpose of the amendment by the 1998 Act was to protect those who made disclosures in the public interest 'not to allow persons to advance personal grudges'.

[2]   ERA 1996, s 43G(4) states 'a subsequent disclosure may be regarded as a disclosure of substantially the same information as that disclosed by a previous disclosure as mentioned in sub-s (2)(c) even though the subsequent disclosure extends to information about action taken or not taken by any person as a result of the previous disclosure'.

2.305   Various factors are considered in determining whether it is reasonable to make the disclosure including the identity of the person to whom disclosure is made; the seriousness of the relevant failure; whether that failure is continuing or is likely to recur; whether the disclosure is made in breach of a duty of confidentiality owed by the employer to any other person; any action taken by the employer or person to whom the disclosure is made, or which might reasonably be expected to be taken as a consequence of previous disclosures. In making a disclosure under s 43G(2)(c)(i) above, regard is to be had to whether in making the disclosure to the employer the worker complied with any procedure whose use by the worker was authorised by the employer.

2.306 Under ERA 1996, s 43H, disclosures of exceptionally serious matters may be protected even though they do not fall within the conditions in the previous sections. There is a good faith requirement, a reasonable belief by the worker that the information etc is substantially true and that it is not made for personal gain. The relevant failure must be exceptionally serious and in all the circumstances it is reasonable for the worker to make the disclosure. In determining 'reasonableness' regard shall be had to the identity of the person to whom the disclosure is made.

2.307 Any term of a contract seeking to prevent a worker from making a protected disclosure is void. This covers employment contracts, or other contracts including settlement agreements. These are commonly referred to as 'gagging clauses'.[1]

[1] Note an employee is not under a duty to inform his employer of a breach of contract by that employee on the facts of the following case: *University of Nottingham v Fishel* [2000] IRLR 471.

2.308 The scope of the phrase 'worker' is defined in s 43K and extends far beyond the scope of employment law. It covers employees and those independent contractors who themselves provide services but not in a professional/client relationship. 'In addition to these, this Act protects certain agency workers, homeworkers, NHS doctors, dentists, ophthalmologists and pharmacists, and trainees on vocational or work experience schemes.'[1] A worker does not lose the protection of the Act where the person receiving the information is already aware of it, ie that there is strictly no 'disclosure'.

[1] Dehn above at p 23–17.

2.309 By ERA 1996, s 47B, a worker has the right not to be subjected to any detriment by any act, or any deliberate failure to act by the employer which has been done on the ground that the worker made a protected disclosure. An employee who is dismissed cannot claim under s 47B but, with one exception, must claim under ERA 1996, ss 103A and 105(6). Complaints may be made to an employment tribunal by a worker – in fact this is the only avenue open (s 14).[1] A declaration of victimisation may be made and compensation awarded. There are limits on awards of compensation to prevent disparities between highly paid workers, and employees, where contracts are terminated. Dismissal because of, or mainly because of, a protected disclosure is automatically deemed an unfair dismissal. Employees are also given new protection against selection for redundancy where they have made a protected disclosure. Claims under this Act are not subject to the minimum qualifying period for unfair dismissal nor to the upper age limit. Regulations may be made covering compensation levels for dismissal under s 8 of PIDA 1998. Interim relief may be claimed by employees but not workers.

[1] On time limits, see note to s 3 in Dehn above.

2.310 In July 2000, an employment tribunal awarded £293,441 to an employee who had been dismissed for justifiable whistleblowing in one of the first cases brought under the Act setting out an early indication of the seriousness of this provision.[1] While compensation levels appear generous, re-employment orders cannot be enforced but employer refusal to comply will lead to additional compensation. However, there are many examples of whistleblowers who have suffered in their employment prospects particularly in relation to health and safety disclosures and those relating to financial irregularity.

[1]   (2000) *Guardian*, 11 July revealed how the government had taken action to reverse a court ruling which allowed detailed facts about employment tribunals to be published. The order significantly reduced the amount of information that could be published. On the procedures to be adopted re evidence by Employment Tribunals, see *ALM Medical Services Ltd v Bladon* (2002) *Times*, 29 August (CA).

2.311   On 1 October 2004, new rules came into effect which enforce secrecy of employment settlements which do not go to an open tribunal. The Employment Tribunals (Constitution and Rules of Procedure) Regulations 2004/1861, it has been claimed, attempt to assist conciliation by avoiding publicity (Sch 1, rule 22). Critics claim that valuable information on whistleblowing will not be made public.

THE LAW RELATING TO THE PROTECTION OF CONFIDENTIALITY

2.312   Almost 40 years ago, the law of confidence was unsuccessfully invoked by the Crown to protect information about Cabinet proceedings (see below). Since then, case law and discussion about the scope of confidentiality have developed considerably. The extent of the obligation makes it a relevant consideration for the whole of the public and private sectors, personal and corporate. It is advantageous to introduce the subject at this stage.

2.313   Under s 163 of the Copyright, Designs and Patents Act 1988, a work made by an officer or servant of the Crown in the course of his or her duties qualifies for copyright protection under the Act and Her Majesty is the first owner of any copyright. This is referred to as 'Crown copyright'[1] and confers a maximum copyright term of 125 years.[2]

[1]   Copyright, Designs and Patents Act 1988, s 163(2); see Copyright Act 1956, s 39.
[2]   Copyright, Designs and Patents Act 1988, s 163(3); see ss 45–50 of the 1988 Act.

2.314   Copyright is not the same thing as confidentiality.[1] Copyright is a property right, a right ad rem although in case law reference has been made to equitable rights to copyright:[2] confidentiality is in essence a right in personam, a right against an individual or individuals to prevent them from perpetrating, or to make them account for, a breach of confidence. '[E]quity intervenes to preserve the confidentiality of information not because information is susceptible of a *proprietary* claim but because its use in the hands of the defendant is unconscionable.'[3] In its simplest sense it is a duty imposed by the civil law to keep a secret. Unlike the law of official secrets the courts, applying the law of confidentiality, cannot treat as secret that which is no longer in fact secret and which has become a matter of public knowledge. It follows that an injunction will not issue to prevent dissemination of information which is already placed in the public domain by others apart from the confidee and where no further damage can be done by publication.[4] What the law can do in such an event is to punish the confidee in breach of his or her duty by way of an award of damages or for an account of profits where s/he has put the information to profitable use. In a classic analysis of the nature of legal protection of confidentiality, Megarry J stated that there has to be information which must be of a confidential nature; the information must have been communicated in circumstances importing an obligation of confidence (and deserving of the protection of confidentiality); and it must be disclosed in breach of that duty to the confidor through unauthorised use.[5]

1   Although the 'public interest' defence in the case of a publication applies to a breach of copyright as well as to a breach of confidence: *Lion Laboratories Ltd v Evans* [1985] QB 526, CA. However, in *Hyde Park Residence Ltd v Yelland* [2001] Ch 143, the Court of Appeal ruled that the two tests were not identical, the copyright test being narrower and therefore less easily invoked. In *Ashdown v Telegraph Group Ltd* [2001] 2 All ER 370, the Vice Chancellor was unwilling to allow a defence to a breach of copyright and confidentiality based on Art 10 ECHR where statutory defences under the 1988 Act were unsuccessful. The Court of Appeal upheld the decision but held that Art 10 rights should be given effect in 'rare' cases where those rights trumped the statutory proprietary rights [2001] 4 All ER 666 (CA). See also *Tillery Valley Foods Ltd v Channel Four News Corp and Another* (2004) 11 May. P.Torremans *Copyright and Human Rights: Freedom of Expression, Intellectual Property, Privacy* (2004). In *HRH Prince of Wales v Associated Newspapers* [2006] EWHC 522 Ch, there is a discussion of various defences against a breach of copyright claim under the 'fair dealing' provisions of the Copyright , Designs and Patents Act 1988, s 30(1) and (2) and the public interest provision in s 171(3). This discussion is hinged upon the usual context of a breach of copyright claim where a newspaper is seeking to justify a breach of copyright under a duty owed by the original author.

2   See in particular Scott J in *A-G v Guardian Newspapers Ltd (No 2)* [1988] 3 All ER 545.

3   Lord Oliver (1989) 23 *Israel Law Review* 407 at 413; *A-G v Guardian Newspapers Ltd (No 2)* [1990] 1 AC 109. See generally, R G Toulson and C M Phipps *Confidentiality* (2nd ed, 2006).

4   Unless, possibly in a case concerning a confidence owed to the Crown further damage to the public interest may be caused, infra.

5   *Coco v A N Clark* [1969] RPC 41.

2.315   The most common use of the law of confidentiality today (although not the most notorious) is in the field of employer/employee relations to protect, in a wide sense, the trade secrets of the employer or to restrict the use of information gleaned by an employee from the course of employment.[1] In such cases the nature of the duty arises from the contractual relationship involving either the interpretation of express provisions[2] or those arising as a matter of necessary implication.[3] Recent litigation has displayed an awareness of the need not to spread too widely the protection given to an employer[4] and also the necessity of enjoining a former employee in breach of the obligation from using information which is in the public domain where his or her prior knowledge or familiarity affords that person an additional advantage over other competitors – the so-called 'springboard' doctrine.[5] But confidentiality may arise in the widest range of circumstances and courts are anxious not to allow its ambit to be too widely drawn. Some contractual relationships are built upon a fiduciary relationship of special trust and terms may be interpreted as protected by confidentiality: principal and agent is often cited. In chapter 1 (paras 1.281 et seq above) it was seen how the stipulations of commercial contracting parties as to what is confidential and where no special relationship exists will not be binding on the courts in terms of the law of confidentiality; in the absence of a duty of confidence any remedies such as they are will be under the law of contract and these may be negligible. In litigation involving a concessions agreement to build a road, it has been held that claims to commercial confidentiality must not be made in an over extensive fashion and in any event a discretion was retained to disclose a compensation clause. Information was sought by a public interest group.[6]

1   *Faccenda Chicken Ltd v Fowler* [1985] 1 All ER 724, affirmed [1986] 1 All ER 617, CA; *Lock International plc v Beswick* [1989] 3 All ER 373; *Intelsec Systems Ltd v Grech-Cini* [1999] 4 All ER 11. See commercial confidentiality: *Helmet Integrated Systems Ltd v Tunnard* [2006] EWCA Civ 1735 and *Crowson Fabrics Ltd v Rider* [2007] EWHC 2942 Ch (on *Faccenda*, etc).

2   See Meagher, Gummow and Lehane *Equity: Doctrines and Remedies* (4th edn, 2002) paras 41.005 et seq for a lucid account.

3   Meagher, Gummow and Lehane, paras 41.005 et seq.

4   *Faccenda Chicken Ltd v Fowler* [1985] 1 All ER 724; affirmed [1986] 1 All ER 617, CA.

5   *Terrapin Ltd v Builders' Supply Co (Hayes) Ltd* (1959) [1967] RPC 375. See, however, Lord Goff in *A-G v Guardian Newspapers Ltd (No 2)* [1988] 3 All ER 545 at 661–662. The doctrine has been held not to apply where a defendant is not involved in any wrongdoing: *Peter Pan Manufacturing Corpn v Corsets Silhouette Ltd* [1963] 3 All ER 402 at 408. See *Vestergad Frandsen A/S v Bestnet Europe Ltd* [2009] EWHC 1456 Ch.

6   *R v Secretary of State for the Environment etc, ex p Alliance Against the Birmingham Northern Relief Road* [1999] Env L R 447. See *R v Department of Health, ex p Source Informatics Ltd* [2000] 1 All ER 786, CA: information required from prescriptions excluding the identity of patients was not confidential.

2.316 An obligation to maintain a confidence may arise independently of contract and had long been the object of appropriate relief in the former Court of Chancery.[1] In 1807, for instance, Lord Eldon, in camera, enjoined the editor of *The Phoenix* from publishing depositions before a Cabinet committee conducting a 'delicate investigation' into allegations that the Princess of Wales had given birth to a child conceived in an adulterous relationship.[2] Subsequent cases display an equitable protection of confidential information which relates to family[3] and intimate relationships.[4] The importance of the equitable jurisdiction is, of course, that it will bind third parties who are not in a contractual nexus with the confidor where they know, or ought to realise, that it is confidential information, or where they have received information without giving valuable consideration,[5] and where there is no possibility of suing for any tortious act such as inducing breach of contract or being a party to a conspiracy. The extent to which relief may be awarded against an innocent third party (ie one without notice actual or constructive) who has provided valuable consideration[6] is a moot point, though such a party ought to be protected from an injunction or action for an account if their conscience is clear; the situation may be different if, initially innocent, s/he subsequently acquires knowledge of the wrong.[7]

1   *Abernethy v Hutchinson* (1825) 3 LJOS Ch 209; *Prince Albert v Strange* (1849) 18 LJ Ch 120; *Morison v Moat* (1851) 20 LJ Ch 513.

2   Meagher, Gummow and Lehane *Equity: Doctrines and Remedies* (4th edn, 2002), para 41.030.

3   *Argyll v Argyll* [1967] Ch 302.

4   Supra. Cf *Lennon v News Group Newspapers Ltd and Twist* [1978] FSR 573, CA.

5   *Saltman Engineering Co Ltd v Campbell Engineering Co Ltd* (1948) 65 RPC 203, CA; *Seager v Copydex Ltd* [1967] 2 All ER 415.

6   See Jones (1970) 86 LQR 463; Meagher etc at 41.005 et seq.

7   Then there may well be an account of profits accruing post the existence of the knowledge of the
     confidence; cf, however, the usual position in equity: viz a good title passes even to a subsequent
     purchaser with notice from a bona fide purchaser: *Wilkes v Spooner* [1911] 2 KB 473 may place
     too much emphasis on proprietorial rather than conscionable aspects of the situation.

2.317   Alongside contractual duties, the law will protect, or rather restrain 'the
publication of confidential information improperly or surreptitiously obtained
or of information imparted in confidence which ought not to be divulged'.[1] The
quotation emphasises the trust and confidence relied upon by the plaintiff: 'or
that the defendant obtained surreptitiously or improperly that which he could
otherwise have obtained either not at all or only on a limited basis'.[2] The quotation
also emphasises the importance of the circumstances in which the defendant
obtained information so that relief is not dependent upon the intrinsic value
or importance of the information itself or upon 'any apprehended damage to
the plaintiff by misuse thereof'.[3] But the latter may be significant. For example,
confidentiality attaches to information which is given to the police during the
course of a criminal investigation, whether it is given by a suspect under caution
or by a potential witness. The weight to be attached to the confidentiality will
depend very much on the particular circumstances in which the material was
obtained.[4] The statement also indicates that the law will protect confidences that
ought not to be divulged: it will not protect every confidence nor, importantly,
will it protect everything marked 'confidential'. Indeed, some confidences ought,
in the public interest, to be disclosed (see below).

1   Swinfen Eady LJ *Ashburton v Pape* [1913] 2 Ch 469 at 475, CA. See: *Douglas v Hello! Ltd* [2001]
     2 All ER 289, CA. See for breach of an implied contractual duty: *Turner v Royal Bank of Scotland*
     [1999] 2 All ER (Comm) 664, CA. It has been suggested *obiter* that under Human Rights Act
     1998, s 12(3) (para 2.349 below) it is arguable that a contractual duty of confidence is stronger
     than an equitable one and the Queen was entitled to an injunction restraining an employee of
     the *Daily Mirror* employed as a royal footman from divulging confidential information: *Attorney
     General v Parry* [2004] EMLR 13. Cf Robert Walker LJ in *London Regional Transport v The Mayor
     of London* [2003] EMLR 4 and Lord Phillips MR in *Campbell v Frisbee* [2003] EMLR 3. Surely a
     claim in contract cannot affect the strength of a *confidentiality*. Contract may help to clarify the
     extent of what is protected. But if information is confidential why should contract make the claim
     'stronger'? However, a contractual claim will subsist within a breach of confidence, so that the
     confidor may terminate the agreement after a confidee has made a disclosure, even one supported
     by a public interest. This was a problem which the Public Interest Disclosure Act 1998 sought to
     address.
2   Meagher, Gummow and Lehane *Equity: Doctrines and Remedies* (3rd edn, 1992), para 41.045.
3   Supra, providing the information is worthy of protection.
4   *Frankson and others v Home Office* [2003] 1 WLR 1953, in particular per Scott Baker LJ at para 35.

2.318   As emphasised in the *Spycatcher* litigation, confidentiality will not protect
trivial or useless information. Further, it is not only information which is obtained
consensually that is protected, ie by a willing confider upon a willing confidee.
Confidential information, even though not 'obtained consensually' nonetheless
'cannot be purloined and freely used'.[1] Information will be protected where
it 'would be just in all the circumstances that [a person] should be precluded
from disclosing the information to others.'[2] The past behaviour of plaintiffs is
important to ascertain whether they are volens or implicitly consenting to the
publication. Their past behaviour towards seeking publicity or selling private
information about themselves may restrict the ambit of confidentiality via

'breaches' by his or her family or coterie;[3] or their behaviour may establish that they do not come to court with 'clean hands'.[4]

1   Meagher, Gummow and Lehane *Equity: Doctrines and Remedies*, para 41.045 and cases cited. The authors are very critical of Megarry VC's observations in *Malone v Metropolitan Police Comr* [1979] Ch 344 at 376 to the contrary.
2   *A-G v Guardian Newspapers (No 2)* [1990] AC 109 at 281 per Lord Goff.
3   *Lennon v News Group Newspapers Ltd and Twist* [1978] FSR 573, CA; or deliberately projecting a public image that was false: *Woodward v Hutchins* [1977] 2 All ER 751, CA. These questions are central to *Campbell v MGN Ltd* and the different approaches taken by the Court of Appeal and House of Lords: [2003] 1 All ER 224 and [2004] 2 All ER 995 respectively.
4   At first instance in the proceedings involving *Spycatcher* in Australia, the judge did not think the 'clean hands' doctrine operated against the government: *A-G for the UK v Heinemann Publishers Australia Pty Ltd* (1987) 8 NSWLR 341, Powell J. On appeal, *A-G for the UK v Heinemann Publishers Australia Pty Ltd* (1987) 10 NSWLR 86 and *A-G (UK) v Heinemann Publishers Australia Pty Ltd (No 2)* (1988) 78 ALR 449.

2.319 Since the previous edition of this work the courts have been forced to address several issues in relation to confidentiality. The most pressing concern has been the impact of Art 8 ECHR and its protection of privacy (para 2.291 above) and the impact the Article will have over the development of the English law of confidentiality. Will it create via the Human Rights Act 1998 a right to privacy in English (and British and Northern Irish) law? Privacy is a theme that is addressed in chapter 7 (see paras 7.185 et seq below). The short answer at this stage is that there remain differences in the approach taken by English courts and the Strasbourg Court of Human Rights and that a free-standing or 'over-arching, all-embracing' right to privacy has not arisen in English law other than those provided by statute such as the Data Protection Act 1998 – which regulates the use of personal information (ch 7) – the Regulation of Investigatory Powers Act 2000 (paras 2.200 above) and, especially, the Human Rights Act 1998.[1] In several cases, the courts have confronted the issue and have given relief where the law of confidentiality would have provided a remedy, or refused to provide relief where on equitable grounds relief was not justified. In no English case has a court given a remedy for a breach of privacy as a tort.[2] Article 8 is, however, directly enforceable by the courts against public bodies and courts are duty bound to uphold that Article and all other Convention rights contained in HRA 1998. Through the use of art 8, the courts have fashioned a legal right to privacy and protection of personal information and the use of superinjunctions making secret the fact that a claimant has used the courts to obtain an injunction, breach of which may amount to a contempt of court, have fomented heated discussion of the re-emergence of prior restraint on freedom of speech. We revisit this subject in greater detail in chapter 7 (para 7.185 et seq).

1   *Wainwright v Home Office* [2003] UKHL 53 and for a breach of art 8 in the ECtHR: *Wainwright v UK* App No 12350/04.

2   *Douglas v Hello! Ltd* [2001] 2 All ER 289 (CA); *A v B* [2002] 2 All ER 545 (CA); *Douglas v Hello! Ltd (No 3)* [2003] 3 All ER 996 (Ch).

2.320 There has also been a recognition that 'aspects of privacy' will be protected because privacy 'lies at the heart of liberty in the modern state. A proper degree of privacy is essential for the well-being and development of an individual'.[1] Although the House of Lords ruled in *Wainwright v Home Office*[2] (a pre-HRA 1998 case) that there is no all encompassing action for 'breach of privacy', it has been suggested that following the incorporation of Art 8 into UK laws, the essence of the tort of breach of confidentiality is 'better encapsulated now as misuse of private information'.[3] Autonomy and dignity are central features of this development. The values inherent in Arts 8 and 10 are now a part of the law of confidence and the protection of private information. Neither article takes pre-eminence over the other which is very important in relation to the 'public interest' – there is no automatic overriding interest in publicity of information or in privacy. If the emphasis is to be placed on the distinction between 'private' and 'public' information, this begs analysis of the method used to distinguish between the two. The test of Gleeson CJ in *Australian Broadcasting Corp v Leach Game Meats Pty Ltd*[4] met with some approval in the case of the supermodel Naomi Campbell, when it was reported that she was seeking therapy for drugs-related addiction together with the nature of the therapy and accompanying photographs:

> 'The requirement that disclosure or observation of information or conduct would be highly offensive to a reasonable person of ordinary sensibilities is in many circumstances a useful practical test of what is private.'

In *Campbell*, the majority in the House of Lords ruled that the above information was protected by confidentiality and art 8 (see para 2.324 below). The courts in England have developed this line of thinking (paras 7.185 et seq).

[1]   Per Lord Nicholls in *Campbell v MGN Ltd* [2004] 2 All ER 995 (HL) at para [12].
[2]   [2003] UKHL 53, [2003] 4 All ER 969 (HL). This involved strip searches of visitors to a prisoner by prison officials. The events in question took place *before* the HRA came into effect. Post-HRA, the claimants in *Wainwright* could have made their claim on the basis of Art 8 by virtue of HRA 1998, ss 6 and 7. Lord Hoffmann believed that it was far from clear that a breach of Art 8 would provide relief for distress where a breach was unintentional; it is unclear why such a limit should be imposed (see para 7.188, note 1, below). In *Wainwright v UK* (para 2.319, note 2 above) the ECtHR found that there had been a breach of art 8 and also art 13 – but not art 3.
[3]   Lord Nicholls in *Campbell v MGN Ltd* [2004] 2 All ER 995 at para [14]. See Lord Hoffmann at paras 50–52, ibid that a right to protection of private information is 'the right to control the dissemination of information about one's private life and the right to the esteem and respect of other people' at para 51. Lord Hope spoke of Ms Campbell's right to *privacy* being infringed at para 125 although the action was framed in confidentiality.
[4]   (2001) 185 ALR 1. Lord Nicholls however, opined that a concentration on 'highly offensive' rather than 'a reasonable expectation of privacy' focused more on a test of proportionality in relation to an interference rather than on the existence of a confidentiality itself.

2.321   Private information may be protected even though it concerns matters that take place in public; and acts in private places may not warrant protection as private information. Context is everything. It is crucial in explaining the way in which confidentiality has been fashioned to protect public sector secrets (below).

2.322   Information to be protected must be capable of being described or defined with sufficient clarity to be the subject of an injunction.[1] Minor breaches of confidence by limited publication will not necessarily defeat the request for an injunction; it is very much a matter of fact and degree and the possibility of extended or additional harm by publication, even reviving public recollection[2] of damaging public controversy, may suffice. Clearly, there comes a point at which even adventitious publicity will defeat an injunction, as the necessary quality of confidentiality or secrecy will have evaporated. Prior publication will not necessarily remove the protection of privacy (para 7.185 et seq). As we shall see, there is a difference between the position of the confidant and third parties where confidences relating to state secrets are involved (paras 2.329 et seq below).

[1]   *O'Brien v Komesaroff* (1982) 56 ALJR 681 (Australia).
[2]   *Schering Chemicals Ltd v Falkman Ltd* [1981] 2 All ER 321.

The public interest defence

2.323   Where there is a public interest in revealing confidential information to the public, ie where it is genuinely in the interest of the public that the information be revealed, and not merely interesting to the public, then the duty of confidentiality will not extend to that information.[1] Originally conceived in the phrase 'there can be no confidence in an iniquity' it has been extended to cover wrongdoing of various degrees,[2] unconscionable behaviour, and now covers that which ought to be made public because of public safety and health and to prevent individuals being misled.[3] This is so even where the disclosure is activated by malice.[4] However, disclosing for personal profit, or making any unnecessarily wide disclosure via the media or internet and not to authorities may remove the public interest protection. The facts have to be carefully assessed. In not automatically negativing malice the common law test is considerably wider than the public interest test contained in the PIDA 1998 (see above). It may not, however, contain the same breadth as the public interest discretionary disclosure test under s 2 of the FOIA 2000 (see paras 1.98 et seq above). It should be recalled that under FOIA 2000, s 41 information may not be disclosed if the disclosure would constitute an actionable breach of confidence. It was observed that the public interest test under the law of confidentiality would be available but the onus of establishing such an interest lay on the requester for information (paras 1.206–1.207).

[1]   *Gartside v Outram* (1856) 3 Jur NS 39.
[2]   *Initial Services Ltd v Putterill* [1968] 1 QB 396, CA; *Hubbard v Vosper* [1972] 2 QB 84, CA.
[3]   *Lion Laboratories v Evans* [1985] QB 526, CA. However, a disclosure may not be justified by publication in the media, but by reporting to the authorities: *Francome v Mirror Group Newspaper Ltd* [1984] 2 All ER 408, CA. See also *W v Egdell* [1989] 1 All ER 1089; affd [1990] 1 All ER 835, CA; *R v Crozier* (1990) 8 BMLR 128, CA; compare *R v Registrar-General, ex p Smith* [1991] 2 All ER 88, CA; and *Re X* [1994] 3 All ER 372, CA.
[4]   *Re a Company's Application* [1989] 2 All ER 248. See also: *Re Smith Kline & French Laboratories Ltd* [1990] 1 AC 64, HL.

2.324   The question of a public interest defence has become increasingly embroiled with the right of freedom of speech under Art 10 ECHR and the right to privacy under Art 8 ECHR, both now parts of UK law. One must be balanced against the other in the context of specific facts and merits. Too much emphasis of one will unjustifiably jeopardise rights under the other.[1] The balancing has taken place in several high profile cases where the courts have ruled that the details of a sexual relationship between a married professional footballer and two casual partners did not merit protection by a court order prohibiting a newspaper from publishing details of the relationships. The footballer was a role model and his 'clay feet' were justifiably exposed. Preventing the press from reporting these facts would interfere with freedom of speech rights under Art 10. Casual sexual relationships did not merit the same degree of protection as marital relationships. Furthermore, while the press will of course publish for profit as a commercial concern, the two females involved wanted to exercise their Art 10 rights in order to make a financial profit.[2] Although the identities of footballers playing sexual 'away games', or those of rock stars and celebrities, have subsequently not always been protected by the courts from disclosure, the growing use of superinjunctions has caused the media to complain about the apparently increasing use of gagging orders to prevent any information at all about sexual or other peccadillos fom being published. Orders have been awarded *contra mundum*. Judicial restraints on publication include the fact that the claimant has gone to court to seek an injunction. The courts have not adopted the robust attitude of Lord Woolf in *A v B* (see note 2 below) especially where there may be some underhand activity by a sexual partner of the person seeking the injunction. Nonetheless, the award in some cases is difficult to understand, especially, for instance, in the case of the disgraced banker Fred Goodwin who was having an affair with a senior colleague at the time of the collapse of RBS bank. Identities have been revealed through Parliament and via social sites such as Twitter, making the court orders practically useless in terms of privacy but raising the possibility of contempt proceedings. This area is the subject of a report by Lord Neuberger MR and we address this in chapter 7 (paras 7.203 and 7.204).[3] Conversely, where Naomi Campbell had publicly declared that she was not a drug addict the press were entitled to publicise the fact that she was and that she was receiving treatment but not the fact that she was attending Narcotics Anonymous, details of the treatment and a 'visual portrayal' (photograph) of the model leaving the NA meetings. These were features of private information which did not warrant publication.[4] They were not publishable simply because they attended items of information which in the public interest could be published.

[1] However, see paras 10.6–10.7 below where, in relation to cases concerning the upbringing of children, the paramountcy principle in Children Act 1989, s 1(1) invariably necessitates secrecy: see for other situations *Re S (a child) (identification: restriction on publication), Re* [2003] 3 WLR 1425. See H.Fenwick (2004) 67 *Mod L.R.* 889.

[2] *A v B* [2002] 2 All ER 545 (CA).

[3] For publication of the existence of an affair but not details see *Ntuli v Donald* [2010] EWCA Civ 1276. For complete anonymity, see *JIH v News Group Newspapers Ltd* [2011] EWCA Civ 42. On the refusal to issue an injunction where a person's identity had entered the public domain: *BBC v HarperCollins Publishers Ltd* [2010] EWHC 2424 (Ch).

[4] See para 2.320, note 3 above. Cf *Fressoz and Roire v France* (1999) 5 BHRC 654 (CHR) where journalists published details of the Managing Director of Peugeot's salary (publicly available information) as well as his tax return (prohibited under French penal law from publication). The ECtHR set ruled that the conviction under French law for publishing the tax return was a denial of Art 10 rights: 'If ... the information about M.Calvert's annual income was lawful and its disclosure permitted, the applicants' conviction for merely having published the documents in which that information was contained, namely tax assessments, cannot be justified under Article 10. In essence, that Article leaves it to journalists to decide whether or not it is necessary to reproduce such documents to ensure credibility' (para 54). Surely they are not free to publish unless there is wrong-doing in the return ie evasion (and avoidance) of tax?

2.325 Lord Steyn in *Re S (a child)* (see para 10.18 below) stated that four propositions emerge from the *Campbell* case:

'First, neither article has *as such* precedence over the other. Secondly, where the values under the two articles are in conflict, an intense focus on the comparative importance of the specific rights being claimed in the individual case is necessary. Thirdly, the justifications for interfering with or restricting each right must be taken into account. Finally, the proportionality test must be applied to each. For convenience I will call this the ultimate balancing test. This is how I will approach the present case.' (para 17)[1]

[1] See *W (Children) (Identification Restrictions on Publication)* [2005] EWHC 1564.

2.326 There has been extensive litigation on the rights of the police to disclose information about known paedophiles to those likely to be affected by their presence in a local area. Although the paedophiles should have been allowed to see the information before it was disclosed, on the facts of the case this had not been a fatal omission and the general policy of disclosure was not unlawful or irrational.[1] The courts will be vigilant to ensure fair procedures in the manner in which such information may be disclosed.[2] Furthermore, naming and shaming members of a teenage gang who terrorised a housing estate when they were the recipients of Anti Social Behaviour Orders under Crime and Disorder Act 1998, s 1 was justified as an invasion of their privacy on the facts.[3]

[1] *R v Chief Constable of the North Wales Police, ex p AB* [1998] 3 All ER 310, CA. See also *Bunn v BBC* [1998] 3 All ER 552; *Woolgar v Chief Constable of the Sussex Police* [1999] 3 All ER 604, CA – disclosure of confidential information to a regulatory authority; *Preston Borough Council v McGrath* (2000) *Times*, 19 May, CA – police entitled to disclose information on corruption to a council; *S v S* [1999] 1 All ER 281, CA; *Pharaon v BCCI SA* [1998] 4 All ER 455; *Hellewell v Chief Constable of Derbyshire* [1995] 4 All ER 473 – confidentiality protected 'mugshots' taken in police custody; see *R (Ellis) v Chief Constable of Essex Police* [2003] EWHC 1321 (Admin), at para 1.277, note 1 above and *R (A) v National Probation Service* [2003] EWHC 2910 (Admin) and disclosure of murder conviction to manager of accommodation. On Art 8 ECHR, see *Z v Finland* (1998) 25 EHRR 371. In another context, note *Brent LBC v N* [2005] EWHC 1676 and refusal to allow disclosure to a foster child's parents that the fosterer was HIV positive.

[2] See note 1 above. See *R (X) v Chief Constable of the West Midlands Police* [2005] 1 All ER 610 (CA). While safeguards and procedures must be followed in *R (X)* – which concerned the Police Act 1997 – this did not require a hearing for the claimant.

[3] *R (Stanley, Marshall and Kelly) v Metropolitan Police Commissioner* [2004] EWHC 2229 (Admin). On protection of art 8 rights and non-disclosure of police information see *A (A child) v Chief Constable of Dorset* [2010] EWHC 1748 (Admin) citing *Al Rawi v The Security Service* [2010] EWCA Civ 482 on refusing closed procedures and special advocates for a civil trial. The decision in *Al Rawi* was appealed to the Supreme Court which ruled that under the common law, the special advocate procedure was not extendible to civil actions (para 9.127): see, however, *Al Rawi v The Security Service and Others* [2011] UKSC 34 where the special advocate procedure could be used in employment vetting cases. See the Cabinet Office/Ministry of Justice Green Paper *Justice and Security* Cm 8194 (2011); see para 10.86 below.

2.327 It is important to realise, however, that the public interest defence is only a defence against an action in breach of confidence; it will not provide the basis of an action for wrongful dismissal, or for a claim of unfair dismissal, against an employer by an employee who is subsequently dismissed after his public interest disclosure. The employee will have to turn, in such a situation, to the PIDA 1998 (para 2.229 et seq above).

2.328   The above can serve as little more than an introduction to a fast developing area of law. We must now examine these basic principles as they have been applied to protect the public secrets of the state.

Public secrets and confidentiality

2.329   The Crown may avail itself of the law of confidentiality to protect its own personal secrets, as can anyone else.[1] In fact in the nineteenth century there were several cases concerning confidentiality which involved the royal family.[2] However, since 1975, the Attorney-General on behalf of the Crown has invoked the law of confidentiality to restrain publication of information about the processes of government – that side of Crown activity that affects the public sphere. It is clear that although the Crown prayed in aid the law of confidentiality in these cases, the courts have modified that law to the particular purposes of government activities. This modification will become more apparent now that the laws of confidentiality focuses more upon private information and human autonomy and dignity.

[1]   For an injunction protecting the personal information of the Queen in her private capacity see: *A-G v Barker* [1990] 3 All ER 257, CA and *A-G v Parry* (para 2.317, note 1 above).
[2]   See para 2.316, note 1 above. These did not involve the Crown, ie sovereign. Actions were brought in a personal, not governmental capacity.

2.330   In *A-G v Jonathan Cape Ltd*,[1] the Attorney-General sought to restrain (unsuccessfully)[2] the publication of the memoirs of the former Secretary of State, Richard Crossman, which contained numerous details of his work as a Cabinet Minister. Lord Widgery at first instance held that not only would the plaintiff have to establish a breach of confidence by publication, but also that the public interest required that publication be restrained and that there was no other competing public interest of greater moment than that relied upon by the Crown which would allow publication. This reasoning was developed by Mason J in *Commonwealth of Australia v John Fairfax & Sons Ltd*:

> 'The equitable principle has been fashioned to protect the personal, private and proprietary interests of the citizen, not to protect the very different interests of the executive government. It acts, or is supposed to act, not according to standards of private interest, but in the public interest. This is not to say that Equity will not protect information in the hands of the government, but it is to say that when Equity protects government information it will look at the matter through different spectacles.
>
> It may be a sufficient detriment to the citizen that disclosure of information relating to his affairs will expose his actions to public discussion and criticism. But it can scarcely be a relevant detriment to the government that publication of material concerning its actions will merely expose it to public discussion and criticism. It is unacceptable in our democratic society that there should be a restraint on the publication of information relating to government when the only vice of that information is that it enables the public to discuss, review and criticise government action.

Accordingly, the court will determine the government's claim to confidentiality by reference to the public interest. Unless disclosure is likely to injure the public interest, it will not be protected.

The court will not prevent the publication of information which merely throws light on the past workings of government, even if it be not public property, so long as it does not prejudice the community in other respects. Then disclosure will itself serve the public interest in keeping the community informed and in promoting discussion of public affairs. *If, however, it appears that disclosure will be inimical to the public interest because national security, relations with foreign countries or the ordinary business of government will be prejudiced, disclosure will be restrained.* There will be cases in which the conflicting considerations will be finely balanced, where it is difficult to decide whether the public's interest in knowing and expressing its opinion, outweighs the need to protect confidentiality.'[3]

This statement has met with general approval in subsequent litigation to which we now turn pausing only to make some points about publications by Ministers and civil servants – the subject of the proceedings in *Jonathan Cape*.

[1] [1976] QB 752.
[2] Too lengthy a period existed between the events in question and the time of application for the injunction.
[3] (1980) 147 CLR 39 at 51. The qualifying nature of the italicised words (not italicised in original) should be noted. On the case and copyright – see Cripps *The Legal Implications of Disclosure in the Public Interest* (2nd edn, 1994), ch 4.

2.331   The whole area of ministerial publications, and those by civil servants, diplomats and special advisers was investigated by the Public Administration Committee in 2006–09 following the publication of memoirs by former diplomats and special advisers. The government believed that existing procedures based on the Radcliffe report were adequate for ministers. Under these, ministers were informed of duties of confidentiality and official secrecy on taking office; that they should sign an undertaking; and that they had to obtain permission from the Cabinet secretary for publication. The secretary had no powers of enforcement, merely persuasion in those situations where no breach of law occurs.[1] The committee wanted a system whereby diplomats and civil servants and advisers were placed under contractual duties of confidentiality and would assign copyright to the Crown with an independent form of arbitration to determine the rights of the Crown and the public interest in publication in the event of a dispute. Formal independent arbitration was rejected by the government and the Radcliffe principles continue to apply to ministers.[2]

[1] *Report of the Committee of Privy Counsellors on Ministerial Memoirs* Cmnd 6386 (1976).
[2] *Whitehall Confidential? The Publication of Political Memoirs* (HC 689 I & II (2005–06); GR HC 91 (2007–08); *Mandarins Unpeeled* HC 664 (2007–08) and GR HC 428 (2008–09).

The Spycatcher litigation

2.332   Peter Wright was a former member of the security service MI5, who wished to publish his memoirs in Australia. These contained a great deal of information acquired while in that service, although much of it was already published, and some of it was subsequently shown to be unreliable. The publication of Wright's memoirs in Australia could not be restrained by an English court.[1]

[1] *A-G v Guardian Newspapers Ltd (No 2)* [1988] 3 All ER 545. See also *Esso Australia Resources Ltd v Plowman* (1995) 183 CLR 10 cited in Toulson and Phipps op cit para 5–05 for a very interesting public interest test.

2.333   It is now established that under the civil law, members or former members of security and intelligence services owe a lifelong duty of confidentiality to the Crown which can be protected by injunction against the member, or former member, to restrain publication, as well as any third party who receives such information.[1] Such a duty of confidentiality 'may also apply to other Servants of the Crown' where presumably they dealt with intelligence information.[2] In all other cases, civil servants owe a duty of confidentiality to the Crown: the precise scope, extent and nature of the duty, and the degree of judicial protection afforded to it, will depend upon the circumstances. They would also be covered by the relevant provisions of OSA 1989 (above).

[1] Per Scott J [1988] 3 All ER 545 at 551.
[2] How relevant 'notification' under OSA 1989, s 1 is in this regard is an interesting question (para 2.176 above). For the unsuccessful attempts to restrain publication in Australia, see para 2.318, note 4 above. Litigation also took place in New Zealand and Hong Kong. See M Fysh (ed) *The Spycatcher Cases* [1989] European Law Centre for the reports of cases.

2.334   Injunctions, ex parte and inter partes, were issued by the English High Court to prevent publication by newspapers of the contents of the memoirs, in so far as these could be contained in an outline of allegations to be made in Australian proceedings, of Wright's book, *Spycatcher*. The Australian proceedings commenced in 1985. The Millett injunction of 11 July 1986 restrained:

'newspapers from publishing or disclosing any information obtained by Mr Wright in his capacity as a member of MI5 or from attributing any information about MI5 to him. There were, however, three important provisos. First, the order permitted the direct quotation of attributions to Mr Wright already made by [another author] in published books … or already made by Mr Wright in a TV programme broadcast in 1984. Second, the order permitted the disclosure or publication of material disclosed in open court in the course of the New South Wales action; and, third, the fair and accurate reporting of proceedings in either House of Parliament in this country or of any public court proceedings in this country was excepted from the scope of the injunctions.'[1]

[1] Per Scott J [1988] 3 All ER 545 at 553.

2.335   On 25 July 1986 the Court of Appeal dismissed an appeal from the judgment of Millett J but slightly modified the injunctions.[1]

[1] Per Scott J at 553.

2.336   There were publications in other newspapers of enjoined material which formed the basis of contempt proceedings (see below). There were also subsequent attempts by the papers enjoined to have the injunctions lifted because of widespread publication of the book in the United States, the lack of an import ban on the book covering travellers coming from the United States, as well as the fact that extracts had been published in *The Sunday Times* in July 1987. The Vice-Chancellor subsequently lifted the injunctions on the basis that the 'secrecy' of the information had gone.[1] This judgment was overruled by the Court of Appeal[2] which held that, although the contents were no longer secret, there was the possibility of further damage being done to the security service and international relations by publication in newspapers of such information. The injunction was modified to allow publication in very general terms of the allegations made by Mr Wright.[3]

> There was then an appeal to the House of Lords (see [1987] 3 All ER 316 at 343–376, [1987] 1 WLR 1248 at 1282–1321). A minority, Lord Bridge and Lord Oliver, would have allowed the appeal and taken the same course as was taken by Sir Nicolas Browne-Wilkinson V-C. Their reasons were, like his, that the interlocutory injunctions, although rightly granted in the first place, had been overtaken by supervening events and could no longer serve any legitimate purpose. Lord Brandon, Lord Templeman and Lord Ackner, on the other hand, took the view, expressed with variations in emphasis, that the Attorney-General had an arguable case for a permanent injunction in that the defendant newspapers had been and would be in breach of duty in publishing extracts from or commenting on information contained in *Spycatcher*, a work published by an ex-officer of MI5 in apparently flagrant breach of the duty of confidence he owed to the Crown. They concluded, therefore, that a temporary injunction, pending trial, should remain.'[4]

[1]   *A-G v Guardian Newspapers Ltd* [1987] 3 All ER 316.
[2]   [1987] 3 All ER 316.
[3]   At 339.
[4]   Per Scott J [1988] 3 All ER 545 at 556.

2.337 However, the modifications introduced into the injunction by the court of appeal were considered unworkable and the reporting of what had taken place in open court in Australia was prohibited.

Permanent injunctions

2.338 The hearings for permanent injunctions against the newspapers[1] restraining them from publishing information obtained directly or indirectly from Peter Wright as well as a general injunction restraining future publication of material derived from Wright or other members of the security service, came before Scott J.[2] It will be useful to look at the decisions on the application for permanent injunctions and then to assess how future interim applications for injunctions restraining publications in breach of confidence, and which concern public secrets, may be dealt with.

[1]   *The Observer, The Guardian* and *The Sunday Times*.
[2]   See para 2.336, note 4 above.

2.339 The court at first instance, and the Court of Appeal and House of Lords, held that:

(1) Wright was under a lifelong duty of confidentiality. That lifelong duty was not relieved by worldwide publication of the material. The injunction on Wright, his agents and servants, would remain. The lifelong duty on security and intelligence officers has been confirmed by subsequent case law. The House of Lords' discussion of the duty under ss 1 and 4 of OSA 1989, Art 10 ECHR and *Shayler* (paras 2.181 et seq above) should be recalled. However, Scott J added obiter 'the duty of confidence would not extend to information of which it could be said that, notwithstanding the needs of national security, the public interest required disclosure.' Reference must be made at this point to *Shayler*, where Lord Bingham stated that if the internal channels refused to take effective action, a 'former officer' could seek permission to disclose to the press from his superior and then ultimately to the Minister and a refusal would be subject to judicial review (para 2.182 above). However, in *R (A) v B* [2009] UKSC 12, the Supreme Court ruled that the RIPA tribunal was the appropriate body to determine disputes between former members of MI5 and the authorities in relation to ECHR, Art 10 rights. The court has noted the tendency for cases involving security matters to read like 'aphabet soup' and principles for anonymising litigants were discussed in *Guardian News and Media Ltd Re HM Treasury v Ahmed* [2010] UKSC 1. Any information compromising safety of agents would be unlikely to be given such an authorisation. But, if the information revealed matters which 'however scandalous or embarrassing' would not damage any security or intelligence interest or impede the services' public functions, 'another decision might be appropriate.'[1] If an authorisation were not forthcoming, that decision could be subject to judicial review (subject to *R (A) v B* above). The response of the court will very much depend on the nature of information which it is sought to disclose. A review of case involving Art 10 ECHR will be rigorous and intrusive. Special counsel may have to be appointed to deal with very sensitive security information. Scott added, 'Nor ... would the duty extend to information which was trivial or useless or which had already been disclosed under the authority of the government.'[2]

(2) The articles in *The Observer* and *The Guardian* were fair reporting of the nature of the case in Australia. No 'pressing social need' (ie national security) was damaged by their publication.[3]

(3) With regard to the routine criminal activities (burglary), references to this in reporting the Australian litigation were permissible, but there 'was no legitimate public interest to be served by disclosure' in any other, or greater detail.

(4) The allegations of iniquity and the plot to assassinate President Nasser were such that 'a duty of confidence cannot ... be used to prevent the press from informing the public that the allegations have been made'.[4] The allegation of attempts to destabilise the Wilson government could not be protected by a duty of confidentiality,[5] nor could the allegations of Soviet attempts to penetrate MI5:

'The press has a legitimate role in disclosing scandals in government. An open democratic society requires that that be so. If an allegation be made by an insider that, if true, would be a scandalous abuse by officers of the Crown of their powers and functions, and the allegation comes to the attention of the press, the duty of confidence cannot, in my opinion, be used to prevent the press from reporting the allegation. I do not think it is an answer to say that the allegation has been investigated and been found to be groundless. Where that is the case, public belief in the allegation will, no doubt, be reduced. Nor is it, in my opinion, necessarily an answer to say that the allegation should not have been made public but should have been reported to some proper investigating authority. In relation to some, perhaps many, allegations made by insiders, that may be the only proper course open to the press. But the importance to the public of this country of the allegation that members of MI5 endeavoured to undermine and destroy public confidence in a democratically elected government makes the public the proper recipient of the information.'[6]

However, 'just excuse' for publication of allegations by an official[7] or their servant or agent cannot be by way of mere assertion.[8]

(5)   *The Sunday Times*, in serialising *Spycatcher*, was in breach of a duty of confidence as it was indiscriminate publication, and an account of profits would be made.[9]

(6)   The newspapers, including *The Sunday Times*, are not under any duty now to refrain from disclosing (by serialisation) or reporting on the information contained in *Spycatcher*. Scott J was not impressed by arguments of further damage to the national interest by harm caused by a third party publishing information from an insider.[10]

(7)   None of the newspapers could be enjoined at the time of Scott J's judgment from publishing future information from Wright or any other security official.[11] The court could not respond to a mere possibility or speculation.

[1]   *R v Shayler* [2002] 2 All ER 477 at para 30.
[2]   Per Scott J, at p 585j. Lord Donaldson MR and Lord Griffiths did not concur on the trivia exception, pp 597–598 and 650 respectively. Lord Goff did. In *R v Shayler* [2002] 2 All ER 477 (HL) Lord Scott obviously felt unease about too wide a protection for the security service: see para 120.
[3]   Lord Donaldson disagreed, p 601. The importance of his remarks for interim applications in future should be noted. Cf HRA 1998, s 12.
[4]   P 588. See, however, Lord Griffiths [1988] 3 All ER at 657 e–j, Lord Goff at p 660 and Bingham LJ's test at p 630. See Lord Donaldson's test at pp 604–605.
[5]   Such acts, if true, would have breached the Maxwell-Fyfe Directive (para 2.221, note 1 above).
[6]   At pp 588–589 per Scott J. And see: *Fressoz v France* 5 BHRC 654 (ECtHR).
[7]   This includes a former official, see OSA 1989, and para 2.176, note 2 above.
[8]   See comments of Lord Keith at pp 641–642.
[9]   Bingham LJ disagreed.
[10]   Lords Donaldson MR and Griffiths dissented vis-à-vis *The Sunday Times*.
[11]   Such an application would be merely speculative.

2.340   In the House of Lords, Lord Keith believed – it was 'common ground' – that neither the defence of prior publication nor the so-called 'iniquity' rule/

defence would have availed Wright if he had sought to publish his book in England. Sporadic and 'low key' prior publication could not conceivably justify detailed publication of his book. The damage, vis-à-vis the press, had already been done by worldwide publication.[1]

[1] At 642. See Lord Woolf in *A v B* [2002] 2 All ER 545 (CA) above, where it was held that reporting to the press (for a profit) was justified on the facts although the judge at first instance had ruled this impermissible, but reporting the facts to friends and the footballer's wife was permissible!

2.341 Lord Goff doubted whether Wright was still bound by a duty of confidence which could be enjoined by injunction when the information was in the public domain. 'The subject matter is gone; the obligation is therefore gone.' All that is left is the remedy or remedies for breach of the obligation. Lord Goff believed Mason J in *Fairfax* supported this although the Law Lord was alone on this point.

2.342 The book itself, it was held, could be published, but not via Wright or his agents or servants. It was in the public domain.

Article 10 ECHR

2.343 In the High Court,[1] Court of Appeal,[2] and House of Lords,[3] there was the clearest of support for the view that the ECHR could be invoked to support freedom of expression in aiding the interpretation of English common law, and the Convention was not restricted to the interpretation of statutory law.[4] In fact, the strength of feeling among the judges in support of this utilisation of the ECHR was appreciable.[5] Since that time, the Convention has been brought into domestic law by the Human Rights Act 1998 (HRA 1998) and the common law has developed through judicial interpretation its own protection of fundamental human rights.[6] Whether with an 'English gloss' or not, the courts will have the highest concern to protect Art 10 rights. But as seen above (para 2.324) and below (paras 2.345 et seq below) such rights have to be balanced with other rights and considerations.

[1] Per Scott J at pp 580–582.
[2] Per Bingham LJ at pp 627–628.
[3] Lord Goff at p 660e–h.
[4] See Megarry VC in *Malone* (para 2.196, note 1 above) at p 13. See also *Brind* (para 2.369, note 2 below), where it was held that the ECHR has no relevance to a statutory instrument where the Act is clear. NB *Chundawadra v Immigration Appeal Tribunal* [1988] Imm AR 161, CA and *R v Central Independent Television plc* [1994] 3 All ER 641, CA. The HRA 1998 has revolutionised this area; but see para 2.369, note 4.
[5] See Lord Bridge in the interlocutory proceedings: [1987] 3 All ER 316. NB *A-G v BBC* [1981] AC 303 at 352 and 362. The European Commission of Human Rights has upheld sanctions on civil servants, in disciplinary proceedings, for unauthorised disclosures to the press: 4274/69, *X v Germany* 35 Collection Dec 158; 9401/81, *X v Norway* 27 Decisions & Reports 228. And see *Civil Service Unions v United Kingdom* (1987) 10 EHRR 269.
[6] See in particular *HM Treasury v Ahmed* [2010] UKSC 2 and 5.

2.344 Article 10 has already been cited at para 2.290 above.

2.345 The European Court of Human Rights (ECtHR) has said that in applying Art 10:

> 'it is faced not with the choice between two conflicting principles but with a principle of freedom of expression which is subject to a number of exceptions which must be narrowly interpreted ... It is not sufficient that the interference involved belongs to that class of exceptions listed in Article 10 which has been invoked; neither is it sufficient that the interference was imposed because its subject-matter fell within a particular category or was caught by a legal rule formulated in general or absolute terms; the Court has to be satisfied that the interference was necessary having regard to the facts and circumstances prevailing in the specific case before it.'[1]

[1] *Sunday Times v United Kingdom* (1979) 2 EHRR 245; *Dudgeon v United Kingdom* (1981) 4 EHRR 149. See *Kelly v BBC* [2001] 1 All ER 323.

2.346 The court has ruled that restraint must be proportionate to the need for restraint.[1] Further, it is unlikely that the court would accept as a blanket justification for restraint reasons of national security on a bare assertion by the government[2] But the ECtHR has shown itself to be tolerant of claims to national security where cause can be shown.[3] A pressing social need would have to be made out on the facts. This would be true not only in relation to the law of confidentiality, but also official secrecy and deciding whether the OSA 1989 complies with obligations under the Convention. Readers are reminded of the discussion of *R v Shayler* (paras 2.181 et seq above) where these questions were examined and of the Law Lords' recognition of the need for probing and invasive reviews where human rights questions are involved.

[1] *Dudgeon v UK*, above. See *Hector v A-G of Antigua and Barbuda* [1990] 2 All ER 103, PC.
[2] See, however, 10078/82 *M v France* 41 Decisions & Reports 103 (Commission) and *Civil Service Unions v United Kingdom* (1987) 10 EHRR 269.
[3] *Leander v Sweden* [1987] 9 EHRR 433 and see *Brind v UK* (1994) 18 EHRR 342. See *Segerstedt-Wiberg v Sweden* at para 2.293 above, and further *Kennedy v UK* [2010] ECHR 26839/05.

Interim injunctions

2.347 The important factors relating to confidentiality and its protection in the operation of governmental bodies by permanent injunction must be seen in the context of a 'confidence' still being confidential, ie a secret or information that still requires protection. If information is no longer a secret, then a permanent injunction cannot be awarded unless, in the case of State secrets, further damage may be caused by repetition. This seems to be the basis of government arguments vis-à-vis security and intelligence personnel and their revelations regarding their work, even when the information is in the public domain. This argument was accepted by the House of Lords in a case in which an interim interdict[1] was sought in Scotland to stop publication of information from a book by a former MI6 member in a Scottish newspaper, even though the contents were accepted by the Crown as 'innocuous'. For that latter reason, and not for the reason that limited publication had taken place,[2] the House of Lords declined to upset the refusal of the lower courts to award the interdict against a third party who was not an agent, servant or 'anyone in the "direct chain from the confidant"'.[3] If the paper had received the book directly from the author, this, it seems, may well have implicated them in the duty of confidence. They could, therefore, have been the subject of a court order. Both Lords Templeman and Jauncey believed that, if not entirely co-extensive, where no prosecution could be brought under the OSA 1989[4] no injunction could be awarded at common law.[5]

[1]   *Lord Advocate v Scotsman Publications Ltd* [1989] 2 All ER 852.
[2]   279 copies of *Inside Intelligence* had been distributed by the author.
[3]   Per Lord Jauncey in *Lord Advocate v Scotsman Publications Ltd* [1989] 2 All ER 852 at 863b.
[4]   Under OSA 1989, s 1 or where a disclosure is 'damaging': paras 2.163 et seq above.
[5]   NB the injunction may not be awarded, but a prosecution may follow as there is no 'public interest' defence (para 2.264 above). See also Lord Templeman at 861g.

2.348   In the interlocutory proceedings involving *Spycatcher*,[1] the Court of Appeal and the House of Lords, by majority, did not accept that publication of the book in the USA and elsewhere, and its importation without official restriction, had brought the contents of the book into the public domain. The potential for damage was still present and restraint prior to publication, or 'prior restraint', was ordered by injunction in the widest of terms.[2] It is tempting to look at the case at the stage of litigation involving the permanent injunction and to say the majority of Law Lords and Court of Appeal were wrong in the interlocutory proceedings. But such a view is facile. While it was true to suggest, as in the first edition of this book that a court at an interlocutory application is asked to decide the balance of convenience and whether or not there is a serious issue in dispute the position has now to be interpreted in the light of HRA 1998, s 12.[3] Any doubt about a plaintiff's rights, especially in an area as delicate as confidentiality involving state secrets and national security, will be protected pending full hearing for a permanent injunction when the overall position may be assessed.

[1]   See para 2.332.
[2]   Ie preventing publication. See *H v N (A Health Authority)* (2002) *Times*, 19 March where a newspaper was enjoined from publicising the name of a health authority where disclosure might lead to the identity of an HIV positive dentist employed by the authority.
[3]   *American Cyanamid Co v Ethicon Ltd* [1975] AC 396, HL; *Cambridge Nutrition Ltd v BBC* [1990] 3 All ER 523, CA.

Section 12 of the Human Rights Act 1998

2.349   Section 12 of HRA 1998 will have a profound effect in this area. It is headed by the expression 'freedom of expression' and states the section applies if a court is considering whether to grant any relief[1] (including injunctions) which, if granted, might affect the Convention right to freedom of expression. Where the respondent (publisher, broadcaster etc) is not present and not represented no such relief (ex parte or without notice injunctions) is to be granted unless the court is satisfied:

(a)   that the applicant has taken all practicable steps to notify the respondent; or
(b)   that there are compelling reasons why the respondent should not be notified.

[1]   'Relief' includes any remedy or order other than in criminal proceedings.

2.350   The section continues (s 12(3)) that no such relief is to be given so as to restrain publication before trial unless the court is satisfied that the applicant is likely to establish that publication should not be allowed. This clearly puts the onus on the applicant for relief. It is no longer a balance of convenience test pending trial but a likelihood that the applicant will win at the final hearing. In many cases it will make a vital difference – it affords an impetus to publication and freedom of speech.[1] There may be a temptation to see the approach as consistent with the that adopted by the courts in defamation proceedings.[2] Courts have, however, insisted that the test for success by a claimant must not be set too high. A claimant for s 12(3) relief may be advancing his or her fundamental rights such as a right to life which the courts will have to give full effect to in dealing with an application. In *Cream Holdings Ltd v Bannerjee*, the Court of Appeal held that 'likely' does not mean 'more probable than not'. The threshold test to apply in deciding whether to award an interim injunction preventing publication is that of a 'real prospect of success, convincingly established.'[3] In applying the test a court is required to consider the merits of the claim for injunctive relief so as to reach a judgment as to the prospects of eventual success. The court should not grant interim relief unless it is satisfied on 'cogent evidence' that the plaintiff does have a real prospect of succeeding at trial 'notwithstanding the defendant's ex hypothesi conflicting right to freedom of expression.' The Court of Appeal felt that this was a lower test which was based on a 'realistic possibility of eventual success in preventing publication' and not 'a probabilistic threshold of a better than even prospect of success, below which interim relief, however necessary for a fair trial, cannot be granted.' On such an application, a judge will be given a wide margin of discretion. On the facts, the court was satisfied this test was established and an interim injunction was rightly awarded by the judge at first instance. Sedley LJ agreed with the interpretation of 'likely' but disagreed with the majority on whether an interim order should have been made. On this point the House of Lords agreed with Sedley LJ. The matters which the newspaper wished to publish were matters of serious public interest. The applicant's prospects of success were not 'sufficiently likely to justify making an interim order.' Lord Nicholls offered the following guidance:

> 'Section 12(3) makes the likelihood of success at the trial an essential element in the court's consideration of whether to make an interim order. But in order to achieve the necessary flexibility the degree of likelihood of success at the trial needed to satisfy section 12(3) must depend on the circumstances. There can be no single, rigid standard governing all applications for interim restraint orders. Rather, on its proper construction the effect of section 12(3) is that the court is not to make an interim restraint order unless satisfied the applicant's prospects of success at the trial are sufficiently favourable to justify such an order being made in the particular circumstances of the case. As to what degree of likelihood makes the prospects of success 'sufficiently favourable', the general approach should be that courts will be exceedingly slow to make interim restraint orders where the applicant has not satisfied the court he will probably ('more likely than not') succeed at the trial. In general, that should be the threshold an applicant must cross before the court embarks on exercising its discretion, duly taking into account the relevant

jurisprudence on article 10 and any countervailing Convention rights. But there will be cases where it is necessary for a court to depart from this general approach and a lesser degree of likelihood will suffice as a prerequisite. Circumstances where this may be so include those mentioned above: where the potential adverse consequences of disclosure are particularly grave, or where a short-lived injunction is needed to enable the court to hear and give proper consideration to an application for interim relief pending the trial or any relevant appeal.'[4]

[1] See *Jockey Club v Buffham* [2003] 2 WLR 178 public interest in disclosure (horse-race scandals) outweighed confidentiality.

[2] *Bonnard v Perryman* [1891] 2 Ch 269; see *Greene v Associated Newspapers Ltd* [2005] 1 All ER 30 where the rule in *Bonnard v Perryman* was confirmed by the CA; *Coys Ltd v Autocherish Ltd* [2004] EWHC 1334.

[3] [2003] 2 All ER 318 (CA). See *Imutran Ltd v Uncaged Campaigns Ltd* [2001] 2 All ER 385; s 12(3) where it was stated that s 12(3) only introduces a 'marginally higher test' than *American Cyanamid*. This seems very restrained and was doubted in *Cream Holdings* above. See *Douglas v Hello! Ltd* [2001] 2 All ER 289, CA.

[4] *Cream Holdings v Bannerjee* [2004] UKHL 44, para 22. On s 12(3) see: *Tillery Valley Foods v Channel Four News* [2004] EWHC 1075 (Ch) and *BBC v HarperCollins Publishers Ltd* [2010] EWHC 2424.

2.351 It is perfectly clear that in exercising its powers under s 12(3) the court must balance rights under Art 10 with other Convention rights. So much is required by HRA 1998, s 3 and 'consistent construction'. Arden LJ pointed out that in Convention jurisprudence, the Court of Human Rights had ruled that a right to freedom of expression should not be constrained unless the need for restriction is 'convincingly' established. We have seen how in protecting privacy of individuals and personal information the courts have awarded superinjunctions preventing any interim disclosure of information in its entirety (above and paras 7.203 and 7.204).

2.352 In national security cases, however, it is likely that courts will tread cautiously and any doubt of danger will be resolved in the applicant's favour. This opinion is reinforced by the wider formulation of 'national security' that has been given by the courts.[1]

[1] *Secretary of State for the Home Department v Rehman* [2002] 1 All ER 122 (HL) (see para 1.124 above). See, however, *M v Secretary of State for the Home Department* [2004] 2 All ER 863 (CA).

2.353 Subsection (4) concerns relief more generally but its subject matter is confined to material as described below. It states that the court must have particular regard to the importance of the Convention right to freedom of expression and where it is claimed by the respondent or appears to the court to be 'journalistic, literary or artistic material' such regard will also be had to the extent to which:
(a) the material has, or is about to, become available to the public; or
(b) it is, or would be, in the public interest for the material to be published.

2.354 The court is also to have regard to any relevant privacy code, such as the press code or broadcasting code.[1] Quite what weight may be given to codes which are the product of one institution as opposed to an association is not clear. In the case of the press code this makes provision for privacy, accuracy, children and harassment amongst other concerns (see paras 7.199 et seq below). It is clear that rights under Art 10(1) are essential considerations, but they do not possess automatic overriding power. They have to be balanced with the variety of considerations spelt out in the subsection. This takes us to matters which are discussed in chapter 7 (see para 7.185) and chapter 10 (see para 10.18).

¹   See HRA 1998, s 12(4)(b) and para 2.353. On Art 10 rights and traditional property rights see: *Appleby v UK* App No 44306/98.

Iniquity and 'just excuse' in publishing

2.355   As regards publication of an iniquity, the House of Lords judgments in the *Spycatcher* permanent proceedings, and in the *Inside Intelligence case*,¹ would offer little² scope for publication by a security or intelligence officer of such iniquities. Their duty is lifelong and, even outside the jurisdiction,³ is prohibited in the widest form without exception by the OSA 1989 (see above). Scott J thought (supra) that it was up to the authorities to decide what information in the hands of security officials should be protected – if they refused 'to draw any line at all, they mistake, in my view, the nature of the duty of confidence they seek to enforce'.⁴ Further, in his belief, a duty of confidentiality did not apply to iniquities: 'If the information was trivial or useless, or if it was public knowledge anyway, or if it was of serious iniquity, the conclusion may follow that the defendant was never under a duty not to disclose the information.'⁵ However, disclosure to the press would only be justified as a last resort – for the most serious of misdeeds and where official avenues had been pursued without response or where it would be justified to ignore them.⁶ Lord Griffiths gave support to this dictum (at 650d). Once again, the decision in *Shayler* (paras 2.181 et seq above) must be recalled. *All* internal channels will have to be pursued and the position is not as robust as Lord Griffiths believed.

¹   *Lord Advocate v Scotsman Publications Ltd* [1989] 2 All ER 852.
²   See also Lord Donaldson MR in *A-G v Guardian Newspapers Ltd (No 2)* [1988] 3 All ER 545 at 598b, and Lord Griffiths at 650c–f.
³   See OSA 1989, s 15. Their absence may prevent a prosecution.
⁴   *A-G v Guardian Newspapers Ltd (No 2)* [1988] 3 All ER 545 at 574g.
⁵   The All ER report at p 583c omits the 'not' from this quotation. The correct version is reported at [1990] 1 AC 109 at 159H.
⁶   See *Francome v Mirror Group Newspapers Ltd* [1984] 2 All ER 408, CA.

2.356   Lord Keith, however, in speaking of the publication of the book but not in making a revelation to, eg, the press, believed:

'The work of a member of MI5 and the information which he acquires in the course of that work must necessarily be secret and confidential and be kept secret and confidential by him. There is no room for discrimination between secrets of greater or lesser importance, nor any room for close examination of the precise manner in which revelation of any particular matter may prejudice the national interest. Any attempt to do so would lead to further damage.' (at 642 c–d)

2.357 Scott's view, which was supported, would accord better with legal principle. There must, theoretically, be items of information over which the duty does not extend. However, the decision in *A-G v Blake* would seem to support Lord Keith's views. But *Blake* was concerned with preventing a wrongdoer profiting from his wrongdoing, not preventing publication of information. As recent court cases have shown, in today's world global village, preventing publication is often idle.[1]

[1] See the case of Richard Tomlinson (para 2.367, note 2 below) where the Court of Appeal refused to prevent publication of his book on MI6 because it was in the public domain. Attention was then directed towards seizing his profits. *A-G v Times Newspapers* [2001] 09 LS Gaz R 38, CA.

2.358 Lord Keith gave his opinion on the position of the press and then on Wright and his agent/licensee:

'As to just cause or excuse, it is not sufficient to set up the defence merely to show that allegations of wrongdoing have been made. There must be at least a prima facie case that the allegations have substance. The mere fact that it was Mr Wright, a former member of MI5 who, with the assistance of a collaborator, had made the allegations, was not in itself enough to establish such a prima facie case. In any event the publication [by *The Sunday Times*] went far beyond the mere reporting of allegations, in so far as it set out substantial parts of the text of *Spycatcher*. For example, the alleged plot to assassinate Colonel Nasser occupies but one page of a book, in paperback, of 387 pages, and the alleged plot to destabilise Mr Wilson's government about five pages. In this connection it is to be noted that counsel for *The Sunday Times* accepted that neither of the two defences would have availed Mr Wright had he sought to publish the text1 of *Spycatcher* in England. There is no reason of logic or principle why The *Sunday Times* should have been in any better position acting as it was under his licence.'[2]

[1] Text of the book, not allegations per se.

[2] *A-G v Guardian Newspapers Ltd (No 2)* [1988] 3 All ER 545 at 644e–g.

2.359 On the issues determined at the interlocutory stage, Scott J believed in the permanent injunction proceedings that the report of proceedings in an Australian court, published by the two newspapers, was permissible,[1] but that the disclosure and report of routine security service activities (bugging of diplomatic missions and meetings) would have to be justified by 'a strong countervailing public interest'.

[1] Cf Lord Donaldson MR at 600–601. Scott J actually allowed more by way of publication than was actually reported in the case in Australia at the relevant time. However, a majority of the Court of Appeal and House of Lords approved Scott J on this point.

2.360 On the serious allegations, viz the plot to destabilise the Wilson government, the plot to assassinate President Nasser, and Russian infiltration of MI5, publication by the press (although not disclosure by the security official or former official who had not gone through the procedures outlined by Lord Bingham) did not constitute a breach of duty:[1]

'I hope the allegation [to kill President Nasser] is untrue. But whether the allegation is true or untrue the duty of confidence cannot, in my opinion, be used to prevent the press from informing the public that the allegation has been made.

None the less the editors contend that if the allegations [re the Wilson Government] are repeated by an insider the press ought to be entitled to report that fact. I agree. The press has a legitimate role in disclosing scandals in government. An open democratic society requires that that be so.[2]

The legitimate purpose of the duty of confidence imposed on members and ex-members of MI5 is to preserve the secrecy of MI5's affairs and thereby to enable it to operate efficiently. The purpose is not to save the government of the day from pressure or embarrassment. Second, and more important, the ability of the press freely to report allegations of scandals in government is one of the bulwarks of our democratic society. It could not happen in totalitarian countries. If the price that has to be paid is the exposure of the government of the day to pressure or embarrassment when mischievous and false allegations are made, then, in my opinion, that price must be paid.

In my judgment, a newspaper which comes into the possession of confidential information known to emanate from a member or ex-member of the security services must ask itself whether and to what extent public disclosure of the information can be justified. Prima facie, the information should not be disclosed. A strong case is, in my view, needed to outweigh the national security interest in the material remaining confidential. The Editors gave me to understand that they did ask themselves this question. I think they came to the right answer. In my view the articles represented the legitimate and fair reporting of a matter that the newspapers were entitled to place before the public, namely the court action in Australia. Further, and for different reasons, disclosure of two of the allegations was, in my view, justified.[3] There was no justification for indiscriminate[4] reporting, however.

To sum up: newspapers may report what is in the public domain; they may report what is "innocuous"; they may report the proceedings of foreign courts and legislatures;[5] they may report what, in the genuine public interest, the public ought to know, which will be determined by the circumstances of particular cases. To emphasise, at the interlocutory stage, once the plaintiff has established the existence of a duty of confidentiality, it is then up to the defendant to prove that the confidential nature of information has been destroyed; that it is "innocuous" if not admitted as such, or that there is an iniquity or item of information which should be published. As Lord Donaldson MR said at the interlocutory stage:

"The second part of their [the newspapers] case is and always has been that Mr Wright has revealed unlawful conduct on the part of the service or some of its officers and that the public interest in the exposure of what is quaintly known as 'iniquity' overrides the public interest in confidentiality, even when the need for confidentiality is so overwhelmingly and obviously necessary in the national interest. Here again I have to remind myself that, whilst I must assume that this might prove to be the case, it might not, and, in any event, mere allegations of iniquity can never override confidentiality. They must be proved and the burden of proof will lie on the newspapers."[6]

In the light of criticism, he amplified this in the later permanent proceedings:

"What I should have said, and what I hope that I meant to say, was that the publication of bare allegations which clearly involve a breach of confidence cannot be justified simply because, if true, they would support a defence based on the public interest in the exposure of 'iniquity'. The greater the degree and importance of the confidentiality which the newspapers would be breaching, and prima facie it can hardly be greater than in the context of revealing matters concerning the security service, the more sure they must be that the allegations are likely to be true before they can justify publication. This involves looking for independent corroboration and, in a national security context, considering what opportunity the government has had of investigating the allegations, what investigations have taken place and the result (if known), the extent to which the opposition is aware of the allegations, the extent to which the opposition accepts the government's conclusions and the extent to which the ordinary process of parliamentary control of the executive is operating and may be relied on to safeguard the public interest. Just as it is not for the media to usurp the constitutional function of the courts, so it is not their right, duty or role to usurp that of Parliament."[7]

[1] Cf OSA 1989, s 1.
[2] Per Scott J in *A-G v Guardian Newspapers Ltd (No 2)* [1988] 3 All ER 545 at 588.
[3] Scott J [1988] 3 All ER 545 at 558–59.
[4] As *The Sunday Times* had reported. Cf Lord Donaldson at 606b–j.
[5] Cf no defence of prior publication under the OSA 1989.
[6] *A-G v Guardian Newspapers Ltd* [1987] 3 All ER 316 at 337d.
[7] [1988] 3 All ER 545 at 604–05.

2.361 Dillon LJ did not believe that an editor had to submit copy to the authorities for clearance. He must act responsibly where he knows the Crown believes national security is involved, 'asking himself the right questions and giving the right answers'. This approach was followed in the case of the former MI6 officer Richard Tomlinson (para 2.367, note 1 above).[1] However, where an editor publishes without warning the authorities, charges under the OSA 1989 may be relevant and applicable (para 2.339 et seq above).

[1] In May 2011 Max Mosley lost his case seeking to guarantee a right for an individual to be warned in advance when the press was about to run a critical story allegedly breaching their privacy rights under art 8: *Mosley v UK* (unreported, 10 May 2011) ECHR.

2.362 Where the government asserts national security as a reason for non-publication by prior restraint, the court will not act on the mere assertion of the government, 'but it does mean that where national security is in issue the court will readily acknowledge the obvious limitations of its own knowledge and expertise'.[1] Bingham LJ would also give 'iniquity' a 'less restricted meaning than [Scott J] did'. For Lord Griffiths, the Treasury Solicitor should be informed.[2] A financial motive in informing would always be suspect.

[1]   [1988] 3 All ER 545 at 628 per Bingham J.
[2]   [1988] 3 All ER 545 at 657f–j.

2.363 It is essential, then, to realise that proceedings for interlocutory and permanent injunctions were very different processes. A decision at the interlocutory stage to hold the ring had no binding quality on a later decision for a permanent injunction.[1] Now, the prospect of success is a factor to consider before awarding interim relief under the HRA. On appeal from the first instance decision, a decision which involves an exercise of discretion, appeal courts are only prepared to overturn the decision on very limited grounds.[2] Section 12 of HRA 1998 places the onus squarely on those seeking an injunction to satisfy the court of the requirements in the section before publication will be halted. If there is any genuine risk to national security put forward by the Attorney-General a judge will be reluctant to allow publication to proceed.

[1]   Pace Lord Bridge in the interlocutory proceedings [1987] 3 All ER at 345 obiter. For a successful interim application against a former MI5 official: *A-G v Turnaround Distribution Ltd* [1989] FSR 169.
[2]   See Lord Diplock in *Hadmor Productions Ltd v Hamilton* [1982] 1 All ER 1042 at 1046, HL.

2.364 The Court of Human Rights ruled when the *Spycatcher* proceedings progressed to Strasbourg that the original injunctions were not in breach of Art 10. However, when the book was published in the USA, the injunction was no longer supportable.[1]

[1]   *Observer and Guardian v UK* (1991) 14 EHRR 153. The first ruling concerned events up until 30 July 1987; the court ruled 14–10 that no breach of Art 10 ECHR had taken place because such prohibition was within the margin of appreciation of domestic bodies. The court was unanimous that after 30 July 1987 the injunction was in breach of Art 10 ECHR. The book was published in the USA on 13 July 1987.

Publication by those not named in the original order

2.365 In the *Spycatcher* proceedings, the publication of information from the book by newspapers that were not enjoined by the Millett injunctions led to the Court of Appeal establishing the possibility of the newspapers being in contempt of court. In overruling the High Court, the Court of Appeal held that an interference with the administration of justice was capable of amounting to a contempt of court. Section 6(c) of the Contempt of Court Act 1981 preserved the power of the court to commit for contempt conduct that was intended to impede or prejudice the administration of justice. Where, as in this case, an order was made to preserve the subject matter of an action, viz confidential information, pending trial, a non-named party who knew of those orders but who destroyed or seriously damaged that subject matter would be guilty of criminal contempt if in doing so s/he intended to impede or prejudice the administration of justice.[1] The intention would need to be a 'specific intention' and not a reckless action and 'such an intent need not be expressly avowed or admitted, but can be inferred from all the circumstances, including the foreseeability of the consequences of the conduct'.[2] Subsequent proceedings established that several of the papers were in fact guilty of contempt and the general thrust of the Court of Appeal judgment was maintained by the House of Lords.[3]

[1] *A-G v Newspaper Publishing* [1987] 3 All ER 276. And see *X County Council v A* [1985] 1 All ER 53; cf *Re Lonrho plc* [1989] 2 All ER 1100, HL.
[2] See Lord Donaldson at 304c.
[3] For the committal hearing: *A-G v Observer Ltd and Guardian Newspapers Ltd* (1989) Times, 9 May; on appeal (1990) Times, CA, 28 February. *A-G v Times Newspapers Ltd* [1991] 2 All ER 398, HL. *Jockey Club v Buffham* [2003] 2 WLR 178 where the court ruled that injunctions binding third parties only applied to interim and not permanent injunctions.

2.366   The decision in *A-G v Punch Ltd*[1] should be noted carefully for the wide protection the Court of Appeal (a decision subsequently reversed by the Law Lords) gave to a publisher who was not named in the original order of the court. The Court of Appeal held that an intention to defeat the purpose of the original order of the court had to be established to amount to a contempt. The wider the original order, the more difficult it may be to establish a contempt. Furthermore, in the case of national security, the case concerned the publication of the Shayler allegations, the evidence required to establish intent on the part of the publisher was that there was knowledge that information had not previously been published. The court was very concerned that to require less than this would run the risk of introducing censorship by the Attorney-General and this would amount to a clear breach of Art 10 of the ECHR.

[1] [2001] 2 All ER 655, CA. See Simon Brown LJ dissenting, however.

2.367   The House of Lords ruled that even where orders were drawn in 'over wide terms' a contempt would be committed where a third party (newspaper editor) wilfully interfered with the administration of justice by thwarting the *purpose* of an interlocutory order issued by the court. The purpose of the order was to protect the confidentiality of information specified in the order pending trial so that at trial the court could adjudicate on those questions of confidentiality meaningfully (ie not after a disclosure destroyed the confidential nature of the information. The editor knew that the order sought to protect the confidentiality of information relating to national security. By publishing the order, he was doing precisely what the order sought to prevent – pre-empting a fair trial on those issues. This constituted a 'knowing' interference with the administration of justice. Any discussion of whether there was an intent to harm national security was besides the point.[1] Where an order was set in broad terms there was nothing objectionable in providing in an order that it does not cover information which the Attorney-General has confirmed in writing is not information that the Crown is seeking to restrain. The court remains the arbiter of what can be published and the order (drafted by the Attorney-General) should set out this safeguard of application to the courts for clarification. The order would have to be a 'justified and proportionate restraint' on freedom of speech.

The Law Lords hoped that the Attorney-General and future judges would draft such orders as carefully as possible to provide necessary protection but not to include unnecessary information.[2]

1   *A-G v Punch Ltd* [2002] UKHL 50 [2002] 1 All ER 289 (HL).
2   And see *A-G v Times Newspapers Ltd* [2001] 1 WLR 885: it was not just to impose on a newspaper publishing information from a former security service officer's memoirs published in the USA, Europe and on the internet the need to obtain confirmation from the Attorney-General or the court that information it wanted to republish was in the public domain so that the cloak of confidentiality had been lifted. It was for the newspaper's editor to judge whether the information should be republished and the existing variation imposed a duty to comply with the law of confidentiality. Anything beyond that was a fetter on the newspaper's freedom of expression.

PRIVACY PROTECTION

2.368   Privacy is an important component of individual integrity, not only in relation to invasive government, central or otherwise, but also in relation to entities such as the press and media. In chapter 7 there is a more prolonged discussion about the development of privacy protection in our law.

BANNING BROADCASTING

2.369   The Secretary of State has power under s 336(5) of the Communications Act 2003 to require the Office of Communications[1] via notice to direct licensed broadcasters to refrain from including in their licensed services any matter, or description of matter. The previous formulation of this power was exercised in relation to prescribed organisations in Northern Ireland in 1988. In the past, the veto may cover any matter or classes of matter and a direction may include a specific broadcast.[2] The exercise of this power previously had not attracted the protection of Art 10.[3] Once more, however, the presence of the Human Rights Act will change the nature of future debate (above). Under s 336(1)–(4) the Secretary of State has broad powers to require the Office to direct holders of licences as specified to publish in their licensed services specified announcements. Powers under the section are in addition to any other powers conferred on the Secretary of State. Section 329 allows the Secretary of State to proscribe foreign 'unacceptable foreign television and radio services'. Section 319 sets out in considerable detail OFCOM's code on standards for the content of TV and radios services. Section 320 provides for special impartiality requirements in relation to service providers in matters of political or industrial controversy or matters relating to current public policy. On Broadcasting Act 1990, s 6 and banning programmes on the grounds of offending taste and decency, the House of Lords decision in *R (ProLife Alliance) v BBC* indicates clearly that Art 10 may not always be a trump card.[4] The case concerned videos for a TV political broadcast of what was involved in abortion processes featuring mutilated foetuses. The ban was not unreasonable. The approach should be compared with the far more rigorous (anxious) scrutiny of the Court of Appeal which was based on proportionality and which ruled the ban a breach of HRA 1998.[5] In *R (on application of Animal Defenders International) v Secretary of State for Culture, Media and Sport* [2008] UKHL 15 the appellant, an animal protection society, sought a declaration under HRA 1998, s 4 that the Communications Act 2003, s 321(2) banning broadcasting of political advertising (animal rights) was incompatible with ECHR, art 10 as given effect in this country by HRA 1998. The section is said to be incompatible as imposing an unjustified restraint on the right to freedom of political expression. The law lords refused to award a declaration despite the strong authority to the contrary of the ECHR's judgment in *VgT*.[6]

[1] Established by the Office of Communications Act 2002.

[2] *R v Secretary of State for the Home Department, ex p Brind* [1991] 1 AC 696, HL. And the courts' power – 'to protect its own process' – to ban broadcasting during the hearing of an appeal in which a retrial was being canvassed: *A-G v Channel 4 Television Co Ltd* [1988] Crim LR 237, CA.

[3] *Brind*, op cit.

[4] [2003] 2 All ER 977 (HL).

[5] [2002] 2 All ER 756. See *VVT v Switzerland* (2001) 10 BHRC 473, ECHR: the *VgT* decision.

[6] Note 5 above.

The Government's War on Terror

2.370 Anti-terrorism legislation since 2000 has placed numerous powers on the authorities to obtain, transfer, swap and use information in the 'war on terror'.[1] There are numerous offences involving use or possession of information.[2] The anti-terrorism efforts have involved secret procedures to hear cases against terrorist 'suspects' in a variety of procedures. We examine these procedures in chapter 9 (paras 9.127 and 9.131–9.132).

[1] See C Walker *The Anti-terrorism Legislation* (2009) for a full treatment.

[2] *R v Zafar etc* [2008] EWCA Crim 184 – Terrorism Act 2006, s 2 possession of terrorist literature; *R v K* [2008] EWCA Crim 185: Terrorism Act 2000 , s 58 and terrorist information.

Chapter 3

The European perspective

3.1 In this chapter, we examine the European perspective to our contemporary government and the use of legal provisions, and legal duties, relating to information. We are not part of a European federalism and, although a form of quasi-federalism seemed to be moving closer to realisation, the failure of the Treaty on the European Constitution (TEC) after the rejection of the French and Dutch voters in their national referenda paved the way for the Treaty of Lisbon (ToL) on the EU (TEU) and the Functioning of the EU (TFEU). The latter treaties were formally ratified by all member states and subsequently took effect in December 2009. ToL played down some of the more obvious moves towards greater federal tendencies: any reference to 'constitution' has gone; the original constitutional treaty provision on the primacy of Union law over national laws (TEC, Art 1.6) has given way to a Declaration in the ToL No 17. The EU Charter of Fundamental Rights is not an integral part of the treaties as it was in the Constitution but it is a legally binding instrument which 'is to have the same legal value as the treaties' according to TEU, Art 6(1). The Minister for Foreign Affairs has given way to a High Representative although a President of the EU for a term of two years has been provided for and appointed. However, nobody should be deceived: the TEU is the TEC in an envelope and many of the major features of the constitution were incorporated in the TEU. The EC and EU are now simply the EU and the three-pillar edifice of the EU has been collapsed into a single-tier structure comprising the former EC, the common foreign and security area and the freedom, security and justice area. The first and third are now covered by a common legislative method with binding effect in national laws but foreign and security policy are dealt with exclusively in the TEU and will have its own *modi operandi* maintaining its intergovernmental character. The UK has elected to be outside much of the freedom, security and justice area unless it opts in.

¹ H Kranenbourg 'Access to documents and data protection in the EU' (2008) CMLRev 1079.

3.2 The impact of the EU on our domestic affairs assumed greater and greater significance not only under the EC pillar but also the former second and third pillars (see para 3.11 below). This impact will remain under ToL. The Conservative opposition leading up to the 2010 election was hostile to the increased role of the EU and when it formed the coalition government in May 2010 with the Liberal Democrats a European Union Bill was published introducing UK national referendum locks before any further transfers of power to the EU.

3.3 While much of the business of government takes place between the UK and devolved governments/executives and the EU Commission, the EU has impinged increasingly on the lives of individuals who might wish to know what lies behind decisions or non-decisions of the EU institutions. Constitutional demands have been placed on the EU by its citizenry so that it operates in a more open and responsive manner. Since our accession to the European Community under the Treaty of Brussels in 1972, implemented in our domestic law by the European Communities Act 1972 and taking effect on 1 January 1973,[1] law-making and decision-making binding upon the UK may be carried out in the institutions of the EU. Treaty provisions and Directives may be directly effective and Regulations are directly applicable within the legal system of a member state. Decisions providing for access to Council and Commission documents, which were supplemented by a joint code on access, were issued in 1993 and 1994, and these have now been replaced by a Regulation following a Treaty amendment at Amsterdam (see paras 3.18 et seq below). The ToL adds to these provisions. The Council of Ministers is the legislative body of the Community although co-decision on legislation with the European Parliament (EP) had become increasingly common and, under ToL, it will become the normal ('ordinary': TFEU, Art 289) method of making legislation along with qualified majority voting (QMV) in the Council, although some items will not be subject to QMV. Complex procedures exist to deal with disagreements between the Council and Parliament under existing arrangements in TFEU, Art 294. The Commission formulates proposals for new Community policies and laws, mediates between member states to secure the adoption of these proposals, co-ordinates national policies and oversees the execution of existing Community policies, and also makes regulations.

[1]   T C Hartley *Foundations of European Community Law* (7th edn, 2010). See also P Craig *The Treaty of Lisbon* (2010).

3.4 As well as the ordinary legislative procedure, there is a 'special legislative procedure' under TFEU, Art 289(2) allowing for adoption of a measure by either the Council or Parliament with the participation of the other body. Acts adopted by both ordinary and special procedures are 'legislative acts' or legal acts. Legislative acts, in specific areas provided for by the treaties, may also be adopted on the initiative of a group of member states, the Parliament, on the recommendation of the European Central bank or at the request of the Court of Justice or European Investment Bank (Art 289(4)). Under Art 296(2) legal acts shall state the reasons on which they are based and shall refer to any proposals, initiatives, recommendations, requests or opinions required by the Treaties.

3.5 The Commission is a politically independent body which meets in private.[1] It has delegated legislative powers and implementing powers. Under TFEU, Art 290 the Parliament and Council may delegate to the Commission the power to adopt 'non-legislative acts of general application' subject to conditions laid down in the article. These delegated regulations supplement or amend non-essential elements of the legislative acts of the Parliament and Council. The conditions in Art 290 are strict. Such regulations are not subject to the comitology procedures (below) but the Commission has undertaken to consult national experts in their making. Many of its proposals on implementing measures (regulations) are formulated through complex committee structures comprising national civil servants and commission officials.[2] The governing article here is TFEU, Art 291. Committees created by the Council which are of both a managerial and regulatory nature may prevent the Commission proceeding with a measure unless the Committees approve. There are also advisory committees. New provisions in 2006 established regulatory committees with scrutiny and allowed the EP to block the measures approved by these committees where they were quasi-legislative in nature and emerged from the co-decision law-making procedure of the EP and Council. Committees other than those established in 2006 were established under Council Decision 1999/468/EC. The 1999 decision has now been replaced by a regulation introduced in March 2011 establishing two procedures for the committees: an examination procedure and an advisory procedure (Regulation (EU) 182/2011 under TFEU, Art 291(2)). The former deals with implementing measures of a general nature and those dealing with a potentially specific impact in important areas such as agriculture, fisheries, environment, health, taxation and trade. Decisions approving the Commission measure are by qualified majority and in the case of rejection the Commission may redraft the measure or appeal to an appeal committee. Advisory committees operate in 'other fields' and the Commission must take the 'utmost account' of its opinion which is reached by simple majority. The new regulation also confers on the E and the Council a right of scrutiny. Where the basic legislative act has been adopted under the co-decision procedure, the EP or the Council may at any time inform the Commission that it considers the draft implementing act to exceed the powers which they conferred on it. In such a case, the Commission must review the draft act and decide whether to maintain, amend or withdraw it. 'In order to achieve greater consistency, the procedural requirements should be proportionate to the nature and impact of the implementing acts to be adopted (Recital No 10).'

[1] See Rules of Procedure of the EU Commission 2010/138/EU, Art 9, 24 February 2010.
[2] G Brandsma et al 'How transparent are EU Comitology Committees in practice?' (2008) 14 ELJ 819.

3.6 A register of committees exists and the list of committees is published with the annual reports of committees. The register contains agendas, draft implementing measures, summaries of papers and voting results. Their deliberations as contained in documents are subject to the Regulation on access (see below).Case law had decided that the committees were covered by the former Code on access (see below) and they are covered by the access Regulation (see below). Commission decisions are taken by simple majority vote.

Under a 'written procedure' draft decisions are frequently circulated among the Commissioners. They are considered adopted if no objections are made within a specified period. Representations from individuals are not encouraged; far more common are representations from collective groups such as trade associations, business lobbies, public interest groups as well as domestic governments. A White Paper and a follow-up paper have made numerous suggestions in relation to law- and rule-making and consultation, openness and other safeguards.[1]

[1]   *European Governance* COM (2001) 428 final, European Commission and COM (2002) 704, 705, 709, 719 European Commission.

3.7   The Council of Ministers of the EU – comprising ministers from each member state, and not to be confused with the European Council, which is the gathering of heads of state or government, the President of the European Council and the president of the Commission (TEU, Art 15) – is a joint legislator with the European Parliament of EU primary legislation (legislative measures), subject to the co-decision procedure within the TFEU, concludes agreements with foreign countries and decides on the Community budget together with the EP. Most Council meetings were held in private although some meetings have been open to the public since 1993 and became more transparent in 2006. Council meetings are regulated by the Council's rules of procedure.[1] The Council is served by a permanent committee of senior national officials known as COREPER which has two operating levels. In relation to legislative committees the Council meets in public when considering and voting on a draft legislative act. The same provision (TFEU, Art 15(2)) states that the Parliament shall meet in public. The Parliament's rules of procedure from March 2011 state that Parliament shall conduct its activities in 'utmost transparency' in accordance with TEU, Art 1, para 2, TFEU, Art 15 and Charter of Fundamental Rights, Art 42.[2] Positions adopted by ministers were not originally revealed by the Council save to the extent that they are covered by the Regulation on access, although ministers may make public their own position. Successive treaties from Maastricht have considerably enhanced the role of Parliament as a legislator as explained above in the ordinary legislative procedure. The Council of Ministers and the Parliament may, where provided for by the Treaties, adopt regulations, directives and decisions by a special legislative procedure under TFEU, Art 289. A legislative act may delegate to the Commission powers to make regulations (non-legislative acts or regulatory acts often described as quasi-legislative) to supplement or amend non-essential elements of a legislative act (TFEU, Art 290) subject to the procedures outlined above in relation to committees.

[1]   Council Decision 1 Dec 2009, 2009/937/EU [2009] OJ L 325/35
[2]   Title III, arts 103 and 104 on the application of TFEU, Art 15 and EC Regulation 1049/2001.

3.8   The Parliament possesses certain opportunities to amend and modify the budget. As a general rule, committees of Parliament will normally sit in public unless, at the time of the presentation of the agenda, business is divided into public and private sessions (Parliamentary Rules of Procedure, Art 103 (March 2011)). The rules continue: 'However, if a meeting is held in camera, the committee may, subject to Art 4(1)–(4) of European Parliament and Council

Regulation (EC) 1049/2001 (below), open documents and minutes from the meeting to public access' (Art 104).

3.9   At the end of meetings, coordinators will sit in private to discuss future agendas and 'household business'. The Committee which deals with members' immunities sits in private session.

3.10   Relationships between member states, and between those states and the institutions of the Union, are governed by a provision in the Treaty on 'good faith' and 'sincere cooperation' (TEU, Art 4(3)), although the phrase 'good faith' is not in the Treaty itself. It was held by the ECJ in *Zwartveld* that this necessitates the sharing of information in the Commission's possession with national authorities to help those authorities carry out inquiries into the operation of markets and alleged malpractices in relation to EC law.[1] Furthermore, Commission officials had to consent to an examination before the domestic judges. Both were subject to *imperative* reasons for non-disclosure that the Commission might advance. The case did not concern a preliminary reference under then EC, Art 234 (TFEU, Art 267) or a point of interpretation of a Treaty or secondary provision of law and the procedure was regarded as innovative. Provisions exist in the Treaty for exchange of information between member states subject to a right of non compliance where a member state considers supply contrary to the 'essential interests of its security' (TFEU, Art 346(1((a)). Exchange of information will be a crucial dimension in freedom security and justice (see below) in relation to combating crime at the EU level.

[1]   Case C-2/88 [1990] ECR I-3365 followed by *S and S Services Ltd v Customs and Excise Commissioners* [2004] Eu.L.R. 1. On cooperation in competition investigations, see: Council Regulation OJ L [04/01/03] arts 11 and 12 and chapter V on investigations.

3.11   One of the most controversial aspects of the operation of the EC, and now the EU, in recent years has been the 'democratic deficit' in the Community. New styles of governance, the growth of comitology and the advent of numerous agencies have all taken place to advance cooperative international governance but have not been accompanied by developed and appropriate accountability and transparency mechanisms or an administrative procedure code. There are codes on good administrative practice produced by the EU Ombudsman and Commission, and regulations exist for agencies and comitology. The Charter of Fundamental Rights includes principles on good administration (Art 41).

3.12   A subject of particular concern has been the residual role that National Parliaments (NPs) play in the implementing of EC legislative provisions and the EU policy-making process, while the role of the European Parliament (EP) in the legislative process has increased. Whatever the EP's democratic legitimacy, the fact that it is not seen as superior to NPs is widely held and accepted. NPs have been poorly provided with information about legislative proposals before the Council and did not have sufficient time to question relevant Ministers.[1] The Amsterdam Treaty provided a Protocol (No 13) on the role of national Parliaments within the EU. The committees of the Westminster Parliament with responsibility for EU affairs were subject to amendments to their remit and titles after the 1998 memorandum of the President of the Council to the select committee on Modernisation of the House of Commons.[2] This identified three main objectives of any changes: strengthening the role of the Westminster Parliament; increasing democratic oversight of new EU legislation; and increasing the transparency and parliamentary awareness of the conduct of EU business.[3] Changes have been made in domestic regimes vis-à-vis Parliamentary oversight of draft legislative measures.[4] Crucially, the ToL has important protocols on both the role of NPs in the EU and on subsidiarity and proportionality.[5] The Commission consults widely before proposing legislative acts. These protocols have strengthened the role of NPs in the legislative process, have increased the information they receive from the Commission in relation to consultation documents and draft measures and their timeliness so that eight weeks must elapse between a draft measure being available to a NP and its being placed on a provisional agenda for the Council for its adoption or for the adoption of a position under a legislative procedure. Exceptions are possible in cases of 'emergency'. A ten-day period, again subject to emergency, shall elapse between the placing of a draft legislative act on the provisional agenda of the Council and the adoption of a position. Each EU institution has to ensure constant respect for the principles of subsidiarity and proportionality under TEU, Art 5. Draft legislative acts as defined have to be justified according to these principles and have to contain a detailed statement making it possible to appraise compliance with the principles. Further requirements including financial impact are in Art 5 of the Protocol on Subsidiarity and Proportionality. The Protocol allows for a reasoned opinion on non-compliance with subsidiarity from a NP of a draft legislative proposal within eight weeks of the transmission of the proposal to NPs. Where a threshold (30 per cent for legislative proposals and 25 per cent for a legislative act under TFEU, Art 76) of votes from NPs (each NP has two votes, one for each chamber in bicameral parliaments) determines that subsidiarity is not conformed with, the proposal must be reviewed by the Commission or proposer of the draft measure. Under the ordinary legislative procedure a vote of a simple majority of NP votes allocated prompts such a review by the Commission. The review may maintain, amend or withdraw the draft or proposal. Reasons have to be given for the decision. The Commission has to give reasons for its decision in the case of a proposal under the ordinary legislative procedure. The reasoned opinions and those of NPs must be submitted to the Union legislator, and the EP and Council must consider before the conclusion of first reading whether the legislative proposal is compatible with subsidiarity. A majority of 55 per cent in the Council or a majority of votes cast in the EP can kill off the proposal. The Protocol provides for judicial review under TFEU, Art 263 of legislative acts because of alleged infringement of subsidiarity. The application may be made by member states 'or notified by them in accordance with their legal order on behalf of their NPs or a chamber thereof'. The Committee of the Regions may also bring such actions on specified grounds. Under the Protocol on Subsidiarity and Proportionality, Art 9 the Commission must submit each year a report to the Council, EP and NPs on the application of TEU, Art 5. It will be forwarded to the Economic and Social Committee and the Committee of the Regions.

[1]   See P Birkinshaw and D Ashiagbor 'National Participation in Community Affairs: Democracy, the UK Parliament and the EU' (1996) *Common Market Law Rev* 499 and the Select Committee on European Legislation *The Scrutiny of European Business* HC 51 xxvii (1995–96).

[2]   Cm 4095. The Commons Committee is now called the European Scrutiny Committee. The House of Lords committee is the Select Committee on the European Union. See the latter's stinging report on the framework directive on discrimination: *Fourth Report* (2000–01).

[3]   See C Kerse (2000) *European Public Law* 81.

[4]   P. Birkinshaw *European Public Law* (2003) ch 7.

[5]   Ibid.

3.13   Two further developments are crucial: the move towards qualified majority voting allowed legislation to be passed in the Council without the specific approval of national Ministers and therefore, it was argued, without the consent or authorisation of the duly elected government of the member state; and, secondly, the secrecy of the conduct of the two inter-governmental pillars covering foreign and security policy, and police and judicial co-operation in criminal matters both of which are part of the post-TEU edifice, as explained above. The former House of Lords Committee on the European Communities had found information on these to be worryingly thin.[1] The business of these two pillars was also conducted through committees and sub-committees that operated in secrecy. Openness is very much a key issue in the future development and legitimation of the EU. Significant reforms are contained in the ToL. Important in the present discussion are further provisions on access and transparency that will be examined below, the collapsing of the pillar structure into one legal edifice with one legal personality, the formal institutional recognition of the European Council (Heads of State) of the EU as an institution of the EU and one which will be within the access regimes for the first time; that the Council as legislator will sit in public under Art 7 of its rules of procedure (para 3.7, note 1), and under Art 8 in other cases where legally binding but non-legislative measures are to be adopted but only for the 'first deliberation';[2] the protocols on the role of national parliaments (above); and crucially, the elevation of the previously intergovernmental Charter of Fundamental Rights as a legally binding part of the ToL. This promotes openness, transparency, access to information, data protection and good administrative process to fundamental constitutional measures along with the more usual subjects of human rights protection.[3]

[1]   HL 105 (1994–95) *The Intergovernmental Conference.* This was the precursor to the EU Committee.

[2]   This covers 'important new measures' as determined by the Presidency. The Council or COREPER may determine otherwise. The Council or COREPER may determine by QMV which important issues affecting the interests of the EU and its citizens shall be the subject of public debates in the Council. It shall be for the Presidency, any member of the Council, or the Commission to propose issues or specific subjects for such debates, taking into account the importance of the matter and its interest to citizens.

[3]   See P Birkinshaw (2004) 10 *European Public Law* 57 and '*Supranationalism, the Rule of Law and Constitutionalism*' in P Eeckhout and T Tridimas *Yearbook of European Law 2004* (2005) OUP, p 199.

3.14   EU institutions should consult widely before taking legislative initiatives. TEU, Art 11 contains three underlying principles: dialogue, transparency and pluralism, the latter as represented by representative associations, citizens and 'parties concerned'.[1] Consultations should be widely published via 'Your Voice in Europe'.[2] Eight weeks are allowed for responses to written consultations and 20 days' notice of meetings should be given. A 2002 communication states that lobbyists must abide by standards such as explaining the interests they represent and how inclusive these are. Failure to abide by these standards means their submission will not be treated as a representative one and will be afforded less weight. Having observed the rather anodyne qualities of these measures, the Commission established a voluntary register for lobbyists. Membership is only allowed for those who observe a code of conduct in the register.[3] Inclusiveness is explained in the 2002 Communication (COM(2002)704, 11–12).

[1] European Commission General Principles and Minimum Standards for Consultation of Interested Parties by the Commission (2002).
[2] http://ec.europa.eu/yourvoice//consultations/index_en.htm.
[3] European Commission European Transparency Initiative: A Framework for Relations with Interest Representatives (Register and Code of Conduct) COM(2008)323.

3.15   These measures have sought to enhance transparency in the EU. Finally, before examining the regulation on access to information it should be noted that the European Parliament and Council of Ministers agreed a Directive on the re-use of public sector information, which is to be implemented by 1 July 2005 (Directive 2003/98/EEC (17/11/03) OJ L 345/90). The UK has implemented this provision as was explained in chapter 2 (para 2.40 et seq).

THE DECISIONS AND THE CODE ON ACCESS

3.16   The Decisions and the Code on Access have now been superseded by the Regulation on access which is discussed below. The provisions of the Code need no longer delay us but some very important case-law was decided under the Code showing the secrecy (and somewhat duplicitous negotiations) that went on in the making of legislation by the Council. This showed that the Council had not balanced all relevant considerations in deciding whether to apply an exemption correctly after a request was made for documents used in the legislative process and crucial evidence came from member states who were not happy with the way the decision was taken.[1] Subsequently, on 2 October 1995, the Council adopted a Code of Practice on Public Access to the Minutes and Statements in the Minutes of the Council Acting as Legislator.[2] In the case of a statement by one or more members of the Council, the Council will seek the agreement of the author(s) before deciding to make it available to the public. Decisions will be taken on whether public access should be allowed to references to documents before the Council and decisions taken or conclusions reached by the Council which are contained in the minutes relating to the final adoption of its legislative acts. The aim is to ensure the widest possible public availability of its minutes save in exceptional cases covered by Art 4(1) of the 1993 Decision. The permission of author(s) of statements in minutes will be sought before taking a decision on publication. It does not say what will happen if the agreement is not forthcoming. Its decision will be taken on advice from COREPER – the permanent committee of the Council of Ministers – and the Code only takes effect after its adoption. A Council Decision (2000/23/EC (13/1/2000) 2000 OJ L 9/22) made additional provision on access. The 2001 regulation now makes provision for access to documents in the legislative process as does the ToL (below).

1   *Carvel v EU Council* Case T-194/94 [1996] All ER (EC) 53.
2   PRES/95/271, 2 Oct 1995.

3.17 Further litigation produced a series of embarrassing set-backs for the Commission usually on technical points under the Code. These cases have covered a failure to give proper reasons and to follow correct procedures for refusing access.[1] This was followed in the *Svenska* decision where the Court of First Instance (CFI) also ruled that it had jurisdiction over third pillar documents in the possession of the Council – subject to exemptions. Again the CFI ruled that clear reasons had to be given for refusing access.[2] Access to second pillar documents was also maintained in *Heidi Hautala v EU Council* where a decision by the Council to refuse consideration of handing over redacted documents to an applicant was annulled by the Court of First Instance and upheld by the ECJ because it was 'disproportionate'.[3] In the *Rothmans* case, the CFI held that 'comitology' (the committees of the Commission above) documents are accessible under the Code on access.[4] Limits have been placed on requests for information so the CFI has said the Commission does not have to comply with every request for information.[5] The CFI has nonetheless insisted that proper procedures are complied with.[6] Partial disclosure could not be evaded by the Council and Commission by finding that 'partial disclosure would be of no use to the applicant'.[7] However, on one major point, the ECJ refused to accept the argument that a right of access to information constituted a constitutional right under the Community framework which was built on openness and the rule of law.[8] Such an approach had been argued for by the Advocate General. The judgment did express the point, however, that there was a trend towards a 'progressive affirmation of individuals' rights of access to documents held by public authorities'. In the *Hautala* decision above, the ECJ declined the invitation to decide whether EC law recognises a general right to information. The CFI described access rights as a 'wide general principle' and any exceptions should be construed 'strictly' ie, in favour of openness. The EU Ombudsman was also very active in pursuing the principles of openness and access to documents and he conducted an own-initiative investigation into the practices of Community institutions.[9] This led to all bodies adopting their procedures to follow the Decisions and the Code, even though they were not covered by the Code. The Council also adopted a register of documents allowing Council documents drawn up after 1 January 1999 to be identified. The EU Ombudsman has also produced a model *Code of Good Administrative Behaviour* which states that institutions should produce information on request subject to permissible exemptions.

1   Case T-105/95 *WWF UK v Commission* [1997] ECR II-313; *Kuijer v EU Council*: Case T-188/98 [2000] 2 CMLR 400 – the Council was in error in failing to carry out an assessment of each document requested in relation to conditions in countries from which the majority of asylum seekers originated. A blanket reason for refusing access where the conditions differed was unlawful and failed to show each document had been individually assessed. See also, *Bavarian Lager Co Ltd v EC Commission*: Case T-309/97 [1999] ECR II-3217.
2   *Svenska Journalistförbundet v EU Council*: T-174/95 [1998] ECRII-2289.
3   Case T-14/98 [1999] 3 CMLR 528; Case C-353/99P 6 December 2001, ECJ.

4   Case T-188/97 *Rothmans International BV v EC Commission* [1999] ECR-II 2463.
5   Case T-106/99 *Meyer v Commission* [1999] ECR II-3273.
6   Case T-105/95 *WWF UK v EC Commission* [1997] ECR II-313.
7   Case C-353/01P *Mattila v Council of EC and Commission* [2004] 1 CMLR 32.
8   See Case C-58/94 *Kingdom of the Netherlands v The Council* [1996] ECR I-2169.
9   OJ 1998 C 292/170; *Annual Report of the European Ombudsman* (1999), p 245.

THE EC REGULATION ON ACCESS (ARTICLE 255 EC)

Background

3.18   In the Commission's explanatory memorandum on the draft Regulation on access, the Commission explained how the Amsterdam Treaty introduced a new Art 255 into the EC Treaty, which grants the citizens and residents of the Union the right of access to the documents of the European Parliament, the Council and the Commission. The governing provision is now TFEU, Art 15, which we address below. The Treaty also included among the general principles of the Union the idea that decisions must be taken as openly as possible and as closely as possible to the citizens.

3.19   Under the terms of the EC, Art 255 (Amsterdam 1999), the Commission had to prepare draft legislation on the general principles and limits governing the right of access to documents of the three institutions (note three institutions – not the coverage that the EU Ombudsman has ensured in his own-initiative inquiries investigating access among EU institutions and which sought to persuade institutions to adopt practices on access based on the Code), which must be adopted under the co-decision procedure within two years of the entry into force of the Amsterdam Treaty, ie before 1 May 2001. Each institution must also lay down specific provisions regarding access to its documents in its rules of procedure (see below).

Scope of the Regulation (Arts 1 and 2)

INSTITUTIONS COVERED BY THE REGULATION

3.20   In accordance with Art 255 of the EC Treaty, the Regulation will apply only to documents of the European Parliament,[1] the Council and the Commission. These institutions and their constituent parts are defined in Arts 1 and 2 and, by virtue of recital 8, include all agencies established by the institutions. The Regulation (recital 7) also applies to third and second pillar documents, subject to exemption within the Regulation.

1   On access to a full report about MEPs' expenses, which the EP had denied and whose disclosure the General Court believed was 'an overriding public interest' see *Toland v EP* Case T-471/08 and judgment of the General Court second chamber (7 June 2011) annulling the EP's decision. EC Regulation 1049/2001, Art 4(2) and (3) were invoked by the EP see para 3.73, note 2 below).

3.21 Articles 28(1) and 41(1) of the Treaty on European Union expressly provide that the right of access also applies to documents relating to the common foreign and security policy and police and judicial co-operation in criminal matters (the second and third pillars). This is confirmed by recital 7 (above). The terms of TFEU, Art 15 are set out below.

3.22 In accordance with the case-law of the Court of Justice, the Regulation must also apply to documents relating to activities under the ECSC (now disbanded) and Euratom Treaties.[1]

[1]   Case: 382/85: *Deutsche Babcock Handel GmbH v Hauptzollamt Lübeck-Ost* [1987] ECR 5119 (Judgment given on 15.12.1987).

DOCUMENTS COVERED BY THE REGULATION

3.23 The legislation will cover all documents held by the three institutions, ie documents drawn up by them or emanating from third parties and in the possession of the institutions. This widening in the scope of the access system was seen by the Commission as a major step forward compared to the current system which only covers documents produced by the institutions.

3.24 Both the EP and the European Ombudsman keenly advocated this approach which was in line with existing legislation in most member states. The formulation of Declaration No 35 in the EC Treaty – which allows a member state to request the Commission or Council not to communicate to third parties documents from that state without its prior agreement – also supports a broader interpretation of Art 255 EC. However, it is understood that access to a document received from a third party will not be granted if the document is covered by one of the exceptions provided for in Art 4(1) and (2). Where there is some doubt on this, the institution will consult the author of the document first, although it reserves the right, if no reply is forthcoming, to take the final decision on whether to hand over the document or not (for the legal effect of a 'request' by a member state, see para 3.78 below). Access to documents from third parties will be limited to those sent to the institution after the date of entry into application of this Regulation so as to enable European citizens to be properly informed of this wider access to documents.

DEFINITION OF THE TERM 'DOCUMENT'

3.25 The term 'document' is defined as any content whatever its medium: paper, electronic, sound, visual or audio-visual recording. It will cover only administrative documents, ie any document on a topic which falls within the institution's remit concerning policies, activities and decisions. Excluded are documents expressing individual opinions or reflecting free and frank discussions or provision of advice as part of internal consultations and deliberations as well as informal messages such as e-mail messages 'which can be considered the equivalent of telephone conversations'. As the Committee of Independent Experts emphasised in its Second Report 'like all political institutions, the Commission needs the "space to think" to formulate policy before it enters the public domain, on the grounds that policy made in the glare of publicity and therefore "on the hoof" is often poor policy'.[1]

[1] Second report by the Committee of Independent Experts, ch 7, para 7.6.6.

COMPATIBILITY BETWEEN THE GENERAL PRINCIPLE OF ACCESS TO DOCUMENTS AND EXISTING SPECIFIC RULES

3.26 Specific rules relating to the access to documents or files already exist in connection with certain procedures. It is therefore important to stipulate clearly that the future rules governing the right of access to documents will not apply where specific rules already exist for certain persons who have a particular interest in information or rules governing the confidentiality of certain documents. However, these rules should be revised as soon as possible in the light of the general principles on transparency.

Beneficiaries of the right of access (Art 3)

3.27 In accordance with Art 255 of the EC Treaty, any citizen of the Union, and any natural or legal person residing or having its registered office in a member state, enjoys the right of access to documents. The applicant is not required to cite a special reason.

Exceptions to the right of access (Art 4)

3.28 The legislation includes a number of exceptions to the right of access to documents. As under the present system, all the exceptions are based on a 'harm test' although the expression used in 'undermine'. This means that access to documents will be granted unless disclosure would undermine certain specific interests, which are spelled out in Art 4 (with reference to specific examples). Compared with the rules laid down in the present Council and Commission code of conduct, the wording of the exceptions has been spelled out more clearly. It is also worthy of note that the harm must be 'seriously undermine' in the case of internal documents or those received from outside the institution or concerning opinions for internal use in deliberations (cf the test of 'prejudice' under the FOIA 2000). In some cases as shall be seen there is an overriding 'public interest in disclosure' test allowing disclosure even though an exception might apply.

Processing of initial and confirmatory applications, remedies, exercise of the right of access and rules on reproduction for commercial purposes or other forms of economic exploitation (Arts 5–8)

3.29 The proposal contains provisions similar to those in force under the former Code – which operated satisfactorily the Commission believed – with a number of adjustments.

3.30 For example, the time-limit for replies may now be extended by one month, provided that the applicant is notified in advance and detailed reasons are given. In accordance with the judgment given by the CFI on 19 July 1999 in Case T-14/98 (*Hautala v EU Council* and upheld in the ECJ Case C-353/99P), the proposal also introduces a requirement that, where a document contains passages covered by one of the exceptions to the right of access, partial access must be granted after the passages covered by the exception have been concealed.[1]

---

[1] See also: *Mattila*, para 3.17, note 7 above.

3.31 The Regulation introduces the principle that no reply to a confirmatory request equals a positive response which strengthens citizen's rights.

Final provisions (Arts 9–13)

3.32 A number of final provisions are proposed, which are designed to:
- commit the institutions covered by the Regulation to take the necessary steps to inform citizens of their rights and to set up public registers of documents; and
- remind the institutions that they must lay down in their rules of procedure specific provisions for the implementation of the general principles and limits laid down in this Regulation.

3.33 The Commission spelt out that the three institutions should undertake to adopt a number of additional measures in order to ensure a consistent approach in the implementation of the new rules governing public right of access to their documents: 'Such measures include training and informing their staff and reviewing existing procedures for registering, filing, archiving and classifying documents'.

3.34 From the Preamble to the Regulation on access, it is important to note the following recitals which add to points already made.

'Article 1(2) of the Treaty on European Union, as amended by the Treaty of Amsterdam, enshrines the concept of openness, stating that "This Treaty marks a new stage in the process of creating an ever closer union among the peoples of Europe, in which decisions are taken as openly as possible and as closely as possible to the citizen".' (recital 1)

3.35 This it could be argued is a constitutional clarion call for openness which must include access to documents:

'Openness enables citizens to participate more closely in the decision-making process and guarantees that the administration enjoys greater legitimacy and is more effective and more accountable to the citizen in a democratic system.' (recital 2)

3.36   This seems self-declaratory:

'The purpose of this Regulation is to give the fullest possible effect to the right of public access to documents and to lay down the general principles and limits on such access in accordance with Article 255(2) of the EC Treaty.'

3.37   The next three recitals from the Preamble state that the European Coal and Steel Community (ECSC) and Euratom treaties are within this Regulation (ECSC no longer exists), the Regulation applies to common foreign and security policy and police and judicial co-operation in criminal matters (freedom, security and justice); and that access to documents should be extended to include all documents held by the three institutions. Recital 6 calls for wider access to documents in cases where the institutions are acting in a legislative capacity including the exercise of delegated powers (see para 3.5 above).

3.38   Where other rights of access exist, these rules will not undermine those; such rights as under the Directive on data protection or procurement. Certain documents 'on account of their highly sensitive content' are to be given special treatment. These concern defence and security (recital 9) (see below). The Regulation will include documents received by the institutions.

3.39   Recital 11 states that, although all documents 'in principle' should be available, 'certain public and private interests should be protected'.

3.40   This sets out the requirement for exceptions or exemptions from access. These are criticised below:

'In order to ensure that the right of access is fully respected, a two-stage administrative procedure should apply, with the additional possibility of court proceedings or complaints to the Ombudsman.' (recital 13)

The right of challenge against an adverse decision is available to the courts (now TFEU, Art 263) and via the ombudsman (TFEU, Art 228).

3.41   This refers to an initial request, a refusal and then a request for a further consideration – the 'confirmatory' stage:

'Each institution should take the measures necessary to inform the public about the new provisions in force; and to train its staff to assist citizens exercising their rights under this Regulation. In order to make it easier for citizens to exercise their rights, each institution should provide access to a register of documents.' (recital 14)

3.42   This is an important provision. An up-to-date register is invaluable in helping to gain access:

'Even though it is neither the object nor the effect of this Regulation is to amend national legislation on access to documents, it is nevertheless clear that, by virtue of the principle of loyal cooperation which governs relations between the institutions and the Member States, Member States should take care not to hamper the proper application of this Regulation and should respect the security rules of the institutions.' (recital 15)

3.43 As we shall see, this provision was heavily criticised by the European Parliament although it was toned down to its present form from a far stronger version which more or less stated that member states had to be 'loyal'.

3.44 Recital 16 states that the Regulation is without prejudice to existing rights of access to documents for member states, judicial authorities or investigative bodies.

'In accordance with Article 255(3) of the EC Treaty, each institution lays down specific provisions regarding access to its documents in its rules of procedure.' (recital 17)

3.45 Each institution covered by the Regulation will have to make rules of procedure containing specific provisions on access. These are very important because the Regulation is not effective until they are made and they will deal with items such as the confidentiality of their own proceedings.[1] In spite of all its protestations advocating greater openness, it was the EP's rules which could lend themselves to greater protection of secrecy.

[1]   The EP rules are: Regulation 2001/2135 13 November 2001 and Bureau Decision on Public Access to EP Documents 2001 OJ C 374/1; Council Decision 29 November 2001 OJ L 313/40 (Council); and 5 December 2001 OJ L 345/94 for the Commission.

3.46 In Council Decision 2000/527/EC of 14 August 2000, the Council incorporated the effects of the Decision of the Secretary General of the Council on classification of documents.[1] This allows for the classification of documents as 'top secret', 'secret', 'confidential', 'restricted' and various internal references for information which is not to be publicly available. Where documents are in the first three classifications and they concern 'military and non-military crisis management within the framework of a strengthened European security and defence policy' they shall be *excluded* from the provisions allowing access under the Decision. Further, to protect classified information, 'It is ... necessary to provide that a Council document from which conclusions may be drawn regarding the content of classified information put out by a natural or legal person, a Member State, another Community institution or body or any other national or international body may be made available to the public only with the prior written consent of the author of the information in question' (recital 4).[1] The public register will contain no reference to the information classified in the manner stated above. As shall be seen, new provisions govern the rules on sensitive documents (below).

[1]   Decision of 27 July 2000, OJ C 239/01.
[2]   OJ L 212, 23/08/2000, p 0009.

3.47 Note that the ECJ and CFI are not included in the Regulation – the ECJ began drawing up a code on access after the EU Ombudsman's own initiative inquiry even though the ECJ and CFI are not within the Ombudsman's jurisdiction when acting in their judicial role.

The Treaty of Lisbon

3.48　One of the motivating desires behind the drafting of the EU Constitution (EUC) by the d'Estaing Convention was a simplification of the existing framework of Union institutions and laws. The creation of a single legal personality into which the three separate pillars would collapse, the formal establishment of the European Council as an institution of the Union and not a nebulous supranational and all-governing quango (quasi-autonomous international governmental organisation), the allocation of competencies and the principles of conferral, subsidiarity and proportionality in the exercise of powers by the EU institutions were all realised in the ToL, but not the simplification of the legislative procedure as set out in the EUC.

3.49　The ToL provides a new legal base for an access regulation in TFEU, Art 15(3). This states that Under TEU, Art 6 the Union recognises the rights, freedoms and principles set out in the Charter of Fundamental Rights of the European Union of 7 December 2000 (as adapted at Strasbourg on 12 December 2007), which has the same legal value as the Treaties. The provisions of the Charter do not extend in any way the competences of the Union as defined in the Treaties. Under Art 42 of the Charter of Fundamental Rights there is a right of access to the documents of the institutions, bodies, offices and agencies of the Union. This was a fundamental right in international law, and much broader in its effect than existing rights, and on the coming into force of the ToL it will effectively become a legally binding part of the Treaties and not simply a matter of intergovernmental agreement. Art 41 of the Charter gives a right to good administration. So, the rights in the Charter to good administration and a right of access to documents are legally binding 'fundamental rights'.[1]

[1]　Case T-3/00 & 337/04 *Pitsiorla v Council* (27/11/07) concerning the European Central Bank.

3.50　Under TEU, Art 10(3) every citizen has the right to participate in the democratic life of the Union. Decisions shall be taken as openly and as closely as possible to the citizen (and see Art 1). This is also present in TEU, Art 1 and repeats provisions in the existing Amsterdam EU Treaty in Art 1.

3.51　TEU, Art 11 provides that the institutions shall, by appropriate means, give citizens and representative associations the opportunity to make known and publicly exchange their views in all areas of Union action. The institutions shall maintain an open, transparent and regular dialogue with representative associations and civil society. The European Commission shall carry out broad consultations with parties concerned in order to ensure that the Union's actions are coherent and transparent. Citizens (not less than a million) may invite the Commission to submit proposals for laws for the purpose of implementing the Treaties.

3.52 The provision on access to documents was in the first part of the TEC which dealt with constitutional basics (TEC, Art I.50) as well as under Part Three of the TEC. It is now (apart from its presence in the Charter above) in the second part of ToL: the TFEU.

3.53 Under TFEU, Art 15 (replacing TEC, Art 255) it states that in order to promote good governance and ensure the participation of civil society, the Union institutions, bodies, offices and agencies shall conduct their work as openly as possible. After provisions about Parliament and the Council meetings being in public, the latter when considering and voting on a legislative act, it states:

'3. Any citizen of the Union, and any natural or legal person residing or having its registered office in a Member State, shall have a right of access to documents of the Union institutions, bodies, offices and agencies, whatever their medium, subject to the principles and the conditions to be defined in accordance with this paragraph.

General principles and limits on grounds of public or private interest governing this right of access to documents shall be determined by the European Parliament and the Council, by means of regulations, acting in accordance with the ordinary legislative procedure.

Each institution, body, office or agency shall ensure that its proceedings are transparent and shall elaborate in its own Rules of Procedure specific provisions regarding access to its documents, in accordance with the regulations referred to in the second subparagraph.

The Court of Justice of the European Union, the European Central Bank and the European Investment Bank shall be subject to this paragraph only when exercising their administrative tasks.'

It should be emphasised that this measure does not confer rights on those who are not 'citizens or resident in the EU'. The position at present is that non-citizens and residents are covered by EC Regulation 1049/2001, as explained above. Secondly, all institutions of the EU are covered. This will include the European Council, which is made an 'institution' under ToL. Because of the collapse of the pillars into one EU edifice there is no formal distinction between what were EC and EU concerns. The coverage of this measure would appear to be much wider that the existing regulation. We await the final detail.

3.54 TFEU, Art 298(1) provides that 'in carrying out their missions, the institutions, bodies, offices and agencies of the Union shall have the support of an open, efficient and independent European administration' and the EP and Council shall establish provisions to that end. Under the TEC it stated that such provisions are subject to staff regulations and conditions of employment on confidentiality, discipline and non-publication of materials acquired from employment.[1]

---

[1] Case C-274/99P *Connolly v EC Commission* [2001] ECR I-1611; Case C-340/00P *EC Commission v Cwik*; see A Biondi (2003) European Public Law 39.

3.55 Finally, the Commission has conducted a review of EC Regulation 1049/2001 on access and its recommendations for amendment and comments are dealt with below (paras 3.99 et seq). The House of Lords EU Committee has examined the subject of access to EU documents (HL 108 (2008–09)).

Regulation (EC) 1049/2001

3.56 The Commission is reviewing Regulation (EC) 1049/2001 (OJ L 145/43)[1] on access, a process which preceded ToL. However, the existing Regulation is likely to be the basis of any future regulation and its details must be addressed along with proposals for its reform. Article 1 of Regulation (EC) 1049/2001 states that the purpose of the Regulation is to establish rules ensuring the easiest possible exercise of the right of access. Article 2 states that any citizen of the Union, and any natural or legal person residing or having its registered office in a member state, has right of access to the documents of the institutions subject to the principles, conditions and limits defined in the Regulation. The institutions may grant access to such documents subject to the same conditions, principles and limits.

[1]   See the 'Report from the Commission on the application in 2008 of Regulation EC No 1049/2001' (COM(2009)331). Applications for access have risen from 3,841 in 2006 to 5,197 in 2008. For the figures and report for 2010 see COM(2011) 492 final (12.08.2011).

3.57 Under Art 2(3) on 'scope':

'(3) This Regulation shall apply to all documents held by an institution, that is to say, documents drawn up or received by it and in its possession, in all areas of Union activity.'

This would include documents from individuals and corporations, other EU institutions and national governments.

3.58 Access to documents from third parties shall be limited to those sent to the institution after the date of entry into force of the Regulation.

3.59 Article 3 sets out the definitions:

'For the purposes of this Regulation:
(a)   "document" shall mean any content whatever its medium (written on paper or stored in electronic form or as a sound, visual or audiovisual recording); concerning a matter relating to the policies, activities and decisions falling within the institution's sphere of responsibility;
(b)   "third party" shall mean any natural or legal person, or any entity outside the institution concerned, including the Member States, other Community or non-Community institutions and bodies and third countries;'

3.60 An earlier draft of the article spelt out the bodies covered by the institutions and various committees.

3.61 These provisions disappeared from the final version after prolonged disputes between the EP and the Council and Commission. The recitals include Comitology committees, agencies, and COREPER is a Council body. Clearly missing is the European Council for which the ToL now makes provision (see below). It should be added that executive agencies are covered by Council Regulation (EC) 58/2003, Art 23 of which concerns access to documents under Regulation 1049/2001.[1]

[1] Council Regulation (EC) 58/2003, OJ L 11/1, laying down the statute for executive agencies to be entrusted with certain tasks in the management of Community programmes; on financial regulation, see Council Regulation (EC) 1605/2002, OJ L 248/1.

3.62 Documents will be accessible to the public following a written application or application in electronic form or through a register. Documents drawn up in a legislative procedure shall be made directly accessible in accordance with Art 12. The register has not been seen as user-friendly and many preparatory legal documents were not registered. If a document is not on the register there should be an indication of where it may be located.

3.63 A written request for access must be sufficiently precise to enable an institution to identify the relevant documents (Art 6(1)). Clarification may be sought where the request is not precise. Assistance should be provided to enable the requester to clarify a request (Art 6(2)), There is a general duty to assist and provide information on how and where to make applications (Art 6(4)). Applications recieved must be acknowledged and a response made in 15 days of either allowing or refusing access with reasons for the latter (Art 7)). Where the request is for a 'very long document' or a large number of documents, informal discussion may take place to settle a fair solution on what should be provided (Art 6(3)). This latter aspect has featured in litigation (below). The applicant is not obliged to state reasons for the application or his interest.

3.64 In Case T-2/03 *Verein fur Konsumenteninformation v Commission* [2005] ECR II-1121 a request was made for documents which would involve an allegedly 'unreasonable amount of work' in reading voluminous documents. The case concerned determining where the balance of interest lay in either granting public access or allowing public disclosure and the institution's right to protect the interest in good administration. However, this latter possibility justifying refusal was 'applicable only in exceptional cases' and the institution had to justify this stance. In Case T-42/05 *Williams v Commission* [2008] ECR II-156 the court emphasised that the possibility of denial in such cases was applicable only in exceptional circumstances. The institution relying on the unreasonableness of the task entailed by the request bears the burden of proof of the scale of that task (para 86). The requester in *Williams* asked for internal communications within the Commission on six pieces of legislation which were the core of its legal regime on genetically modified organisms. The Commission availed itself of the possibility under Art 6(3) of the Regulation of dividing the applicant's initial request into six. The Commission replied only to the first request on preparatory documents relating to a Directive – the request was not 'wide-ranging'. Nothing in the other requests suggested an 'unreasonable amount of work' likely to be detrimental to good administration. The Commission could not rely on the unreasonable work test to justify non-consideration of the disclosure of each and every document held by it relevant to the request. The principle of transparency had to be observed. If files are identifiable, they should be considered. The test is an onerous one.

Exceptions

3.65 Article 4 establishes exceptions and exemptions. Settled case law of the courts states that the exceptions must be interpreted and applied 'restrictively' so as not to defeat the right of access[1] although a wide discretion will apply in some exceptions (below). The Regulation deals with access to 'third party documents' held by an institution. 'Third party' means any natural or legal person other than one of the three institutions covered by the Regulation. Unless it is clear that the document shall or shall not be disclosed, there has to be consultation by the institution with the third party with a view to assessing whether one of the exceptions is applicable.

[1]   Case T-211/00 *Kuijer v Council* [2002] ECR II-485, para 55; Case T-194/04 *Bavarian Lager v Commission* [2007] ECR II-4523, para 94. See D Adamski (2009) 46 CMLR 521 and P Leino (2011) 48(4) CML Rev 1215.

3.66 Article 4 states:

'1. The institutions shall refuse access to documents where disclosure could undermine the protection of:
(a)   the public interest as regards:
(i)   public security,
(ii)   defence and military matters,
(iii) international relations;
(iv) the financial, monetary or economic policy of the Community or a Member State

3.67 Article 4(1) does not contain an overriding public interest allowing disclosure as regards the relevant exceptions. It provides a mandatory exception where protection of a public interest in one of the stated areas would be undermined by disclosure.

3.68 Under Art 4(1)(a) (specifically sub-paras (i) and (iii)) the ECJ ruled in *Sison* that the Council must be recognised as enjoying a 'wide discretion' for the purpose of determining whether the disclosure of documents would undermine the public interest.[1] The review of the legality of such a decision was limited to verifying whether the procedural rules and duty to state reasons had been complied with, whether the facts had been accurately stated, and whether there had been a manifest error of assessment or misuse of powers. In assessing the exceptions the Council was not obliged to take account of the applicant's particular interests in seeing the documents. Even though the reasons were brief for the decision in question they were 'adequate' [81]. A statement of reasons under TFEU, Art 296 (formerly TEC, Art 253) must be appropriate to the act in issue. Case T-264/04 *WWF European Policy Programme v Council* [2007] ECR II-911 concerned a request for documents related to international trade negotiations taking place within the WTO. These covered WTO and states' positions and minutes of meetings. It was reasonably foreseeable that disclosure would undermine the proceedings thereby undermining the public interest regarding international interests and the Community's financial, monetary and economic policy. One should note, however, Case T-211/00 *Kuijer v Council* [2002] ECR II-485 where access to human rights reports prepared by the Centre for Information, Reflection and Exchange on Asylum was refused. They covered asylum and reports on other countries. The court overruled the Council in *Kuijer*. Each report had to be considered and they contained general statements that had already been published and were not politically sensitive. Where a Member State invokes Art 4(5) (below) it too must be given a 'broad discretion in assessing exceptions under Art 4(1)(a). In Case T-362/08 *IFAW Internationaler Tierschutz-Fonds gGmbH* (which concerned Art 4(1)(iii)–(iv), 4(3) and 4(5); below) in which it was claimed that disclosure of the documents in question would undermine Germany's international relations and economic policies. The risk of undermining a protected interest must be reasonably foreseeable and not purely hypothetical and the reasoning must not be based on 'manifestly erroneous' grounds (*IFAW*, para 124). The test for non-disclosure was satisfied in *IFAW* (below).

[1]   Case C-266/05 P *Sison v Council of the EU* (1 February 2007). The case concerned specific restrictive measures directed against certain persons and entities to combat terrorism in Decision 2002/848/EC. In Case C-402/05P and C-415/05P *Yassin Abdullah Kadi and Al Barakaat International Foundation v Council of the European Union and Commission of the European Communities* and Case T-85/09 *Kadi v Commission* the ECJ and General Court ruled unlawful EU regulations which breached the human rights protection of the EU – an 'autonomous legal order' – and which had implemented UN Security Council resolutions. The General Court found that the review by the UN Security Council committee of inclusion of individuals on a list of suspected terrorists was inadequate to allow for a 'searching review' by the EU courts. See also Case T-318/01 *Othman v Council and Commission*.

3.69   Article 4(1)(b) states: [the public interest as regards] 'privacy and the integrity of the individual, in particular in accordance with Community legislation regarding the protection of personal data' (see ch 7, and para 1.269). Article 4(1)(b) has been widely discussed and much litigated. The leading case of *Bavarian Lager* saw the Court of First Instance (CFI) rule that the Data Protection Regulation (EC 45/2001) does not trump the access Regulation to prevent disclosure of personal data.[1] The case concerned a meeting between EU officials, British civil servants and representatives of a beer-brewing trade organisation which discussed matters relevant to the applicant who was not allowed to attend the meeting. Proceedings commenced against the UK under then TEC, Art 226 for alleged breaches of TEC, Art 28 before the meeting took place. The applicant requested the names of those from the organisation who had attended the meeting as well as names of companies making submissions to the Commission. In determining whether Art 4(1)(b) applies, 'it is necessary to examine whether public access to the names of the participants at the meeting … is capable of actually and specifically undermining the protection of the privacy and the integrity of the persons concerned' (para 120). The participation of the names as 'representatives' of organisations did not affect their private lives the CFI determined (para 125).

¹   Case T-194/04 *Bavarian Lager v Commission* [2007] ECR II-4523; see Case C-465/00 Österreichischer Rundfunk and Others [2003] ECR I-4989.

3.70   In her opinion for the ECJ in the appeal by the Commission against the CFI decision in *Bavarian Lager*, the Advocate General accepted that the case concerned two 'fundamental rights of equal value': access and privacy. The Advocate General agreed with the destination of the CFI but not with its method of travel. The CFI had given insufficient weight to the Community legislation on protection of personal data. However, the Commission's decision was correctly annulled because the governing provision was Regulation 1049/2001. The claim was for access to an official document which incidentally contained personal data; it was not a request for data involving *processing* of personal data. The latter would be governed by the provisions of EC Regulation 45/2001. That was not the case here. Although the Advocate General believed the decision should be upheld there is clearly a very grey area in the Opinion between requests for documents incidentally containing personal data (governed by EC Regulation 1049/2001 including Art 4(1)(b)) and those containing a large quantity of personal data and 'processing' (governed by the provisions of EC Regulation 45/2001).¹

¹   Case C-28/08 *P*, 15 October 2009.

3.71   The ECJ on appeal, however,¹ ruled that names of individuals was personal data and therefore protected under EC Regulation 45/2001. The ECJ ruled that the Commission was within its rights to restrict disclosure in this way. In its judgment the ECJ sidestepped the 'big questions' that many were hoping to have resolved in this case. The ECJ confined its ruling to the point that Bavarian Lager had failed to show why it needed to know the names and that, in the absence of any credible claim of a need to know, the data protection/privacy rights in EC Regulation 45/2001 took precedence as of right over the access provisions in EC Regulation 1049/2001. However, the fact that this point had not been raised in argument means that it is open in the future for a requester to show good reasons why disclosure is justified. EC Regulation 45/2001 is not an automatic trump card. The court's judgment contrasts sharply with that of the CFI and with the Opinion of the Advocate General, who wrestled with the wider issues of principle.

¹   Case C-28/08 *P*, 2 July 2009.

3.72   Article 4(2) states:

'The institutions shall refuse access to a document where disclosure would undermine the protection of:
–   commercial interests of a natural or legal person including intellectual property,
–   court proceedings and legal advice,
–   the purpose of inspections, investigations and audits,
unless there is an overriding public interest in disclosure.'

For the exceptions in para 2, but not for those in para 1 above, there is a public interest override (para 3.73 below). The Court or Ombudsman will be able to make a decision on the balance of the merits. 'Commercial interests' is a very broad formulation (see para 1.215 above).[2]

[1]   Case T-36/04 *API v Commission* (12/9/07).
[2]   Case T-237/02 *Technische Glaswerke Ilmenau Gmbh v Commission* [2007] 1 CMLR 39 where a strict test in favour of disclosure was applied by the CFI. Case T-308/04 *Terezakis v Commission* (30/1/08); and Case T-237/02 *Franchet v Commission* [2006] ECR II-2023. On audits into MEPs' expenses and disclosure of the report, see Case T-471/08 *Toland v European Parliament* (judgment of second chamber General Court, 7/06/11).

3.73   Some criticisms are made of these provisions below. It should be observed that under Art 4(2) there is now a public interest override allowing the courts or the Ombudsman to allow access where a greater public interest is served by disclosure than by secrecy. The institutions will have to prove that disclosure would undermine the protection of: the public interest and the specified subject areas under Art 4(1); disclosure would undermine the privacy and personal integrity of the individual under Art 4(1); or disclosure would undermine the interests under para 2 of Art 4 but with a public interest override in the latter case only.

3.74   Under Art 4(2) an overriding public interest in disclosure may also be applied although a harm test is made out. In *Turco* (concerning the legal advice exception, see below) the ECJ ruled that an overriding public interest in disclosure need not be distinct from the general principles of openness and transparency that underlie the Regulation.[1] The onus is on the applicant for documents. However, the ECJ *Turco* judgment has assisted requesters by requiring an institution to ascertain, if it takes the view that disclosure would undermine the protection of legal advice in the legislative process, as in *Turco*, whether there is any overriding public interest justifying disclosure despite the fact that its ability to seek legal advice and receive frank, objective and comprehensive advice would thereby be undermined. The institution has to balance the particular interest to be protected by non-disclosure of the document concerned against, inter alia, the public interest in the document being made accessible in the light of the advantages stemming from increased openness. This 'enables citizens to participate more closely in the decision-making process and guarantees that the administration enjoys greater legitimacy and is more effective and more accountable to the citizen in a democratic system.' The institution must explain the basis of the exception and its reasoning on the public interest (paras 45 and 49). As things stand, nothing constrains the institutions to make the balance in favour of the public interest in disclosure where a harm test is established. In *Turco* the harm test was not established, the court believed. Where a harm test is made out by an institution, applicants have to argue for the public interest, but their arguments unavoidably face the considerable difficulty of not having seen the relevant document. In 2009, the EU Ombudsman's office dids not know of a case where officials had identified a public interest in disclosure where a harm test has been established.[2] The EU institution has to establish a harm test and determine and reason on the public interest. Although *Turco* assists requesters under the EU Regulation the requester still faces considerable difficulties.

[1]   Joined Cases C-39/05 P and C-52/05 P, *Turco v Council*, judgment of 1 July 2008, paragraphs 67 and 74.
[2]   See I Harden (2009) EPL 239.

3.75   A general and abstract argument from an institution that disclosure would lead to doubts as to the lawfulness of a legislative act did not suffice to establish that the protection of legal advice would be undermined where the legal advice and opinion exception involved the institution's own legal service and advice they had provided. There would be no compromise of independence by disclosure of legal opinions where there were no reasonably foreseeable, as opposed to purely hypothetical, risks of frank and reliable advice being undermined. An assessment of where the public interest lay had to be made by the institution. Disclosure of an institution's legal advice documents from its legal service on legal questions arising when legislative initiatives were being debated increased transparency and strengthened the democratic right of European citizens to scrutinise the information on which a legislative act is based. Non-disclosure may be justified in cases of particular sensitivity or where it went beyond the legislative process. In this case, a 'detailed statement of the institution's reasons' had to be given.[1]

[1]   Case C-39/05 *Sweden v Council of the European Union* [2007] I-11389. See also Case T-36/04 *Association de la Presse Internationale ASBL v Commission* [2007] CMLR 51.

3.76   Article 4, para 3 continues that firstly, access to a document, drawn up by an institution for internal use or received by an institution, which concerns a matter where the decision has not been taken by the institution, shall be refused if disclosure of the document would seriously undermine the institution's decision-making process, unless there is an overriding public interest in disclosure. Secondly, access to documents containing opinions for internal use as part of deliberations and preliminary consultations within the institution concerned shall be refused even after the decision has been taken if disclosure would seriously undermine the decision-making process unless, once again, there is a public interest override. 'Shall' connotes a mandatory refusal, but the institution would have to give cogent reasons why it 'would' 'seriously' undermine the decision-making process. 'Seriously' connotes a higher degree of harm than in the previous tests. The deliberative stage of decision-making is not excluded. Access may be had to documents containing internal discussions. In a request for such documents, access must be allowed unless the institution can show that serious harm to its decision-making process is reasonably foreseeable and not purely hypothetical[1] and the requester cannot establish that there is an overriding public interest in disclosure.

[1]   Case T-403/05 *MyTravel v Commission*, judgment of the CFI of 9 September 2008. See paras 51–54. See Case T-144/05 *Muniz v Commission* (18/12/08) and Case T-471/08 *Toland v European Parliament* above.

3.77   In Case T-233/09 *Access Info Europe v Council*, the General Court ruled that the Council had acted unlawfully in refusing to disclose documents revealing the identities of the member states and their proposals and positions on redrafting Regulation 1049/2001 on access. The Council objected to the identities being revealed because of the grounds stated in Art 4(3)(i). The court emphasised the importance of transparency in the legislative process in ruling against the Council. The Council's arguments, basically protecting the identities of those member states in favour of restricting the scope of Regulation 1049/2001 did not accord with full accountability in 'a system based on the principle of democratic accountability' (para 69).[1] The content of the Commission's proposed reforms of Regulation 1049/2001 is addressed below.

[1]   http://www.access-info.org/documents/Access_Docs/Advancing/EU/Secret_State_of_EU_Transparency.pdf.

3.78   Third parties shall be consulted to assess whether a para 1 or 2 exception applies 'unless it is clear that the document should or should not be disclosed' (Art 4(4)). It should be noted that this does not cover the exceptions in para 3 of Art 4, although in the case of a member state the following is highly relevant. A member state may request the institution not to disclose a document originating from that member state without its prior agreement under Art 4(5). The effect of such a request when it is made by a member state was not originally entirely clear: is it binding on the institutions or merely persuasive? Clearly it would be diplomatically insensitive not to follow the wish of a member state, and in the spirit of EU cooperation the article would imply a duty to comply with the member state's wish. It was not initially clear whether the reasonableness of that wish would be important. In a controversial and much critised decision in December 2004, the CFI made it clear that Art 4(5) placed the member state in a different position to a third party under Art 4(4). A 'request' from a member state to the Commission not to disclose constituted an instruction not to disclose, the CFI held and was therefore mandatory. The member state was under no obligation to state the reasons for its refusal and the institution had no power to question whether disclosure could be made on eg public interest grounds. Where no request was made by the member state after it had been consulted, the institution remained obliged to see whether the document should be disclosed under Art 4(4). It would then be for national authorities to determine any application for access under any relevant national measures. Other third parties have a right to be consulted by the institution involved. But their wish is not binding on the institution.[1]

[1]   See Case T-168/02 *Internationaler Tierschutz-Fonds GmbH v The Commission* (2004) *Times*, 20 December. The Commission was supported by the UK, the applicant by Sweden, Denmark and the Netherlands.

3.79   This judgment was not followed by the ECJ on appeal.[1] The ECJ ruled that a 'document originating from a Member State' covers any document that a member state transmits to an institution regardless of the author. Article 4(5) does not give the member state a 'general and unconditional right of veto to access'. Furthermore, the Article gives a member state an opportunity to participate in a decision by the institution. The ECJ ruled that decisions should involve a 'genuine dialogue' discussing the possibility of invoking exceptions in Art 4 above. Dialogue should be commenced without delay and time limits (below) should be observed. Following the dialogue, where the member state objects to disclosure, it has to state reasons for the objection with reference to the exceptions set out above in Art 4(1) to (3). If the member state does not provide reasons for its refusal upon request the institution should allow access where it believes none of the exceptions above applies. Where a reasoned refusal is forthcoming, the institution should deny access. The institution has to explain the reasons for the member state refusing access under one or other of the exceptions above. The validity of reasons provided by a member state may be reviewed by EU courts.

1 Case C-64/05 P, *Sweden (IFAW) v Commission* [2007] ECR I-11389.

3.80 In Case T-362/08 *IFAW Internationaler Tierschutz-Fonds gGmbH*, which concerned Art 4(1)(iii)–(iv) and 4(3) second paragraph, the Commission relied upon reg 4(5) to deny access. This was a decision in the case discussed above (para 3.68) after it had been remitted to the General Court by the ECJ after that court heard appeal on the preliminary points (above). The facts involved a request for a letter from the German Chancellor to the Commission President involving a proposed development of an environmentally protected site concerning natural habitats and wild fauna. Many documents given to the Commission by German authorities had been disclosed. In relation to the contested letter, the court accepted that the examination of the applicability of the exceptions must be clear from the institution's reasons and these must be based on clear reasons from the member state as to why the exceptions are applicable. The reasoning of a member state adopted by the institution must disclose in a clear unequivocal manner the reasoning followed by the institution adopting the measure.[1] The member state's reasons must comply with the duty to provide reasons in TEC, Art 253 (now TFEU, Art 296(2)). The relationship between the member state and institution must respect the duty of loyal cooperation now set out in TFEU, Art 4(3). The requester must be allowed to understand the origin and grounds of the refusal and the court must be allowed to exercise its review. Although the court did not want to make a specific ruling on the nature of the Commission's review of the member state decision (para 84) – such a distinction would have been relevant had the Commission disagreed with the member state (para 86) – it is clear that the review by the court is not limited to a prima facie or 'cursory' review as suggested by the Commission (para 87). But nor could the court second guess the decision of the Commission and member state by engaging in a review of the merits and a de novo decision. The refusal must be based on the duty to give reasons and on a substantive assessment made by the member state of the applicability of the exceptions which has been accepted and properly explained by the Commission. On this basis, the reasoning of the Commission revealed no errors in the member state's reasons and the decision was lawful. Three levels of review seem to be possible: cursory or prima facie review; complete or detailed review, and merits review, the latter of which is not invoked. The court noted the institution enjoys a broad discretion to determine whether the public interest in Art 4(1)(a) exceptions 'could' (para 104) be undermined. The word used in Art 4(1) is 'would'. The discretion relates to a 'complex and delicate nature which calls for the exercise of particular care and that the criteria in Art 4(1)(a) ... are very general' (para 104) (*Sison*, paras 34–36). A member state making a political assessment must also be afforded a broad discretion. The documents in question were 'confidential' and the letter concerned a confidential matter regarding the economic policy of Germany and other member states. Although the statement of reasons was brief it was still 'adequate' in the light of the context of the case and it was sufficient to enable the requester to ascertain the reasons for refusal and for the court to review those reasons. There had been a prolonged history of communications with the requester over the proposed development in Germany which the Commission had approved on grounds of public interest within the relevant environmental legislation (para 113).

1   Case C-266/05 P, *Sison v Council* [2007] ECR I-1233.

3.81   The European Ombudsman has requested the European Commission to release documents originating from Spain concerning the construction of an industrial port in Granadilla, Tenerife. This followed a complaint from the European Environmental Bureau (EEB), a federation of environmental citizens' organisations. Having inspected the documents, the Ombudsman concluded that the Commission should release them, unless the Spanish authorities gave valid arguments against disclosure. Furthermore, he did not agree that the disclosure of all but one of the internal documents would undermine the Commission's decision-making process. The Commission explained its refusal by referring to objections to disclosure from the Spanish authorities. The Ombudsman pointed out, however, that if member states request the Commission not to release documents it receives from them, they must give convincing arguments based on EU transparency rules. He noted that Spain has yet to provide such convincing arguments. The Ombudsman had also called on the Commission to release internal documents concerning the construction of the Granadilla port. The Commission accepted this recommendation and released the documents, thus 'demonstrating its willingness to improve the transparency of its procedures'.[1]

1   http://www.ombudsman.europa.eu/en/cases/decision.faces/en/5515/html.bookmark.

3.82   Serious problems could be produced were it not for the Council's practice of treating the written positions of delegations and documents summarising the oral statements by member states of the Council, or those held by one of its preparatory bodies, as Council documents. They are then within the Regulation.[1]

1   See B Driessen, 'The Council of the European Union and access to documents' (2005) *European Law Review* 675 at p 687.

3.83   Documents may be redacted to allow access to parts not covered by exceptions. Usually exceptions apply for 30 years but in the case of privacy, commercial interests or sensitive documents, the period of exception may be extended for longer. Separate provisions exist to deal with archives of the Union.[1]

1   These are documents that are more than 30 years old: see para 3.98, note 1 below.

3.84   The courts and the Ombudsman will require reasons for refusals which make plain the basis on which refusal is being maintained. If these are inadequate, it has been explained how the courts and Ombudsman will adopt a strict approach and, if adequate reasons cannot be provided, order disclosure. The Regulation (Art 8) states that an applicant has to be informed of rights to challenge under Arts 230 and 195 of the EC Treaty (TFEU, Arts 263 and 228) to the courts and ombudsman. The ombudsman has been a champion on openness.

3.85 For documents in the possession of a member state, originating from an institution, the member state shall consult with the institution concerned to ensure that no decision is made jeopardising the objectives of the Regulation 'unless it is clear a document shall, or shall not, be disclosed' (Art 5).

3.86 The provisions under Art 6 concerning applications for access are dealt with above (paras 3.29–3.30).

3.87 Art 7 has been dealt with above. In the institution's written statement of the reasons for the total or partial refusal the institution must inform the applicant of their right to seek a 'confirmatory application', ie an internal review. It has been seen how the period may be extended beyond 15 days. Failure to reply within the prescribed time limit entitles the applicant to make a confirmatory application. This is a higher level of internal review of the initial decision. Such an application must be made within 15 working days of the initial refusal.

3.88 Article 8 concerns confirmatory applications. This again has to be handled promptly. The same time limits of 15 days are repeated to grant access or to deny access with a written statement of reasons for total or partial denial. The applicant must be advised of remedies.

'2. In exceptional cases (eg large documents etc) , the time-limit provided for in paragraph 1 may be extended by 15 working days, provided that the applicant is notified in advance and detailed reasons are given.

Failure to reply within the prescribed time-limit shall be equivalent to a negative reply entitling the applicant to proceed to the court or EU Ombudsman.'

3.89 Article 10 concerns the exercise of the right to access:

'1. The applicant shall have access to documents either by consulting them on the spot or by receiving a copy, including, where available, an electronic copy, according to the applicant's preference.'

3.90 The cost of producing and sending the copies may be charged to the applicant inferring a discretion. The cost shall not exceed the 'real charge'. On the spot consultation, copies of less than 20 A4 pages and direct access in electronic form or through the register shall be free. Article 10(2) allows the institution to inform the applicant on obtaining documents already released and which easily accessible to the applicant. The format of documents shall include electronic, Braille, large print or tape.

3.91 Article 9 deals with the treatment of sensitive documents. These are documents originating from the member states, institutions, third countries or international organisations classified as 'Très secret/Top secret, secret or confidentiel/confidential' in accordance with the rules of the institution concerned protecting essential interests under Art 4(1)(a), especially public security, defence and military matters. Information does not have to fall within Art 9 to be treated as confidential or sensitive. Reasons do not have to be given justifying non-disclosure of information which would themselves reveal sensitive or confidential information that is not within Art 9. (see para 111 of the *IFAW* decision above). Applications for these documents may only be dealt with by those who are vetted and cleared to deal with them. These persons may also assess which references to sensitive documents could be made in the public register. It is clear that sensitive documents shall only be released or recorded in the register 'only with the consent of the originator'. This is an exclusion and not an exception. Reasons should be given for refusal in a manner which does not compromise the interests protected in Art 4. Member states shall take appropriate measures to ensure that, in handling applications for sensitive documents, the principles in Arts 9 and 4 are complied with in relation to sensitive documents. The rules of the institutions concerning sensitive documents shall be made public. The most recent rules on classification have been published. They are voluminous documents and have been amended on a variety of occasions.[1] Also published are rules on handling sensitive documents between the Council, Commission and EP.[2]

[1] Council Decision 19 March 2001 [2001] OJ L 101/1; Commission Decision 29 November 2001 [2001] OJ L 317/1 and on access by the EP to sensitive documents: (2002) OJ C 298/1. See Council Decisions 2004/194/EC, 10 February 2004; 2005/571/EC, 12 July 2005; 2005/952/EC, 20 December 2005; and 2007/438/EC, 18 June 2007.
[2] 20 November 2002, [2002] OJ C 298/1.

3.92 Article 11 deals with registers of documents which institutions have to provide including in electronic form. Documents shall be recorded without delay. The register had to be operational by 3 June 2002 and must provide details on referencing but not so as to undermine the exceptions. Documents should, as far as possible, be directly available through electronic form especially legislative documents and 'where possible' documents relating to policy or strategy development (Art 12). The register should indicate where the document is located if direct access is not available. Article 13 specifies the documents that shall be published in the Official Journal of the EU. Institutions must take the requisite measures to inform the public of their rights under this measure, and member states shall cooperate in providing information to citizens. Article 15 deals with good administrative practice within the institutions to facilitate access rights under the Regulation and an inter-institutional committee shall be established to examine best practice and discuss future developments. Existing copyright laws limiting rights of reproduction or exploitation are not affected. Annual reports shall be published by each institution with details on refusals to grant access, reasons for such, and the number of sensitive documents not recorded in the register. The Commission was to report on implementation by 31 January 2004 (see para 3.99 note 3 below on recent reports). The Regulation was implemented by rules of procedure by each institution and was applicable from 3 December 2001.[1]

[1] See para 3.45 note 1 above.

3.93 The EU Ombudsman has been very critical of an earlier version of the access Regulation.[1] In a valuable report, the House of Lords Committee on the EU reported on a draft of the Regulation.[2] It was critical of the Commission's failure to consult before the adoption of the draft Regulation. The Lords committee noted: 'Extensive external consultation would have demonstrated a commitment to openness' (para 46). It criticised an original recital which stated that 'Member States shall take care not to hamper the proper application of this Regulation.' It was seen as going far beyond the requirements of co-operation in then Art 10 of the EC Treaty and seemed to impose a requirement on member states' FOI laws not to be more liberal than the EC regime. Sweden and Scandinavian countries pride themselves on their openness and many member states are seeing the benefits from greater transparency. The 'Community system should not create any unnecessary restrictions, especially where national FOI regimes are more liberal.' (para 53). The final version removed many of these objectionable provisions. Secondly, the Lords Committee felt that all the institutions and bodies covered by Art 255 of the EC Treaty should be expressly stated in the Regulation (as in the UK Freedom of Information Act 2000) and should include not only committees and working groups but all agencies created by the institutions. This should include Europol, albeit with a transitional period. Those institutions not covered, eg the Central Bank, should be reminded that as a matter of good administration[3] they could follow the principles of this Regulation.

[1] See *Wall Street Journal* (2004) 24 February, p 11 and reply from Romano Prodi *Wall Street Journal* (2000) 9 March.
[2] HL 109 (1999–2000) *Sixteenth Report*. See also HL 221 (2006–07) *Behind Closed Doors – G6 Meeting*.
[3] Article 41 of the EU Charter of Fundamental Rights.

3.94 Thirdly, in principle, all documents should be accessible and exceptions to the right should be limited as far as possible. The harm test should be applied on a case by case basis. Where third party documents are sent to the institutions with a request for confidentiality there should, where necessary, be an arbitration procedure between the third party and institution concerned. This might involve the ECJ, the EU Ombudsman or the Data Control Authorities in the institutions. Documents on security from eg NATO cannot be treated in the same way as company documents. However, the EP was critical of the security reviews on classification made by the Council in the summer of 2000. Detailed rules now govern these matters.

3.95 Fourthly, the term 'document' should be interpreted broadly. This will include internal documents of the institutions although 'informal documents' ie purely personal documents involving personal opinions and 'brain-storming' will not be included. This provision if enacted will be difficult to operate but it has not caused overwhelming problems in eg the USA where the distinction is made. The Commission proposal actually reduces access to internal documents.

3.96 Fifthly, modes of access should be made as easy as possible, especially in the case of legislative documents. The register should contain 'mostly the documents relating to the legislative procedures and including all proposals, opinions, working documents, agendas, documents for discussion at formal meetings, minutes, declarations and positions of Member States'.[1] Classified documents should also be listed so that a challenge may be made to their classification as non-public. Information officers should replace Secretary-Generals as the arbiter on access for confirmatory decisions. Electronic versions of the Official Journal and of internal registries should be available in reading rooms everywhere in the Union. Under Art 10 of the EC Treaty (co-operation) local authorities could be asked to arrange this facility. Access should be user friendly.

[1] European Parliament Final A5-0318.2000, 27 October 2000 and Final A5-0318/2000 Part 2, 3 November 2000, the Cashman Report.

3.97 Sixthly, where a member state is asked for documents of an EU institution, national rules should prevail subject to a spirit of loyal co-operation entailing that member states should inform institutions of the request and fully take into account their views. It is important not to prejudice the development of Community policy.

3.98 Finally, Art 18 refers to the Regulation on archives.[1]

[1] Regulation (EEC) 354/83; and see Council of Europe 2002/0203 (CNS) COM (2002) 462 final (4 September 2002) on a proposal to amend 354/83.

THE COMMISSION PROPOSALS FOR 'RECASTING' REGULATION 1049/200

3.99 In 2007, the Commission commenced[1] a public consultation on access to documents[2] followed by a Commission proposal to 'recast' the Regulation.[3] The Commission proposed that the existing distinction between citizens and residents (who enjoy the right of access) and other natural and legal persons (who 'may' be granted access – see above) should be removed. All natural and legal persons should have the right of access.

[1] This section relies heavily on Ian Harden's article in (2009) EPL 239. The EU Committee of the House of Lords reported on the Commission's recommendations in HL 108 (2008–09).
[2] Public Access to Documents held by institutions of the European Community: a Review, COM(2007) 185 final.
[3] COM(2008) 229 final. Recasting is a special legislative technique which is not best suited to the Regulation in that it placed constraints on Parliament's manoeuvrability. The most recent Commission report on the application of the Regulation in 2008 is COM(2009) 331 Final (2 July 2009).

3.100 The Commission proposed amendments to assist applicants requesting documents that are not clearly stated or that cannot be identified. The period for responding would only commence from the time clarification is received. Some of the difficulties here may relate to an institution's incomplete indexing.

3.101 The Commission also proposes extending the normal deadline for handling a confirmatory application to 30 working days. This may be extended for a further 15 working days. The 15-working-day deadline, the Commission has argued, is far too short and creates insuperable burdens.

3.102 The definition of 'document' would be amended to include only those 'formally transmitted to one or more recipients or otherwise registered.' The Commission proposal would mean that no application for access to a document drawn up by an institution could be made unless so transmitted or registered.[1] If not formally transmitted it would have to be registered. This would give the Commission wide powers of inclusion and exclusion.

[1] Article 3(a).

3.103 The Commission further proposed excluding access to investigation files or proceedings of an 'individual scope' until they were 'closed' or an act had become 'definitive', ie completed. Where documents were obtained or taken from natural or legal persons in such investigations these would be permanently excluded even if any harmful effect had been removed by the passage of time.[1] This amendment would remove the consideration of an overriding public interest consideration.[2] According to Harden a literal reading of the proposed new text would allow a 'whole document' to be 'permanently excluded' 'even if the relevant information were contained only in a footnote.[3] There are also implications for the use of databases and data search engines and how the expression 'documents' is defined. Search engines and electronic databases might have been designed with internal management needs only in mind and may need to be redesigned with regard to the needs of transparency.

[1] Article 2(6).
[2] In particular, Art 4(2), first indent, and Art 4(3).
[3] Harden (2009) EPL 239.

Proposals for exceptions

PROTECTION OF THE ENVIRONMENT

3.104 Protection of 'the environment, such as breeding sites of rare species' would be added. There would be no possibility of an overriding public interest in disclosure.[1] This is consistent with the Aarhus Convention.[2] Further alignment of the Access Regulation and the Environmental Information Regulation would include emissions into the environment.

[1] As under Article 4(1). See Regulation 1367/2006 European Parliament and Council of 6 September 2006 and application of Åarhus Community institutions and bodies 2006 OJ L 264, p 13.

COURT PROCEEDINGS AND LEGAL ADVICE

3.105   To the existing exception covering court proceedings and legal advice in Art 4(2) would be added 'arbitration and dispute settlement proceedings'. The Commission propose this as a 'clarification'. Given that the European Ombudsman has ruled that the WTO dispute resolution1 is not covered by this exception, this has the appearance of a considerable extension, not clarification. In Turco, which preceded the Commission's proposalsm,² the ECJ reversed the ruling of the CFI. The Regulation imposes an obligation to disclose the opinions of the Council's legal service in connection with a law-making process, the ECJ ruled. This would include cases where the service had expressed doubts about a draft legislative instrument. The Commission argued if the service had subsequently to advise on the measure's legality this would place the service in an invidious position. The ECJ ruled unequivocally that such sensitivity could not justify an exception to openness within the Regulation. The Council should attend to any improper pressure on the service to influence its published advice. Sensitivity should not be an excuse for non-transparency.

¹   See Case 582/2005/PB: http://www.ombudsman.europa.eu/decision/en/050582.htm
²   Joined Cases C-39/05 P and C-52/05 P, *Turco v Council*, judgment of 1 July 2008.

INDIVIDUAL PRIVACY

3.106   The Commission proposed a change to the exception concerning privacy and integrity of the individual presently in Art 4(1)(b). This reform has been drafted very much with the ruling by the CFI in the Bavarian Lager case in mind, although we saw above how the ECJ quashed the CFI's ruling.¹ The proposal (a new Art 4(5)) seeks to allow the names, title and functions of public-office-holders, officials and private-interest representatives in relation to their professional activities to be disclosed. An exception would apply where, 'in the particular circumstances, disclosure would adversely affect those persons'. In addition:

> 'Other personal data shall be disclosed in accordance with the conditions regarding lawful processing of such data laid down in EC legislation on the protection of individuals with regard to the processing of personal data.'

This suggests that for 'other personal data' the Regulation on access would not be the governing provision; it should be Regulation 45/2001 on the regulation of personal data. The CFI in *Bavarian Lager* in fact decided the opposite: the access Regulation should be the governing provision.² The ECJ made no finding on priority; simply that Regulation 45/2001 had not been complied with as it should, and it may allow disclosure. In its judgment, the CFI emphasised that the Art 4(1)(b) exception only applies to data 'capable of actually and specifically undermining the protection of privacy and the integrity of the individual'. It does not apply to all personal data. The ECJ did not accept this.

¹   Case T-194/04, *Bavarian Lager v Commission* [2007] ECR II-4523.
²   See especially paragraphs 98–100 of the judgment.

DECISION-MAKING

3.107 The Commission proposed that the exception for the decision-making process should be widened by extending the range of papers protected to include 'all documents in that process'. This should be seen in the context of the narrowing of 'documents' that are covered by the amended Regulation (above) and the exclusion of documents forming part of the administrative file of an investigation or of proceedings concerning an act of individual scope. Taken together there would be a considerable extension of this exception.

MEMBER STATE DOCUMENTS

3.108 For multi level governance, the Commission proposes that a member state may give reasons to an institution for withholding documents based on exceptions in Reg 4(5) 'or on specific provisions in its own legislation preventing disclosure of the document concerned.' The 'adequacy of these reasons ... shall be appreciated by the institution ... insofar as they are based on exceptions laid down in this regulation'. The ECJ ruled in IPAW that while national laws may identify an interest deserving protection an exception cited by the institution had to be consistent with Reg 4.[1]

[1] Case C-64/05 P, *Sweden (IFAW) v Commission* [2007] ECR I-11389. See paras 83–84, 86 and 88.

MISCELLANEOUS

3.109 Proposals from the Commission on contract selection procedures seem to make it easier to refuse documents opening up decisions involved with awarding contracts. Amendments are proposed for staff selection procedures. Suggested amendments to copyright seem to confuse copyright and access protecting papers covered by copyright from access. The proposal requires clarification. It appears to treat copyright as a means of defeating access and not simply the unauthorised re-use of information. Re-use is covered by its own Directive (2003/98/EC).

OVERALL IMPACT

3.110 While some of the Commission's suggested reforms seek to reduce the overall administrative burden of access regimes and should be seen against a background of claims to inadequate resourcing for transparency and access, the Commission nonetheless emerges as very defensive. The European Parliament has rightly argued that if a right to access and transparency are given, their realisation should be adequately resourced. Many of the proposals possess a spirit of secrecy and 'Big Brother knows best'. This sits most uneasily with the plaudits for transparency accompanying the EU Constitution and ToL fanfares of recent memory. The approach is in marked contradiction to the Commission's

'European Transparency Initiative' and its 'drive towards more transparency' which was launched in November 2005 and which included a review of the Regulation.[1]

[1]   Minutes of the Commission's meeting No 1721 of 9 November 2005.

3.111   The sum result of the proposals is a risk of enhancing the opportunities for networked favouritism and the thwarting of a wider public involvement in administration. The Commission has consistently taken a less than positive approach to genuine transparency and access. The EP proposals for amendment to the Regulation are below. One proposal is that a statement that an inter-institutional register of lobbyists and interested parties is a 'natural tool for the promotion of openness and transparency' should be placed in the recitals to the Regulation. How has the EP sought to promote its view of openness and transparency and the public interest?

THE EUROPEAN PARLIAMENT'S PROPOSALS[1]

3.112   The EP debated the proposals for reform on 11 March 2009 following a report by a committee under Michael Cashman MEP.[2] The concern of the EP is far more consistent with the principles of transparency and openness than the Commission proposals. Information officers should be appointed to ensure compliance witin each Directorate General

[1]   See P Birkinshaw 'Transparency and Access to Documents' in P Birkinshaw and M Varney (eds) *The European Union Legal Order after Lisbon* (2010).
[2]   The Committee on Civil Liberties, Justice and Home Affairs 2008/0090(COD) (5 January 2009): http://www.europarl.europa.eu/sides/getDoc.do?pubRef=-//EP//NONSGML+COMPARL+ PE-415.164+02+DOC+PDF+V0//EN&language=EN.

3.113   A new recital 4 states:

'Transparency should also strengthen the principles of good administration in the EU institutions as provided for by Article 41 of the Charter of Fundamental Rights of the European Union ('the Charter'). Internal procedures should be defined accordingly and adequate financial and human resources should be made available to put the principle of openness into practice.'

The detailed proposals frequently diverge from the position of the Commission.[1] In March 2011, the Commission put forward more limited proposals to amend reg 1049 basically seeking to introduce the amendments introduced under TFEU, Art 15.[2]

[1]   For details, see http://www.europarl.europa.eu/sides/getDoc.do?type=TA&language=EN&refer ence=P6-TA-2009-0114#BKMD-16.
[2]   http://www.statewatch.org/news/2011/mar/eu-com-access-reg-1049-proposal.pdf. This the the site of Statewaytch which is very critical of the Commission's proposals, arguing that they do not address the question of transparency of the legislative process and Art 4(3) of the regulation (above).

THE COUNCIL OF EUROPE

3.114 The Committee of Ministers of the Council of Europe adopted a Recommendation of 25 November 1981 on access to information held by public authorities.[1] This reflects a degree of international agreement on the desirability of access to information, but it does not form part of our domestic law because it is not a part of the Convention incorporated into domestic law in October 2000. Furthermore, 'one or more of its principles' may be modified or excluded in the interests of 'good and efficient administration'. They are also subject to 'such limitations and restrictions as are necessary in a democratic society for the protection of legitimate public interests' (such as national security, public safety, public order, the economic well-being of the country, the prevention of crime, or for preventing the disclosure of information received in confidence) and for the protection of privacy and other legitimate private interests, having, however, 'due regard to the specific interest of an individual in information held by public authorities which concerns him personally'.[2]

[1] R(81)19. A further instrument is currently being drafted.
[2] R(81)19, Art V.

3.115 A new Recommendation (Rec(2002)2) on access to official documents was adopted by the Committee of Ministers on 21 February 2002, referring amongst other matters to the UN Convention of Access to Information and Recommendation No. R (2000) 13 on a European policy on access to archives. Article IX speaks of public authorities 'as far as possible' making information available by drawing up lists or registers of documents they hold.

3.116 in June 2009 a convention from the Council of Europe on access to official information was opened to signature.[1]

[1] Council of Europe Convention on Access to Official Documents Treaty Series 205 (18 June 2009).

3.117 The ECHR, which the UK has incorporated into domestic law, though not completely, by the HRA 1998 and which remains an international as well as a domestic legal obligation, also has relevant Articles: these are Art 2 on the right to life, Art 3 on the prohibition on torture and inhuman and degrading treatment, Art 6 (fair and public hearings), Art 8 (respect for private and family life) and Art 10 (freedom of expression), and are examined elsewhere (chs 1, 7 and 9).

Chapter 4

Local government as providers and keepers of information

INTRODUCTION

4.1 We saw in ch 2 that, until the Freedom of Information Act 2000 (FOIA 2000), many of the duties on central government to provide information to Parliament or the public were non-legal duties. For local government there has been an Access to Information Act since 1985[1] so the legal position is, ostensibly, significantly different. First, however, we have to indicate what is meant by local government. The following offers a brief outline.

[1] Local Government (Access to Information) Act 1985, effective from 1 April 1986. It is an amendment to the Local Government Act 1972 (LGA 1972), Sch 12A. See *Access to Information in Local Government* Office of the Deputy Prime Minister (September 2002).

4.2 In England the expression covers the county authorities, unitary authorities, district authorities and parish councils existing within some districts. Under the Local Government (Wales) Act 1994, Wales is divided into unitary authorities. London comprises the unitary boroughs both inner and outer.[1] The City of London is administered by a non-statutory corporation.[2]

[1] London Government Act 1963. The provisions of the 1963 Act were incorporated with slight modification in the LGA 1972.
[2] SH Bailey *Cross on Principles of Local Government Law* (3rd edn, 2004).

4.3 From 1 April 1986, the Greater London Council and metropolitan county authorities (there were six) were abolished by virtue of the Local Government Act 1985 (LGA 1985). The Act provided for the transfer of their functions to other authorities. Most of such functions went to London borough councils and metropolitan district councils. Part IV of the LGA 1985 provided for separate 'joint authorities' to be established to act as police, fire, civil defence and passenger transport authorities in the former metropolitan counties and as the fire and civil defence authority for London. Changes to the regime for fire services has been brought about by the Fire and Rescue Services Act 2004. A 'residuary body' was established by Part VII for each area to deal with residual affairs concerning abolished authorities. An Inner London Education Authority established under Part III of the LGA 1985 was abolished by the Education Reform Act 1988.[1]

[1]   Education Reform Act 1988, s 162. It had a non-statutory existence from 1965.

4.4   An authority for Greater London was re-established by the Greater London Authority Act 1999, and provision was made for the election of a mayor.

4.5   The areas of counties, districts, unitary authorities[1] and London boroughs are designated as 'principal areas' and their councils are known as 'principal councils' (PCs). Parishes and communities have parish and community meetings and they may have parish and community councils.

[1]   Local Government Act 1992, Part II.

4.6   Authorities have duties and powers assigned to them by public and private Acts of Parliament and by statutory instruments. They are also exhorted, cajoled, advised, etc by ministerial circulars, departmental rules and administrative communications. The relevant duties and powers will be dealt with on a subject-by-subject basis throughout the book. There is also an extensive network of quasi local authorities and private contractors who carry out functions on behalf of authorities. These functions are likely to be designated functions for the purposes of the FOIA 2000 bringing such contractors within the terms of the Act but the FOIA 2000 will only apply to such functions as are designated.[1]

[1]   See paras 1.86 et seq above.

4.7   Plans for the creation of regional assemblies or authorities in England were ultimately not carried through as they failed to be supported in the referendums in which they were put forward. The regional development agencies, which offered a degree of regional government focused in particular on economic development in the regions, are being phased out by the present government as part of the cuts to NDPBs. The local government legislation does provide for attendance at meetings of principal authorities, committees and sub-committees, as will be seen.

4.8   The Localism Bill (2010–2011) proposes some significant changes to local government in England. The proposed Sch 2 of the Bill makes some changes to the governance arrangements presently provided for in the Local Government Act 2000 (addressed in greater detail below where the changes are material). Significant changes are also proposed for the regime on standards, involving the abolition of much of the present regime; this is addressed in greater detail in ch 5. There are also measures which aim to deliver pay accountability in local government, allowing the Secretary of State to offer guidance to local authorities on appropriate levels of remuneration and requiring each local authority to produce a senior pay policy statement. The Bill also creates the ability (already included to an extent in the Local Government and Public Involvement in Health Act 2007 (LGPIHA 2007)) for local people to petition for a local referendum on a particular issue. There is further provision for local referendums where councils are seeking to secure an increase in council tax. The Bill is also notable for its plan to remove the ultra vires rule for local authorities, allowing far greater freedom of action than is presently permitted by the law. Chapter 4 of Part 4 of the Bill deals with assets of community value and requires a list of such assets to be produced and published. Changes are also proposed in relation to certain aspects of social housing provision, which are noted insofar as they are relevant to this work in ch 8. These changes are significant and will make changes to many area of the law that are examined by this book.

NEW MODEL EXECUTIVES FOR AUTHORITIES

4.9   In *Modern Local Government: In Touch With the People*,[1] the government set out its plans for modern local government and appropriate forms of councils for such authorities which were responsible for spending about a quarter of all public expenditure (in 1998, approximately £95–98 billion). Such councils were to be built on a 'culture of openness and ready accountability' (para 1.2). Pointing out the pathetically low turnout at local elections the paper believed that councillors did not sufficiently reflect their communities (only a quarter of councillors were women) and that the structures within which local authorities operated were the result of nineteenth-century legal philosophy. The committee structure was 'inefficient and opaque' with councillors spending 'too many hours on often fruitless meetings' (para 1.15). 'Above all, the committee system leads to the real decisions being taken elsewhere, behind closed doors, with little open, democratic scrutiny and where many councillors feel unable to influence events' (para 1.15). It set forth an agenda for change involving new organisational frameworks to run councils, the creation of opportunities for giving local people a greater say in the running of the council and its service provision – by establishing 'beacon councils', improving local services, reforming business rates, improving local financial accountability, capital finance and providing a new ethical framework. The subject of standards and organisation had been heavily influenced by the Nolan Committee on Standards report on local government.[2]

[1]   Cm 4014 (1998).
[2]   Cm 3702 (1997).

4.10   The question of organisation was taken forward in *Local Leadership: Local Choice* ('*Local Leadership*')[1] and has now found its way into the Local Government Act 2000 (LGA 2000).[2]

[1]   Cm 4298 (1999).
[2]   See SI 2000/2850, 2000/2851, 2000/2852, 2000/2853. For Wales, see SI 2001/2277 (W 167), 2007/397 (W 173) and SI 2002/802 (W 175), SI 2007/399. Note also the further changes and amendments to be brought about by the Local Government (Wales) Measure 2011.

4.11   The government sought to produce a regime of governance that would promote efficiency, transparency, accountability and high standards of conduct, enhance decision-making and be appropriate to local circumstances.[1] It was hoped the legal changes will provide strong leadership, powerful roles for *all* councillors and high standards of conduct. The way forward was for councils – which under new arrangements will remain single legal entities – to consult the local community on how they wish to be governed with referendums on whether there should be a directly elected mayor as in London. Detailed guidance on local consultation has been provided.[2] This referendum could be initiated by a petition of 5 per cent of the electorate or a proposal from the Council. Statutory guidance would provide details on content and timing of referenda and regulations would contain the rules of conduct for a referendum paying regard to the Neill report (Nolan's successor) on party political funding.[3] A majority decision in favour of change would be binding on the council. The government would be able to say what detailed proposal for a new form of local governance must be drawn up following a petition; how the proposal must reflect any intention or preferences of the petitioners; when the referendum should be held; and must ensure fair conduct. The detailed proposal when implemented will become the council's constitution.

[1]   LGA 2000, ss 11 and 12, and with reference to additional forms of executive.
[2]   Modern Local Government: Guidance on Enhancing Public Participation DETR (1998). The Local Government Act 2000 New Council Constitutions – Guidance Pack DETR (2000) has further guidance on Consultation Guidelines for English Local Authorities. See Local Authorities (Conduct of Referendums) (England) Regs 2004, SI 2004/226.
[3]   Cm 4057 (1998).

4.12   If the proposal is not supported, it cannot be implemented. The council could, after further consultation, move to another form of operating which does not involve a mayor. After a five-year moratorium a further referendum for a mayor would be possible. The government want the issue to be raised locally and it does not want councils to continue with traditional patterns of administration. If no referendum is put to the people, and no new form of organisation is put into effect (see below) the Secretary of State may direct a referendum within a specified period on a question determined by the Secretary of State. The present government has expressed disappointment with the limited uptake of new governance arrangements and particularly the small number of authorities that have moved to have an elected mayor, as only 12 elected mayors are presently in place.[1] It is suggested that the government will use powers in the Localism Bill, once passed (via the insertion of new ss 9N–9ND into the LGA 2000) to designate leaders of authorities in big cities as 'shadow mayors' once the Bill is passed and then to require a referendum to determine whether there should be a permanent move to an elected mayor at the time of the council elections in 2012.

[1]   DCLG (2011) *A Plain English Guide to the Localism Bill: Update*, p 8.

4.13   The three models of management presently in place are:
(1)   A directly elected mayor with a cabinet.
(2)   A cabinet with a leader.

(3)   A directly elected mayor and a council manager (restricted to Wales by LGPIHA 2007 and then repealed for Wales by the Local Government (Wales) Measure 2011.

The Localism Bill (2010–2011) proposes that these arrangements should remain the same, with only types (1) and (2) available in England.

4.14   These models presently in place seek to provide a 'clearly identified and separate executive to give leadership and clarity to decision-taking' and 'powerful roles for all councillors to ensure transparency and local accountability.'[1] Such forms of governance will provide for a separation of the executive and will be efficient, transparent, and accountable:

> 'All councillors will have powerful roles, acting together in the council, or as members of the executive or powerful overview and scrutiny committees. People will know who is responsible for decisions, and communities will have a clear focus for leadership. Decisions will be scrutinised in public, and those who take them and implement them will be called publicly to account for their performance.' (para 3.3)

[1]   *Local Leadership etc*, para 3.1.

4.15   *Consultative Drafts of proposed Guidance and Regulations on New Constitutions for Councils* were published in May 2000.[1] In England, the regime for changing executive arrangements was altered by the LGPIHA 2007, which introduced the new ss 33A–33I to the LGA 2000. These sections are broadly similar to those previously in place under the 2001 Regulations. The arrangements in Wales were provided for by the Local Authorities (Changing Executive Arrangements and Alternative Arrangements) (Wales) Regulations 2004, SI 2004/3158. These Regulations were repealed for Wales with some transitional provisions by the Local Government (Wales) Measure 2011, Part 3.

[1]   DETR, May 2000. See para 4.10, note 2 above.

4.16

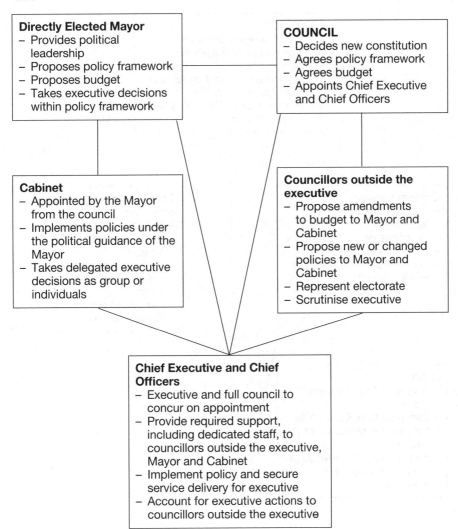

Figure 4.1 Directly elected mayor with cabinet

4.17

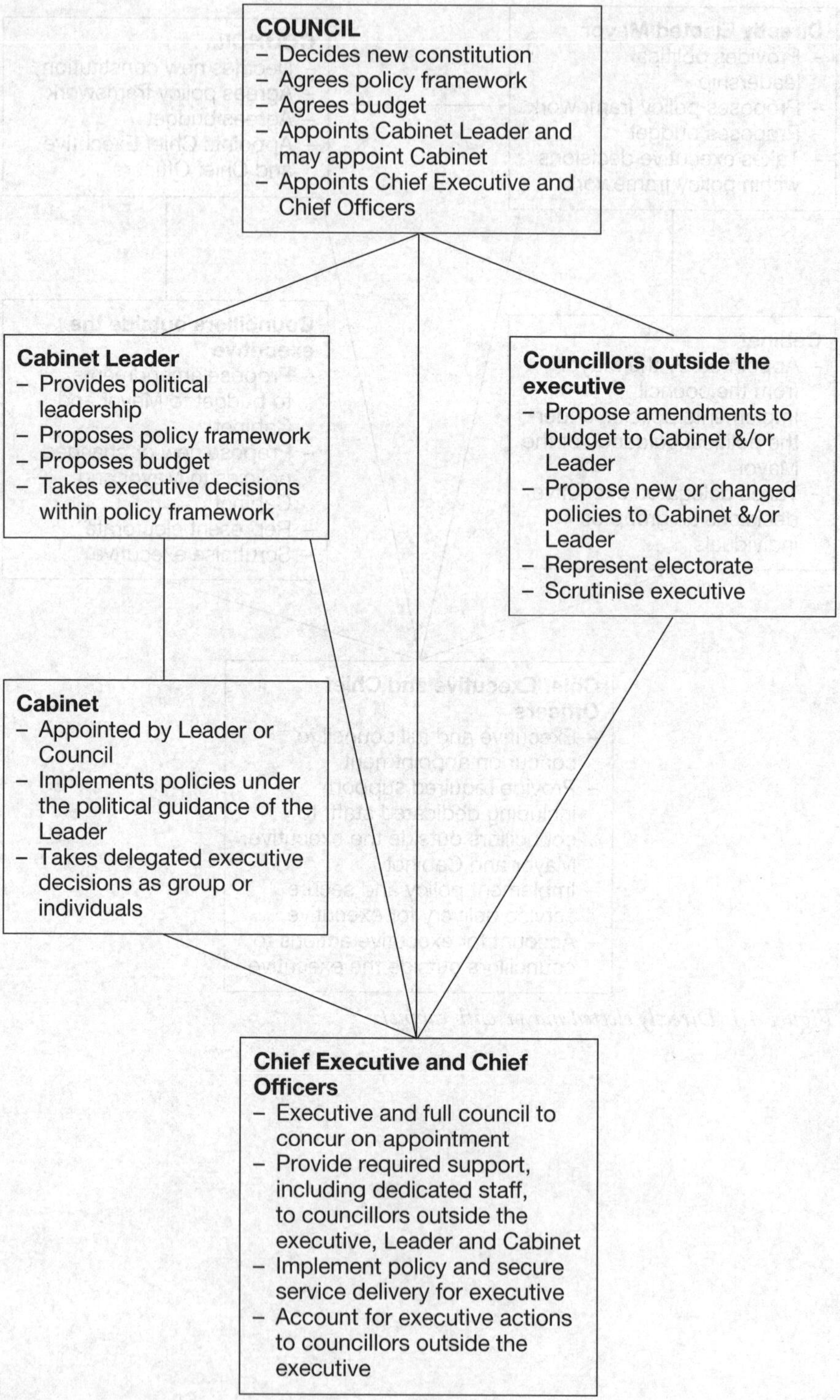

COUNCIL
– Decides new constitution
– Agrees policy framework
– Agrees budget
– Appoints Cabinet Leader and may appoint Cabinet
– Appoints Chief Executive and Chief Officers

Cabinet Leader
– Provides political leadership
– Proposes policy framework
– Proposes budget
– Takes executive decisions within policy framework

Councillors outside the executive
– Propose amendments to budget to Cabinet &/or Leader
– Propose new or changed policies to Cabinet &/or Leader
– Represent electorate
– Scrutinise executive

Cabinet
– Appointed by Leader or Council
– Implements policies under the political guidance of the Leader
– Takes delegated executive decisions as group or individuals

Chief Executive and Chief Officers
– Executive and full council to concur on appointment
– Provide required support, including dedicated staff, to councillors outside the executive, Leader and Cabinet
– Implement policy and secure service delivery for executive
– Account for executive actions to councillors outside the executive

Figure 4.2 Cabinet with a leader

4.18

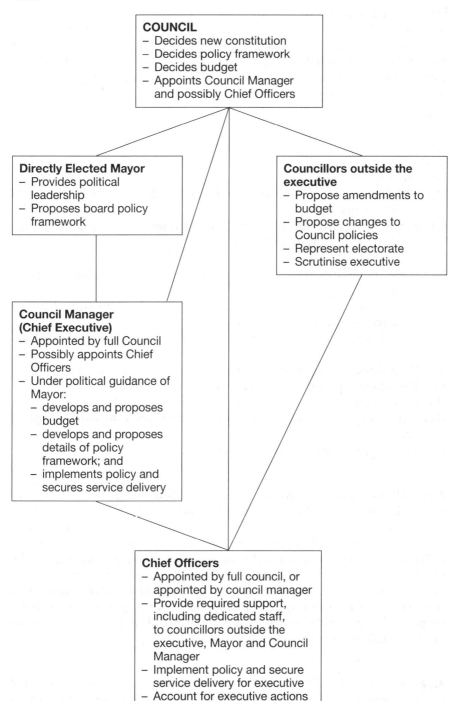

Figure 4.3 Directly elected mayor and council manager

4.19   The details on these points are contained in Part II of the LGA 2000 including the minutiae of executive functions and their discharge. They are supplemented by Regulations and guidance.[1] A resolution of an authority is required in order for the executive arrangements which must be available at principal offices for public inspection (LGA 2000, s 29). The usual provisions apply in terms of notices in two newspapers circulating in the area providing the details of arrangements.

[1]   See para 4.10, note 2 above.

4.20   Before adopting its new constitution, a council should address:
(1)   The model for its new constitution.
(2)   The functions of the executive and whether they should be subject to conditions and limits.
(3)   How the executive should be structured and which groups or individuals should have which responsibilities.
(4)   How the overview and scrutiny role should be structured.
(5)   What committees there should be for functions not discharged by the executive.
(6)   What standing orders there should be to define the relationship between executive and the rest of the council.
(7)   How changes to the new constitutional arrangements will be developed and agreed.
(8)   What should be the relationship between councillors and officers.
(9)   Who should appoint the chief executive and other officers.
(10) How appointments to other bodies should be determined.
(11) Direct support for mayoral or scrutiny functions from small groups of officers.
(12) Transitional arrangements and timetabling.

4.21   All councillors will agree or approve key plans and decisions. Regulatory responsibilities such as licensing and planning will not be functions of the executive but will be carried out by the full council or delegated to committees and other matters may be taken by the full council or delegated in accordance with a council's new constitution. A chair is elected from the councillors and by the full council and that person may not be a member of the executive, or the overview and scrutiny committee (see paras 4.123 et seq below). It is hoped that these arrangements will allow councillors more time to give direction to the council and local services such as local performance plans, fundamental reviews of best value or community safety.

4.22   All new forms of local governance must have one or more overview and scrutiny committees (OSCs): see LGA 2000, s 21 and Sch 1, para 7. They are to have the same political balance as the full council and will meet in public with the current rules on public access (see below ch 6) applying. Details on size, number etc would be for local choice. They would be required to cover all aspects of the executive's responsibilities. The constitution would provide for details such as co-opted members (non-voting) and chairs, and requesting a full debate in council before a decision is taken or implemented. Constitutions will be required to provide that OSCs would be:

(a) able to require members of the executive and officers to attend their meetings and to invite others to attend;

(b) required to meet and examine these people in public (current rules on access to apply);

(c) able to have all necessary support and information and training to discover what their local community wants and to represent them effectively; and

(d) required to ensure the Standing Orders protect minority interests on the committee to get their concerns onto the agenda.

4.23 The Local Government Act 2003 (LGA 2003) provides for voting rights for co-opted members of OSCs (LGA 2003, s 115). These have to comply with a published scheme. Under LGA 2003, s 116 local polls may be conducted to ascertain the views of those polled about any matter relating to services provided in pursuance of an authority's functions or expertise on such services including powers under LGA 2000, s 2. Details on polls are left to authorities subject to guidance.

4.24 The constitution will provide for the existence of other committees and sub-committees, membership, chair appointments, and role and responsibility. They are required to have the same political balance as the council and current rules on public access and conduct of business will apply. Social services committees are to be abolished. Councils will also be able to decide on area committees and neighbourhood forums.

4.25 The Localism Bill (2010–2011) retains OSCs and their functions in their present form with no radical changes. The functions and composition of OSCs in Wales will be altered by the full coming into force of the provisions of Part 6 of the Local Government (Wales) Measure 2011, although this does not appear to bring about significant changes to the operation of the present system.

4.26

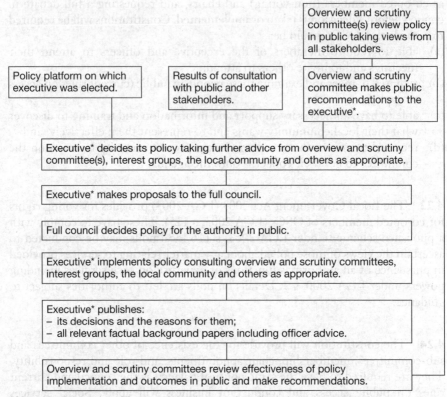

Policy platform on which executive was elected.

Results of consultation with public and other stakeholders.

Overview and scrutiny committee(s) review policy in public taking views from all stakeholders.

Overview and scrutiny committee makes public recommendations to the executive*.

Executive* decides its policy taking further advice from overview and scrutiny committee(s), interest groups, the local community and others as appropriate.

Executive* makes proposals to the full council.

Full council decides policy for the authority in public.

Executive* implements policy consulting overview and scrutiny committees, interest groups, the local community and others as appropriate.

Executive* publishes:
– its decisions and the reasons for them;
– all relevant factual background papers including officer advice.

Overview and scrutiny committees review effectiveness of policy implementation and outcomes in public and make recommendations.

* Mayor, another member of the executive or the executive collectively, as the case may be.

Figure 4.4 Policy formulation and implementation in a new constitution[1]

[1]   From the Local Government Bill Consultative Document, May 2000, p 11.

4.27 The executive should take the lead on all policy and strategy issues, including the budget, searching for best value and decisions on resources and priorities. It is the focus for forging links and partnerships outside the council. The expected size of executives is 15 per cent of the council or ten councillors, whichever is the smaller. They may be smaller but where there is a cabinet with a leader or elected mayor there should be at least three members. The constitution should set out membership but the executive does not usually reflect the political balance on the council. It will comprise majority or coalition members. Specific members would be given portfolios – this was the preferred option with the government because it 'speeds up decisions and clarifies responsibilities, improving accountability' (para 3.47). Decisions would either be taken by the whole cabinet, in sub-groups, as individuals or as combinations of these. In a cabinet with a leader, appointments would be made by either the leader or the council and in the latter case it would by majority vote decide the make-up of the cabinet under its constitution.

4.28 Formal co-option is not allowed, but a mayor could benefit from a political adviser paid for by the council in addition to those advisers serving the three largest groups. S/he could attend but not vote at executive meetings.

EXECUTIVE MEETINGS AND ACCESS TO INFORMATION

4.29 It is envisaged that 'at a minimum' any provisions on access to information will need to comply with the FOIA 2000 (ch 1). An executive must ensure that a record of all decisions taken, and the reasons for those decisions is produced, and that record, along with factual and background papers (excluding that information which is currently exempt under Sch 12A to the LGA 1972 (see ch 6) relating to those decisions must be made public. Once a decision is taken by an individual, the record of that decision and the reasons for the decision and additional items must be made public. The LGA 1972 (as amended by the Local Government (Access to Information) Act 1985 (LG(ATI)A 1985)) will continue to apply to meetings of the full council, committees and sub-committees including the overview and scrutiny committee (OSC). The same provisions on openness that apply to committees will apply to cases where the executive consults with an OSC. The OSC will also have the right to see, but not make public, any information relating to their responsibilities which would be exempt to the public by virtue of Sch 12A to the LGA 1972. Regulations spell out qualifications (see below). The OSC is under the provisions on access set out in the amended 1972 legislation and is also within the provisions of s 15 of the Local Government and Housing Act 1989 (LGHA 1989) (duty to allocate seats to political groups (see paras 4.113 et seq below). Political advice to the executive remains private. Meetings of the executive may be open to the public [or press] or private (see below and LGA 2000, s 22(1)).

4.30 The OSC would have the right to demand the attendance of the mayor or leader, along with members of the executive or council officers to answer questions or to contribute to a debate on policy with an implied right to call for papers from those parties (this latter right is not specifically mentioned in LGA 2000, s 21 but must be implicit in the power of effective scrutiny and was indeed provided for in regulations). The government was minded to make advice from officers public along with factual material. It realised that officers might be placed in a sensitive position when it was seen that their advice was not being followed and the regulations excluded access to their advice. Reports and background papers will be provided as explained below. The duty to create a record of decision and the reasons would lie on an officer when it is the decision of all or some of the executive. If made by an individual member of the executive, it is their responsibility to create the record and to make it available to the proper officer. The 1999 White Paper said the monitoring officer (MO) (see paras 4.101 et seq below) is under a duty to ensure it becomes publicly available as described below and failure to create or make it available is a criminal offence. 'Papers and records of decisions will subsequently be kept open for public scrutiny in the same way as those relating to non-executive decisions'. The OSC will also be able to ask for any additional factual information it requires to support its work. Effective discharge of its role requires 'regular and open dialogue' with the executive. No further provision on access may be required.[1] The full discussion and approval by the council of policy proposals and the budget will ensure openness! All officers will be accountable to the council in its overview and scrutiny role and may be called to give evidence to OSC. The council manager will have the right to attend and speak at all meetings of the authority except OSC. All officers will have to adapt to the new situation where consultation directly with local people and stake-holders will replace servicing and attending committees. The government believed that a veto power in the mayor over council or committee decisions 'could be appropriate'.[2]

[1] *Local Leadership*, para 3.65.
[2] Ibid, para 3.66.

4.31 In LGA 2000, s 22(1) meetings of the executive or its committees, joint committees and sub-committees of the latter may be held in public or private. The decision on openness is taken by the executive. This seems at first to cut across the thrust of the 1985 legislation on access but that legislation has been used as a basis for the regulations on openness and access (see chs 5 and 6 below). A written record must be kept of *prescribed* decisions made by executives and their committees held in private and by individual members which must include reasons for decisions. These records, together with 'such reports, background papers or other documents 'as may be prescribed' must be made available to the public in accordance with regulations made by the Secretary of State. The whole or any part of a document may be held back on specified grounds. The regulations may make provision as to the circumstances in which meetings are to be held in private in whole or in part; the information to be included in written records; on the reasons to be included; those responsible for the records; on the requirement that such records may be made available to members of authorities and to OSC; their availability by electronic means; to confer rights on members of the public, members of local authorities or OSC in relation to records or documents; and to create offences in respect of rights or 'requirements' under the section. Further Regulations may be made concerning access to joint committees or written records where held in private etc (see s 22(12)).

4.32 Regulations made under LGA 2000, s 22,[1] while containing rights for the public to see papers relating to forthcoming decisions, require executive meetings or part of meetings to be held in public when taking 'key decisions'. There are three further situations requiring public meetings. Meetings, or a part of a meeting, must also be held in public when a matter likely to be discussed at a meeting, or that part of a meeting, relates to a decision included in the current forward plan – a central feature of the new executive arrangements – (see regs 13 and 14 below) and where that decision is likely to be made at a meeting of the decision-making body within 28 days of the meeting. This will only apply where an officer is to be present at that meeting where the matter is discussed who is not a political adviser or assistant or council manager. Secondly, meetings etc must also be held in public where a matter relating to a key decision to be made by the decision-making body concerned is to be discussed with an officer present at that meeting or part of the meeting other than a political adviser or assistant. Thirdly, a public meeting must be held where a decision is made in relation to which a notice under reg 15 has been given. Regulation 15 concerns situations where the inclusion of a matter in a forward plan is impracticable and it relates to a key decision. In the case of the second and third grounds requiring public meetings, a 'meeting' does not include a meeting the principal purpose of which is for an officer to *brief* a decision-making body or members of a decision-making body on matters connected with the taking of an executive decision – ie when giving advice. 'Principal purpose' may be interpreted in the light of guidance issued by the Secretary of State. The requirement for a public meeting is subject to reg 21 concerning confidentiality and other matters (below). Meetings held in public must have reports, agendas and background papers published five clear days in advance.

¹ Local Authorities (Executive Arrangements) (Access to Information) (England) Regulations 2000, SI 2000/3272, amended by SI 2002/716 and SI 2006/72.

4.33 Key decisions are decisions which, in the opinion of the decision-taker, are likely to result in a local authority incurring expenditure which is, or the making of savings which are, significant having regard to the local authority's budget for the service or function to which the decision relates; or are likely to be significant in terms of its effects on communities living or working in an area comprising two or more wards or electoral divisions in the area of the local authority. In determining 'significant', regard shall be had to guidance issued by the Secretary of State (which does not seem to have been created since the coming into force of the Regulations). The intention may be good, but reg 8 bristles with subjective judgements. This does not prevent *discussion* of key decisions by executives in secret (a 'private meeting') where the officer is not in attendance or is offering advice. Executives will decide what is a key decision. Where it is not a key decision, or otherwise not within reg 7, the authority can meet in private and papers will not have to be available in advance. Key decisions may be delegated to individuals and only discussed at meetings and this will produce less publicity although reports on decisions taken by individual executive members must be publicly available in advance for at least three clear days before making a key decision. The member or officer shall ensure it is publicly available as soon as possible after the member or officer receives it. This is subject to confidential and other items in reg 21 (see para 4.38 below). Background papers for reports or part of reports must also be available in sufficient number.¹ In Standing Committee, the Minister stated that 'an executive may meet as a group of executive members, each of whom will have personal responsibility for an area of decision taking'.² If a decision is based on a *draft* report are these excluded from the publicity provisions? One would expect that a decision based on a *draft* report converts the report into a final report. The regulation states that 'report' does not include a draft report and 'document' does not include a draft document. Reports submitted to an individual executive member or officer with a view to it being considered when he makes a key decision must be sent by the person submitting the report to the Chair, or every member in the absence of the former, of a relevant OSC.

4.34   Executives must publish 'forward plans' with details of key decisions due to be taken in the coming four months (reg 13(2)) the documentation available about them, and the proposed consultation arrangements. A plan, other than the first, shall have effect from the first day of the second month for which the immediately preceding plan has effect – they are updated on a monthly basis. Regulation 14 concerns the contents of plans. These include the matter in respect of which the decision is to be taken, details of individual decision takers, dates or periods of decisions, all those to be consulted and the means of such consultation, steps and details to be taken by those who wish to make representations to the executive about decisions to be taken, and a list of documents submitted for consideration to the decision-taker but not those only available in draft form.

4.35   The taking of a 'key executive decision' must be preceded by the publication of a reg 12 notice. Regulation 12 provides for an instruction to be given to the proper officer (monitoring officer – para 4.101 below) to publish a notice of key decisions, that a forward plan with particulars of those decisions has been prepared, the period for which the forward plan is to have effect, that the plan may be inspected free of charge and at all reasonable hours at the authority's offices, that the plan contains a list of documents submitted to the decision takers for consideration in relation to the matters in respect of which decisions are to be taken, addresses from which copies of listed items are available, that other relevant documents may be submitted, procedures for requesting those documents (if any) as they become available, the dates in each month in the following 12 months on which each forward plan will be published and made available to the public at the local authority's offices. This must be published in one newspaper circulating in the authority's area not later than 14 days before the first day on which the forward plan is to have effect.

4.36   There is a general exception to this requirement in reg 15 – publication is 'impracticable' – but, subject to reg 16, no decision shall be taken until the decision-taker, either an individual or a chairman of a body, has informed the chair of a relevant OSC or each member thereof of the matter to which the decision is to be taken (reg 15(1)(a)). This must be by notice in writing. Furthermore, s/he must instruct the proper officer to make available at the offices of the authority for public inspection a copy of such notice (reg 15(1)(b)) which has been publicly available for five clear days (reg 15(1)(c), as amended). Regulation 16 concerns exceptions from reg 15 on grounds of urgency. In such cases the decision maker obtains the agreement of the chair of the OSC, the chair or vice-chair of the local authority in descending order of availability. Where a key decision has been taken and it was not treated by the decision maker as a key decision, the OSC may require a report to be submitted by the executive to the local authority within such time as specified. This must include details of the decision and reasons for it, the body or individual who made the decision, and reasons for the executive's opinion that it was not a key decision, provisions of regulation. The executive leader or appropriate person must submit a quarterly report on decisions taken under reg 16 in the preceding three months, the number of such decisions and a summary of their subject matter. Obstruction of rights of public access is an offence (reg 23).

4.37 In the final stages of the LGA Bill (24 July 2000) the government made it clear that executives would be open to the public when discussing 'key decisions' made by authorised individuals and not simply when making a collective decision. They will be open unless the public are excluded under reg 21(1), ie whenever it is likely that, if the public were present, confidential items would be disclosed to them in breach of the obligation of confidence. The definition of confidentiality is that available under the LG(ATI)A 1985. The public may be excluded by resolution from an executive meeting whenever it is likely, in view of the nature of the business to be transacted or the nature of the proceedings, that if members of the public were present during that item there would be disclosure to them of exempt information. This means information exempt under the 1985 Act (see paras 6.29 et seq below). The public may be excluded where advice is given by a political adviser/assistant. The public may also be excluded to maintain public order. Further provisions on resolutions, public notice ('five clear days', and see para 6.37 below) and public attendance and facilities for 'duly accredited members of the press' echo those in the 1985 legislation. These provisions also cover meetings of committees of executives.

4.38 Under SI 2000/3272, reg 3, the proper officer shall, as soon as reasonably practicable after a private meeting or a public meeting, produce a record of every decision taken at that meeting and, as respects each decision, a statement of (a) the record of the reasons for the decision; (b) any alternative options considered and rejected; (c) any conflict of interest declared by any member of the decision making body; and (d) any note of dispensation granted in respect of such a declaration. This should be compared with ss 35 and 36 of FOIA 2000 (paras 1.164 et seq above). Regulation 4 provides for similar rights to records of executive decisions of individuals. Regulations make provision for the inspection of documents after executive meetings of authorities and executives' committees, as well as inspection of background papers, additional rights of access to documents for members of local authorities which are similar to some of the provisions contained in the LG(ATI)A 1985 (see paras 5.88 and 6.3 et seq below). Nothing in the Regulations confers a right of access to confidential or exempt information or to 'advice provided by a political adviser' (reg 21). Where a copy of a report or part of a report accompanying agenda items at a meeting is withheld, the report shall be marked 'nor for publication' and a statement to that effect specifying that it contains confidential information, by reference to the descriptions in Sch 12A to the LGA 1972 (see paras 6.29 et seq below) the description of exempt information applicable to that report; or that the report contains advice of a political adviser or assistant. The public may be excluded from meetings on similar grounds as above by resolution which has to identify the part or parts of meetings from which the public are excluded. The public may be excluded to maintain public order. Records and reports must be publicly available for six years beginning on the date on which the decision relating to the record or report was made. Background documents are available for four years from the date of the meeting; any longer period is discretionary.

4.39 The additional rights of members to access covers 'any document, which is in the possession, or under the control of the executive of a local authority and contains material relating to any business to be transacted at a public meeting' other than a document which is in the form of a draft (see SI 2000/3272, reg 2).[1] Certain exemptions under Sch 12A to the 1972 Act are grounds for refusing access to documents and parts of documents; these are the same as under the rights of members for access to committee documents under the LG(ATI)A 1985, which amends the 1972 legislation (see ch 5). Rights to documents are also subject to this proviso and, in addition, where access by a member would involve disclosure of advice provided by a political adviser. The above rights are in addition to any other rights, eg common law, or under the LG(ATI)A 1985. Regulation 9 dealing with decisions of individual members of executives largely repeats these provisions. The original regulation provided that, where a record and statement prepared by an individual member does not fairly and accurately reflect the matters required to be recorded and stated, the proper officer shall prepare a record and statement of those matters, and destroy, or make arrangements for the destruction of, the record and statement prepared by the individual member. This was removed. The OSC and its sub-committees are given extensive powers of access to documents but not to documents available only in draft form. This access does not include exempt or confidential information 'unless that information is relevant to an action or decision that they are reviewing or scrutinising or to any review contained in its programme of work'. There will be interesting arguments as to 'relevance' as well as who has the final decision. No such qualification attaches to advice of political advisers so this is effectively excluded from OSC oversight (SI 2000/3272, reg 18).

[1]　For more detail see paras 5.100 et seq.

4.40 The Regulations add a new exemption: 'advice from political advisers'.[1] Although such advisers may participate in discussions of political groups, they can take no role in formal meetings. As the Campaign for Freedom of Information (FOI) states the point, 'by formally encouraging the involvement of political advisers – but allowing all traces of their advice to be deleted from the published record – the government may be undermining its own claim that the new arrangements will provide greater transparency and accountability than at present.'[2]

[1]　DETR 3 July 2000; SI 2000/3272, reg 7(3)(c) and see LGHA 1989, s 9.
[2]　Local Government Bill: Briefing for Report Stage, Campaign for FOI.

4.41 Regulations dealing with duties to publish information in a register of the name and address of every member of the executive and the ward or division they represent, as well as information about committee members and details of executive functions exercisable by individual members, were not included in the final regulations. SI 2000/3272, reg 22 covers details of publicity and provision for copying information. Details of offences of obstruction and failure to comply with these duties are contained in reg 23.

4.42   The 2000 Act also provides for new offences relating to the unauthorised disclosure of information which are very broad. Section 63(1) of the LGA 2000 permits ethical standards officers (ESOs) (see paras 4.131 et seq below) to disclose information for limited purposes. Under s 63(2) the Secretary of State or a local authority may serve a notice on an ESO stating that in their opinion disclosure of any specified information or class of information 'would be contrary to the public interest'. Unauthorised disclosure is an offence with a maximum punishment of two years in prison (s 63(4)). This does not appear to be limited to confidential information. It applies not only to ESOs once notice has been given, but to 'any person' who discloses the information regardless of how they obtained it. No harm or damage has to be established unlike the situation under the Official Secrets Act 1989 (OSA 1989) (see para 2.163 above). As the Campaign for FOI points out, government policy since the 1993 White Paper on *Open Government* is that new offences involving unauthorised disclosure of information should contain a specific test of harm. The offences appear to be without a defence. Under the OSA 1989, the defendant may establish a defence that he did not know and had no reasonable cause to know that the information was information to which the Act applied. As drafted, the prohibition undermines the disclosure provision in sub-s (1), ie information disclosed to the Standards Board, where it is publicly available, provided with consent to publish it or the disclosure is for the purpose of criminal proceedings.

LOCAL GOVERNMENT AND ADMINISTRATIVE PRACTICE ON ACCESS

4.43   In its White Paper of 1993, the government stated that local government would be covered by a code on access like central government. It is with local government that most people have regular contact in the UK, not central or even devolved government. In 1995 the government resiled from this position and left it to authorities to devise their own guidance on access. This was produced in June 1995 and basically advises authorities to have in place a policy on access to documents.[1] This is a weakening of the original concept of a central government code which in turn is a weakening of a statutory code. The FOI Campaign has been very critical of this development, arguing that such guidance produces only the weakest of frameworks to guide local authorities' actions on openness. The position of the local ombudsman may not be quite so limp. Where guidance exists as a recommended practice, failure to follow the guidance depends upon whether the guidance has been adopted. Where adopted and not followed this may amount to maladministration where no justifications are given for the departure. Even if not adopted the authority may still be asked to justify why they have not adopted such guidance in refusing a request for information and the manner in which they have refused access may well amount to maladministration. It should be added that legislation does exist on access to local authority committee and sub-committee documents, background papers and the law allows access to meetings by the public – a 'Government in the Sunshine' provision.[2] The Commission for Local Administration has produced its own guidance on 'Access to Information' (1997, revised March 2000) which deals with requests to the Commission for information. It is based on the government's revised code (ch 2). After 1 January 2005, the FOIA applies to *all* public authorities covered by the Act to allow individual access within its terms (ch 1).

[1]   AMA, ACC, ADC *Open Government – a Guidance Note* (June 1995).
[2]   LG(ATI)A 1985, an amendment to the LGA 1972.

Publication of information

4.44   There are duties upon principal councils in numerous statutes to publish information for the public. The Local Government (Inspection of Documents) (Summary of Rights) Order 1986 lists those enactments until May 1986 which conferred rights to attend meetings and to inspect, copy and be furnished with documents. The most important of these is the LGA 1972, as amended by the LG(ATI)A 1985, and which is described in detail in chs 5 and 6. The duties as updated are as follows, and must be available in written summary form at the offices of every council:

Enactment	Subject matter	Authorities outside London, in London, each borough
Commons Registration Act 1965, s 3(2) (NB Commons Act 2006 in force for some areas)	Register of common land	Counties and unitaries
Local Government Act 1972, s 60(2)(c), (4)(b), (5)(b) (Wales only)	Copies to Local Government Boundary Commission proposals, recommendations and amendments	Counties, metropolitan districts and unitaries
Local Government Act 1974, s 30(4)	Copies of reports of ombudsman	All authorities
Control of Pollution Act 1974, s 64(7)	Register of recorded noise levels in noise abatement zones (copies and fee)	Districts and unitaries
Local Land Charges Act 1975, s 8	Register of local land charges (prescribed fee)	Districts and unitaries
Noise Insulation Regulations 1975, SI 1975/1763, reg 6(3)	Map or list of buildings eligible for insulation works	Highway authorities

Enactment	Subject matter	Authorities outside London, in London, each borough
s 96(4)	Register of land held not currently in use (copies and fee)	All authorities
Sch 32, para 3(5)	Enterprise Zone Planning scheme (copies)	Districts and unitaries
Highways Act 1980, s 36(7)	List of highways maintainable at public expense	Counties, metropolitan districts and unitaries
s 37(5)	Certificates of highways dedicated to public use and magistrates' courts order to similar effect	Counties, metropolitan districts and unitaries
Wildlife and Countryside Act 1981, s 57(5)	Definitive map of public rights of way	Counties, metropolitan districts and unitaries
Sch 15, para 3(8)(a)	Documents which are taken into account in modification of definitive map (within notice period) (copies)	Counties, metropolitan districts and unitaries
Representation of the People Act 1983, s 89(1)	Returns of election expenses in local government elections (copies and fee)	Returning officers
Housing Act 1985, s 105(5) and (6)	Scheme of housing management including housing association schemes lodged with housing authorities	Districts and unitaries
s 106(2)–(5)	Allocation of rules and (for the applicant only) records of information supplied by the applicant	Districts and unitaries
s 414(3)	Copies of entries in register of common lodging houses	Districts and unitaries
Local Government Act 1988, s 12	Information as to external bids competing for functional work in competition with authorities direct l abour	'defined authorities'

Enactment	Subject matter	Authorities outside London, in London, each borough
Local Government Finance Act 1988, Sch 9	Property Rating Valuation List (Business Rates)	
Children Act 1989, s 17 and Sch 2	Information about services and assistance etc, under the Act	Counties, metropolitan districts and unitaries
s 71(1)	Register of child minders and premises	Counties, metropolitan districts and unitaries
s 83, as amended by Children Act 2004, s 54	research and returns on children	
Control of Pollution (Amendment) Act 1989, s 2(4)	Register of Waste Disposal Licences (copies and fees)	Counties and unitaries
Local Government and Housing Act 1989, s 92	Information regarding proposals, actions taken and available assistance for declared renewal areas	Counties, metropolitan districts and unitaries
Town and Country Planning Act 1990, s 69(5)	Register of planning applications and decisions	Districts and unitaries (or counties where national park)
s 188(3)	Registration of enforcement and stop notices	Districts and unitaries (or counties where national park)
s 198(4)(a)	Register of applications for consent to works under TPOs and decisions	Districts and unitaries (or counties where national park)
s 214	Register of notices of intention to carry out works to trees in conservation areas	Districts and unitaries (or counties where national park)
Planning (Listed Buildings and Conservation Areas) Act 1990, s 2(4)	List of buildings of special architectural or historic interest	Counties, metropolitan districts and unitaries
Environmental Protection Act 1990, s 20(7)	Register of information on integrated pollution and air pollution control	Counties, metropolitan districts and unitaries
s 64(6)	Register of information on waste recycling and disposal (copies and fee)	Counties, metropolitan districts and unitaries

Enactment	Subject matter	Authorities outside London, in London, each borough
Water Industry Act 1991, s 200(2)	Map of public sewers and drains	Districts and unitaries
Town and Country Planning (Control of Advertisement) Regulations 1992, SI 1992/666, reg 21(6)	Register of application for and decisions on, consent to display advertisements	Districts and unitaries
Town and Country Planning (Enforcement) (Inquiries Procedure) Rules 1992, SI 1992/1903, r 8(8)	Statements and documents prior to appeal against enforcement notice (copies where 'practicable')	All authorities
Clean Air Act 1993, s 38(5)	Registration of information on atmospheric pollution (copies and fee)	Districts and unitaries
Highways (Inquiries Procedure) Rules 1994, SI 1994/3263, r 6(7)	Statements of highway authority and documents prior to public enquiry (copies where practicable)	Highway authorities
Environment Act 1995, Sch 11	Exchange of information between authorities	Counties, unitaries and districts
	Public access to information about air quality	
Housing Act 1996, s 136(1)	Information regarding introductory tenancies and arrangements as to their management, etc	Districts and unitaries (and Housing Action Trusts)
Local Government (Publication of Staffing Information) (Wales) Regulations 1996, SI 1996/1899	Quarter staffing statistics	All Welsh authorities
Housing Act 1996, s 166(1)(a) (substituted by Homelessness Act 2002, s 15)	Copies of entries on housing register (relating to applicant only)	Districts and unitaries (and Housing Action Trusts)

Enactment	Subject matter	Authorities outside London, in London, each borough
s 168(2)	Information as to local housing authority's allocation scheme (copies and fee)	Districts and unitaries (and Housing Action Trusts)
Education (School Information) (England) Regulations 2008, SI 2008/3093, regs 8 and 9 (for Wales see SI 1999/1812)	Information as to maintained schools and admission arrangements (copies to parents of affected children)	Counties, metropolitan districts and unitaries
Audit Commission Act 1998, s 13(2)	Immediate reports made by the auditor (copies and fee)	Counties, metropolitan districts and unitaries
s 15(1)	Inspection of documents and questions at audit	Counties, metropolitan districts and unitaries
Town and Country Planning (Trees) Regulations 1999, SI 1999/1892, reg 3(3)	Register of TPOs and any modifications	Districts and unitaries
Town and Country Planning (Inquiries Procedure) (England) Rules 2000, SI 2000/1624, r 6(13)	Statements and documents referred to prior to public inquiry on planning appeal (copies available where practicable)	All authorities
Town and Country Planning Appeals (Determination by Inspectors) (Inquiries Procedure) (England) Rules 2000, SI 2000/1625, r 6(13)	Written submissions and documents (copies available where practicable)	All authorities
Housing Act 2004 s 232(4) and (5)	Register of licences for houses in multiple occupation and other properties subject to registration (copies and fee)	Local housing authorities

Enactment	Subject matter	Authorities outside London, in London, each borough
Town and Country Planning (Inquiries Procedure) (Wales) Rules 2003, SI 2003/1623, r 6(13)	Statements and documents referred to prior to public inquiry on planning appeal (copies available where practicable)	All authorities
Town and Country Planning Appeals (Determination by Inspectors) (Inquiries Procedure) (Wales) Rules 2000, SI 2003/1267, r 6(13)	Written submissions and documents (copies available where practicable)	All authorities
Childcare Act 2006, s 12 (s 27 in Wales)	Information to parents on the provision of childcare and other services relevant to parents	All authorities
Childcare Act 2006, s 13 (England only)	Information and advice to childcare providers	All authorities
Commons Act 2006, s 20 (NB the Commons Registration Act 1965 (above) is still in force for some areas)	Register of common land	Counties and districts
Local Government and Public Involvement in Health Act 2007, ss 35, 41 and 52	Explanatory document if change from partial council elections to full council elections or vice versa is proposed	Districts
Compulsory Purchase (Inquiries Procedure) Rules 2007, SI 2007/3617, r 7(4)	Acquiring authority's statement and documents prior to public enquiry	All authorities
Electricity Generating Stations and Overhead Lines (Inquiries Procedure) Rules 2007, SI 2007/841	Statements and documents of authority prior to enquiry into authority's objections to siting of generating stations, overhead cables and pipelines	All authorities

4.45   To the above duties must be added duties under the Local Government Acts 1999 and 2000, the Greater London Authority Act 1999, the Homelessness Act 2002, ss 3(9), 15 and 17, the Local Government Act 2003 and the Planning and Compulsory Purchase Act 2004.

4.46   The provisions relating to compulsory competitive tendering (CCT) in s 12 of the Local Government Act 1988 (LGA 1988) have been replaced by 'best value' duties and provisions under the Local Government Act 1999 (LGA 1999). Under LGA 1999, s 3 a best value authority (see ss 1 and 2) must make arrangements to secure improvement in the way in which its functions are exercised, having regard to a combination of economy, efficiency and effectiveness. Authorities have to consult various representative bodies to decide how to fulfil the duty arising under sub-s (1) and they must have regard to guidance issued by the Secretary of State on whom to consult and the form, content and timing of consultations. LGPIHA 2007 inserts a new s 3A into the LGA 2007, offering the potential for best value authorities to facilitate the involvement of representatives of local persons (or classes therof) in the exercise of best value functions. This might be done via the provision of information, consultation or the taking of other steps, offering a broad discretion over the steps to be taken to the authorities concerned. Police authorities are excluded from s 3A, and the Secretary of State can exempt other authorities by Order. Section 3A(5) provides that where guidance is issued by the Secretary of State, the authority must have regard to it. Guidance was issued in 2008.[1] The provisions in the Act which required authorities to draw up a best value plan and carry out best value reviews were repealed in England by LGPIHA 2007 and in Wales by the Local Government Measure 2009, removing what was a considerable obligation on authorities to publish information in this area. Best value activities remain subject to audit (described as a 'best value inspection' (BVI)), and the powers of inspection under the Audit Commission Act 1998 (ACA 1998) apply (see paras 4.64 et seq below). A copy of the auditor's report sent to the authority (it is also sent to other parties) may also be published by the auditor. The Audit Commission must also send a copy to the Secretary of State if there is a recommendation of a direction by the latter under s 15. Where the Audit Commission carry out an inspection under s 10 into an authority's compliance with the relevant duties, the inspector has a right of access at all reasonable times to any premises of the BVI concerned and to any document relating to the BVI which appears to him to be necessary for the purposes of inspection. He may require those holding or accountable for such documents to give him such information and explanation as he thinks necessary and he may require the person to attend before him in person to give the information or explanation or to produce the document. Failure to comply without reasonable excuse is a criminal offence. The inspector must give three days' notice of any requirement under this section and, if required, produce documents identifying himself. An inspection report shall be published by the Audit Commission.[2] Section 20 of the LGA 1999 adds best value authorities to those listed under s 2(1) of the Local Government Planning and Land Act 1980, which lists authorities subject to duties in codes to produce information.

---

[1]   DCLG (2008) *Creating Strong, Safe and Prosperous Communities: Statutory Guidance*, paras 2.12–2.27.

²   And see ACA 1998, s 51 on general powers of Audit Commission to publish information. See
LGA 2003, ss 107–108.

4.47   To encourage Public Private Partnerships LGA 2003 provides for
business improvement districts (BIDs), which have to be approved after a ballot
of non-domestic rate-payers in the proposed district (LGA 2003, Part 4).

4.48   Section 17 of and Sch 2 to the Children Act 1989 impose a duty upon
authorities to publish information about services and assistance etc for children
under that Act.

4.49   Under LGHA 1989, s 92 where local housing authorities have declared
an area to be a 'renewal area'[1] under Part VII of the Act, they must publish
information, from time to time, in such manner as appears to them best designed
to ensure that residents or owners of property in the area are informed:
(a)   of the action the authority is proposing to take;
(b)   of the action they have taken; and
(c)   what assistance is available for carrying out works in the area.

[1]   These replaced housing action areas and general improvement areas under Housing Act
1985, Part VIII. It covers an area of a local housing authority consisting primarily of housing
accommodation where the living conditions are unsatisfactory.

4.50   By s 95(4), notice of the resolution identifying the renewal area, describing
its effect, stating where it may be inspected 'at all reasonable times' etc, has to
be published in two or more newspapers circulating in the locality (one of which
being, where practicable, a local newspaper).[1] The renewal area replaces housing
action areas and general improvement areas.

[1]   See s 95(5) on further steps on publicity.

4.51   The duties contained in statutes and regulations concerning access to
personal information have not been included at this stage but are treated in detail
below (see ch 7).

4.52   As well as duties to the public, there are duties to the following bodies.

Central government

4.53   Again, there are numerous duties to provide central government, usually
a Secretary of State, with information, or in some instances duties to provide
information to government inspectorates.[1] To some extent, one might argue
that the amount of provisions requiring such information to be provided have
reduced in recent years, partly due to a desire on the part of central government to
reduce the burden on local authoriities (an example here is the revocation of the
requirement to maintain details of undeveloped land) or in some cases because
functions traditionally exercised by local authorities have been transferred to
central government agencies. Duties under LGA 1999 in relation to best value
were described above, as were duties under LGA 2000. Duties to provide

information to the Secretary of State include: financial returns to the Secretary of State;[2] information relating to education;[3] council-house sales;[4] slum clearance and redevelopment, housing conditions, housing action areas[5] as superseded by renewal areas;[6] housing revenue account subsidies;[7] trade descriptions;[8] child care;[9] regional strategies and development plans (paras 8.109 et seq below);[10] or, after a notice from the Secretary of State, to obtain information where s/he believes an authority has broken requirements as to competition. A more general duty is contained in s 230 of LGA 1972 (and see LGHA 1989, s 157(9)). Under LGA 1972, s 230:

> 'Every local authority, every joint board and every joint committee of local authorities shall send the Secretary of State such reports and returns, and give him such information with respect to their functions, as he may require or as may be required by either House of Parliament.'[11]

[1]   Eg Police Act 1996, s 54; Fire and Rescue Services Act 2004, s 28; Children and Young Persons Act 1933, s 103.
[2]   LGA 1972, s 168; see SI 1996/88, Art 6. See LGHA 1989, s 65.
[3]   Education Reform Act 1988, s 158 repealed in part; Education Act 1996, s 408.
[4]   Housing Act 1985, s 169.
[5]   Housing Act 1985, s 246.
[6]   LGHA 1989, Part VII.
[7]   LGHA 1989, s 85.
[8]   Trade Descriptions Act 1968, s 26(2).
[9]   Children Act 1989, s 83.
[10]   Planning and Compulsory Purchase Act 2004, Part II and Local Democracy, Economic Development and Construction Act 2009, s 78. Note that regional plans will be removed and the relevant provisions of the Local Democracy, Economic Development and Construction Act 2009 concerning the plans will be repealed if clauses 89–93 of the Localism Bill (2010–2011) come into force.
[11]   See: SI 1996/88, Art 7; SI 1996/1243, Art 11, Sch 7, para 9.

4.54   In spite of the ostensibly copious nature of this provision, local government legislation since 1980 is replete with duties to provide information which became more attuned to hedging in potential defaulters[1] under statutory duties. An example was the Local Government Finance Act 1988 which concerned the long-departed community charge/poll tax.[2] This was replaced by s 64 of the Local Government Finance Act 1992 (LGFA 1992) (and see also LGFA 1992, ss 28, 29 and LGA 2003, Part 6) and the LGA 1999 which sought to improve relations between central and local government in relation to capping powers over local government, powers which produced various *causes célèbres* in litigation in the early 1990s. It is worth quoting in full. This concerns the amount calculated by the authority for its budget requirement (see also LGFA 1992, ss 38 and 52). Under the relevant provisions, authorities have to calculate budget requirements for a financial year. Where this is believed by the Secretary of State (or National Assembly in Wales – s 52Z) to be excessive he may designate (cap) or nominate (warn) the authority for producing an excessive budget requirement. This involves copious procedures which may lead to the authority being capped and having financial targets set.

[1]   Eg Rates Act 1984, s 8.
[2]   Local Government Finance Act 1988, s 72.

4.55 LGFA 1992, s 52Y(1): 'An authority shall notify the Secretary of State in writing of any amount calculated by it as its budget requirement for a financial year, whether originally or by way of substitute.'

4.56 LGFA 1992, s 52Y(2) and (3) deal with notification of aggregate amounts for any financial year of any precepts and time-limits for making notifications.

'(4) The Secretary of State may serve on a charging authority or precepting authority a notice requiring it to supply to him such information as is specified in the notice and required by him for the purpose of deciding whether to exercise his powers, and how to perform his functions, under this Chapter ie to limit council taxes and precepts.

(5) The authority shall supply the information required if it is in its possession or control, and shall do so in such form and manner, and at such time, as the Secretary of State specifies in the notice.

(7) If an authority fails to comply with subsection (2) above the Secretary of State may assume the information required to be such as he sees fit if he informs the authority concerned of his intention to make the assumption; and in such a case he may decide in accordance with the assumption whether to exercise his powers, and how to perform his functions, under this Part.

(8) In deciding whether to exercise his powers, and how to perform his functions, under this Part the Secretary of State may also take into account any other information available to him, whatever its source and whether or not obtained under a provision contained in or made under this or any other Act.'

4.57 Where information – not being personal information (see sub-s (6)) – is requested in a notice on an authority or relevant officer and is required by the Secretary of State to decide whether to exercise relevant powers under this Part of the Act and not just designating, then ,where the information is not supplied, the Secretary of State may by s 68(3) simply make assumptions about the information required and the authority and, on those assumptions, decide how to act.

4.58 Under LGFA 1992, s 68(2) the authority shall supply the information required, and shall do so in such form and manner, and at such time, as the Secretary of State specifies in the notice.

4.59 Under s 68, the Secretary of State may act on any assumptions and estimates s/he deems fit where the authority fails or refuses to supply information. The rate-capping 'saga' in 1985 offers interesting analogies,[1] and the provisions were tested in the House of Lords.[2]

[1] See Grant *Rate Capping and the Law*.
[2] *R v Secretary of State for the Environment, ex p Hammersmith and Fulham London Borough Council* [1990] 3 All ER 589, CA.

4.60 Authorities designated for capping under the Rates Act 1984 wanted the Secretary of State to disclose the assumptions which formed the basis of his determination of their proposed maximum rate or precept. The High Court refused to award discovery against him for the production of documents relating to his assessment of the proposed maximum for ILEA, as the 'relevant' material was before the court.[1] Were that not so, the court 'would not necessarily have upheld the Secretary of State's alternative defence on grounds of public interest'. The Court of Appeal upheld this decision, adding that there was no valid ground for arguing that the production of the documents would advance the applicant's case 'which had to be directed to the objective reasonableness of what the Secretary of State had done, not to a subjective examination of why he had done it'.[2]

[1]   *R v Secretary of State for the Environment, ex p Greater London Council and Inner London Education Authority* (26 February 1985, unreported).
[2]   (1 March 1985, unreported).

4.61 When leave to apply for judicial review was awarded in April 1990 to the Labour-controlled authorities which had been charge-capped, discovery of documents relating to the Secretary of State's decision was not allowed. However, an undertaking was given by the Secretary of State that he would volunteer relevant information. The authorities argued that they had a right to have disclosed to them 'any information which he intends to take into account received from a source other than the authority in question and of which the authority might not be aware':

> 'Finally, it was submitted for the appellant authorities that the Secretary of State is under a legal obligation before submitting a draft order for approval by the House of Commons under s 110 to disclose to the authority affected any information which he intends to take into account received from a source other than the authority in question and of which the authority might not be aware. Both courts below accepted the view that the requirements of fair procedure imposed such an obligation, but the court of appeal rejected the complaint … that there had been any breach of obligation. The position taken on behalf of the Secretary of State in relation to this submission was that it was the practice to inform an authority of any factual information on which the Secretary of State proposed to act which contradicted the case put forward by the authority, but that the reason for this practice was simply to ensure so far as possible that the information on which the Secretary of State proposed to act was accurate. It was not accepted that there was any legal obligation in the matter … To read into the statute a legal obligation on the Secretary of State to disclose to an authority challenging his proposed cap all relevant information before him and then to give the authority the opportunity to comment on or counter that information … would introduce such delays into a procedure which is meant to operate with the greatest expedition and I cannot believe that this is what Parliament intended.'

4.62 The matter should be resolved by 'sound administrative practice' and not 'nice legal definitions' in this non-adversarial process.[1]

[1]   Lord Bridge at [1990] 3 All ER 589, 639f.

4.63 These are some of the major provisions concerning the duties to provide information to central government. Other duties fall under legislation on eg capital finance (borrowing) under LGA 2003, s 14. Further areas which relate to complaint, appeal etc to the Secretary of State – and in which provision of information is ancillary – are examined in ch 9.

The Audit Commission and the auditor

4.64 The provisions relating to the Audit Commission and audit are to be found in ACA 1998, which consolidated the extensively amended LGFA 1982, Part III, which in turn re-enacted, with some amendments, the audit provisions of Part VIII of LGA 1972. The LGFA 1982 also established the Audit Commission which is appointed by the Secretary of State. The accounts of local authorities are not audited by the Comptroller and Auditor-General under the National Audit Act 1983 (see ch 11).

4.65 The accounts subject to audit are specified in ACA 1998, s 2 and Sch 2 and include health bodies listed in para 1 of Schedule 15 to the National Health Service Act 2006 (NHSA 2006). The Commission appoints auditors to audit the accounts of any body whose accounts are required to be audited. Codes of Practice are prepared and kept under review by the Commission.[1] These Codes prescribe the way in which auditors are to carry out their functions under the Act. Codes, which represent best professional practice, have to be approved by both Houses of Parliament at five-yearly intervals and are read in conjunction with relevant regulations under ACA 1998, s 27.

[1]   For local government, see Audit Commission: *Code of Audit Practice: Local Government Bodies*, March 2010; see also Code of Practice Annex. NHS bodies are covered by Audit Commission: *Code of Audit Practice: Local NHS Bodies*, March 2010. See SI 2011/817 (England) and 2005/368 (Wales), and SI 1997/2747.

4.66 Under ACA 1998, s 6, an auditor has the right of access at all reasonable times to all such documents relating to a body whose accounts are required to be audited under the Act and which appear to the auditor to be necessary for the purposes of his functions under the Act. S/he shall be entitled to require from any person holding or accountable for any such document such information and explanation as s/he thinks necessary for those purposes. If s/he thinks it necessary, s/he may require any such person to attend before the auditor in person to give the information or explanation or to produce any such document. S/he may require any officer or member of a body whose accounts are to be audited to give such information or explanation as s/he thinks necessary for the purposes of the audit and, again if s/he thinks necessary to require any such officer or member to attend before the auditor in person to give the information or explanation (s 6(4)). The body audited must provide the auditor with every facility and all information which s/he may reasonably require for the purposes of the audit. Failure to comply without reasonable excuse is a punishable offence (s 6(6)). Section 6 of the ACA 1998 was added to and revised significantly by the

LGPIHA 2007. The major additions are s(6)1A, which makes it clear that that auditors' right of access to a document includes the right to inspect, take away or copy the document concerned. Section 6(4A)–(4C) are also added, and concern enhanced rights to receive and inspect copies of electronic documents and the computer equipment on which such documents are stored.

4.67 Under earlier similar provisions, it was clearly settled that the auditor's powers were not restricted to officers or documents of the authority; contractors and their documents were included.[1] Oaths are rarely considered necessary and decisions on the auditor's inability to take evidence upon oath under previous legislation would no longer appear to be conclusive as earlier legislation did not confer a power to 'hear, receive and examine evidence'.[2]

[1]   *Re Hurle-Hobbs Decision* [1944] 2 All ER 261, CA; *R v Hurle-Hobbs, ex p Simmons* [1945] KB 165. On the former LGFA 1982, s 20, see *Porter v Magill* [2002] 1 All ER 465 (HL).
[2]   Evidence Act 1851, s 16; *R v Roberts* [1908] 1 KB 407 at 419, 439, CA. See Lords Keith and Templeman in *Lloyd v McMahon* [1987] AC 625 at 697E and 716G–H, HL.

4.68 Changes between s 6(1) and (2) and previous legislation[1] 'appear to be intended to make clear that the auditor's powers are not restricted to being tied too closely to the accounts. There is an overall limitation to the purposes of the audit, but this includes such questions as the effectiveness of the use of resources[2] in respect of which it may not be possible to point to a specific item in the accounts'.

[1]   LGA 1972, s 158(1).
[2]   On the former s 15(1)(c). R Jones *Current Law Statutes Annotated* (1982) ch 32, p 20.

4.69 The new provisions apply to officers and members whether or not they possess or are accountable for documents. Section 6(3) of the Act was repealed by LGPIHA 2007 and was replaced by the insertion of more detailed provisions on access to computerised information in s 6(4A)–(4C) as noted above. Section 6(4A) empowers the auditor to require that a computerised document is produced in a legible from that can be taken away. Section 6(4B) permits the auditor to inspect computer equipment on which documents have been created and to require the assistance of the users of such computer equipment.

4.70 Under s 20 of ACA 1998 (as enacted), an auditor had the power to issue a prohibition order if s/he believes the body or an officer is about to make or has made a decision which involves unlawful expenditure, unlawful action likely to cause loss or deficiency, or is about to enter an unlawful item of account. Sections 21–23 qualify and set out additional features in relation to the power to issue a prohibition order. The power to issue a prohibition order has been removed by LGA 2000 and replaced with an advisory notice allowing the auditor to ventilate his concerns on the grounds that an item of account is contrary to law, but leaving it to the courts to take necessary action. LGA 2000, s 91 adds a new s 19A to ACA 1998 and ss 20–23 are repealed. ACA 1998, s 19B sets out the effects of advisory notices.[1]

[1]   And note their effects on contracts and third parties under ACA 1998, s 19C.

4.71   Rights for electors etc to inspect the auditor's report, and other rights, are dealt with elsewhere (see paras 8.17 et seq below).

4.72   The Audit Commission is under a duty to carry out its own, or to promote, comparative studies to enable it to make recommendations for improving the economy, efficiency and effectiveness of authority services and financial or other management (s 33) and/or the impact of statutory provisions or directions or guidance given by a minister of the Crown on economy, efficiency and effectiveness in the provision of services or on financial management (s 34). Reports are published. This does not apply to health service bodies.[1] The Commission may assist the Secretary of State in studies related to housing benefit administration and registered providers of social housing. The Commission may require any body, or officer or member of such, whose accounts are required to be audited, to make available for inspection by the Commission or any person authorised by it documents which relate to the authority and which are needed for the purposes of the study. The authority shall make the documents available.[2] Section 37 previously contained provisions for the Commission to become involved in the production of reports in relation to health, social care and a number of other matters including prisons, police and probation through the provision of assistance to the relevant regulator or inspectorate. Section 37 was repealed by LGPIHA 2007.

[1]   See the Health and Social Care Act 2008, which creates the Care Quality Commission (CQC). Chapter 5 of Part I of the Act provides that the CQC may engage in studies into the economy, effectiveness and efficiency of services covered by the Act. Section 55 of the Act requires that the findings and recommendations in these reports must be published. Section 56 of the Act sets out the role of the Audit Commission in any studies – the CQC may act jointly with the Audit Commission, or may request that the Audit Commission carries out a study on its behalf. Sections 62–65 of the Act cover powers of entry, inspection of documents and the power to require explanations of documents. Sections 76–80 cover the use of personal information, including an offence of disclosure of personal information by CQC employees and a range of defences and permitted disclosures and uses of information.

[2]   ACA 1998, s 38(4).

4.73   The Commission may require any such body, or its officers or members, whose accounts are audited under the Act to make available for inspection by or on behalf of the Commission the accounts concerned and such other documents relating to the body as might reasonably be required by the Commission or that person for the functions under the Act or for the purposes of any study under s 33 or 34.[1] This is to assist the Commission in maintaining proper standards in the auditing of accounts. Under s 48(4) penalties are imposed on 'persons' for failure to comply with a requirement under sub-s (1)(b). The Commission may require the body to make available for inspection by or on behalf of the Commission, in order to assist the Commission to maintain proper standards in the auditing of the accounts of a body subject to audit, the accounts concerned and 'such other documents relating to the body as might reasonably be requested by an auditor for the purpose of the audit'.

[1]   ACA 1998, s 48(1).

4.74   Information received by the Commission or auditor for purposes under the Act or audit or a study shall not be disclosed – on pain of imprisonment or fine or both – except: with the consent of the body or person to whom the information relates; for the Commission's or auditor's functions etc under the Act; or for the purposes of criminal proceedings.[1] New sections 49(2C) and 49ZA have been added by the LGPIHA 2007, which provide for disclosure under FOIA 2000 in appropriate circumstances. Specific provisions apply to health service bodies and the functions of the Secretary of State, Comptroller and Auditor General or Care Quality Commission under NHSA 2006.

[1]   ACA 1998, s 49 and see *Bookbinder v Tebbit (No 2)* [1992] 1 WLR 217. Note also s 50 on supply of housing benefit information to the Commission by the Secretary of State.

4.75   LGA 2003, Part 8 places the Audit Commission's Comprehensive Performance Assessment on a statutory basis and his reports are now published by virtue of the Act (LGA 2003, s 99).

4.76   It must be noted at this point that there are proposals to abolish the Audit Commission and transfer its functions to other bodies or to the private sector. In March 2011 the DCLG produced a consultation paper.[1] In the paper, the government suggests that the Audit Commission has grown too large and its audits and other reporting functions are too focused on providing information to central government, rather than on the localism agenda that is being pursued, inter alia by the Localism Bill. It is proposed that for all bodies presently covered by the ACA 1998 with a turnover greater than £6.5m independent auditors will need to be appointed from the private sector. In local government, this should be done by the full council. It is also recommended that each local authority should look to create an audit committee (some have this in place already) which should be involved in the oversight of the council's audit function. It is acknowledged that many other bodies covered by the ACA 1998 already have some kind of audit committee, which could work with the appointed auditor to secure effective financial oversight. The paper proposes to retain the power of the auditor to make reports in the public interest and other relevant disclosures where this is felt to be necessary. The National Audit Office (NAO) will take over the Audit Commission's role in producing guidance on audit for the bodies concerned. For bodies with income and expenditure below £6.5m it is proposed that the requirement for audit be removed and replaced with a process of light-touch inspection. This regime applies already to certain bodies with income and expenditure of less than £1m.

[1]   DCLG (2011) *Future of Local Public Audit: Consultation.*

4.77   The Audit Commission has produced a document in response to the proposals in which it outlines some concerns over the proposals.[1] In particular, it argues that the NAO's role in creating guidance for local audit which is then interpreted by the private firms undertaking the audit could lead to considerable fragmentation in the system. The paper also casts some doubt that the reforms will deliver significant savings and suggests that it is possible that the independence of the audit process may be reduced as firms become increasingly reliant on the income from local audits. The government has not yet responded to consultation responses. It is anticipated that legislative proposals might be brought forward late in 2011.

[1]   Audit Commission (2011) *Future of Local Public Audit.*

Public Audit (Wales) Act 2004

4.78   Under this Act, new functions are conferred on the Auditor General for Wales. Most significantly, the Auditor General will exercise most of the functions currently exercised in Wales by the Audit Commission for Local Authorities and the National Health Service in England and Wales. The result is a single public audit body for Wales, headed by the Auditor General. It is intended that the Auditor General and his staff will be known collectively as 'the Wales Audit Office' in English and 'y Swyddfa Archwilio Cymru' in Welsh. The Wales Audit Office will be responsible for the financial and performance audit of the Assembly; its sponsored bodies and a number of other publicly funded bodies; health bodies (primarily NHS Trusts and Local Health Boards) and local government bodies in Wales. Provisions aimed at safeguarding the constitutional independence and democratic accountability of local government in Wales are also included. The Act possesses powers for cooperation for cross-border purposes.

4.79   Part 2 of the Act relates to the arrangements for auditing the accounts of local government bodies in Wales; carrying out studies into the way in which they exercise their functions, provide services or are managed; and ensuring that information about their performance is published. Schedule 1 amends, in relation to Wales, the best value regime set out in the Local Government Act 1999. The classes of bodies comprising local government bodies in Wales are set out in s 12. Chapter 1 of Part 2 of the Act largely comprises equivalent provisions to those in Part 1 of the Audit Commission Act 1998 and, before that, in the Local Government Finance Act 1982. Responsibility for making the arrangements just referred to, in respect of Wales, is transferred from the Audit Commission to the Auditor General. According to the explanatory notes: 'It does so in a way that is intended to acknowledge and preserve local government democratic accountability'.

4.80   There are duties of cooperation between the Auditor General and the Audit Commission (primarily in s 43), and numerous provisions on access to and publication of information (particularly in Chapter 4 of Part 2).

Part VIII of the Local Government Finance Act 1988

4.81   We have seen above how individual officers[1] have been placed under greater and more specific duties to provide information to central government. It is worth highlighting the Local Government Finance Act 1988 (LGFA 1988).

[1]   Eg under Housing Act 1988, s 90.

4.82   Part VIII of this Act makes provision for financial administration of local authorities[1] and combined police authorities and combined fire and rescue authorities.[2] The most salient feature is the strengthening (or underlining) of the functions of the chief finance officer – the 'responsible officer'.

[1]   For which see LGFA 1988, s 111. See also eg Serious Organised Crime and Police Act 2005, s 20.
[2]   LGFA 1988, s 112.

4.83　The responsible officer must, after the coming into effect of the relevant Part of the Act (29 September 1988), hold certain professional qualification requirements (unless in office immediately before that date).

4.84　Under LGFA 1988, s 114, the responsible officer must make a public report in specified cases of actual or anticipated financial misconduct. In relation to local authorities operating executive arrangements, the provisions of s 114A are also relevant. This duty should be read in conjunction with the power of the auditor to issue advisory notices under LGA 2000 (see above). This provision grew out of the notorious cases of the audit, surcharge and disqualification involving councillors of rate-capped authorities, and the 'creative accounting'[1] techniques of other authorities as well as capped ones to 'minimise the short-term effect of' income limitation.[2] The government was convinced such devices were storing up long-term problems for such authorities' finances.[3] In *Lloyd v McMahon*,[4] the Court of Appeal criticised members of two authorities who had acted 'with blatant recklessness in disregarding the principal officer's advice'.[5] However, were that officer simply to toe a council line, or that of a ruling party, that would probably involve a breach of duty to the council and ratepayers.[6]

[1]　Involving new methods of budgeting, transferring money between funds and across financial years, etc.
[2]　Grant *Current Law Statutes Annotated* (1988) vol 3, ch 41, p 151.
[3]　Cmnd 9714 (1986) paras 7.15–25.
[4]　[1987] 1 All ER 1118 (CA and HL).
[5]　Per Dillon and Woolf LJJ.
[6]　For a brief history of the treasurer in local government see Grant *Current Law Statutes Annotated* (1988) vol 3.

4.85　The responsible officer shall make a report if it appears to him/her that the authority etc:
(a)　has made or is about to make a decision which involves or would involve the authority incurring expenditure which is unlawful;
(b)　has taken or is about to take a course of action which, if pursued to its conclusion, would be unlawful and likely to cause a loss or deficiency on the part of the authority; or
(c)　is about to enter an item of account, the entry of which is unlawful.

4.86　The government believed this formula 'requires the chief finance officer only to concern himself with the lawfulness of a course of action and the likelihood that it will cause the authority to incur a loss, and not with the intentions or state of mind of those responsible'.[1]

[1]　Lord Hesketh 498 Official Report (5th Series) HL col 196 (14 June 1988).

4.87　Under LGFA 1988, s 114(3) the responsible officer shall make a report under this section if it appears to him that the expenditure of the authority incurred (including expenditure it proposes to incur) in a financial year is likely to exceed the resources (including sums borrowed) available to it to meet that expenditure. This is especially relevant given the authority's duty to budget under s 95. Where such a report is made it shall be sent to the person who has the duty at the time to audit the authority's accounts; and to every member of the authority (s 114(4)). The authority's head of service and monitoring officer shall be consulted as far as reasonably practicable in preparing the report (LGHA 1989, Sch 5, para 66; for Wales, see SI 2001/2281 (W 171)).

4.88   Section 114(5) provides that the duties under sub-ss (2) and (3) are to be performed by the responsible officer personally. Where unable to act because of absence or illness, the duties under sub-ss (2) and (3) shall be performed in accordance with sub-s (6) by properly qualified subordinates. By sub-s (7) a relevant authority shall provide its chief finance officer with such staff, accommodation and other resources as are, in the officer's opinion, sufficient to allow his or her duties under this section to be performed.

4.89   Where copies of a report are sent as above, the authority shall consider the report at a meeting where it shall decide whether it agrees or disagrees with the views contained in the report and what action (if any) it proposes to take in consequence of it (s 115(2)). This meeting must be held not later than the end of the period of 21 days, beginning with the day on which copies of the report are sent, and the meeting must be of the council, not a committee or sub-committee or officers.[1] During the 'prohibition period' the course of conduct which led to a report under s 114(2), or any agreements leading to a report under s 114(3), shall not be pursued or entered into respectively. If these sections are not complied with, any payment or contract will be considered ultra vires,[2] although the consequences for third parties are not spelt out. LGA 2003, s 30 introduced some flexibility into s 115 by allowing the chief finance officer to authorise the entering into an agreement to improve the situation or prevent it deteriorating or recurring. His authorisation must be in writing and be accompanied by the CFO's explanations.

[1]   Cf LGA 1972, s 101; LGFA 1988, s 115(3).
[2]   LGFA 1988, s 115(7) and (8). The authority is taken not to have had the power to make the payment or enter into the agreement. This, it is submitted, relates to the vires of a public body rather than to private law capacity. Presumably, the contract etc will be unenforceable. See the Local Government (Contracts) Act 1997 and LGA 2000, s 91 adding new ss 19A, 19B and 19C to the ACA 1998 (above).

4.90   The 'prohibition period' means the period beginning with the day on which copies of the report are sent (LGFA 1988, s 115(9)(a)) and ending with the first business day (s 115(2)) to fall after the day (if any) on which the authority's consideration of the report under sub-s (2) above is concluded (s 115(9)(b)). Non-compliance with the 21-day period is immaterial for the purposes of s 115(9)(b), as are the nature of the decisions made at the meeting.

4.91   The report does not have to be made public under ACA 1998, nor does it have to be kept confidential, but the provisions of the LG(ATI)A 1985 apply to such meetings.[1]

[1]   Excepting 'confidential' and exempt information.

4.92   It should be noted that the authority does not have to desist from its action; the report and accompanying procedure constitute a *locus poenitentiae*. But the auditor, who has to receive a report, may act under s 8 of the ACA 1998 (above). S/he has a duty to consider whether, in the public interest, s/he should issue a special report in the course of audit for the consideration of the body under audit or to inform the public, and further to consider whether an immediate report is required in the public interest. Auditors have a statutory right of access to current accounts 'and both they and the Audit Commission have taken the view that the s 8 power is exercisable at any time and is not confined to the statutory audit process which commences when the authority's accounts are completed and submitted for audit'.[1] LGA 2003, ss 107–108 reduce the time-limit for an authority's consideration of a public interest report from four months to one month, and the auditor's power of extension is likewise reduced.

[1]   Grant *Current Law Statutes Annotated* (1988) vol 3.

4.93   Although the relationship between this Part of the Act and s 8 is 'unclear', Grant believes the auditor may exercise his power:

'(1)   to report on issues falling outside the scope of a chief finance officer's report;
(2)   to report in default of any report from the chief finance officer;
(3)   to report on the same issue as is contained in a chief finance officer's report, but to different effect.'

4.94   Further, the auditor's powers to issue advisory notices under LGA 2000 may well come into effect.[1]

[1]   LGA 2000, s 91 amending ACA 1998, s 19A.

4.95   Where it is proposed to hold a meeting under s 115 above, the authority's proper officer shall as soon as is reasonably practicable notify its auditors of the date, time and place of the proposed meeting (s 116(1)). S/he has to inform the auditor as soon as reasonably practicable after a s 115 meeting of any decision taken (s 116(2)).

4.96   It should be added that LGA 2003, ss 25–30 contain provisions on reports from chief finance officers to authorities (including the Greater London Authority) on the 'robustness of estimates' for calculations under LGFA 1992 or the Greater London Authority Act 1999 and on the adequacy of proposed financial reserves.

Members[1]

4.97   Chapter 5 contains a detailed discussion of the duties of an authority to provide information to members under common law and the LG(ATI)A 1985. The LGHA 1989 will significantly affect the position of the member, and groups of members, and their powers in relation to certain matters. These can be dealt with now, although the discussion does not directly concern the giving of information to members.

[1] See Birkinshaw *Open Government, Freedom of Information and Local Government* (1986) Local Government Legal Society Trust.

THE LOCAL GOVERNMENT AND HOUSING ACT 1989

Designated and monitoring officers

4.98   Under the LGHA 1989[1] every relevant authority has to 'designate' one of its officers as the head of their paid service 'and must provide that officer with such staff accommodation and other resources as are, in that officer's opinion, sufficient to allow the officer's duties under this section to be performed' (s 4(1)(b)).

[1] See Greater London Authority Act 1999, s 72 and SI 1996/323, Sch 2, Art 4.

4.99   The 'designated officer' (DO) shall, where s/he considers it appropriate, prepare a report to the authority in respect of any proposals of the DO, as specified, on:
(a)   the manner in which the discharge by the authority of their different functions is co-ordinated;
(b)   the number and grades of staff required by the authority for the discharge of their functions;
(c)   the organisation of the authority's staff; and
(d)   the appointment and proper management of the authority's staff (s 4(3)).

4.100   As soon as practicable after s/he has prepared a report under this section, s/he shall arrange for a copy of it to be sent to each member of the authority. This report must be considered by the council (non-delegable) not more than three months after copies of the report are first sent to members.

4.101   Under s 5 of the LGHA 1989[1], authorities must designate an officer as a 'monitoring officer' (MO), with the same provisions as under s 4(1)(b) above as regards the DO. Section 5A deals with the role of the MO in authorities operating executive arrangements – the role and powers are in all material aspects the same as under s 5 as described below, except that the executive rather than the authority or relevant committee is under the obligation to consider the MO's reports. The MO may not be the head of the paid service. The MO has to prepare a report for the authority on any proposal, decision or omission by the authority, committee, sub-committee or officer of the authority, or any joint committee on which the authority is represented (s 5(4)(a)–(c)), which appears to the MO to constitute, to have given rise to, or which is likely to, or would give rise to a contravention by the authority etc of any enactment, or rule of law [or of any code of practice made or approved by or under any enactment,] or any maladministration or injustice under Part III of the Local Government Act 1974 (the ombudsman provisions).

[1] Amended by LGA 2000, Sch 5, para 24(3) and LGA 2003, s 113.

4.102 The MO is under a duty as soon s practicable after preparing a report to arrange for a copy of it to be sent to each member of the authority.[1] In preparing such a report the MO has to consult, so far as practicable, with the head of the authority's paid service and the chief finance officer (s 5(3)).

[1]   Or each member of the committee under s 5(4).

4.103 The authority, or committee under s 5(4), must consider the report at a meeting held not more than 21 days after copies of the report are first sent to the authority or committee. In the case of the authority the duty is non-delegable to one of its committees (s 5(5)). The authority is under a duty to ensure that no step is taken, before the report is considered, for giving effect to any proposal or decision to which it relates.[1]

[1]   And without prejudice to any duty imposed by virtue of LGFA 1988, s 115: see para 4.89 above.

4.104 The MO must perform these duties personally, or, in the event of absence or illness, through deputies nominated by the MO.

4.105 It should be noted that the authority is not bound by the report; it only has to consider it. Clearly, the reports under the LGHA 1989 and LGFA 1988 have as their objectives the provision of a 'cooling off period' before any potentially unlawful or maladministrative practice is perpetrated. The reports may strain relationships between the respective officers and their authorities, and are clearly aimed at preventing some of the 'excesses' caused by authorities trying to circumvent previous government legislation. The relevant meeting will fall within the terms of the LG(ATI)A 1985 (see chs 5 and 6).

4.106 Further, Regulations made by the Secretary of State may require a relevant authority's standing orders to require the MO to prepare a report to the authority in respect of every proposed appointment of a person to a 'politically restricted post'[1] stating whether in the MO's opinion the proposed appointment can be made without contravening the Act and without considering any matter which could not properly be taken into account. The MO may, in accordance with regulations, have to state reasons if the appointment cannot be so made.[2]

[1]   LGHA 1989, s 2 for definition.
[2]   LGHA 1989, s 8(3)(c) and (d). These will be incorporated in the standing orders.

Staff appointments

4.107 These measures are in s 8 of the LGHA 1989 (and see s 7, as amended by SI 2003/1673, reg 31, at para 5.34 below) and impose a duty upon an authority to adopt prescribed provisions in standing orders in relation to the appointment of staff so as to restrict the freedom of authorities in the manner of appointment and in the directions which authorities can give to persons making appointments. The report by the MO on every proposed appointment to a politically restricted post is not sent to all members as above, but to the authority. In addition, the regulations may prohibit the authority or committee or sub-committee or other person acting on their behalf from acting towards an employee, ie dismissing or disciplining, except in accordance with recommendations contained in a report made to the authority by an independent person of such a description as is prescribed by the regulations. As this report concerns an employee, the LG(ATI)A 1985 and its exemptions vis-à-vis public access and members' access come into play, although a member may be able to establish a 'need to know' at common law (paras 5.70 et seq below).

Appointment of political assistants

4.108   Two further provisions which are of relevance concern the appointment of assistants to members of a political group to which members of the authority belong. Such an appointment is permissible providing it is within the terms of the statute.[1] No appointment can be made until the authority have allocated a post to each of the groups qualifying for one; appointments which do not qualify are prohibited as is more than one allocation to any one political group. To qualify as a group under LGHA 1989, s 9, membership of the group must comprise at least one-tenth of the authority's membership; the number of other groups, if any, which are larger than that group does not exceed two; or, if there are more than two other qualifying groups, the authority has determined the group in question (of which in total there must be no more or less than three) to be the group to receive an allocation, the only safeguard presumably being judicial review on the *Wednesbury* principles.[2] Special provision is made where only one group has one-tenth or more membership. The maximum number is then two groups (s 9(7)). Powers cannot be delegated to advisers under this section by use of LGA 1972, s 101 or the Scottish equivalent. Regulations provide for a variety of details[3] including whether a person is or is not a member of a political group and the manner in which such a determination is to be made.

[1]   LGHA 1989, s 9(2): one of not more than three posts; each falls to be filled by the wishes of a political group to which the post has been allocated under standing orders; the salary is within the relevant amount (see s 9(4)). See Greater London Authority Act 1999, s 68.

[2]   *Associated Provincial Picture Houses Ltd v Wednesbury Corpn* [1948] 1 KB 223, CA.

[3]   See LGHA 1989, s 9(10). By s 9(9) an authority's employees cannot be directed by such an adviser except to provide secretarial or clerical services.

4.109   The LGA 2000 has important implications for the use of political advisers (see para 4.30 above).

Voting rights of members

4.110   The other relevant provision affects the voting rights of members of certain committees. Members of committees etc who are not members of the authority are to be treated as non-voting members for the purposes of designated powers under s 13 of the LGHA 1989.[1] However, if the committee is one enumerated within s 13(4) or its sub-committee, s/he shall not be treated as a non-voting member unless not also a member of the parent committee in the case of a sub-committee.

[1]   By LGHA 1989, s 13(2) the section applies to powers conferred by LGA 1972, s 102(1); those exercisable under Education Act 1996, Sch 33, Pt I.

4.111 The Secretary of State may prescribe by Regulations members of sub-committees as voting members even when not members of the appointing committee.

4.112 Section 102(3) of the LGA 1972 has been amended,[1] omitting the necessity that two-thirds of the members of certain committees are to be members of an appointing authority or authorities.

¹   See LGHA 1989, Sch 12.

Political balance of bodies

4.113 The LGHA 1989 makes provision for the political balance of bodies of a relevant authority, the latter of which are under a duty to review the representation of different political groups on that body after divisions occur on party lines within that body,[1] and the committees[2] of which are under a similar duty where they have power to make appointments from time to time to a body covered by the section.[3] The authority or committee must determine[4] the allocation to the different political groups, into which the members of the authority are divided, of all the seats which are to be filled by appointments[5] made by the authority or committee.[6] Membership of committees and sub-committees is thereby regulated. These provisions do not apply to executive arrangements under the LGA 2000 and accompanying Regulations (paras 4.29 et seq above).

¹   LGHA 1989, s 15(1)(a)–(d) sets out the 'relevant times' of reviews, and such other times as prescribed. See Greater London Authority Act 1999, s 57.
²   Except as prescribed by regulations made by the Secretary of State.
³   LGHA 1989, s 15. And see LGHA 1989, Sch 1 on the bodies covered.
⁴   At the 'relevant times'.
⁵   The duty arises as soon as practicable after the review.
⁶   LGHA 1989, s 15(3).

4.114 In making appointments, effect must be given, so far as reasonably practicable, to the following principles:
(a)   that not all the seats on the body are allocated to the same political group;
(b)   that the majority of the seats on the body is allocated to a particular political group if the number of persons belonging to that group is a majority of the authority's membership;
(c)   subject to the above, that seats on ordinary committees are allocated to each political group in proportion to the total number of seats on the ordinary committees of the authority as is borne by the number of members of that group to the membership of the authority; and
(d)   subject to paras (a) to (c) above, that the number of the seats on the body which are allocated to each political group bears the same proportion to the number of all the seats on that body as is borne by the number of members of that group to the membership of the authority (s 15(5)).

4.115 Basically, s 15 amends the common law which is described in ch 5 (para 5.59).

4.116 Under Sch 1, there are further provisions concerning the political balance on local authority committees. Subject to exceptions as may be made by regulations, s 15 applies to counties, districts, boroughs, their committees and:

(a) ordinary committees and sub-committees of the authority;
(b) advisory committees and sub-committees appointed by such advisory committees; and
(c) any body falling within para 2 of the Schedule which is a body at least three seats on which fall from time to time to be filled by appointments made by the authority or committee.

4.117 Regulations may be made providing for the circumstances in which members of a relevant authority are to be treated as divided into different political groups; who is to be treated as a member of such a group and when membership ceases, and setting down a procedure to determine disputes on membership; and specifying the manner in which, and the times at which, the wishes of such a group are to be expressed and the consequences of a failure by such a group to express its wish.

4.118 On appointments and vacancies, the wishes of the political group allocating seats must be followed.

4.119 Section 17 concerns exemptions to and extensions of political balance requirements.[1] Breach of s 15 does not invalidate proceedings (s 16(3)).

[1] In a manner prescribed by regulations and subject to no dissenting vote of the authority or committee. This does not defeat a duty under LGHA 1989, s 15(1)(c), (d) or (e) or (2).

4.120 By s 20, the Secretary of State may require, by regulations, authorities to incorporate into standing orders provisions regulating their proceedings and business and to make, or refrain from making, such other modifications of any such orders as may be prescribed (s 20(1)).

4.121 Section 20(2) empowers regulations to require standing orders to contain, notwithstanding any enactments or relevant decisions of the authority or its committees or sub-committees, an authorisation for members to requisition meetings of the authority, its committees or sub-committees, to require the review of decisions by the authority or a committee, and to require that a vote of the authority etc is taken in a particular manner.

4.122 Section 20(3) provides:

'Regulations under this section may contain such incidental provision and such supplemental, consequential and transitional provision in connection with their other provisions as the Secretary of State considers appropriate.'

4.123 Many of the details of this Part have been supplemented by Regulations.[1] The impetus for change came from the Widdicombe Report[2] and the government reply to that Report. Opinion was divided on whether the abuse of a small minority of authorities justified such wholesale legislative regulation of committee proceedings. By the late 1990s, the question of standards had become inseparable from new styles of management in local government.

¹   Eg Local Authorities (Standing Orders) Regulations 1993, SI 1993/202.
²   *The Conduct of Local Authority Business* Cmnd 9797 (1986); Cm 433 (1988) (reply).

STANDARDS OF CONDUCT

4.124   Standards of conduct in local government formed the subject of Lord Nolan's third report. It was also a concern of the Widdicombe Report in 1986 on *Conduct in Local Government* which led to developments such as the introduction of the Monitoring Officer and Reporting Officer (see above). The subject was also a central feature of events in several authorities including Westminster.¹ The present government set out its plans for a new ethical framework in *Modern Local Government: In Touch with the People*² (1998) (ch 6). Following this report, many councils started to develop systems such as standards committees, panels or benches to address matters of conduct relating to members to ensure openness and honesty in their activities. These vary in detail between size, independent membership, political balance and arrangements for chairs.

¹   Involving Dame Shirley Porter: see *Porter v Magill* [2002] 1 All ER 465 (HL). For indemnities relating to local government members (including mayors) and officers, see LGA 2000, s 101 and SI 2004/3082: special provisions apply to breaches of the code. The SI makes provision for repayment of indemnities to authorities: it does not cover criminal or wilfully wrongful acts, fraud or recklessness; nor does it apply to bringing defamation actions but it does apply to their defence.
²   (1998) ch 6, Cm 4014.

4.125   The above White Paper had three basic components:
(1)   A requirement upon every council to adopt a code of conduct that all members would have to sign up to.
(2)   A requirement for most authorities to set up standards committees to oversee ethical issues and provide advice and guidance on the code and its implementation.
(3)   The establishment of an independent body, the Standards Board, which will investigate alleged breaches of a council's code (see paras 4.131 et seq below).

4.126   The government intended to replace the National Code of Local Government Conduct (s 31 of the LGHA 1989 and Joint Circular) with a statutory requirement for every council to adopt a code of conduct covering the behaviour of elected members.¹ Each one would have to agree to abide by the code. The code would be based on a general set of principles approved by Parliament in a model code. These are: community leadership; duty to uphold the law; supporting constituents' interests but not putting them above the general interest; selflessness; integrity and propriety; hospitality – ie recording of gifts etc; making decisions on one's judgment; objectivity in decision-making; accountability; openness; confidentiality; stewardship – ensuring proper use of public resources; participation; declarations of private interests; respect for officers and employees (para 6.7).

1   *R v Local Comr for Administration, ex p Liverpool City Council* [1999] 3 All ER 85; affirmed [2001]
     1 All ER 462, CA and the ombudsman's reliance on the Code which set higher standards in
     establishing an interest in a decision than the law: ombudsman upheld by the Court of Appeal on
     challenge by the council.

4.127 The Local Government Association was invited to develop these principles which in turn develop Nolan's famous principles for those in public life. The mandatory elements – setting common standards – will have to be adopted by authorities with opportunity to modify further details to their own requirements. Town, parish and combined authorities will be subject to uniform national codes. A draft *Model Code of Conduct* was published in February 2001 (see SI 2001/3575) and was then modified and re-published in 2007 as SI 2007/1159. The Code had to be adopted within six months. Any mandatory provisions apply regardless of the adoption of the Code by an authority. The government believed that the new structures will counter any dangers to secrecy that the new executive arrangements might bring insofar as they achieved a greater concentration of power. The new ethical framework will minimise the risk of unethical practice in all councils. To some this sounded over optimistic.

4.128 All principal councils will have to establish a Standards Committee (SC) (LGA 2000, s 53; see SI 2003/1483). The SC will advise on the adoption of a local code, monitoring and updating it as necessary (s 54(2)(a)). It will have a remit to organise training and deal with less serious allegations of impropriety handed over to it by the Standards Board. It will act in an advisory capacity on ethics and its role may not be restricted to this area but it will have no executive powers. There should be at least one independent co-opted voting member and at least two councillors who are members. Not more than one member of the council executive should be a member and the SC should not include a directly elected mayor. That latter member from the executive should not chair the SC. Section 55 deals with SCs for parish councils and s 56 for community councils in Wales.

4.129 LGA 2003, s 113 provides that a Standards Committee may appoint one or more sub-committees. These are not to perform functions under LGA 2000, s 55 or 56 for which provision already exists.

4.130 It was envisaged that the monitoring officer (MO) will play a key role in supporting the SC: 'The MO will have an enhanced role in providing advice and assistance on ethical standards issues to members, officers and also to the SC and in maintaining the public register of interests' (see above). The MO is given power to delegate functions under LGA 2000, ss 60(2), 64(2), 70(4) and 71(2).[1]

1   By virtue of a new LGA 2000, s 82A, added by LGA 2003, s 113.

4.131 The Standards Board (SB) deals with alleged breaches of the new code of conduct for local government (LGA 2000, s 57). The SB pursues complaints in a rigorous and impartial manner. Though funded by grant in aid from the government it will be independent of central and local government and the Secretary of State will provide a copy of the SB's audited accounts to Parliament.[1]

Responsibility for receiving, investigating and reporting on alleged breaches of a local authority's code is placed with ethical standards officers (ESOs) who are appointed by the Secretary of State (ss 59–62). ESOs are given wide powers of investigation and information gathering under s 62 including information relating to communications passing between the authority and a government department. ESOs may or must produce reports on investigations under the terms of s 64 and he must send a copy to the MO of the authority concerned. Section 65 allows for interim reports in the 'public interest'. Section 66 enables a MO to investigate any matters so referred and to report or make recommendations to the Ethical Standards Committee. Regulations under s 66 may provide for the publicity to be given to any reports, recommendations or action. SI 2004/2617 sets out procedures for monitoring officers and the treatment of their reports by standards committees. The SB will comprise the ESOs together with some non-executive members appointed by the Secretary of State 'some of whom may represent local government and related organisations'. It will have a minimum of three members and will be assisted by staff. The ESOs will investigate allegations of breaches of the code but an Adjudications Panel independent of the ESOs will establish whether an allegation is true (ss 75–80). Its members will be appointed by the Lord Chancellor (the National Assembly for Wales in the case of the Welsh Panel) and it will sit in panels 'case tribunals' or 'interim case tribunals' (for interim reports) of at least three members to hear individual adjudications. The Panel will be within the jurisdiction of the Council on Tribunals. The work of the Panel and SB may be brought within one organisation while ensuring independence of functions.

[1]   Like the Audit Commission, Commission for Local Administration, Local Government Commission.

4.132 Complaints will have to be made in writing to the SB and may come via the public, councillors, officers, police, ombudsmen and auditors. The MO or SC must refer complaints on such matters to the SB. Guidance may be given by the SB to these bodies and police authorities in Wales on certain matters (SI 2004/2618). Cases will be allocated to the ESOs individually, and the ESO may decide that the MO or SC can deal with the case or that an SB investigation is appropriate. The White Paper stated that if the ESO believes for good reason that an allegation is true and could lead to disqualification he may recommend suspension of a member from membership of the Council for up to six months where he considered that it was in the public interest to suspend the member concerned before the conclusion of a full investigation.[1] ESOs will be given similar investigatory powers to auditors and failure to co-operate will be a criminal offence and they may authorise similar powers to persons assisting their investigations. There would have to be appropriate co-ordination with ombudsmen and auditor investigations and criminal investigations would take precedence (see LGA 2000, s 67). The ESO publishes a report which is handed to the person who is the subject of the report, the SC or adjudication panel (AP) as appropriate. The report will determine that the allegation is unsubstantiated, that no further action is necessary, or that it be referred back to the SC or forwarded to the AP. Case Tribunals would comply with all legal procedural requirements including legal representation, and would be empowered to require attendance of witnesses, administering of evidence on oath, and production of documents. The panel could, where the allegation is substantiated, make one of three penalties: censure; suspension from council meetings and its committees for up to one year; disqualification from membership of an authority for up to five years for the most serious of breaches. For interim case tribunals the penalties are suspension or partial suspension from membership details of which are specified and which can last for up to six months (ss 79 and 78 respectively). An appeal would lie to the High Court under both sections.

¹ See LGA 2000, s 65(3) which does not spell this out.

4.133 In its *Tenth Report* the Committee on Standards in Public Life found that the centralised system for dealing with complaints at national level first of all produced many complaints about the proportionality of the system which the committee believed justified (Cm 6407, 2005, ch 3). Too many 'minor, vexatious and politically motivated complaints caused long delays'. Centralisation ran against the culture of localism and was counter to the advice of the Committee in 1995. Similar problems had been avoided in Scotland and Wales. Procedures should move to locally based arrangements initially, and the composition of local standards committees should be strengthened.

4.134 The Localism Bill (2010–2011) proposes a dismantling of the standards regime for England. The changes are outlined in para 5.47 below.

'WHISTLEBLOWER' ARRANGEMENTS – PUBLIC INTEREST DISCLOSURE ACT 1998

4.135 We have dealt with these provisions in ch 2 (paras 2.299 et seq above).

COMMISSIONS FOR LOCAL ADMINISTRATION

4.136 The last major source of request for information from authorities, apart from the public, is made by the commissions for local administration – the ombudsmen. These were subject to Cabinet Office discussion involving the establishment of a new commission to cover all the major public sector ombudsmen (see para 2.132 above). They were also subject to two-stage investigations and reports about the Commission's future conducted by the Department of the Environment in 1996. Established by Part III of the Local Government Act 1974 (LGA 1974), the commissions have been the subject of considerable statutory amendment. The contents of 'maladministration' can be deferred until a later chapter (see ch 10 below). It is pertinent to point out at this stage that the LGA 1988 allows a complainant to complain directly to a local ombudsman. The complaint must be in writing. A substantial increase in complaints followed this reform.

4.137 There are three offices of local commissioners for England[1] and one for Wales. Northern Ireland has a commissioner for complaints. The Scotland

Act and Wales Act provide for ombudsmen for devolved matters and, under the Scottish Public Services Ombudsman Act 2002, a combined Ombudsman service for Scottish public authorities was established. In the past, a Welsh Administration Ombudsman existed for the Welsh National Assembly and for bodies dealing with devolved administration in Wales. The Public Services Ombudsman (Wales) Act 2005 (PSO(W)A 2005) unifies ombudsmen in Wales. The Commission for Local Administration in Wales and the Welsh Administration Ombudsman have been abolished and a new Public Services Ombudsman for Wales has been created. Each commission in England under LGA 1974, Part III has to publish information about the procedures for making complaints. Every commissioner must submit an annual report to his commission.[2] In Wales, PSO(W)A 2005, Sch 1, para 14 contains similar requirement, with the report to be laid before the Welsh Assembly. The commission shall prepare a general report on the discharge of their functions and must formally submit it to the appropriate representative persons and authorities[3] despite the commission having arranged for its publication. These are persons representing authorities, or authorities not so represented. LGPIHA 2007 has amended s 23A by inserting LGA 1974, s 23A(3) in order to require the laying of the annual report before Parliament. After consulting the representative persons and authorities, each Commission for Local Administration (CLA) may provide to authorities 'such advice and guidance' about good administrative practice as appears to the CLA to be appropriate. The CLA may arrange for the information to be published (LGHA 1989, s 23). The commissions are now funded by central government exchequer grant but are independent of central government. Additional non-investigatory advisory commissioners may be appointed. For information see: www.lgo.org.uk.

[1]   The three areas have become less distinct geographically so that all three Ombudsmen cover parts of London, in the case of one ombudsman only one borough. See HC 458 (2004–05) on *The Role and Effectiveness of the Local Government Ombudsmen.*

[2]   LGA 1974, s 23(11). The commissioners also conduct a triennial review of the investigation of complaints, s 23(12): see Commission for Local Administration (2009) *Review of the Operation of Part III of the Local Government Act 1974.* The requirement for a triennial report is not in place in PSO(W)A 2005.

[3]   The representative persons must be given a reasonable time to make their comments: LGHA 1989, s 25(2) (LGA 1974, s 23A).

4.138   The commissioner's investigations shall be conducted in private, the procedure being determined by the commissioner as appropriate in the circumstances. The local commissioner (LC) may obtain information from such persons and in such manner, and make such enquiries, as s/he thinks fit, and determine whether any person should be represented.[1] Those furnishing information may be paid expenses[2] and allowances for loss of time. Similar provisions can be found in PSO(W)A 2005, s 13.

[1]   LGA 1974, s 28(2).
[2]   LGA 1974, s 28(3).

4.139   By s 29 of the LGA 1974, upon investigation a commissioner may require any members or officer of the authority concerned, or any other person who in his or her opinion is able to furnish information or produce relevant documents, to furnish any information or produce any such relevant documents.[1] S/he is given, for such investigation, the powers of a High Court judge in respect of the attendance and examination of witnesses and in respect of the production of documents. S/he may require, under s 29(3), any person to furnish information concerning communications between the authority concerned and any government department, or to produce any correspondence or other documents forming part of any such written communication. Similar provisions can be found in PSO(W)A 2005, s 14.

[1] Reports eg in 1989, have highlighted difficulties in obtaining information.

4.140 The Official Secrets Acts and other provisions enjoining secrecy on HM officials do not apply to requests from the ombudsman for information – no breach of the law is perpetrated by complying.[1] Nor, where LGA 1974, s 29(3) applies, may the Crown rely upon any such secrecy provision or privilege such as 'public interest immunity' to withhold information[2] although subject to that subsection, viz s 29(4), no person shall be compelled for the purposes of an investigation under the Act to give any evidence or produce any document which s/he could not be compelled to give or produce in civil proceedings before the High Court. In other words, an individual can plead a personal privilege providing s 29(4) does not override that claim. Similar, though less detailed provisions can be found in PSO(W)A 2005, s 15.

[1] LGA 1974, s 29(2).
[2] Information disclosed by a government department under the LGA 1974, s 29(3) shall not be made public in a commissioner's report unless the department is given not less than one month's written notice.

4.141 Where without lawful excuse a local commissioner, or his or her officer, is obstructed in his or her functions, or a person acts or obstructs his or her investigation so that if it were a proceeding in the High Court that would constitute a contempt, the commissioner may certify the offence for the High Court which can deal with the matter.[1] Similar obligations and powers are contained in PSO(W)A 2005, s 15.

[1] LGA 1974, s 29(8) and (9).

4.142 Under LGA 1974, s 32, as amended by LGPLA 1980, s 184, notice may be given to the commission by the minister of the Crown or any of the authorities mentioned in s 25(1) which has the effect of instructing the commissioner not to disseminate information or documents as specified beyond the commissioner or the staff assisting the commissioner. All publications as specified in s 32 are absolutely privileged.[1] Information obtained by local commissioners or their officers, during or for investigations, shall not be disclosed except for reports under ss 30, 31 and 31B, or for the purposes of an investigation being carried out by the PCA or Health Service Commissioner for England, for the purposes of an investigation under the new LGA 1974, Part 3A (investigations into privately arranged or funded adult social care – inserted by the Health Act 2009), proceedings under the Official Secrets Acts 1911–1989, for perjury or for inquiries conducted with a view to taking such proceedings or for proceedings under s 29(9).[2] Otherwise, the information is privileged in legal proceedings.[3] The courts have upheld the local ombudsman where there have been challenges to his their powers to obtain information and early in their career, their powers had to be amended to prevent authorities resisting requests for information.[4] The High Court has ruled that where an ombudsman decided not to investigate a complaint formally – and where the reasons were flawed, the ombudsman should have shown his interview notes to the complainant in the absence of any good reasons preventing this. These covered meetings with an official and the chair of the planning committee.[5] Section 32(2) of the Act did not prohibit disclosure of the notes which in the circumstances were required in the interests of fairness. The local ombudsman should respect any request for confidentiality but he must not adopt a blanket test of non-disclosure. This decision does seem to be desirable on the grounds of fair procedure but it does seem to disregard the strict wording of s 32(2). Similar provisions can be found in PSO(W)A 2005, ss 26–27 and 32.

[1]   There are four kinds of publication that are protected involving communications between the commission and members, complainants, etc. The LGPIHA 2007 adds publication under s 31B (power of the Commissioners to publish reports). SI 2007/1889, Art 9 adds a further protection of publication where this results from collaboration between the Local Commissioners and the PCA or Health Service Commissioner for England.
[2]   Contempt proceedings.
[3]   LGA 1974, s 32(2).
[4]   *Re a Subpoena (Adoption: Comr for Local Administration)* [1996] 2 FLR 629 and access by the ombudsman to adoption files.
[5]   *R (Turpin) v Commissioner for Local Administration* [2001] EWHC Admin 503.

4.143   Section 33 concerns consultation between local commissioners, the parliamentary commissioner (who is an *ex officio* member of the Commission for Local Administration) and the health service commissioner where a complaint involves more than one ombudsman.[1] Section 32(2) above does not apply to inhibit such consultation.[2] It was noted in ch 1 how ombudsmen may exchange information with the Information Commissioner and vice versa. Similar provisions can be found in PSO(W)A 2005, s 25.

[1]   He may, if necessary, inform the person initiating the complaint of appropriate steps.
[2]   Which otherwise restricts disclosure of information.

Reports of the commissioners into investigations

4.144   The provisions relating to reports have been amended by legislation in 1988, 1989, 2000, 2007 and 2009. The authority concerned, inter alia, in a complaint receives a copy of the report.[1] Such authority shall make copies of the report available, for a period of three weeks, for inspection by the public without charge, at all reasonable hours at one or more of their offices. Any person is entitled to take copies of, or extracts from, the report when so made available (LGA 1974, s 30(4)). Not later than two weeks after the report is received by the authority the 'proper officer' (s 30(7)) shall give public notice, by advertisement and such other ways as appear to him or her appropriate, that copies of the report will be available as under s 30(4). S/he shall specify the date, being a date not more than one week after the public notice is first given, from which the period of three weeks (above) will begin. The authority shall supply a copy of the report to any person on request, if s/he pays such charge as the authority may 'reasonably require'.[2] The publicity etc provisions may be waived at the commissioner's discretion on the grounds of the public interest and those of the complainant and third persons (s 30(7)). Obstruction of these rights by a person with custody of the reports is a criminal offence punishable summarily (s 30(6)). The Court of Appeal has ruled that under LGA 1974, s 30(1), the LGO is only required to report *after* an investigation is completed; anything else, such as a decision not to continue, only requires a statement of reasons.[3] These provisions are mirrored in PSO(W)A 2005, ss 16 and 17.

[1]   As do the complainant, referring member and others alleged to have taken or authorised action complained against: see ch 6. NB the introduction of a new s 30(1B) by LGPIHA 2007. This section permits the Commissioner to refuse to provide copies of the report if he is satisfied with the action that the authority under investigation has taken or proposes to take and he believes that it is not appropriate to prepare and send a copy of the report. If the Commissioner decides to do this he must prepare a statement of reasons for his decision and copy it to the persons concerned.
[2]   LGA 1974, s 30(4A); LGA 1988, Sch 3, para 6.
[3]   *R (Maxhuni) v Commissioner for Local Administration* [2002] EWCA Civ 973, (2002) NLJ 1172 (CA).

4.145   Section 31 of the LGA 1974 has been the subject of recent amendment by LGPIHA 2007. In particular, s 31(1) is modified to apply whenever there has been maladministration in connection with the exercise of the authority's administrative functions, a failure in a service which it was the function of an authority to provide or when there is a failure to provide such a service. This application is clearly broader than the old wording of s 31, which applied the section only where a commissioner reports a case of injustice caused to a person aggrieved in consequence of maladministration.

4.146   In addition to the publicity outlined above, the report has to be laid before the authority; it has to be considered by the authority; and the authority must notify the commissioner of its actions thereon or proposals within three months of receiving the report or such longer period with the written agreement of the commissioner.[1]

[1]   LGA 1974, s 31(2) as added by LGHA 1989, s 26.

4.147   If this notification is not received within the requisite period; or the commissioner is not satisfied with the authority's actions or proposals; or s/he does not receive confirmation from the authority that they have taken action, as proposed, to his or her satisfaction – this has to be within a three-month period after the end of the period allowed – s/he may issue a 'further report'.[1] This will set out the facts above and will make recommendations.[2] These, by virtue of LGA 1974, s 31(2B), are such as the local commissioner thinks fit to make with respect to action which, in his or her opinion, the authority concerned should take to remedy the injustice to the person aggrieved and to prevent similar injustice being caused in the future, ie it is a prophylactic device. A new s 31(2BA) is added, creating a similar regime should there be a report in relation to a failure in a service or a failure to provide a service in order to support the modifications made by the LGPIHA 2007 noted above. Similar provisions can be found in PSO(W)A 2005, ss 19 and 22, although with the 'old' 'persons aggrieved' wording.

¹   LGA 1974, s 18(2A)(c), as amended.
²   LGA 1974, s 18(2A).

4.148   The section makes clear that s 30 supra and s 31(2) apply to further reports under s 31(2A) as they do to a report under s 30 – with necessary modifications.¹ This repeats the requirement of a notification for a further report, which if not received within the requisite period (three months), or if the commissioner is satisfied before the expiry of that time that the authority concerned has decided to take no action, or s/he is dissatisfied with the action or proposals of the authority, or no confirmation is forthcoming as under s 18(2A)(c)² or for an extended period in writing, then s/he may, by notice to the authority, require them to arrange for a statement to be published in accordance with s 31(2E) and (2F).³

¹   LGA 1974, s 31(2C), as amended.
²   Confirmation of action to the commissioner's satisfaction.
³   LGA 1974, s 31(2D).

4.149   This statement, in a form agreed by the authority and the commissioner, consists of:
(a)   details of any action recommended by the local commissioner (LC) in his or her further report which the authority have not taken;
(b)   such supporting material as the LC may require; and
(c)   if the authority so requires, a statement of the reasons for their having taken no action on, or not the action recommended in, the report.¹

¹   LGA 1974, s 31(2E).

4.150   'Publication' of a statement is satisfied where it is in any two editions within a fortnight of a newspaper circulating in the area of the authority agreed with the LC, or, in default of agreement, nominated by the commission and publication in the first such newspaper arranged for the earliest practicable date.¹

¹   LGA 1974, s 31(2F).

4.151   Failure on the authority's part to arrange for publication or to agree within a specified period¹ shall lead to the LC arranging for such a statement under LGA 1974, s 31(2E) to be published in any two editions within a fortnight of a newspaper circulating within the authority's area (s 31(2G)). The authority will have to reimburse on demand any reasonable expenditure incurred by the LC under s 31(2G). The section only applies to reports made after the section comes into force.

¹   One month beginning with the date on which they receive the notice under s 31(2D), or such longer period as the commissioner agrees in writing.

4.152   A new s 31A is added to the LGA 1974 by LGHA 1989, Part II. This provision has been significantly amended by the LGPIHA 2007, although the thrust of the provisions remains the same. This specifies that the authority itself must have referred to it consideration of a further report under s 31(2A) if it is proposed that the authority should take no action on, or not the recommended action in, a report.[1] Consideration of such reports by committees specified in LGA 1972, s 101(9)[2] or by an appeal committee constituted under Education Act 1980, Sch 2, para 1 'shall be subject to a corresponding restriction', ie the authority itself must have the report referred to it.[3]

[1]   LGA 1974, s 31A(1).
[2]   Including education, police and social services committees. The latter will not operate where authorities have adopted executive arrangements: LGA 2000, s 102.
[3]   LGA 1974, s 31A(2).

4.153   These restrictions do not apply where the report recommends that action be taken by a joint committee established under LGA 1972, s 101 or any committee referred to in an enactment specified in s 101(9)(c), (d) or (h).[1]

[1]   LGA 1974, s 31A(3).

4.154   Where the authority, in considering a LGA 1974, s 31(2A) report, takes into account a report by a person or body with an interest in the LC's report, it must also consider a report by a person or body with no interest in the LC's report, ie an independent assessment must be made.[1]

[1]   LGA 1974, s 31A(4).

4.155   Any member of an authority or of a committee as specified in s 31A(2) and (3), and who is named and criticised in a report or further report of an LC, shall not vote on any question relating to such report.

4.156   LGPIHA 2007, s 177 inserts a new LGA 1974, s 31B giving the Local Commissioner express powers to publish reports and statements under LGA 1974, ss 30 and 31 and summaries thereof if he believes that it is in the public interest to do so after taking account of the interests of the complainant and other persons. The Commissioner may also provide a report or part of it to anyone who requests it and charge a reasonable fee for doing so.

4.157   A provision added by LGHA 1989, s 32 allowing a member to be identified in a report where there was action amounting to maladministration by the member which breached the national code of conduct was repealed by LGA 2000, Sch 5, para 15.

4.158   Finally on reports, the LGOs have initiated the practice of issuing special reports which bring together the experience and information of several investigations into one subject area. These have covered funding of aftercare under Mental Health Act 1983, s 117, delays in referring housing benefit appeals to the Appeals Service, school admissions and appeals and administrative pitfalls, and parking enforcement by local authorities (www.lgo.org.uk/special-reports/htm).

4.159 The LGA 2000 provides for communications between ethical standards officers (ESOs) and the local ombudsmen about complaints where one of them believes it raised issues of relevance to the other as specified (s 67). LGA 2000, ss 68–74 provide that, in Wales, the role of ESOs will be taken by the local ombudsman. There is no Standards Board for Wales (see, however, SI 2004/2618 which enables the Standards Board to issue guidance to monitoring officers and standards committees of relevant authorities in England and police authorities in Wales in respect of certain matters referred to them by the Standards Board's ESOs or, in Wales, Local Commissioners). The Public Services Ombudsman (Wales) Act 2005 now contains detailed provisions on these and other matters concerning the unified ombudsman scheme in Wales.

RESTRICTING PUBLICITY BY AUTHORITIES

4.160 In ch 2 (paras 2.100 et seq above) it was observed how the provision of information by central government for publicity purposes was restricted by conventions. A series of confrontations between central government and local government in the 1980s ended in legislation restricting the use of information by authorities for publicity purposes. This followed a report from a committee of inquiry under David Widdicombe QC published in July 1985.[1] The specific terms of reference were to clarify:

> 'the limits and conditions governing discretionary spending, including the use of ss 137 and 142 of the LGA 1972 and Scottish equivalents for political purposes in local government, or in relation to bodies set up, and largely financed by, local authorities.'

[1] Local Authority Publicity (1985) HMSO.

4.161 Under the Local Government Act 1986 (LGA 1986), as amended by LGA 1988, a local authority shall not publish any material which, in whole or in part, appears to be designed to affect public support for a political party.[1] In determining whether material falls within the prohibition, regard shall be had to the content and style of the material, the time and other circumstances of publication and the likely effect on those to whom it is directed and, in particular, to the following matters:

(a) whether the material refers to a political party or to persons identified with a political party or promotes or opposes a point of view on a question of political controversy which is identified as the view of one political party and not of another; and

(b) where the material is part of a campaign, the effect that the campaign appears to be designed to achieve.[2]

[1] LGA 1986, s 2(1).
[2] LGA 1986, s 2(2) as amended by LGA 1988, s 27; effective from May 1988.

4.162 Under LGA 1986, s 2(3), an authority shall not give financial or other assistance to a person for the publication of material which the authority are prohibited by this section from publishing themselves, ie it prohibits publication through an agent or indirectly.

4.163 Section 3 of the LGA 1986 is a voluminous section amending LGA 1972, ss 137 and 142 and Local Government (Scotland) Act 1973, ss 88 and 83. LGA 1972, s 142 concerns the provision of information relating to local government within authorities' respective areas as well as films, lectures, seminars and displays to the same effect. The sections had featured in various celebrated episodes, including the abolition of the Greater London Council (GLC), and regularly in litigation causing the auditor to opine that s 142 should be concerned more with 'information rather than persuasion'.[1] The Scottish and English case-law established that: the provision did not confine a council to publishing purely factual information. It allowed explanation and justification. Nor was the authority prevented from selecting information projecting the controlling party in a favourable light[2] but attempting to persuade the local inhabitants to adopt a course of action advocated by an authority, against the effects of rate-capping, and employing an advertising agency to effect such persuasion, were unlawful. The authority was adopting an unlawful objective viz, persuasion or proselytisation which had materially influenced its decision. Permitted objectives within 'information relating to local government' would be an explanation of legislation such as the Rates Act 1984 as well as a description of how far the authority's activities and facilities would be contracted if the Secretary of State's directions on maximum expenditure were adhered to.[3] The GLC was restrained by injunction from engaging advertisers to help its campaign against abolition. It was not a case of information dissemination but persuasion.[4]

[1]   *R v Inner London Education Authority, ex p Westminster City Council* [1986] 1 All ER 19; *R v Greater London Council, ex p Westminster City Council* (1985) Times, 22 January.
[2]   *Meek v Lothian Regional Council* 1983 SLT 494.
[3]   *R v Inner London Education Authority, ex p Westminster City Council* [1986] 1 All ER 19.
[4]   *R v Greater London Council, ex p Westminster City Council* (1985) *Times*, 22 January.

4.164 LGA 1972, s 142 is now amended and concerns publicity 'relating to the functions of an authority' and not 'as to local government matters affecting the area' – ie it is drawn more tightly and relates to functions which must be statutorily based – and to services available in the area provided by other authorities as mentioned in sub-s (1B). The Communications Act 2003 amends s 142 to allow for an electronic communications network or electronic communications service to broadcast or distribute information falling within the amended section, but not to do anything which would be a contravention of the 2003 Act or a number of other Acts which concern licensing of broadcasting and electronic communications networks. An arrangement may be made with the provider of such a network. Information concerns information relating to services within an authority's area provided by the authority or by other authorities mentioned in sub-s (1B) or information relating to the functions of an authority.

4.165 LGA 1972, s 137 confers a power upon authorities to spend up to the product of various charges[1] which in their opinion is in the interests of the area or any part of it or some or all of its inhabitants, provided that the object of expenditure is not the subject of other statutory provision. Widdicombe in 1985 found that some authorities had used this section to finance publicity campaigns.

Section 3 of the LGA 1986 amends the section to limit its scope. A local authority may incur expenditure under s 137(1) on publicity only:

(a) for the purpose of promoting the economic development of the authority's area where the publicity is incidental to other activities undertaken or to be undertaken by the authority for that purpose; or

(b) by way of assistance to a public body or voluntary organisation where the publicity is incidental to the main purpose for which assistance is given.[2]

[1] See now LGHA 1989, Sch 2 and the replacement of the 2p rate: s 137(4) and (4AA). LGA 2003, s 118 provides for differences to formulae calculating sums.

[2] LGA 1972, s 137(2C); LGA 1986, s 3(3).

4.166 LGA 1972, s 137(2C) also provides that expenditure under s 142 on information as to services provided by local authorities shall be subject to s 137(2D)–(9) so that expenditure under s 142 will be included in the financial limit under s 137.

4.167 Finally, LGA 1972, s 137(2D) defines 'publicity' as 'any communication, in whatever form, addressed to the public at large or to a section of the public', and 'voluntary organisation' as 'a body which is not a public body but whose activities are carried on otherwise than for profit'.

4.168 Part I of the LGA 2000 contains powers for local authorities as defined to promote the economic, social or environmental well-being etc of their areas (s 2). Limits are set in s 3 which prevent an authority doing anything prohibited etc in any enactment although these may be repealed by an order of the Secretary of State under s 5. LGA 2000, s 7 makes further provision for the definition of local authorities by a slight amendment to LGA 1972, s 137. Clause 1 of the Localism Bill (2010–2011) introduces a new 'general power of competence', giving local authorities the same power to act that an individual generally has. This general power of competence is subject to the boundaries contained in clause 2, one of which is that: 'If the exercise of a pre-commencement power of a local authority is subject to restrictions, those restrictions apply also to exercise of the general power insofar as it is overlapped by the pre-commencement power'. The precise result of this interplay between clause 1 and clause 2 is not entirely clear. The explanatory notes to the Bill state that: '…if an existing power requires a particular procedure to be followed, the same procedure will apply to the use of the general power to do the same thing'. It also applies any express prohibitions, restrictions and limitations within primary or secondary legislation, to the use of the general power. Schedule 1 of the Bill also proposes a slight amendment of LGA 1972, s 137(9) to provide for a definition of local authorities in accordance with the provisions of the Bill. It is clear that this change would expand the powers of local authorities to a considerable degree beyond those described above in LGA 2000. At the same time, limitations and prohibitions such as those contained in LGA 1972, ss 137 and 142 would seem to continue to apply.

4.169 LGA 1972, s 142(2A) allows authorities to assist voluntary organisations to provide advice and information to individuals about their rights and duties as well as providing assistance by making communications or providing representation.

4.170   Section 4 of the LGA 1986, as amended, empowers the Secretary of State to issue one or more codes of recommended practice on the content, style, distribution and cost of local authority publicity and such other related matters as s/he thinks appropriate, and local authorities 'shall have regard to the provisions of any such code in coming to any decision on publicity'.[1] This does not mean follow, even less slavishly adhere to, but the authority, to be safe, must provide evidence, eg a minute, that they regarded the code.

[1]   'Shall have regard to': *De Falco v Crawley Borough Council* [1980] QB 460, CA. See also *R (Beale) v Camden LBC* [2004] EWHC 6 (Admin), [2004] HLR 48.

4.171   Codes may deal with different kinds of publicity or different kinds of local authority or the same kind of local authority in different circumstances or different areas and the code may be revised or withdrawn. A code, which shall be subject to consultation[1] before issue or revision or withdrawal, shall be laid in draft and approved by both Houses. Revisions of a code are subject to more prolix procedures. The Code was revised and republished in 2011, partly in order to address certain issues, particularly local authority publication of local newspapers, which the incoming government felt were a problem. The major provisions of the Code are as follows. It states[2] that nothing in the Code overrides the prohibition found in LGA 1986, s 2 (see para 4.161) but that some guidance is offered on publications which may contain or have links to party political material. The major focus of the Code is 'paid advertising and leaflet campaigns, publication of free newspapers and newssheets and maintenance of websites – including the hosting of material which is created by third parties.[3]

[1]   With local authority associations appearing to be concerned and with any authorities as appear to the Secretary of State to be desirable.
[2]   DCLG Circular 01/2011, para 3.
[3]   DCLG Circ 01/2011, para 2.

4.172   There are some key principles for all local government publications in the code. All publications should be lawful, cost-effective, objective, even-handed, appropriate, have regard to equality and diversity and should be issued with care during periods of heightened sensitivity.[1] The Code further notes that 'local authorities should not use public funds to mount publicity campaigns whose primary purpose is to persuade the public to hold a particular view on a question of policy.' It is permissible, however, for an authority to publish material that corrects erroneous material that has been published by other parties.[2]

[1]   DCLG Circ 01/2011, para 4.
[2]   DCLG Circ 01/2011, para 16.

4.173   The Code is clear that all local authority publicity that is paid for must abide by the ASA's Code, and any broadcast material must be sure to avoid contravening the prohibition on political advertising in the Communications Act 2003 and also legislation on elections and referendums.[1] All publicity relating to policies should be balanced and factually accurate and all paid-for advertising by LAs should be clearly marked as such.[2] The Code further prohibits the paying of lobbyists in order to publish material designed to change the views of public officials, MPs, etc and provides that LAs should not spend money on having stands at the conferences of political parties which seek to influence members of that party to take a particular view on a certain issues or issues.[3] One particular feature of the new Code, as noted above, is that it aims to prevent any publication of communications which 'seek to emulate commercial newspapers in style or content'.[4] Furthermore, where LAs seek to publish newspapers or similar publications, these should not be published more frequently than on a quarterly basis, or a monthly basis in the case of parish councils.[5] The content of such publications should be limited to information about the 'business, services and amenities of the council or other local service providers'. All information that is produced should be freely available to anyone who requests it, and should be 'in a format readily accessible and understandable by the person making the request or by any particular group for which services are provided'.[6] All local authority publications should seek, insofar as is possible, to further the authority's obligations in terms of combating discrimination and promoting equality and diversity.

[1]   DCLG Circ 01/2011, paras 5–9.
[2]   DCLG Circ 01/2011, paras 15–18.
[3]   DCLG Circ 01/2011, paras 26 and 27.
[4]   DCLG Circ 01/2011, para 28.
[5]   DCLG Circ 01/2011, para 28.
[6]   DCLG Circ 01/2011, para 29.

4.174   The Code has guidance on advertising, which should not be used as a means of subsidising a voluntary, commercial or industrial organisation, and which should be cost-effective. Local authorities should generally avoid publications which do nothing more than seek to echo central government publicity. Where there is a question of value for money, LAs ought to seek advice from appropriately qualified analysts.[1]

[1]   DCLG Circ 01/2011, paras 10–14.

4.175   The code contains a section on the use of publicity at times of heightened sensitivity, and addresses publications at the time of elections and referendums. The basic thrust is that publications on politically controversial issues should be avoided at this time and no publication should seek to influence voters.[1] The Code was the subject of a report by the Communities and Local Government Select Committee.[2] The Committee expressed some dissatisfaction with the Code's limitations on the ability of LAs to produce newspapers as it was felt that the complaints of the local and regional press that these publications were unfair competition were not generally supported by evidence. Furthermore, the report notes that although there is need for regulation of the use of lobbyists by local government, the Code on publicity, particularly given its lack of direct enforceability, is perhaps not the best place for this to be done.

[1]   DCLG Circ 01/2011, paras 33–35.
[2]   HC 666 (2010–2011)

4.176 Under s 5 of the LGA 1986, local authorities are required to keep a separate account of expenditure for publicity. This applies to publicity expressly or impliedly authorised by any statutory provision. Any interested person may at any reasonable time and without payment inspect the account and make copies of it.[1] Intentional obstruction of this right is a criminal offence triable summarily. Power to make regulations governing rights of inspection of accounts under LGFA 1982, s 23(1)(e) applies to the right of inspection under s 5(2).[2] The Secretary of State may exclude by order prescribed descriptions of publicity or expenditure.[3]

[1] LGA 1986, s 5(2).
[2] LGA 1986, s 5(4).
[3] LGA 1986, s 5(5); see also sub-ss (6) and (7).

4.177 The provisions of LGA 1986 do not apply to information provided under LGA 1972, Part VA (LG(ATI)A 1985) and its Scottish analogue. Local authorities are defined in s 6(2) to include those in s 6(3). The LGA 1986 also covers any such publicity expressly or impliedly authorised by any statutory provision including:

- s 111 of the LGA 1972 – general subsidiary powers;[1]
- s 141 of the LGA 1972 – research and collection of information; and
- s 145(1)(a) of the LGA 1972 – provision of entertainment etc.

[1] *R v Greater London Council, ex p Westminster City Council* (1985) *Times*, 22 January.

4.178 A new s 2A was added to LGA 1986 by LGA 1988, s 28. This prohibits the intentional promotion of homosexuality or the publication of material with the intention of promoting homosexuality by a local authority.[1] The section continues that a local authority shall not promote the teaching in any maintained school (s 2A(4)) of the 'acceptability of homosexuality as a pretended family relationship'.[2] In any proceedings connected with the application of this section a court shall draw such inferences as to the intention of the local authority as may reasonably be drawn from the evidence before it. The evidence before the court, and inferences from that evidence alone, must be viewed objectively (s 2A(2)). However, 'nothing in sub-s (1) above shall be taken to prohibit the doing of anything for the purpose of treating or preventing the spread of disease' providing there is not, presumably, an ulterior motive as inferred under s 2A(3).

[1] LGA 1986, s 2A(1)(a).
[2] LGA 1986, s 2A(1)(b).

4.179 The provisions in LGA 1988, s 28 sparked off further controversy when attempts were made in Scotland to repeal this provision and hostile reaction ensued from church leaders and businessmen. The government also sought, initially unsuccessfully, to repeal the provisions in England and Wales. Under LGA 2000, a provision was added stating that the above ban did not prevent the headteacher or governing body of a maintained school, or a teacher employed by a maintained school, from taking steps to prevent any form of bullying. LGA 1986, s 2A was repealed by LGA 2003, s 122.

QUASI LOCAL GOVERNMENT

4.180 A member of that family of beasts known as 'quangos' is a 'qualgo' – a quasi autonomous local government organisation. In general terms these are bodies which are not local authorities according to statutory definitions, but which are either government agencies – the urban development corporations under the Local Government Planning and Land Act 1980 is an example – or else they are created by local authorities – such as local authority companies – or they may form partnerships between central and local government, eg, local enterprise agencies. To these may be added a wide variety of programmes and agencies initiated by central government but operating locally. Lord Nolan's committee on standards also investigated local spending bodies such as higher education institutions, further education institutions, grant maintained schools, Training and Enterprise Councils, local enterprise councils in Scotland and housing associations.[1]

[1]   *Local Public Spending Bodies* Cm 3270 I and II (1996).

4.181 To what extent are these bodies bound to provide information to the public about their activities? The bodies in question are not formally within the terms of the LG(ATI)A 1985 and so are not covered by that legislation unless items of their business are present on the agenda of authority meetings.[1] Even here, they would be subject to exclusion on grounds of confidentiality or exemption. Apart from this eventuality, the information and meetings of such bodies do not have to be available to the public or open to the public, though they may be available to other bodies such as the Comptroller and Auditor-General, the parliamentary or local commissioner, or they may have to report to the Secretary of State or to Parliament. With companies, the provisions of company law apply, although the information available under the Companies Acts will be limited largely to details of directors, etc and accounting information.[2] If the bodies or their functions are identified or designated for purposes of FOIA 2000, then they will be under that legislation (see ch 1). It is interesting to note that Chapter 3 of Part 2 of the Local Democracy, Economic Development and Construction Act 2009 provides that all companies, limited liability partnerships and industrial and provident societies connected to local authorities in England should be notified to the Audit Commission, which will then appoint an auditor. There is provision for the auditor's access to all relevant information from the body concerned and the auditor is empowered to publish 'public interest reports'. These provisions have not been brought into force and the relevant regulations to support their operation do not seem to have been drawn up. In light of the present government's proposals to abolish the Audit Commission it seems impossible that these provisions will be brought into force in their present form. The provisions appear to serve a valuable function to the extent that they seek to deliver further accountability and openness in what is one of the least regulated areas of local authority activity and it may be that their spirit might be maintained in the future as the impact of the proposed changes in the Localism Bill (2010–2011) to local authority powers becomes apparent.

[1]   See chs 5 and 6.
[2]   See the Companies Act 2006.

4.182 Government legislation has given local authorities a specific power to carry out economic development; they will not use LGA 1972, s 137. 'The power introduced under the LGHA 1989 will be a general, but circumscribed, power to engage in economic development initiatives at the discretion of the authority'.[1] These provisions have now been repealed by LGA 2000 (see paras 4.187 et seq below). Other powers for such expenditure, including that under s 137, were to be removed but survived the 2000 Act. The Conservative government also believed that some activities were not appropriate to local government, eg some commercial trading activities and equity participation in commercial companies. Legislation (infra) would attend to the consideration of priorities across the whole field of economic development; co-ordination with other activities by the authority and with the agencies in the public and private sectors; and proper scrutiny, and special provision for consultation with the business community. On local authority interests in companies a consultation paper was issued by the DoE in June 1988.

[1] Cm 433 (1988), para 7.14.

SECTION 137 EXPENDITURE

4.183 New limits for expenditure under LGA 1972, s 137 were proposed even after the removal of economic development expenditure from the section. Section 137 is widely used for funding voluntary organisations, charities and bodies providing a public service otherwise than for gain and for contributions to special appeals. Section 137 need only be used:
(a) where an authority is contributing to the general running costs of a charity working in the UK – eg Marriage Guidance Council;
(b) for some activities in certain types of advice-giving organisations, eg law centres;
(c) for an appeal by another local authority; and
(d) to fund other organisations, where specific powers or s 137 do not apply, but where they consider such expenditure to be in the interests of the area or some of its inhabitants.

4.184 While accepting the desirability of funding of voluntary bodies, the government agreed with Widdicombe that there should be clear arrangements for assuring the accountability and monitoring of bodies that benefit from grants. A list of grants to bodies and their purpose should be made available – these would be those in excess of £2,000. Voluntary bodies should send an annual report to the authority saying how the grant has been used; this should be publicly available. The code of practice on annual reports is to be amended to give the public more detailed information about s 137 spending 'which by definition is spending on matters not approved by Parliament'.

4.185 Section 137 is further amended[1] and a new s 137A is added by LGHA 1989, s 37. This provides that where in any financial year a local authority provides financial assistance to a voluntary organisation (s 137(2D)) or a body or fund falling within s 137(3), and the amount provided equals or exceeds the relevant minimum (£2,000 or such sum as specified by order (s 137(3)), the body has to furnish to the authority a statement in writing of the use to which the amount has been put.[2] Such a statement has to be furnished within the period of 12 months beginning on the date when the assistance is provided (ie, the date on which the grant or loan is made, or on which a guarantee was entered into). Under s 137(4) it is sufficient to furnish to the local authority an annual report or accounts containing the required information which shall be deposited with the 'proper officer'.[3] 'Local authority' includes the common council of the City of London. LGA 2003, Sch 8, Part I repealed s 137(4AA) and (4C).

[1]   And see LGA 1972, s 137 as amended by LGHA 1989, Sch 2, and Audit Commission Act 1998, Sch 3, para 3(4).
[2]   LGA 1972, s 137A, added by LGHA 1989, s 37.
[3]   Available as accounts and under the LG(ATI)A 1985 but cf exemptions, infra.

ECONOMIC DEVELOPMENT

4.186   The powers associated with the promotion of economic development are now contained in Part I of LGA 2000. If the proposed changes in the Localism Bill (2010–2011) come into force, authorities will enjoy expanded powers in this area along with many others. Before examining these provisions it should be noted that LGA 2003, ss 41–59 make provision for business improvement districts (BIDs). Reference has already been made to BIDs (para 4.47 above) and how they are subject to approval by non-domestic rate-payers.

4.187   The provisions of LGA 2000 define 'local authorities', give wide powers to authorities to promote or improve the economic well-being of the area as well as social well-being and economic well-being of the area (s 2). Specific powers are given under s 2(4) and the power is subject to legal prohibitions and restrictions and does not include a power to raise money. It may also be subject to restrictions set out in Standing Orders and authorities must have regard to guidance from the Secretary of State. Community strategies must be prepared. Powers inhibiting authorities may be revoked, repealed, disapplied or amended by Order (s 5). Under s 6 the Secretary of State may by order revoke etc any enactment requiring a local authority to prepare, produce or publish any plan or strategy relating to such a matter.[1] The Localism Bill (2010–2011) will apply LGA 2000, s 2 only to Wales, as the powers of LAs in England will be expanded in the manner described in para 4.168 above.

[1]   See amendments in LGA 2003, s 100 and Sch 3, para 12.

Companies as 'alter egos' of local authorities

4.188   LGA 2003, s 127 and Sch 8, Part I repealed LGHA 1989, Part IV (ss 39–66) which concerned revenue accounts and capital finance of local authorities, which were enumerated within s 39.

4.189   LGA 2003, s 18 makes provision for the bodies described and seeks to ensure that local authorities do not evade capital controls. This applies to

Passenger Transport Executives, companies under LGHA 1989, Part V subject to local authority influence or control, and trusts subject to local authority influence.

LOCAL AUTHORITY LOANS

4.190   A new regime for capital finance, credit and accounts was introduced by LGA 2003, ss 1–24.[1] These provisions replace the controls in LGHA 1989, Part IV and seek to introduce a national framework of standards and accountability, devolution, diversity, flexibility and greater choice of 'customers'. Credit arrangements (loans) must not exceed the affordable borrowing limit set by an authority under s 3 and any limits under s 4 concerning national limits or limits set by direction in relation to a particular authority. The Secretary of State has certain reserved powers under s 8(3). Under s 14, a local authority shall supply the Secretary of State with such information relating to any of the matters dealt with in this Chapter, and at such time, as he may request. Although the Localism Bill (2010–2011) expands the powers of authorities, as noted in para 4.168 above, existing limitations on powers and processes are maintained, so the provisions in the LGA 2003 on borrowing will retain relevance.

[1]   See *Modernising Local Government Finance* (September 2000) and *Strong Leadership: Quality Public Services* Cm 5237 (2001). LGA 2003, Part 7 seeks to simplify the housing revenue account and subsidy system. It contains powers on borrowing and freedom to establish 'high-performing' arms length management organisations (ALMOs). The *Local Government Ombudsman Annual Report 2003–04* stated that ALMOs are within the LGO jurisdiction but detailed advice would be provided in guidance on 'Partnerships'.

LOCAL AUTHORITIES AND CONTROLLED COMPANIES

4.191   LGHA 1989, Part V (ss 67–73) concerns companies in which local authorities have interests. Section 68 concerns companies under the control of a local authority and how control is constituted. Section 68(6) stipulates that notwithstanding that a company is a controlled company, it will be deemed an 'arm's length' company if all of eight conditions apply at the time it is controlled. Section 69 concerns companies subject to local authority influence – this will include 'almost all housing associations' – the provisions of which may be extended to non-charitable trusts subject to local authority influence. Different provisions may be made for trusts and companies under s 70 (the substantive provision governing the actions of authorities over controlled and influenced companies) (s 72(2)). Where a company is an 'authorised' company, ie specified as such by regulations, then by s 71(5) in any case where a member or officer is an authority's representative at an annual general meeting of an authorised company or is a member of an authorised company mentioned in s 71(7), the authority has to make arrangements (by SO or otherwise) allowing members to put questions to the representative about the company's activities.

> '(6) Nothing in subsection (5) above shall require the representative (as defined in that subsection) to disclose any information about the company which has been communicated to him in confidence.'

4.192   Section 73 makes special provisions for the situation where authorities are acting jointly in controlling companies, or do so by committees. The effect of LGA 2003, s 18 was outlined above. Part V is the subject of repeal by the Local Government and Public Involvement in Health Act 2007, s 216, but the repeal has not yet been brought into force. Part V would be replaced by the provisions of Part 12 of the 2007 Act and relevant secondary legislation which has not yet been made. It is presently unclear whether the repeal is likely to be brought into force.

URBAN DEVELOPMENT CORPORATIONS

4.193   Urban development corporations (UDCs) were public corporations established by statutory order under LGPLA 1980, s 135 for designated areas of land by the Secretary of State if s/he is of the opinion that it is expedient in the national interest to do so. In 1990, UDCs existed in the following areas: London Docklands, Merseyside, Trafford Park, Teesside, Tyne and Wear, Cardiff, Bristol, Leeds, Central Manchester and Sheffield. These UDCs have now lapsed. New UDCs were created in Thurrock in 2003, London Thames Gateway in 2004 and Northamptonshire West in 2006. At the present time, these are the only three active UDCs. Details of their operations may be found in the first edition of this book.[1]

[1]   *Government and Information: The Law Relating to Access, Disclosure and Regulation* (1st edn, 1990), ch 2.

HOUSING ACTION TRUSTS

4.194   Housing action trusts (HATs) were intended to take over local authority housing powers and duties. They are public corporations. They are not subject to the LG(ATI)A 1985. Their impact on housing is dealt with later in this book (paras 8.94 et seq below).

COUNCIL TAX

4.195   Schedule 2 to the LGFA 1992 and Regulations thereunder set out details on administration of the collection of council tax, which replaced the notorious poll tax provisions, and include: supply of information to authorities; supply of information by authorities; and use of information by authorities.[1] Schedule 3 lists penalties for failing to supply information to either billing or levying authorities.[2]

[1]   Numerous regulations have been made under this schedule, see eg SI 1992/613 as amended. See LGA 2003, Part 6.
[2]   See SI 1992/613, as amended.

NON-DOMESTIC RATING

4.196   Under LGFA 1988, Sch 9, para 5 valuation officers (VOs) may serve a notice on an owner or occupiers of an hereditament requesting information as specified and which the officer reasonably believes will assist him/her in carrying out his/her statutory functions. The LGHA 1989 has added a new para 1A requiring the officer to state why s/he believes the information requested will assist him/her in carrying out his/her functions. Further provisions added by that Act relate to the supply to the VO of information as prescribed by regulations, and to access to valuation lists by 'a person' whether as against the VO (if the VO maintains it), the charging authority,[1] or the Secretary of State.[2] Compliance must be within a reasonable time and place without payment; information may be in documentary or other form as the person or authority requested thinks fit.[3] Copies of information in documentary form may be made by the person given access and photocopies may be requested; where not in documentary form transcripts may be made of or from the information, or a person having control of access to the information may be required to supply him/her with a copy in documentary form of, or extracts from, the information.[4] A reasonable charge may be requested, compliance depending upon payment. Intentional obstruction is an offence. Under LGFA 1988, Sch 9, para 9,[5] a person may, at a reasonable time and without making payment, inspect any proposal made or notice of appeal given under regulations made under s 55 of the LGFA 1988, if made or given as regards a list which is in force when inspection is sought or which has been in force at any time in the preceding five years. Copies of, or extracts from, documents may be made, or photographic copies requested from a person with custody (para 9(2)). A reasonable charge may be requested, compliance depending upon payment. Intentional obstruction is an offence.

[1]   Where the authority has deposited a copy of the list under LGFA 1988, s 41(6B).
[2]   Where the Secretary of State has deposited it under LGFA 1988, s 52(6B).
[3]   LGFA 1988, Sch 9, para 8(6) as amended by LGHA 1989, Sch 5. And see revised paras 5 and 6.
[4]   LGFA 1988, Sch 9, para 8(7), (8).
[5]   As amended by LGHA 1989, Sch 5.

4.197 National non-domestic rating is based upon two rating lists: the local list compiled under LGFA 1988, s 41 by the VO; and the central list, compiled by the central VO under LGFA 1988, s 52. The latter concerns centrally owned property, eg nationalised industries, privatised utilities. Both lists were to be compiled on 1 April 1990, and on 1 April of every fifth year thereafter.

4.198 The LGA 2003 makes some significant developments in relation to non-domestic rates. Briefly these affect rate relief and crucially, a power for the Secretary of State to prescribe a system for the local retention of non-domestic rates (s 70). This is part of the move to greater flexibility in local provision of services and should be seen alongside the provisions on BIDs (para 4.186 above).

LOCAL ACCESS FORUMS

4.199 The Local Access Forums (England) Regulations 2007, SI 2007/268, made under Countryside and Rights of Way Act 2000, s 94, require Highway Authorities and National Park Authorities to establish advisory bodies – local access forums – to advise on improved access to land for open-air recreational purposes. These Regulations include consultation requirements and public access to meetings of forums.

POLICE

4.200 Outside the Metropolitan Police District and City of London Police Area, police were traditionally organised on a local basis. The movement towards a national legal framework for policing has been a dramatic development in the last ten years as will be seen. There are also specific forces covering British Rail and the Ministry of Defence.[1] Earlier legislation was consolidated in the Police Act 1996 which established police areas. Each police area shall have police authorities which are committees based on county councils with necessary modifications after the introduction of unitary authorities. Combined police authorities are appointed where two or more county areas have been combined.[2] The size of the authority must be at least 17, with a majority made up from elected councillors appointed by the relevant council(s), five are independent members appointed by the authority from a short-list drawn up by the Secretary of State, and three are JPs. Until the Greater London Authority Act 1999, the police authority for the Metropolitan Police was the Home Secretary (see below); for the City of London Police, the police authority is the Court of Common Council. Strategic priorities and performance targets for police authorities may be set by the Home Secretary.[3] Police authorities must establish objectives for the policing of the authority's area during the year, establish local plans setting out proposed arrangements for the policing of the authority's area during the year and must publish annual reports.[4] Under the LGA 1999, police authorities are responsible for conducting 'best value' reviews. The Government has presented the Police Reform and Social Responsibility Bill (2010–2011) to Parliament. This Bill proposes enormous changes to the present regime of police governance. Outside of London, police authorities are to be replaced by police and crime commissions, led by a police and crime commissioner, with the remainder of the elected members constituting a police and crime panel. The commissions are to be elected through the procedure outlined in Chapter 6 of Part 1 of the Bill and then the police and crime panel will choose one of their number to be the commissioner (clause 1). In the Metropolitan Police district, the Mayor of London will serve the function of commissioners elsewhere in the country. The police and crime commissioner will issue a police and crime plan in the financial year in which each ordinary election of commissioners takes place, though the plan may be varied (clause 6 or 7 in London). Any strategic priorities set down by the Secretary of State must be had regard to. Once the plan is issued, the commissioner must have regard to it in the exercise of his functions, as must the Chief Constable of each force. Clauses 12–15 set out provisions for the elected body to publish information specified in regulations, produce annual reports and provide information to police and crime panels. Clause 15 amends the route through which public views on policing can be sought, amending the relevant provisions in the Police Act 1996. Chapter 4 of Part 1 of the Bill deals with accountability of the commissioner, including the power to require attendance and information in clause 30. It is also proposed that the Secretary of State's power to issue performance targets for the police be repealed (clause 83). Clause 80 of the Act proposes significant amendment of s 37A of the Police Act 1996, which presently allows the Secretary of State to set strategic priorities for police authorities. If the amendments proposed in clause 80 come into force, the

Secretary of State will be empowered to issue a document known as the 'strategic policing requirement', which sets out the Secretary of State's view of national threats at the time of issue and the appropriate national policing capabilities to counter the threats identified. Chief officers will be required to have regard to this in the exercise of their functions. It is perhaps strange that there is no requirement for commissioners or panels to have regard to these when setting priorities.

[1]   Metropolitan Police Acts 1829 et seq; Police Act 1964; Ministry of Defence Police Act 1987; Transport Act 1947; cf Police Officers (Central Service) Act 1989.
[2]   See LGA 1985, ss 24 and 25 for arrangements after the abolition of the metropolitan counties.
[3]   PA 1996, ss 37A and 38.
[4]   PA 1996, ss 7, 8 and 9.

4.201   The legal relationship between the authority and chief officer of police – in the Metropolitan force the commissioner,[1] in the counties and combined forces the chief constable,[2] and in the City the commissioner[3] – is contained in the Metropolitan Police Acts 1829–1839, and for county forces in the Police Act 1964 (which also has some provisions relating to the Metropolitan force) as consolidated in the Police Act 1996. The basic informing idea behind the police in England and Wales is that they should operate free from executive or political control. In the Metropolitan force it has usually been said that the Home Secretary assumes a wide responsibility to Parliament for the general policies of the Metropolitan Police, while denying himself any opportunity to direct the detailed operations of the force which is the preserve of the commissioner,[4] a position accepted by the Parliamentary Commissioner and a Lord Justice of Appeal,[5] although 'this forthright view is not in full accord with the history of the Metropolitan Police'.[6] Should the Police Reform and Social Responsibility Bill (2010–2011) be enacted in its present form, the control of the police, at least at the local level, is likely to become considerably more politicised.

[1]   Appointed by the Crown on the advice of the Home Secretary.
[2]   Appointed by the police authority subject to the Home Secretary's approval.
[3]   As above.
[4]   The Parliamentary Commissioner for Administration has accepted that the Home Secretary has no power to give instructions to the Metropolitan Police on the manner in which they should carry out their duties: HC 6 (1967–68) p 25, HC 350 (1967–68) pp XIII, 56–58 cited in Bradley and Ewing (formerly Wade and Bradley) *Constitutional and Administrative Law* (1997) pp 528 et seq.
[5]   Per Salmon LJ *R v Metropolitan Police Comr, ex p Blackburn* [1968] 2 QB 118 at 138, CA.
[6]   Bradley and Ewing, above, p 529.

4.202   This traditional balance has now been formally influenced by the Police Reform Act 2002. This Act places a duty on the Home Secretary to prepare a National Policing Plan each year setting out strategic priorities for the next three years. The Home Secretary may now issue codes of practice to chief officers of police as well as police authorities, although this power is proposed for repeal by the Police Reform and Social Responsibility Bill (2010–2011), clause 83. Her Majesty's Inspectors of Constabulary are responsible for reports on various inspections into police forces including those on the National Criminal Intelligence Service, National Crime Squad and the Police National Computer (see below). These provisions will be amended by the Police Reform and Social Responsibility Bill (2010–2011) as presently proposed to allow local policing boards to request inspections by Her Majesty's Inspectorate of Constabulary (HMIC) and empowers HMIC, rather than the Secretary of State, to publish the reports that are produced (clauses 85 and 86). Adverse reports on efficiency and effectiveness of forces maintained under s 2 of the Police Act 1996 (local police forces and the Metropolitan police) may lead to a Home Secretary's direction under the 2002 Act, s 5 directing a police authority to take specified remedial measures. The authority may be required to submit an 'action plan' setting out the action proposed to be taken in relation to the remedial measures. The 2002 Act extended the powers of police authorities to require senior officers to resign on the grounds of efficiency and effectiveness and it gives new powers to the Home Secretary to require police authorities to request the resignation or retirement of senior police officers on those grounds (s 33). Section 32 provided new powers to authorities to suspend senior police officers (with the Home Secretary's approval).[1] These provisions will be amended should the Police Reform and Social Responsibility Bill (2010–2011) come into force to transfer these powers to the relevant local police and crime commissioner, though the Secretary of State will retain a power to instruct the commissioner to remove chief constables or the Commissioner and Deputy Commissioner of the Metropolitan Police (clause 84).

[1]   *R (Secretary of State for the Home Department) v Humberside PA* [2004] EWHC 1642.

4.203   Outside the metropolis, the Police Act 1996 (PA 1996) places each police force under the chief constable's direction and control, or, in their absence, that of their deputy.[1] The force is not under the control of the police authority (PA) for operational purposes. The PA provides the requisite premises and equipment (PA 1996, s 4). It, subject to Home Secretary approval, has power of appointment over chief constables or deputy or assistant chief constables, and may require, subject to similar approval, the same officers to retire in the interests of efficiency or effectiveness.[2] The PA may institute disciplinary proceedings against the chief constable and the Home Secretary may require the PA to retire the chief constable (s 42). Note the changes outlined above should the Police Reform and Social Responsibility Bill (2010–2011) be brought into force.

[1]   PA 1996, s 10(1).
[2]   PA 1996, ss 11(2) and 12(3) in relation to Assistant Chief Constables.

4.204   The Greater London Authority Act 1999 established a police authority for the Metropolitan Police (s 310). This will replace the Home Secretary as the PA in London (s 312). The Commissioner and Deputy Commissioner are appointed by the Crown. Assistant Commissioners are appointed by the authority, subject to the Secretary of State's approval (s 319). The authority may call upon the Commissioner, Deputy Commissioner or Assistant Commissioners to retire on the grounds of economy and efficiency, acting with the Secretary of State's approval (ss 318 and 319). Note the changes outlined above should the Police Reform and Social Responsibility Bill (2010–2011) be brought into force.

4.205   The Police Act 1997 created a national policing service: the National Criminal Intelligence Service whose role is the provision of intelligence to other police forces and national law enforcement agencies including the National Crime Squad set up under Part II of the Police Act 1997 and which brings together the regional crime squads. These bodies were disbanded by the Serious Organised Crime and Police Act 2005. The Police Information Technology Organisation set up under Part IV of the Act was responsible for advising the police on information technology, but was disbanded by the Police and Justice Act 2006. Part V of the Act creates a new legislative framework for the disclosure of criminal records for employment purposes (see paras 7.239 et seq below).

4.206   The Serious Organised Crime and Police Act 2005 reformed the national policing agencies significantly, disbanding the National Crime Squad and the National Criminal Intelligence Service as described above and creating the Serious Organised Crime Agency (SOCA), bringing together the two previous bodies. The following passage is taken from the explanatory notes accompanying the Bill:

'The White Paper *One Step Ahead: A 21st Century Strategy to Defeat Organised Crime* (CM 6167) in March 2004 proposed the establishment of a single powerful agency to lead the fight against organised crime – the Serious Organised Crime Agency. SOCA will bring together the National Crime Squad (NCS), the National Criminal Intelligence Service (NCIS), the investigative and intelligence work of Her Majesty's Customs and Excise (HMCE) on serious drug trafficking, and the Immigration Service's responsibilities for organised immigration crime. SOCA will be an intelligence-led organisation. Its core objective will be to reduce the harm caused by organised crime. To achieve this objective SOCA, working with others, will use a variety of strategies, including the investigation and prosecution of criminals involved in serious organised crime, the disruption of supply networks, the confiscation of criminal assets, the taxation of undeclared earnings and improving the defences of the financial sector and others against attack by organised criminals. In discharging its functions, SOCA will co-operate closely with the police, intelligence agencies, Asset Recovery Agency (ARA), Her Majesty's Revenue and Customs (HMRC) (which under the Commissioners for Revenue and Customs Bill is expected to take over the functions of the Inland Revenue and the Commissioners for Customs and Excise during 2005), financial regulators, international partners and many others.

SOCA's remit will extend throughout the United Kingdom, but with special arrangements in place in recognition of the devolution settlement in Scotland and the particular circumstances of Northern Ireland. In carrying out its functions in Scotland and Northern Ireland, the Agency will work in partnership with the Scottish Drug Enforcement Agency and the Police Service for Northern Ireland respectively.'

4.207   The Serious Organised Crime and Police Act 2005, ss 9 and 10 allow the Secretary of State to set strategic priorities and lay down Codes of Conduct for SOCA. Numerous sections of the Act cover various informational issues. Sections 6 and 7 of the Act require SOCA to produce annual plans and annual reports respectively and s 11 gives the Secretary of State the power to require that SOCA submits a report to him on issues related to the exercise of its functions. Sections 32–35 of the Act concern SOCA's use of information. Section 32 permits SOCA to use information that it has acquired in the exercise of one of its functions in relation to any of its other functions. Sections 33–35 of the Act set out the ways in which SOCA might disclose information to other parties and the restrictions on disclosure. Finally, s 36 requires other police forces to pass information to SOCA.

4.208 The Government proposes to disband SOCA and create a National Crime Agency (NCA), designed to offer an integrated approach to the tackling of national and organised crime. The NCA will have a number of different operational commands, including a border policing command and an economic crime command, which will work alongside the Serious Fraud Office, the FSA and the OFT. There is no draft legislation on this issue in the public domain at the time of writing,[1] so the informational framework is not yet clear, although the NCA's powers are likely to be similar to those of SOCA. The NCA should come into operation in 2013 according to current plans.

[1]   The general outline of the NCA is set out in a statement by the Home Secretary (Theresa May) to Parliament. See HC Deb, 8 June 2011, c 232.

The police authority's power to obtain information

4.209 The opportunities for the PA to extract information from the chief constable are circumscribed. Its responsibilities cover an 'efficient' and 'effective' police force, but general standards are laid down by the Home Secretary. The Home Secretary may give directions to authorities after adverse reports by inspectors of constabulary and as to a minimum budget (PA 1996, ss 40–41). On operational matters, the chief constable has control. The chief constable sends a copy of his annual report to the PA and the authority may request the chief constable to make a report on specific matters connected with the policing of his area (s 22). The chief constable may withhold, however, with the support of the Home Secretary, information which in the public interest ought not to be disclosed (s 22(5)). The relationship between a PA and the chief constable will be coloured by a wide variety of factors, the formal legal details accounting for only one part of that relationship. While chief constables have often displayed a greater degree of candour with their PAs, the law gives them the right to withhold information on those matters which they believe should remain confidential. They retain control over operational matters and information thereon. Difficulties have arisen in detailed questioning by PAs on the application of general policy, rather than on specific cases which very often relate to complaints,[1] or which anticipate requests for discovery in litigation.[2] The PA has to keep itself informed about the manner in which complaints about the police from the public are dealt with by the chief constable. At county council and analogous local authority meetings, members of a police authority can be questioned by county councillors or other members about the discharge of the authority's functions (s 20). The impact of the LG(ATI)A 1985 is examined in chs 5 and 6. The FOIA 2000 applies to police authorities and chief officers of police. The Police Reform and Social Responsibility Bill (2010–2011) proposes that HMIC be added as a designated body to FOIA 2000 (clause 89).

¹   See Part II of the Police Reform Act 2002 on complaints.
²   See ch 10 on discovery (disclosure).

4.210   *Ex p Northumbria Police Authority*¹ emphasised the special relationship between the Home Secretary and chief constables. The Court of Appeal held that a chief constable could provide plastic baton rounds and CS gas to the force under either s 41 of the Police Act 1964 or under a prerogative power to maintain the peace as an officer of the Crown.² The issue of a Home Office circular advising that the chief constable did not have to consult the PA on their provision was ruled not to be ultra vires as it did not replace an exclusive power of the PA under s 4(4), but expressed rather a surviving prerogative power relating to public security.³

¹   *R v Secretary of State for the Home Department, ex p Northumbria Police Authority* [1988] 1 All ER 556, CA.
²   To provide equipment to maintain efficiency and public order.
³   The Police Act 1964 had not filled all the space occupied by the former prerogative under the principle of *A-G v De Keyser's Royal Hotel* [1920] AC 508, HL. See also *R v Secretary of State for the Home Department, ex p Fire Brigades Union* [1995] 2 All ER 244 HL.

4.211   The case is, it is submitted, unsatisfactory, as many basic constitutional points are not given sufficient analysis. What, for instance, is the extent of this prerogative? When will it come into play to remove the safeguard provided by the PA?

4.212   Police information is covered by the Official Secrets Acts, whereas local authority information is not per se so covered.¹ Employees of a police authority, ie therefore employed by a county council where a committee of the council, are covered by the OSA 1989.² One of the most frequent uses of Official Secrets Act 1911, s 2 concerned unauthorised use and sale of information from the police national computer, or police files.³

¹   Unless it otherwise falls under the OSA 1989 as 'Crown information' (paras 2.163 et seq above).
²   This would cover solicitors employed by forces.
³   As occurred with regularity in Northern Ireland.

Police national computer (PNC)

4.213   The PNC 1 was introduced in 1974 and is based at Hendon in North London. It serves all police forces in England and Wales. It was described by the Bichard inquiry as an 'effective system' giving 'over 138,000 police officers instant access to critical policing information'.¹ The PNC and police practices in relation to data retention were investigated by the Bichard inquiry which reported in June 2004. A more detailed analysis is to be found with an examination of the Data Protection Act 1998 (see para 7.233 below). Requests for data increased

10 per cent to 65 million for the year ending March 1999. This did not include 25 million vehicle checks using ANPR systems. The daily record is 241,788 requests for information from forces. In 1999, the 500,000th criminal record was converted from microfiche onto an online database. Changes have included installation of larger mainframes and wider access to PNC through mobile data terminals. As long ago as 1990, a new computer, PNC 2, was expected to be operating by the end of 1990 and it was hoped to incorporate full criminal records on five million people (on microfiche in 1990). The PNC code of practice of 1982 was not published although a more recent replacement by the Association of Chief Police Officers (ACPO) incorporating the Data Protection Act 1998 was, but it was only in general terms.

¹   *The Bichard Inquiry* HC 653 (2003–04) following the conviction of Ian Huntley for the murders of Jessica Chapman and Holly Wells and the considerable confusion surrounding retention of files under the Data Protection Act 1998.

4.214   The National Strategy for Police Information Systems, launched in November 1994, seeks to set out greater co-ordination between forces in England and Wales in computerised holding and retrieval practices. Police Information Technology Organisation (PITO) is a body set up to develop IT support with the police and involves a tripartite structure of ACPO, police authorities and the Home Office/Scottish Office. It oversees the Police National Network and the National Automated Fingerprint Identification System.

4.215   Information on the PNC, or other police computers, is protected by the Official Secrets Acts where it falls within a relevant category (paras 2.163 et seq above). However, data subjects may have access under the Data Protection Act 1998 although various items relating to police information on individuals will be exempt (see ch 7). A problem with the PNC or other computers will be the fact that one does not know how information is classified and stored, eg, subversives, unwarranted complaint against police, etc. The Home Affairs Committee has criticised police practices in disclosing manual personal records to government and employers and has recommended an independent statutory body to replace police control over record-holding through such bodies as, eg, the National Identification Bureau.¹ The Criminal Records Bureau has such functions delegated to it by the Secretary of State. The details are now in Part V of the Police Act 1997 and are examined in ch 7 (para 7.239 below).

¹   HC 285, 1989–90; and see *On the Record* Cm 3308 (1996) and the earlier Home Office consultation paper *Disclosure of Criminal Records for Employment Vetting Purposes* Cm 2319 (1993).

Police complaints

4.216   Provisions concerning the supervision of police complaints by the Police Complaints Authority and access to investigations generated a great deal of controversy. Many of the complaints which had sought access to information fell under the law concerning public interest immunity (ch 10 below) but not all did. Investigating officers' reports were not available but the position relating to information generated by the investigation and held by the police was altered by the House of Lords when it ruled that such information could only be protected on a contents basis.[1] Under Police Act 1996, s 80 the Police Complaints Authority was prevented from disclosing information received by it in connection with its functions.[2] The position is now governed by the Police Reform Act 2002. Part 2 of, and Schs 2 and 3 to, this Act established the Independent Police Complaints Commission (IPCC). This body will be able to conduct independent investigations into the most serious complaints against the police as well as supervise or manage police investigation of complaints and hear various appeals from local resolution of disputes (a complainant has to consent to a local resolution) and investigations by chief officers or police authorities including where it is alleged inadequate information has been provided (Sch 3, para 25(2) in the latter case). Complaints relating to death or serious injury must be referred to the IPCC, other complaints may be referred under regulations and the IPCC can direct a reference to it of a complaint. The IPCC will have jurisdiction under regulations over the National Criminal Intelligence Service and the National Crime Squad. The system does not deal with complaints relating to direction and control of a police force. There is a duty on the IPCC to keep the complainant informed of the progress of an investigation, provisional findings of the person conducting an investigation, information about relevant reports and action thereunder and the outcome of such action. Regulations may provide for the detail (Police (Complaints and Misconduct) Regulations 2004, SI 2004/643) and for exceptions to disclosure where information may be used for actual or prospective criminal proceedings, where disclosure may be premature or inappropriate and amongst other grounds for the protection of national security, to prevent crime or apprehend offenders, to prevent a disproportionate adverse effect in relation to any benefits or which is otherwise necessary on public interest grounds (s 20 and reg 12). Section 21 imposes a duty on a chief officer, a police authority or the IPCC to keep 'interested' parties (apart from a complainant) informed of matters under the section. This will cover relatives and those suffering serious injury as an alleged result of conduct investigated and those who satisfy s 21(3). It might cover those who withhold their consent for the matter to be dealt with as a complaint leading to the circumstances being dealt with as a 'conduct matter'. The latter may lead to an investigation even though there has been no complaint. It is restricted to matters which are potentially a breach of discipline or a criminal offence (Sch 3, Part 2). Investigations may lead to disciplinary or criminal action (Sch 3, Part 3).

---

[1]   *R v Chief Constable of the West Midlands ex p Wiley* [1994] 3 All ER 420 (HL).
[2]   *R (Green) v Police Complaints Authority* [2004] 2 All ER 209 (HL). Section 80(1)(a) did not, in the circumstances, require disclosure of witness statements and other materials sought by the claimant.

Chapter 5

Restrictions on the use of, and access to, information by public officials and representatives

CENTRAL GOVERNMENT

5.1 The subject of the restriction on information within central government has been examined in ch 2. Such restrictions may also be placed expressly, or by the operation of law, on Crown information covered by the Official Secrets Act 1989 (OSA 1989) which is communicated to officials in other tiers of government, ie local government, public corporations, non-departmental bodies and so on, as well as members of the public, regardless of the fact that the recipients have not signed the OSA. Given the existence of the Freedom of Information Act 2000 (FOIA 2000), it would be possible to plead a defence to charges under the latter Act where a recipient of information had no reason to believe that it had been handed over in contravention of the OSA 1989. Indeed, a proper consideration of an FOIA request may well constitute authorisation under the OSA 1989. Readers are referred to chs 1 and 2.

MPs, Lords and ministers

5.2 The ability of MPs to extract information from departments has been examined above in ch 2. When not protected by parliamentary privilege[1] in the course of parliamentary proceedings, MPs are subject to the same rules of law on the use of information as any other citizen. Under s 13 of the Defamation Act 1996 a Member of Parliament or a peer may waive any protection 'so far as concerns him' of any enactment or rule of law which prevents proceedings in Parliament being impeached or questioned in any court or place outside Parliament and where his conduct in or relating to proceedings in Parliament is in question in defamation proceedings. This was introduced in the Lords to circumvent the decision in *Prebble v Television New Zealand*[2] whereby defamation actions could be staid by a court if the invocation of parliamentary privilege by an MP or peer would cause an injustice to the other party whose ability to defend an action would thereby be seriously undermined by his inability to examine and cross-examine on the basis of privileged material. In *Hamilton v Al Fayed*[3] which concerned the notorious episode in which Neil Hamilton MP was accused by Mohamed Al Fayed of taking bribes for asking parliamentary questions and who subsequently sued Al Fayed for defamation, the House of Lords ruled that s 13 was a 'complete answer' to the application to stay proceedings because it allowed the plaintiff MP to waive the privilege of the whole House, although he could not waive the privilege for another MP in legal proceedings; he could only waive the privilege for himself.[4]

[1] Wade and Ewing *Constitutional and Administrative Law* (2010, 15th edn) ch 11. Article 9 of the Bill of Rights is part of a wider manifestation of privilege in which 'the courts and Parliament are both astute to recognise their respective constitutional roles': Lord Browne-Wilkinson in *Prebble v Television NZ* [1995] 1 AC 321, PC. See also *Toussaint v Attorney General of St. Vincent and the Grenadines* [2007] UKPC 48, [2007] 1 WLR 2825, where the Privy Council found that s 16 of the House of Assembly (Privileges, Immunities and Powers) Act 1966 (of St. Vincent and the Grenadines), which sought to prevent the use of Parliamentary statements as evidence in legal proceedings without the permission of the Speaker of the House did not prevent T from using a statement by the Prime Minister in judicial review proceedings relating to expropriation of his property. This was the case because there was an established practice that ministerial statements in Parliament could be used in judicial review proceedings and also because in a case such as that of T (which concerned appropriation of his property) s 16 had to be read down in light of the constitutional right of protection for private property, thus requiring the statement to be admitted as evidence in order to facilitate such judicial review. In *A v UK* App 3573/97 (2002) *Times*, 28 December, the ECtHR ruled that absolute privilege from defamation for a legislature was not beyond the 'margin of appreciation' and was proportionate; and in *McVicar v UK* App No 4631/99, the ECtHR ruled that unavailability of legal aid for defamation actions was not a breach of Art 6 ECHR. However, the unavailability of legal aid in this case was a breach of Art 6 in *Steel and Morris v UK* (the McDonald libel case) Application 68416/01 (15 February 2005), ECtHR.

[2] [1995] 1 AC 321, PC.

[3] [2000] 2 All ER 224, HL.

[4] Defamation Act 1996, s 13(3). See *Buchanan v Jennings* [2004] 3 WLR 1163 (PC) on repetition of parliamentary statement on non-privileged occasion; record of parliamentary proceedings could be relied upon to confirm the making of a statement and subsequent confirmation of it, even if not repeated, and could lead to a liability in defamation.

5.3 In this case, the Parliamentary Commissioner for Standards (PCS) – appointed as a consequence of Lord Nolan's first report – had investigated complaints against Neil Hamilton and had made an adverse report against him to the Select Committee on Standards and Privileges. The House of Lords doubted the correctness of the Court of Appeal's decision in this case. The Court of Appeal had held that the questioning of the evidence before the Committee on Standards and Privileges, which had upheld the critical report on Neil Hamilton by the PCS, was not interfering with Parliamentary privilege because it was not questioning their conclusion but merely allowing the evidence to be questioned by a different process to the committee's in a court of law.[1] The Court of Appeal had come to the same conclusion as the Law Lords on s 13. Lord Browne-Wilkinson's criticism seems well directed.[2] The route taken by the Court of Appeal would have allowed that very questioning of parliamentary proceedings which the privilege denies. In 2002, the incumbent Commissioner's appointment ceased in circumstances suggesting retribution from MPs who disliked the investigatory thoroughness of the then Commissioner. The episode seriously undermined public credibility in the ability of Parliament to regulate itself.[3]

1   [1999] 3 All ER 317, CA.

2   It was Jonathan Aitken's ability to waive his privilege which led to his famous trial against *The Guardian*, his loss of that action and his subsequent trial and conviction for perjury.

3   See *Standards of Conduct in the House of Commons* Cm 5663 (Nov 2002) Committee on Standards in Public Life. This made numerous recommendations in relation to the Commissioner, including a fixed-term appointment of between 5 and 7 years, and that there should be an investigatory panel chaired by an independent lawyer to handle serious contested cases. There are numerous recommendations on procedure. See HC Debs 26 June 2003 for the Parliamentary Debate. See also HC 1055 (2003–04) on protection of witnesses who have given evidence before select committees.

5.4   Unlike elected councillors, MPs are under no statutory regulation to declare their financial interests, although they should not ask questions in the House where they have such an interest; nor are there rules of law preventing them voting on matters in the House in which they have an interest. Serious impropriety may be a matter for the Committee on Standards and Privileges which applies various resolutions of the House of Commons.

5.5   A 'compulsory'[1] register of MPs' interests has existed since a Resolution of the House on 22 May 1974 (and see the Resolution of 12 June 1975). In July 1996, a Code of Conduct and a Guide to the Rules Relating to the Conduct of Members was approved by the House of Commons and was most recently significantly revised in 2009, with a further update in 2010.[2] This applies to ministers who are MPs and they are additionally under a code of practice qua Ministers (see para 2.99 above). It does not apply to the House of Lords which, since 1995, has had its own register of Lords' interests which contains two mandatory entries and one discretionary entry. Lord Neill began an enquiry in June 2000 into the Lords' register of business interests and to establish whether peers should operate under an ethical code of conduct; and the House of Lords agreed to a Code of Conduct and mandatory register of interests on 2 July 2001 (HL Debs 2 July 2001 col 630; and see HL 69 (2003–04) on the Code of Conduct and Members Interests, paras 46–47). The Code was subject of a major revision and strengthening in 2009 and now operates on a basis which is broadly equivalent to that which applies to the House of Commons.[3]

1   Enoch Powell persistently refused to register his interests. See *Rost v Edwards* [1990] 2 All ER 641 which has subsequently been doubted in *Prebble* above; and HC 115 (1989–90).

2   *The Code of Conduct* May 2010 HC 735 (2008/2009) (available at http://www.publications. parliament.uk/pa/cm200809/cmcode/735/735.pdf).

3   *Code of Conduct for Members of the House of Lords* November 2009 (available at http://www. publications.parliament.uk/pa/ld/ldcond/code.pdf).

5.6   There are 12 categories of registrable interests[1] for MPs covering: directorships; remunerated employment, office, profession etc; clients; sponsorships; gifts, benefits and hospitality (UK); overseas visits; overseas benefits and gifts; land and property other than the MP's home; shareholdings; controlled transactions under the Political Parties, Elections and Referendums Act 2000, Sch 7A;[2] miscellaneous, ie, any relevant interests not falling within the above; and declaration of any family members who are employed and remunerated through parliamentary allowances. Registration is required for 'financial interests or any other material benefit'. Unremunerated interests which might be thought by others to influence his actions in a manner similar to remunerated interests may be registered, although the decision to do this rests with the MP concerned.

[1]   There are ten categories in the Code applicable to the House of Lords, including all those which must be declared by MPs except the controlled transactions and declaration of employment of family members.

[2]   The controlled transactions are loans or other credit agreements over £500 offered to members which relate to political activities.

5.7   An employment agreement which involves the provision of his services in his capacity as an MP must conform to the Resolution of the House of 6 November 1995 and subsequently amended, most recently on 9 February 2009. A copy of any agreement for the provision of such services must be placed with the PCS. The Nolan Committee recommended that paid advocacy should be prohibited, ie acting as a representative for another as an MP for pay or reward.[1] Resolutions against paid advocacy go back as far as May 1695. Paid advocacy was prohibited by the Resolution of 15 July 1995. The rules on this issue are now contained in Chapter 3 of the Code. When adopted in 1995, the Code drew a distinction between initiation of Parliamentary proceedings on the one hand and speaking in support of a subject after declaration of interest on the other, with the former strictly prohibited. Since 2002, the Code has not drawn this distinction, but prohibits a Member from doing anything in Parliament with the objective of conferring a benefit exclusively on an individual or body from whom the member has received or expects to receive a financial benefit. Members are free to speak or initiate proceedings which relate to interests of such individuals or bodies provided that the relationship between them and the Member is properly registered and declared. Guidance is given on the parameters of the advocacy rule (paras 95–98) and in difficult cases the advice of the PCS should be sought. The rules do not prohibit sponsorship, or acting as a director, adviser or consultant, and the line is difficult to draw in some cases. Further guidance is contained in paragraph 100 of the Code for Members who hold such positions. The rules on lobbying for reward or consideration cover advocacy or initiation of any cause or matter on behalf of any outside body or individual or urging any other Member of either House including Ministers to do so in any speech, PQ, Motion, or introduction of a Bill or Amendment. Chapter 2 of the Code of Conduct concerns Declaration of Members' Interests and dates from the Resolution of 22 May 1974. For Divisions in the House or its committees, registration of an interest in the Register is sufficient. The Code has detailed provisions on declarations at other procedures: debates, written notices, select committees etc.

[1]   And see recommendations 9 and 10 of the Neill Committee's report: *Reinforcing Standards* Cm 4557 (2000).

5.8   As already explained, a PCS exists who compiles the register on MPs, and also investigates complaints, from the public or other MPs, of breaches of the code. The office is non-statutory.[1] The PCS reports to the Select Committee on Standards and Privileges. Communications between a member of the public and the PCS are not covered by Parliamentary privilege and are not legally privileged until the Commissioner decides the case 'has some substance to merit further enquiry.'[2] Such communications may, however, be given a qualified privilege especially in the light of the House of Lords judgment in *Reynolds v Times Newspapers*[3] where the Law Lords, in a case concerning the press it should be noted, although not prepared to accept 'political information' as a generic category of information attracting qualified privilege, nonetheless adverted to the common law of misstatements of fact and the elasticity of the common law of qualified privilege to give protection to the press where necessary to protect freedom of expression and the genuine public interest. Reynolds, the former Irish Prime Minister, claimed to have been defamed by *The Sunday Times*. Disclosures made by the press would be covered by the *Reynolds* decision in appropriate circumstances.[4] That decision has no direct relevance to those mentioned in the code who are not members of the press, or MPs, the latter of whom would be covered by parliamentary privilege if engaged in 'proceedings in Parliament'. But it would appear anomalous if the more liberal framework of *Reynolds* were not extended to public spirited individuals where parliamentary privilege did not protect them. Presumably the PSC would treat the communications as confidential and the office would not be subject to orders of the court enjoining disclosure.[5] The PSC is not susceptible to attack by way of judicial review, the Court of Appeal has held, because his work is inherently involved with the internal work of Parliament unlike the ombudsman, whose work is citizen-directed.[6]

---

[1] For Scotland, see the Scottish Parliamentary Standards Commissioner Act 2002, and SI 2003/2278 extending powers of investigation to witnesses and documents in England, Wales and Northern Ireland, and SSI 2003/135 on the manner in which devolved and local authorities in Scotland perform their duties. The Public Bodies and Public Appointments etc Scotland Act 2003 provides for an office of Commissioner for Public Appointments to prepare and publish and keep under review a code of practice in respect of Scottish Ministers appointing to offices named in Sch 2.

[2] Code of Conduct, para 107.

[3] [1999] 4 All ER 609, HL. See also *McCartan Turkington Breen (a firm) v Times Newspapers Ltd* [2000] 4 All ER 913, HL and *Mahon and Another v Rahn and Others (No 2)* [2000] 1 WLR 2150.

[4] If a statement about an individual is false it is defamatory because the law implies malice. Qualified privilege provides a defence. Where qualified privilege applies to cover a statement or more correctly an occasion when the statement was made, malice in fact has to be proved by the plaintiff. This can be proved where the statement was made with knowledge of its falsity, with recklessness as to its truth or where the respondent was negligent as to its truth. This is in contradistinction to the USA where a false statement about a politician attracts a qualified privilege unless made knowing it was false, or with reckless disregard as to its truth (the 'public figure' defence: *New York Times Co v Sullivan* 376 US 254 (1964). The Law Lords emphasised the elasticity of the common law on qualified privilege allowed an appropriate weight to be given to the importance of free speech by the media on all matters of public concern and confined interference with that freedom to what was necessary in the circumstances of the case. These circumstances were not to be considered separately from the duty-interest test – was there a duty to inform and a public interest in knowing – but were to be taken into account in determining whether the test was satisfied or whether the public was entitled to know the allegation. The following were offered as 'illustrative' examples of circumstances to consider in taking into account whether qualified privilege protects a statement: The seriousness of the allegation. The more serious the charge the public is misinformed and the individual damaged if the charge is

untrue. The nature of the information and its concern to the public. The reliability of the source. Steps taken to verify the information. The status of the information – does it command respect? The urgency of the situation – news is a perishable commodity. Was comment sought from the plaintiff although this may not always be necessary? Did the article cover the 'gist' of the plaintiff's version? The tone of the article – a newspaper may invite questions or investigations rather than make assertions. The circumstances of publication including timing. 'This list is not exhaustive' per Lord Nicholls at 626 b–e. Freedom of speech is the basis of true democracy, but should newspapers be compelled to publish a declaration of falsehood if a statement was false but privileged? See Lord Hutton's strictures in formulating the duties of investigative media reporters prior to publication in his investigation into the death of David Kelly: HC 247 (2003–04) pp 212–214. See *Loutchanksy v The Times (No 2)* [2002] 1 All ER 652 (CA) on the public interest in publishing an article 'true or false'. See further: *Galloway v Telegraph Group Ltd* (2005) *Times*, 13 January; *Miller v Associated Newspapers Ltd* [2003] EWHC 2799; *Oliver v Chief Constable of Northumbria* [2003] EWHC 2417; and for a strict application of the 'responsible journalism' by the Court of Appeal: *Jameel v Wall Street Journal Europe No 3* [2005] EWCA Civ 74. The House of Lords overturned the decision of the Court of Appeal on the issue of 'responsible journalism' in *Jameel*, finding that the Court of Appeal's finding that the qualified privilege defence did not apply as the newspaper had not delayed publication frustrated the intent of the House in *Reynolds* to liberalise the requirements of qualified privilege. See [2006] UKHL 44, [2007] 1 AC 359. The courts have not been generous to journalists. See *Dow Jones and Co Ltd v Jameel* [2005] EWCA Civ 75 on 'the legal presumption that publication of a defamatory article about an identifiable individual caused that individual to suffer damage, without the need to prove that the publication had in fact damaged that individual's reputation, was not incompatible with the right to freedom of expression under the Human Rights Act 1998, Sch 1, Part 1, Art 10' from the headnote. This issue was not appealed to the House of Lords in *Jameel*, but the Law Lords, in their opinions, appear to approve of the Court of Appeal's approach to this issue.

5   See eg Contempt of Court Act 1981, s 10 (ch 10) and the Public Interest Disclosure Act 1998 (ch 2). On cases of absolute privilege regarding evidence to the Office for the Supervision of Solicitors, see *Gray v Avadis* [2003] EWHC 1830 (QB) and *Baxendale-Walker v Middleton* [2011] EWHC 998. For a case on qualified privilege between the Bar Council and members of the Bar, see *Kearns v General Council of the Bar* [2003] EWCA Civ 331, [2003] 1 WLR 1357.

6   *R v Parliamentary Comr for Standards, ex p Al Fayed* [1998] 1 All ER 93.

5.9   The recent expenses scandal which has affected both the Commons and the Lords led to substantial reform of the system for the claiming of Parliamentary expenses, including considerable enhancements to the openness of the process. Expenses claims were governed by the *Green Book*[1] in the House of Commons. A guide is in place on allowances in the House of Lords. The scheme for allowances in the House of Lords was revised considerably in 2010.[2] Both Houses have now published details of expense claims made by members, with the House of Commons publishing detailed information about claims made from 2004/2005 until the third quarter of 2010. Following the expenses scandal, partly brought about by a number of successful FOIA requests and appeals,[3] significant changes in the expenses scheme in the House of Commons were brought about. The Parliamentary Standards Act 2009 sets out a new regime for dealing with MPs' expenses and creates the Independent Parliamentary Standards Authority (IPSA). The Act requires the IPSA to create a scheme for the payment of MPs' allowances (s 5) along with appropriate guidance (s 7). By virtue of Sch 1 of the Act, IPSA is required to produce an annual report and is subject to FOIA 2000. IPSA adopted a publication scheme under FOIA 2000, s 19 in 2010[4] and augmented this with further guidance on its approach to publishing MPs' expense claims in 2011.[5] The guidance outlines a broadly proactive approach to the publication of MPs' expense claims, broken down into categories and also in terms of total expenses claimed. There is a searchable database, which allows the public to make searches by individual MP, category of expense, etc. The guidance makes it clear that digitised copies of receipts and other documentation supporting expense claims will not ordinarily be made available, primarily on grounds of the expense of doing so. The guidance also sets out what information will not be published routinely – generally MPs' personal information, such as addresses, bank account details, etc.

1   House of Commons (2009) *Green Book*.
2   House of Lords (2010) *Guide to Financial Support for Members*.
3   See eg FS50074144 and EA/2006/0015-16 *Corporate Officer of the House of Commons v Information Commissioner and Norman Baker* and EA 2007/0061-63, 0122-123 and 0131 *Corporate Officer of the House of Commons v Information Commissioner (Leapman, Brooke and Thomas)*.
4   IPSA (2010) *Publication Consultation Response*, Annex B. Available at: http://www.parliamentarystandards.org.uk/transparency/Our%20consultations/June%202010%20-%20Publication%20Scheme%20Consultation/Publication%20Consultation%20Response.pdf.
5   IPSA (2010) *Publication Consultation Response*, Annex B. Available at: http://www.parliamentarystandards.org.uk/transparency/Our%20consultations/June%202010%20-%20Publication%20Scheme%20Consultation/Publication%20Consultation%20Response.pdf.

5.10   IPSA took over the publication of MPs' expense claims from 7 May 2010. IPSA has maintained the database outlined above from that date and the database is available to be searched via IPSA's website. In addition to the data that IPSA makes available in line with the guidance outlined in the previous paragraph, it has also received a considerable number of FOIA claims. These, along with any responses, are available on IPSA's website.[1]

1   See http://www.parliamentarystandards.org.uk/transparency/Pages/Freedom%20of%20information-requests-and-Responses.aspx.

5.11   The regime for the House of Lords is comparatively less stringent, with the Parliamentary Standards Act 2009, s 2 specifically excluding the House of Lords from the regime. There have, however, been substantial reforms to the system of allowances in the Lords and the transparency of claims. Rule 10(c) of the recently adopted Code of Conduct[1] states that failure to comply with the rules in respect of the financial support to members is a breach of the Code and is subject to investigation by the newly created House of Lords Commissioner for Standards, which has taken over the investigation of such complaints from the Clerk of the Parliaments. Details of members' claims for allowances and expenses are published on Parliament's website,[2] and the House of Lords Committee for Privileges and Conduct has considered a number of recent cases of improper claims and has made reports accordingly.

1   Code of Conduct for Members of the House of Lords and Guide to the Code of Conduct.
2   See   http://www.parliament.uk/mps-lords-and-offices/members-allowances/house-of-lords/holallowances/hol-expenses04/.

5.12   In addition, conventions govern the use by present and past Ministers of former ministerial documents and Cabinet documents which formed part of their duties while in office or which cover their current field of responsibility.[1] These are now codified in the Ministerial Code,[2] which provides that former Ministers should have reasonable access to their papers from the period when they were in office, including having access to the Cabinet Office or Cabinet Committee papers which were issued to them when in office or which they were known to have handled (r 2.9). Ministers are supplied with guidelines on avoiding a conflict of interest between personal and public duties while in office (see para 2.99). The Code prohibits any Minister from writing a book on their experience as a Minister while in office, or entering into a contract to do so (r 8.9). Former Ministers must submit a copy of the manuscript of any book written about their experiences after their time in office to the Cabinet Secretary 'in good time before publication' and must also abide by the guidance contained in the Radcliffe report (r 8.10). The law of confidentiality, which was examined in ch 2, applies to the use by Ministers or former Ministers of official information, although except in the most blatant and serious of breaches it may prove difficult to invoke. An injury to the public interest would have to be established to award an injunction preventing publication, and the provisions of the Human Rights Act 1988 would have to be brought into consideration, especially s 12 and Art 10 ECHR (see para 2.349). The situation where this is most likely to arise relates to publication of memoirs. Certainly, there has been no successful case brought by or on behalf of the government which has prevented publication by a Minister of his or her memoirs. In the spring of 2000, when it became publicly known that Stella Rimington, the former Head of the Security Service MI5, was planning to publish her memoirs, no steps were taken to prevent publication. David Shayler, it will be recalled, was prosecuted under the OSA 1989.[2] For a discussion of the Parliamentary Affairs Select Committee investigation into political memoirs and possible unauthorised disclosure, see para 2.331 above.

[1] Hunt (1982) *Public Law* 514.
[2] Cabinet Office (2010) *Ministerial Code*.
[3] From 1983, it is suggested that seven books have been published by former security and intelligence officials about their work: Norton Taylor (2000) *The Guardian*, 27 July.

5.13 It is surprising, perhaps, that public opinion has not forced a more detailed regulation by law on the abuse by MPs and ministers of their official position and information derived therefrom. In this respect, the Nolan Reports and those of his successors (currently Sir Christopher Kelly), in spite of their significant advances, have largely continued the traditions of self-regulation and internal control over standards in public life in central government, in contradistinction to legal regulation. Those traditions came under further strain when the Committee investigated a report by the PSC into Keith Vaz MP and a junior Minister. There had been significant obstruction of the PSC in her investigation of alleged breaches of the Code (HC 314 (2000–01), paras 65–72). It is evident that the public opprobrium driven by the expenses scandal led to increased legal regulation and intervention into the system of Parliamentary expenses, including some criminal prosecuations and a clarification of the position in relation to Parliamentary privilege where criminal offences may have been committed in relation to expense claims.[1] Expenses are now undoubtedly dealt with in a more transparent way and the rules for both Houses have been modified significantly. More broadly, however, other than the introduction of the House of Lords Commissioner for Standards, relatively few changes have been introduced to prevent abuses other than in relation to expenses. In fact, it is arguable that the rules in relation to initiation of Parliamentary proceedings as a result of an employment relationship are more permissive now than they have been in the past.

¹   *R v Chaytor* [2010] UKSC 52, [2010] 3 WLR 1707.

Civil servants

5.14   As well as the OSA 1989 and other specific statutes prohibiting the disclosure of information, the civil service code sets out a series of prohibitions aimed at preventing conflicts of interest. There was no statute governing the civil service although a Bill was before the House of Lords in 2003–04 (see below). They were governed under a prerogative power and orders, although Lord Neill and others suggested that the time is ripe for a Civil Service Bill which amongst other things would prevent them being dragged into the political arena (see para 2.152 above). The governance of the Civil Service was put on to a statutory footing by the Constitutional Reform and Governance Act 2010, noted above in chapters 1 and 2. Breaches of confidentiality and conflicts of interest are largely a matter of internal discipline and domestic hearings with the occasional *cause célèbre* such as the Ponting trial elevating matters to the criminal courts.¹ The provisions governing confidentiality have been examined in ch 2. Further provisions cover Crown copyright. Specific prohibitions covering corruption – which might involve the sale on one's own behalf of information or advantages or opportunities while on official business² – in the public sector, and the public and private sector, are contained in the Public Bodies Corrupt Practices Act 1889 and the Prevention of Corruption Acts 1906 and 1916.³ These are not restricted to Crown servants, and the 1889 Act does not cover an agent of the Crown. Nolan in his first report recommended clarification by Parliament of the law relating to bribery, or receipt of bribes by MPs and furthermore that the statute law on bribery should be consolidated. The Bribery Act 2010 is now in force and has repealed the legislation outlined above. The Act creates new offences of bribing another person and a number of new offences in relation to receipt of bribes which results in improper performance of a function or activity. It is clear that the Act also envisages circumstances in which the receipt of a bribe may constitute improper performance of a relevant activity in and of itself without the need for further action or inaction on the part of the recipient. Section 3 of the Act defines the functions or activities that are subject to the Act's provisions. All public functions are covered by the Act, provided that the person performing the function or activity is expected to do so in good faith, with impartially, or is in a position of trust. Section 16 of the Act extends its application to 'individuals in the public service of the Crown'. In order for an offence to be committed, s 4 requires that the function or activity is performed 'in breach of a relevant expectation', or that the failure to perform a particular function or activity is itself a breach of a 'relevant expectation'. The test of what is expected is outlined in s 5(1) as 'what a reasonable person in the United Kingdom would expect in relation to the performance of the type of function or activity concerned'. In the case of MPs and civil servants it seems likely that this test would at least in part be informed by the standards codes outlined above.⁴ Despite considerable discussion and a number of proponents, the Bribery Act did not create a new offence of misuse of public office and it seems unlikely that such an offence will be created in the near future.

1   See paras 2.281 et seq above, and the codes referred to. Rules exist requiring under-secretaries and above (and their equivalent) to seek government assent before accepting employment in business and other bodies within two years of resignation or retirement. Government departments apply similar rules where officials below that rank have had contact with the prospective employer. See Treasury and Civil Service Committee: Acceptance of Outside Appointments by Crown Servants HC 216 (1980–81). See also: HC 44 (1988–89) on Parliamentary Lobbying Committee on Privileges. See Nolan First Report Cm 2850, recommendations 15, 17, 29, 30 and 31, and Neill Cm 4557, ch 11. Revised rules came into effect on 1 April 1996. The rules were extended to Ministers and special advisers only after the Committee's first report in 1995. An Advisory Committee on Business Appointments provides advice on appointments and the First report's recommendation that its reasons should be published 'was not fully implemented' Neill (above), para 11.8.

2   *Reading v A-G* [1951] AC 507, HL; *A-G v Blake* [2000] 4 All ER 385, HL.

3   The essence of the offence is the receipt, or agreement to receive a reward etc or 'advantage whatever' (Public Bodies Corrupt Practices Act 1889, s 1(1)) or 'any gift or consideration' (Prevention of Corruption Act 1906, s 1(1), and see s 1(2)) in return for doing or forbearing to do anything … in which the public body (1889 Act) or principal (1906 Act) is engaged or concerned. Section 2 of the 1916 Act allows corruption to be presumed where any money, gift or other consideration has been paid, given to or received by a public sector employee. See *R v Braithwaite* [1983] 1 WLR 385, CA, on 'consideration'; and *R v Calland* [1967] Crim LR 236 on dishonesty and corruption and cf *R v Smith* [1960] 1 All ER 256, and CCA, *R v Lindley* [1957] Crim LR 321. See Salmon Commission *Standards of Conduct in Public Life* Cmnd 6524 (1976) on a proposed offence of corruption at p 102. Can a leak in the public interest, albeit for reward, be corruption?

4   The guidance on the application of the Act produced by the MoJ can be found at http://www.justice. gov.uk/downloads/guidance/making-reviewing-law/bribery-act-2010-guidance.pdf. It is important to note that this guidance applies to commercial organisations, as required by s 9 of the Act, but is likely to have relevance to public authorities due to the effects of s 16 of the Bribery Act 2010.

5.15   In ch 2 there was a discussion of the ninth report of the Committee on Standards on *Ministers, Special Advisers and the Permanent Civil Service* and the Government Response and the Code for Special Advisers (see paras 2.99 and 2.151).

EU

5.16   Article 339 of the Treaty on the Functioning of the European Union (TFEU) provides that members of the institutions of the EC and officials and servants shall be required, even after their duties have ceased, not to disclose information covered by professional secrecy about undertakings, business relations and cost components. Staff regulations (interpretation of which is now dealt with by the European Union Civil Service Tribunal) specify restrictions on the use of information, and the case law of the General Court and ECJ has examined cases involving publication of works by officials in alleged contravention of the regulations.[1]

1   Case C-274/99P *Connolly v EC Commission* [2001] ECR I-1611; Case C-340/00P *EC Commission v Cwik*; see A Biondi (2003) *European Public Law* 39.

LOCAL GOVERNMENT[1]

5.17   The most important restrictions will be those operating to restrict disclosure on the use of information by members of authorities and by officers.

1   For Scotland, see the Ethical Standards in Public Life etc (Scotland) Act 2000 which covers councils and devolved bodies.

5.18 Legislation aimed at preventing corruption seeks to restrict the use of official, or other, positions for personal gain or profit and these will apply to officials in local government. See paragraph 5.14 above for a discussion of the impact of the Bribery Act 2010 in this area. Members who have extensive rights to information (see below) are bound by legal restrictions and there was a Department of the Environment code of guidance which was provided for under the LGHA 1989 and has now been replaced by a code of conduct provided for under the Local Government Act 2000 (LGA 2000) (see below). Such restrictions have been the subject of extensive investigation by government-appointed bodies and by government replies since the late 1960s.

5.19 The former national code of local government conduct constituted guidance and was not thought to be legally binding upon members. However, the local ombudsman has regard to the code when considering whether action, and specifically a failure to comply with the code, constitutes maladministration. In *R v Local Comr for Administration, ex p Liverpool City Council* the ombudsman was ruled to have acted lawfully when she applied the code's test of 'interest' to establish bias on the part of councillors in making a planning decision. The councillors argued that the more relaxed test of bias in administrative law should have been the determinant of bias and in this case the maladministration of which the ombudsman found them guilty.[1] The code provided that a member's overriding duty was to the whole local community with a special duty to constituents. Councillors should not be influenced by private or personal factors in any decision which they had to make. They should avoid any occasion for suspicion or the appearance of improper conduct. It is a councillor's duty alone to decide what view to take on a council matter. The code emphasised that non-pecuniary interests such as kinship, friendship, membership of or association with a society, trade union, freemasons,[2] or voluntary bodies can be as important as pecuniary interests. Unless insignificant, such an interest should be disclosed and the member should decide whether it is clear and substantial. If s/he so decides, s/he should withdraw, pending consideration by the meeting, unless one of four circumstances or other dispensation obtains (para 12).

---

[1]   [1999] 3 All ER 85; affirmed [2001] 1 All ER 462. See *R v Broadland District Council, ex p Lashley* (2000) 2 LGLR 933, CA.

[2]   See *R v Newham London Borough Council, ex p Haggerty* (1986) 85 LGR 48, in which it was ruled a mandatory requirement that councillors declare whether they were inter alia freemasons before being allocated to committees was intra vires. The decision was reversed by the LGHA 1989.

5.20 This code has been replaced by a new model code of conduct for members and co-opted members of relevant authorities in England made by the Secretary of State by order under LGA 2000, s 50.[1] The National Assembly for Wales has done likewise (SIs 2001/2276 and 2008/788). The following provisions replace those under Local Government and Housing Act 1989 (LGHA 1989), s 19 and Local Government Act 1972 (LGA 1972), ss 94–97.

---

[1]   See Local Authorities (Model Code of Conduct) Order 2007, SI 2007/1159. The separate code of conduct for police authorities was revoked by the 2007 order and the provisions of SI 2007/1159 apply to police authorities and fire and rescue authorities as they do to other local government bodies.

5.21   Under LGA 2000, s 49 the Secretary of State may specify the principles which are to govern the conduct of members and co-opted members (sub-s (7)) of relevant local authorities (sub-s (6)) in England. These principles will be contained in an order. The National Assembly for Wales may make orders likewise. Both bodies must engage in consultation with listed bodies (subs-ss (3) and (4) respectively). The code is enforceable via an authority's standards committee (see ch 4).

5.22   The model code must be consistent with the principles for the time being specified in an order under s 49(1) or (2). It may include mandatory and optional provisions. Consultation as required under s 49 has to take place before an order is made under s 50. Furthermore, the Secretary of State may invite a representative of local government in England to send to him a proposed model code. As well as requiring certain formalities and consultation by the representative body, the invitation may require different codes, or different provisions of a code for different authorities or descriptions of authorities.

5.23   Where an order under s 50 is made, each relevant local authority must pass a resolution within six months from the day on which the order applying to it under s 50 was made, or as soon as reasonably practicable thereafter, which adopts a code as covering the behaviour expected of their members and co-opted members (s 51(1)). The code, or revised code, as well as containing mandatory provisions and possibly optional ones may also contain other provisions consistent with the model code. Whether or not a code is adopted in time, mandatory provisions are nonetheless to apply to members and co-opted members. The code must be made available at an authority's principal office for inspection at specified times by the public as soon as reasonably practicable after adoption or revision. At least one notice must also be published in a local newspaper which includes required statements. The authority may also give additional publicity to the adoption or revision of a code. Copies must be sent to the Standards Board for England by an English authority and in the case of a Welsh authority to the Commission for Local Administration in Wales (see paras 4.124 et seq above). A declaration by a member on accepting office, the form of which may be prescribed by LGA 1972, s 83, may include a declaration that in performing his duties he will observe the authority's code of conduct (LGA 2000, s 52). Even where an authority adopts or revises a code after a declaration of acceptance, within two months of the code being adopted or revised, a member must give a written undertaking to the authority that he will observe the code in the performance of his duties. If the undertaking is not given, the office is to be vacated. Where a person is elected as a member of an authority to which LGA 1972, s 83 does not apply, he may not act in that office until he has given such an undertaking as above. Similar provisions apply to codes adopted or revised after a member has begun to act in office. Similar provisions also apply to co-opted members.

5.24   The Local Authorities (Model Code of Conduct) (England) Order 2007, SI 2007/1159 provides for general obligations and personal interests; and Sch 1, para 12 concerns withdrawing from meetings in the event of an interest.[1] Schedule 1, Part 3 has provisions on a register of interests. The scope of the

Code has been construed broadly, catching a number of actions that councillors have argued were undertaken in a personal, rather than an official, capacity.[2]

[1]   *R (Richardson) v North Yorkshire CC* [2003] EWCA Civ 1860, [2004] 2 All ER 31 (CA) has ruled that the regulation and para 12 of the Code refer to members of the Council as a whole and not simply members of the committee in question, and members must withdraw from a meeting where s/he has a prejudicial interest (see para 10). A member of the Council attending a council meeting could not, simply by declaring that s/he was attending in a private capacity, thereby divest him or herself of their official capacity as a councillor. Only by resigning could the official role be shed.

[2]   See eg *R (Mullaney) v Adjudication Panel for England* [2009] EWHC 72 (Admin), [2010] BLGR 354. In this case, M trespassed on land belonging to a third party and filmed the third party and some of his buildings, then posted the video on the Internet. M argued that he had taken these steps due to a public interest, as he was seeking to force council officers to take action against the owner of the buildings, whom he alleged had undertaken works without necessary planning and building consent. The court found that the adjudication panel had not erred in finding that M was acting in an official capacity and that his actions were a breach of the Code.

5.25   Authorities, but not parish and community councils, must establish Standards Committees whose duties include advising on adoption and revision of codes of conduct and their monitoring and training on items raised by the code. They also promote high standards of conduct and assist members and co-opted members to observe the code. Sub-committees of the Standards Committees of district or unitary authorities may perform that role for parish councils. Significant changes to this process are to be brought about if the Localism Bill (2010–2011) comes into force in its present form. See 5.47 below for further details.

5.26   A Standards Board for England is also established as a corporate body whose members are appointed by the Secretary of State. They will appoint Ethical Standards Officers and may issue guidance on the conduct of members etc which they may arrange to make public. The Commission for Local Administration in Wales will perform analogous functions in Wales. A person may make a written allegation to the Board that a member etc has, or may have, failed to comply with the authority's code of conduct. The details on these points were covered in ch 4 (paras 4.124 et seq above).

5.27   Under LGA 2000, s 81 every relevant authority must establish and maintain a register of interests of the members etc of the authority. This duty is discharged by the Monitoring Officer. Interests will include those of spouses or partners (s 81(8)). This will be available for public inspection. Each member etc must be required by virtue of the mandatory provisions of the code to register such financial and other interests as specified in the mandatory provisions of the code. The mandatory provisions must also require any member etc to disclose such interests before taking part in the business of the authority relating to that interest and also prevent or restrict the participation of a member in any business to which such an interest relates. A dispensation from a prohibition from participation by the authority's standards committee will not constitute a breach of the code by the member. The circumstances in which a dispensation may be given may be set out in regulations. SI 2007/1159 (The Model Code),

Sch 1, para 14 sets out one possible dispensation. Where information relating to personal interests could be considered to be 'sensitive' (defined as creating, or being likely to create, a serious risk that the member or a person who lives with the member will be subject to violence or intimidation) then, subject to the agreement of the authority's monitoring officer, such an interest need not be included on the register.

The law on officers' duties

5.28   Like members, officers are subject to the civil law of confidentiality, although the latter qua an employment relationship, the former qua membership (see paras 5.50 et seq below). Councillors and officers should show 'mutual respect' to each other. Section 82 of the LGA 2000 allows the Secretary of State, and the Welsh National Assembly, to issue a code on the conduct which is expected of qualifying employees of relevant authorities. Consultation must take place with local authority representative bodies, trade unions, the Audit Commission and the Commission for Local Administration. The Welsh Government introduced a code of conduct for employees in the Code of Conduct (Qualifying Local Government Employees) (Wales) Order 2001, SI 2001/2280. This order applies to all local government employees in Wales with the exception of teachers and firefighters. In England, consultation has been undertaken since 2001 regarding the possible adoption of a code of conduct for employees, but no such code has ever been adopted. The most recent consultation took place in 2008.[1] The Localism Bill (2010–2011) as it presently stands will remove the power of the Secretary of State to adopt such a Code for England, so it appears unlikely that there will be any future adoption of a code for employees in England.[2]

[1]   DCLG (2008) *Communities in control: Real people, real power Codes of conduct for local authority members and employees.*
[2]   LGA 2000, s 82(8) for qualifying employees.

5.29   The LGHA 1989 deals with perceived abuse on the appointment and use of officers and advisers in local government. This is known as 'twin-tracking'.

5.30   Sections 115–117 of the LGA 1972 deal with a variety of relevant themes on officers' duties. Section 116 – which has been applied and referred to in numerous regulations – prohibits an officer of an authority being a member of the employing authority. Section 1 of the LGHA 1989[1] has extended the prohibition to those holding politically restricted posts under any other local authority in Great Britain. These sections were augmented by the Local Government Officers (Political Restrictions) Regulations 1990.[2] LGHA 1989, s 2(1) defines holders of politically restricted posts as:
(a)   the person designated under s 4 below as the head of the authority's paid service;
(b)   the statutory chief officers; see s 2(6);
(c)   a non-statutory chief officer; see s 2(7). This does not include those whose duties are solely secretarial or clerical or are 'support services';
(d)   a deputy chief officer; see s 2(8); again secretarial etc duties are excluded;

(e)   the monitoring officer designated under s 5;
(f)   any person holding a post to which s/he was appointed in pursuance of s 9;[3]
(g)   any person not falling within paras (a) to (f) above whose post is for the time being specified by the authority in a list maintained in accordance with s 2(2) and according to directions under LGHA 1989, s 3 or 3A or with LGA 1972, s 100G(2) or Local Government (Scotland) Act 1973, s 50G(2) (list of officers to whom powers are delegated).

[1]   See Cm 433 (1988) ch 5 for the reasons behind the government's reform.
[2]   See SI 1990/851 and SI 1990/1447.
[3]   This concerns assistance for political groups.

5.31   Under s 2(2) an authority has to prepare and maintain a list of posts, duties of which fall within s 2(3) (below) and are not exempted. They will be listed and deposited with the 'proper officer'.[1] The list in s 2(2) will be deposited within two months of the section coming into force and any modifications to the list will also be notified. Previously, all officers in full-time posts (or part-time posts where the remuneration, if the officer worked full-time, would have exceeded the prescribed amount) whose remuneration exceeded an amount prescribed in Regulations were included on the list of those who were subject to political restrictions. This requirement was removed by the Local Democracy, Economic Development and Construction Act 2009, s 30. The result of this is that posts are no longer included on the list of politically restricted posts only by virtue of the level of remuneration, but remain to be listed by local authorites if it is determined that LGHA 1989, s 2(3) applies.

[1]   See LGA 1972, s 270(3).

5.32   Under LGHA 1989, s 2(3), the duties of the post under a local authority fall within s 2(2) if they consist of or involve any one or more of the following tasks:

'(a)   giving advice on a regular basis to the authority themselves, to any committee or sub-committee of the authority or to any joint committee on which the authority are represented;
(b)   speaking on behalf of the authority on a regular basis to journalists or broadcasters.'

5.33   Head teachers, principals of schools, colleges etc maintained or assisted by LEAs are excluded, as are teachers or lecturers in such establishments.[1] In England, the recently introduced LGHA 1989, s 3A (inserted by the Local Government and Public Involvement in Health Act 2007) allows the holder of a post listed under s 2(3) to apply to the standards committee of a local authority to have that post exempted from the list and for any person to apply to the standards committee to have a post which is not presently listed to be included on the list. Under the Localism Bill 2010–2011, the head of paid service in a local authority will take over this role from the standards committee. In Wales, persons shall be appointed by the Secretary of State to consider, inter alia, applications for exemption from political restriction and to advise on the determination of questions arising under s 2(3), supra (s 3). A local authority must give such a person all information as is reasonably required for the statutory functions, and must comply with that person's directions. The post-holder must be informed where that post is included in a list by the person. In the case of *Ahmed v UK*[2] the European Court of Human Rights ruled that the regulations made under the statute were not in breach of Arts 10 (freedom of expression), 11 (freedom of association), and Art 3 of Protocol 1 (right to participate fully in the electoral process).

[1] LGHA 1989, s 2(10).
[2] [1999] IRLR 188.

Staff appointments on merit

5.34 The LGHA 1989 also makes provision in relation to the appointment of staff (and assistants for political groups). All staff appointments of local authorities, or parish or community councils in England and Wales, shall be made on merit (s 7(1)), whether appointed by the authority etc or a committee and whether made under s 112 of the LGA 1972 (s 7(2)). This provision is subject to legislation on employment for the disabled;[1] genuine occupational requirements relating to sex, pregnancy and maternity, marriage and civil partnership, gender reassignment and race;[2] and the necessary qualifications of those responsible for the administration of the financial affairs of certain authorities (LGHA 1989, s 113). The section came into force at the expiry of the period of two months beginning on the day of enactment (16 November 1989).

[1] Equality Act 2010, ss 39, 40 and 49–51, and Sch 8.
[2] Equality Act 2010, Sch 9, para 1.

Staff and standing orders

5.35 Under LGHA 1989, s 8, regulations may require relevant authorities to incorporate in Standing Orders (SOs) prescribed provisions relating to staff, subject to modification or non-modification as specified. SOs relate to staff if they make provision for appointments to paid office or employment by the authority or the dismissal or disciplining of such persons.[1]

[1] SI 2001/3384 (England) and SI 2006/1275 (Wales).

5.36 The SOs restrict the manner of exercising the power of selection for, or of, appointment so as to make it exercisable only by the authority itself, or a committee or sub-committee, or by particular officers of the authority and to restrict an authority and its committees/sub-committees giving directions on whom to appoint or 'otherwise to interfere with the making of appointments by such persons'.[1] Further, regulations may require the monitoring officer (MO) to prepare a report to the authority in respect of every proposed appointment of a person to a politically restricted post[2] stating whether in his or her opinion the proposed appointment can be made without contravening any statutory provision in Part I of the LGHA 1989 and without considering matters 'which could not properly be taken into account'. If it cannot be so made, s/he must state the reasons.[3] The regulations may provide that SOs:

'prohibit the authority or any committee, sub-committee or other person acting on their behalf from dismissing or taking other disciplinary action against a person holding office or employment under the authority except in accordance with recommendations contained in a report made to the authority by an independent person of such a description as is prescribed by the regulations.'[4]

[1]   LGHA 1989, s 8(3)(a)–(b).
[2]   LGHA 1989, s 8(3)(c).
[3]   LGHA 1989, s 8(3)(d).
[4]   LGHA 1989, s 8(3)(e).

5.37   LGHA 1989, s 8(4) empowers these regulations to contain a wide variety of incidental provisions. These concern delegations; reports of MOs on sub-s (3) (c) above; the consequences of any contraventions of SOs under the regulations:

'(i)   in relation to any appointment or contract of employment;
(ii) in relation to any proceedings on a complaint to an industrial tribunal; and
(iii) in relation to any expenditure incurred by the authority,'

and in relation to the appointment of persons under s 9 of the LGHA 1989; and the appointment of persons for the purposes of joint committees on which 'relevant authorities' (s 8(5)) are represented.

5.38   The White Paper stated that councillors should be excluded from participating in the appointment of officers who are not within the proposed politically restricted category.[1]

[1]   Cm 433, para 5.40.

Political advisers and exemptions

5.39   LGHA 1989, s 9 says that appointments under that section, viz assistants for political groups, may be made regardless of s 7 or any SO or rule of law rendering it unlawful to have regard to any person's political activities or affiliations in determining whether s/he should be appointed. Such appointments are those:

'...   made for the purpose of providing assistance, in the discharge of any of their functions as members of a relevant authority, to the members of any political group to which members of the authority belong;
(b)   the terms of the appointment comply with subsection (3);
(c)   the appointment is to one of not more than three posts which a relevant authority have decided to create for the purposes of this section; and
(d)   each of those posts falls, under the standing orders of the authority, to be filled from time to time in accordance with the wishes of a political group to which the post has been allocated under those standing orders.'[1]

[1]   See para 4.108 above, on political advisers.

5.40 SOs of relevant authorities whose members are in different political groups shall, by virtue of s 9(5):

(a) prohibit the making of an appointment to any post allocated to a political group until the authority have allocated a post to each of the groups which qualify for one;

(b) prohibit the allocation of a post to a political group which does not qualify for one; and

(c) prohibit the allocation of more than one post to any one political group.

5.41 LGHA 1989, s 9(6) caters for the situation where members of a relevant authority are split into different political groups. A group shall qualify for a post if:

'(a) the membership of that group comprises at least one-tenth of the membership of the authority;

(b) the number of the other groups (if any) which are larger than that group does not exceed two; and

ᐧ (c) where the number of the other groups which are the same size as or larger than that group exceeds two, the authority have determined that that group should be a group to which a post is allocated;

and it shall be the duty of a relevant authority, before making any allocation for the purposes of this section in a case in which there are groups which would qualify for posts if paragraph (c) above were disregarded, to make such determinations under that paragraph as secure that there are no more nor less than three groups which do qualify for a post.'

5.42 Powers cannot be delegated for the discharge of the authority's functions to a s 9 appointment (LGHA 1989, s 9(8)). Further provisions stipulate that officers or employees shall not act under the direction of a s 9 appointment (except secretarial or clerical services). Further, SOs may specify, under regulations which may be made:

'(a) the circumstances in which the members of a relevant authority are to be treated as divided into different political groups;

(b) as to the persons who are to be treated as members of such a group and as to when a person is to be treated as having ceased to be a member of such a group;

(c) requiring the question whether a person is or is not a member of a political group to be determined in such manner as may be provided for by or under the regulations;

(d) requiring a relevant authority from time to time to review allocations made for the purposes of this section;

(e) specifying the manner in which, and times at which, the wishes of a political group are to be expressed and the consequences of a failure by such a group to express its wishes;

and regulations under this section may contain such incidental provision and such supplemental, consequential and transitional provision in connection with their other provisions as the Secretary of State considers appropriate.'

5.43 LGHA 1989, s 10 limits the amount of paid leave which may be given by the latter authority to an officer who is a member of another authority.

5.44 It is necessary to spell out the above provisions to comprehend the far greater degree of regulation of officers and political advisers and, inter alia, their use of local authority information, or political group information. The 1990 Code stated that officers are responsible to the council and are appointed according to legal rules and SOs. An officer's job is to advise councillors and the council, and to carry out the council's work under the direction and control of the council and its committees. The government made such copious provision in law, to be amplified by regulations and SOs, because they felt, contrary to the 1986 Widdicombe report, that a statutory chief executive would be an inappropriate person to arbitrate on the detailed application of rules for party balance on committees, or deciding whether a councillor needs to see a document or attend a meeting. It would impose a uniform pattern of organisation at the highest level on all authorities and it required a detailed definition of the role of the chief executive in relation both to members and other chief officers. This the then government found ill-advised. The changes introduced for members in the LGA 2000 continue with the process of statutory norms backed up by codes and regulations.

5.45 At the time of the first edition of this work, that approach seemed hard to square with the role of the MO and the officer designated under s 4 as the head of the paid service, with access to all necessary resources and with a duty to report to the council and all members, as well as the changes relating to the chief financial officer. It now seems unavoidable.

5.46 A draft consultation paper from the Office of the Deputy Prime Minister in August 2004 queried whether a separate code of practice from that for employees, dealing specifically with conduct of political advisers, should be produced.

5.47 The Localism Bill (2010–2011) proposes enormous changes in the regime in England outlined above. Clause 14 of the Bill provides that Sch 4 of the Bill will have effect. Schedule 4, which spans some eight pages of the Bill, removes the power of the Secretary of State to provide a set of principles for the conduct of members of relevant authorities in LGA 2000, s 49 and also deprives the Secretary of State of the power to issue a model code of conduct. The Bill removes the requirement for authorities to create standards committees. If the Bill is passed in its present form, the system for standards in councils will become almost entirely self-regulatory. Clause 15 requires that each relevant authority 'promote and maintain high standards of conduct by members and co-opted members of the authority'. Clause 16 provides that an authority may adopt a code of conduct for its members if it wishes to do so. Investigation of the breaches of any code that is adopted and any penalty that might be applied for a breach of the code is left entirely to the discretion of the authority. The register of members' interests remains in clause 17, with provision for criminal sanctions for failure to disclose in clause 18. These changes, while delivering considerable freedom to local authorities, seem to have the disadvantage of opening up the potential for considerable inconsistency between authorities. Given that some elements of the previous code were designed to offer protection to third parties who may have been subject to inappropriate behaviour from members of authorities, this may lead to some individuals suffering disadvantage. Sch 4, Part 2, para 1 of the Bill provides that any code of conduct adopted by an authority under the LGA 2000 ceases to have effect.

Attendance of officers at party groups

5.48   In relation to the attendance of officers at party groups and meetings, the government stated:

'The Government agree broadly with the Committee's proposals which, they consider, give necessary recognition to the forum in which many major issues of council policy are now formulated in many local authorities, and the need for officers to act effectively in giving advice to councillors. The Government propose therefore to recommend the Local Authorities' Conditions of Service Advisory Board to amend the terms and conditions of service to local government officers to make clear that no special inhibition is placed on officers' attendance at party groups. In addition, the Government will encourage local authorities to set out in local conventions details of their arrangements for officer attendance at party group meetings, together with safeguards to ensure that all requests for officer attendance are addressed to the chief executive or appropriate chief officer, who would have responsibility for deciding which officers should attend, and that all substantial party groups on the council are notified and offered this facility. Subject to satisfactory arrangements being made by local authorities, the Government do not propose to legislate on this matter.'[1]

[1]   Cm 433, para 5.30.

5.49   The position of officers being present at new style executive meetings was discussed in ch 4 (paras 4.27 et seq above).

Legal restrictions on officers' use of information

5.50   Section 117 of the LGA 1972 restricts an officer's use of information:

'(1) If it comes to the knowledge of an officer employed, whether under this Act or any other enactment, by a local authority that a contract in which he has any pecuniary interest, whether direct or indirect (not being a contract to which he is himself a party), has been, or is proposed to be, entered into by the authority or any committee thereof, he shall as soon as practicable give notice in writing to the authority of the fact that he is interested therein.

For the purposes of this section an officer shall be treated as having indirectly a pecuniary interest in a contract or proposed contract if he would have been so treated by virtue of section 95 above had he been a member of the authority (see above).

(2) An officer of a local authority shall not, under colour of his office or employment, accept any fee or reward whatsoever other than his proper remuneration.[1]

(3) Any person who contravenes the provisions of subsection (1) or (2) above shall be liable on summary conviction to a fine.'

[1] See, on corruption, para 5.14 above.

5.51 Section 115 is relevant as it places a duty on local authority employees:

'   ... at such times during the continuance of his office or within three months after ceasing to hold it, and in such manner as the local authority direct, [to] make out and deliver to the authority, or in accordance with their directions, a true account in writing of all money and property committed to his charge, and of his receipts and payments, with vouchers and other documents and records supporting the entries therein, and a list of persons from whom or to whom money is due in connection with his office, showing the amount due from or to each.

(2) Every such officer shall pay all money due from him to the proper officer of the local authority or in accordance with their directions.'

Officers' access to information

5.52 It would be presumed that an officer has access to all necessary and relevant information to perform his or her duties in advising the council and its relevant members. Such questions would fall under the rubric of employment law. Unlike the position with members (see paras 5.56 et seq below), officers' grievances have not caused a litany of litigation on this point. Section 117 of the LGA 1972 above deals with an officer's duty to provide notice of an interest. Consultations took place on a code of conduct for employees (above). The provisions of the LGHA 1989 seek to ensure the political neutrality of appointments and aim to reduce the scope for improper interference by members in appointments, dismissals and discipline, thereby seeking to reduce occasions for refusing, on irrelevant grounds, access to information.

5.53 Legally, improper refusal to give access could justify a finding of constructive dismissal in appropriate circumstances. If relief were sought to obtain the document or information per se, would an officer proceed by judicial review or under private law process? Judicial review would probably be the better option but would an officer be interpreted as enforcing contractual rights? In reality such a problem is unlikely to remain unresolved to the extent that it would require the intervention of a court or tribunal.

5.54 Where a claim for access was made by an officer below the level of a chief officer of a department, the matter would be resolved by an internal 'appeal' to the head of department. Further recourse in the case of a dispute involving the head of a department would have to be made as a matter of practice to the chief executive,[1] usually in conclave with the leader of the council. In the event of non-resolution, it would be a matter for the full council – an unlikely and undesirable scenario. Where a disciplinary aspect is present, the provisions in LGHA 1989, s 8(3)(e) would have to be complied with.

[1]   Not as a matter of law – there is no statutory office of chief executive: see LGHA 1989, s 4, and Head of Paid Service.

5.55   We look at the effects of the law of confidentiality below.

Access by members to information and meetings

COUNCIL MEETINGS

5.56   In ch 4, we saw how provisions for the new executive arrangements for authorities had brought with them their own provisions on access. This passage should be read in conjunction with the relevant section of ch 4 (paras 4.27 et seq above). The point was noted that these were built on the model of the Local Government (Access to Information) Act 1985 (LG(ATI)A 1985). There is also an abundance of common law principles on access which will remain relevant as well as statutory provisions for access outside executive arrangements.

5.57   Every councillor has a common law right to attend every part of all meetings of the full council by virtue of being elected and under LGA 1972, Sch 12, para 4(2)(b), and 'a summons to attend the meeting, specifying the business proposed to be transacted thereat … shall … be left or sent by post' to the home of every councillor.

5.58   Councillors must be summoned to the meeting and be given the agenda three clear days in advance of it taking place;[1] only business specified in the summons may be transacted at the meeting, with the sole exception of the AGM, at which statutory business or urgent matters under SOs may also be conducted. 'Any other business' is unlawful where notice of the business is not specified. By LGA 2000, s 98(2) this period of three clear days may be extended by order to 'such greater number of days as may be specified'.

[1]   The day on which the notice is given and the day of the meeting are to be excluded: *R v Herefordshire Justices* (1820) 3 B & Ald 581. On council meetings see LGA 1972, Sch 12 as amended by Local Government Act 1985, Sch 14, para 35 and Sch 17. See LGA 2000, s 98.

MEMBERSHIP OF COMMITTEES AND SUB-COMMITTEES

5.59   The provisions in the LGHA 1989 relating to the party balance of committees and sub-committees will substantially affect this topic. Within the provisions of ss 15–17, there has to be a proportional representation of political parties in relation to the parties' membership of the council on committees and sub-committees. This is novel and amends the common law position.[1] We looked at the provisions in ch 4 (paras 4.111 et seq above).[2] Membership of the full council and their finance committee must comprise elected members alone. We also looked at the limits placed on co-option on to committees of non-elected members, of which in 1988 there were 6,000 compared with 24,000 elected councillors. The provisions seek to ensure that co-opted members have relevant experience and expertise, that they do not vote on decision-making committees, though this prohibition would not apply to advisory committees. Certain committees, eg police, are exempted.

[1] *R v Rushmoor Borough Council, ex p Crawford* (1981) *Times*, 28 November – council may exclude opposition members from committee membership; *R v Greenwich London Borough Council, ex p Lovelace* [1990] 1 All ER 353; cf *R v Sheffield City Council, ex p Chadwick* (1985) 84 LGR 563 and ultra vires action vis-à-vis sub-committees; *Manton v Brighton Corpn* [1951] 2 KB 393. The council cannot delegate the power to remove from committees: *R v Brent London Borough Council, ex p Gladbaum* (1989) 88 LGR 627. See *R v Warwickshire County Council, ex p Dill-Russell* (1990) 89 LGR 640.

[2] See *R v Portsmouth City Council, ex p Gregory* (1990) 89 LGR 478, DC.

5.60 The government did not accept that one-party policy groups should be exempted from the provisions of the LG(ATI)A 1985 or pro rata representation as Widdicombe suggested, making them special status 'deliberative committees'. If committees, they are committees:

'Instead the Government considered that such groups should retain an informal status and that the provision of officer advice (in so far as there is any doubt on the question) should be secured through appropriate amendments to officers' terms and conditions of service and through published conventions adopted by individual councils to suit their own requirements. Officers would also be enabled to give advice to minority party groups. These proposals are subject to the reservation that officers should not be required to attend and advise such groups where party members other than councillors are present.'[1]

[1] Cm 433, para 2.17.

DELEGATION TO A SINGLE MEMBER

5.61 The government White Paper has a helpful passage:

'Under the present law a council can delegate decisions to a committee, sub-committee or an officer. Decisions cannot be delegated to a single member,[1] although the rule appears to be broken in some cases.[2] The Committee recommended that this practice, often known as 'chairman's action', should be made lawful. The Government do not agree since this would breach the principle of corporate decision making and the principle of pro rata representation on decision making committees which is proposed above. An urgency committee of, say, three members ought to be able to deal with the limited number of circumstances in which major urgent decisions are necessary while less important urgent decisions can be delegated to officers. The government will consider whether guidance to local authorities would be helpful.'[3]

1   *R v Secretary of State for the Environment, ex p Hillingdon London Borough Council* [1986] 1 All ER
    810 affirmed, [1986] 2 All ER 273n CA; and cf *R v Brent Health Authority, ex p Francis* [1985] 1 All
    ER 74; *R v Port Talbot Borough Council, ex p Jones* [1988] 2 All ER 207.
2   *Ex p Francis*, above; and *Fraser v Secretary of State for the Environment and the Royal Borough of
    Kensington and Chelsea* (1987) 56 P & CR 386.
3   Cm 433, para 2.18.

5.62 This must now be seen in the light of the LGA 2000 where single-person decisions may be made. See, for example, LGA 2000, s 14(1), (2) and s 15(4)(b) (ii).

5.63 Powers are conferred upon executives by virtue of LGA 2000, ss 10–13 and functions so allocated may 'not be discharged by the authority' (s 13(10)(a)) and are not covered by LGA 1972, s 101(1) which concerns the arrangement for the discharge of functions by the authority. Functions may be discharged by the elected mayor or by arrangement of the mayor 'by another member of the executive' (s 14(2)(a), (b)(ii)). This facility is also afforded to executive leaders in non-mayoral executives where executive arrangements do not allocate functions under s 15(2) and s 15(4)(b). Where an executive consists of an elected mayor and an officer – 'a mayor and council manager executive' – functions may be discharged by the council manager who is an officer of the authority either alone or with the mayor but not by the mayor alone (s 16(2)(a) and (b)). The Secretary of State may by regulations arrange for the discharge of functions which may include their discharge by area committees (ss 17 and 18) or another local authority (s 19).

5.64 The Court of Appeal has held that where a member votes simply on the grounds of 'blind party allegiance' s/he is abandoning a duty to make up his or her own mind on how to vote on a particular issue. The issue in question involved setting a rate.[1] The councillor was entitled to give weight to the views of colleagues in his party and to the party 'whip'. However, the person challenging the resolution of the meeting on the grounds of 'blind allegiance' would have to establish as much, and this would not be established where councillors, albeit following a party line, nevertheless retained an unfettered discretion[2] on the issue and a free choice. Even this case shows the difficulty involved in getting a court to look behind the record.[3]

1   *R v Waltham Forest London Borough Council, ex p Baxter* [1987] 3 All ER 671, CA; on misfeasance
    of office present in the votes of some members of a committee, see *Jones v Swansea City Council*
    [1989] 3 All ER 162, CA. In the *Waltham Forest* case, SOs made a distinction between committees
    dealing with general business and those dealing with quasi-judicial business: in the latter category
    an independence of judgment was required.
2   On the independence of a school governor: *ILEA v Brunyate* [1989] 1 WLR 542, HL. On fixed
    policies and manifesto promises, see *Bromley London Borough Council v Greater London Council*
    [1983] 1 AC 768, HL; cf *Secretary of State for Education and Science v Tameside Metropolitan Borough
    Council* [1977] AC 1014, HL and more recently, *R (Island Farm Development Ltd) v Bridgend CBC*

[2006] EWHC 2189 (Admin), [2007] BLGR 60. The Court of Appeal recently overturned a decision of the High Court which found that the making of a planning decision in a pre-election period (contrary to the council's own guidelines) was unlawful due to the appearance of bias in some of the councillors. See *R (Lewis) v Redcar and Cleveland BC* [2008] EWCA Civ 746, [2009] 1 WLR 83.

³   This was not the case, however, in *Bromley London Borough Council, supra.*

5.65   In the case of a casting vote by a mayor, there was no duty on the mayor to use the casting vote to maintain a status quo, as that would continue a deadlock. A casting vote, where exercised, had to be exercised 'honestly and according to [a] perception of what was in the public interest'.[1] The Court of Appeal has added that a casting vote may be used as the voter thinks fit and in favour of the political party to which s/he belongs. Impartiality is not required.[2]

¹   *R v Bradford City Metropolitan Council, ex p Wilson* [1989] 3 All ER 140.
²   *R v Bradford City Metropolitan Council, ex p Corris* [1989] 3 All ER 156, CA.

INSPECTION OF DOCUMENTS AND ATTENDANCE AT MEETINGS

5.66   The government rejected Widdicombe's proposals making the chief executive the arbiter of contested cases involving members, usually of minority parties, and decisions to refuse them access to documents or to allow them to attend a meeting. The government did not intend to remove from the courts the ultimate resolution of such disputes.

5.67   Two further points are relevant before we look at the law on access.

5.68   First, a problem arises from the LG(ATI)A 1985. Widdicombe observed that it enables councillors to have access to documents not available to the public and in which they have a pecuniary interest. The government proposed to amend the law to correct the anomaly.[1]

¹   Cm 433, para 2.19.

5.69   Second, however, a proposal that councillors' rights of access and attendance should be codified in statute and the common law provisions subsumed within such a codification did not eventuate in the LGHA 1989. The problem was identified with exclusion of minority parties which the provisions in the LGHA 1989 sought to redress.

Common law

5.70   The following discussion on the common law must be seen in conjunction with the LG(ATI)A 1985 rights and the changes on party political balance introduced by the LGHA 1989. The common law will also have to be assessed in the light of arrangements made for access to executive committees which were discussed in ch 4.

5.71   What is the law? A corpus of precedents going back to the eighteenth century establishes the rights of members of corporations to see the books or documents of the corporation of which they are members, providing they have no ulterior or improper motive in wishing to see them. A similar right existed for copy-holders to examine the muniments held by the lord to establish the terms of their tenancies – sometimes expressed in forceful language.[1] Mandamus (mandatory order) would issue to enforce the duty on the body at the discretion of the court. A series of judgments of less appreciable antiquity has established the following propositions. A member has a prima facie right to inspect documents which are addressed to the council of which s/he is a member. S/he has this right because s/he is under a duty to keep himself or herself informed of council business which touches upon his or her role as an elected representative. But this right is not absolute. If s/he has an indirect motive, then the council may raise this as a bar to inspection. As a corollary of this limitation, a member is not afforded a roving commission through council documents. The most important manifestation of this last restriction is present in the fact that council administration is conducted through committees and post-LGA 2000 coming into effect, through new-style executives. If a member is also a member of a committee, then a fortiori, s/he has a prima facie right to inspect documents coming before that committee.[2] If s/he is not a member of the committee then s/he has to show cause why sight of them is necessary to perform his or her duties adequately: in common parlance s/he must establish a 'need to know'. This would appear to be the case at common law as regards documents before the executive. If a member of a committee, the right is not absolute, but can be qualified on the ground that there is some other good cause to refuse access established by the committee.[3] Dicta suggest that good cause can be established by the committee if inspection might lose the benefit of qualified privilege attaching to documents in relation to defamation proceedings: where there might be a risk of unnecessary replication of 'gossip and hearsay'; or where documentation or reports relate to matters before the committee prior to the appointment of the member to the committee and it is not necessary for the new member to be apprised of the information to perform his or her duties.[4]

[1]   *R v Fraternity of Hostmen in Newcastle-upon-Tyne* (1745) 2 Stra 1223; *R v Allgood* (1798) 7 Term Rep 746; *R v Tower* (1815) 4 M & S 162; *R v Merchant Tailors' Co* (1831) 2 B & Ad 115; *R v Governor & Co of Bank of England* [1891] 1 QB 785.
[2]   *Birmingham City District Council v O* [1983] 1 All ER 497, HL.
[3]   *Bank of Bombay v Suleman Somji* (1908) 99 LT 62, PC; *R v Southwold Corpn, ex p Wrightson* (1907) 97 LT 431; *R v Hampstead Borough Council, ex p Woodward* (1917) 116 LT 213; *R v Barnes Borough Council, ex p Conlan* [1938] 3 All ER 226. But not to defeat rights under the LG(ATI)A 1985.
[4]   *R v Lancashire County Council Police Authority, ex p Hook* [1980] QB 603, CA.

5.72   The member's right to inspect is a strong one, but it is not absolute even when s/he is a member of a committee, and Lord Brightman's emphatic words in *Birmingham City District Council v O*[1] about no secrecy existing between a member of a social service committee and the social workers of the department have to be seen in the context of the member's position or the request being above-board and not for any ulterior or improper motive. The basic point is that if the committee, or if necessary the council, show cause, the onus transfers to the member to establish that that cause and the decision which represents it are unreasonable, on the test established by Lord Greene MR in *Associated Provincial Picture Houses Ltd v Wednesbury Corpn*.[2] If the council establishes a good cause, the onus on the member then becomes a difficult one to shift as in favour of the council or committee omnia praesumuntur rite esse acta.[3] A reasonable decision of a committee or council which has considered all relevant matters and not considered irrelevant ones will stand. Where the arguments are of equal weight, the bias may, be in favour of disclosure. These basic propositions were illustrated by *R v Hackney London Borough Council, ex p Gamper*.[4]

[1] In '*O*'s case, Lord Brightman said where a councillor had a bona fide and reasonably based concern ... not a mere busybody ... the bias should be in favour of access, not concealment.
[2] [1948] 1 KB 223, CA.
[3] *Hook's* case above.
[4] [1985] 3 All ER 275.

5.73 In *Gamper*, Lloyd LJ held that in a Labour-controlled authority, a member of the minority Liberal party who was a member of the public services and housing committees was entitled to see documents going before a Direct Labour Organisation (DLO) sub-committee of the first committee and he was entitled to attend meetings of the sub-committee by virtue of his membership of the parent committee:

'The committee of which the applicant was a member had a residual responsibility for the matters delegated to the sub-committee, and was answerable in its turn to the Council by virtue of its terms of reference. On that, if no other ground, he had demonstrated a "need to know".'

5.74 Lloyd LJ further stated that the applicant councillor could not perform his duties as a member of the council, nor as a chairman of an unrelated, ie to the Public Services' Committee, housing services sub-committee without sight of the agenda and working papers of the DLO sub-committee. These latter grounds turned very much on the individual facts, but the former ground is a strong authority to suggest that a member of a committee has a prima facie right of access to its sub-committees. The authority had not considered the councillor's legitimate need to know in refusing to let him inspect the documents or attend the sub-committee and had therefore failed to consider a relevant factor. Had they considered this and still maintained that the councillor could not have sight of documents and access, their decision, Lloyd LJ believed, would be unreasonable and ultra vires on the basis of the residuary test in *Associated Provincial Picture Houses Ltd v Wednesbury Corpn* (above). Attempts to evade the impact of this decision by the committee creating a working party rather than a sub-committee would be looked at with scepticism and there would be a strong tendency for courts to look at the substance of what was established and not the mere appellation.[1]

[1] See *Moffat's* case below.

5.75 The following are important indications of the ambit of the right:

'Counsel for the council argued that the Birmingham case was concerned only with a single document, or file of documents, whereas here Mr Gamper is asking for access to committee documents generally. I can see no difference in principle, provided the documents come within the scope of Mr Gamper's "need to know". Mr Gamper cannot perform his duties properly or effectively as a member of the council, or the public services committee, or as chairman of the Shoreditch district housing committee, without having access to the agenda, minutes and other documents of the DLO sub-committees. There may be, I know not, documents which are so confidential that they cannot be disclosed without passages in those documents being covered up or deleted.'[1]

[1]   [1985] 3 All ER 275 at 281.

5.76   On attendance at meetings, as distinct from access to documents:

'Counsel rightly drew my attention to the fact that neither the Birmingham case, nor any of the previous reported cases, were directly concerned with attendance at a meeting as distinct from access to documents. Nor was anything said in any of the cases, which anyone has been able to find, about the right to attend committee or sub-committee meetings. But there is no logical distinction between access to documents and attendance at meetings. As in the case of access to documents, the answer must depend on whether the councillor needs to attend the meeting in order to perform his duties properly as a member of the council. In the end this point was conceded by counsel for the council. It may be, as counsel submitted, that the councillor must show a more urgent need to know in the case of attendance than in the case of access to documents. But it is unnecessary to decide that point now. As in the case of access to DLO sub-committee documents, the council's decision to exclude Mr Gamper from sub-committee meetings must, in my view, be quashed on two grounds: that the council asked itself the wrong question, and that it reached a conclusion which no reasonable council could have reached if properly directed in law. Obviously, the right to attend DLO sub-committee meetings does not carry with it the right to take part in the discussions, unless invited to do so, or to vote.'[1]

[1]   [1985] 3 All ER 275 at 283.

5.77   Where information was 'confidential', that would not *ipso facto* destroy the right, but:

'Members of the council are, by virtue of Standing Order 24(6) and other references in the standing orders, under an obligation not to disclose confidential information. I will assume in favour of the council, though I find it difficult to imagine, that there are some matters which come before the sub-committee, such, perhaps, as prices at which it is proposed to tender or at which rival contractors have tendered, that are so highly confidential that they cannot be disclosed even to members of council. That cannot, in my view, justify blanket denial of access to all sub-committee documents. If there are indeed such highly confidential matters, then they can be dealt with in the usual way, as I have already mentioned, by covering up what needs to be kept confidential. The very width of the prohibition in the present case shows to my mind conclusively that no reasonable council directing itself in accordance with the principles stated in the Birmingham case, could have reached the decision to exclude access to all sub-committee documents.'[1]

[1]   [1985] 3 All ER 275 at 283. See Donaldson LJ in *ex p O* [1982] 1 WLR 679, CA, on the need to apply a 'screening' process with great strictness in child care cases and adoption.

5.78   Further, councillors seeking access are well advised to be as specific and clear as possible as to why they have a need to know. Reasons must be spelt out in most cases.[1]

[1]   See, eg [1985] 3 All ER 275 at 281 b–c.

5.79   The theme of *Gamper's* case was developed in *R v Sheffield City Council, ex p Chadwick*.[1] The applicant was a leader of a minority party on the city council and a member of the policy committee, the principal committee of the authority. A sub-committee of that committee was the budget sub-committee, a recommendatory committee all the members of which were members of the ruling party alone.[2] Chadwick sought a declaration that the council acted unlawfully by refusing to allow him to attend meetings of the budget sub-committee and by refusing to supply him with copies of reports made to that sub-committee. He considered it necessary to attend and receive information because of the Secretary of State's decision to rate-cap Sheffield City Council's expenditure and his need 'to reach a reasonable judgment on those [budget] decisions' made at a future policy committee and city council meeting called for that purpose. His attendance was denied, although certain amounts of financial information were to be provided by the Treasurer 'according to conventions', but agenda papers were excluded. The council's case was that exclusion of opposition members was necessary because of the sensitive proposals for a budget examined and worked out in such a sub-committee, and attendance of opposition members would make it difficult for members to seek the advice of officers without inhibition. The aim was to protect the secrecy of the party's deliberative process.

[1]   (1985) 84 LGR 563.
[2]   NB the LGHA 1989 and pro rata membership according to political strength: see paras 4.111 et seq above.

5.80   Woolf LJ held that it was not permissible for the council, by allowing the sub-committee to be used for party political purposes, to justify a need for confidentiality and secrecy which would not otherwise arise, ie it was unlawful to use a sub-committee for party political purposes in this way. It was possible for them to establish an ad hoc group outside the council structure, and even to consult officers of the council. But the confidential nature of the party political deliberations taking place was an unlawful consideration for the council to adopt in denying access and the council could 'not reasonably take the view that he did not have a need to know' to understand the recommendation behind resolutions on which he was to vote. There was no justifiable reason for confidentiality. If attendance was a convenient way for a councillor to obtain information, then absent special circumstances of confidentiality 'there would in the ordinary way be no rational basis for refusing attendance'. Nor would a councillor with a need to know be expected to exhaust all other channels to get information, providing he did not act unreasonably. He had a need to know and the committee had no good reason to exclude him.

The case law and executives

5.81   Nothing in principle precludes the operation of the common law principles in relation to executives under the LGA 2000, but the fact that most members will not be on such executives, that they have no roving commission through council documents and that in terms of accountability an overview and scrutiny committee (OSC) will be appointed militate against a wide interpretation of their right to access. Where meetings are held in private, a need to know will have to be established to gain access to documents and members may find it more useful to rely upon the FOIA 2000 or regulations under the LGA 2000, whichever are more favourable. Special provision is made in LGA 2000, s 21 for access by the public to executive information (see below) and these are drafted in order to be consistent with the FOIA 2000. The case-law had actually adopted a more subtle and flexible approach when dealing with the rights of members of a corporate body represented through the council and committees. The LGA 2000 emphasises the division more along Whitehall lines where MPs have no right to know executive information apart from that under the FOIA 2000 and SOs of the House and other legal provisions (see ch 2). Local authorities are still corporate bodies but the executive arrangements could easily facilitate an enhanced secrecy in deliberations and decision-making. It will be interesting to see how courts will respond to the challenge.

5.82   In terms of presence at meetings, LGA 2000, Sch 1, para 5 provides that a member of a local authority who is not a member of the authority's executive is entitled to attend, and speak at, a meeting of the executive, or of a committee of the executive, which is held in private only if invited to do so. This seems fairly conclusive in terms of attendance. Could it be argued that, because statute has removed any right of attendance, it has also removed any claim to a right to know?

When is it council information?

5.83   A question often raised is whether or not documentation or reports are addressed to the council or whether they are or are not committee papers. If not, then it was reasoned that they are not documents prima facie within the scope of the case-law, so that there is no basic presumption of a right to inspect. This is important where there are one party working groups, or budgeting 'groups' of leading members of the ruling party planning the council budget. Are such documents or is such information council information? A budgeting sub-committee in *Chadwick*'s case was dealing with council information to which he had a need to know. Further, meetings outside the formal council structure may still be within the realm of what a councillor 'needs to know' to perform his duties. It is a question of fact and degree. The more informal, extraneous or the less directly related to council business, the less likely are documents to be relevant, or council information.

5.84 In *R v Hyndburn Borough Council, ex p Strak*[1] for instance, there were informal meetings of political leaders of the two leading groups, in collaboration with senior officers, where, councillor Strak complained, decisions were effectively taken on behalf of the council, de facto if not de lege. It was accepted that it was in order for senior officers to consult members of particular political groups, and where the initiative came from officers it should be exercised reasonably. Where officers had delegated powers, there was nothing improper in their exercising those powers after consulting members or groups of members. In respect of decisions taken by officers, the rights of members to be informed was the same as that which operated as against committees. It was also accepted that, normally, there was no right to obtain information or be present in consultations between officers and members when they were consulted as members of a political group. There would not normally be a need to know, although it is submitted one may be established on the facts of a case.

[1]   CO/918/85 (17 December 1985, unreported).

5.85 Minutes of the meetings, Strak suggested, showed that the meetings were not part of an informal administrative consultation process before official organs of the council made decisions. They were decision-making meetings on behalf of the council, a claim with which Woolf LJ was not inclined to disagree, and therefore Strak was justified in seeking access. It would seem, however, too unguarded to offer this as authority for the proposition that a member cannot establish a need to know and be present in the consultation process between a political group and officials. It is an arguable proposition depending upon the facts of each case, unlikely though it may be to achieve success in a large majority of consultative processes. The extent of the legitimate official interest and responsibility of the councillor will need to be assessed.

Working parties[1]

5.86 It has been decided that local authorities have power to establish working parties (White Papers) to proffer advice to committees.[2] In *R v Eden District Council, ex p Moffat*,[3] councillor Moffat was excluded from the meetings of a working party which he claimed in fact was a sub-committee, and under SOs and common law he had a right to attend. On the facts, which included membership of the committee of chief officers,[4] it was held that the body was a working party, with consequently no right for Moffat to attend under the SOs.

[1]   On funding officers' time to serve political parties see: *Leicester City Council v District Auditor for Leicester* [1989] RVR 162, CA.
[2]   Pursuant to the power in LGA 1972, s 111(1) and not under the exercise of functions through the council, committee, sub-committee or officers under s 101(1). The case concerned 'confidential' items about appointments and restructuring.
[3]   *R v Eden District Council, ex p Moffat* (15 April 1987, unreported) CO/803 86; on appeal 8 November 1988 667/87 and (1988) *Times*, 24 November, CA.
[4]   Officers cannot be members of committees: LGA 1972, s 104. They can be a member of a 'mayor and council manager' executive: LGA 2000, s 11(4).

5.87 At first instance, Webster J believed that there was no reason in principle why a common law 'need to know' argument on behalf of a councillor could not be made out in relation to information before a working party of which s/he was not a member.[1] This, respectfully, must be correct, although in Moffat's case no need to know was established. The fact that Moffat was a member of the council establishing the WP would have been influential, although membership of the parent will not confer automatic right of admission to its progeny. His presence might inhibit frank discussion in a forum discussing tentatively provisional and sensitive matters, and he had no right to attend,[2] even though he may have benefited from being present in later council meetings discussing the report. Nourse LJ on appeal believed this benefit constituted a 'need to know' and argued that a right to attend is not a right to participate, 'nor may it generally be objected that his presence there will inhibit others from speaking out as they would otherwise do' where he has a need to know. His right can only be defeated where his presence would cause injury to the public interest by eg breaching a confidence. 'It is not to be defeated by vague generalisations and the sensitivities of those who might feel more comfortable if he was excluded from their discussions'. The two other judges did not believe there was a need to know, or a need to attend.[3]

[1] On appeal, Nourse LJ agreed, Croom-Johnson LJ and Sir Denis Buckley seemed not to, but Croom-Johnson LJ appeared to be arguing to the particular facts, not making a general principle.
[2] However, Webster J at first instance believed the authority had acted unfairly and unlawfully in not allowing Moffat to explain why he had a bona fide right or need to attend. This refusal was unlawful, he held. The Court of Appeal, however, did not agree. There was no right to attend, and therefore no right to explain why a right to attend might be established!
[3] Croom-Johnson LJ and Sir Denis Buckley.

Access for members under the Local Government (Access to Information) Act 1985

5.88 This Act, which adds to LGA 1972, s 100, is dealt with exhaustively in ch 6. It confers rights on the public, including the press, and members to attend local authority meetings, committee and sub-committee meetings and the right to receive notice of meetings, to inspect and copy the agenda of any council, committee or sub-committee meeting three clear days before the meeting takes place – the three clear days period has been extended to such longer period as the Secretary of State may prescribe by order (LGA 2000, s 98(2)) and the period has been extended to five days;[1] to inspect and copy any reports being considered during the public part of such a meeting; to inspect the minutes of any such meeting except where the minutes of the private part of a meeting themselves reveal the information which led to the meeting being closed in the first place. In the latter case only a summary giving a 'reasonably fair and coherent record' of the proceedings needs to be provided. Also conferred is a right to inspect background papers used in the preparation of the reports to be discussed in public at any council, committee or sub-committee meetings.

[1] This was done by SI 2002/715.

5.89 There are exemptions and exclusions from these rights (see para 6.29).

5.90   Under the Act, councillors are in a stronger position than members of the public. LGA 1972, s 100F (as inserted) states that a councillor may see any documents 'in the possession or under the control' of the council which contain material relating to any business to be transacted at a meeting of the council, committee or sub-committee, unless those documents contain exempt information as defined in LGA 1972, Sch 12A, Part I, paras 1–6, 9, 11, 12 and 14 (as inserted by LG(ATI)A 1985, Sch 1). These rights are wider than the public's rights in four ways:[1]

(i)   the public's rights only apply to the public parts of meetings, whereas the member's rights are not so restricted, although certain exemptions apply;

(ii)   not all the exemptions which apply to the public apply to members;[2]

(iii) the member has access to background documents that relate to the business conducted at the meeting, ie they are not restricted to those that disclose facts or matters on which the report of an officer is based and which have been relied on to a material extent in the report, as is the case with the public;

(iv)   documentation available to the public, it has been argued, need only relate to 'the business' being transacted, not to a report about the business which is being discussed, ie 'facts, reports, counter evidence to that used by an officer, contrary opinions of other officers etc which may have been ignored, forgotten … or simply not known by the officer writing the report will not be available to the public but will be available to members'. Other documents which relate to the business being transacted, apart from those available to the public, should be asked for.

---

[1]   These points were made by Ron Bailey *Guide to Councillor's Rights To Information*; see paras 6.29 et seq below for the provisions.

[2]   Quaere the position of members of the authority who are not members of the committee which is dealing with 'confidential' information according to the LG(ATI)A 1985? Are they members of the public and thereby automatically excluded? Presumably not if they have a need to know.

5.91   Further, only the public are excluded, under the statute, from meetings where 'confidential' items are to be discussed. This means they will not have access to related documents. The statute does not exclude members, though as a matter of practice they probably will be.

5.92   The rights under this section are in addition to the common law rights above. The statutory rights cannot be defeated by common law restrictions.

5.93   If a member who is not on a committee establishes a need to know, then s/he will be entitled to obtain the document, even if it falls within one of the exempt categories.[1]

---

[1]   *Birmingham City District Council v O* [1983] 1 All ER 497, HL.

5.94   That is the common law position. Once such a need is established, it overrides third party rights to confidentiality, or immunities of local authorities unless ulterior motives be established. The Act will be important for routine information; the common law will be important for exempt information, or information not covered by the Act where there is a need to know. Controversial questions likely to arise under the Act are: (1) when is a document in the possession or under the control of a principal council? and (2) what is a meeting of the council, or committee or sub-committee of the council, or a committee or sub-committee, under LGA 1972, ss 101(9) and 102?

5.95 As regards possession or control, information collected by officers for their official duties would seem to be covered; with members there must be an opportunity to acquire information which could concern council business but which is their private property. Once again, in difficult cases it is a question of fact and degree. Useful questions may be: by whom was it collected or acquired? In what capacity? for what purpose? How closely related is it to council business? The discussion above on committees etc is relevant here (paras 5.59 and 5.07 et seq above). Executive bodies of a council are now provided for under LGA 2000, s 13 and their executive functions under s 14. The LG(ATI)A 1985 has no relevance to them as shown above. The Act will have relevance to functions effected by the council, committees, sub-committees and officers and by OSCs (s 21(11) for the latter). Officers cannot be members of the council, committees or sub-committees. A council can establish deliberative/advisory committees – these will be covered by the Act. A council can establish a working party (see above) – these will be purely tentative or advisory and will not be covered. However, the information or documentation before these working parties will eventually often come before the official organs of the council; it will then be covered by the Act unless, crucially that body is the executive. FOIA 2000 will clearly apply to information from the executive body.

5.96 The Local Authorities (Executive Arrangements) (Access to Information) (England) Regulations 2000, SI 2000/3272, provide for access to documents and proceedings of executive bodies as set out in Part II of the LGA 2000.[1] The Regulations provide that records must be kept of all decisions made at private or public executive meetings. Under reg 3 the records should include inter alia a record of the decision, reasons for the decision, details of any alternative options considered and rejected, and details of any conflicts of interest that were declared. Similar provisions apply in reg 4 to decisions taken by individual members. Regs 5 and 6[2] generally require these records and any background documents to be accessible to the public at the offices of the authority 'as soon as is reasonably practicable'. Newspapers may request the records of decisions made (but not background documents), which must be provided on payment of postage, the cost of copying or any necessary charge for transmission. The Regulations give the public access to executive meetings and certain documents (primarily the agenda and related documents and 'forward plans') for these meetings which relate to 'key decisions' (ie those which involve expenditure or cost savings which are significant in regard to the authority's budget, or those which are significant in terms of their impact in an area comprising two or more electoral wards of the authority). Members of the local authority enjoy a broader right of access. It is useful to set out the full details of reg 17 (as amended):

(1) Subject to paragraphs (3) to (4) , any document which—

(a) is in the possession, or under the control, of the executive of a local authority; and

(b) contains material relating to any business to be transacted at a public meeting,

shall be available for inspection by any member of the local authority.

(2) Subject to paragraphs (3) to (4) any document which—

(a) is in the possession, or under the control, of the executive of a local authority; and

(b) contains material relating to—

(i) any business transacted at a private meeting;

(ii) any decision made by an individual member in accordance with executive arrangements; or

(iii) any key decision made by an officer in accordance with executive arrangements,

shall be available for inspection by any member of the local authority when the meeting concludes or, where an executive decision is made by an individual member or a key decision made by an officer, immediately after the decision has been made.

(3) Paragraphs (1) and (2) do not require a document to be available for inspection if it appears to the proper officer that it discloses exempt information of a description falling within Part 1 of Schedule 12A to the 1972 Act (descriptions of exempt information: England)3.

(3A) But paragraphs (1) and (2) do require (despite paragraph (3)) the document to be available for inspection if the information is information of a description for the time being falling within—

(a) paragraph 3 of Schedule 12A to the 1972 Act (except to the extent that the information relates to any terms proposed or to be proposed by or to the authority in the course of negotiations for a contract); or

(b) paragraph 6 of Schedule 12A to the 1972 Act.

(4) Where it appears to the proper officer that compliance with paragraph (1) or (2) in relation to a document or part of a document would involve the disclosure of advice provided by a political adviser or assistant, that paragraph shall not apply as regards that document or part.

(5) The rights conferred by paragraphs (1) and (2) are in addition to any other rights that a member of a local authority may have.

---

[1] Amended by SI 2002/716 and 2006/69. For Wales, see SI 2001/2290 The Local Authorities (Executive Arrangements) (Decisions, Documents and Meetings) Regulations. These were amended by SI 2002/1385 and 2007/951.

[2] In reg 6, there is a requirement that background papers to a report or part of a report before the executive should be made available to the public for public inspection. In reg 2, 'background papers' are defined as in relation to a report or part of a report, means those documents other than published works, that: (a) relate to the subject matter of the report or, as the case may be the part of the report; and (b) in the opinion of the proper officer—(i) disclose any facts or matters on which the report or an important part of the report is based; and (ii) were relied on to a material extent in preparing the report.

In *Trillium (Prime) Property GP Ltd v London Borough of Tower Hamlets* [2011] EWHC 146 (Admin), Ouseley J found that there had been a breach of the regulations when the council had failed to include certain documents, including a report from English Heritage and a list of groups who supported a particular position in relation to a planning application. The council had argued that these documents were 'published' (and thus not within the scope of reg 6) as they were publicly available. Ouseley J rejected the idea that all documents which were publicly available were 'published'. He said at [167]: 'Although the documents which should have been listed as background papers were to some degree public, and Trillium certainly knew of some of them, they were not in my view published documents within the statutory definition. They were not the sort of documents deliberately made available to the general public, or to the informed but relevant public. They are not such that it can be assumed that the public or would-be participants would know of them or have ready access to them. Listing should alert members to them, and the public is entitled to see them.' In *Trillium*, this omission was not sufficient to invalidate the decision at issue in the case as a whole, but the decision was found to be unlawful due to various other inadequacies in the report which led to the decision.

5.97 Regulation 18 provides that members of the OSC of a local authority is entitled to copies of any document in the possession or under the control of the local authority that contains material relating to a public or private meeting of a decision-making body, or which relates to any decision that has been made by a member of the executive or an officer of the local authority under executive arrangements. The only exceptions to this are where the document contains confidential or exempt information (see below), although the member of the OSC can still require access to such document where the information relates to a decision or action s/he is scrutinising, or which is contained in the programme of work of the OSC. Members of the OSC may not have access to any document or part of a document which contains advice provided by a political adviser or assistant. The Regulations further provide that the OSC may require the executive to submit a report on any decision that was not treated as a 'key decision' if the OSC is of the opinion that it should have been treated as being such. The report should contain details of the reasons for the decision, the body or individual who made the decision and the reasons why the decision was felt not to be a key decision (reg 19). Regulation 20 requires the executive leader to submit a quarterly report of executive decisions taken including the particulars of the decision and a summary of the matters to which the decision relates.

5.98 SI 2000/3272 contains, in reg 21, a number of exceptions to the requirements set out above. The public can be excluded from meetings where their presence would lead to the disclosure of confidential information, exempt information (under LGA 1972, s 100I and Sch 12A), where attendance at the meeting would reveal the advice of a political adviser or assistant or where lawful power is used to maintain orderly conduct at a meeting. The exclusion must apply only to the parts of the meeting where such information is likely to be discussed or revealed. Similar provisions apply to documents, which may not be made available for inspection by the public if such availability would lead to the disclosure of confidential or exempt information, or would lead to the revealing of the advice of a political adviser or assistant.

5.99 The provisions of SI 2000/3272 appear to be broadly in line with the approach taken in FOIA 2000, although it seems possible that members of the public would need to have recourse to FOIA 2000 to obtain documents, etc relating to those decisions that are not 'key decisions' in the majority of cases. The applicable exemptions appear to be broadly similar.

Working practice

5.100   Under the common law, the decision not to allow inspection of committee, etc documents will invariably be made by the committee, though in constitutional theory the council has a right to make a final decision.[1] Many authorities have devised procedures, either de lege in standing orders or de facto to resolve such disputes. Executives under the LGA 2000 will make decisions on access relating to their activity and deliberations vis-à-vis members. They will be subject to judicial review.[2]

[1]   See Lord Brightman in *Birmingham v O* above. There were subtle differences between committees with referred, as opposed to delegated, powers.
[2]   For members of the public, there will be judicial review and possible resort to the ombudsman. What will the role of the OSC be in such cases?

5.101   The examples in existence often followed the standard model of standing orders, viz inspection of any document which has been considered by a committee, sub-committee or by the council and supply of a copy if available.

> 'Provided that a Member shall not knowingly inspect and shall not call for a copy of any document relating to a matter in which he is professionally interested or in which he has directly or indirectly any pecuniary interest within the meaning of the Local Government Acts for the time being in force and provided that this Standing Order shall not preclude the Director of Administration from declining to allow inspection of any document which is or in the event of legal proceedings would be legally protected by privilege or other claim confidentiality.'

5.102   SOs will invariably refer to rights under the LG(ATI)A 1985.

5.103   Some authorities spell out in guidelines for chief officers of departments how to react if a request is made to them for access to files or documentation. Basically in the case of any difficulty the matter should be referred to the appropriate committee chairman and/or the director of administration or his equivalent. If the director of administration is seised of the issue, a regular pattern is for the director to contact the chair and for them to make an informal ruling. A significant number of authorities believe that is adequate. In some cases provision is made for further 'appeal' to the chief executive, possibly in conclave with the leader of the council, with a final appeal to the full council or in some cases the policy and resources committee. Although these possibilities exist, resort to them in practice is extremely rare. The government refused to give the Chief Executive a statutory role to resolve such disputes. Executives will make their own decisions.

5.104   On attendance at committee meetings, a common SO provides:

> 'Any member of the Council shall be permitted to attend a meeting of any Committee of which s/he is not a member and will only be permitted to speak with the prior consent of the Chair but in no circumstances will such member be enabled to move, second or vote upon any motion before

the meeting. Any such member shall be bound by any decision of the Committee as to the confidentiality of any information whether written or oral discussed at that meeting.'

5.105 The same provision often applies to sub-committees. SOs cannot reduce statutory or common law rights and those in the LGHA 1989 should be recalled. If they attempt this they are ultra vires.[1] Where they provide rights in excess of the law, but not contrary to it, they must be complied with.[2]

[1]   See de Smith, Woolf and Jowell *Judicial Review of Administrative Action* (6th edn, 2007) and *Supplement* (2009).
[2]   *R v Hereford Corpn, ex p Harrower* [1970] 1 WLR 1424.

Revised standing orders

5.106 The Widdicombe Committee and the government believed that SOs need clarifying and amending to safeguard the rights of minority parties. Unlike Widdicombe, the government preferred voluntary guidance,[1] reserving powers to enable a statutory core of SOs to be prescribed should that be judged desirable. The following were to be included in the guidance:

'(a)   the right of a minority party to put a matter on the agenda of the council or one of its committees or sub-committees;
(b)   the circulation of agendas and papers to members and officers;
(c)   the suspension of the council's standing orders;
(d)   the right of a minority party to require a committee or sub-committee with delegated powers to take decisions to refer matters to full council or a parent committee;
(e)   the delegation of decisions to officers;
(f)   provision to give the chief executive or chief officer the right to advise either orally or in writing on any matter coming before the council or a committee for decision;
(g)   the requirements for calling special meetings of the council;
(h)   the duty[2] of the chairman of a council, committee or sub-committee meeting to clear the public gallery in the case of disorder.

They do not think that councils should be expected to provide for a compulsory "question time", which would be inappropriate in many councils, for example, where there is no controlling group seeking to answer for council policy. Any standing orders governing the membership of committees would need to reflect the proposed statutory requirements which are set out.

The government agree with the Committee's conclusion that authorities should draw up, and make available publicly, conventions about the working relationships between political groups and between councillors and officers. They commend such conventions to authorities. They do not consider that such conventions should be required by statute.'[3]

[1]   Prepared by local authority associations and government departments.
[2]   *R v Brent Health Authority, ex p Francis* [1985] 1 All ER 74.
[3]   Cm 433, paras 2.27–2.28.

5.107 Section 20 of the LGHA 1989 empowers regulations to require SOs to allow members to requisition meetings of an authority and its committees, etc. In the case of new executive meetings, the government has placed its faith in access regulations and the Overview and Scrutiny Committees.

5.108 Provision on SOs is now made by the Local Authorities (Standing Orders) (England) Regulations 2001, SI 2001/3384. These Regulations require certain local authorities in England to make or modify SOs so that they include the provisions set out in the Regulations, or provisions to the like effect.

5.109 Part II of the LGA 2000 provides for local authorities to draw up proposals for the operation of executive arrangements (under which certain functions of the authority are the responsibility of an executive) or, in the case of certain authorities, for the operation of alternative arrangements (see ch 4). In the case of executive arrangements, the local authority's executive must take one of the forms specified in LGA 2000, s 11.

5.110 Under the Regulations, a county council, district council or London borough council which is operating executive arrangements must have SOs relating to its staff which include the provisions set out in Sch 1 (on staff), and must have SOs for regulating its proceedings and business which include the provisions set out in Sch 2 (regulating business and proceedings), or provisions to the like effect. The SOs must be the appropriate ones for the particular form that the executive takes (as set out in different Parts of Schs 1 and 2) and, if that form changes, the SOs must be varied accordingly (reg 3).

5.111 A county council, district council or London borough council which is operating alternative arrangements must have SOs relating to its staff which include the provisions set out in Sch 1, Part IV, or provisions to the like effect (reg 4).

5.112 A county council, district council, London borough council, the Common Council of the City of London and the Council of the Isles of Scilly must, in respect of disciplinary action against the head of the authority's paid service, its monitoring officer and its chief finance officer, make SOs incorporating the provisions set out in Sch 3 to the Regulations (disciplinary action), or provisions to the like effect. Such SOs must be made no later than the first ordinary meeting of the local authority falling after the day on which the Regulations came into force (reg 6).[1]

---

[1] For a case on the interpretation of Sch 3, see *Leatham v Hillingdon LBC* [2006] EWHC 2283 (QB), [2007] BLGR 45.

5.113 SI 2001/3384, reg 7 prescribes a procedure for investigation by an independent person, which is to be followed where there is alleged to have been misconduct by the head of the authority's paid service (unless he is the authority's council manager), its monitoring officer or its chief finance officer. Similar provisions were included in the Local Authorities (Standing Orders) Regulations

1993 ('the 1993 Regulations') in relation to the head of the authority's paid service; and reg 8 revokes the similar provisions in the 1993 Regulations in so far as they extend to England (but not in relation to a National Park authority in England to which the 1993 Regulations apply by virtue of the National Park Authorities (England) Order 1996).

Inspection of the accounts

5.114   Under LGA 1972, s 228(3) as amended,[1] a member has the right to inspect the accounts of the authority or any proper officer of the authority. S/he has the right to copy them or take an extract from them.[2]

[1]   By LGA 1985, Sch 14, para 24.
[2]   See also ACA 1998, ss 8–13.

Confidentiality

5.115   The law of confidentiality has been examined in ch 2. It may be invoked to restrain members, officials, or third party recipients of confidential information from breaking the confidence on the principles already discussed. There is no law of official secrecy protecting local authority information in the way that Crown information is protected by the OSA 1989. Indeed, in evidence to the Franks Committee on the former OSA 1911, s 2 it was claimed that such legislation in local government was unnecessary.[1] The law of confidentiality has been successfully invoked to protect confidential council reports, as well as papers on the accounts of controversial works.[2]

[1]   Association of Metropolitan Authorities' submission to the Franks Report on OSA 1911, s 2.
[2]   See eg, *The Guardian* 12 December 1998.

5.116   However, several points need to be addressed in relation to local government.

5.117   First, it is likely that authorities will find it difficult to justify the award of an interim injunction restraining breach of confidence where it concerns the secrets of a public body such as a local authority. It is unlikely that such a body will be able to invoke national security[1] or other reason why a 'public secret' should be maintained. It is more likely that a court will look to see if the information concerns an individual, eg a child[2] or, of increasing importance, an item of commercial confidentiality which is given very wide protection under the FOIA 2000.

[1]   Although Margaret Thatcher's government discussed the possibility of amending the LG(ATI) A 1985 to cover national security. The Attorney-General would be the appropriate plaintiff for civil law applications.
[2]   See *Re M and N (minors)* [1990] 1 All ER 205; *Re A (Minors) (Child Abuse: Guidelines), Practice Note* [1991] 1 WLR 1026. For developments (of which there have been many) regarding litigation, see paras 10.6 et seq below.

5.118 Secondly, the confidential nature of much of a member's business is emphasised in official publications, circulars and SOs. These, however, will not necessarily be conclusive in persuading a court to award an interim injunction and the considerations in the preceding paragraph are relevant. Section 12 of the Human Rights Act 1998 and applications to the courts for interim orders imposing 'prior restraint' will also be of crucial significance here (para 2.349 above). It is a problem which is likely to be resolved by peer group and administrative pressure/redress from within the authority.

5.119 Thirdly, officials are employees of the authorities and the nature of their contracts of employment, implicitly if not expressly,[1] will contain terms of confidentiality. These will be of especial importance in relation to commercial and trade 'secrets'[2] though the ambit of the law will not be restricted to such areas. It must also be recalled that we are dealing with principles under confidentiality and the courts will wish to see damage to the public interest before restraining publication by third parties. The terms of the Public Interest Disclosure Act 1998 should be recalled (para 2.299 above).

[1]   'No officer shall communicate to the public proceedings of any committee ie meeting etc, or the contents of any documents relating to the authority unless required by law or expressly authorised to do so.' National Joint Council Conditions of Service, section 7, para 72.

[2]   See *Faccenda Chicken Ltd v Fowler* [1986] 1 All ER 617, CA. The courts have shown reluctance to protect confidential information after a contract is terminated unless it constitutes a trade secret or is so highly confidential it amounts to such. The Court of Appeal examined this issue further in *Lancashire Fires* v *SA Lyons & Co Ltd* [1997] IRLR 113.

OTHER PUBLIC BODIES

5.120 The FOIA 2000 has now affected every public authority and those private bodies which are designated for the purposes of the Act. This was covered in ch 1 (and see Annex A below).

5.121 All public bodies, and private Data Controllers are covered by the Data Protection Act 1998 and their personal records will have to be available in accordance with the terms of that Act (ch 7 below). Where the employees of such bodies are not Crown servants as defined in the OSA 1989, they will not be under the 'direct' duties within ss 1–4 of that Act, but they may become liable under s 5 and they may be notified of liability for unauthorised disclosure where they are contractors dealing with relevant information or are researchers covered by the terms of the Act. As we saw in ch 1, a wide range of statutes imposes specific criminal offences upon individuals not to release information without authority, usually received in confidence by government or its agencies (see Annex B for a list of such statutory provisions). Under the FOIA 2000 these are subject to ministerial review under s 75.

5.122 For most employees, the most significant inhibition to maintain effective secrecy will be that of dismissal, the withdrawal of benefits and the blighting of career prospects should they betray their employers' confidences, not to mention the risk of black-listing by private agencies as a troublemaker.

It is common practice to restrict any public comments, media interviews, etc among former nationalised industries' employees and other public bodies by a code of conduct with contractual force.[1] Guidelines on conduct, basically to avoid a conflict of interest are common for chairmen of public corporations but unless incorporated into contracts of employment they are not likely to be legally binding.[2] Readers are also referred to the discussion on confidentiality in ch 2 and above and also to the discussion on the Public Interest Disclosure Act 1998 in that chapter.

[1]   The British Medical Journal has published allegations of a strictly enforced 'tight-lipped policy by management in the NHS' (*New Statesman*, 10 June 1988). It has been claimed that city analysts' research was controlled and 'disciplined' prior to the electricity flotation by a 'centralised committee of government experts': *The Guardian*, 29 September 1989. This was to help create a good impression for investors. It remains a widespread practice. What will the impact of Art 10 and the Human Rights Act 1998 be? Article 10 can take horizontal effect, ie between private actors.

[2]   They may articulate duties of confidentiality and duties to account which will be incorporated into the contractual nexus expressly or implicitly although it is true that such duties will operate independently of contract where there is a fiduciary or trust relationship: see *Reading v A-G* [1951] AC 507, HL, and Goff and Jones *The Law of Restitution* (6th edn, 2002).

PUBLICATION OF INFORMATION

5.123 Where publication is not practised voluntarily or is not of a type covered by the FOIA 2000, one has to look at the statute, if it is a body created by statute, to see what the duties and powers are in relation to publicity and information. There is a frequent duty to publish annual reports which are laid before Parliament, accounts which may be examined by the Comptroller and Auditor-General (see ch 11) and other information as required. Guidance has been given on the establishment of non-departmental bodies, formerly by the Treasury, now the Cabinet Office.[1] This contains guidelines on, inter alia, accountability and information flows for managerial efficiency.[2] More recent versions have offered guidance on provision of information and guidance on annual reports and audits.[3] Advice is given on public meetings, and departments and public bodies should hold such meetings at least annually. Publication of minutes should be considered, stakeholders and 'interested parties' should be invited and wide publicity for such meetings should be made, although due regard must be had to sensitive, commercial and political information. Members of Non-Departmental Public Bodies (NDPBs) must abide by a Code of Practice.[4] The internal flow of information within the executive, rather than the public provision of information, has characterised the world of public corporations such as those that ran nationalised industries.[5] Today, notwithstanding the FOIA 2000, it is common to have a regulatory commission (formerly a non-ministerial department) with responsibility for collecting information about performance and standards from a range of private, public and privatised concerns. The bodies in question, eg the Gas and Electricity Markets Authority under the Utilities Act 2000, will be under a duty to provide information to the public (see para 8.331 below). Behind such agencies will be select committees of Parliament conducting examinations and the ombudsman may be allowed to investigate the commissions.

1. *Public Bodies: A Guide for Departments* (2006). Available at: http://www.civilservice.gov.uk/about/resources/public-bodies.aspx.

2. *Public Bodies: A Guide for Departments* (2006), chapter 8, which is concerned with openness and accountability.

3. *Public Bodies: A Guide for Departments* (2006), chapter 8, para 3.1.

4. Available at: http://www.hm-treasury.gov.uk/psr_governance_gia_guidance.htm.

5. A Prosser (1986) *Nationalised Industries and Public Control*. See Sir R Reid (1990) *The Times*, 9 January.

REGULATORY AGENCIES

5.124 The agencies which have been established to regulate telecommunications, gas, electricity and water markets are dealt with elsewhere (ch 8). As is common with many investigatory, regulatory or supervisory public bodies, there are criminal restrictions on the disclosure of information by officials within those bodies.

EXECUTIVE AGENCIES

5.125 The government announced in February 1988 a plan to allocate the executive functions of government to units designated as agencies headed by a chief executive.[1] By December 1998, 138 agencies had been established and four departments were operating on Next Steps Lines (employing in all 383,290 staff).[2] By 2002, there were 127 agencies, 92 reporting to Whitehall departments[3] – these figures do not include Scottish, Welsh and Northern Irish bodies. The major thrust of the initiative is for greater accountability and efficiency. The parent department and the Treasury must be satisfied 'that the proposed Agency will have a robust management structure with appropriate financial, accounting and management information systems'. In 2009 the number of agencies had grown to 192. The newly elected coalition Government pledged to reduce the number of such bodies and undertook a review process that has led to recommendations to merge a number of executive agencies and to abolish a number of others, returning their functions to government departments.[4] Some other bodies are to be privatised or converted to charitable status. The Public Bodies Bill (2010–2011) is presently passing through Parliament and is primarily designed to give Ministers the power to abolish the bodies listed in Sch 1 of the Bill and to order the merger of those listed in Sch 2. The Government has argued that the reduction in the number of agencies will deliver greater accountability as a larger proportion of government functions will be exercised by government departments and thus will be subject to greater democratic accountability. The Public Administration Select Committee has cast a degree of doubt on the efficacy of these changes in delivering greater accountability, as much depends on the detail of the way in which functions are taken back into Departments of State.[5] Furthermore, many of the accountability measures described below will no longer apply, yet these arguably provide a reasonably clear set of goals and principles upon which to judge the performance of agencies.

1. Under *The Next Steps Initiative*: announced in February 1988.

2. The agencies employed 331,010, staff of whom 304,645 were civil servants: *Next Steps Report 1997* Cabinet Office (1998). The departments made up the difference. The latest reports include

only staffing of 'executive' NDPBs, which numbered 111,129 in 2009. For the most recent statistical account, see Cabinet Office (2009) *Public Bodies 2009*.

³   *Better Government Services – Executive Agencies in the 21st Century.*
⁴   For the latest information on which bodies are to be retained, merged or abolished, see Cabinet Office (16 March 2011) *Public Bodies Reform – Proposals for Change.*
⁵   HC 537 *Smaller Government: Shrinking the Quango State* (5th Report of 2010–2011), pp 27–32.

5.126   Each agency will be required to produce every year on a rolling basis a medium-term corporate plan and an annual operating plan with detailed performance targets for the year ahead. As these will be a part of the annual public expenditure survey they will not be published as a part of that process, although annual reports of the agencies will normally be published. Agencies will generally remain Crown bodies and staff will be civil servants. Ministers will be responsible for overall policy, objectives, targets and resourcing of agencies. The chief executive will normally be better placed to deal with operational matters. The chief executive's responsibilities and authority will be set out in a 'framework document' which will normally be published. These will contain whatever details exist in relation to 'reporting arrangements' for the public. The Comptroller and Auditor-General will audit their accounts (see ch 11). The Parliamentary Commissioner for Administration will have jurisdiction over them. There have been some notorious episodes involving Ministers and Agency Chief Executives where the public picture of their relationship was not a true reflection of private reality.[1]

¹   D Lewis *Hidden Agendas: Politics, Law and Disorder* (1997).

5.127   After so many years, the excitement generated by the appearance of the agencies has evaporated. The discussion moved on to focus on 'joined-up government and joined-up services' – a joining of public-sector providers together with voluntary and private-sector bodies in which information sharing and greater use of information technology is the key to effective public service for the future. Debate now appears to have moved further on to look at the potential for the 'Big Society', in terms of shifting certain aspects of service delivery to charities and community groups. A White Paper on *Open Public Services*[1] has been published which outlines proposals for delivering greater competition and diversity in public service delivery, with greater potential for service provision by private and community or voluntary sector organisations. From the perspective of this volume, the most important proposals are those which suggest that there will be an endeavour to provide greater access to open data on public services (para 3.17) and also to deliver increased transparency via publication of business plans and spending data (para 5.23). Some of these policies are already in the process of being implemented, whereas the broader plans on open data are still in an early stage. As noted above, some agencies will be dissolved and their tasks returned to government departments or they will be merged. Exemptions in FOIA for issues such as policy-making may lead to some concerns about this process. There may also be challenges for the FOIA regime if delivery of public services is shifted to the private, charitable or voluntary sectors as these bodies are not currently subject to the FOIA regime. The White Paper notes that FOIA has been extended to academy schools[2] and certain private providers of healthcare services, but does not set out further plans to extend the Act's horizons.

[1] Cm 8145, July 2011.
[2] This was done by the Academies Act 2010, Sch 2, para 10 as FOIA 2000, Sch 1, para 52A.

APPOINTMENTS TO PUBLIC BODIES AND TERMS OF CONDUCT

5.128 We saw earlier how heavily regulated by the law appointments to local government have become. The civil service code contains prohibitions on the political activities of civil servants.

5.129 Public appointments, and the associated power of ministerial patronage, was investigated by the Nolan Committee and his recommendations led to the establishment of the Public Appointments Commissioner in December 1995. The operation of this body was reviewed by the Neill Committee on Public Standards in its report of January 2000. This reported that there were concerns with the use of procedures for making appointments which did not reflect the different levels of importance, status, responsibility and remuneration for the posts. There was a lack of proportionality in approaches adopted. The remit of the Commissioner was extended in October 1998 to cover nationalised industries, public corporations, utility regulators and advisory non-departmental public bodies. A concern in NHS bodies was with delays in making appointments and insensitivity in treatment of, for instance, volunteers.[1] Government departments are required to follow the Commissioner's principles and code of practice in making over 11,000 ministerial appointments in 'England, Scotland and Wales'.

[1] Cm 4557 (2000), ch 9.

5.130 The work of the Commissioner was again investigated by the Committee on Standards in its *Tenth Report*. While a culture of appointment on merit had been introduced, there were still examples of 'unregulated ministerial interventions' which differed from practices in devolved regimes. The Commissioner should be given a power, like the Scottish Commissioner, of halting appointments in breach of the code, and recruitment and training of independent assessors should be further standardised.[1] There was still public disquiet about 'cronyism'.

[1] See ch 2.

Chapter 6

Public access to information and access to meetings

GENERAL ACCESS UNDER THE LOCAL GOVERNMENT (ACCESS TO INFORMATION) ACT 1985

6.1 This chapter examines the major legal provisions which open up the meetings of public authorities to the public and which allow inspection of a public authority's documents alongside the Freedom of Information Act 2000 (FOIA 2000).

6.2 The major legislation involves local government, viz the Local Government (Access to Information) Act 1985 (LG(ATI)A 1985) which in fact is an amendment to the Local Government Act 1972 (LGA 1972).[1] The 1985 Act has been extended to other public bodies, as we shall see. It will also be necessary to examine the Public Bodies (Admission to Meetings) Act 1960, as that Act applies to public bodies as listed in the Act, including health authorities. Central government has already been examined in ch 1, and general duties requiring information and openness in local government were looked at in detail in ch 4 and duties to provide access to meetings or otherwise under the Local Government Act 2000 (LGA 2000) were also examined. In ch 8 there will be a comprehensive survey of the access provisions relating to particular areas of administration. The present chapter will not repeat such discussion, but will concentrate on public access to information and meetings under the two pieces of legislation identified above. Agencies of central government may be showing increasing tendencies towards open meetings; this is true of the Food Standards Agency and the Office of Communications (and for non-departmental bodies, see paras 5.120 et seq above).

[1]   LGA 1972, s 100. The new provisions are known as Part VA.

LOCAL AUTHORITY MEETINGS

6.3   The LG(ATI)A 1985 amended and added to s 100 of the LGA 1972. Section 100 itself extended the provisions of the Public Bodies (Admission to Meetings)

Act 1960, which opened up council meetings to the public and press, to cover committee meetings of local authorities. Until the 1960 Act only the press had access to local authority meetings following legislation in 1908.[1] However, the High Court has held that LGA 1972, s 100A (inserted by LG(ATI)A 1985) did not require the public to be admitted to the 'pre-decision deliberations' of a council's sub-committee dealing with the grant or renewal of licences for sex establishments. The proceedings were 'quasi judicial' in nature and it accorded with neither experience nor expectation that pre-decision deliberations would take place, or could reasonably take place, in public.[2] This is an unhelpful decision. The public should only be excluded if grounds for exclusion are made out under the Act, eg confidentiality, and not for additional reasons.

[1]   Local Authorities (Admission of the Press to Meetings) Act 1908; and see *Tenby Corpn v Mason* [1908] 1 Ch 457, CA.
[2]   *R v Wandsworth London Borough Council, ex p Darker Enterprises Ltd* (1999) 1 LGLR 601.

6.4 The LG(ATI)A 1985, which was extended to health service joint consultative committees (the Act's effect in relation to these was repealed by the Health Act 1999) and to community health councils (these were removed in England in 2003, but are retained in Wales) is important not only in allowing access to documents, but also in being an open meetings law.[1] Since 2002, the NHS in England has seen what is an astonishing number of different methods for public involvement. The National Health Service Reform and Health Care Professions Act 2002, ss 15–22 introduced patients' forums and the Commission for Patient and Public Involvement in Health, which had the function of advising NHS bodies on public involvement. This structure was extended to NHS Foundation Trusts by the Health and Social Care (Community Health and Standards) Act 2003. This regime was then substantially modified to create a system of patients' forums, supported by the Commission for Patient and Public Involvement in Health (which also appointed members of patients' forums) by the National Health Service Act 2006. Patients' forums and the Commission for Patient and Public Involvement in Health were then abolished by the Local Government and Public Involvement in Health Act 2007 and have been replaced by local involvement networks under the Local Government and Public Involvement in Health Act 2007. The Health and Social Care Bill (2010–2011) proposes further changes, including the renaming of local involvement networks as 'local Healthwatch organsations'. There is also a proposal to create a new committee of the Care Quality Commission known as the Healthwatch England Committee. The present regime is considered in more detail below.

[1]   Note the US Government in the Sunshine Act 1976 and the Federal Advisory Committee Act 1972 and the Australian Freedom of Information Act 1982 which have open meetings' dimensions.

6.5 The LG(ATI)A 1985 opens up the meetings of a principal council, its committees and sub-committees to the public. It also allows public access to the agenda and connected officers' reports of meetings in advance of meetings, inspection of minutes and other documents after meetings, the inspection of background papers before and after meetings, and the Act places duties upon councils to publish additional information. The Act, as we saw in ch 3, confers additional rights on the members of principal councils. It also sets out material which is excluded from access and that which is exempt. The Act extends to Scotland.[1]

[1]   Local Government (Scotland) Act 1973, s 50 with differences, not all of which were intended.

6.6   In what follows, the provisions are referred to as sections of the LGA 1972, as inserted by LG(ATI)A 1985.

Principal councils

6.7   As well as county, unitary and district councils and London boroughs, s 100J of the LGA 1972 includes (amongst others) the following bodies as principal councils:

(1)   The Assembly of the Greater London Authority.[1]
(2)   A joint authority.[2]
(3)   The Common Council of the City of London.
(4)   A joint board or joint committee constituted as a body corporate under any enactment, and it discharges functions of two or more principal councils which includes bodies under (1)–(3) above.
(5)   A combined police authority which is a body corporate. Police authorities which are committees of councils were covered by the LGA 1972; to avoid doubt, a specific inclusion has been made for combined police authorities. The 1985 amendment covers not only rights to attend meetings, but rights to documentation. The Act does not alter the existing legal relationship between members of police authorities and chief constables and the rights the former have to be informed of police administration.[3] In London the Home Secretary was replaced by the Metropolitan Police Authority as the authority (para 4.200 above) and s 313 of the Greater London Authority Act 1999 applies the relevant parts of LGA 1972, Part VA (LG(ATI)A 1985) to the authority. As we shall see, both members of a constituent council who are non-members of the police authority and the public may be excluded from meetings when items which contain exempt information are taken, although not all the exemptions apply to the former.[4] The public must be excluded when items are 'confidential' within the statute, which would include information under the Official Secrets Act 1989 (OSA 1989) which a chief constable is not authorised to disseminate beyond his authority's membership.[5] Under Police and Criminal Evidence Act 1984, s 106 arrangements have to be made, including for London, to obtain the views of the community on policing and to establish local police liaison groups. These groups are not included in the 1985 Act and are under no legal duty to give the general public rights of admission or to documentation.
(6)   A fire and rescue authority.

[1]   Greater London Authority Act 1999, s 58. This makes some amendments to LG(ATI)A 1985: see s 58(3), (4) and (5). And see ss 45–48 (as amended by the Greater London Act 2007) – the latter providing for an annual report from the Mayor, a public meeting once in every financial year (s 424(1)) to engage in the State of London debate, and a People's Question Time twice a year in public with the Mayor and Assembly.

² See LGA 1985, Parts III and IV.
³ See para 4.209 above.
⁴ See, specifically, LGA 1972, Sch 12A, para 14.
⁵ Or, indeed, *to* that membership, unless authorised.

6.8 In relation to the above bodies, special provisions apply for the posting of notices of meetings where they are not held at the offices of a local authority but at other premises. Notice will be posted at those other premises. Special provisions also apply to take account of the fact that the membership of the above bodies (1)–(6) is not directly elected.

6.9 Where bodies are not specified as principal councils, eg urban development corporations, local authority companies, trading partners or bodies such as the former London Residuary Body, they are not covered by the statute.

Committees, sub-committees and working parties

6.10 The LG(ATI)A 1985 applies to all the committees and sub-committees of principal councils (s 100E). Section 100E makes detailed provision on the committees included, but it does not deal with the question of what is excluded. The major problem has concerned bodies referred to as working parties, advisory groups, one party groups, etc. Widespread evasion of the Act could take place by frequent resort to such bodies as we saw in ch 5.

6.11 Although the courts will look at what has been created, and, it is submitted, look to the essence rather than the mere form or appellation,[1] there are limits on what they can do. Readers will recall the discussion in chs 4 and 5 of reforms of committee membership and powers which touch upon the present subject.

[1]   *Southwark London Borough Council v Peters* (1972) 70 LGR 41; *R v Brent London Borough Council, ex p Gladbaum* (1989) 88 LGR 627. See now Local Government and Housing Act 1989 (LGHA 1989), Sch 11, para 26. See also *Lillie v Newcastle CC* [2002] EWHC 1600 (QB), (2002) 146 SJLB 225 where it appears to be accepted that an independent review body created by a council may not fall within s 100E.

6.12 First, officers cannot in law be members of committees or sub-committees.[1] They are frequently made members of such working parties. Further, it is not possible to have a committee of one person;[2] and members cannot act in an executive capacity alone outside the provisions concerning executives under the LGA 2000 (see paras 4.29 et seq above). They may advise an officer to whom powers are delegated.

[1]   LGA 1972, ss 80(1)(a) and 104(1). They may be members of an executive, as specified.
[2]   *R v Secretary of State for the Environment, ex p Hillingdon London Borough Council* [1986] 1 All ER 810; see *Fitzpatrick v Secretary of State for the Environment* (1988) *Times*, 29 December, CA, and sub-delegation to officers under the Chief Officer.

6.13 It has also been held, as we saw in ch 5, by the High Court and by a unanimous Court of Appeal, that a local authority has power to establish working parties which are not committees or sub-committees. It was accepted that a local authority's members, outside the executive, can only exercise the functions of a local authority via a committee or sub-committee (LGA 1972, s 101(1)). However, a distinction was drawn between the functions of a local authority and its powers. Its functions are set out in ss 180–215 of the LGA 1972:

> 'Section 111 of the LGA gives it power to do anything which is calculated to facilitate or is conducive or incidental to the discharge of its functions. The exercise of a power can therefore be distinct from the discharge of a function ... the setting-up of the working party and the working party's activities constituted things done pursuant to the power conferred by s 111(1), not the discharge by the authority of any of its functions.'[1]

[1]   Webster J *R v Eden District Council, ex p Moffat* (15 April 1987, unreported) CO/803/86 (QBD). On s 111(1) generally, see: *Hazell v Hammersmith and Fulham London Borough Council* [1991] 1 All ER 545, HL, and *Akumah v Hackney LBC* [2005] 2 All ER 148, HL. See *R v Broadland District Council, ex p Lashley* (2001) *Times*, 20 March, CA.

6.14   Power to establish such bodies was possessed by the council, its committees or sub-committees under LGA 1972, s 111(1). However, a point not dealt with by the judge but raised on appeal[1] concerned s 101(12), which provides:

> 'References in this section and section 102 below (which concerns the appointment of committees), to any of the functions of a local authority, include references to the doing of anything which is calculated to facilitate or is conducive, or incidental to, the discharge of any of those functions.'

[1]   See CO/803/86 (QB), Croom-Johnson LJ; affirmed No 667/87 and (1988) *Times*, 24 November.

6.15   In other words, the 'doing' of anything under s 111(1) is a 'function'.

6.16   On appeal, it was not accepted that this provision meant that such bodies would be involved with the functions of an authority, and ipso facto had to be a sub-committee etc. It would seem that, where a working party is closely involved with the performance of a function, it is really a committee in another guise with officers in attendance advising. However, this merely begs the question.

6.17   Where, however, it is a genuine advisory body, proffering tentative advice – not recommendations – to the sub-committee etc, then it will not be a body falling within the 1985 amendments. No power will be delegated to it.

6.18   Nourse LJ believed that:

> 'The functions of a local authority are not confined to the acts which they are expressly or impliedly required or empowered to perform by [the LGA] ... The setting up of the working party was calculated to facilitate the discharge of the Council's function of improving their structure and efficiency.'

6.19   They therefore had power to set it up under s 111(1), and the LG(ATI)A 1985 does not cover such bodies.

6.20 The power of the authority to appoint sub-committees and advisory committees under LGA 1972, s 102 has been provided by LGHA 1989, Sch 11, para 25.

Excluding the public[1]

(1) MANDATORY

6.21 Under LGA 1972, s 100A(2) the public must be excluded from a meeting during an item of business whenever it is likely, in view of the nature of the business to be transacted or the nature of the proceedings, that, if members of the public were present during that item, confidential information would be disclosed to them in breach of the obligation of confidence. Nothing in that Part of the Act (LGA 1972, Part V) authorises or requires disclosure of confidential information.

[1] An injunction has been issued to prevent an admission by ticket only to a meeting pending a judicial review: *R v Bradford Metropolitan City Council, ex p Gasson* (1988) *Guardian*, 22 October, Farquharson J.

6.22 LGA 1972, s 100A(3) defines confidential information as:
(a) information furnished to the council by a government department upon terms (however expressed) which forbid the disclosure of the information to the public. This might also involve a breach of the OSA 1989 (see ch 1) if one of the relevant categories of information is involved and the disclosure is damaging (and unauthorised); and
(b) information the disclosure of which to the public is prohibited by or under any enactment (eg, OSA 1989) or by the order of a court (see paras 10.2 et seq below).

6.23 It should be noted that confidential under the statute is not the same as that under the judicially developed doctrine under common law. As the former Department of Environment pointed out, those writing to local authorities 'in confidence' are not protected by this section. Where such correspondence is received, authors should be advised that their written representations cannot be considered unless they are prepared to allow them to be disclosed.[1]

[1] DoE Circ 6/86, para 14.

6.24 The Greater London Authority Act 1999 has expanded the definition of 'confidentiality' for the purposes of that Act (s 58(3) and (4)). It includes disclosure 'in breach of the obligation of confidence' without the consent of the relevant body and includes financial or business affairs of any particular person acquired in the course of a relationship between that person and a relevant body (Transport for London and the London Development Agency); amounts of expenditure proposed to be incurred by a relevant body under a particular contract where this would confer an advantage on a body seeking to enter a contract with that relevant body whether against the relevant body or another; any terms proposed or to be proposed by or to a relevant body in the course of negotiations for any particular contract if it would prejudice that body in those or other negotiations; identities of tenderers to the relevant body for contracts for goods or services.

(II) DISCRETIONARY

6.25   Under LGA 1972, s 100A(4) a council may by resolution[1] exclude the public from a meeting during an item of business whenever it is likely, in view of the nature of the business to be transacted or the nature of the proceedings, that if members of the public were present during that item there would be disclosure to them of exempt information as defined (see below).

[1]   Which would have to be in public; cf *R v Brent Health Authority, ex p Francis* [1985] 1 All ER 74.

6.26   As with confidential documents under sub-s (3), the documents ought to be marked before the meeting by the committee clerk that they are exempt. He is usually the 'proper officer' for the purposes of this Part of the Act.[1]

[1]   LGA 1972, s 270(3).

6.27   The resolution may be upset if unreasonable, or otherwise unlawful, but the onus would be on the applicant.[1] The public, it should be noted, do not have to be excluded: it is at the council/committee/sub-committee's discretion.

[1]   For attempts to impugn the proper officer's classification, see para 6.50 below.

6.28   The resolution must identify the proceedings, or the part of the proceedings to which it applies, and state under what category of exempt information the resolution is being made. Where a resolution is passed, the section does not require the meeting to be open to the public during proceedings to which the resolution applies.[1]

[1]   LGA 1972, s 100A(5): 'resolution ... shall'. Given the importance of a resolution to exclude the public, it is expected that there will be strict compliance with the provisions of this subsection and that the courts will, if called upon, interpret 'shall' as imposing a mandatory duty. In *R v Liverpool City Council, ex p Liverpool Taxi Fleet Operators' Association* [1975] 1 All ER 379 Lord Widgery CJ, in a case concerning the interpretation of Public Bodies (Admission to Meetings) Act 1960, s 1(2), interpreted the instruction to give reasons in the minute of the resolution excluding the public as directory only, so non-compliance would not necessarily vitiate the meeting in law. Here, the direction is written in mandatory language, however, and should be interpreted accordingly.

The categories of exempt information

6.29   The categories of 'exempt information' are provided in LGA 1972, Sch 12A, Part I (inserted by LG(ATI)A 1985, Sch 1) which has to be read in conjunction with Sch 12A, Part II (the qualifications). It will be convenient to spell out the categories at this juncture. Schedule 12A provides that exempt information, which the Secretary of State can add to or delete by statutory instrument (negative resolution procedure: s 100I(2) and (4)). Schedule 12A was replaced in its entirety by The Local Government (Access to Information) (Variation) Order 2006, SI 2006/88, Sch 1. It is notable that there is now a considerable difference in the provisions between England and Wales. In England, Parts I, II and III of Sch 12A apply, whereas in Wales Parts IV, V and VI apply.

6.30 In England, exempt information is that:
(1) relating to any individual;
(2) which is likely to reveal the identity of an individual;
(3) relating to the financial or business affairs of any particular person (including the authority holding that information);
(4) relating to any consultations or negotiations, or contemplated consultations or negotiations, in connection with any labour relations matter arising between the authority or a Minister of the Crown and employees of, or office holders under, the authority;
(5) in respect of which a claim to legal professional privilege could be maintained in legal proceedings;
(6) which reveals that the authority proposes:
   (a) to give under any enactment a notice under or by virtue of which requirements are imposed on a person; or
   (b) to make an order or direction under any enactment; or
(7) relating to any action taken or to be taken in connection with the prevention, investigation or prosecution of crime.

6.31 The exemptions for England relate to information that is required under certain enactments (listed at point (7) in para 6.35 below) and information where 'it relates to proposed development for which the local planning authority may grant itself planning permission pursuant to regulation 3 of the Town and Country Planning General Regulations 1992'. Schedule 12A, Part II, para 10 provides that the exemptions listed above are qualified exemptions in a similar sense to FOIA 2000, ie information 'is exempt information if and so long, as in all the circumstances of the case, the public interest in maintaining the exemption outweighs the public interest in disclosing the information'. It is interesting to note that the English approach is a significant change to the previous approach under LGA 1972, Sch 12A, offering a much shorter list of exemptions that are qualified, although it is evident that the exemption relating to 'information relating to any individual' along with 'information which is likely to reveal the identity of any individual' is potentially broader than the more detailed list of exemptions in place prior to the amendements in 2006 and still in place for Wales.

6.32 In Wales, exempt information is that relating to:
(1) Employees and office-holders of the authority (past, present or applicants to become); 'employee', 'office-holder': Sch 12A, Part VI, para 1(1).
(2) Employees and office-holders (past, present or applicants to become) of a magistrates' court committee or probation committee (see Courts Act 2004, ss 4 and 5 and Probation Act 1993 and Criminal Justice and Court Services Act 2000).
(3) Any particular occupier (past or present) or applicant for accommodation provided by or at the expense of the authority.
(4) Applicants for or recipients of (past or present) any service[1] provided by the authority.

(5) Applicants for or recipients of (past or present) any financial assistance provided by the authority.[2] (By Sch 12A, Part V, para 1, information relating to a person of a description specified in any of paras (1)–(5) supra is not exempt information by virtue of that paragraph unless it relates to an individual[3] of that description in the capacity indicated by the description.)

(6) Information relating to the adoption, care, fostering or education of any particular child; 'child' is defined (Sch 12A, Part VI, para 1(1).

(7) Information relating to the financial or business affairs (Sch 12A, Part VI, para 1(1)) (whether past, contemplated or current) of any particular person (other than the authority), although it is not exempt information if it is required to be registered under:
  (a) the Companies Acts 1985–1989;
  (b) the Friendly Societies Act 1974;
  (c) the Industrial and Provident Societies Acts 1965–1978;
  (d) the Building Societies Act 1986; or
  (e) the Charities Act 1960 as amended.

(8) The amount of any expenditure proposed to be incurred by the authority under any particular contract for the acquisition of property or the supply of goods or services. Such information is exempt if and so long as disclosure to the public of the amount there referred to would be likely to give an advantage to a person entering into, or seeking to enter into, a contract with the authority in respect of the property, goods or services, whether the advantage would arise as against the authority or as against other such persons.

(9) Any terms proposed or to be proposed by or to the authority in the course of negotiations for a contract for the acquisition or disposal (Sch 12A, Part VI, para 1(1)) of property or the supply of goods or services. Such information is exempt if and so long as disclosure to the public of the terms would prejudice the authority in those or any other negotiations concerning the property or goods or services.

(10) The identity of the authority (as well as of any other person, by virtue of para (7) above) or the person offering any particular tender for a contract for the supply of goods or services; 'tender for a contract' is defined (Sch 12A, Part VI, para 1(1)).

(11) Information relating to any, or any contemplated, consultation or negotiations in connection with a labour relations matter arising between the authority or a Minister of the Crown and employees of, or office-holders under, the authority and is exempt information if and so long as disclosure to the public would prejudice the authority in the respective matters; 'labour relations matter' is defined (Sch 12A, Part VI, para 1(1)).

(12) Any instructions to counsel and any opinion of counsel (whether or not in connection with any proceedings) and any advice received, information obtained or action to be taken in connection with:
  (a) any legal proceedings by or against the authority; or
  (b) the determination of any matter affecting the authority,
  (whether, in either case, (a) or (b), proceedings have been commenced or are in contemplation).
  The 'determination' referred to in (b) is to administrative hearings such as inquiries. Of crucial significance under this exemption will be the

interpretation of 'or are in contemplation' in relation to legal proceedings. Could this mean that advice on a sensitive matter which touches upon possible ultra vires action or decision-making will make it proper to presume that proceedings are 'contemplated' at the suit of the auditor, a member of the public or a government department? Presumably more than a 'vague anticipation' and more of a probable likelihood would be required (see the discussion of legal professional privilege in ch 10). Opinions of and instructions to counsel are given a complete exemption which is not dependent upon litigation being in progress or contemplated.

(13) Information which, if disclosed to the public, would reveal that the authority proposes:

(a)   to give under any enactment a notice under or by virtue of which requirements are imposed on a person; or

(b)   to make an order or a direction under any enactment, and remains exempt if and so long as, basically, disclosure to the public might afford a person affected by the notice etc an opportunity of defeating the purpose, or a purpose of, the notice etc. Where, for instance, action might be taken in advance of a building preservation notice.

(14) Any action taken or to be taken in connection with the prevention, investigation or prosecution of crime.

(15) The identity of a 'protected informant' which is a person giving the authority information which tends to show that a criminal offence; a breach of statutory duty; a breach of planning control, as defined in s 171A of the Town and Country Planning Act 1990; or a nuisance has been, is being, or is about to be committed.

[1]   'Service' ought not to include, it is submitted, a statutory duty and attendant powers to regulate such as planning or licensing.

[2]   This would only relate to an individual (LGA 1972, Sch 12A, Part II, para 1), so a company would presumably not be covered.

[3]   Quaere corporations? Unlikely. The Scottish equivalent says 'person'.

6.33   This is a considerable corpus of exemptions, complicated by the differing regimes in England and Wales.[1] One point to note is that the exemptions as drafted will exclude a member of the public being in attendance, even where s/he has been the provider of exempt information. It is common practice for authorities to deal with 'appeals' from officers' decisions by referring 'appellants' to committees and sub-committees of the authority. Some allow the appellants to be present; others do not.[2] Where such cases fall within one of the categories, the appellant's presence will still be discretionary. This was one of the issues which the DoE undertook to deal with in guidance on the Act – it was not. No guidance appears to have been issued more recently by the DCLG. This is an important point as the presence of an 'appellant' could be vital, especially given the High Court's sanction for the receipt of hearsay evidence in housing homeless cases by authorities which may be dealt with at committees or by officers.[3]

[1]   See the comments of R Squire MP, Standing Committee C, col 86, 20 March 1985.

[2]   Birkinshaw *Grievances, Remedies and the State* (2nd edn, 1995) ch 3.

[3]   *R v Southampton City Council, ex p Ward* [1984] FLR 608; *R v Nottingham City Council, ex p Costello* [1989] Fam Law 469. See ch 6.

6.34 We shall deal with the requirements allowing access to documents in a moment, and readers are referred to the details of the regulations concerning 'manual' (paper) education, social services and housing files in ch 7 (paras 7.156 et seq below), now under the provisions of the Data Protection Act 1998.

6.35 It was expected that authorities would establish their own methods to deal with disputes concerning access and classification. The possibility of an 'appeals committee' was suggested (R Squire MP, Standing Committee, col 17, 13 March 1985). Specific provision in the Bill for an appeal procedure within authorities was dropped. This territory has now been heavily influenced by the Citizen's Charter programme and the Labour government's 'Better Government' initiative (see ch 9 below).

Access under LG(ATI)A 1985 and FOIA 2000

6.36 While the FOI Bill was going through Parliament, the government believed that an applicant for information, if defeated under one Act, should be able to apply under the other – in other words s/he would get the benefit of the more generous provision. There are many situations where the local government legislation applied but where FOIA does not – meetings for instance. The right of the public to be present at meetings of principal authorities is determined by the 1985 legislation. Furthermore under FOIA 2000, s 21(1) information required to be communicated upon request under another statute will be exempt under FOIA. The following sets out a diagram from the Office of the Deputy Prime Minister on the relationship between the two schemes.

CURRENT REGIME COVERED BY PART VA OF THE LOCAL GOVERNMENT ACT 1972 AND ACCESS TO INFORMATION REGULATIONS	FREEDOM OF INFORMATION ACT 2000
Right of access to information	
Public has right of access to meetings and documents connected with decisions a local authority makes. ● Full council, its committees and sub-committees, background papers, agendas and reports for those meetings (Part VA of LGA 1972) ● Executive and their committees where a key decision is to be taken, documents relating to executive and key decisions (Access to Information Regulations, SI 2000/3272)	**General right of access** to **all recorded information** held by public authorities. ● Information which is already required to be made available must continue to be made available ● Duty of a public authority to provide advice and assistance to those seeking information

CURRENT REGIME COVERED BY PART VA OF THE LOCAL GOVERNMENT ACT 1972 AND ACCESS TO INFORMATION REGULATIONS	FREEDOM OF INFORMATION ACT 2000
	• Right of access applies to any written request for information whether it mentions FOI or not. General right of access to all recorded information held by public authorities
How information is released	
Local authorities are **required** to make information available to the public, even in the absence of specific requests. • Papers must be made available **five clear** days before meetings take place • **Designated officers** decide whether information is exempt and if it should be released • Local authorities take a **proactive** stance	The public makes a **request for information**. • Authorities have **20 days** to respond to the request • Authorities may charge a **fee** for dealing with requests • **Any officer/member** who receives a request for information will have to decide whether to disclose • Local authorities take a **responsive** stance
Forward plans and publication schemes	
Authorities operating executive arrangements must set out a **forward plan** showing what key decisions they plan to take over the next four months	All authorities must produce a **publication scheme** – a guide to information the authority publishes or intends to publish.
Exemptions	
Seven exemptions in Schedule 12A of LGA 1972 (England) and 15 exemptions (Wales) **tailored to local government** including: • Information relating to individuals • Details of financial and business affairs • Instructions to counsel • Information relating to the investigation or prosecution of crime	23 exemptions listed in FOIA 2000 applying to all **public bodies. Eight of these are absolute exemptions**, meaning information in these categories is automatically exempt, including: • Information dealing with national security matters • Personal information (dealt with under DPA 1998) • Court records **Information accessible through the publication scheme** is exempt, since it is already publicly available.

CURRENT REGIME COVERED BY PART VA OF THE LOCAL GOVERNMENT ACT 1972 AND ACCESS TO INFORMATION REGULATIONS	FREEDOM OF INFORMATION ACT 2000
A council **may** by resolution exclude the public from a meeting during an item of business, if in its view exempt information is likely to be disclosed An officer **may** choose not to disclose exempt information contained in background papers/ agendas/ reports/ minutes. If, after the exclusion of exempt information, minutes do not provide a fair and reasonable view of proceedings the proper officer must provide a **summary of proceedings**. Individual local authorities will have established **their own procedure for dealing with complaints** regarding the classification of exempt information. The Monitoring Officer often plays a key role.	A **public interest test** must be applied to the remainder of the exemptions – information must be released unless the public interest in not disclosing is greater than the public interest in disclosing. The exemptions this test applies to include: ● Commercial interests ● Legal professional privilege ● Health and safety A dissatisfied applicant may appeal to the Information Commissioner about an authority's decision on where the public interest lies or if they think information has been wrongly withheld. The Commissioner may require disclosure.

Figure 6.1 Comparison between current regime and FOIA 2000

Public notice and other provisions

6.37 Public notice of the time and place of the meeting shall be given by posting it at the offices of the council (Assembly in London)[1] at least five clear days before the meeting (three clear days in Wales), or, if the meeting is convened at shorter notice,[2] at the time it is convened. As we shall see below, background documents are also available under LGA 1972, s 100D.

[1] See LGA 1972, ss 100E(2) and 100J(3).
[2] See para 6.38.

6.38 It has been held that five 'clear days' excludes the day on which notice is given and the day of the meeting.[1] It is submitted that to keep within the spirit of the legislation, and indeed the letter, viz 'public notice' (LGA 1972, s 100A(6)), these days would not include days on which council offices were closed to the public.[2] Such an interpretation would also accord with LGA 1972, s 243.[3]

1   *R v Herefordshire Justices* (1820) 3 B & Ald 581; *Alexander v Simpson* (1889) 43 Ch D 139: notice must be clear and unconditional. On specifying the business, see: *Longfield Parish Council v Wright* (1918) 16 LGR 865; *R (Fitzgerald) v McDonald* [1913] 2 IR 55; *R v Dublin Corpn* [1911] 2 IR 245. Rules on voting for principal councils are usually governed by SOs. For parish and community councils there are express provisions in the LGA 1972 where SOs do not apply. A resolution will be void if there is non-compliance with SOs: *R v Educational Services Committee of Bradford City Metropolitan Council, ex p Professional Association of Teachers* (1986) *Independent*, 16 December; but contract awards will not be void. SOs are usually in public libraries and every member possesses a copy. See also *R v Flintshire CC, ex p Armstrong-Braun* [2001] LGLR 1.
2   Sundays and public holidays; see also *Carey, Smithers v DPP* [1989] Crim LR 368, DC.
3   Which concerns, inter alia, computation of time.

6.39   The LGA 2000 has amended LGA 1972, ss 100A(6)(a) and 100B(3) and (4), by allowing the Secretary of State to substitute a longer period of days for notice of meetings of councils and the Assembly in London and access to their agenda and connected reports. This applies to council and Assembly meetings as well as committees and sub-committees (LGA 1972, s 100E). This power has been exercised for England, extending the period from three to five days (SI 2002/715).

6.40   While the meeting is open to the public, the council shall not have power to exclude members of the public from the meeting (LGA 1972, s 100A(6)(b)). However, this has to be read in conjunction with sub-s (8). The latter preserves the common law power of the chairperson of a statutory body to exclude the public if it was clear that members of the public were intent on causing such disruption that the transaction of business was being, or would be, prevented.[1] As the chairperson may take preventive action before the meeting, it was held that the resolution excluding the public did not have to be made in public.[2] However, doubts about the correctness of this decision have been expressed in so far as the chairperson was acting alone – and there cannot be a committee of one.[3] The actual wording of sub-s (8) says that the section 'is without prejudice to any power of exclusion to suppress or prevent disorderly conduct or other misbehaviour at a meeting', which is broad enough in scope to cover anticipated disturbance. It has been held, however, that the exercise of the power of exclusion must be reasonably conducted and that excluded persons should be provided with an opportunity to put their case.[4] If the level of (anticipated) disturbance is such that this is impossible, the chairperson should formally resolve, with other members of the committee (possibly acting as a sub-committee), to exclude the public in advance.

1   *R v Brent Health Authority, ex p Francis* [1985] 1 All ER 74 and the Public Bodies (Admission to Meetings) Act 1960. See *R v Bickenhill Parish Council, ex p Secretary of State for the Environment* [1987] JPL 773.
2   'A decision relating to the internal affairs of the authority' per Woolf J in *R v Secretary of State for the Environment, ex p Hillingdon London Borough Council* [1986] 1 All ER 810.
3   Cf the Court of Appeal in *Hillingdon* [1986] 2 All ER 273n.
4   *R v Brent London Borough Council, ex p Assegai* (1987) *Times*, 18 June.

The press

6.41 Duly accredited representatives of the newspapers[1] attending the meeting for the purposes of reporting proceedings for their newspapers while the meeting is in progress shall, so far as practicable, be afforded reasonable facilities for making their report and, unless the meeting is held in premises not belonging to the council or not on the telephone, for telephoning the report at their own expense (LGA 1972, s 100A(6)(c)). Bob Neill (Parliamentary Undersecretary of State in the DCLG) wrote to all council leaders and monitoring officers in February 2011 reminding them of their duties under the LGA 1972 and also encouraging councillors to permit 'bloggers' to enjoy the same facilities as newspapers, to permit blogging and 'tweeting' from council meetings and also to permit filming.[2] Despite the DCLG's wish to ensure that such opportunities are offered, it is clear that this is not presently mandated by the legislation and there do not appear to be legislative proposals to put such access on a legislative footing. One question, to which the answer is not entirely clear, is whether journalists from accredited newspapers could be prevented from blogging and 'tweeting' from council meetings, or whether this would be considered to be part of the activites of modern news-gathering and dissemination.

[1] LGA 1972, s 100K(1) and see s 100E(2)(b). Note that the definition of newspaper is limited to newspapers, news agencies and broadcasters.

[2] See http://www.communities.gov.uk/documents/localgovernment/pdf/1850773.pdf.

6.42 The Act does not require authorities to permit the taking of photographs, or the televising or broadcasting of proceedings (LGA 1972, s 100A(7)).

Access to documents

6.43 The LGA 1972 defines information to include 'an expression of opinion, any recommendations and any decisions taken' (s 100K(1)).

6.44 Copies of agendas and copies of officers' reports relating to items on the agenda (reports for the meeting) shall be[1] open to inspection by members of the public at the offices of the council (not libraries) at least five clear days (as amended by LGA 2000, s 98, see above) before the meeting.[2] Where, however, the meeting is convened at shorter notice, eg because of emergency, copies of both agenda and reports shall be open from the time the meeting is convened. Where an item is added to an agenda (see LGA 1972, s 100B(4)(b) below), copies of which are open to inspection by the public, then copies of that item and any related report shall be open to inspection from the time the item is added.[3] Section 100B(3) adds, tantalisingly, that nothing in the subsection requires that items, agendas or reports should be publicly available on inspection before copies are available to members of the council. This must be read subject to the three-day requirement (as amended) or the convening of a meeting if shorter notice, or the adding of an item to the agenda where such apply; otherwise the provision appears nonsensical.[4] Copies may be made available to the public before members of the council. The principal council and its committees etc are not free to abandon the five-day or longer period required under LGA 2000, s 98 but must only convene meetings at shorter notice[5] or add items to the agenda where permitted.[6] Section 100H states that committee reports and committee agendas must be open to inspection at all reasonable hours.

[1] This is mandatory. The subsection refers to any reports but this will not preclude speaking to the item; but a full oral report could not be used to defeat the section.
[2] LGA 1972, s 100B(1) and (3), see supra. What of a meeting in the evening? The provisions apply to committees and sub-committees.
[3] LGA 1972, s 100B(3)(a) and (b). Under different legislation viz Education Act 1944, Sch 1, Part II, para 7, it has been held that a bare recommendation cannot constitute a report: *R v Inner London Education Authority, ex p F* [1988] COD 100; and *R v Cornwall County Council, ex p Nicholls* [1989] COD 507.
[4] And, on a matter of construction, the primary duty is to inform the public by statutory notice; this would be defeated if authorities deliberately delayed notice so as to inform members first, ie it was a ploy.
[5] As in an emergency.
[6] See LGA 1972, s 100B(4)(b) below.

6.45 This view is reinforced by s 100B(4) which states that an item of business may not be considered at a meeting of a principal council unless either a copy of the agenda including the item (or a copy of the item) is open to public inspection for three clear days (or longer period) before the meeting or, where the meeting is convened at shorter notice, from the time the meeting is convened. This refers to items, not reports. However, it would not be lawful to publicise an agenda and items with the expression 'report to follow' alongside any item, and then to provide the reports to the public in breach of the three clear day (or longer) rule. The report must comply with the above provisions, subject, it is submitted, to reasonable and limited additions such as necessary updating.

6.46 Under s 100B(4)(b) the chairperson of the meeting, where s/he is of the opinion that an item should be considered at the meeting as a matter of urgency, may allow the item to be considered even though the notice provisions have not been complied with. This must be because of 'special circumstances' which shall be 'specified in the minutes'. Because of the importance of this incursion into the principles of the Act, courts will look carefully at this mandatory requirement and will expect more than cursory references to vague circumstances,[1] even though the judgment is that of the chairperson.[2] The word 'specify' would suggest reasons which would support a reasoned justification in an affidavit, although the minute would not itself be a reasoned justification.

[1] For an example of directory wording see: *R v Liverpool City Council, ex p Liverpool Taxi Fleet Operators' Association* at para 6.28, note 1 above.
[2] On reviewing a subjective discretionary opinion see: *Associated Provincial Picture Houses Ltd v Wednesbury Corpn* [1948] 1 KB 223, CA. *Padfield v Minister of State for Agriculture, Fisheries and Food* [1968] AC 997, HL; *Secretary of State for Education and Science v Tameside Metropolitan Borough Council* [1977] AC 1014, HL; *Lonrho plc v Secretary of State for Trade and Industry* [1989] 2 All ER 609, HL; *R v Secretary of State for the Environment, ex p Hammersmith and Fulham London Borough Council* [1990] 3 All ER 589, HL.

6.47 There is an incompatibility – there are several – between LGA 1972, s 100B(4) and Sch 12, Part I. Schedule 12, para 4(5) restricts the business of a council meeting itself (but not the annual meeting) to those items specified[1] in the summons. Additional items can be taken at the annual meeting and include, inter alia, matters of urgency in accordance with the council's standing orders, but it does not allow matters to be taken because of urgency as under s 100B(4). Paragraph 4(5) would appear, on the face of it, to prevail. A compromise would be to incorporate the chairperson's powers under s 100B(4) into the standing orders.

[1] See para 6.36, note 1 above, and *R v Lambeth London Borough Council, ex p Boston* (25 April 1986, unreported) CO/610/186.

Exempt documents

6.48 The public inspection provisions of LGA 1972, s 100B(1) may be disapplied by the proper officer, if s/he thinks fit, to the whole of any report, or any part, which relates only to items during which, in his or her opinion, the meeting is likely not to be open to the public (s 100B(2)).

6.49 The provision can only refer to exempt documents and not the excluded confidential category, as these must be dealt with in a closed meeting.

6.50 The phrases 'if ... fit' and 'in his opinion' both relate to a subjective discretion on the part of the proper officer. Case-law shows that such phrases as these and their analogues do not create an inviolable power. It would be open to a party with sufficient interest to seek judicial review of the proper officer's decision, but the applicant would have to be expeditious to have a decision altered before a meeting. Under the Civil Procedure Rules 1998, Part 54 new procedures for judicial review have been operative since October 2000. The court is given power to 'take the decision itself' if no purpose is served by remitting the matter to the body against which a 'quashing order' (certiorari) is sought. This may not be possible where the power is reposed by statute in a specific person or body (r 54.19). Where permission to proceed is given to an applicant, a stay of proceedings may also be ordered by the court (r 54.10(2)).

6.51 Discovery (disclosure) of documents can be applied for, but usually discovery is used as an aid to proving one's case; here, obtaining the documents constitutes the very reason for making the application. The court, presumably, could not order discovery to the applicant if the documents fell within one of the exempt descriptions, as the decision on disclosure is for the relevant meeting of a principal council in such a case. The applicant would be using the court to stand in judgment upon the 'proper officer's' classification. If access is applied for under the FOIA 2000, the Information Commissioner will be the appropriate authority to deal with complaints once the local authority has been through its internal procedures (para 1.233 above).

6.52 The judge, if doubt existed, could examine the documents to be satisfied that the discretion was wrongly or correctly exercised: the burden on the applicant would be a heavy one.

6.51 Where under LGA 1972, s 100B(2) the whole, or any part, of a report is not open to public inspection under sub-s (1), every copy of the report, or relevant part, shall be marked 'Not for publication'. On every such report, or relevant part, there must be stated the category of exempt information according to Sch 12A under which the council is likely to exclude the public during the item to which the report relates (sub-s (5)).

At the meeting

6.53 Where a meeting, or part of a meeting, of a council etc is required to be open to the public,[1] a 'reasonable number of copies of the agenda and of reports for the meeting must be available for the public who are present. LGA 1972, s 100B(2) applies to such reports.

---

[1] Or if at the authority's discretion, the exemptions do not apply.

The press

6.54 Representatives of a newspaper (LGA 1972, s 100K(1)) may make a request for and, on payment of postage or other necessary charge for transmission,[1] be supplied with:

(a) a copy of the agenda for a meeting of a principal council and its committees and sub-committees and a copy of its reports, subject to the s 100B(2) qualification above;

(b) such further statements or particulars, if any, as are necessary to indicate the nature of the items included in the agenda; and

(c) if the proper officer thinks fit in the case of any item, s/he shall supply[2] copies of any other documents supplied to members of the council in connection with the item.

---

[1] This does not appear to contain a discretion not to charge.
[2] Mandatory where the proper officer thinks fit.

6.55 The s 100B(2) qualification can only apply to reports, and not to the statements, documents etc under items (b) and (c) above.

Background papers

6.56 Under LGA 1972, s 100D background papers[1] may be inspected.

---

[1] See LGA 1972, s 100D(5). The inclusion of sub-s (5) was conceded by the proponent of this Private Member's Bill to ensure the Bill's passage.

6.57 This is an important provision in the Act. Section 100D concerns the right of the public to inspect 'background papers' to reports which are to be made available under ss 100B and 100C. The papers are to be available if and so long as copies of the whole or part of a report for a principal council are required by the sections to be open to inspection by members of the public, though after the meeting the relevant period for public inspection of background papers is four years, not six. Those copies of reports will have to include a copy of a list of background papers of the report, or part of the report, compiled by the proper officer. These will have to be available for inspection at the offices of the council or London Assembly.[1] A copy of the list and documents required to be made available shall be taken ... to be so open if arrangements exist for its production to members of the public as soon as is reasonably practicable after the making of a request to inspect the copy. Nothing in the section requires the inclusion of 'exempt information' and nothing requires or authorises the inclusion of a document containing confidential information within the meaning of s 100A(2). Basically sub-s (5) leaves the definition of 'background papers' up to the opinion of the proper officer on whether they disclose any facts or matters on which the report or an important part of the report is based, and, again in his or her opinion, have been relied on to a material extent in the definition. The courts have given a wide discretion to what officers include either in reports or in background documents in drafting reports for committee.[2]

[1] This Part was amended by LGA 2000, s 97.
[2] *Maile v Wigan MBC* [2001] Env.L.R. 11: a database dealing with potentially contaminated sites in the council area. See now the application of the Environmental Information Regulations 2004, SI 2004/3391 (paras 8.204 et seq below).

6.58 If discovery were applied for, it will be with a view to obtaining documents, and not simply to have a classification changed as under s 100B(2) (see discussion above).

Inspection after the meeting

6.59 Under LGA 1972, s 100C the minutes, or copy of the minutes, of the meeting of a principal council and committees and sub-committees (s 100E) shall be open to inspection by members of the public for six years after the meeting at the offices of the council. Time runs from the date of the meeting. Minutes disclosing 'exempt information' where the public were excluded are excluded (and see s 100A(2)). A copy of the agenda for the meeting and copies of reports for the meeting relating to items during which the public were allowed to be present shall be open to inspection likewise. Also available will be a summary under sub-s (2). Where parts of the minutes are excluded because of the 'exempt information' provision and the minutes available do not provide a reasonably fair and coherent record of the whole or part of the proceedings, 'the proper officer shall make a written summary of the proceedings or the part ... which provides such a record without disclosing the exempt information' (s 100C(2)). This will require some skill.

6.60 Prior to this Act coming into effect only the minutes of councils and committees exercising referred powers were open to inspection by law; those of committees exercising delegated powers were not open to inspection.[1] The minutes of sub-committees likewise were not open to inspection; the authority had discretion.

¹   *Wilson v Evans* [1962] 1 All ER 247.

Additional information

6.61   A principal council has to maintain a register containing:

(1)   The name and address of every member of the council for the time being and the ward or division which s/he represents; as well as the name and address of every member of each committee or sub-committee of the council for the time being (and see LGHA 1989, Sch 11, para 24).

(2)   A list of powers delegated to officers under statute stating the officers' title. It does not require a power to be listed 'if the arrangements for its discharge by the officer are made for a period not exceeding six months'.¹

(3)   At the office of every principal council there shall be kept a written summary of the rights to attend the meetings as specified in the Act and to inspect, copy and be furnished with documents as specified in the Act, and under LGA 1972, Part XI and such other enactments as the Secretary of State specifies by order. The respective 'register', 'list' and 'written summary' shall all be open to inspection at the offices of the council.

¹   See LGA 1972, Part VI.

6.62   Similar provisions were included in the first draft of the regulations providing access to new executive meetings. They were removed (paras 4.29 et seq above).

A miscellany

6.63   Section 100H of the LGA 1972 contains supplemental provisions and establishes the offences which relate to the intentional obstruction, or refusal to comply with the rights created by this Act, by those having the custody of documents which are required to be open to inspection by virtue of s 100B(1) or 100C(1). Offences are triable summarily by fine. Documents shall be open to inspection for all reasonable hours, and for documents under s 100D(1) upon payment of such reasonable fee as may be required for the facility. Copies or photocopying facilities may be required upon payment of reasonable fees.¹

¹   This has led to abuse: Birkinshaw 'Open Government – Local Government Style' in *Public Policy and Administration* (1988) p 46.

6.64   Section 100H(5) provides for qualified privilege for any 'accessible' documents (s 100H(6)) available for inspection or supplied to the public, or which is supplied to a newspaper.¹

¹   The case of *Lillie v Newcastle CC* [2002] EWHC 1600 (QB) held that the publication of a report by an independent review body set up to investigate allegations of child abuse by certain council employees was covered by s 100H as the report was made available at a council meeting and that the independent review body, as it was acting in accordance with its contractual arrangement

with the council in making the report available to the council, enjoyed the protection of qualified privilege at common law. Ultimately, however, the independent review body was found to be liable for defamation in its production of the report as there was evidence of malice.

General comments

6.65   The above is an account of the legal provisions introduced into LGA 1972 by the LG(ATI)A 1985. Various points call for comment.

6.66   First, there are various anomalies and inconsistencies arising from the fact that the 1985 Act amends LGA 1972, s 100 and Sch 2, Part I but without all the necessary dovetailing taking place. We examined, in particular, the relationship between para 4(5) of the Schedule and s 100B(4)(b).

6.67   Secondly, a variety of items, such as 'any other business' or discussion of the minutes of a previous meeting, will have to be avoided unless they are brought within the notice provision of s 100B.

6.68   Thirdly, the Act provided for no internal enforcement mechanism with rights of appeal to designated officers. It was hoped that authorities would provide grievance procedures for such disputes, but a requirement in the Bill that they be provided was dropped (see above). Those disgruntled by refusals will have to rely upon the local ombudsman, judicial review or political support via a councillor, although there is a far greater consciousness of the necessity for effective grievance procedures now than there was in past decades.

6.69   Fourthly, too many provisions in the Act are either vague or unclear, eg 'reasonable charges' is a term which has been abused and is ambiguous, and the notice provisions relating to councillors being informed before the public need clarification.

6.70   Fifthly, the LG(ATI)A 1985 in basic terms exempts personal information from public access. However, s 17(1) of the Local Government Finance Act 1982 (LGFA 1982) allowed inspection of the accounts to be audited by the auditor and all the relevant books, deeds etc by 'any person interested'. The auditor is bound by confidentiality under the Act, but the member of the public who inspects is not so bound. In *Oliver v Northampton Borough Council*[1] a member of the public wished to see a computer print-out of a wages book for a project carried out by the authority. As this contained confidential personal information on employees, the authority objected, and refused access to the complete record, offering instead a summary. The result was that the authority was convicted. On appeal to the High Court, it was held that the duty was 'compulsive' and access had to be given to the complete record of what was before the auditor – however undesirable that might be because of confidential information being present. If this information were presented to a meeting covered by the 1985 Act it would be exempt, but LGFA 1982, s 17 is a separate provision existing in its own right. *Oliver* was subsequently reversed by LGHA 1989, s 11 which exempts personal information on employees.[2] There would also today be Human Rights Act implications.

¹   (1986) 151 JP 44.
²   And see Audit Commission Act 1998, s 15(3) and (4).

6.71 Sixthly, the Act's operation was the subject of extensive discussion between the local authority representative bodies and the then DoE, and certain matters were a cause of concern for the respective interests.¹

¹   The DoE considered the inclusion of a national security exclusion. Local authorities have encountered difficulties with the 'three clear days' formulation now extended by powers of the Secretary of State (above), and the application of the law to quasi-judicial committees.

6.72 Seventhly, the practices of a number of authorities, before the Act was passed and since, have been exemplary in responding to or surpassing the Act's requirements.¹ The DoE left it to a circular to encourage good practice to assist those who are disabled to make use of the Act.

¹   See eg *Charter for Open Government* Association of London Boroughs (1986).

6.73 Finally, where the FOIA 2000 gives greater rights of access than LG(ATI) A 1985, or where amendments to the LGA 1972 prove more liberal, the applicant may use whichever is the more generous. The 1985 Act is an open meetings law, whereas FOIA is not. These points were examined above.

Access to information etc of executives under the Local Government Act 2000

6.74 This was dealt with in detail in ch 4.

PUBLIC BODIES (ADMISSION TO MEETINGS) ACT 1960

6.75 The LG(ATI)A 1985 did not, as described above, apply to the meetings or documents of parish councils, or community councils. These are covered by LGA 1972, Sch 12 as regards meetings (Parts II–IV) and by the Public Bodies (Admission to Meetings) Act 1960 (PB(ATM)A 1960) since 1 April 1986. The PB(ATM)A 1960 also applies to the council of the Isles of Scilly and joint committees and joint boards discharging the functions of parish councils; community councils or the council of the Isles of Scilly inter alia, to the committees of parish or community councils and parish meetings; the land authority for Wales; Strategic Health Authorities; special health authorities where the order establishing such an authority so provides; Primary Care Trusts (except in relation to the exercise of functions under the National Health Service (Service Committees and Tribunal) Regulations 1992; and a number of other bodies dealing with healthcare functions, including the Care Quality Commission and the Council for Healthcare Regulatory Excellence, and other bodies with power to levy a rate, other than bodies subject to LGA 1972, Part VA.¹ NHS trusts are under a duty to meet in public at an annual meeting and are now generally subject to the provisions of the Act, although this was not always the case. Water authorities were removed from the requirements of the 1960 Act in 1983, and no provision similar to the PB(ATM)A 1960 allowing public attendance at meetings of water companies was incorporated in the Water Act 1989. Regional Committees of the Consumer Council for Water under the 1991 Act are covered by the PB(ATM)A 1960.

¹   Bodies to which LGA 1972, ss 100A to 100D apply, whether or not by virtue of LGA 1972, s 100E or s 100J.
²   National Health Service and Community Care Act 1990, Sch 2, Part II, para 7 (and Sch 6, Part II, para 7 for Scotland).

6.76   In straightforward terms, public access is allowed to the meetings of the bodies as scheduled in the 1960 Act. Public notice must be given on similar terms as under LGA 1972, Part VA. Newspapers are given similar rights as under the LGA 1972, as well as reasonable facilities for taking their report and telephoning the report at their own expense, unless the meeting is held in premises not belonging to the public authority or not on the telephone. Similar provisions are made for press agents and broadcasters, with a qualification as under LGA 1972, s 100, and for qualified privilege.

6.77   The 1960 Act contains the prototype of LGA 1972, s 100A(8) which was discussed above (para 6.40) and need not be revisited here.

6.78   Under s 1(2) of the 1960 Act, power is given to exclude the public whenever publicity would be prejudicial to the public interest because of the confidential[1] nature of the business or for other special reasons stated in the resolution excluding the public and arising from the nature of the business. In particular, and without prejudice to the foregoing, the section covers the power to treat the need to receive or consider recommendations or advice from sources other than members, committees or sub-committees of the body as a special reason why publicity would be prejudicial to the public interest. This is regardless of the subject or nature of the recommendations or advice. Advice from officers would, therefore, be protected by this exemption. This provision has been the subject of judicial interpretation. In *R v Liverpool City Council, ex p Liverpool Taxi Fleet Operators' Association*,[2] 40 members of the public wished to attend a committee meeting, at which only 14 seats were available for the public, the press and those attending to make representations. The chair decided to exclude the public because of the limited seating and because of the need to hear those making representations privately. Those were the reasons, but they were not minuted adequately. Lord Widgery held that the reason for exclusion amounted to 'special reasons' within the Act but that the legal requirement that the reasons be stated in the resolution was directory, not mandatory and would only be set aside if a party suffered injury! The vagueness of the reason[3] did not therefore invalidate the resolution. In fact, the court supplied the reasons which the public authority had omitted.

¹   Not as per LGA 1972, Part VA but as is ordinarily understood.
²   [1975] 1 All ER 379.
³   'So that the business of the committee may be carried out satisfactorily'; 'limitations of space' was also mentioned.

EXTENSION OF LOCAL GOVERNMENT (ACCESS TO INFORMATION) ACT 1985

6.79 The relevant provisions of the LG(ATI)A 1985[1] apply to community health councils in Wales[3] and their committees, with necessary modifications to account for differences in their organisation and administration. This extension was effected by the Community Health Councils (Access to Information) Act 1988. Access has to be allowed to registers of members of the bodies covered at all reasonable hours free of charge. Copies may be made, or requested,[4] on payment of a reasonable fee.

[1]   LGA 1972, ss 100A–100D, 100H and 100I.
[2]   Amended by Health and Social Care (Community Health and Standards) Act 2003, Sch 4, para 25 and Sch 14, Part I.
[3]   National Health Service (Wales) Act 2006, s 182.
[4]   And must be received within three days, including the day of request, under the Community Health Councils (Access to Information) Act 1988.

6.80 In the 1988 Act, the list of exemptions is extended to include two new paragraphs:

'6A. Information relating to the physical or mental health of any particular person.
6B. Information relating to –
(a)   any particular person who is or was formerly included in a list of persons undertaking to provide services under Part II of the National Health Service Act 1977 or is an applicant for inclusion in such a list;[1] or
(b)   any particular employee of such a person.'

[1]   General medical, dental, ophthalmic and pharmaceutical services.

6.81 NHS bodies will make representations to local authority 'overview and scrutiny committees' (OSCs) concerning the views of members of the public about healthcare. OSCs were extended to health care matters by the Health and Social Care Act 2001, s 7, amended by the National Health Service Act 2006 and the National Health Service (Wales) Act 2006. The role of the OSC is further set out by The Local Authority (Overview and Scrutiny Committees Health Scrutiny Functions) Regulations 2002, SI 2002/3048.

6.82 As noted above, the regime for public involvement with NHS bodies in England has been and continues to be the subject of enormous reform. The recent history of the changes is set out above in para 6.4. The present provisions which apply are those which are found in the Local Government and Public Involvement in Health Act 2007 (LGPIHA 2007), although it was noted above that the public also enjoys access to meetings of many NHS bodies via the PB(ATM)A 1960. The LGPIHA 2007, Part 14 requires each local authority to enter into contractual arrangements to allow local people to participate in the commissioning, provision and scrutiny of local care services – to be known as a local involvement network. 'Local care services' and 'care services' are defined in s 221(6) and include health services provided by the NHS and social services provided by local authorities. Under s 227, each local authority must, when reaching contractual arrangements, require the local involvement network to deliver an annual report detailing its activities thoughout the year and its expenditure. Section 224 requires that service providers should respond to the reports and actions of local involvement networks. Section 225 provides that service providers should allow authorised persons from local involvement networks to have access to this report in order to view and observe the carrying on of service provision in their local authority facilities. Further details on rights of access and other matters in relation to local involvement networks can be found in the Local Involvement Networks (Duty of Services-Providers to Allow Entry) Regulations 2008, SI 2008/915 and the Local Involvement Networks Regulations 2008, SI 2008/528.

CONCLUSION

6.83   The PB(ATM)A 1960 is an interesting example of open government in a wider sense than simply providing access to documents. Its spread is, however, very limited. The same cannot be said of laws relating to access to personal documents. It is to that subject that we now turn.

Chapter 7

Access to personal information and privacy

7.1 The first part of this chapter discusses the Data Protection Act 1998 (DPA 1998), as amended by the Freedom of Information Act 2000 (FOIA 2000); the DPA 1998 basically allows the subjects of computerised and 'structured' files to access such files (or more precisely the personal data within them) which are held on them. The FOIA 2000 covers access to a less-structured range of personal information than does the DPA 1998 but it only applies to public authorities as defined under FOIA (para 1.85). There then follows a discussion on particular statutes dealing with access to personal information. In the White Paper on FOI in December 1997,[1] the government stated its desire to bring as much of the existing legislation on access to personal information as possible under the new FOIA 2000, so far as the latter statute covered public authorities. In the result, however, the DPA 1998 is the governing statute on access to personal information, although it was extended by FOIA 2000 as shall be explained. The Access to Personal Files Act 1987 was repealed by the DPA 1998, which came into force on 1 March 2000 (SI 2000/183). The provisions of the FOIA 2000 allowing individual access to personal records came into effect on 1 January 2005. There may be areas where knowledge of the earlier legislation allowing access may be helpful.[2]

[1] *Your Right to Know: The Government's Proposals for a FOIA* Cm 3818 (1997).
[2] Consumer Credit Act 1974; Access to Personal Files Act 1987 and Social Services, Housing Regulations 1989 and Scottish equivalents; Access to Medical Reports Act 1988; Education (School Records) Regulations 1989 and Scottish equivalents; Access to Health Records Act 1990; Human Fertilisation and Embryology Act 1990. See paras 7.156 et seq below. See generally, *Encyclopedia of Data Protection* Sweet and Maxwell Vols I–IV.

7.2 Data protection involves: restrictions on the use or 'processing' of personal data; access by the person who is the subject of the data to the data; and supervision by an independent adviser. There may be exemptions from the provisions of the Act.

7.3 Sensitivity about use of personal data is a widely shared concern. Wrongful loss and disclosure of personal data on a massive and frequent scale – facilitated by the introduction of the memory stick – have been a reiterating feature of public and private commercial enterprises. The details have been collected by the House of Lords Constitution Committee in its review of surveillance.[1] Google in the private sector engaged in highly criticised practices.[2] Despite widespread concerns about data security, the Labour government nonetheless pressed ahead with its identity cards bill, which became law in 2006.[3] The Act deals with eleven main topics – Registration and a National Identity Register; ID cards; maintaining accuracy of the Register and other items;. provision of information from the Register for verification purposes; required identity checks; other permitted uses of registered information; supervision of operation of the Act; offences; civil penalties; fees and charges; and provisions relating to passports. The scheme was introduced and an Identity Commissioner was established. However, on coming to power in 2010, the coalition government took steps to dismantle the scheme under the Identity Cards Act 2010 which requires the destruction of all data on the National Register within one month of enactment. The Office of National Statistics investigated prospects for a population register. Discussion has taken place on making the electoral register a national database and various identifier databases have been suggested and databases have been established for children and for health and numerous other areas including student loans. In June 2011, the National Police Improvement Agency launched the police national database allowing the police nationally to share and access locally held information and intelligence. Reforms to retain data taken from those in police custody have been introduced following an adverse ruling from the ECtHR (para 7.256 below).[4] In 2009, the government abandoned plans for the creation of a national database on communications (para 2.200 et seq). We shall encounter in this chapter numerous problems associated with subjects such as data transfer, data retention, data , etc.

[1]   HL 18 (2008–09) and GR Cm 7616;.and see HC 702 (2010–11) IC's report to the House of Commons pursuant to Home Affairs Committee's report 'A surveillance society' by the Surveillance Studies Network. The IC has stated that the UK was sleepwalking into a 'surveillance society' on the report of the surveillance society in 2006. For the 2011 update see: http://www. surveillance-studies.net/?p=385.

[2]   The Information Commissioner issued a critical report on 3 November 2010: www.ico.gov. uk/.../google_inc_street_view_press_release_03112010.ashx.

[3]   See Cm 5557, 6019, 6020, 6178, 6358 and 6359 as well as the Home Affairs Committee HC 130 (2003–04) on the background.

[4]   See on the National DNA Database HC 472 (2009–10) HAC.

DATA PROTECTION ACT 1998[1]

7.4   The DPA 1998 is a tortuous and very important piece of legislation. It has been blamed for many ills – often unjustifiably. The first such legislation appeared in the UK in 1984, prompted by our membership of the Council of Europe and the European Convention of Data Protection of 1981.[2] The present legislation arose from the necessity of complying with the requirements of Directive 95/46/EC[3] on data protection. Data protection falls within the EU competence and is a reserved matter under devolution legislation. By virtue of Art 286 EC (Amsterdam) the Directive was binding on the institutions of the EC from 1 January 1999 although this was then effected under Regulation

(EC) 45/2001 of the European Parliament and Council, and Council Decision 2004/644/EC. Separate arrangements were made for the EU pillars and under Freedom, Security and Justice (FSJ) the relevant provisions were based on the Council of Europe convention. Data sharing was allowed under special treaties agreed by member states such as Schengen (to which the UK did not sign up and did not benefit from) and the Prum convention dealing with police transfer between signatories of data on fingerprints, DNA and vehicles (para 7.219). The Article 29 working party advises the Commission on data protection. Under the ToL there is a common legislative model for the former EC and FSJ pillars – now of course collapsed into one EU edifice. Lisbon TFEU, Art 16 provides for data protection and laying down of rules by the ordinary legislative procedure. The special nature of data protection in the area of freedom security and justice is acknowledged under Declaration 21 and provision is made for special treatment for data affecting national security under Declaration 20. Under Lisbon TEU, Art 39 a derogation from art 16 is allowed in relation to Common Foreign and Security personal data which will have its own regime. In May 2006, the ECJ ruled that an agreement to transfer personal data on flight passengers between the EU and US authorities was unlawful and relevant decisions of the Council and Commission were annulled.[4] A modified agreement operates.

[1] There are numerous free publications and Guidelines from the Office of the Information Commissioner: www.informationcommissioner.gov.uk. The European Commission has been critical of the DPA 1998 as the implementing measure for the DP Directive: see for an EU ombudsman complaint amberhawk.typepad.com/files/dp_infraction_reasons.pdf. See S Charlton and S Gaskill *Encyclopaedia of Data Protection* (2008); and R Jay and A Hamilton *Data Protection Law and Practice* (3rd edn, 2007); P Carey *Data Protection Handbook*.

[2] Lloyd, I *Information Technology Law* (4th edn, 2004) Butterworths. See also M Chissick and J Harrington *E-government: A Practical Guide to the Legal Issues*.

[3] [1995] OJ L 281/31; D Bainbridge *EC Data Protection Directive* (1996) Butterworths.

[4] *European Parliament et al v Council of the European Union et al* Cases-317/04 and 318/04 (30 May 2006). Subsequently, new regimes came into effect: see *The EU/US Passenger Name Record Agreement* House of Lords European Union Committee HL 108 (2006–07). A new agreement (Passenger Name Record) was signed in July 2007 and data on foreigners are excluded from US Privacy Act protection and the US has no Data Protection Act equivalent (OJ L 204 4/08/2007 p 18). The agreement is to last for seven years. A planned PNR allowing retention by the US authorities for 15 years has run into difficulties with member states and Commission lawyers. Any redress is discretionary only and regulated by the US authorities, retention is arguably disproportionate and breaches human rights.

7.5   The extent of the present Directive's ambit can be seen in *Lindqvist*[1] where it was held by the ECJ that the posting of personal data on the internet amounted to the processing of personal data for the purposes of the Data Protection Directive. L was a voluntary worker at a Swedish parish who referred to the health and other items of gossip of other members of the group on an internet page stored on her personal computer at home. These were identified by name or other means. L had not notified the relevant national supervisory authority under the terms of the Directive of the processing, including that relating to sensitive personal data (below) and she was therefore in breach of its terms. Case C-524/06 *Huber v Germany* discusses the subject of discrimination between member states in data protection. Important points of privacy protection in relation to personal data and investigating breaches of copyright are provided in

Case C-275/06 *Productores de Musica de Espana (Promusicae) v TDES* where the ECJ ruled that under the EU Charter of Fundamental Rights rights to privacy and data protection had to be properly balanced against rights to property and access to justice in breaches of copyright litigation. No right automatically prevailed. Implementation of Directives had to respect that balance and operate proportionately. Case C-28/08P *Bavarian Lager v Commission* discusses the relationship between the EU data protection regime and access to EU documents and was examined in chapter 3 (para 3.69 et seq). Directives may not only determine the interpretation of domestic laws; they may also be directly effective under specified and long established principles.[2]

[1]   Case C-101/01 [2004] 2 WLR 1385.
[2]   See Cases C-465/00, C-138/01 and C-139/01 *Neukomm v Österreichischer Rundfunk* (ECJ, 20 May 2003) and the discussion on the relationship between ECHR, Art 8 and Directive 95/46/ EC. Also, Case C-92/09 and C-93/09 *Volker und M Schecke etc v Land Hessen*.

7.6   As the UK Act's long title makes clear, it is not just an access statute but an Act which provides for the 'regulation of the processing of information relating to individuals, including the obtaining, holding, use' as well as disclosure of such information. Matching the two statutes – the DPA 1998 and the FOIA 2000 – was not easy because of the perceived conflict between disclosure under the FOIA 2000 and regulation under the DPA 1998. The House of Lords has spoken of the undoubted importance of FOIA but emphasised that FOIA operates so as not to override privacy and data protection.[1] After a good deal of uncertainty, the government amended the DPA 1998 by FOIA 2000 in a manner which has caused some very difficult provisions. At the suggestion of the Select Committee on Public Administration, requests by individuals for their own personal information will be made under the DPA 1998. Requests for information about other individuals will be made under the FOIA 2000 but subject to the DPA 1998 requirements where the Act operates. The Data Protection Commissioner (DPC)) became the Information Commissioner and is responsible for the administration of both statutes. The IC's rulings in relation to access under s 40 have exposed the DPA 1998 to interpretation on a regular basis. The DPA has been the subject of some controversial rulings from the Court of Appeal. However, case law from the courts is sparse and the IC is not an enforcement mechanism for the DPA as he is for the FOI, as will be explained.

[1]   *Common Services Agency v Scottish Information Commissioner* [2008] UKHL 47.

7.7   The Data Protection Act 1984 (DPA 1984) only applied to computerised personal information. The DPA 1998 has a much wider coverage and applies to personal information, 'data', which is being processed by means of equipment operating automatically in response to instructions given for that purpose (DPA 1998, s 1(1)(a)); information which is recorded with the intention that it should be processed by means of such equipment (s 1(1)(b)); is recorded as part of a relevant filing system or with the intention that it should form part of a relevant filing system – this involves 'structured information' which is stored by reference to a number or code for instance (s 1(1)(c);[1] crucially this may include paper or 'manual records'; finally information which does not fall within the above but forms part of an 'accessible record' under DPA 1998, s 68. This defines an accessible record as: a health record which consists of information relating to the physical or mental health or condition of an individual and has been made by or on behalf of a health professional in connection with the care of that individual; an educational record as defined in Sch 11, para 2 (for England and Wales), para 5 (Scotland) or para 7 (Northern Ireland) (this does not cover private schools, although they will qualify if they fall within the first three groups (s 1(1)(a)–(c) above); an accessible public record as defined by Sch 12 which basically covers housing and social services records). These are records which were covered by their own legislation or regulations on access to personal records and crucially they cover manual (non-electronic and non-structured) records. These have now been effectively incorporated within the DPA 1998 but form a distinct category of data.

[1] See below on 'relevant filing system'.

7.8 FOIA 2000, s 68 adds *recorded* information held by a public authority which does not fall within any of the above provisions. By this means the DPA 1998 rights of subject access and data accuracy are extended to all personal information held by public authorities as defined. The first four categories, however, apply regardless of whether the data is held by a public or private body. The latter only applies to data held by a public authority covered by the FOIA 2000. By this means, the wider areas of personal information covered by the FOIA 2000 are not extended to private holders of such information. A chart relating to the interrelationship of the two systems drafted by the DPC's office is set out at para 7.14 below.

7.9 Finally, the Privacy and Electronic Communications Directive (Directive 2002/58/EC of the European Parliament and Council) has been implemented into UK law by SI 2003/2426. These regulations are examined below (paras 7.279 et seq below). An e-Privacy Directive 2009/136/EC is operative from May 2011.[1]

[1] Para 7.296 below.

DATA PROTECTION ACT 1998 AND THE FREEDOM OF INFORMATION ACT 2000

7.10 While the FOIA 2000 states that all personal information held by public authorities is included within the DPA 1998, it cancels all the effects of being within the DPA 1998 for this last category of information added by FOIA 2000, s 68 apart from subject access rights and accuracy. Even these will not apply to non-designated functions of public authorities – those basically which are not of a public nature – and personal information held by those bodies falling under this last group of information. This means therefore that the DPA 1998 applies to public authorities' non-automated records even though they are not part of a relevant filing system and not part of an 'accessible record' as defined in the Act and as explained by the Court of Appeal in *Durant v Financial Services*

Authority (paras 7.15 et seq below). 'An example of this might be incidental personal information on a policy file, or in loose papers.'[1] Section 69 of the FOIA 2000 adds a further qualification to subject access rights to the group of personal information introduced under the FOIA 2000. Where the information is, although not part of a relevant filing system or part of an accessible record, nonetheless structured to a certain extent by reference to individuals eg 'a case file about an individual which contains correspondence about a number of matters relating to that individual and is indexed by reference only to the dates of the correspondence'[2] it is treated for subject access purposes as any other personal information under the DPA 1998.

[1]   *FOI Consultation on Draft Legislation* (1999) Cm 4355, para 169.
[2]   Cm 4355, para 170.

7.11   Where it is not 'relatively structured' ie 'relatively unstructured', additional rules apply on access requests. Firstly, unstructured personal data will not be given unless the information is *expressly* described in the request. Requests for information covered by the DPA 1998 will usually be met by giving the subject all of their data without them having to specify any part of it. 'No part of the residue of relatively unstructured personal information, however, will be included in response to a subject access request unless the data subject has expressly described it.'[1] Requests will therefore have to be more specific for this kind of information. Secondly, the authority may refuse an access request in so far as it relates to that information where to allow it would cost more than is provided for in a 'prescribed cost ceiling'.[2]

[1]   Cm 4355, para 170.
[2]   See paras 1.72 et seq above. FOIA 2000, s 13 gives a discretion to allow access but subject to a different fees schedule.

7.12   FOIA 2000, s 70 strips away all the substantive rights under the DPA 1998 to the group of personal information introduced under the FOIA 2000 apart, as we have seen, from subject access and inaccuracy. It further adds that the extension of access and accuracy rights does not apply to personnel records within that group of information held by public authorities and this follows the FOI White Paper of 1997. In the White Paper, this group was to be excluded. They are now covered by an exemption. It is basically an absolute exemption (para 1.105).

7.13   The DPA 1998 provides that where there is a statutory duty to provide information to the public it is exempt from subject access, accuracy and certain other restrictions on disclosure. This is because such access provisions eg marriage, births, death registers and the Land Registry, make their own detailed provisions. If the provision stood without more, it would also embrace and thereby exempt those duties under the FOIA 2000. The FOIA 2000 is therefore not included within these provisions.[1]

[1]   Without this provision, the FOIA 2000 would dominate the DPA 1998 re subject access.

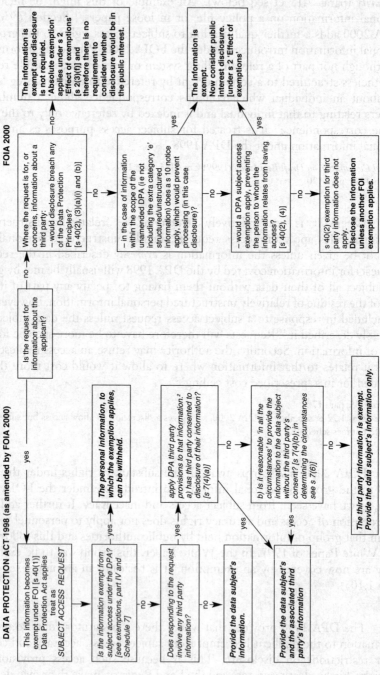

7.14

FREEDOM OF INFORMATION ACT 2000[1]

PROVISIONS GOVERNING ACCESS TO PERSONAL INFORMATION HELD BY PUBLIC AUTHORITIES

DATA PROTECTION ACT 1998 (as amended by FOIA 2000) | **FOIA 2000**

This information becomes exempt under FOI [s 40(1)] Data Protection Act applies treat as *SUBJECT ACCESS REQUEST*

Is the request for information about the applicant?

— yes →

Is the request is for, or concerns, information about a third party: – would disclosure breach any of the Data Protection Principles? [s 40(2), (3)(a)(i) and (b)]

→ no →

– in the case of information within the scope of the unamended DPA (ie not including the extra category 'e' structured/unstructured information) does a s 10 notice apply, which would prevent processing (in this case disclosure)?

→ no →

– would a DPA subject access exemption apply, preventing the person to whom the information relates from having access? [s 40(2), (4)]

→ no →

s 40(2) exemption for third party information does not apply.
Disclose the information unless another FOI exemption applies.

— no →

(yes) ↑ The information is exempt and disclosure is not required. 'Absolute exemption' applies under s 2 'Effect of exemptions' [s 2(3)(f)] and therefore there is no requirement to consider whether disclosure would be in the public interest.

(yes) ↑ The information is exempt.
Now consider public interest disclosure [under s 2 'Effect of exemptions'].

— yes →

Is the information exempt from subject access under the DPA? [see exemptions, part IV and Schedule 7]

→ yes → **The personal information, to which the exemption applies, can be withheld.**

→ no →

Does responding to the request involve any third party information?

→ no → **Provide the data subject's information.**

→ yes →

apply DPA third party provisions [s 7(4)/(a)]
a) has third party consented to disclosure of their information? [s 7(4)/(a)]

→ yes → **Provide the data subject's and the associated third party's information**

→ no →

b) Is it reasonable 'in all the circumstances' to provide the information to the data subject without the third party's consent? [s 7(4)(b); in determining the circumstances see s 7(6)]

→ yes ↑

→ no →

**The third party information is exempt.
Provide the data subject's information only.**

[1] ISBN 0–10–543600–3 (30 November 2000).
[2] Nb: However, where the information does not *identify* the third party, or it can be edited so as not to identify the third party, it should be provided.

DURANT V FINANCIAL SERVICES AUTHORITY[1]

7.15 *Durant* has been the most influential, and controversial, decision from domestic courts on the ambit of the DPA 1998 in relation to 'personal data' and 'structured filing systems'. The claimant applied to the Financial Services Authority (FSA) under DPA 1998, s 7 for disclosure of personal data relating to him held by the FSA. Access to some information was provided but the FSA refused further disclosure. The court was provided with all the information or documents under DPA 1998, s 15(2) that the FSA did not wish to disclose to Durant. The court reiterated the approach adopted by Lord Phillips MR in *Campbell v MGN*[2] who observed that, as the DPA 1998 implements a Directive, it should be interpreted in a manner consistent with the Directive. 'A purposive approach to making sense of the provisions is called for.' It was not 'appropriate' to look for the 'precision in the use of language that is usually to be expected from parliamentary draftsman' (*Campbell*, para 96). The Court of Appeal, echoing previous case law, identified the conflict at the heart of data protection laws: the protection of fundamental human rights to privacy and accuracy of personal data held by others under the terms of the DPA 1998 and the facilitation of the free flow of such data between the EU member states.

[1] [2003] EWCA Civ 1746, [2004] I P & T 814. See also *Johnson v Medical Defence Union* [2005] 1 All ER 87 on CPR disclosure re DPA claims: para 7.125, note 1 below.
[2] [2003] QB 633.

7.16 The background to the case was litigation between the claimant and Barclays Bank in which the claimant had been unsuccessful. D had attempted to obtain documents from the Bank with a view to further litigation and he wished to know what information the defendant possessed on the Bank in its capacity as a regulator under the Financial Services Act 1987. The FSA declined these requests although it did investigate D's complaints against the Bank. It did not inform D of its outcome pursuant to confidentiality under ss 82–85 of the 1987 Act. D therefore invoked his rights under DPA 1998, s 7. He sought documents that were both in electronic form and manual documents.

7.17 The FSA disclosed data in computerised form – beyond *Durant*'s strict DPA entitlements according to the Court of Appeal – having redacted some information to erase the names of others. The FSA refused the request for the unredacted computerised files as well as the paper documents on the grounds that these did not constitute personal information within the terms of the expression 'personal data' under DPA 1998, s 1(1). Even if it did, it did not constitute data within the separate definition of that word in s 1(1)(c) in the sense of forming a 'separate filing system'. It was accepted by the FSA that some of its manual files were basic. These included a file relating to systems controls arranged in date order which contained some information relating to D in part about his complaint against the Bank. The second manual file was a 'Complaints file' about complaints to the FSA by customers of the Bank about the Bank. These had 'sub-dividers ordered alphabetically by reference to a complainant's name, containing behind a divider marked "Mr Durant" a number of documents relating to D, filed in date order.' The third group was the Bank Investigations

Group file maintained by the FSA's Regulatory Enforcement Department. This was related to and organised by reference to issues or cases concerning the Bank 'but not necessarily identified by reference to an individual complainant.' (*Durant*, para 15) The last file was the Company Secretariat papers 'a sheaf of papers in an unmarked transparent plastic folder held by the FSA's Company Secretariat' concerning D's complaint about the FSA's refusal to hand to D details of its investigation into D's complaints against the Bank and its outcome. These were not organised by date or any other criterion.

> 'The FSA has acknowledged in correspondence that each of the files in question contains information in which D features, that some of them identify him by reference to specific dividers within the file and that they contain such documents as: copies of telephone attendance notes, a report of forensic examination of documents, transcripts of judgments, hand-written notes, internal memoranda, correspondence with the Bank ... with other individuals ... and between the FSA [and D].' (Para 17)

7.18 The Court of Appeal concentrated on four questions:[1] what makes data in manual or electronic files personal? What is a 'relevant filing system' in the definition of 'data' in DPA 1998, s 1(1) that makes personal information in a manual system 'personal data' disclosable to the subject under s 1(1)? Was the manual filing system such that the FSA were under a duty to disclose it had it been a computerised system? Further questions concerned when it was reasonable in all the circumstances to comply with the request to disclose even though the personal data contains personal information about another who has not consented to disclosure? Lastly, by what principles should a court be guided in exercising its discretion under s 7(9) to order a data controller, who has wrongly refused to comply with a request under s 1(1), to comply with the request?

---

[1] The two latter questions not dealt with in this section concerned: first, redaction of computerised files that the FSA argued did not contain personal data and files that did contain such data on other individuals. The latter raised the question of the reasonableness of disclosing the data to the applicant (para 7.64 below). The fourth question concerned the court's powers under DPA 1998, s 7(9) which was, by the time of the Court of Appeal's hearing, no longer live.

'Personal data'

7.19 The court preferred a narrow interpretation of personal data: the term 'is not an automatic key to any information, readily accessible or not, of matters in which he may be named or involved'. Nor is it a form of assistance for disclosure of documents for litigation (see ch 10). 'Ready accessibility' though important is not a starting point. Not all information obtained from a 'computer search against a person's name or unique identifier is personal data within the Act' (para 27). Two 'notions' may be of assistance in determining whether it is personal data: is the information 'biographical' in a significant sense? Is it recording information of a putative data subject's 'involvement in a matter or an event that has no personal connotations, a life event in respect of which his privacy could not be said to be compromised' (para 28). Secondly, does the information focus on the subject and not on 'some other person with whom he may have been involved' or some event in which he may have had an interest (para 28) eg, as in this case, an investigation into another person's or body's conduct that he may have complained of. This narrow interpretation is reinforced, the court felt, by the concentration on the 'data subject' in terms of rights under the Act and expressions in the Act. In short, the information which D sought was not personal data whether it was sought from an electronic system or a manual system. In relation to his complaints about the Bank and the FSA's investigation of his complaints, information generated by such complaints made by D could not render such information 'personal data'(para 30). In para 31, Auld LJ believed that what was sought by virtue of the DPA 1998 was 'third party discovery' for further litigation an 'exercise ... unrestricted by considerations of relevance'.

'Relevant filing system'

7.20 The court believed that the DPA 1998 and Directive contained no material differences on the provisions relating to 'a relevant filing system' (Directive 95/46/EC, Art 2(2)(c), recitals 15 and 27; DPA 1998, s 1(1)). The court believed that the intention of these provisions 'is to provide, as near as possible, the same standard of sophistication of accessibility to personal data in manual filing systems as to computerised records. It is not a question of obtaining information easily: it is a question of 'structuring' information in a set or part of a set in such a way that specific information about an individual is 'readily accessible'. Several factors influenced the court to adopt the narrower interpretation of 'relevant filing system' urged on behalf of the FSA so that, firstly, ease of retrieval of information from filing systems 'with minimal time and cost through clear referencing mechanisms within any filing system potentially containing personal data [which may be] the subject of a request for information (para 45)' would have to be evident. The Act's intention cannot have been to impose a 'disproportionate effect on the property rights of data controllers' whose administrative section would have to 'leaf through files to see what [information], and whether information qualifying as personal data of the person who has made the request, is to be found there [and which] *would bear no resemblance to a computerised search*.' (para 45 – emphasis added). When seen in the context of the narrow meaning identified by the court for 'personal data' the required easy access to such data 'must be on a par with that provided by a computerised system' and the need for a restrictive meaning to 'relevant filing system' is plain (para 47). 'Parliament intended to apply the Act to manual records only if they are of sufficient sophistication to provide the same or similar ready accessibility as a computerised filing system' (para 48).

> 'That requires a filing system so referenced or indexed that it enables the data controller's employee responsible to identify at the outset of his search with reasonable certainty and speed the file or files in which specific data relating to the person requesting the information is located and to locate the relevant information about him within the file or files, without having to make a manual search of them.' (para 48)

7.21   Files are part of a relevant filing system if they are structured in such a way clearly to indicate at the outset of the search whether specific information capable of amounting to personal data of an individual requesting it under DPA 1998, s 7 is 'held within the system, and, if so, in which file of files it is held' (para 50). Secondly and conjunctively, the phrase is limited to a system 'which has, as part of its own structure or referencing mechanism, a sufficiently sophisticated and detailed means of readily indicating whether and where in an individual file or files specific criteria or information about the applicant can be readily located' (para 50). The FSA files in question did not satisfy these tests.

7.22   When one considers the description of unstructured personal data that public authorities will have to disclose under FOIA, it may well reinforce this restrictive interpretation of 'personal data' and 'relevant filing system' (above). However, it could be argued that the narrow definitions adopted by a unanimous Court of Appeal will provide scope for abuse of data holding of such a kind that led to the calls for reform in the 1970s and 1980s to safeguard an individual's integrity. It should be remembered that the courts have the power of inspection to see whether the statutory definitions are satisfied and it is to be hoped that they will exercise such powers appropriately to protect individuals against abuse.[1]

[1]   See *Johnson v Medical Defence Union* [2005] 1 All ER 87 (para 7.125, note 1 below).

DPA definition of personal data

7.23   Personal data means data which relates to a living individual – the data subject – who can be identified from that data (or from that data and other information in the possession of the holder of information, or which is likely to come into the possession of the data controller) including an expression of opinion about the individual and any indications of the intentions of the data controller in respect of the individual. Previously where opinions on employees were processed and were not exempt they would have to be disclosed to the employee, but not the intentions of the employer, ie to dismiss or to promote. Such data will now be disclosable. The narrow interpretation of this term in relation to both electronically and manually stored data was discussed above under *Durant*.

7.24   The words 'or from that data and other information in the possession of the holder of information, or which is likely to come into the possession of the data controller' were discussed by the House of Lords in *Common Services Agency v Scottish Information Commissioner* [2008] UKHL 47. In a complex case dealing with barnardised (subject to distortion) data the law lords ruled that the Scottish Information Commissioner would have to establish clearly whether a child's identity could be established by other data and information in the possession of the authority. If so, it was personal data and the safeguards and protection provided by the Act applied. The Scottish Information Commissioner (SIC) had not established whether it was personal data according to this provision. Surely a crucial question would be whether the requester would have access to the *other data or information*.[1]

[1]   See *Magharafelt v IC* EA/2009/0047 (para 7.107 below).

7.25   The controller and processor of data are referred to as the 'data controller' (DC) and 'data processor' (DP). The DC means a person who either alone or jointly or in common with others determines the purposes for which and the manner in which any personal data are, or are to be, processed – it covers an intention to process data.[1] Data may be controlled by an individual, in tandem with others via an intranet as a part of a group using groupware.[2] A DP is 'any person' who processes the data on behalf of the DC – but it does not include a DC's employee. An example of such a person is an independent contractor, such as the company Electronic Data Systems (EDS) (from 2009 HP Enterprise Services), which processes data on behalf of both public and private organisations.

[1]   DPA 1998, s 1(1).
[2]   A Charlesworth *Annotation to Data Protection Act Current Law Statutes* (1998) ch 29.

7.26   Processing in relation to data or information means obtaining, recording or holding the information or data or carrying out any operation or set of operations on the information or data, including:
(a)   organisation, adaptation or alteration of the information or data;
(b)   retrieval, consultation or use of the information or data;
(c)   disclosure of the information or data by transmission, dissemination or otherwise making it available; or
(d)   alignment,[1] combination, blocking, erasure or destruction of the information or data.

[1]   This phrase is not explained.

7.27   This is a much wider definition than under the DPA 1984 and includes obtaining and recording data.[1] Processing no longer has to take place with reference to the data subject as under the DPA 1984. 'It is a compendious definition and it is difficult to envisage any action involving data which does not amount to processing within this definition.'[2] The section also circumvents the decision of the House of Lords in *R v Brown*[3] which held that where a defendant was charged with using personal data then accessing or retrieval of information on a computer so that it could be read either on screen or by means of a print-out was not 'using' the information but simply transferring the information into a different form prior to possible use being made of it. The Court of Appeal has ruled that where a DC was responsible for the publication of 'hard copies' (newspapers) which reproduced data (photographs) that had previously been processed by means of equipment operating automatically, that publication formed part of the processing and thereby fell within the scope of the DPA 1998. There was no reason why the obtaining and using of information should not fall within the scope of 'processing' within the DPA 1998.[4]

[1]   DPA 1998, s 1(2) and (3).
[2]   Data Protection Commissioner, *Introduction to the 1998 Act* ch 2.
[3]   [1996] 1 All ER 545, HL.
[4]   *Campbell v Mirror Group Newspapers* [2002] EWCA Civ 1373, [2003] 1 All ER 224 (CA). See *Douglas v Hello! (No 3)* [2003] 3 All ER 996 at para 230: '*Campbell* ... fortunately ma[de] an understanding of the Act easier than do the unvarnished provisions of the Act itself'.

7.28 Despite the width of this definition, the Court of Appeal nonetheless ruled by majority that selecting data to make a decision in relation to the data subject was not processing.[1] The strong dissent of Arden LJ is, we submit, in better accord with the intentions of the DPA 1998.

[1] *Johnson v Med Def Union No 2* [2007] EWCA Civ 262.

7.29 The Act defines a 'relevant filing system' (above) to mean any set of information relating to individuals to the extent that, although the information is not processed by means of equipment operating automatically in response to instructions nonetheless the set is 'structured' either by reference to individuals or criteria relating to individuals (eg, code numbers) in such a way that specific information relating to a specific individual is readily accessible. This last phrase is crucial as is the word 'set' – a collection of information with a common theme or purpose. The precise scope of what manual files are included has led to conflicting interpretations with the DPC interpreting the provision more broadly than the government.[1] Does it cover a file on which the subject's name is on the front but the information in loosely assorted papers is not readily extractable? If not part of a 'set' it could fall under the personal data added by the FOIA 2000 rather than under this heading but only when held by a public authority. It seems that where applicable it will cover card indexes, rollerdex, microfiche. The discussion of the Court of Appeal in *Durant v FSA* in which a narrow interpretation was given to this term was examined above.

[1] See the DPC's *Introduction to the 1998 Act.* This was the view of the DPC when she gave evidence to the Select Committee on Public Administration in its inquiry into the White Paper: HC 398 I (1997–98) Qu 220.

Sensitive personal data[1]

7.30 Section 2 of the DPA 1998 defines sensitive personal data which consists of information as to the data subject's racial or ethnic origin; their political opinions; their religious or other similar beliefs; whether a member of a trade union;[2] their physical or mental health or condition, their sexual life; the commission or alleged commission of any offence by the data subject; or proceedings for any offence committed or alleged to have been committed by the subject and their disposal or any sentence. This group of data is important in relation to the data protection principles and whether data are processed fairly and lawfully (Sch 3 and para 7.55 below). DPA 1998, Sch 3 imposes very strict conditions of the processing of sensitive personal data. In the *Common Services Agency* litigation [2008] UKHL 47, para 37 the law lords ruled that 'sensitive personal data' should be read as a subset of 'personal data' so that data qualifying as personal data and subject to the descriptions for sensitive personal data are subject to the personal data definitions and restrictions.

[1] See generally SI 2000/417 on processing of sensitive data and SI 2068/2006 likewise and SI 2002/2905 on processing of sensitive personal data concerning elected representatives. Note also Employment Relations Act 1999, s 3 and Employment Relations Act 1999 (Blacklist) Regulations 2010, SI 2010/493.
[2] See Trade Union and Labour Relations (Consolidation) Act 1992, s 1.

The special purposes

7.31 The Act also defines 'special purposes' to include the purposes of journalism; artistic purposes; and literary purposes. This is important in relation to exemptions from duties under the Act to protect freedom of speech rights under ECHR, Art 10 and the Human Rights Act 1998 (HRA 1998) and enforcement and compensation for distress.[1]

[1]   See paras 7.85 and 7.122 below.

Various

7.32 DCs have to comply with the data protection principles in relation to all personal data over which they are the controller. These principles, the detailed instructions on their interpretation (both in Sch 1) and the conditions that are relevant for the first principle in relation to all personal data processing (Sch 2) and processing of sensitive personal data (Sch 3), are central to an understanding of the DPA 1998 (see paras 7.42 et seq below). The DPA 1998 applies to DCs established in the UK, and DCs outside the UK and EEA under certain conditions (see para 7.40 below).

7.33 The DPA 1998 renamed the Data Protection Registrar the DPC and also established the Data Protection Tribunal. As we have seen, the FOIA 2000 renames these bodies the Information Commissioner and Information Tribunal respectively. A Chairman of the Tribunal will be assisted by a person representing the interests of information (including data controllers) holders and information (including data subjects) requesters.

Notification

7.34 Under the DPA 1984, every data user holding personal data had to register. Now the duty is for data controllers to 'notify' the Commissioner of their wish to be placed on the register of those intending to process personal data. There are some exemptions from notification. Fees are payable and possibly refundable (DPA 1998, ss 18(5), 19(4)). Since 2009 there are two levels of fee. For private enterprises with a turnover of £29.5 million and 250 or more members of staff, and for public authorities with over 250 members of staff, the notification fee is £500 from 1 October 2009. Under these threshholds the fee is £35 unless the DC is exempt[1] Even though not registered when they should be or where exempt from registration, DCs will still be liable for breaches of the data protection principles. Details relating to notification are in regulations.[2]

[1]   Data Protection (Notification and Notification fees) (Amendment) Regulations 2009, SI 2009/1677.
[2]   SI 2000/188 as amended, including by SI 2009/1677.

7.35 The user's register entry is compiled from information provided in the user's application. DCs will have to provide a general description of measures to be taken for the purpose of complying with the seventh DP principle concerning appropriate security (below). The information that registrable particulars for controllers will contain, and the detail and form of these, is subject to the Commissioner's determination (DPA 1998, ss 16 and 18 as amended by Coroners and Justice Act 2009, s 175 and Sch 20 concerning information about verification of fees payable under s 18(5)). These include:

(1)   Their name and address or that of their nominated representative.

(2)   A description of the personal data being or to be processed by or on behalf of the DC and the category(ies) of data subject to which they relate.

(3)   A description of the purpose(s) for which they are or are to be processed.

(4)   A description of any recipient(s) to whom the DC intends or may wish to disclose the data.

(5)   The names, or a description of, any countries or territories outside the EEA to which the DC directly or indirectly transfers, or intends or may wish directly or indirectly to transfer, the data.

(6)   Where data is not assessable (sic) data under s 22 (basically, data particularly likely to cause substantial damage or distress to data subjects or otherwise significantly to prejudice their rights and freedoms: see para 7.37 below), it may be processed without registration if the processing is not by means of equipment operating automatically in response to instructions given for that purpose or, the data was not recorded with the intention that it should be processed by means of such equipment; where the data may be processed within a particular category of processing which the Secretary of State feels will not prejudice the rights and freedoms of data subjects, it may be exempted by regulations from registration but the non-inclusion on the register must be stated in the notification. Article 18.2 of the EC Directive allows for the simplification of and exemption from notification. The DPA 1998 was intended to promote this development to achieve simplification. The DPR certainly felt that too many data users were legally bound to register under previous legislation making non-registration of defaulters a serious problem. In the year ending 31 March 1999, there were 90,205 renewals and new registrations. By 2009–10, the figure was 328,164 (IC AR HC 220 (2009–10) p 41).

7.36   DPA 1998, s 19 contains details on the register of notifications and, by sub-s (6), the Commissioner shall provide facilities for making the information in the register available at all reasonable hours to the public free of charge in visible and legible form. The Commissioner may provide such other facilities to allow public access to the entries as she considers appropriate and on payment of a prescribed fee, if such a fee is required, shall supply any member of the public with a duly certified copy in writing of the particulars of any entry. DCs who are public authorities must register that fact.[1] By s 20, DCs are under a duty to make sure that their entries are as up to date as possible and the Commissioner is under a duty to make such changes as are notified as are necessary. Processing in breach of the registration requirement is a criminal offence as is failure by the DC to keep their entry up to date although a defence of 'all due diligence' is allowed (s 21).

---

[1]   DPA 1998, s 16(1)(ff) (added by FOIA 2000, s 71). On notification, see http://www.ico.gov.uk/ for_organisations/data_protection/notification.aspx.

7.37   The Commissioner has to assess whether any notification under s 18 or under s 20 involves 'assessable processing'. This means processing which is likely to cause substantial damage or substantial distress to data subjects or otherwise significantly prejudice the rights and freedoms of data subjects (s 22). An order made by the Secretary of State was to specify 'assessable processing'. Three types of data have been identified as relevant: processing of genetic data; data matching (para 7.208 below); and processing by inquiry agents. Within 28 days of receipt of a notification as above of assessable processing, the Commissioner must give a notice to the DC stating the extent to which the Commissioner is of the opinion that the processing is likely or unlikely to comply with the Act's provisions. This period may be extended by special circumstances for one period of 14 days. No assessable processing may take place before the effluxion of these periods unless the DC has received a notice from the Commissioner. Contravention by the DC is a criminal offence.

7.38   DCs may appoint data protection supervisors to monitor in particular and in an independent manner the DCs' compliance with the duties in the Act. Even where certain personal data are exempt from the notification process and particulars have not been filed by the DC, the data subject may still have access to that information unless otherwise exempted under notification regulations. Failure to comply is an offence, subject to a defence of showing all due diligence to comply (DPA 1998, s 24). The Commissioner may submit proposals for notification regulations to the Secretary of State and is under a duty to keep their operation under review and may submit proposals for amendment. Section 26 concerns fees.[1] As explained above, there are now at two levels of fee for notification.

[1]   SI 2009/1677. The maximum fee under s 7(2) for access by a data subject is £10 (SI 2000/191), and for requests to credit reference agencies, limited to a requester's financial standing, £2. Special provisions relate to medical records and education records: see para 7.151 below.

7.39   The register is maintained by the Commissioner. The Commissioner is a regulator and enforcer of the legislation and acts as a sort of ombudsman for data subjects – there were 'over 49,000 assessments completed (complaints) in 2009–10 (*Annual Report 2009–10* HC 220 p 34). Assessments are at the request of those covered by DPA 1998, s 42 (see para 7.120 below). However, the IC is not an enforcement mechanism under DPA 1998 as under FOIA, and cases of assessments are not individually reported and the matter is usually resolved by correspondence pointing out possible breaches of the Act.[1] The register will allow subjects to assess, in general terms, whether a DC is likely to hold information upon them, eg as employer, customer, etc. The subject can then ask the DC whether the DC has information on the subject, and if so – with exemptions – the subject has a right of access under s 7. A DC who is unhappy with a decision of the IC may appeal to the First Tier Tribunal Information Rights (below). The Coroners and Justice Act 2009, Part 8 and Sch 20 create new powers for the IC to carry out assessments following notorious episodes concerning loss of data (para 7.58 below).

[1]   http://www.ico.gov.uk/complaints.aspx.

Data held outside the UK

7.40 The DPA 1998 applies to data controllers established in the UK where the data are processed in the context of that establishment. DCs outside the UK and EEA who use equipment in the UK for processing data otherwise than for the purposes of transit through the UK are covered by the Act.[1] By virtue of the Crime (International Co-operation) Act 2003, ss 81 and 94 and SI 2004/786, s 54A was added to the DPA 1998, under which the IC may inspect any personal data recorded in:

(a) the Schengen information system;

(b) the Europol information system;

(c) the Customs information system.

[1]   DPA 1998, s 5(2) and (3).

The Commissioner's duties

7.41 The Commissioner has a variety of duties under the DPA 1998 including the promotion of good practice by DCs and to promote the observance of the Act by DCs. S/he shall arrange for the publication of information about the Act and good practice as well as advice as appears appropriate. S/he shall also prepare and disseminate to such persons as she considers appropriate codes of practice for guidance on good practice. Guidance has been produced for public and private sector bodies on CCTV, the Child Support Agency, Council Tax, the Electoral Register, on Notification/Registration (FAQ), Exam Results Disclosure, Subject Access (FAQ), Health Data, Inland Revenue (disclosures under the Taxes Management Act), for Local Authorities, sale of planning applications to local traders, promotion of Political Parties, Registration Officers and rights to inspect Local Authority records, Vehicle keepers information, Violent warning markers and Website (FAQ) Guidance for the private sector covers Legal Guidance, Compliance Advice, Subject Access and third party information and Internet: protection of Privacy. Guidance may be produced by order of the Secretary of State or at the Commissioner's discretion. This will follow consultation with trade associations, data subjects and their representatives as s/he considers appropriate. No doubt many such codes will be produced but one of special interest relates to *Users of Closed Circuit TV*[1] which sets out, inter alia, rights of subjects, ie those caught on security camera and access by third parties. An *Employment Practices Data Protection Code* is in various parts covering: *Recruitment and Selection; Records; Monitoring at Work; Small Business Code* and *Workers' Health* (www.informationcommissioner.gov.uk).The Commissioner may encourage the making of codes by trade associations for their members and s/he may consider any code after consulting with data subjects or representatives and may advise whether the code promotes features of good practice including compliance with the DPA 1998.[2] S/he may disseminate certain EU 'findings' and Commission decisions and information on processing outside the EEA. S/he may with the DC's consent assess processing of personal data to see if good practice is followed. The DC will be informed of the results. She may charge for services provided (DPA 1998, s 51(8)). Annual reports and other reports shall be laid before each House of Parliament as well as any codes prepared under s 51(3). The IC has published widely on data and privacy protection issues and publications include: CCTV, employment, data sharing, privacy notices and electronic communications.[3] There are also sector guides for businesses, education, local government, health, etc.[4] Guidance is also available on subjects including: bankrupcy, credit, criminal records, DVLA, electoral register, health, housing, identity theft, junk mail, marketing calls/texts/faxes, radio-frequency identification tags, schools/universities/colleges, spam emails, social networking and wi-fi security.[5]

[1]   See Wadham (2000) New LJ 1173 and 1236.
[2]   See eg the Code of Practice for Fire Brigades. Codes have been prepared by ACPO and the Association of Chief Probation Officers.
[3]   http://www.ico.gov.uk/for_organisations/data_protection/topic_guides.aspx.
[4]   http://www.ico.gov.uk/for_organisations/sector_guides.aspx.
[5]   See http://www.ico.gov.uk/for_the_public.aspx for links.

THE DATA PROTECTION PRINCIPLES

7.42   The principles which govern the holding etc of data are set out in DPA 1998, Sch 1, Part I and are to be interpreted in accordance with Part II of that Schedule. DPA 1998, s 4(4) places a duty on DCs to comply with the principles unless exempted from doing so. Schedule 1, Part I provides as follows:

'1   Personal data shall be processed fairly[1] and lawfully and, in particular, shall not be processed unless–
   (a)   at least one of the conditions in Schedule 2 is met, and
   (b)   in the case of sensitive personal data, at least one of the conditions in Schedule 3 is also met.
         As will be seen this principle has featured regularly in IC and tribunal reports.
2   Personal data shall be obtained only for one or more specified and lawful purposes, and shall not be further processed in any manner incompatible with that purpose or those purposes. Disclosure under FOIA does not have to be specified (para 7.109).
3   Personal data shall be adequate, relevant and not excessive in relation to the purpose or purposes for which they are processed.
4   Personal data shall be accurate and, where necessary, kept up to date.
5   Personal data processed for any purpose or purposes shall not be kept for longer than is necessary for that purpose or those purposes. This principle featured prominently in *Chief Constable of Humberside etc v IC* [2009] EWCA Civ 1079 where the Court of Appeal reversed a decison of the information tribunal in EA/2007/0096 (para 7.235).
6   Personal data shall be processed in accordance with the rights of data subjects under this Act.
7   Appropriate technical and organisational measures shall be taken against unauthorised or unlawful processing of personal data and against accidental loss or destruction of, or damage to, personal data. This principle has featured in numerous infamous cases involving

public and private DCs. Breaches of the principle led to reforms in the Criminal Justice and Immigration Act 2008, s 144 (DPA 1998, s 55); Data Protection (Monetary Penalties) Order 2010, SI 2010/910 and Coroners and Justice Act 2009, Part 8 and Sch 20 (paras 7.136 and 7.207 et seq below).

8   Personal data shall not be transferred to a country or territory outside the European Economic Area unless that country or territory ensures an adequate level of protection for the rights and freedoms of data subjects in relation to the processing of personal data.'

We saw above how special arrangements were made between the EU and USA regarding passenger information (para 7.4).

1   See the DPR's Annual Report for 1999, pp 58–66 for a report of an appeal to the tribunal concerning Midlands Electricity plc and processing unfairly in that the company was using information about customers without their consent: *Midlands Electricity plc v DPR* [1998–99] Info TLR 217. On blacklisting in employment see Employment Relations Act 1999 (Blacklist) Regulations 2010, SI 2010/493. Contravention of this last principle will be an offence and subject to the Commissioner's remedies. It should be noted, however, that there is no power for the Commissioner in the 1998 legislation to issue a transfer prohibition notice (TPN) preventing the transfer out of the UK as under the DPA 1984. In fact under the DPA 1984 only one TPN was issued by the DPR. And see 7.40 above on inspection of EU data-holding.

Interpretation of the principles

7.43   Under DPA 1998, Sch 1, Part II in relation to the first principle, when determining for the purposes of the first principle whether personal data was obtained fairly, regard is to be had to the method by which they were obtained, including in particular whether any person from whom they are obtained is deceived or misled as to the purpose(s) for which they are processed.

7.44   DPA 1998, Sch I, Part II, para 1(2) states that, subject to para 2 below, data are treated as obtained fairly under the first principle if they consist of information obtained from a person who:
(a)   is authorised by or under any enactment to supply it; or
(b)   is required to supply it by or under any enactment or by any convention or other instrument imposing an international obligation on the UK.

7.45   Any disclosure authorised by such statute, or required by such convention or instrument shall be disregarded in determining whether information was obtained fairly.

7.46   The DPC will need to consider all the circumstances behind the obtaining of information to assess whether it was obtained unfairly. Was there a full explanation by the user to the subject of why information was required and how it was to be used, in response to questions or otherwise? Could the subject reasonably have been expected to understand the explanation etc? Intended uses and disclosures should be revealed. The DPC has expressed the hope that codes of practice prepared by users will encourage the provision of full and helpful explanations to individuals.

7.47   DPA 1998, Sch I, Part II, para 2 states that, subject to para 3, for the purposes of the first principle in the case of data obtained from the data subject, data are not to be treated as processed fairly unless (a) the subject has information specified in para 3 (which states the identity of the DC or his representative, the purpose(s) or intended purpose(s) of processing or any further information which is necessary in the circumstances to allow processing to be fair) or (b) is provided with it, or it is made readily available to him 'so far as practicable' and in any other case, the DC ensures as far as practicable that before the relevant time or as soon as practicable after that time the data subject has, is provided with or has readily made available to him specified information (in sub-para 3). The sub-para spells out the relevant time. In relation to (b) above, where the provision of that information would involve a 'disproportionate effort' or the recording or disclosure of information is required by a legal provision binding on the DC except one imposed by contract the provisions in para 2(1)(b) do not apply. Other provisions may be added by the Secretary of State.

7.48   Special provisions apply to personal identifiers.

7.49   In relation to the second principle, DPA 1998, Sch I, Part II states that the purpose(s) for which personal data are obtained may be specified in a notice from the DC to the subject or in a notification given to the Commissioner under Part III of the DPA 1998. Regard is to be had to the purpose(s) for which personal data are intended to be processed by any person to whom they are disclosed in determining whether any disclosure of personal data is compatible with the purpose(s) for which the data were obtained.

7.50   In relation to the fourth principle, DPA 1998, Sch I, Part II sets out when the fourth principle is not to be regarded as contravened by reason of inaccuracy in personal data which accurately record information obtained by the DC from the subject or a third party ie the DC has taken reasonable steps to ensure the accuracy of the data having regard to the purpose(s) of obtaining and further processing the data, and the subject has notified the DC of their inaccuracy and the data indicate that fact.

7.51   In relation to the sixth principle, a person is to be regarded as contravening the sixth principle if, but only if, he contravenes provisions of ss 7, 10(1) and (3), 11(1), 12(1), (2)(b), (2)(a) or (3). These concern rights of access, processing for direct marketing and processing data for automated decision-taking.

7.52   In relation to the seventh principle, which concerns levels of security appropriate to the degrees of harm that might follow from the events in the seventh principle, regard shall be had to the nature of the data to be protected, the DC ensuring reliability of employees, ensuring reliability of data processors and forms for contracts for processing and stipulated terms ie compliance with the seventh principle.

7.53   As regards interpretation of the eighth principle, criteria are set out on adequate levels of protection for data transferred out of the UK and include the nature of the personal data. The criteria require that the level of protection is one which is adequate in all the circumstances of the case having particular regard to: the country or territory of origin of the information contained in the data; the country or territory of final destination of that information; the purposes for which and period during which the data are intended to be processed; the law in force on the country or territory in question; international obligations of that country or territory; any relevant codes of conduct or other enforceable rules in that country or territory; and any security measures taken in respect of the data in that country or territory.

Conditions for processing

7.54 DPA 1998, Sch 2 sets out conditions relevant for the purpose of the first principle. These must be complied with to ensure compliance with the first principle. The conditions are that the subject either has to give his consent to the processing; or the processing is necessary for a variety of grounds. These include situations where processing is necessary[1] for the performances of a contract to which the data subject (DS) is a party, for compliance with legal obligations other than a contract to which the DC is subject, to meet the vital interests of the DS, for the administration of justice, or for statutory, Crown, Ministerial or departmental functions etc. Last of all processing is necessary for the purposes of the legitimate interests of the DC or third parties or parties to whom the data are disclosed except where prejudicial to the DS.[2] This condition is very important in relation to FOIA requests for personal data belonging to another individual, as will be explained. One of the above needs to be satisfied for the lawful processing of personal data. It is an extensive list and needs to be consulted.

[1] See *A-G v Walker* 3 Ex 242: 'necessary' includes that which is 'reasonably required or legally ancillary to the accomplishment of specified purposes'. 'Necessary' is interpreted to mean unavoidable.
[2] See *R v Chief Constable of Essex ex p Ellis* [2003] EWHC 1321 and the Offender Naming Scheme: photographs of convicted criminals were displayed in areas of the commission of the crime. The High Court refused to award a declaration that the scheme was disproportionate and unlawful under Art 8 ECHR and HRA 1998: see para 1.277, note 1 above.

7.55 DPA 1998, Sch 3 sets out conditions for the first principle and sensitive personal data (and see SI 2000/417). Sensitive personal data were explained above (para 7.30). The subject has to give his *explicit* consent to the processing; or processing is necessary for a variety of reasons or is carried out for 'legitimate activities'. These include: the purposes of exercising or performing any right or obligation which is conferred or imposed by law on the data controller in connection with employment; the processing is necessary (a) in order to protect the vital interests of the data subject or another person, in a case where—(i) consent cannot be given by or on behalf of the data subject, or (ii) the data controller cannot reasonably be expected to obtain the consent of the data subject, or (b) in order to protect the vital interests of another person, in a case where consent by or on behalf of the data subject has been unreasonably withheld; the processing (a) is carried out in the course of its legitimate activities by any body or association which—(i) is not established or conducted for profit, and (ii) exists for political, philosophical, religious or trade-union purposes, (b) is carried out with appropriate safeguards for the rights and freedoms of data subjects, (c) relates only to individuals who either are members of the body or association or have regular contact with it in connection with its purposes, and (d) does not involve disclosure of the personal data to a third party without the consent of the data subject. The information contained in the personal data has been made public as a result of steps deliberately taken by the data subject. Further conditions include legal advice and legal rights, medical treatment, anti-fraud investigations, medical treatment, assessing equal treatment among different racial or ethnic groups and so on. There is considerable power of modification by the Secretary of State and the Secretary of State is given power by order to provide for additional safeguards. This is an extensive list.

7.56 DPA 1998, Sch 4 describes case where the eighth principle does not apply. It covers consent by the subject to transfer and necessary transfers.

7.57 DPA 1998, s 33 makes provision for data processed for 'research purposes' which includes statistical or historical purposes. Such data are exempt from certain of the data protection principles. The purpose of the research processing must not be in the form of measures or decisions targeted at particular individuals and the processing does not cause harm or distress. Where the 'relevant conditions' are complied with, processing for the above purposes is exempt from the second and fifth data protection principles, and they are exempt from s 7 (access rights). The research must be made available through results in a way which does not identify individuals.

ASSESSMENT NOTICES UNDER CORONERS AND JUSTICE ACT 2009, PART 8, S 173 AND SCH 20

7.58 The Coroners and Justice Act 2009, s 173 adds a new s 41A to the DPA 1998 in relation to assessment notices made by the IC. It is easiest simply to set out the section. The Commissioner may serve a data controller within sub-section (2) with a notice (in this Act referred to as an 'assessment notice') for the purpose of enabling the Commissioner to determine whether the data controller has complied or is complying with the data protection principles. The provisions apply to government departments, and to PAs and 'persons of a description' in both cases where designated by order of the Secretary of State.

'(2) A data controller is within this subsection if the data controller is—
(a) a government department,
(b) a public authority designated for the purposes of this section by an order made by the Secretary of State, or
(c) a person of a description designated for the purposes of this section by such an order.

(3) An assessment notice is a notice which requires the data controller to do all or any of the following—
(a) permit the Commissioner to enter any specified premises;

(b) direct the Commissioner to any documents on the premises that are of a specified description;

(c) assist the Commissioner to view any information of a specified description that is capable of being viewed using equipment on the premises;

(d) comply with any request from the Commissioner for—
  (i) a copy of any of the documents to which the Commissioner is directed;
  (ii) a copy (in such form as may be requested) of any of the information which the Commissioner is assisted to view;

(e) direct the Commissioner to any equipment or other material on the premises which is of a specified description;

(f) permit the Commissioner to inspect or examine any of the documents, information, equipment or material to which the Commissioner is directed or which the Commissioner is assisted to view;

(g) permit the Commissioner to observe the processing of any personal data that takes place on the premises;

(h) make available for interview by the Commissioner a specified number of persons of a specified description who process personal data on behalf of the data controller (or such number as are willing to be interviewed).

(4) In subsection (3) references to the Commissioner include references to the Commissioner's officers and staff.

(5) An assessment notice must, in relation to each requirement imposed by the notice, specify—
(a) the time at which the requirement is to be complied with, or
(b) the period during which the requirement is to be complied with.

(6) An assessment notice must also contain particulars of the rights of appeal conferred by section 48.

(7) The Commissioner may cancel an assessment notice by written notice to the data controller on whom it was served.

(8) Where a public authority has been designated (as a public authority) by an order under subsection (2)(b) the Secretary of State must reconsider, at intervals of no greater than 5 years, whether it continues to be appropriate for the authority to be designated.

(9) The Secretary of State may not make an order under subsection (2)(c) which designates a description of persons unless—
(a) the Commissioner has made a recommendation that the description be designated, and
(b) the Secretary of State has consulted—
  (i) such persons as appear to the Secretary of State to represent the interests of those that meet the description;
  (ii) such other persons as the Secretary of State considers appropriate.

(10) The Secretary of State may not make an order under subsection (2)(c), and the Commissioner may not make a recommendation under subsection (9)(a), unless the Secretary of State or (as the case may be) the

Commissioner is satisfied that it is necessary for the description of persons in question to be designated having regard to—

(a)   the nature and quantity of data under the control of such persons, and

(b)   any damage or distress which may be caused by a contravention by such persons of the data protection principles.

(11) Where a description of persons has been designated by an order under subsection (2)(c) the Secretary of State must reconsider, at intervals of no greater than 5 years, whether it continues to be necessary for the description to be designated having regard to the matters mentioned in subsection (10).

(12) In this section—

"public authority" includes any body, office-holder or other person in respect of which—

(a)   an order may be made under section 4 or 5 of the Freedom of Information Act 2000, or

(b)   an order may be made under section 4 or 5 of the Freedom of Information (Scotland) Act 2002;

"specified" means specified in an assessment notice.'

7.59   DPA 1998, s 41B: Assessment notices: limitations

'(1) A time specified in an assessment notice under section 41A(5) in relation to a requirement must not fall, and a period so specified must not begin, before the end of the period within which an appeal can be brought against the notice, and if such an appeal is brought the requirement need not be complied with pending the determination or withdrawal of the appeal.

(2) If by reason of special circumstances the Commissioner considers that it is necessary for the data controller to comply with a requirement in an assessment notice as a matter of urgency, the Commissioner may include in the notice a statement to that effect and a statement of the reasons for that conclusion; and in that event subsection (1) applies in relation to the requirement as if for the words from "within" to the end there were substituted "of 7 days beginning with the day on which the notice is served".

(3) A requirement imposed by an assessment notice does not have effect in so far as compliance with it would result in the disclosure of—

(a)   any communication between a professional legal adviser and the adviser's client in connection with the giving of legal advice with respect to the client's obligations, liabilities or rights under this Act, or

(b)   any communication between a professional legal adviser and the adviser's client, or between such an adviser or the adviser's client and any other person, made in connection with or in contemplation of proceedings under or arising out of this Act (including proceedings before the Tribunal) and for the purposes of such proceedings.

(4) In subsection (3) references to the client of a professional legal adviser include references to any person representing such a client.

(5) Nothing in section 41A authorises the Commissioner to serve an assessment notice on—

(a) a judge,

(b) a body specified in section 23(3) of the Freedom of Information Act 2000 (bodies dealing with security matters) [see para 1.117 et seq], or

(c) the Office for Standards in Education, Children's Services and Skills in so far as it is a data controller in respect of information processed for the purposes of functions exercisable by Her Majesty's Chief Inspector of Eduction, Children's Services and Skills by virtue of section 5(1)(a) of the Care Standards Act 2000.

(6) In this section "judge" includes —

(a) a justice of the peace (or, in Northern Ireland, a lay magistrate),

(b) a member of a tribunal, and

(c) a clerk or other officer entitled to exercise the jurisdiction of a court or tribunal;

and in this subsection "tribunal" means any tribunal in which legal proceedings may be brought.

7.60 DPA 1998, s 41C: Code of practice about assessment notices

(1) The Commissioner must prepare and issue a code of practice as to the manner in which the Commissioner's functions under and in connection with section 41A are to be exercised.

(2) The code must in particular—

(a) specify factors to be considered in determining whether to serve an assessment notice on a data controller;

(b) specify descriptions of documents and information that—

(i) are not to be examined or inspected in pursuance of an assessment notice, or

(ii) are to be so examined or inspected only by persons of a description specified in the code;

(c) deal with the nature of inspections and examinations carried out in pursuance of an assessment notice;

(d) deal with the nature of interviews carried out in pursuance of an assessment notice;

(e) deal with the preparation, issuing and publication by the Commissioner of assessment reports in respect of data controllers that have been served with assessment notices.

(3) The provisions of the code made by virtue of subsection (2)(b) must, in particular, include provisions that relate to—

(a) documents and information concerning an individual's physical or mental health;

(b) documents and information concerning the provision of social care for an individual.

(4) An assessment report is a report which contains—

(a) a determination as to whether a data controller has complied or is complying with the data protection principles,

(b) recommendations as to any steps which the data controller ought to take, or refrain from taking, to ensure compliance with any of those principles, and

(c) such other matters as are specified in the code.

(5) The Commissioner may alter or replace the code.

(6) If the code is altered or replaced, the Commissioner must issue the altered or replacement code.

(7) The Commissioner may not issue the code (or an altered or replacement code) without the approval of the Secretary of State [see para 7.61 below].

(8) The Commissioner must arrange for the publication of the code (and any altered or replacement code) issued under this section in such form and manner as the Commissioner considers appropriate.

(9) In this section "social care" has the same meaning as in Part 1 of the Health and Social Care Act 2008 (see section 9(3) of that Act)."

7.61 The Protection of Freedoms Bill 2011 removes the requirement in s 41C that guidance issued by the IC has to be approved by the Secretary of State.

RIGHTS OF DATA SUBJECTS AND OTHERS

7.62 These rights are contained in DPA 1998, Part II (ss 7–15).[1] Basically, an individual is entitled after making a request in writing and paying the prescribed fee, to be informed by any data controller whether personal data of which that individual is the data subject are being processed by or on behalf of that data controller (s 7(1)(a)). If so, then they shall be given by the DC a description of:

(a) personal data of which that data is the data subject;

(b) the purposes for which they are being or are to be processed; and

(c) recipients or classes of recipient to whom they are entitled to be disclosed (s 7(1)(b)).

[1] http://www.ico.gov.uk/for_the_public.aspx.

7.63 The subject is entitled to have communicated to them in an intelligible form:

(a) the information constituting any personal data of which that individual is the data subject (see s 8(2)); and

(b) any information available to the DC as to the source of those data,

and the subject is entitled to know the logic involved in decision-making (although this will not cover a trade secret) where the data is processed automatically and is likely to form the sole basis for any decision significantly affecting the subject such as work performance, credit-worthiness, reliability or conduct (s 7(1)(d)).

7.64 A DC is not obliged to comply with the request under this section unless the DC is supplied with such information as they may reasonably require in order to be satisfied as to the identity of the requester and to locate information which that person seeks.[1] Where disclosure to a requester would allow disclosure of information about another individual who can be identified from that information, the DC does not have to comply unless the other person consents to that disclosure to the requester or it is reasonable in all the circumstances to comply with the request without consent.[2] Another individual can be identified from the information being disclosed 'if he can be identified from that information, or from that and any other information which, in the reasonable belief of the DC, is likely to be in, or come into, the possession of the data subject making the request' (s 8(7)). These provisions were discussed in *Durant v FSA* (paras 7.15 above). The balancing process involved in DPA 1998, s 7(4)–(6) and s 8(7) between the rights of the DS and a third party only come into play if the information relating to the other person necessarily forms a part of the personal data of the data subject. A presumption of non-disclosure without the other party's consent applies unless the DC considers disclosure reasonable in all the circumstances (s 7(4)). It must be *reasonable* for the DC to comply with a request for information notwithstanding that it contains information about another. This seems to place the onus of justifying reasonableness on the DC. DPA 1998, s 7(6) highlights factors that a DC should consider in assessing what is 'reasonable': eg any duty of confidentiality owed to a third party, steps taken by the DC to obtain consent from the third party, the third party's capability to give consent and any express refusal of consent by the third party.

[1] Where personal data added by the FOIA 2000 is requested the onus on the requester to provide additional identifying criteria is greater (see paras 7.11 et seq above).
[2] See DPA 1998, s 7(5) on the duty of supplying redacted information where the identity of the third party can be omitted.

7.65 Paras 56 and 57 of *Durant* have interesting examples of situations where the FSA asked other individuals whether they might disclose the personal data with their names on it in an unredacted form and where in other cases the FSA exercised its discretion to disclose. Where information was not disclosed the Court of Appeal held that it was the DC who was the primary decision-maker on the merits under the DPA 1998 and not the courts, whose function was restricted to one of review. Fundamental rights of individuals are present in this balancing and a court should display an 'anxious scrutiny' of the legitimate interests involved, but a detailed examination of documents under DPA 1998, s 15(2) was not called for unless a judge's reasoning on the issue *and* the factual issues raised on appeal to the Court of Appeal demand it. The DS's right to privacy may have a powerful impact where the third party is going to act on the information to the DS's disadvantage (s 7(1)(b)(iii)) and obligations of confidentiality to a third party may appear weaker. Likewise, if the third party has supplied information which is inaccurate, that may well have a bearing on the question (*Durant*, para 66).

7.66 A request must be complied with promptly and in any event before the end of the prescribed period beginning with the relevant day. The prescribed period is 40 days or such other period as may be prescribed by regulations. A court may order a DC to comply with the request (DPA 1998, s 7(9)). In *Durant*, the Court of Appeal seemed to suggest that seeking access to correct errors might be a good reason to order compliance, but seeking information for an ulterior motive may not. Regulations under s 8 may state that, if a DC receives a request for information under s 7(1), he must also supply other pieces of information described in s 7(1) as well. There are safeguards against repetitious requests. Data supplied must be that held at the time the request is received subject to any deletions or amendments between that time and the time of supply that were going to be made regardless of the request. Section 9 contains modifications to s 7 requests where the DC is a credit reference bureau and covers requests under Consumer Credit Act 1974, s 159.

7.67 DPA 1998, s 10 provides a right to the DS to give a notice to a DC requiring the DC at the end of a period which is reasonable in the circumstances to cease, or not to begin, processing etc data of which the DS is the subject where the processing etc is likely to cause or is causing substantial damage or substantial distress to him or to another which is or would be unwarranted. This provision does not apply where any of the conditions in DPA 1998, Sch 2, paras 1–4 is met or in cases prescribed by regulations. Within 21 days of receipt of the written notice, the DC must give the person sending the notice their own written notice stating that he has complied or intends to comply with the DS notice or stating reasons why the DC regards the notice as unjustified and the extent to which he intends to comply with it. The court may take such steps as it thinks fit to ensure compliance with a notice served on a DC where there is a failure to comply.

7.68 DPA 1998, s 11 confers a right on an individual to prevent or to cease processing for the purposes of direct marketing by serving a written notice and the court may take such steps as it sees fit to enforce the notice where satisfied that the DC has failed to comply. 'Direct marketing' means the communication (by whatever means) of any advertising or marketing material which is directed to particular individuals (s 11(3)).[1]

[1] See the discussion in *R (Robertson) v Wakefield MDC* [2001] EWHC Admin 915, [2002] QB 1052 and *R (Robertson) v Secretary of State* [2003] EWHC 1760 at para 7.221, note 2 below on the sale of data on the electoral register to commercial bodies. There was an interesting discussion of s 11. There are now two versions of the register: a full version and an edited version but the provisions are convoluted: see http://www.ico.gov.uk/for_the_public/topic_specific_guides/electoral_register.aspx. A controversy arose in June 2011 concerning the sale of insurance personal data details to intermediaries to sell on to solicitors to encourage personal injury claims.

7.69 DPA 1998, s 12 deals with the individual's right to prevent decisions taken by the DC which significantly affect that individual being based solely on the processing by automatic means of personal data in respect of which that individual is the DS. This involves evaluations of the subject's performance at work, creditworthiness, reliability or conduct. These matters are specifically referred to but are not exclusive. It has been pointed out that under the DPA 1984, such processing was 'effectively controlled'[1] and although widely known in relation to credit-worthiness, less known but increasing use of psychometric testing for employment decisions is covered.[2] The individual has the right where such a decision has been made by such processing to require the DC to reconsider or take a new decision 'otherwise than on that basis'. This may be enforced by the court. There are time limits of 21 days from receipt of the notice to set out the steps taken by the DC to comply with the DS notice. These provisions do not apply to exempt decisions. These exemptions cover decisions as specified which satisfy certain conditions or are otherwise prescribed by regulations. The specified conditions are those decisions relating to the entering or performing of a contract with the DS, those authorised or required by any enactment, and the effect of the decision is to grant a request of the DS, or steps have been taken to safeguard the legitimate interests of the DS, eg by allowing representations to be made.

1   *Equifax Europe Ltd v DPR* (unreported, 1992, Data Protection Tribunal).
2   Charlesworth *Data Protection Act 1998 Current Law* ch 29, 29–21 (1998).

7.70   Individuals who suffer damage by reason of any contravention by a DC of any of the requirements of the DPA 1998 are entitled to compensation from the DC for that damage (s 13). This is much broader than the right under the DPA 1984. The Act further provides that distress by reason of any contravention by a DC of any of the requirements of this Act is also compensable by the DC if the individual suffers damage by reason of the contravention, or the contravention relates to the processing of personal data for the special purposes in which case 'distress' is sufficient in itself for compensation without proof of damage.[1] A defence is available to a DC that he took such care as was reasonable in all the circumstances to comply.

1   See *Douglas v Hello! (No 3)* [2003] 3 All ER 996, and a minimal award under DPA 1998, s 13, at para 239 on the facts. See paras 7.117 et seq and 7.192 et seq below.

7.71   Where a court is satisfied on the application of a DS that personal data of which the applicant is the subject are inaccurate, the court may order the DC to rectify, block,[1] erase or destroy those data and any other personal data in respect of which he is the DC and which contain an expression of opinion which appears to the court to be based on the inaccurate data. This applies whether or not data accurately record information received from the DS or a third party. Where it does accurately record such information and DPA 1998, Sch 1, Part II, para 7 is satisfied[2] then instead of making the above order the court may require the data to be supplemented by such statement of the true facts relating to the matters dealt with by the data as the court may approve (s 14(2)(a)). Where any provisions in para 7 is not complied with it may make such an order to secure compliance with or without the above statement. Courts may also take steps to prevent further contraventions of the Act. DCs may also be required to notify third parties to whom they have passed inaccurate personal data, where it considers it reasonably practicable (ie the extent of the numbers involved (s 14(6)), of any rectification etc.

1   'Blocking' is not defined. It seems to suggest that data is made inaccessible although it may be held: see R Jay and A Hamilton *Data Protection Law and Practice* (2007) paras 1–14, 20–15 and 17–15.
2   This concerns the fourth principle, see above.

7.72 The jurisdiction is exercised by the High Court or county court in England and Wales and the Court of Session and sheriff court in Scotland. The court has wide powers of inspection but not of disclosure to applicants pending the determination of that question in the applicant's favour.

Exemptions

7.73 The DPA 1998 is a comprehensive code but is subject to exemptions contained in DPA 1998, Part IV, which should be read in conjunction with Sch 7. The Secretary of State also has power to make additional exemptions under s 38, although wider exemption-making powers were removed from the Bill in the Lords.

7.74 DPA 1998, s 27 specifies two basic provisions from which personal data may be exempted: subject information provisions and the non-disclosure provisions. Other provisions may be exempted so each exemption must be examined closely. The first exemption dealing with national security illustrates an exemption with a variety of rights and provisions making it very close to an exclusion from DPA 1998.

SUBJECT INFORMATION PROVISIONS

7.75 These contain two central features. If this exemption applies, the processing of data is exempted from the following. First, an exemption from the requirement that data may only be treated as processed fairly when certain safeguards are followed – disclosure to the DS of the DC's identity or that of his representative; the purposes for which the data are to be processed; and any such information as would be required to make the processing fair. Under the exemption the DC will not have to provide this information where the DS has supplied the data. Where the DS did not supply the data, the information does not have to be supplied to the DS before the data are processed or disclosed to a third party (DPA 1998, Sch 1, Part II, para 2). Secondly, an exemption from the provision that the DS has the right of access to the personal data under s 7.

THE NON-DISCLOSURE PROVISIONS

7.76 These have three basic features from which data may be exempt 'to the extent to which they are inconsistent with the disclosure in question' (DPA 1998, s 27(3) ie, the purpose of a disclosure would be undermined by maintenance of the relevant principles or safeguards): from the fair processing of data in the first principle, except to the extent to which processing requires compliance with the conditions in Schs 2 and 3 (above: concerning conditions that are relevant for the first principle of fair and lawful processing regarding consent or processing is necessary for specified purposes); that any disclosure of personal data must take place in conformity with the second to fifth principles (see above); and that any disclosure of personal data must take account of the right of the DS to object to processing likely to cause damage or distress, the right of the DS to have inaccurate personal data of which he is the subject rectified etc (see above), and to have third parties to whom the data have been notified informed of that rectification etc.

7.77 Where either of these phrases is used to describe an exemption, the above items will be exempt in relevant disclosures covering those phrases. Other provisions of the Act may also be exempted as explained below.

7.78 The specific exemptions cover the following subject areas.

National security

7.79 By virtue of DPA 1998, s 28, national security is exempted from the data protection principles, Parts II (rights of DS), III (notification) and V (enforcement, and see s 28(11)), and s 55 which concerns criminal offences of unlawfully obtaining etc personal data. Its exemption is in fact an exclusion from the Act where all the exemptions apply. A certificate signed by a Minister of the Crown stating that the exemption from all or any of the above provisions 'is or at any time' was required for national security shall be conclusive evidence of that fact. The certificate under s 28(2) may identify the personal data to which it applies by means of a general description and may have prospective effect. The person affected by the certificate may appeal to the Information Tribunal and that body, applying the principles applied by a court on an application for judicial review, may allow the appeal and quash the certificate if it finds that the Minister did not have reasonable grounds for issuing the certificate. One should note the similarity to FOIA 2000, ss 23(2) and 24(3) which were discussed in ch 1. It should be noted how circumscribed the powers of the Tribunal are.[1] However, it is not true to say, as the DPR did in the past, that the courts have no power to question such a certificate. Their powers are clearly circumscribed since the statute stipulates that the certificate is 'conclusive evidence' of the fact that data is exempt for the purpose of safeguarding national security. Recent pronouncements by the courts that a bare assertion of national security by the executive is not sufficient to bar judicial inquiry are not to the point as the certificate is 'conclusive' evidence. However, the certificate must be related to the statutory purpose; and it must not bear illegality upon its forehead, ie, bad faith, abuse of process or ulterior intent. As the facts are completely within the control of the executive, judicial intervention is unlikely except in the most blatant of cases. Nor should it be overlooked that national security has been afforded a more expansive meaning in rulings of the higher courts (para 1.124 above). However, the Information Tribunal has ruled a certificate under DPA 1998, s 28(5) was invalid where, in response to the claimant's request for access to his personal data under s 7, the security service provided non-committal replies 'neither confirming nor denying' (NCND) their processing of such data. Were the certificate valid, such replies would have been authorised. The Home Secretary considered that there were reasonable grounds for the certificate because this was necessary to safeguard national security. The claimant, supported by the Information

Commissioner, accepted that the NCND response would be justified if s 7(1) (a) requests for information made to the service were responded to by a lawful determination that a positive response would be harmful to national security. 'The validity of the Certificate in question was disputed ... on the ground that its terms were wide enough to relieve the Service from any obligation to decide whether or not national security would be harmed by a positive response to the particular request.' Replying in such wide terms would not be justified where a positive response would not be harmful to national security. The Tribunal made no findings on the merits of the individual case nor did it investigate whether the Service held any information on the subject. But it concluded, by applying principles applicable to judicial review, that the Minister did not have reasonable grounds for issuing the Certificate which had the unnecessarily wide effect of allowing the service not to respond to a request regardless of whether or not national security would be harmed by a positive response in the particular case. The Certificate was drafted with the purposes for which and circumstances in which data were acquired or are held 'rather than the consequences for national security if data were released or their existence acknowledged at the time of the request' (para 15).[2] In *Kennedy v UK* the Strasbourg court ruled that there had been no breaches of ECHR, arts 6, 8 or 13 by the Investigatory Powers Tribunal when it simply stated that no determination had been made in favour of Kennedy's complaints about processing of data by MI5 and GCHQ. The tribunal sat in private.[3]

[1] See SI 2000/206 and SI 2000/731.
[2] *Norman Baker MP v Secretary of State for the Home Department* [2001] UKHRR 1275. See also *R (Secretary of State for the Home Department) v IC* [2006] EWHC 2958 (Admin).
[3] *Kennedy v UK* [2010] ECHR 26839/05. Cf *Uzukauskas v Lithuania* [2010] ECHR 1060.

7.80 Any other parties may appeal to the Upper Tribunal against the alleged effects of a certificate in relation to general descriptions of data applying to personal data. The Tribunal may determine that the certificate does not so apply. The power to issue a certificate must be exercised by a member of the Cabinet or Attorney General or Lord Advocate (see also s 28(8) and (9)).

7.81 Relevant principles under Art 8 were discussed in *Segerstendt-Wiberg v Sweden* [2007] EHRR 2 by the ECtHR (see para 2.253 above).

Crime and tax

7.82 Where under DPA 1998, s 29 data are processed for the purpose of:
(a) the prevention or detection of crime;
(b) the apprehension or prosecution of offenders; and
(c) the assessment or collection of any tax or duty or of any imposition of a similar nature,

then the data are exempt essentially from the subject information provisions and the non-disclosure provisions. It also allows for the disclosure of such data to bodies like the police performing their statutory functions so that they can process it free from the subject access provisions. There is also a provision which allows government departments, local authorities or any other authority administering housing benefit or council tax benefit to have the benefit of an exemption from s 7 where they have classified personal information with a view to assessing risk assessments of DSs from the perspective of tax or duty assessment or collection, or preventing or detecting crime or apprehending or prosecuting offenders where the offence consists of unlawful claims or unlawful applications for payments out of public funds.

Health, education and social work

7.83 DPA 1998, s 30 covers these items. The Secretary of State may by order exempt from the subject information provisions, or modify those provisions in relation personal data consisting of information as to the physical or mental health or condition of the DS. Similar provisions may be made covering school pupils including past pupils. Exemptions may also cover processing of personal data for social work 'in relation to the data subject or other individuals conducted by government departments, local authorities or voluntary bodies'. These are examined below (para 7.99).

Listed relevant functions of a regulatory nature under s 31

7.84 These personal data may also be exempted from the subject information provisions. These include: seeking to protect members of the public against financial loss due to dishonesty, malpractice or other seriously improper conduct by or unfitness or incompetence of persons in banking, insurance, investment or other financial services or in the management of corporate bodies. Bankrupts and professional persons are also included. Further provisions cover protecting charities against misconduct; protecting the property of charities; securing the health, safety and welfare of persons at work. Relevant functions include: any statutory function; any function of the Crown, Minister of the Crown, government department or 'any other function which is of a public nature and is exercised in the public interest' (DPA 1998, s 31(3)(c)). The various duties and powers of public sector ombudsmen may also be exempt from the subject information provisions in relation to personal data acquired by them. The Director General of Fair Trading is likewise exempt in relation to personal data and functions seeking to protect the public and to regulate competition in the form of both agreements and abuses of dominant position.[1]

---

[1]   And see Financial Services and Markets Act 2000, s 233.

Exemptions concerning the 'special purposes'

7.85 It will be recalled that special purposes were mentioned in DPA 1998, s 3 and covered the use of personal data for journalism, literary purposes and artistic purposes. Personal data processed only for special purposes are exempt from any provision to which this subsection (s 32(1)) relates where the processing is undertaken with a view to the publication (s 32(6)) by any person of any journalistic, literary or artistic material. This provision was included in order to give protection to freedom of expression. The DC has to 'reasonably believe' that having regard in particular to the special importance of the public interest in freedom of expression, publication would be in the public interest. The DC has also to reasonably believe in all the circumstances that compliance with the provision is incompatible with the special purposes. The provisions for which there are exemptions are the data protection principles excepting the seventh (security); s 7 (right of access); s 10 (right to prevent processing likely to cause damage or distress); s 12 (rights in relation to automated decision-making); s 14(1)–(3) (rights to rectification, blocking etc). In assessing whether the belief of the DC in the publication in the public interest is a reasonable one regard may be had to compliance with any code of practice which is relevant to the publication in question and is designated by order of the Secretary of State for the purposes of this section. Section 32(4) provides a means of avoiding a prior restraint injunction against impending publication where proceedings are brought against a DC under various provisions[1] and it is claimed or appears to the court that data in question are being processed only for the special purposes and with a view to publication by any person of any journalistic etc material which, at the time 24 hours immediately before the relevant time (and relevant time means at any time in the proceedings) had not previously been published by the data controller. The court shall stay proceedings until either of the following is met: that the Commissioner makes a determination under s 45 – that a DC is not processing data for any journalistic purposes – which takes effect (as to special purposes see below); or where proceedings were stayed on the making of a claim, the claim was withdrawn.

[1] DPA 1998, ss 7(9), 10(4), 12(8) or 14 or by virtue of s 13.

7.86 In *Campbell v MGN Ltd*, it was held that DPA 1998, s 32 applied not only to the period before publication, but also protected journalists in relation to proceedings for infringement once publication had taken place.[1] 'A conclusion to the contrary would render the exemption purposeless' (paras 107–127). It was illogical, the court ruled, (as the first instance judgment had) to exempt the DC from the obligation, prior to publication, to comply with provisions which he reasonably believed to be incompatible with journalism, but to leave him exposed to a claim for compensation the moment that the data had been published. Section 32 therefore also exempted the 'publication' (paras 128–130). This aspect of the Court of Appeal's judgment concerning s 32 was *not* overruled by the House of Lords on appeal.[2]

[1] [2002] EWCA Civ 1373, [2003] 1 All ER 224 (CA).
[2] The House of Lords concentrated on the confidentiality rulings: [2004] 2 All ER 995; for the first instance judgment on the DPA aspects holding that s 32 applied *only* before publication: [2002] EWHC 499 (QBD).

7.87 Section 12 of the HRA 1998 also provides protection for freedom of speech, journalism, artistic and literary endeavours. This was discussed in chapter 2 (paras 2.257 et seq above).

Research

7.88 Data may also be exempt for certain research purposes including statistical and historical research (s 33). This has been covered already (see para 7.57).

Statutory duty to publish

7.89 Where data consist of any information which the DC is obliged to make available to the public by or under any enactment, which includes an 'enactment passed under the DPA' (s 70(1)) and whether by publication, inspection or otherwise and whether free or by charge, DPA 1998, s 34 provides it is exempt from the subject information provisions, the non-disclosure provisions and the fourth data protection principle and s 14(1)–(3). FOIA 2000 is not such an enactment: access to personal data/documents under the FOIA 2000 is subject to an absolute exemption from the provisions of the FOIA 2000 in the case of access by data subjects (paras 7.10 et seq above). The position of third-party requesters for data on another is dealt with below (para 7.107).

Disclosure required by legal duty

7.90 Personal data are also exempt from the non-disclosure provisions where the disclosure is required by or under any enactment, any rule of law or court order (DPA 1998, s 35). This would cover public interest immunity (para 10.64 below) although the court may redact personal confidential information. The area of competition law may pose considerable difficulties where personal information is concerned. In *France Telecom*, the Cour de Cassation (top civil court in France) ruled that France Telecom (FT) had to provide its directory of unlisted telephone numbers to a rival marketing services' company notwithstanding FT's data protection concerns.[1] They are also similarly exempt where disclosure is necessary for the purposes of or in connection with any legal proceedings (including prospective legal proceedings) or for the purpose of obtaining legal advice.

[1] *France Telecom v Lectiel* Judgment No 2030, CC, Chambre Comm 4 December 2001. Doubtless, undertakings of confidentiality may have to be given but even these may not prove inviolable. See further on information dissemination *RTE v Commission* Cases C-241 and 242/91 P [1995] ECR I-743.

Personal and family affairs

7.91 Where data are processed by an individual only for the purposes of that individual's personal, family or household affairs (including recreational purposes) they are exempt (DPA 1998, s 36) from the data protection principles and the provisions of Parts II and III (rights of data subjects and notification). Where, however, data are entered on the internet, this exemption does not apply (see *Lindqvist*: para 7.5 above).

Additional exemptions

7.92 We have already noted that DPA 1998, s 38 confers powers on the Secretary of State to make additional exemptions. A power to make additional exemptions in the FOI Bill was removed from the Bill.

7.93 DPA 1998, Sch 7 contains further miscellaneous exemptions, as follows.

Confidential references

7.94 Where confidential references are given by the DC, they are exempt from s 7 if given for: education, training, employment of the DS including prospective; appointments to an office; or provision of any service by the DS. Where a DC is the prospective employer who holds the reference and the reference has come from another, the wording in para 1 does not exempt that reference because it has not been *given by the DC*. The identity of the referee may be protected, however, and this may justify non-subject access under s 7(4)–(6) (para 7.64 above).

Armed forces

7.95 Where disclosure of personal data would be likely to compromise the combat effectiveness of any of the armed forces of the Crown they are exempt from the subject information provisions (Sch 7, para 2).

Judicial appointments

7.96 Personal data processed for assessing suitability for judicial appointments including QCs and conferring any honour by the Crown are exempt from the subject information provisions (Sch 7, para 3).

Crown employment

7.97 Personal data processed for the purposes of Crown employment and appointments to offices by the Crown, Ministers or Northern Ireland departments may be exempted by order from the Secretary of State from the subject information provisions (Sch 7, para 4).

Management forecasts, corporate finance, negotiations, examination marks, etc

7.98 Personal data used for management forecasts or planning to assist in business or other activity are exempt from the subject information provisions and corporate finance are exempt from the subject information provisions where the application of those provisions would be likely, or would have, respectively specified consequences. Further exemptions cover: prejudicing negotiations; examination marks,[1] examination scripts; data which could be subject to a claim of legal professional privilege or where disclosure would lead to self incrimination for an offence other than one under the DPA 1998.

¹   This provision is to prevent access before results are published. Some universities have stopped
    publication of class lists unless those included have consented to prevent allegations of substantial
    damage or distress if the DS's whereabouts were revealed.

Data Protection (Subject Access Modification) Orders

7.99   A series of access modification orders has been approved by Parliament.
These cover: the Data Protection (Miscellaneous Subject Access Exemptions)
Order 2000, SI 2000/419, as amended; the Data Protection (Subject Access
Modification) (Social Work) Order 2000, SI 2000/415; the Data Protection
(Subject Access Modification) (Social Work) (Amendment) Order 2011,
SI 2011/1034; the Data Protection (Subject Access Modification) (Education)
Order 2000, SI 2000/414; and the Data Protection (Subject Access Modification)
(Health) Order 2000, SI 2000/413. To these can be added the Data Protection
(Subject Access Modification) (Social Work) (Amendment) Order 2005,
SI 2005/467, which provides exemptions in relation to children's guardians, as
well as data processed by the Children and Family Court Advisory and Support
Service.

7.100   The Data Protection (Subject Access Modification) (Health) Order 2000,
SI 2000/413 applies to personal data consisting of information as to the physical
or mental health or condition of the of the data subject. This does not apply to
data exempted from DPA 1998, s 7 by an order made under s 38(1) of the Act.
Data falling within s 4(2) are exempt from the subject information provisions.
This concerns data processed by a court and consisting of information supplied
in a report or other evidence given to the court by a local authority or other body
listed in the regulation.¹ Personal data are exempt from s 7 in any case to the
extent to which the application of that section would be likely to cause serious
harm to the physical or mental health or condition of the data subject or any
other person (Art 5(1)). A DC who is not a health professional (Art 2(a), (b)) shall
not withhold information constituting data to which this order applies on the
ground that the exemption in Art 5(1) applies with respect to the information,
unless the DC has first consulted the person who appears to the DC to be the
appropriate health professional on the question of whether or not the exemption
in Art 5(1) applies to the information. Under Art 7(1) this article does not apply
where the data has, before the request, been the subject of a written opinion
from the appropriate health professional that the exemption in Art 5(1) applies
to all the information which is the subject of the request. This in turn does not
apply where the opinion was obtained six months before the relevant day (DPA
1998, s 7(10)) or was obtained within that period but it is reasonable in all the
circumstances to re-consult the appropriate health professional.

¹   Health and Social Services Board etc.

7.101   Any person under SI 2000/413, Art 5(4) – a person with parental
responsibility (responsibilities in Scotland) for the data subject where the subject
is a child (or under 16 in Scotland); or the data subject is incapable of managing
their own affairs and that person has been appointed by a court to manage those

affairs – is entitled to make a request for access on behalf of a data subject and who has made such a request, then the personal data will be exempt from DPA 1998, s 7 in any case where the application of that section would disclose information:

(a) provided by the data subject in the expectation that it would not be disclosed to the person making the request;

(b) obtained as a result of any examination or investigation to which the data subject consented in the expectation that the information would not be disclosed; or

(c) which the data subject has expressly indicated should not be disclosed provided that in paragraphs (a) and (b) disclosure shall not be prevented where the data subject has expressly indicated that he no longer has the expectation referred to (Art 5(3)).

7.102 Where DCs are not health professionals they shall not disclose data under this provision unless the DC has first consulted the person appearing to the DC to be the appropriate health professional on whether or not the exemption in Art 5(1) above applies to that information (Art 6(1)). This does not apply where the data has already been seen or is known to the subject. Article 6(1) does not apply to any request where the opinion of a relevant health professional has been sought by the DC prior to receiving the request and the opinion states in writing that Art 5(1) does not apply to all of the information which is the subject of the request.

7.103 Under Art 2 of the Health Order (SI 2000/413), the 'appropriate health professional' means:

'(a) the health professional who is currently or was most recently responsible for the clinical care of the data subject in connection with the matters to which the information which is the subject of the request relates; or

(b) where there is more than one such health professional, the health professional who is the most suitable to advise on the matters to which the information which is the subject of the request relates; or

(c) where there is no health professional available falling within sub-paragraph (a) or (b) above, or the DC is the Secretary of state and the data are processed in connection with his functions under the Child Support Act 1991, the Child Support Act 1995 or in relation to social security or war pensions a health professional who has the necessary experience and qualifications to advise on the matters to which the information which is the subject of the request relates.'

7.104 The Data Protection (Subject Access Modification) (Social Work) Order 2000, SI 2000/415 applies to data falling under paras 1 and 2 of the Schedule to the Order. It does not apply to data falling under the education or health exemption order. Personal data covered by para 2 of the Schedule are exempt from the subject access provisions. Data under para 1 of the Schedule are exempt from DPA 1998, s 7(1)(b)–(d) where their disclosure would be likely to prejudice the 'carrying out of social work' (see Art 5(2)) by reason of the fact that serious harm to the physical or mental health or condition of the data subject or any other person would be likely to be caused. Article 5(3) has a similar provision to the Health Order (SI 2000/413), Art 5(3) (see above). It is to be amended by SI 2011/1034 in relation to exemptions for Welsh ministers and officials.

7.105   The Data Protection (Subject Access Modification) (Education) Order 2000 (SI 2000/414) applies to personal data consisting of information constituting an educational record as defined in DPA 1998, Sch 11, para 1. Special provisions apply to data which may be claimed on behalf of a child who has been the subject of or may be at risk of child abuse.

Transitional relief

7.106   Schedule 8 to the DPA 1998 contains very detailed transitional relief by way of exemptions. These operate in addition to the exemptions already discussed. The aim was to provide a smooth transition from the regime existing under the 1984 DPA to the 1998 regime. The first transitional period exemptions ended on 23 October 2001 and the second on 23 October 2007.

The exemption in FOIA 2000, s 40

7.107   The FOIA 2000 exemptions were examined in chapter 1. However, the pre-existence of a comprehensive legal code on data protection meant that the UK was legally obliged to accommodate FOIA 2000 into the DPA 1998. The pervasive nature of DPA 1998 concepts, principles and technicalities in the discussion of FOIA 2000, s 40 meant that a reader would have to have knowledge of the DPA 1998 to understand how the s 40 exemption works. Moreover, s 40 is the most heavily used of the exemptions. Readers are reminded that where a DS request involves their own data, the DPA 1998 is the governing provision and the exemption in s 40 is absolute. When a FOI request involves data belonging to a third party, the exemption will be absolute where disclosure breaches specified data protection principles (DPP). However, this does not mean protection of data is absolute. The principles invariably require judgment and interpretation and it may, for instance, be 'fair and just' and 'necessary' to disclose personal data on specific facts. As will be seen, the cases frequently have to make such judgment calls. Central to such judgments is DPA 1998, Sch 2, para 6: 'The processing is necessary for the purposes of legitimate interests pursued by the data controller or by the third party or parties to whom the data are disclosed, except where the processing is unwarranted in any particular case by reason of prejudice to the rights and freedoms or legitimate interests of the data subject.' (See FS 50088977.) It is perfectly clear from numerous cases that where a requester seeks to utilise this provision, the burden of proving the legitimate interest is on the requester. The DS should be consulted under the terms of the FOI Code of Practice. FS 50082768 states that the IC's *Awareness Guidance* has advice about requests concerning access to information about third parties: would it cause unnecessary or unjustified distress or damage to the person who the information is about? Would a third party expect such information to be disclosed to others? Has the person been led to believe that the information would be kept secret? Has that third party expressly refused consent? Furthermore, under Sch 2, para (6) it is up to the claimant to prove that it is in the PI for the data to be disclosed (reversing the FOIA 2000 PI test). Numerous cases have established that a person's name is personal data (*Turcotte v IC and LB Camden* EA/2007/0129; although see the strange decision in *T Harcup v IC and Yorkshire Forward (YF)* EA/2007/0058). FS 50150598 makes it clear that in relation to the records of a telephone conversation in which names were mentioned, the IC thought that the s 40(1) exemption would apply, and imported the definition of personal data from the DPA 1998. Where names are present on documents held by a PA, and a FOIA request is made for that document or information, the DPA 1998 will come into play. In many cases this may well be incidental; but very often a requester might wish to know who precisely was present at, say, a meeting, eg for commercial reasons. This was the reason for wanting access in the most famous litigation on the relationship between the access to documents regulation and the data protection provisions in EU law. The EU courts and Advocate General all came to different conclusions by different processes on which legal regime took precedence (para 3.69 et seq). There is also the possibility of sinister motives in making a request. Two major themes have emerged in the case law. Firstly, when might it be possible to identify data subjects from information which appears anonymised but which may allow identification from that information and other information in the possession of the DC? This was the central issue in *Common Services Agency v Scottish Information Commissioner* [2008] UKHL 47. Here, information relating to childhood incidences of leukemia in the Dumfries and Galloway area by census ward was requested. The information had been barnardised (distorted) to prevent identification. But the law lords ruled that the SIC had erred in law in failing to ask whether this data was personal data under DPA 1998, s 1(1) and, if so, whether its disclosure would breach the DPP. The reason for the error was because the definition of 'personal data' comprises both the data requested and whether from that and any other information in the possession of the DC or which is likely to come into the DC's possession a person can be identified. Lord Hope made it clear that it may be possible to do something to both sets of data which make it impossible to identify an individual and in which case it is not personal data protected by the DPA 1998. In *Magherafelt DC v IC* EA/2009/0047 there was a request for information on the disciplinary record of council employees. Information about numbers disciplined and numbers dismissed was given. The IC had decided that a summarised schedule in which no one was identified but with more details should be disclosed but, on appeal, the tribunal overruled the IC. Even though the information had been barnardised it would still be possible to identify individuals from the information in the schedule. The data was not anonymous in the context of a small workforce working closely in a 'family situation'. It would have been all too easy for a reporter to establish the identities of those involved by seeking information from council employees. The information constituted personal data under DPA 1998, s 1(1)(b); its disclosure would breach the first DPP; and the data was protected by FOIA 2000, s 40(2). One might ask whether there may not be a good reason under DPA 1998, Sch 2, para 6 for disclosing details of disciplinary breaches if they were serious. The PA had been in breach of FOIA 2000, s 17 by not explaining why it relied on s 40(2). The case is on appeal to the Upper Tribunal (see FS50133250 in relation to correct non-disclosure at school level of identities of those subject to school exclusions after 'drug finds'. There was a risk of identifying individuals and the consequences for them could be very serious. The council had correctly invoked s 40). In *Department of Health v IC and the Pro-Life Alliance* EA/2008/0074 it was explained that up until 2003 the DoH published comprehensive statistical information relating to abortions. The information was provided by doctors and patients and was entered into frequency tables, each data cell representing the number of respondents that fell into that cell. The provision of the information by the doctors and patients was compulsory. After 2003 the published information was significantly reduced and certain data was excluded. The Pro-Life Alliance made a request for the missing information under FOIA, but the DoH claimed that: (a) disclosure was prohibited by the Abortion Regulations 1991, SI 1991/499; and (b) FOIA 2000, s 40 applied. The DoH sought to rely additionally on FOIA 2000, s 44. The IC found that ss 40 and 44 did not apply to the information. The main issue for the tribunal to decide was whether either of these two exemptions should apply. In relation to s 40, the tribunal found that the information did constitute personal data, but that the nature of the information did not give rise to a realistic possibility of identifying either the doctor or the patient. Section 44 is discussed in chapter 1 (para 1.224) The IT ordered disclosure of the information (and see *All Party Parliamentary Group on Extraordinary Rendition v IC and MoD* [2011] UKUT 153 (AAC)). In FS50243084 involving the Department of Health, Social Services and Public Safety the complainant requested information in relation to previously released abortion statistics for hospitals in Northern Ireland for the years 2003–2007. The Department of Health, Social Services and Public Safety (DHSSPS) refused to disclose some of this information under s 40(2) and (3)(i)(a) (personal data of third parties) as a basis for non-disclosure. The IC did not find that these exemptions were engaged and the DHSSPS was required to disclose the information in question.

7.108 In relation to Sch 2, para 6 considerations – processing necessary for purposes of the legitimate interests of the DC or a third party to whom data are disclosed, except where processing is unwarranted in any particular case by reason of prejudice to the rights, freedoms or legitimate interests of the DS – the factors involved in arriving at judgment have been well rehearsed. In a case involving Cambridge University (FS 50110885; below at para 7.109) the general question is: is disclosure fair? DPA 1998, Sch 2(6) was satisfied. The IC did not believe in this case that a specific notification to data subjects that their data may be disclosed under FOIA 2000 is necessary (para 47). There was no high expectation of privacy attached to this data (para 50). But this may not be the case in other circumstances. In *William Thackeray v IC and the GMC* EA/2009/0063 the tribunal considered the DS's reasonable expectations as to disclosure and privacy; his seniority in the GMC; whether the information that was already in the public domain would reduce the expectation of privacy; whether disclosure would cause unnecessary or unjustified damage to the DS; and the legitimate interests of the public. They concluded that the processing of the information would be fair. The case concerned a fitness-to-practice hearing of a doctor before the GMC. The IC was overruled (FS50241410). While the IC and tribunal have been vigilant to protect data held by the police under s 40 (*C Colliass v IC* EA/2010/0084), in *J Bryce v IC* EA/2009/0083 the tribunal was prepared to distinguish between different classes of information. The case concerned a request for information about a criminal investigation report; the report was requested. The DN was amended by the tribunal. Not all information constituted personal data which would be protected therefore under s 40(1) and (2). The focus of the tribunal's analysis is on the way the public authority (PA) conducted the inquiry and their actions. It was not about an individual. Information about police practices and procedures was disclosable, but some information about an offendee (therefore personal data) was not disclosable by virtue of DPA 1998, Sch 2(6). Information about witnesses was not disclosable, nor was information about an eight-year-old daughter of the offender. In FS50141015 the complainant requested information from the Department for Work and Pensions (DWP) as to whether there were any compliments or complaints recorded about a doctor employed by a third party. The DWP eventually (there was a question as to who held the information) responded that even if it were held by the third party on their behalf, it would be exempt from disclosure by s 40(5). However, in accordance with s 40(5), the DWP was correct to neither confirm nor deny the existence of the requested information; had it confirmed, the DWP would have contravened the first of the DPPs. The IC considered the consequences of disclosure on the doctor and decided that release of information regarding complaints would be unfair. The information requested belonged to a category of information whose nature was such that normally it would remain confidential between an employee, his employer and even possibly a regulatory professional body. *Mr Rob Evans v Information Commissioner and Ministry of Defence* EA/2006/0064 is a case that was examined under FOIA 2000, s 36 where some disclosure of formal background notes of lobbying meetings had been disclosed – but not informal notes (para 1.164). In this case on somewhat tortuous grounds the tribunal did not consider that there had been a breach of Part II of Sch 1, para 2(1)(b). The IT then considered a possible breach of the first principle on the basis of the conditions contained in DPA 1998, Sch 2. Under para 6 of that provision, '[t]he processing must be necessary for the purposes of legitimate interests pursued by ... the third party'. It was decided that Mr Evans had a legitimate interest as a reporter, which had to be balanced against the prejudice to the data subject (Mr Wood). It was recognised that legitimate interest is not always the same as public interest, but that in the instant case they amounted to the same thing. The public interest in disclosure was minimised as the information would not have been of 'much interest to anyone'. However, the prejudice which would have been suffered by Mr Wood could have been very damaging both for the company and for him personally. The IT therefore concluded that the public interest weighed in favour of non-disclosure (and see *Dundass v IC and Bradford MDC* EA/2007/0084 where Sch 2(6) militated against disclosure). In *BERR v IC and FoE* EA/2007/0072, Friends of the Earth wanted information about meetings (lobbying) between CBI and a the Department for Trade and Industry on a variety of subjects, with dates, participants, minutes and correspondence. Disclosure was ordered and in some cases material was redacted (see *P Dun v IC*

EA/2010/0060 and disclosure of senior civil servant's details not breaching the first DPP).

7.109   An important point to bear in mind is that the date of a request may be of vital importance in s 40 requests. FS 50088853 concerned a complainant who sought the background papers relating to the 1993 Memorandum of Understanding on Royal Finances (the 'MOU') under which the Queen and the Prince of Wales would voluntarily pay income tax. The treasury refused to release the information, citing s 40. The Commissioner made a distinction between private and public finances. Information relating to the former would fall within s 40(2), which is an absolute exemption. The important and decisive point the IC ruled in denying access because public finances were not involved was that at the time of the MOU there were no FOI provisions and therefore it was not expected that the information would be disclosed. In another IC case (FS 50119963), the complainant requested the names of doctors who had previously worked in a particular hospital department between the years 2000 and 2004. The public authority refused to disclose the information citing s 40. The IC concluded that the public authority was correct to withhold the information on the basis of s 40. The important point in this case was that the applicant had harassed a registrar with correspondence and this was likely again if names were released. While the motives of an applicant are not relevant under FOI requests, disclosure to the world would include the applicant. Although any 'harassment' would be minor – involving correspondence (quaere) a more significant factor was that registrars in the relevant period had a legitimate expectation of confidentiality and no legitimate purpose of the requester was served under Sch 2(6) (on this point see next paragraph). In FS50099923 the IC also believed that in ordering disclosure of information concerning film footage of trials at sea on biological warfare agents which had been used to infect animals in the early 1950s the current climate of openness is very different to 1996 when a similar disclosure caused distress, the MoD alleged. Individuals would be indentifiable from the film. In this case the PA also claimed that the second DPP concerning notification for 'specified and lawful purposes' prevented disclosure because FOIA was not notified as a 'purpose' for processing. The IC did not feel that the second DPP concerning notification was relevant because the drafter of s 40 had in mind that such data could be disclosed and to bar it under the second DPP would effectively bar all claims under FOIA 'on the basis that data were not originally obtained for that [FOIA] purpose'. This ruling is crucial in facilitating access to personal data providing the relevant principles and DPA 1998, s 10 – concerning 'disclosure likely to cause distress' – are not breached. FS50110885 was a request for information to Cambridge University for numbers and gender statistics of pupils from the same school who had successfully applied for a course. This had been withheld. The IC stated that the 'purposes of processing' for DPA purposes, which have to be stated, are 'broad'. The request concerned the collation of statistics. Disclosure of personal data under FOIA is not a 'specific purpose for which such information is processed. In responding to a request made under the Act the PA is not fulfilling one of its business purposes; it is simply complying with a legal obligation [under FOIA]' (para 44). The IC believed that it would be difficult to argue that compliance with a legal rule would be incompatible with other purposes for which personal data may be processed.

7.110 It must also be noted that the 'neither confirm nor deny' (NCND) provision in s 40(5) may come into play where responding to a FOI request would itself reveal personal data. In FS50178633 the complainant made a request for all correspondence between the General Medical Council (GMC), a named doctor and his employers. The GMC went through confirmation or denial. However, the IC found that the GMC was not obliged to respond to the request under s (1)(1)(a) by virtue of s 40(5)(b)(i). The IC considered that responding with a confirmation or denial was a disclosure of information which constituted personal data under DPA 1998, s 1 and which would breach the first DPP; the doctor would have a reasonable expectation of privacy. The public interest was in favour of non-disclosure because whilst there was a legitimate public interest in ensuring the competence of doctors, the existing safeguards were sufficient to ensure such competence. See also FS50298086 concerning a request by Lord Ashcroft's solicitors to the Cabinet Office for information about Lord Ashcroft and his nomination to a working peerage in 1999. The IC concluded that all of the requested information is Lord Ashcroft's personal data and therefore the Cabinet Office was correct to refuse to disclose this information under s 40(1). The Commissioner also concluded that in light of the effect of s 40(5) the Cabinet Office was not in fact obliged to confirm or deny whether it held such information.

7.111 In cases dealing with financial fraud, deception or improper conduct, the IC and tribunal have sought to establish: (a) whether the person about whom information is sought and who will be named is acting in a private or public capacity; and (b) the seniority of the person named and whether this makes a difference. In FS 50116822 there was a request to a NHS Trust for a copy of an internal report into allegations of financial irregularity made against a former director of research governance. Section 40(2) was invoked. 'Seniority of individual' should be taken into account in deciding whether to disclose. Information about someone acting in an official or work capacity should normally be disclosed unless there is some risk to the individual concerned (from IC's *Guidance*) (para 42). In *Corporate Officer of House of Commons v IC* EA/2006/0074-0076 (below) the tribunal approved the IC guidance: does it apply to the public or private life of data subject (see below)? Would disclosure cause unnecessary or unjustified distress or damage to the individual? Would the individual expect information to be disclosed to others? Was the individual led to believe information would be kept secret? Has express refusal to consent been declared? The IC believed disclosure of the internal report would be fair and lawful. Disclosure of third parties named in the report would be unfair and breach the first DPP, but it could be disclosed if anonymised. Disclosure on these terms did not involve a breach of s 40.

7.112 It was under the heading of 'financial irregularity' that requests were made for information on MPs' expenses – the most high-profile investigations and the most important constitutionally conducted under FOIA 2000. There have been many MPs' expenses cases and, in the most important, the position of the IC and tribunal have been upheld by the High Court. FS 50071451 witnessed the IC issuing an information notice (IN) to the House of Commons! The information was examined at the House of Commons. The request was for the receipts, rental agreements or mortgage interest statements of six MPs under the Additional Costs Allowance (ACA – second homes). The House of Commons' corporate officer claimed that disclosure over and above that in the Publication Scheme would breach the DPA 1998 (para 18). The IC decided that the requested information is personal data and that its fully itemised disclosure would be unfair. However, he ruled that it would not contravene the DPA, Sch 2, para 6 to disclose the information showing the totals paid under specified headings within the ACA. This was ordered to be disclosed. The corporate officer appealed the DN which led to even wider disclosure ordered by the tribunal and the ruling was upheld by the court (below). There is an irony in that had the Commons not resisted the original DN, not so much information would have been published. The appeals were heard in *Corporate Officer of House of Commons v IC and Leapman, Brooke and Thomas* EA/2007/0061-63, 0122-23, 0131. The Corporate Officer's arguments on the appeal to the IC were rejected but the IC did set limitations on what was disclosable. The IC's ruling excluded 'sensitive personal data of MPs, personal data of third parties, but not the name of those in receipt of rents/mortgage interest, and bank statements, loan statements, phone numbers and other matters'. The tribunal in its ruling held that more data should be made public than the IC had determined in its application of Sch 2, para 6 considerations and the public interest. The rules on which ACA operated were secret and unknown to MPs themselves in order not to encourage maximum claims. Self-denial had not been manifest. Lack of transparency did not encourage accountability and honesty in the system which was overseen by the National Audit Office and Commons Committee on Privileges. The tribunal's ruling was appealed to the High Court which upheld the tribunal's decision. The questions involved had 'a wide resonance throughout the body politic bearing on public confidence in our democratic system at its very pinnacle' (*Corporate Officer of the House of Commons v IC, Brooke and Leapman* [2008] EWHC 1084 (Admin) para 15). The case led to an overhaul of the MPs' expenses system, the resignation of the Speaker and two ministers in disgrace and the resignation of numerous MPs as well as criminal convictions and imprisonment of MPs.[1] FS 50070469 concerned a request for Tony Blair's ACA details. The IC asked for information from the Commons on 9 September 2005. An IN was issued on 6 June 2006 and information given to IC on 14 July 2006. The outcome was similar to the previous case. In FS 50067986 information requested was on the travel expenses of MPs including an MP's spouse on official business. By way of defence, the Commons sought to establish motives for the request and use of information. This was irrelevant and not permitted under FOIA 2000, the IC ruled. If it were possible to establish a pattern of travel (ie specific routes) that might constitute a security risk. But this was not a problem here. DPA 1998, Sch 2(6) justifies disclosure. However, disclosure of 'detailed routes, times or dates of those journeys' would not be justified. FS 50073128 involved a request for the names and salaries of MPs' staff. Section 40(2) could protect relatively junior staff appointments and details of salaries of assistants insofar as disclosure might breach the DPP. The information was 'held' by the Commons for the purposes of FOIA 2000, s 3(2), the IC ruled, in rejecting the arguments of the Commons. Section 40(2) did not in itself protect the names of staff (however, FOIA 2000, s 36(7) is absolute in relation to the Commons and names of staff and its invocation could not be questioned where it was properly claimed). The question of MEP expenses, and a report thereon, was the subject of a request under the EU access regulation. Following an initial refusal to publish a detailed report, the General Court ruled that disclosure was 'an overriding public interest'.[2]

1   R v Chaytor [2010] UKSC 52. An independent Parliamentary Standards Authority was established under the Parliamentary Standards Act 2009 'to bring independent oversight and control over MPs expenses'.
2   Case C-471/08 Toland v European Parliament.

7.113   *Corporate Officer of House of Commons v IC and N Baker (AP)* EA/2006/0015 and 0016 concerned one of 167 FOIA requests for travel expenses claimed by MPs. Information was sought on MPs' travel expenses including the 'total amount claimed for each MP for modes of travel by rail, road, air and bicycle'. These included: European travel; extended travel and family travel. Section 40 was invoked. Since the autumn of 2004, publication schemes had published general sums on such expenses and indeed the Scottish Parliament had led the way in disclosing more information on this subject than Westminster. The IC argued that the DPA's operation had to be affected by a 'culture of openness'. Information about someone acting in an official or work capacity should normally be provided on request unless there is some risk to the individual concerned. Family and private life information involve different considerations. For the purposes of fair processing, the IC's guidance was accepted by the tribunal: does data belong to public or private life of the individual? The private interests of an MP are not 'necessarily first and paramount consideration in a case such as this' where the 'personal data relates to their public lives' (para 79). Sch 2(6) involves a balancing of competing interests, namely those of the DS and the requester's legitimate interests. However, under the PI considerations in the qualified exemptions, the PI in secrecy or non-disclosure has to be greater than that in disclosure to maintain secrecy, as seen in chapter 1 above. Under Sch 2(6) the processing must be 'necessary' for the legitimate interests of members of the public to apply. It is only where it is established that the requester's interests outweigh or are greater than the data subject's interests that the personal data should be disclosed. This emphatic ruling set the benchmark. The appeals in *Corporate Officer of the HC v IC* EA/0074 and 0076 concerned information requested about an individual MPs' travel expenses and not collective data: the House of Commons held information collectively on MPs. The request was to try and identify 'green and environmental' aspects of travel. The arguments in favour of non-disclosure were that this would involve an 'invasion of privacy and family life, diverts MPs and the House of Commons from other Parliamentary business, MPs only consent to aggregate disclosure, not individual disclosure, and MPs subject to media scrutiny' and so on. Section 40 was invoked by the corporate officer although it was agreed that s 40(3)(a)(i) did not apply. This was about 'public life', not private life, and so Sch 2(6) applied. Disclosure of individuals' aggregate figures should be disclosed, but not 'disclosure of travel details which could reveal the times, origins and destinations of journeys and the modes of transport likely to be used at particular times and circumstances' as such information could be of potential assistance to those with evil intentions, 'especially where such information was not otherwise available to them'.

7.114 Details of salaries of named individuals are frequently requested.1 The coalition government announced on coming to power that as well as providing details of 'new' contracts, tender documents of central government over £10,000, new items of central government expenditure over £25,000, and salaries of local government senior management staff would be published. In FS50294798 the complainant made a request under FOIA 2000 to the Department for Transport (DfT) for information relating to the latest bonus of the chief executive of an agency of the DfT. The DfT explained that some of the information requested was publicly available; that the annual reports of the DfT and the relevant agencies contain salary and bonus information relating to the individual concerned within a £5,000 band. The complainant was directed to this information. The specific information about the bonus was refused under the exemption contained at FOIA 2000, s 40(2). The Commissioner considered that the DfT correctly applied the s 40(2) exemption to withhold the information relating to the bonus of the individual concerned and required no further action to be taken. In FS50142539 salaries of senior academics at a university were withheld and were exempt under s 40(2). In FS50267001 information was requested about the head teacher's salary. This information should have been provided but refusing to supply details of his bonus was correct. Bankers' bonuses have become a notoriously heated topic given the astronomical sums of taxpayers' money that have been spent on bailing out banks after 2007, thereby causing huge public debt and cuts in public financing for public services and financial support. Some UK banks (at the time of writing) are publicly owned but are not within FOIA 2000. The stated aim of government is for banks to publish the names of recipients of bonuses and their amount. There is no legal power to force banks to disclose such information although if they were publicly owned it would seem that there could be ways other than via legislation to achieve this. Terms would have to be negotiated. Privately owned banks have argued that publishing such information would have implications for the law of employment, human rights and data protection, which would prevent such disclosures. We doubt that this information is confidential under the law of confidentiality or that it would be impossible to use the DPA 1998 to require disclosure. For ECHR, Art 8 to come into play, the nature of the 'private interest' in receiving huge sums by way of bonus while operating in regulated markets and by taking risks that could have a profound impact on the public interest as was seen after 2008 all raise arguments on the nature of the 'private' interest in question. Is this 'private' or 'public' life? The so-called Merlin agreement on remuneration between the Lord Chancellor and senior bankers is available at http://www. hm-treasury.gov.uk/d/bank_agreement_090211.pdf.

1   See incidentally, PAC HC 472 (2009–10) Top Pay in the Public Sector.

7.115 Many of the 'salary' requests have involved payments by the BBC either in the form of fees, salaries or expenses. As we saw in chapter 1 (para 1.90) the question of what information was covered by the 'journalism, art or literature' proviso and which was thereby excluded from FOIA 2000 led to extensive litigation and a ruling from the courts that the IC's 'preponderant purpose' ruling was unlawful. Several decisions may be decided differently today after the court of appeal's ruling (para 1.94). FS 50067416 was a request for the highest earner in BBC Northern Ireland. The 'journalism etc' exclusion was ruled not to operate. On the basis of s 40 the IC stated that while it would breach DPA 1998 to disclose the exact salary, this would not be the case in relation to the pay band and individual's name. Other requested information related to the cost of producing a show and fees for 'talents'. The question under s 40 was: is this private or public business? Sch 2(6) was satisfied in relation to the highest earner in terms of the pay band. It was reasonable to expect that BBC would keep information about 'talent' fees confidential and s 40 protected this. The 'talents' were not in a position to influence policy choices affecting expenditure. FS 50102474 was a request to BBC for the cost of the 'Children in Need' programme in 2005. In relation to s 40, the request concerned a one-off fee payment for a presenter, not a salary. The IC found that there was a widespread perception that performers would perform for free. 'The IC considers that individuals who hold such high-profile and public-facing roles should expect information about them to be available to the public. This is especially so in a climate where the public are constantly alerted by the media to the high earnings of its programme presenters and in a society where the requirement for scrutiny of public spending is increasingly expressed' (para 42). Applications for information on expenses' payments (to Alan Yentob) have been rightly refused (FS50068026). Amounts spent by the BBC on taxis have not been exempt under s 43(2).

7.116 The tribunal upheld the IC in *Guardian News and Media Ltd* EA/2008/0084, which concerned the Ministry of Justice (MoJ) and details of the disciplinary action taken against judges including their names, the reasons for the action and the dates of action. The MoJ refused to disclose on the basis of s 40. The MoJ had provided inadequately reasoned responses (which were out of time) under s 40, which amounted to a breach of s 17. The IC found that the information came within the definition of personal data in DPA 1998. The legitimate interests of the public were important but the tribunal agreed that the individuals' reasonable expectations regarding the information were that it would not be disclosed. Important factors also included the data subjects' seniority and whether disclosure would cause unjustified damage to the individuals. On balance the information should not be disclosed because the internal disciplinary procedures in place were sufficient to assess suitability and provide scrutiny. The data subjects would not expect these matters to be made public and disclosure would cause 'unwarranted damage and distress'. The procedures involved in disciplining judges are explained in some detail by the tribunal.

ENFORCEMENT

7.117 DPA 1998, Part V (ss 40–50) covers enforcement. In particular, s 40(1) provides that the Commissioner, where satisfied that a DC has contravened or is contravening any of the data protection principles, may serve on that person an enforcement notice (EN). This requires that person to take, or refrain from taking, specified steps within a certain period and/or to refrain from processing any personal data or specified data or processing them in a manner or for a purpose as specified and after such time as may be specified. The DPC must consider, in deciding whether to serve an enforcement notice, whether the contravention has caused or is likely to cause any person damage or distress. In relation to breaches of the fourth principle, the EN may require rectification, erasure, blocking or destruction of other data held by the DC which contains an opinion which appears to the Commissioner to be based on the inaccurate data. The EN in relation to the fourth principle may also require the preceding rectification where data accurately record information received or obtained by the DC from the DS or a third party or require the DC to take steps to comply with para 7 of Part II of Sch 1 and if the Commissioner thinks fit for supplementing the data with such statement of the true facts relating to the matters dealt with by the data as the Commissioner may approve. An EN may require the DC to notify third parties of the rectification etc if reasonably practicable regard being had in particular to the number of persons involved. An EN must contain (s 40(6)):

'(a) a statement of the principle or principles which the Commissioner is satisfied have been or are being contravened and his reasons for reaching that conclusion; and

(b) particulars of the rights of appeal conferred by section 48 below.'

7.118 The time given for compliance is usually longer than the time allowed for appeal and its determination if made. An EN may provide that steps should be taken as a matter of urgency.

7.119 There is a period of informal negotiation, and following that oral or written representations may be made before service of an EN. The approach of the DPC in relation to ENs in transitional periods was indicated above. An EN may be cancelled or varied by written notice. A person on whom an EN is served may apply in writing after the period of appeal has expired requesting a cancellation or variation of the EN because of changed circumstances so that all or any of the provisions need not be complied with in order to comply with the data protection principles.

7.120 The Commissioner may be requested by or on behalf of any person who is or believes s/he is directly affected by any processing of personal data to make an assessment as to whether it is likely or unlikely that the processing is or has been carried out in compliance with the DPA 1998's provisions (s 42). 'Directly affected' is a limiting expression although the IC enjoys some discretion in interpretation. The Commissioner may make an assessment in a wide manner unless s/he lacks necessary information about the requester's identity or to identify the processing in question. The Commissioner may have regard to specific matters in determining in what manner it is appropriate to make an assessment. These are: the extent to which the request appears to the IC to raise a matter of substance; any undue delay in making the request; whether the requester may make a s 7 application in relation to the data. Where a request is received, the IC shall notify the requester whether an assessment has been made as a result and of any view formed or action taken but only to the extent that she considers appropriate with regard especially to any s 7 exemption in relation to the personal data. See para 7.73 et seq.

7.121 To assist enforcement, the Commissioner may serve an information notice (IN) under DPA 1998, s 43 where s/he has received a request for an assessment under s 42 or where s/he reasonably requires information to establish compliance with the data protection principles. This contains requests for specified information which may be required in a specified time and form and the provision has been amended by the Coroners and Justice Act 2009, Sch 20, para 8 so that the place at which it must be furnished may be specified. An IN must contain certain statements in relation either to a request being made under s 42 or in relation to the information's relevance to assess compliance with the principles and the reasons for its relevance. The IN must also contain details of the right of appeal. There are similar provisions on the expiry of time limits so as to protect rights of appeal and their hearing and in a case of urgency 'by reason of special circumstances' the IN may take effect within seven days starting with the day on which the notice is served. The IN must include a statement of reasons for the belief that the matter is one of urgency. There are exemptions for legal professional privilege (see s 43(7)) and self-incrimination as amended by Sch 20, para 10. An IN may be cancelled.[1]

---

[1]   This section is subject to DPA 1998, s 46(3).

7.122 There are also special information notices (SINs) similarly amended as above by the Coroners and Justice Act 2009, Sch 20, para 9. These are used where a request has been made under the DPA 1998, s 42 or the Commissioner has reasonable grounds for suspecting that where proceedings have been stayed under s 32 (journalism, literature and art) the personal data to which the proceedings relate are not being processed for the special purposes or are not being processed with a view to the publication by any person of any journalistic etc material which has not previously been published by the DC. The SIN must contain similar provisions to the IN above but in addition the Commissioner may request information for the following purposes, ie to ascertain:
(a)   whether the personal data are being processed only for the special purposes; or
(b)   whether they are being processed with a view to the publication by any person of any journalistic etc material which has not previously been published by the DC.

7.123 The SIN must contain a s 42 statement as for INs or a statement as to why the Commissioner does not believe the data are being processed for journalistic etc purposes. Similar provisions apply as for an IN in relation to expiry times for replies, situations of urgency, protecting legal professional privilege, savings for self-incrimination other than for offences under the DPA 1998 and cancellation. The Commissioner may, whether as a result of service of an SIN or otherwise, make a determination that personal data are not being processed for the special purposes or are not being processed with a view to publication of any journalistic etc material which has not previously been published by the DC. The determination will be written and served on the DC. It will contain particulars of rights of appeal and will not take effect until appeal rights have expired or appeal has been determined (s 45).

7.124   An EN may not be served on a DC with respect to the processing of data for the special purposes until a determination under s 45(1) in relation to those data has taken effect and the court has granted leave for the notice to be served. The court shall not grant leave unless satisfied that the Commissioner has reason to suspect a contravention of the DPP which is of substantial public importance and except where the case is one of urgency and the DC has been given notice of the application for leave in accordance with rules of court. An SIN must not be served on a DC in relation to processing of data for the special purposes unless a determination under s 45 in relation to those data has taken effect.

7.125   An individual who is an actual or prospective party to proceedings under DPA 1998, s 7(9), 10(4), 12(8) or 14 or by virtue of s 13, and which concern special purposes data, may apply to the Commissioner for assistance in relation to those proceedings. These provisions concern: failure to comply with a request for access to information; failure to comply with a notice objecting to processing that may cause substantial damage or distress; failure to reconsider a decision made via automated decision taking or to make a new decision; failure to rectify, block, erase or destroy inaccurate personal detail; compensation for failure to comply with certain requirements of the Act. It has been ruled that, where a DS is refused access under s 7(9), the DS may apply for disclosure of personal data and other documents under ss 10, 13 and 14 where the DS is claiming a breach of the Act under those provisions. The power of the court to view data under DPA 1998, s 15(2), and which gives no rights to the DS unless successful under the s 7 claim on access, does not restrict disclosure rights under the Civil Procedure Rules for the other claims.[1] 'Assistance' may take the form of assistance with litigation (see DPA 1998, Sch 10). This will not be granted unless it involves a matter of substantial public importance. The IC will inform the applicant of the decision and what he will do or, if he intends to do nothing, the reasons why (s 53).

[1]   *Johnson v Medical Defence Union Ltd* [2005] 1 All ER 87 Ch D. Laddie J was vigilant to point out that he was not ruling on the merits of the disclosure claim and confidentiality within the terms of s 15(2), and s 7(4)–(6) would have to be respected. See also [2004] EWHC 347 (Ch).

7.126   Non-compliance with an EN, IN or SIN is a criminal offence although a defence of 'all due diligence' is permissible. It is also an offence to make knowingly or recklessly a false statement in a material respect in response to a IN or SIN.

APPEALS[1]

7.127   Appeals against ENs, INs, SINs and an assessment notice may be made to the Information Tribunal.[2] Appeals may also be made against the

Commissioner's refusal to cancel or vary a notice under DPA 1998, s 41(2). Appeal may be made against inclusion of statements under or their effect as respects any part of the notice under s 40(8), 43(5) or 44(6). An appeal may also be made against a determination under s 45.

¹   See SI 2000/189.
²   DPA 1998, s 48 as amended by Coroners and Criminal Justice Act 2009, Sch 20.

7.128   Schedule 6 to the DPA 1998 governs the procedure. Appeal shall be allowed where notice was not in accordance with the law or on the basis that the DPC should have exercised discretion differently,¹ or the Tribunal may substitute such other decision or notice as could have been made or served by the Commissioner. Otherwise the Tribunal shall dismiss the appeal. Determinations of fact on which a notice is based may be reviewed by the Tribunal. The Tribunal may vary or cancel ENs, remove statements or their effects in notices making such modifications as necessary, it may cancel determinations under s 45.

¹   Provisions which anticipate the FOIA 2000.

7.129   An appeal on a point of law may be made by any party to the appeal to the High Court, the Court of Session in Scotland if the appellant's address is in Scotland, or the High Court (Northern Ireland) if that address is in Northern Ireland. Both the Tribunal and the Commissioner are under the supervision of the Council on Tribunals.

Internal reviews

7.130   Regulations made under the Access to Personal Files Act 1987 made reference to the provision of internal review procedures to review refusals to provide access to personal files. These are not specifically referred to in the DPA 1998 nor in regulations made thereunder. For personal records covered by the FOIA 2000, concering third parties and which are not absolutely exempt, internal review will have to be provided under that Act (see para 1.233 above). It might appear anomalous if such procedures did not cover rights under the DPA 1998 so far as public bodies are concerned. The FOIA 2000 does not apply to private bodies unless they or their functions are designated by the Secretary of State.

SEARCH AND SEIZURE

7.131   Under Sch 9 to the DPA 1998, the Commissioner may apply to a circuit judge for a warrant for search and inspection and seizure, and operation and testing, of equipment and documents. This can happen where the judge has reasonable grounds for suspecting that an offence under the DPA 1998 has been or is being committed, or that the data protection principles have been or are being contravened by a DC and that relevant evidence is to be found on premises named in the Commissioner's information upon oath. The powers may be exercisable by the Commissioner or the IC's officers or staff. A judge shall not issue a warrant for special purposes data unless a determination under s 45 has been made. The judge must be satisfied of other matters including proper notice to the occupier and access was demanded at a reasonable hour and refused, or entry was granted but permission to inspect etc was refused. There are details on execution of warrants. Intentionally obstructing persons in the execution of warrants or failing without reasonable excuse to give such persons assistance as they may reasonably require are criminal offences. The Coroners and Criminal Justice Act 2009, Sch 20, para 14 amends this provision specifying powers of entry, search and seizure; and see the Criminal Justice and Immigration Act 2008 below.

7.132   Matters exempt from search and seizure are personal data exempt, under s 28 of the DPA 1998 (national security), from any provisions under the Act, and:

'(1) (a)   any communication between a professional legal adviser and his client in connection with the giving of legal advice to the client with respect to his obligations, liabilities or rights under this Act; or

(b)   any communication between a professional legal adviser and his client, or between such an adviser or his client and any other person, made in connection with or in contemplation of proceedings under or arising out of this Act (including proceedings before the Tribunal) and for the purposes of such proceedings.

(2) Sub-paragraph (1) above applies also to
(a)   any copy or other record of any such communication as is there mentioned; and
(b)   any document or article enclosed with or referred to in any such communication if made in connection with the giving of any advice or, as the case may be, in connection with or in contemplation of and for the purposes of such para 1 of Schedule 11 to the DPA. Special provisions apply to data which may be claimed on behalf of a child who has proceedings as are there mentioned.

(3)   This paragraph does not apply to anything in the possession of any person other than the professional legal adviser or his client or to anything held with the intention of furthering a criminal purpose.

(4)   In this paragraph references to the client of a professional legal adviser include references to any person representing such a client.'

7.133   No enactment or rule of law prohibiting or restricting the disclosure of information shall preclude a person from furnishing the Commissioner or the Tribunal with any information necessary for the discharge of their functions (DPA 1998, s 58). Furthermore, the Commissioner and staff and agents, past and present in all cases, are bound by a confidentiality provision in s 59 vis-à-vis information obtained or furnished under the Act and relating to identifiable individuals or businesses. This may be disclosed with lawful authority including those necessary for the discharge of functions under the Act, is made with the individual's consent or under provisions of the Act, or it is a public interest disclosure but otherwise a knowing or reckless contravention of the section is a criminal offence. The Registrar before becoming the Commissioner claimed that this provision was too broad and may punish disclosures which are harmless but not strictly necessary.

OFFENCES AND MONETARY PENALTY NOTICES

7.134 The power to issue monetary penalty notices was noted above. Under DPA 1998, s 55, it is an offence knowingly or recklessly to obtain or disclose personal data or information therein without the DC's consent. Likewise procuring the disclosure to another person of the information is an offence. There are provisos covering the prevention or detection of crime or where disclosure was authorised by law, where a person acted under reasonable belief that he had the right to act as he did or it was in the public interest. It is no longer provided as it was under the DPA 1984 that where data are lost, or destroyed without the authority of the user or bureau – it does not include authorised destruction – or are disclosed or made accessible to a person, in both cases without authority, the subject shall be entitled to compensation from the user or person carrying on a bureau.

7.135 A new provision was added in the Criminal Justice and Immigration Act 2008, s 78. This adds a defence to an offence under s 55 where a person acted for the special purposes with a view to the publication by any person of any journalistic, etc material and in the reasonable belief that in the particular circumstances the obtaining, disclosing or procuring was justified as being in the public interest.

Monetary penalty notices

7.136 The Criminal Justice and Immigration Act 2008, s 144 has added a power for the IC[1] to make a monetary penalty notice and adds a new s 55A to the DPA 1998. The power has been further modified by the Coroners and Justice Act 2009, Part 8 and Sch 20. It is simplest to set out the provisions in full.

'(1)The Commissioner may serve a data controller with a monetary penalty notice if the Commissioner is satisfied that:
(a) there has been a serious contravention of section 4(4) (duty to comply with DPP) by the data controller,
(b) the contravention was of a kind likely to cause substantial damage or substantial distress, and
(c) subsection (2) or (3) applies.

(2) This subsection applies if the contravention was deliberate.

(3) This subsection applies if the data controller—
(a) knew or ought to have known —
   (i) that there was a risk that the contravention would occur, and
   (ii) that such a contravention would be of a kind likely to cause substantial damage or substantial distress, but

(b)   failed to take reasonable steps to prevent the contravention.

(4) A monetary penalty notice is a notice requiring the data controller to pay to the Commissioner a monetary penalty of an amount determined by the Commissioner and specified in the notice.

(5) The amount determined by the Commissioner must not exceed the prescribed amount.

(6) The monetary penalty must be paid to the Commissioner within the period specified in the notice [28 days under SI 910/2010, reg 6 (below)].

(7) The notice must contain such information as may be prescribed.

(8) Any sum received by the Commissioner by virtue of this section must be paid into the Consolidated Fund.

(9) In this section—

> "data controller" does not include the Crown Estate Commissioners or a person who is a data controller by virtue of section 63(3);

> "prescribed" means prescribed by regulations made by the Secretary of State.'

1   For the IC's guidance on penalty notices, see http://www.ico.gov.uk/~/media/documents/library/ Data_Protection/Detailed_specialist_guides/ICO_GUIDANCE_MONETARY_PENALTIES. ashx. The IC has been criticised for not 'utilising the potential of increased fines for DP breaches' say ViaSat. The IC stated that ViaSat had misinterpreted figures: https://www.privacyassociation. org/publications/2011_04_22_numbers_show_many_data_breaches_few_fines.

7.137   DPA 1998, s 55B: Monetary penalty notices: procedural rights

'(1) Before serving a monetary penalty notice, the Commissioner must serve the data controller with a notice of intent.

(2) A notice of intent is a notice that the Commissioner proposes to serve a monetary penalty notice.

(3) A notice of intent must—
(a)   inform the data controller that he may make written representations in relation to the Commissioner's proposal within a period specified in the notice, and
(b)   contain such other information as may be prescribed.

(4) The Commissioner may not serve a monetary penalty notice until the time within which the data controller may make representations has expired.

(5) A person on whom a monetary penalty notice is served may appeal to the Tribunal against—
(a)   the issue of the monetary penalty notice;
(b)   the amount of the penalty specified in the notice.

(6) In this section, "prescribed" means prescribed by regulations made by the Secretary of State.'

7.138 DPA 1998, s 55C: Guidance about monetary penalty notices

'(1) The Commissioner must prepare and issue guidance on how he proposes to exercise his functions under sections 55A and 55B.

(2) The guidance must, in particular, deal with—
(a) the circumstances in which he would consider it appropriate to issue a monetary penalty notice, and
(b) how he will determine the amount of the penalty.

(3) The Commissioner may alter or replace the guidance.

(4) If the guidance is altered or replaced, the Commissioner must issue the altered or replacement guidance.

(5) The Commissioner may not issue guidance under this section without the approval of the Secretary of State although under the Protection of Liberties Bill 2011 the IC only has to consult the secretary of state and the requirement of approval is removed (clause 102(3)).

(6) The Commissioner must lay any guidance issued under this section before each House of Parliament.

(7) The Commissioner must arrange for the publication of any guidance issued under this section in such form and manner as he considers appropriate.[1]

(8) In subsections (5) to (7), "guidance" includes altered or replacement guidance.'

[1] See para 7.136, note 1 above.

7.139 DPA 1998, s 55D: Monetary penalty notices: enforcement

'(1) This section applies in relation to any penalty payable to the Commissioner by virtue of section 55A.

(2) In England and Wales, the penalty is recoverable—
(a) if a county court so orders, as if it were payable under an order of that court;
(b) if the High Court so orders, as if it were payable under an order of that court.

(3) In Scotland, the penalty may be enforced in the same manner as an extract registered decree arbitral bearing a warrant for execution issued by the sheriff court of any sheriffdom in Scotland.

(4) In Northern Ireland, the penalty is recoverable—
(a) if a county court so orders, as if it were payable under an order of that court;
(b) if the High Court so orders, as if it were payable under an order of that court.'

7.140 DPA 1998, s 55D: Notices under sections 55A and 55B: supplemental

'(1) The Secretary of State may by order make further provision in connection with monetary penalty notices and notices of intent.

(2) An order under this section may in particular—

(a)   provide that a monetary penalty notice may not be served on a data controller with respect to the processing of personal data for the special purposes except in circumstances specified in the order;

(b)   make provision for the cancellation or variation of monetary penalty notices;

(c)   confer rights of appeal to the Tribunal against decisions of the Commissioner in relation to the cancellation or variation of such notices;

(d)   make provision for the proceedings of the Tribunal in respect of appeals under section 55B(5) or appeals made by virtue of paragraph (c);

(e)   make provision for the determination of such appeals;

(f)   confer rights of appeal against any decision of the Tribunal in relation to monetary penalty notices or their cancellation or variation.

(3) An order under this section may apply any provision of this Act with such modifications as may be specified in the order.

(4) An order under this section may amend this Act.'

7.141   The Data Protection (Monetary Penalties) (Maximum Penalty and Notices) Regulations 2010, SI 2010/31 lays down a maximum penalty of £500,000. It sets out the prescribed information for notices of intent and monetary penalty notices. Under the Data Protection (Monetary Penalties) Order 2010, SI 2010/910, the IC must consider any written representations made in relation to a notice of intent to issue a monetary penalty notice (MPN). Regulation 3 states that the period for making such representations must not be less than 21 days beginning with the first day after service of notice of intent. An MPN may not be served six months later than service of a notice of intent. An MPN may be varied (reg 4) or cancelled (reg 5) and the Regulations set out procedures. Limits on enforcing MPNs are set out in reg 6. This includes the expiration of the 28-day period and non-payment of all or any of the payment, conclusion of appeals and expiry of the appeal period. The Protection of Freedoms Bill 2011 removes the requirement in s 55C that guidance issued by the IC has to be approved by the Secretary of State.

7.142   Section 60 deals with prosecutions and specifies that the consent of the DPP or Commissioner is necessary for a prosecution. Directors as well as bodies corporate may be guilty of offences.

PROHIBITING THE REQUIREMENT TO PRODUCE CERTAIN RECORDS

7.143   Section 56 of the DPA 1998 concerns situations where relevant records are required to be produced by or for an individual. Generally, this is prohibited, but it is subject to important exceptions. A 'relevant record' means any record which has been or is to be obtained by a DS from any DC specified in the first column of the Table set out below in the exercise of a right under DPA 1998, s 7 and, secondly, it contains information relating to any matter specified in relation to the DC in the second column. It includes a copy of such a record or any part of a record. The Table may be amended by the Secretary of State.

7.144

Data controller	Subject matter
1. Any of the following persons—	(a) Convictions.
(a) a chief officer of police of a police force in England and Wales.	(b) Cautions.
(b) a chief constable of a police force in Scotland.	
(c) the Chief Constable of the Royal Ulster Constabulary.	
[(d) the Director General of the Serious Organised Crime Agency.]	
2. The Secretary of State.	(a) Convictions.
	(b) Cautions.
	(c) His functions under [section 92 of the Powers of Criminal Courts (Sentencing) Act 2000], section 205(2) or 208 of the Criminal Procedure (Scotland) Act 1995 or section 73 of the Children and Young Persons Act (Northern Ireland) 1968 in relation to any person sentenced to detention.
	(d) His functions under the Prison Act 1952, the Prisons (Scotland) Act 1989 or the Prison Act (Northern Ireland) 1953 in relation to any person imprisoned or detained.
	(e) His functions under the Social Security Contributions and Benefits Act 1992, the Social Security Administration Act 1992 or the Jobseekers Act 1995.
	(f) His functions under Part V of the Police Act 1997.
	[(g) His functions under the Safeguarding Vulnerable Groups Act 2006] [For the Safeguarding Vulnerable Groups (Northern Ireland) Order 2007].

Data controller	Subject matter
3. The Department of Health and Social Services for Northern Ireland.	Its functions under the Social Security Contributions and Benefits (Northern Ireland) Act 1992, the Social Security Administration (Northern Ireland) Act 1992 or the Jobseekers (Northern Ireland) Order 1995.

7.145   One person may not require another person or a third party to produce a relevant record or to supply a record to him in connection with the following situations:

(a)   the recruitment of another person as an employee;

(b)   the continued employment of another person; or

(c)   any contract for the provision of services to him by another person.

7.146   Under s 56(2) a similar prohibition applies where a person who is concerned with the provision (for payment or not) of goods, facilities or services to the public or a section of the public must not as a condition of providing or offering to provide any goods, facilities or services to another person, require that other person or a third party to supply him with a relevant record or to produce a relevant record to him.

7.147   These provisions do not apply where the requirement was authorised by law or court order or was in the particular circumstances in the public interest.

7.148   There is a special provision in relation to Part V of the Police Act 1997 (certificates of criminal records etc) whereby the imposition of the above requirement is not to be required as being justified in the public interest where access may be requested on the ground that it would assist in the prevention or detection of crime (and see Police Act 1997, ss 112–113 and 115). Under the 1997 Act, employers (via applications made by employees) can access criminal records in relation to those involved with the care of children, the vulnerable and others (see paras 7.239 et seq below). Individuals may have access to their own files which are to be used by others, but the information may be limited. Section 115 of the 1997 Act concerning provision of 'enhanced criminal records' (para 7.239 below) must be exercised fairly and in conformity with natural justice and Art 8 ECHR; but the Court of Appeal has ruled that this did not mean that an applicant had to be given a hearing by the chief officer of police where the former disputes evidence of a sexual offence which did not lead to a conviction. Section 117 allows the applicant to seek an amended certificate from the Secretary of State (Criminal Records Bureau).[1]

---

[1]   *R (X) v Chief Constable West Midlands* [2005] 1 All ER 610 (see para 7.239 below) and *R (L) v Met Police Com'r* [2007] EWCA Civ 168. For the Criminal Records Bureau, see www.crb.gov.uk.

7.149   Contravention of DPA 1998, s 56(1) and (2) is a criminal offence.

HEALTH RECORDS

7.150 Any term or condition in a contract will be void insofar as it seeks to require an individual to produce all or part of a record obtained under data access rights by that individual and which contains information about that individual's mental or physical health made by a health professional in the course of caring for the individual (DPA 1998, s 58). The *GMC Guidance* (July 2000) concerns patient confidentiality and the Information Commissioner has produced guidance: *Guidance and Confidentiality NHS Code of Practice* (2009). The NHS *Code of Practice Confidentiality* was revised in 2006 and see the Department of Health's website at www.dh.gov.uk). Protecting patient confidentiality is a core value of the NHS and emphasised in the NHS constitution (2010).

FEES, AND OTHER REGULATIONS

7.151 Fees have been set by the Data Protection (Subject Access) (Fees and Miscellaneous Provisions) Regulations 2000, SI 2000/191. A maximum of £10 is payable for applications under DPA 1998, s 7(2)(b)[1] except where the request comes under reg 4, 5 or 6. The Schedule sets out rates for written documents according to page lengths. The maximum that may be charged is £50 for manual health records and for education records. Separate Regulations have been made to cover: notification by DCs and fees (Data Protection (Notification and Notification Fees) Regulations 2000, SI 2000/188); the processing of sensitive personal data (Data Protection (Processing of Sensitive Personal Data) Order 2000, SI 2000/417); functions of designated authority (Data Protection (Functions of Designated Authority) Order 2000, SI 2000/186); and designated codes of practice (Data Protection (Designated Codes of Practice) Order 2000, SI 2000/418 (as amended)). See also SI 2001/3214 and SI 2001/3223. A request for 'unstructured personal data' under DPA 1998, s 9A(3) (as introduced by FOIA 2000) is subject to the 'appropriate limit' set out in SI 2004/3244, ie £600 and £450 (see para 1.74 above).

[1] See para 1.74 above. The fee is £2 if the request is for limited information from a credit reference agency.

7.152 In 2009, two levels of fees were introduced for DC notification (para 7.34 above).

THE CROWN

7.153 DPA 1998 binds the Crown. Each government department shall be treated as a person separate from any other government department. Each will have to notify the Commissioner of their processing. Neither the DC of the Royal Household, Duchy of Lancaster or Duchy of Cornwall nor any government Department shall be liable to prosecution under the Act but Crown servants may be prosecuted for various matters: unlawfully obtaining and disclosing personal data, unlawfully procuring the disclosure to another person of information contained in personal data, or selling unlawfully obtained personal data. Sch 20, para 7 of the Coroners and Justice Act 2009 includes within 'government departments' any part of the Scottish administration, a Northern Ireland department, Welsh Assembly government and any body or authority exercising statutory functions on behalf of the Crown.

7.154 An order on Crown appointments exempts certain appointments from the subject access provisions of the DPA 1998.[1]

[1]   Data Protection (Crown Appointments) Order 2000, SI 2000/416.

7.155 The Department for Constitutional Affairs has expressed the view that for the law of confidentiality, departments are 'different legal persons' but without supporting argument. Secretaries of State are a one and indivisible office.[1]

[1]   *Public Sector Data Sharing* Nov (2003) p 11, DCA.

ACCESSIBLE DATA (DPA 1998, S 68 AND SCH 12)

7.156 'Accessible records' are records that were available under the Access to Health Records Act 1990, personal information held for social work purposes and personal information relating to public sector tenancies under the Access to Personal Files Act 1987. Rights of access to educational records under the Education (School Records) Regulations 1989 (see Education Reform Act 1988, ss 218 and 232) and Scottish and Northern Ireland analogues are also 'accessible records' under the DPA 1998 (see para 7.7 above). Until the combination of the DPA 1998 and the FOIA 2000 Britain had not, in general terms, gone as far as other common law jurisdictions in allowing access to personal documents by the data subject (the individual concerned). In other respects, Britain had gone further. While there was very comprehensive coverage of automated files by holders who were public bodies or private bodies, access to paper documents was not comprehensive but was covered by statutes for specific subject areas. These invariably made a distinction between private and public bodies – so that in the case of housing, housing authorities were covered but not housing associations. In health, coverage was more comprehensive. The principal statutes were the Access to Personal Files Act 1987, the Access to Medical Reports Act 1988, Access to Health Records Act 1990 and the Human Fertilisation and Embryology Act 1990 as well as Consumer Credit Act 1974, s 158. The DPA 1998 now covers manual documents, as defined ie 'structured filing systems', held by both public and private bodies within the terms of that Act. Rights to accessible records were incorporated within the DPA 1998. The FOIA 2000 also extends the range of manual documents held by public bodies, and 'public bodies' may of course be added to by order of the Secretary of State (see paras 1.85 et seq above).

7.157 The Access to Personal Files Act 1987 was repealed by the DPA 1998 and the regulations made under that Act as well as access provisions not under that Act but referred to above were phased out so that they only covered applications made to the court before the repeal took effect.

7.158   As originally drafted, the Access to Personal Files Bill covered manual files relating to: health records; educational records (including those maintained by 'any school, college, polytechnic, university, or any other educational establishment as defined in the Education Act 1944, s 77' and education authorities); housing records; benefit or other records (eiusdem generis); social services and welfare records; employment records held by any employer; bank, building society and credit records (cf Consumer Credit Act 1974, s 158) and immigration records. The debates in Parliament on the Bill and the campaign for freedom of information literature were punctuated by examples of numerous cases where personal information of the above kind had been inaccurate, misleading, erroneous and, potentially or actually, extremely damaging to innocent victims. A particularly notorious episode has concerned the use of personal records by employment reference agencies which provide information on the alleged political sympathies of individuals.[1]

[1]   And, allegedly, on their relatives; see Hollingsworth and Norton-Taylor *Blacklist* (1988); Employment Relations Act 1999, s 3; and Employment Relations Act 1999 (Blacklists) Regulations 2010, SI 2010/493.

7.159   The government pressed its own Bill upon the proponents which was restricted to local authorities which the proponents reluctantly accepted to ensure passage to the statute book. The education bodies covered by the education regulations were not as broad as those contained in the original Bill. Many of these anomalies have now been swept away by the combined effects of the 1998 and 2000 legislation. But, crucial differences will still operate between private and public DCs. So, for access to a housing record held by a non-public sector landlord as defined the records would have to fall under the 'electronic' or 'manual' provisions of the DPA 1998 and not the 'accessible' provisions.

STATUTORY PROHIBITIONS OR RESTRICTIONS ON DISCLOSURE

7.160   The rights under the DPA 1998 prevail against any other statutory prohibitions or restrictions on the disclosure of information. The most obvious statute is the Official Secrets Act 1989. Police information, or categories of it, is likely to be so protected and may be relevant in social services cases. Rights under the present Act will therefore override the prohibitions etc in the 1989 Act unless these are re-incorporated in 'any exemptions or restrictions prescribed in the regulations'.

RECORDS AND THE COMMON LAW

7.161   The common law witnessed some interesting developments in relation to applications for records that were not covered by the DPA 1998. The decision in *Durant* has placed a restricted meaning on 'structured files' and 'personal data' (paras 7.15 et seq above) and FOIA only applies to public authorities. Resort may have to be made to the common law. In *ex p Martin*[1] a person suffering from psychiatric problems applied to two medical authorities for the disclosure of his medical records to establish more information about specific incidents in the past. Because the records were not on computer and were made before 1991, they were not subject to the existing statutory provisions. The first authority refused to make disclosure stating it had no authority to do so. The second authority made disclosure subject to conditions that an assurance had to be given by the applicant that no litigation was contemplated by him. This assurance the applicant refused to give. The second respondent subsequently refused access after the responsible consultant psychiatrist determined that disclosure to the applicant was not in his best interests and would be detrimental to him. After applying for a judicial review of this decision, the second respondents' solicitor wrote stating that the applicant's nominated medical adviser could have access to the documents to decide whether and to what extent disclosure could be made to the applicant without causing him harm. The Court of Appeal upheld the High Court's decision to refuse access stating that access could be denied by the owner of the patient's records (the authority) if it was in his best interests not to see them, ie where they could cause detriment to his health. The court felt that on the facts, the offer by the Board was a complete answer to the request and it was, one might add, a generous offer. Because the respondent had done all that was necessary to comply with their duty, judicial review was rightly denied. One might suspect that had the offer not been made the approach of the Court of Appeal may have been less generous to the authority. Nourse LJ for instance stated that a health authority no more than a private doctor does not have an absolute right to deal with medical records in any way it chooses and has at all times to act in the best interests of the patient. 'Those interests would usually require that a patient's medical records should not be disclosed to third parties; conversely, that they should usually … be handed on by one doctor to the next or made available to the patient's legal advisers if they are reasonably required for the purposes of legal proceedings in which he is involved.'[2]

---

[1]   *R v Mid Glamorgan Family Health Services Authority ex p Martin* [1995] 1 All ER 356, CA; see *Sidaway v Bethlem Royal Hospital Governors* [1985] 1 All ER 643, HL and *McInerney v MacDonald* (1992) 93 DLR (4th) 415, Canada. In *A Health Authority v X* [2001] 2 FLR 673 it was held that disclosure of a GP's records relating to children to a health authority was subject to conditions of confidentiality.

[2]   *Martin* at 363j. See the Caldicott Committee on *Patient Identifiable Information* December 1997.

7.162   Where personal information is held by 'holders' of a kind not specified by the DPA 1998 – cases do not spring readily to mind – and where their possession of information is not otherwise prohibited by the law, eg Official Secrets Act 1989, it will be well to remember that the possibility of a breach of confidence, trespass or wrongful interference with personalty (documents) under the Torts (Interference with Goods) Act 1977 may have occurred in the manner in which the information was obtained. In the absence of a breach of confidence, or breach of copyright or patent or such protection over intellectual property, British law does not provide for the protection of personal information per se unless an action, eg for defamation, can be maintained. It is of course well to remember the impact of the Human Rights Act 1998 on this area and the application of Art 8 ECHR, which have added to privacy protection and which we examine below. Further, the dealing with inaccurate information which causes harm – financial or physical/emotional – could on the facts amount to negligence as well as being defamatory. The proximity of the holder to the subject ought to be sufficient to satisfy a duty of care situation[1] – in spite of recent attempts to limit the range of victims.[2] The comprehensive nature of the DPA 1998 will make the residual role of the common law less useful in those areas where the Act protects data.

[1]   *Spring v Guardian Assurance plc* [1994] 3 All ER 129, HL, duty between referee and job applicant; see also *Cox v Sun Alliance Life Ltd* [2001] IRLR 448 and *Bullimore v Pothecary Witham Weld* [2011] IRLR 18.
[2]   See also the Malicious Communications Act 1988.

7.163   Health and Social Care Act 2001, s 60 allows 'patient information' to be passed on without consent in prescribed circumstances for improving patient care or in the public interest. Provision may be made to disclose prescribed information to the person to whom the information relates by health service bodies. There are limits on the confidential patient information that may be prescribed (s 60(5)). Details are in regulations, and a Patients Information Advisory Group is established under s 61 (see SI 2001/2836).[1]

[1]   See *R v Department of Health ex p Source Informatics Ltd* [2000] 2 WLR 940 where a company wished to gather information about GPs' prescribing habits from pharmacists for a fee. They wished to sell this to pharmaceutical companies. Providing the information was not confidential in itself, ie revealing a patient's identity, there was nothing unlawful in this practice. This section seeks to avoid any complications resulting from that decision but only on the specified grounds. See Health Service (Control of Patient Information) Regulations 2002, SI 2002/1438.

7.164   Disclosure (discovery) may be applied for to obtain the 'offending' or relevant documents, but in the nature of the action such a claim is likely to appear speculative unless the allegations are itemised, and may meet with little sympathy at the interlocutory stage before pleadings, eg for an interim injunction[1] unless the applicant can satisfy the court on application that they are necessary to dispose fairly of the case and not merely to substantiate a suspicion.[2] *Anton Piller* orders (now renamed search orders) may be invoked where there is a risk of destruction or interference with essential evidence.[3] Specificity will be required. However, judges may be less sympathetic to bodies which peddle in personal information for profit than to statutory bodies collecting information in the exercise of their public duties and powers and where confidentiality is often required.[4] In terms of personal document it is difficult to see how the DPA 1998 will not govern the situation.

[1]   RSC Ord 24, r 1(1); cf *Gaskin v Liverpool City Council* [1980] 1 WLR 1549, CA; for prohibitory injunctions and the balance of convenience: *American Cyanamid Co v Ethicon Ltd* [1975] AC 396, CA; *Cambridge Nutrition Ltd v BBC* [1990] 3 All ER 523, CA; *National Mutual Life Association of Australasia Ltd v GTV Corpn Pty* [1989] VR 747. Cf *Bonnard v Perryman* [1891] 2 Ch 269, CA; *Gulf Oil (GB) Ltd v Page* [1987] Ch 327, CA. See para 2.321, note 2 above.
[2]   *RHM Foods Ltd v Bovril Ltd* [1982] 1 All ER 673, CA: a case concerning property rights of the plaintiff.
[3]   See paras 10.119 et seq below, and *Anton Piller KG v Manufacturing Processes Ltd* [1976] Ch 55.
[4]   Cf *Campbell v Tameside Metropolitan Borough Council* [1982] 2 All ER 791, CA.

ACCESS TO MEDICAL REPORTS ACT 1988

7.165   The Access to Medical Reports Act 1988 (ATMRA 1988) confers a right on an individual to have access, in accordance with the provisions of the

1988 Act, to any medical report relating to that individual which is to be, or has been, supplied by a medical practitioner for employment purposes or insurance purposes.

7.166 The 'applicant' means the person referred to in ATMRA 1988, s 3(1). This is the person who applies to a medical practitioner for a medical report relating to any individual to be supplied to him for employment or insurance purposes.

7.167 An application must not be made unless the applicant has notified the individual of his or her proposed application and the applicant has the individual's consent. Such notification must inform the individual of his or her right to withhold consent to the application and of his or her rights under the Act, as well as the effect of s 7 (exemptions).

7.168 Under the Act (s 2(1)):

'"care" includes examination, investigation or diagnosis for the purposes of, or in connection with, any form of medical treatment;

"employment purposes", in the case of any individual, means the purposes in relation to the individual of any person by whom he is or has been, or is seeking to be, employed (whether under a contract of service or otherwise);

"health professional" has the same meaning as in the Data Protection (Subject Access Modification) (Health) Order 1987;

"insurance purposes", in the case of any individual, means the purposes in relation to the individual of any person carrying on an insurance business with whom the individual has entered into, or is seeking to enter into, a contract of insurance, and "insurance business" and "contract of insurance" have the same meaning as in the Insurance Companies Act 1982;

"medical practitioner" means a person registered under the Medical Act 1983;

"medical report", in the case of an individual, means a report relating to the physical or mental health of the individual prepared by a medical practitioner who is or has been responsible for the clinical care of the individual.'

7.169 Supply of a medical report for employment or insurance purposes shall be construed as for the purposes of the person who is seeking to be supplied, or who was so supplied for such purposes in the case of a report which has already been supplied (s 2(2)).

7.170 On giving consent to an application under ATMRA 1988, s 3, an individual has the right to express his or her wish to have access to the report before it is supplied. The applicant has to notify the practitioner of that fact when the application is made and simultaneously notify the individual of the making of the application (s 4(1)). Each notification must contain a statement on the effect of s 4(2). This basically imposes a duty on the notified practitioner to allow access to the individual before supply. The report must not be supplied before access is allowed and s 5 is complied with, or 21 days have elapsed from the date of the making of the application without a communication from the individual 'concerning arrangements for the individual to have access to it'.

7.171 Similar provisions apply where the applicant does not notify the practitioner under s 4(1) above, but before supplying the report the individual notifies the practitioner that s/he wishes to have access before supply.

7.172 By ATMRA 1988, s 4(4) references to giving an individual access to a medical report are references to:
(a) making the report or a copy of it available for his or her inspection; or
(b) supplying the individual with a copy of it. A reasonable fee may be charged by the practitioner to cover the cost of supplying a report.

7.173 Where access is given to an individual, the report shall not be supplied to the applicant without the individual's consent (s 5(1)). The individual, before s/he consents to supply, may request in writing (s 5(3)) that the practitioner amends any part of the report that the individual considers incorrect or misleading. If agreeable, the practitioner can amend the report 'to the extent that s/he is prepared to accede to the individual's request' (s 5(2)(a)). If not agreeable to an amendment, s/he shall, upon the individual's request, attach a statement to the report of the individual's views relating to any part of the report which s/he is declining to amend (s 5(2)(b)).

7.174 The practitioner has to retain reports under the Act for at least six months from the date of supply (s 6(1)) and access has to be given to an individual upon request to relevant reports supplied within the previous six months (s 6(2)). Access can be by way of supplying a copy or making a copy available and reasonable fees to cover the cost of supply may be charged (s 6(3)).

7.175 Section 7 concerns exemptions. Individual access does not have to be given under ss 4(4) or 6(3) to any part of a medical report whose disclosure would in the opinion of the practitioner be likely to cause serious harm to the physical or mental health of the individual or others or would indicate the intentions of the practitioner in respect of the individual. Intentions would cover proposed treatment, recommendations, etc.

7.176 Under s 7(2) a medical practitioner shall not be obliged to give an individual access to any part of a medical report whose disclosure would be likely to reveal information about another person, or to reveal the identity of another person who has supplied information to the practitioner about the individual, unless:
(a) that person has consented; or
(b) that person is a health professional who has been involved in the care of the individual and the information relates to or has been provided by the professional in that capacity.

7.177 Where the exemptions are applicable to any part (but not the whole) of a medical report, the individual, who shall be notified of that fact, will be allowed access to the remainder of the report.

7.178 Where the exemptions cover the whole of the report, the individual has to be notified of that fact; but the report shall not be supplied to the applicant unless the individual consents. The individual has no right of access and the restrictions imposed by s 4(2) and (3) on supply do not take effect.

7.179 Relief is via the county court, or, as the Act extends to Scotland, the sheriff's court, where an individual satisfies that court that a person is not likely to comply or has failed to comply with duties under the Act (s 8).

7.180 All notifications required or authorised to be given under the Act must be in writing and may be given by post (s 9).

ACCESS TO HEALTH RECORDS ACT 1990

7.181 For several years the government expressed its support for a patient's legal right of access to his/her medical files. In 1990, the above Act was passed after earlier setbacks and significant opposition from the medical profession and medical insurers. The Act has been taken over by the DPA 1998. However, personal representatives or a deceased person's dependants may apply for records relating to the cause of death where eg, a negligence action is possible.

CONSUMER CREDIT ACT 1974, S 158

7.182 These rights are now brought within the DPA 1998. Section 158 provides that a credit reference agency must give a consumer a copy of the file relating to the consumer kept by the agency, within the prescribed period after receiving:
(a) a request in writing to that affect from any individual (the consumer);
(b) such particulars as the agency may reasonably require to enable them to identify the file; and
(c) the relevant fee.

7.183 When giving a copy of the file under s 158(1), the agency shall also give the consumer a statement in the prescribed form of his or her rights under s 159 (below). If the agency does not keep a file relating to the consumer it shall give the consumer notice of that fact, but need not return any money paid. A contravention by the agency of any provision of this section is an offence.

7.184 Section 159 rights include correction or removal of an entry if incorrect and which would be likely to cause prejudice. The agency must, under s 159(2), notify the consumer within 28 days of receipt of the notice of its action complete with the amended entry where it has been amended, with a further right for the consumer to serve on the agency an accompanying notice or correction to be provided with the entry. This notice must be complied with. The consumer, or the agency, may apply to the Director-General of Fair Trading for his order. Failure to comply with this order is a criminal offence.

PRIVACY PROTECTION

7.185 Until the incorporation of the ECHR under the Human Rights Act 1998 (HRA 1998), which took effect from 2 October 2000, there was no doubt that our law fell short of the protection of privacy envisaged in Art 8 ECHR. There was no statutory or common law right to privacy as such.[1] There was no right to control the use of information about oneself or one's image other than through limited legal rights then existing.[2] There is, simply, no absolute right to be left alone. The DPA 1998, and the law of confidentiality, are the closest we get to such protection (on the latter, see para 2.312 above). Now, however, statutes and regulations must be read wherever possible to be compatible with the Convention and, in particular in relation to our present discussion, Art 8. This states that everyone has the right to respect for his private and family life, his home and his correspondence and the Article was set out in ch 2 (para 2.291 above). Public authorities act unlawfully if they breach this Article without a legal justification and victims of such breaches will be entitled to remedies. The Article does not establish direct liability for breaches on individuals in their relationships under private law. As will be seen, the courts are under a duty to apply existing obligations in common law or statute as *modified* by Arts 8 and 10, and this can produce legal effects between individuals – horizontality.

[1] See para 7.188, note 2 below.
[2] See *Aubry v Editions Vice-Versa Inc* [1998] 1 SCR 591 for the position in Quebec.

7.186 Some important points were raised in pre-HRA litigation. In *R v Broadcasting Standards Commission, ex p BBC*[1] it was held by the High Court that a company had no right to privacy as set out in the code under which the BBC operated because in conformity with Art 8 ECHR (see para 2.291 above) that Article only applied to individuals and not corporate bodies. This decision was reversed by the Court of Appeal who held that corporate bodies are entitled under the code to protection of their privacy.[2] This was not a decision on confidentiality but on the code under which the BBC operated and Broadcasting Act 1996, ss 107(1) and 110(1). The question was raised in many quarters whether the HRA 1998 would lead to the development of a law of privacy along the lines of that in the USA. A legal right for privacy means a right to have personal information, and not simply that which would be protected by confidentiality, including film or photographs, protected by court orders or by award of damages where wrongly invaded. There is a considerable body of jurisprudence on Art 8 and the domestic courts will have to have regard to the decisions and opinions of the ECtHR, Commission and Committee of Ministers when interpreting statutes, regulations and developing the common law.[3] Case-law from the ECtHR has ruled that English legislation outlawing consensual homosexual conduct between more than two males in private, group activities which had been video-taped, was a breach of their right to privacy under Art 8.[4] It was seen how the ECtHR has gone further in its protection of privacy than have domestic courts although in the latter there was a more recent concentration on 'private information' as the central organising concept which deserved judicial protection. The ECtHR will be influential. The right of action was still based in confidentiality as supported by the provisions of the HRA 1998; they were not based on any free-standing tort of privacy.[5] There shall be no interference with these rights by a public authority except that which is in accordance with the law and is necessary to protect itemised desiderata. This interference must be necessary and must be proportionate in an objective sense. In *Gaskin v UK*[6] the ECtHR ruled that the absence of an independent arbiter to rule on claims for access to personal files (in this case concerning a child in care) was a breach of Art 8. Furthermore, it has been accepted by the same court that the failure by the state to provide protection against Art 8's infringement by a private party is a breach of Art 8. The state had failed in its duty of protection even though the invasion of private life was by a private citizen.[7] We have seen in ch 2 and will see in ch 10 how Art 8 has been interpreted to provide a right to information where such access is necessary to protect those rights (see paras 2.295 et seq above). To this extent, as we saw, it has gone further than the court's interpretation of Art 10 which was ruled to be of no assistance to *Gaskin*. However, as seen in ch 2, Art 10 rights are frequently in a balance with Art 8 rights (paras 2.324 et seq and 2.354 above).[8]

---

1   [1999] EMLR 858.

2   [2000] 3 All ER 989, CA; and see Sir S Sedley *Freedom, Law and Justice* (1999) ch 2.

3   HRA 1998, ss 2 and 3. It refers to the interpretation of a Convention right coming before the courts which would include the common law.

4   *ADT v UK* [2000] 2 FLR 697, ECtHR. For further discussion on the reach of Art 8, see *R (Razgar) v Secretary of State for the Home Department* [2004] UKHL 27.

5   *Campbell v MGN Ltd* [2004] 2 All ER 995 (HL) and *A v B* [2002] 2 All ER 545 (CA). For confidentiality protection in private relationships see: *D v L* [2004] EMLR 1 and a lovers' tiff; *Lady Archer v Williams* [2003] EMLR 38; and *Mills v News Group* [2001] EMLR 41 where a private address of a property being purchased by a friend of Paul McCartney was not protected.

6   (1989) 12 EHRR 36.

7   *X and Y v Netherlands* 8 EHRR 235 (ECtHR). Guidance was given in *A v B* [2003] QB 195 (see para 2.324 above) on balancing of interests, which many believe to be over-generous to the press. *A v B* has been heavily qualified subsequently (below).

8   See *A Local Authority (Inquiry: Restraint on Publication)* [2003] EWHC 2746 (Fam), [2004] 1 All ER 480 and the balancing of Art 8 ECHR rights of children and adults and a local authority's rights to publish under Art 10. The Family Division granted an injunction against the local authority preventing publication of a 's 7 Local Authority Social Services Act 1970 inquiry' into a children's and vulnerable adults' home. See now chapter 10 below.

7.187 The ECtHR has subsequently ruled that breaches of Art 8 may well be committed in circumstances where an English court could not award a remedy under provisions existing at the time of judgment. In *Peck v UK*[1] an individual had been filmed by CCTV attempting suicide in a public place by cutting his wrists. The film and photographs from it were subsequently publicised in a number of ways including national TV coverage. No attempt was made to conceal the applicant's identity. Peck's application to English courts for relief was unsuccessful, although it should be noted that the relevant facts took place before the Human Rights Act 1998 came into effect. The ECtHR ruled that there had been a breach of Art 8 and also Art 13 because there had been no remedy in domestic courts for the breach. It should be noted that the defendant in the domestic proceedings was a local authority and the situation would now be covered by the HRA. It may well be very difficult to maintain that not maintaining anonymity in similar circumstances for the claimant was not a breach of Art 8 on the authority's part. It should not be forgotten that, under HRA 1998, s 2, domestic courts must take into account any judgment of the ECtHR; and s 3 states that, in so far as it is possible to do so, 'primary and secondary legislation must be read and given effect in a way which is compatible with Convention rights'.

1 *Peck v United Kingdom* Application no 44647/98 (2003) 13 BHRC 669; the events occurred in 1995 and 1996 and the first instance judge noted the future impact of the HRA. The authority had acted under Criminal Justice and Public Order Act 1994, s 163 and Local Government Act 1972, s 111(1).

7.188 In a further development, Princess Caroline was found to have been a victim of a breach of Art 8 when photographs of her in public places were published by the press in Germany, publications which were not actionable under German law.[1] It was observed above how the English law of confidentiality has had to absorb the Art 8 and Art 10 rights in the development of the case-law (para 7.186 and paras referred to). The law of confidentiality has moved from a quasi-proprietorial basis (though this should not be exaggerated) to a more humanistic approach where the protection of private information (including photographs) is becoming the object of judicial protection. But the courts in the UK have shied away from the creation of a comprehensive tort of privacy itself as *Wainwright* shows (para 2.320 above). In *Wainwright v Home Office*[2] the Law Lords ruled that there was no common law tort of invasion of privacy. The case concerned events involving the strip search of prisoners to a prisoner occurring before the HRA came into effect. If their rights to family and private life under HRA 1998 were breached, then this would be actionable although the courts have shown reluctance to award tortious levels of damages for breaches of the HRA (especially when effectively it was maladministration that was causing a breach; see para 9.61 below), but it must be questioned whether it is correct to suggest, as Lord Hoffmann did, that for damages a breach of Art 8 would have to be intentional. Intentionality may go to quantum but not liability. Surely, Lord Hoffmann's approach is the test for misfeasance of public office? In *Wainright v UK* the ECtHR found a breach of Art 8 ECHR by the UK on the facts pleaded before the English courts.[3] Courts have relied upon the law on confidentiality, defamation or trespass and other torts as modified by Arts 8 and 10 where they wish to apply common law protection. That protection has become ever more apparent. These points were discussed in relation to *Campbell v MGN Ltd* (paras 2.324 et seq above). It is clear that important developments have been made by the English courts in advancing the 'protection of private information' by reformulating the law of confidentiality. Will it be extended to cover personal files that are not protected by the DPA? On what basis and to what extent could protection be given?

1 *von Hannover v Germany* Application 59320/00. This concerned Princess Caroline and photographs taken in public places over a sustained period of time by paparazzi; German law

had drawn a distinction between public places and a 'secluded place' to which the claimant had withdrawn. See *Sciacca v Italy* (2006) 43 EHRR 20 on publication of an identity photo taken by Italian inland revenue police; and *Paulik v Slovakia* [2006] 3 FCR 323 (ECtHR) on art 8 rights. In an English case, a female DJ, Sara Cox, was awarded an injunction to prevent publication of photographs of her sun bathing in the nude with her newly married husband: The Guardian, 7 June 2003. See Sexual Offences Act 2003, s 67 and the offence of 'voyeurism' re the recording of 'private acts' by third parties without their consent for the sexual gratification of others.

2   *Wainwright v Home Office* [2003] 4 All ER 969 (HL) was discussed above (para 2.320). Concerning intention to breach a right, this has been doubted by Lord Lester QC citing *Halford v UK* (1997) 24 EHRR 523 at para 76 – improper purpose made breach more serious; *Darnell v UK* (1993) 18 EHRR 205 at para 24; *McMichael v UK* (1995) 20 EHRR 205 at para 103 – claimant not disqualified from compensation because breach unintentional and at common law; *Entick v Carrington* (1765) 19 *State Trials* 1029. See also *Kaye v Robertson* [1991] FSR 62, CA. Cf *Shelley Films Ltd v Rex Features Ltd* [1994] EMLR 134; and *R v Khan* [1996] 3 All ER 289, HL. See R Wacks *Personal Information, Privacy and the Law* (1993) *Privacy* (1993). In *Earl Spencer v UK* (1998) 25 EHRR CD 105 the European Commission of Human Rights was not convinced that the English law of confidentiality was an inadequate remedy for breaches of Art 8 ECHR. See also *Z v Finland* (1998) 25 EHRR 371.

3   [2007] 44 EHRR 40 UK in breach of Art 8. *I v Finland* (2009) 48 EHRR 31 on duties under Art 8 regarding failures to protect medical records from unnecesary disclosure to hospital staff other than those treating. See *Mak v UK* [2010] 2 FLR 451 and breach of Art 8 where a minor was subject to medical tests without authorisation and *AD v UK* (2010) *The Times*, April 6 and breach of Art 8 in relation to disproportionate action by authority in care orders.

7.189   As the HRA 1998 proceeded through Parliament, fears were expressed that the incorporation of Art 8 would undermine freedom of the press and media. In *R v Broadcasting Complaints Commission, ex p Granada TV* for instance, the Court of Appeal upheld a complaint concerning a broadcast which featured a photograph of a murdered child which was broadcast without the parents' consent. This had interfered with the parents' right to privacy and family life.[1] Would politicians, the powerful and famous who are in the public eye, or the corrupt and criminal, use Article 8 to prevent any discussion of events which the public should know about? What was the public entitled to know? Special provisions were therefore introduced in the Act under s 12 to protect freedom of expression. We have seen the content of these provisions above (paras 2.349 et seq above). Special regard is to be had to the public interest in publication and any relevant privacy codes such as exist for the press and media. The onus is on the person claiming relief from the court. Clearly, Art 8 has to be balanced with Art 10 rights to freedom of expression. An interesting early example of the benefits of Art 10 was seen in the case of *Kelly v BBC*[2] where the High Court refused to prevent the broadcast of an interview with a 16-year-old who was a ward of court and who had left home to live with a religious cult (see para 10.6 below). These were not proceedings concerned with the upbringing of a child. In such cases, a stricter approach to secrecy of proceedings is usually enforced.

1   [1995] EMLR 163.
2   [2001] 1 All ER 323. See *JIH v News Group Ltd* [2011] EWCA Civ 42.

7.190   The conflict that may emerge where the principles of freedom of speech and privacy clash was graphically illustrated in the case of Jon Venables and Robert Thompson, the notorious murderers of James Bulger, when the two youths sought to continue injunctions protecting them as children[1] to prevent the revelation of their identities now that they were adults after their release from prison (they would be given new identities) or their whereabouts. Such an order protecting adults was then unprecedented.[2] The courts had to balance their right to privacy, confidentiality, to rehabilitation and to life – in the fear of threats of serious violence to them – and the right of the press to inform the public of their identity and whereabouts. The judgment of the court[3] was given by the President of the Family Division and she held that an injunction would be issued in the broadest terms prohibiting the publication of any information leading to the identity of either claimant or their future whereabouts. This would cover their present whereabouts, 'any information about their present appearance and similar information.' The injunction would cover any attempts by the media to solicit information from past or present carers , staff or co-detainees at their secure units until the claimants were released from prison. The injunction would also seek to prohibit further publication in [England or Wales] of information published on the internet or outside the UK. It remains to be seen how practicable this last feature will be. The injunction was also described as 'contra mundum', against the world at large.[4] While the rights to freedom of expression and a free press under Art 10 were given especial importance in s 12 of the HRA 1998, that right had to be balanced against other rights, including those under the Convention such as Art 2 (right to life), Art 3 (prohibition of torture) and Art 8 (right to privacy and family life). The court's task was to apply the Convention to the interpretation and development of the common law and although that did not seem to create a free standing cause of action by one private party against another, it did include a positive obligation on the court as well as a negative one. In other words the court must give positive expression to the rights of the claimants under the influence of the Convention and common law. The court is a public authority under s 6(3) of the HRA 1998 and is under a duty to act in a way which is compatible with the Convention.

[1]   The injunctions were issued under Children and Young Persons Act 1933, s 39 in November 1993.
[2]   See also *X County Council v A* [1985] 1 All ER 53 where extensive protection was given to an adult (the murderess Mary Bell who had murdered when she was 11) under wardship jurisdiction to protect her child. See also *X (formerly M Bell) v O'Brien* [2003] EWHC 1101 where an injunction was issued to protect the anonymity of the same person who had now achieved adulthood. On 24 February 2005, an injunction was issued by Eady J in the High Court protecting the anonymity for life of Maxine Carr, former partner of child murderer Ian Huntley. The order was unopposed by the media and was issued because of the serious threat of bodily injury or death to Ms Carr.
[3]   *Venables v News Group Newspapers Ltd* [2001] 1 All ER 908 (Fam D). And see *Glaser v UK* [2000] 3 FCR 193 where the ECtHR outlined the 'positive obligations' under the Convention in relation to Art 8.
[4]   *A-G v Times Newspapers Ltd* [1992] 1 AC 191, HL. See also *X County Council v A* [1985] 1 All ER 53 above. See *A-G v Greater Manchester Newspapers Ltd* [2001] All ER (D) 32 and contempt proceedings concerning breaches of Butler-Sloss P's injunction.

7.191   The court was satisfied of the requirement of such protection given the 'uniquely notorious' circumstances of this 'exceptional case', and that there was compelling evidence of the risk of death or serious injury possibly in the form of torture if the information were revealed. Indeed, were Art 8 alone in risk of being breached, the judge was doubtful whether injunctions 'to restrict the Press in this case' would be issued. It was also clear that the basis of the injunctions was the law of confidentiality as influenced by the duty to act compatibly with Convention rights when interpreting the common law.

7.192 It has been seen that English courts were initially resistant to the development of a law of privacy. The DPA 1998 (above) and the RIPA 2000 (paras 2.200 et seq above) both seek to provide, if not protection of privacy, then safeguards in the use of private information. In the latter case, protection as balanced with the intrusive powers of the state, although intrusion by private parties is as big a threat to privacy. But the common law, in the area of privacy as in other areas concerned with fundamental rights, is rapidly developing principles protecting privacy. In *Douglas v Hello! Ltd*[1] the Court of Appeal believed that two famous film stars arguably had a remedy for breach of confidence and privacy when a magazine, *Hello!*, published photos – which they had obtained from an unauthorised source – of their wedding and which the plaintiffs had already contracted to sell exclusively to a rival journal. In refusing to continue an injunction issued by the High Court to prevent further publication of the defendant journal after publication of 15,750 copies, the judges nevertheless spoke in emphatic terms of the couple's right to confidentiality and privacy. There was also, it should be noted, the possibility of an unlawful interference with the plaintiffs' contractual rights.

[1]   *Douglas v Hello! Ltd* [2001] 2 All ER 289, CA; Keene LJ thought that *Kaye v Robertson* would be decided differently today (in 2001). By 2011 this is an absolute certainty. See also *A v B* [2002] 2 All ER 545 (CA) which now has to be qualified. In the House of Lords foe *Douglas* see para below 7.193 and note 1.

7.193 The Court of Appeal based its judgment on the basis of confidentiality – in the circumstances a commercial confidentiality seems more appropriate and this is how the judge in the trial of *Douglas v Hello!* interpreted the relationship[1] – although the court spoke of 'a right of privacy which we will today recognise and protect and which was grounded in equity and the common law.' The case gave 'the final impetus to the recognition of a right to privacy in English law.' It has been influential in litigation before the law lords including in *Campbell v MGN Ltd* [2005] UKHL 61 (para 2.324 above and see *MGN Ltd v UK* Application No 39401/04, January 18, 2011 ECtHR) and subsequent case law. In *Campbell*, the law lords applied the law of confidentiality as modified by the need to protect personal private information under Art 8 ECHR although not all the personal information about the famous model was protected (paras 2.320 and 2.324). The court in *Douglas* was unanimous in lifting the injunction that had been imposed by the High Court because damages or an account of profits would be an adequate remedy at full trial for the plaintiffs (events proved otherwise) whereas an injunction could cause unquantifiable harm to the defendant in the event of their being successful. Were the pictures to be published, that would probably lead to a breach of cl 3 of the Press Complaints Commission Code of Practice protecting privacy to which under s 12(4)(b) of the HRA 1998 the court was to have particular regard. The court was also to have particular regard to the Convention right of freedom of expression but this was not a trump card which automatically overrode every other consideration. A series of factors had to be balanced. The court felt that if a breach of cl 3 of the Code of Practice were established at trial this would probably deprive *Hello!* of its reliance on Art 10 at the full trial. There was no public interest, one might add, in *their* publication of the photographs. The photos had also become available to the public. The case was persuasive for the development of a free-standing Art 8 right of privacy in English law which takes 'direct horizontal effect' between private individuals. In *Hello!* Sedley LJ expressed the point as follows: 'The law no longer needs an artificial relationship of confidentiality …: it can recognise privacy itself as a legal principle drawn from the fundamental value of personal autonomy.' The HRA 1998 and the Convention do not, as Butler-Sloss P said in *Venables*, 'establish new law. They reinforce and give greater weight to the principles already established in our case law.' One might add they have become part of the common law. And the courts are under a duty by virtue of HRA 1998, s 6 to apply the Articles to disputes before them, including those disputes between private parties. And the common law's method is development of principle. As in *Venables*, the case reveals the court applying the Convention to the interpretation and development of common law and equity in the form of confidentiality and protection of personal information. It shows that development, however, becoming ever more robust.[2] The decision at the trial of *Douglas v Hello! (No 3)*[3] where Lindsay J stated that the Convention comes into play even in cases involving only private parties and *Campbell* (para 2.324 and above) reveal how that process continues. The court of appeal in *D v H (No 3)* upheld the claims of the Douglases for breach of confidence and protection of their private information. The fact that they had authorised publication of approved photos of 'a private occasion' did not remove their right to confidentiality in seeking reparation for publication of unapproved photos. Furthermore, a prior publication of personal information may not remove the necessity of preventing or punishing further publication.

[1]   *Douglas v Hello!* [2003] 3 All ER 996: 'akin' to a trade secret or a hybrid which was dealt with 'unconscionably' by the defendants. The Douglases received £14,600 for distress and incidental costs; *OK!*, which was wrongfully denied the scoop were awarded £1,047,756 for lost sales from *Hello!* The court of appeal [2005] EWCA Civ 595 upheld the claim of the Douglases noting that the award of the amount of damages to them did not represent an 'adequate and satisfactory' remedy when considered against the initial refusal of the court of appeal in the 2000 proceedings to award an interim injunction because damages would be an adequate remedy. The decision in relation to the claimant *OK!* was reversed on the grounds that it had no right to commercial confidentiality. In the House of Lords in *Douglas v Hello! Ltd (No 3)* [2007] UKHL 21 the issue concerned the claimant *OK!* only – there was no appeal against the ruling in favour of the Douglases – and by a majority of 3–2 *OK!* won its appeal and the original award of damages was reinstated.

[2]   There has been an interesting debate between those who argue that the HRA 1998 does not create direct horizontal effect between individuals: Sir R Buxton (2000) 116 LQR 48, those who argue that it does precisely that: Sir W Wade (2000) 116 LQR 217, and those who argue that horizontal effect is produced indirectly: M Hunt (1998) Public Law 423. On damages under HRA 1998 see: *Anufrijeva and Another v Southwark LBC* [2004] 1 All ER 833 (CA).

[3]   [2003] 3 All ER 996.

7.194   The protection of private information featured more prominently in the Court of Appeal's judgment in *Douglas*.

7.195   The discussion of the emerging principles in *Campbell* have been developed in a series of English judgments. These display a growing sensitivity to privacy protection. In *R (Axon) v Secretary of State for Health* [2006] EWHC 37 (Admin) the High Court ruled that a girl under the age of 16 was entitled to communicate confidentially with her doctor about advice on sexual matters and without her mother having a right to be informed. In *HRH Prince of Wales v Associated Newspapers* [2006] EWCA Civ 1776, confidential journals written by the Prince of Wales regarding the handover of Hong Kong to China, alleged to have been sent to between 50–75 contacts, and which were given to the press by a servant in breach of a contractual term of confidence, were protected by personal privacy and confidentiality.[1] These portayed participants in a less than flattering light. No public interest was present in their disclosure and injunctions preventing publication were rightly awarded by the High Court. 'What is the nature of "private information"? It seems to us that it must include information that is personal to the person who possesses it and that he does not intend shall be imparted to the general public. The nature of the information, or the form in which it is kept, may suffice to make it plain that the information satisfies these criteria'. The Court of Appeal has considered that these observations remain sound. They are in no way 'discordant' with the statement of Lord Nicholls of Birkenhead in *Campbell v MGN Ltd* [2005] UKHL 61 at para 21:

'Essentially the touchstone of private life is whether in respect of the disclosed facts the person inquestion had a reasonable expectation of privacy.'

Lord Hope of Craighead at para 85 advanced a similar test:

'... a duty of confidence will arise whenever the party subject to the duty is in a situation where he knows or ought to know that the other person can reasonably expect his privacy to be protected.'

Lady Hale at para 134 advanced the same test and Lord Carswell at para 165 endorsed this. Lord Hoffmann at para 51 made the following statement in agreement with the principles of protection of personal information, although he disagreed on their application to the facts in question:

'Instead of the cause of action being based upon the duty of good faith applicable to confidential personal information and trade secrets alike, it focuses upon the protection of human autonomy and dignity-the right to control the dissemination of information about one's private life and the right to the esteem and respect of other people.'

[1]   *Cambell v Frisbee* [2002] EWCA Civ 1374 on support for *contractual* duties of confidentiality being more important than simple confidentiality. We doubt this to be the case.

7.196   In *McKennitt v Ash* [2005] EWHC 3003 (QB), (appeal dismissed in [2007] 3 WLR 194) the High Court protected personal information contained in a publication by the singer Loreena McKennit's personal assistant and friend declaring the information to be protected by personal privacy and confidentiality and injuncting it from further publication. The information covered: (i) Ms McKennitt's personal and sexual relationships; (ii) her personal feelings and, in particular, in relation to her deceased fiancé and the circumstances of his death; (iii) matters relating to her health and diet; (iv) matters relating to her emotional vulnerability; and (v) the details of an unhappy financial dispute between Ms McKennitt and the defendants. The court made an assessment itemising 34 classes of information and identified those that were deserving of protection under personal privacy and confidentiality and therefore needed to be protected by an appropriate injunction and damages for injured feelings. It was clear that the authority of older cases such as *Woodward v Hutchins* [1977] 2 All ER 751 and the availability of a public interest defence to a defendant based on misdemeanours of the plaintiff were today of limited worth. In *Murray v Express Newspapers plc* [2007] EWHC 1908 Ch the issue concerned a photograph of JK Rowling and her husband and their baby son in a buggy in a public place. The photo was taken covertly with long-range lense. This was published by a newspaper together with some information from JK Rowling previously published in a newspaper. It was an application to strike out the action by Rowling for showing no cause of action. 'The reality of the case is that the Claimant's parents seek through their son to establish a right to personal privacy for themselves and their children when engaged in ordinary family activities wherever conducted' (para 7). From Lord Hope in *Campbell* (para 122): 'The taking of photographs in a public street must, as Randerson J said in *Hosking v Runting* [2003] 3 NZLR 385, 415, para 138, be taken to be one of the ordinary incidents of living in a free community. The real issue is whether publicising the content of the photographs would be offensive: Gault and Blanchard JJ in the Court of Appeal [2004] NZCA 34, para 165. A person who just happens to be in the street when the photograph was taken and appears in it only incidentally cannot as a general rule object to the publication of the photograph, for the reasons given by L'Heureux-Dubé and Bastarache JJ in *Aubry v Éditions Vice-Versa Inc* [1998] 1 SCR 591, para 59. But the situation is different if the public nature of the place where a photograph is taken was simply used as background for one or more persons who constitute the true subject of the photograph. In England, people do not have a right to protect their image as such where photos are taken in a public place. It is the use to which the photos may be put that interests the law. The use of Naomi Campbell's photo in a public place was not objectionable; it was the use of her photo at a very private occasion – seeking medical assistance through a narcotics anonymous group that was an invasion of her privacy.' The first instance judgment rejected the claimant's claim holding that he (baby Rowling) had no reasonable expectation of privacy. The court of appeal reversed this ruling and held that there was a triable issue which had to go before a trial judge: [2008] EWCA Civ 446.

7.197   In *Mosley v Ass News* [2008] EWHC 1777 (QB) the former boss of Formula One racing and son of Sir Oswald Mosely brought proceedings against the defendant for publishing in one of their newspapers, and videos on their web, pictures of the claimant participating in sadomasochism, including bondage, beatings and domination, with prostitutes at a party which he had organised. Mosley claimed he had been ruined by this exposure. The defendant claimed was in the public interest because, they alleged, of anti-semitic overtones to the behaviour and, failing that, a public interest in knowing that a celebrity was engaging in such immoral conduct. Eady J decided that the claimant had a reasonable expectation of privacy in relation to sexual activities (albeit unconventional) carried on between consenting adults on private property. He found that there was no evidence that the gathering was intended to be a simulation of Nazi behaviour or adoption of any Nazi attitudes. Nor was it in fact, he held: 'I see no genuine basis at all for the suggestion that the participants mocked the victims of the Holocaust.' There was bondage, beating and domination, which seem to be typical of sadomasochism. But there was no public interest or other justification for the clandestine recording, for the publication of the resulting information and still photographs, or for the placing of the video extracts on the *News of the World* website – all of this on a massive scale. Of course, the judge accepted 'that such behaviour is viewed by some people with distaste and moral disapproval, but in the light of modern rights-based jurisprudence that does not provide any justification for the intrusion on the personal privacy of the Claimant.'[1] Damages of £60,000 were awarded and the judge refused to award exemplary damages. Mosely then proceeded to the ECtHR, but he was unsuccessful in his attempts to obtain a ruling of a right for a person in his position to be informed by the media or press of a warning before publication. Mosley's case was an important development in privacy protection and the courts have awarded superinjunctions to prevent any disclosure at all by the press of private information or even information about the proceedings themselves (below).

[1] See *Wood v Commissioner of Police* [2009] EWCA Civ 414 which concerned the taking of photographs by police and breach of Art 8. *R (B) v Stafford Combined Court* [2006] EWHC 1645 (Admin), which was a sex offence case. The medical records of a 14-year-old girl were ordered to be disclosed to the defendant. There was a wrongful interference with the girl's Art 8 rights because of inadequate protection and who was not represented. *A v C* [2006] CL Nov 129 concerned the disclosure of commendation about police officers – they must expect publicity – and see *R (Harper) v Aldershot Magistrates Court* [2010] EWHC 1319 (Admin); *C v AB* [2006] EWHC 3083 QB; and *T v BBC* [2007] EWHC 1683 QB – balancing Art 8 and 10 rights. See *X v Unnamed Persons* [2006] EWHC 2783 which concerned John Doe injunctions against 'persons unknown' to protect identities. *White v Withers LLP* [2008] EWHC 2821 (QB) was a case concerning alleged misuse of 'private information' – the application was unsuccessful.

7.198 There is no doubt that the Convention may be invoked to develop the common law and there has been widespread comment about the impact the Act has had on affecting legal relations between private parties by the doctrine of indirect horizontal effect. Only public bodies or those exercising functions of a public nature are directly bound by the Act's imposition of a duty to act in accordance with the Convention. Because courts are themselves under such a duty, this could well encourage the invocation of Convention rights into private relationships to prevent intrusive contractual terms or secrecy clauses in contracts being enforced. The Act cannot, however, bind private parties directly: it has no direct horizontal effect. But, insofar as the courts are bound and must enforce the law in accordance with Convention rights, the Articles may be indirectly horizontally effective. Section 12 of the Human Rights Act 1998 makes special provision for the application of Art 10 in litigation including private or public parties (paras 2.349 et seq above).[1]

The press and media[1]

7.199 A Protection of Privacy Bill narrowly failed in the Commons as long ago as 1988–89. This would have given wide protection to individuals against unauthorised disclosure of information about them, basically by the press, even though true. They would have been given a right of action, even though there was nothing defamatory in what was published: it was simply an invasion of privacy. A defence for the press or media would exist where 'the subject matter was of public concern and that the publication was for the public benefit'. The prime minister has revived the discussion of a need for a privacy law in 2011.

1   M Tugendhat and I Christie *The Law of Privacy and the Media* (2nd ed, 2011); G Robertson and A Nicol *Media Law* (5th edn, 2007); R Clayton and H Tomlinson *Privacy and Freedom of Expression* (2009).

7.200   In November 1989, every major newspaper agreed a voluntary code of practice to cover invasion of privacy and complaints. In June 1990, the Calcutt Report on privacy[1] recommended the creation of a Press Complaints Commission, initially on a non-statutory basis. After repeated chances at the 'last chance saloon' the Commission's Code of Practice and the Commission still operate on a non-statutory basis. The most recent version was ratified by the Press Complaints Commission in April 2004 (with effect from January 2011: http://www.pcc.org. uk/cop/practice.html). The Commission has 17 members, a majority of whom have no connection with the press 'ensuring its independence'. The chair is press-appointed. It is a self-regulatory mechanism financed by a levy on the press and magazines. Membership is voluntary. Too often, some newspapers simply ignore its rulings. At the time of the cessation of the *News of the World* in the phone-hacking scandal in 2011, its abolition was widely predicted, predictions encouraged by the Prime Minister. An inquiry was established under Leveson LJ to investigate the 'culture, ethics and practice' of the press (www.levesoninquiry.org.uk). Some form of statutory regulation was anticipated. Despite the scandal engendered by the *News of the World* and other sectors of the press, a free press is a bastion of democracy, a point repeated many times in recent years by senior judges. Regulation must not lead to censorship or political interference with the press. Public-interest journalism must be protected, but so too must individual integrity and dignity. The successor body needs to be completely independent of the press, although it will be paid for by levies on the press. Its budget will have to increase significantly to ensure its effectiveness. It is understoof that membership by the press will be compulsory. The body will have to be equipped with full powers of investigation and enforcement. The Commission publishes guidance on its complaints process which does not cover legal or contractual matters, advertising, taste and decency and the choice of what is published, subject to the Code. Guidance is given on accuracy, opportunity to reply, as well as comment, conjecture and fact, listening devices, hospitals, misrepresentation, harassment, payment for articles, intrusions into grief or shock, innocent relatives or friends, photographs or interviews of children, children in sex cases, victims of crime, financial journalism, confidential sources and the 'public's interest' in exposing wrongdoing. On privacy the Code states:

'3. Privacy

Everyone is entitled to respect for his or her private and family life, home, health and correspondence, including digital communications.

Editors will be expected to justify intrusions into any individual's private life without consent. Account will be taken of the complainant's own public disclosures of information.

It is unacceptable to photograph individuals in private places without their consent.

Note – Private places are public or private property where there is a reasonable expectation of privacy.'

[1]   Cm 1102. See J.Rosenburg *Privacy and the Press* (2003) and M Fenwick and G Phillipson *Media Freedom under the Human Rights Act* (2006).

7.201   Under HRA 1998, s 12(4) in dealing with cases where the respondent claims or it appears to the court that the material in question concerns journalistic, literary or artistic material and relief is sought which might affect the exercise of the Art 10 right if granted, the court is to have regard to any code on privacy in deciding whether to grant relief affecting the Convention right of freedom of expression as well as having 'particular' regard to the Art 10 right. This could be important both in terms of breaches of the code and awards of injunctions and damages.

7.202   A statutory Broadcasting Standards Commission existed for broadcasting, having been established under the Broadcasting Act 1996 and which replaced the Broadcasting Standards Council and Broadcasting Complaints Commission of the Broadcasting Act 1990. It has now been replaced by provisions under the Communications Act 2003 which place the Office of Communications under a duty to set, review and revise 'such standards for the content of programmes' to be included in TV and radio programmes to secure the 'standards objectives' set out in s 319(2) of the 2003 Act. Section 324 specifies the procedures, including the publication of a draft code, that OFCOM must go through in setting and publicising standards. As well as these provisions, OFCOM will be bound to comply with the HRA and it is under a statutory obligation to take account of such international obligations as the Secretary of State may notify to them. The courts have ruled that the erstwhile Commission was correct to criticise a programme which broadcast a photograph of a child who had been murdered several years previously after a complaint by the parents whose privacy had been unjustly interfered with.[1] The Court of Appeal has also ruled that a company has a right under the code not to have its privacy infringed when concealed cameras took pictures in the company's shop after various accusations of selling second-hand goods represented as new. This was in spite of the fact that, under Art 8 of the ECHR, companies, it is presumed, cannot enjoy human rights.[2] The BBC has its own internal complaints procedures for complaints about accuracy and impartiality and these arrangements have been criticised by the Lords Communications Committee (para 9.3).

[1]   *R v Broadcasting Complaints Commission, ex p Granada TV Ltd* [1995] EMLR 163, CA.
[2]   *R v Broadcasting Standards Commission, ex p BBC (Liberty Intervening)* [2000] 3 All ER 989, CA; *Niemietz v Germany* (1992) 16 EHRR 97.

Injunctions and super-injunctions

7.203   The use of super-injunctions to protect privacy and confidentiality has been widely reported as a serious infringement on freedom of speech. Certainly attempts to prevent reporting of Parliamentary debates raising issues involved in litigation were clearly misguided.[1] A typical form of such an injunction is: 'The Defendants must not disclose the identity of the Claimant in this action or the nature of the action or the relief sought and granted, save for the purpose of this action.' Additionally, the fact that proceedings are taking place may be prohibited from disclosure: see *Terry v Persons Unknown* [2010] EWHC 119 (QB) for a discussion of principles.[2] There are also orders for anonymised injunctions to prevent the reporting of parties' identities. The use of super-injunctions generated a great deal of controversy: it was revealed in Parliament and on Twitter who had been awarded such injunctions including the failed RBS banker Fred Goodwin and footballer Ryan Giggs. The leaks by Twitter provoked the seeking of orders from the courts requiring the release of the identities of those responsible (para 10.53 et seq). The Lord Chief Justice highlighted the dangers of outright war between the press and media and the courts. Lord Neuberger was appointed to set up a committee to enquire into the use of super-injunctions and the report ('Report of the Committee on Super-Injunctions: Super-Injunctions, Anonymised Injunctions and Open Justice') was published in May 2011.[3] A practice direction has been issued under the name of the Master of the Rolls on 'Super-Injunction and Anonymised Injunction Data Collection and Practice Guidance for Non-Disclosure Injunctions'.[4] The report's terms of reference cover practice and procedure bearing in mind HRA 1998, s 12, the impact on open justice, a clear definition of 'super-injunction' and makes proposals for reform especially to the Civil Procedure Rules and Practice Directions. The report states that open justice is fundamental but not absolute and derogations may be made to the extent 'strictly necessary' to secure the proper administration of justice. Injunctions have to be supported by clear and cogent evidence and cannot be awarded to 'become in practice permanent' (p v). Practice guidance should be issued setting out principles on 'interim non-disclosure orders'. The guidance will deal with HRA 1998, s 12 and 'state that it will be a very rare case where advance notice of such an application to media organisations … can be justifiably withheld' (p v). Draft model orders are set out in the annex. Use of specialist judges to hear such applications in not justifiable or practicable. The feasibility of a data collection system for all interim non-disclosure orders on an annual basis and its publication should be considered. The MoJ, Her Majesty's Courts and Tribunals Service and the House authorities should consider the feasibility of a streamlined system for answering *sub judice* queries from the Speakers' offices (p vi). No court order could interfere with Parliament's absolute privilege of freedom of debate under Art 9 Bill of Rights 1689; such an attempt would be unconstitutional. On newspaper reports of Parliamentary proceedings, we quote at length:

> 'Media reporting of Parliamentary proceedings is protected by the Parliamentary Papers Act 1840, which provides an absolute immunity in respect of civil or criminal proceedings for Hansard and any other publication made by order of Parliament. It also provides an absolute privilege for any individual who publishes a copy of Hansard.

> The 1840 Act also provides a qualified privilege in civil or criminal proceedings for individuals who publish a summary of material published in Hansard.

Qualified privilege arises where such a summary is published in good faith and without malice. There is no judicial decision as to whether a summary of material published in Hansard which intentionally had the effect of frustrating a court order would be in good faith and without malice.

Where media reporting of Parliamentary proceedings does not simply reprint copies of Hansard or amount to summaries of Hansard or parliamentary proceedings they may well not attract qualified privilege.

Where media reporting of Parliamentary proceedings does not attract qualified privilege, it is unclear whether it would be protected at common law from contempt proceedings if it breached a court order. There is such protection in defamation proceedings for honest, fair and accurate reporting of Parliamentary proceedings. There is no reported case which decides whether the common law protection from contempt applies. There is an argument that the common law should adopt the same position in respect of reports of Parliamentary proceedings as it does in respect of reports of court proceedings.' (p vii)

1   *RJW and SJW v The Guardian newspaper and persons unknown* (Claim No HQ09).
2   See http://www.judiciary.gov.uk/Resources/JCO/Documents/Speeches/mr-speech-jsb-lecture-march-2011.pdf; *Nutuli v Donald* [2010] EWCA Civ 1276; *Grey v UVW* [2010] EWHC 2367 QB; *JIH v News Group Newspapers Ltd* [2011] EWCA Civ 42; *A v Independent News and Media Ltd* [2010] EWCA Civ 343.
3   http://www.judiciary.gov.uk/Resources/JCO/Documents/Reports/super-injunction-report-20052011.pdf.
4   http://www.judiciary.gov.uk/publications-and-reports/guidance/super-injunction-and-anonymised-inj-data-collection-and-guidance-non-disclosure-inj.

7.204   The failure of the injunctions in several cases to 'hold the ring' and the apparent inability of the threat of contempt proceedings against the bloggers and others impelled the Prime Minister to set up a joint Parliamentary committee to examine privacy protection, regulation of online social networks and the role of the Press Complaints Commission (below).

7.205   There is a genuine fear among the press that the use of super-injunctions is reintroducing the draconian 'gagging writ' preventing free speech. A careful balance has to be struck between an individual's right to privacy under Art 8 ECHR, even for those engaging in dubious but lawful practices, and the rights of the press and media to report under Art 10 ECHR on hypocrisy, double standards by the setters of public opinion, politicians, those in positions of trust and special influence or where there is a genuine public interest, as opposed to a salacious or prurient interest, in knowing of 'private' activity. It may be that the law can only set general guidelines on the balance that has to be struck between privacy and freedom of speech, even if the principles were in legislation, a move which has been supported by David Cameron. A general rule would be dangerous and case-by-case application of the principles may be the only workable way forward to prevent one right automatically trumping the other.

7.206   It has been observed (paras 2.349 and 7.85 above) that both the Human Rights Act 1998 and the DPA 1998 seek to protect freedom of speech in relation to journalism, literature and art. The Court of Appeal has ruled that the rule in *Bonnard v Perryman*[1] is not changed by HRA 1998, s 12(3). That rule stated that once a defendant in a libel trial had verified that he would justify allegedly defamatory comments which he intended to publish at trial, the court would only exceptionally issue an injunction in prior restraint.[2] Privacy protection claims have undermined that robust approach.

[1]   [1891] 2 Ch 269.
[2]   *Greene v Associated Newspapers Ltd* [2005] 1 All ER 30. In *Greene*, the CA assumed that reputation was protected by Art 8 (*Radio France v France* App No 53984/00, 30 March 2004). However, reputation was not as perishable a commodity as personal privacy/confidentiality 'which once breached is lost for ever' and applying the test: is the court satisfied that the claimant is likely to establish at full trial that publication should not be allowed (as explained in *Cream Holdings* [2004] 4 All ER 617 (HL – see para 2.350 above) was too restrictive of freedom of speech in defamation actions. The test in s 12(3) was not suited to the procedures of defamation actions but is appropriate for confidentiality litigation. The s 12(3) test was intended to strengthen the protection for the media in interlocutory proceedings, the inadequacy of which was represented by the decision in *American Cyanamid* [1975] 1 All ER 504 (HL) (para 7.164, note 1 above). See *CDE v MGN Ltd* [2010] EWHC 3308 (QB).

DATA MATCHING AND INFORMATION SHARING AND OTHER PROBLEMS

7.207   Before examining this issue one should note FS50177136 which concerned a request to the Cabinet Office for information regarding a Cabinet Committee that was formed in order to consider data sharing within the public sector. Some information was provided, but the request for minutes of certain meetings and the name and job titles of the members of the Cabinet Committee were refused under FOIA 2000, ss 35 and 40 respectively. In relation to the request for minutes, the Commissioner found that ss 35(1)(a) and 35(1)(b) were engaged because: (1) Cabinet Committees provide a framework for government to consider major policy decisions; (2) the minutes record suggestions and proposals to improve data sharing and no firm policy decision had been taken at the time of the request; (3) the minutes were recorded for the purpose of providing ministers with an accurate account of the meetings; (4) s 35(5) explicitly makes reference to proceedings of any committee of the Cabinet. The public interest favoured non-disclosure because it was important to protect the convention of collective responsibility. To disclose the information would lead to government time being spent commenting on, and defending, individual views expressed in a Cabinet Committee rather than the position of the government (good analysis on this point: paras 33–42). As regards the request for names, etc, the Commissioner found that s 40 was engaged and the information was protected under the first DPP.

7.208   Various statutes and regulations allow for the sharing of information by public authorities: Social Security Administration Act 1992, s 110 gives powers to require information about employees from employers. Powers are provided to obtain information, and pass information on, in the Child Support, Pensions and Social Security Act 2000, ss 13 and 42 respectively (and see Immigration, Asylum and Nationality Act 2006 (Data Sharing Code of Practice) (Review) Order 2007, SI 2007/3447). The Welfare Reform and Pensions Act 1999, ss 72 and 80 allow for sharing of information between governmental bodies, as do the Social Security Administration (Fraud) Act 1997, s 1; Social Security Act 1998, s 3; and Social Security Fraud Act 2001 (SSFA 2001), ss 5 and 6, as well as Finance Act 1997, s 110. The SSFA 2001 provides additional powers for authorities to obtain information and deals with electronic access to information, provides for a code of practice on the use of information powers for exchange of information with overseas authorities and the exchange of information between authorities administering benefit. Finance Act 2003, ss 197 and 198 concern the exchange of information between taw authorities of member states under the Mutual Assistance Directive (Council Directive 77/799/EEC, as amended). Crime and Disorder Act 1998, s 115 and the protocol from the Home Office are examined below (paras 7.239 et seq below). The Children Act 2006 has provisions in ss 37, 56, 64, 69, 90, 92 and 104 (and see Childcare (Supply and Disclosure of Information) (England) (Amendment) Regulations 2008, SI 2008/961 and Childcare (Early Years and General Childcare Registers) (Common Provisions) Regulations 2008, SI 2008/976. The Statistics and Registration Service Act 2007, ss 42 to 46 (with Sch 2) allow existing information flows to continue between the board, as the legal successor body to the Office of National Statistics, and: the General Register Office (s 42); the relevant Secretary of State, and Welsh Ministers, for patient registration data (ss 43 and 44); HMRC (ss 45 and 46, Sch 2); the Bank of England and the Department for Environment, Food and Rural Affairs (s 46 and Sch 2). Supplementary powers are in ss 47–54. The area of criminal justice and anti-terrorism provides numerous examples. This is just a sample.

[1]   With regard to police: *Marcel v Commissioner of the Police of the Metropolis* [1992] 1 All ER 72, but cf *Frankson and others v Home Office; Johns v Same* [2003] EWCA Civ 655 (8 May 2003), CA.

7.209 The Information Commissioner (IC) has expressed concern that the use of such provisions should protect privacy rights. Joined-up government encourages information sharing as under the Crime and Disorder Act 1998 and the Children Act 2004. In the White Paper *Modernising Government*,[1] departments and public bodies are urged to work closely with the IC, to carry through the commitment to openness, to use the IC's powers in relation to assessments and to promote codes of practice, to deploy privacy-enhancing technologies and to provide a proper and lawful basis for information sharing and matching. The DSS, DETR and local authorities have discussed developments concerning 'high-level guidance on data matching'.[2] Following much debate, the Coroners and Justice Act 2009 provides for a code of practice on data sharing.

[1]   Cm 4310 (1999).
[2]   DPC *Annual Report* 2000 ch 5.

7.210 Section 174 of the Coroners and Justice Act 2009 provides for a duty on the IC to prepare a data sharing code of practice. The provisions are set out below. They add a new s 52A to the DPA 1998.

7.211 DPA 1998, s 52A: Data-sharing code

'(1) The Commissioner must prepare a code of practice which contains—

(a) practical guidance in relation to the sharing of personal data in accordance with the requirements of this Act, and

(b) such other guidance as the Commissioner considers appropriate to promote good practice in the sharing of personal data.

(2) For this purpose "good practice" means such practice in the sharing of personal data as appears to the Commissioner to be desirable having regard to the interests of data subjects and others, and includes (but is not limited to) compliance with the requirements of this Act.

(3) Before a code is prepared under this section, the Commissioner must consult such of the following as the Commissioner considers appropriate—

(a) trade associations (within the meaning of section 51);

(b) data subjects;

(c) persons who appear to the Commissioner to represent the interests of data subjects.

(4) In this section a reference to the sharing of personal data is to the disclosure of the data by transmission, dissemination or otherwise making it available.'

7.212 DPA 1998, s 52B: Data-sharing code: procedure

'[(1) When a code is prepared under section 52A, it must be submitted to the Secretary of State for approval.

(2) Approval may be withheld only if it appears to the Secretary of State that the terms of the code could result in the United Kingdom being in breach of any of its Community obligations or any other international obligation.

(3) The Secretary of State must—

(a) if approval is withheld, publish details of the reasons for withholding it;

(b) if approval is granted, lay the code before Parliament.]¹

(4) If, within the 40-day period, either House of Parliament resolves not to approve the code, the code is not to be issued by the Commissioner.

(5) If no such resolution is made within that period, the Commissioner must issue the code.

(6) Where—

(a) the Secretary of State withholds approval [see (2) above], or

(b) such a resolution is passed,

the Commissioner must prepare another code of practice under section 52A.

(7) Subsection (4) does not prevent a new code being laid before Parliament.

(8) A code comes into force at the end of the period of 21 days beginning with the day on which it is issued.

(9) A code may include transitional provision or savings.

(10) In this section "the 40-day period" means the period of 40 days beginning with the day on which the code is laid before Parliament (or, if it is not laid before each House of Parliament on the same day, the later of the 2 days on which it is laid).

(11) In calculating the 40-day period, no account is to be taken of any period during which Parliament is dissolved or prorogued or during which both Houses are adjourned for more than 4 days.'

[1]   Important changes are made to these provisions by the Protection of Freedoms Bill 2011. This removes the requirement in s 52B(1)–(3) that guidance issued by the IC has to be approved by the Secretary of State. The Secretary of State has to be consulted in its preparation and the final version has to be submitted to the Secretary of State (clause 102).

7.213   DPA 1998, s 52C: Alteration or replacement of data-sharing code

'(1) The Commissioner—
(a)   must keep the data-sharing code under review, and
(b)   may prepare an alteration to that code or a replacement code.

(2) Where, by virtue of a review under subsection (1)(a) or otherwise, the Commissioner becomes aware that the terms of the code could result in the United Kingdom being in breach of any of its Community obligations or any other international obligation, the Commissioner must exercise the power under subsection (1)(b) with a view to remedying the situation.

(3) Before an alteration or replacement code is prepared under subsection (1), the Commissioner must consult such of the following as the Commissioner considers appropriate—
(a)   trade associations (within the meaning of section 51);
(b)   data subjects;
(c)   persons who appear to the Commissioner to represent the interests of data subjects.

(4) Section 52B (other than subsection (6)) applies to an alteration or replacement code prepared under this section as it applies to the code as first prepared under section 52A.

(5) In this section "the data-sharing code" means the code issued under section 52B(5) (as altered or replaced from time to time).'

7.214   DPA 1998, s 52D: Publication of data-sharing code

'(1) The Commissioner must publish the code (and any replacement code) issued under section 52B(5).

(2) Where an alteration is so issued, the Commissioner must publish either—
(a)   the alteration, or
(b)   the code or replacement code as altered by it.'

7.215   DPA 1998, s 52E: Effect of data-sharing code

'(1) A failure on the part of any person to act in accordance with any provision of the data-sharing code does not of itself render that person liable to any legal proceedings in any court or tribunal.

(2) The data-sharing code is admissible in evidence in any legal proceedings.

(3) If any provision of the data-sharing code appears to—
(a)   the Tribunal or a court conducting any proceedings under this Act,
(b)   a court or tribunal conducting any other legal proceedings, or
(c)   the Commissioner carrying out any function under this Act,

to be relevant to any question arising in the proceedings, or in connection with the exercise of that jurisdiction or the carrying out of those functions, in relation to any time when it was in force, that provision of the code must be taken into account in determining that question.

(4) In this section "the data-sharing code" means the code issued under section 52B(5) (as altered or replaced from time to time).'

7.216   The IC has produced after public consultation his Statutory Code on Data Sharing, which explains what is meant by data sharing; data sharing and the law; deciding to share data; responsibility, data sharing agreements, privacy impact assessments, data standards and reviewing data sharing arrangements – the latter all under 'governance'. It continues with the rights of individuals and complaints, things to avoid, the IC's powers, and penalties and checklists. The Code has been approved by the Secretary of State and has been laid before Parliament.[1]

---

[1]   http://www.ico.gov.uk/for_organisations/data_protection/topic_guides/~/media/documents/library/Data_Protection/Detailed_specialist_guides/data_sharing_code_of_practice.ashx.

7.217   There is also a European and international dimension to data sharing. At the European level, several law enforcement agencies have been established including Europol, which handles criminal intelligence relating to serious international organised crime. A European Joint Supervisory Body supervises data protection. Provision for data protection is made by the conventions or instruments establishing these bodies. Eurojust is a judicial cooperation organisation aimed at improving coordination and cooperation between investigators concerned with serious international crime. A Eurojust Joint Supervisory Body supervises data protection. A Customs Information System (CIS) exists, supervised by the CIS Joint Supervisory Authority and the European Data Protection Supervisor; and there is Eurodac which is a database of finger prints of applicants for asylum and aliens illegally present in the EU. There is the

Schengen Information System (SIS) linked to the abolition of internal border controls and free movement within the EU and to which the UK did not sign up to but which it intends to join. This has increasingly become a source of criminal information for police forces throughout the member states. In Case C-482/08 *UK v Council of the EU* [2011] 1 CMLR 45 ECJ (Grand Chamber) it was ruled that the UK was rightly denied data on the SIS under Council Decision 2008/633 because the UK had not signed up to the common visa system.

7.218 The EU Convention and Protocol on Mutual Assistance (Cm 7054, 2007 entered into force for the UK on 21 December 2005) places considerable constraints on the exchange of personal data, showing how sensitively member states treat this subject. The Protocol covers serious crime.

Prüm Convention and other measures

7.219 As well as legislation on the sharing of tax data with EU partners, there are wide-ranging developments affecting transfer of personal data in other subject areas. Another instrument with equally complex, but different, data protection provisions is the 2005 Prüm Convention on cross-border cooperation against crime, terrorism and illegal immigration. This is now agreed to by all member states and it adopts much of the wording of the Prüm Convention and became a Framework Decision under the Amsterdam TEU. Originally seven states were a party to it, although only three were operating it: Germany, Austria and Spain. The Convention has been the subject of an extremely critical report by the House of Lords European Union Committee (HL 90 Eighteenth Report para 52 (2006–07) which was fearful of yet another EU instrument with potentially conflicting provisions. It raises serious questions in relation to safeguards about the use of such data. The Convention involves sharing national police access to car registration data banks and supplying DNA and fingerprint information on suspects to other national police forces upon request. These powers are exercised under Art 12 'for the prevention and investigation of criminal offences and in dealing with other offences coming within the jurisdiction of the courts or the public prosecution service in the searching Member State, as well as in maintaining public security.' It raises the question of whether it applies to decriminalised offences. Furthermore, Art 15(a) states: 'In the implementation of Article 12, Member States may decide to give priority to combating serious crime bearing in mind the limited technical capacities available for transmitting data.' Further examples include the 1999 Decision of the Schengen Executive Committee on the Agreement on Cooperation in Proceedings for Road Traffic Offences and the Enforcement of Financial Penalties allowing for the exchange of vehicle information and other matters. At the beginning of this chapter we set out the relevant provisions from the Treaty of Lisbon, which in due course should lead to measures under EU legislation replacing the above measures (para 7.4).

7.220 The Crime (International Cooperation) Act 2003 is concerned with international mutual support and assistance between police forces. Section 81 amends the DPA 1998 and through a new DPA 1998, s 54A gives the UK IC powers to inspect data in Europol, CIS and SIS, and to test and operate equipment used for the purpose of data processing. It allows the IC to inspect personal data recorded in the UK sections of three European information systems (Europol, CIS and SIS) without a warrant. The Conventions require the supervisory authority to have free access to the national sections of the systems. There are savings for data required for the purposes of safeguarding national security.

7.221 The IC has also indicated that information from the major registers in use in the UK concerning individuals can all too easily be used for unintended or undesirable purposes – marketing and commercial exploitation, or watching and besetting to highlight practices that one disagrees with eg animal experimentation, genetically modified crops, or persecution of paedophiles.[1] The Representation of the People Act 2000 allows for two versions of the electoral register – a full unabridged version and a partial version with details left out. The latter version may be publicly purchased.[2] The Privacy and Telecommunications Regulations are examined below and these concern the processing of personal data and the protection of privacy in the telecoms sector. Readers are referred to the discussion on the Regulation of Investigatory Powers Act 2000 in ch 2 (paras 2.200 et seq above). The IC has also noted the difficulties associated with processing data over the internet and guidance has been produced on this subject. For e-commerce, accreditation of online codes of practice is encouraged through Trust UK Ltd comprising the Alliance of Electronic Business and the Consumers' Association which is endorsed by the government. Codes require subscribers to comply with the DPA 1998! Measures are being adopted to develop effective grievance procedures for consumers.

[1]   There is a massive demand for publication of the sex offenders' register following the murder of Sarah Payne in July 2000, along the lines of 'Megan's law' in the USA. In some states pictures, names and other details can be downloaded from a police website. See, for the UK, the Sex Offenders Act 1997 and Sexual Offenders Act 2003, Part 2.

[2]   *R (Robertson) v Secretary of State* [2003] EWHC 1760. The following is extracted from the headnote. The Representation of the People (England and Wales) Regulations 2001, reg 114, which allows the sale of the full electoral register to credit reference agencies, is not unlawful and does not breach voters' human rights. R sought judicial review of reg 114, as amended, which allowed the sale of the full electoral register to credit reference agencies. The Regulations had been amended following the decision in *R (on the application of Robertson) v Wakefield MDC* [2001] EWHC Admin 915, in which it was held that the sale of the register to commercial concerns was unlawful. R contended that reg 114 was (1) inconsistent with the decision in *Robertson*, which made it clear that all sales of the full register to commercial concerns were unlawful, and (2) incompatible with the right to free elections under HRA 1998, Sch 1, Part II, Art 3. Refusing the application, that (1) the judge in *Robertson* had decided that the individual's right to respect for private life under Art 8 was infringed disproportionately by the sale of the electoral register to commercial concerns who utilised it for direct marketing purposes. Although credit reference agencies were commercial concerns, they did not use the register for direct marketing purposes and sales to such agencies were therefore lawful, *Robertson* distinguished. And (2) reg 114 permitted the dissemination of information which was a matter of public record to a narrow group of recipients for a limited purpose, subject to conditions. It represented a balance struck by Parliament following a process of consultation. Selling the register under reg 114 would only cause slight interference with the right to vote under Art 3 whereas the policy pursued a legitimate purpose in the public interest by helping to minimise fraud and the cost of credit,

while maximising access to credit. Accordingly, the approach adopted by Parliament fell within the wide margin of appreciation applicable to Art 3, *Mathieu-Mohin v Belgium* (19 (A/113) 88) 10 EHRR 1 applied. See also *I-CD Publishing Ltd v The Secretary of State and the Information Commissioner* [2003] EWHC 1761 – I-CD argued that the restrictions on selling copies of the register were unlawfully selective and irrational. I-CD owned 192.com, a website that enables its users, on a fee basis, to search for names on its database, which is mainly compiled on the basis of individual local authorities' edited registers. If a high proportion of a council's residents opt out of the edited register, the effectiveness of such a service will clearly be reduced. I-CD thus sought judicial review of the decision that they were not eligible to buy copies of the full register. Mr Justice Kay ruled that the regulations were neutral as to the number of credit reference agencies who could purchase the full register as long as they complied with the conditions imposed by the regulations. If I-CD at any time altered its business so as to comply with the conditions, it would be entitled to purchase the full register.

7.222   The topic of data and information sharing had clearly been at the forefront of the Lord Chancellor's Department and its successor. It is to be hoped that the recent initiatives will help to bring some coherence to this vast practice. A consultation paper *For Your Information: How can the Public Sector Provide People with Information on, and Build Confidence in, the Way it Handles their Personal Details* was prepared in April 2003 (see www.lcd.gov.uk/consult/datasharing/datashare.htm). See also the Government Data Standards Catalogue (www.govtalk.gov.uk).

7.223   This followed a Cabinet Office paper *Privacy and Data Sharing: the Way Forward* (2002). The Home Office has produced a *Framework for Data Sharing* under the Crime and Disorder Act 1998, and guidance exists for those working to safeguard children (*Working Together to Safeguard Children* under Local Authority Social Services Act 1970, s 7).

7.224   The LCD paper has three annexes on a draft public services trust charter, a statement on how public authorities will hold data, and a data-sharing protocol framework. New technology has to comply with ISO 17799 (BS 7799) on standards of information security management which is compulsory for health and social services. The introduction of electronic data record management systems is seeking to assist the implementation of FOIA and build a comprehensive security for data.

7.225   The Department for Constitutional Affairs also published *Privacy and Data Sharing: the Way Forward for Public Services: Guidance on the Law* (November 2003) (www.dca.gov.uk/foi/sharing/toolkit/lawguide.htm#part1) The DCA has suggested a general enabling data sharing power which would be implemented by specific regulations. This is concerned with the *vires* for swapping and relevant considerations (see Figures 7.2 and 7.3 at paras 7.231 and 7.232 respectively).

7.226   The DCA *Guidance* explains how data sharing may be made through 'gateways'. These may be express and permissive, such as the Road Vehicles (Registration and Licensing) Regulations 2002 and under Crime and Disorder

Act 1998, s 115 which enables any information deemed necessary for the compilation of reports in connection with anti-social behaviour orders, sex offender orders and drug treatment and testing orders to be disclosed to any or all of the authorities mentioned in s 115(2). The Children Act 2004 establishes powers to enable information sharing between those services working with children. Local Safeguarding Children Boards will encourage children's services to work together to promote children's welfare. Section 63 of the 2004 Act allows the Inland Revenue to provide information to local authorities for the purposes of child welfare, and adds to the provisions on disclosure contained in Tax Credits Act 2002, Sch 5.

7.227 Express mandatory provisions include Criminal Appeal Act 1995, s 17 allowing the Criminal Cases Review Commission to require a public authority to allow access to, or to give to the Commission documents in its possession especially in relation to criminal investigations (see s 18 for limitations), and National Audit Act 1983, s 8 (see para 11.19 below).[1]

[1]   See *Morris v Director of Serious Fraud Office* [1993] Ch 372, where compulsory powers in a criminal investigation to obtain documents from auditors did not authorise their disclosure to liquidators or others.

7.228 Gateways, the *Guidance* continues, may be implied. They may be implied as a matter of construction. Power may be implied in the public interest.[1] They may be implied by common law or, the *Guidance continues*, under prerogative powers. In relation to the Consultancy Service List – a list of those on whom there are doubts as to their suitability to work with children – there was at the relevant time no statutory authorization to pass information on. Operation of the List was lawful but representations were allowed from those included and were made available to prospective employers in the child-care only after an offer of employment was made.[2] In relation to local authorities wide powers may be implied by Local Government Act 1972, s 111(1) and LGA 2000, s 2(1). A local authority possessed authority to communicate its conclusions resulting from an investigation where it reasonably and genuinely believed that a communication was necessary to protect a child at risk of sexual abuse. A (a headteacher) was dismissed for gross misconduct following investigations pursuant to Children Act 1989, s 47. Such a power, though not express, arose by implication of ss 17, 27, 47 of, and Sch 2 to, the 1989 Act.[3]

[1]   *Woolgar v Chief Constable of Sussex Police* [1999] 3 All ER 604 (CA); *R v Chief Constable of North Wales Police ex p AB* [1998] 3 All ER 310 (CA) (see para 1.276, note 1 and para 2.326, note 1). The cases concern publicity for the whereabouts of convicted paedophiles but with safeguards. See *R (A) v Herts CC* (note 3 below). See also Criminal Justice Act 2003, s 327 and the Criminal Justice and Immigration Act 2008, s 140 and Sch 24 on disclosure of information about convictions for child offenders. See IC case FS50300157 where the complainant requested information concerning the most prolific offender aged ten to 15 within the area covered by the public authority. Initially, the public authority refused the request under the exemptions provided by the following sections of the Freedom of Information Act: s 40(2) (personal information), s 44(1) (statutory prohibitions to disclosure), s 30(1) and (2) (information held for the purposes of investigations) and s 38(1) (endangerment to health and safety). During the Commissioner's investigation, the stance of the

public authority changed and it cited s 12(1) of the Act as it believed that compliance with the requests would exceed the cost limit of £450. The Commissioner found that it was reasonable for the public authority to estimate that the cost of the requests would exceed the limit and so it was not obliged to comply with these requests. However, the Commissioner also found that the public authority failed to comply with s 17(5) of the Act in that it did not cite s 12(1) within 20 working days of receipt of the requests.

2   In *R v Worcester CC and Secretary of State ex p SW* Case CO/4550/99, Newman J stated obiter that the list was compatible with Art 8. See now powers under the Protection of Children Act 1999.

3   *R (A) v Hertfordshire CC* [2001] EWHC Admin 211; *L (Minors) (Sexual Abuse: Disclosure) Re* [1999] 1 WLR 299 distinguished.

7.229   In *Peck v UK*[1] the claimant was a person whose attempted suicide in a public place had been filmed by CCTV. This was sold inter alia to a national TV broadcasting company who, without any attempt to conceal his identity relayed the broadcast on national TV. LGA 1972, s 111(1) allowed disclosure to media, but an unanonymised broadcast was 'disproportionate' interference with Art 8 rights to privacy, the ECtHR held.

1   Application No 44647/98. In *R (A) v Herts CC* [2001] All ER (D) 259 (CA), it was accepted that an implied data sharing power existed under the Children Act 1989; no reliance was made on LGA 1972, s 111(1). An authority informed another authority that a headteacher posed a risk to pupils – relying on *AB* at para 7.228, note 1 above and *R v A Local Authority and Police Authority in the Midlands ex p LM* [2000] 1 FLR 612, disclosure should only be made where there was a 'pressing social need'. Local Government Finance Act 1992, Sch 2, para 17 allows for the supply of information (council tax data) but not personal data. See, on electoral registers, *R (Robertson) v City of Wakefield* [2002] 2 WLR 889 (para 7.68, note 1 and para 7.209, note 2 above). On disclosure between authorities, see *MS v Sweden* App No 00020837/92, *X v UK* 30 DR 239 (1982), *X v Belgium* 31 DR 231 (1982) – all justified on facts. See *Campbell v UK* (1993) 15 EHRR 137: blanket opening of prisoners' letters a breach of Art 8; see also *R v Secretary of State for the Home Department ex p Leech* [1993] 4 All ER 539 (CA). Under the Criminal Justice and Court Services Act 2000, orders disqualifying adults working with children may be made. These are not 'penalties' re Art 7 ECHR and so they may be awarded retrospectively to offences committed before the 2000 Act came into effect: *R v Field* 2 December 2002, (CA).

7.230   The chart below represented government guidance on data transfer. It will have to be seen now in the context of the IC's code above.

7.231

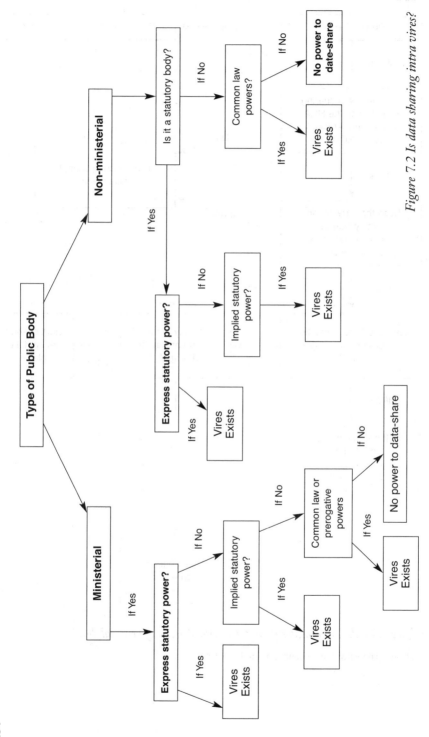

Figure 7.2 Is data sharing intra vires?

7.232

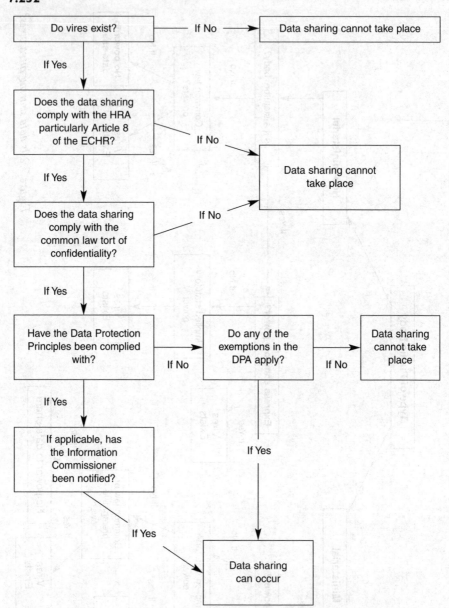

Figure 7.3 Relevant considerations for lawful sharing of personal data *

*Personal data within the meaning of the DPA 1998

DATA HELD BY THE POLICE, AND THE BICHARD INQUIRY

7.233 The report of the Bichard Inquiry was published in June 2004 (HC 653 (2003–04)). The inquiry followed the conviction of Ian Huntley, a school caretaker, for the murder of two young girls and the discovery that police checks failed to disclose an 'extensive history of allegations of sexual offences' by Huntley where there was no conviction. Information held on Huntley had been deleted. The police force in question blamed the DPA 1998 for a lack of searchable records. This allegation was subsequently retracted. Police may hold such information where this is justified by an 'ongoing policing need'. Factors to consider include: the nature of the allegation(s), the strength of evidence supporting an allegation(s) and the seriousness of an allegation(s). But detriment to the individual and the possibly harmful effect of disclosure of inaccurate information, possibly founded upon malicious allegations, to third parties have to be considered. The Association of Chief Police Officers (ACPO) also alleged that two cases subject to action by the IC had undermined the ability of the Criminal Records Bureau to retain records which would assist employers in protecting the interests of children, ie in cases like Huntley's. The IC denied this, pointing out that the two cases in question involved very old conviction records held by the Police National Computer for crimes lacking 'any degree of seriousness'. Huntley's case concerned non-conviction data held by local police forces.[1] The problem arises in relation to rules on the 'weeding' of records. ACPO had devised rules on weeding: in DPP 5 ('data ... shall not be kept for longer than is necessary') there are eight pages of guidance on this topic. Some records are retained for life: those relating to crimes of violence or a sentence of six months or more. The IC's point was that while rules on standard retention are unavoidable, there should be a discretion to depart from them where particular circumstances warrant it. ACPO has suggested that all conviction records should now be retained indefinitely. A Home Office Working Group is reviewing the subject.

[1]   *Annual Report 2003–04*, pp 30–31. The quotations in this paragraph come from the annual report. See also on CJA 1987, s 3(5): *R (Kent Pharmaceuticals Ltd) v Director of the SFO* (2004) *Times*, 18 November.

7.234 The ACPO guidance then operative on weeding suggests that in the case of acquittals and 'cases discontinued without caution' records should not be retained by local police forces normally beyond a 42-day period. Two exceptions were: cases involving acquittal of unlawful sexual intercourse by a male with a female under 16 and acquittal or discontinuance because of a lack of corroboration. More extensive periods of retention were recommended. Guidance is given on the relevant criteria for extended retention in this case (see Bichard, para 3.74.3). These weeding guidelines were re-incorporated within the 2002 ACPO Code on the DPA. The 2002 Code also has guidance on 'criminal intelligence records' ie non-conviction data. Each force produced its own guidance based on the ACPO documents – these varied widely. A new code was introduced in 2008.

7.235   The operation of the Police National Computer (PNC) was described in Bichard.[1] The Phoenix database forming the core of the PNC, was launched in 1995. It includes all details of all persons convicted or cautioned for recordable ie imprisonable offences together with some minor offences set out in regulations made under Police and Criminal Evidence Act 1984, s 27(4). 'Details include the individual's name, known aliases, sex, age, height and distinguishing features.'(para 3.43) Other details of a person's contact with the police and criminal justice system may be entered. Responsibility for placing information on the PNC and its quality and timeliness rests with the Chief Officer of Police of the 43 forces in England and Wales although information is accessible by other forces in the UK. The Court of Appeal in *Chief Constable of Humberside v IC* [2009] EWCA Civ 1079 overruled the Information Tribunal in ruling that data held on five individuals from as long ago as 1981 and which involved minor offences did not breach the DPP and were therefore disclosable. The police position was that conviction data should not be erased except in 'very rare circumstances'. The ACPO *Guidance on the Management of Police Information* (2nd edn, 2010) covers review, retention and disposal in chapter 7.

7.236   The first entry on the PNC is called the 'arrest/summons' report. However, except in exceptional cases such as anti-terrorism, a first report is not usually entered until a person is charged. A first recording generates a unique PNC identification number. Problems have persisted especially in relation to timeliness of reports and these difficulties have been investigated at least five times. The HMIC has described the performance as 'abysmal' although Bichard found that practices were improving. (para 3.50). In November 2003, ACPO published a draft *Code of Practice for Use of the Police National Computer*. This had been finalised by June 2004 and came into effect from 1 January 2005. The Code required 'that details of 90 per cent of a police force's recordable offences must be put on the PNC within 24 hours of a person being arrested, charged, reported, summonsed, cautioned or given a fixed penalty notice.' (para 3.52) One hundred pc must be on within three days. Court results should be entered within seven days of a case's conclusion in at least 50 per cent of cases. Various software applications are in use and a violent and sex offenders' register exists. A Criminal Justice Information Technology Group reviewed the IT systems needed to provide a 'joined-up' criminal justice system. Bichard reported that there was no common IT system for managing criminal intelligence. In March 2005, he reported that such a system was by no means guaranteed although England was on course for a set of protection principles 'unrivalled anywhere in the world'. Guidance on retention and erasure of files was produced in 2006 although this was not endorsed by the IC and the most recent guidance is dated 2008. Guidelines issued by the Association of Chief Police Officers ('the ACPO guidelines') entitled 'Exceptional Case Procedure for Removal of DNA, Fingerprints and PNC Records' (16 March 2006) state that under the guidelines removal of data was to be 'exceptional'. The indefinite retention of such data caused a body of adverse decisions in the courts, led to legislative reform (examined below) and the ACPO guidance was ruled unlawful (para 7.256 note 1). A fourth progress report on Bichard was published in May 2007 by which time 21 of the 31 recommendations had been realised.

7.237 Eight of Bichard's recommendations fell to the Department for Education for action. Recommendation 16 led to the development of an online training package on safer recruitment for headteachers, school governors and other school staff involved in recruitment, to ensure staff recruitment practices – including interviews – reflect the importance of safeguarding children. Safer recruitment training became mandatory for the recruitment of school staff from 1 January 2010. A recruitment panel must have at least one member who has completed the training or, where an individual is in charge of recruitment, that individual must have completed the training. It is the responsibility of schools to comply.

[1] HC 653 (2003–04), p 115 et seq. PNC cannot be relied on as authority re convictions if contested *R v Ainscough (Zane Roy)* [2006] EWCA Crim 694.

7.238 It was seen in 7.3 above that in June 2011, the National Police Improvement Agency launched the police national database allowing police forces to share and access locally held information and intelligence on a national basis. Bichard found that for local police systems there was no uniform approach. Interfaces between forces were 'almost non-existent'. (para 3.63) This should now change. ACPO has taken the lead in implementing and promoting the National Intelligence Model (NIM) – a management framework that requires police forces to analyse and address the methods by which intelligence is obtained, created, used and stored. NIM was expected to be implemented by all forces by April 2004 as defined minimum standards in accordance with the Secretary of State's National Policing Plan. ACPO produced a Code of Practice on the DPA in 2002 and guidance on management of police information in 2010 (2nd edn).[1]

[1] http://www.npia.police.uk/en/15637.htm.

CRIMINAL RECORDS BUREAU

7.239 The Criminal Records Bureau (CRB) came into operation in June 2001. Part V of the Police Act 1997 (PA 1997 as amended) created the CRB which is part of the legislative framework for the disclosure of criminal records. It provides for a system of registration of employers and licensing bodies, and disclosure to them of criminal records; controls to protect confidentiality and an offence of improper disclosure.[1] Certificates would be of three kinds: Criminal Conviction Certificates (Basic Disclosure) under PA 1997, s 112; Criminal Records Certificates ('standard disclosure' (SD) under s 113 – including cautions and spent convictions under the Rehabilitation of Offenders Act 1974 and which must be accompanied by a statement from the prospective employer that the certificate is required for an 'exempted question' under the 1974 Act, ie it is excluded by order from the relevant provisions of the 1974 Act (PA 1997, s 113(2), (5))); and Enhanced Criminal Records Certificates ('enhanced disclosure' (ED) and the most detailed search), where the employment involves 'regularly caring for, training, supervising or being in sole charge of people under 18' (and see SI 2011/719 and note the Protection of Vulnerable Groups Act 2006 below).[2] ED includes not only data from the PNC but also local police force data. Distinctions between SD and ED are 'subtle and unclear' (Bichard, para 4.74). Employers of those involved with the care and education of children and vulnerable adults, those who work in the criminal justice system and those with responsibilities in awarding certain licences and permits may request an individual applying for a position (the applicant) to apply for disclosure of a certificate under the Act. The 1997 provisions have been amended (by the Criminal Justice Act 2003 and Serious Organised and Crime Act 2005 and amendments are proposed in the Protection of Freedoms Bill 2011; below). The information will be provided to the prospective employer. Access is also allowed for national security vetting. The provisions cover data on the PNC, the National Identification Service (microfiche) and those of some local forces. Information provided will not be subject to the provisions on spent convictions under the Rehabilitation of Offenders Act 1974 and regulations thereunder.[3] The Court of Appeal has ruled that the police do not owe a subject of a criminal record a duty of care under common law in formulating records in relation to their completeness and accuracy. Other remedies were available, the court emphasised: judicial review, Art 8 ECHR, HRA 1998, DPA 1998. 'There could also on appropriate facts be possible remedies for misfeasance in public office, for maladministration to an ombudsman, or under the Police Conduct Complaints Procedure.'[4]

[1]   On disclosure of police information generally, see Police Act 1997, s 124. *R v O'Leary GP* [2007] EWCA Crim 186 – punishment for disclosure of police confidential information. See HC 1264 (2010–12) for the Bureau's annual report.

[2]   See the Police Act (Criminal Records) (Amendment) Regulations 2011, SI 2011/719: increasing the fee for an application for an ECR certificate from £36 to £44.

[3]   While the Police Act 1997, Part V does not display a parliamentary intention to overrule common law tests of fairness in disclosing information which did not follow a conviction and identity is in issue, fairness did not on the facts in question necessitate that the Chief Constable provide a hearing to the subject of the record: *R (X) v Chief Constable of West Midlands Police* [2005] 1 All ER 610 (CA) overruling [2004] 2 All ER 1. The applicant can apply to the Secretary of State (CRO) for a new certificate if the former believes it is inaccurate: the Secretary of State will decide (PA 1997, s 117). The Secretary of State may request the chief officer to provide additional information which may be relevant and which should be included in the interests of preventing crime and which can be shown to the employer but not the applicant (s 115(8)) or which will be in the certificate and therefore seen by the applicant under s 115(7). Some reforms are introduced under the Protection of Freedoms Bill (below). On disclosure at the Chief Officer of Police's discretion, see *R (L) v Commissioner of Police of the Metropolis* [2009] UKHL 3 (disclosure did not breach Art 8 ECHR). However, on a breach of Art 8 ECHR where no review of having one's details entered for life on the sex offenders register, see *R (F) v Secretary of State for the Home Department* [2010] UKSC 17. See also *R v Local Authority and Police Authority in the Midlands ex p LM* [2002] 1 FLR 612 and *X v Y (Employment sex offender)* [2004] EWCA Civ 662 (CA) on disclosure of cautions relating to a consenting homosexual act in a public toilet. Employer should have been notified of caution and Art 8 rights were not engaged. In *C v Chief Constable of Greater Manchester Police* [2011] EWCA Civ 175 the court assessed the importance of maintaining a 'proper balancing exercise' in disclosures and whether representatives are required. See also *Criminal Records Bureau – Delivering Safer Employment* HC 453 (2003–04).

[4]   *Desmond v Notts Police* [2011] EWCA Civ 3.

7.240 As well as disclosures under the Police Act 1997, there were the Protection of Children Act 1999 List maintained by the DfES and the Protection of Vulnerable Adults List under the Care Standards Act 2000 run by DfES on behalf of the Department of Health. These lists are 'exclusionary with sanctions' and decisions were made by the departments concerned. Under the Police Act, decisions on employment are made by employers. Under the

Protection of Children Act 1999, the Secretary of State was under a duty to keep a list of individuals who are considered unsuitable to work with children. Names of individuals will be provided by organisations, including child care organisations, where individuals fall within criteria under s 2. Individuals may be transferred from the Consultancy Service Index maintained by the Secretary of State to the list. Employment in education may also be restricted. There are appeal provisions. Decisions on provisional listing without a hearing were ruled a breach of Art 6 ECHR under the then operative Care Standards Act 2000, s 82(4)(b).[1] The provisions in both statutes were replaced by the Safeguarding Vulnerable Groups Act 2006 (para 7.248 below).

[1]   *R (Wright) v Secretary of State for Health* [2009] UKHL 3.

7.241   Bichard recommended a central body to be responsible for a nationally administered register for those who wished to work with children or vulnerable adults. It could be supported by a card or license. The decisions on refusing or permitting registration and in assessing the relevance of police intelligence would lie with the central body. The police could identify, in conformity with current practice, information that should not under any circumstances be given to the job applicant. Employers would take the initial decision on whether a post required registration and would retain the ultimate right of making an appointment. The central body would have the right to ignore any conviction information not deemed relevant to the post and the applicant for registration would have a right pf appeal against refusal of registration. This would be exercised before any information is handed to a third party. The scheme would be phased in to avoid the deluge of applications to the CRB when SDs were introduced and the register would be continually updated. In his March 2005 Report, Bichard stated that the barring system for those working with children was not guaranteed.

7.242   Clause 77 of the Protection of Freedoms Bill (2011) repeals ss 113A(4) and 113B(5) and (6) of the 1997 Act. The explanatory material accompanying the Bill makes the following points. When a person applies for a standard certificate or an enhanced certificate, the CRB simultaneously issues the relevant certificate to the applicant but also, by virtue of ss 113A(4) and 113B(6), sends a copy of the certificate to the registered body which countersigned the application. A registered body will usually be the applicant's employer or prospective employer or other organisation acting on behalf of an employer. The applicant does not have the opportunity to review the certificate and, if desired, challenge the information contained within it, before it is released to an employer. The repeal of ss 113A(4) and 113B(6) removes the provisions that require a copy of a certificate to be sent to the registered body so that the certificate is issued to the applicant only, allowing the applicant to make appropriate representations to the CRB regarding the information released without the disputed information first having been seen by the employer.

7.243   Section 113B(5) of the 1997 Act enables sensitive (non-conviction) information which might be relevant to an employer to be provided to a registered body without being copied to the applicant. Such a procedure is adopted, for example, 'where the police are engaged in an ongoing criminal investigation and the premature release of the relevant information to an applicant for an enhanced criminal records certificate might compromise that investigation'. The repeal of s 113B(5) removes the statutory obligation to disclose the relevant information to the registered body in such circumstances. However, the explanatory material points out that 'it would remain open to the police, using their common law powers to prevent crime and protect the public, to pass such information to a potential employer where they considered it justified and proportionate'. The age of requesters for certificates is set at 16 and for those countersigning applications the age is 18.

7.244　Changes are made in relation to enhanced criminal records and the test to be applied by a chief officer when determining whether additional, non-conviction, information should be included in an enhanced criminal records certificate. In place of the current test of information which, in the opinion of the chief officer 'might be relevant' and ought to be included in the certificate, subsection (1) substitutes a slightly higher test of information which the chief officer 'reasonably believes to be relevant' and which in the chief officer's opinion ought to be included in the certificate.[1] A new s 113B(4A) enables the Secretary of State to issue guidance to relevant chief officers about the discharge of their functions under s 113B(4) to provide relevant non-conviction information about an applicant for an enhanced criminal records certificate; a relevant chief officer is required to have regard to any such guidance.

[1]　*R (L) v Commissioner of Police of the Metropolis* [2009] UKHL 3.

7.245　Sub-section (4) inserts new sub-ss (2A) to (2C) into s 117 of the 1997 Act. These make further provision about disputes concerning the accuracy of the information contained in a certificate. The explanatory material explains that under s 117(2), an applicant in receipt of a criminal conviction certificate, criminal record certificate or enhanced criminal record certificate who disputes the accuracy of the information contained in such a certificate, may make an application to the Secretary of State for a new certificate. New s 117(2A) provides that such an application may, in particular, request a review of the non-conviction information supplied by a relevant chief officer. On receipt of such a request, the Secretary of State must ask an appropriate chief officer of a police force (which will, in practice, be a different chief officer from that who made the original decision to provide non-conviction information to be included in the disputed certificate) to review the relevancy of the disputed non-conviction information.

7.246　New s 116A of the 1997 Act introduces a procedure for updating certificates on a continuous basis:

'An applicant (or a registered or other person authorised by the applicant) for a criminal conviction certificate, criminal record certificate or enhanced criminal record certificate must subscribe to the updating arrangements at the time an application for a certificate is submitted and thereafter re-subscribe to those arrangements on an annual basis. The update arrangements will only be put in place in respect of an applicant for a certificate and thereafter renewed on payment of an initial fee and subsequently of an annual fee to be prescribed by regulations made under new section 116A(5) (by virtue of section 125 of the 1997 Act such regulations are subject to the negative resolution procedure). The annual fee will be set at a level necessary to recover the costs of the service and will be offset by the removal of the need to make repeat applications for a criminal records certificate. Under the update arrangements the CRB will not, as such, provide any new conviction or other relevant information to the subscriber to the updating arrangements. Instead, by virtue of the definition of 'up-date information' in new section 116A(7), in response to a request for update information, the CRB will advise the person making the request either that there is no new information that would be include on a new certificate or that a new certificate should be applied for (which would imply that a new certificate would contain new information).'

7.247   Provision is made in the Bill for conditional cautions and for a person to have offences of buggery or gross indecency between men under the 1956 Sexual Offences Act or earlier legislation to have convictions or cautions disregarded by application to the Secretary of State.

Safeguarding of Vulnerable Groups Act 2006

7.248   This Act (to be amended by the Protection of Freedoms Bill (2011); below) followed a number of episodes where persons with convictions for sexual offences were allowed by civil servants to work with children. It replaces the legislation set out above (para 7.240) The Act provides that there will be two 'barred' lists – one for those who are barred from engaging in regulated activity with children (the 'children's barred list'), and one for those who are barred from engaging in regulated activity with vulnerable adults (the 'adults' barred list'). The Act also establishes an Independent Barring Board (IBB). The IBB will maintain the children's barred list and adults' barred list and will make decisions about whether an individual should be included in one or both barred lists. The Act contains a right of appeal to the Care Standards Tribunal, with the permission of the Tribunal, against inclusion in a barred list on a point of law or on a finding of fact made by the IBB. The Act provides for four routes to inclusion on one or both of the barred lists. These are:

'automatic inclusion as a result of receiving a caution or conviction for specified offences, or other criteria which may be specified (such as orders, foreign orders or directions, and inclusion on a foreign barred list). There will be no right for the individual to make representations nor a right of appeal in these cases. There will be automatic inclusion on one or both of the barred lists as a result of receiving a caution or conviction for certain other specified offences or as a result of having met some certain other specified criteria. There will be a right to make representations and a right of appeal following inclusion. Specified behaviour ("relevant conduct") that leads to consideration for inclusion on one or both of the barred lists. This includes, for example, conduct which harms a child in the case of the children's barred list, or conduct which harms a vulnerable adult in the case of the adults' barred list, or conduct involving child pornography for both lists. Finally, risk of harm where evidence suggests that an individual may present a risk of harm to children or vulnerable adults, this will lead to consideration for inclusion on the appropriate list'.

7.249   An individual who is included in the children's barred list must not engage in regulated activity in relation to children. An individual who is included in the adults' barred list must not engage in regulated activity in relation to vulnerable adults. Generally speaking, 'regulated activity will cover a range of specified activities that provide an opportunity for close contact with children or vulnerable adults, other activities in key settings such as schools and care homes which provide an opportunity for contact, and key positions of responsibility such as the Children's Commissioner and the Director of Adult Social Services'.

7.250   Various criminal offences prevent barred individuals from engaging in regulated activity in relation to children or vulnerable adults; ensure that people permitted to engage in regulated activity in relation to children or vulnerable adults with the permission of a 'regulated activity provider' are subject to monitoring; and ensure that relevant employers check an individual's status in the scheme before permitting an individual to engage in regulated activity in relation to children or vulnerable adults. An individual will become subject to monitoring by making an application to the Secretary of State (CRB). This involves a search of the Police National Computer for cautions and convictions and making enquiries with local police forces to obtain other relevant information.

7.251   The Act also confers power on the Secretary of State to make regulations about controlled activity. This covers certain activity other than regulated activity. There are many holes to be filled in by regulations. 'There is no current intention to prevent a barred individual from engaging in controlled activity. But in part the regulations will be used so as to require employers (and others with responsibility for managing controlled activity) to put in place appropriate safeguards to manage the risks posed by barred individuals'. In broad terms, controlled activity covers support work in 'general health settings, further education settings and adult social care settings. It also covers work which gives a person the opportunity for access to sensitive records about children and vulnerable adults, including education and social services records'.

7.252   Everyone engaging in what the Act refers to as 'regulated activity' with the permission of a 'regulated activity provider' will be subject to monitoring. This covers those who are closely working, or applying to work, with children or vulnerable adults. They will be required to make an application to the Secretary of State to be 'subject to monitoring'. Monitoring will also cover employers engaging individuals in 'controlled activity' and employers will in most cases need to ensure that they are subject to monitoring. Provisions will be spelt out in regulations. The Act allows for the phasing in of applications from existing members of the workforce.

7.253 Where the Secretary of State's enquiries reveal that a person satisfies one of the criteria that lead to automatic inclusion in a barred list, he will refer the matter to the IBB so that the person can be included in the relevant barred list. The Secretary of State will also pass details of relevant cautions and convictions together with all information received from local police forces to the IBB, which the IBB can then consider in relation to inclusion in a barred list. Under the 2006 Act where a person is included in a barred list, he ceases to be subject to monitoring (if he was previously) and is not able to engage in regulated activity. Some modifications are now planned (below). Except in the most serious cases, opportunities to make representations will exist to allow individuals to explain why they should not be barred on the basis of this information.

7.254 The Secretary of State must repeat these searches and enquiries at appropriate intervals. If new information comes to light about a person who is subject to monitoring, the Secretary of State will give the information to the IBB (see above). The IBB may also 'have cause to consider including a person in a barred list on the basis of referrals from employers, local authorities, professional bodies and supervisory authorities'. An employer may register to be notified if an employee ceases to be subject to monitoring. Where this is the case the employer will then be informed of this by the Secretary of State through the CRB.

7.255 No claim for damages may be made in relation to action under s 1 unless the action is done with malice.

CRIME AND SECURITY ACT 2010

7.256 The Crime and Security Act 2010 contains provisions to give additional powers to the police to take fingerprints and DNA samples from people who have been arrested, charged or convicted in the UK, and from those convicted overseas of serious sexual and violent offences. The Act has not come into force but the coalition government intends to repeal the Act under the Protection of Freedoms Bill 2011 (below). The 2010 Act was a response to the ECtHR judgment in the case of *S and Marper v United Kingdom* [2008] ECHR 1581, in which it was held that indefinite retention of DNA samples of unconvicted individuals breached their Art 8 ECHR rights. The 2010 Act sets out a statutory framework for the retention and destruction of biometric material, including DNA samples, DNA profiles and fingerprints, that have been taken from an individual as part of the investigation of a 'recordable offence'.[1] These powers were subject to consultation in the *Keeping the Right People on the DNA Database* published in May 2009. The following provisions had not come into force at the time of writing but in any event were overtaken by the provisions set out below in the Protection of Liberties Bill. It should be added that the 2010 Act amended the powers to enable biometric data (fingerprints and non-intimate samples respectively) to be taken from people and related powers.

¹   The ECHR judgment in *Marper* overruled the House of Lords judgment in *R (S) v Chief Constable of the South Yorkshire Police* [2004] 1 WLR 2196 where the retention in question was permitted by Art 8(2) ECHR it was ruled. In *R (GC) v Com'r of the Police of the Metropolis* [2011] UKSC 21, the Supreme Court ruled by majority that the ACPO guidance authorising indefinite retention was ultra vires the powers in PACE s 64 as amended.

Retention, destruction and use of fingerprints and samples, etc

7.257   Section 14 of the Crime and Security Act 2010: Material subject to the Police and Criminal Evidence Act 1984. According to the explanatory notes accompanying the Act, s 14 substitutes a new s 64 into the Police and Criminal Evidence Act 1984 (PACE 1984) and inserts 14 new sections immediately after it. Section 64 (destruction of fingerprints and samples) currently sets out the purposes for which fingerprints, impressions of footwear and samples may be retained but permits them to be retained after they have fulfilled the purposes for which they were taken without reference to a retention period. The effect of s 14 is to establish a framework for the retention and destruction of such material, following the decision of the ECtHR in *S and Marper v United Kingdom* [2008] ECHR 1581. The new provisions require the destruction of DNA samples once they have been profiled and loaded satisfactorily on to the national database. In any event, all *samples* (whether biological DNA material or other samples, such as dental or skin impressions) are required to be destroyed within six months of their being taken (see new s 64ZA(2)).

7.258   The retention periods for the various categories of data depend on a number of factors including the age of the individual concerned, the seriousness of the offence or alleged offence, whether the individual has been convicted and, if so, whether it is a first conviction. The different categories are summarised as follows:

- Adults, convicted: indefinite retention of fingerprints, impressions of footwear and DNA profile (see substituted s 64(2)).
- Adults, arrested but unconvicted: retention of fingerprints, impressions of footwear and DNA profile for six years (see new s 64ZD).
- Under 18 year olds, convicted of a serious offence or more than one minor offence: indefinite retention of fingerprints, impressions of footwear and DNA profile (see substituted s 64(2)).
- Under 18 year olds, convicted of single minor offence: retention of fingerprints, impressions of footwear and DNA profile for five years (see new s 64ZH).
- 16 and 17 year olds, arrested for but unconvicted of serious offence: retention of fingerprints, impressions of footwear and DNA profile for six years (see new s 64ZG).
- All other under 18 year olds, arrested but unconvicted: retention of fingerprints, impressions of footwear and DNA profile for three years (see new ss 64ZE and 64ZF).
- Persons subject to a control order: retention of fingerprints and DNA profile for two years after the control order ceases to have effect (see new s 64ZC).
- All DNA samples: retained until profile loaded onto database, but no more than six months (see new s 64ZA).

7.259 For the purposes of these provisions, the concept of 'qualifying offence' is used to distinguish between serious and minor offences. Qualifying offence is defined in s 7. The substitution of new s 64 also has the effect of removing the existing right of a person to witness the destruction of their fingerprints or impressions of footwear as, with the increasing use of technology, there are often no physical prints to destroy. However, a person still has the right to request a certificate from the police confirming that their data have been destroyed (see new s 64ZM). There is a new provision in s 64ZB for material which has been given voluntarily to be destroyed as soon as it has fulfilled the purpose for which it was taken, unless the individual is subsequently convicted, has previous convictions or consents to its retention. In addition, where fingerprints or DNA profiles would otherwise need to be destroyed because of the expiry of a time limit set out in the above sections, new s 64ZK enables a responsible chief officer of police to determine that, for reasons of national security, those fingerprints or DNA profiles may be retained for up to two further years on that basis. They may be retained for longer 'where the necessity continues to exist'.

7.260 Section 15 makes provision for Northern Ireland equivalent to that made for England and Wales by s 14, and s 16 makes provision for Scotland for the retention and use of relevant physical data or samples.

7.261 Section 17: Material subject to the Terrorism Act 2000. The Terrorism Act 2000, Sch 8, para 14 currently provides for the retention of fingerprints and samples (and DNA profiles derived from samples) taken from persons detained under s 41 or Sch 7 to the Terrorism Act 2000 (that is persons arrested as a suspected terrorist or persons detained under the ports and borders provisions in Sch 7). Sch 8, para 14 sets out the purposes for which these fingerprints, samples and profiles may be used while they are retained, but permits retention without reference to a retention period.

7.262 Section 17 substitutes for para 14 new paras 14 to 14I, making provision for a destruction and retention regime broadly equivalent to that in the amendments to PACE 1984.

7.263 As in relation to the PACE 1984 provisions, where fingerprints or DNA profiles would otherwise need to be destroyed because of the expiry of a time limit set out in the new provisions, if a chief officer of police (or chief constable in Northern Ireland) determines that it is necessary to retain that material for the purposes of national security, those fingerprints or DNA profiles may be further retained for up to two years (new para 14G). It is open to that chief officer to make further determinations to retain the material, which have effect for a maximum of two years.

7.264 Paragraph 14I largely replicates the existing provision in para 14 (as prospectively amended by s 16 of the Counter-Terrorism Act 2008) in relation to the use to which retained material may be put: it may be used in the interests of national security, in a terrorist investigation, for the investigation of crime or for identification-related purposes (sub-paras (1) and (4)). Sub-paragraph (2) replicates the existing provision in para 14 about the material against which fingerprints and samples taken under the Terrorism Act 2000 may be checked. Sub-paragraph (3) is new, and provides that, once the new requirement to destroy material applies, the material cannot be used in evidence against the person to whom it relates or for the purposes of the investigation of any offence.

7.265   Section 18 provides for a new regime for the retention, destruction and use of biometric material taken in Scotland under the Terrorism Act 2000, Sch 8, para 20. Paragraph 20 currently provides for the retention of biometric material, including fingerprints, DNA samples and DNA profiles taken from persons detained under the Terrorism Act 2000, s 41 or Sch 7 in Scotland. It sets out the purposes for which this material may be used while they are retained, but permits retention without reference to a retention period.

7.266   The time limits for retention depend on the age of the person, whether the person has previous convictions and whether the person is detained under s 41 (arrest on suspicion of terrorism) or under Sch 7 (detention at ports and borders). Where a person is convicted of a recordable offence in England and Wales and Northern Ireland or an offence punishable by imprisonment in Scotland (or where the person already has such a conviction, other than a conviction for a minor offence committed when they were under 18), the material need not be destroyed. Where fingerprints or DNA profiles would otherwise need to be destroyed because of the expiry of a time limit set out in the new provisions, if a chief constable of police determines that it is necessary to retain that material for the purposes of national security, those fingerprints or DNA profiles may be further retained for up to two years (new para 20G). It is open to a chief constable to make further determinations to retain the material, which have effect for a maximum of two years. Paragraph 20I covers the use to which retained material may be put, replicating those for England and Wales or Northern Ireland in s 17.

7.267   Section 19: Material subject to the International Criminal Court Act 2001. Fingerprints and samples may be taken from a person under the International Criminal Court Act 2001, Sch 4 if the International Criminal Court (ICC) requests assistance in obtaining evidence of the identity of a person (who will usually be a person suspected of committing an 'ICC crime' such as genocide or war crimes). Section 19 amends Sch 4 to make provision about the retention and destruction of material taken under that Schedule, so that all material must be destroyed within six months of it being transferred to the ICC, or, if later, as soon as it has fulfilled the purposes for which it was taken.

7.268   Section 20 concerns material subject to the Counter-Terrorism Act 2008 (Scotland). The main area of difference between the provision for England, Wales and Northern Ireland and the provision for Scotland is that any samples that are retained in Scotland may be used only in the interests of national security or for the purposes of a terrorist investigation. This difference is necessary in order to avoid making provision in areas that are within devolved competence.

7.269 Section 21 concerns other material. In essence, s 21 amends s 18 of the 2008 Act to introduce the requirement to destroy any DNA sample referred to in s 18 as soon as a profile has been derived from it or, if sooner, within six months of the sample coming into the authority's possession (new sub-s 18(3A)). New sub-s 18(3B) provides that fingerprints or DNA profiles ('material') relating to an identifiable individual aged under 16 at the time they came into the authority's possession must be destroyed within three years. New sub-s 18(3C) provides for destruction of such material relating to a person aged 16 or over within six years of that material coming into the authority's possession. In each case, where the person is convicted of a recordable offence in England and Wales or Northern Ireland (or where the person already has such a conviction, other than a conviction for a minor offence committed when they were under 18), the material need not be destroyed.

7.270 Where fingerprints or DNA profiles would otherwise need to be destroyed because of the expiry of a time limit set out in the new provisions, if the 'responsible officer' determines that it is necessary to retain that material for the purposes of national security, those fingerprints or DNA profiles may be further retained for up to two years (new sub-ss 18(3E) and (3F)). The responsible officer may make further determinations to retain the material, which again have effect for a maximum of two years. 'Responsible officer' is defined in new sub-s (3G) as the chief officer of the police force or organisation which obtained or acquired the material. New sub-ss section 18(3H) and (3I) replicate the provisions in PACE 1984 (as amended by this Act) about the destruction of copies of fingerprints and DNA profiles, and new sub-s 18(3J) and substituted sections (4) and (4B) (inserted by s 18(5)) make provision about the uses to which the material may be put (which largely reproduces what is currently in s 18(2) and (4)). Section 22 deals with destruction of material taken before commencement. Powers will be contained in regulations. This will enable the Secretary of State to ensure that the retention and destruction regime set out in this Act is applied to existing material, while recognising that this exercise may take some time to complete; there are some 850,000 profiles of unconvicted persons on the National DNA Database. The statutory instrument will be subject to the negative resolution procedure.

Protection of Liberties Bill 2011

7.271 The coalition government set out plans to remove 'unnecessary restrictions' on essential freedoms and these took shape in the Protection of Liberties Bill 2011. A table comparing the retention rules in respect of fingerprints, DNA samples and profiles and footwear impressions as they are before reform, as they would have been under the provisions of the 2010 Act, as they currently operate in Scotland and as they would be under the provisions of the Bill, is set out below. In relation to national security retention a commissioner is to be appointed with powers to order destruction of DNA and fingerprint profiles. The Secretary of State is given powers to issue a code of guidance. Clause 23 inserts a new s 63AA into PACE 1984 which places on a statutory footing the existing National DNA Database. The new section requires DNA profiles taken under PACE or in connection with an investigation to be recorded on the relevant database. The National DNA Database is maintained and operated by the National Police Improvement Agency on behalf of the police; as at 31 July 2010 it contained 6.3 million DNA profiles (representing 5.41 million individuals). The National DNA Database Strategy Board will be placed on a statutory footing. The Bill makes provision for parental consent (of both parents but with exceptions) before a child's (under 18) biometric data can be processed. A child may also object to such processing. There are exceptions and, in the case of objection by a child, processing or continuing processing suitable alternatives have to be in place. The duty is placed on proprietors of schools or governing bodies of colleges. The Bill also provides for a code to be issued by the Secretary of State on CCTV cameras (including automatic number plate recognition) and a Surveillance Camera Commissioner. Amendments are also made to the Safeguarding of Vulnerable Groups Act 2006 The overall effect of the amendments is to reduce the scope of work from which barred individuals are prohibited. Amendments are made to the definition of 'vulnerable adult' and 'regulated activities'. Amendments are also made to the processing of referrals from the Secretary of Sate to the Independent Safeguarding Authority for barring entries on the barred list. Representations may be made. Provision is made for information on barred persons and duties are placed on regulated activity providers to establish whether persons are barred before allowing them to engage in a regulated activity.

7.272 Comparative tables (From explanatory notes)

DNA profile retention periods: comparison between current rules under PACE 1984, the rules applicable in Scotland and the rules that would apply under the provisions in the 2010 Act and in Chapter 1 of Part 1 of the Bill.

Occurrence	Current System (England and Wales)	Crime and Security Act 2010 (England and Wales)	Scottish system	Proposed changes under the Bill
Adult, conviction, all crimes	Indefinite	Indefinite	Indefinite	Indefinite
Adult, non-conviction, serious crime	Indefinite*	Six years	Three years plus possible two-year extension(s) by court	Three years plus possible single two-year extension by court

Occurrence	Current System (England and Wales)	Crime and Security Act 2010 (England and Wales)	Scottish system	Proposed changes under the Bill
Adult, non-conviction, minor crime	Indefinite*	Six years	None	None†
Under 18s, conviction, serious crime	Indefinite	First conviction: five year; second conviction: indefinite	Indefinite	First conviction: five years (plus length of any custodial sentence); second conviction: indefinite
Under 18s, non-conviction, serious crime	Indefinite*	Three years	Three years plus possible two-year extension(s) by court	Three years plus possible single two-year extension by court
Under 18s, non-conviction, minor crime	Indefinite*	Three years	None	None†
Terrorist suspects	Indefinite*	Six years plus renewable two-year period(s) on national security grounds	Not covered (reserved matters)	Three years plus renewable two-year period(s) on national security grounds
Biological DNA samples	Indefinite*	Within six months of sample being taken	As per destruction of profiles	Within six months of sample being taken

*　Destruction of DNA profiles and biological samples is available under 'exceptional circumstances'. This requires an application to the Chief Constable of the relevant police force; removal from the database is then at his/her discretion in accordance with guidelines issued by the Association of Chief Police Officers.

†　In all cases, a speculative search of the DNA and fingerprint databases may be conducted before destruction.

The Bill will be accompanied by an overarching impact assessment and a further ten impact assessments on individual provisions. The impact assessments, signed by Ministers, will be published and placed on the Bill website.[1]

[1]　http://www.homeoffice.gov.uk/publications/legislation/protection-freedoms-bill.

DUTIES TO DISCLOSE INFORMATION

7.273 In a book of this nature it would be impossible to describe the duties which exist in law concerning private bodies or individuals and their disclosure of information. The existing provisions cover convictions;[1] those who work with children as we have seen above;[2] and a host of legal duties to provide information to law enforcement agencies or regulatory authorities. Police and Criminal Evidence Act 1984 (PACE 1984 as amended), ss 8–16 and Sch 1 impose a duty upon a wide range of individuals holding information to disclose the information to the police, upon production of a warrant, even though the relationship is 'confidential'. PACE 1984, s 64(1A) (inserted by Criminal Justice and Police Act 2001, s 82 and further amended as explained above) allows for the retention of fingerprints and DNA samples after an acquittal or decision not to prosecute, a provision which the Law Lords ruled does not engage Art 8(1) ECHR and retention of finger-prints and DNA samples in such cases 'save in exceptional circumstances' was therefore lawful.[3] The subsequent developments reversing this position have been described above. Power of surveillance under Part III of the Police Act 1997 allow surveillance of sensitive confidential and legally privileged information and the extensive powers of the RIPA 2000 were noted in ch 2. Section 15 of the Crime and Disorder Act 1998 is another example, as well as the duties of notification under the Sexual Offences Act 1997 and Sexual Offences Act 2003, Part II. Police Act 1997, s 115 was referred to above (para 7.139) and concerns the scheme to obtain criminal records. Recent developments have been outlined above.

[1]   Rehabilitation of Offenders Act 1974 and orders thereunder.
[2]   On child protection registers, see *R v Norfolk County Council Social Services Department, ex p M* [1989] 2 All ER 359; *R v Harrow London Borough Council, ex p D* [1990] Fam 133, CA; *R v Hampshire County Council, ex p H* [1999] 2 FLR 359, CA; *R v Devon County Council, ex p L* [1991] 2 FLR 541; *R v Lewisham London Borough Council, ex p P* [1991] 3 All ER 529. On disclosure of information re abuses of children: Children Act 1989, ss 47 and 19 do not impose a duty on the local authority, but see *Re EC (Disclosure of Material)* [1996] 2 FLR 725, CA; *Re L; Re V (sexual abuse: disclosure)* [1999] 1 FLR 267, CA. See paras 10.22 et seq below. See further: *R v Secretary of State for Health, ex p C* [2000] 1 FCR 471, CA.
[3]   *R (S) v Chief Constable of South Yorkshire* [2004] UKHL 39. Lord Steyn stated that 'it is of paramount importance that law enforcement agencies should take full advantage of the available techniques of modern technology and forensic science' [para 1]. 'Cultural traditions' in the UK in the state storing information on individuals was a material factor in considering objective justification under Art 8(2), they were not material in considering whether Art 8(1) was engaged!

7.274 In the field of immigration there is the Immigration and Asylum Act 1999, ss 18–21.The provisions under Nationality, Immigration and Asylum Act 2002, Part 6 concerning the provision of 'physical data' by travellers on a voluntary or compulsory basis should be noted, as well as the disclosure provisions relating to public authorities and private persons.

7.275 The Terrorism Act 2000 has various powers including those imposing duties (as soon as reasonably practicable) and powers to disclose information to the police in relation to financial offences supporting terrorism including money laundering (ss 19 and 20 respectively). Section 20 overrides any countervailing statutory duties not to disclose. Under Sch 7, para 17, powers to request in writing information from the owners of ships or aircraft is given, and Anti-terrorism, Crime and Security Act 2001, s 17 inserts a new duty on a variety of bodies in listed statutes to disclose information to the security service. Including Northern Ireland there are 66 statutes included as so affected and covering such bodies in Sch 4. The Terrorism Act 2000, ss 37–39 and Schs 5 and 6 concern powers to obtain information (including financial information) and evidence, and the Anti-terrorism, Crime and Security Act 2001 has forfeiture provisions on terrorist cash and property (ss 1–3), and provisions on freezing orders (ss 4–8). Freezing orders in relation to terrorism have been introduced under powers contained in the United Nations Act 1946 and these were ruled unlawful by the Supreme Court but its decision was revered by temporary legislation and then addrssed in the Terrorist Asset Freezing etc. Act 2010. The Prevention of Terrorism Act 2005 concerned control orders and so on (see para 9.132) which are to be removed under the Terrorism Prevention and Investigation Measures Bill 2011.

7.276   The Competition Act 1998 confers powers of investigation on the Office of Fair Trading under ss 25–31, 61–65, and the Financial Services and Markets Act 2000 is replete with duties to provide information to regulators and others.[1] The Fair Trading Act 1973 and Competition Act 1998 were amended by the Enterprise Act 2002. This Act places on the OFT general duties to acquire information relating to its functions on mergers, market investigations and consumer protection (s 5). Under s 6, the OFT is under a duty to provide information to the public. Amendments are also made to the Competition Commission. Section 203 of the 2002 Act allows IT experts to accompany OFT officials on investigations. Enterprise Act 2002, ss 237 et seq concern restrictions on disclosure of information under the Act. In relation to banks there are over 20 statutes which impose a duty upon, or called upon a bank to disclose information about a customer in the public interest, eg Criminal Justice Act 1988, s 98 and Drug Trafficking Offences Act 1986, s 27.[2] The circumstances requiring, or permitting, such disclosures include insider dealing, company fraud and insolvency, breaches of the Consumer Credit Act 1974, tax evasion, inquiries into the affairs of charities, extradition and mental incapacity.[3] To these may be added s 17 of the Bank of England Act 1998. The duty between a banker and a customer is one of confidentiality,[4] but that duty may be overborne by a public interest defence for the bank under the civil law of confidentiality (see ch 2) or in the legitimate interests of the bank, though the extent of such an immunity for banks, particularly in the latter case, is far from certain.[5] Revenue authorities have sought a 'random search power' into current accounts via the Finance Acts 2008 and 2009 and the Customs and Excise Management Act 1979 as amended in 2011.

[1]   Financial Services and Markets Act 2000, ss 13, 82, 147, 161, 165, 175, 230, 231; and see Anti-terrorism, Crime and Security Act 2001, s 17.

[2]   On ss 93A–93C of the Criminal Justice Act 1988 (as amended by the Criminal Justice Act 1993) and dilemmas facing banks, see: *Governor and Company of the Bank of Scotland v A Ltd* [2001] EWCA Civ 52, [2001] 1 WLR 751.

3 Cm 622 (1989), ch 5 and see App Q for the list. See the Television Licences (Disclosure of Information) Act 2000.
4 *Tournier v National Provincial and Union Bank of England* [1924] 1 KB 461, CA; see R Toulson and C Phipps *Confidentiality* (2006), ch XIV. See *Jackson v Royal Bank of Scotland* [2005] UKHL 3 for damages for a breach of confidence by a bank.
5 See Cm 622 (above) and cf *Bank of Tokyo Ltd v Karoon* [1987] 1 AC 45n, CA; *Re State of Norway's Application* [1989] 1 All ER 745, HL; and *Barclays Bank plc v Taylor* [1989] 3 All ER 563, CA: no breach of confidentiality in bank failing to challenge an application for 'special procedure material' under the Police and Criminal Evidence Act 1984.

7.277   The DPA 1998 will, of course, apply to such holders of data covered by that Act although many of the exemptions and subject access restrictions will operate.

7.278   Duties to allow access, or to disclose information, to regulatory or other authorities would soon take us into the complexities of the regulatory state: eg under the Financial Services and Markets Act 2000, Banking Act 1987, Companies Act 2006, the Taxes Management Act 1970 as amended and the Income and Corporation Taxes Act 1989,[1] VAT Act 1987, Finance Acts and so on as well as the provisions above. Some of these duties are noted elsewhere in this book, but the treatment constitutes a passing reference only (see para 11.1).[2]

1 See *R (Morgan Grenfell & Co Ltd) v Special Commissioner of Income Tax* [2002] 3 All ER 1 (HL) and also note SI 2001/404.
2 See Gender Recognition (Disclosure of Information) (England, Wales and Northern Ireland) Order 2005, SI 2005/635.

PRIVACY AND ELECTRONIC COMMUNICATIONS REGULATIONS

7.279   The Privacy and Electronic Communications (EC Directive) Regulations 2003, SI 2003/2426 (as amended by SI 2004/1039), implement Articles 2, 4, 5(3), 6 to 13, 15 and 16 of Directive 2002/58/EC of the European Parliament and of the Council of 12 July 2002 concerning the processing of personal data and the protection of privacy in the electronic communications sector ('the Directive').[1]

1 See also Electronic Communications Code (Conditions and Restrictions) Regulations 2003, SI 2003/2553, made under Communications Act 2003, ss 109 and 402, on the general duties of providers of networks re operations.

7.280   The Directive repeals and replaces Directive 97/66/EC of the European Parliament concerning the processing of personal data and the protection of privacy in the telecommunications sector, which was implemented in the UK by the Telecommunications (Data Protection and Privacy) Regulations 1999. Those Regulations are revoked by reg 3 of these Regulations.

7.281 Regulation 2 sets out the definitions which apply for the purposes of the Regulations.

7.282 Regulation 4 provides that nothing in these Regulations relieves a person of any of his obligations under the DPA 1998.

7.283 The explanation accompanying the Regulations states that:

'Regulation 5 imposes a duty on a provider of a public electronic communications service to take measures, if necessary in conjunction with the provider of the electronic communications network by means of which the service is provided, to safeguard the security of the service, and requires the provider of the electronic communications network to comply with the service provider's reasonable requests made for the purposes of taking the measures ("public electronic communications service" has the meaning given by section 151 of the Communications Act 2003 and "electronic communications network" has the meaning given by section 32 of that Act). Regulation 5 further requires the service provider, where there remains a significant risk to the security of the service, to provide subscribers to that service with certain information ("subscriber" is defined as "a person who is a party to a contract with a provider of public electronic communications services for the supply of such services").

Regulation 6 provides that an electronic communications network may not be used to store or gain access to information in the terminal equipment of a subscriber or user ("user" is defined as "any individual using a public electronic communications service") unless the subscriber or user is provided with certain information and is given the opportunity to refuse the storage of or access to the information in his terminal equipment.

Regulations 7 and 8 set out certain restrictions on the processing of traffic data relating to a subscriber or user by a public communications provider. "Traffic data" is defined as "any data processed for the purpose of the conveyance of a communication on an electronic communications network or for the billing in respect of that communication". "Public communications provider" is defined as "a provider of a public electronic communications network or a public electronic communications service".'

7.284 Regulation 9 concerns provision of non-itemised bills by public electronic communications services.

7.285 Regulations 10 and 11 concern providers of a public electronic communications service and safeguards in relation to the presentation of calling line identification on a call-by-call basis and connected line identification. This regulation is subject to regs 15 and 16.

7.286 Regulation 14 imposes certain restrictions on the processing of location data, which is defined as 'any data processed in an electronic communications network indicating the geographical position of the terminal equipment of a user of a public electronic communications service, including data relating to the latitude, longitude or altitude of the terminal equipment; the direction of travel of the user; or the time the location information was recorded.'

7.287 Regulation 15 makes provision in relation to the tracing of malicious or nuisance calls. Regulation 16 makes provision in relation to emergency calls ie 999 or European emergency call number 112.

7.288 Regulation 17 concerns automatic forwarding of calls.

7.289 Regulation 18 applies to directories of subscribers, and sets out requirements that must be satisfied where data relating to subscribers is included in such directories. It also gives subscribers the right to verify, correct or withdraw their data in directories.

7.290 Regulation 19, 20, 21, 22 and 23 concern direct marketing.

7.291 Regulation 27 provides that terms in certain contracts which are inconsistent with these Regulations shall be void.

7.292 Regulation 28 exempts communications providers from the requirements of these Regulations where exemption is required for the purpose of safeguarding national security and further provides that a certificate signed by a Minister of the Crown to the effect that exemption from a requirement is necessary for the purpose of safeguarding national security shall be conclusive evidence of that fact. It also provides for certain questions relating to such certificates to be determined by the Information Tribunal referred to in s 6 of the DPA 1998.

7.293 Regulation 29 provides that a communications provider shall not be required by these Regulations to do, or refrain from doing, anything if complying with the requirement in question would be inconsistent with a requirement imposed by or under an enactment or by a court order, or if exemption from the requirement is necessary in connection with legal proceedings, for the purposes of obtaining legal advice or is otherwise necessary to establish, exercise or defend legal rights.

7.294 Regulation 30 allows a claim for damages to be brought in respect of contraventions of the Regulations.

7.295   Regulations 31 and 32 make provision in connection with the enforcement of the Regulations by the Information Commissioner (who is the Commissioner appointed under s 6 of the DPA 1998).

7.296   These provisions are to be amended by the e-Privacy Directive (2009/136/ EC) which was operative from May 2011 (SI 2011/1208). These amend the 2003 Regulations especially in relation to personal data breaches. These Regulations implement Ars 2 and 3 of Directive 2009/136/EC amending Directive 2002/22/ EC on universal service and users' rights relating to electronic communications networks and services, Directive 2002/58/EC concerning the processing of personal data and the protection of privacy in the electronic communications sector and Regulation (EC) No 2006/2004 on cooperation between national authorities responsible for the enforcement of consumer protection laws by making amendments to the Privacy and Electronic Communications (EC Directive) Regulations 2003 ('the 2003 Regulations'). The ICO has provided guidance on 'cookies technology' and other matters protecting privacy rights dealt with under the Directives.[1] Consent has to be given to the use of cookies – devices to track users' computer activity ('spyware') – on the basis of clear and comprehensive information about the purpose of the processing and use of cookies. Service providers are, from May 2011, given 12 months to install the necessary technology.

[1]   http://www.ico.gov.uk/for_organisations/privacy_and_electronic_communications/the_guide. aspx.

COMPUTER MISUSE AND 'HACKING'[1]

7.297   It will be helpful to say a little about the relationship between data protection law and the law relating to computer misuse, although the DPA 1998 is not restricted to computerised information. Computer-related crimes have seen a steady increase as the personal computer has become ubiquitous in the workplace, and increasingly common in the home. As we observed in chapter 2 (para 2.207) such 'hacking' practices have become a preoccupation of security and intelligence services and have developed the epithet of 'cyber warfare'. In the case of many computer-related crimes, such as frauds, the computer is often simply a new means of attaining an existing criminal goal, and such crimes can be, and are, largely prosecuted under existing technology-neutral laws. However, there are a range of undesirable activities, primarily involving unauthorised access to computer systems, and the information held on them, where the nature of the technology requires a more focused and specific legislative response. In the UK, after a series of failed[2] or unsatisfactory[3] prosecutions under existing criminal laws, of defendants who had accessed and used computer systems without permission causing financial losses and breaches of privacy, there was a call for specific legislation to deal with such activities. Within two weeks in June 2011, the victims of ever-sophisticated hacking activities included the IMF, the CIA, Sony, the US Senate, the Turkish government and Citibank.

The prominent informal networks perpetrating these crimes were two groups in particular – Anonymous and LulzSec – whose invariably young members are driven by suspicions of state and corporate institutions and attempts to police or own the web.[4]

[1]   See HC 907 (2010–12) and Government Reply Cm 8182 (2011) on unauthorised tapping and hacking.
[2]   For example, *R v Gold and Schifreen* [1988] 2 All ER 186, HL involving unauthorised access to the Prestel computer system (unsuccessful use of Fraud and Counterfeiting Act 1981 – Interception of Communications Act 1985, s 1(1) was also raised, but not considered by the court).
[3]   *Cox v Riley* (1986) 83 Cr App R 54 involving the deletion of programs from a computerised saw; *R v Whitely* (1991) 93 Cr App Rep 25, (1990) *Times*, 25 May, 8 June (CA), involving unauthorised access to the JANET academic computer network (both cases involved successful use of the Criminal Damage Act 1971, but this was thought by many commentators to be an unsuitable approach in the long run, due to the difficulty of proving 'tangible damage').
[4]   M Glenny *DarkMarket: CyberThieves, CyberCops and You* (2011).

7.298   In 1988–89, the Law Commission published two papers recommending that certain kinds of computer fraud and computer hacking[1] – ie unauthorised entry into a computer, should be criminalised. The Commission did not recommend a 'comprehensive computer crime statute' as this was regarded as neither necessary nor appropriate in England or Wales. The new crimes would cover computer use generally, and would not specifically pertain to the holding of personal information. The reports were followed in short order by legislative action in the form of the Computer Misuse Act 1990 (CMA 1990). Under the CMA 1990, three basic offences have been created: securing unauthorised access to any programme or data held on a computer; obtaining such access to a computer with a view to committing or facilitating a serious criminal offence; and causing an unauthorised modification (including a temporary one) of the contents of any computer which impairs the operation of the computer, any software or the reliability of any data.[2] The Police and Justice Act 2006, s 35 introduced amendments in relation to computer misuse and consent to mail bombing to interrupt the computer system was discussed in *DPP v Lennon* [2006] EWHC 1201 Admin. Papers in October 2010 on national security including cyber security were produced by the Cabinet Office, and the National Security Council will oversee its implementation.[3]

[1]   *Computer Misuse* Working Paper No 10 (1988); *Criminal Law Computer Misuse* Law Commission Report No 186, HMSO (1989).
[2]   Most of the relevant case-law is unreported: *R v Goulden* (1992, unreported); *R v Strickland and Woods* (1993, unreported); *R v Pile* (1995, unreported); *R v Raphael Gray* (2001, unreported); *R v Caffrey* (2003, unreported).
[3]   http://www.cabinetoffice.gov.uk/news/national-security-strategy.

7.299   In the early 1990s, however, there remained a potential lacuna in the overlapping protection provided to personal data by the DPA 1984, and the protection afforded against unauthorised access to data generally by the CMA 1990. This was demonstrated by two cases involving police officers and the Police National Computer system. In *R v Brown*,[1] a police officer was authorised to use the Police National Computer for the registered purpose of policing as agent of his chief constable, who was a registered user under the DPA 1984.

However, he twice caused checks to be made on vehicles owned by debtors from whom the agency had been engaged to recover debts, in order to assist a friend who ran a debt-collection agency. The information was displayed on a computer screen. The first search did not reveal any personal data as the vehicle corporately owned. The second search revealed personal data but there was no evidence that any subsequent use was made of the information obtained. The defendant was charged with two offences of using personal data held within the memory of the computer for a purpose other than that described in the register, contrary to s 5(2)(b), (3) and (5) of the DPA 1984. As noted above, it was held on appeal that a person who merely retrieved information from the database of a computer in the form of a display on a screen or of a printout did not 'use' the data for the purposes of the Act. Shortly afterwards, in *R v Bignall*,[2] two officers serving in the Metropolitan Police had instructed police computer operators to extract details of the registration and ownership of two cars from the Police National Computer for their own personal use. As a result they were charged with offences contrary to CMA 1990, s 1. However, on appeal the court held that that the primary purpose of the CMA 1990 was to protect the integrity of computer systems by criminalising the 'hacking' of computer systems and not the integrity of the data stored on them. Thus no offence under CMA 1990, s 1 was committed as the officers had caused the computer to perform a function to secure access to information held at a level to which they were entitled to gain access, even if they intended to secure access for an unauthorised purpose. We await to see the full fall-out from the hacking scandals.

[1]   [1996] AC 543 HL.
[2]   [1998] 1 Cr App R 1, QBD.

7.300   This lacuna was overcome in the late 1990s by the significant broadening of the definition of 'processing' in the DPA 1998, which closed the *Brown* loophole, and the judgment in the case of *R v Bow Street Metropolitan Stipendiary Magistrate and Another ex parte Government of United States of America*,[1] where an employee who was authorised to access certain data as part of her job accessed the data for use in a complicated fraud. The House of Lords disapproved the decision in *Bignall*, stating that it was erroneous to suggest that, just because a person had authority to access data for one purpose, this meant the person also had authority to access it for an unauthorised purpose. The employee's access was unauthorised, because she had no authority to access the data for the purpose of a fraud. In principle, it currently appears that an individual who processes personal data by means of unauthorised access to a computer system, or with authorised access for an unauthorised purpose, will be in breach of both the DPA 1998 and the CMA 1990.

[1]   [2000] 1 Cr App R 61, HL.

7.301   While the CMA 1990 provides for criminal penalties for computer misuse, it is important for DCs to remember that the DPA 1998 seventh principle requires that 'appropriate technical and organisational measures shall be taken against unauthorised or unlawful processing of personal data and against accidental loss of, or damage to, personal data' and that the appropriateness of measures will vary according to both the sensitivity of the personal data, and any developments in the technology available. Failure to take reasonable precautions against hacking and other forms of misuse may result in a DC facing civil actions from DSs under DPA 1998, s 13, and/or action by the IC including assessment audit and enforcement action. Amendments to these provisions have been examined above (para 7.58).

Chapter 8

Information and open government – specific areas

8.1 This chapter examines specific areas where there are existing duties or powers to publish information. It will be recalled that the FOIA 2000 does not prevent public authorities from exercising existing powers to disclose information. Under FOIA 2000, s 21 information which an authority is *obliged* by or under any enactment (apart from FOIA) to communicate is an absolute exemption under FOIA. One has to obtain it from an authority under that other enactment, whether free of charge or on payment of a fee (para 1.111 above).

POLICY AND FINANCE IN LOCAL GOVERNMENT

8.2 The general provisions of law applicable to meetings, documents and the public, as well as the rights of members to information apply in this area as elsewhere. Because of the sensitivity of this area, political groups in authorities where party politics are active may wish to keep proposals in the policy-making process confidential for as long as possible. However, as we have seen, there are limits imposed on secrecy by the law affecting authorities' meetings, documentation, composition of membership of meetings and members' access.[1] This area is also significantly affected by the Local Government Acts 2000 (LGA 2000) and 2003 (LGA 2003). See chs 4 and 5.

[1] See chs 4, 5 and 6 above.

8.3 In policy formulation, a frequent ploy is to create a one-party group, working group or advisory group which is outside the formal committee structure of an authority,[1] and so not covered by the Local Government (Access to Information) Act 1985, but which nevertheless the authority has power to create as we described above. These will be within the common law duties of authorities to allow access to documents and if necessary to allow a member to be present where the member can establish a right to know based upon a 'need to know'.[2] Such a need would have to relate not only to the subject-matter but also the timing of access. The effects of the Local Government and Housing Act 1989 (LGHA 1989) have been discussed.[3] The reforms which we outlined in ch 4 concerning new-style executives seek to address some of these points (paras 4.29 et seq above). There are dangers that we could end up with executive processes that are more resistant to openness than the present structures. The government hoped that removal of the antagonism that surrounded tax capping and the development through legislation of best value in the provision of local services emphasising participation of service recipients would help open up financial decisions. How successfully we shall see.

[1]   See chs 4 and 5 above.
[2]   See paras 5.70 et seq above.
[3]   See ch 4 above.

8.4   As regards financial planning or budgeting, the position has been affected by the Local Government Finance Act 1988 (LGFA 1988). As we saw in ch 4, this Act has recast the law relating to local authority financial planning. Authorities now impose a council charge, as well as a national business rate set by central government, a change which necessitated a reformulation of the system for re-allocating central government grants to local authorities. It will be recalled from ch 4 that reforms to the business rate were introduced by the LGA 2003. Furthermore, the chief finance officer shall make a report[1] if it appears to him that the authority,[2] a committee or officer of the authority or a joint committee on which the authority is represented:

(a)   has made or is about to make a decision which involves or would involve the authority incurring expenditure which is unlawful;

(b)   has taken or is about to take a course of action which, if pursued to its conclusion, would be unlawful and likely to cause a loss or deficiency on the part of the authority; or

(c)   is about to enter an item of account the entry of which is unlawful.

[1]   LGFA 1988, s 114. See paras 4.81 et seq above.
[2]   LGFA 1988, s 111 for the authorities.

8.5   Section 114 of LGFA 1988 continues:

'(3) The chief finance officer of a relevant authority shall make a report under this section if it appears to him that the expenditure of the authority incurred (including expenditure it proposes to incur) in a financial year is likely to exceed the resources (including sums borrowed) available to it to meet that expenditure. [The head of the authority's paid service and Monitoring Officer shall be consulted as far as reasonably practicable.]

(4) Where a chief finance officer of a relevant authority has made a report under this section he shall send a copy of it to–

(a)   the person who at the time the report is made has the duty to audit the authority's accounts, and

(b)   each person who at that time is a member of the authority.

(5) Subject to subsection (6) below, the duties of a chief finance officer of a relevant authority under subsections (2) and (3) above shall be performed by him personally.

(6) If the chief finance officer is unable to act owing to absence or illness his duties under sub-ss (2) and (3) above shall be performed–

(a)   by such member of his staff as is a member of one or more of the bodies mentioned in s 113(3) above and is for the time being nominated by the chief finance officer for the purposes of this section, or

(b)   if no member of his staff is a member of one or more of those bodies, by such member of his staff as is for the time being nominated by the chief finance officer for the purposes of this section.

(7) A relevant authority shall provide its chief finance officer with such staff, accommodation and other resources as are in his opinion sufficient to allow his duties under this section to be performed.

(8) In this section–

(a)   references to a joint committee are to a committee on which two or more relevant authorities are represented, and

(b)   references to a committee (joint or otherwise) include references to a sub-committee.'

8.6   The authority must consider the report made under s 114 at a meeting of the whole authority, which must be held within 21 days of the sending out of copies of the report. Temporary prohibitions exist regarding the proposed course of conduct which is the subject of the report and new agreements which may involve the incurring of expenditure.[1]

[1]   LGFA 1988, s 115; and see paras 4.89 et seq above.

8.7   Under LGFA 1988, s 116(1), where it is proposed to hold a s 115 meeting, the authority's proper officer shall as soon as is reasonably practicable notify its auditor of: the date, time and place of the proposed meeting; and, after the meeting, what decisions were made. The power of the auditor to issue prohibition orders under LGA 1988, Sch 4 have now been replaced by powers to issue advisory notices. Clearly LGFA 1988, ss 114–116 are aimed more at the final stage of decision-making than the early deliberative stages.

8.8   We have seen how the provisions in the LGA 2000 on standards seek to build on these safeguards (para 4.124 et seq above), and how some changes were introduced by the LGA 2003.

8.9   The powers of the Secretary of State to obtain local authority financial information are described elsewhere (paras 4.54 et seq above).

Inspecting the accounts

8.10   Section 14 of the Audit Commission Act 1998 (ACA 1998) governs the law relating to inspection of the accounts. It applies to all bodies audited under that section but not to health service bodies.

8.11 Under s 14, at each audit 'a local government elector' may inspect and make copies of any statement of accounts prepared by the body pursuant to regulations under s 27. The copy of the report other than an 'immediate report' (under s 8) made by the auditor to the body may be inspected and copied. The elector may require copies of any such statement or report to be delivered to him on payment of a reasonable sum for each copy. Obstruction by the person with custody is a summary offence punishable by fine. Section 15 allows the accounts of a body to be audited, again excluding health service bodies, to be inspected by any person interested[1] as well as all books, deeds, contracts, bills, vouchers and receipts relating to them, and make copies of all or any part of the accounts and those other documents. 'Interest' has been taken to mean a financial or legal interest rather than an idle curiosity and a person so interested has been held to be entitled to employ a skilled agent. Application forms for bursaries have been held not to be vouchers.[2] The Court of Appeal has recently considered the scope of s 15 in *Veolia ES Nottinghamshire Ltd v Nottinghamshire County Council*[3] and determined that it should be construed widely. In this case, Veolia sought to prevent the council from disclosing certain elements of a contract, including details of the formulae for calculating payments to be made as part of the council's contract with Veolia, details of deductions to be made in case of Veolia's default and a performance scorecard. The council also proposed to disclose the key performance indicators that were used to determine if deductions could be made. Counsel for Veolia sought to argue that the documents should not be disclosed to the individual who had made the request under s 15 (the fact that the individual was a local government elector for the purpose of s 15 was not in dispute) as the contract concerned was not expressly included in the council's audited accounts. This argument was rejected by the Court of Appeal where it was held that the reference in s 15(1)(a) to '…the accounts to be audited and all books, deeds, contracts, bills, vouchers and receipts relating to them' should be construed widely as referring to all materials pertinent to the council's annual accounts, regardless of whether they were referred to explicitly in the final summary accounts published by the council. The case then considered whether the requirements in s 15 ought to be 'read down' in light of either the duty of interpretation in s 3 of the Human Rights Act 1998 insofar as the contract could be said to be covered by Veolia's right to private property contained in Art 1 of the First Protocol to the ECHR. The court held that the information did constitute property under the Convention, and therefore the statute ought to be read accordingly in order to deny access to the information in this case.[4] A final issue considered by the case was whether, if the information was disclosed under s 15, Veolia could seek to restrain the party to whom the information was disclosed to use it only for the purpose of audit. Rix LJ felt that it could, whereas the other two judges in the case declined to determine this point as it was not at issue in the appeal given that the case at hand was not one where Veolia had brought private law proceedings in order to claim an injunction.[5]

---

[1] On person interested, see *R (HTV Ltd) v Bristol City Council* [2004] 1 WLR 2717: broadcasting company was a 'person interested' by virtue of its position as a non-domestic rate-payer but not as a media operator, and 'person interested' did not mean someone who found the issue interesting: see *Marginson v Tildsley* (1903) 67 JP 226; *R v Bedwelty UDC* [1934] 1 KB 333; *Stirrat v City of Edinburgh* (1998) SCLR 973 at 978.

[2] *R v Monmouthshire County Council, ex p Smith* (1935) 51 TLR 435. On contracts see: *Hillingdon London Borough v Paulssen* [1977] JPL 518. See *Oliver v Northampton Borough Council* (1986) 151 JP 44 and LGHA 1989, s 11.

[3] [2010] EWCA Civ 1214.

[4] *Ibid* at [143] (Rix LJ) and [162] (Etherton LJ).

[5] *Ibid* at [160] (Rix LJ) and [164] and [166] (Etherton LJ and Jackson LJ respectively).

8.12 By ACA 1998, s 15(2) a local government elector for any area to which the accounts relate may request, and the auditor shall give the elector or any representative of his or hers, an opportunity to question the auditor about the accounts. By virtue of s 15(3), nothing in the section entitles a person to inspect accounts or other documents containing personal information about a member of staff or to require the disclosure of such information in response to questions. Information is personal information as described when it relates specifically to a particular individual and is available to the body audited because the individual held or holds an office or employment under that body; or that payments or other benefits in respect of an office or employment have been or are being made to that individual by the body. Under this latter provision is included so-called 'severance payments' which have caused considerable notoriety (s 15(4)).

8.13 The elector, as above, is given the right under ACA 1998, s 16(1) to attend before the auditor and make objections. Any such meeting between the auditor and the elector should be considered as a 'hearing' for the purpose of the rules of natural justice:[1]

(a) as to any matter to which the auditor can take action under ACA 1998, s 17;[2]

(b) as to any matter on which the auditor could make an immediate report under s 8 of ACA 1998.

[1] As amended by LGA 2000, s 90.

[2] *R (Moss) v KPMG* [2010] EWHC 2923 (Admin) at [11]–[12] (Ouseley J).

8.14 Written notice must be given to the auditor of the objection and the grounds on which it is to be made, and a copy must be sent to the body audited.

8.15 By s 17(4), any person who has made an objection under s 16(1)(a) above and is aggrieved by a decision of an auditor not to apply for a declaration under s 17 (that an item of account is unlawful) has the right to require the auditor to state the reasons in writing for that decision. It must be required within six weeks of the decision. The person may also appeal against that decision to the court. The court hearing the appeal has the same powers as if the auditor had applied for a declaration, powers which are contained in s 17. Lord Nolan recommended in his third report that powers of surcharge of members and officials should be abolished and replaced by orders of the court on the application of the auditor allowing compensation and imposing disqualification from office (Cm 3702–I, Rec 27). He also recommended a new statutory offence of misuse of public office applying to all holders of public office. Furthermore, the right of a local elector to challenge an authority's accounts should be recast to avoid abuse of the process. In June 2000, details of new offences concerning corruption across the public and private sector spectrum were published by the Home Office. Anti-terrorism legislation addressed certain of these issues (see paras 5.14 above).[1]

Section 2 of the Bribery Act 2010 will extend the potential for holders of public office and public sector employees to be prosecuted should they engage in improper conduct and receive a benefit for so doing. The opportunity to create a statutory offence of misuse of public office was not taken in the Bribery Act 2010. The Law Commission, in its report which led to the Bribery Act,[2] noted that the new offence in the Bribery Act would complement, but not replace, the present common law on misconduct in public office. The above items replacing surcharge were contained in the LGA 2000 (ss 90 and 91 on 'advisory notes': see para 4.70 above).

[1]   *Raising Standards and Upholding Integrity: The Prevention of Corruption* Cm 4579, 20 June 2000. See Anti-terrorism, Crime and Security Act 2001, ss 108–110.
[2]   HC 928 (2008–2009) *Reforming Bribery* Law Commission No 313.

8.16   The Accounts and Audit Regulations 2003, SI 2003/533, and the *Code of Audit Practice*[1] provide further details on the auditor's role. The regulations extend the period of public inspection of the accounts to a whole year (previously 15 working days).

[1]   Audit Commission (2010) and see *Statement of Responsibilities of Auditors and Audited Bodies* (2010).

8.17   The above regulations specify the degree of public notice that the authority must give by advertisement before the beginning of the period for public inspection – this must be at least 14 days. Statements of accounts, with an auditor's opinion wherever possible, should be published within the publication period of (originally) nine months (but with reduced periods thereafter) from the end of the period to which the accounts relate. The code says that where appropriate the person inspecting the accounts should be reminded of his or her right to make objection. There is no statutory duty to hold nor any right to insist on, an oral hearing with all the parties to determine an objection, although the auditor must consider[1] whether oral hearings ought to be conducted and, if so, whether the public should be given the right to attend. The public should be excluded 'if it becomes apparent that injustice may be caused by allegations made without due notice' (code, para 22).

[1]   *Lloyd v McMahon* [1987] 1 All ER 1118, CA and HL; *R v District Auditor Chelmsford, ex p Judge* (1988) *Times*, 26 December.

8.18   Section 228(2) of the Local Government Act 1972 (LGA 1972) allows a local government elector for the area of a local authority to inspect and make a copy of, or extract from, an order for the payment of money made by the local authority. Photographic copies may be produced. Failure to comply with the section is a criminal offence.[1]

[1]   See *Brookman v Green* (1983) 82 LGR 228: did not cover allowances under now SI 1986/724, reg 6. See s 228(8) for parish councils.

8.19   Section 14 of the ACA 1998 repeats, with minor amendments, LGA 1972, s 228(4), (6) and (7). This allows any local government elector for an area of a body whose accounts are required to be audited (other than a health service body) under Part III:

(a) to inspect and make copies of any statement of accounts prepared by the body pursuant to regulations under s 27 of the Act and any report (other than an immediate report) made to the body by an auditor; and

(b) to require copies of any such statement or report to be delivered to the elector on payment of a reasonable sum.

8.20 Inspection of documents covered is free and may take place at all reasonable times. Obstruction by a person with custody of the documents is a criminal offence.

EDUCATION

8.21 From the Education Act 1980, the area of education has seen an immense growth in the duties on schools, local education authorities (LEAs) and governors to inform parents in particular of a variety of factors. There have been ten major statutes in that period. The Education Act 2002 is the latest to make provision for new legal frameworks to maintain schools, regulation of independent schools, the national curriculum in England and Wales and other matters.

School Standards and Framework Act 1998, as amended by the Education Act 2002

8.22 Part III of the School Standards and Framework Act 1998 (SSFA 1998, as amended by the Education Act 2002 and the Education and Inspections Act 2006) concerns admission arrangements for maintained schools and, under s 84, the Secretary of State shall issue and from time to time revise a code containing such practical guidance as he thinks fit on the discharge by local authorities,[1] governors of maintained schools, appeals panels and adjudicators of their duties in relation to admissions.[2] A School Admission Appeals Code (2009) came into effect on 10 February 2010 and includes provisions on who must have regard to the Code, disability discrimination, recruitment to appeals panels, venues for hearings, bias, evidence and the conduct of hearings. The Code may include guidelines setting out aims, objectives and other matters in relation to these functions.[3] The persons mentioned above and any other person when exercising relevant functions are under a duty to have regard to any relevant provisions of the Code. The Secretary of State is under a duty to publish the code. There are familiar provisions relating to consultation in the making of the Code and it is subject to negative resolution approval before both Houses. Sections 46–53 of the 2002 Act make provision for admissions, exclusions and attendance and amend various of the provisions contained in the SSFA 1998. There are provisions dealing with the number of pupils to be admitted to maintained schools in any one year and on the coordination of admissions arrangements. SSFA 1998, s 86 provides for the making of arrangements by LEAs to provide for the parents of a child in the area of the authority to express their preference for a school for their child and to state their reasons, though not in relation to sixth-form education or education for children beyond compulsory school age by virtue of s 86(1ZA), inserted by the Education and Skills Act 2008. Section

86A of the SSFA 1998 deals with choices in relation to sixth-form and other non-compulsory education. Authorities are under a duty to comply with the preference unless their preference would interfere with a variety of factors.

¹ See the amendments made by SI 2010/1158 on the integration of functions between LEAs and Childrens' Services departments.

² See DCSF (2010) *School Admissions Code 2010* (available at: http://www.dcsf.gov.uk/sacode/ downloads/admissions-code-feb10.pdf) and Welsh Assembly Government (2009) *School Admissions Code* (available at: http://wales.gov.uk/docs/dcells/publications/090721SchoolAdmissi onsCodeEN.pdf).

³ *School Admission Appeal Code* DCSF 2010 (available at: http://www.dcsf.gov.uk/sacode/downloads/ SchoolAdmissionAppealsCodeWEB060309.pdf.) and Welsh Government 2009 (available at: http://wales.gov.uk/docs/dcells/publications/090716AdmissionAppealsEN.pdf). See also SIs 1998/3130; 1998/3165; 2008/3089 (as amended by SI 2009/1099 (England) or 2006/174 (Wales) and SI 2008/3093 on the publication by local authorities of a composite prospectus of admissions information for schools in their areas. See *R v Stockton-on Tees Borough Council, ex p W* [2000] ELR 93, CA.

8.23 Section 85A of the SSFA 1998 (originally introduced by the Education Act 2002 and heavily modified by the Education and Inspections Act 2006) requires each local authority to create an admissions forum for the purpose of advising the authority on such matters as are prescribed in Regulations and, in particular, under SSFA 1998, s 85A(1)(b) advising on matters relating to admissions. In England, the admissions forum may make reports on prescribed matters and may require the local authority for which it was created, adjoining local authorities and the governors of maintained schools in the area for which the forum is established to provide it with information prescribed in Regulations for that purpose. Section 85A(1C) requires the provision of the requested information by the relevant bodies. The constitution of the admissions forum, its functions and the reports that it is expected to produce are all set out in secondary legislation.¹ The admissions forum should report on whether the admissions arrangements within its area ensure fair access to educational opportunity and also make recommendations for any improvements that might be made. The forum should be provided with any information that it requires in order to exercise its functions. The report made by the forum should be sent to the adjudicator provided for in SSFA 1998, s 25. The Education Bill 2011 proposes to restrict the requirement for an admissions forum to Wales only and proposes the repeal of the requirements in ss 85A(1A)–(1C).

¹ See SI 2008/3091, Parts 3 and 4.

8.24 Under SSFA 1998, s 88P, local authorities are required to produce a report on school admissions giving details of all maintained schools, academies, City Technology Colleges and City Technology Colleges of the Arts. The report should contain, as required by SI 2008/3091, regs 4 and 5, an assessment of the extent to which looked-after and disabled children's interests are served by admissions arrangements, and the extent to which the present admissions arrangements accord with the fair access code, including details of the number of children admitted to each relevant school in its area. Details must also be provided of the number of appeals made. The local authority must also make a statement that the maintained schools in its area will conform to the Schools

Admission Code. Section 88Q of the SSFA 1998 requires information to be provided to the local authority by the schools, admissions forums, members of appeals panels and owners of Academies in order that the report might be produced. This report must be sent to the adjudicator provided for in SSFA 1998, s 25.

8.25   Under SSFA 1998, s 92, local authorities are to publish for each school year prescribed information about:

(a)   the admission arrangements for each of the following: the maintained schools (SSFA 1998, s 20), academies, City Technology Colleges and City Colleges for the Technology of the Arts in their area. If regulations provide such maintained schools outside their area as may be determined by or in accordance with regulations;

(b)   the authority's arrangements for the provision of education at schools maintained by another LEA or not maintained by a local authority;

(c)   arrangements made in relation to expression of parental preferences (s 86(1)), or admission appeals under s 94(1);[1] and

(d)   such other matters of interest to parents or pupils seeking admission as may be prescribed.

[1]   SIs 2008/3089 and 2008/3093 (as amended by SI 2009/1099) (England) or 2006/174 and 1999/1812 (as amended) (Wales); and see *School Admission Appeal Code* DCSF 2010 (available at: http://www.dcsf.gov.uk/sacode/downloads/SchoolAdmissionAppealsCodeWEB060309.pdf). and Welsh Government 2009 (available at: http://wales.gov.uk/docs/dcells/publications/090716AdmissionAppealsEN.pdf). See also SIs 2008/3089 (as amended by SI 2009/1099 (England) or 2006/174 (Wales).

8.26   Foundation and voluntary aided schools are under similar duties, but only in relation to their own schools.

8.27   The governing body of a school maintained by a local authority have to publish information respecting their school as required by regulations and such other information as they think fit in relation to the school. Information about the school includes that relating to employment or training by pupils on leaving school, and about continuing education.

8.28   The Education (School Information) (England) Regulations 2008, SI 2008/3093 specify the information to be published by local authorities and governing bodies including that on special education provision. Under the 2008 Regulations, local authorities are only required to publish details about admission arrangements in a composite prospectus (see Part 2). A school prospectus must be made available for distribution free of charge to parents. This information must contain an explanation of the local authority's fair access protocol and should include particulars of arrangements for co-ordinated admissions (Sch 2, paras 7 and 8) and details of the school's admissions number or numbers and the number of preferences expressed for that school in the previous admissions year (Sch 2, para 13). It is notable that the information that is now mandated to be included in school prospectuses is much reduced in the 2008 Regulations when contrasted with the 2002 Regulations. The school prospectus must now contain only information relating to special needs provision and any other general information that the governing body sees fit (SI 2008/3093, reg 10). The Regulations no longer require information about arrangements for appeals against admission decisions to be published in any document containing the notification to parents of an admission decision: this requirement is now contained in the Education (Admissions Appeals Arrangements) (England) Regulations 2002, SI 2002/2899. Governing bodies have to provide authorities with specified information to assist with publication of a composite prospectus (SI 2008/3093, reg 7). Information to be published by local authorities in respect of transport to and from schools and further education institutions must be published (Sch 3, paras 9–11). There is a further duty, applicable only to children of compulsory school age, to publish information on the arrangments and policies in place on the transport of children with special educational needs to maintained, non-maintained and independent special schools (Sch 3, para 15). The local authority must make available the composite prospectus by displaying it on its website and also making copies available on request at local authority offices and at each maintained school in the local authority's area (reg 6). The information that local authorities are required to publish under Sch 3 must be published in a similar manner, but there are additional requirements that a copy is provided to parents of children in maintained schools in the area and at every academy, City Technology College and City Technology College of the Arts and for reference in public libraries (reg 9).

Reports on pupils and information about pupils

8.29   Teachers are under an obligation to provide assessments, reports and records relating to pupils.[1] The latter concerns curricular and educational records and the duties of head teachers of maintained schools. Records of pupils must be transferred to educational institutions which they subsequently attend by the school governing body if requested. Under the Education Reform Act 1988, ss 218 and 232, the Secretary of State had the power to make regulations concerning the retention and disclosure of records. Regulations were issued in July 1989 but these duties now fall under the Data Protection Act 1998 (DPA 1998) (see ch 7). The Education (Information About Individual Pupils) (England) Regulations 2006, SI 2006/2601 also provide details of the information about pupils that governing bodies of schools are required to supply to local authorities. The Regulations apply to all schools maintained by a local authority, iincluding schools with sixth forms providing education to pupils over compulsory school age, but only if these schools also provide education to pupils of compulsory school age (regs 3 and 4). City Technology Colleges, City Colleges for the Technology of the Arts and academies are also included in the requirements (reg 5). Information must ordinarily be provided within 14 days of the local authority's request. The principal requirements (contained in Sch 1) provide that, in relation to all pupils (other than sixth-form pupils), the information which schools are required to provide includes: the student's personal details, including date of birth, gender, surname and preferred surname; the derivation of information about ethnicity; whether the pupil is or has been looked after by a local authority; whether the pupil has special educational needs; whether the pupil is eligible for free school meals; whether the student has been identified as gifted and talented; and information relating to absences. In relation to excluded pupils, schools must provide alongside the personal details outlined above, details of whether the pupil had special educational needs or was looked after by a local authority and the details of the exclusion and reasons for it (Sch 1, Part 2). For sixth-form students at institutions covered by the Regulations, Sch 2 provides that the information to be provided includes the personal details outlined above for pupils covered by Sch 1 and details of the qualifications that are being pursued.

[1]   See most recently SI 2005/1437 and SI 2006/2601. For Wales see: SI 2004/1026 and 2007/3562. For information to be provided by independent schools see SI 2010/2919 (England) and SI 2003/3230 (as amended by SI 2007/947) (Wales).

Access to records

8.30 Regulations on individual pupils' achievements are to be found in The Education (Pupil Information) (England) Regulations 2005, SI 2005/1437. These Regulations do not apply to independent schools and there are no requirements at present for similar disclosure. The governing body of every school is under an obligation to ensure that a 'curricular record', defined as 'a formal record of a pupil's academic achievements, his other skills and abilities and his progress in school', is kept. Schools are not required to keep records on behaviour and personality, although they remain free to keep such records if they wish. Regulation 3 also defines the concept of an 'educational record':

(1) Subject to paragraph (4), in these Regulations 'educational record' means any record of information which—
(a)   is processed by or on behalf of the governing body of, or a teacher at, any school specified in paragraph (2);.
(b)   relates to any person who is or has been a pupil at any such school; and
(c)   originated from or was supplied by or on behalf of any of the persons specified in paragraph (3),

other than information which is processed by a teacher solely for the teacher's own use.

(2) The schools referred to in paragraph (1)(a) are—
(a)   any school maintained by a local authority; and
(b)   any special school which is not so maintained.

(3) The persons referred to in paragraph (1)(c) are—
(a)   any employee of the local authority which maintains the school or former school attended by the pupil to whom the record relates;
(b)   in the case of—
    (i)   a voluntary aided, foundation or foundation special school; or
    (ii)   a special school which is not maintained by a local authority,

any teacher or other employee at the school or at the pupil's former school (including any educational psychologist engaged by the governing body under a contract for services);

(c)   the pupil to whom the record relates; and.

(d)   a parent of that pupil..

(4) In addition to the information referred to in paragraph (1), an educational record includes—

(a)   any statement of special educational needs; and

(b)   any personal education plan,

relating to the pupil concerned.

(5) For the purposes of this regulation, 'processed' shall be construed in accordance with the definition of 'processing' in section 1(1) of the DPA 1998.

The Regulations cover the keeping, disclosure and transfer of school records and cover all key stages of education.

8.31   The provisions cover educational progress reports; and behaviour records either held separately or which were passed on from year to year. Regulation 3(1)(c) draws a distinction between formal records and a teacher's note for 'personal use' which would be regarded as the teacher's property and therefore excluded, but not if they were passed on to other teachers, orally or otherwise. Regulation 3(3)(a) covers material provided by education welfare officers and other local authority employees. Information provided to or from outside bodies, eg social services departments, local authorities, medical practitioners, etc on suspected child abuse is not to be disclosed to parents or children (see below). Nor were reports prepared for proceedings to which the Magistrates' Courts (Children and Young Persons) Rules 1992, SI 1992/2071 apply.

8.32   Under reg 5(2), parents have the right to inspect a pupil's educational record free of charge within 15 school days of the parent's written request. The parent may also request a copy of the educational record, for which a fee no greater than the cost of production may be charged (reg 5(3)). The Regulations include, for the first time, any statement of special educational needs in the definition of 'educational record', along with the personal learning plan for any pupil in local authority care. The governing body must not supply any information that it could not lawfully disclose to the pupil under the DPA 1998, which the pupil would have no right to access under the DPA 1998 or any order made under s 30(2) or 38(1) of the Act (see below). The primary exemptions relate to information which would seriously harm the pupil physically, mentally or emotionally, or where the information disclosed would reveal that the pupil is or has been the subject of child abuse or is considered to be at risk of child abuse and this disclosure would not be in the pupil's best interests.[1] The pupil him or herself may request access under the DPA 1998 and has no right to request the information set out above under the Regulations, which apply only to parents. The position under the DPA 1998 is discussed below and in ch 7. It is notable that academies are not covered by the Regulations.

[1]   See Data Protection (Subject Access Modification) (Education) Order 2000, SI 2000/414.

8.33   Regulation 5(5) of SI 2005/1437 provides that where a pupil is under consideration to another school (including independent schools), further education institution or higher education institution, the governors should transfer the curricular record upon request. Note that this obligation extends to the curricular record only and excludes details of any assessment of the pupil's achievement (reg 5(6)).

8.34   The governing body is responsible for making arrangements for the keeping and disclosure of records. Day-to-day responsibility rests with the staff and teachers. Disclosure of references remains voluntary as references are exempted by DPA 1998, Sch 7, para 1 and thus by reg 5(4) of the Regulations. Many authorities allow for disclosure of references to parents.

8.35   The Regulations also require the headteacher of every school covered by SI 2005/1437 to produce an annual report, supplied either to the parent or to the pupil in cases where the pupil is an 'adult pupil'.[1] The information which must be provided is set out in Sch 1, which primarily relates to educational progress and attainment. There is a further requirement that a similar report be provided to each school-leaver.

[1]   As defined in SI 2005/1437, reg 6(7)(a).

8.36   SI 2005/1437 also creates the concept of a 'common transfer file' which must ordinarily be transferred to the new school at which a pupil becomes registered if the pupil changes school (reg 9). The contents of the 'common transfer file' are set out in Sch 2.

8.37   Access provisions for pupils are now governed by the DPA 1998 as amended by FOIA 2000. No time limit is imposed on reports to which access may be had but the FOIA 2000 took over four years for access rights to be implemented. Where reports are computerised, or constitute structured files or other 'accessible' paper files covered by the DPA 1998 or the FOIA 2000 amendments to the data protection legislation, the access and other provisions of the DPA 1998 as amended (see ch 7) will apply. 'Accessible record' under DPA 1998, s 68 means an educational record as defined by Sch 11. This covers any record of information, but not that processed by a teacher solely for the teacher's own use, which:
(1)   is processed by or on behalf of the governing body of, or a teacher at, any school (ie a maintained school or a special school under Education Act 1996, s 6(2)) in England and Wales;
(2)   relates to any person who is or has been a pupil at the school; or
(3)   originated from or was supplied by or on behalf of the persons mentioned in para 4, ie employees of the local authority maintaining the school, for other schools as covered a teacher or other employee at the school including an educational psychologist engaged by the governing body under a contract for services, the pupil to whom the record relates and a parent of that pupil (as defined by Education Act 1996, s 576(1)). Separate provisions apply to Scotland and Northern Ireland and there are transitory provisions for England and Wales concerning grant maintained etc. schools.

8.38 By virtue of DPA 1998, s 30 the Secretary of State may exempt educational records[1] from subject information provisions or may modify those provisions in relation to access (see paras 7.135 et seq above). Under the FOIA 2000, schools will not need to count school holidays when calculating response times under the FOIA.

[1] See DPA 1998, s 30(5) for definitions of 'educational authority' and 'proprietor'. The Regulations on exemptions are The Data Protection (Subject Access Modification) (Education) Order 2000, SI 2000/414.

8.39 Section 9 of the Children and Young Persons Act 1969 obliges local authorities in care proceedings to provide such information about the school record of any child or young person as appears to the authority likely to assist the court.

Governors' reports

8.40 Governors of maintained schools in England are no longer under an obligation to produce an annual report on their work. The requirement, which was most recently found in the Education Act 2002, s 30, was repealed for England in 2005, other than for maintained nursery schools. In Wales, governors must still produce an annual report as required by the Education Act 2002, s 30. The detail of the report that must be produced is set out in The School Governors' Annual Reports (Wales) Regulations 2001, SI 2001/1110. Governors of maintained schools in England are under an obligation to produce a 'school profile' by virtue of the Education Act 2002, s 30A. This must contain the information that is prescribed by the Secretary of State. The school profile has three parts: information on school performance provided by the Department of Education; a summary of the latest Ofsted report; and information in the form of a narrative provided by the school. The school profile is then published on a government website.[1] The Government proposes to remove the requirement to produce a school profile during the 2011/2012 academic year as part of the programme to reduce statutory requirements that are imposed on schools.[2]

[1] The profiles can be accessed at http://schoolsfinder.direct.gov.uk/schoolsfinder/.
[2] See Education Bill 2011, cl 32.

8.41 The report required of governors in Wales which may be produced in languages other than English, must give the names of all the governors, their terms of office, details of how they were appointed and whom they represent, the school's examination results, financial statements, and information about steps to improve community links. The governors also have to prepare a statement containing a financial statement, National Curriculum assessments, security for pupils and staff, numbers of registrations, pupils' attendance, pupils' achievements, and so on. They also have to prepare a separate written statement setting out their views on whether sex education should be part of the curriculum, and if it is taught, how it should be taught. Information has to be provided about school syllabuses and other educational subjects.

Reports on academies

8.42 The Secretary of State is required by the Academies Act 2010, s 11 to produce an annual report on academy arrangements entered into during the year and the performance of academies over the year. The report must include information that the Secretary of State might require by creating Regulations under the Education Act 1996 (EA 1996), s 537 or through the Academy Agreement. Academy agreements contain a clause[1] allowing the Secretary of State to request information on a wide range of matters including, inter alia, the curriculum, assessment of students, teaching staff, class sizes and numbers of pupils excluded. The Academies Act 2010, s 11(4) requires the Secretary of State to lay the report produced before Parliament.

[1] The numbering of the clauses in academy agreements is not consistent throughout all of those that are published, though in those published for academies to open in September 2010, the clauses are generally found in paras 117–118.

Inspectors' reports

8.43 The Secretary of State had, as a practice, published HM Inspectors' (of schools) reports, involving local authorities and schools and the effects of expenditure policies on the education service in England and Wales. Inspections are also carried out in the private independent sector, and for further education and other colleges. In the independent sector, the inspection bodies (ISI, the Bridge Schools Inspectorate and the Schools Inspection Service) are all required to publish the reports that they produce by virtue of the agreement letters that they have in place with the Department for Education.[1]

[1] The agreements can be found at http://www.education.gov.uk/schools/leadership/typesofschools/independent/a009053/registration-of-independent-schools.

8.44 The Education and Inspections Act 2006 (amended for England by the Education and Inspections Act 2006, Part 8 in particular)[1] sets out the statutory framework including the functions of the Chief Inspector for England and another for Wales, as well as HM Inspectorates – again, one for England and Wales. The schools that are subject to inspection are set out in the Education Act 2005, s 5. In England, schools may be inspected by a Chief Inspector, one of the appointed HM Inspectors or 'additional inspectors' as provided for in ss 113–114 and Sch 12 of the Education and Inspections Act 2006. In Wales, schools may be inspected by registered inspectors (who enjoy various rights of appeal to a tribunal against adverse decisions concerning their registration under s 27) although a school may be inspected by a member of the Inspectorate. In England, the Education Act 2005, ss 14, 14A and 15 (maintained schools) and 16, 16A and 17 (non-maintained schools) deal with destination of reports. Copies of reports are to be made available to the public, and parents of registered pupils at the school must be sent a copy of the report. If special measures are proposed the local authority (maintained schools) or proprietor (non-maintained schools) must prepare a written statement of the action they propose to take, which must be sent to the Secretary of State, the Chief Inspector and any other person that the Secretary of State may specify. Further details on the procedure in relation to provision of reports and statements can be found in SI 2005/2038. Similar provisions apply to Wales, as set out in the Education Act 2005, ss 37–42 and SI 2006/1714. In Wales, ss 39(7) and 42(5) of the 2005 Act set out the requirements for local authorities or proprietors to make copies of their statements available to the public and parents. In England, the Act does not set out requirements for the statement itself to be provided to members of the public or parents, but each statement that is produced must set out the way in which the school will inform parents of the action that is proposed and how the views of parents will be sought.[2] Clause 40 of the Education Bill 2010–2011 proposes some modifications to the material to be included in the reports produced by inspection teams.

[1]   The main purpose of the amendments in Part 8 of the Education and Inspections Act 2006 is to create the Office for Standards in Education, Children's Services and Skills in England, offering an integrated approach to inspection of local authority childcare and school and further education in England. The bulk of the framework for school inspections remains unchanged and is found in the Education Act 2005.

[2]   For further information see DFES (2008) *Statutory Guidance on Schools Causing Concern*, ch 4.

8.45   The Education and Inspections Act 2006 introduced a power, contained in ss 11A–11C of the Education Act 2005, for the Chief Inspector to investigate complaints made about schools by parents. Section 11A provides that the Chief Inspector may investigate a 'qualifying complaint' if he thinks it appropriate to do so. Section 11A(2) defines a 'qualifying complaint' as one which falls within a prescribed definition, is made in writing and is made by a person who satisfies the prescribed conditions. The Regulations which elaborate on this are to be found in The Education (Investigation of Parents' Complaints) (England) Regulations 2007, SI 2007/1089. Regulation 3 sets out the matters which might be subject to complaint and include the quality of education provided at a school, the standard of educational attainment and the quality of leadership. Regulation 5 provides that before a complaint can be considered, the complainant should have followed any complaints process that this is in place, although reg 6 permits the Chief Inspector to waive this requirement if it is deemed appropriate. Section 11B of the Education Act 2005 requires that schools and local authorities (where relevant) should provide all necessary information to allow a complaint to be investigated and, if necessary, arrange for a meeting of parents in order to facilitate the investigation. Section 11C allows the Chief Inspector to publish a report on the outcome of the investigation if this is deemed to be appropriate. The Chief Inspector must provide a copy of any such report to the school, to the local authority in case of a maintained school, and the Chief Inspector may also direct that the report is provided to parents.

8.46   Also published is a list of spending totals in league form of each local authority.

Admissions and exclusion appeal procedures under the SSFA 1998

8.47   We have seen how under the SSFA 1998 and the Education Act 2002 the local authority has to 'make arrangements' allowing the parents to express a preference of school for their child, with specified exceptions. By SSFA 1998, s 94 every local authority has to make arrangements allowing the parents of a child to appeal against the allocation of a particular school to their child. Governing bodies of a foundation or voluntary aided school shall make arrangements allowing for appeal against refusing to allow admission to the school. Joint arrangements may be made by the governing bodies of two or more such schools. An appeal panel is established under regulations under the SSFA 1998 as amended which does not allow for members of the authority to be appointed as members of the panel (see SI 2002/2899 as amended). The same provision allows membership from those who have 'experience in education, are acquainted with the educational conditions in the area of the authority or are parents of registered pupils at a school' along with lay members. Panels are to consist of three or five members. Decision is by simple majority, the chairman possessing a casting vote. No one employed by the authority other than as a teacher may be on the panel and a teacher cannot sit on a panel hearing an appeal on his school. The procedure is spelt out in SI 2002/2899, Sch 2 and includes opportunity for: parents to present their child's case orally; parents to be represented by friend or otherwise; private hearings except when otherwise directed; and written communication of the decision stating the grounds upon which it is made. The panel shall consider, inter alia, parental preferences under s 94, and arrangements for the admission of pupils published by the local authority or governors. The decision of the panel is binding on the local authority. For the Regulations in Wales (which are largely identical) see SI 2005/1398.

8.48   Panels fall under the Tribunals and Inquiries Act 1992. Local authorities have to publish information about admissions under s 92 (see above).

8.49   The forerunner to these provisions was the subject of numerous investigations by the local ombudsman who may also investigate admissions matters relating to governors. In one case he was criticised by the High Court for overstepping his proper powers of investigation (see paras 9.53 et seq below). There are a variety of cases dealing with the earlier legislation.[1]

[1]   *R v South Glamorgan Appeals Committee, ex p Evans* (10 May 1984, unreported); see Tweedie (1986) Public Law 407; and *R v Greenwich London Borough Council, ex p Governors of John Ball Primary School* (1989) 88 LGR 589, CA; followed in *R v Kingston upon Thames Royal Borough, ex p Kingwell* [1992] 1 FLR 182 and *R v Governors of the Bishop Challoner Roman Catholic Comprehensive Girls' School, ex p Choudhury* [1992] 2 AC 182, HL.

8.50   Pupils excluded from maintained schools have a right of appeal against exclusion or reinstatement to the above appeal panels which are to operate with some modifications (see Education Act 2002, s 52 and SI 2002/3178 (England) or SI 2003/3227 (Wales)).

Special educational needs and the Education Act 1996

8.51   The Education Act 1981 introduced distinct legal provisions concerning a local authority's assessment of the 'special educational needs' (SEN) of a child.

The relevant provisions now are in EA 1996, Part IV, Chapter 1, re-enacting Part III of the Education Act 1993 (and, for Wales, see Education Act 2002, ss 191–195). The Secretary of State is under a duty to issue and revise a code of practice to which LEAs are under a duty to have regard.[1] Briefly, a local authority is under a duty to provide special needs children with placements in mainstream schools providing this is not incompatible with the parents' wishes or with a variety of other factors. The local authority has to notify a parent that they propose to make an assessment of the SEN of a child where it is of opinion that a child has SEN and it is necessary to determine the SEN; of the procedure; of an officer from whom information may be obtained and of the parents' right to make representations and submit written evidence within a time-limit of not less than 29 days beginning with the date of the service of notice. If an assessment is then made, the decision with reasons (in writing) must be notified to the parent. The local authority must keep a statement of the SEN of a child if it determines SEN after an assessment under EA 1996, s 323. The statement under s 324 may include provision excluding the application of the national curriculum (Education Act 2002, s 92).[2] In England, appeal lies to the First Tier Tribunal[3] by the child's parent against refusal by the LEA to make a statement. In Wales, the appeal lies to the SEN Tribunal (Wales).[4] The parent may also appeal against the contents of a statement. Parents may request an LEA to make an assessment and appeal lies to the Tribunal against refusal to do so.

[1] Department for Education (2001) *Special Education Needs: Code of Practice* DFES 0581/2001.
[2] See also: Education Act 2002, s 93 on temporary exceptions for individual pupils in relation to the national curriculum; s 94 on the provision of information about s 93 exceptions to the parent SI 2008/2833, reg 3. The appeal previously lay to the Special Educational Needs Tribunal. See *H v Kent County Council* [2000] ELR 660 and *H v East Sussex CC* [2009] EWCA Civ 249, [2009] ELR 161 on giving adequate reasons. See also the Special Educational Needs and Disability Act 2001.
[4] See EA 1996, ss 333–336, SI 2001/600 and SI 2002/2787.

8.52   Section 332D of the EA 1996 (as inserted by the Special Educational Needs (Information) Act 2008) requires the Secretary of State to publish information obtained under powers in the EA 1996, s 332C that 'would, in the opinion of the Secretary of State, be likely to assist the Secretary of State or other persons in improving the well-being of children in England with special educational needs'. The information must not include the names of the children concerned and can be published in whatever manner the Secretary of State thinks fit. The Secretary of State may levy a charge, not exceeding the cost of supply for any document published.

8.53   The Special Educational Needs (Provision of Information by Local Authorities) Regulations 2001, SI 2001/2218, deal with details on publication of information about SEN.[1] These Regulations place a duty on local authorities to publish information about matters relating to the provision of education for children with special educational needs. In particular they are required to publish an explanation of that part of special educational provision that they expect maintained schools to fund from their budget shares, and that element that the authority expect to fund themselves. They must also publish information about the broad aims of their policy on special educational needs, as well as specific action the authority is taking on SEN issues.

1   See SI 2006/2601 (England) and SI 2004/1026 and 2007/3562 (Wales) on information about individual pupils.

8.54   The provisions on appeals from the Education Act 1980 onwards, and the meetings, representations, and appeals of the 1981 Act as developed may well have the quality of overkill about them. Parental power, local pluralism and popular support all helped to dictate the necessity of more apparent and regular procedures to deal with school allocation disputes etc though it is of interest to point out that prior to the Education Act 1980 local authorities had often provided detailed informal procedures for education disputes.

Provision of Information on the National Curriculum and s 409 (formerly s 23) complaints

8.55   Section 408[1] of the EA 1996 concerns provision of information in relation to that part of the Act and in relation to the National Curriculum (see SI 1989/954), syllabuses, and educational achievement of pupils.[2]

1   Under EA 1996, s 406, LEAs, head teachers and governing bodies must forbid the pursuit and promotion of partisan political activities in schools and s 407 imposes a duty to secure a balanced treatment of political issues.
2   And see eg SI 2007/2324.

8.56   Section 409 concerns complaints about the national curriculum and provision of information, and was originally introduced under Chapter I of the Education Reform Act 1988. EA 1996, s 409 provides:

'(1) A local authority shall, after consultation with governing bodies of foundation and voluntary aided schools, make arrangements for the consideration and disposal of any complaint to which subsection (2) applies.

(2) This subsection applies to any complaint which is to the effect that the authority, or the governing body of any community, foundation or voluntary school maintained by the authority or any community or foundation special school so maintained which is not established in a hospital—
(a)   have acted or are proposing to act unreasonably in relation to the exercise of a power conferred on them by or under a relevant enactment, or
(b)   have acted or are proposing to act unreasonably in relation to the performance of, or have failed to discharge, a duty imposed on them by or under a relevant enactment.'

8.57   Subsection (3) defines 'relevant enactment' to include:

'(a) any provision which by virtue of section 408(4) is a relevant provision of this Part for the purposes of section 408(1) (aa) any provision which by virtue of section 408(4A) is a relevant provision of the Education Act 2002 for the purposes of section 408(1), and

(b) any other enactment (whether contained in this Part or otherwise) so far as relating to the curriculum for, or religious worship in, maintained schools.

(4) The Secretary of State shall not entertain under section 496 (power to prevent unreasonable exercise of functions) or 497 (powers where a local authority or governing body fail to discharge their duties) any complaint to which subsection (2) applies, unless a complaint concerning the same matter has been made and disposed of in accordance with arrangements made under subsection (1).'

8.58   DES circular 1/89 (which is still in operation) sets out guidance for the local arrangements for the consideration of complaints. Local authority proposals had to be submitted for the agreement of the Secretary of State. This saw the benefits of the following 'model':

(1)   Informal discussion with teachers and the 'head'; not all such expressions of concern should be considered as 'complaints'.

(2)   A formal complaint to the governors dealt with by those with direct responsibility for the matters involved, with procedures securing 'full and fair consideration' for the views of the complainant. A further stage might involve further consideration by 'responsible persons' who have no direct involvement in the issues complained about.

(3)   Reference to the local authority where the complaint is not satisfactorily resolved for the complainant.

(4)   Only *after* the previous procedures are exhausted will a complainant's case be considered by the Secretary of State under EA 1996, s 496 or 497.

8.59   Section 29 of the Education Act 2002 further sets out a requirement that the governing body should establish a complaints procedure for all maintained schools and publicise the availability of that procedure. This procedure may have some bearing on the handling of a national curriculum compaint at the level of the school. Non-statutory guidance was issued in 2003 to aid governors in the promulgation of a complaints process, though the guidance is broadly in line with that in circular 1/89.[1]

---

[1]   Under EA 1996, s 406, local authorities, head teachers and governing bodies must forbid the pursuit and promotion of partisan political activities in schools and s 407 imposes a duty to secure a balanced treatment of political issues.

8.60   These arrangements will not cover the actions of individual teachers or the headteacher. The arrangements will *not* apply in respect of complaints relating to grant-maintained schools. If specific statutory appeals procedures apply to a complaint and allow for appeal to the governors, that procedure should be followed before invoking s 409. If it involves an appeal to the Secretary of State, s 409 has *no relevance*.

8.61   The duties covered by the complaints arrangements are:

'i.   the provision of a curriculum, including religious education and worship, which meets the general requirements of the Education Act 2002;

ii.   the implementation of the National Curriculum and compliance with Orders and Regulations made about its requirements and exceptions to its provisions;

iii.   provision to pupils of compulsory school age of courses leading to an external qualification, only if that qualification and the associated syllabus or syllabus criteria have been approved;

iv.   provision of religious education and worship as required by the Act and other enactments;

v.   in the case of a local authority, establishment of a Standing Advisory Council on Religious Education (SACRE) and review of the agreed syllabus for the area if the SACRE so requires;

vi.   the need to act reasonably in deciding whether or not to be associated with an application for exemption from all or part of the National Curriculum in order to carry out developmental work;

vii.   in the case of a governing body, consideration of appeals by parents about the temporary withdrawal of pupils from part or all of the provisions of the National Curriculum;

viii.   operation of charging policies in relation to the curriculum;

ix.   compliance with regulations about the provision of information (s 408); and

x.   compliance with any other enactments relating to the curriculum.'

8.62   The arrangements need to include:

'(i)   a clear first point of contact in the local authority for formal s 409 complaints from where complaints will be fed into the appropriate level of the formal machinery;

(ii)   a mechanism to identify all *relevant* complaints and weed out those not within the scope of s 409;

(iii)   a mechanism to identify urgent complaints, and procedures to consider them appropriately;

(iv)   a series of distinct stages through which complaints would progress, and arrangements to ensure that these are followed;

(v)   provision for the complainant (accompanied if so desired, and if necessary with the assistance of an interpreter) to make representations in person at each stage;

(vi)   clear criteria for the identification of the end point of each stage, which will normally be after a report has been made to the complainant, and a mechanism for ensuring that the complainant is kept fully informed of progress during, as well as at the end of, each stage;

(vii)   the involvement of the governing body, or members acting on its behalf, at the first formal stage of complaint. The governing body should satisfy itself that the complaint has been fully investigated and a decision taken before it is referred to the local authority for consideration;

(viii) the involvement of elected members of the local authority. The authority should establish procedures to satisfy itself that the complaint has been fully investigated and a decision taken before it is referred to the Secretary of State; and

(ix) at the end of each stage of the procedure, arrangements for the complainant to be informed of:

    (a) the decision taken and the reasons for it;

    (b) any action taken or proposed, including details of any request to those complained against to take particular actions to resolve the complaint; and

    (c) the further recourse available – eg the next stage of the local authority arrangements, or complaint to the Secretary of State.'

Information about complaints' arrangements

8.63 The circular (DES Circular 1/89, para 6) advises that: '[local authorities] should show that they have plans for general publicity about their complaints' arrangements, in addition to the requirements to be established in regulations under [s 408 of the Education Act 1996] for reference to be included in school prospectuses, and full copies of the complaints arrangements to be available in each school'.

Monitoring

8.64 Paragraph 7 of the circular states that the arrangements should provide for regular reports to full governing bodies and to the Education Committee giving, as a minimum, summary data on the number of complaints dealt with at the various formal levels, the time taken to deal with them, and their outcomes. There should be an annual return to the Department for Education giving the number of formal complaints dealt with and their outcomes.

School closures

8.65 There are statutory provisions[1] which cover these items. In the past, predecessors to these provisions concerning duties to consult before closing a school have been heavily litigated.[2]

---

[1] Education and Inspections Act 2006, ss 15–17 and SI 2007/1288 (England) or SSFA 1998, ss 28–35; Sch 6 and SI 1999/1671 (Wales).

[2] *R v Brent London Borough Council, ex p Gunning* (1985) 84 LGR 168; *R v Sutton London Borough Council, ex p Hamlet* CO/1657/85 (1986) Lexis Enggen Library, Cases file; *Nichol v Gateshead Metropolitan Borough Council* (1988) 87 LGR 435, CA; *R v Kirklees Metropolitan Borough Council, ex p Molloy* (1987) 86 LGR 115, CA on consultation and provision of information. And see *Harvey v Strathclyde Regional Council* 1989 SLT 612, HL.

Designation of grammar schools and subsequent issues

8.66 The SSFA 1998, ss 104–109 allows the Secretary of State to designate any school which had selective admissions arrangements as a grammar school.

In order to be so designated, a school had to have admissions arrangements that had the objective of selecting students only on the basis of high academic ability. Provisions are in place (ss 105–109) to allow parents to petition so that a ballot might be held for the school to cease to have selective admissions arrangements. The Education (Grammar School Ballots) Regulations 1998, SI 1998/2876 set out the requirements for the petition that parents must submit and the process for a ballot if a valid petition is submitted. Section 107 of the SSFA 1998 places restrictions on the ability of local authorities and governing bodies of schools to engage in expenditure to provide information in relation to petitions or ballots.

Conversion to academies

8.67   The Academies Act 2010 creates a framework through which governors of maintained schools can apply to the Secretary of State for an order transferring the school to academy status. Section 5 of the Act requires that the governors consult with '…such persons as they think appropriate.' Section 5(2) provides that the consultation 'must be on the question of whether the school should be converted into an Academy.' Section 5(3) allows the consultation to take place at any time before the academy arrangements are entered into, ie either before or after the application for an academy order has been made. There is considerable potential for litigation over this process of consultation, perhaps similar to that on the closure of school outlined in para 8.65 above.

HIGHER EDUCATION ACT 2004

8.68   Part 3 of the Higher Education Act 2004 (HEA 2004) concerns student fees for higher education courses and fair access to universities. When making awards to funding bodies, the Secretary of State may make conditions in relation to these awards to the Higher Education Funding Council and the Training and Development Agency for Schools. These may in turn set limits to fees for qualifying courses in universities and training colleges. Penalties may be imposed where such limits are not maintained. A Director of Fair Access to Higher Education has been appointed by the Secretary of State. The duties of the Director include identifying good practice relating to the promotion of equality of opportunity in connection with access to higher education (whether full-time or part-time), and giving advice about such practice to publicly-funded institutions. The Director must perform his functions under Part 3 of the Act in such a way as to promote and safeguard fair access to higher education (including part-time higher education in so far as his functions are exercisable in relation to it). He is under a duty to protect academic freedom.

8.69   Institutions are under duties to produce plans specifying levels of fees for qualifying courses and must also include such provisions relating to the promotion of equality of opportunity as are required by regulations to be included in the plan. Regulations (under HEA 2004, s 33(5)) may set out provisions:

'(a) requiring the governing body to take, or secure the taking of, measures to attract applications from prospective students who are members of groups which, at the time when the plan is approved, are under-represented in higher education,

(b) requiring the governing body to provide, or secure the provision of, financial assistance to students,

(c) requiring the governing body to make available to students and prospective students information about financial assistance available to students from any source,

(d) setting out objectives relating to the promotion of equality of opportunity and, in relation to Wales, the promotion of higher education,

(e) relating to the monitoring by the governing body of-
    (i) its compliance with the provisions of the plan, and
    (ii) its progress in achieving any objectives set out in the plan by virtue of paragraph (d), and

(f) requiring the provision of information to the relevant authority.'

8.70   The Student Fees (Approved Plans) (England) Regulations, SI 2004/2473 set out the requirements for the content of the plans that are to be submitted to the Director of Fair Access to Higher Education. The Regulations provide that each plan submitted to the Office for Fair Access must contain details of the measures to be taken to attract applications from groups that are under-represented in higher education, to provide details of the bursaries and other financial student available to prospective students, to provide details of plans to make the information on financing available to students and prospective students and to provide information to prospective student on the aggregate amount of fees to be charged to complete the course in advance of a firm commitment on the part of the student to undertake the course of study (reg 3). Regulation 6 requires that once a plan is approved, it must be published in a manner which makes it easily accessible to students and prospective students. The Office for Fair Access also publishes all agreements on its website.[1] Regulation 3 also provides that the plan must set out proposals for the institution to provide the director with information that he may reasonably require.

[1]   These are available at http://www.offa.org.uk/access-agreements/.

8.71   Universities and colleges must apply to the director for approval of their plan. SI 2004/2473 sets out the procedure for the approval of plans in reg 5, which provides that the director must make a decision over whether to approve the plan within a reasonable time. If the director determines that the plan should not be approved, he must inform the institution concerned and the institution may either make representations as to why the plan should be approved in its present form or modify the plan. The director must then consider the representations or modifications and make a decision over whether to approve the plan within a reasonable period. Regulation 8 provides for a similar procedure should an institution seek to vary its plan. Regulations 15–22 set out the process for review of a provisional decision of the director (defined in reg 15). Review may only be sought on three grounds – that there is a material factor that was not drawn previously to the director's attention for a good reason, that the director has failed to take account of a material factor or that the director's decision is disproportionate in light of the facts that the director considered (reg 19). The review is to be undertaken by a person or panel appointed by the Secretary of State and the governing body of the institution concerned must apply for a review within 20 calendar days of the provisional decision. In Wales the panels will be appointed by the Welsh Assembly and separate provisions apply for Wales.[1] Plans may be in force for a maximum of five years. Section 40 of the 2004 Act provides for the handing over of information as follows: 'If so requested by the Director, the Higher Education Funding Council for England and the Training and Development Agency for Schools must provide the Director with any information which is in its possession and is reasonably required by the Director for the purposes of his functions. Section 40(2) states: 'If so requested by the Higher Education Funding Council for England or the Training and Development Agency for Schools, the Director must provide the Council or the Agency with any information which is in his possession and is reasonably required by either of those bodies for the purposes of its functions'. Under s 46, the university visitor loses jurisdiction over disputes concerning staff as follows: there will be no jurisdiction in respect of:

(a)   any dispute relating to a member of staff which concerns his appointment or employment or the termination of his appointment or employment,

(b)   any other dispute between a member of staff and the qualifying institution in respect of which proceedings could be brought before any court or tribunal, or

(c)   any dispute as to the application of the statutes or other internal laws of the institution in relation to a matter falling within paragraph (a) or (b).

[1]   In Wales, the Higher Education Funding Council for Wales is the authority charged with policing access plans. This is by virtue of SI 2011/658. The arrangements for the approval of the plans are very similar to those for England and can be found in SI 2011/884. It is also notable that SI 2011/658 adds s 40A to the HEA 2004, requiring the designated bodies in Wales to produce an annual report on the exercise of their functions each year.

8.72   Part 2 of the 2004 Act and Schs 1–4 provide for a system for dealing with students' complaints made in relation to acts or omissions of qualifying institutions by students or former students. The Office of the Independent Adjudicator for Higher Education is the designated complaints body for England and Wales. 'Qualifying complaints' may be considered by the Office and a set of rules to govern the compaints process has been created.[1] Procedures concerning review of complaints are protected by absolute privilege by virtue of HEA 2004, s 17. The visitor's jurisdiction to hear student complaints is removed as a result of the creation of the Office of the Independent Adjudicator.

[1]   Available at http://www.oiahe.org.uk/downloads/OIA-RulesMay2008.pdf.

SOCIAL SERVICES

8.73   On 1 April 1989, the Access to Personal Files (Social Services) Regulations 1989, SI 1989/206, came into force. These were referred to in ch 7 (para

7.156) when access to personal records, both on paper and computerised, was discussed. They were made under the Access to Personal Files Act 1987. With the coming into effect of the DPA 1998, the Access to Personal Files Act 1987 and regulations thereunder were repealed, and records became available under the DPA 1998, as 'accessible records', as amended by the FOIA 2000. Social work records are accessible public records for the purposes of the DPA 1998 by virtue of Sch 12 to that Act. By virtue of DPA 1998, s 30, social work records processed by government departments, local authorities, voluntary organisations or other bodies designated under the order, along with health and education records, may be exempted by the Secretary of State from the subject information (access) provisions, or such access may be modified. Such power shall not be exercised unless subject access 'would be likely to prejudice the carrying out of social work' (see paras 7.99 et seq above).

8.74   On one point, the former regulations covered an area which is not dealt with by the new DPA 1998 or regulations thereunder. Under reg 11 of the former access regulation an individual who is the subject of information held by a local social services authority and who is aggrieved by any decision of that authority concerning the individual's access to, or rectification or erasure of, that information, may within 28 days of being notified of the decision require that decision to be reviewed. The review was by a committee of three members of that authority appointed for that purpose, not more than one of whom may be a member of the committee established under s 2(1) of the Local Authority Social Services Act 1970. The individual could make representations to the committee's members either in writing or orally. The committee was not specifically empowered to override the wish of a health professional (cf reg 8(5) (a) or (b)).

8.75   In ch 9 (para 9.90) there is a discussion of the complaints procedures for social services authorities introduced under the Health and Social Care Act 2008. Paragraph 9.113 below discusses changes proposed by the Health and Social Care Bill 2011.

Child care

8.76   The provisions of the DPA 1998 which replaced the access regulations under the Access to Personal Files Act 1987 concern *all* aspects of a social services' department's holding of personal files. The Butler-Sloss Report, 'Child Abuse in Cleveland',[1] contained recommendations for greater emphasis upon 'informing and consulting' parents on major decisions in all spheres of the child care legislation and an Office of Child Protection to scrutinise the local authority's application in care proceedings and to call for any reports. The relevant recommendations continued (p 246):

> 'Parents should be informed and where appropriate consulted at each stage of the investigation by the professional dealing with the child, whether medical, police or social worker. Parents are entitled to know what is going on, and to be helped to understand the steps that are being taken.

Social services should confirm all important decisions to parents in writing. Parents may not understand the implications of decisions made and they should have the opportunity to give the written decision to their lawyers.

Parents should always be advised of their rights of appeal or complaint in relation to any decisions made about them or their children.

Social services should always seek to provide support to the family during the investigation. Parents should not be left isolated and bewildered at this difficult time.

The service of the place of safety order on parents should include a written explanation of the meaning of the order, the position of the parents, their continuing responsibilities and rights and advice to seek legal advice.

Records related to the use of statutory powers on an emergency basis should be kept and monitored regularly by social services departments.

A code of practice for the administration by social workers of emergency orders for the purposes of child protection including the provision of information to parents defining their rights in clear simple language should be drawn up.

Parents should be informed of case conferences and invited to attend for all or part of the conference unless, in the view of the Chairman of the conference, their presence will preclude a full and proper consideration of the child's interests.

Irrespective of whether parents attend the conferences, social workers have a primary responsibility to ensure that the case conference has information relating to the family background and the parents' view on the issues under consideration.'

Arrangements for parental access should be made unless there are exceptional reasons in the child's interests why they should not take place. A qualified lawyer should be called where needed.

Senior managers in social services departments should develop efficient systems to allow accurate monitoring of service activity alerting them to problem areas.

Police should ensure there is an adequate communication network with other child protection agencies and medical reports should be full and accurate, and there should be specialist assessment teams for cases of particular difficulty, each member of which will have direct access to all relevant information.

The Divisional Court has held that parents of a child in care proceedings are entitled to the information, viz police medical reports, on their child held by the social services department where there are suspicions of sexual abuse. The authority ought also to help parents arrange an independent medical inspection.[2]

---

[1]   Cm 412 (1988). Regarded by the High Court as 'recommended reading': *Re E (A Minor) (Child Abuse: Evidence)* [1991] 1 FLR 420. On child protection registers, see para 7.273, note 2.

[2]   *R v Hampshire County Council, ex p K* [1990] 2 All ER 129 (care proceedings); see *Re M (a minor) (disclosure of material)* [1990] FCR 485, CA: general discovery by list not appropriate in wardship

proceedings, but the immunity of social work records was not absolute and the need for secrecy had to be balanced against the requirements of justice to all the parties, including parents. See also: *Re E (a minor) (child abuse: injunctions)* [1990] FCR 793, and *R v Sunderland Juvenile Court, ex p G* [1988] 2 All ER 34, CA. See *Practice Direction* [1995] 1 FLR 456, *Re M (disclosure)* [1999] 1 FCR 492, *Re M and A* [1999] 1 FLR 443 and *Re D (minors)* [1996] AC 593.

Children Act 1989

8.77   Section 42 of the Children Act 1989[1] gives a guardian ad litem appointed under the Act the right, at all reasonable times, to examine and take copies of any records of, or those held by, a local authority which were compiled in connection with any application under the Act relating to the child concerned.[2]

[1]   *Manchester City Council v T* [1994] 2 All ER 526, CA.
[2]   Public Interest Immunity does not arise in relation to such a report: *In re J (a Child) (Care Proceedings: Disclosure)* [2003] EWHC 976 (Fam), [2003] 2 FLR 522.

8.78   The 1989 Act has provisions in ss 22(4) and 26(2)(d)(i) to ascertain, inter alia, the wishes of the child, parents and those with parental responsibility in relation to decisions and reviews of children in care or provided with accommodation. Section 26(3) stipulates that local authorities establish procedures for representations, including complaints, by children, parents, those with parental responsibility and foster parents. Regulations have been made.[1] These require the authority to appoint one of their officers to coordinate all aspects of their consideration of the representations, to allow representations to be made orally but to be put in writing as a record and sent to the person making the representations to comment on their accuracy. They require the appointment of an independent person to take part in the consideration of the representations. The person making the representations – the complainant – has the right to refer the matter to a panel. The regulations set out the procedure and the panel's power to make recommendations. Authorities must monitor procedures. These provisions apply to accommodation provided by voluntary organisations.[2] Children who are being looked after or provided with accommodation by local authorities have the right to have their cases reviewed in accordance with schedules set out in the regulations. Before conducting any review the local authority shall, unless it is not practically reasonable to do so, seek and take into consideration the views of the child, his parents, any person other than parents having parental responsibility for the child and any other person whose views are considered relevant by the authority including in the latter case relevance to any particular matter which is to be considered in the course of the review. Details of information from the review and any decisions must be recorded. Sections 22, 24, and 26 of the 1989 Act were amended by the Adoption and Children Act 2002, which concerns reviews of 'looked after children' (2002 Act, s 118). This section arose from judicial criticism that authorities may be breaching Art 8(2) ECHR in failing to follow care plans which formed a part of the court's decision to make a care order. The Care Planning, Placement and Case Review (England) Regulations 2010, SI 2010/959 set out the requirements for care plans and the review of them, including requirements for the recording of the various review processes, the keeping of a care record and the keeping and confidentiality of the care record.[3] Further duties to record and inform are in the Children (Secure Accommodation) Regulations 1991, SI 1991/1505 and the Children's Homes (Regulations) 2001, SI 2001/3967,[4] in particular Part III and Schs 2 and 3.[5]

[1] Representations Procedure (Children) (England) Regulations 2006, SI 2006/1738 (England) or SI 2005/3365 (Wales).

[2] See *Lost in Care: Bryn Estin Home* HC 201 (1999–2000). In England, The Arrangements for Placement of Children by Voluntary Organisations and Others (England) Regulations 2011, SI 2011/582 set out detailed requirements for the planning and monitoring of care for children placed in care homes operated by the voluntary sector. The Regulations require that records in relation to the care are kept, set out provision for the retention and confidentiality of the records and also require that written records of review processes are kept.

[3] For Wales, similar, if less detailed, provisions can be found in SI 2007/307 and SI 2010/1700.

[4] For Wales, see SI 2002/327.

[5] See SIs 2010/959 and 2001/582; 1991/893; 1991/910. See also SI 2007/722 on childcare disclosure functions, and Childcare Act 2006, ss 82–84.

8.79 Complaints relating to social services under the Health and Social Care (Community Health and Standards) Act 2003 are examined in ch 9 (para 9.90). Under the Children Act 1989, s 17 and Sch 2, local authorities are to publish information about services provided under ss 17, 18, 20, 23A and 23B and 24A and 24B by the authority and, where they consider it appropriate, by others. They are to take such steps as are reasonably practicable to ensure that those who might benefit from the services receive the information relevant to them.

8.80 Children Act 1989, s 88 and Sch 10 added s 51A to the Adoption Act 1976. This established the Adoption Contact Register, which was held by the Registrar-General. These provisions have now been replaced by those in the Adoption and Children Act 2002 (see below).

8.81 The Children Act 1989 also provides for registers covering disabled children (Sch 2, para 2); the making of regulations on, inter alia, records kept by the authority for children placed with foster parents (Sch 2, para 12); and opportunities for specified parties to be notified of arrangements for providing accommodation and maintenance, with opportunities for such parties to make representations.[1]

[1] See the Care Standards Act 2000, and the Fostering Services Regulations 2011, SI 2011/581.

8.82 Section 83 of the Children Act 1989 (which has been subject to significant amendment by a number of pieces of later legislation) permits the Secretary of State or local authorities to carry out or commission research into their functions under the Act and also those of Local Safeguarding Children Boards (LSCBs). There can also be research into adoption and care homes. In order to facilitate this research, the Secretary of State may require local authorities, voluntary organisations and magistrates courts to provide him with information, including information relating to and identifying particular children. Any information requested by the Secretary of State must be laid before Parliament in a classified abstract.

Children Act 2004

8.83 This Act creates a Children's Commissioner for England to look after the interests of children. Commissioners exist for Wales, Scotland and Northern Ireland. The 2004 Act follows the Climbié inquiry (Cm 5860, and Cm 5861 and Government Reply Cm 5992). The Children's Commissioner is required under s 8 to produce an annual report on his activities, findings and programme of work for the next year. The Act contains provisions on co-operation between local authorities and other service providers to improve well-being and to promote and safeguard the welfare of children. Section 12 of the Act permits the creation of information databases to facilitate co-operation and the safeguarding of the welfare of children, either under ss 11 and 12 of the 2004 Act or s 175 of the Education Act 2002. The information that can be held in the database is defined very broadly in s 12, but specifically excludes medical and personal records. The database (known as 'ContactPoint') was ultimately brought about in 2007, after considerable debate and some scaling back of the data to be held.[1] The Children Act 2004 Information Database (England) Regulations 2007, SI 2007/2182 provide the detail of the information to be held in the database, the procedures for ensuring its accuracy and the requirements in terms of who must provide information for inclusion in the database and who might have access to the information in the database. Regulation 8 provides that upon the satisfaction of certain conditions, the information on the database becomes 'archived information' and may usually only then be retained for six years from the date on which it becomes 'archived information'. Certain exceptions to this provision, primarily in order to allow local authorities and LSCBs to undertake child protection investigations.

[1]   See N Parton (2008) 35(1) *Journal of Law and Society*, pp 181–184 for an account of the debates over the creation of the database.

8.84 LSCBs have been established in England in accordance with the requirements of the Children Act 2004, ss 13–16 of the Act. The boards are under an obligation to publish an annual report concerning the safeguarding and welfare of children within its area. Section 14B, inserted by the Children, Schools and Families Act 2010 and not yet in force, allows a LSCB to require individuals or bodies holding information that will enable or assist the LSCB to exercise its functions to provide information to it. The information so provided must be used only to assist the LSCB in the exercise of its functions.[1]

[1]   See also SI 2006/90.

Gaskin v United Kingdom[1]

8.85 This is a case concerning a former foster child in the care of a local authority. He sought access to his social services records and was denied them. This refusal was upheld by the Court of Appeal[2] on an application for discovery. The case was concerned with the law prior to the changes introduced by the Access to Personal Files Act 1987 and later developments. The case proceeded to the European Court of Human Rights, Gaskin claiming a breach of Art 8 of the Convention which provides:

'1.   Everyone has the right to respect for his private and family life, his home and his correspondence.

2.   There shall be no interference by a public authority with the exercise of this right except such as is in accordance with the law and is necessary in a democratic society in the interests of national security, public safety, or the economic well-being of the country, for the prevention of disorder or crime, for the protection of health or morals or for the protection of the rights and freedoms of others.'

1   *Gaskin v United Kingdom* [1990] 1 FLR 167; see also: *Brown v Matthews* [1990] Ch 662, CA; and M.G. v UK (2002) *Times*, 11 October, ECtHR. For a case where the local authority met the requirements in Arts 2 and 8 ECHR (parent wanted access to a 16-year-old dead son's file): *R (Addinell) v Sheffield City Council* [2001] ACD 61.

2   *Gaskin v Liverpool City Council* [1980] 1 WLR 1549, CA.

8.86   By eleven votes to six, the European Court upheld Gaskin's claim, holding that, while the confidentiality of public records was important for receiving reliable and objective information and also to protect third parties, persons in Gaskin's position had a vital interest in obtaining such information, a right protected by the Convention, to know about their past and early development. The British system existing at the relevant time could, in principle, have been compatible with Art 8 *but* there must be a safeguard where a contributor, *including a doctor*, wrongfully withholds consent to access to records to which he or she has contributed. The principle of proportionality required that an independent authority must be in existence to determine the respective claims to confidentiality and to access. The absence of such a procedure amounted to a violation under Art 8 and the automatic preference given to the contributors' views was disproportionate to the aims pursued and were not necessary in a democratic society.

8.87   This has implications for the regulations on access above, as the views of medical staff must be sought before access is given and, under the regulations, no independent means of challenge is provided.

ADOPTION

8.88   Under the Adoption Agency Records Regulations 1983, SI 1983/1964, an adoption agency has a power to 'provide access to its case records … as it thinks fit'. This discretion, like all such powers, must not be fettered by a rigid policy. A rigid policy refusing access to adopted children would be subject to judicial review.[1] Sections 56–65[2] of the Adoption and Children Act 2002 make provision for information to adopted children on reaching the age of eighteen and restrictions on access where access to an original birth certificate might endanger a 'birth relative'. Sections 125–131 are concerned with the Adoption and Children Act Register which is maintained by the Secretary of State. This contains information about children who are suitable for adoption and prospective adopters. An arrangement may be entered into whereby an 'organisation' may exercise powers in relation to the register. The register is only accessible within the terms of the statute to agencies acting on behalf of prospective adopted children and prospective adopters and is not open for public inspection or examination (see SI 2005/389).

[1]   *Gunn-Russo v Nugent Care Society and Another* [2002] 1 FLR 1. NB *R v Registrar General, ex p Smith* [1991] 2 All ER 88, CA; and *Re X* [1994] 3 All ER 372, CA. See: *R v Derbyshire County Council, ex p E* (1989) *Guardian*, 25 May, on Adoption Act 1976, s 19 – duties to inform parents of failed placement of a child. Cf Human Fertilisation and Embryology etc Act 1990. On Child Protection Registers see para 7.273 above and para 9.123, note 1 below, and case-law. See *Odievre v France* [2003] FCR 621, ECtHR: no breach of Art 8 in refusing access by an adopted child to information about her natural mother's identity. The mother was also entitled to protection under Art 8 and the approach adopted by France was within the state's margin of appreciation.

[2]   Further requirements on the holding and disclosure of information can be found in SI 2005/888 The Disclosure of Adoption Information (Post-Commencement Adoptions) Regulations. For Wales see SI 2005/2689.

HUMAN FERTILISATION

8.89   The Human Fertilisation and Embryology Authority (Disclosure of Donor Information) Regulations 2004, SI 2004/1511, prescribes information that may be supplied to an adult who was, or may have been born, as a result of treatment under the Human Fertilisation and Embryology Act 1990. This concerns information about the donor of the sperm, eggs or embryos entered on the register under the Act. Disclosure of the donor's identity is restricted to information supplied by the donor after 1 April 2005. The Human Fertilisation and Embryology Act 2008 introduces a number of new provisions on information and also creates a clearer regulatory framework for disclosures. Of particular importance is the new right given to donors to discover how many children may have been born as a result of the donation and their genders and years of birth (though these may not be disclosed if it may enable the donor to discover the identity of the children concerned). Section 33D of the 1990 Act (introduced by the 2008 Act) allows the Secretary of State to authorise the processing of information stored by the Human Fertilisation and Embryology Authority to be used for the purposes of medical or other research. Regulations provide the broader detail of what the information may be used for and how it might be disclosed.[1]

[1]   The Human Fertilisation and Embryology (Disclosure of Information for Research Purposes) Regulations 2010, SI 2010/995.

HOUSING

Housing records

8.90   Until the DPA 1998 came into effect in March 2000, the provisions of the Data Protection Act 1984 applied to computerised personal records. For paper records, regulations covering housing were made under the Access to Personal Files Act 1987. These regulations came into force on 1 April 1989 (and see DoE circ 13/89). The 1987 Act was repealed by the DPA 1998 and the regulations were therefore rescinded also. The DPA 1998 now governs the situation and readers are directed to the discussion in ch 7. One point to note has been the duty on sellers of residential property under Housing Act 2004, Part 5 to prepare a complete information pack about the property.

8.91 The 1989 regulations covered public housing authorities; they did not apply to housing associations (see DoE Circ 13/89, para 9) but they did apply to housing action trusts established under the Housing Act 1988. The FOIA 2000 provisions cover housing action trusts and the Housing Corporation, but not individual housing associations unless they are designated under the FOIA 2000. If designated under the FOIA 2000 (s 5) the situation will be on a par with housing authorities. Under the DPA 1998, local authority housing authorities are covered in relation to information held for the purposes of any of the authority's tenancies. These are accessible public records (see DPA 1998, Sch 12).

Housing administration

8.92 Since 1980, the efforts of the government to off-load public housing on to the private sector have been obvious and widely reported. The first step was the 'right to buy' policy under the Housing Act 1980. Housing and Planning Act 1986, ss 7 and 8 encouraged and facilitated the disposal to private sector landlords of tenanted properties held by local authorities, with consultation provisions for tenants where tenants were to lose their security of tenure. The Secretary of State was not to give his or her consent if it appeared to him or her that a majority of the tenants to which the application relates do not wish the proposal to proceed. S/he may have regard to any information available to him/her 'and the local authority shall give him such information as to the representations made to them by tenants and others ... as he may require'. However, the 'Secretary of State's consent to a disposal was not invalidated by a failure on his/her part or that of the local authority to comply with the requirements of this Schedule'. These provisions must now be read in the light of the Housing Act 1996 (HA 1996) which repealed many relevant provisions of the Housing Act 1988 (HA 1988). For England, a number of provisions of the Housing Act 1996 have been repealed or amended by the Housing and Regeneration Act 2008 (HRA 2008).

8.93 There has been increasing reliance on the provision of housing via housing associations registered under the Office for Tenants and Social Landlords (OTSL) and the Welsh Assembly Ministers, particularly after the HA 1988. In England, this area is now governed by HRA 2008, Parts 2 and 3, which deal with the social rented sector where social landlords, ie housing associations, have to be registered with the OTSL (operating as the Tenant Services Agency) on a register which is made available to the public.[1] The OTSL has a general power to obtain information, which it can enforce, and it also has powers to receive and disclose information under HRA 2008, ss 107–109). The OTSL may publish information, advice and guidance as part of its role by virtue of HRA 2008, s 97. Furthermore, under Chapter 6 of the HRA 2008, the OTSL has the power to set and monitor standards for social housing in England and to issue Codes of Practice on standards after consultation with relevant parties. Under s 204, the OTSL may require each registered provider to produce an annual report on its performance in respect of the standards that are set by the OTSL, which must be sent to the regulator. The OTSL must publish an annual report on the performance of registered providers, with particular focus on information that would be useful to local authorities, tenants and potential tenants. If the OTSL issues a penalty notice to a registered provider or requires a registered provider to pay compensation then under ss 228(3) and 240(3) of the 2008 Act respectively the OTSL may require the registered provider to publish information about the penalty or compensation award in a specified manner. In Wales, the Welsh ministers enjoy similar powers to seek and disclose information, granted by ss 30–33 of the HA 1996. Information about levels of performance is collected by the Welsh ministers from 'registered social landlords' and this is to be publicised as the ministers considers appropriate: at least once a year for tenants and prospective tenants (HA 1996, ss 34 and 35). The Welsh ministers may issue guidance for registered social landlords. In both England and Wales, registered social landlords must belong to a scheme for the investigation of complaints which can be enforced via the High Court (HA 1996, s 51 and Sch 2 (as amended)). The scheme involves an independent ombudsman, the Housing Ombudsman, and various other matters set out in the Schedule.

[1]   The register is available to be searched on the Tenant Services Agency's website at http://portal. tenantservicesauthority.org/FindAndCompare.aspx.

8.94   The HA 1988 introduced housing action trusts (HATs)[1] to which local authority housing stock may be transferred together with housing and a variety of other powers including planning powers. Their basic objectives are found in s 63. These include repair and improvement and 'proper and effective management and use' of property, and to encourage diversity in the identity of landlords, which can be achieved either by disposal[2] and/or by use of their grant-aid/financial assistance powers in s 71.

[1]   A public corporation.
[2]   HA 1988, s 63(1); see ss 63(3) and 79: Arden *Current Law Annotated Statutes Vol 4* (1988), pp 50–124.

8.95   HATs' principal powers are to provide and maintain housing, and to facilitate the provision of shops, advice centres and other such facilities for the benefit of the community or communities in their areas, not merely those living in their accommodation. They possess power to acquire, hold, manage, reclaim and dispose of land and other property, carry out building and other operations, seek to ensure the provision of utilities and similar services and carry on 'any' business or undertaking, together with a general ancillary power[1] to do anything 'necessary or expedient' for the purposes of the objects and powers or purposes incidental thereto.[2]

[1]   LGA 1972, s 111.
[2]   HA 1988, s 63(3).

8.96   By HA 1988, s 63(5) a transaction is not to be treated as invalid – ultra vires – because of a failure to observe the objects or to exercise their powers for stated purposes.

Consultation and publicity

8.97 The Secretary of State shall, under HA 1988, s 61, consult every local housing authority any part of whose district is to be included in the proposed designated area before making a designation order for a HAT.

'(2) Where the Secretary of State is considering a proposal to make a designation order, he shall use his best endeavours to secure that notice of the proposal is given to all tenants of houses in the area proposed to be designated who are either secure tenants or introductory tenants or tenants of such description as may be prescribed by regulations.

(3) After having taken the action required by subsection (2) above, the Secretary of State shall either–

(a) make arrangements for such independent persons as appear to him to be appropriate to conduct, in such manner as seems best to them, a ballot or poll of the tenants who have been given notice of the proposal as mentioned in that subsection with a view to establishing their opinions about the proposal to make a designation order; or

(b) if it seems appropriate to him to do so, arrange for the conduct of a ballot or poll of those tenants in such manner as appears to him best-suited to establish their opinions about the proposal.

(4) If it appears from a ballot or poll conducted as mentioned in subsection (3) above that a majority of the tenants who, on that ballot or poll, express an opinion about the proposal to make the designation order are opposed to it, the Secretary of State shall not make the order proposed.'

8.98 HA 1988, s 90 provides that an authority shall provide 'any document' or information to the Secretary of State to carry out his tasks under s 90(3).

8.99 A variety of duties upon housing authorities exist under the Housing Act 1985 (HA 1985) concerning information on improvement grants, assistance for owners of defective premises; repair notice; improvement notices and slum clearance; duties to report to the Secretary of State on overcrowding in their area and to report on particular houses or areas. HA 1996, Part VII concerns duties to the homeless. This is further amended by the Homelessness Act 2002, which imposes new duties on local housing authorities. These include rights for information and guidance, as well as allocation schemes (ss 15, 16).

8.100 HA 1985, s 104 concerns provision of information about tenancies. It imposes a duty on every body which lets dwelling-houses under secure tenancies[1] to publish information 'about its secure tenancies in such form as it considers best-suited to explain in simple terms and so far as it considers appropriate, the effect of' express terms of secure tenancies; Parts IV of the HA 1985; and ss 11–16 of the Landlord and Tenant Act 1985.[2] The information 'so far as is reasonably practicable' shall be kept up to date and the secure tenant shall be supplied with a copy of information published by the authority under the section and terms of the tenancy in so far as not expressed in the lease or written tenancy agreement ... nor implied by law. The written statement shall be supplied on the grant of the tenancy or as soon as practicable afterwards.

1   See Leasehold Reform, Housing and Urban Development Act 1993, s 123.
2   See HA 1996, Sch 15, para 2 – landlord's repairing obligation.

8.101 Section 105 of the HA 1985 (as amended) provides that every landlord authority covered by the section shall make and maintain 'such arrangements as it considers appropriate to enable those of its secure tenants who are likely to be substantially affected by a matter of housing management' to inform the tenants of its proposals and to make their views known to the authority within a 'specified period'. The authority is under a duty to consider representations so made and to publish its arrangements which are to be available for inspection, free of charge, at all reasonable hours at the authority's principal office, or which can be furnished, on payment of a reasonable fee, to any member of the public asking for a copy etc. Section 114 defines landlord 'authority' and s 105(2) and (3) define 'housing management'. It is the latter if 'in the opinion of the landlord authority concerned it:

(a) relates to the management, improvement, or demolition of dwelling houses let by the authority ... or to provision of services or amenities in connection with such dwelling-houses; and
(b) represents a new programme of maintenance, improvement or demolition or a change in the practice or policy of the authority; and
(c) is likely substantially to affect its secure tenants as a whole or a group of them.'

8.102 Rent payable under secure tenancies or charges for services etc are not matters of housing management. The section also defines 'group'.

8.103 A landlord authority which is a registered housing association shall, instead of making the documents available at its principal office under HA 1985, s 105(6)(a), send copies to the OTSL or Welsh ministers and to the council of any district or London borough in which there are dwelling-houses let by the association as secure tenancies. The council shall publish them as under sub-s (6) (a) but there is no duty to provide copies for a charge.

8.104 HA 1985, s 106 states that every landlord authority (see s 114) shall publish a summary of its rules on determining priority on application, exchanges and transfers, and it is under a duty to maintain a set of those rules and allocation procedure rules and make them available at its principal office for inspection at all reasonable hours without charge by members of the public.[1] A copy of the summary of the rules is available without charge, and a copy of a set of the rules 'shall be furnished on payment of a reasonable fee, to any member of the public who asks for one'. The requirement to keep a housing register has gone (Homelessness Act 2002, s 14). Rights for access to personal documents under the HA 1985 are subsumed within the access rights under the DPA 1998 (paras 7.156 et seq above), although s 106(5) gives the right for applicants for social housing to require that the housing authority provide 'details of the particulars which he has given to the authority about himself and his family and which the authority has recorded as being relevant to his application for accommodation.'[2]

[1]   See HA 1996, Sch 16, para 1.
[2]   And see SI 2002/3264 and SI 2006/1294 on allocation of Housing in England. In Wales see SI 2003/239.

8.105   Sections 121AA and 121B of the HA 1985 (added by the Housing Act 2004) require information to be provided to secure tenants by the relevant body on their right to buy. The information should assist tenants in making a decision over whether they wish to exercise the right to buy or not. The information that is to be provided to tenants is found in an Order,[1] and includes the circumstances in which the right can and cannot be exercised, the exceptions to the right, the procedure for exercising the right and the cost of so doing. Information must also be provided on the initial costs that might be faced, the risk of repossession and advice on the other costs that a homeowner might face. The risk of repossession must also be publicised. The information must be kept up to date insofar as is reasonably practicable. Section 121B provides that the document must be published and copies of it must be supplied to secure tenants of the body concerned. The Order promulgated under s 121AA provides that the document must have been published within two months of the Order coming into force and, whenever it is revised, within one month of that revision. In addition to providing a copy to each of its tenants, s 121B also requires that the document must be supplied free of charge to anyone requesting it, and that it must make copies available at its principal offices and other places it considers appropriate at reasonable hours. The fact that the document is available from these locations must be publicised to the secure tenants of the body.

[1]   SI 2005/1735 (England) and SI 2005/2681 (Wales).

8.106   The Housing and Regeneration Act 2008 creates, for England, the Homes and Communities Agency (HCA). The objectives of the Agency are set out in s 2 of the Act and include improving the supply and quality of housing and securing the redevelopment of land or infrastructure and encouraging sustainable development. Section 36 provides that the Secretary of State might require the HCA to provide information about the homes supplied by it as social housing. Sections 38–40 give the HCA power to publish ideas and information, etc, provide education and training and also to publish guidance. If the HCA wishes to provide guidance, it must consult before doing so.

PLANNING AND THE ENVIRONMENT

8.107   The governing provisions relating to planning are in the Town and Country Planning Act 1990, as amended by the Planning and Compensation Act 1991. The Planning and Compulsory Purchase Act 2004 has made some important innovations that will be described where relevant. Once again, the reader must be directed to the provisions of the Local Government (Access to Information) Act 1985 (LG(ATI)A 1985) (amending the LGA 1972), and the provisions of the LGA 2000 for those duties dealing with access to executive meetings, committee meetings, reports and background papers and the more general provisions of the FOIA 2000 (see chs 1 and 4–6). Notwithstanding the developments to local authority administration ushered in by the LGA 2000 (see ch 4), it was intended that authorities would retain planning committees. In planning, certain decisions can be delegated to officers.[1] These decisions, and the information relating to them, will be covered by the LG(ATI)A 1985 unless exempt, insofar as the decisions have to go back to a committee for report and notification or for formal approval, and details of delegation have to be published under the Act.[2] The intention behind the FOIA 2000 was that the more liberal regime between the LG(ATI)A 1985 and the FOIA 2000 would prevail (paras 6.33 et seq above).

[1]   LGA 1972, s 101 and eg SI 1992/1492, reg 10.
[2]   LG(ATI)A 1985: LGA 1972, s 100G(2).

8.108   However, planning permission has to be consistent with guidelines laid down by central government for development plans and development control issued through circulars and, from 1988, by way of policy guidance notes. Circulars are to be used for administrative details, not for guidance on policy. Regional guidance is also published by the Secretary of State, eg SERPLAN for the south-east, in planning policy guidance notes. Development plans as produced by local planning authorities (LPAs) below constitute the basic background for decisions on planning and land use. Regional Development Agencies established under the Regional Development Agencies Act 1998 are also be responsible for policy decisions with implications for planning and development, although note the discussion below of the Localism Bill's proposed changes in this area, which will remove most aspects of regional involvement. Furthermore, the Regional Development Agencies themselves will be abolished once the Public Bodies Bill (2010–2011) comes into force as the Regional Development Agencies are contained in Sch 1 of the Bill and the Government has indicated its intention to use the powers in clause 1 of the Bill to abolish them.

Statements of planning policy

8.109   In the past, county planning policy was formulated through structure plans[1] which involved publicity and public participation exercises. These plans were then replaced by the provisions of the Planning and Compulsory Purchase Act 2004. The provisions of the Planning and Compulsory Purchase Act 2004 were then replaced by the provision in Part V of the Local Democracy, Economic Development and Construction Act 2009. The following paragraphs will outline the changes made first by the Planning and Compulsory Purchase Act 2004 and then the changes and modifications made by the 2009 Act. The regional spatial strategies (RSS) and regional strategies under the 2009 Act were relatively short-lived, as the regional strategies have now been revoked by the Secretary of State. The final part of this section will outline the proposed changes to be made by the Localism Bill (2010–2011) should it come into force in its present form.

[1]   TCPA 1990, Pt II, and Planning and Compensation Act 1991, s 27 and Sch 4.

8.110 The Planning and Compulsory Purchase Act 2004 introduced RSS for each region, and regional planning bodies (RPB) that were assisted by local authorities. The RSS set out the Secretary of State's policies in relation to the development and use of land within the region. RPBs were recognised by a Secretary of State direction and were required to contain at least 60 per cent of members of local authorities or prescribed authorities. The RPB was required to keep the RSS under review (s 3) and monitor the implementation of the RSS throughout the region. RPBs were required to seek the assistance of local authorities for various statutory responsibilities. The RSS was to be be revised in accordance with s 5. For the purposes of s 5, the RPB must prepare and publish a statement of its policies as to the involvement of persons who appear to the RPB to have an interest in the exercise of those functions. Section 8 applied if the Secretary of State decided that an examination in public was to be held of a draft revision of a RSS. The decision was his, it should be noted. The person to conduct the examination is appointed by the Secretary of State and 'no person has a right to be heard at an examination in public' (s 8(3)). Regulations for procedure could be made after consultation between the Secretary of State and the Lord Chancellor.[1] The person appointed reported to the Secretary of State (s 8). Section 9 had notice and comment type procedures in relation to changes the Secretary of State proposes to make either after an examination or where none is held. Section 11 provided for regulations to be made in relation to statutory procedures; giving notice and publicity; public inspection of draft revisions or other documents; the extent of consultation and participation by the public in anything in relation to that part of the statute; for making and considering representations; publication of drafts or reports produced; monitoring of RPBs; and reasonable charges for copies of documents.

[1] See Town and Country Planning (Initial Regional Spatial Strategy) (England) Regulations 2004, SI 2004/2206.

8.111 Part I of the Planning and Compulsory Purchase Act 2004 was repealed by the Local Democracy, Economic Development and Construction Act 2009, Part V. This Act removes the notion of a RSS and replaces it with the 'regional strategy'. The regional strategy sets out the policies in relation to the sustainable economic development of a region and the policies in relation to the development and use of land in a region (s 70(2)(a) and (b)). Strategies might apply to the region or any part of it (s 70(3)) and must include policies on reducing and adapting to climate change (s 70(4)). The Act makes it clear that the regional strategy at the time of the Act passing into law would be the RSS in place prior to the passage of the Act (s 70(6)). The review and revision of the regional strategy is the responsibility of the regional authorities (s 74), which are the RDA for the region and a new body, known as a Leaders' Board. Provision for the Leaders' Board is in s 71. Each 'participating authority' (for most areas, district and county councils) are required to create a scheme for the operation of a Leaders' Board. Section 71 requires consultation with appropriate persons prior to the adoption of the scheme and schemes must then be approved by the Secretary of State. Section 73 of the Act places sustainable development as an important part of the strategy process, requiring both the Secretary of State and the regional authorities to exercise their powers under Part V of the 2009

Act with the objective of contributing to sustainable development. Section 74 of the Act requires the authorities set out above to keep the regional strategy under review and to revise it when expedient or necessary. The Act places some focus on public participation and public examination of plans. Section 75 of the Act requires the responsible regional authorities to draw up and abide by a policy statement on the involvement of interested persons in the revision of the regional strategy. This policy statement must be published. Section 76 allows the regional authorities to carry out an examination in public of the revisions proposed to a regional strategy. It is clear that the regional authorities have a discretion to do this and are not required to do so, but the exercise of this discretion is constrained by s 76(2), which states that in making the decision whether or not to examine in public the authorities should have regard to the scale of the revisions and the level of interest in the revision process, along with other factors that the authorities deem relevant. Once the authorities have decided to hold an examination in public, they must inform the Secretary of State of their decision and he must then appoint a person to hold it. Should the authorities decide not to hold an examination in public, the Secretary of State may choose to require this by virtue of s 76(5). Section 77 of the Act sets out the matters to be considered when revising the plan, which are mainly other relevant planning policies, particularly of adjoining regions. Section 78 of the Act requires that the revised regional strategy is approved by the Secretary of State and sets out a process for revision if not approved. Section 79 provides the Secretary of State with reserve powers to consider revisions to a regional strategy should the regional authorities fail to do so. Once the plan is approved it becomes part of the development plan for the purposes of s 38 of the Planning and Compulsory Purchase Act 2004 (s 84). Policy guidance on regional planning under Part V of the 2009 Act, including guidance on the constitution of Leaders' Boards has been published.[1]

---

[1]   See Town and Country Planning (Initial Regional Spatial Strategy) (England) Regulations 2004, SI 2004/2206.

8.112   The discussion of the provisions of Part V of the Local Democracy, Economic Development and Construction Act 2009 describes the current law in force, but is already largely academic. On 6 July 2010 the Secretary of State acted to revoke regional plans and all references to them in other planning policy documents.[1] Clause 89 of the Localism Bill (2010–2011) will revoke Part V of the 2009 Act. The Court of Appeal has recently found that the revocation of regional strategies by the Secretary of State using powers under s 79(6) of the 2009 Act is lawful, and that local planning authorities are thus entitled to take account of the revocation in the making of decisions on planning applications.[2]

---

[1]   See the letter from the Chief Planning Officer to local authorities of 6 July 2010, found on the DCLG website at http://www.communities.gov.uk/documents/planningandbuilding/pdf/1631904.pdf.

[2]   *R (Cala Homes South Ltd) v Secretary of State for Communities and Local Government* [2011] EWCA Civ 639 (27 May 2011).

8.113   There has been some concern expressed about the removal of regional planning from the planning process. The Communities and Local Government

Select Committee has recently published a report[1] which notes that the immediate revocation of regional plans leaves a significant lack of regional input into the planning process, with particular problems in relation to certain strategic issues such a traveller sites and mining.

[1]   HC 517 (2010–2011) *Abolition of Regional Spatial Strategies: A Planning Vacuum* (2nd report of 2010–2011).

8.114   The Localism Bill (2010–2011) proposes a new 'bottom up' approach to regional planning, where local planning authorities will be encouraged to co-operate with one another in order to adopt a co-ordinated approach at the regional level. Clause 90 of the Localism Bill seeks to insert a new s 33A into the Planning and Compulsory Purchase Act 2004 in order to require such co-operation in relation to sustainable development, but the committee notes in its report that there is no sanction for a failure to co-operate. More broadly, the witnesses to the committee are generally sceptical that ad hoc arrangements for co-operation between local planning authorities are likely to deliver the coherence of the regional strategies that were previously in place.

8.115   Under Part II of the Planning and Compulsory Purchase Act 2004, local planning authorities must conduct surveys of their area in relation to development or the planning of its development: s 13 of the 2004 Act provides details. County councils are to conduct surveys where development affects a 'county matter'. LPAs are to produce local development schemes (s 15) specifying local planning documents, development plan documents, jointly prepared documents, and timetables for the preparation and revision of documents. Procedural matters may be made by regulations and will deal with publicity, public inspection of schemes and other items. Section 17 provides details on local development documents and under s 18 a LPA must prepare a statement of community involvement. Local development documents must be prepared in accordance with the local development scheme and s 19(2) lists the matters to which an LPA must have regard in preparing a local development document. Every development plan document must be submitted to the Secretary of State for independent examination. Persons making representations seeking to change a development plan document must be given the opportunity to appear before and be heard by the conducting the examination who is appointed by the Secretary of State. That person makes recommendations to the Secretary of State giving reasons (s 20). Local development documents must be in 'general conformity' with RSSs or spatial development strategy in relation to a London borough. The opinion of the RPB will be sought by the LPA (s 24). The part of the Act has details on revocation and revision of local development documents and default powers by the Secretary of State, joint local development documents and joint committees, annual monitoring reports and regulations covering similar items in relation to RSSs under s 11 (above).

8.116   Under s 38 of the 2004 Act, development plans are in relation to Greater London the spatial development strategy and development plan documents; in relation to other authorities in England the RSS and development plan documents.[1] Note that the RSS is no longer a relevant part of a development plan due to the revocation outlined above, but all other plan documents created under Part II of the Planning and Compulsory Purchase Act 2004 remain in force, as do all published planning policy statements, other than the regional strategy.[2] The Government has committed to reforming the present system of planning policies with a consolidated National Planning Framework. Work on this process is presently at an early stage, although the commitment has appeared in a work plan for the DCLG.[3]

[1]   See SIs 2004/2203 to 2004/2209 on the new arrangements under the 2004 Act.
[2]   See the letter from the Chief Planning Officer to local authorities of 6 July 2010, found on the DCLG website at http://www.communities.gov.uk/documents/planningandbuilding/pdf/1631904.pdf.
[3]   DCLG (2011) *Major Infrastructure Planning Reform: Work Plan*, para 35.

Register of planning applications

8.117   Every planning authority must keep a register of planning applications and decisions, containing information as prescribed including information as to the manner in which such applications have been dealt with.[1]

[1]   TCPA 1990, s 69. See also ss 188, 214.

8.118   Section 69(3) of the TCPA 1990 states that a development order may make provision for the register to be kept in two or more parts, each part containing such information relating to applications for planning permission as may be prescribed by the order, and may also make provision:
(a)   for a specified part of the register to contain copies of applications and of any plans or drawings submitted therewith; and
(b)   for the entry relating to any application, and everything relating thereto, to be removed from that part of the register when the application (including any appeal arising out of it) has been finally disposed of, without prejudice to the inclusion of any different entry relating thereto in another part of the register.

8.119   Every register kept under s 69 shall be available for inspection by the public at all reasonable hours.[1]

[1]   See also SI 1995/419, Art 25.

Publication of notices of applications

8.120   Under s 65 of the TCPA 1990, as amended by Planning and Compensation Act 1991, s 16 there has to be compulsory publicity for all planning applications. There are statutory requirements for different classes of development. An accompanying circular (DoE Circ 15/92) defines 'publicity' as giving notice of a planning application so that neighbours and other interested parties can make their views known in the case. Publicity may require 'consultation', ie inviting the views of specialist bodies for particular types of development. 'Notification' requires developers to notify owners and agricultural tenants of a planning application they intend to submit in relation to the owner's or tenant's land. There are details on notification forms and certificates which have to be filled. Responsibility falls primarily on LPAs (parish or community councils (Wales) may assist). The GDO was amended and consolidated in 1995 (SIs 1995/418 and 1995/419), 1999 (SI 1999/293), 2003 (SI 2003/956) and 2005 (SI 2005/85).

8.121   The types of publicity involve: publishing a notice in a local newspaper; posting a site notice, visible to the general public; neighbour notification to occupiers and owners of adjoining properties. It is courteous to advise third parties of decisions and to exercise 'judgment' on how best to do this. The table below sets out the statutory publicity requirements.[1]

---

[1]   And see SI 1995/418; and SI 1995/419. For a requirement of legibility of a notice under the Telecommunications Act 1984, Sch 20, para 18(2), *Lloyd Jones and Others v T Mobile (UK) Ltd* [2003] EWCA Civ 1162 – a notice on private land did not have to be 'accessible' from neighbouring land!

8.122

'TABLE – STATUTORY PUBLICITY

Nature of Development	Publicity Required	GDO or other statutory provisions
Development where application accompanied by environmental statement	Advertisement in newspaper and site notice	Article 12B of the GDO
Departure from development plan		
Affecting public right of way		
Major development	Advertisement in newspaper and either site notice or neighbour notification	Article 12B of the GDO
Minor development	Site notice or neighbour notification	Article 12B of the GDO
Development affecting the setting of a listed building	Advertisement in newspaper and site notice and use of website	Section 67 of the Planning (Listed Buildings and Conservation Areas) Act 1990 and SI 1990/1519
Development affecting the character or appearance of conservation area	Advertisement in newspaper and site notice and use of website	Section 73 of the Planning (Listed Buildings and Conservation Areas) Act 1990 and SI 1990/1519
Permitted development requiring prior notification to local planning authority	Site notice posted by developer	Relevant part of Schedule 2 to the GDO'

8.123   Prior to these changes, the ombudsman had spent a great deal of time investigating 'neighbourhood notification' schemes. Outside the statutory requirements, notification or consultation is a matter of local discretion. The Association of District Councils (ADC) had advised its members to avoid making formal resolutions committing the authority to undertaking specified non-statutory neighbour or general public consultation in connection with planning applications. It advised that officers should be formally authorised to undertake 'such informal consultation entirely at their discretion, having due regard to prior circulars and that planning staff should never give firm commitments to consult over future planning applications'. There is authority to suggest that breach of an undertaking could be remedied through the courts[1] and could on the facts amount to a breach of a legitimate expectation; be that as it may, the ADC felt that if no formal undertaking were given, maladministration was unlikely to arise in a refusal to consult. Failure to consult, to inform, to meet or to advise have all been held to constitute maladministration, even in the absence of a formal undertaking. What upset the Commission for Local Administration (CLA) was that the advice from the ADC was given without consulting the CLA. The statutory changes are therefore desirable. Under SI 1990/1519 as amended by SI 2004/2210, special provisions apply to Camden LBC.

[1]   *R v Liverpool Corpn, ex p Liverpool Taxi Fleet Operators' Association* [1972] 2 QB 299, CA; *A-G of Hong Kong v Ng Yuen Shiu* [1983] 2 All ER 346, PC; *R v Secretary of State for the Home Department, ex p Khan* [1985] 1 All ER 40, CA. For publication of planning applications where the authority has an interest see: *Steeples v Derbyshire County Council* [1984] 3 All ER 468; *R v Sevenoaks District Council, ex p Terry* [1985] 3 All ER 226; *R v St Edmundsbury Borough Council, ex p Investors in Industry Commercial Properties Ltd* [1985] 3 All ER 234.

Appeals

8.124   Where permission is not given, either after a planning agreement[1] or otherwise, or the application is not called in by the Secretary of State,[2] or is subject to conditions which the applicant does not accept, the applicant may appeal.[3] The rules governing town and country planning inquiries have been reformulated and developed. In addition, detailed guidance is provided on these procedures by the Planning Inspectorate in PINS 01/2009. This emphasises, consistency, fairness, openness and cooperation between the various parties. It hopes for the speeding up of decisions while ensuring public participation.

[1]   TCPA 1990, s 106; the authority allows development in return for an undertaking from the developer to comply with specifications or make provision for the authority's wishes in the development. See also ss 106A and 106B (added by the Planning and Compensation Act 1991). NB the rather complex interaction between s 106 agreements and the 'Community Infrastructure Levy' found in Part 11 of the Planning Act 2008 and SI 2010/948, regs 122 and 123, which place limits on the extent to which s 106 agreements can be used.
[2]   Under TCPA 1990, s 77.
[3]   On appeal under TCPA 1990, s 78 or referral under s 77. See *Making Your Planning Appeal* The Planning Inspectorate (2011). See also for enforcement procedures: SIs 2002/2682, 2002/2683, 2002/2684, 2002/2685 and 2002/2686 and SI 2003/390 (W 52), 2003/394 (W 53) and 2003/395 (W 54).

8.125   A variety of hearings is possible for the appeal, including: an informal hearing now accompanied by regulations (para 8.185 below); an appeal by way of written representation, decided by the Secretary of State or an appointed person; or a public inquiry with the final decision made by the Secretary of State or the appointed person.

8.126   For public inquiries where the Secretary of State determines the appeal, SI 2000/1624 applies. We will concentrate on these Regulations, although there are three or four times the number of written representation inquiries than there are public inquiries.[1]

[1]   Planning Inspectorate (2010) *Planning Inspectorate Statistical Report 2009/2010*, Table 2.3.

8.127   The position of the Secretary of State was thrown into some confusion by the declaration of the Divisional Court that his role as an appellate authority is inconsistent with Art 6 ECHR insofar as he is an 'interested party'.[1] This judgment was reversed by the House of Lords which held that, although the Secretary of State was not an impartial tribunal for the purposes of the HRA 1998 and Art 6, the totality of the procedures, including a judicial challenge under statute, had to be examined in their entirety and the possibility of a statutory review in the courts did provide the necessary independence and impartiality to comply with Art 6.[2] The Planning Act 2008 introduced a new Infrastructure Planning Commission (IPC) to determine planning applications for large infrastructure projects, guided by national policy statements on the development of infrastructure concerned. The Secretary of State had only limited powers to intervene or give directions in the process, which were found in ss 109–113. This process arguably removed the concerns which led to the judicial review claims above in many cases where the Secretary of State might be said to be an interested party. The Localism Bill abolishes the IPC and transfers its functions back to the Secretary of State; the IPC was ultimately very short-lived and up to April 2011 had not made any decisions to grant development consent for a project.

[1]   See *R (on the application of Holding & Barnes plc) v Secretary of State for the Environment, Transport and the Regions* [2001] NLJR 135.
[2]   *R (Alconbury) v Secretary of State for the Environment, Transport and the Regions* [2001] 2 All ER 929.

Preliminary information to be supplied by local planning authority

8.128   Rule 4 of the Town and Country Planning (Inquiries Procedure) (England) Rules 2000, SI 2000/1624, provides that a LPA shall, on receipt of a notice from the Secretary of State of his intention to cause an inquiry to be held ('the relevant notice'), forthwith inform him and the applicant in writing of the name and address of any statutory party[1] who has made representations to them; and the Secretary of State shall as soon as practicable thereafter inform the applicant and the local planning authority in writing of the name and address of any statutory party who has made representations to him.

[1]   See SI 2000/1624, r 2 for definition of a 'statutory party'. For the Welsh rules, see: SIs 2003/1266, 2003/1267, 2003/1268, 2003/1269, 2003/1270 and 2003/1271.

8.129   Rule 4(2) applies where:

'(a)   the Secretary of State or any local authority has given to the local planning authority a direction restricting the grant of planning permission for which application was made; or

(b) in a case relating to listed building consent, the Commission has given a direction to the local planning authority pursuant to s 14(2) of the Listed Buildings Act as to how the application is to be determined; or

(c) the Secretary of State or any other Minister of the Crown or any government department or any body falling within rule 11(1)(c) has expressed in writing to the local planning authority the view that the application should not be granted either wholly or in part, or should be granted only subject to conditions; or

(d) any person consulted in pursuance of a development order has made representations to the local planning authority about the application.'

8.130   Where r 4(2) above applies, the LPA shall forthwith after the date of the relevant notice ('the relevant date') inform the person of the inquiry and, unless they have already done so, that person or body shall thereupon give the local planning authority a written statement of the reasons for making the direction, expressing the view or making the representations, as the case may be.

8.131   A new r 4(4) under the 2000 Rules states that the LPA shall ensure that, within two weeks of the starting date, the Secretary of State and the applicant have received a completed questionnaire together with a copy of the documents referred to in it, as well as ensuring that any statutory party and 'other person' who made representations to the local planning about the application occasioning the appeal has been notified that an appeal has been made, along with the address to which and period within which they may make representations to the Secretary of State. These do not apply to referred applications under r 3(1).

Pre-inquiry hearings

8.132   SI 2000/1624, r 5 allows for a pre-inquiry meeting to be held unless the Secretary of State believes it unnecessary in the case of an inquiry lasting for more than eight days or if he believes it necessary in the case of shorter inquiries. A statement of matters about which he particularly wishes to be informed for the purposes of his consideration of the application or appeal in question will be served where a pre-inquiry meeting is to be held.

8.133   The LPA shall cause to be published in a newspaper circulating in the locality in which the land is situated a notice of the Secretary of State's intention to cause a meeting to be held and of the statement served as above in such form as the Secretary of State may specify (r 5(3)). Statements under r 4(2)(c) will also be served (above) and will be copied to the Minister or department concerned. The LPA has to publish in a local newspaper in relation to the land in question a notice of the Secretary of State's intention for a meeting to be held.

8.134   The LPA and the applicant shall ensure that within eight weeks of the starting date two copies of their outline statement have been received by the Secretary of State. The latter then forwards a copy of the relevant report to the other party.

8.135   Where r 4(2) above applies, the LPA shall:

'(a) include in their outline statement the terms of–
  (i)   any directions given together with a statement of the reasons therefor; and
  (ii) any view expressed or representation made on which they intend to rely in their submissions at the inquiry; and
(b) within the period mentioned in para (2), supply a copy of their outline statement to the person or body concerned.' (r 5(4))

8.136   The Secretary of State may in writing require any other person who has notified him or her of an intention or a wish to appear at the inquiry to serve, within four weeks of being so required, an outline statement on the Secretary of State, the applicant and the LPA.

8.137   The meeting (or, where there is more than one, the first meeting) shall be held no later than 16 weeks after the relevant date.

8.138   The Secretary of State shall give not less than three weeks' written notice of the meeting to the LPA, the applicant, any person known at the date of the notice to be entitled to appear at the inquiry and any other person whose presence at the meeting seems to be desirable; and s/he may require the local planning authority to take, in relation to notification of the meeting, one or more of the steps which s/he may under r 10(6) require them to take in relation to notification of the inquiry (r 5(8)).

8.139   The inspector shall preside at the meeting and shall determine the matters to be discussed and the procedure to be followed, and s/he may require any person present at the meeting who, in his or her opinion, is behaving in a disruptive manner to leave and may refuse to permit that person to return or to attend any further meeting, or may permit him or her to return or attend only on such conditions as s/he may specify (r 5(9)).

8.140   Where a pre-inquiry meeting has been held pursuant to para (1), the inspector may hold a further meeting. Paragraph (9) applies to such a meeting which is designed to obtain any additional information required (r 5(10)). Rule 5(10) makes provision for further information. A code of practice on preparing for major planning inquiries contained at DoE Circ 15/96, Annex 4 has now been superseded by Annex 4 of DCLG Circ 05/2000. DCLG Circular 05/2000 has now been superseded by the Planning Inspectorate's guidance in PINS 01/2009 which contains no Annex on major planning inquiries, perhaps because most of these inquiries would have been envisaged to be undertaken by the IPC under the procedure set out in the Planning Act 2008. This may need to be revisited if the IPC is abolished by the Localism Bill.

Service of statements of case etc[1]

8.141   SI 2000/1624, r 6(1) states that the LPA shall ensure, not later than–

(a)   six weeks after the starting date; or

(b)   where a pre-inquiry meeting is held pursuant to r 5, four weeks after the conclusion of that meeting,

two copies of their statement of case have been received by the Secretary of State, and a copy by any statutory party.

---

1   In the past, inspectors have complained that pre-inquiry submissions were unhelpful and not sufficiently related to the inquiry.

8.142   Rule 6(2) concerns the duty on a LPA to include in their statement of case details of the time and place where the opportunity to inspect and take copies described in rule 6(13) shall be afforded and where r 4(2) applies the matters mentioned in r 5(4)(a)(ii) unless already notified in an outline statement. A new r 6(13A) was intoduced in 2009 and provides that the opportunity referred to in r 6(13) will be satisfied if a person is notified of publication of the documents on a website, the address of that website and details of how to access the documents concerned on that website.

8.143   Under r 6(3), the applicant has to ensure that two copies of their statement of case have been received by the Secretary of State within various time schedules depending upon whether a per-inquiry hearing was held or not. A copy of the LPAs statement is sent by the Secretary of State to the applicant and a copy of the applicant's to the LPA.

8.144   The applicant and LPA may in writing each require the other to send a copy of any document or the relevant part of any document referred to in the list of documents comprised in that party's statement of case. This shall be sent as soon as practicable.

8.145   The Secretary of State may in writing require any other person who has notified the former of an intention or a wish to appear at an inquiry to serve three copies of their statement of case, within four weeks of being so required, on the Secretary of State and a (or any other) statutory party (r 6(6) and see para 8.127, note 2). The Secretary of State shall send these as soon as practicable to the LPA and applicant.

8.146   The Secretary of State shall supply any person from whom s/he requires a statement of case in accordance with para (6) with a copy of the LPA's and the applicant's statement of case and shall inform that person of the name and address of every person on whom his or her statement of case is required to be served. The Secretary of State or an inspector may require in writing any person who has served a statement of case in accordance with this rule to provide such further information about the matter contained in the statement as s/he may specify and within specified times (r 6(8)). The LPA or applicant so required must supply the relevant number of copies of information in writing to the Secretary of State or inspector as well as to any statutory party. The rule carries on to deal with 'any other persons' and their provision of information as well as statements by 'any persons'.

8.147 Any person serving a statement of case on the LPA shall serve with it a copy of any document, or of the relevant part of any document, referred to in the list comprised in the statement .

8.148 Unless s/he has already done so, the Secretary of State shall not later than 12 weeks from the starting date, serve a written statement of the matters referred to in r 5(2)(a)(ii) on the applicant, the LPA, any statutory party and any person from whom s/he has required a statement of case (r 6(12)).

8.149 The LPA shall afford to any person who so requests a reasonable opportunity to inspect and, where practicable, take copies of any statement of case, written comments, information or other document which, or a copy of which, has been sent to them in accordance with this rule, and the LPAs completed questionnaire and statement of case together with a copy of any document, or of the relevant part of any document, referred to in the list comprised in that statement and any written comments, information or other documents sent by the LPA pursuant to this rule. Safeguards exist where any person who sends a statement to the Secretary of State wishes to comment upon the case of another party. Copies of such comments must be passed to the Secretary of State and any statutory party the former passing them on to the applicant and LPA.

8.150 Under former rules, if a LPA failed to comply with the relevant requirement and presented uninspected documentation at the inquiry, the inspector had a discretion to allow new documents to be introduced, so long as s/he gives the relevant parties an adequate opportunity to consider such new documents. In *Performance Cars Ltd v Secretary of State for the Environment*[1] a LPA had circulated details of proposed development to neighbours, who then lodged a series of objections which the applicant wished to see. The LPA refused to hand them over to him. They were finally given to the applicant at the beginning of the inquiry itself. The inspector allowed the applicant one hour and forty minutes adjournment to peruse the documents, and the applicant was successful in having the Secretary of State's decision, upholding the LPA and the inspector, quashed on the grounds of breach of former rr 6(4) and 10(5). A nice test was spelt out in a case decided by Kerr J:[2]

> 'The court must consider the nature of evidence or information received, its importance to the issues as they stood at the time of its receipt, the extent to which it had already been the subject of cross-examination or comment by the other side, its relationship to the ultimate decision and in effect whether in all the circumstances a reasonable person would consider that there was any risk of injustice or unfairness having resulted.'

[1] *Performance Cars Ltd v Secretary of State for the Environment* [1977] JPL 585, CA. See *South Oxfordshire DC v Secretary of State for the Environment etc* [2000] 2 All ER 667 and *R (Jeffery) v First Secretary of State* [2007] EWCA Civ 584 on introducing new evidence at the appeal. In *Jeffery*, the Court of Appeal was clear that and challenge to the validity of a decision of the Secretary of State on grounds that not all relevant evidence had been considered with an endeavour to raise new points of evidence at the judicial review stage would not be permitted otherwise than in circumstances when there awas a good reason for failure to raise the evidence at the inquiry stage.

[2]   *Lake District Special Planning Board v Secretary of State for the Environment* [1975] JPL 220, *Reading Borough Council v Secretary of State for the Environment and Commercial Union Properties (Investments) Ltd* [1986] JPL 115.

8.151   In *Performance Cars* the adjournment was not adequate opportunity to examine the documents fairly.

8.152   Parties should provide in their statements the data, methodology and assumptions used to support their submissions.

8.153   If no pre-inquiry hearing is held under r 5, the inspector may hold one if s/he it necessary (r 7(1)). Parties are given two weeks' written notice of a pre-inquiry meeting and as well as obvious parties, this includes 'any person whose presence at the meeting appears to him to be desirable'. Further rules deal with inquiry timetable; notification of the appointment of an assessor; and date and notification of an inquiry (rr 8, 9 and 10). Under r 10(3), the period of notice for an inquiry is reduced from not less than 42 days to not less than four weeks. In 2009, r 10(3A) was added to permit written notice to be provided via publication on a website. Under r 10(6) the Secretary of State may require the LPA to take one or more of the following steps:

'(a)   not less than two weeks before the date fixed for the holding of an inquiry to publish a notice of the inquiry in one or more newspapers circulating in the locality in which the land is situated;

(b)   to serve a notice of an inquiry on such persons or classes of persons as he may specify within such period as he may specify;

(c)   to post a notice of an inquiry in a conspicuous place near to the land, within such period as he may specify.'

8.154   Where the land is under the control of the applicant s/he shall, if so required by the Secretary of State, affix firmly to the land or to some object on or near the land, in such manner as to be readily visible to and legible by members of the public, such notice of the inquiry as the Secretary of State may specify; and s/he shall not remove the notice, or cause or permit it to be removed, for such period before the inquiry as the Secretary of State may specify (r 10(7)). Rule 10(8) contains details of what has to be specified in such notices.

8.155   As well as the applicant and the LPA, a variety of public authorities and statutory parties, 'any other person who has served a statement of case in accordance with r 6(6) or an outline statement under r 5(5)' is entitled to appear. Any other person may appear at the inspector's discretion. Legal representation is allowed.

8.156   Representatives of government departments and other specified public bodies may, by written application to the Secretary of State not later than two weeks before the date of an inquiry, be requested to attend and be made available. This concerns cases where the Secretary of State, or the New Towns Commission, has given a direction under r 4(2)(a) or (b); or the Secretary of State or any other Minister of the Crown or other government department has expressed a view under r 4(2)(c) which the LPA have included in a statement served under rr 5(2) or 6(1); or another Minister or any government department has expressed such a view under r 4(2)(c) and the Secretary of State has included its terms in a statement served under r 5(2) or 6(12). The representative shall give the reasons for the direction or expression, shall give evidence and be subject to cross-examination to the same extent as any other witness (r 12(3)) but nothing shall require a representative to answer any question which in the opinion of the inspector is directed to the merits of government policy.

8.157 The procedural rules have become more obviously legalistic, which doubtless reflects the development of inquiry procedures in practice over the last 20 or so years. This legalism has led to excessive delays causing the government to introduce amendments to the appeal process (see paras 8.186 et seq below).

Statements or proofs of evidence

8.158 By SI 2000/1624, r 13, a person entitled to appear at an inquiry who proposes to give, or to call another person to give, evidence at the inquiry by reading a proof of evidence shall send the required number of copies of the proof to the Secretary of State – who passes them on to the LPA and applicant – together with a written summary of that evidence although no summary is required where the proof contains no more than 1,500 words (r 13(2)). A copy is sent to any statutory party. Where a written summary is provided only that summary shall be read at the inquiry, unless otherwise permitted or directed by the inspector.

8.159 The proof and summary shall be received by the Secretary of State no later than four weeks before the date fixed for the inquiry, or by the date of any timetable agreed under r 8 (r 13(3)). The Secretary of State shall send to the inspector as soon as practicable after receipt any proof of evidence together with any summary sent to him in accordance with this rule and received within the specified period if any.

8.160 Any person required by this rule to send copies of a proof of evidence to Secretary of State shall send with them the same number of copies of the whole, or the relevant part, of any documents referred to in the proof, unless copies of the documents or parts of documents in question have already been made available by the local authority pursuant to r 6(13).

8.161 Local authorities must allow any person a reasonable opportunity to inspect and copy documents sent to or by them under r 13(7). A new r 13(8), introduced in 2009, provides that this requirement is complied with if the documents are published on a website and the address and location of the documents on the website are publicised.

8.162 Rule 14 states that LPAs and applicants shall together prepare an agreed statement of common ground and ensure that the Secretary of State and any statutory party receive a copy. The LPA must make this available for public inspection and copying.

Procedure at inquiry

8.163 Procedure at an inquiry is under the control of the inspector unless otherwise provided by the rules (SI 2000/1624, r 15(1)). The inspector has to identify at the start of the inquiry the main issues as they appear to the inspector and any matters on which the inspector requires further elucidation by parties entitled or permitted to appear. This does not preclude reference by the parties to other matters which they regard as relevant and which are not identified by the inspector. Usually, the applicant shall begin and shall have the right of final reply; and the other persons entitled or permitted to appear shall be heard in such order as the inspector may determine (r 15(4)). Section 321 of the TCPA 1990 provides that all inquiries must be held in public and the public should have access to the inquiry documents, other than where disclosure of the information would compromise national security or reveal the measures to be taken in order to secure any premises or property and this disclosure would be contrary to the national interest.[1]

[1] See also SI 2006/1284 (England) or SI 2006/1387 (Wales).

8.164 A person entitled to appear at an inquiry shall be entitled to call evidence and the applicant, the LPA and a statutory party shall be entitled to cross-examine persons giving evidence. However, subject to the foregoing and paras (6) and (7) of r 15, the calling of evidence and the cross-examination of persons giving evidence shall otherwise be at the inspector's discretion (r 15(5)).

8.165 Rule 15(6) provides that the inspector may refuse to permit:

'(a) the giving or production of evidence,
 (b) the cross-examination of persons giving evidence, or
 (c) the presentation of any other matter'

which s/he considers to be irrelevant or repetitious; but where s/he refuses to permit the giving of oral evidence, the person wishing to give the evidence may submit to the inspector any evidence or other matter in writing before the close of the inquiry. Evidence given in summary may still be subject to cross-examination on the proof.

8.166 The inspector may direct that facilities shall be afforded to any person appearing at an inquiry to take or obtain copies of documentary evidence open to public inspection (r 15(8)).

8.167 The inspector may require any person appearing or present at an inquiry who, in the inspector's opinion, is behaving in a disruptive manner to leave and may refuse to permit that person to return, or may permit that person to return only on such conditions as s/he may specify; but any such person may submit to the inspector any evidence or other matter in writing before the close of the inquiry.

8.168 The inspector may allow any person to alter or add to a statement of case served under r 6 so far as may be necessary for the purposes of the inquiry; but s/he shall (if necessary by adjourning the inquiry) give every other person entitled to appear who is appearing at the inquiry an adequate opportunity of considering any fresh matter or document (r 15(9)). The inspector may proceed with an inquiry in the absence of any person entitled to appear at it (r 15(11)).[1]

---

1 See *Ostreicher v Secretary of State for the Environment* [1978] 1 WLR 810, CA. Though see eg: *Lucy v Royal Borough of Kensington and Chelsea* [1997] COD 191 or, more specifically in the planning context: *West Lancashire DC v Secretary of State for the Environment, Transport and the Regions* [1998] JPL 1086.

8.169 The inspector may take into account any written representation or evidence or any other document received by him from any person before an inquiry opens or during the inquiry provided that s/he discloses it at the inquiry (r 15(12)). Inquiries may be adjourned subject to safeguards and where an inquiry lasts for eight or more days any closing submissions must be shown to the inspector by the close of the inquiry.

8.170 Rule 16 concerns site inspections.

Procedure after inquiry

8.171 After the close of an inquiry, the inspector shall make a report in writing to the Secretary of State which shall include conclusions and recommendations or the reasons for not making any recommendations. The inspector does not have to make specific 'findings of fact' any longer.

8.172 Where an assessor has been appointed s/he may, after the close of the inquiry, make a report in writing to the inspector in respect of the matters on which s/he was appointed to advise (SI 2000/1624, r 17(2)).

8.173 Where an assessor makes a report in accordance with the above the inspector shall append it to his or her own report and shall state in that report how far s/he agrees or disagrees with the assessor's report and, where s/he disagrees with the assessor, the reasons for that disagreement (r 17(3)). When making his decision the Secretary of State may disregard any written representations, evidence or other document received after the close of the inquiry. The Secretary of State does not have to disregard it. But where he regards it, the following provision is crucial. If, after the close of an inquiry, the Secretary of State:

'(a) differs from the inspector on any matter of fact[1] mentioned in, or appearing to him to be material to, a conclusion reached by the inspector, or

(b) takes into consideration any new evidence or new matter of fact[2] (not being a matter of government policy)'[3]

and is for that reason disposed to disagree with a recommendation made by the inspector,[4] the Secretary of State shall not come to a decision which is at variance with that recommendation without first notifying the persons entitled to appear at the inquiry who appeared at it of the disagreement and the reasons for it; and affording to them an opportunity of making written representations to the Secretary of State within three weeks of the date of the notification, or (if the Secretary of State has taken into consideration any new evidence or any matter of fact, not being a matter of government policy) of asking within that period for the re-opening of the inquiry (r 17(5)).

1   *Lord Luke of Pavenham v Minister of Housing and Local Government* [1968] 1 QB 172, CA; *Brown v Secretary of State for the Environment* (1978) 40 P & CR 285 on fact/value distinction, ie opinion on the merits.

2   *Buxton v Minister of Housing and Local Government* [1961] 1 QB 278. See also *R (Hughes) v First Secretary of State* [2006] EWCA Civ 838, where it was held that acknowledgement of a legal obligation incumbent on a local authority which was not mentioned in the inspector's report was not a fresh finding of fact to engage the procedure in r 17(5).

3   *Bushell v Secretary of State for the Environment* [1981] AC 75, HL; *R v Secretary of State for Transport, ex p Gwent County Council* [1986] 2 All ER 18; reversed [1987] 1 All ER 161, CA; see *Innisfil Township v Vespra Township* (1981) 123 DLR (3d) 530.

4   *R v Secretary of State for the Environment, ex p Greater London Council* [1986] JPL 32: conditions imposed on inspector's recommendations after subsequent consultation with another department: not a disagreement.

8.174 The Secretary of State may, as s/he thinks fit, cause an inquiry to be re-opened to afford an opportunity for persons to be heard on such matters relating to an application or appeal as s/he may specify, and s/he shall do so if asked by the applicant or the LPA in the circumstances and within the period mentioned in the preceding paragraph; and where an inquiry is re-opened (whether by the same or a different inspector):

'(a) the Secretary of State shall send to the persons entitled to appear at the inquiry who appeared at it a written statement of the specified matters; and

(b) paragraphs (3) to (8) of rule 10 shall apply as if the references to an inquiry were references to a re-opened inquiry'. (r 17(7))

Notification of decision

8.175 The Secretary of State shall notify his decision on an application or appeal, and the reasons for it, in writing to all persons entitled to appear at the inquiry who did appear, and to any other person who, having appeared at the inquiry, has asked to be notified of the decision (SI 2000/1624, r 18(1)). There has been extensive litigation of the requirement to provide 'reasons' which is examined in ch 9 (paras 9.125 et seq below). Rule 18(1A) was added in 2009 to permit notification by website if the persons entitled to notice agree to this as a method of communication.

8.176 Where a copy of the inspector's report[1] is not sent with the notification of the decision, the notification shall be accompanied by a statement of the conclusions and of any recommendations made by the inspector, and if a person entitled to be notified of the decision has not received a copy of that report, s/he shall be supplied with a copy of it on written application made to the Secretary of State within four weeks of the date of the determination (r 18(4)). 'Report' includes an assessor's report; other documents not included may be inspected by any person receiving a copy of the report on a written application within six weeks of the date of the Secretary of State's decision. Rule 18(3A) allows this requirement to be met by publishing the documents concerned in a website and providing details to the persons concerned.

1 'Report' includes any assessor's report appended to the inspector's report but not any other documents so appended, see below and SI 2000/1624, r 18(3).

Procedure following quashing of decision

8.177 SI 2000/1624, r 19 stipulates that where a decision of the Secretary of State on an application or appeal in respect of which an inquiry has been held is quashed in proceedings before any court, the Secretary of State:

'(a) shall send to the persons entitled to appear at the inquiry who appeared at it a written statement of the matters with respect to which further representations are invited for the purposes of his further consideration of the application or appeal; and

(b) shall afford to those persons the opportunity of making, within three weeks of the date of the written statement, written representations to him in respect of those matters or of asking for the re-opening of the inquiry; and

(c) may, as s/he thinks fit, cause the inquiry to be re-opened (whether by the same or a different inspector) and if he does so paragraphs (3) to (8) of r 10 shall apply as if the references to an inquiry were references to a re-opened inquiry.'

8.178 Representations and requests under para (b) must be received within three weeks of the date of the written statement under para (a).

8.179 The Secretary of State may allow further time for the taking of any steps required or enabled under these rules. Extensive amendments are also provided to cater for the role of the mayor under the executive regimes introduced by the LGA 2000.

8.180 The main objective of the rules is 'to make an inquiry process at all stages as efficient and effective as possible, while impairing neither the fairness and impartiality of the proceedings, nor the ability of participants to make representations which are relevant to the decision'.[1] The rules are aimed at speeding up the inquiry, allowing 'no place for surprise tactics'. The latest guidance in PINS 01/2009 is the result of a consultation which took place in 2007. The objectives of the 2007 consultation were primarily to enhance proportionality, customer focus and efficiency within the system.[1] The changes introduced included the reduction of some time limits, the ability of the Planning Inspectorate (on behalf of the Secretary of State) to choose an appeal procedure[2] and the potential to introduce a fee for appeals (which has not yet been introduced at the time of writing). There were further reforms in 2009, noted above where relevant, which enable the use of electronic communications to satisfy the various requirements for participants to be notified in writing at various stages of the appeals process.

1 See DoE Circ 10/88, para 6.
2 DCLG (2007) *Improving the Appeal Process in the Planning System – Making it Proportionate, Customer Focused, Efficient and Well Resourced.*
3 On which, see the guidance in PINS 01/2009, Annex C.

8.181 The above rules, with modifications, are virtually identical in all procedural respects to inquiries where inspectors make the decisions.[1]

1 SI 2000/1625. Procedures for simplified planning zones are contained in SI 1992/2414: see TCPA 1990, s 83 and Sch 7.

Written representation procedures

8.182 These procedures were made statutory in 1986 under the Housing and Planning Act 1986 (now in the Planning (Consequential Provisions) Act 1990 and the details are in the Town and Country Planning (Appeals) (Written Representations Procedure) (England) Regulations 2000, SI 2009/452).[1] Appellants are invited by the department to waive the right to a hearing and to have the appeal decided on written representations only, saving time and expense. The 2009 Regulations have two distinct parts: Part One relating to householder appeals and Part Two which relates to appeals in all other cases. Written notice of the hearing shall be given to 'interested parties' ie any person notified or consulted in accordance with the Act or a development order about the application which has given rise to the appeal or any other person who made representations to the LPA about the application. The notice must specify the matters in SI 2009/452, regs 6(2) (householder appeals) or 13(2) (other appeals). A questionnaire relating to the proceedings must be completed by the LPA who submit this to the Secretary of State and the appellant. The LPA must also include all documents referred to in the questionnaire when it is sent to the Secretary of State and the appellant. The questionnaire requests a range of information from the LPA and requires the inclusion of the reasons for the refusal of planning permission, any policies that are replied upon in order to refuse the application, reports prepared during review of the application and relevant minutes from the LPA's Planning Committee.[2] The questionnaire provides the basis of the LPA's representations in householder appeals (r 7(2)) and may constitute its sole input into a Part Two procedure (r 14(2)). If the LPA is to treat the questionnaire as being its sole representation, it should inform the Secretary of State and the appellant accordingly (r 14(2)).[3] If the LPA wishes to make additional representations it may do so within six weeks of the starting date of the appeal. The appellant's notice of appeal and accompanying documents will constitute the basis of his appeal in householder appeals cases (r 7(1)), and also in a Part Two procedure (r 14(1)), though in a Part Two procedure the appellant may make further written representations within six weeks of the start of the appeal. The householder appeal in Part One is designed to be rapid and offers no potential to offer further representations on the part of the appellant and the LPA beyond those submitted under r 7, though the Secretary of State may request further information from the parties if this is considered necessary. The Secretary of State serves the representations made under r 7, though under the Part One householder procedure there is no opportunity to comment on these unless further information is sought. Third parties notified under reg 6 will have their written representations served on the appellant and LPA. They will receive information setting out the application and other matters but no provision is made to receive the appeal notice of the applicant and the questionnaire of the LPA. An application may be made under the FOIA 2000 if they are not otherwise forthcoming.

1   And see PINS 01/2009, Parts 3 and 4.
2   See also PINS 01/2009, paras 3.3 and 4.3.
3   See PINS 01/2009, paras 3.3.3 and 4.3.1 respectively.

8.183   The Part Two procedure in SI 2009/452 offers a greater potential for reponses to be made to submissions by the parties. Rule 14 of the Regulations requires, as noted in the previous paragraph, the appellant to provide a notice of appeal and the LPA to provide its questionnaire and allows a six-week period after the start of the appeal for either party to make additional representations (though note that the LPA may not do so if it has indicated under r 14(2)) that the questionnaire will be its sole representation in the appeal). If the parties make further representations, the Secretary of State must send these to the other party and each party has the opportunity to make further comments upon any representations that are made, though the Secretary of State has the right to ignore these unless they are made within nine weeks of the start of the appeal (r 14(7)).

8.184   Site visits are not catered for in the rules in either Part One or Part Two procedures, but it is clear they may be conducted by the inspector.[1] It is made clear that no discussions can take place in relation to the case with any party during the site visit.[2] The decision notice is made public and sent to the parties in the appeal and a request can be made for a reasoned decision.[3] The process may have serious disadvantages for third parties such as neighbours and interest groups. Under the Part One procedure, no provision is made for their views, let alone participation – even if they fall within those persons who made representations at the application stage. In the Part Two procedure, r 15 allows for third parties to make representations within six weeks of the start of the appeal, but only if they fall within the class of persons required to be notified in r 13 (those persons required to be notified under the provisions of an Act or Order, or those who made representations at the initial stage). Third parties should where possible have access to documents submitted by the principal parties, facilitated by the LPA and not the Planning Inspectorate.[4] A majority of appeals are now conducted by the written representation procedure.

1   PINS 01/2009, 3.5 or 4.7. Site visits may be carried out wherever it is deemed to be necessary.
2   PINS 01/2009, 3.5.1 and 4.7.1.
3   *South Bedfordshire District Council v Secretary of State for the Environment and Boyle* [1987] JPL 507. See also PINS 01/2009, 3.6 and 4.8. The decision will be published on the Planning Inspectorate's website.
4   PINS 01/2009, 1.17.2.

Hearings[1]

8.185 The Town and Country Planning (Hearings Procedure) (England) Rules 2000, SI 2000/1626 provide for what is an intermediate procedure, somewhere between the full inquiry and a system of written representations. Guidance has been produced for hearings (PINS 01/2009, Part 5). In Annex C of PINS 01/2009 there is a table of guidance on the suitability of the procedures, which emphasises that hearings will be suitable if: the proceedings are unlikely to take more than one day; little or no third party interest is involved; no technical, legal or policy questions are involved; and formal cross-examination will not be required. If cross-examination is deemed necessary, the inspector must consider whether a formal inquiry is more suitable (r 11(3)). Publicity for a hearing will be given as the LPA thinks advisable, and those with an interest in the land and any person who wrote to the LPA at the application stage will be notified of the time of a hearing. Three weeks before the hearing the LPA and appellant will provide a written statement of their case containing full particulars and a list of any documents to which they wish to refer. Representation is not essential. The provisions in relation to third party access to information and attendance are relatively liberal (rr 6(6), 6(6A) and 9(2)).

[1] See *Dyason v Secretary of State for the Environment* (1998) 75 P & CR 506, CA, on judicial criticisms of informal proceedings hearings becoming too 'informal' and which may lead to unfairness. *Joy v Secretary of State for Transport etc* (12/11/02 QBD), draft planning conditions sent to developer and planning authority but not to all parties who had participated: a fatal breach of fairness and SI 2000/1626, r 14(3).

Major planning inquiries

8.186 The Town and Country Planning (Major Infrastructure Project Inquiries Procedure) (England) Rules 2005, SI 2005/2115, replace SI 2000/1624 for major infrastructural inquiries held by the Secretary of State before he determines applications referred to him under TCPA 1990, s 76A(4)(a), required in respect of a major infrastructure project. The major features of these Rules to apply to major infrastructure project inquiries are as follows. Rule 3 provides for the use of electronic communications. Rule 5 provides for persons wishing to participate in the inquiry to register their interest and the part they wish to play. Rule 6 requires the Secretary of State to hold a pre-inquiry meeting, and enables the inspector to hold meetings other than pre-inquiry meetings. Rule 8 provides for an inquiry timetable to be agreed by the Secretary of State, and that the agreed timetable is not to be varied without his consent. Rule 10 enables the appointment of a technical adviser to assess expert evidence and report to the inspector on areas of disagreement. Rule 11 enables the appointment of a mediator to assist parties to reach agreement on matters relevant to the inquiry, or to define and narrow areas of disagreement. Rule 17 enables the inspector to curtail cross-examination if he considers that permitting cross-examination or allowing it to continue (as the case may be) would have the effect that the timetable agreed under r 8(1) could not be adhered to.

8.187 A Regulatory Impact Assessment has been prepared in relation to the Rules. This is placed in the libraries of both Houses of Parliament and is available from the Department. A Code has been produced for *Planning Inquiries into Major Projects* (ODPM Circ. 07/2005). See also the DETR's Code of Practice on the *Dissemination of Information during Major Infrastructure Developments* (1999).

Costs

8.188 DCLG Circ 3/09 outlines the opportunities for costs to be awarded against parties at inquiries where 'unreasonable behaviour' on one side has incurred unnecessary expense on the other.[1] The potential to make an award of costs arises from LGA 1972, s 250(5) as applied in various pieces of planning legislation as set out in Annex F of DCLG Circ 3/09. See DCLG Circ 3/09 on current guidance.

1   *Barking and Dagenham London Borough Council v East London Housing Association* (1988) 3 PAD 154. *R v Secretary of State for the Environment ex p Rochford DC* [2000] 3 All ER 1018. NB charges for information and advice before a formal planning application: *McCarthy & Stone (Developments) Ltd v London Borough of Richmond upon Thames* [1992] 2 AC 48, HL, reversing *R v Richmond-upon-Thames London Borough Council, ex p McCarthy & Stone (Developments) Ltd* [1992] 2 AC 48, CA.

Environmental impact assessments

8.189 Planning authorities shall not grant planning permission where an environmental impact assessment (EIA) application has been made by a developer until they have considered the environmental information relating to such application. They have to state in their decision that they have done so.[1] The relevant regulations are now SI 1999/293 and DETR Circular 2/99. These regulations extend the projects covered by EIAs and make a small number of procedural changes. These regulations have details on procedure and publicity requirements for EIAs.

1   TCPA 1990, s 71A; EC Council Directive 85/337/EEC, as amended by Directive 97/11/EC, 2003/35/EC and 2009/31/EC.

8.190 The House of Lords has treated compliance with the Directive as a strict requirement so there had been no EIA where a 'disparate collection of documents, produced by parties other than the developer and traceable by a process with a good deal of energy and persistence as satisfying the requirement to make available to the public the Annex III [of the Directive] information' had been made available. The EIA was an accessible compilation of the relevant environmental information and a summary in non-technical language, produced by the developer at the very start of the application process.[1]

1   *Berkeley v Secretary of State for the Environment* [2000] 3 All ER 897, HL. And see *R v Durham City Council, ex p Huddleston* [2000] 1 WLR 1484, CA, and the impact of the Directive on domestic law possessing indirect horizontal effect. A planning authority's decision that an EIA was not required was challengeable only on grounds of unreasonableness: *R (Jones) v Mansfield DC* [2003] EWCA Civ 1408, [2004] Env LR 21.

PUBLIC HEALTH, SAFETY AND ENVIRONMENTAL HEALTH

Emissions and discharges

8.191 Information and results about environmental quality, such as results from monitoring programmes for *some* air and water pollutants are available. These show national trends and local details. Levels of radioactive emissions are available, as are the volume of sewage dumped into the sea and the level of pesticides in shellfish taken from British waters. And there are public registers concerning planning decisions involving hazardous substances,[1] pesticides,[2] carriers of controlled waste[3] and environmental permitting.[4] The Pollution Prevention and Control Act 1999 (as amended by the Waste and Emissions Trading Act 2003 in relation to emissions trading schemes, and penalty provisions of UK Greenhouse Gas Emissions Trading Scheme 2005: see SIs 2005/925, 2005/2903 and 2010/1996 on the schemes, including the new aviation emissions scheme) has important provisions concerning prevention and control of pollution by regulation (and see Sch I, Part I). Special provision is made for emissions under exemptions under the Environmental Information Regulations 2004 (paras 8.204 et seq below).

[1] Planning (Hazardous Substances) Act 1990, s 28; The Planning (Hazardous Substances) Regulations 1992, SI 1992/656, especially reg 23; and DCLG Circ 04/00. See generally: *Garner's Environmental Law* (looseleaf, LexisNexis) and T Hayward *Constitutional Environmental Rights* (2004).
[2] On approved substances and other official notices.
[3] Control of Pollution (Amendment) Act 1989, s 2 and SI 1991/1624; cf Control of Pollution Act 1974, s 94.
[4] SI 2010/675 Environmental Permitting (England and Wales) Regulations 2010, Part 5 and Sch 24.

8.192 The difficulty with discharges concerns the secrecy surrounding pollution covered by individual discharges. The law provided protection to safeguard the trade and commercial secrets of polluters – but characteristically in such wide terms that the secrecy extended well beyond such a legitimate objective. As long ago as 1864, the Chief Alkali Inspector publicly expressed the view that 'every information regarding any work must be considered private, unless the publication is demanded by the Act or permitted by the owner'. The Alkali Inspectorate operates under a secrecy clause in the Health and Safety at Work etc Act 1974 (s 28(7)) prohibiting it from disclosing any information about air pollution from works which it controls (see below). A close relationship often exists between the inspectorate and the industry it polices, whereby secrecy has to be maintained to obtain the necessary level of information to make the inspectorate's existence viable in a 'co-operative venture'.

8.193 The Government in its Environmental Protection Act 1990 (EPA 1990) obliges enforcing authorities to disclose considerable information about the regulation of all activities which require an authorisation. SI 1991/507, regs 15–17 provide that a considerable amount of information should be made available regarding the activities of those who have sought authorisation under the EPA 1990, including details of any enforcement processes that have been undertaken.

The information must be available for inspection by the public at reasonable times and, on the payment of a reasonable fee, it must be possible to take copies. There are a number of circumstances in which information may be excluded, including commercial confidentiality and national security. The Act introduced an 'integrated pollution control' policed by HM Inspectorate of Pollution. The Environment Act 1995 (EA 1995) established the Environment Agency (EA) (and the Scottish Environment Protection Agency) which now carries out the Alkaline Inspectors' functions. They publish details of board meetings including meetings and discussions and agreed action. Only information on registers is publicly available[1] and much raw data, including some data displayed on maps, is made available via the Pollution Inventory and 'What's in Your Backyard?' system maintained by the EA.[2] EA 1995, Sch 11, para 4(1), (2) has provisions on public access to information about air quality held by local authorities.[3]

[1] This will include applications for authorisation; authorisations and any conditions attached; variation notices; information summary of operator's compliance record; enforcement of any prohibition notice served; information about completed court actions against operators; indications, where appropriate, of omitted information from the registers.

[2] The EA's power to require the provision of information on the discharge of pollutants is now to be found in reg 60 of the Environmental Permitting (England and Wales) Regulations 2010, SI 2010/675. The 'What's in Your Backyard' system can be found at http://maps.environment-agency.gov.uk/wiyby/wiybyController?ep=maptopics&lang=_e.

[3] See also: Pollution Prevention and Control Act 1999, s 2 and Sch 1, para 11. The US Environmental Protection Agency has power to gather, and make publicly available, information on air toxin emissions by industries, including emissions of CNCs. These relate to individual industries under a 1986 law. See UKELA on 'Freedom of Access to Information on the Environment' (1989) *Environmental Law* p 3.

8.194 Prosecutions under existing legislation for air pollution had averaged less than one a year.

8.195 EPA 1990, Part I (ss 1–28) concerns integrated pollution control and air pollution control by local authorities. Sections 13–19 deal with enforcement by means of enforcement and prohibition notices and appeals [against notices] as well as provision of information by authorities to the Secretary of State. Sections 20–22 deal with publicity (see also SI 1991/507) via public registers of authorisations and variation, enforcement and prohibition notices. Part II (ss 29–78) concerns waste on land and ss 64–66 deal with publicity via public registers with the exclusion of national security and confidential items. Part IIA (added by Environment Act 1995, s 57) concerns contaminated land, ss 78A–78V deal with remediation notices and appeals therefrom and duties of remediation and registers with the usual exclusions. Part VI concerns genetically modified substances. Sections 114–115 allow for inspections, ss 116–121 for enforcement powers and ss 122–123 for publicity.

8.196 The Clean Air Act 1993, Part II covers emissions of grit and dust from furnaces. Part V in ss 34–40 has detailed provisions on information about air pollution and Part VII has various miscellaneous provisions concerning unjustified disclosures of information (s 49) rights of entry and inspection (s 56) powers of a local authority to obtain information (s 58) and inquiries (s 59).

Water

8.197 The Water Act 1989, Part III which dealt with the control of water pollution was largely repealed by the Water Resources Act 1991 (WRA 1991)[1] and itself amended by the EA 1995. The responsibilities of the National Rivers Authority (NRA) were taken over by the Environment Agency (for regulation of water industries, see paras 8.303 et seq below). The NRA had responsibility for various registers transferred to it including water abstraction and impounding licences; water quality objectives, discharged consents to controlled waters and sampling results and waste management licences. These are now under the control of the EA.

[1]   See the Anti-Pollution Works Regulations 1999, SI 1999/1006.

8.198 The Water Act 2003 amends the Water Industry Act 1991 (WIA 1991) and has created the Water Services Regulation Authority (2003 Act, s 34 and Sch 1) to replace the DG of Water Supply, and further establishes the Consumer Council for Water (s 35 and Sch 2). The latter may have regional and other committees. Section 39 amends the statement of objectives and duties of the Authority, and s 40 concerns the issuing of guidance by the Secretary of State or Welsh Assembly to the authority on social and environmental matters. Sections 43–47 amend the WIA 1991 to set out the general functions of the Council, the provision of information to the Council , provision of statistical information to consumers, consumer complaints and Council investigations in water service.

8.199 Information about water pollution is now contained in the WRA 1991 as amended by the Water Act 2003. WRA 1991, Part VIII (ss 187–206) relates to information provisions: ss 187–188, as amended by Sch 22 to the EA 1995, concern annual reports and publication of information; ss 189–195 cover registers; ss 196–203 deal with provision of information by the authority to the Secretary of State, water undertakers etc, the EA's powers to obtain information and exchanges of information relating to pollution incidents; ss 204–205 impose restrictions on disclosure of information; and s 206 provides for making false statements. Furthermore, information concerning water or effluent samples taken by persons other than the authority may now be included (eg a discharger). Regulations set out the procedure to be followed in relation to consents under WRA 1991, Part III and where a discharge consent is granted by the agency without an application and appeals to the Secretary of State under WRA 1991, ss 91 and 191B in respect of consents under Chapter II, Part III of the Act and over information which the Agency has determined is not commercially confidential. Provision is further made in relation to pollution control registers under s 190 of the Act (see SI 1996/2971 and 2010/675).

General environmental provisions including the Environmental Information Regulations

8.200 The EA 1995 contains provisions concerning provision of information to the Minister and annual reports by the EA 1995 (ss 51–52), public inquiries (s 53), and provisions relating to the mutual disclosure of information between the EA, Ministers and local authorities (s 113).[1] EA 1995, Sch 11 concerns air quality reviews and other matters in relation to local authorities.

[1]   See EA 1995, Sch 11, para 4 on air quality and Sch 22 on amendments to the WRA 1991.

European law

8.201   The European Commission in October 1988 recommended a Directive introducing a wide-ranging public right of access to environmental information (9182/88 (Com) 484). This became Council Directive 90/313/EEC (7 June 1990). Member states would have to implement this within their own law within a specified period. This has now been superseded by Directive 2003/4/EC (OJ L 41/26) on public access to environmental information.

8.202   In 1992, the Houses of Parliament approved the Environmental Information Regulations 1992, SI 1992/3240 (as amended by SI 1998/1447) implementing the 1990 Directive.[1] The regulations applied to any information that relates to the environment (reg 2(2) held by a relevant person (reg 2(3)). There is an obligation to make such information available to any person who requested it and no restriction imposed on disclosure by any other law applies to disclosure under the regulations apart from reg 4. Regulation 4 concerns restrictions on disclosure relating to 'confidential' information which is expansively defined including information supplied voluntarily or in confidence and the person supplying does not consent to disclosure. These Regulations are now replaced by new 2004 Regulations implementing the 2003 Directive (below).

[1]   See *Freedom of Access to Information on the Environment* HL 9 (1996–97) First Report Select Committee on the European Communities.

8.203   The Consultation Document on the Freedom of Information (FOI) Bill[1] stated that the existing regulations would be repealed and replaced with an FOI access right. The general right will be modified to give effect to Directive 90/313/ EEC and the Aarhus Convention (the United Nations Economic Commission for Europe) on access to information, public participation in decision-making and access to justice in environmental matters signed by the UK in 1998.[2] Section 73 of the FOIA 2000 contains a power to make such a provision. The regulations will form a free-standing provision giving access to environmental information. Information available under these provisions will be exempt from access under the FOIA 2000. The regulations may provide for a code of practice to apply to bodies covered by the regulations and for the application of the Information Commissioner (IC)'s powers. The IC's enforcement powers and the use of the Information Tribunal have largely been applied (see ch 1). The Regulations will not apply to Scottish bodies under s 80; they will be covered by Scottish regulations.[3]

[1]   Cm 4355, May 1999, para 54.
[2]   See *Aarhus Convention*: Cm 4736, June 2000. See M Pallemaerts (ed) *The Aarhus Convention at Ten* (2011).
[3]   SSI 2004/520.

The Environmental Information Regulations 2004

8.204 The Environmental Information Regulations 2004 (EIR 2004), SI 2004/3391, came into effect on 1 January 2005 – the same date as the access provisions in FOIA 2000 (see ch 1). They implement Council Directive 2003/4/EC (OJ L 41/26).[1] Any directly enforceable rights under the Directive will be enforceable through domestic courts if such rights have not been properly implemented into UK laws. The regulations will operate in tandem with FOIA 2000, but information available under the regulations is exempt from FOIA 2000. Crucially, the power of ministerial veto under FOIA 2000, s 53 is retained under the regulations (reg 18(6)). Requests for information do not have to be in writing as under FOIA 2000. The range of bodies covered by EIR 2004 is wider than that in FOIA 2000. The regulations apply to all information held by a public authority (PA) covered by the regulations and there is no exemption where the cost of compliance exceeds an 'appropriate limit' as under FOIA 2000, s 12 (para 1.71 above). There are no absolute exemptions. There is a 20-working-day period for responding to all requests including those involving consideration of the public interest, although an extension from 20 to 40 days is allowed for complicated and high-volume requests. Bodies covered by the regulations must have a complaints and reconsideration procedure for allegations of non-compliance. All exemptions are subject to a public interest test and special provisions relate to emissions (below). The 'exceptions' (exemptions) differ from FOIA 2000 exemptions although similarities and differences have been discussed in case law.

[1] On the regulation for EU institutions see Regulation EC 1367/2006 EP and Council 6 September 2006 (OJ L 264/13 (25.9.06). Also relevant are the INSPIRE Regulations 2009, SI 2009/3157, which transposed the 2007 EU INSPIRE Directive, which aims to improve environmental policy-making in Europe. Member states are required to make available in a consistent format spatial data sets within the scope of the Directive, and create services for accessing these data sets. Doing so will enable data sets to be more easily shared and facilitate the development and monitoring of environmental policy and practice in member states and across the EU.

8.205 According to guidance prepared by Defra (the sponsoring authority), 'any request, wherever it comes from, and whatever form it takes, will be a valid request for environmental information so long as the information requested is environmental'. If the information is not environmental, another governing regime such as FOIA 2000 will have to be considered. The authority, and not the applicant, has to identify which regime is operable and relevant where a request is made for information. An applicant may specify that the request is under the EIR 2004 but this is not conclusive on the public authority (PA) if it is not correct. Chapter 6 of the updated guidance on EIR 2004 has details on processing applications.[1] Procedures for dealing with requests must be published, and chapter 6 of the guidance also provides detailed guidance on transferring requests to other PAs and what should be done in the event of a request for records transferred to the National Archives or NI Public Records Office.

[1] http://archive.defra.gov.uk/corporate/policy/opengov/eir/guidance/full-guidance/pdf/guidance-6.pdf.

8.206 There are numerous cases where the IC or tribunal has ruled that the PA has dealt with a request for information under the wrong regime: in FS50227038, which concerned the Office of the First Minister and Deputy First Minister, the request should have been decided under EIR 2004, not FOIA 2000, s 35, See also FER50092316 and *B Archer v IC and Salisbury DC* EA/2006/0037.

8.207 The draft guidance has contains the following chapters: Who is covered?; What is covered?; What do the EIR 2004 require public and other authorities to do?; Proactive dissemination; Handling requests; Refusals; Complaints, Reconsideration and Appeals; Records Management and Offences; and Monitoring and Reporting.

8.208 There is also a code of practice issued in accordance with EIR 2004, reg 16. This gives advice on 'desirable' practice. It is not legally binding: failure to follow the code will render it difficult for bodies to comply with their legal obligations, the foreword to the code advises. It may be departed from for good reasons which can be justified to the Information Commissioner. The code offers advice on training, advice and assistance to requesters, on clarifying the request while indicating that requesters are unlikely to have identifiers such as file reference numbers. Because there is no equivalent of FOIA 2000, s 12 (para 1.71 above), an authority is expected to deal with all requests for environmental information 'regardless of the cost'. 'Unreasonable' requests may be refused under an exception (below). There are no provisions dealing with organised campaigns as under FOIA 2000 (para 1.74 above). The code offers advice on charges, timely responses and has detailed provisions on transfers of requests to other authorities (see para 1.96 above). The foreword to the code spells out the powers of the IC to issue practice directions and information notices (paras 1.20, 1.147 and 1.165 above). The code provides guidance on copyright, which is likely to be very important in some environmental information: www.hmso. gov.uk/copyright/managing_copyright.htm and www.hmso.gov.uk/copyright/ guidance/gn_19.htm on advice on licensing under FOIA 2000 requests.

8.209 The code also gives advice on requests for information shared with third parties: there is no duty to consult third parties but a commitment to do so may be made. There is also advice on public sector contracts which mirrors that in the earlier FOIA code under FOIA 2000, s 45. Authorities should refuse to enter agreements that purport to restrict rights of access under EIR 2004 (code, para 47). Confidentiality clauses should be rejected where they relate to contractual terms, a contract's value and performance. The public interest test should be explained to contractors and, as in FOIA 2000, a schedule may be used to identify information which should not be disclosed (paras 1.188 et seq above). But such schedules are not immune from EIR 2004 obligations and rights (para 48). 'In any event, PAs should not agree to hold information 'in confidence' which is not confidential in nature' (para 49). This looks like the more robust version of the earlier s 45 code. Commercial confidentiality and voluntarily supplied data (below) are not excepted (exempt) when the information relates to emissions, although the non-exception is not restricted to these categories (below). The PA should not agree to accept and hold information from third parties 'in confidence' unless it is confidential in nature (para 51).

SCOPE

8.210 The regulations implement the Directive's definition of environmental information (EI),[1] which is very wide and includes written, electronic, visual or audio information on:

1. the state of the elements of the environment, such as air, atmosphere, water, soil, land, landscape and natural sites, biological diversity and its components, including genetically modified organisms and the interaction among these elements;

2. factors affecting or likely to affect the environment referred to in 1 above such as substances, energy, noise, radiation or waste, including radioactive waste, emissions, discharges and other releases;

3. measures (including administrative measures) such as policies, legislation, plans, programmes, environmental agreements, and activities affecting or likely to affect the elements and factors in 1 and 2 above as well as measures or activities designed to protect those elements;

4. reports on the implementation of environmental legislation;

5. cost–benefit and other economic analyses and assumptions used within the framework of environmental measures and activities referred to in 3 above;

6. the state of human health and safety, including the contamination of the food chain, where relevant, conditions of human life, cultural sites and built structures in as much as they are or may be affected by the state of the environment, or factors, measures or activities affecting the environment.

[1] Directive 2003/4/EC OJ L 41/26 (14.2.03), recital 10 and Art 2(1). For case-law under the 1992 Regulations, see: *R v British Coal Corporation ex p Ibstock Building Products Ltd* [1995] JPL 836 (a strange decision re informers) and *R v Secretary of State for the Environment etc ex p Alliance against the Birmingham Northern Relief Road and Others* Case No: CO/4553/98 QBD. See also Case C-321/96 17/6/1998.

8.211 The definition does not include 'non-existent information ... which could be created by manipulating existing information' or information that does not exist until further research is carried out' (Defra guidance, para 3.7). There is no time limit on historical data. The regulations cover EI 'no matter when the information was created or gathered' (para 3.9).

8.212 There appear to be no geographical limitations to these definitions of EI. The code of practice and the draft guidance have helpful advice on the definition and scope.

PUBLIC AUTHORITIES

8.213 Definitions of public authorities (PA) are those used in FOIA 2000, s 3(1) (para 1.85 above) but Scottish authorities are defined by Scottish measures (SSI 2004/520). The Scottish regulations make modifications for the devolved regime, but the general framework is the same – implementation is an EU requirement. The definition in the UK measures initially included 'any other body or authority exercising statutory functions on behalf of the Crown' but this disappeared from the final regulations. The definition of 'public authorities' in the Directive, Art 2.2 is quite broad. A government department is to be treated as a person separate from any other government department for the purposes of EIR 2004, Parts 2, 4 and 5. There are special provisions for those listed in FOIA 2000, Sch 1 as 'designated bodies' under s 5 so that such bodies designated and falling within a 'specified description', or only covered by FOIA 2000 in relation to 'information of a specified description', are not public authorities under these regulations. The exclusions relating to the intelligence and security services under FOIA 2000 seem to apply unless they are caught by the expression: a body carrying out 'functions of public administration' (EIR 2004, reg 2(2)(c)). Presumably this will not cover operations and security-sensitive items. The draft guidance specified that the services are covered, but in a passage that is rather opaque (para 2.9). This was removed from the final version. An exception may be claimed on grounds of national security. The exclusion in FOIA 2000, Sch 1, para 6 relating to the special services and those units providing assistance to General Communications HQ is specifically removed. The definition includes any other body, office holder or person (except a Scottish public authority which are to be covered by Scottish measures: SSI 2004/520) 'that carries out functions of public administration' (reg 2(1)). The definition includes any other body, office holder or person (except Scottish public authority) that is under the control of a body, office holder or person falling within the above definitions and that in relation to the environment:

i)   has public responsibilities
ii) exercises functions of a public nature
iii) provides public services.

8.214 Would this latter definition include utilities as providers of public services and which are under licence from the state and which are state regulated? It would appear to cover private companies in which public bodies hold majority or controlling shares and arguably those bodies or individuals under contract with government to perform public duties. There will doubtless be much testing of these points before the Information Commissioner, the tribunal and the courts. The guidance dated July 2010 (which offers 'guidance' and not legally binding instructions) says in para 2.22 that the EIR 2004 include private companies and certain PPPs engaged in water, waste, transport and energy sectors. Utility companies are covered. It may also cover environmental consultants. The code of practice also describes 'control' as a 'relationship constituted by statute, regulations, rights, licence, contracts or other means which either separately or jointly confer the possibility of directly or indirectly exercising a decisive influence on a body' (code, para 2.4). Private companies 'sufficiently associated' with the activities of the government so that they owe similar environmental obligations 'have responsibilities under EIR 2004' (ibid). A contractual relationship is not decisive per se: it will depend upon the terms and nature of the contractual relationship: 'the merits'. On transparency and reporting on sustainability issues, see www.defra.gov.uk/environment/envrp/index.htm.

8.215 In *Network Rail Ltd v IC and NRI Ltd* EA/2006/0061-62 the tribunal, overruling the IC (FER 0087031) ruled that Network Rail is not a PA under the EIR 2004. Under FOIA 2000 PAs are identified in the Schedule to the Act.

This is not the case under EIR 2004 because it is open to the IC or tribunal to use the EIR criteria to argue that a body not covered by FOIA is a PA under the EIR. The case concerned EIR 2004, reg 2. The tribunal was influenced by case law concerning Network Rail under the HRA 1998, which raises different points to the case in question. In its initial statements of FOIA developments, the coalition government stated that Network Rail was a prime candidate for designation as a PA under FOIA. If designated as a PA under FOIA this would also make it a PA under EIR 2004. As of writing this commitment has not been acted upon. In *Port of London Authority (PLA) v IC & another* EA/2006/0083 the tribunal decided that the Port of London Authority was a PA for EIR purposes even though not scheduled under FOIA 2000. The UN Economic Commission for Europe's Implementation Guide to the Aarhus Convention and DEFRA's guide were adverted to for guidance. The cases have distinguishing features on the merits and there was a statutory underpinning to the PLA's functions and a notable influence by government in appointments and in its loans. The PLA refers to itself in its contracts as a PA. The relevant function was public and was covered by statute. The IC has also decided that a housing association is a public authority under EIR 2004 (FER149772). The tribunal has ruled that the Duchy of Lancaster is not a PA for the purpose of EIR 2004 (*J Cross v IC* EA/2010/0101). However, in *M Bruton v The IC and The Duchy of Cornwall* EA 2010/0182 the tribunal ruled that the Duchy was a PA for the purposes of the EIR. In *Smartsource v IC etc* [2010] UKUT 415 (AAC) the Upper Tribunal (on a case transferred from the First Tier Tribunal to the Upper Tribunal) ruled that privatised water and water and sewerage companies in England and Wales are not PAs under EIR 2004. The Upper Tribunal heard the appeal although technically it was an appeal from a decision letter, not a decision notice. The Aarhus Convention: An Implementation Guide (ECE (UN) (2000) stated that, 'The Convention tries to make it clear that such innovations (privatising the provision of public services) cannot take public services out of the realm of public involvement, information and participation.' The tribunal was heavily influenced by case law under HRA 1998.[1] The fact that the water companies had to provide a universal continuing service under special conditions, have special public interest powers and were restricted in stopping a service for non-payment of rates did not promote them into a service providing public administrative services. Although highly regulated, they were not subject to control by PAs. They were not subject to the EIR 2004. Given the objective of transparency in the EIR 2004, we submit that this ruling is deficient and the policy of the Directive and Aarhus would be better served by treating providers of universal public services connected to the environment as covered by EIR 2004 whatever their legal status. The concern should not be on formal definitions of the 'state' but on transparency in the provision of essential services.

[1]   *Cameron v Network Rail Infrastructure Ltd* [2006] EWHC 1133 (QB) and *YL v Birmingham City Council* [2007] UKHL 27.

'HISTORICAL RECORDS' AND 'WORKING DAY'

8.216   These terms have the same meaning as in FOIA 2000 (see paras 2.64 and 1.75). Data, data subject, data protection principles and personal data have the same meanings as in the DPA 1998 (see ch 7). The Code of Practice and the guidance provide advice on dealing with records transferred to National Archives or the NI Public Records Office.

HOLDING INFORMATION

8.217 EIR 2004 apply to a PA that 'holds' environmental information. It is not confined to information in its possession but includes that which it may hold on behalf of another (cf para 1.85). It holds information which is in its possession but which it has produced or has received from another or which is held by another person (not simply an authority) on behalf of the authority. The guidance states that the Regulations do not apply to privately owned archives deposited in a public sector archives office for preservation where those archives, if not so deposited, would not be subject to the EIR 2004 (Guidance, para 6.19). The Regulations do not apply to any public authority to the extent that it is acting in a judicial or legislative capacity. This will cover the courts and presumably tribunals, and Parliament. The guidance includes, inter alia, ombudsmen, the Planning Inspectorate, the Council (sic) for Racial Equality and Social Services Complaints panels. Non-application should not be taken to cover administrative functions. These bodies are not a part of the 'judicial arm of the state'.[1] The Regulations do not apply to either House of Parliament 'to the extent required for the purpose of avoiding an infringement of their privileges'. The case law has shown that PAs may have to engage in onerous exercises to establish who holds information under EIR 2004: *I Bickford Smith v IC* EA/2010/0032.

[1]   *A-G v BBC* [1981] AC 303.

PRO-ACTIVE AVAILABILITY

8.218 Public authorities shall, in respect of EI that they hold, progressively make the EI available to the public by electronic means which are easily accessible,[1] and take reasonable steps to organise the information relevant to its functions with a view to the active and systematic dissemination to the public of such information. EIR 2004, reg 4 states this will not apply to excepted information under reg 12 (below). The information will include that referred to in Art 7(2) of the Directive: texts of international treaties, conventions or agreements, and of Community, national, regional or local legislation, on or relating to the environment; policies, plans and programmes relating to the environment ; progress reports on the implementation of the previous two items when held or prepared in electronic form; state of the environment reports from national, regional or local bodies which should be conducted at least every four years and which deal with the quality and pressures on the environment; data or summaries of data derived from the monitoring of activities affecting or likely to affect the environment; authorisations with a significant impact on the environment and environmental agreements or a reference to the place where such information can be requested or found in the framework of Art 3 of the Directive (the access provision); environmental impact studies and risk assessments concerning the environmental elements referred to in Art 2(1)(a) or a reference to where the information may be found. The information has also to include the facts and analyses of facts which the public authority considers relevant and important in framing major environmental policy proposals. Guidance has been published on the use of publication schemes to make information pro-actively available.[2]

¹   This will not apply to information collected before 1 January 2005 in non-electronic form.
²   http://www.defra.gov.uk/corporate/policy/opengov/eir/pdf/article7report.pdf.

REQUESTS

8.219   EIR 2004, reg 5 provides that public authorities are under a duty to provide on request environmental information that they hold. This is subject to reg 12(3) which states that, where the applicant is seeking personal data on him or herself, the duty does not apply; an applicant will have to invoke the DPA 1998 (ch 7 above). The duty is in accordance with stipulations laid down in the Regulations as well as exceptions. Information shall be made available as soon as possible and not later than 20 days after the date of receipt of the request. By reg 7 this period may be extended to 40 working days 'if [the PA] reasonably believes that the complexity or volume of the information requested means that it is impracticable either to comply with the request within the earlier period or to make a decision to refuse to do so'. The applicant must be informed of this as soon as possible and not later than 20 working days after the receipt of the request. Information compiled by the authority shall be up to date, accurate and comparable 'so far as the public authority reasonably believes'. Where the information made available comprises 'factors such as substances, energy, noise, radiation or waste, including radioactive waste, emissions, discharges and other releases into the environment, affecting or likely to affect the elements of the environment' set out in reg 2(1)(a) then, if the applicant so requests, the public authority must inform the applicant of the place where information can be found on the measurement procedures, including methods of analysis, sampling, and pre-treatment of samples, used in compiling the information, or refer the applicant to the standardised procedures used. This duty is subject to the capability of the authority 'to do so'.

8.220   As is common elsewhere, any enactment or rule of law that would prevent disclosure of information under these regulations – apart from the exceptions within the regulations – shall not apply. This would include the 1989 Official Secrets Act.

8.221   Information shall be made available in the format requested unless it is reasonable to make the information available in another format or form, or the information is already publicly available and easily accessible to the applicant in another form or format. The guidance states that information may be requested in writing, by email, orally over the telephone or during a meeting or by sign language although no advice is offered on the latter (Guidance, chapter 6, introduction). Where information is not made available in the form or format requested, the PA shall explain the reason for its decision as soon as possible and not later than 20 working days after date of the receipt of the request for the information (extendable to 40 days under reg 7 (above)); provide the explanation if the applicant so requests and inform the applicant of the contents of reg 11 to make representations and to engage in a reconsideration (below) and also of the enforcement and appeal provisions in reg 18. Under reg 14, a refusals notice in writing must be issued where information is denied under reg 12(1) or 13(1). These must state the reasons for refusal and any exceptions under regs 12(4), (5) or 13, matters considered in reaching a public interest decision under reg 12(1) (b) or under regs 13(2)(a)(ii) or 13(3) where applicable.

CHARGES

8.222 Charges may be made for making the information available. Details on charging provisions are contained in the Code of Practice (pp 13–14) and in the guidance (ch 6). Charges do not have to be imposed but, where they are, they should be 'reasonable'.

8.223 PAs shall not charge for allowing an applicant to access any public registers or lists of environmental information held by the PA such as on the Pollutant Release and Transfers Register. The Sustainable Development Unit maintains a register of Environmental Registers as required under EC Directive 2003/4/EC, Art 3(5)(c). Nor can PAs charge for making information available for examination on their premises. Any charges shall not exceed an amount which the PA is satisfied is a reasonable amount. This would be stricter than the *Wednesbury* test as developed by the *Tameside* decision: 'reasonable amount' connotes objective criteria.[1] An advance payment may be requested and the PA shall notify the applicant of the amount required. If such a notification is given, the PA is not required to make the information requested available or to comply with EIR 2004, reg 6 (form or format) or reg 14 (requirements when refusing information and issuing a refusal notice), unless the charge is paid no later than 60 working days after the date on which the PA gave the notification. In computing the 20-day period, the day of giving a notice and the day on which payment is received by the PA are disregarded. PAs must make available a schedule of its charges and information on the circumstances in which a charge may be levied or waived.

[1] *Associated Provincial Pictures Houses Ltd v Wednesbury Corporation* [1948] 1 KB 223; *Secretary of State for Education and Science v Tameside MBC* [1977] AC 1014.

8.224 In FER0314876 the complainant submitted a request to Chichester District Council ('the council') for information from environmental records held on a property in Chichester. The complainant specified that he wished to view the records in person. The council agreed to provide the information requested but only on the provision of a set fee. The Commissioner's decision is that the council failed to comply with reg 5(1) as it failed to make information available on request, and reg 5(2) as it failed to make it available within the statutory time for compliance. The council breached reg 6(1) by failing to comply with the complainant's request to make the requested information available in a particular format. The council has also breached reg 8(2)(b) by attempting to impose a charge for allowing the complainant to inspect some of the requested information. The Commissioner required the council to make the requested information available for the complainant to inspect within 35 days of this notice. In *East Riding of Yorkshire Council v Information Commissioner and Stanley Davis Group Limited t/a York Place* EA/2009/0069, York Place was a company specialising in the obtainment of information for home buyers/sellers. It, like many other such companies, would often obtain information by making requests about planned activities in the vicinity of a client's property (eg road changes, planning consents, etc). In this respect the Law Society developed a standard from known as Form CON29R which could be sent to councils to request the relevant information. The request in this instance was to make arrangements in order to inspect the records for highways and traffic schemes within 200 metres of the property. The request was rejected and the appellant argued that it should be treated as a request under either FOIA 2000 or EIR 2004. Later, all parties accepted that the EIR applied. The IC decided that the information did fall within the EIR and that none of the exceptions applied. However, because the information was not in a form which enabled it to be inspected without further collation by the council, it argued that it was entitled to provide the information in a collated document and impose a reasonable charge for doing so, relying on EIR 2004, regs 6(1), 8(1) and (2). The IC did not agree: the council was required to allow inspection and could make no charge for doing so. The council appealed to the tribunal. It argued that the reasonableness test contained in reg 6 should be applied to a request to inspect, not just the information needed to answer the questions on the form. Further, it was reasonable for it to make the information available in another format. The issues were: (a) whether the request was for inspection of all council records relating schemes in the 200m vicinity; (b) whether York Place had an unqualified right to inspect; (c) whether reg 6 permitted the council to check, collate and redact the information and provide a hard copy if there was no unqualified right to inspect; and (d) whether it was reasonable to charge for a hard copy. On the first issue, considering the factual matrix and the nature of the CON29R form, the tribunal found that the request was for the information which was required to answer the questions. As regards the unqualified right of inspection, on reading the EIR as a whole and notwithstanding the wording of EU Directive 2003/4 ('the establishment and maintenance of facilities for the examination of the information required'), there was no such right. Regulation 8(2) allows the requestor to express a preference which may be overridden by the public authority under reg 6. The council made several arguments as to why it was unreasonable for York Place to inspect: (a) personal data would be visible on inspection; (b) the security and integrity of the network would be put at risk; (c) some of the records would be unintelligible to an untrained reader; (d) the software licence was limited to ten users at any particular time, which covered only use by council staff. The tribunal rejected all of these arguments as either not evidenced, or not having been sufficiently investigated for alternatives. The council was not entitled to force York Place to accept the information in a documentary format; it should have allowed inspection free of charge (see also *Castle Point BC v IC* EA/2010/0040).

8.225 As under FOIA 2000, PAs shall provide advice and assistance to applicants and prospective applicants 'so far as it would be reasonable to expect the PA to do so' (EIR 2004, reg 9). Where requests are formulated too generally, the PA may request the applicant to provide more particulars in relation to the request, again the PA request should be 'as soon as possible' and not later than 20 days after date of receipt of the request and it must assist the applicant. Compliance with a Code of Practice under EIR 2004, reg 16 by a PA shall be taken as compliance with this regulation.

8.226 EIR 2004, reg 10 allows for the transfer of requests between PAs, including Scottish PAs, as well as supply of relevant addresses to the applicant. The date of receipt of a transferred request by a PA for the purposes of regs 5(2), 6(2)(a) and 14(2) is the date on which it receives the request. The code of practice and guidance have advice on these matters.

THE RELATIONSHIP BETWEEN FOIA 2000 AND EIR 2004

8.227 The belief was that the EIR 2004 created, as a result of EU obligations, a self-contained code dealing with environmental information (EI). Where EI was involved, the Regulations and not FOIA 2000 would operate. This made good sense. Under FOIA 2000 s 9, EI is not an absolute exemption, but as EIR contains its own PI test for all exceptions there is no room for the operation of the PI test under FOIA. Section 39(3) does not limit the 'generality of FOIA 2000, s 21(1) – information applicable to applicant by other means (para 1.111 et seq) – so s 21 can apply in EIR cases. The tribunal has had difficulties in understanding the relationship between the two codes (*Rhondda Cynon Taff CBC v IC* EA/2007/0065) and has argued that FOIA still has a role to play over and above s 21. If this were the case, a form of ping-pong would take place under different regimes involving, very likely, the same officials. The sensible and accurate position here is that the EIR 2004 governs the situation regarding EI.[1] In FER0359156, a local authority claimed FOIA 2000, s 42 in relation to a paper that had been before a planning committee held in public. Any confidentiality and privilege had been lost by the paper becoming public and that the EIRs governed the case. Breaches of regs 5 and 14 were establsihed.

[1]   P Birkinshaw *Freedom of Information: the Law, the Practice and the Ideal* (4th edn, 2010) pp 245–256.

EXCEPTIONS TO DUTY OF DISCLOSURE

8.228 The exceptions to disclosure are contained in EIR 2004, reg 12. The Defra draft guidance has some constructive comments on the exceptions. The exceptions are to be construed restrictively in accordance with Directive 2003/4/EC, Art 4 (and see reg 12(2) below). The code of practice also advises that in stating an exception PAs should not simply 'paraphrase the wording of the exception' like the earlier version of the s 45 code. Regulation 20 amends FOIA 2000, s 39 to take account of the existence of the Regulations – information available under the Regulations, subject to exceptions, is exempt under FOIA 2000 (para 8.227 above). A PA may refuse to disclose EI requested if an exception identified in reg 12(4) and (5) (below) is present and 'in all the circumstances of the case, the public interest in maintaining the exception outweighs the public interest in disclosing the information (reg 12(1)). The PI applies in all exceptions under reg 12(1)(b). As with FOIA, the case for secrecy has to outweigh that for disclosure, so in an even balance, disclosure prevails. The guidance provides advice on weighing the public interests (paras 7.102–7.111) recommending that information should be redacted wherever possible. It will also be very important to consider any human rights aspects of access to information under the HRA 1998 (see paras 9.146 et seq below). Regulation 12(2) states that 'A PA shall apply a presumption in favour of disclosure.' Personal data referring to the applicant are dealt with under the DPA. Personal data requested which do not refer to the applicant are dealt with in accordance with reg 13 (below).

Regulation 12(4)

8.229 A PA may (it possesses a discretion) refuse to disclose EI under EIR 2004, reg 12(4) where:

- it does not hold that information when an applicant's request is received (reg 12(4)(a));
- the request for information is 'manifestly unreasonable' – this would suggest a test that is satisfied immediately and unchallengeably. It would have to be a blatant abuse on the part of the applicant and not simply a difficult request (reg 12(4)(b));
- the request is formulated in too broad a manner and reg 9 (above) has been complied with (reg 12(4)(c));
- the request refers to documents in the course of completion, that are 'unfinished' or are incomplete data. In other words the documents are premature and need to be finalised; there is no requirement that disclosure would be misleading. In short, a policy is still being developed or the statistics or material are not complete. Even where documents are incomplete, it may be possible to disclose information that is finalised. This will raise difficult questions(reg 12(4)(d));
- the request is for disclosure of 'internal communications'; the exception does not require the reasonable opinion of a qualified person to be sought but FOIA 2000, s 36 should be followed (see paras 1.182 et seq above). For the purposes of this exception 'internal communications' includes communications between government departments (reg 12(8)). In FS50261661 the IC ruled that reg 12(4)e does not protect info received from other councils (reg 12(4)(e)).

8.230 Case law (i) In FER0112249 the complainant requested information regarding the distribution of European Union Common Agricultural Policy subsidies by DEFRA. The public authority refused disclosure, arguing that reg 12(4)(b) applied because the request was manifestly unreasonable in that it required extensive and costly extraction. However, the complainant had expressed a willingness to extract the information himself; therefore the Commissioner found that reg 12 was not engaged. *Stephen Carpenter v IC and Stevenage Borough*

Council EA/2008/0046 concerned FOIA and EIR. Mr Carpenter requested information from the council regarding the council's sale of land to a company which then obtained planning permission and resold the land for a significant profit. The requests were refused on the grounds that they were vexatious for the purposes of FOIA 2000, s 14 or manifestly unreasonable under EIR 2004, regs 12(1) and 12(4)(b). The tribunal decided that the requests were manifestly unreasonable because: (i) they were far too frequent – there were ten requests within 12 days; (ii) the requests were very similar in nature; (iii) the requests were 'threatening, intemperate and harassing'; (iv) much of the documentation had already been provided and the requests were therefore evidence of an obsessive and unreasonable attitude. In *Dr K Little v IC* EA/2010/0072 information was correctly denied under reg 12(4)(b) when the Welsh Assembly refused to disclose information about wind farms.

8.231   Case law (ii) In FS50156849, reg 12(4)(d) did not apply because the information was not 'material in the course of completion'; the final version of the study had already been completed. *Cabinet Office v IC* EA/2010/0027 discussed a request for information relating to the policy on nuclear new-build that was initially raised in a white paper in 2003 and which featured eventually in the high court decision in the *Greenpeace* case (para 8.271). The Government was ruled to have acted unlawfully because of inadequate consultation and information.

8.232   Case law (iii) Information was refused under FOIA 2000, s 40 and EIR 2004, reg 12(4)(e) – in the latter case to protect ministerial communications and collective responsibility and civil servant advice (internal communications). The tribunal ruled that information had to be released subject to some redactions and removal of written comments on the papers. *DEFRA v IC* EA/2009/0011 concerned a request for the minutes of meetings between Lord Hunt and Mayor Johnson of London on air quality. Regulation 12(4)(e) was invoked. Information was released but some was withheld. Counsel for an additional party wished to see the redacted material in order to participate effectively in the closed session of the tribunal. This would be subject to a 'confidentiality ring', ie he would not pass on the information or its contents to anyone else including his client. This, although permissible under the tribunal's rules, was denied and the decision is subject to an appeal to the Upper Tribunal. In *Friends of the Earth v IC & Export Credit Guarantee Dept* EA/2006/0073 (ECGD) information was requested on whether EIR 2004 properly implemented Directive 2003/4/EC in relation to 'internal communications' in reg 12(4)(e). This provides an exception where 'the request involves the disclosure of internal communications'. By 12(8) it is provided 'internal communications includes communications between government departments.' Friends of the Earth requested from ECGD information about the application of credit in respect of the Sakhalin project and specifically correspondence circulating among departments about the 'sensitive' project concerning oil and gas development off a Russian island north of Japan and the risk presented thereby to the Western Grey Whale. Evidence to the Information Tribunal spelt out the huge environmental and social concerns in addition to concern about the whales themselves. The request was denied on the basis of reg 12(4)(e) to protect confidentiality and collective decision-making in government. The IC in his DN held that internal communications covered communications within a department as well as between departments. He upheld their decision on PI grounds. The IT accepted that the exemption applied to a public authority comprising several departments. The IT believed that the PI in withholding the information did not outweigh that in disclosure. The IT did not want to engage in a comparative discussion of FOIA 2000, s 35 and EIR 2004, reg 12(4)(e): 'the onus being to specify clearly and precisely the harm or harms that would be caused were disclosure to be ordered. If no such harm can clearly be made out given the effect and terms of Reg 12(2), the balance must fall in favour of disclosure under the test in Reg 12(1)(b)' (para 53). The PI put forward by ECGD included collective responsibility and candour. The former is not a 'trump card'. The 'touchstone is the public interest' (para 57). 'Life after FOIA has changed and had to change' (para 61). The minister is accountable but it is not only his final decision which has to be scrutinised. Timing of a request is a factor to be considered. 'Arguably EIR may set a higher test in establishing an exception [than FOIA] and a general resort to the "chilling effect" on record keeping. The IT observed "officials in all public authorities as well as Ministers in government should now be fully aware of the risk that in a given case their notes and records, and indeed all exchanges in whatever form, are in principle susceptible to a request or order for disclosure" (para 61). The project was not in its infancy or in any way preliminary and there was an undisputed public debate regarding all issues in the project. However, showing disunity in government would be unlikely to add weight to the PI in disclosure. No real prejudice was shown to decision-making and there was a genuine public interest in the discussion and the information would enable the public better to understand an important issue. Two years had passed between the request for comments and the request for information. No evidence was presented of harm arising in 2005 of discussions in 2003. The existence of a large amount of published evidence/information was not relevant in this case – the requested information itself was not in the public domain. An appeal to the High Court from the tribunal was unsuccessful (*ECGD v Friends of the Earth* [2008] EWHC 638 (Admin)). See *South Gloucestershire Council v IC and Bovis Homes Ltd* EA/2009/0032 (below) on reg 12(4)(e) and FS50224707.

8.233 Case law (iv) *Lord Baker v IC and DCLG* EA/2006/0043 also involved EIR 2004, reg 12(4)(e). There had been a request for information relating to officials' submissions made to the Deputy Prime Minister following the report of the inspector in the application to build Vauxhall Tower. The Deputy Prime Minister allowed permission to build and did not accept the inspector's recommendation. In *Bushell v Secretary of State for the Environment* [1981] AC 75 the House of Lords ruled that it was not unfair for the minister to take into account new factual evidence from within his department and to refuse to re-open the inquiry where the new evidence was part of the underlying reason for making a decision and there was no disagreement between the inspector's recommendations and the minister's decision. The advice in *Baker* from officials was received before the Deputy Prime Minister overruled the inspector. The IC said submissions as a whole should have been disclosed but officials' advice should not be. There were familiar arguments from the department about a loss of candour if disclosure were allowed. The tribunal ruled that disclosure of advice and opinions after a decision was made public would not undermine to any significant extent the proper and effective performance of officials' duties. The PI did not weigh in favour of non-disclosure. Local government has been used to openness and access to information and has worked effectively; why should central government be treated differently queried the tribunal? In FER50092316 the complainant requested information relating to Luton Airport and the South East and East of England Regional Air Services Study ('SERAS'). Specifically he requested any information provided to ministers as a basis for decisions on which options to take forward for Luton Airport for appraisal in stage two of the SERAS study, together with any records of the ministers' decisions and the reasons for them. After some correspondence the Department for Transport (DfT) informed the IC that it was relying upon reg 12(4)(e) to withhold the information in question. The IC decided that reg 12(4)(e) was correctly relied upon. He then considered the public interest as required by reg 12(1)(b). The arguments of the DfT were as follows:

(a) That reg 12(4)(e) recognised the need for 'self-contained space' for consideration of different policy options; that disclosure would be unhelpful and prejudicial because some of the issues were of a highly sensitive and controversial nature; that disclosure could reveal confidential policy and commercial priorities which might limit impartiality and collective responsibility. All of these arguments were rejected by the IC who acknowledged that the timing of a request is an important consideration (the instant case being four years). Once a decision has been made, the risk of disclosure prejudicing the policy process is likely to be reduced.

(b) That public consultation and debate were only appropriate before policy-making. However, the IC thought that disclosure would help inform a necessary continued debate.

(c) That part of the information may have had a doubtful veracity and disclosure could have undermined other government policy. On the contrary, the IC prioritised transparency and the correction of false assumptions.

(d) That the information may have misrepresented more contemporary government thinking. This was rejected because the fact that information may be misleading or inaccurate is not a legitimate basis for withholding it.

(e) That the commercial interests of both the then current and future airport's operator would be protected by non-disclosure. The lapse of time was considered to negate this.

In para 41, the IC stated: 'The IC acknowledges that the timing of a request is a very important consideration in this type of situation where different policy options are being examined and debated … once a decision has been made on the policy … the risk of disclosure prejudicing the policy process is likely to be reduced.' Information relates to meetings occurring in 2001. No detailed evidence was given to the IC of harm from disclosure. Disclosure of information can still be useful after a policy has been announced to inform continuing debate. There is no PI in not revealing information because it may disclose that government assumptions were misplaced. Disclosure would help 'ensure transparency' (para 48). The IC was unpersuaded that commercial interests of airport operators would be detrimentally affected or that disclosure would lead to future lack of co-operation. The IC considered that where the government policies 'could have such wide-ranging and serious implications on people's lives, the environment and the economy', that the public interest was clearly in favour of disclosure. Disclosure would allow a 'more informed debate' on important issues (para 65). The balancing test came down in favour of non-disclosure in a case involving Nirex – the former adviser on nuclear waste and now brought within the Nuclear Decommissioning Authority: see FER0178729. In FS50156849, reg 12(4)(e) on internal communications did not apply because the adviser was considered to be an external independent advisor. The IC referred to Art 4.2 of Directive 2003/4/EC on this point ('grounds for refusal ... shall be interpreted in a restrictive way'). He did, however, accept that in some circumstances information provided by an independent advisor may be an internal communication if there was a contractual relationship or if the advisor was carrying out a function of the public authority. (See *Chichester DC v IC* EA/2010/0153.)

Regulation 12(5)(a)–(e)

8.234 The exceptions in EIR 2004, reg 12(5)(a)–(g) are as follows, and PAs may (again, the discretionary nature of this power should be noted) refuse to disclose EI to the extent that disclosure would adversely affect (not, it should be noted, 'could', so a greater degree of certainty and supporting justification is required, and 'would' is used throughout FOIA 2000):

- international relations, defence, national security or public safety. Regulation 15 makes provision for ministerial certificates stating that an exception is required for national security and the public interest does not favour disclosure (reg 12(5)(a)) (para 1.124 above, and below). The certificate may be appealed against to the tribunal (reg 18(7)). FER 0280033, a case involving a request for a digital version of a weather station data set from the Climactic Research Unit at UEA to Georgia Tech, was part of a notorious episode involving UEA. Reg 12(5)(a), and 12(5)(c) and (f) below did not apply. See also FER 0282488 on a similar complaint;[1]
- the course of justice (eg law enforcement), the ability of a person to receive a fair trial, or the ability of a PA to conduct an inquiry of a criminal or disciplinary nature (reg 12(5)(b));
- intellectual property rights (below) (reg 12(5)(c));
- the confidentiality of the proceedings of that or any other PA where such confidentiality is provided by law (reg 12(5)(d)) (see paras 2.312 et seq above); para 7.5.5.4 of the Guidance advises that exemptions imposed by the local government access laws do not override EIR 2004. Confidentiality will have to satisfy 'confidentiality' under the law, presumably the common law: see FS 50094124. The views of the courts on the words 'in confidence' were noted (para 1.203 et seq). Confidentiality suggests the legal test in the law of confidentiality;
- the confidentiality of commercial or industrial information where such confidentiality is provided by law to protect a legitimate economic interest (reg 12(5)(e)). There has been very little case law on this exception so some

additional comments are in order. This is a narrower exception than the commercial interests exemption in FOIA 2000, s 43. The reference is to information protected by commercial confidentiality (paras 1.215 et seq above). The Guidance states that where information has been kept off a register under the Environmental Protection Act 1990, s 22 this may be a relevant factor. In *Amway Corpn v Eurway International Ltd*: Case No CO/4553/98, [1974] RPC 82 ('the BNRR case'), legitimate economic interest also implies that the exception may be invoked only if disclosure would significantly damage the interest in question and assist its competitors (Guidance, para 7.5.6.2). From 1 December 2005, the Guidance notes that all central government departments and executive agencies are obliged to have an environmental purchasing policy properly integrated with departmental procurement practices. Mechanisms must be introduced to monitor and report on progress. The environmental implications and impacts of all government contracts must be considered. Once these are known, 'the PA will be readily able to determine the extent to which information they hold is environmental' (Guidance, para 7.55). The Procurement Strategy for Local Government lays out the approach to strategic procurement implementation in local government. The guidance on contracts was examined above. There must be a legitimate economic interest to protect. It might involve 'costs, prices or insight into a company's operating strategies. Confidentiality per se is not determinative – it must also relate to the protection of legitimate economic interests' (Guidance, para 7.5.6.5). The guidance from the Ministry of Justice on FOIA 2000, s 41 may be relevant but EIR 2004 is not restricted to information obtained by the PA from the other contracting party and a breach of confidence is not referred to as 'actionable'. The environmental implications and impacts of all government contracts will have to be considered including mandatory central government environmental purchasing policies and procurement practices. The Environmental Protection Act 1990, s 22 allows information to be kept off a register and this may be a factor to consider. The Procurement Strategy for Local Government covers local government.

● the interests of the person who provided the information where that person:
  (i)   was not under, and could not have been put under, any legal obligation to supply it to that or any other PA – the information was volunteered or possibly returned as a quid pro quo but without compulsion on the part of the PA;
  (ii) the person did not supply it in circumstances such that that or any other PA is entitled apart from these Regulations to disclose it – this is not entirely clear. The obvious power of disclosure would be FOIA 2000, but EI is given an exemption under that statute so it would not be disclosable. In spite of that exemption, does the PA still retain a discretion to disclose the information under FOIA (para 1.198 – it is not an absolute exemption under FOIA)? FOIA 2000, s 39 suggests not. EI is dealt with by the EIR 2004 regime. Information protected by the law of confidentiality or by a permissible agreement would not be disclosable by a PA subject to the public interest test and the provision on emissions under EIR 2004;

(iii) and the person has not consented to its disclosure, and it appears therefore to be confidentiality that is protected. In the BNRR case, the court found that information contained in a concession agreement following negotiations between the parties is not fairly described as information 'supplied' by one party to another (reg 12(5)(f));

• the protection of the environment to which the information relates, eg where disclosure might lead to some exploitation of the environment which is damaging to the environment (reg 12(5)(g)).

[1] See the Commons Science and Technology Committee HC 444 (2010–12) and HC 496 (2010–12), also containing the government response.

8.235   Case law (i) Under reg 12(5)(a) see *Office of Communications v IC and T-Mobile (UK) Ltd* EA/2006/0078 below (para 8.237). FER 0280033 involved a request for a digital version of a weather station data set sent from the Climactic Research Unit at UEA to Georgia Tech (above).

8.236   Case law (ii) In *Mersey Tunnels Users Association v IC and Halton Borough Council* EA/2009/0001 the Mersey Tunnels Users Association made a request to the council for information. This was the second stage of appeal and was necessary because the council located further information relevant to the request but was exempt from disclosure under FOIA 2000, s 42 or EIR 2004, regs 12(5)(b), 12(5)(e), 12(4)(d) or 12(5)(f). The IT had already decided that all of the information should be dealt with under the EIR and therefore went on to consider whether any of the exemptions applied to the additional information and, where relevant, whether the public interest favoured disclosure or non-disclosure. The public interest test was to be considered as at the time of the request, not the time of the appeal. The council was permitted to rely on additional exemptions, notwithstanding the late assertion of them, because it could not have previously raised the exemption, as the information had not been located at that time. This served to disadvantage the appellant, but the IT found that it should not penalise the council and should consider the exemptions in deciding whether or not the information should be disclosed. Regulation 12(4)(d) was relied upon in respect of three draft documents. The IT agreed that the exemption was engaged because a draft document is unfinished. The IT found that the public interest favoured non-disclosure because there was little public interest in disclosing a draft document, the final version of which was likely to be made public. The council purported that reg 12(5)(b) covered 21 of the documents. The IC had decided that the documents were covered by legal professional privilege because they referred to legal advice that was given to the council. The IT considered the case of *Three Rivers District Council and Others v Governor and Company of the Bank of England* [2004] UKHL 48 and followed *Rudd v IC and the Verderers of the New Forest* EA/2008/0006 and *Creekside Forum v IC and the Department for Culture, Media and Sport* EA/2008/0065. The IT found that information which was privileged fell within reg 12(5)(b), but only if the document *would* adversely affect the course of justice (an additional requirement to FOIA 2000). Some of the documents were found to fall within the exemption because disclosure would prejudice the public authority from adopting a more favourable or an alternative position and disclosure of legal advice in general would prejudice public authorities in obtaining advice on their legal rights, obligations and liabilities. However, notwithstanding this finding, it was in the public interest for some of the information to be disclosed. The factors in favour of disclosure were: (a) transparency and accountability; (b) informing the public that advice was sought and that the council acted properly and lawfully; (c) enabling the public to challenge decisions; (d) ensuing debate improve the quality of future decision-making; and (e) significant local public interest. The factors against disclosure were: (a) strong public interest in maintaining legal professional privilege; (b) public authorities should be able to give and receive full information from its legal advisors; (c) confidentiality is key to the lawyer–client relationship; and (d) the legal advice was 'live' at the time of the request and the procurement exercise had not begun. On reg 12(5)(e), relating to 17 documents, the IT followed the decision in *South Gloucestershire Council v IC and Bovis Homes Ltd* EA/2009/0032 that, 'wherever, because of the sensitive nature of the information, the law recognises the confidentiality of the information as deserving of legal protection, the confidentiality is provided by law'. The exemption is not limited to circumstances where a duty of confidentiality is owed by or to the council. Some of the documents were held to fall within reg 12(5)(e), and, of those, the public interest favoured non-disclosure. A schedule attached to the DN details the individual findings relating to each document. In *G Plumbe v IC* EA/2009/0117 the tribunal upheld the claim involving the protection of legal privilege on PI grounds. *Mr Christopher Boddy v Information Commissioner and North Norfolk District Council* EA/2007/0074 was an appeal to the IT from a decision of the IC. Mr Boddy sought disclosure of counsel's legal advice obtained by the council concerning the development of certain land. However, he stated that the exception in reg 12(5)(b) would apply; the council was exempt from disclosure by way of legal professional privilege (LPP). The IT considered the matters as follows:

- Cessation of legal professional privilege. The IT applied the House of Lords case *Three Rivers District Council and Others v Governor and Company of the Bank of England* [2004] UKHL48 on LPP. The IT decided that LPP had not ceased.

- Application of reg 12(5)(b). In *Kirkaldie v The Information Commissioner and Thanet District Council* EA/2006/001, reg 12(5)(b) was applied to information subject to LPP. The test in this respect is whether the course of justice would be adversely affected by disclosure. The IT considered that it would be so affected because the possibility of litigation existed and it would not have been fair for there not to have been a level playing field; disclosure would have revealed the strengths and/or weaknesses of the case to the opposing side and would have adversely affected the course of justice.

- The public interest test. Regulation 12(1)(b) provides for consideration of the public interest. It was noted that each case must be considered on its facts and that there is a presumption in favour of disclosure. There were several complaints from Mr Boddy, for example, that the council was breaking restrictive covenants and deceiving the public. However the IT rejected these arguments because they could all be dealt with through private or public legal proceedings. Further, if anybody wished to challenge the council over its actions, they would be able to take their own legal advice.

M Watts v IC EA/2007/0022 involved reg 12(5)(b).The tribunal ruled the prospect of a public enquiry following an outbreak of E. coli was not for criminal or disciplinary matters and so reg 12(5)(b) and its exception did not apply. LPP had not been waived in *R Burgess v IC & Stafford BC* EA/2006/0091 when a barrister's report had been given by the council to a councillor. The tribunal believed not and repeated points concerning the limits of waiver under FOIA 2000, s 42 (para 1.209 et seq).

8.237 Case law (iii) The most important discussion concerning reg 12(5)(c) is in *Office of Communications v IC and T-Mobile (UK) Ltd* EA/2006/0078. It was unsuccessfully appealed to the High Court but was partially successful on appeal to the Court of Appeal. The case has been referred to the ECJ by the Supreme Court (*Office of Communications v IC* [2010] UKSC3). The requester asked Ofcom for information concerning the location, ownership and technical attributes of mobile-phone cellular base stations. There was concern about radio frequency radiation in the form of electromagnetic waves. Information had been provided to Ofcom by each company offering a mobile phone service. The location of the stations could be found using maps on a website, but this did not show the whole database such as address, location and postcode, or whether each station is mounted on a particular kind of building or structure. The IC had ordered disclosure of these details in his DN. The primary concern was the health considerations of operating such base stations. The Stewart Report recommended that a database be set up giving details of all base stations and their emissions. This was issued in 1999. The details were to include: 'the name of the company, the grid reference, height of antennae, date transmission commenced, frequency range and signal characteristics of transmission, transmitter power and maximum legislative power output'. Stewart recommended a national database that should be 'readily accessible' by the public allowing easy identification of all base stations within a defined geographical area. A voluntary scheme was brought into effect but mobile network operators (MNOs) did not want specific information about various items published. 'The Sitefinder website was duly set up by the Government and has been operated since the end of 2003 by the respondent, the Office of Communications ("Ofcom"). The site is constructed from information voluntarily provided by mobile network operators from their databases. It has enabled individuals, by inputting a postcode, town or street name, to search a map square for information about the base stations within it', according to Lord Philips. This agreement represented a 'modest dilution' of the Stewart proposals, the tribunal believed. The MNOs wanted protection of commercially sensitive information arguing this was not detrimental to Stewart's proposals. The information available through the website was also available from local planning authorities. A request was made for information on base stations and Ofcom refused relying on reg 6(1)(b) – information already publicly available. Grid references were not available. Subsequently Ofcom relied upon reg 12(5)(c) – intellectual property rights – arguing under reg 12(1)(b) that the PI favoured non-disclosure. An appeal was made to the IT on basis that under reg 12(5)(c) disclosure would have an adverse effect on Ofcom's database right or copyright in data on the website. Other exemptions under FOIA 2000 were also said to apply. The MNOs withdrew from the cooperative scheme when the IC found against Ofcom. Recital 10 of the Directive was important for helping to define environmental information. Radio waves are an emission, the tribunal believed, thereby introducing the nullification/disapplication of the exception by virtue of reg 12(9) – as explained, this provides that some exceptions do not apply to protect information about emissions. The names of the MNOs were within EIR 2004 and so subject to a reg 12(9) disapplication. The tribunal found that the PI favoured disclosure and arguments that disclosure would increase vandalism, etc although substantiated to some extent they was not forceful arguments and did not outweigh the public interest in favour of publication – a position supported by the 1999 report. The PI, in respecting commercial interests of intellectual property rights, preventing the increase of criminal activity and the withdrawal of MNOs from the voluntary arrangements were all relevant factors to consider in balancing the PI (modification of licences may make voluntary arrangements a 'legal obligation' although MNOs would challenge this). However, the tribunal ruled that the PI for one exception could not be aggregated and transferred to another exception. They were not cumulatively applicable to assess whether the PI in disclosure was outweighed by non-disclosure – can, in other words, the interests served by different exceptions be combined and then weighed against the public interest in disclosure? The PI in non-disclosure did not outweigh the PI in disclosure. Although there was an unsuccessful appeal to the High Court by Ofcom, the appeal was partially successful in the Court of Appeal ([2009] EWCA Civ 90). The CoA found that the exceptions could be weighed cumulatively in assessing the public interest in disclosure and they did not have to be considered singularly, ie the sum is bigger than its parts. The CoA disagreed with the tribunal and Laws LJ on this and the case was remitted to the tribunal to reconsider this point noting that the tribunal could very well reach the same result. Looking at the exceptions in the aggregate would allow the overall public interest to be assessed. The CoA did rule in favour of the tribunal that public benefit from the disclosure can be weighed against possible breaches of third-party IP rights. Third-party IP rights to databases set out in the 1997 Regulations could not of themselves defeat rights of access. Copyright does not defeat access rights. But using material in breach of copyright is still actionable and may involve criminal offences. The CoA also agreed with the IT and High Court that the names of the MNOs were environmental information and the public interest in disclosure extended to these. In the reference from the Supreme Court the majority believed that the exceptions could be cumulated to assess the strength of the PI in non-disclosure:

'The majority view is that, since all the facets of the public interest in disclosure go into one side of the scales, it makes sense to put all the aspects of the interests served by refusal to go into the other side. These latter interests may be highly diverse and without any common factor (as in the present case, where the arguments against disclosure under the public safety and intellectual property rights exceptions are separate, one being concerned with public, the other with private protection). But that, in the majority view, can be seen as a positive reason why it is permissible to accumulate them.

If, in some future case, it was possible to identify some overlap, then some allowance might perhaps be appropriate to eliminate double counting. The majority further point out that some of the heads of article 4(2), particularly (b), already involve different interests under which different factors could arise which could, they consider, presumably be cumulated.' (para 13)

The Advocate General on the reference to the ECJ gave an opinion supporting the majority of the Supreme Court and the CoA's decision (Case C-71/10, 10 March 2011). The ECJ supported the Advocate General ruling that PAs may 'evaluate cumulatively the grounds for refusal to disclose' (para 28) while a number of separate interests may, cumulatively, 'militate in favour of disclosure' (Case C-71/10 *Ofcom v IC* [2011] ECJ (28.07.11), para 25). FER0279668 also concerns reg 12(5)(c). The complainant submitted a request to Walsall Council to inspect building control information. The complainant specified that he wished to view the records in person. The council withheld the information under the exception at reg 12(5)(c), on the grounds that disclosure would be detrimental to the council's intellectual property rights. The Commissioner's decision was that reg 12(5)(c) was not engaged. During the course of the investigation, the council decided to rely on the exception at reg 12(4)(b) (manifestly unreasonable). The Commissioner has upheld this exception. The council also breached reg 14(2) by failing to provide a refusal notice within the statutory time for compliance, and reg 14(3) by failing to cite an exception that it later relied upon in its refusal notice. The council also breached reg 9(1) by failing to offer the complainant appropriate advice and assistance.

8.238   Case law (iv) FER0280033 (above) was a case involving a request for a digital version of a weather station data set sent from the Climactic Research Unit at UEA to Georgia Tech. Regulation 12(5)(c) was raised by the UEA. In rejecting the UEA's invocation of the exception, at para 97, the IC stated, citing the Defra guidance:

'Copyright does not prevent authorities releasing information they hold. However, where such information is subject to copyright, it should be made clear to applicants that the copyright still exists.' (para 7.5.4.1 page 12)

'The Commissioner is of the view that this exception is not intended to protect intellectual property rights in themselves but is intended to protect the interests of the holders of intellectual property rights. Accordingly, in order to engage the exception, it is necessary to demonstrate that the public authority or other interested parties held intellectual property rights in respect of the withheld information and that those rights would have been adversely affected had the information been disclosed. The Commissioner highlights the Information Tribunal decision in Ofcom (EA/2006/0078), paragraph 47:

"The Information Commissioner's case was that he had been right in his Decision Notice to say that infringement of an intellectual property right was not sufficient to trigger the exception. He considered that the expression 'adverse effect' required something more in terms of actual harm to commercial or other interests. Ofcom and T-Mobile, on the other hand, argue that the question of loss or harm should be taken into account when carrying out the public interest balance required by EIR regulation 2(1)(b), but not at the stage of determining whether the exception has been engaged... However we believe that, interpreting the exception restrictively requires us to conclude that it was intended that the exception would only apply if the infringement was more than just a purely technical infringement, (which in other circumstances might have led to a court awarding nominal damages, or even exercising its discretion to refuse to grant the injunction that would normally follow a finding of infringement). It must be one that would result in some degree of loss or harm to the right holder. We do not therefore accept that such harm should only be taken into consideration when carrying out the public interest balance.'"

8.239   Case law (v) In relation to reg 12(5)(d) FER0086108 was a request for information about two contractors cleaning up after a foot-and-mouth epidemic. Regulation 12(5)(d) – confidentiality of proceedings – was properly invoked for the second contractor. The reg 12(5)(d) exception concerned a settlement at which information had been prepared exclusively for discussion at the meeting. The PI favoured non-disclosure because DEFRA's trustworthiness would be called into account if it breached undertaking. Disclosure may also have serious implications for DEFRA and their exposure to legal suits (see *Chichester DC v IC* EA/2010/0153).

8.240   Case law (vi) FS50206320 deals with reg 12(5)(e) – confidentiality of commercial or industrial information. The PA entered into a public finance initiative contract with Veolia Environmental Services (Veolia) to outsource certain waste management functions in order to enable the PA to discharge its statutory waste management obligations. The complainant asked to see the contract and related documents. The PA eventually provided much of the information requested but withheld some citing reg 12(5)(e). The IC decided, following decisions in earlier leading cases, that the reg 12(5)(e) exception had been correctly engaged by Nottinghamshire County Council for some of the information. For some of information withheld under reg 12(5)(e) the balance of the public interest in maintaining the exception did not outweigh that in disclosure. The remaining information was correctly refused as the balance of the public interest in maintaining the exception outweighed that in disclosing the information. In a separate legal process, the complainant asked the PA for some of the relevant information under the provisions of the Audit Commission Act 1998. The High Court granted access. In *South Gloucestershire Council v IC and Bovis Homes Ltd* EA/2009/0032 Bovis made two planning applications to the council and was informed that the council was to use an independent development appraisal via a consultant. Bovis requested a copy of this information, but the council refused, citing the exceptions for internal communications (reg 12(4)(e)) and confidentiality (reg 12(5)(e)) under the EIR. The IC decided that neither of these exceptions were engaged and ordered disclosure; the council appealed to the IT. The council submitted that the IC took too narrow an approach to the exceptions. The IC maintained that the information was not part of internal communications because it involved third-party consultants, and the duty of confidentiality was not provided by law because it was not to protect a legitimate economic interest. The IT found that the information was not part of an internal communication because of the third-party nature of the consultants. In relation to the confidentiality exception, the IC submitted that the words 'provided by law' should be interpreted as 'imposed on the public authority by law'; the council in this case made a choice to treat the information as confidential, but could, if it so chose, have disclosed it at any time. The IC referred the IT to *Office of Communication v IC* EA/2006/0078. The IT did not accept this interpretation of the wording of the Regulations: '[w]herever, because of the sensitive nature of the information, the law recognises the confidentiality of the information as deserving of legal protection, the confidentiality is provided by law'. The IT therefore considered the exception to be engaged. They went on to consider the public interest and found that the factors submitted in favour of disclosure (eg accountability, transparency, public understanding and the role of external consultants) were very limited considering the amount of information already in the public domain. The IT found that the public interest favoured non-disclosure. (See also FER0079969 and *North West etc Fisheries Committee v IC* EA/2007/0133). See also *North West Bath and NE Somerset Council* EA/2010/0045 for a lengthy discussion where information was disclosed in a redacted form (and see *Chichester DC v IC* EA/2010/0153).

8.241   Case law (vii) There has been little case law under reg 12(5)(f), but see *Elmbridge BC v IC* EA/2010/0106 and *Staffordshire CC v IC* EA/2010/0015, [2010] UKFTT 573 GRC.

8.242 Information that is subject to exceptions should be retained along with copies of information handed to the requester. This information is needed for quality control management and also in case appeals are launched to the IC.

Regulation 12(6) and 'neither confirm nor deny' (NCND)

8.243 Regulation 12 continues by stating that a PA may respond to a request for the purposes of reg 12(1) by 'neither confirming nor denying whether such information exists and is held by the PA, whether or not it holds such information, where that confirmation or denial would involve the disclosure of information which would adversely affect any of the interests referred to in [reg 12(5)(a)] above and would not be in the public interest under [reg 12(1)(b)]'. The confirmation or denial may be overridden in the public interest. The NCND provision has a far more restricted application for exemptions than under FOIA 2000, where it applies in most exemptions. For the purposes of the preceding sentence, whether information exists and is held by a PA is itself the disclosure of information (reg 12(7)).

EMISSIONS

8.244 By virtue of EIR 2004, reg 12(9) where the EI to be disclosed relates to emissions, the exceptions above from reg 12(5)(d)–(g) may not be relied upon by a

PA. For the purposes of paras (b) and (d) and (f) above, references to a PA includes a Scottish PA. Finally, reg 12(11) stipulates that nothing in the regulations allows EI to be withheld where it is held with other EI that is properly withheld under the regulations 'unless it is not reasonably capable of being separated from the other information' so as to make the EI available. Parts of documents not covered by an exception should be disclosed where it is reasonably severable. In FER0085500 the complainant requested a report into an application for a grant towards a proposed biomass generation plant. This was initially refused under ss 41 (information provided in confidence) and 43 (commercial interests) of the Act. The information withheld fell within the definition of EI in the EIR and the PA should consider what exceptions from the EIR may apply. The public authority cited regs 12(5)(d) (confidentiality of proceedings of public authorities provided by law), (e) (commercial confidentiality) and (g) (environmental protection). The Commissioner found that the information is on emissions and, therefore, reg 12(9) applied. As reg 12(9) provides that information on emissions cannot be subject to any of the exceptions provided in regs 12(5)(d) to (g), the Commissioner found that the exceptions cited by the public authority were not engaged. The public authority was required to disclose to the complainant the information withheld.

SEVERENCE OF NON-EXCEPTED MATERIAL

8.245 Regulation 12(11) stipulates that nothing in the Regulations allows EI to be withheld where it is held with other EI that is properly withheld under the Regulations 'unless it is not reasonably capable of being separated from the other information' so as to make the EI available. Sections of documents not covered by an exception should be disclosed where it is reasonably severable.

PERSONAL DATA

8.246 Personal data of which the requester is the data subject must be requested under the DPA as is the case for requests for such data under the FOIA regime (paras 1.200 and 7.10 et seq above). Personal data about another person within paras (a)–(d) within the definition of data within DPA 1998, s 1(1) (para 7.7 above) shall not be disclosed to the requester if one of two conditions is satisfied (reg 13). First of all where disclosure would breach the data protection principles in the DPA 1998 (para 7.42 above). It also provides that personal data shall not be disclosed if the individual who is the subject of the data has *properly* given notice that disclosure would cause *unwarranted* substantial damage or distress and there is no overriding public interest in disclosure. The italicised words are qualitative and would have to be supported by evidence and reasons. Furthermore, there is, in the second case an overriding public interest. In the case of manual data added by FOIA 2000, where disclosure to the public other than under these regulations would contravene any of the data protection principles but for DPA 1998, s 33A(1), such data shall not be disclosed (paras 7.10 et seq above). The second condition is that data is exempt under DPA 1998, Part IV and the subject would not have access under s 7(1) and in 'all the circumstances of the case' the public interest in not disclosing the data outweighs the case for disclosure. The transitional exemptions under DPA 1998, Part III shall be disregarded. PAs may respond by neither confirming nor denying the existence or holding of such data where doing so would either contravene any of the data protection principles or s 10 or would do so if s 33A(1) (above) were ignored; or where the data is exempt under DPA 1998, Part IV from s 7(1)(a) – the access provision. In relation to reg 12(3) in FS50282532 it was held that information about a s 106 planning agreement was correctly withheld. In FER0112249 the complainant, DEFRA, requested information regarding the distribution of EU Common Agricultural Policy subsidies. The public authority refused disclosure on the basis of EIR 2004, regs 12 and 13. As regards reg 13, the public authority claimed that the information could not be disclosed under the first DPP. The IC rejected this argument. He accepted that the complainant had a legitimate interest, both as a member of the public and as a member of the press, in knowing how agricultural subsidies were distributed. Further, even though the information related to 'individuals' being paid the subsidy, they were not individuals in a personal capacity, but in a business capacity. In this case, communicating the details of the subsidy paid to a person in a business capacity was deemed justified (see *W Young v IC and DOE NI* EA/2007/0048; see also the *Volker Eifert* Case C-93/09 (ECJ on this point). A planning officer's report was wrongly withheld under reg 13 when it was claimed that it constituted personal data. Some personal data were contained and were redacted but it was important that those affected by public decisions should know of the background: *Surrey Heath Borough Council v IC* EA/2010/0034.

REFUSALS UNDER REG 12(1) OR 13(1)

8.247 These refusals shall be in writing and must be explained (specify reasons not to disclose) to the applicant not later than 20 days after date of receipt of the request. Reasons include a refusal under EIR 2004, reg 12(4), (5) or 13 (see *G Freeze v IC* EA/2010/0112 on reg 13). They must include the matters the PA considered in reaching its decision on the public interest. If EI is refused because of the exception relating to unfinished or incomplete documents (reg 12(4)(d)), the PA must also specify, if known to it, the name of any other PA preparing the information and the estimated time within which the EI will be finished or completed. The refusal shall contain advice to the applicant on their rights to make representations and of the enforcement and appeal provisions under reg 18 (below) which, with modifications, are those under FOIA 2000 (paras 1.234 et seq above).

MINISTERIAL CERTIFICATES

8.248 A Minister (FOIA 2000, s 25(3)) or his designate may certify (EIR 2004, reg 15(1)) that disclosure under reg 12 would adversely affect national security (para 1.282 et seq above) and would not be in the public interest under reg 12(1) (b). Similarly to FOIA 2000, a certificate is conclusive evidence of the matters within reg 12(1) and may identify information in general terms. A document purporting to be such a certificate shall be received in evidence and deemed such a certificate until the contrary is proved. Provision is made for true copies.

8.249 A code of practice has been issued by the Secretary of State in terms similar to those under FOIA 2000, but with important distinctions as explained above, and this may make different provision for different PAs. The Information Commissioner has to be consulted before issuing or revising any such code. Powers of the Commissioner under FOIA 2000, ss 47 and 48 (general functions and practice recommendations, paras 1.164 et seq above) apply to the Regulations subject to reg 16(6) which allows for cross-referencing. Regulation 17 concerns requests for historical records (para 8.216 above), which are those over 30 years old (s 62), and for transferred public records by appropriate records authorities and responsible authorities (s 15 and para 1.96 above).

REPRESENTATIONS AND RECONSIDERATION

8.250 EIR 2004, reg 11 allows an applicant to make representations to a PA in relation to the applicant's request for environmental information if it appears to the applicant that the PA has failed to comply with a requirement of the Regulations in relation to the request. The representations shall be made in writing to the PA no later than 40 working days after the date on which the applicant believes that the public authority has failed to comply with the requirement. The PA must, free of charge, consider any representations together with any supporting evidence. It has to publicise its complaints procedure on the publication scheme. It will decide whether there has been compliance with any requirement. Internal reviews should be undertaken by parties who were not involved in the original decision (Guidance, ch 8, and code of practice). Any written reply from an applicant expressing dissatisfaction should be treated as a complaint. It should be possible to reverse or otherwise amend decisions previously taken. Where the organisation is small, or the decision is made at a level of seniority that it cannot be reviewed, the organisation should consider waiving the internal review, the guidance advises, although the code is less precise. Paragraph 67 of the code states that, where the outcome of a complaint is that information should be disclosed that was previously withheld, the information in question should be disclosed as soon as possible and within the time limit. Procedural defects should prompt an apology from the PA. Notice of the PA's decision has to be given to the applicant as soon as possible and no later than 40 days after the date of receiving the representations. Timescales should be set out in the complaints procedure. If these cannot be met, the complainant should be informed. Records should be kept for monitoring and amending procedures. Complainants should be informed of target dates for the determination of complaints. If it decides there has been such a failure by the PA, it shall include in its notification a statement of the failure to comply; the action the authority has proposed to take to comply with the requirement and the period within which such action will be taken. Where the decision refusing information is upheld, the requester must be informed of rights of appeal to the IC.

ENFORCEMENT AND APPEAL PROVISIONS

8.251 Where an applicant has made representations to a PA under EIR 2004, reg 11 and the applicant believes that the PA has failed to comply fully with the requirements of that provision, the enforcement and appeal provisions (involving the Tribunal) of FOIA (FOIA 2000, Parts IV and V and Sch 3) apply with modifications (reg 18). FOIA 2000, Part IV shall not apply in a case where a ministerial certificate concerning national security has been issued under reg 15(1) – this refers to the powers of enforcement and search and seizure residing in the IC under FOIA 2000, ss 50–56 and Sch 3. Presumably these powers would be restored if a certificate were quashed by the tribunal under FOIA 2000, s 60(3) (para 1.283). Necessary cross-referencing in the FOIA enforcement and appeal provisions to the regulations is effected under reg 18 so that a reference to a public authority in FOIA is a reference to a PA under these regulations. Reference to the code of practice, general rights of access to information in s 1(1), means by which communication is to be made (s 11), refusals of request (s 17) and contents of decision notices (s 50(4)) in FOIA are to be treated as references to EIR 2004, regs 5(1), 6 and 14. The reference to the offence of altering records etc under FOIA 2000, s 77 in Sch 3, para 1 shall be treated as an offence under reg 19, and that regulation establishes an offence in relation to EI requests where an official or other person covered by the regulation erases, blocks, defaces, destroys or conceals any record with the intention of preventing its disclosure wholly or partly. Prosecution has to be by the Information Commissioner or Director of Public Prosecutions, or with the latter's consent.

8.252 FOIA 2000, ss 23(1) and 24(1), which refer to exemptions for bodies dealing with security matters and national security, shall be treated as a reference to information whose disclosure would adversely affect national security. The veto power under s 53 (paras 1.150 et seq above) applies to decision and enforcement notices under the regulations. Section 60 on appeals against national security notices applies with modifications so that reg 15(1) replaces s 24(3), and s 60(2) has no application to the regulations in relation to bodies listed under s 53(1)(a) (paras 1.150 et seq above). A government department is not liable to prosecution in relation to an offence under FOIA 2000, Sch 3, para 12 relating to execution of warrants, but the prosecution provisions apply to persons in the public service of the Crown or acting on behalf of either House of Parliament or the Northern Ireland Assembly.

8.253 It will be recalled that the Aarhus Convention was concerned not only with access rights to information but also with access to justice. It was thought at one stage that this would encourage more public participatory mechanisms for decision making on the environment. The government was of the view that existing mechanisms involving inquiries and registers were adequate and Directive 2003/4/EC, Art 6 on access to justice is implemented by EIR 2004, regs 11 and 18. Representations may be made under Art 15 of the UNECE Convention on Access to Information, Public Participation in Decision-making and Access to Justice in Environmental Matters via a complaints procedure set up under the Convention where the Convention has not been properly implemented, but all domestic and EU avenues would have to be explored. The Directive may well offer directly effective rights which may be pursued initially through domestic courts.

Costs under EIR cases

8.254 Costs orders may be awarded against appellants for manifestly unreasonable, frivolous, vexatious or improper behaviour. In *M Fowler v IC and Brighton and Hove City Council* EA/2006/0071 the IT made the point that there would be no costs order against a party reasonably pursuing appeals. *Milford Haven PA v IC and Third Parties* EA/2007/0036 contains a discussion of costs order under IT rules. 'Manifestly unreasonable, frivolous' etc behaviour under reg 29 of the IT Rules. The case also has discussion of earlier authorities. The basis for awarding costs was changed at the beginning of 2010 (para 1.253) but the basic test is the Tribunals, Courts and Enforcement Act 2007, s 29 and the Tribunal Procedure Rules 2009, SI 2009/1976, r 10 and involves 'acting unreasonably'.

Pesticides

8.255 In the use of pesticides the government has in the past relied heavily on a self-regulatory framework by the industry concerned which operated a pesticide safety precaution scheme (see www.pesticides.gov.uk). However, the scheme was believed to conceal practices concerning excessive use, and secrecy protected toxicity studies on pesticides so that it was unclear why particular decisions had been reached and also which products were turned down. Such information could prevent illicit export to Third World countries. Under the Food and Environment Protection Act 1985, as amended by the Pesticides Act 1998,[1] the Ministry of Agriculture, Fisheries and Food (MAFF – now DEFRA) will make public an evaluation of the safety test data submitted by manufacturers seeking approval for a new pesticide. Initially, only summaries were to be published, not the full studies as is the practice under law in the USA.[2] Only summaries of those approved after the provisions come into force were to be published; existing pesticides and their studies prior to that date were not published. An amendment to the Control of Pesticides Regulations 1986, SI 1986/1510 in 1997 states that ministers may now disclose full evaluations and reports pertaining to the evaluations to a member of the public at his request. Copies may be made of these documents. However, members of the public who obtain such access are prohibited from making commercial use of the information and may not publish the information unless expressly permitted to do so in writing by the relevant minister (reg 8). In November 1988, MAFF announced that secret files on pesticide safety were to be opened to manufacturers but not to the public. The old excuse for not informing the public – commercial confidentiality – was to be swept aside as an incentive to competition. But the abandoning of that excuse preventing public access in the past was not to benefit the public. The MAFF also admitted to the Commons Agriculture Committee that safety data on many older pesticides was deficient by modern standards. The Trade Association representing pesticide producers saw itself still exercising a central role in the administration of the relevant legislation. Close co-operation between the regulators and those regulated is seen in other cases and does not always operate in the public interest.

¹ Food and Environment Protection Act 1985, Pt III, ss 16–19; see the Pesticides (Fees and Enforcement) Act 1989. There is a monthly listing of approvals and announcements on the MAFF *Pesticides Register*.
² Freedom of Information Act (USA) 1966, as amended.

8.256 The Pesticides Act 1998 allowed for the provision of information given at any time as well as information provided under s 16 of the 1985 Act (s 1(4)). Information may be provided 'subject to any condition that the Ministers consider appropriate' (s 1(3)). This relates to control of pesticides, the UK Pesticides Safety Precautions Scheme or the Agricultural Chemicals Approval Scheme. Section 2 of the 1998 Act conferred new powers for an environmental officer to question persons whom s/he has reasonable cause to believe is able to give the officer useful information to carry out his functions. Answers so given are excluded from the rules of self-incriminatory statements but are not admissible in subsequent criminal proceedings against the maker of the statement or their spouse. Information on pesticides will now generally be covered by the EIR 2004 (above).¹ The Court of Appeal considered a case on pesticides in 2009.² In this case, Mrs Duffy argued that the Government's present approach to the regulation of pesticides was not compatible with Directive 91/414/EC. Much of the analysis in the case is not related directly to information about pesticides, but part of the discussion considers submissions over the Government's refusal to follow recommendations from a Royal Commission which would have preferred to see more information provided to those affected by pesticide spraying. The Court of Appeal found that the Government's present approach to the provision of information was not unlawful.

¹ Regulation 8 of SI 1986/1510 (as amended) specifically notes that its provisions are without prejudice to the EIR.
² *Downs v Secretary of State for the Environment, Food and Rural Affairs* [2009] EWCA Civ 664, [2009] 3 CMLR 46.

Waste disposal

8.257 EPA 1990, Part II, as amended by EA 1995, Schs 22 and 24 (and see SI 1996/593), contains provisions dealing with 'Waste on Land', and s 64 deals with public registers which each waste regulation authority (WRA) must maintain containing prescribed particulars. These relate to current or recently current (s 64(3)) licences granted by the authority; current or recently current applications to the authority for licences; applications for licence modifications under s 37 and notices issued by the authority; notices under s 38 effecting the revocation or suspension of licences or imposing requirements on the holders of licences; appeals under s 43; certificates and notices under ss 39(9) and 42(5); convictions of licence holders granted by the authority in relation to any matter in Part II; occasions when the authority has discharged certain functions under s 42 or 61; directions given to the authority under this part by the Secretary of State; any other prescribed matters. Waste collection authorities which are not WRAs must maintain prescribed matters on a register maintained under the above provision which 'relates to the treatment, keeping or disposal of controlled waste in the area of the authority' (s 64(4)). Authorities have to secure that registers as described are open to public inspection at its principal office free of charge and at all reasonable hours affording reasonable opportunities for the public to copy entries on payment of a reasonable charge.

8.258 EPA 1990, s 65 allows for the exclusion at the Secretary of State's discretion of information relating to national security. Section 66 allows for 'commercially confidential' information to be excluded where it relates to the affairs of an individual or business and they have not consented to its inclusion on the register. To be commercially confidential, it has to be determined as such by the authority or on appeal, by the Secretary of State. The sections contains provisions relating to procedures as well as objections and appeals for 'any person or business'. The determination of confidentiality may last for four years and can be renewed. Information is commercially confidential in relation to any person or individual if its being contained in the register would prejudice to an unreasonable degree the commercial interests of that person or individual.

8.259 Further provisions deal with supervision and enforcement by inspectors with powers of entry etc; powers to deal with imminent danger of serious pollution; to obtain information from persons and authorities; and default powers of the Secretary of State.[1]

[1] Re fines under EPA 1990, s 71, see: *R v Hertfordshire County Council, ex p Green Environmental Industries Ltd* [1998] Env LR 153, CA, [2000] 2 AC 412, HL; see also SI 2006/1380.

8.260 Outside London, information about waste disposal is available at county (or unitary authority) level.[1]

[1] See the Planning (Hazardous Substances) Act 1990, especially s 28 on registers and SI 1992/656 on the publication of notices of applications, inspection of applications as well as an enforcement register and consents' register. See further the Waste and Emissions Trading Act 2003 on landfills, monitoring authorities, provision of information and public registers, waste management in England and Wales.

Health and Safety at Work etc Act 1974, s 28(7)

8.261 In 1986, the Health and Safety at Work Commission (HSWC), at ministerial bidding, found that, contrary to the view it had held for 11 years, s 28(7) of the Health and Safety at Work etc Act 1974 (HSWA 1974) did not prohibit publication to the public of information they had received from those inspected unless the disclosure was with the consent of the person from whom the information was obtained. Because the HSWC believed hitherto that only employees of sites inspected could receive information, it had failed adequately to acknowledge the effects of other sections requiring them to make arrangements to provide information to anyone concerned with the general purposes of the Act. These included protection of the public from factory hazards and air pollution. Strict secrecy was relaxed but this only represents an administrative concession in interpretation. Details, data and quantities of information given are purely a matter of discretion, not legal right. However, HSWC undertook to:

(a) inform complainants of the results of investigation; and

(b) reveal details of chemical leaks after accidents if the firms involved do not;

(c) provide the names and addresses of firms licensed or covered under various statutory schemes on public registers and also those convicted of criminal offences.

8.262 The policy did not include publication of details of enforcement notices served on firms who failed to meet safety standards. HSWC dropped this idea. However, under the Code on Access 1994 which was examined in ch 2, the HSWC undertook to publish information on a large variety of matters including names and addresses of firms on whom improvement and prohibition notices have been served. The FOIA 2000 applies to the Commission and Executive as to all other scheduled bodies and several of the FOIA 2000's provisions have special relevance to health and safety.[1]

[1] Eg FOIA 2000, ss 28, 29, 36, and 38 and see ch 1. See also the Management of Health and Safety at Work Regulations 1999, SI 1999/3242.

Environment and Safety Information Act 1988

8.263 This legislation constituted a considerable fillip for environmental information. It was a Private Member's Bill which was enacted in July 1988. The Environment and Safety Information Act 1988 requires authorities responsible for environment, safety and fire laws to establish public registers of enforcement notices they serve when premises fail to meet legal safety standards. These cover: the HSWA 1974 and dangers to the public and employees from activities such as asbestos stripping, demolition, industrial air pollution, chemical explosions and the risks of accidents in shops, offices, railways and other premises; the Food and Environment Protection Act 1985 dealing with pesticides; the Fire Safety and Safety of Places of Sport Act 1987 dealing with fire precautions at public premises and safety precautions at sports grounds. More than 14,000 enforcement notices were served each year, yet until 1 April 1989 when the Environment and Safety Information Act 1988 came into force, these did not have to be published. Consequently the public did not know that warnings by safety authorities had been ignored.

8.264 Not only will the Act ensure that a register is established to record breaches of safety laws, but also that notices are complied with promptly – over 100 prosecutions a year were brought by the Factory Inspectorate for failure to comply with notices. In about 10 per cent of enforcement notices that were served, a factory inspectorate survey showed in 1979 that the problem was continuing or had recurred four years later. Provision is made to exempt trade secrets information.

Nuclear energy and waste

8.265   Nuclear energy production is, understandably, an area that has attracted widespread controversy. A variety of statutes protect such information, on pain of criminal prosecution. The Anti-terrorism, Crime and Security Act 2001, Part 8 (ss 76–81) addresses the security of the nuclear industry and amends earlier legislation: the powers of the UK Atomic Energy Authority constabulary are expanded, powers are conferred on the Secretary of State to regulate for the safety of the civil nuclear industry; it introduces specific crimes (intentionally or recklessly) of disclosing any information or thing the disclosure of which 'might prejudice the security of any nuclear site or of any nuclear material' (s 79). The offence has an extra-territorial dimension when committed by UK citizens. Nuclear material includes that 'anywhere in the world which is being transferred to or from a nuclear site or carried on board a British ship including nuclear material which is expected to be so held, transported or carried. This would cover the use of trains through densely populated urban areas.

8.266   Section 80 of the 2001 Act creates a new offence of making a prohibited disclosure of uranium enrichment technology. The other major provisions are: Atomic Energy Act 1946, s 13; Radioactive Substances Act 1960, s 13(3) (repealed by the Radioactive Substances Act 1993; and see s 34 of the 1993 Act); and European Communities Act 1972, s 11(2). These latter provisions are not directed to national security but rather *all* information obtained under the Acts, eg trade secrets and processes. But for the events of 11 September 2001, they were likely to be reviewed with a view to possible repeal or amendment under the provisions of FOIA 2000, s 74. The Office for Civil Nuclear Security (DTI) has drawn up guidelines for nuclear power managers on what the public should be told in relation to the nuclear generation of power. On 'safety cases ... details of the potential hazards ... or details of the impacts of releases' are deemed, according to the *Guardian*, 'not releasable' because of possible assistance to terrorists. The body responsible for investigating and advising on the disposal of intermediate and some low-level radioactive waste, Nirex, has since 2001 operated under a voluntary code on openness which allows for access to information and resolution of any complaints about denial of access by an independent Transparency Panel. With the coming into effect of the EIR 2004, Nirex will come under that regime.

8.267   Under the Energy Act 2004, a Nuclear Decommissioning Authority (NDA) has been established to decommission and clean up nuclear sites. A Civil Nuclear Police Authority and Constabulary are established. A committee on radioactive waste management has also been established to advise on disposal of radioactive waste both for the safety of people and the environment. and reported to the Secretary of State (Defra) in July 2006. The committee made a number of recommendations supporting geological storage, but noted that further research was needed into the most appropriate methods for storing the material concerned. The Government accepted many of the committee's proposals in a White Paper[1] The committee's work is ongoing[2] and it publishes its proceedings and documents on its website, including an e-bulletin of recent activities and developments. The committee has conducted and continues to conduct open meetings around the country. The NDA is subject to FOIA and it is under an obligation to keep records of all its proceedings by virtue of the Energy Act 2004, Sch 1. Access to certain elements of nuclear energy policy has also been sought and granted under the EIR 2004.[3]

¹   Cm 7386 (2008) Managing Radioactive Waste Safely: A Framework for Implementing Geological Disposal.
²   See http://corwm.decc.gov.uk/.
³   See FER50132239.

8.268   The European Parliament has in the past published a critical report from its Energy, Research and Technology Committee on the agreements reached by the British government and the European Commission which allowed the government to redesignate civil nuclear material as non-civil, thereby removing the requirement of safeguards. The Commission refused to publish details of the agreements concerning the right of inspectors to look at nuclear reprocessing works, while not giving them full access contrary to the Euratom Treaty. The Parliament has called for a right of access because of widespread allegations of chronic mismanagement and corruption.[1]

¹   And packing of advisory committees. The Radioactive Substances Act 1960 was amended in 1993 and further amended by the Environment Act 1995 which places the issue of authorisations in the hands of the Environment Agency. Under EA 1995, s 39 the agency has certain duties to make documents and records accessible by the public. See *R v Secretary of State for the Environment, ex p Dudley Metropolitan Borough Council* [1989] COD 441; and also *R v HM Inspectorate of Pollution, ex p Greenpeace (No 2)* [1994] 4 All ER 329. In *EC Commission v United Kingdom* (12 April 2005), the ECJ ruled that military information on nuclear disposal plans did not fall under the Euratom Treaty.

8.269   The Energy Select Committee of the Commons recommended a full debate in the Commons on new rules for public inquiries which curtail the rights of objectors to nuclear power stations[1] including the right to present written evidence instead of oral evidence where it was allegedly against the 'public interest'. In fact, at the Hinkley Point Inquiry into a pressurised water reactor, certain secret instructions to the inspector from the government restricting the taking of evidence were published. Safety issues are not ruled out of order at nuclear inquiries as they were at early inquiries into Magnox reactors. However, at the Sizewell inquiry, access to original safety reports and data on safety was refused 'on commercial grounds' – the summaries merely provided an 'official consensus'. At Hinkley, evidence which had been leaked without the Central Electricity Generating Board's (CEGB) permission was ruled inadmissible by the Inspector – a ruling more suitable for a court of law than an inquiry into objections.[2]

¹   Environment Committee, First Report (1987–88); SI 1987/2182 repealed by SI 1990/528.
²   See also Public Information for Radiation Emergencies Regulations 1992, SI 1992/2997 and DoE Circ 21/90 on local authorities responsibilities for public access to information under the Radioactive Substances Act 1960, as amended by the EA 1995, and DoE Circ 22/92.

8.270   The Nuclear Safeguards Act 2000 also has many important information provisions in relation to safeguards connected with treaties on non-proliferation of nuclear weapons. Under the Planning and Compulsory Purchase Act 2004 there is a provision allowing the representation of interested parties by an appointed person where the Secretary of State decides to close an inquiry from public attendance on the grounds of national security and where those interested parties would not otherwise be able to see or hear evidence or read documents.

8.271   The Energy Act 2008 requires each operator of a licensed nuclear plant to submit to the Secretary of State a 'Funded Decomissioning Plan' to come into operation when the plant reaches the end of its operating life. Section 52 of the Act give the Secretary of State powers to request further information and documents from an applicant prior to the approval of a plan, or when the plan stands to be modified. Section 53 gives the Secretary of State broad powers to require information to be given about the progress of a plan once it comes into operation. Section 59 creates a specific offence of 'further disclosure of information', where any information obtained by ss 52 or 53 or regulations under the Act cannot be further disclosed unless one of the exceptions in s 54 (concerned with the sharing of information for regulatory purposes) applies. Section 60 creates the offence of supplying false information, though by virtue of s 60 such proceedings can only be instituted by the Secretary of State or the DPP. The Nuclear Decommissioning and Waste Handling (Finance and Fees) Regulations 2011, SI 2011/134, reg 5 sets out that information must be provided on the costs of the plan at the time of initial application and any changes that might result if a modification is applied for. These must be accompanied by a 'verification report', which is an examination of whether the costs and financing of the plan are prudent. The verification report must be produced by an independent party. It is perhaps important to note that the legislative process prior to the Energy Act 2008, and in particular the White Paper and consultations which led to the Act, resulted in litigation which required further disclosure of information to interested parties and a further consultation process, resulting from a finding of a legitimate expectation to fuller consultation than was orignially undertaken.[1]

[1]   *R (Greenpeace) v Secretary of State for Trade and Industry* [2007] EWHC 311 (Admin), [2007] Env LR 29.

8.272   The NDA has produced a policy document, dated August 2008, which applies to nuclear sites that are privately, rather than publicly, owned.[1] These private companies are not subject to FOIA. The contract between the NDA and the company concerned provides that these private companies must assist the NDA in achieving compliance with its FOIA obligations, including passing any requests received that could be considered to be FOIA or EIR requests to the agency and providing any information necessary to assist the NDA in responding to these requests. The document is clear that the ultimate decision over whether to disclose information lays with the NDA, though any material that may be released will be shown to the operator for comment in advance.

[1]   Nuclear Decommissioning Agency Document IAG01, Rev 1.

FOOD PRODUCTION

8.273 The network of advisory groups, inside interest groups, lop-sided domination by the regulated industries and government secrecy has been a feature in the process of food production. Throughout the 1980s and 1990s, the Food Advisory Committee, the Committee on Medical Aspects of Food Policy etc, their departmental sponsors and the food industry were embroiled in a variety of sagas involving sensational revelations of poisoned food, suppression of information and Treasury forestalling – because of cost – of an independent inquiry into salmonella in egg production. The episode led to the resignation of a Minister, enormous public disquiet and a select committee investigation. Further sensations covered listeria in cheese and contaminated meat as well as the 'Mad Cow Disease' saga. It culminated in the tragedy of Bovine Spongiform Encephalopathy (BSE), the banning of beef exports into Europe and elsewhere and an extensive inquiry into the events surrounding BSE and its human form new variant Creutzfeldt-Jakob Disease. This inquiry under the Law Lord, Lord Phillips, published its report in 16 volumes in October 2000. It was very critical of government secrecy. It found a 'team failure' in MAFF to evaluate food risks properly.[1] MAFF was subsequently disbanded and a new department, the Department for the Environment, Food and Rural Affairs (Defra), was established.

[1]   HC 887 Vols I–XVI (1999–2000).

8.274 A White Paper in 1998[1] recommended an autonomous Food Standards Agency to restore public confidence in food. The Food Standards Agency was created by the Food Standards Act 1999 (FSA 1999) to protect public health in relation to food and which would operate as openly and transparently as possible according to guiding principles whose aim was the protection of the public interest. The Agency will prepare and publish a statement of general objectives and practices including an undertaking that its activities are the subject of consultation with those affected or with 'where appropriate' members of the public. In protecting the public interest and taking proportionate action, the agency should ensure that the public have adequate and clearly presented information to enable consumers to make an informed choice and its decision-making processes should be as 'open, transparent and consultative' as possible 'so that the public and other interested parties could: make their views known; see the basis on which decisions had been taken; reach an informed judgment about the quality of the Agency's processes and decisions' consulting widely before deciding.[2] The members are appointed by the Secretary of State (4–8), and by Scottish Ministers (2), the Welsh Assembly (1), the NI Department of Health and Social Services. The agency is a body corporate exercising its functions on behalf of the Crown (FSA 1999, s 1(3) and Sch 1, para 1). The Agency has various advisory committees, makes annual and other reports and develops or helps develop policy in relation to food safety and consumer aspects and provides advice, assistance and information to public authorities on such matters (s 6).

[1]   *The Food Standards Agency: A Force for Change* (Cm 3830, 1998).
[2]   C Andrews *Current Law Statutes* c 28 1999.

8.275   Under FSA 1999, s 7 the Food Standards Agency has the function of providing advice and information to the general public (or any section of the public) on the above maters as well as providing advice, information or assistance on such matters to any person who is not a public authority. Informing the general public is for the purpose of ensuring that they are kept adequately informed about and advised in respect of matters which the Agency considers significantly affects their capacity to make informed decisions about food. It has a broad function to keep itself informed of matters connected with food safety by monitoring scientific, technological and other fields of knowledge to ensure that the Agency has sufficient information to enable it to take informed decisions and to carry out other functions effectively (s 8). It may carry out 'observations' to obtain information about food supply or production and use of feeding-stuffs etc, for which powers of entry are provided under ss 10 and 11. It monitors the activities of various enforcement authorities (between 300 and 400 local authorities) and may require bodies to provide information about enforcement for which powers of entry are given after various procedural requirements.

8.276   The Agency may publish its advice under FSA 1999, s 6, 7 or 9 (s 9 concerns feeding-stuffs) and from its observations and monitoring and any other information.[1] This power of publication is subject to any restrictions set out in the DPA 1998 and any statutory prohibitions (see s 19(8)) or incompatible Community obligations or where publication would be a contempt of court (s 19). The Agency must also balance the public interest in disclosure as against confidentiality. Guidance may be issued (s 20) to public authorities on 'food-borne' diseases, ie BSE and other variants (s 20(5)).

[1]   See *R (Friends of the Earth) v Food Standards Agency* [2007] EWHC 558 (Admin), [2008] Env LR 35 for an example of a judicial review case where Friends of the Earth sought to obtain a declaration requiring the FSA to use its powers to advise local authorities of a risk in long grain rice that could contain genetically modified organisms. The declaration was refused by the court.

8.277   Section 25 provides that where an enactment prevents the disclosure to the agency of information which would facilitate the Agency's functions (see s 25(2) for Scotland) or prevents publication by the agency under s 19, the Secretary of State may by order modify such enactments allowing disclosure and publication. A rule of common law (confidentiality) may also be modified but only to allow disclosure, not to publish information.[1] Regulations may also provide for the notification of tests of samples taken from individuals (s 27).

[1]   Quaere whether the common law public interest in disclosure is broader than this? – see paras 2.294 et seq above.

8.278   The legal provisions relating to disclosure of information are to be found in the Food Safety Act 1990 (repealing large portions of the Food Act 1984), and eg s 45C of the Public Health (Control of Disease) Act 1984 on the provision of information in food poisoning cases.[1] The 1990 Act introduced compulsory registration of all food premises, more training for those handling food and greater power of inspection for environmental health and trading officers.[2] There are a very large number of Regulations in place on various aspects of food labelling, many of which are created under s 26 of the Food Safety Act 1990.

1   See SIs 2010/657; 2010/658 and 2010/659 for England and SIs 2010/1544; 2010/1545 and
    2010/1546 for Wales.
2   See Food Safety Act 1990, s 26: and also eg Quick Frozen Foodstuffs Regulations 1990,
    SI 1990/2615 on labelling; SI 2009/1584 (England) and 2009/1795 (Wales) on irradiation
    licences; SI 2009/3238 (England) and 2009/3378 (Wales) on labelling of food additives and the
    Genetically Modified and Novel Foods (Labelling) (England) Regulations, SI 2000/768 and
    SI 2000/1925 (Wales).

8.279   Milk production and dairies are regulated by a variety of regulations.

LICENSING RESPONSIBILITIES

8.280   In a work such as this it would take far too much time to discuss the
provisions relating to licensing functions. Licensing authorities must act fairly,
sometimes in accordance with stricter interpretations of natural justice, must
exercise their discretion fairly and reasonably, consider relevant factors and not
consider irrelevant factors.[1] Refusing to award a licence on grounds that are
malicious or knowingly unauthorised is an actionable wrong; recklessness as to
authorisation will suffice.[2] Further, the courts may expect interested parties to be
consulted and their representations listened to where they stand to be affected by
the grant of a licence, especially where assurances have been made to that effect.[3]
It has been held that a licensing or registration process engages a 'civil right' and,
as such, ECHR, Art 6 applies to actions taken as part of the process.[4]

1   *Associated Provincial Pictures Houses Ltd v Wednesbury Corpn* [1948] 1 KB 223, CA, and related
    cases.
2   *Dunlop v Woollahra Municipal Council* [1982] AC 158, PC; *Bourgoin v Ministry of Agriculture,
    Fisheries and Food* [1985] 3 All ER 585, CA; *Roncarelli v Duplessis* (1959) 16 DLR (2d) 689; *Three
    Rivers District Council v Bank of England (No 3)* [2000] 3 All ER 1, HL.
3   See paras 9.99 et seq below; *R v Liverpool Corpn, ex p Liverpool Taxi Fleet Operators' Association*
    [1972] 2 QB 299, CA and *R v Brent London Borough Council, ex p MacDonagh* (1989) 21 HLR 494.
    However, it has been held that a sub-committee hearing a sex-establishment application is not
    covered by the LG(ATI)A 1985 when dealing with pre-decisional matters because it is quasi-
    judicial: *R v Wandsworth London Borough Council, ex p Darker Enterprises Ltd* (1999) 1 LGLR 601.
    See further the Private Security Industry Act 2001 on the Security Industry Authority, licence
    requirements, licensing functions, registers for approved contractors and powers of entry,
    inspection and information.
4   *R (Wright) v Secretary of State for Health* [2009] UKHL 3, [2009] 1 AC 739. Cf *R (G) v Governors
    of X School* [2011] UKSC 30, where the court held that a teacher who was the subject of internal
    disciplinary proceedings by a school could not require that he be represented in these proceedings
    by a solicitor as Art 6 was not engaged, despite the fact that his dismissal would then lead to his
    registration as a person fit to work with young people coming under scrutiny. The majority in
    the court held that the Independent Safeguarding Authority (ISA) was independent from the
    school's disciplinary process and was required to reach an independent judgment on the issue of
    G's suitability to work with children. Lord Kerr dissented, noting the difficulty caused by this
    approach given that much of the fact-finding and testing of evidence against the claimant would
    be done at the disciplinary proceedings in the school, and the ISA was necessarily going to need
    to rely on some of this material.

8.281   However, some statutes spell out the degree of notice and publicity
and opportunities to object to the application for a licence. Licensing of sex
establishments under the Local Government (Miscellaneous Provisions) Act

1982 is replete with particularly copious provisions. Schedule 3, Para, 10, paras 7–18 provide as follows:

'(7) An applicant for the grant, renewal or transfer of a licence under this Schedule shall give public notice of the application.

(8) Notice shall in all cases be given by publishing an advertisement in a local newspaper circulating in the appropriate authority's area.

(9) The publication shall not be later than 7 days after the date of the application.

(10) Where the application is in respect of premises, notice of it shall in addition be displayed for 21 days beginning with the date of the application on or near the premises and in a place where the notice can conveniently be read by the public.

(11) Every notice under this paragraph which relates to premises shall identify the premises.

(12) Every such notice which relates to a vehicle, vessel or stall shall specify where it is to be used as a sex establishment.

(13) Subject to sub-paragraphs (11) and (12) above, a notice under this paragraph shall be in such form as the appropriate authority may prescribe.

(14) An applicant for the grant, renewal or transfer of a licence under this Schedule shall, not later than 7 days after the date of the application, send a copy of the application to the chief officer of police.

(15) Any person objecting to an application for the grant, renewal or transfer of a licence under this Schedule shall give notice in writing of his objection to the appropriate authority, stating in general terms the grounds of the objection, not later than 28 days after the date of the application.

(16) Where the appropriate authority receive notice of any objection under sub-paragraph (15) above, the authority shall, before considering the application, give notice in writing of the general terms of the objection to the applicant.

(17) The appropriate authority shall not without the consent of the person making the objection reveal his name or address to the applicant.

(18) In considering any application for the grant, renewal or transfer of a licence the appropriate authority shall have regard to any observations submitted to them by the chief officer of police and any objections of which notice has been sent to them under sub-paragraph (15) above.'

8.282   However, the objector is not specifically given a right to attend.

8.283   The statutory framework within which licensing operates has to be examined for the precise details of opportunities to make objection, to be informed, to challenge decisions by way of appeal to the courts, or Secretary of State etc. In some instances, registers available to the public will be kept.[1] A list of statutory schemes for licensing is available in practitioners' works on eg local government.[2] Licensing by central government may often involve 'notice and comment' procedures, but few participating rights.[3]

1   Eg residential homes (see Health and Social Care Act 2008, Ch II), planning applications, under the Control of Pollution (Amendment) Act 1989 and SI 1991/1624; and Children Act 1989, Sch 5, and ss 60(4), 63(11) and Sch 6, s 66(5) and Schs 7, 8 and 9.
2   Bailey, *Cross on Principles of Local Government Law* (3rd edn, 2004), App D.
3   See the utilities below and duties to provide information and allow access of the public in the allocation and modification of licences within the regulator's powers.

8.284 The Licensing Act 2003 provides for a unified system of regulation of the activities of the sale and supply of alcohol, the provision of regulated entertainment (see Sch 1), and the provision of late night refreshment (see Sch 2). In the Act, these activities are referred to collectively as 'the licensable activities' and are the responsibility of local authorities (s 3 and see SIs 2005/43 and 2005/44). Section 8(1) provides that each licensing authority – local authorities and see SIs 2005/43 and 2005/44 – must maintain a register which records details of the authorisations it issues, the temporary event notices it receives, other notices and applications to it as set out in Sch 3, and any other information which the Secretary of State prescribes. Under s 8(2) the Secretary of State is given the power to make regulations as to how that register must be maintained. Section 8(3)–(5) provides that the information contained in the register must be made available for inspection by the public during office hours, free of charge, and that a copy of that information must be supplied on request (for a fee). Section 8(6) and (7) makes provision for the Secretary of State to arrange, through administrative action, for the establishment of one or more central registers, in which case the licensing authorities may be required to pay for the cost of such arrangements.

TRADING STANDARDS AND CONSUMER PROTECTION

8.285 This is now the common appellation for what were 'weights and measures' and 'public control' departments. Section 69 of the Weights and Measures Act 1985 defines weights and measures authorities. They enforce locally a series of statutes designed to protect the consumer[1] and to pursue grievances. They invariably work in a close relationship with the Office of Fair Trading (OFT) and provide that office with information on local enforcement, often on a voluntary basis, but there are legal duties also.[2] Under s 69(5), a local weights and measures authority may make, or assist in the making of, arrangements to provide advice to or for the benefit of consumers of goods and services within the area of the authority. This is buttressed by LGA 1972, s 142 (see ch 4), and LGA 1972, s 137 (see ch 4) authorising expenditure. Consumer advice centres are common features of consumer protection departments to provide information about consumer affairs, assist complainants and offer advice. A Local Authorities Co-ordinating Body on Trading Standards has existed since 1976.

1   Weights and Measures Act 1985; Trade Descriptions Acts 1968 and 1972; Consumer Credit Act 1974; Competition Act 1998; Hallmarking Act 1973; and the Consumer Protection Act 1987; and the Consumer Protection from Unfair Trading Regulations 2008, SI 2008/1277.
2   In relation to proposed proceedings. The Public Accounts Committee has criticised local trading standards authorities and the OFT for over caution and timidity in their approach which had endangered consumers' lives in relation to standards: *Financial Times*, 30 August 2000.

8.286 The OFT is responsible for numerous regulatory and enforcement functions. It publishes many advisory booklets and hand-outs, and its very informative annual report has information and details about enforcement and regulation. Some of the information obtained under consumer credit licensing has been made publicly available through disclosure on the consumer credit licensing public register for several years.

8.287 The OFT's annual report for 1998 emphasised the importance of information for consumers to help in providing adequate protection. Industry in the UK spends about £12 billion pa on advertising its own interests – a reflection of its appreciation of the value of information. In recent years, information and its availability has become a key focus for consumer protection. The European Commission's most recent consumer protection strategy emphasises the need for consumers to be provided with adequate information about products and services.[1] Similarly, the OFT's recent statement on enforcement of consumer protection also emphasises the importance of the availability of information.[2]

[1] COM(2007) 99 *EU Consumer Policy Strategy 2007–2013.*
[2] OFT 1214 (2010) *Statement of Consumer Protection Enforcement Principles.*

COMMERCIAL ENTERPRISE AND CONTRACTING

8.288 The provisions of the LGHA 1989 were examined in ch 2. These followed the Widdicombe Report and White Paper[1] on local authority commercial undertakings. Local authorities were under duties to engage in compulsory competitive tendering under Part I of the Local Government Act 1988 (LGA 1988). These duties have since been overtaken by the 'best value' regime introduced under the Local Government Act 1999 (LGA 1999).

[1] Cmnd 9797 (1986); Cm 433 (1988).

8.289 Part I of the LGA 1999 lists 'best value authorities' (BVA), a list which may be amended. A BVA must make arrangements to secure continuous improvement in the way in which its functions are exercised, having regard to a combination of economy, efficiency and effectiveness. It has to engage in widespread consultation in deciding how to fulfil its duty. The Local Government and Public Involvement in Health Act 2007 abolished the requirement for authorities to draw up best-value plans and carry out best-value reviews and also the ability of the Secretary of State to set performance indicators and performance standards for best-value objectives in England. These requirements remained in place for Wales, but have now been repealed by the Local Government (Wales) Measure 2009. The Secretary of State has copious powers to issue specifications and 'guidance', which must be taken into account by local authorities in the performance of their activities by virtue of the modified LGA 1999, s 3(4).

8.290 The Audit Commission can inspect BVAs to ensure compliance and LGA 1999, s 11 gives the inspector wide powers of access to premises and documents. Fees may be charged for such inspections, and reports must be issued by the Audit Commission after inspection. The reports may be published by the Commission. The Secretary of State has considerable sanction powers under s 15, including power to issue directions. The duty to publish information under Local Government Planning and Land Act 1980, s 2(1) applies to BVAs.[1]

[1] LGA 1999, ss 20 and 22. Regulation (EC) No 213/2008 of the European Parliament and Council on the Common Procurement Vocabulary.

8.291 Under Part II of the LGA 1988 duties are placed upon local authorities and other public bodies as defined in Sch 2 of the Act in relation to contracts for the supply of goods, materials or services or the execution of works. Under s 17 a duty is imposed on such bodies to exclude from relevant supply or works contracts any consideration of matters which come within the definition of non-commercial matters within the section. Authorities under Sch 2 must not discriminate against a contractor by invoking political or 'irrelevant' considerations.[1] It covers decisions to include or exclude, from approved lists of contractors or from 'invitation to tender' lists, a selection of contractors and sub-contractors. Section 17(5) specifies the non-commercial matters.[2] Section 19 of the LGA 1999 empowers the Secretary of State to remove certain of the matters specified in LGA 1988, s 17(5) as 'non-commercial matters' by order. No such orders have yet been made.

[1] Much more specific than the common law test of relevance: *R v London Borough of Enfield, ex p F Unwin (Roydon) Ltd* (1989) 46 BLR 1; *R v Islington London Borough Council, ex p Building Employers Confederation* [1989] IRLR 382. See also, more recently, *R (A) v B Council* [2007] EWHC 1529 (Admin), [2007] BLGR 813 (a case which also discusses the application of Art 8 ECHR to s 17 in light of the circumstances involved in the case) and *R v Bristol CC, ex p D L Barrett and Sons* (2001) 3 LGLR 11.
[2] Terms and conditions of employment of employees; self-employment; involvement in irrelevant fields of central government policy; conduct in industrial disputes; restricting the territorial activities of contractors; affiliation or interests of a political, industrial or sectarian nature, contribution to a political party.

8.292 Section 155(2) of the Equality Act 2010 gives a Minister of the Crown power to make regulations which 'may impose duties on a public authority that is a contracting authority within the meaning of the Public Sector Directive in connection with its public procurement functions.' The Equality Act 2010 repeals LGA 1988, s 18, which permitted local authorities to take account of certain issues pertaining to race relations in their procurement process. Section 155(2) of the Equality Act 2010 must be viewed in the context of the public sector equality duty contained in Part 11 of the 2010 Act. As of yet, no regulations or official guidance have been produced on the impact of the 2010 Act on procurement activities.[1]

[1] For more information see Wadham et al *Blackstone's Guide to the Equality Act 2010* (2010) ch 8.

8.293 Interestingly, duties under LGA 1988, s 17(1) create a sufficient interest for judicial review for a potential or, where made, former potential contractor,[1] and a failure to comply with the provisions in the section is actionable (s 19(7)) by any person who, in consequence, suffers loss or damage.[2]

[1] *R v Hereford Corpn, ex p Harrower* [1970] 1 WLR 1424.
[2] See LGA 1988, s 19(9) allowing judicial review proceedings on grounds other than non-commercial matters.

8.294 Section 20 concerns the giving of reasons. It provides:

'(1) Where a public authority exercises a function regulated by section 17 above by making, in relation to any person, a decision to which this section applies, it shall be the duty of the authority forthwith to notify that person of the decision and, if that person so requests in writing within the period of 15 days beginning with the date of the notice, to furnish him with a written statement of the reasons for the decision.[1]

(2) This section applies to the following decisions in relation to any person, namely:

    (a) in relation to an approved list, a decision to exclude him from the list,

    (b) in relation to a proposed public supply or works contract—

        (i) where he asked to be invited to tender for the contract, a decision not to invite him to tender,

        (ii) a decision not to accept the submission by him of a tender for the contract,

        (iii) where he has submitted a tender for the contract, a decision not to enter into the contract with him, or

        (iv) a decision to withhold approval for, or to select or nominate, persons to be sub-contractors for the purposes of the contract, or

    (c) in relation to a subsisting public supply or works contract with him—

        (i) a decision to withhold approval for, or to select or nominate, persons to the sub-contractors for the purposes of the contract, or

        (ii) a decision to terminate the contract.

(3) A statement of reasons under subsection (1) above shall be sent to the person requesting it within the period of 15 days beginning with the date of the request.'

---

[1] The period may be amended by order.

European directives

8.295 European directives seek to ensure open competition in public procurement, and in 1989 a Directive was adopted on enforcement procedures for the directives. The present rules can be found in Directive 2004/17/EC[1] (as amended), which covers contracts for works, supplies and services in the utilities sector (ie post, water, energy and transport) and Directive 2004/18/EC[2] (as amended) which applies to public contracts for works, supply and services. The new regime is simplified and pulls together provisions which used to be spread across a number of different directives and regulations. The two new directives encourage the use of electronic means, particularly for providing information about the contracts that are available. Some contracts and purchasing processes which were concluded under the previous legislative regime may still be covered by those rules, but the number of such contracts is becoming progressively fewer. In addition to the two directives noted above, there is also a Remedies

Directive[3] and a directive which modifies the regime in the two directives above in cases of defence procurement.[4] The bulk of the provisions in the directives are implemented in the UK by The Public Contracts Regulations 2006, SI 2006/5.

[1]   [2004] OJ L 134/1
[2]   [2004] OJ L 134/114.
[3]   Directive 89/665/EEC for the public sector and Directive 92/13/EEC for the utilities sector. Both of these directives were substantially amended by Directive 2007/66/EC, [2007] OJ L 335/31.
[4]   Directive 89/665/EEC for the public sector and Directive 92/13/EEC for the utilities sector. Both of these directives were substantially amended by Directive 2007/66/EC, [2007] OJ L 335/31.

8.296   It should be added that Regulation (EC) 213/2008 of the European Parliament and Council concerns the Common Procurement Vocabulary (CPV). The CPV is an important tool in the publicity process for public contracts, as it permits each contract to be classified according to its subject matter. Potential bidders may then search for public contracts in fields that are of interest to them as defined by the CPV.

8.297   These measures set out the procedures that are to be followed in awarding contracts by bodies covered by the Regulations: open, restricted, negotiated. Directive 2004/18/EC applies to contracts above a specific threshold: supplies £101,323 (central government contracting authorities with some variance for defence contracts) or £156,442 (sub-central contracting authorities); services £156,442 (in certain cases £101,323) (central government) or £156,442 (local government); and works £3,927,260. For utilities, the limits are £3,297,260 for works contracts and £313,694 for all other contracts. There are also thresholds for prior information notices listing the contracts to be awarded in the coming year. The Directives require EU-wide publication of contracts, use of non-discriminatory technical specifications and use of objective criteria for selection of participants in tendering and contract award. In *Telaustria v Telekom Austria* (Case C-324/98 [2000] ECR I-10745) the ECJ ruled that, even where the Directives do not apply, fundamental rules of the EC Treaty such as non-discrimination, which includes an obligation of transparency, do apply. This will cover 'a degree of advertising' by the contracting authority to enable both competition in tendering and a review of 'impartiality of procurement procedures' (paras 60–62). Some guidance on contracts that fall outside of the thresholds required by the Directives or are otherwise excluded from the regime is now available.[1]

[1]   [2006] OJ C 179/2.

8.298   In the case of the vast majority of contracts, the contracting authority is required to publicise its intention to seek tenders in the *Official Journal of the European Communities* (OJEC) except in certain specified circumstances. Specifications cover the form of advertisement and information which it must contain, which should usually be submitted via the electronic tools discussed below. UK press advertisements must be limited to information contained in the

OJEC and must not be published before notice is sent to the Publications Office of the EU. Regulations provide for response times by contractors and their access to documents and other information. Regulation 32 of SI 2006/5 requires a contracting authority to submit various statistical and other reports in respect of each contract awarded by it, including a record containing information on the awardee and the reasons why the contract was awarded. The Commission may request these records and reports if it so wishes. Where technical specifications are to be applied, these must be contained in the contract documents and are subject to strict controls to avoid discrimination.

8.299   Each contracting authority is required to produce a statistical report giving details of the number of contracts awarded, the type of contracts (whether service, supply or works), the process through which contracts were awarded, the value of the contracts and other information, such as the nationality of contract awardees and the subject matter of each contract according to the CPV. This requirement is implemented in the UK in reg 10 of SI 2006/5.

8.300   Electronic systems have now largely superseded paper-based publications for the notification of public contracts. The SIMAP system provides the necessary forms for contracting authorities to notify the publications office of a contract that is to be advertised. There are two possible routes that might be used – either the e-Notices system, where individual contracting authorities provide the information to the publications office by entering data online, or the e-Senders system, where approved third parties prepare the necessary information and send it to the publications office directly. Once notification is received by the publications office, the contract is publicised online on the Tenders Electronic Daily (TED) system, which has replaced the S series of the Official Journal. There is a desire on the part of the European Commission to increase the amount of contracts that are concluded using e-Procurement, and a Green Paper has been produced (COM(2010) 571) to examine what needs to be done in order to increase the usage of electronic means to conclude public contracts.

Local Government (Contracts) Act 1997

8.301   This Act was passed following litigation which ruled that local authorities could not enter – or at least not with legal effect – and could not have enforced against them ultra vires contracts.[1] In order to encourage various initiatives, not least the PFI and PPPs, the Act sought to remove uncertainties arising from the litigation by allowing self-certification under the Act which produces a strong presumption that the contract is lawful and the contract can therefore be performed. Any challenge may only be made by a public law or audit review process, not by private law. If the courts by such public law process determine that a contract is unlawful, in spite of a presumption and explicit discretion to allow an unlawful contract to be performed then there are special discharge terms which may be agreed or imposed allowing payment to the contractor, or those financing the contractor, of compensation.[2] Under s 4, a copy of the certificate has to be open for inspection by members of the public during the period for which the contract operates. It is to be available for all reasonable times without payment and the public are to be provided with facilities for obtaining copies on payment of a reasonable fee.

1   The Local Government (Contracts) Act 1997 is silent about rights in restitution: *Westdeutsche Landesbank Girozentrale v Islington London Borough Council* [1996] 2 All ER 961, HL; *Kleinwort Benson Ltd v Lincoln City Council* [1998] 4 All ER 513, HL.

2   See *Burgoine v Waltham Forest London Borough Council* (1996) 95 LGR 520 for personal liability of officers.

CIVIL DEFENCE AND EMERGENCIES

8.302   The Civil Contingencies Act 2004 confers civil defence functions on ministers, local authorities and a number of other authorities and providers of public services, including health authorities, police, fire services, ambulance services, utilities and transport providers. The detail of the bodies covered can be found in Schs 1 and 2 of the Act. Section 2(1)(f) of the Act requires the plans and assessments that are produced by the bodies covered by Schs 1 and 2 to be published insofar as the publication might prevent an emegency, reduce the impact of an emergency or enable action to be taken in relation to an emergency. The bodies covered by the Act must also maintain araangements to warn the public and offer advice if an emergency has occurred or is likely to occur by virtue of s 2(1)(g) of the Act. Section 6 of the Act allows the promulgation of Regulations to facilitate the provision and transfer of information between the bodies coverd by the Act. The Civil Contingencies Act 2004 (Contingency Planning) Regulations 2005, SI 2005/2042, Part 8 deals with the issue of information. This part classifies certain information as 'sensitive information' and makes provision for the transfer of that information and prohibits the publication or disclosure of such 'sensitive information' acquired under the Act and Regulations otherwise than in accordance with the provisions of the Regulations. Part 8 also provides for the procedure for bodies covered by the Act to request and transfer information that is required for the exercise of functions under the Act.

REGULATION OF WATER INDUSTRIES

8.303   The Water Act 1989 established a National Rivers Authority, which has been superseded by the Environment Agency under the EA 1995. Under s 1 of the Water Industry Act 1991 (WIA 1991), a Director-General of Water Services operated.[1] Both the Environment Agency and Director-General of Water Services were subject to the Parliamentary Commissioner's jurisdiction, although flood defence and land drainage functions of the EA will be subject to the local ombudsman. The Water Act 2003 introduces provisions for the better operation and regulation of the water industry by amending the WIA 1991. The Director-General of Water Services is replaced by the Water Services Regulatory Authority ('the Authority'). A Chief Inspector of Drinking Water and a Drinking Water Inspectorate are established. The 2003 Act also establishes a new independent Consumer Council for Water ('the Council'), known as WaterVoice, to replace the Customer Service Committees and the Ofwat National Consumer Council. The Council shall establish regional committees for Wales and England as the relevant authorities direct. The Council will deal with customer complaints – unless they are to be dealt with by the Authority and it may conduct investigations into matters 'relating to the interests of consumers'. The Act requires the Authority and the Council to consult on and publish forward work programmes and annual reports. Furthermore, it provides both the Authority and Council with a new duty to contribute to sustainable development and gives the Authority a duty to further the consumer objective wherever appropriate through the promotion of effective competition. The Act includes provisions which aim to increase the opportunities for competition in the supply of water services. This will be achieved by setting up a system to license new entrants to supply water to large commercial and industrial customers based on a water consumption threshold. To further this objective the Authority will be provided with new regulatory powers to administer the competition framework.

[1] Water Act 1989, s 5.

8.304 The 2003 Act adds a new s 192A to the WIA 1991 which requires both the Authority and, separately, the Council to publish before each financial year a forward work programme (FWP). FWPs should contain a general description of projects apart from routine activities, which the Council or Authority plans to undertake during the year. They will include associated objectives and an estimate of the overall expenditure for the year. The Authority and the Council must both consult on drafts of the programmes. A new s 192B requires the Authority to produce, for the Secretary of State, an annual report on its activities, and those of the Competition Commission in respect of any references made by it which the Authority makes during the previous financial year. The report shall include a general survey of development of matters falling within the scope of its functions, a report on progress of projects described in the forward work programme for that year, a summary of orders and penalties imposed and a report on any matter which it is required to report on as a result of a requirement by the Secretary of State or the Assembly.

8.305 Section 40 of the 2003 Act, concerning guidance to the Authority on social and environmental matters, adds a new s 2A to WIA 1991. Similar provision was made in the Utilities Act 2000 for the gas and electricity industries (see below). The section allows the Secretary of State or, for water and sewerage undertakers whose areas are wholly or mainly in Wales, the Assembly to issue statutory guidance to the Authority. The guidance will be on how the Authority might contribute to social and environmental policies. WIA 1991, s 2A(2) requires the Secretary of State and the Assembly, where practicable, to have regard to the costs and benefits which may be expected to result from the guidance. Section 2A(3) requires the Authority to have regard to any such guidance when discharging its statutory functions.

8.306 Companies may be appointed by the Secretary of State, or the Water Regulator with the Secretary of State's consent or authorisation, to be water or sewerage undertakers for any area of England and Wales. WIA 1991, s 6 contains details of the appointment of undertakers; s 7 concerns the provisions for the continuity of and replacement of appointments; s 8 contains the procedure including public notice and comment provisions in relation to a replacement appointment; s 11 covers conditions of appointment; and s 12 their determination. Appointment conditions may be modified by agreement; or they may be referred to the Competition Commission if existing conditions are adversely affecting the public interest. Section 15 deals with the contents of reports on modification references, and ss 16 and 17 concern the modification of conditions, the latter section under Chapters I and II of the Competition Act 1998. Enforcement orders to secure compliance may be made by the Secretary of State or the regulator, and objections may be made (WIA 1991, ss 18 and 19–22).

The register[1]

8.307 Part VII of the WIA 1991 on information provisions deals with reports by the DG (for which read 'regulatory authority') and reports by customer service committees. Under WIA 1991, s 195 the DG shall maintain a register, at such premises and in such form as s/he may determine for the purposes of Part II (appointment and regulation of undertakers as above). Section 31 provides that the register is to be publicly available subject to such times and payment of such charges as specified by order of the Secretary of State. Copies of extracts may be obtained by any person on payment of such fee as is designated, and the DG will certify the copy etc as a true copy. The register will contain:

(a) every appointment under Chapter I of Part II of this Act, every termination or transfer of any such appointment, every variation of the area for which any company holds any such appointment and every modification of the conditions of any such appointment;

(aa) every licence under Chapter 1A of Part 2 of this Act, every variation or revocation of any such licence and every modification of the conditions of any such licence;

(b) every direction, consent or determination given or made under any such appointment by the Secretary of State, the Competition Commission or the Authority itself;

(bb) every direction, consent or determination given or made under any such licence by the Secretary of State, the Authority, the Assembly or the Environment Agency;

(bc) every determination made by the Authority under section 17E or 66D(1) above [or regulation 5(1) of the Water Supply Licence (New Customer Exception) Regulations 2005];

(c) every final enforcement order made under section 18 above, every provisional enforcement order made or confirmed under that section and every revocation of such a final or provisional enforcement order;

(d) every undertaking given to and accepted by the Secretary of State or the Authority for the purposes of subsection (1)(b) of section 19 above and every notice under subsection (3) of that section; […]

(e) every special administration order and every discharge of such an order;

(f) every penalty imposed under section 22A(1) or (2) above and every notice under section 22A(6) above; and

(g) every designation made by the Authority under section 66G or 66H above.

(3) If it appears to the Secretary of State that the entry of any provision in the register would be against the public interest, he may direct [the Authority] not to enter that provision in the register; and the Authority shall comply with any such direction.'

---

¹ See Water Industry Act 1991, ss 196, 197 200 on duties to keep registers etc by water and sewerage undertakers.

Information to the Secretary of State and regulatory authority

8.308 By WIA 1991, s 202(1), undertakers are under duties to supply all such information to the Secretary of State relating to any matter which:

'(a) is connected with, or with any proposals relating to, the carrying out by that company of the functions of a water undertaker or sewerage undertaker; or

(b) is material to the carrying out by the Secretary of State of any of his functions under this Act'

as the Secretary of State may reasonably require.

8.309 Information required under the section shall be furnished in such form and manner, and be accompanied or supplemented by such explanations, as the Secretary of State may reasonably require (s 202(2)).

8.310 The information which a company may be required to furnish to the Secretary of State under this section shall include information which, although it is not in the possession of that company or would not otherwise come into the possession of that company, is information which it is reasonable to require that company to obtain (s 202(3)).

8.311 A requirement for the purposes of this section shall be contained in a direction which–

'(a) may describe the information to be furnished in such manner as the Secretary of State considers appropriate;

(b) may require the information to be furnished on a particular occasion, in particular circumstances or from time to time; and

(c) may be given to a particular company, to companies of a particular description or to all the companies holding appointments under

Chapter I or II of this Act or licences under Chapter 1A of that Part'.
(s 202(4))

8.312   The obligations of a water undertaker or sewerage undertaker under this section shall be enforceable by the Secretary of State.[1]

[1]   Water Act 1989, s 20.

8.313   In carrying out enforcement powers the Secretary of State and the Authority are given wide powers to require information from companies (s 203). Failure to supply the information without reasonable excuse is a criminal offence, so too is intentional destruction, suppression or alteration of information although no-one is compelled to produce information which could not be compelled in civil proceedings in the High Court.[1]

[1]   See also WIA 1991, ss 204–205.

8.314   Under s 203(2), a notice under this subsection is a notice signed by the Secretary of State or the Director and:

'(a)   requiring the person on whom it is served to produce, at a time and place specified in the notice, to
(i)   the Secretary of State or the Director or
(ii)   any person appointed by the Secretary of State or the Director for the purpose,
(iii)   any documents which are specified or described in the notice and are in that person's custody or under his control; or
(b)   requiring that person, if he is carrying on a business, to furnish, at the time and place and in the form and manner specified in the notice, the Secretary of State or the Director with such information as may be specified or described in the notice.'

8.315   Under WIA 1991, s 201(1) the Secretary of State may arrange for the publication, in such manner as he considers appropriate, of such information relating to any matter which is connected with the carrying out by a company holding an appointment under Part II, Chapter I of the Act of the functions of a water undertaker or sewerage undertaker as it may appear to him to be in the public interest to publish. Section 202 imposes a duty on undertakers to furnish the Secretary of State with information. Section 206 places restrictions on disclosure of information.

8.316   Information and advice may contain that which it is expedient to give to any customer or future customer but not so as to prejudice an individual or body.

8.317   Annual reports to the Secretary of State by the DG are presented to both Houses. The Water Act 2003 places a duty of cooperation on the Secretary of State, the Welsh Assembly, the Environment Agency and the Authority to cooperate and provide information to each other (s 52).

The Environment Agency's register

8.318 By s 190 of the WRA 1991, as amended, the EA maintains, in accordance with regulations, a register with prescribed particulars of:

'(a) any notices of water quality objectives or other notices served under section 83 of that Act;
(b) [...];
(c) [...];
(d) [...]
(e) the following, that is to say–
   (i) samples of water or effluent taken by the authority for the purposes of any of the water pollution provisions of this Act;
   (ii) information produced by analyses of those samples;
   (iii) such information with respect to samples of water or effluent taken by any other person and the analyses of those samples as is acquired by the Authority from any person under arrangements made by the Authority for the purposes of any of those provisions; and
   (iv) the steps taken in consequence of any such information as is mentioned in sub-paragraph (i) or (iii) above.'

8.319 The EA is under a duty to secure that the contents of registers maintained by the Authority under this section are available, at all reasonable times, for inspection by the public free of charge; and to afford members of the public reasonable facilities for obtaining from the Authority, on payment of reasonable charges, copies of entries in any of the registers.

Duties upon the Environment Agency and water undertakers to provide information

8.320 We have seen how the EA (which assumed the responsibilities of the National Rivers Authority) has to supply the appropriate minister, as reasonably required, with all such advice and assistance as appears to it to be appropriate for facilitating the performance of their functions. Part VIII of the WRA 1991 concerns provision of information and annual reports on a wide variety of matters. Notices requiring information may be served by the minister or EA.

8.321 Formerly, the National Rivers Authority was under a duty to provide a water undertaker with all such information to which this section applies as was in its possession and is reasonably requested by the undertaker for purposes connected with the carrying out of its functions relating to water pollution. Section 203 of the WRA 1991 concerns exchanges of information between the Authority and water undertakers in relation to pollution incidents. Information provided to a water undertaker or the EA under s 203(1) shall be provided in such form and in such manner and at such times as the undertaker or authority may reasonably require.

8.322 Information provided under WRA 1991, s 203(1) or (2) above to a water undertaker or to the EA shall be provided free of charge (s 203(4)). Section 203 applies to information about the quality of any controlled waters or of any other waters or about any incident in which any poisonous, noxious or polluting matter or any solid waste matter has entered any controlled waters or other waters. The EA is under a wide duty to supply the Secretary of State or minister with information about their property and functions. The EA's annual report is presented to the Secretary of State and is laid before both Houses (WRA 1991, s 187).

Prohibitions on disclosure

8.323 Section 204 of the WRA 1991 imposes a very wide prohibition on the disclosure of information. No information with respect to any particular business which: '(a) has been obtained by virtue of any of the provisions of this Act; and (b) relates to the affairs of any individual or to any particular business' shall, during the lifetime of that individual or so long as that business continues to be carried on, be disclosed without the consent of that individual or the person for the time being carrying on that business. There are a variety of exceptions.

8.324 Disclosure in contravention of the section is a criminal offence. Nothing shall preclude the disclosure of information made by one government Minister or department to another or to assist or enable designated public authorities to carry out functions specified by order.

REGULATION AND INFORMATION FROM UTILITIES IN ELECTRONIC COMMUNICATIONS, GAS AND ELECTRICITY[1]

8.325 In the case of electronic communications, gas and electricity and water, regulatory agencies have been established to regulate a former nationalised industry on privatisation. The regulatory bodies were, technically, designated as 'non-ministerial departments of state'.[2] They are now regulatory commissions. There is a Postal Services Commission established under the Postal Services Act 2000. The regimes for gas and electricity were fundamentally affected by the Utilities Act 2000 (see below). The Competition and Service (Utilities) Act 1992 (CS(U)A 1992) made some amendments to WIA 1991, s 38 to allow for the collection and publication of information about levels of performance and compensation payments as well as overall performance. Similar provisions apply to sewerage undertakers.

---

[1] On utilities, see C Graham *Regulating Public Utilities: a Constitutional Approach* (1999). See ss 24 – 29 of the Consumers, Estate Agents and Redress Act 2007 on the powers of the consumer body for energy and post to require the provision of information.

[2] We will not deal with railways apart from informing readers that there is a Rail Regulator, the Office of Rail Regulation (ORR) established by the Railways and Transport Safety Act 2003. The ORR licenses those rail companies who are franchised and enforces license conditions. Following the Transport Act 2000, the Strategic Rail Authority was established under Part IV

of that Act and it assumed responsibility for rail franchising and has some responsibility for consumer affairs including the financing of consumer committees. Network Rail took over Railtrack and is essentially owned by the government. The Strategic Rail Authority is responsible for a variety of purposes and objectives including promoting the use of the rail network for the carriage of passengers and goods and an integrated system of transport. While contributing to sustainable development, promoting efficiency and economy, competition in passenger services is no longer an objective for the SRA but competition is a responsibility of the ORR. The SRA will have responsibility for track accessibility and charges as well as safety, the latter of which will necessitate close liaison with the Health and Safety Executive. The SRA franchises passenger services according to various objectives and criteria and awards are made 'on the best overall value for money'. This involves subsidy as well as fee. Network Rail is responsible for the track and its maintenance and the railway infrastructure. By Transport Act 2000, ss 227 and 228 the Central Rail Users' Consultative Committee became the Rail Passengers' Council and the Rail Users' Consultative Committees became the Rail Passengers' Committees and their terms of reference were extended (see Schs 22 and 23). Under the Railways Act 2005, the SRA was abolished and its functions transferred to the Secretary of State. A Rail Passengers' Council was created, together with committees. The Rail Passengers' Users Council has now been renamed as the Passengers' Council as a result of additional functions relating to other modes of transport. These changes were introduced by the new s 19A of the Railways Act 2005, introduced by the Local Transport Act 2008. See also SI 2010/439. The National Lottery was regulated by a single-person regulator but this was renamed the National Lottery Commission when the regulator was forced to resign after receiving gifts from the company which ran the Lottery, Camelot. In the summer of 2000, the National Lottery Commissioner resigned after a finding of acting unfairly in a judicial review brought by Camelot when she discontinued negotiations with Camelot for the renewal of the licence in favour of further discussions with Richard Branson's Virgin group alone: *R v National Lottery Commission, ex p Camelot Group plc* (2000) *Times*, 12 October.

8.326   The utility regulators and utilities are covered by the FOIA 2000, the latter with regard to their functions which have been designated as 'public' under FOIA 2000, s 4 or where they are providing a service under a contract with a public authority, the provision of which is a function of the authority. As with the case of the water and sewerage industries, there are specific statutory duties and powers allowing the regulator to have access to an industry's documents or information. The CS(U)A 1992, as well as placing duties vis-à-vis standards of performance and service on industries, also imposed a tripartite complaints structure with complaints being redressed by a procedure within each industry, by customer service committees and finally by the DG (as he then was). Special provision was made for a variety of disputes, for disconnections and to increase competition in gas and water industries. The water industry and electricity regulators had features which made them more consumer-friendly and the CS(U)A 1992 sought to approximate the position of all regulators to whom that legislation applied. The DGT was obliged to collect information about compensation paid by designated operators and levels of overall service achieved in providing relevant services. The DG possessed a power to direct that information be given to the DG by an industry in relation to compensation payments and on levels of performance achieved by operators. This information which had been collected or furnished to the DG had to be published by the DG at least once a year. Information could be excluded from publication where its publication might seriously and prejudicially affect an individual or 'body of persons', whether corporate on not, and which relates to that individual or body of persons (Telecommunications Act 1984, s 27C, inserted by CS(U)A 1992, s 2). These provisions were based on Electricity Act 1989, s 42. Under s 27D of the 1984 Act (inserted by CS(U)A 1992, s 3), information had to be given to customers of designated bodies about overall performance at least once every 12 months. The Energy Act 2011, Pt 1, Ch 5 (not yet in force) introduces a power for the Secretary of State to modify licences in order to require providers to supply more detailed tariff information to consumers.

8.327 In the case of telecommunications, the then Director General of Telecommunications also acted as a consumer complaints body. The DGT maintained the registers of licences and orders under the Act,[1] of approved contractors and approved apparatus,[2] and these are publicly available. All operators of public telecommunications systems had to be licensed by the Secretary of State,[3] other systems may be licensed by the DGT. The licence may specify that information services are to be provided[4] and the issue of a licence and its modification was subject to 'notice and comment' provisions.[5] The DGT had the duty of collecting information on telecommunications' activities[6] and to publish information and advice 'in such form and in such manner ... as it may appear to him to be expedient to give to consumers, purchasers and other users of telecommunication services'[7] excluding, as far as is practicable, information on the private affairs of an individual or corporate bodies that might unjustifiably prejudice those persons if disclosed.[8] Under s 53, the DGT had power to obtain information by demand with a saving for that which could not be compelled in civil proceedings.[9] Obstruction was a criminal offence. The DGT had power to establish advisory bodies, and has to establish certain advisory bodies.[10] OFTEL, then the regulatory body, developed policy and conducted licence reviews under very open and transparent consultation procedures and hearings.[11] The DGT published annual and other reports.

[1] See SI 1995/232.
[2] Telecommunications Act 1984, ss 19, 21, 23 respectively.
[3] This may be delegated.
[4] CS(U)A 1992, ss 7 and 8(2), (3).
[5] CS(U)A 1992, ss 8(5) and 12(2). The Competition Commission may be involved in licence modification references.
[6] CS(U)A 1992, s 47(2).
[7] CS(U)A 1992, s 48(1).
[8] CS(U)A 1992, s 48(2) and (3).
[9] Codes of practice have been produced by the relevant associations.
[10] See CS(U)A 1992, s 54 and sub-s (4) for the relevant bodies.
[11] *Improving Accountability* OFTEL 1997; and *Improving Accountability – Further Steps* OFTEL 1998.

8.328 The CS(U)A 1992 repeats provisions on individual and overall standards of performance in the case of gas. For the regulation of gas suppliers, the regulator was the DG of Gas Supply. The Gas Act 1986, and the CS(U)A 1992 above, were significantly amended by the Gas Act 1995, adding gas transporters and shippers to the regulatory framework. In this case a separate body exists for consumer complaints – the Gas Consumers' Council (GCC) with 11 regional offices. Tariffs were originally fixed under statute.[1] The DG and GCC are given powers to investigate their respective 'matters'[2] and the DG is under similar duties to the DG of Telecommunications to keep a register[3] and publish information[4] and has a similar power to demand information.[5] Gas Act 1986, s 42 contains a criminal prohibition on the disclosure of information obtained under the Act relating to the affairs of an individual or any particular business (see SI 2000/1122). It lasts for the lifetime of that individual or duration of that business. The Gas Act 1995 increased powers of the DG to demand information from licence holders where their licences were being revoked, suspended, or had expired or were expiring (see Gas Act 1995, Sch 3, paras 45–51).

1   Gas Act 1986, s 14. This ceased to have effect on the passage of the Gas Act 1995.
2   Gas Act 1986, ss 31 and 33, as amended by the CS(U)A 1992 and the Gas Act 1995.
3   Gas Act 1986, s 36, amended by the Gas (Exempt Supplies) Act 1993 and Gas Act 1995, Sch 3, para 42.
4   Gas Act 1986, s 35, as amended by the Gas Act 1995.
5   Gas Act 1986, s 38, similarly amended.

8.329   Under the Electricity Act 1989, a DG of Electricity Supply was established who was the regulatory and licensing authority,[1] and under s 2 there were established consumers' committees for authorised areas of a public electricity supplier or authorised areas of two or more such suppliers. Licences were subject to notice and comment provisions on their award,[2] modification (with possible references to the Competition Commission), and the DG had power to require information.[3] The DG had power to make regulations specifying standard of performance for tariff customers, and what information should be given to individuals by suppliers.[4] S/he may determine the standard of overall performance of suppliers; s/he shall collect information, from time to time, with respect to levels of performance[5] which has to be given by suppliers and which is to be published. The DG had duties of investigation into supply matters, including complaints which may be referred for arbitration, and the consumers' committees had duties to make representations to, and consult with suppliers on matters affecting the consumer interest. Individual disputes may be referred to them by the DG. Enforcement disputes are investigated by the DG; 'other matters' by the committees.

1   Electricity Act 1989, s 1.
2   Electricity Act 1989, s 6(4).
3   Electricity Act 1989, s 28, as amended by the CS(U)A 1992.
4   Electricity Act 1989, s 39, as similarly amended.
5   Electricity Act 1989, s 40, as similarly amended.

8.330   The general duties of the DG were similar to those of the other DGs. As has already been explained the DGs have all been replaced by regulatory commissions and the provisions outlined above are largely historical in nature, with the new procedures outlined in the discussion below.

Utilities Act 2000

8.331   The Utilities Act 2000 (UA 2000) combined the regulatory authorities for gas and electricity in the Gas and Electricity Markets Authority and created the Gas and Electricity Consumer Council, which has now been superseded by the National Consumer Council (NCC) created by the Consumers, Estate Agents and Redress Act 2007 (CEARA 2007). Both bodies are to publish a document setting out a description of the projects they are planning to undertake during the year. This does not cover routine projects. The authority, which performs functions on behalf of the Crown, must publish annual and other reports. UA 2000, s 6 substitutes a new s 35 of the Gas Act 1986 on the publication of information and advice about consumer matters. The authority and the council shall make arrangements with a view to securing co-operation and exchanges of information between them and 'consistent treatment of matters which affect them both' (UA 2000, s 7). In the gas market, the Secretary of State's and the authority's principal objective is to 'protect the interests of consumers' in relation to gas conveyed through pipes wherever appropriate by promoting effective competition between persons engaged in, or in commercial activities connected with, the shipping, transportation or supply of gas so conveyed (s 9).[1] In performing this duty, regard is to be had to the interests of the disabled or chronically sick, pensioners, those on low incomes and those residing in rural areas. This does not allow the interests of other consumers not to be considered (Gas Act 1986, s 4AA(3), as substituted). Similar provisions with necessary modifications apply to generation, transmission, distribution or supply of electricity.[2] The Act made numerous amendments to the licensing provisions concerning electricity and gas supply etc. It also added considerably to the provisions on individual and overall standards of performance and their publication and enforcement.

[1]   Which adds a new s 4AA to the Gas Act 1986.
[2]   UA 2000, s 13 adding a new s 3A(1) to the Electricity Act 1989.

8.332 The NCC[1] has to obtain and keep under review information about consumer matters including those from different areas of the UK as well as information about the views of consumers in different areas. To assist in these tasks the NCC must set up territorial committees for Wales, Scotland and Northern Ireland whose tasks include providing advice and information to the council on consumer matters. The NCC may issue advice or guidance to any person with a view to improving standards of service and promoting best practice in connection with the handling of complaints made by consumers or any other matter affecting the interests of consumers (CEARA 2007, s 19). Information shall not be disclosed – although this does not apply where the recipient is the authority, Secretary of State, Competition Commission or any other public authority – where the information relates to any particular individual or body of persons (corporate or unincorporated) unless the body etc has consented, it is publicly available from another source (the FOIA 2000), or its disclosure would not in the opinion of the council 'seriously and prejudicially affect the interests of the individual or body'. This latter point involves consultation with the individual and regard has to be had to the authority's opinion on the desirability or otherwise of disclosure.

[1]   Under CEARA 2007, s 6 in connection with the interests of consumers, the council shall have regard to the interests of the disabled, chronically sick, those of pensionable age, etc.

8.333 The NCC has the function of providing information to consumers of gas and electricity as defined by publishing information as the NCC deems appropriate or by responding to requests or otherwise. For details, see CEARA 2007, ss 19 and 24.

8.334   Section 45 of CEARA 2007 imposes a duty on the NCC to publish statistical information about standards of performance and complaints made by consumers about any matter relating to the activities of such suppliers, etc and the handling of such complaints. The NCC also has a power (under CEARA 2007, s 19) to publish advice and information about consumer matters where it appears to the council that publication would promote the interests of consumers. It may publish in such manner as it thinks fit. The provisions also apply to the giving of advice, etc to public authorities.

8.335   Finally, there are general provisions (CEARA 2007, s 24) relating to the supply of information to the NCC by GEMA as the NCC may require for the purpose of exercising its functions. The NCC has similar powers in relation to energy suppliers and the OFT. The bodies concerned should comply with a request as soon as reasonably practicable and in a manner and form as is reasonably specified by the NCC although the NCC has to regard the desirability of minimising costs or other detriments to the body concerned, etc. If a body refuses to provide the information that has been requested, it must give reasons for doing so. A refusal by a licence-holder to supply information may be referred to GEMA by the NCC and the authority has to determine whether the licence holder is entitled to resist supply. If not, then information must be supplied. Where the authority makes such a determination, or where it itself refuses information, it must supply a notice of its reasons to the NCC. The latter may publish such a notice subject to the above safeguards (CEARA 2007, ss 24–25).

8.336   The NCC is also under a duty to provide information to GEMA on a similar basis. The NCC must give notice of reasons for any refusal which the authority may publish in such manner as it considers appropriate.

8.337   The Electricity (Trading and Transmission) Bill 2003–04 became the Energy Act 2004, Part 3 and establishes a UK-wide market for trading and transmission of electricity. The Act increases the licensing responsibilities of the Gas and Electricity Markets Authority (GEMA) and seeks to ensure competitive and reliable energy supplies.

8.338   The Utilities Bill of 1999/2000 originally created a Telecommunications Authority to replace OFTEL and a Telecommunications Consumer Council. With necessary modifications, the provisions relating to gas and electricity which have been outlined from the Act applied to telecommunications. Although the DG of Water Supply retained his position in the Bill, the Bill created a Water Advisory Panel and a Consumer Council for Water. Again the Bill set out provisions, with necessary modifications, for information etc as above. These provisions covering telecommunications and water were removed from the eventual Act. These matters were dealt with in the Water Act 2003, as seen above, and in the Communications Act 2003. For the purpose of completeness, the Office of Fair Trading was also made a commission by virtue of the Enterprise Act 2002.

8.339 There has been considerable EU action in the fields of gas, electricity and electronic communications in recent years. The EU has acted to create a more open internal market in gas[1] and electricity[2] and in 2002 delivered its 'New Regulatory Framework' for electronic communications services, which has since been modified in 2009.[3] Consumers are not generally directly affected by the EU action in the field of gas and electricity, but the action in relation to electronic communications services has a much greater impact on end users, including requiring greater provision of information about services and service quality to consumers.

[1] See Directives 2009/73/EC (internal market in natural gas) and 2008/92/EC (transparency of gas prices to industrial end users). These should be considered alongside Regulation 2009/715/EC on access to natural gas transmission networks and Regulation 2010/994/EU on security of gas supply.

[2] See Directive 2009/72/EC (internal market for electricity). This Directive should be considered alongside Regulation 714/2009 on access to electricity networks for cross border transmission of electricity and Regulations 774/2010/EU and 838/2010/EU which concern aspects of charging for use of electricity transmission networks.

[3] Directives 2002/17/EC – 2002/21/EC. This suite of Directives covers a wide range of aspects, including competition, licensing and universal service in electronic communications markets. The Directives were amended in 2009.

COMMUNICATIONS ACT 2003

8.340 The Office of Communications Act 2002 established OFCOM which has the regulatory responsibilities for communications and broadcasting, replacing a variety of other bodies. It has duties to promote the interests of citizens in communications matters and of consumers in relevant markets 'where appropriate' by competition and to promote 'media literacy'. The details of regulatory powers and responsibilities are in the Communications Act 2003. The functions, transferred functions and duties are set out in ss 1–31 of the 2003 Act. Amongst other things, OFCOM is under a duty to publish and take account of consumer research and to consult consumers. A Consumer Panel will be appointed by OFCOM and advisory committees exist for different parts of the UK and for the elderly and disabled. OFCOM is subject to various 'general information functions' (2003 Act, ss 24–26) and has to maintain a publicly accessible register of those who have who have sent notification of their wish to provide a communications network and service (licensing has been removed: s 147). Universal service conditions are provided for in ss 61–72, and ss 135–146 contain details on 'information provisions'. Details on disputes and appeals in relation to providers are contained in ss 185–197. The Broadcasting Standards Authority has gone and its functions are taken over by OFCOM (ss 319–328). Sections 106–119 and Sch 3 deal with the electronic communications code (amending Telecommunications Act 1984, Sch 2). Licensing will continue for independent TV broadcasting. The BBC, Channel Four, the Welsh Authority and the Gaelic Media Service will carry on broadcasting under existing arrangements, as amended by the 2003 Act, and will be regulated by OFCOM. OFCOM has to produce a standards code (ss 319–328, and see para 2.369 above). Broadcasters may be directed to transmit a statement of findings when they have breached any licence conditions, and financial penalties may be imposed (ss 344, 345). Section 393 has the usual restrictions on disclosing information in the performance of OFCOM's duties under the Act.

FINANCIAL SERVICES AND MARKETS ACT 2000

8.341   This Act replaces the Financial Services Act 1986. It provides for the Financial Services Authority (FSA) to act as the regulator of financial markets covered by the Act. There are numerous powers and duties in relation to regulation and information-gathering in the Act and the provisions covering auditors should be noted.[1] Part XVI establishes the Ombudsman Scheme[2] for activities to which the compulsory jurisdiction rules of the Act apply and which are conducted by an authorised person (s 226). There is also a 'voluntary jurisdiction' (s 227). The ombudsman is given wide powers to obtain information and refusal to comply may be referred to the High Court or Court of Session for it to deal with as a contempt if satisfied that the defaulter has no reasonable excuse for the default (ss 231–232). Section 233 amends DPA 1998, s 32 to make data processed by the ombudsman exempt from the subject access provisions where access would prejudice the proper discharge of the ombudsman's functions. Chapter 11 (para 11.1, note 6) has some details on the FSA's compulsory powers of obtaining information and evidence.

[1]   Financial Services and Markets Act 2000, ss 341–344. See Companies (Audit, Investigations and Community Enterprise) Act 2004.
[2]   See Financial Services and Markets Act 2000, Sch 17.

Chapter 9

Information, redress of grievance and judicial review

INTRODUCTION

9.1 The purpose of this chapter is to provide a practical overview of the way that internal and more formal grievance procedures, ombudsmen and judicial review help to open up the decision-making process of public institutions and to make them more responsive to the public. Interest in informal resolution of grievances has grown substantially in the last three decades. So too has interest in, and the number of offices of, ombudsmen. In fact, in the past an Ombudsman Commission has been suggested by a Cabinet Office research paper as a way of providing a one stop or linked-up ombudsman to deal with linked-up public services. The Scottish have created such a commission in Scotland under the Scottish Public Services Ombudsman Act 2002 (para 2.132 above). The Public Services Ombudsman (Wales) Act 2005 has established a unified ombudsman scheme in Wales although the Commissioner for Older People (Wales) Act 2006, s 20 introduced a complaints procedure for older people. It may be that linked-up justice is an equally pressing need in the era of joined-up government[1] and offloaded and downsized government.[2] This has been addressed to some extent by the Department for Constitutional Affairs in a White Paper response to the Leggatt review on tribunals (see below) which laid the foundation for the Tribunals, Courts and Enforcement Act 2007 (TCEA 2007). The Law Commission has reported on *Public Sector Ombudsmen* and we were able to make brief reference to this report in this chapter.[3] In the area of fair procedure the courts have made significant contributions in the area of judicial review since the early 1960s in the terrain covered by jurisdictional review, review for irrationality and procedural impropriety. In more recent years the growing European influence on our public law has added to the judicial armoury especially in human rights protection.

---

[1] *Modernising Government* Cm 4310 (1999).

[2] *The Coalition: Our Programme for Government: Freedom, Fairness, Responsibility* (May 2010) HM Government.

[3] Law Commission Paper No 329 HC 1136 (2010–12). See para 9.57 below. On the pre-appointment hearings for the post of Parliamentary and Health Service Ombudsmen see HC 1220 I & II (2010–12).

9.2   What follows will extract the practical implications for openness and the obtaining of information from these developments.

INTERNAL COMPLAINTS AND GRIEVANCE PROCEDURES

9.3   The movement towards widespread provision of internal complaints grievance procedures in public bodies, and more latterly in privatised industries and bodies under contract with public bodies to provide publicly financed services, has its origins in the mid-1970s in the UK. Over 20 years ago, the Organisation for Economic Co-operation and Development (OECD) noted that 'equal access by all citizens to the public administration and to the established complaints system – a basic right in the constitutional principles of OECD Member countries – is not always, nor necessarily, ensured by the structures of representative democracy'.[1] The OECD referred to the need to establish mechanisms to deal with complaints before ombudsmen or courts are invoked ie, internal mechanisms. We shall see that these may take very different forms. This message was reinforced by a detailed report from the National Audit Office in March 2005 which found that government complaints' processes were slow, complex and expensive. The 1.4 million complaints that were known cost £510 million to process and involved 9,300 staff. (National Audit Office: Citizen Redress HC 21 (2004–05); Appendix 1 of the report has details of scales and costs of redress systems in agencies and departments, and Appendix 2 has examples of case studies in agencies.) The Administrative Justice and Tribunals Council (AJTC) established under the TCEA 2007 has referred to internal complaints procedures in its newsletters.[2] A publication in June 2011, 'Right First Time', addresses a core concern for all involved in the delivery of public services: how to get more decisions right first time. The AJTC reports on how over a million appeals and other challenges to governmental decisions are now made each year to tribunals, ombudsmen and other dispute-resolution bodies: 'These result in surprisingly high success rates and each appeal involves significant processing costs as well as strain on the individual whose rights are affected.' The report identifies the scope to make 'substantial savings through a concerted effort to improve original decision-making within government departments, agencies and other public bodies'. Despite the obvious advantages for citizens and public authorities in getting things right first time currently there are 'few incentives or policies directed at such an outcome', the AJTC reports.[3] The AJTC has also published 'Principles of Administrative Justice' (2010). In *Securing Fairness and Redress: Administrative Justice at Risk* (2011) the AJTC examined mistakes, complaints and independence in administrative justice, asking, 'What is happening in the era of austerity and cutback?' In June 2011, the House of Lords Communications Committee reported on BBC internal complaints mechanisms covering complaints about impartiality and accuracy with the Corporation's programmes. Media regulator Ofcom, rather than the BBC, should have the final say over such complaints, the Committee recommended (HL 166 (2010–12). The Lords Communications Committee's inquiry into BBC governance and regulation also said 'the convoluted and overly complicated complaints process at the BBC' must be improved. Although effective internal complaints procedures are essential, we argue, in the case of the BBC leaving complaints on impartiality and accuracy in journalistic judgement to the Corporation made the BBC 'judge and jury in these matters'.[4]

[1] OECD *Administration as Service: The Public as Client* (Paris, 1987).
[2] *Adjust Newsletter* (2008) at: www.ajtc.gov.uk/adjust/adjust_ latest.htm. The Council has been earmarked as a 'quango' to be chopped in the 2010 review of quangos. Its responsibilities included oversight of the administrative justice system and state accountability.
[3] http://www.justice.gov.uk/ajtc/docs/AJTC_Right_first_time_web(7).pdf.
[4] House of Lords Communications Committee HL 16 (2010–12).

9.4 Many commentators noted in former years how unresponsive public bodies were to citizens or recipients of such bodies' services when there was a perceived shortcoming or failure in service. It was commonplace, indeed almost universal, not to have identified personnel or procedures to deal with complaints and to provide no information about how complaints that were made were processed. This was in marked contradiction to employee/personnel complaints where procedures were far more apparent in public bodies. Answers to queries were in the most perfunctory of forms and redress of any kind rarely forthcoming. Any success in registering a complaint invariably owed more to persistence, stamina and sheer cussedness on the part of a complainant which may have resulted in the 'noisy wheel getting the grease' outcome rather than one based upon just desert, strength of case and merits. Most bodies were content to rely upon ombudsmen, tribunals – of which there are many in the UK[1] – and courts to remedy wrongs. Any internal mechanisms were superfluous.

[1] A review of tribunals was conducted by Sir Andrew Leggatt and a White Paper has been produced: see para 9.7, note 1 below.

9.5 Some authorities on the contrary developed highly effective complaints procedures during the 1980s and many of the examples from these local authorities were used as suggestions for good procedures by central government. The Alternative Dispute Resolution movement had its influence encouraging means of redress other than through courts or formal adjudicatory bodies. In 1991 there was the Citizen's Charter (CC) initiative from Prime Minister John Major. The principles that the Charter sought to advance were: explicit standards; openness; information; choice; non-discrimination; accessibility; and finally, when things went wrong, a 'good explanation', an 'apology' and 'well publicised and readily available complaints procedures'.[1] The Commons select committee on public administration re-emphasised the Charter's message of 'putting the user first' and using complaints procedures as learning devices. The report, which concentrated on central government delivery of services to the public, also identified that difficulties were present in identifying 'complaints', distinguishing between complaints and appeals and the assistance required in using complaints procedures when available.[2] The Cabinet Office was seen as the place to champion good complaints practice. The Parliamentary and Health Services Ombudsmen were seen as a source of information on problems with public services and the number of complaints upheld should reflect a level of quality control. The Cross-Government Complaints Handlers Network was established in 2006, the report noted, and this self-organised body could be developed into a more formal body. The committee recommended a single access point for all public services in central government providing information and advice on complaining. Government departments should publicise their complaints procedures in their publication schemes under the Freedom of Information Act 2000 (FOIA 2000) (para 1.48).[3] These are not confined to FOIA complaints. More recently the Cabinet Office has published guidance on establishing internal ombudsman-like schemes within departments which builds on the work of the British and Irish Ombudsman Organisation guidance (below). It recommends avoidance of the word 'ombudsman', consultation with the Ministry of Justice where a tribunal may be more appropriate and special regard to the need to safeguard Art 6 ECHR rights where an individual's civil or political rights are in issue.[4]

[1] *Citizens Charter* p 5. These were established under statutory regulations in schools, utilities and elsewhere; see now eg Complaints against Schools (England) Regulations 2010, SI 2010/853.

[2] Select Committee on Public Administration *When Citizens Complain* 5th report HC 409 (2007–08) and GR HC 997 (2008–09). See PAC and HC 1147 (2007–08) *From Citizen's Charter to Public Service Guarantees*. See the National Audit Office *Handling Customer Complaints* HC 995 (2007–08) and HC 853 (2007–08) *Feeding Back: Learning from Complaint Handling in Health and Social Care*. There are some very useful chapters in M Adler ed *Administrative Justice in Context* (2010). See H Genn *Judging Civil Justice* (2009) ch 3.

[3] See for an example from local government: http://www.communities.gov.uk/corporate/foi/complaintsprocedure/.

[4] Cabinet Office Ombudsman schemes – guidance for departments (2009).

9.6 Specific areas in local government have been the subject of developments in terms of grievance redress such as social services and education (below) and in health there have been statutory initiatives put in place which were modified in 2009.[1] In Scotland, the Crerar report in 2007[2] reviewed complaints procedures covering all authorities under the Scottish administration including Scottish local authorities. This report led to a government report recommending standardisation of procedures for Scottish local authorities and a greater role for the Scottish Public Services Ombudsman acting as an independent complaints handler.[3] This only covered Scottish bodies and not UK bodies dealing with tax or social security complaints. The Commission for Local Administration and the Welsh ombudsman have provided guidance on complaints handling by local authorities, discussed below, and the local ombudsman can hear complaints about the work of the local standards committees that were examined in paras 5.24 and 5.47.

[1] http://www.nhs.uk/choiceintheNHS/Rightsandpledges/complaints/Pages/NHScomplaints.aspx.

[2] L Crerar 'Report of the Independent Review of Regulation, Audit Inspection and Complaints Handling in Scotland' (2007) Scottish Government.

[3] Fit-For-Purpose Complaints System Action Group 'Report to Ministers' Scottish Government (2008).

9.7 Prime Minister Blair stated in *Leading from the Front Line* (2003, Office of Public Service Reform) that he wished to see services that were not only universal but which treated people as individuals and, in response to the Leggatt review on tribunals, which recommended a unified system of tribunals provided by central government,[1] the Department for Constitutional Affairs published 'Transforming Public Services: Complaints, Redress and Tribunals' (Cm 6243,

2004). This included as one of its key elements in a five year plan: 'moving out of courts and tribunals disputes that could be resolved elsewhere through better use of education, information, advice and *proportionate dispute resolution*. 'Transforming Public Services' concentrated on a range of policies and services that, so far as possible, will help people avoid problems and legal disputes and where they cannot a system that 'provides tailored solutions to resolve the dispute as quickly and cost-effectively as possible' (para 2.2). These may use the full spectrum of well-known devices such as adjudication, arbitration, conciliation, early neutral evaluation, mediation, negotiation and ombudsmen.

[1] *Tribunals for Users – One System, One Service* (2001) www.tribunals-review.org.uk; and see M.Partington ed *The Leggatt Review of Tribunals: Academic Seminar Papers* Faculty of Law, University of Bristol (2001). M Adler (ed) *Administrative Justice in Context* (2010).

COMPLAINTS

9.8 A complaint (whether written or oral) is a statement that something has gone wrong regardless in fact of whether anything has gone wrong. It is the complainant's perception that is important though that does not mean that anyone who complains will get what they seeking. It is also distinguished from a simple request for information or clarification. A grievance is an unresolved complaint or one that is not resolved to the satisfaction of the complainant. There can be complaints about maladministration: delay, inaccuracy, oversight, rudeness, bias, inappropriate behaviour. The Parliamentary Ombudsman has provided a list that has been added to over the years (see para 2.133, note 1 above). Complaints may have serious and widespread implications where a change in decision may effect not simply one complainant but potentially thousands. Complaints may also be directed not at the rights or wrongs of an individual decision but at the policy lying behind a decision. There is usually a reluctance for complaints procedures being allowed to address policy complaints, but feeding information about such complaints back to policy makers is increasingly regarded as a vital component of the complaints' industry.

Government and other initiatives

9.9 The Directgov website provides details on complaining about public and private bodies.[1] Many complaints arise from poor communication or/and inadequate information and publicity. Very often the quality of service or what is provided is not clearly set out so recent years have seen increasing attempts to set out service and performance criteria, sometimes in the form of a 'contract' between authorities and citizens. Complaints about a reduction in service are likely to increase in a period of austerity.

[1] http://www.direct.gov.uk/en/Governmentcitizensandrights/Yourrightsandresponsibilities/ Makingcomplaints-yourrights/index.htm.

9.10 The Major government set up within the Citizen's Charter (CC) Unit a CC Complaints Task Force in 1993 which has been superseded by the Better Government initiative and Service First of the Labour Government. This published advice for public-sector bodies on: access to complaints systems; simplicity and speed in the operation of a complaints system; achieving fairness covering items such as monitoring fairness in responses and investigations and treatment of complainants, getting second opinions where necessary, independence in complaints procedures and use of outside individuals, use of mediation and conciliation services, treatment of difficult and vexatious complainants, protection of confidentiality. Further papers dealt with staff training and motivation so as to engender a constructive approach to complaints and to integrate complaints resolution into an overall service/consumer programme. Much depended upon ethos and positive culture. This meant giving high visibility to complaints processes and ensuring that those working in such processes were not regarded as 'also rans' in terms of career development.

9.11 Advice was offered on learning the lessons from complaints which included guidance on recording complaints including informal complaints eg oral expressions of dissatisfaction and the best ways of extracting information from complaints to feed it into the management and policy-making processes. It also had advice on complaints about policies themselves for although there was no, or at best limited scope, to change policy on taxation, excise, competition it may be that the complaint was really about explanation of policy or an exercise of discretion within a given policy on eg social security payments. The last paper covered remedies. Today, government departments and public authorities will be expected to possess well-publicised complaints procedures via publication schemes under the FOIA, through websites and otherwise. Public authorities will also have to possess internal complaints avenues to deal with challenges under FOIA 2000 (para 1.233 above).

9.12 The Parliamentary and Health Service Commissioners has produced 'Principles of Good Complaint Handling' (2009).[1] This counsels on: getting it right, including acting in accordance with the law and relevant guidance and the rights of others including their human rights; being customer-focused; being open and accountable; acting fairly and proportionately; and putting things right and seeking continuous improvement. All of those have specific points of supporting detail. Like the Commission for Local Administration (below), the ombudsman has produced 'Principles of Good Administration' (2009) and 'Remedy' (2009).[2] All operate under the same basic principles as those proposed for complaint handling.

[1]　http://www.ombudsman.org.uk/__data/assets/pdf_file/0005/1040/Principles-of-Good-Complaint-Handling.pdf.
[2]　http://www.ombudsman.org.uk/improving-public-service/ombudsmansprinciples. The Administrative Justice and Tribunals Council has also published *Principles for Administrative Justice: the AJTC's Approach* (November 2010).

9.13 The Commission for Local Administration (CLA) produced guidance on good practice for authorities within the local ombudsmen's jurisdiction. One of these was entitled 'Running a Complaints System', which was revised by the CLA in 2009.[1] This has a wealth of good advice to give local authorities – who are likely to be the tier of government that most citizens come into contact with. The guidance states that from April 2009, local ombudsmen will expect complainants to use the internal procedures before they will take up a complaint, although there may be exceptions. It defines a complaint as an 'expression of dissatisfaction' whether provided by the council, a contractor or a partner that requires a response. Distinctions between formal and informal complaints should not be made. 'Local Partnerships and Citizen Redress' provides guidance on complaints procedure operated by partners.[2] Guidance exists on 'Unreasonably Persistent Complainants and Unreasonable Complainant Behaviour' (2010).[3] 'Listening, Responding, Improving: a Guide to Better Customer Care'[4] from the Department of Health contains guidance on statutory procedures for adult social care. Separate procedures exist for child care. The main reasons for having a complaints system are:

(a)   individuals are now more aware of their right to voice critical comments and suggestions for improvement;

(b)   increasing emphasis is being given by public bodies to providing services of the highest affordable standard;

(c)   greater emphasis is being given to the importance of promoting and developing customer care;

(d)   as an integral part of customer care policy and quality assurance programme a complaints system can show that an authority cares about their constituents;

(e)   complaints systems need not be defensive but can be positive ways of improving customer satisfaction and enhancing services; and

(f)   well-publicised complaints procedures are part of government and opposition philosophy on the rights of citizens.

[1]   http://www.lgo.org.uk/publications/guidance-notes/
[2]   www.lgo.org.uk/publications/special-reports.
[3]   Ibid.
[4]   Department of Health 2009: www.dh.gov.uk.

9.14   'Running a Complaints System' gives detailed guidance on what are complaints, a checklist of questions for officials setting up procedures to ensure efficacy and a checklist of their responsibilities. The guidance gives added emphasis to the development of information technology. It does not advocate *one* procedure but offers advice on best principles for complaint handling. The principles are: accessibility, communication, timeliness, fairness, credibility and accountability. The variety of channels other than internal procedures through which it might be better to pursue complaints of a criminal, financial or disciplinary matter. There are checklists on good investigative practices and on awarding compensation. An effective complaints procedure will help to resolve the dissatisfaction of citizens about the service they should have, or believe they should have, received. To be effective it will provide: a straightforward means for customers or their representatives to make a complaint – it will be accessible and conspicuous, simple to use; a procedure for investigating a complaint objectively which will be as speedy as possible working according to pre-determined time limits though these may, and with explanation, have to be waived but a target of 12 weeks should be aimed for; keep the complainant informed about progress and eventual outcome; offer redress where required; ensure that action is taken to avoid recurrence; feedback necessary information to officials, managers and politicians to ensure relevant information is taken into account when decisions are taken on resource allocation, benefit conferral, prioritisation, quality assurance and forward planning. A National Audit Office report in 2008 found feedback in social care and health complaints to be undeveloped.[1] The guidance recommends that a member of senior management should 'own' the procedure and reports should be made to that person on complaints and outcomes and who should disseminate best practice lessons. Responses should be proportionate.

[1]   National Audit Office 'Feeding Back? Learning from complaints handling in health and social care' HC 583 (2007–08).

9.15   The CLA guidance no longer recommends procedures involving three distinct stages. Two stages should be adequate and kept within the timescale. The CLA document speaks of complaint resolution by frontline staff. If that fails, there should be reference to a specific person who displays independence and authority within the council. This is not clear. Liaison with partners and contractors should be effectively and timeously pursued. A third stage might involve a person outside the section becoming involved, perhaps as part of a review panel, but this may cause delay and is not encouraged. The review panel has been removed from adult-care complaints. In the field of complaints about medical treatment in the NHS, services complaints are made to service staff and employing organisations/trusts will appoint a complaints officer. A second stage for more resistant complaints, which was dealt with by an independent panel comprising independent members, has been removed under changes introduced in 2009. The second stage now involves the Health Service Ombudsman whose statutory powers have been considerably extended and who can question the clinical judgement of doctors and other specialists; however, the courts have been quick to remind the ombudsman that he cannot investigate matters at large – the subject of investigation must be in the complaint.[1] Patient Advice and Liaison Services are available in all hospitals. Police complaints and complaints against privatised utilities involve a three-tier structure; these begin with complaints being resolved by the utilities themselves who provide their own procedures and which progress through ever-increasing degrees of formality.

[1]   *Cavanagh v Health Service Commissioner* [2005] EWCA Civ 1578.

9.16   The 1997 Labour Government developed thinking on complaints procedures which was initially contained in a 1998 publication from the Cabinet Office.[1] The PM's Office of Public Service Reform and the Department for Constitutional Affairs carried on a variety of initiatives since 2003. This built on the recommendations of the Complaints Task Force whose work was given support by the Parliamentary Public Service Committee in its report on the CC in 1997[2] and replaces the Task Force's Guidance and the Charter Unit's Complaints Review Arrangements in Public Services (May 1997). In particular, it emphasises the desirability of internal complaints procedures, a further review procedure where the first stage is not successful and which should be separate 'from line management' and then advising complainants of where to go should they remain dissatisfied viz, ombudsmen or other statutory procedures. Additional items included publishing information at least once a year on:

(a)   the number and type of complaints;

(b)   how quickly they were dealt with;

(c)   users' satisfaction; and

(d)   actions taken as a result.

¹   *How to deal with complaints* (June 1998, *Service First – the New Charter Programme*).

²   HC 78-I (1996–97), pp xxvii–xxx.

9.17 Further points included putting details of complaints procedures on the Internet. Freephone numbers should be used. It emphasises necessary precautions to avoid discrimination against complainants: make clear they will not suffer any adverse consequences, allow access to necessary documents and personnel but allow complaints to be made confidentially where this is required – although confidentiality should not be used to prevent important information for service improvement being disclosed – monitoring services provided to those who have complained and allowing complaints to be made to others who are not dealing directly with complainants and carrying out surveys of those who have made a complaint.

9.18 The second-stage 'review arrangements' which it urges upon public authorities concern complaints about maladministration and failures to meet service aims and targets. It does not cover formal appeals about decisions based on statutory requirements or complaints about policy (p 3). However, for internal complaints staff should be trained to deal with complaints about policy even if 'they cannot change things' (p 37). I will say more about the relationship of different redress mechanisms below. There is certainly a greater emphasis on all staff knowing about effective complaint redress mechanisms.

9.19 Building on existing work and procedures, it gives examples of best practice. One city housing authority uses a complaints form with a tear-off slip for the complainant to send in. The rest of the form the complainant keeps and explains in simple language how the complaint will be dealt with and includes deadlines and a section on the reverse which allows them to record all relevant dates. Some authorities include a stamped addressed envelope for complaints. Other authorities use business cards for their employees to give to those who wish to complain while they are travelling locally.

9.20 Another city authority had the following procedure which was fairly typical:

STAGE 1

You will receive an acknowledgement within 7 working days of receipt of your complaint, telling you who is dealing with it. A full reply will follow within 14 working days of receipt, or you will be advised of any delay.

STAGE 2

If you are not happy with the outcome, please write back within one month (there's no need to send a new form). A Departmental Complaints Manager will acknowledge your letter within 7 working days of its receipt and arrange a review of your complaint. You will be sent a reply within 14 working days of receiving your letter, or be advised of any delay.

STAGE 3

If you are still unhappy with the situation, please write back to the Departmental Complaints Manager within one month. Your complaint will then be referred to the Director of Legal and Administrative Services for a final review. You will be sent an acknowledgement within 7 working days of receiving your letter and a full reply will be sent within 14 working days of its receipt or you will be advised of any delay.

9.21 One other public authority provides the following service to those who have complained:

A 20 per cent check of the service provided to those who have complained is carried out. A questionnaire asks: Did you find it easy to complain? Were you given an apology?

Were you satisfied with any explanation given? Was you complaint dealt with quickly enough? Would you like further contact with the Customer Service Manager?

9.22 The checklist to follow in setting up a complaints system is: set out service standards; inform the user about complaints systems; remove barriers to complaining; explain the stages of the procedures; meet any special needs; provide support and assistance to those who need it; obtain the views of those who use the procedures.

9.23 The document sets out a series of 'dos' and 'don'ts' in terms of good practice. To help monitor complaints there might be sense in a departmental complaints manager who will prepare a departmental procedure for monitoring and dealing with complaints received by the department – increasingly these are spoken of as being 'owned' by employees and users who will contribute towards their design. S/he will make sure all staff are familiar with the procedures and that procedures are properly publicised. One authority has spelt out guidance for its employees. This explains why the authority needs a complaints procedure; what a complaint is; who can complain; how the separate stages of the procedure work; other assistance that should be available for consumers; the authority's comments and suggestions scheme; how to deal with complaints against the authority's employees; a detailed list of good and bad practice in relation to complaints.

9.24 The principles for good procedures follow much of what has been discussed already, but they should be written in clear simple language and in *all relevant languages* (the CLA guidance above states that complaints leaflets should be written in plain English) and cover complaints about operations and policy and should be subject to regular review. They should spell out clearly when a complaint should go to the next stage. These stages are: on the spot reply (informal); referral, investigation and reply; internal review; external review. It might be advisable to use an easily identifiable colour for complaints forms to ensure they are not misplaced.

9.25   Replies should: aim to answer all the points of concern appropriately; be factually correct; avoid jargon; be signed by the officer responsible; contain a contact number; and inform the person what to do next if still not satisfied. In difficult cases, visits at the home of the complainant may be made. A willingness to meet with complainants may be useful and is certainly good practice.

9.26   The guidance was written in a period that was not subject to recession and huge reduction in public expenditure. These factors will clearly have an extensive impact on levels and quality of service. There is also pressure to remove services from local government control, as with schools under the school academy programmes. Nonetheless, there are important lessons which it would be fatal to ignore. In 2007–08, the Public Administration Select Committee has expressed its support for the enduring influence of the 1991 Citizens Charter on the provision of public services in England and Wales.[1]

[1]   *From Citizen's Charter to Public Service Guarantees: Entitlements to Public Services* HC 411 (2007–08).

REMEDIES

9.27   A separate CLA publication has been published on 'Remedies' (2005). Guidance is offered on a wide range of local authority responsibilities including bad neighbours, time and trouble payments and housing repairs and management, education admissions and special needs, social services, the environment and planning. Compensation has been a vexed issue in the UK. In a report into 'Maladministration and Redress',[1] the Parliamentary Commissioner for Administration investigated the total confusion of practice and procedures for making compensatory payments. The situation verged on anarchy. In central government, the position is discretionary and governed by Treasury Guidance, known as 'Dear Accounting Officer' letters. Those issued prior to 2008 have largely been disbanded.[2] 'Managing Public Money' (2011)[3] is the present Treasury account of good financial practice. Chapter 4.13 and 14 and Annex 4.14 deal with complaints, remedy and transparency. Annex 6.3 advises on when charges may be made for information.[4] The available guidance states that staff should provide information which will allow complainants to identify whether a service is below par. Suitable remedies should be offered and ensure that staff are aware of the options; try to give remedies that complainants wish for though within reason and obvious constraints; survey complainants to see whether they received the remedy they wanted. Remedies might include:

(a)   an apology;
(b)   an explanation;
(c)   correction of the error or other remedial action;
(d)   an undertaking to improve procedures or systems; and
(e)   financial compensation, ie one-off or structured settlement.

[1]   HC 112 (1994–95); *Government Reply* HC 316 (1994–95).

²   http://www.hm-treasury.gov.uk/psr_governance_dao_letters.htm.
³   http://www.hm-treasury.gov.uk/psr_managingpublicmoney_publication.htm.
⁴   http://www.hm-treasury.gov.uk/psr_mpm_annexes.htm.

9.28   Great care should be taken in devising financial compensation, especially if a precedent is being set. Novel, unusual, or complex cases require consultation with the Treasury as do those where limits of delegation are in issue as well as implications for other service deliverers. Guidance is provided on these matters including interest awards. Financial awards should have estimates cover and be approved by a Parliamentary vote. They score as special payments in departments' resource accounts. Annual reports should indicate through 'summary information' what payments have been made for maladministration. In local government, the CLA has produced detailed guidance on remedies and financial compensation (above). There are also greater legal restrictions on making compensatory payments because of the statutory basis of local government administration, but the Local Government Act 2000, s 92 makes provision to pay compensation (or provide some other benefit) where a person has been adversely affected by maladministration.

Encouraging good practice

9.29   To encourage the right attitude among staff, and in addition to what has been said already, managers should send notices to all staff stressing the importance of complaints and the benefits of handling them well. 'Chief executives or equivalents in all public services should be held personally responsible for effective complaints handling. And this would be reflected in job descriptions and performance appraisals, including decisions on performance related pay.' It would, as the Select Committee said, be a contractual undertaking by senior officers. In turn managers should recognise and reward staff who handle complaints well. Some authorities have made handling complaints a part of formal appraisal of staff:

> 'For staff who deal direct with the public, the assessment of their ability to handle customers well is a major determinant of their appraisal. More importantly, the appraisal itself reaffirms the authority's commitment to customer care and provides these staff with the opportunity to say what they feel is going well or badly in this area and what help they need to do the job better.' (*How to deal with complaints*, p 43)

9.30   Complaints procedures should be separated from disciplinary procedures. Greater publicity, provision of information, consultation with representatives of user groups and staff and delegation for complaints handling to 'the lowest possible level' (ie most accessible) will help reduce the cost of administering such schemes and any consequential demand for more resources.

9.31   Recording complaints should be done in a consistent and detailed fashion. It should be simple, practical and not onerous and should be useful for monitoring complaints. There are details on the minima that should be recorded and these include: name, address and telephone number of complainant; date of receipt; details of the complaint, putting it into a category depending upon the subject; remedy requested; immediate action to be taken. Advice on complaint analysis is provided and an example from a police headquarters is given:

> 'the HQ produce a six monthly management report on complaints. This shows: the number and type of complaint broken down into departments and districts; complaints that have been sorted out into type and result; and management issues arising from complaint investigations. The report is reviewed each year with feed-back from those who receive it.' (Ibid, p 51)

9.32   The following information about complaints should be published: the numbers and types or categories of complaints received; the speed with which they were dealt with compared with target times; levels of customer satisfaction with your replies; action taken to improve services as a result of complaints.

9.33   It might also be useful to consider setting up networks of authorities who provide complaints procedures to compare best practice etc.

9.34   The London-Wide Complaints Network was set up in March 1997 although it no longer seems active. Its membership involved 20 London Boroughs. Its aims were to:
(a)   exchange ideas and information on all areas of local authority complaints procedures with maximum encouragement for the sharing of information;
(b)   agree on features of good practice where possible;
(c)   act as a support group for officials engaged in complaints procedures;
(d)   identify any network-wide training/conference needs and develop common approaches where appropriate to meet them; and
(e)   provide effective liaison and representation of the views of the network and institutions/directorates it represents to relevant bodies such as ombudsmen.

9.35   The group met every three months.

9.36   There has also been increasing contact between public and private sector bodies such as retailers to gain relevant experience and cross-fertilisation of ideas. The review of complaints procedures themselves to see how fairly etc they are working may well benefit from having an outside element on it to help bring impartial and fresh ideas. The review process should have access to all staff and relevant papers. It should have power to enforce its decisions on the authority.

9.37   As well as the internal review with a possible independent element, authorities should consider the creation of formal external arrangements for reviewing complaints after internal processes have been exhausted. Complaints review means an arrangement for reviewing individual complaints or complaints systems that is separate from line management. Details will obviously relate very closely to the needs of the authority and its users. It might be completely external – as is increasingly common in UK central government (see below) and some services in local government, eg social services. In other cases it might utilise the office of a senior manager who has not been involved with the service area or complaint. These reviews might review difficult complaints, systems of complaints' handling or both. There may be some confusion with internal monitoring mechanisms if not careful. The existence of external review mechanisms may well help to persuade the public that complaints are being taken seriously and the authority aims to deal with them fairly.

> 'In 1995 … the Citizen's Charter Complaints Task Force reported that people felt there was a gap between internal investigations by line management and an external ombudsman.' (Ibid, p 68)

9.38 The term 'ombudsman' should not be used for this body to avoid confusion with statutory models (see below).

9.39 Reviewers should respect confidentiality but they should also report on their work publicly after an investigation is concluded and be free to contact the press in a responsible manner. Their independence should be guaranteed and they should be properly resourced. Complaints that reviewers will deal with should be clearly defined eg does it include relatives of users/service recipients or advisers/ representatives? Those entitled to complain should be able to reach the reviewer directly without having to obtain approval from the service or authority. Review arrangements should be fully advertised and explained.

9.40 Adjudicators have been appointed for investigation of complaints by many departments and public bodies. Some are statutory like the Office of the Independent Adjudicator for Higher Education under the Higher Education Act 2004. Others are non-statutory such as the Independent Complaints Adjudicator for Ofsted and the Adult Learning Inspectorate, the Independent Complaints Reviewer dealing with the Land Registry, the National Archives, the Charity Commission, the Audit Commission (to be disbanded) and the Homes and Community Agency and Waterways ombudsman. An interesting example of an external review is that of the Adjudicator's Office in the areas of Inland Revenue, Customs and Excise and the Contributions Agency (National Insurance):

> 'The Adjudicator's Office (AO) do not investigate a complaint until the user has been through the relevant organisation's internal complaints system. Before they investigate a complaint, they make sure that the organisation has the chance to sort out the problem at a senior level. If a senior manager has not had this opportunity the AO refer the complaint to that manager to deal with. The AO make sure that the user knows they can come back to them if they are not happy with the reply they get from the organisation. If someone goes to the AO with a complaint or question about an organisation other [than bodies within the AO's remit] they try to help these people and give them information about where they should go to get things sorted out.' (Ibid, p 75)

9.41 Reviewers should offer the opportunity for conciliation if necessary and the procedure should separate out these two functions. The Independent

Case Examiner of the Child Support Agency (an agency of central government) provides a conciliation function as well as a complaints review service. Reviewers will be expected to follow the points of good practice recommended for complaints procedures and should have their own complaints procedures for those dissatisfied with their service. Even ombudsmen may be guilty of maladministration. Reviewers should have access to the staff and papers they require – in the case of the Prisons Ombudsman (sic) information has been refused.

9.42 The reviewer should be able to monitor responses to complaint recommendations to ensure compliance and bodies covered by such reviews should enforce their decisions unless they have very good reasons for not doing so which they should explain in public. Reviewers should identify trends in complaints referred; repeated failures of service or standards; weaknesses in institutions' complaints procedures or organisation. They should have a fast track to senior managers and chief executives. While they cannot overrule policy or law, they should be able to comment on the impact of policy and law – not unlike the UK ombudsmen. They are expected to advise on further recourse to statutory ombudsmen. They will publish individual reports and annual reports and other reports as required. These reports should be widely circulated publicly.

9.43 For central government and its agencies, reviewers, adjudicators, commissioners, case examiners cover: Inland Revenue (including tax credit and child benefit), the Valuation Office Agency, Customs and Excise (now combined with the Inland Revenue as HMRC), the Public Guardianship Office and the Insolvency Service – all within the Adjudicator's Office; the Vehicle Licensing Authority, the Driving Standards Agency, the Highways Agency, the Vehicle Inspectorate, the Child Support Agency (an agency which was the subject of a deeply critical report of the Parliamentary Ombudsman)[1] together with the Northern Ireland Social Security Agency, prisons and probation (both private and public prisons through the prisons' ombudsman), the Immigration Services Commissioner, War Pensions, HM Land Registry, the Office for Standards in Education; and they exist in various local authorities, probation services and educational institutions such as the Office of the Independent Adjudicator for Higher Education. There are usually limits on such bodies, such as the Adjudicator's Office, dealing with matters that can be brought before an independent tribunal or which might have already been investigated by the ombudsman.

[1] HC 20 (1995–96).

Attitudes towards complaints procedures

9.44 To some, additional grievance procedures are not self-evidently justified. There may be other more effective routes through which to make complaint (see below). They may be specifically suited to an Anglo-Saxon culture, a mix of individualism and anti-state sentiment and where the absence of a defined sphere of public law and, until recently, a public law tradition have encouraged the burgeoning of grass-roots legal systems and domestic avenues for maintaining social order. Other legal/political traditions within Europe have no need for such mechanisms, it may be argued. Germany is a leading example.

9.45 To others they appear as anti-public sector; a means of encouraging captious anti-public service sentiments and supporting advocates of a minimal state. The Labour Government (1997–2010) nevertheless gave full support to complaints mechanisms supporting the existence of at least one internal complaints procedure within public bodies serving the public as one of the 'six Whitehall standards' of public service. Such a complaints procedure is also included as one of the nine principles of public service delivery. The *Better Government* programme has embarked upon a wide-ranging and continuing process of consultation and participation by all relevant parties to enhance public service and to shape the service that people want. Proposals cover: People's Panels (which it claims to be the first *national* initiative of its kind in the world, although local initiatives have occurred in Germany and the USA), Quality Networks involving managers at national level, charters (200 national, 10,000 local) and a commitment to place the key public service principles in legal provisions and an interactive use of the Internet to discuss best practices in public service were early initiatives.[1] FOIA 2000 requires bodies covered by the Act to make publicly available information on how services are run; the service they provide; standards of service and performance against them; and complaints procedures[2] – all part of an attempt to make the programme more bottom up and less top down. We saw in ch 8 how 'best value' was seen as relying upon full consultation with local citizens and how detailed guidance on consultation had been published by the DETR.[3] The most recent code on consultation was published by the Cabinet Office in 2008.[4] There is nothing to indicate a change in philosophy in the coalition government. When a record number of complaints (over 100,000) was recorded against the NHS in 2009–10, the minister responsible stated: 'The Coalition Government is determined to put patients at the centre of everything the NHS does. Quality and outcomes will be the measures by which the service is judged.'[5] The Government was forced in June 2011 by the strength of professional and public opinion to modify its plans for greater competition and private delivery of health care by making procedures more participatory and transparent (para 9.106 below).

[1] *The Citizen's Charter: A consultation exercise: the Government's response.*
[2] *Service First: the new charter programme.*
[3] *Guidance on Enhancing Participation in Local Government* (October 1998); *Strong Local Leadership – Quality Public Services* Cm 5327 (2001) and *Code of Practice on Consultation* Cabinet Office 2004: www.cabinet-office.gov.uk/regulation/consultation/code.htm on consultation by central government, and *Public Participation in Local Government: a Survey of Local Authorities* ODPM (2002). The latter found that take-up of traditional methods of engaging the public had slowed significantly in recent years whereas take-up of innovative and deliberative approaches such as interactive websites, citizens' panels and focus groups have increased since 1997.
[4] http://www.bis.gov.uk/files/file47158.pdf.
[5] http://www.bbc.co.uk/news/health-11083236. And see HC 482 (2010–11) *Listening and Learning: Ombudsman Review of NHS Complaints Handling.*

Preparation

9.46 Before establishing a complaints procedure, officials and management should be committed to its introduction. Staff will have to be properly motivated and receive adequate training. This has been repeated in the guidance noted above from the Parliamentary ombudsman and CLA. A senior official should be identified as the person having overall responsibility for introducing the procedure. S/he may well head a working group. Consider any resource implications and how they can be met. Will additional staff be required with obvious limits in straightened times? Epmployee whistleblower provisions are now mandatory. Consult all relevant bodies: the ombudsman, user groups and trade associations, employees' associations, trade unions, legal officers, financial controllers, national bodies as appropriate and groups with special problems. Define a complaint and what is not included. Who can complain? Details of how to complain: all addresses including e-mail, phone and fax numbers. Stages of any procedure. Recording of complaints, any form that they should be in – whether informal at first but thereafter in writing but without pedantic obstacles. Who takes action? Political involvement and how to respond. Time limits. How to deal with special cases: eg very senior officials as subjects of complaint, financial impropriety. What to do about anonymous complaints? Remedies available. Advice on other remedies and next steps. Establish a senior officer to co-ordinate and manage complaints arrangements to ensure consistency, promote efficiency and facilitate monitoring. Don't call this person an ombudsman. How will the complaints procedures tie in with any existing procedures required by law or currently in operation eg disciplinary procedures? How can procedures be best publicised and most widely disseminated: make maximum use of the Internet and up-to-date software.

INTERNAL COMPLAINTS PROCEDURES, OMBUDSMEN, TRIBUNALS AND COURTS

9.47 There have been three significant reviews in the area of administrative justice in the UK within the last 15 years. These were the review of the public sector ombudsmen schemes undertaken by the Cabinet Office, the review of tribunals undertaken by Sir Andrew Leggatt and the review of judicial review procedure by Sir Jeffery Bowman which led to the new Part 54 of the Civil Procedure Rules 1998. To a great extent, all three reviews have been conducted discretely with no attempt to interrelate their investigations and findings and the relationship between different approaches to justice in the joined-up state.[1] The joined-up state has lost its currency but downsizing should not be an excuse for uncoordinated anarchy. The threatened removal of the Administrative Justice and Tribunals Council in plans annnounced in 2010 did not did not inspire confidence in maintaining overall coherence in administrative justice.

[1]   See N Lewis and P Birkinshaw *When Citizens Complain: Reforming Justice and Administration* (1993).

9.48 How do complaints procedures relate to other bodies or procedures that may be resorted to? Complaints procedures have proliferated. But there may be formal processes of internal review which concentrate on the correctness of the initial decision. The object is not to see whether discretion may be exercised differently. In a UK context and commonly elsewhere, if internal processes exist, the ombudsman will expect them to be resorted to unless there is a compelling reason why not. The complaints procedures will, as already stated, cover basically the same ground as the ombudsmen – maladministration – and UK ombudsmen supply copious guidance for authorities within their jurisdiction on what good and bad practice are.[1] Ombudsmen are increasingly the last or very often third stage in a complaints process after the internal procedures are finalised. Ombudsmen are also subject to changes in the areas that they cover; the Localism Bill 2011 transfers complaints about local authority social housing from the loval government ombudsmen to the housing ombudsman. The latter is approved under Housing Act 1996, s 51 by the Secretary of State and social landlords are under a contractual duty to implement the housing ombudsman's recommendations.[2]

[1]   Above para 9.12 and see PCA *The Ombudsman in Your Files.*
[2]   See HC 1343 (2010–12) for the annual report.

9.49   One point that has arisen in the UK, and this arose from the very early days of the Citizen's Charter, concerns the overlap between such procedures and established ombudsmen. The concerns relating to confusion have continued. Indeed, ombudsmen felt threatened by their existence for a variety of reasons: they might be a deliberate attempt to undermine ombudsmen by taking work away from them and giving it not to *independent* persons but to bodies that were inherently a part of the body that was complained against. They could confuse the public into believing that they were the ombudsmen and deprive the real ombudsmen of the benefit of their service.[1] In tune with the appeal to the market driven philosophy of the then government in the UK, it was suggested that ombudsmen should enter the market of dispute resolution mechanisms and compete with other bodies for the custom of citizens. This did not come to fruition and ombudsmen very clearly are hierarchically superior to internal mechanisms.

[1]   See the Select Committee on the Parliamentary Commissioner's report at: HC 158 (1991–92).

9.50   However, the British and Irish Ombudsmen Association (BIOA) – a representative body – did seek to control the use of the name 'ombudsmen' and established criteria which had to be satisfied before the appellation could be used and refused to admit to the Association anyone who did not satisfy the criteria of independence. There have been difficulties with the Prisons Ombudsman and the Revenue etc Adjudicator and their perceived lack of independence. The Parliamentary Commissioner for Administration (PCA) also advised that the expression 'ombudsman' should not be used by internal bodies. This has not been respected in some cases. Furthermore, ombudsmen have stated that not possessing an internal procedure may indicate evidence of maladministration. The BIOA has produced guidance to assist in setting up internal complaints regimes.

9.51 A difficulty that has arisen in the UK is the question of what the promises under the Citizen's Charter and its successors amount to. Are they legally binding under private or public law or are they merely exhortatory? In the case of the utility regulators, standards and compensation schemes are written in formal published documents, sometimes in the form of regulations as occurred originally in the case of electricity. Elsewhere, they do not take the form of legal rules. The Parliamentary Ombudsman (PO) has written that where they are firm promises, a claim for compensation where they are not met is very strong. If they are 'indicators of performance' they are persuasive but not guarantees entitling one to compensation as a right. Meeting targets does not rule out maladministration; failure to meet them does not automatically mean maladministration.[1]

[1]   PCA *Annual Report* 1993.

9.52 In relation to courts, an important development has been the use of the existence of internal procedures to reduce opportunities for legal remedies. First of all where they exist, courts will expect parties seeking judicial review to use them *before* they can come to court unless the remedies internal procedures offered were inadequate or there were other serious shortcomings.[1] Limitation periods would run from the date of the final decision of a complaints body. More importantly, under English law, where a statute lays down a remedy for an aggrieved party, and where a duty is not owed to a restricted group of individuals, this has been taken by the courts as a good reason for not creating a duty owed to the individual from a breach of the statute and a right for compensation to a party allegedly injured by the breach. This has been illustrated in some dramatic case-law where the courts relied upon the existence of internal complaints procedures as one reason to deny a right to compensation for breaches of statutory duties.[2] Furthermore, statutory rights in public law eg for access to a solicitor for those in custody are remediable by judicial review and did not carry a right to damages where there was a breach of a statutory provision.[3] That having been said, this area has been subject to considerable European influence, both via the EU and the ECHR.[4] It is also feeling the considerable impact of the Human Rights Act 1998 and the duty to take into account the relevant jurisprudence of the Convention on Human Rights under HRA 1998, s 2 and the duty of compatible construction of statutes and regulations under s 3. As the FOIA 2000 places a duty upon authorities to publicise complaints procedures in publication schemes, this could be seized upon by the courts as a reason for not creating a compensatable right in private law for a breach of statutory duty. Article 13, which concerns an effective remedy for breaches of convention rights, was not implemented by the HRA but it remains an obligation under the Convention in international law. To avoid further criticism the ombudsmen and the courts will have to provide robust investigations and remedies. The fact that the ombudsmen could not enforce their decisions undermined their efficacy in relation to Art 13, the ECtHR believed. This comes close to short-changing ombudsmen regimes because they are not based on adjudicatory procedures. That would still leave any actions in negligence to be addressed by the courts. Complaints procedures under FOIA to deal with FOI complaints are dealt with by the code issued under the FOIA 2000 (para 1.22).

1   *R v Falmouth and Truro Port Health Authority, ex p South West Water Services Ltd* [2000] 3 All ER 306, CA.

2   See *X v Bedfordshire County Council* [1995] 2 AC 633, HL and note *Barrett v Enfield London Borough Council* [1999] 3 All ER 193, HL, and *Phelps v Hillingdon London Borough Council* [2000] 4 All ER 504, HL – in the latter two cases there is strong evidence that the courts are more relaxed about allowing actions to proceed. In *Lawrence v Pembrokeshire CC* [2007] EWCA Civ 446 the court noted comments that Art 8 ECHR may well have changed the position of a duty of care to children in relation to decisions affecting children. See, however, *Osman v United Kingdom* (1998) 5 BHRC 293 where the ECtHR ruled that denying a right of action in negligence on policy grounds (action against the police investigating crime) was a breach of Art 6 ECHR; the English case law followed *Hill v Chief Constable of the West Yorkshire Police* [1989] AC 53, itself followed in *Brooks v Commissioner of the Metropolitan Police* [2005] UKHL 24 and *Van Colle and Smith* [2008] UKHL 50. The case of one of the litigants in *X* above successfully challenged the ruling of the House of Lords: in *TP v United Kingdom* (2000) 2 LGLR 181 the ECmHR ruled that there had been a breach of Art 6 when the English courts ruled that an action in negligence could not be maintained against a decision by social services to take a child into care. A failure to provide video evidence in good time was also ruled to be a breach of Art 8. The ECtHR did not believe a breach of Art 6 had occurred but there had been a breach of Art 8: [2001] 2 FCR 289. See *Z v UK* [2000] 2 FCR 245, ECmHR upheld on this aspect by the ECtHR in relation to Art 3 but not Art 6: [2001] 2 FCR 246. In *E v UK* App No 33218/96 [2002] 3 FCR 700 the ECtHR held that a local authority's failure to protect step-children from being sexually abused by a step-father amounted to a breach of Arts 3 and 13 ECHR – no further issue concerning a breach of Art 8 arose. In *DP v UK* [2002] 3 FCR 385 there were breaches of Art 13 ECHR because of an absence of 'effective domestic procedure of enquiry' for allegations of abuse via the local ombudsman and the courts. See *A v Essex CC* [2003] EWCA Civ 1848 where it was held that local authorities owe prospective adopting couples who are also parents a duty of care to take reasonable steps to provide all relevant information about children being considered for adoption including information about problematic behaviour. See also *JD v East Berkshire Community Health NHS Trust* [2005] 2 AC 373 – no duty of care owed by health care officials tp parents accused of abuse of their children; *Lawrence v Pembrokeshire* above had not advanced the position re a duty to parents by virtue of Art 8 ECHR. This would be 'a step too far' in relation to removing or registering children. Note also *EJ Connor v Surrey CC* [2010] EWCA Civ 286.

3   *Cullen v Chief Constable of the RUC* [2004] 2 All ER 237 (HL) concerning Northern Ireland (Emergency Provisions) Act 1987, s 15(1). There were very strong dissenting judgments from Lords Bingham and Steyn who felt that a breach of s 15 was actionable per se but following EU law, proof of a 'sufficiently serious breach' is required for a damages action, at para 21. See incidentally: *Watkins v Secretary of State for the Home Department* [2004] 4 All ER 1158 (CA) and general damages for interference with fundamental rights by misfeasance of public office. The Law Commission in its 2008 paper 'Administrative Redress:Public Bodies and the Citizen' recommended a public law of tortious liability but this was widely criticised and not pursued in its 2010 paper No 322.

4   See P Birkinshaw *European Public Law* (2003), ch 10.

9.53   A problem that has arisen between courts and ombudsmen in the UK ought not to interfere with relationships between complaints procedures and courts, viz a cross-over of jurisdiction. Public sector ombudsmen in the UK are prevented from investigating and recommending in cases where there is a legal or statutory administrative remedy unless this route is unreasonable in the circumstances for the complainant. The wording differs between schemes but that is the end result. They have a discretion to investigate but the courts have reminded ombudsmen that this must be exercised carefully. The same is not true for private sector ombudsmen many of whom may investigate legal disputes but a conflict in jurisdiction has arisen.[1] Most ombudsmen in other jurisdictions are not so limited. Some unfortunate decisions from the courts have reminded the ombudsmen of their limitations and that they are subject to judicial review, which is understandable, although a very exacting standard of review has been imposed.[2] Furthermore, one judicial decision has stated that where there is a legal remedy before the courts, the ombudsman should hand the case over to the courts where the courts have suitable forms of relief and the fact that the complainant is unlikely to obtain a legal remedy ought not to constrain the ombudsman's decision even though a remedy may be available on the grounds of maladministration.[3] However, if the ombudsman exercised his discretion and investigated, the judgment stated that the court would not give a remedy on that basis, suggesting judicial deference. It has been repeated that difficulty in obtaining judicial review may not be enough to give the ombudsman solid grounds to launch an investigation.[4] In cases of doubt, the High Court has advised complainants that where there is overlap, the ombudsman should be approached first so as to avoid the operation of the statutory mechanism depriving the ombudsman of jurisdiction after judicial review proceedings have been initiated.[5]

[1] Dr Julian Farrand was particularly disgruntled at the approach of some judges towards his office when he was the Pensions Ombudsman. Some judges, he said in a press release in July 1997, were 'inimical to the idea of the ombudsman'.

[2] *R v Parliamentary Comr for Administration, ex p Balchin* [1997] JPL 917 and *ex p Balchin (No 2)* (2000) 2 LGLR 87; *R v Comr for Local Administration, ex p Croydon London Borough Council* [1989] 1 All ER 1033. See *R (Hughes) v Local Government Ombudsman* [2001] EWHC Admin 349 where the High Court did not believe it was open to the ombudsman to find 'no injustice' on the evidence, but where it was inappropriate for the court to rule on a finding that should be made when the ombudsman reconsidered the matter.

[3] *R v Comr for Local Administration, ex p Croydon London Borough Council* [1989] 1 All ER 1033.

[4] *R (on the Application of UMO) v Commissioner for Local Administration in England* [2003] EWHC 3202 and *R v Commissioner for Local Administration ex p Field* [2000] COD 58.

[5] *UMO*, ibid.

9.54   The ombudsmen have said that these decisions have not had an inhibiting effect. Indeed, in a Court of Appeal decision in March 2000, a more relaxed attitude was taken by the court to an ombudsman investigation where there was a legal remedy available. Part of the complaint was about the fact that the ombudsman had used a less demanding test for a finding of bias than that required by the courts. This, it was held, was not impermissible. Maladministration and unlawful activity are not synonymous, although there may be overlap. Indeed, the fact that the ombudsman had full investigatory powers and in a judicial review the applicants may not have obtained necessary evidence to get their case started was a serious factor swaying the case the ombudsman's way.[1] Nonetheless, when ombudsmen were introduced into the UK, the law of judicial review was nowhere near as developed and as sophisticated as it is today, and its sophistication owes much to European influence. Maladministration, which to repeat is what internal complaints procedures basically deal with, was a much wider and more nebulous concept covering mistakes, errors, oversights, delay, rudeness, incompetence, inaccuracy, failing to explain or give adequate information or advice, bias, bad procedures and inadequate monitoring of existing procedures, disproportionate redress and failing to advise on rights of appeal or other remedies. The list is endless. Maladministration allows the ombudsman to examine the full range of information on which the decision-maker acted, or failed to act, and their practice of sending the draft report to the department or authority investigated allows the ombudsman to discover additional information. Only very rarely has the local ombudsman felt that the body investigated has not been forthcoming with all the relevant information,[2] although in the case in question it was the default of an individual officer, not the authority's policy.

[1]   *R v Local Comr for Administration, ex p Liverpool City Council* [1999] 3 All ER 85 and on appeal [2001] 1 All ER 462, CA.
[2]   Inv87/A/203.

9.55 In the case of the PO a developing relationship of constructive cooperation has been witnessed since the last edition of this work. This has been seen in some prolonged and difficult cases involving persons interned by the Japanese in the Second World War and the claims to a compensation fund (*R (Elias) v Secretary of State for Defence* [2006] EWCA Civ 1293), the complaints concerning occupational retirement pensions (*R (Bradley) v Secrtary of State for Work and Pensions* [2008] EWCA Civ 36) and on the investigation and reports involving Equitable Life and the loss suffered by those holding policies with the assurance company (*R (EMAG) v HM Treasury* [2009] EWHC 2495). The claims of the internees were originally rejected by the court (*R (ABCIFER) v Secretary of State for Defence* [2003] EWCA Civ 473) but the PO found maladministration in the way the claims were dealt with and the manner in which the scheme was administered. The PO was concerned not only with the complainant's case and those in a similar position but sought to draw attention to the way compensation schemes were introduced by the Government. All relevant questions should be considered before an announcement by government and any changes to a scheme should be publicised and explained (HC 324 2005–06). In *Bradley*, the Government had rejected the findings and recommendations of the PO. The court, while making no ruling on the recommendations, held that the Government had acted with irrationality because in rejecting the PO's findings it had failed to provide cogent reasons for the rejection. It could not simply reject them out of hand (*Bradley v Secretary of State*). In EMAG the divisional court again held that the Government had failed to produce cogent reasons for rejecting a number of the Ombudsman's findings of maladministration and injustice, and quashed its decision to reject the findings. The Government's application for permission to appeal was refused. The court has also required the Government to provide a written response to the judgment within 21 days (*R (EMAG) v HM Treasury*).[1] In both cases, this judicial criticism and increasing Parliamentary scrutiny led to a government reconsideration and implementation (though not complete) of the PO recommendations. However, in *Cavanagh v HS Commissioner* [2005] EWCA Civ 1578 the court of appeal reminded the ombudsman (health) that he is not free to examine complaints at large; there is no roving commission and the ombudsman can only investigate matters raised in a complaint. The Local Government Ombudsman's (LGO) powers were amended to allow investigation of a matter that comes 'to his attention during the course of an investigation' where it appears an injustice may have been caused (LGA 1974, ss 24A(5) and 26D). *Bradley* and *EMAG* have helped establish the constitutional position of redress through the ombudsmen.[2]

[1]   See *R (Gallagher) v Basildon DC* [2010] EWHC 2824 for the test involved when a local ombudsman'd recommendations are not followed.

² T Buck et al 'The Ombudsman Enterprise and Administrative Justice' (2011). See PAC HC 781 Work of the Ombudsman (2010–12).

9.56 The whole question of the relationship between the courts and ombudsmen has been the subject of Law Commission investigations and reports.[1] The LGO rejected 352 complaints in 2008–09 because of the statutory bar, the Parliamentary and Health Service Ombudsman (PHSO) 39, and the Public Services Ombudsman for Wales eight. It is not an idle matter. The Commission in its consultation paper found the 'default position in favour of judicial review was no longer sustainable'.[2] The Commission provisionally proposed relaxing the bar where the interests of justice required this. This entailed questions of whether a court seized of a case should stay proceedings to allow the ombudsman to investigate beyong those currently available in civil procedure rules to allow recourse to alternative dispute resolution (ADR).[3] The Commission proposed such a power. It also proposed specific powers in ombudsmen to rely upon methods of resolving complaints other than by investigation, ie via negotiation. The PHSO should be able to dispense with the requirement that a complaint be in writing it was proposed. The local ombudsman has this power (LGA 1974, s 26B(3); Local Government and Public Involvement in Health Act 2007, Part 9). The 2007 Act made a variety of changes to the local ombudsman scheme in relation to matters subject to examination, including some contractual matters, and methods of complaining. The filter should be amended it was proposed to allow a dual track access to the PO via an MP or directly by a complainant similar to practices involving the local ombudsmen.[4] Further proposals for consultation include allowing the public sector ombudsmen to dispense with the requirement to investigate in private where this seems appropriate. A power to refer a legal point for the determination of the administrative court was proposed and it was asked whether there should be a requirement for a legal opinion before referral.

¹ *Administrative Redress: Public Bodies and the Citizen* (2008) Consultation Paper No 187. Ditto Paper No 322 (2010) and on judicial review and public liability and Public Services Ombudsmen Law Commission Consultation Paper No 196 (2010).
² No 196 para 4.24.
³ CPR 26.4(2).
⁴ Select Committee on Public Administration *Parliament and the Ombudsman* HC 107 (2009–10) para 6 and Further Report HC 471 (2009–10) para 3.

9.57 In July 2011, the Law Commission published its report 'Public Service Ombudsmen'.[1] Among its recommendations are:
(a) the creation of a specific power to stay an application for judicial review, so that suitable matters are handled by ombudsmen rather than the courts;
(b) improved access to the ombudsmen by modifying the 'statutory bar' – the rule that recourse may not be had to the ombudsmen if the complaint has or could be pursued in a court of law;
(c) a power for the ombudsmen to refer a question on a point of law to the courts; and
(d) the removal of the MP filter in relation to the Parliamentary Commissioner for Administration.

¹ Law Commission Paper No 329 (July 2011) HC 1136 (2010–12).

9.58 Where ombudsmen deal with *legal* disputes, as is common on the continent and in UK private law regimes, the courts in the UK have been assertive in holding their decisions to be legally incorrect when the ombudsman has attempted to mitigate the rigors of the law to do what they believe was just in the circumstances. The Pensions Ombudsman was particularly outspoken in his criticism of judges whom he believed had not understood the purpose of ombudsmen, part of whose job was to mitigate the rigours of the law.[1] It is hard to avoid the conclusion that there have been jurisdictional jealousies driving this debate. It is also interesting to note that in its guidance to local authorities on good administrative practice, many of the points raised are clearly statements of proper legal practice arising from judicial decisions.

[1]   See para 9.53, note 1 above.

9.59 The presence of the ombudsman has had a beneficial impact on bureaucratic decision-making. Their practice of commenting on aspects of good administration, and deploring those which, while not maladministration, are in need of criticism is encouraging of improved performance.

9.60 It is now accepted that courts will not treat complaints procedures with suspicion. They are more likely to be seen by judges as a sensible and welcome attempt by public authorities to settle disputes before the necessity of resorting to expensive and over-worked courts or the ombudsman. If complaints procedures are driven by an ideology or are invested with too much power, then in a UK context this may well attract an exacting standard of review.

9.61 Furthermore, although ombudsmen are not duty bound like courts to have regard to the principles of the Convention on Human Rights' institutions in its interpretations, it has nonetheless been confirmed by the Court of Appeal that complainants should usually turn to the ombudsman and not the courts where they are claiming damages for a breach of human rights caused by maladministration. The case concerned the breach of a positive duty to act under Art 8 ECHR. The compensation was comparable to ombudsman awards and ombudsmen are a free service. In the same case, the court ruled that where damages were sought under the HRA for maladministration then the local ombudsman's recommendations can be looked at for guidance.[1] A suggestion by Lord Woolf that damages under the HRA should be on the low side has been disapproved and not followed; but the approach adopted when calculating damages for breaches of duty under the civil law was not to be followed. In the judgment in *Anufrijeva*, there was support for the award of modest damages where maladministration was complained of. The House of Lords has since ruled that decisions of the ECtHR on damages under Art 41 ECHR in relation to breaches of Art 6 should not be followed 'inflexibly' but neither should they be 'significantly more or less generous' than those judgments in awards under HRA 1998, s 8. The HRA was not a 'tort statute' said Lord Bingham (*R (Greenfield) v Secretary of State for the Home Department* [2005] UKHL 14). The finding of a breach in the case of Art 6 and a rehearing were usually adequate. Claims involving maladministration should be brought in the Administrative Court,

Lord Woolf believed, and before giving any permission to apply for judicial review the Administrative Court judge should require the claimant to explain 'why it would not be more appropriate to use any available internal complaints procedure' or proceed to the Police Complaints Authority or Local Government Ombudsman where relevant. Damages claims may be best dealt with by such a process and the court would restrict itself to any other relief required. The court wanted to encourage alternative forms of relief without wishing to be prescriptive (see para 81). The use of prolix and highly expensive judicial procedures for such claims was not encouraged.[2]

1   *Anufrijeva and Another v LB of Southwark* [2004] 1 All ER 833 following *R (Bernard) v LB Enfield* [2002] EWHC 2282 (Admin). In the light of *Anufrijeva* and LGA 2000, s 92 allowing local authorities to give compensation for maladministration, the Commission has rewritten its guidance on remedies (paras 9.13–9.14 above). See *Andrews v Reading BC* [2004] EWHC 970 where some dicta of Lord Woolf are clarified. Max Mosley was awarded £60,000 damages in his successful suit under Art 8 ECHR and confidentiality (para 7.197). He proceeded to the ECHR initiallly arguing that such an award breached his rights under Art 13 ECHR but subsequently sought to establish that he had a right to be forewarned by the press of a publication breaching his privacy in order to allow him to seek an injunction before publication. He was unsuccessful.

2   See eg the complaints procedures available for qualifying schools under the Apprenticeship. Skills, Children and Learning Act 2009, Part 10, ch 2.

THE RESPONSE TO LEGGATT[1]

9.62   The White Paper *Transforming Public Services: Complaints, Redress and Tribunals* (Cm 6243, July 2004) from the Department for Constitutional Affairs (DCA) sets out a wholly revised agenda for administrative justice in modern Britain and Northern Ireland. The WP recognises the advantages to government and management of effective grievance and complaints mechanisms in terms of information for reform and enhanced delivery of service and to complainants of having greater transparency and access to decision-making channels and an enhanced sense of justice and equity when they are working effectively.

1   See para 9.7, note 1 above.

9.63   The WP, it will be recalled, aimed to promote policies that empower the citizen to enhance their lives in both a communal and individual sense, to reduce the need for courts and tribunals through *proportionate dispute resolution*, ensuring that remedial devices, and constitutional arrangements are 'fit for their purpose and cost effective', and finally to re-shape the DCA to meet the needs of the public. The aim, as we saw above, is for problem avoidance in the first place and where disputes arise, to provide 'tailored solutions' to remedies. The White Paper notes that the existence of departmental schemes for resolution of complaints is 'patchy' and there is 'scope for greater government involvement in establishing a consistent and co-ordinated policy on the role and benefit of independent complaint handling schemes' (para 3.17).

9.64   Within a unified tribunal system a new type of organisation should be created which 'will not only provide formal hearings and authoritative rulings where these are needed but will have as well a mission to resolve disputes fairly and informally either by itself or in partnership with the decision-making department, other institutions and the advice sector (para 4.21). The WP recommends a commitment across government to better handling of complaints and 'faster, friendlier and cheaper solutions'; a unified tribunal service aimed at promoting proportionate dispute resolution in central government and an Administrative Justice and Tribunals Council to replace the Council on Tribunals but 'with an expanded remit' (para 6.1). It is, as the WP says, aiming at linked-up justice at the central government level. The objectives are: improvements in the original decisions on service affecting an individual; better explanation of decisions; enhanced resolution of disputes 'without external intervention'; and better availability of information to the public about how to seek redress (para 6.33). There will be a two-tier structure of tribunal hearings, the proposed 'judges' for which will be subject to recommendation by the Judicial Appointments Commission. There will be a Senior President of Tribunals of Lord Justice of Appeal level; Sir Robert Carnworth was the first president. The administrative support for the new structure of tribunals will be provided by an executive agency of the DCA (now Ministry of Justice) known as the Tribunals Service. In 2011 HM Courts and Tribunals Service was established. This is an integrated executive agency providing support for the administration of courts and tribunals in criminal, civil and family jurisdictions in England and Wales and non-devolved tribunals in Scotland and Northern Ireland. It uniquely operates as a partnership between the Lord Chancellor, the Lord Chief Justice and the Senior President of Tribunals as set out in a Framework Document. It publishes an annual business plan (2011–15) and it publishes an annual report with published accounts. The Tribunals Service has published annual performance targets against key performance indicators. Powers to make procedural rules will be transferred to the Secretary of State for Constitutional Affairs/Lord Chancellor and these will aim for accessibility, fairness and efficiency both for tribunals and for less formal processes.

9.65 With some exceptions there will be a two-tier structure for tribunals including an appellate level within the new structure. The exceptions will include the Special Immigration Appeals Commission (SIAC) and the Proscribed Organisations Appeals Commission. There are six 'first tier' chambers of tribunals comprising: general regulatory, health, education and social care, immigration and asylum, social entitlement, tax, and war pensions and armed forces compensation. From the new appeals tribunals appeal will lie to a newly created Administrative Appeals Tribunal – now the Upper Tribunal (Administrative Appeals Chamber together with other specialist divisions). From here any supervisory/appellate jurisdiction would be exercised by the Court of Appeal. Judicial review in the High Court would therefore seem to have little place where these new structures are operative although unappealable decisions of the Upper Tribunal may be subject to limited review in the Administrative Court.[1] Anxious to minimise cost, the WP did not want to recommend funding for full scale representation in every administrative dispute or tribunal case. Clearer initial procedures, greater transparency and fuller explanations and advice should reduce the need for legal representation. In cases where representation would assist, the WP spoke of 'enhanced advice project' for fact finding assistance and advice on presentation and the merits of a case. The hope was that most tribunal cases would be free of legal representation so that, as Leggatt suggested, with improved procedures and clearer channels and advice from tribunal staff, 'the vast majority of appellants' will be able to put their cases properly themselves (Leggatt, para 4.21). The Law Society was not so sanguine arguing that representation was increasingly necessary. Funding already exists for representation before some tribunals but legal aid is subject to severe cuts.[2]

[1]   *R (Cart) v Upper Tribunal* [2011] UKSC 28, [2010] EWCA Civ 859. The Supreme Court likened review to existing statutory grounds of appeal from the Upper Tribunal to the Court of Appeal.

[2]   Eg the EAT, Mental Health Review Tribunal, the Lands Tribunal, Special Immigration Appeals Commission, the Proscribed Organisations Appeal Commission, the Immigration Appeal Tribunal or proceedings before an adjudicator in immigration. See Asylum and Immigration (Treatment of Claimants etc) Act 2004 and the Asylum and Immigration Tribunal. So also are proceedings before the Protection of Children Act Tribunal, and some proceedings before the VAT and Duties Tribunal and General and Special Commissioners of Income Tax are supportable through the Community Legal Service. The Legal Services Commission runs the legal aid scheme in England and Wales through the Community Legal Services (civil) and the Criminal Defence Service.

9.66   Finally, and crucially, the WP recommended that the Council on Tribunals be replaced by an Administrative Justice and Tribunals Council. It would cover the whole of the administrative justice sector reporting to the Secretary of State/Lord Chancellor and the Administrative Justice Council might make suggestions for departmental review of decisions, for proportionate dispute resolution, for balance between different parts of administrative justice, and would ensure that 'the relationships between the courts, tribunals, ombudsmen and other ADR routes satisfactorily reflect the needs of users' (para 11.12). Some of its reports have been identified above. The AJTC was one of the bodies to face abolition in the quango cull announced in 2010.

ADR AND THE COURTS

9.67   There has been some confusion over the relationship between alternative dispute resolution (ADR) and the role of the courts. Active case management should encourage the use of ADR within Civil Procedure Rules 1998 (CPR 1998), rr 1.4(2)(e) and 26.4(1).[1] In *R (Cowl) v Plymouth City Council* the Court of Appeal ruled that a council's willingness to follow a statutory complaints procedure rightfully deprived the applicant of an opportunity for judicial review. The court stated that it was of paramount importance that litigation should be avoided between public authorities and members of the public, and courts were under a duty to use their powers under the CPR 1998 so that such disputes were resolved, or issues of conflict reduced, with the minimum of judicial intervention.[2]

[1]   *Dunnett v Railtrack plc* [2002] 2 All ER 850. Rule 1.4(2)(e) defines 'active case management' as including 'encouraging the parties to use an alternative dispute resolution procedure if the court considers that appropriate and facilitating the use of such procedure'. Rule 26.4(1) provides that 'a party may, when filing the completed allocation questionnaire, make a written request for the proceedings to be stayed while the parties try to settle the case by alternative dispute resolution or other means'.

[2]   [2002] 1 WLR 803 (CA).

9.68   In *Halsey* the Court of Appeal was prepared to accept that there are many disputes that are suitable for mediation. This was consistent with the Woolf reforms on civil procedure. The view of the court, however, was that when the government had given a pledge that ADR would be used in litigation involving public authorities, it was no more than an undertaking that ADR would be considered in appropriate cases. The court offered helpful advice on when mediation should be considered. The court believed that a party could not be compelled into ADR: the court's role was one of encouragement. The court believed it:

> 'would not be right to stigmatise as unreasonable a refusal by the successful party to agree to a mediation unless he showed that a mediation had no reasonable prospect of success. That would be to tip the scales too heavily against the right of a successful party to refuse a mediation and insist on an adjudication of the dispute by the court. It seems to us that a fairer balance is struck if the burden is placed on the unsuccessful party to show that there was a reasonable prospect that mediation would have been successful. This is not an unduly onerous burden to discharge: he does not have to prove that a mediation would *in fact* have succeeded. It is significantly easier for the unsuccessful party to prove that there was a reasonable prospect that a mediation would have succeeded than for the successful party to prove the contrary'. (para 28)

9.69   H, quoting from the headnote in *Halsey*, 'appealed against an award of costs in favour of M'. H had brought a claim against M arising from the allegedly negligent treatment of her husband while in hospital. Her husband had subsequently died. M disputed liability and refused H's invitation to take part in alternative dispute resolution. Following the dismissal of the claim at trial, the judge awarded M its costs on the grounds that it had successfully defended the claim and that the CPR 1998 were not designed to compel parties who had a good defence to settle claims that they ultimately went on to win. In dismissing the appeal, that the judge had been right to conclude that M should not be deprived of any of its costs by reason of the fact that it had refused to accept H's invitations to mediate, since M had not acted unreasonably by refusing. The judge had also been justified in finding that H's approaches to M on the subject of mediation had been 'somewhat tactical'. M had been reasonable in taking the view that the costs of a mediation would have been disproportionately high compared with the actual value of the claim and M's costs of a trial. In the circumstances, H had not discharged the burden of proving that mediation had a reasonable prospect of success.'[1]

1   *Halsey v Milton Keynes General NHS Trust* [2004] EWCA Civ 576 (CA). See *Burchell v Bullard* [2005] EWCA Civ 358.

9.70   To hold parties bound to use ADR may breach Art 6 ECHR. On the other hand, where a satisfactory internal procedure exists and this has not been resorted to, this may be a ground for refusing judicial review. The Court of Appeal could see no good ground for discriminating against public bodies which had been successful in litigation by way of adverse cost orders.

9.71   Readers are referred to the discussion of *Anufrijeva* in the Court of Appeal (para 9.61 above).

REDRESS OF GRIEVANCE WITHIN AUTHORITIES AND OPENNESS AND INFORMATION

Central government

9.72   The most successful route in pressing a grievance was traditionally seen to be by invoking an MP's assistance. Approximately three million letters a year are sent to MPs from constituents.[1] Departments invariably have a hotline to the minister's office and 'fast reply' services in response to MP's letters. Indeed the level of ministerial reply can itself be dictated by the status of the MP, eg Secretary of State response to Privy Councillor and so on. There are frequently internal hierarchical appeals through a department which can end up with the Cabinet. This is so in the field of procurement, for instance. Many formalised internal procedures have been established since the beginning of the 1990s as we have seen, especially in executive agencies, and these will doubtless have a very marked impact on redress of grievance. It was noted above how the DCA's WP highlighted the 'patchy' nature of internal mechanisms.

1   C Harlow and R Rawlings *Law and Administration* (3rd edn, 2009) p 445.

9.73   What is of interest is that the end response is rarely more than a routine reply. However, the internal inquiries may well generate a voluminous file of documentation and correspondence, none of which will be shown to the MP or the complainant s/he is sponsoring.

9.74   A few basic points must be made. First, it would be otiose to expect departments to have uniform procedures although these are now available online and are relatively easy to negotiate (and see Directgov at 2.32 above). Departments differ enormously, not only between themselves and their size and organisation, the topics they deal with and the level of contact they will have with the public, but also the internal organisation within a department will vary between divisions of a department. A good starting place will be the website of a department or agency or non-departmental body or the manual, *Civil Service Yearbook* (47th edn), to identify divisions and organisations within departments and government agencies in order to make personal contact.

9.75   Secondly, the sort of response one is likely to receive will vary according to its perceived importance. The MP connection outlined above is an obvious factor, but so too will be civil service perceptions of whether the grievance has political implications, whether it is a potential lawsuit or whether it will find its way to the ombudsman. In many cases, all three avenues may potentially be involved.

9.76   Grievances with obvious political implications will see the involvement of politicians at the highest of levels. So much is unremarkable. Action will be coloured by the potential public reaction and making of ministerial statements.

Where a lawsuit is expected, the involvement of the legal division will mean that a wary eye will be kept on the privilege attaching to documents and the guarded nature of statements. The investigatory powers of the ombudsman will, indeed, have inculcated a defensive attitude to make sure that all responses, internal procedures and time taken for action are up to scratch – not necessarily open and helpful to the complainant, but up to scratch internally.

9.77 Delivery of services through local, area or regional offices has attracted much parliamentary attention from select committees and the Public Accounts Committee in particular. Some agencies have been severely criticised for shortcomings in service. Deficiencies in service have been highlighted in a variety of reports.[1] At the same time, the drive towards cash limits, greater efficiency, effectiveness and economy in administrative operations is itself generating many of the grievances among the recipients or non-recipients of such programmes.

[1]   Eg HC 319 (1986–87); HC 736 (1987–88); HC 451 (1987–88); HC 498 (1987–88) the Child Support Agency HC 20 (1995–96), the *Individual Learning Accounts* HC 633 (2002–03) and more generally Treasury Committee HC 340 I (2001–02) and HC 149 (2002–03) *Parliamentary Accountability of Departments*.

9.78 In many areas of governmental and private activity there are special agencies which are government appointed and which deal specifically with the promotion of rights in particular areas, eg the Equality and Human Rights Commission for the promotion of equality and human rights,[1] the Independent Police Complaints Commission under the Police Reform Act 2002 and regulations thereunder or bodies whose regulatory activities will involve some degree of grievance redress, eg the Office of Fair Trading, or the agencies appointed to regulate privatised industries and consumer bodies. The move towards executive agencies in central government has been accompanied by a greater awareness of the need for effective grievance procedures. These agencies are subject to the Parliamentary Ombudsman (see ch 2 and 2.132 above).

[1]   HL 78 (2003–04) HC 536 (2003–04); HL 156 and HC 998 ditto Joint Committee on Human Rights on the Commission and Cm 6185 (2004) *Fairness for All: a New Commission for Equality and Human Rights* on the government proposals and the Equality Act 2010.

9.79 Where a complaint concerns the activities of these bodies, in the first instance it may well be more advantageous to address the matter to the chief executive of the agency concerned. A complaint to a sponsoring department may well be deflected with the answer that it does not fall within the department's responsibilities. Further complaint may well be made to the Parliamentary Ombudsman or the local ombudsman: the amended Schedules to the Acts establishing these bodies will have to be examined to establish that they are within their respective jurisdictions. Publication schemes under the FOIA 2000 should have details of internal processes.

9.80 There are literally thousands of rights of appeal to an 'independent' body under statute in addition to informal methods of grievance redress, or informal requests for information. These may be dealt with by way of a tribunal hearing, some other kind of administrative hearing as in the case of disappointed applicants under the Social Fund, or by an inquiry. The DCA proposals for reform of the 'administrative justice system' was outlined above. A Special Immigration Appeals Commission was established to conduct appeals where the Secretary of State has directed that a person be deported on the grounds of national security or for the public good. This replaced the 'three wise men' procedure. A 'special advocate' may be appointed by the Attorney General to represent the appellant who may well be absent from proceedings.[1] The procedures involving possible deportation and then those on control orders involving house arrest of suspected terrorists under the Prevention of Terrorism Act 2005 have spawned an impressive catalogue of case law.[2] Statutes, statutory instruments and circulars and codes of practice should all be consulted as they invariably have important provisions on the supply of information or the giving of reasons for decisions.[3] Further, case-law may well set the parameters of fair procedure (paras 9.114 et seq below) and dictate what the interpretation of crucial provisions actually means, what factors or information should be considered by a decision-maker and what weight should be given to them.

[1] This followed criticism by the ECtHR of the decision in *R v Secretary of State for the Home Department, ex p Chahal* [1995] 1 WLR 526, CA: *Chahal v United Kingdom* (1996) 23 EHRR 413. Special Immigration Appeals Commission Act 1997 and SI 2003/1034 and SI 2007/1285. As Blake describes it in his essay, the SIAC was introduced under the SIAC Act 1997 to 'resolve the dichotomy between a fair hearing for the suspect and the preservation of secrecy for informer material and other intelligence data that could not be disclosed to suspects without compromising future operations' based, it appears on Canadian procedures. In the UK a special advocate (SA) or counsel is appointed where the Home Secretary intends to use sensitive material. The deportee will have his own lawyers and the SA operates on behalf of his interests but he does not represent the deportee. The SA can discuss the case personally with the deportee and obtain information from that person. But the SA cannot communicate with the proposed deportee after the sensitive or 'closed' material has been served on the SA. 'Thereafter the SA cannot communicate with the appellant of his lawyers about the case, for fear that questions may inadvertently disclose the nature of the closed material. Submissions are then made that some closed material should be disclosed in whole or in gist to achieve as fair a hearing as possible and commensurate with the public interest. The substantive appeal then proceeds to an open and closed part with the state's case for exclusion tested by the SA in the absence of the appellant.' From R Dyzenhaus (ed) *The Unity of Public Law* (2004) at 240–241. In *A,B, etc v Secretary of State for the Home Department* (para 9.132, note 4 below) the SIAC heard evidence that was not given to the Court of Appeal or House of Lords. It needs only to be added that the same SA has, allegedly, acted for both the government and the appellant: R. Norton-Taylor *Guardian*, 22 December 2004. See, further, Commons Constitutional Affairs Committee *Seventh Report* HC 323 I and II (2004–05) on special advocates and suggested reforms; and *Secretary of State for the Home Department v AF* [2009] UKHL 28 following *A v UK* [2009] ECRR 301 where it was ruled by the law lords, following the ECHR, that denying sufficient information to the defendant to make an effective challenge to an allegation against him was a denial of Art 6 ECHR rights. The procedure was allowed in hearings by the Parole Board: *Roberts v Parole Board* [2005] UKHL 45. See *Al Rawi v The Security Service* [2011] UKSC 34 and the refusal of the Supreme Court to allow an appeal by the government against the Court of Appeal's ruling that the closed material/special advocate procedure could not be extended to ordinary civil actions at common law; see, however, *Tariq v Home Office* [2011] UKSC 35 decided the same day as *Al Rawi* where there was no breach of Art 6 ECHR or EU law in allowing the closed procedure/SA procedure before the employment tribunal in a security vetting employment case. On fairness and national security see also *R (AKH) v Secretary of State for the Home Department* [2009] 1 WLR 2049. See the *Kadi* etc cases in the EU (para 3.68).

[2] See *A v Secretary of State* [2004] UKHL 16; *Secretary of State v MB* [2007] UKHL 46; *Secretary of State v AF (FC) and another* [2009] UKHL 28.

[3] See, eg on inquiries, paras 8.124 et seq above.

9.81 Again there are numerous rights of appeal, opportunity to make objection or complaint to the Secretary of State or Minister or some other body. In the course of this book we have dealt with numerous examples and those on education spring readily to mind (paras 8.47 et seq above). In form, such opportunities are often contained in default powers residing in central government to issue orders or take action when a local or other authority is failing to perform its statutory responsibilities. The duties may be enforceable by a mandatory order. The flow of information from the exercise of such statutory powers in relation to local government was examined in ch 4.[1] A party representing a complainant should make full inquiries to establish what opportunities there are to meet or deal with officials/Ministers at an appropriate level; what details of any existing processes are available; and what can be provided in the way of background material and information to effect an acceptable resolution.

[1] In April 1984, a list of default powers residing in Secretaries of State and ministers was given in Hansard: 58 HC Official Report (6th series), col 249 (11 April 1984). More recent examples include: LGA 1985, Sch 1, para 13; Children Act 1989, s 84; see also Water Act 1989, ss 33(2), (6) and 146: power to give directions to the National Rivers Authority under the latter; TCPA 1990, Sch 1, para 13 and Care Standards Act 2000, s 113.

9.82 The more aggressive a complainant becomes, the greater the risk that the officials will become more cautious and retentive. Although departments can be very accommodating in their pursuit of openness and fairness, where this operates to their detriment they will draw obvious conclusions. Further, the courts may well prompt them to draw such conclusions. This was graphically illustrated in the litigation involving *Lonrho plc* and the attempts of its managing director to get publication of a report by inspectors into the take-over of Harrods by an opposing interest group. The Secretary of State's reluctance arose from the possibility of criminal proceedings, which were still under consideration, in which the report might be crucial. The Lonrho group was attempting to pressurise the Secretary of State to refer the bid to the Monopolies and Mergers Commission (MMC). There were extensive internal negotiations between the Department of Trade and Industry, the Director General of Fair Trading and Lonrho's representatives. Lord Keith describes in vivid terms one of the meetings at the Department of Trade and Industry at which there was the fullest opportunity for points and counter-points to be made and for all the views on publication that were made by Lonrho to be considered seriously, which he was satisfied they were. Lonrho was represented by three counsel, two solicitors and three directors at the meeting. A representative of the Serious Fraud Office was cross-examined by counsel for Lonrho.[1]

[1] *Lonrho plc v Secretary of State for Trade and Industry* [1989] 2 All ER 609 and 613e–h.

9.83 Lord Keith's warning is worth quoting in full:

'The only effect of Lonrho's conduct is to discourage decision-makers from affording oral interviews. In some cases an oral interview will remove misunderstandings and provide clarification and new information. In the present case there never was excuse or justification for a meeting, let alone four meetings, although the DTI was understandably anxious to demonstrate its fairness. It was clear from beginning to end that the Secretary of State intended to publish the report as soon as possible and took the view that the public interest in early publication of the report was outweighed by the risk that early publication might hamper or prevent the institution, or prejudice the outcome, of a criminal prosecution. Lonrho's arguments that early publication would have no adverse effect and that there were overwhelming public interest reasons in favour of early publication could be and were fully set forth and explained in written submissions of inordinate length to which oral representations added nothing.'[1]

[1]   [1989] 2 All ER 609 at 617a–c. Cf Companies Act 1989, s 68.

9.84   This is far removed from the usual processes of internal grievance redress, but it offers useful illustrations of what can take place before formal statutory or legal processes begin.

9.85   The presence of the Parliamentary Commissioner has doubtless assisted in enhancing an appreciation of procedural fairness, as have judicial decisions. The introduction of the FOIA 2000 should give greater emphasis to effective means for resolving disputes and assuaging anxieties.

Local government

9.86   A substantial volume of research has been conducted on the area of redress of grievance within local authorities. More recent work has located such procedures within participatory mechanisms.[1] The role of members here is not as immediately effective in general terms as the role of the MP, and indeed MPs are often resorted to on problems concerning local government.[2] This is not to say that authorities do not treat members' complaints with care, and often internal procedures will be triggered only after the intervention of a member.

[1]   See para 9.45, note 3 above.
[2]   Lewis, Seneviratne and Cracknell *Complaints Procedures in Local Government* (1987), pp 4 et seq.

9.87   The position of the member and his/her ability to obtain information has been examined in ch 5. It must be pointed out that if a member is seeking information to assist a person with a grievance against the authority, this *may* cause the authority to interpret the request as being for an ulterior, improper or unreasonable motive. On the other hand, it falls within the duties of a member to represent the interests of his constituents including those with a grievance about the authority's administration.

9.88   In 1974, the Redcliff–Maud report[1] recommended the adoption by all authorities of 'clearly established and well publicised machinery for the reception and investigation of complaints' from the public. In 1978, a code of practice on such complaints was issued by the Commission for Local Administration. A fully revised code came into existence in 1992 and has itself been revised (http://www.lgo.org.uk/publications/guidance-notes/). The general impression gained from a detailed research programme into complaints procedures in local government over a decade ago found that in spite of very good practice in some authorities, much was still wanting from the perspective of good and open procedures, accessibility and responsiveness. Complaints are very often dealt with in an 'unpatterned and uneven' way. The existence of good procedures is often deceptive as they are really little more than defensive mechanisms to the existence of the ombudsman and the possibility of a complaint ending up in that office. The task of locating appropriate officers can be very difficult. Only one authority had full-time complaints' officers, and even then their existence was not publicised.[2] In other authorities most complaints' officers, typically in the chief executive's office, are there essentially to respond to ombudsmen complaints that have been referred back to the authority. In some areas statute has taken the lead as in s 202 of the Housing Act 1996, which provides for an internal review procedure within the authority for an applicant under the homeless persons provisions. Section 204, as amended by the Homelessness Act 2002, provides a right of appeal to the county court on a point of law.[3] Regulations set out the procedures to be followed (SI 1999/71 and see 2006/1294), and a code of practice on homelessness has been published (2006, ODPM).

[1]   *Conduct in Local Government* Cmnd 5636 (1974), vol 1.
[2]   Para 9.86, note 2 above.
[3]   *Francis v Kensington and Chelsea LBC* [2003] 2 All ER 1052. On review of these procedures, see *Hall v Wandsworth LBC* [2004] EWCA Civ 1740. *Runa Begum v London Borough of Tower Hamlets* [2003] UKHL 5; *Tomlinson and Ors v Birmingham City Council* [2010] UKSC 8 and see para 9.123, note 1 below on the right for an applicant to demand an oral hearing.

9.89   Authorities have made efforts to publicise their procedures and services – in part a response to consumer awareness and the necessity of selling themselves. And expenditure on such items is lawful providing it relates to publicity and information, not political proselytism. Quite how publication schemes under the FOIA 2000 will affect local authorities we shall have to wait and see. There has also been the Local Government (Access to Information) Act 1985. The 1985 legislation does seem to have some impact on local authority administration.[1] The original Bill's inclusion of a procedure to deal with disputes over entitlement to documents was dropped. The government and local authorities preferred voluntary procedures. They will be available under the FOIA 2000. Where, as increasingly is the case, service provision is outsourced to private providers, the specifications should indentify clear complaints processes within the provider. Those not resolvable by such a process will have to be made to the local authority outsourcer (see eg Draft Contracting Out (Local Authorities Social Services Functions) Order 2011, SI 2011/1568). The action of the local authority will be subject to the ombudsman procedure.

[1]   J Steele *Public Access to Information: An evaluation of the Local Government (Access to Information) Act 1985*, Policy Studies Institute and DoE 1995, and *Access to Information in Local Government* Office of the Deputy Prime Minister (2002): see para 6.36 above.

9.90   The Health and Social Care (Community Health and Standards) Act 2003 made provision for the Secretary of State to make regulations about the handling and consideration of complaints in relation to the functions of English NHS bodies, the provision of health care by or for such bodies, and also about the discharge of social services functions by English local authorities and the provision of services in the discharge of those functions. The Act provides regulation-making powers covering the procedures that are to be followed. Under the Health and Social Care Act 2008 the Care Quality Commission is an independent regulator of health and social care providers in England, Scotland, Wales and Northern Ireland whether in the NHS, local government, private bodies or voluntary arrangements. Complaints procedures are contained in the Local Authority and National Health Service Complaints Regulations 2009, SI 2009/309 and their amending Regulations, SI 2009/1768 for adult social care complaints. The Regulations 'align' complaints procedures for adult social and health care into a single set of arrangements. Bodies covered by the Regulations have to have arrangements in place to deal with complaints. A 'responsible person' must ensure compliance with the arrangements. Those who may make complaints are identified. The Regulations apply to complaints made after 1 April 2009. Complaints must be dealt with efficiently and properly investigated. Complainants must be treated with courtesy and respect; receive assistance on understanding relevant procedures and where such assistance is available; receive a timely and appropriate response; and be informed of the outcome of any investigation. Arrangements have to ensure any action is taken if necessary in the light of the outcome of the complaint. There are two stages for the making of complaints. For social care complaints the second stage involves the local ombudsman. Regulations 13 and 14 deal with procedures for making a complaint about social services or care; reg 15 deals with communications; reg 16 with publicity arrangements, reg 17 with monitoring; and reg 18 with annual reports by bodies covered.

9.91 New powers have come into force for the LGO to investigate complaints from people who arrange their own care. 'Self-funders' will now have the same access to the independent complaints service as those people who have had their care arranged and funded by local authorities. The Health Act 2009 amended the Local Government Act 1974 to give the LGO service its new powers from 1 October 2010.

9.92 Children's social services complaints procedures involve a three-stage procedure under the Children Act 1989 Representations Procedure Regulations 2006, SI 2006/1738. These regulate the procedure which local authorities are to follow in the consideration of representations made to them about the discharge of certain functions under the Children Act 1989 (CA 1989) and under the Adoption and Children Act 2002 (ACA 2002). The Regulations specify some of the matters about which a person may make representations using this procedure. They also apply the procedure, with modifications, to representations made to voluntary organisations providing accommodation for children and about fostering limits. The explanation to the Regulations sets out procedures as follows.

9.93 Part 2 is concerned with the subject matter of representations. As well as providing a procedure for making representations about the discharge by a local authority of its functions under CA 1989, Part 3, the Regulations provide a procedure for considering representations about specified local authority functions under CA 1989, Parts 4 and 5 (reg 3), functions under ACA 2002 (reg 4), and functions related to special guardianship support services (reg 5).

9.94   Part 3 makes general provision about representations. Regulation 8 allows a local authority not to consider representations, in whole or in part, if the local authority decide that to do so might prejudice any of the proceedings falling within para 1. By reg 9 a complainant may make his representations to the local authority no later than one year after the grounds to make the representations arose. However, if the representations are made outside that time limit the local authority may still consider them if they think that it would not be reasonable to expect the complainant to have made the representations within a year, and that it is still possible to consider the representations effectively and fairly.

9.95   Local authorities have to give complainants information about the representations procedure when they first make representations and they must also give information about advocacy services (reg 11) where relevant, ie where the complainant is a looked-after child or a child in need and so is entitled to an advocate under CA 1989, s 26A.

9.96   Regulation 12 sets out how local authorities are to deal with representations which are made by persons falling within CA 1989, s 26(3)(e), (3B)(b) or (3C) (c). Each section requires local authorities to consider representations from persons whom the local authority considers to have sufficient interest in the child concerned to warrant their representations being so considered. Local authorities must decide whether to consider the representations and are required to take into account the views of the child if they think it appropriate to do so.

9.97   Part 4 sets out the procedure for considering representations. Unless the complainant and the local authority agree otherwise, the first stage involves an informal attempt to resolve the problem (regs 14 and 15). This stage usually begins when the local authority receive the representations, when they decide to consider representations from someone falling within CA 1989, s 26(3)(e), (3B) (b) or (3C)(c), or when, in appropriate cases, an advocate has been appointed for a child. The complainant may ask for the start date to be a later date as agreed with the local authority. This stage should be concluded within ten working days of the start date, but that period can be extended where the local authority consider that the representations are complex.

9.98   Before progressing to the second stage, whether the representations have been considered under stage one or not, they must be writen down where they have only been made orally (reg 16).

9.99   The second stage of the procedure is governed by reg 17 and involves consideration of the representations by an independent person. The local authority must consider the representations and send a notice of response within time limits set out in paras (3) to (5).

9.100   The third stage of the procedure involves consideration of the representations by a panel of three (reg 19), which can be requested by the complainant or his advocate in accordance with reg 18. All three members of the panel must be independent. The panel has to make recommendations within five working days of considering the representations and the local authority has 15 working days to consider the recommendations and make a decision (reg 20).

9.101 Part 5 is concerned with representations to voluntary organisations and about fostering limits. Regulation 21 requires voluntary organisations who are providing accommodation for a child to have a procedure (set out in reg 22) for considering representations made to them by the persons specified in paras (a) to (d).

9.102 Under CA 1989, Sch 6, para 6, every local authority is required to establish a procedure for considering any representations made to them about the discharge of their functions under Sch 6, para 4 which allows a local authority to exempt people from the limit on the number of children they may foster. Regulation 23 sets out the procedure local authorities must follow in carrying out consideration of such representations.

Ad hoc inquiries

9.103 One point that should be referred to is the position of local authority ad hoc inquiries – those that are not provided for under any specific statutory provision. The Law Commission has investigated the subject of ad hoc local inquiry reports. The Law Commission investigation followed an inquiry report into abuse of children in care in North Wales in 2000.[1] The inquiry chairman was concerned that local authorities might not act in the wider public interest after such reports for fear of defamation actions[2] or loss of insurance cover. Such fears may cause authorities not to publish reports, others could not learn from mistakes and improve procedures and facts would not become known. The Commission's investigation was not limited to abuse of children but covered 'any serious failure in the delivery of local authority services'. Among the Law Commission's recommendations were that the guidance issued by the Society of Local Authority Chief Executives on ad hoc inquiries and the code of practice issued jointly by the ABI and LGA should be refined to ensure that local authorities can act in the public interest without putting their insurance cover at risk; the law relating to qualified privilege should be amended to protect fair and accurate inquiry procedures and reports in the absence of malice. 'Fair' means conclusions are based on findings of fact from evidence as presented and any parties criticized are given notice of any criticisms, an opportunity to respond and their response is fairly represented in the report. Joint local authority reports would also be likewise protected but where reports are made by a local authority and another public authority the statutory defence recommended by the Commission would protect the local authority but the other body would rely on any common law defence of qualified privilege. Where there is a serious failure to deliver a service, there should be a statutory power to establish a new form of special inquiry. These may be required where parties are or may be reluctant to produce information or evidence. Powers to require information or evidence may be enforceable through a High Court order.[3]

1   *Lost in Care* HC 201 (1999–2000). This was established under the Tribunals of Inquiry (Evidence) Act 1921.
2   In *R (Comninos) v Bedford DC* [2003] EWHC 121 a council had powers under the Local Government Act 1972 to fund its legal officers' legal costs or to indemnify them in libel actions: see also *Jameel v Wall Street Journal Europe* [2003] EWHC 2945 and [2006] UKHL 44.
3   *In the Public Interest: Publication of Local Authority Inquiry Reports* Law Commission No 289 Cm 6274 (2004).

Inquiries Act 2005

9.104   The Department for Constitutional Affairs has published a consultation paper *Effective Inquiries* (May 2004) in response to the Select Committee on Public Administration's report.[1] The report was not confined to local government. Non-statutory inquiries have been resorted to on numerous and notorious occasions by central government or other authorities, including the Scott Inquiry, the Hutton Inquiry and the Butler Inquiry. The Inquiries Act 2005 seeks to provide a statutory framework for formal, independent inquiries into events causing, or which could cause, public concern, or 'where there is public concern that particular events may have occurred', according to the Act's explanatory text. The Act makes provision on how inquiries held under its remit are to be conducted. An inquiry chairman will have powers to require the production of evidence and for either or both the establishing minister and the chairman to be able to place restrictions on both public access to the inquiry, and publication of evidence, where appropriate. These provisions were seen as controversial. The chairman may sit with a panel. The inquiry will not determine either civil or criminal liability. The Act also makes provision for expenses and legal fees. One of the reasons for introducing the Bill was the huge cost of the Saville Inquiry into 'Bloody Sunday', estimated at £150 million but finally alleged to have cost in the region of £400 million.[2]

1   HC 606 (2003–04). See by the same committee: HC 51 (2004–05) *Government by Inquiry*.
2   http://report.bloody-sunday-inquiry.org/.

9.105   Under devolution arrangements, devolved authorities have their own powers to conduct inquiries into subjects relevant to the exercise of their powers: see eg Government of Wales Act 1998, s 35. The Bill will have a UK-wide remit although matters within devolved administration will be the responsibility of ministers from those administrations.

NHS complaints and the NHS Constitution[1]

9.106   Prior to the Health and Social Care (Community Health and Standards) Act 2003, the NHS complaints procedure was set out in various directions and guidance. It could sometimes take 18 months or more to exhaust all existing elements of the complaints procedure and therefore the purpose of legislation was to ensure that complaints were investigated rigorously and resolved as quickly as possible. The PHSO's report 'Making things better? A report on reform of the NHS complaints procedure in England' highlighted weaknesses in the current approach to complaints handling in health and social care, some of which were: complaints systems being fragmented within the NHS, between the NHS and private health care systems, and between health and social care; and the complaints system not being centred on the patient's needs. The PO's findings were supported by the Healthcare Commission in 'Spotlight on Complaints' (2006). The LGO also identified problems in complaints handling and redress within health and social care partnerships. 'When the procedural frameworks are different, it is much more difficult to provide a seamless service.' The Department of Health believed that retaining the current arrangements was simply not on the agenda. It would not meet government commitments and it would not improve local handling of complaints. Furthermore, changes to the current legislation were needed in any event with the dissolution of the Healthcare Commission.

[1]   http://www.nhs.uk/choiceintheNHS/Rightsandpledges/NHSConstitution/Pages/Overview. aspx.

9.107 Following consultation the Department of Health published 'Making experiences count. The proposed new arrangements for handling health and social care complaints. response to consultation' (February 2008). As explained above, the Local Authority and National Health Service Complaints Regulations 2009 cover adult social care and health complaints. The explanatory note to the Regulations states:

> 'The Department considered whether to make prescriptive regulations that set out in detail what organisations must and must not do. This option would require organisations to operate within narrow and restrictive procedures, which would limit the flexibility needed for a more personalised approach to delivery of complaints arrangements at local level. These regulations align adult social care and health complaints processes into a single set of arrangements. They require the complainant to be involved in the way in which the complaint is handled, by requiring the body dealing with the complaint to offer to discuss this with the complainant. They also remove prescription around the timescale to be followed in terms of investigating a complaint. Less prescription around timescales allows organisations to assess and deal appropriately with all complaints, allowing these arrangements to meet the needs of the individual case and for proper consideration of learning and service development issues. Specifically in relation to complaints about NHS care, the regulations remove the second tier (the Healthcare Commission reviewing individual complaints cases) from the arrangements, with the Health Service Ombudsman providing independent review of cases unresolved at local level.'

A two-tier complaints model has been introduced.

9.108 Regulation 7 of the 2009 Regulations provides:

> '(1) This regulation applies to a complaint which is—
> (a)   made to a Primary Care Trust in accordance with these Regulations on or after 1st April 2009;

(b) about the services provided by a provider under arrangements with
     the Primary Care Trust; and
(c) not specified in regulation 8(1).

(2) In this regulation, "provider" means an NHS body, primary care
provider or independent provider.

(3) Where a Primary Care Trust receives a complaint to which this
regulation applies—
(a) the Primary Care Trust must ask the complainant whether the
     complainant consents to details of the complaint being sent to the
     provider; and
(b) if the complainant so consents, the Primary Care Trust must as soon
     as reasonably practicable send details of the complaint to the provider.

(4) If the Primary Care Trust considers that it is appropriate for the
Primary Care Trust to deal with the complaint—
(a) it must so notify the complainant and the provider; and
(b) it must continue to handle the complaint in accordance with these
     Regulations.

(5) If the Primary Care Trust considers that it is more appropriate for the
complaint to be dealt with by the provider, and the complainant consents—
(a) the Primary Care Trust must so notify the complainant and the
     provider;
(b) when the provider receives the notification given to it under
     sub-paragraph (a)—
     (i)   the provider must handle the complaint in accordance with these
           Regulations; and
     (ii) the complainant is deemed to have made the complaint to the
           provider under these Regulations.'

Regulation 8 covers complaints not to be dealt with under the procedure and
reg 9 deals with cooperation between responsible bodies where more than one
is involved.

9.109   The former PHSO, Ann Abraham, has published the report 'Listening
and Learning' (HC 482 (2010–2011)) which assesses the NHS's performance
over the previous year in responding to and learning from complaints from
patients and their families. The overall conclusion is that the NHS needs to
listen more attentively and learn more from complaints. The report is the first
of what will be an annual series of reports examining NHS complaint handling.[1]

---

[1] See NAO 853 (2007–08) Feeding Back: Learning from Complaints' Handling in Health and
     Social Care. See also Commons Health Committee Complaints and Litigation HC 786 (2010–12
     and Government Reply Cm 8181 (2011)).

9.110   Where complaints result in disciplinary proceedings before the GMC,
the High Court has requested a greater degree of openness and the desirability
of conducting proceedings in public.[1] In the screening process complainants
should receive confidential documents unless there were strong grounds against

this and an undertaking of confidentiality could be extracted. This introduces us to the role of the courts in securing greater openness through the doctrine of natural justice or fair procedure.

[1] *R v General Medical Council, ex p Toth* [2000] 1 WLR 2209. See SIs 2000/2051 and 2000/2034.

9.111 Nevertheless, there are significant drawbacks, not least the low public awareness of the procedures. More still needs to be done in this area. And public uncertainty over the role of the ombudsmen is not assisted by the constant changing of bodies over whom they have jurisdiction. This has been a constant theme since the 1987 legislation affecting the PCA, and the inclusion under the LGO's jurisdiction of housing action trusts but not housing associations, the planning and housing functions *only* of English Partnerships and housing only for the Commission for New Towns, and whether new bodies created by local authorities are within jurisdiction, eg Housing Arms Length Management Organisations.[1] The jurisdictional division in the operation of ombudsmen is baffling, even to the expert! Changes under the Local Government and Public Involvement in Health Act 2007 were outlined above (para 9.56).

[1] See *LGO Annual Report 2003/04* p 11. The LGO believed they were within jurisdiction.

9.112 The NHS (Redress) Act 2006 provided for schemes for redress of grievances through non-judicial processes under civil justice arising from medical negligence claims. It sets out the cases to which a scheme may apply. A scheme may only apply to cases involving liabilities in tort arising out of qualifying services provided as part of the NHS in England, whether provided in England, in another part of the UK or abroad (s 1(2) and (5)). This means that a scheme may cover people with claims in tort arising out of hospital treatment as part of the NHS wherever that hospital treatment might be provided. Redress could include an offer of compensation, apologies, explanations and reports stating how action would not be repeated. The scheme was to be implemented by regulations which would contain the details of schemes which could involve the provision of free legal advice and representation and an emphasis on resolution to avoid litigation. Provision was to be made for the making and dealing with complaints of maladministration in the operation of schemes, who may make complaints and about what. The ombudsman could investigate complaints that were not resolved. The NHS Redress (Wales) Measure 2008 Commencement Order 2011 covers schemes operating in Wales.

9.113 The Health and Social Care Bill 2011 sets in place a dramatic reorganisation of health and social care in England. Strategic Health Trusts and Primary Care Trusts are to be abolished. Part 3 of the Bill establishes an independent regulator of the NHS known as the monitor and services from licensed providers will be commissioned through a NHS Commissioning Board authorising commissioning consortia to commission services. The monitor's duties include ensuring that competition and patient choice operate effectively. Complaints may be made about designation of services and representations may be made about licensing decisions. Information standards will be the duty of the Health and Social Care Information Centre (Part 9, ch 2) and a body called Healthwatch England (s 178) will oversee public involvement, and there are to be local healthwatch orgainsations (ss 179–186). Part 5, ch 2 deals with the health scrutiny functions of local authorities and makes provision for the establishment of health and well-being boards in each upper-tier local authority area. It sets out their role in preparing the joint strategic needs assessment, the joint health and well-being strategy and in promoting integrated working between NHS, public health and social care commissioners. This chapter also contains provisions to make it possible for foundation trusts and commissioning consortia to be designated as Care Trusts. Annual public meetings of the NHS Foundation Trusts and Trusts will have to take place (s 154) and there are further provisions on Health Service Commissioner reports and to whom they may be sent (s 198). Certain provisions of the Bill extend to Scotland and Northern Ireland as well as Wales. The Bill was subjected to widespread professional and public criticism and in June 2011 the NHS Future Forum, a body appointed by the Government to make recommendations for modifications reported.[1] The major recommendations included:

(a)   the pace of the proposed changes should be varied so that the NHS implements them only where it is ready to do so;

(b)   the Secretary of State for Health should remain ultimately accountable for the NHS;

(c)   nurses, specialist doctors and other clinicians must be involved in making local decisions about the commissioning of care – not just GPs – but in doing this the NHS should avoid tokenism, or the creation of a new bureaucracy;

(d)   competition should be used to secure greater choice and better value for patients – it should be used not as an end in itself, but to improve quality, promote integration and increase citizens' rights;

(e)   the drive for change in the NHS should not be based on monitor's duty to 'promote' competition, which should be removed, but on citizens' power to challenge the local health service when they feel it does not offer meaningful choices or good quality;

(f)   all organisations involved in NHS care and spending NHS money should be subject to the same high standards of public openness and accountability.

The government response promising a 'drive for transparency' and acceptance of many of the recommendations is at: http://offlinehbpl.hbpl.co.uk/News Attachments/PG/WMS.pdf (Cm 8113, 2011).

[1]   http://healthandcare.dh.gov.uk/future-forum-report/.

FAIR PROCEDURE, INFORMATION, OPENNESS AND THE COURTS

9.114   It must be emphasised that what follows is directed towards extracting what case-law has contributed towards the task of obtaining information, reasons and openness in the administrative process. What follows is not an exposition, detailed or otherwise, of the law of judicial review, fair procedure and natural justice.[1] Nor can the chapter offer an analysis of those matters that are properly susceptible to judicial review.[2] A few preliminary words are necessary to explain how the information basis on which judicial review takes place and which are relevant to our discussion. Judicial review generally has increased phenomenally (10,548 applications in 2010 – see www.judiciary.gov.uk – up from 160 in 1974 and 5,439 in 1998).[3]

[1]   See de Smith, Woolf and Jowell *Judicial Review of Administrative Action* (6th edn, 2007) ; Wade and Forsyth *Administrative Law* (10th edn, 2009); P Craig *Administrative Law* (6th edn, 2008).
[2]   *R (Campaign for Nuclear Disarmament) v the Prime Minister* [2002] EWHC 2777 – legality of war in Iraq non-justiciable; *R (Abassi) v Secretary of State for Foreign and Commonwealth Affairs* [2002] EWCA Civ 1598 – failure to exercise diplomatic powers in respect of British national subject to alleged breaches of human rights in a foreign state was susceptible to judicial review because judicial review could supervise prerogative powers and a legitimate expectation that the government would not ignore the matter had been established by government statements but A had received all the assistance he could legitimately expect; *R (Marchiori) v The Environmental Agency* [2001] EWCA Civ 03: merits of defence policy were for the government and not the courts to decide, and a court could not question a statutory discharge of radioactive waste authorisation in the production of nuclear weapons. See also *R (Gentle) v Prime Minister* [2008] UKHL 20. On the scope of review of fact, as distinct from law, see *E v Secretary of State for the Home Department* [2004] 2 WLR 1351 and *R (Assura Pharmacy Ltd) v NHS Litigation Authority* [2008] EWHC 289 (Admin).
[3]   *The Judge over your Shoulder* (3rd edn, 2000) Tr Sol.

9.115 Traditionally, judicial review is a review on a point of law or legality. It is not concerned with the facts or the merits of a decision. The latter means that a court on judicial review cannot second-guess the judgment of an official or tribunal which is concerned solely with a judgment on the merits or inherent quality of the subject on which that official or tribunal has to make judgment. The court cannot swap its opinion or judgment for that of the official. The reluctance to question mistakes of fact was also coloured by the very limited fact-finding capabilities of the reviewing court. Evidence was filed on affidavit and cross-examination and disclosure of documents were rarely used. In addition, the applicant had the burden of establishing any allegations. Questions of fact seem initially straight forward: A is 6ft 2 ins tall. B is female, C is a British national. When a question of fact is involved, the courts set out the limits of their review powers many years ago.[1] However, a question of fact is not always straightforward. If a judgment requires an inference from fact, this could be treated as a question of mixed fact and law and to some extent reviewable if, for instance, the inference drawn is not justified or if there is simply inadequate evidence for the inference. An absence of evidence supporting a finding of fact could become a question of law.[2] Where a condition precedent has to be established before a power can be exercised the courts regard this as a question of jurisdictional fact and a question of law which they are empowered to correct or establish.[3] A clear mistake in fact is reviewable: S is a safe country to deport D when clearly this is wrong and can be shown to be so. A striking development in recent years has been the extension of the scope of review for mistakes of fact. In *E v Secretary of State for the Home Department*, the Court of Appeal ruled that a mistake of fact 'giving rise to unfairness' was a ground for review providing that a mistake of fact could be proved by available evidence and that the mistake can be objectively established, must not have been induced by the applicant or his advisers, and played a material part in the decision, even if it was not a decisive factor.[4] Crucially, a poor process of reasoning to a decision may lead to a quashing of a decision and a remit to the decision maker where a factual basis is not adequately explained.[5] Greater powers of disclosure of documents allowed by the courts in judicial review applications (para 10.59), and the possibility of obtaining documents under FOIA 2000, may well provide more factual material to challenge the reliability of a decision. Much depends upon how far the courts will, on the limited judicial review procedures, excavate the evidential basis of a decision. In human rights cases, the courts are themselves under a duty to abide by the Convention rights entailing an assessment of the proportionality of a decision-maker's exercise of power where a human right is engaged. In such cases, a merits review may seem unavoidable.[6]

'These provisions, read purposively and in context, make it plain that the task of the appellate immigration authority, on an appeal on a Convention ground against a decision of the primary official decision-maker refusing leave to enter or remain in this country, is to decide whether the challenged decision is unlawful as incompatible with a Convention right or compatible and so lawful. It is not a secondary, reviewing, function dependent on establishing that the primary decision-maker misdirected himself or acted irrationally or was guilty of procedural impropriety. The appellate immigration authority must decide for itself whether the impugned decision is lawful and, if not, but only if not, reverse it.'[7]

[1]   *Edwards v Bairstow* [1956] AC 14. See incidentally *MA (Somalia) v Secretary of State HD* [2010] UKSC 49 on 'safe country guidance' for deportation.
[2]   *Coleen Properties Ltd v MHLG* [1971] 1 WLR 433 now has wide acceptance.
[3]   *Secretary of State for Education v Tameside MBC* [1977] AC 1014.
[4]   *E v Secretary of State for the Home Department* [2004] EWCA Civ 49 and *R v CICB ex p A* [1999] 2 AC 330; cf *Shaheen v Secretary of State for the Home Department* [2005] EWCA Civ 1294.
[5]   *Hatungimana v Secretary of State for the Home Department* [2006] EWCA Civ 231.
[6]   *Huang v Secretary of State for the Home Department* [2005] EWCA Civ 105; upheld on this point in [2007] UKHL 11 para 11.
[7]   [2007] UKHL 11 para 11.

9.116   A general overview of the development of judicial review raises the question of proportionality review which has been addressed elsewhere (para 2.292).[1] Furthermore, the courts on judicial review now have powers to make new decisions within the terms of s 15 and s 141 of the Tribunals, Courts and Enforcement Act 2007 as well as to issue interim declarations under CPR r 54 as amended. The courts have extended the ambit of irrationality review in cases that do not involve a human rights aspect[2] and review on legitimate expectation[3] and equality have all made significant strides in providing judicial protection.[4]

[1]   *R (Daly) v Secretary of State for the Home Department* [2001] UKHL 26.
[2]   Development of judicial review outside human rights: *Eisai Ltd v NICE* [2008] EWCA Civ 438; *R (Bristol Myers Squibbs Pharmaceuticals Ltd v NICE)* [2009] EWHC Civ 2722.
[3]   Recent cases on legitimate expectation: *R (Merritt) v Peterborough Magistrates' Court* [2009] EWHC 467 and *R (HSMP Forum UK Ltd v Home Secretary* [2009] EWHC 711).
[4]   See below para 9.168.

9.117   Such is the flexibility of the development of the concept of natural justice into fair procedure since the decision of *Ridge v Baldwin*[1] in 1963 that it would today be idle to attempt to draw out with particularity the distinction between the two. The influence of Art 6 ECHR has also been profound, as discussed below, although it may carry some technical limitations. Fair procedure represents the extension of the concept of natural justice into a looser, more discretionary framework in the administrative sphere. It is what fairness demands in a particular context. It is a continuum of natural justice. The fact that an administrative decision has procedural rules to structure its progress does not rule out the application of the principles of fair procedure, viz a fair hearing and an absence of bias,[2] to supplement those rules if need be. Similarly, the labelling of a decision as political, non-legal or administrative does not *automatically* dictate the attitude of the courts and whether they should or should not intervene on the basis of a breach of fair procedure. Whenever a person's rights, liberty, privileges,[3] interests, livelihood, good name or occupation are at risk of being lost, taken away or otherwise destroyed, or indeed where they stand to suffer a detriment,[4] the strongest presumption will exist that such an occurrence ought not to take place without that person being given the opportunity to know why a course of action is being proposed and to address their comments, orally or in writing, to the decision-maker. An oral hearing may be dispensed with where the party has already been heard orally and the deciding body is in possession of all the facts.[5]

[1] [1964] AC 40, HL.

[2] *Audi alteram partem* and *nemo iudex in sua causa*. For detailed statutory codes see the TCP rules (paras 8.124 et seq above) and the Immigration and Asylum Appeals (Procedure) Rules 2000, SI 2000/2333, as amended. On judicial supplementation of a statutory procedure see *Lloyd v McMahon* [1987] 1 All ER 1118, CA and HL. On bias see: *Porter v Magill* [2002] 1 All ER 456 (HL) and *Lawal v Northern Spirit Ltd* [2004] 1 All ER 187 (HL) and *Davidson v Scottish Ministers* [2005] UKHL 74 – judicial involvement in legislative proceedings by a judge. For the ever more demanding application of the bias test: *R (Al-Hasan) v Secretary of State for the Home Department* [2005] 1 All ER 97 (HL) and prison discipline. For the question of whether judicial review survives a statutory review under Nationality, Immigration and Asylum Act 2002, s 101 see: *R (G) v IAT etc* [2004] 3 All ER 286 – per Collins J. Only 'exceptionally' would it survive; upheld on appeal [2005] 2 All ER 165 (CA). Art 6 ECHR lay behind the reforms leading to the creation of the United Kingdom Supreme Court in 2010 in order to separate the legislative and judicial functions of the UK's top court: Constitutional Reform Act 2005.

[3] Privileges have been 'transmuted' into public law rights: *R v Board of Visitors of Hull Prison, ex p St Germain* [1979] QB 425, CA was a watershed.

[4] See Lord Roskill in *Council of Civil Service Unions v Minister for the Civil Service* [1984] 3 All ER 935, HL; and *R v Secretary of State for the Environment, ex p Brent London Borough Council* [1982] QB 593. See *R (U) v Commissioner of Metropolitan Police* (29/11/02) (QBD) it was a breach of the fair trial provisions guaranteed by Art 6 for a young person accused of an offence of indecent assault to be given a formal warning without being told that his admission of guilt and consequent warning would cause his name to be recorded on the sex offenders' register: Crime and Disorder Act 1998, ss 65–66.

[5] *R v Immigration Appeal Tribunal, ex p Hussain* (1989) *Times*, 9 October, CA: a case which should be treated with caution. Likewise *R (Smith) v Parole Board* [2003] EWCA Civ 1269: recall to prison of a life prisoner; no right to an oral hearing on the facts was reversed by the House of Lords [2005] UKHL 1 (para 9.121 below). An oral hearing should be ordered where there was a disputed issue of fact which was central to the Board's assessment and which could not fairly be resolved without hearing oral evidence, *R (on the application of West) v Parole Board* [2002] EWCA Civ 1641 applied. Cf *Waite v UK* (2003) 36 EHRR 54 (ECtHR): recall from licence for a life prisoner after expiry of the tariff was a breach of Art 5(4) where an oral hearing allowing legal representation and calling of witnesses was not given. Unavailability of compensation was a breach of Art 5(5).

9.118   Where a person's 'civil rights and obligations' are determined (or where criminal charges are brought) the protection offered by Art 6 ECHR and the HRA 1998 which guarantees a 'fair and public hearing within a reasonable time by an independent tribunal established by law' and the requirement for a reasoned judgment will come into play. What constitutes civil rights and obligations is not always patently clear but they include rights under the Convention[1] but not where deportation is in question and no other convention rights are involved.[2] Article 6 will be crucial in its impact upon administrative decision-making for those decisions falling within its remit; many do not. In prison disciplinary cases involving hearings by the governor or controller, and who had not allowed legal representation, the adjudicators were not sufficiently independent of the Home Office, and the proceedings were a breach of Art 6, the ECtHR has ruled (*Whitfield v United Kingdom* (2005) *Times*, 27 April – Application 46387/99 CHR).[3] Because of the involvement of ECHR rights in control order cases the House of Lords has ruled unreservedly that those subject to orders must have access themselves to information which is crucial for their case (*Secretary of State for the Home Department v AF (FC) and another* [2009] UKHL 28 applying *A v UK* [2009] ECHR 301). Even where the HRA did not apply, the denial of access to an open court and a right to judicial protection was a denial of the principle of legality in relation to the property rights of an individual (*HM Treasury v Ahmed & Ors* [2010] UKSC 2 & 5). The English courts are also adjusting Art 6 to a common law culture which gives a high priority to informality and avoidance of excessive legalism where possible. The basic test is: what does fairness demand? Regardless of Art 6 there has been a considerably enhanced perception of the requirements of justice in a wide range of administrative contexts. In disciplinary proceedings involving a solicitor the Court of Appeal held that civil rights and obligations were not engaged unless the proceedings were 'directly decisive of those rights' in that they could lead to the discontinuation of a solicitor's right to practice. Where as in this case, the proceedings could lead to the award of a 'reprimand' which could lead to an increase in the cost of a solicitor's indemnity insurance, that did not determine the solicitor's legal rights. From that decision there was an appeal with a right to a public hearing. Basically a right did not come into question until a binding decision with legal effect was to be made. In the process of deciding whether such a decision should be made, eg by the Solicitors' Disciplinary Tribunal, the claimant solicitor's rights under Art 6 would be engaged.[4] Where the rights protected by Art 6 are involved, the court may have to look at the totality of the procedures in operation in an administrative context to see whether adequate protection is present (see paras 9.132 et seq below).

[1]   See HRA 1998, s 1 for 'Convention rights'.
[2]   *RB (Algeria) v Secretary of State for the Home Department* [2009] UKHL 10. Reliance was placed on *Maaouia v France* (2001) 33 EHRR 42.
[3]   See *Tangey v Gov of Elmley Prison* [2005] EWCA Civ 1009 on Art 6 and prison discipline; *R (Gardner) v Parole Board* [2006] EWCA Civ 1222 on exclusion of prisoner from a hearing and fair process; *Ezeh v UK (2003);* R (Napier) v SoS HD [2004] EWHC 936 (Admin) and prison discipline; and *R (King) v Secretary of State for Justice* [2010] EWHC 2522 (Admin) and disciplinary proceedings in a young offender institution before a governor adjudicator. No breach of Art 6 ECHR and judicial review would oversee legality and fairness.
[4]   *R (Thompson) v Law Society* [2004] 2 All ER 113. The Bar Council's disciplinary process has been ruled a breach of Art 6 ECHR by the Visitors to the Inns of Court because of insufficient independence. See *R (Argles) v Visitors to the Inns of Court* [2008] EWHC 2068 and reluctance to invalidate proceedings on the basis of the de facto appointment to an adjudicating office. See *R (G) v Governors of X School* [2011] UKSC 30 (para 9.130 below). On Art 8 ECHR rights and the judicial process see: *Principal Reporter v K (Scotland)* [2010] UKSC 56.

9.119 In decisions of an administrative character, where a body is empowered to proceed by way of a written procedure and not an oral one, it should not be inflexible as to the manner in which it exercises discretion and it should be prepared to hear evidence orally where fairness requires this; where for instance there are substantial disputes of fact.¹ The broader the discretionary framework in which a decision is being taken, and the more it involves a matter of policy affecting a wide range of interests, the less scope there is to structure formally a decision-making process with the principles of fair procedure, although the requirement of fairness, like reasonableness,² is implicit in the exercise of public power and will have to be applied.³ In some contexts, however, the judges have found it difficult or unnecessary to construe fairness as requiring a right to be heard or consulted, or to know, in other than general terms, why a course of action is being pursued. However, where the circumstances and context require the principles of a fair procedure, or where a 'legitimate expectation' has been created in the mind of a person affected by a decision or non-decision that his or her view will be canvassed, or that a warning will be given before a state of affairs is altered, then in such circumstances procedural restraints and safeguards have been applied.⁴ A notable decision involved a decision by the Minister to change his policy in relation to the production and sale of oral snuff where although the applicant manufacturers who had been induced by government grants to manufacture in the UK could not claim a substantive legitimate expectation that the Minister would not change policy in relation to the manufacture of the product. However, he was in breach of his statutory duty to consult when he refused to divulge independent medical reports on the substances. The 'high degree of fairness and candour owed to the applicants was due in part to the catastrophic effect that the ban would have on their financial interests'.⁵

¹ *R v Army Board of the Defence Council, ex p Anderson* [1992] QB 169; and see *R v Department of Health, ex p Gandhi* [1991] 1 WLR 1053: 'administrative convenience must not override exigencies of a particular case' at 1063; see also *R v Manchester Metropolitan University, ex p Nolan* [1994] LR 380, cited in de Smith's *Judicial Review*, 7th edn, para 7-055; *R v Secretary of State for the Home Department, ex p Venables* [1997] 3 All ER 97, HL.

² *Associated Provincial Picture Houses v Wednesbury Corpn* [1948] 1 KB 223, CA.

³ Byles J in *Cooper v Wandsworth Board of Works* (1863) 14 CBNS 180; Lord Reid in *Ridge v Baldwin* [1964] AC 40, HL; Lord Denning in *R v Liverpool Corpn, ex p Liverpool Taxi Fleet Operators' Association* [1972] 2 QB 299. And see *R v British Coal Corpn, ex p Price* [1993] ICR 720.

⁴ *R v Secretary of State for the Home Department, ex p Ruddock* [1987] 2 All ER 518 and *R (Greenpeace) v Secretary of State for Trade and Industry* [2007] EWHC 311. For an absence of an oral hearing see: *R (Dudson) v Secretary of State for the Home Department* [2005] UKHL 52 – no breach of Art 6 ECHR when the Lord Chief Justice reviewed minimum terms of a sentence imposed on a child or 'young person' murderer. The process was more akin to an appeal and not a primary review of fact.

⁵ *R v Secretary of State for Health, ex p US Tobacco International Inc* [1992] 1 All ER 212. On legitimate expectation interests, see *ex p Coughlan* etc at para 9.124 below.

9.120 Generally the courts are increasingly concerned to ensure that justice and administration are conducted under sufficient levels of openness. However, anonymity of witnesses at an inquiry may be ordered in order to protect a fundamental right to life.¹ Where a source of evidence may be put at risk if revealed to a prisoner whose case was being heard by the Parole Board, the evidence may be withheld from the prisoner and his legal representatives. The

Parole Board has power, through the specially appointed advocate procedure, to mitigate any unfairness.[2] The case caused a notable division of opinion between the majority and the dissenting judges.

1   *R v Lord Saville of Newdigate, ex p A* [1999] 4 All ER 860, HL, the inquiry into 'Bloody Sunday'. On anonymity of witnesses in criminal trials see Criminal Evidence (Witness Arrangements) Act 2008 reversing *R v Davis* [2008] UKHL 36 which prohibited anonymous witnesses in criminal trials.

2   *R (Roberts) v Parole Board* [2005] UKHL 45.

9.121   The House of Lords has ruled that the Parole Board is under a duty, by virtue of Art 5(4) ECHR, when considering the case of a prisoner serving a determinate sentence whose release on licence has been revoked, to afford the prisoner an oral hearing. Furthermore, the common law may require an oral hearing in the particular context of a case (*R (Smith) v Parole Board* [2005] UKHL 1).

Opportunities to be heard

9.122   The basic principle is a right to be heard before an adverse decision is taken. As well as a hearing, opportunities can be built to obtain information, allow examination and obtain reasons. A right to a hearing does not always imply a right to an oral hearing: a person is 'entitled to an oral hearing where fairness requires that there should be such a hearing but fairness does not require that there should be such a hearing in every case'.[1] Where facts are in issue which could affect the decision or where an oral hearing would otherwise make a contribution to a just result.[2]

1   *R (Ewing) v Department for Constitutional Affairs* [2006] EWHC 504; and see *R (West) v Parole Board* [2005] UKHL 1.

2   *R (West) v Parole Board* [2005] UKHL 1.

9.123   Whenever a decision is going to affect adversely an individual, the presumption will be that that individual, absent special reasons, will be entitled to a hearing.[1] The same ought to apply to an identifiable or ascertainable group which stands to be adversely affected *unless*, the courts have maintained, the change is going to be effected by the making of legislative provisions or rules.[2] However, where the adverse effect is serious,[3] or where the decision-maker has informed the person affected that they will be heard before a decision is taken, and even though it does not affect their 'rights' but their 'privileges' such as welfare payments, licences, grants or state concessions, then a legitimate expectation to be heard may be implied on the facts.[4] Therefore a representation that a group of affected parties would be heard before new licences were allocated; or that an opportunity to make a special case out even with regard to the exercise of a discretion; an undertaking to confer a right of audience before the exercise of legal duty,[5] or a regular practice of consultation before decision-taking in the past,[6] have all been said to have created a right to be heard because of legitimate expectation in the minds of the recipients.[7]

¹   See *R v Harrow London Borough Council, ex p D* [1990] Fam 133, CA: placing children on child abuse register; see *R v United Kingdom* [1988] 2 FLR 445 on termination of parental rights and Arts 6 and 8 of the ECHR; *R v Wandsworth London Borough, ex p P* [1989] COD 262: right to a hearing before removal from list of 'approved foster parents'. In *R v Secretary of State for the Home Department, ex p Allen* (12 November 1999, unreported), the Court of Appeal held that a prisoner had not been unfairly treated when he had not been given a hearing and had not seen relevant information relating to his early release assessment. A hearing, and any access rights, would arise on an appeal to the Governor. Cf *R v Secretary of State for the Home Department, ex p Harry* [1995] 3 All ER 360. For dispensing with an oral hearing in reviewing a young offender's tariff: *R (Smith) v Secretary of State for the Home Department* (2004) Times, 18 February. See *R (Williams) v Secretary of State for the Home Department* [2002] 4 All ER 872 (CA): documents disclosed to a review team reviewing a post tariff sentence for a discretionary life prisoner should, subject to public interest immunity (paras 10.64 et seq below) be available to the prisoner and an oral hearing should be provided in 'exceptional circumstances'. *R (Hammond) v Secretary of State for the Home Department* [2005] UKHL 69 – Criminal Justice Act 2003, Sch 22, para 11(1) is incompatible with Art 6(1) ECHR and should be read with an implied condition for an oral hearing if necessary in a decision concerning sentencing and tariff setting. See *Roberts v Parole Board* [2005] UKHL 45 on use of 'special advocates' in prison above and note paras 9.127 and 9.141 below. For assessing an applicant's age for entitlement to support under Children Act 1989, Part III (whether asylum seeker under 18 years old): *R (B) v Merton LBC* [2003] 4 All ER 280 – question did not require a trial and full judicialisation of proceedings. See *Makisi v Birmingham City Council* [2011] EWCA Civ 355 and a right for a homeless housing applicant to demand an oral hearing under SI 1999/71, regs 6 and 8; see *Lambeth LBC v Johnston* [2008] EWCA Civ 690.

²   See, however, *R v British Coal Corporation and Secretary of State for Trade and Industry, ex p Vardy* [1993] ICR 720.

³   Depriving individuals of eg trade unions' rights: see para 9.127, note 1 below; cf *Bates v Lord Hailsham* [1972] 3 All ER 1019.

⁴   In *R (Adlard) v Secretary of State for Transport, Local Government and the Regions* [2002] EWCA Civ 735 the Court of Appeal ruled that a refusal to call in a planning application by the Secretary of State did not require an opportunity for oral hearings and refusal of such did not engage Art 6 rights.

⁵   See cases at para 9.125, note 4 below and *R v Birmingham City Council, ex p Sheptonhurst Ltd* [1990] 1 All ER 1026, CA.

⁶   *CCSU* case para 9.127, note 1 below, Lord Roskill; *R v IRC, ex p Unilever plc* [1996] STC 681, CA.

⁷   And see *R v Devon County Council, ex p Baker* [1995] 1 All ER 73, CA, where there was insufficient notice given to residents of an old people's home to allow proper representations or complaints.

9.124   In *ex p Coughlan*[1] the Court of Appeal, developing earlier and much criticised (in certain quarters) decisions,[2] established that a substantive legitimate expectation – that is, an expectation to a thing, a position or something of substance – could be established where a representation to do or not do a certain thing, and then to go back on that representation, would be so unfair that it amounted to an abuse of power. In such a situation, the court could itself having established the legitimacy of the representation balance the requirements of fairness against any competing interest relied upon by the authorities for the change of policy and could make appropriate orders. This was the strongest of three positions discussed by the court. The first was where the authority's representation was merely a factor to consider and which it gave the weight which it felt appropriate and no more. Its decision here could only be overturned on grounds of *Wednesbury* unreasonableness.[3] The second case was where the authority promised or represented that it would consult parties before making a decision. The representation may be express or implied from prior conduct but the representee must, it appears, have knowledge of it[4] although not necessarily have acted in reliance of it,[5] and must not behave in a manner which is less than even-handed; they must put all their 'cards face up on the table'.[6] A representation should be 'clear, unambiguous and devoid of relevant qualification'.[7] Consultation must take place unless the court is convinced there is a countervailing reason why it should not. What is represented must be within the authority of the representor (*R (Bloggs 61) v Home Secretary* [2003] 1 WLR 2724) and for representations by one ministry binding on another (see *R (BAPIO Action Ltd) v Home Secretary* [2008] UKHL 27).

[1]   *R v North and East Devon Health Authority, ex p Coughlan* [2000] 3 All ER 850, CA.
[2]   *R v Ministry of Agriculture, Fisheries and Food, ex p Hamble (Offshore) Fisheries Ltd* [1995] 2 All ER 714.
[3]   *R v Secretary of State for the Home Department, ex p Briggs, Green and Hargreaves* [1997] 1 All ER 397, CA.
[4]   *R v Secretary of State for the Home Department, ex p Hindley* [2000] 2 All ER 385, HL.
[5]   *R (Bibi) v Newham LBC* [2002] 1 WLR 237 (CA) although reliance is a relevant factor. In *R (Begbie) v Secretary of State for Education* [2000] 1 WLR 1115 (CA), absence of reliance was 'an exception rather than the rule'. The representation must be intra vires: *Al Fayed v Adv Gen Scotland* (2004) SLT 798 (IH). The courts have emphasised that legitimate expectation is not to be supported lightly: see, Wade and Forsyth *Administrative Law* (10th edn, 2009) pp 455–456.
[6]   Bingham LJ in *R v IRC, ex p MFK Underwriting Agencies Ltd* [1990] 1 WLR 1545.
[7]   Per Bingham LJ, ibid. See *R v Falmouth and Truro Port Health Authority, ex p South West Water Services Ltd* [2000] 3 All ER 306, CA.

9.125   Over 30 years ago, Megarry V-C helpfully analysed[1] a typical decision in an administrative framework as:

(1)   Removal of a benefit conferred. Here, a right to be heard would usually obtain, and may still be insisted upon, though where a solicitor acting for the applicant has negligently prevented the applicant being present at an earlier hearing that may not constitute a breach of natural justice.[2]

(2)   Non-renewal of a benefit conferred. Here, a legitimate expectation is often created that non-renewal will only be for a cause; and where there is such a cause it ought, in fairness, to be communicated to the individual where benefit is not being renewed.[3]

(3)   Allocation of a benefit. Here, Megarry V-C held that no right to be heard existed. This was for a number of reasons. First, the numbers involved may well make hearings impossible. Second, a reason for non-conferral of a benefit may not be because of a detriment attaching to an applicant such as a blemish on a record; it may not be awarded simply because the strength of the application is not sufficient. Also, by implication, in this case no legitimate expectation of a hearing has been created – unless the conferring body has indicated otherwise.[4] And conferral of benefits may involve an exercise of wide discretion and subjective judgment which courts traditionally have been reluctant to expose to detailed scrutiny in the absence of an obvious vitiating factor.[5]

[1]   *McInnes v Onslow Fane* [1978] 3 All ER 211.
[2]   *Al Mehdawi v Secretary of State for the Home Department* [1989] 3 All ER 843, HL.
[3]   See *R v Birmingham City Council, ex p Sheptonhurst Ltd* [1990] 1 All ER 1026, CA; cf *Stevenson v United Road Transport Union* [1976] 3 All ER 29.
[4]   *R v Liverpool Corpn, ex p Liverpool Taxi Fleet Operators' Association* [1972] 2 QB 299, CA; *A-G of Hong Kong v Ng Yuen Shiu* [1983] 2 All ER 346, PC; *R v Secretary of State for the Home Department, ex p Khan* [1985] 1 All ER 40, CA; *R v Great Yarmouth Borough Council, ex p Botton Bros Arcades Ltd* (1987) 56 P & CR 99.

⁵   *Roncarelli v Duplessis* (1959) 16 DLR (2d) 689 at 705; see *Jones v Swansea City Council* [1989] 3 All ER 162, CA. The Court of Appeal has re-affirmed this reluctance in *R (Khatun) v Newham LBC* [2005] QB 37.

9.126   Nevertheless, statute frequently supplements the omission of the common law to allow hearings before conferral of a benefit, as in planning where a decision is 'called in' by the minister,[1] and appeals or reviews after an adverse decision.[2]

¹   Town and Country Planning Act 1990, s 77. NB Structure and Development Plans and their replacement: see paras 8.109 et seq above.
²   As in social security; cf the Social Fund and administrative review: Social Security Act 1986, Pt III; SI 1988/34; see *R v Social Security Fund Inspector, ex p Stitt* (1990) *Times*, 23 February. For a list of social security legislation see: http://www.dwp.gov.uk/docs/c-0021.pdf.

9.127   Reasons of national security,[1] emergency action[2] or the greater public good[3] in the past have defeated a right to a hearing, but not to fair treatment.[4] Even in cases of national security, special procedures may have to be devised using 'special counsel', as under the Special Immigration and Asylum Commission appeals, to ensure that procedures are not unlawful. However, the requirements of the ECHR must not be overlooked, in particular the requirements of judicial control of detention under Art 5 and a fair hearing before an independent tribunal under Art 6.[5] These requirements are reinforced in the UK by the Human Rights Act 1998 which came into effect on 2 October 2000. In *ex p Turgut*, the Court of Appeal emphasised that where a decision to deport an applicant for political asylum was challenged for breaching Art 3 ECHR prohibiting torture and inhuman and degrading treatment, and there were allegedly no grounds to award exceptional leave to stay, the court's role was not that of primary fact finder. But the court had to subject the decision to 'rigorous examination' and examine the underlying factual material. No special deference to the Secretary of State's view of the facts would be given. The right under Art 3 was 'absolute and fundamental'. The area of judgment to which deference was to be shown to the Secretary of State was a 'decidedly narrow one' in such a case. The case was decided before the HRA 1998 took effect. The decision was not overturned.[6] But it now looks dated and rather threadbare. The decisions of the courts have extended this concept of anxious scrutiny so that it mat be very difficult to discern any real difference between a primary decision-maker and the courts in cases concerning rights under Art 3 ECHR. The most difficult of cases have involved national security detentions and deportations and although the courts have given a wide berth to statutory definitions of national security and the information the Secretary of State may use to satisfy statutory definitions (para 1.124) a justification for detention will have to be made out.[7] In December 2004, the House of Lords, in a court of nine Law Lords, ruled that detention under Anti-terrorism, Crime and Security Act 2001, s 23 for an indefinite period without trial was a breach of the HRA 1998 and Art 5 ECHR. The rule of law demanded limits to executive detention.[8] The law lords followed this judgment with a further judgment involving the same claimants who argued that it was not permissible for a judicial tribunal (SIAC was the tribunal in question) to hear evidence that was extracted under torture overseas by foreign parties. The law lords ruled such a practice was repugnant to the common law, although the party alleging torture had to prove the case (*A etc v Secretary of State for the Home Department* [2005] UKHL 71). The further development involving disclosure of relevant evidence to a person subject to judicial proceedings involving special counsel was outlined above (para 9.80). The Supreme Court has ruled that the special advocate procedure is not extendible to civil litigation under the common law[9] although its use in security vetting procedures and employment did not involve a breach of Art 6 ECHR. As we point out in para 10.86 the government is seeking suggestions on the balance to be struck between 'justice' and 'security' in the handling of sensitive evidence.[11]

1 *Council of Civil Service Unions v Minister for the Civil Service* [1984] 3 All ER 935, HL; *R v Director Government Communications Headquarters, ex p Hodges* [1988] COD 123.

2 *R v Secretary of State for Transport, ex p Pegasus Holdings (London) Ltd* [1988] 1 WLR 990.

3 *R v Gaming Board for Great Britain, ex p Benaim and Khaida* [1970] 2 QB 417, CA; *Norwest Holst Ltd v Secretary of State for Trade* [1978] Ch 201, CA; *R v Secretary of State for the Environment, ex p London Borough of Southwark* (1987) 54 P & CR 226.

4 See Megarry V-C in *McInnes* (at para 9.125 note 1 above). See *R v Secretary of State for the Home Department, ex p Cheblak* [1991] 1 WLR 890, CA.

5 Note in particular the decision in *Chahal*, para 9.80, note 1 above and the criticism from the ECtHR in *Chahal v UK* (1996) 23 EHRR 413. And under Art 8, see *Smith v UK* [1999] IRLR 734, ECtHR.

6 *R v Secretary of State for the Home Department ex p Turgut* [2001] 1 All ER 719, CA. See also *R v Secretary of State for the Home Department, ex p Javed* [2001] 3 WLR 323 (CA). Post-HRA, see re Art 8 ECHR, *Huang v Secretary of State for the Home Department* [2005] EWCA Civ 105 – deference to Secretary of State's view on proportionality not permissible in non-policy questions. See also *R (Razgar) v Secretary of State for the Home Department* [2004] UKHL 27.

7 *M v Home Secretary of State for the Home Department* [2004] 2 All ER 863 (CA).

8 *A (FC) and others (FC) (Appellants) v Secretary of State for the Home Department (Respondent)* [2004] UKHL 56. The derogation was a disproportionate and discriminatory measure. However, eight Law Lords ruled that the declaration of a state of emergency by the government under Art 15 ECHR – 'an essentially political decision' – was not unlawful.

9 *Al Rawi v The Security Service and Others* [2011] UKSC 34 at common law.

10 *Tariq v Home Office* [2011] UKSC 35 and see *Kennedy v UK* [2010] ECHR 26839/05 and compare *Uzukauskas v Lithuania* [2010] ECHR 1060.

11 *Justice and Security* Cm 8194 (2011).

9.128 The ECtHR had ruled that not providing a tenant with a procedural opportunity to challenge a factual ground for serving a notice to quit was a breach of Article 8 ECHR (*Connors v UK* [2005] 40 EHRR 9). In *Harrow London Borough Council v Qazi* [2003] UKHL 43, it was held by the majority that the contractual and proprietary rights to possession of a public authority landowner could not be defeated by a defence based on Art 8 ECHR. In *Kay and others v Lambeth London Borough Council* [2006] UKHL 10, it was held by the majority, affirming *Qazi*, that the county courts, when faced with a defence to a claim to possession by a public authority landlord which is based on Art 8, should proceed on the assumption that domestic law strikes a fair balance and is compatible with the occupier's Convention rights. But it was recognised that there might be cases of a special and unusual kind, of which *Connors* was an example, where it would be incompatible with Art 8 for the occupier not to be permitted to challenge the factual allegations that were made against him which were the basis for the claim for a possession order. If the legal framework denied him that opportunity it would fall to be regarded as incompatible with the Convention right. There are several ways in which such a procedural challenge may be made. The House of Lords had to revisit the decision in *Kay*[1] and held that a decision by an authority to terminate a right to possession of land by travellers should be challengeable on judicial review which would be more exacting than the usual form of review. It would include assessment of fact, and reasons for possession and whether the decision was 'disproportionate'.[2] In *Kay v UK* [2011] HLR 2 the ECtHR ruled there had been a breach of Art 8 by the UK in *Kay* because the proportionality of the authority's action had not been assessed.

[1]   And also had to consider the effect of the ECtHR judgment in *McCann v United Kingdom*, application no 19009/04; see now *Kay v UK* App No 37341/06 21 Sept 2010 (ECtHR).
[2]   *Doherty v Birmingham City Council* [2008] UKHL 57 at paras 52, 53–55, 68, 70 and more emphatically Lord Mance at 161–164 who argued Convention principles should apply. See also *Manchester City Council v Pinnock* [2010] UKSC 45 where it was held that the proportionality of a possession order must be judicially assessed and *Hounslow LBC v Powell etc* [2011] UKSC 8.

Preliminary hearings

9.129   A difficult issue concerns a preliminary hearing before a more formal determination at which the individual will be heard.

9.130   As a general rule of thumb, a hearing will not be necessary at the preliminary[1] (investigatory) stage, but one should be held where serious consequences follow immediately to the detriment of the individual, ie stoppage of earnings,[2] and the purpose of the investigation will not be defeated or unduly frustrated by a hearing. The House of Lords has ruled that Art 6 ECHR was breached where a provisional listing under the Care Standards Act 2000 did not afford a right to a hearing so depriving a worker of employment in care pending a full hearing. The consequences were very serious and a full hearing could take months to hear (*R (Wright and others) v Secretary of State for Health* [2009] UKHL 3).[3] A fair procedure will not require that the person investigated be given the earliest opportunity to be fully informed of *all* relevant information and it will not require a hearing at the preliminary stage, especially where that may well hinder the investigation or run the risk of intimidating witnesses or destroying evidence. However, an outline of adverse information should be provided, orally if need be.[4] It is now clear that a mere advisory body is subject to judicial review[5] where it abuses its powers or acts unfairly, although fair procedure would be unlikely to involve a hearing as a legal requirement before such a body. This might be otherwise, perhaps, where the nature of the recommendations require hearings because they are damning and are de facto binding. Even then, the hearing would be investigatory rather than adversarial.[6] It is also clear that a non-public body exercising powers on behalf of the state or acting in the public interest as a surrogate for the state may also be subject to public law review under CPR 1998, Part 54[7] and the principles of fair procedure apply likewise to such bodies. The courts have been careful not to extend this jurisdiction too widely.[8] They have nonetheless been prepared to advance the boundaries of review or to dovetail the tests for review of private bodies and public bodies exercising disciplinary procedures.[9]

[1]   *Wiseman v Borneman* [1971] AC 297, HL; *Pearlberg v Varty* [1972] 1 WLR 534, HL; *Furnell v Whangarei High Schools Board* [1973] AC 660, PC. See *R v General Medical Council, ex p Toth* (para 9.100, note 1 above).

2   Though a hearing was not necessary in *Furnell* above. See *Re HK* [1967] 2 QB 617; *Re Pergamon Press Ltd* [1971] Ch 388, CA; *R v Agricultural Dwelling-House Advisory Committee, ex p Brough* [1987] 1 EGLR 106. *R v P Borough Council, ex p S* [1999] Fam 188: suspension from child minder's register without providing an opportunity to make representations during investigation was unfair. See also *Wright and others* in the following text.

3   See *R (G) v X School of Governors* [2011] UKSC 30; para 9.141 below.

4   See *Fayed v UK* (1994) 18 EHRR 393; and see Lord Slynn in *Rees v Crane* [1994] 1 All ER 833, PC.

5   See *R v ADHAC, ex p Brough* [1987] 1 EGLR 106; *R v Eden District Council, ex p Moffat* (15 April 1987, unreported) CO/803/86; on appeal 667/87 (1988) *Times*, 24 November, CA. *R v Boundary Commission, ex p Foot* [1983] QB 600, CA; see *R v Ethical Committee of St Mary's Hospital, ex p Harriott* [1988] 1 FLR 512.

6   On the provision of information in an investigation of the former Monopolies and Mergers Commission, see: *R v MMC, ex p Elders IXL Ltd* [1987] 1 All ER 451; *R v MMC, ex p Matthew Brown plc* [1987] 1 All ER 463; and on not allowing further comment: *R v MMC, ex p Air Europe* (1988) 4 BCC 182. See *Interbrew SA v Competition Commission* [2001] EWHC Admin 367. See also: *Unichem Ltd v Office of Fair Trading* [2005] CAT 8.

7   *R v Panel on Take-overs and Mergers, ex p Datafin* [1987] 1 All ER 564, CA; *R v Panel on Take-overs and Mergers, ex p Guinness plc* [1989] 1 All ER 509, CA; *R v Advertising Standards Authority, ex p Insurance Service plc* (1989) 133 Sol Jo 1545; *R v General Council of the Bar, ex p Percival* [1991] 1 QB 212; cf *R v FIMBRA, ex p Cochrane* [1991] BCLC 106; *R v Disciplinary Committee of the Jockey Club, ex p Massingberd-Mundy* [1993] 2 All ER 207: Jockey Club not judicially reviewable under Ord 53. Cf *R v Jockey Club, ex p Ram Racecourses* [1993] 2 All ER 225. For a private law employment case *R (K) v Middlesbrough BC* [2010] EWHC 1035 (Admin) and for public law process in an employment case: *R (Shoesmith) v Ofsted* [2011] EWCA Civ 642.

8   *R v Football Association Ltd, ex p Football League Ltd* [1993] 2 All ER 833; *R v Insurance Ombudsman Bureau, ex p Aegon Life Assurance Ltd* [1994] COD 426; *R v Panel of the Federation of Communication Services Ltd, ex p Kubis* [1998] COD 5.

9   See *R (Beer) v Hampshire Farmers Market Ltd* [2004] 1 WLR 233; *Bradley v Jockey Club* [2004] EWHC 2164.

The content of a fair hearing

9.131 Generally, the person entitled to a fair hearing has the right to know the case against him or her; to be given fair and timely warning; to know the impression of the decision-maker; to examine the evidence; to cross-examine witnesses and to know the identity of those making accusations,[1] although clearly the law of defamation and other qualifications will be important in this respect.[2] However, the courts have acknowledged that procedures aimed at achieving speedy resolution of disputes may not be required to make such a full disclosure of evidence; this was so in a case which concerned a Special Adjudicator established under the Asylum Appeals (Procedure) Rules 1993, SI 1993/1661 where the Home Secretary was not obliged to hand to the adjudicator the material on which the former had based a 'safe country certificate'.[3] Given the importance of the certificate to the outcome the decision appeared regrettable. In *R v Secretary of State for the Home Department, ex p Turgut* in another asylum case where ill-treatment under Art 3 of the ECHR was alleged, the court stated it was under an obligation to subject the Secretary of State's decision to a rigorous examination by considering the underlying factual material.[4] The attitude of the courts, shaped by decisions of the ECtHR, has become more demanding in relation to the human rights' aspects of such cases so that information crucial to the case against the suspect cannot be denied in a manner inconsistent with Art

6 ECHR rights (*Secretary of State v AF (FC) and another* [2009] UKHL 28; above at para 9.118).

¹ Cf *Local Government Board v Arlidge* [1915] AC 120, HL. It was unfair not to disclose evidence of one pupil against another in a decision to exclude a child from a grant maintained school: *R v Head Teacher and Independent Appeal Committee of Dunraven School, ex p B* [2000] ELR 156, CA.
² And the absence of absolute privilege. Decisions on procedure, within the bounds of reasonableness, are for the tribunal alone: see *A v Southwark London Borough Council* (1987) Guardian, 21 October.
³ *R v Secretary of State for the Home Department, ex p Abdi* [1996] 1 All ER 641, HL. See *RB (Algeria) v Secretary of State for the Home Department* [2009] UKHL 10.
⁴ See para 9.127, note 6 above. See *Re Application of Officer O's Application for Judicial Review* [2008] NIQB 52 – a request for a police officer's medical file – Art 8 ECHR in issue – notice to be given and representations allowed. *Szuluk v UK* App 36936/05 CHR – reading of prisoner's medical correspondence – Art 8 breached.

9.132 The courts would now have to be additionally vigilant that such an approach is consistent with Art 6 ECHR as applied by the HRA 1998. The individual must be given the opportunity to present his or her own case, to present evidence and not to face improper or constant interruption. These are decisions made by administrative bodies and are not decisions made by courts of law,¹ so hearsay evidence is usually admissible subject to the evidence being of reliable 'probative' value² and an opportunity is provided to comment on it by the party concerned who should be allowed to argue on the whole case. However, where serious disciplinary consequences may follow, hearsay evidence ought not to be taken.³ If such cases involve civil rights and obligations as outlined above, Art 6 ECHR will apply (see *Whitfield v UK*, para 9.118 above). Where the government had exercised a power to derogate from the HRA 1998 (Art 5 ECHR) in order to detain persons suspected of being terrorists without charge on evidence which, it was claimed, had been extracted under torture, a majority of the Court of Appeal refused to vitiate either the decision of the Secretary of State to detain or proceedings before the Special Immigration Appeal Tribunal upholding the decision. Guilt was not in question, but suspicion. The Home Secretary had to act on a wide range of materials which he could not verify as conforming with Art 3 ECHR. To require him to do so would be inconsistent with his power to act on a suspicion and a belief. The dissenting judge believed any party bringing an appeal before the commission could not be said to have had a fair trial, within Art 6(1) ECHR, if evidence obtained by torture had been used against him. The court accepted that, in the context of Anti-terrorism, Crime and Security Act 2001, s 21, a reasonable belief justifying detention could be held on the basis of the receipt of information which had not been proved and suspicion could reasonably arise from unproved facts.⁴ This decision was reversed by the House of Lords (para 9.118 above) unanimously. This was not a matter concerning technical rules of evidence; it was a matter of constitutional principle. Receipt of evidence before a judicial body in the UK that had been obtained by torture was prohibited. However, the person making the allegation of torture had to prove that fact. In the circumstances of SIAC procedures this could invariably prove to be inmpossible. Sections 21 to 32 of the Anti-terrorism, Crime and Security Act were repealed by s 16 of the Prevention of Terrorism Act 2005 (itself given a 12-month life). The 2005 Act introduced the highly controversial 'control order' regimes approved by, or taken under, judicial authority. The Schedule to the 2005 Act provides that the details of procedures in control orders are to be in rules of court. These will include: dispensing with hearings, conducting hearings in the absence of 'relevant persons', non-disclosure of full details of reasons for decisions relating to the proceedings to the relevant person, for modes of proof, for legal representation, for non-disclosure provisions, for disclosure of summaries of material by the Secretary of State, non-use of material, for anonymity, use of advisers and special representation. It has already been explained how the procedures have led to a corpus of case law.[5] Control orders are to be repealed under the Terrorism Prevention and Investigation Measures Bill 2011 and are to be replaced by Terrorism Prevention and Investigation Measures. These, according to the explanatory note, would be a 'civil preventative measure intended to protect the public from the risk posed by suspected terrorists who can be neither prosecuted nor, in the case of foreign nationals, deported, by imposing restrictions intended to prevent or disrupt their engagement in terrorism-related activity. The regime would be capable of imposing less intrusive restrictions than those available under control orders, and there would be increased safeguards for the civil liberties of those subject to the measures. There would be no provision in the replacement system for derogation from the ECHR' as under control orders. The Government's difficulties with control orders involved non derogating measures.

[1] The Court of Appeal ruled that hearsay evidence could be taken in wardship cases, but not in custody or access cases: *Re W* [1990] FCR 286 and *H v H* [1990] Fam 86, CA, on access. The Children Act 1989 allows for the reversal of decisions on the exclusion of evidence: s 96(3).

[2] See *R v Deputy Industrial Injuries Comr, ex p Moore* [1965] 1 QB 456, CA; *Mahon v Air New Zealand* [1984] AC 808, CA.

[3] See *R v Board of Visitors of Hull Prison, ex p St Germain (No 2)* [1979] 3 All ER 545; NB *Mahon's* case where the proceedings became a trial of fact and the strict test applied.

[4] *A etc v Secretary of State for the Home Department* [2004] EWCA Civ 1123 reversed by [2005] UKHL 71.

[5] On secret hearings under Employment Tribunals (Constitution and Rules of Procedure) Regulations 2004, SI 2004/1861, Sch 1 para 54(2), *B v Secretary of State for Defence* [2010] ICR 54 adverted to the limits of a tribunal's expertise in national security. *Coles v Barracks* [2006] EWCA Civ 1041 provided a different emphasis in security vetting cases. See *Tariq v Home Office* [2010] ICR 223 and para 54, compliance with the ECHR. In *Tariq v Home Office* [2011] UKSC 35, the Supreme Court ruled in favour of the Home Office that the closed material/special counsel procedure was permissible before employment tribunals deciding security vetting cases; see para 9.127 above.

9.133 The tendency in British public administration to informalise administrative procedures could face serious consequences if Art 6 was readily invokable in informal resolution processes (see *Whitfield v UK*, para 9.118 above). The field of land use and planning regulation was thrown into panic some years ago when the Divisional Court ruled that the system for dealing with planning and compulsory purchase, railway and highway appeals where a Secretary of State called in an application or otherwise made a decision in a case in which he notionally had a governmental interest in applying policy breached Art 6 because he was not an independent and impartial tribunal. The House of Lords ruled in *Alconbury* that the whole decision-making process had to be seen in its entirety. There were usually public inquiries before inspectors. The Secretary of State's decision was controllable in the courts by an application by a 'person interested' under eg Town and Country Planning Act 1990, s 288 on a point of law rather like judicial review. There was no review of facts or merits. The House of Lords held that although the Secretary of State was not an independent tribunal, the fact that his decision was reviewable in a court of law provided the necessary compliance with Art 6. Indeed, it was not appropriate for courts to become involved in the merits of government policy in land use regulation or related matters, and ECtHR jurisprudence did not require an appeal on the merits.[1]

[1] *R (Alconbury) v Secretary of State for the Environment* [2001] 2 All ER 963 (HL) reversing the Divisional Court at ditto 934. The Law Lords did not decide on the extent to which proportionality might be available in English law in such a case, though see Lord Slynn at para [51]. For the ECtHR: *Albert v Belgium* (1983) 5 EHRR 533; *Bryan v UK* (1995) 21 EHRR 342; and *Chapman v UK* (2001) 10 BHRC 48. See, further, P Craig (2003) *Public Law* 753.

9.134 In *Runa Begum v Tower Hamlets* the question was whether an internal local authority review dealing with homeless cases under Housing Act 1996, s 202 complied with Art 6. The review was conducted by an officer of the authority. The procedure left by itself did not comply because the officer was not an 'independent and impartial tribunal' for Art 6 purposes, but the Law Lords ruled that an appeal to the county court (on a judicial review basis) under s 204 of that Act did bring the overall procedure within Art 6. The absence of full fact-finding powers by the appeal court did not deprive that procedure of Art 6 qualities assuming, without deciding, that the right in question was a civil right.[1] In *Tomlinson* (below) the Supreme Court decided that determining 'homelessness decisions' under the relevant procedures does not involve Art 6 rights. Although judicial review in the past has not offered a sufficient review of facts to satisfy cases where Art 3 was engaged[2], the UK courts have been more persuaded by the heightened levels of scrutiny that may apply when human rights are engaged, or situations which impose a serious detriment on claimants. The courts are prepared to see whether the process of decision-making as a whole, including judicial review, offers adequate opportunity for challenge.[3] Where a decision-making process is tainted by unfairness and clearly cannot be remedied by judicial review because the court cannot establish the basis on which a decision-maker made a decision affecting civil rights, judicial review did not offer adequate safeguards for Art 6.[4] The case concerned refusal of assistance to an asylum seeker under Nationality, Immigration and Asylum Act 2002, s 55 which the Secretary of State refused after inadequate enquiries as to why claims for assistance by the claimants had not been made 'as soon as reasonably practicable'. The process had not been adequately explained to the claimants, what the purpose of interviews (eligibility for support) was for, inadequate information had been given to them, insufficient thought had been given to statutory formulations such as 'reasonably practicable', relevant factors such as the claimant's state of mind and could asylum reasonably have been claimed earlier had been overlooked? The questions put to claimants at the time did not allow 'a sufficiently full picture for a fair decision to be made' (para 90). More than a standard form questionnaire was required. Nor were there sufficient inquiries by the authorities to satisfy themselves adequately in law of whether they are complying with the claimant's rights under eg Arts 3 and 8 ECHR.

The interviewer, furthermore, was not the person who made the decision. Nor had the claimant been given the 'gist of the case against him'. All will depend on specific circumstances. On the facts, a request for further review by the Secretary of State would not have satisfied fairness. Where these standards as suggested but the court were satisfied, judicial review would provide a procedure compliant with Art 6 because an proper scrutiny could be had by the court of the decision.

¹   [2003] 1 All ER 731 (HL) considering *Bryan v UK* (1996) 21 EHRR 342, ECtHR. See *Feld v Barnet LBC* (CA) 18/10/04 and *Hall v Wandsworth LBC* [2004] EWCA Civ 1741 on the tests and procedure to be applied by the reviewing officer: a 'housing authority is not a court'; 'its primary task is that of investigation'. It must act fairly, but does not have to engage in indefinite exchange and counter-exchange of evidence and comment.

²   *Vilvarajah v UK* (1991) 14 EHRR 248; *Chahal v UK* (1996) 1 BHRC 405.

³   See *Alconbury* below. See also: *R (Beeson) v Dorset CC* (2003) *Times*, 2 January: no reason to question the integrity of a decision on the facts and judicial review could rectify any errors; *R (L) v Secretary of State for the Home Department* [2003] 1 All ER 1062 – judicial review could rectify any shortcomings under Nationality, Immigration and Asylum Act 2002, s 115; see, on the role of clerks in Scottish District courts (analogue of magistrates' courts), *Clark v Kelly* [2003] 1 All ER 1106 (HL); and, on assessors sitting with a judge under Race Relations Act 1976, s 67(4), *Ahmed v Governing Body of Oxford University* [2003] 1 All ER 915.

⁴   *R (Q) v Secretary of State for the Home Department* [2003] 2 All ER 905 (CA) – on the proviso that a 'fair' sysyem was in place to question asylum seekers about welfare payments.

9.135   The *Runa Begum* decision has raised important questions. The impact of the HRA 1998 may have led to an increasing judicialisation of our public services but the courts have shown that they will not require public service providers or state agents to set up procedures satisfying the strict tests of Art 6 ECHR for internal review of rights protected by Art 6 where somewhere in the process there is an opportunity for appropriate judicial challenge of primary facts and the decision is made by parties who are independent – this is not strictly interpreted – of the initial authority. The House of Lords in *Runa Begum* stressed that although the housing officer in a homeless case had been called upon to resolve some disputed factual issues, these findings of fact were, per Lord Bingham, 'only staging posts on the way to the much broader judgments' concerning local conditions and the availability of alternative accommodation, which the housing officer had the specialist knowledge and experience to make. Although the housing officer could not be regarded as independent, since she was employed by the local authority which had made the offer of accommodation which Runa Begum had rejected, statutory regulations provided substantial safeguards to ensure that the review would be independently and fairly conducted, free from improper external influences. Any significant departure from the procedural rules would have afforded a ground of appeal.

9.136   Where a decision complained against ultimately rests on broad discretionary determinations of policy or expediency a full review on the merits is not necessary or appropriate. Where internal review procedures do exist and where they establish questions of primary fact and determine civil rights protected by Art 6, there would have to be an appeal capable of reviewing facts to an independent body acting judicially. The principles have been developed in the following case law. In *Tsfayo* ((2007) ECHR 656 App No 60860/00) the ECtHR had before it a case from England involving a Housing Benefit and

Council Tax Benefit Review Board (HBRB) comprising five councillors from the council. Housing benefit is a means-tested assistance for rented accommodation. It was an Art 6 protected human right (unlike a decision on homelessness per *Tomlinson* below). Not only did the HBRB lack any independence from the council executive, it was directly connected to one of the parties to the dispute. Any procedural safeguards were not adequate to 'overcome this fundamental lack of objective impartiality' (para 47). The High Court had previously ruled in another case involving a HBRB that it 'did not have jurisdiction to rehear the evidence or substitute its own views as to the applicant's credibility. Thus, in this case, there was never the possibility that the central issue would be determined by a tribunal that was independent of one of the parties to the dispute' (para 48). The procedure constituted a breach of Art 6. *Tsfayo* was decided in England before the HRA 1989 came into effect. The limited nature of judicial review over the procedures in question at the relevant date had already been established (*R (Bewry) v Norwich City Council* [2001] EWHC Admin 657, Moses J). Review cannot upset findings on the *weight* of evidence as opposed to an absence of evidence or a clear error. The lack of independence and its effect may not be sufficiently scrutinised by the court. Would bias in the composition of a board itself not be subject to review?

9.137 The ECtHR held that the decision-making process in *Tsfayo* was significantly different. In contrast to *Alconbury* and *Rena Began*[1], in *Tsfayo* the HBRB was deciding a simple question of fact: was there 'good cause' for the applicant's delay in making a claim? The HBRB found the applicant's explanation to be 'unconvincing' and rejected her claim for back-payment of benefit. No specialist expertise was required to determine this issue. The factual findings in *Tsfayo* cannot 'be said to be merely incidental to the reaching of broader judgments of policy or expediency which it was for the democratically accountable authority to take' (para 45), as in *Alconbury*. In *Tomlinson v Birmingham City Council* [2010] UKSC 8, in ruling that when determining cases of homelessness under statutory provisions, the governing procedures for such a determination do not attract Art 6 protection (and the strict application of impartiality), the justices stated (para 49):

> 'That being the present state of the authorities, I would be prepared now to hold that cases where the award of services or benefits in kind is not an individual right of which the applicant can consider himself the holder, but is dependent upon a series of evaluative judgments by the provider as to whether the statutory criteria are satisfied and how the need for it ought to be met, do not engage article 6(1). In my opinion they do not give rise to "civil rights" within the autonomous meaning that is given to that expression for the purposes of that article. The appellants' right to accommodation under section 193 of the 1996 Act falls into that category. I would hold that article 6 was not engaged by the decisions that were taken in the appellants' cases by the reviewing officer.'

See also *Makisi* at para 9.123, note 1 above.

[1] In *Ali v Birmingham City Council* [2008] EWCA Civ 1228 it was stated that *Rena Began* covered questions of primary fact as well as decisions resting on the special expertise of the decision-maker.

9.138 Requests for all relevant documents and information should be made. If they are denied and relied upon by the decision-maker, the denial will have to be justified.[1] In a wide range of circumstances, such a practice may well be questioned successfully in the courts.[2] The Divisional Court has held that in cases concerning allegations of child abuse parents are entitled to information held by social services departments on their children. The information concerned official police medical reports. The authority should also have helped to arrange for the parents to make their own independent medical inspection (see para 10.22 below).[3] Unreasonable and speculative demands would not have to be met. A recent judgment of a majority of the House of Lords was prepared to accept the ex parte (to one party only) notification of information to one party which was not revealed to the other side in environmental regulation despite the misgivings of some of the law lords.[4] Such communications are generally prohibited under American law.

[1] *Chief Constable of North Wales Police v Evans* [1982] 1 WLR 1155, HL; *R v Assistant Metropolitan Police Comr, ex p Howell* [1986] RTR 52, CA; *Kanda v Government of the Federation of Malaya* [1962] AC 322, PC; *Fraser v State Services Commission* [1984] 1 NZLR 116: *R (Bentley) v HM Coroner for Avon* [2001] EWHC 170 Admin. See *Lloyds Bank plc v Cassidy* (2005) *Times*, 11 January.

[2] *R v Secretary of State for Health ex p United States Tobacco International Inc* [1992] 1 All ER 212. In *Lewis v A-G of Jamaica* [2000] 3 WLR 1785 the Privy Council overturned death sentences where there had been a failure to disclose materials to petitioners for mercy. See also, *R v Chelsea College of Art and Design, ex p Nash* [2000] Ed CR 571.

[3] *R v Hampshire County Council, ex p K* [1990] 2 All ER 129 – juvenile care proceedings.

[4] *R (Edwards and another) v Environment Agency and others* [2008] UKHL 22 and EIAs: Lords Mance and Brown disagreed on this point.

9.139 Nor will the following:

(1) Where there are security reasons for withholding information, especially on the grounds of national security.[1] However, where English courts refused to balance national security considerations and the security of the individual involved by refusing to review the evidence on which the Secretary of State based a decision to deport an Indian national 'for reasons of a political nature' that would run foul of Art 5(4) ECHR. C's liberty had not been subject to any effective judicial control. While respecting the legitimate requirements of national security and evidence from informers, the courts must provide the individual with an appropriate level of procedural justice.[2] The SIAC procedures were introduced to deal with this problem in respect of those facing deportation on national security grounds. One should also refer to the procedures involved in 'control orders' under the Prevention of Terrorism Act 2005 (para 9.132 above). We have seen how the courts have insisted, largely by ECtHR prompting, that these procedures must comply with the open and fair justice requirements of Arts 5(4) and 6 ECHR (above).

(2) Where the identity of informers (and consequential risk of harm to them) may be established by giving detailed information.[3] Even here, although there is no need to quote 'chapter and verse', an outline of the allegations will be required.[4]

(3) Where there is an apprehension that the party involved requires detailed information to invoke the law of defamation where qualified privilege may not apply or to intimidate witnesses or to present others giving evidence.[5]

(4)   Where the request is really part of a frustrating exercise or is unnecessary in the circumstances.[6]

[1]   See *Council for Civil Service Unions* (para 9.117, note 4). NB *R v Secretary of State for the Home Department, ex p Ruddock* [1987] 2 All ER 518.

[2]   *R v Secretary of State for the Home Department, ex p Chahal* [1995] 1 All ER 658 and *Chahal v United Kingdom* (1996) 23 EHRR 413. See *R (Tucker) v DG National Crime Squad* [2003] EWCA Civ 2 and seeking disclosure of sensitive intelligence reports.

[3]   See *R v Gaming Board for Great Britain, ex p Benaim and Khaida* [1970] 2 QB 417, CA; *Re Pergamon Press Ltd* [1971] Ch 388, CA.

[4]   As above. And see: *R v Secretary of State for the Home Department, ex p Duggan* [1994] 3 All ER 277; and *R v Secretary of State for the Home Department, ex p Hickey (No 2)* [1995] 1 All ER 490.

[5]   Ibid and *Maxwell v Department of Trade and Industry* [1974] QB 523, CA.

[6]   *Public Disclosure Commission v Isaacs* [1989] 1 All ER 137, PC; cf *Bushell v Secretary of State for the Environment* [1981] AC 75, HL and refusal to allow cross examination of departmental representatives on what was alleged to be 'policy'.

9.140   A committee entitled to sit in closed session does not have to disclose legal advice from its officers to persons with a right to be heard or to disclose its advice.[1] The High Court has ruled that the PCA has not acted unfairly in sending a draft report of his investigation to the department complained against but not to the complainant, because it was the department that was being investigated and not the complainant.[2]

[1]   *R v Royal Borough of Kensington and Chelsea, ex p Stoop* [1992] PLR 58, HL.

[2]   *R v Parliamentary Comr for Administration, ex p Dyer* [1994] 1 All ER 375.

THE RIGHT TO LEGAL REPRESENTATION

9.141   A fair procedure may necessitate legal representation. In cases where a disciplined organisation is concerned, eg the police or a prison, the courts have denied the automatic right to legal representation for parties involved in disciplinary hearings.[1] The parties have therefore been denied the presumed benefits that representation will bring for forensic examination of evidence and eliciting of information as well as interpretation of possibly complex rules. But the courts have insisted that legal representation should be allowed if reasonably required in the circumstances because of the seriousness of a charge and potential penalties; whether any points of law are likely to arise; the capacity of the party to conduct his or her own case; whether procedural difficulties are likely to arise; the need for a reasonably speedy dispatch of a disciplinary matter in an institution such as a prison; and the need for fairness between all the parties involved.[2] In other cases the courts have held that although legal representation before a domestic body was discretionary, it may well be mandatory where serious consequences follow.[3] The Court of Human Rights has ruled that whether offences in prison were criminal or disciplinary was only a starting point in an inquiry; disciplinary proceedings before the governor attended by forfeiture of remission was a criminal matter and proceeding after refusing legal representation for a prisoner was a violation of Art 6 ECHR.[4] This decision must put under question a previous ruling of the House of Lords that the mere fact that a disciplinary charge may also be the grounds for bringing a criminal charge will not, ipso facto, be a sufficient ground for insisting upon legal representation.[5] The Prison

Rules have been amended (SI 2002/2116) by providing an adjudicator approved by the Secretary of State to inquire into charges of serious offences against of discipline. A governor who determines that a charge is sufficiently serious must refer the charge to the adjudicator. At an inquiry by the adjudicator, a prisoner is given the opportunity of legal representation. Elsewhere, in *Kulkani v Milton Keynes Hospital Trust* [2009] EWCA Civ 789 a doctor at a disciplinary hearing was entitled to representation by a Medical Protection Society lawyer. Art 6 ECHR required legal representation in disciplinary cases with serious implications if a ruling was adverse. In *R (G) v X School Governors* [2009] EWHC 504 refusal of legal representation before school governors dealing with a serious disciplinary subject and serious consequences if a finding was adverse necessitated legal representation even though it was not a criminal matter according to Convention law as in *Engel*.[6] This ruling was upheld by the Court of Appeal but reversed by majority in the Supreme Court, which reasoned that Art 6(1) rights were not in play in this case because this was an internal disciplinary matter and the decision on barring the teacher from working with children would be determined on appeal by the Independent Standards Authority where legal representation would be allowed. It has to be said that this case reveals a limited approach to the fairness in issue under Art 6(1) and how the common law may have provided fuller protection.[7] Lord Kerr dissenting stated: 'The overall process involving the determination of the claimant's civil right must be fair. In light of this, it is mistaken to concentrate substantially or exclusively on an individual stage in that process. In this case, the disciplinary proceedings were critical in testing the evidence against the claimant. To recognise his right to be legally represented at that stage is consonant with the proper safeguarding of his article 6 rights.'[8] We respectfully agree.

[1] See *Fraser v Mudge* [1975] 1 WLR 1132, CA; *Maynard v Osmond* [1977] QB 240, CA, per contra *Joplin v Chief Constable of Vancouver* (1985) 20 DLR (4th) 314. Police regulations in England and Wales were amended to allow legal representation. In prison disciplinary proceedings, see *Whitfield v UK* (para 9.117above).

[2] *R v Board of Visitors of Wormwood Scrubs Prison, ex p Anderson* [1984] 1 All ER 799.

[3] *Manchanda v Medical Eye Centre Association* [1986] LS Gaz R 3673, CA; see *Pett v Greyhound Racing Association Ltd* [1969] 1 QB 125, CA; *Enderby Town Football Club Ltd v Football Association Ltd* [1971] Ch 591.

[4] *Ezeh and Connors v UK* [2004] 39 EHER 1. See *Tangney v Governor of HMP Elmley and Home Secretary* [2005] EWCA Civ 1009. See *R (Cannon) v Governor of Full Sutton Prison* (30/1/03): the permission of the governor was required before a prisoner could exchange legal documents with a legal adviser – requirement was held proportional.

[5] *Hone v Maze Prison Board of Visitors* [1988] 1 All ER 321, HL.

[6] *Engel v Netherlands* (1979–80) 1 EHRR 647, ECHR.

[7] Cf *Al Rawi v The Security Services* [2011] UKSC 34 and *Tariq v Home Office* [2011] UKSC 35, para 9. And para 9.127 above.

[8] *R (G) v Governors of X School* [2011] UKSC 30 citing *Ringeisen v Austria (No 1)* (1971) 1 EHRR 455 and *Le Compte, Van Leuven and De Meyere v Belgium* (1981) 4 EHRR 1.

9.142 In disciplinary, and non-disciplinary, administrative decision-making, although legal representation is not uncommon,[1] in the absence of the above considerations there would appear to be no legal duty to allow representation.[2] Statements do exist that in the absence of specific statutory or other prohibitions an individual who has a right of appearance before a statutory tribunal is entitled to be represented by a legal adviser or other appropriate spokesperson.[3] To interfere with a prisoner's right of access to legal advice by reading his correspondence to lawyers has been interpreted as a denial of a prisoner's right of unimpeded access to the courts.[4] The House of Lords has ruled that preventing a journalist conducting an interview with a prisoner may amount to an interference with a prisoner's right to freedom of expression and the right to have his case investigated to establish the safety of his conviction.[5] These are further examples of recently discovered fundamental human rights under the common law and which exist independently of the HRA 1998.[6]

[1] See *Lonrho plc v Secretary of State for Trade and Industry* [1989] 2 All ER 609, HL.

[2] Legal aid for representation is extremely limited and covers those bodies referred to above (para 9.65, note 2).

[3] de Smith's *Judicial Review*, Woolf, Jowell and Le Sueur (6th edn, 2007), at para 7.075 and seq (see para 9.114, note 1 above) and ibid for interpreters and litigation friends at 7.081–2. See Lord Hutton HC 247 (2003–04), ch 13.

[4] *R v Secretary of State for the Home Department, ex p Leech (No 2)* [1994] QB 198, CA.

[5] *R v Secretary of State for the Home Department, ex p Simms* [1999] 3 All ER 400, HL. In *R (Hirst) v Secretary of State* (2002) *Times*, 10 April, a policy (based on regulations) which prohibited a prisoner the right to contact media whenever his purpose was comment on matters of legitimate public interest was lawful. See also *Broadmoor Hospital Authority v R* [2000] 2 All ER 727 (CA): unsuccessful attempts to stop publication of a book by an inmate of a special hospital of his book about his crime; *R (Nilson) v Governor of Full Sutton Prison* [2004] EWCA Civ 1540, 2 February: refusal to hand back to a prisoner autobiographical writings under Prison Standing Order 5 was not a breach of Art 10 ECHR and (2004) *Times*, 23 November.

[6] Note HRA 1998, s 11 which states that rights under the Convention do not restrict any other rights conferred on an individual by any other laws including common law and EC law. NB *HM Treasury v Ahmed and ors* [2010] UKSC 2 and 5.

9.143 Wider-ranging inquiries such as those conducted into the Hillsborough football disaster by Sir Peter Taylor and into prison riots by Lord Woolf have adopted more restricted approaches to the conduct of the inquiry than might be usual in eg planning inquiries. The editors of *de Smith* put the matter as follows:

> 'only those persons whose actions were at risk of being criticised were allowed to be represented, witnesses were normally only called by counsel to the inquiry, who exercised his discretion as to who should be called, and cross-examination was strictly limited. Different techniques were used for different classes of evidence, only part was given orally (not all in public) .... And in the case of the Prison Inquiry even seminars were employed to canvass issues of a wide-ranging nature.'[1]

[1] *De Smith's Judicial Review*, above, para 7.130. See *Effective Inquiries* (DCA, May 2004) and Inquiries Act 2005. See Lord Hutton's inquiry into the death of the WMD expert David Kelly HC 247 (2003–04).

9.144 These approaches were adopted to save time and resources and to prevent the inquiry being overwhelmed by material. This allowed for the expeditious production of reports without complaint of unfairness say the editors. Sir Richard Scott adopted a more restrictive approach to the representation of witnesses before his famous *Matrix Churchill* inquiry.[1]

[1] HC 115 (1995/96) and Blom-Cooper (1994) PL 1.

9.145 Where a person in police custody was refused access to a lawyer for the first 48 hours in detention there was a breach of a right to a fair trial, the ECtHR has held.[1]

[1] *Murray v UK* (1996) 22 EHRR 29. See also *Magee v UK* (2000) *Times*, 20 June.

Cross-examination

9.146 Like legal representation, cross-examination may well in the circumstances be necessary for the realisation of a fair procedure. It may also serve to intimidate those taking part in the proceedings so as to prevent a fair procedure.

9.147 The general principle would seem to be that if a witness is called, especially in a disciplinary hearing, then s/he should be cross-examined, perhaps with the questions being put through the chairperson. When a witness is not called, and hence cannot be cross-examined, then whether this amounts to a denial of fair procedure depends on the circumstances which were discussed above in relation to hearsay evidence. Where for instance, in school exclusion appeals a witness is fully aware of the case against him, an absence of witnesses at an oral hearing did not undermine the adequacy of the procedure.[1] A prisoner appearing before a prison disciplinary tribunal following a positive mandatory drug test was not allowed to cross-examine the relevant laboratory scientist provided that he had been informed about the tests that had been used and the safeguards to ensure accuracy. This is an important proviso.[2] Where a witness has given oral evidence and a request to cross-examine the witness is made by a party, especially where there is a dispute of fact with important consequences, cross-examination should, it is submitted, be allowed.[3] In *R (Al-Sweady) v Secretary of State for Defence* [2009] EWHC 2387 (Admin) on cross-examination and judicial review proceedings the court commented on the lamentable level of disclosure in a case of killings by the UK military in Iraq. The use of cross-examination in judicial review applications is considered below (para 10.60).

[1] *R (J) v School and College Head Teacher* [2003] EWHC 1747. See *R (S) v Knowsley NHS PCT etc* [2006] EWHC 26 where serious disputes of fact will require cross-examination.
[2] *R v Governor of Swaleside Prison, ex p Wynter* (1998) *Times*, 2 June.
[3] *Knowsley* above and *R (Sim) v Parole Board* [2003] EWCA Civ 1845.

9.148 Where there are opportunities for full written *and* oral representations before the taking of adverse decisions, and where these may be put through a legal representative, then the absence of the opportunity to cross-examine a witness making accusations may not be fatal to a fair procedure.[1] Where serious consequences flow from a decision, then the right to cross-examine should be presumed. In one case, the classification of a non-discrimination notice served by the Commission for Racial Equality as an administrative matter, and not as a penalty, justified the conclusion that there was no implied right to cross-examination.[2] The crucial finding of such an issue turning on a mere appellation is unfortunate: what is of significance is the seriousness of the consequences. The same case also held that as the Commission, with powers of subpoena,[3] has power to delegate its function of formal investigation to its officers, then its officers' reports are necessarily hearsay if no direct evidence is taken at a hearing. As it is proper to delegate its functions in such a way, it is proper to act on such reports.[4] For the purpose of administrative convenience, one would not expect every hearing in the administrative process to be fully confrontational, adversarial and judicialised. On the other hand, the seriousness of the consequences may dictate that a party making a serious allegation should be cross-examined, and where no improper motive on the part of the requester can be discerned or suspected such examination should be permitted.[5] All that the rules of natural justice mean are that the proceedings must be conducted in a way which is fair in all the circumstances. The presence of matters covered by Art 6 will involve degrees of procedural fairness consistent with that provision. Disputes of fact would have to be subjected to cross examination where there would be serious consequences for an individual's civil rights and obligations.

[1] *R v Commission for Racial Equality, ex p Cottrell and Rothon* [1980] 3 All ER 265: the proceedings were classified as more investigative than judicial: sed quaere.

[2] *R v Commission for Racial Equality, ex p Cottrell and Rothon* [1980] 3 All ER 265.

[3] For a 'named' investigation, ie into 'persons' as identified; for a general investigation, the subpoena powers are those of the Secretary of State: Race Relations Act 1976, s 50 and *Re Prestige Group plc, Commission for Racial Equality v Prestige Group plc* [1984] 1 WLR 335.

[4] *R v Commission for Racial Equality, ex p Cottrell and Rothon* [1980] 3 All ER 265, and NB *R v Hull Prison Board of Visitors ex parte St Germain (No 2)* [1979] 3 All ER 545.

[5] See, however, *Benaim and Khaida* etc, para 9.139, note 3 above.

9.149 The courts have given wide leeway to bodies carrying out administrative inquiries to conduct their procedures in a way which the bodies deem appropriate. The matter is within their discretion unless Parliament determines otherwise. They have shown reluctance to interfere with situations where cross-examination, and also final submissions, were not allowed on the grounds that the hearing, by a regional passenger committee, was not 'justiciable'[1] but purely fact-finding and recommendatory. Again the test should be, what does fairness require in the circumstances? If there is any possibility that 'facts' are being proffered which are not facts, then one could argue that cross-examination should be allowed.

[1] *R v London Regional Passengers Committee, ex p Brent London Borough Council* (1985) *Financial Times*, 29 November, CA. See *Effective Inquiries* (DCA, May 2004) and the Inquiries Act 2005; para 9.104 above.

9.150 However, where the facts are concerned with the formulation of government policy, and where the 'facts' can be ascertained by the Minister and his advisers, then cross-examination at an inquiry into objections will not be required as a matter of fairness.[1] Nor indeed might discussion of complex facts justifying a policy. If such has taken place at an inquiry, then it need not as a matter of law form part of the report to the Minister by the person holding the hearing.[2] There are more appropriate fora for the examination of government policy.[3] The FOIA 2000 allows for the release of factual information related to the policy formulation process (para 1.170 above). We discussed in chapter one the impact of this measure.

[1] *Bushell v Secretary of State for the Environment* [1981] AC 75.

² R v Secretary of State for Transport, ex p Gwent County Council [1987] 1 All ER 161, CA; reversing QBD.
³ Eg, Parliament.

9.151 Where as a result of a complaint an investigation into alleged malpractices by a high-ranking official is instigated, the complainant has no right to question or rebut the case of the investigating commission where it decides, after investigation, that the complaint has not been made out.[1] It is submitted that this is not so much a question of fairness as an attempted and improper assumption by an individual of an official body's responsibilities and duties.

¹ Public Disclosure Commission v Isaacs [1989] 1 All ER 137, PC.

Reasons for decisions

9.152 It remains true as a statement of general principle, though for how much longer remains debatable, that there is no obligation for administrators to give reasons for their decisions, whether adverse or favourable, in English or Scottish law.[1] Numerous decisions have formerly emphasised the fact that it is neither a rule of law nor, therefore, a component of natural justice.[2] Without reasons for decisions, a right of challenge or a right of appeal may well be little more than illusory.[3] The Privy Council has acknowledged the growing trend in the law to require reasons for decisions a 'trend that was consistent with current developments towards an increased openness in matters of government and administration.' It was also a position that will be affected by the HRA 1998 and Art 6 of the ECHR where an individual's civil rights and obligations are concerned.

¹ Stefan v General Medical Council [1999] 1 WLR 1293, PC. See R v DPP, ex p Manning [2000] 3 WLR 463: it is good administrative practice to give reasons for not prosecuting. Mousaka Inc v Golden Seagull Maritime Inc (2001) Times, 3 October: refusing permission to appeal under Arbitration Act 1979, s 69 did not breach Art 6 if no reasons were given! For a contrary approach in Canada: a common law presumption that reasons will be given for adverse decisions: Baker v Canada (Minister of Citizenship and Immigration) [1999] 2 SCR 817 and D Dyzenhaus (ed) The Unity of Public Law (2004). R (Hasan) v Secretary of State for Trade and Industry [2008] EWCA Civ 1312: FOIA 2000 has not changed the general rule that there is no duty to provide reasons for decisions. Culkin v Wirral Independent Appeal Panel [2009] EWHC 868 (Admin) – an adequate explanantion of school exclusion had been given.
² Wade and Forsyth Administrative Law (10th edn, 2009) p 436ff; Justice/All Souls Administrative Law: Some Necessary Reforms (1988).
³ See Minister of National Revenue v Wright's Canadian Ropes [1947] AC 109, PC; see also: English v Emery Reimbold & Strick Ltd [2002] 1 WLR 2409 (CA) judges must give adequate reasons: so too must tribunals: Burns v Royal Mail Group plc and Another (2004) Times, 24 June. See further R (Cunningham) v Exeter Crown Court [2003] 2 Cr App R (S) 64: reasons must be given for costs order refusing defendant's costs and also Lavelle v Lavelle (9/3/04) (CA). NB statutory provision and Coleen Properties Ltd v Minister of Housing and Local Government [1971] 1 WLR 433, CA. On reasons in planning decisions, Oxford City Council v Secretary of State for Communuties and Local Government [2007] EWHC 769 (Admin); R (Wall) v Brighton and Hove City Council [2004] EWHC 2582 (Admin); R (Persimmons Homes Ltd) v Secretary of State for Communties and Local Government [2007] EWHC 1985 (Admin); Halifax Life Ltd v Eagle Life Assurance Society [2007] EWHC 503 (Comm): reasons under Arbitration Act 1996 regarding expert determination.

9.153 To this opening bold statement of general principle, however, may be added several caveats. First, the courts will insist that a decision is made on the basis of relevant evidence before a decision-maker, and they are prepared to strike down a decision which is not justified by the factual evidence.[1] Such an approach has been facilitated by the extension of the concept of the record in judicial decisions providing more material for a court's scrutiny.[2] However, in the absence of information before the court, it is up to the party alleging illegality to substantiate his or her case. In judicial review procedure courts are empowered to make orders for disclosure and cross-examination but are usually cautious in invoking this power (see para 10.59 below).

[1]   See *R v Secretary of State for Transport, ex p Cumbria County Council* [1983] RTR 129, CA; *Ashbridge Investments Ltd v Minister of Housing and Local Government* [1965] 3 All ER 371, CA; and see *ex p Turgut* (para 9.127 note 6 above). See also *OFT v IBA Healthcare* [2004] 4 All ER 1103. See also the Competition Appeal Tribunal in *Unichem Ltd v OFT* [2005] CAT 8. On submission of new evidence by a claimant, see *E v Secretary of State for the Home Department* [2004] EWCA Civ 49 acknowledging, but not slavishly following, *Ladd v Marshall* [1954] 1 WLR 1489.
[2]   Tribunals and Inquiries Act 1992, s 10(6). See Admin Decisions (Jud Rev) Act 1977 (Australia).

9.154 Secondly, the courts will not allow the statutory purpose of legislation to be defeated or overborne by an improper motive on the part of the minister or other official.[1] In the cases illustrating this proposition, there has been evidence of improper motive on the part of the Minister.[2] However, the case would have to be a flagrant one for the courts to intervene, and a decision of the Law Lords in 1989 shows that they are sympathetically disposed to ministerial pleas of the complexity of regulatory regimes in legislation and that they will usually be slow to find bad faith in a failure to give reasons.[3] However, the circumstances should be carefully noted. The case concerned a report by DTI inspectors into a take-over and the failure of the Secretary of State to publish that report; to refuse to make a reference to the Monopolies and Mergers Commission; and a refusal to give reasons for his decision. Of constraining influence in the judges' minds was the fact that a criminal investigation into the contents of the report was still being conducted with a possibility of prosecutions. Also, the Secretary of State had been advised by, not constrained by, a report from the Director-General of Fair Trading which recommended that a reference should not be made.

[1]   *Padfield v Minister of Agriculture Fisheries and Food* [1968] AC 997, HL. See *R v Ministry of Defence, ex p Murray* [1998] COD 134, for a general statement.
[2]   As above.
[3]   *Lonrho* case (para 9.82, note 1 above).

9.155 Thirdly, the judiciary have shown a preparedness to accept that where a situation calls out for, or begs, a reasoned justification, they may well insist that one should be given even though no statute requires one, or they may draw inferences which are adverse to the decision-maker.[1] The common law will supplement the omission of the legislature. Several important decisions have put a gloss on this developing duty. In *Cunningham*[2] the Court of Appeal held that where a judicialised tribunal (acting analogously with industrial and employment tribunals) was making decisions affecting an individual's rights and even though under a prerogative power relating to civil servants, it must nonetheless give reasons for decisions which revealed how it directed its mind giving an indication of whether its decisions are lawful. Failure to provide such reasons was a breach of natural justice on the facts. The absence of reasons hindered opportunities to challenge the decision. In a dramatic development in *Doody*,[3] the House of Lords held that facilitating a right of challenge or appeal was but one feature behind a right to reasons. Another would be where serious adverse consequences followed a decision and where to leave it without a reasoned explanation is an affront to justice and fairness. *Doody* concerned the setting of the tariff period of imprisonment of a life prisoner. The courts have made it clear that a finding that a body is acting 'judicially as in *Cunningham*' is not essential to establish a duty to give reasons. What is crucial is the impact of the decision on individuals' lives. However, this point was made in a case where the courts refused to impose a duty to give reasons in a situation where it was felt they lacked expertise to interfere with the subject matter in question, ie 'pure academic judgements' relating to the quality of research upon which decisions were made vis-à-vis state funding. It might be different if evidence were present of discrimination or unfairness or a decision is 'inexplicable' or 'aberrant'.[4]

[1] *R v Lancashire County Council, ex p Huddleston* [1986] 2 All ER 941, CA; *Lonrho* at 620c; *New Zealand Fishing Industry Association Ltd v Minister of Agriculture Fisheries and Food* [1988] 1 NZLR 544, NZ CA. See also: *R v Tower Hamlets London Borough Council, ex p Rouf* (1989) 21 HLR 294 and *R v Nottingham City Council, ex p Costello* (1989) 21 HLR 301 for fairness in homelessness inquiries.
[2] *R v Civil Service Appeal Board, ex p Cunningham* [1991] 4 All ER 310, CA.
[3] *R v Secretary of State for the Home Department, ex p Doody* [1994] 1 AC 531, HL.
[4] *R v Higher Education Funding Council, ex p Institute of Dental Surgery* [1994] 1 All ER 651.

9.156 As dramatic was the Court of Appeal decision which heard Mohamed Al Fayed's appeal from the High Court against the refusal of the Home Secretary to allow him British nationality. Although under s 44 of the British Nationality Act 1981 nothing required the relevant authorities to give reasons for decisions, nevertheless fairness may require that the applicant was provided with sufficient information relating to any concerns or misgivings the Home Secretary may have about the application and which it was not contrary to the public interest to divulge.[1] The Home Secretary subsequently undertook to provide reasons in nationality cases. Where disagreement arose between a local authority and an inspector of an inquiry into a development plan, the authority was under a duty to give reasons for its insistence that a site's green belt merits outweighed the worst case analysis of a housing shortage. Such a balancing exercise was not a matter of purely subjective planning opinion but its absence was a failure to identify overriding objective considerations leading to a decision. Its decision could not therefore stand.[2]

[1] *R v Secretary of State for the Home Department, ex p Fayed* [1997] 1 All ER 228, CA, and see *R v Secretary of State for the Home Department, ex p Venables* [1997] 3 All ER 97, HL. And in *Stefan v GMC* above, the absence of a statutory requirement to give reasons nonetheless did not rule out the necessity of brief reasons.
[2] *Peel Investments (North) Ltd v Bury Metropolitan Borough Council* [1999] PLCR 307, CA.

9.157 In spite of these advances, the basic principle holds again and again and a substantial body of case-law exemplifies the proposition that where there is no duty to give reasons imposed by statute, the courts will not, and should not, require them.[1] Decisions appear inconsistent.[2] Nor will the courts require 'reasons for the reasons' where it is argued that the reasons as provided (under statutory regulations) are no more than standardised responses.[3] However, in refusing to allocate a child to a school of his parents' first choice, a standard letter was not sufficient and had to contain some more precise reasons.[4] Contrariwise, reasons for not giving a capital grant may be 'brief even though an explanation of a rejection had been promised.[5] In prison administration a denial of reasons when refusing to accept the Parole Board's recommendation to release a prisoner[6] and a failure either to hear a prisoner before, or to give him adequate reasons within a reasonable time, for his removal from association under r 43 of the Prison Rules 1964 have not constituted a denial of fair procedure.[7] The former decision must now be read in the light of *Doody* and *Smith* and other decisions where the courts have upgraded the fairness of proceedings even in a custodial context. These earlier decisions are unlikely to be followed today and the impact of ECtHR decisions should be noted.[8] Such cases from the past can be explained by the overall desire to maintain security and safety in prison administration but more recent decisions have shown that such arguments must not be too readily accepted where fundamental rights are in issue.[9] Good order and safety may be decisive in cases where those suspected by the Secretary of State of being terrorists are detained under Anti-terrorism, Crime and Security Act 2001, s 21 (upheld by the Special Immigration Appeal Commission and who were allowed access to reporters from the BBC and *Guardian* but only within earshot of officials). The detainees claimed a breach of their rights under Art 10 but the court was satisfied that the safeguard, which had been agreed to by the reporters, was necessary for the maintenance of prison order.[10] Where an individual is affected by the exercise of the royal prerogative, viz refusal of a passport, s/he is entitled to be informed of reasons for the refusal[11] but not where *ex gratia* payments were refused under the royal prerogative although in a recent case the decision was explained.[12]

[1]   See eg *R v Secretary of State for Social Services, ex p Connolly* [1986] 1 WLR 421, CA; *R v Criminal Injuries Compensation Board, ex p Moore* [1999] 2 All ER 90; *R v Secretary of State for the Environment etc, ex p Marson* (1999) 7 P & CR 202, CA; *R v University College London, ex p Idriss* [1999] Ed CR 462 – refusal to admit to a course.

[2]   See eg *R v Islington London Borough Council, ex p Trail* [1994] 2 FCR 1261 and *R v Bristol City Council, ex p Bailey* (1994) *Times*, 23 November.

[3]   *R v Secretary of State for the Home Department, ex p Swati* [1986] 1 All ER 717, CA; see *R v Secretary of State for the Environment, ex p Hackney London Borough Council* (1983) 81 LGR 688.

[4]   *R v Birmingham City Council, ex p M* (1998) *Times*, 13 October. In *R (Reading BC) v Admissions Appeal Panel for Reading BC* [2005] EWHC 2378 an admissions' appeal panel had to give reasons in an appeal where it branded the authority's decision as unreasonable.

[5]   *R (Asha) v Millennium Commission* [2003] EWCA Civ 88. In *S. Bucks DC & Another v Porter* the House of Lords held that planning reasons (by an inspector) may be brief – substantial prejudice must be shown in failing to provide an adequately reasoned decision. See *OFT v IBA Healthcare* [2004] 4 All ER 1103 at 1134–35 per Carnwath LJ: requirement for reasons does not mean the detail of a legal judgment or an inquiry report.

[6]   *R v Secretary of State for the Home Department, ex p Gunnell* [1984] Crim LR 170; *Weeks v UK* (1987) 10 EHRR 293; *R v Parole Board, ex p Bradley* [1990] 3 All ER 828.

[7]   *R v Deputy Governor of Parkhurst Prison, ex p Hague* [1992] 1 AC 58; on appeal [1992] 1 AC 58, CA; *Re Hales* (1990) *Times*, 8 May.

[8]   *Doody* above. See also: *R v Secretary of State for the Home Department, ex p Hickey (No 2)* [1995] 1 WLR 734; *R v Secretary of State for the Home Department, ex p McAvoy* [1998] 1 WLR 790; *R v*

Secretary of State for the Home Department, ex p Duggan [1994] 3 All ER 277 – an outline of reasons for security categorisation may be sufficient; and *R v Governor of Maidstone Prison, ex p Peries* [1998] COD 150 – standards of Duggan not applicable in all categorisation decisions – reasons should be given for decision but no entitlement to prior notification of materials. On the ECtHR, see *Ezeh* (para 9.141, note 4 above). See also *R (Ali) v Director of High Security Prisons* [2009] EWHC 1732 (Admin): classification of prisoner as high-risk meant provision of reasons and an opportunity of a hearing to review decision, but not a prior disclosure of material considered.

9 See eg *R v Secretary of State for the Home Department, ex p Simms* [1999] 3 All ER 400, HL. *R (Daly) v Secretary of State for the Home Department* [2001] 2 AC 532.

10 *R (A) v Secretary of State for the Home Department* [2004] HRLR 12.

11 *R v Secretary of State for Foreign and Commonwealth Affairs, ex p Everett* [1989] QB 811, CA, reasons actually known to applicant.

12 *R v Secretary of State for the Home Department, ex p Harrison* [1988] 3 All ER 86; see *Re McFarland* [2004] UKHL 17 where an explanation was given.

9.158 In cases where an authority has removed a contractor from a list of approved contractors[1] and removed peoples' names from a local authority's list of potential foster parents[2] the courts have ruled that the parties have the right to know why and to rebut any 'allegations'. Similarly, a juvenile court must state its reasons for refusing an application to discharge a care order in respect of a child.[3] Where there is a duty to provide reasons, but the information has been communicated to the individual via another source, a failure to give reasons may well not be fatal.[4]

1 *R v Enfield London Borough Council, ex p T F Unwin (Roydon) Ltd* (1989) 46 BLR 1.

2 *R v Wandsworth London Borough Council, ex p P* [1990] FCR 89.

3 *R v Worcester City Juvenile Court, ex p F* [1989] 1 All ER 500; and see *W v Greenwich London Borough Council* [1989] 2 FLR 67: reasons for refusing parental access.

4 See *ex p Everett* above.

9.159 Since the 1989 judgment of the Court of Appeal in *Cunningham* there has been a growing judicial awareness of the content of fairness, and the courts have spelt out more and more clearly the duty of judges themselves to give adequate reasons for decisions.[1] But the position is still blemished by inconsistency. The inconsistency is not purely domestic. Under EC law, for instance, a general duty to give reasons for decisions has been developed by the courts (ECJ and CFI) and has followed from the duty to give reasons for their legislative decisions under Art 253 (previously 190, now TFEU 296(2)) EC and from general principles of law.[2] However, in *Sodemare* the ECJ ruled[3] that the requirement to give reasons for a legislative decision in Art 253 did not apply to the laws of a member state which fell within the purview of Community law. The Community courts have ruled that, where reasons should be given, they should be provided at the time of decision and not subsequently.[4] Important guidance on the timing or reasons is contained in *Nash v Chelsea College.*[5]

1 *Flannery v Halifax Estate Agencies Ltd* [2000] 1 All ER 373, CA; *English v Emery Reinbold & Strick Ltd* [2002] 3 All ER 385 (CA). In *Baird v Thurrock BC* (2005) App LR 11/07, (2005) Times (15 November): county court judges should give judgments with sufficient reasons on conflicts of evidence.

2 *UNECTEF v Heylens:* 222/86 [1987] ECR 4097; *EC Commission v Italy:* 7/61 [1961] ECR 317.

3 Case C-70/95: [1998] 4 CMLR 667.

4 Case 195/80 *Michael v European Parliament* [1981] ECR 2861; see also in a domestic setting *R (S) v Brent LBC* [2002] EWCA Civ 693.

5　[2001] All ER D 133. See also *VK v Norfolk CC* (2005) *Times*, 6 January – inadequate SEN reasons
cannot be substantially supplemented. See also, *R (Wall) v Brighton and Hove City Council* [2004]
EWHC 2582. See, however, *OFT v IBA Healthcare* (para 9.157, note 5 above).

Section 10 of the Tribunals and Inquiries Act 1992

9.160　This section, which was first enacted in 1958 following the wake of the
Franks Report, imposes a duty on tribunals listed in Sch 1 to the Act to furnish
a statement (written or oral) of the reasons for a decision. The duty only arises
if a request for reasons is made[1] on or before the giving or notification of the
decision. Reasons may be refused or curtailed on grounds of national security.
Reasons may be refused to persons not primarily concerned with the decision
if the tribunal is of the opinion that to furnish them would be contrary to the
interests of any person primarily concerned.[2] A statement of reasons is part of
the decision and will be incorporated into the record.[3] The section is silent about
providing a statement of established facts.

1　Specific rules usually impose an unqualified duty.
2　Tribunals and Inquiries Act 1992, s 10(3).
3　Tribunals and Inquiries Act 1992, s 10(6).

Failure to provide reasons

9.161　It is probably correct to say that a failure to provide *adequate* reasons
is not, under the above provisions of the 1992 Act, an automatic error of law
justifying judicial intervention.[1] However, if inadequate reasoning reveals
erroneous or irrational decision-making, or such can be inferred from the
reasoning, then the courts will intervene.[2] Perfunctory reasons per se may not
be a ground for invalidating a decision but may be the grounds for awarding
a mandatory order (mandamus) to supply adequate reasons.[3] The courts have
shown more recent signs of a readiness to strike down decisions in breach of
statutory duties to provide reasons or to treat failures to provide reasons as
breaches of fair treatment.[4] Industrial (now employment) tribunals may give
reasons in summary form only ([Employment Tribunals] (Constitution and
Rules of Procedure) Regulations 1993, SI 1993/2687, r 10, Sch 1 as amended by
SI 2004/1861, Sch 1) except in four cases.[5]

1　*Crake v Supplementary Benefits Commission* [1982] 1 All ER 498; see *R v Northants CC ex p Marshall*
[1998] COD 457. Cf *Re Poyser and Mills' Arbitration* [1964] 2 QB 467 and *R v Mental Health
Review Tribunal, ex p Pickering* [1986] 1 All ER 99.
2　*Crake* supra and *Meek v City of Birmingham District Council* [1987] IRLR 250, CA.
3　*Elliott v London Borough of Southwark* [1976] 2 All ER 781, CA.
4　*R v Westminster City Council, ex p Ermakov* [1996] 2 All ER 302, CA; *R v City of London Corpn, ex p
Matson* [1997] 1 WLR 765, CA; *R (Wall) v Brighton and Hove CC* [2004] EWHC 2582 (Admin).
5　Two of the cases allow a party to request full reasons. The Court of Appeal has also allowed
exiguous reasons, though cf *Meek*'s case, note 2 above. *William Hill Organisation Ltd v Gavas*
[1990] IRLR 488, CA. See SI 2004/1861, Sch 2 for procedures in national security cases.

9.162　Secretaries of State are under the duty, in s 10 of the Tribunals and
Inquiries Act 1992, to give reasons for their decisions after an inquiry into

planning or compulsory purchase appeals and after the inspector has reported to him. Such a duty is now contained in procedural rules.[1] Although judicial decisions have treated benevolently a planning authority's failure to comply with statutory duties to provide reasons,[2] the duties under the procedural regulations have on occasions been very strictly interpreted to the detriment of the authorities.[3] Reasons must be clear and intelligible and must reflect the substance of relevant arguments that were adumbrated. The House of Lords has refused to hold in a planning case that a court must first decide whether reasons were adequate and then assess whether any inadequacy could reveal a shortcoming in the decision-making process.[4] Does a decision leave 'genuine as opposed to forensic doubt' as to what was decided and why?[5] In planning also, reasons by a Secretary of State which seem sparse may be given a helpful gloss by matters raised at an inquiry and the inspector's reasons in the recommendations.[6] On application to the courts to quash compulsory purchase orders, there is some reason to believe that the courts will examine the factual basis of a decision with more than their customary degree of scrutiny to establish a 'sufficient justification' for a ministerial decision on the merits.[7]

[1]   See paras 8.124 et seq above and eg TCP (Inquiries Procedure) Rules 2000, SI 2000/1624, r 18; and see for major infrastructure project inquiries SI 2005/2115.

[2]   *Brayhead (Ascot) Ltd v Berkshire County Council* [1964] 2 QB 303, and see: *Save Britain's Heritage v Secretary of State for the Environment* [1991] 2 All ER 10, HL; *Bolton MDC v Secretary of State for the Environment* (1995) 71 P&CR 309 (HL) and *S. Bucks DC v Porter (No 2)* [2004] UKHL 33 reversing [2003] EWCA Civ 687.

[3]   See *Volvox Establishment v Secretary of State for the Environment* [1988] 1 PLR 49; the leading case is *French Kier Developments v Secretary of State for the Environment* [1977] 1 All ER 296; *London Residuary Body v Secretary of State for the Environment* [1988] JPL 637. See the House of Lords in *Save Britain's Heritage* above and *Givaudan & Co Ltd v Minister of Housing and Local Government* [1967] 1 WLR 250.

[4]   *Save Britain's Heritage v Secretary of State for the Environment* (above, note 2).

[5]   *Clark Homes Ltd v Secretary of State for the Environment* [1993] 66 P&CR 263 per Bingham MR.

[6]   *Save Britain's Heritage v Number 1 Poultry Ltd* [1991] 1 WLR 153, HL; *Elliott v Southwark London Borough Council* [1976] 1 WLR 499, CA; see de Smith, paras 9.049–9.053.

[7]   See: *R v Secretary of State for Transport, ex p de Rothschild* [1989] 1 All ER 933, CA; see *Coleen*, para 9.152, note 3. See the wide berth given to 'material considerations' in granting planning permission and TCPA 1990, s 70(2) and agreements under s 106: *R v Westminster City Council, ex p Monahan* [1989] 2 All ER 74, CA and *Tesco Stores Ltd v Secretary of State for the Environment* [1995] 2 All ER 636 (HL).

Reasons for decisions under the FOIA 2000

9.163   FOIA 2000 contains provisions concerning the giving for reasons for decisions. The provision is in s 19(3)(b) and will be incorporated in publication schemes, although duties to provide reasons for decisions under FOIA 2000 are present in the Act and were strengthened as the Bill progressed through Parliament. Such duties occur in s 17(1)(c) to state why an exemption applies and s 17(3) on claiming public interest grounds for maintaining an exemption. In fact, there are numerous duties to provide reasons for decisions in statutes and regulations which in some cases require detailed reasons to be given as a legal requirement.[1] It is a matter of regret that such a general duty was not contained in the primary FOIA 2000 itself rather than to be left in publication schemes, and that the view of the government was that it only applied to reasons for decisions published in a publication scheme (see paras 1.288 et seq above). It is also to be hoped that a general duty to provide reasons will not act to undermine those duties in statutes and regulations where they provide for the giving of more specific duties in statutes and regulations. We saw in chapters 1 and 8 how the Information Commissioner and tribunal had insisted on full and proper reasons being given for refusals to provide information under the Act (see eg FER0313870).

[1] A LeSueur (1999) *Current Legal Problems* 150.

General points

9.164 Under the court's powers of judicial review in Part 54 of the CPR 1998 (formerly RSC Ord 53), the more draconian a decision affecting an individual, the more likely the court will be to conduct a probing inquiry to establish an adequate evidentiary basis and that a decision was not irrational or otherwise oppressive.[1] Examples include *ex p Turgat*.[2] Under the HRA 1998, however, the courts will impose demanding standards in reviewing decisions interfering with rights protected under that Act; the standard of review may vary according to the importance of the right or where interference has to be 'necessary' to protect other legitimate interests or rights.[3] The courts have refused to set rigid formulae for the test to be applied, but numerous cases have set out quite clearly the more intrusive into a person's liberties and rights a decision is, the more careful will the courts be in scrutinising the legal and factual basis for a decision, even in cases of detention of suspected terrorists under Anti-terrorist, Crime and Security Act 2001, s 21 and in the case of control orders and whatever may replace such orders.[4] Reference should be made to the obligation under Art 6 of the ECHR which guarantees to everyone an entitlement to a fair and public hearing before an independent tribunal within a reasonable time in the determination of one's civil rights and obligations as well as any criminal charges laid against an individual. The interpretation of the Article has in the past been somewhat limited, thereby reducing the range of administrative decision-making against which the Article will provide protection.[5] UK courts must take into account the decisions of the ECtHR, some of which which have been listed above, in determining questions concerning convention rights. Further, UK courts must, 'so far as is possible', read and give effect to domestic measures in a manner consistent with Convention rights. This legislative mandate has transformed the domestic judicial approach to questions of administrative fairness generally, if not invariably, for the good.

[1] *R v Secretary of State for the Home Department, ex p Gaima* (1988) *Guardian*, 6 December: political asylum; cf *Bugdaycay v Secretary of State for the Home Department* [1987] AC 514, HL; *R v Ministry of Defence, ex p Smith* [1996] 1 All ER 257, CA.

[2] See para 9.127.

[3] *R (Daly) v Secretary of State for the Home Department* [2001] UKHL 26; *International Transport Roth GmbH v Home Secretary* [2002] 3 WLR 345.

[4] *M v Secretary of State for the Home Department* [2004] 2 All ER 863: refusing to overrule SIAC's decision that the Secretary of State did not have *reasonable* suspicion that the claimant was linked to named terrorist organisations. *Ex p Smith*, above; *Simms*, para 9.157, note 9 above. See *A v Secretary of State for the Home Department* [2004] UKHL 56.

⁵ *Le Compte v Belgium* (1981) 4 EHRR 1; *Kaplan v UK* (1980) 4 EHRR 64 and *Feldbrugge v Netherlands* (1986) 8 EHRR 425; *Deumeland v Germany* (1986) 8 EHRR 448; Bradley *Public Law* (1987) p 3. See further Bradley (1995) *European Public Law* 347.

9.165   Also the Committee of Ministers of the Council of Europe, to which the UK is a party, has passed a resolution – Resolution (77)31 – recommending that governments of member states should be guided in their law and administrative practice by five principles: the fourth principle concerns a statement of reasons where an administrative act adversely affects the rights, liberties or interests of the person concerned.

9.166   The other principles cover: a right to be heard; access to information on which an administrative act is based; assistance and representation; and the nature of remedies available for the persons concerned, ie both natural and artificial persons. The Charter of Fundamental Rights of the EC (now incorporated within the draft EU Constitution) and the code of good administrative practice of the EU Ombudsman contain a duty to provide reasons for decisions.

Consultation

9.167   Numerous statutes impose duties to consult and the duty generally has been the subject of extensive interpretation.[1] The presence of a duty to consult can give third parties a locus to come to court who otherwise would not have standing to challenge a decision on allocation of contracts of medical service.[2] Guidance has been issued by the government on consultation (para 1.238). The Department for Business Innovation and Skills (BIS) code on written consultation names the bodies that have signed up to its principles (2008) in which formal consultations on Green Papers but not WPs or independent reviews or impact assessments may be supplemented by public hearings.[3]

[1] Usually, but not exclusively, before the making of statutory regulations and orders: for a strict interpretation in another context, see *Grunwick Processing Laboratories v ACAS* [1978] AC 655, HL. For a general and useful test of the criteria of consultation, see Webster J *in R v Secretary of State for Social Services, ex p Association of Metropolitan Authorities* [1986] 1 All ER 164.
[2] *R (Smith) v N.E. Derbyshire PC Trust* [2006] EWCA Civ 1291; see also Local Government and Public Involvement in Health Act 2007, Part 14 ss 221–234 on local involvement networks. See the discussion on NHS reforms at para 9.106 above.
[3] http://www.bis.gov.uk/policies/better-regulation/consultation-guidance.

9.168   The courts have established under common law principles[1] that the person engaging in the consultation must, with a receptive mind, seek and welcome the aid and advice which those with local or specialised knowledge may be in a position to proffer in regard to a plan or proposals which the decision-maker has tentatively evolved.[2] The decision-maker must supply sufficient information to those consulted to enable them to tender advice, and, on the other hand, a sufficient opportunity must be given to those consulted to tender that advice.[3] In meeting requests for information, however, the decision-maker is not required or expected to formulate detailed plans for the future administration of a large scheme or point the way to the solution of all new problems.[4] Sufficient time must be given by the consulting body to those consulted to enable them to offer helpful advice to be considered by the consulting party.[5] 'Sufficient' means sufficient to allow the purpose to be fulfilled. Even where urgency is present, this will not allow the consulting party to offer so little time and such little information that those consulted were not sufficiently informed, and their views insufficiently considered. However, in the specific statutory context, the question of whether there was sufficient consultation may have to be decided by looking at the facts as they appeared to the Secretary of State or other decision-maker. The form and substance of regulations and the time for consultation may well depend on matters of a political nature, of which the Secretary of State etc was the best judge. But this would not absolve the minister of the duty to consult.[6] Further, where a decision-maker is adequately informed of *all* relevant aspects of a decision, s/he may be excused in law the necessity of consulting every interest.[7] A very powerful statement on the legal requirements of a duty to consult was provided in the *Greenpeace* case where the Government had promised the fullest consultation before progressing on any changes in relation to a policy not to build new nuclear power generators. The policy was changed. The consultation was seriously flawed: it lacked vital information on disposal of nuclear waste and economic costs, and this amounted to a breach of a legitimate expectation by the Government. The announcement of a change of policy was unlawful.[8] In *Eisai Ltd v NICE* the courts insisted on disclosure in a consultation process of the 'fully executable version of data' relied upon by NICE in issuing guidance on drug use despite NICE's claims to confidentiality. The claimant stood to be disadvantaged in a commercial capacity by the guidance and would be placed at a disadvantage if it could not subject the data to its own testing.[9] The limits on what the House of Lords by majority was prepared to allow access to in relation to ex parte notifications by a party in planning regulation was noted above.[10] The cases emphasise that fairness must be seen in context. Where a stated basis of consultation was altered by a minister who adopted new approaches without warning and without opportunities for consultees to address those approaches, he acted unfairly and unlawfully even though the changed criteria were not irrelevant.[11]

[1]   A nice discussion is in *R v Brent LBC ex p Gunning* [1986] 84 LGR 168.

[2]   *Rollo v Minister of Town and Country Planning* [1948] 1 All ER 13, CA, per Morris J. On the continuing nature of consultation: *Fletcher v Minister of Town and Country Planning* [1947] 2 All ER 496.

[3]   *Rollo* per Bucknill LJ.

[4]   *Port Louis Corpn v A-G of Mauritius* [1965] AC 1111, PC, per Lord Morris.

[5]   *R v Secretary of State for Social Services, ex p Association of Metropolitan Authorities* [1986] 1 All ER 164.

[6]   Above. However, although the resulting regulations were made in breach of a mandatory requirement and theoretically ultra vires, they had become law and would not be invalidated because of widespread reliance upon them.

[7]   *R v Secretary of State for Wales, ex p Glamorgan County Council* (1988) *Times*, 25 June – school closure. See, however, *R (Goldsmith) v Wandsworth LBC* [2004] EWCA Civ 1170 – all evidence *must* be considered in local; authority welfare decision.

[8]   *R (Greenpeace) v Secretary of Sytate for Trade and Industry* [2007] EWHC 311.

[9]   [2008] EWCA Civ 438 and see para 66 and reversing the High Court. See *R (Bristol Myers Squibbs Pharmaceuticals Ltd) v NICE* [2009] EWHC 2722 (Admin).

[10] *R (Edwards and another) v Environmental Agency* [2008] UKHL 22 concerning EIAs.

[11] *Devon County Council v Secretary of State for Communities and Local Government* [2010] EWHC 1456 (Admin).

9.169   Unless a hearing is required by statute, consultation is usually satisfied by written communications, representations or comments. The High Court has interpreted a statute as conferring a right to a public hearing in the form of an inquiry where there was a conflict of testimony, although none was expressly provided for under the relevant sections. The decision was doubted on this point by the Court of Appeal.[1] The usual form of a duty to consult is to consult such interests as the Secretary of State, or named official or body, believes relevant. It is a mandatory duty to consult followed by a discretion as to those whom s/he deems appropriate. It is the decision-maker's discretion on who is appropriate and could usually only be upset on the grounds of unreasonableness or irrationality. Where a body *is* deemed appropriate for consultation by the decision-maker, but through no fault of the consulting person is not presented with the information, consultation has not taken place and that body may be excluded from the scope of a subsequent decision or regulations.[2] Where, as a matter of discretion, a body is not consulted, the courts have been reluctant to make good the omission of the person consulting; and they have gone so far as to say that no right to consultation exists before a policy is changed by rule-making or delegated legislation,[3] or where a policy or principle is being evolved, even for those who stand to be significantly affected. The scope of the protection has widened, it is true, and courts are more sensitive to procedural fairness even of a collective nature. But courts still tread most surely where the rights of individuals are involved.

[1]   *R v Secretary of State for Wales, ex p Emery* [1996] 4 All ER 1; affd [1998] 4 All ER 367, CA. Provisions for hearings were provided for in other parts of the statute: Wildlife and Countryside Act 1981, Schs 14 and 15. See *R (Ashbrook) v Secretary of State etc* [2005] 1 All ER 166.

[2]   *Agricultural, Horticultural and Forestry Industry Training Board v Aylesbury Mushrooms Ltd* [1972] 1 WLR 190.

[3]   *Bates v Lord Hailsham* [1972] 3 All ER 1019 is the clearest statement; *Re Findlay* [1985] AC 318, HL; *R v Crown Court at Aylesbury, ex p Chahal* [1976] RTR 489. Cf *ex p Ruddock*, para 9.139, note 1 above; *R v Secretary of State for the Environment, ex p Hammersmith and Fulham London Borough Council* [1990] 3 All ER 589, HL.

9.170   The decisions suggest that, where a party stands to lose an important right or privilege, the courts will infer a right to consultation.[1] Indeed the language of consultation is being used interchangeably with the language of fair procedure, and a right to a hearing where there is a 'legitimate expectation' of consultation taking place. A right to consultation is frequently observed by an opportunity to make written representations:

> 'As the two cases show, the principle [of legitimate expectation] is closely connected with "right to be heard". Such an expectation may take many forms. One may be an expectation of prior consultation. Another may be an expectation of being allowed time to make representations, especially where the aggrieved party is seeking to persuade an authority to depart from a lawfully established policy adopted in connection with the exercise of a particular power because of some suggested exceptional reasons justifying such a departure.'[2]

The courts have developed the law of legitimation expectation – both substantive and procedural (see para 9.119 above).[3] The High Court has ruled that disabled persons had a legitimate expectation in being consulted in decisions affecting them under the Disability Discrimination Act 1995 as amended.[4] The decision in *Bancoult* set limits to the scope of legitimate expectation in the special circumstances of not allowing the British Indian Ocean Territory (BIOT) islanders to return to their native home which had become a US naval base. The majority was not persuaded that a legitimate substantive expectation was established on the facts. The dissent of two law lords has more legal conviction in its reasoning.[5] However, where the representations are clear and precise, they have been upheld by the courts.[6]

[1] See the *CCSU* case, para 9.117, note 4 above and at first instance [1984] IRLR 309 and *Ruddock*, para 9.139, note 1 above; the courts will look for a particular detriment to an identifiable and restricted group but this test does not satisfy all the cases.

[2] Lord Roskill in the *CCSU* case [1984] 3 All ER 135 at 954, HL. See *R v Tameside Metropolitan Borough Council, ex p Governors of Audenshaw High School* (1990) *Times*, 27 June.

[3] *R (Nadarajah) v Secretary of State for the Home Department* [2005] EWCA Civ 1363, Laws LJ.

[4] *R (Boyjo) v Barnet LBC* [2009] EWHC 3261 (Admin), DDA 1995, ss 49A(1) and 49D(2).

[5] *R (Bancoult) v Secretary of State for Foreign Affairs* [2008] UKHL 61.

[6] *R (HSMP Forum UK Ltd v Home Secretary* [2009] EWHC 711 and *R (BAPIO Action Ltd) v Secretary of State for the Home Department* [2007] EWCA Civ 1139, [2008] UKHL 27; *R (Luton BC and others) v Secretary of State for Education* [2011] EWHC 217 (Admin), paras 94–96 on duty to consult via a legitimate expectation.

9.171 However, where consultation has taken place on proposals for changes in a health authority area, and such proposals are subsequently revised in the light of the consultation, there is no duty to repeat the consultation process unless the revised proposals are so different that they constitute fresh proposals. Whether the revised proposals constitute fresh proposals is a question of fact and degree in each case.[1] It has also been ruled that persons who had not participated in a consultation should not be denied *locus standi* to challenge a decision after the consultation.[2]

[1] *R v Shropshire Health Authority, ex p Duffus* (1989) *Times*, 16 August.

[2] *R (Edwards) v Environmental Agency and Another* [2004] 3 All ER 21, *R (Edwards) v Environmental Agency and Another (No 2)* [2006] EWCA Civ 877: no point in quashing decision on which data is out of date.

The remedy

9.172 Where a duty to consult is mandatory the resulting instrument, order, decision *ought* to be ultra vires and challengeable in direct or collateral proceedings. However, the courts have frequently resiled from such straightforward logic and where the duty has not been complied with, have either excluded the affected party from the operation of the order,[1] or have let the subsequent regulations stand, declaring merely that consultation did not take place.[2] Some judgments have suggested that administrative decisions ought not to be impeached collaterally, but only in direct proceedings.[3] This would appear to have been thwarted by subsequent case-law, and the House of Lords established that although there is no rule confining the range of collateral challenge, there may be limitations to collateral challenge making it unsuitable where a detailed statutory code for appeal is set out.[4] In their desire to promote expedience at the expense of strict logic, the courts are turning their backs on the full consequences of a decision or action being ultra vires and have held, for instance, that a decision in breach of natural justice is not void in a complete sense[5] but may be rectified by a later internal hearing or may be acted on until declared void by a court. However, in this latter respect it must be remembered that relief under CPR 1998, Part 4 is discretionary, not as of right, and relief may be refused when because of undue delay it would cause substantial hardship to, or substantially prejudice the rights of, any person or would be detrimental to good administration.[6]

[1]   See *Aylesbury Mushrooms*, para 9.169 above.
[2]   *Ex p AMA*, para 9.167 above.
[3]   *Quietlynn Ltd v Plymouth City Council* [1988] QB 114; *Bugg v DPP* [1993] QB 473.
[4]   *R v Wicks* [1997] 2 All ER 801, HL and *Boddington v British Transport Police* [1998] 2 All ER 203, HL.
[5]   *Calvin v Carr* [1980] AC 574, PC; *London and Clydeside Estates Ltd v Aberdeen District Council* [1980] 1 WLR 182, HL.
[6]   Supreme Court Act 1981, s 31(6); see: *R v Dairy Produce Quota Tribunal, ex p Caswell* [1989] 3 All ER 205, CA, affd, [1990] 2 All ER 434, HL; *R v Swale Borough Council, ex p Royal Society for the Protection of Birds* [1991] 1 PLR 6; *Hardy v Pembrokeshire County Council* [2006] EWCA Civ 240. Note under EU procurement directives and implementing regulations: Case C-406/08 *Uniplex v NHS BSA* (ECJ 28/01/10).

9.173   A court has held that a byelaw made by the Defence Secretary may be both bad and good simultaneously, even though in breach of a statutory provision in the enabling statute.[1] A court has a discretion whether to strike down the whole of the subordinate instrument or to enforce only the valid parts of it.[2] The decision represented part of a growing trend favouring administrative convenience rather than strict individual entitlement. Such discretion will not attend decisions where human rights are involved. However, the House of Lords allowed an appeal holding that where a vitiating factor in subordinate legislation was of a nature that it could not successfully be severed from the regulations without substantially altering the subject matter of the remaining regulations, the regulations were ultra vires.[3]

[1]   *DPP v Hutchinson* [1989] QB 583; Military Lands Act 1892, s 14(1) and SI 1985/485.
[2]   See *R v Secretary of State for Transport, ex p Greater London Council* [1986] QB 556 and *R v North Hertfordshire District Council, ex p Cobbold* [1985] 3 All ER 486.
[3]   *DPP v Hutchinson* [1990] 2 AC 783, HL. Note *R (National Association of Health Stores & Anor) v Department of Health* [2005] EWCA Civ 154 and the filling in of omissions by the courts.

Fact-finding inquiries

9.174   In the next chapter we shall see the extent to which the courts may facilitate access to information. A right to freedom of information had not been established at common law. However, in a remarkable decision in *Shipman*, the Divisional Court upheld a challenge by families of the victims of Dr Shipman, who murdered numerous female victims in Manchester, against the decision of the Secretary of State to hold the inquest in private. Kennedy LJ held that the decision to sit in private was irrational and contravened the principle of freedom of speech in Art 10 ECHR. It constituted an unjustified government interference with the free communication of information. The exceptions to free expression must be narrowly interpreted and the necessity for any restrictions must be convincingly established. It is, he continued, incumbent on the press to impart information and ideas on matters of public interest. Free expression was a fundamental right of common law as well as being enshrined in the ECHR. In this point he reiterated the House of Lords decision in *Derbyshire County Council v Times Newspapers Ltd* in which it was held that a public authority has no capacity to sue in defamation because of the inhibiting effect this would have on freedom of speech under common law.[1] A public inquiry must proceed in public 'unless there are persuasive reasons for taking some other course'. The Minister had failed to give persuasive reasons for excluding the press and public and, for this reason, he had exceeded his powers.[2]

[1]   [1993] AC 534, HL. See *McLaughlin v Lambeth LBC* [2010] EWHC 2726 (QB). See also *A v Independent News Media Ltd* [2010] EWCA Civ 343.
[2]   *R v Secretary of State for Health, ex p Wagstaff* [2000] 1 WLR 292, DC.

9.175   The decision in *Wagstaff* has subsequently not been followed where Art 10 has been invoked to attempt to insist that an inquiry held to establish facts should be held in public. The courts have reminded litigants that Art 10 confers a right to pass on information, not a right of access to information.[1] Inquiries into deaths under Art 2 ECHR (the 'right to life' provision) where there has been a state involvement have met with a more positive response from the courts that such inquiries should be in public. The cases have concerned inquiries into racist murders in prisons in disturbing circumstances where an investigation must be 'independent, effective, reasonably prompt, have a sufficient element of public scrutiny, and involve the next of kin to an appropriate extent'.[2] In *Khan*, a young child of three had died in hospital after being the victim of gross negligence and after suspicions of a cover-up. Internal inquiries by the police and the hospital trust had not been in public and had not involved the parents. In these circumstances, a public inquiry involving the effective participation of the parents through legal representation was called for. A statutory inquest *might* satisfy this test but not if the father was unfit to participate because of his grief at the child's death and its circumstances, and if legal representation was not provided.[3] Readers are reminded of the discussion on *Effective Inquiries* and the Inquiries Act 2005 above (para 9.104).The judgment placed doubts on the suitability of inquests to conduct investigations consistent with the requirements of Art 2 ECHR. This view was heavily influenced by case-law of the ECtHR on Art 2 and deaths suffered under the responsibility of state organs – whether deliberately or through other culpable or questionable behaviour.[4] The House of Lords has ruled that, to satisfy the requirements of Art 2, inquests should allow a jury to express its factual conclusion on the events leading up to a death in custody so that the word 'how' [the deceased came by death] should mean 'by what means *and in what circumstances*'.[5] A further House of Lords decision confirmed that there has to be a proper examination and analysis of disputed facts, the events leading to a prisoner's suicide, steps taken or not taken to prevent it, and precautions necessary to avoid or reduce the risk to other prisoners.[6] Case law has added profusely to the application of relevant principles.[7]

[1]   *R (Persey) v Secretary of State* [2003] QB 794 – foot and mouth disease inquiry; *R (Howard) v Secretary of State for Health* [2003] QB 830 – National Health Service Act 1977, s 2 – a general

provision. Specific powers exist under s 84 of the 1977 Act and some inquiries have been held partially in private, with relatives and participants admitted but not the general public.

2   *R (Amin) v Secretary of State for the Home Department* [2003] 4 All ER 1264 (HL).
3   *R (Khan) v Secretary of State for Health* [2003] 4 All ER 1239 (CA).
4   *Edwards v UK* (2002) 12 BHRC 190; *Jordan v UK* (2001) 11 BHRC 1; *Finucane v UK* (2003) 37 EHRR 29.
5   *R (Middleton) v West Somerset Coroner* [2004] 2 All ER 465 (HL) and Coroners Act 1988, s 11(5) (b)(ii) and regulations under the Act.
6   *R (Sacker) v West Yorkshire Coroner* [2004] UKHL 11. Also *R (Stanley) v Inner North London Coroner* [2003] EWHC 1180 – failure to provide adequate reasons in relation to the achievement of the aims of an inquest amounted to a breach of Art 2. See, however, *Re McKerr* [2004] 2 All ER 409 (HL) and G. Anthony (2005) *European Public Law* cf *Re McCaughey* [2011] UKSC 20 – the obligation to inquire into death resulting from 'shoot to kill' policy in Northern Ireland could pre-date the incorporation of the ECHR under the HRA 1989: *Silih v Slovenia* [2009] 49 EHRR 37and *Varnava v Turkey* [2010] 50 EHRR 21. For inquiries and litigation into deaths of prisoners in British military custody in Iraq under Arts 2 and 3 after hostilities had ceased: *R (Al-Skeini) v Secretary of State for Defence* [2007] UKHL 6. The HRA 1998 applied to actions of forces in those circumstances where an individual was under British military detention but not otherwise and *R (Al Jeddah) v Secretary of State for Defence* [2007] UKHL 58 on displacement of the HRA 1998 by Security Council resolutions and which is on appeal to the ECtHR. The ECtHR allowed the appeals in *Al Skeini v UK* [2011] ECHR 1093 and in *Al Jeddah v UK* [2011] ECHR 1092 holding in the first that the ECtHR (and therefore HRA 1998) was breached in relation to those killed by UK forces in Iraq, even when not detained, where there had been no independent inquiry into their deaths. The second case decided that the UN Security Council resolutions did not *implicitly* authorise displacement of the ECHR in Iraq. Any displacement would have to be *explicit*. How would explicit displacement square with *Kadi Nos 1 and 2* (para 3.68)?
7   *R (on the application of P) v Secretary of State for Justice* [2009] EWCA Civ 701: death in custody and compliance with Art 2 ECHR. *R (on the application of D) v Inner South London Assistant Deputy Coroner* [2008] EWHC 3356 (Admin) and Art 2. *R (Smith v Oxfordshire Assistant Deputy Coroner* [2009] EWCA Civ 441 and *Savage v South Essex Partnership NHS Foundation Trust* [2008] UKHL 74; *R (Platts) v HM Coroner for South Yorkshire* [2008] EWHC 2502 on Art 2. *R (Scholes) v Secretary of State for the Home Department* [2006] EWCA Civ 1343 – no right to a public inquiry into young offender's suicide. *R (Gentle) v The Prime Minister* [2008] UKHL 20 – no duty under Art 2 not to commence unlawful war and therefore no public inquiry into the war. *R (Canning) v HM Coroner for Northampton* [2005] EWHC 3125 (Admin) – no reasonable cause to suspect culpable failing re death. R (L) v Secretary of State for Justice [2009] EWCA Civ 2416. *Brecknall v UK* (2008) 46 EHRR 42 – Art 2 and a death in Northern Ireland involving breaches of Arts 2 and 13. R (JL) v Secretary of State for Justice [2008] UKHL 68 – independent investigation into near suicide in prison. *R (Hurst) v London North District Coroner* [2007] UKHL 14: death prior to HRA 1998 coming into effect (HRA 1998 only affects inquests after 2 October 2000); McKerr correct (but see *Re McCaughey* above, note 6). *Bubbins v UK* (App 50196/99): breaches of Arts 2 and 13 in lack of remedy over police killing. *R (Lawrence) v HM Coroner for West Somerset* [2008] EWHC 1293 (Admin) on test for judicial review. *R (Allen) v HM Coroner for Inner London (North)* [2009] EWCA Civ 623. Also: *R (Mcleish) v HM Coroner for the North District of Greater London* [2010] EWHC 3624 (Admin); *R (Hair) v HM Coroner for Staffordshire (South)* [2010] EWHC 2580 (Admin) and *Re Chief Constable of NI's Application for Judicial Review* [2010] NIQB 66.

9.176   The Coroners and Justice Act 2009 introduced major reforms into investigations (inquests) into deaths.[1] The explanatory memorandum accompanying the Act states that the purpose of the Act 'is to establish more effective, transparent and responsive justice and coroner services for victims, witnesses, bereaved families and the wider public. It seeks to achieve this by:

(a)   updating parts of the criminal law to improve its clarity, fairness and effectiveness;

(b)   giving vulnerable and intimidated witnesses, including those in respect of
       gun and gang-related violence, improved protection, from the early stages
       of the criminal justice process;
(c)   introducing a more consistent and transparent sentencing framework;
(d)   improving the service bereaved families receive from a reformed coroner system;
(e)   giving those who are suddenly or unexpectedly bereaved opportunities to
       participate in coroners' investigations, including rights to information and
       access to a straightforward appeals system; and
(f)   putting in place a unified system of death certification that includes
       independent scrutiny and confirmation of the causes of death given on
       death certificates.

Section 5 establishes the matters to be ascertained and the purpose of a senior
coroner's investigation. The two purposes of an investigation are: (i) to establish who
the deceased was and how, when and where the deceased came by his or her death;
and (ii) to establish the details needed to register the death (such as the cause of
death). These purposes were previously contained in r 36(1) of the Coroners Rules
1984, and in section 11(5)(b) of the Coroners Act 1988. Section 5(2) requires the
scope of the investigation to be widened to include an investigation of the broad
circumstances of the death, including events leading up to the death in question,
where this wider investigation is necessary to ensure compliance with the ECHR),
in particular Article 2. Article 2 relates to the State's responsibility to ensure that its
actions do not cause the death of its citizens. The Act does not define the precise
circumstances under which a coroner should conduct an Art 2 investigation. This will
allow for flexibility in the future should case law determine that Art 2 inquests should
extend to cover additional matters. Such information could, however, be contained
in guidance issued by the Chief Coroner. The Act deals with juries and in general
an inquest must be held without a jury. Section 7(2) and (3) of the 2009 Act set out
the exceptions to this rule. A jury must be summoned where the deceased died while
in custody or otherwise in state detention, and the death was violent or unnatural,
or of unknown cause; where the death was as a result of an act or omission of a
police officer or member of a service police force (defined in s 48) in the purported
execution of their duties; or where the death was caused by an accident, poisoning
or disease which must be reported to a government department or inspector. This
includes, for example, certain deaths at work. Although a jury is not required in
any other case the coroner will be able to summon one in any case where he or she
believes there is sufficient reason for doing so. The Government will in secondary
legislation make further, more detailed provision about the conduct of inquests (in
the Coroners Rules to be made under s 45).

[1]   J Cooper *Inquests* (2011). NB powers in relation to criminals' publications is covered in the last
      part of the Act.

9.177   The next chapter investigates the role of the courts in extracting
information from parties in litigation and other relevant matters.

Chapter 10

Litigation and information

10.1 In this chapter there will be an examination of the opportunities that may be provided to obtain information through the process of litigation and the obstacles that may be placed in the path of a litigant wishing to obtain information. There will not be an exhaustive treatment of the practice and procedure of litigation and rules of evidence, nor will there be any discussion of the law of contempt[1] and how orders and penalties for contempt may be used to pre-empt discussion of matters that are sub judice.[2] The major preoccupation will concern the process of discovery, or disclosure of documents as it is known following the Woolf reforms, and especially the legal immunities which may prevent disclosure or inspection.

[1] Contempt of Court Act 1981; see Arlidge, Eady and Smith *Law of Contempt* (3rd edn, 2005); Borrie and Lowe *The Law of Contempt* (4th edn, 2010); Miller *Contempt of Court* (3rd edn, 2000); the Salmon Report on *Tribunals of Inquiry Cmnd* 4078 (1969); the Phillimore Report Cmnd 5794 (1974); *Sunday Times v United Kingdom* (1979) 2 EHRR 245; *In the Public Interest: Publication of Local Authority Inquiry Reports* Law Commission No 289 Cm 6274 (2004). See further: J Jaconelli *Open Justice: Reappraising the Public Trial* (2002) and J Jacob *Civil Justice in the Age of Human Rights* (2007). We are grateful to our colleague, Martin Parry, for assistance on the family law aspects of this chapter and to Joe Jacob for advice on openness of judicial proceedings.

[2] See Birkinshaw *Freedom of Information: The Law, The Practice and The Ideal* (4th edn, 2010), ch 11.

IN CAMERA OR PRIVATE HEARINGS

10.2 Under Part 39 of the Civil Procedure Rules 1998 (CPR 1998), the general rule is that a 'hearing' is to be in public subject to a number of provisos. That principle of the common law was stated in constitutional terms in *Scott v Scott*.[1] Hearings may be in private if publicity would defeat the object of the hearing, it involves national security, confidential information or where publicity might damage the interests of a child or patient, and other matters as identified or 'the court considers this necessary, in the interests of justice'.[2] Article 6 ECHR provides an entitlement to a 'fair and public hearing' in the determination of civil rights and obligations, or any criminal charge against an individual.[3] This Convention right is subject to exceptions similar to CPR 1998, Part 39.

¹ [1913] AC 417 (IIL). The Privy Council has ruled that at common law the trial judge has no power to make orders preventing publication of proceedings in open court, but a *warning* may be given that publication could lead to contempt proceedings: *Independent Publishing Co Ltd v Att Gen of Trinidad and Tobago* [2005] 1 All ER 499. See *Att Gen v Leveller Magazine Ltd* [1979] AC 440. The Court of Appeal has recently considered the scope of openness of hearings in relation to proceedings brought to restrain publication of private information in *H v News Group Newspapers* [2011] EWCA Civ 42, [2011] 1 WLR 1645, with a discussion of the need to balance ECHR, Arts 8 and 10 alongside the requirements of Art 6. For the general principles set out, which begin with the premise that the names of the parties should be included in all orders and judgments of the court and that any departure from that principle is a derogation from the principle of open justice. See para [21] of the judgment.

² *A v Times Newspapers Ltd* [2003] 1 All ER 587 and principles relevant to open or private hearings involving children under the Children Act 1989. See *B and P v UK* (App Nos 36337/97 and 35974/97): 'upbringing' (custody) proceedings in private and unpublished judgments did not breach Art 6 ECHR, ECtHR. In October 2004, the case of Charlotte Wyatt (11 months old and seriously ill and debilitated) was heard in public so that 'informed debate' could help discussion of controversial matters concerning life support. See *Blunkett v Quinn* (2004) *Times*, 7 December where judgment was given in public in a case concerning parental responsibility and contact orders in order to overcome widespread misinformation in the media. The case involved the then Home Secretary.

³ *Axen v Germany* (1983) 6 EHRR 195, para 25.

10.3   The presumption in favour of publicity is, amongst other things, there to assist free reporting and freedom of speech. In *Reynolds v Times Newspapers Limited*¹ Lord Nicholls of Birkenhead expressed the view:

> 'It is through the mass media that most people today obtain their information on political matters. Without freedom of expression by the media, freedom of expression would be a hollow concept. The interest of a democratic society in ensuring a free press weighs heavily in the balance in deciding whether any curtailment of this freedom bears a reasonable relationship to the purpose of the curtailment.'

¹ [2001] 2 AC 127 at 200G–H. See also *Jameel v Wall Street Journal Europe SPRL (No 3)* [2006] UKHL 44, [2007] 1 AC 359, where the House of Lords overturned the Court of Appeal's finding that the *Wall Street Journal* had lost its right to claim qualified privilege as it did not delay and give the claimant the opportunity to comment on a story prior to publication. The Privy Council case of *Seaga v Harper* [2008] UKPC 9, [2009] 1 AC 1 then extended this to expression beyond the newspaper medium. In the context of super injunctions see *H v News Group Newspapers* [2011] EWCA Civ 42, [2011] 1 WLR 1645, especially [19]–[25]. CPR PD 51F has now been issued and concerns the collection and publication (in anonymised form) of information about non-disclosure injunctions.

10.4   One point to note immediately, however, is the power of a court to sit in camera when it is deemed appropriate; an obvious example would be a trial under s 1 of the Official Secrets Act 1920 (OSA 1920) where sensitive information is to be examined.¹ Another may be where confidential industrial or commercial information is involved. Even when proceedings are in chambers or are in camera, that does not mean that judgments in those proceedings are secret. 'The concept of a secret judgment is one which I believe to be inherently abhorrent'². Secrecy would depend upon the subject matter. It has been held that a judge may decide to keep a judgment secret in cases where the court is hearing an arbitration claim pursuant to s 68 of the Arbitration Act 1996 in private under CPR r 62.10, although there should be no automatic presumption of such secrecy.[3] Under the Contempt of Court Act 1981 (COCA 1981), and a wide variety of other statutes, courts have a range of powers to restrict or defer publication of information[4] and to exclude the press or public or to restrict reporting.[5] The principle of a public hearing does not apply to cases in family proceedings involving children or mentally disordered persons. Administration of Justice Act 1960, s 12 concerns the publication of information in proceedings held in private. This is not in itself a contempt of court except in five areas specified below (para 10.8).

[1]   OSA 1920, s 8: sentence must be passed in open court.
[2]   Per Jacob J in *Forbes v Smith* [1998] 1 All ER 973. See also *Hodgson v Imperial Tobacco Ltd* [1998] 1 WLR 1056 at 1071C–1072C, CA. I am grateful to Joe Jacob for reference to these cases. See further on confidentiality: *Cream Holdings v Bannerjee* [2004] 4 All ER 617 (HL) below. Pronouncement of judgment in public after an in camera hearing is in conformity with Art 6 ECHR: *Pelling v Bruce-Williams* [2004] 3 All ER 875.
[3]   *Department of Economics, Policy and Development of the City of Moscow v Bankers Trust Co* [2004] EWCA Civ 314, [2005] QB 207.
[4]   Contempt of Court Act 1981, ss 4(2), 11. On 'secret witnesses' see *R v Lord Saville of Newdigate, ex p A* [1999] 4 All ER 860, CA, and Marcus (1990) Public Law p 207. See CPR 1998, r 39.2(3); on the three-stage test to follow, see: *R v Sherwood ex p The Telegraph Group plc* [2001] 1 WLR 1983 (CA): 'The questions to be posed were firstly whether any press reporting would give rise to a substantial risk of prejudice in the relevant proceedings, secondly, in the event that such a risk was found to exist, whether an order under s 4(2) of the 1981 Act would dispose of that risk, and thirdly, if an order would dispose of that risk, whether it was the best method by which to eliminate it having regard to the competing public interest considerations exemplified by Human Rights Act 1998, Sch 1, Part I, Arts 6 and 10. A judge might conclude that the risk of prejudice identified should nevertheless be regarded as bearable on the basis that it constituted the lesser of two evils. On the facts of the instant case, severance of the trials had been necessary in the public interest and any media reports would have undermined the aim of such an order, *R v Beck Ex p Daily Telegraph Plc* [1993] 2 All ER 177 distinguished'.
[5]   See eg, Criminal Justice Act 2003, ss 71 and 72. See *R v Waterfield* [1975] 2 All ER 40, CA, and discretion to allow reporters to remain. See also *R (on the application of Guardian News and Media Ltd) v City of Westminster Magistrates' Court* [2010] EWHC 3376 (Admin), [2011] 1 WLR 1173 where the court found that the *Guardian* could not invoke ECHR, Art 10 to give it a right to inspect documents referred to by the parties in extradition proceedings as the documents concerned had been subject to detailed oral representations in open court. 'We do not consider that there is any basis or any justification for extending the Article 10 rights of the Guardian so as to entitle it to inspect additional documents merely because its journalists have a genuine concern to see them. In addition, if the Guardian's case was correct and its journalists had a genuine desire to inspect documents which had been made available for the purpose of criminal proceedings (including unused material), such documents would then automatically become open for inspection even if they had not been relied on and even though they had been produced solely for the purpose of the criminal proceedings. This extension of Art 10 sought by the Guardian cannot be justified.' at [33], per Sullivan LJ. See *Re Crook* (1989) *Times*, 13 November, CA: information received privately in chambers in criminal matters – when the public are excluded, the press should be excluded; and *Re London and Norwich Investment Services Ltd* (1987) *Times*, 16 December. On the now repealed SI 1983/942, see *Pickering v Liverpool Daily Post and Echo Newspapers plc* [1990] 1 All ER 335, CA (mental health review tribunals) and reversing in part [1991] 1 All ER 622 (HL): name of patient making application to Mental Health Review Tribunal and directions as to discharge not a part of 'proceedings' and latter like formal order of court excluded from protection under Administration of Justice Act 1960, s 12(2). Mental health cases have now been transferred to the Health, Education and Social Care Chamber of the First Tier Tribunal and the rules for mental health cases can be found in Part 4 of SI 2008/2699. The principle in the case does not appear to have been affected by the revised rules as r 14(7) of the 2008 Rules is very similar to r 21(5) of the 1983 rules. On press reports of proceedings in public: *Barlow Clowes Gilt Managers Ltd v Clowes* (1990) *Times*, 2 February. The EAT has ruled that both it and Employment Tribunals

have power to order restricted reporting orders: *X v Metropolitan Police Commissioner* (2003) New LJ 719. Note also that the Supreme Court has recently held that the 'closed material procedure', where a special advocate might represent the claimant where the claimant and his representatives is compatible both with EU Law and the ECHR when used in Employment Tribunals. See *Home Office v Tariq* [2011] UKSC 35. See also Employment Tribunals (Constitution and Rules of Proceedings) Regulations 2004 and criticism of government attempts to keep 'whistleblower' proceedings secret until the tribunal hearing: HL Debs, 27 October 2004 (para 2.311 above).

10.5 The following offers a brief description of some of the more important examples.

10.6 The public are excluded from the youth court, although the press are admitted and may publish certain particulars. They must not publish names and addresses which might identify the family involved.[1] Section 97 of the Children Act 1989 states that rules under s 144 of the Magistrates' Courts Act 1980 may provide for those courts to sit in private when dealing with proceedings under the Children Act 1989.[2] Publication of information identifying children is prohibited.[3] Children Act 2004, s 62 makes provision for a wide range of proceedings in which publication may be allowed. Privacy may be dispensed with by order of the court or Secretary of State in the child's welfare. A defence to a prosecution is available where the defendant did not know and had no reason to suspect that publication was intended, or likely, to identify the child. The section defines 'publish' (s 97(5)). The section is without prejudice of any other power of a magistrates' court to sit in private. The Court of Appeal has ruled that there is no duty under s 17 or 47 of the Children Act 1989 on local authorities to inform other authorities of the addresses of those found guilty of sexual abuse in care or other family proceedings. Information may be disclosed to the police or a defendant in a criminal trial but not to authorities to pass on.[4] Children Act 1989 proceedings in the magistrates' courts, county (circuit) court and High Court and wardship hearings are in private, with both the press and public excluded. It has been held that, in the absence of a specific injunction, facts in the public domain and not covered in the wardship proceedings may be published.[5]

[1] Children and Young Persons Act 1933, ss 47 and 49; and *Re M and N (Minors)* [1990] 1 All ER 205, CA a balancing of the right of the media and the need to protect the welfare of the child in cases of genuine public interest involving children where information is not statutorily barred under the Administration of Justice Act 1960, s 12. See Children Act 1989, s 97 (as amended by the Access to Justice Act 1999). Note that s 97 will be repealed when Part 2 of the Children, Schools and Families Act 2010 comes into force. Part 2 sets out in greater detail than the present s 97 and is designed to allow greater access to family proceedings. The changes follow Cm 7131 *Confidence & Confidentiality: Openness in Family Courts – A New Approach* and Cm 7502 (2008) *Family Justice in View*.

[2] And see Family Procedure Rules 2010, SI 2010/2955, r 12.73 and *Re W* (below); *Re A (a minor) (disclosure of medical records to the GMC)* [1999] 1 FCR 30; and *A Health Authority v X (No 1)* [2001] EWCA Civ 2014, [2002] 2 All ER 780. On the relationship with ECHR, Art 6, see *B v UK* [2000] 2 FCR 97 and *B and P v UK*, para 10.2, note 2 above.

[3] See *Kent County Council v K* [1994] 1 WLR 912; *Re G (Social Worker: Disclosure)* [1996] 1 FLR 276; *Re EC (Disclosure of Material)* [1996] 2 FLR 725, CA; *Oxfordshire County Council v L and F* [1997] 1 FLR 235. For more recent cases see *Re X (Children) (Disclosure for Purposes of Criminal Proceedings)* [2008] EWHC 242 (Fam), [2008] 3 All ER 958 and *M (A Child) (Children and Family Reporter: Disclosure)* [2002] EWCA Civ 1199, [2003] Fam 26. See *Re Z (A Minor) (Freedom of Publication)* [1997] Fam 1; *Re C (a minor) (Care Proceedings: Disclosure)* [1997] Fam 76, CA; and *Re W (minors) (social worker: disclosure)* [1998] 2 All ER 801, CA; *Re M (A Child) (Children and*

Family Reporter: Disclosure) [2002] EWCA Civ 1199. [2003] Fam 26; and *Re H (Children) (Care Proceedings: Disclosure)* [2009] EWCA Civ 704, [2009] 2 FLR 1531 for a discussion of balancing confidentiality and disclosure. In the *Re H* case the Court of Appeal held that changes to the Family Proceedings Rules 1991 (since repealed and replaced by the Family Procedure Rules 2010 (above)) and in particular the repeal of r 4.23 and its replacement by r 10.20A in 2005 may tip the balance in favour of disclosure in a larger number of cases than in the past. Rule 12.73 of the Family Proceedings Rules 2010 contains a similar list of parties to whom information might be disclosed as that which was contained in r 10.20A of the old rules. The courts have treated requests by police for documents arising in child proceedings more generously and have emphasised the cooperation that must exist between the various agencies involved in child welfare: see 'Working Together to Safeguard Children' Dept of Health (1999). In another context, the courts have also discouraged applications to them for orders under Family Law Act 1986, s 33 directing the police to disclose the whereabouts of a child who was in the custody of one parent in a refuge: *S v S* [1999] 1 All ER 281, CA. Also: *Re K (A Child)* [2000] NLJR 1538 and *Re X* (above).

4   *Re L and Re V (Minors: sexual abuse: disclosure)* [1999] 1 FLR 267, although cf *R (on the application of A) v Hertfordshire CC* [2001] EWCA Civ 2113, [2001] BLGR 435. See *R (A Child) (Care Proceedings) (Disclosure), Re* (2000) *Times,* 18 July, CA and disclosure under Children Act 1989, s 42(1)(b). In *Re W and Others (Children)(Care Proceedings: disclosure)* [2004] 1 All ER 787 the court ordered the police to disclose information about a suspected drugs dealer to a solicitor of the mother of a child in care proceedings, but not to pass on to the clients without permission.

5   *Re W (Publication of Information)* [1989] 1 FLR 246: the order, enforceable against newspapers and editors but not, on facts, journalists; see *Re C (No 2)* [1989] 2 All ER 791; *Re L* [1988] 1 All ER 418. For wardship proceedings and local authorities, see Children Act 1989, s 100. Stephen Brown P has included, for a ward of court, the name and address and indication of the identity of a ward as publishable where such publication is not specifically enjoined and does not form part of the proceedings: *Re W.* See *Cumbria County Council v X* (1990) *Times,* 25 June. In *Kelly v BBC* [2001] 1 All ER 323, the High Court refused to prevent the broadcast of a programme, with an interview, about a 16-year-old ward of court who had left his family home to live with a religious sect. Article 10 of the ECHR was crucial in allowing the broadcast. There was no breach of Administration of Justice Act 1960, s 12 nor of Children Act 1989, s 97(2) nor any question of the custodial jurisdiction of the court. See also *X (a Child)* [2001] FCR 541; *Medway Council v BBC* [2002] 1 FLR 104; and *BBC v Rochdale MBC* [2005] EWHC 2862 (Fam), [2006] EMLR 6 where the court held that two social workers in a particular case could be identified, finding that the Art 10 right to freedom of expression held greater weight than the Art 8 rights either of the social workers concerned or the children who might have been identified from the disclosure of the social workers' identities. It should be noted, however, that the disclosure was to take place some time after the original intervention by social services.

10.7   Where the 'upbringing' of a child is concerned the principle that the welfare of the child is paramount deriving from Children Act 1989, s 1(1) has been used to impose secrecy for the proceedings.[1] In cases where the care and upbringing of the child were not, or were not directly, in question the courts had been prepared to allow press reporting of facts which might reveal the identity of children involved in proceedings because of the public interest of free speech and a free press.[2] Or reports may be allowed, but not identifying the children.[3] The subject is now dominated by the decision in *Re S* which held that the position was governed by the rights, and Convention methodologies, under Arts 8 and 10 of the Convention by virtue of the Human Rights Act 1998 (below).

1   *In re Z (A Minor) (Identification: Restrictions on Publication)* [1995] 4 All ER 961 (CA) – a TV programme about the daughter of Cecil Parkinson and Sarah Keays and her special educational needs: injunction prohibiting commentary identifying child maintained. See: *A and Byrne and Twenty-Twenty TV v UK* (1998) 25 EHRR CD 159 before the EComHR. See Lord Steyn in *Re S (a child)* [2004] UKHL 47 at para 37 where this view is maintained obiter.

[2] *Re W (A Minor) (Wardship: Freedom of Publication)* [1992] 1 All ER 794 (CA); *R v Central Independent Television* [1994] 3 All ER 641, CA.
[3] *Re W (A Minor) (Wardship: Restrictions on Publication)* [1995] 2 FLR 466 (CA).

10.8 The secrecy of proceedings involving the upbringing of children has brought increasing criticism that parties involved in the litigation may find it impossible to be treated fairly.[1] Furthermore the courts have been prepared to allow proceedings to be heard in public, for identities to be released or for judgment to be published where this is clearly in the public interest because of the important questions raised.[2] Section 12(1) of the Administration of Justice Act 1960 and formerly the common law prohibited publication of details of the proceedings[3] held in private; however, publication of the name of a sex offender who had made an application to the Mental Health Review Tribunal did not concern *proceedings before* the tribunal. Section 12 states that the publication of information relating to proceedings before any court sitting in private (including in camera or in chambers) shall not of itself be contempt of court. There are five exceptions to this including proceedings involving the inherent jurisdiction of the court with respect to minors, under the Children Act 1989 or which otherwise relate wholly or mainly to the maintenance or upbringing of a minor. The second category concerns proceedings under Part VIII of the Mental Health Act 1959 and any other provision of that Act authorising applications or references to a Mental Health Review Tribunal or county court. The last three deal with national security, secret processes and inventions, and last of all where the court has the power and expressly prohibits publication of all information relating to the proceedings or of information of the description which is published. Section 12(2) allows the publication of the text or a summary of the whole or part of an order made by a court except where the court with power to do so expressly prohibits publication.[4]

[1] Commons Constitutional Affairs Committee HC 1247(i) (2003–04). See Cm 6507 *Family Justice*.
[2] Where questions relating to the continuing life of a child in serious physical distress on a life support machine or where a 'miracle baby' born to an infertile mother was in fact the product of child trafficking: in the latter case, identities were not released.
[3] See *Pickering v Liverpool Daily Post and Echo Newspapers plc* [1991] 1 All ER 622 (HL) on 'proceedings' before Mental Health Review Tribunals.
[4] *Re G (Minors) (celebrities: publicity)* [1999] 3 FCR 181, CA.

10.9 In relation to a child, the section is not concerned with protecting information about the child or that s/he is a ward of court and is the subject of wardship proceedings.[1] Nor does the section apply to documents held by social services which have not been filed with or used in the proceedings.[2] The Family Division has ruled that there is a publication whenever the law of defamation would treat there as having a publication: subject to exceptions of communication of information to a professional where both the communicator and the recipient were acting in furtherance of protection of the children. In essence, a distinction is drawn between 'the nature of the dispute' and the publication of evidence, even in summary form. The former may be permissible; the latter will not.[3]

[1] *X v Dempster* [1999] 1 FLR 894 at 898. See *Kelly* above.
[2] *Re W* [1998] 2 All ER 801, CA. Such documents will be covered by the Data Protection Act 1998 and by the law of confidentiality.
[3] *Re B (a child) (disclosure)* [2004] 2 FLR 200. Munby J provided examples of what cannot be published.

10.10 Part 2 of the Children, Schools and Families Act 2010 has the potential to significantly change the regime outlined above. It proposes the repeal of s 97 of the Children Act 1989, which provides anonymity for children in relevant cases and is intended to encourage transparency and openness in family justice and to increase media access to family proceedings. Part 2 of the Act has not yet been brought into force and no decision on its implementation will be made prior to the publication of the final report of the Family Justice Review, which is due in late 2011.[1] Section 11 of the Act reads as follows:

'(1) This section applies in relation to any relevant family proceedings at which the public are not (or, in the case of proceedings which have already taken place, were not) entitled to be present.

(2) The publication of information relating to the proceedings is a contempt of court committed by the publisher unless the publication of the information is—

(a) an authorised publication of the text, or a summary, of the whole or part of an order made or judgment given by the court in the proceedings (see section 12),

(b) an authorised news publication (see section 13), or

(c) authorised by rules of court.

(3) Nothing in this section makes it a contempt of court to publish information with the permission of the court.'

[1] Written statement by Jonathan Djangoly HC Deb 11 October 2010 c7WS. The final report, at paras 2.234–2.235, supports the recommendation that the provisions of Part 2 of the Children, Schools and Families Act 2010 should not be implemented. See Family Justice Review (2011) *Family Justice Review: Final Report.*

10.11 It has been observed that the restrictions in place in ss 11 and 12 of the 2010 Act are in some respects more restrictive than the present law. In particular, the 2010 Act applies to a greater number of cases than s 12 of the Administration of Justice Act 1960 and removes the present freedom to publish orders and judgments presently in place.[1] Section 12 of the Act creates a default position of publication, both for orders and judgments in family cases covered by the Act, provided that any 'identification information' is redacted. 'Identification information' is defined in ss 21(1) and (2) of the Act and covers the issues that one might anticipate, including details of names, addresses, friends and relatives and schools, etc. Information may only be published in certain cases relating to parental orders under the Human Fertilisation and Embryology Act 1990 and certain adoption cases with the permission of the court. Likewise, any publication of court orders or reports which contain identification information can only be done within the parameters laid down by the court. It has been noted that the pilot project on publication of county court judgements in certain public law cases led to considerable differences in the quality of judgments published, with a common problem being that the reports frequently referred to documents in the court bundle, which were not available to the public.

[1] Mummery LJ, 'Lost Opportunities: Law Reform and Transparency in the Family Courts' [2010] CFLQ 273.

10.12 Section 13 of the 2010 Act provides a framework for media reporting of family proceedings covered by the Act. The provisions of s 13 are as follows:

(1) A publication of information is an authorised news publication if the following conditions are met.

(2) Condition 1 is that the information was obtained by an accredited news representative by observing or listening to the proceedings when attending them in exercise of a right conferred on accredited news representatives by rules of court.

(3) Condition 2 is that the publisher of the information—
(a) is the accredited news representative,
(b) publishes the information with the consent of, or pursuant to a contract or other agreement entered into with, that representative, or
(c) has obtained the information from a publication of information which is an authorised news publication.

(4) Condition 3 is that—
(a) the information is not—
   (i)   identification information relating to an individual involved in the proceedings,
   (ii) sensitive personal information relating to the proceedings, or
   (iii) restricted adoption information or restricted parental order information,
(b) the information is information within paragraphs (i) to (iii) of paragraph (a) and the publication is permitted by the court for the purposes of this Condition, or
(c) the information is identification information relating to an individual involved in the proceedings (but not restricted adoption information or restricted parental order information) and the individual is a professional witness in the proceedings.

(5) Condition 4 is that if the publication is—
(a) a publication of the text, or a summary, of an order made by a court in adoption proceedings or parental order proceedings, or
(b) a publication of the text, or a summary, of a judgment given by a court in relevant family proceedings,
the publication is permitted by the court for the purposes of section 12.

(6) Condition 5 is that the publication is not prohibited by, and does not breach any restriction imposed by, the court for the purposes of this condition or section 12.

(7) The court may permit the publication of information for the purposes of Condition 3 or prohibit or restrict the publication of information for the purposes of Condition 5 on its own initiative or on the application of any interested person.

10.13 Lord Justice Mummery has criticised the provisions of s 13 of the 2010 Act as being unduly restrictive on the media – information relating to the proceedings may only be reported if it was gleaned by 'observing or listening to the proceedings', according to s 13(2). This creates a burden on the media that did not always exist in the past, as the wording of s 13 suggests that if the media obtain exactly the same information but not via the method set out in the section, it cannot be published.[1] Sections 14, 15 and 16 of the Act lay down the consideration to be taken account of by the court when deciding whether to permit or prohibit publication of certain matters. Factors include the public interest, the interests and safety of the children involved in the case and, in relevant circumstances, whether the parties consent to disclosure.

[1] Mummery LJ, 'Lost Opportunities: Law Reform and Transparency in the Family Courts' [2010] CFLQ 273.

10.14   It may be that Part 2 of the 2010 Act will not be brought into force. A recent report of the Justice Select Committee notes that, 'While united against the scheme set out in the CSFA 2010, our witnesses disagreed as to the way forward.'[1] The Committee recommended that Part 2 should not be implemented and the government should consider fresh legislation on the issue.

[1] HC 518-I (6th Report of 2010–2011 session) *Operation of the Family Courts*, para 282. See also para 10.10, note 1.

10.15   Section 39 of the Children and Young Persons Act 1933 (CYPA 1933) – amended by Youth Justice and Criminal Evidence Act 1999, s 45 – protects the anonymity (in relation to press reports) of children in criminal courts in respect of name, address, identifying particulars, photographs and moving picture.[1] The court may make a direction suppressing publication of the matters set out above. The High Court may grant an injunction achieving the same end. Section 49 of the CYPA 1933 (which applies to publication of proceedings in youth courts) contains an automatic restriction on publication of the matters set out above, although under s 49(4A) the court may dispense with the restrictions if it considers it in the public interest to do so.[2] It should be noted that the CPS has issued fresh guidance to prosecutors on the seeking of orders under ss 39 and 49 of the CYPA 1933 in August 2011 as a result of the riots and disorder which took place in that month. The new guidance suggests that prosecutors should be discouraged from seeking a s 39 order and may wish to seek dispensation of the restrictions contained in s 49 in circumstances where the crimes committed relate to serious public disorder, serious offences which undermine the public's confidence in the safety of their communities; and hate crimes.[3] The guidance makes it clear that these considerations must always be balanced against the interests of the defendants in such cases. A person aggrieved may appeal, with permission of the Court of Appeal, to that court against an order of the Crown Court restricting or preventing reports or restricting public access under the following orders contained in s 159(1) of the Criminal Justice Act 1988:

'(a) an order under section 4 or 11 of the Contempt of Court Act 1981 made in relation to a trial on indictment;

(aa) an order made by the Crown Court under section 58(7) or (8) of the Criminal Procedure and Investigations Act 1996 in a case where the Court has convicted a person on a trial on indictment;

(b) any order restricting the access of the public to the whole or any part of a trial on indictment or to any proceedings ancillary to such a trial; and

(c) any order restricting the publication of any report of the whole or any part of a trial on indictment or any such ancillary proceedings; and the decision of the Court of Appeal shall be final.'

1   The Divisional Court can review the lifting of a reporting ban: *Re H* (1999) *Times*, 13 August.
2   And see *R v Central Independent Television plc* [1994] 3 All ER 641, CA, for limitations on a court's specific powers of restriction. See CYPA 1933, s 49(4A), added by Crime (Sentences) Act 1997, s 45, and *McKerry v Teesdale etc Justices* (2000) 164 JP 355, CA.
3   Crown Prosecution Service (2011) *Guidance on Imposing and Lifting Reporting Restrictions in Cases Involving Youths who are Convicted.* Available at: http://www.cps.gov.uk/legal/p_to_r/reporting_restrictions_-_cases_involving_convicted_youths/.

10.16 Section 159 allows the appeal judge to give directions ordering the transfer to that judge of any transcript or note of proceedings or other document and to stay proceedings in any other court until the appeal is dispensed of, and related matters.[1]

1   Criminal Justice Act 1988, s 158 concerns anonymity in rape cases.

10.17 Rules allow for the above appeals to be heard in private. Readers are reminded of the powers of publicising anti social behaviour orders but in a manner which is reasonable and proportionate (para 2.326, note 3).[1]

1   *R (Stanley etc) v Metropolitan Police Commissioner* [2004] EWHC 2229 (Admin).

10.18 Article 8 of the ECHR and the Human Rights Act 1998 (HRA 1998) may also be invoked by those who have protective orders preventing reporting or publication of information about them as children to continue after they achieve adulthood. Convention rights will now dominate the situation and the former wardship case-law will have to be re-examined in the light of the Convention and the framework provided by those rights. The former case-law may be of some use in exercising a balance between rights under Arts 8 and 10. Such injunctions preventing reporting were requested by the murderers of the young child, James Bulger, after their release from prison and after they had achieved adulthood. Orders prohibiting such publication were granted by the High Court (see paras 7.169 et seq above). Such orders are 'exceptional', but have been used in the case of Mary Bell until she achieved the age of 18, and injunctions were issued on her reaching that age on the grounds of protecting confidentiality (para 7.169, note 91 above).[1] However, in *Re S* under inherent powers, the court refused to prohibit publication of the identities of a child's mother and her alleged murder victim (the child's brother) in criminal proceedings to protect the identity of her son who was involved in care proceedings, but a balance will have to be struck between Arts 8 and 10 ECHR.[2] These criminal proceedings were not concerned *directly* with the upbringing of the child. Both Articles must be considered in their own right and balanced proportionately. The majority held, agreeing with the judge at first instance, that the injunction should be discharged and reporting allowed. This decision, but not the reasoning, was upheld by the House of Lords. In giving the judgment for the appeal committee, Lord Steyn stated:

'The House unanimously takes the view that since the 1998 Act came into force in October 2000, the earlier case law about the existence and scope of inherent jurisdiction need not be considered in this case or in similar cases. The foundation of the jurisdiction to restrain publicity in a case such as the present is now derived from convention rights under the ECHR. This is the simple and direct way to approach such cases. In this case the jurisdiction is not in doubt. This is not to say that the case law on the inherent jurisdiction of the High Court is wholly irrelevant. On the contrary, it may remain of some interest in regard to the ultimate balancing exercise to be carried out under the ECHR provisions. My noble and learned friend Lord Bingham of Cornhill invited the response of counsel to this approach. Both expressed agreement with it. I would affirm this approach. Before passing on I would observe on a historical note that a study of the case law revealed that the approach adopted in the past under the inherent jurisdiction was remarkably similar to that to be adopted under the ECHR. Indeed the ECHR provisions were often cited even before it became part of our law in October 2000. Nevertheless, it will in future be necessary, if earlier case law is cited, to bear in mind the new methodology required by the ECHR as explained in *Campbell*.'[3]

[1] *Re X (A Minor)* [1984] 1 WLR 1422 and *W, Y v SO, News Group Newspapers Ltd* [2003] 2 FCR 686.
[2] *Re S (a child) (identification: restriction on publication)* [2003] EWCA Civ 963, [2003] 3 WLR 1425 (CA).
[3] *Re S (a child) etc* [2004] 4 All ER 683, HL, at para 23; for *Campbell*, see paras 2.295 and 7.172 above. See *Blunkett v Quinn* (2004) *Times*, 7 December, para 10.2, note 2 above. More recently, the court has granted injunctions to prevent the publication of any material that might identify birth parents of children who had been adopted. The parents wished to give interviews to the media in order to highlight what they believed were miscarriages of justice which ultimately led to the adoption of their children. The court found that although the birth parents were pursuing a legitimate objective, there was an overriding interest in the protection of the adopted children and thus granted injunctions in broad terms, prohibiting publication of any information that could lead to the identification of the children or the interference in their family life. See *Re B (Children)* [2010] EWHC 262 (Fam), [2010] 1 FLR 1708. Conversely, injunctions have been refused where the guardian of a child sought to restrict publication of proceedings in coroner's inquest investigating the death of the chiild's sister. It was argued that reports of proceedings could lead to identification of the surviving sibling, but the court held that the public interest in the free reporting of legal proceedings outweighed the child's Art 8 rights – *Re LM (A Child) (Reporting Restrictions: Coroner's Inquest)* [2007] EWHC 1902 (Fam), [2007] CP Rep 48.

10.19 A factor that weighed heavily with openness was the large number of exceptions to openness provided by Parliament (above) and that further judicial inroads would pile 'exception upon exception to the principle of open justice'. The child was not a participant in a criminal trial for which specific provision is made.

10.20 In appeals otherwise from decisions of courts which sat in private, the appeal court has the same power to sit in private for all or part of the appeal, though the decision, and reasons for the decision, must generally be in public.[1]

[1] Domestic and Appellate Proceedings (Restriction of Publicity) Act 1968, s 1.

10.21 Nevertheless, the general presumption is that justice will be done in public.[1] However, proceedings in chambers are in private but judgments will usually be public documents unless the nature of the proceedings requires secrecy[2] and the Court of Appeal (Criminal Division) has laid down guidelines on when information should be received privately in chambers by the judge in criminal matters. Where the public were excluded, the press should usually be excluded.[3] It should be observed that interim proceedings in the Queen's Bench Division for injunctions are in chambers, in contradistinction to the Chancery Division where proceedings are in open court. Court proceedings in England and Wales may not be broadcast or recorded publicly but discussions are taking place with a view of allowing limited broadcasts. In November 2004, filming of proceedings in the Court of Appeal was allowed but for internal consumption only. The Department for Constitutional Affairs launched a consultation exercise on broadcasting court proceedings, which has not ultimately led to a change in the law, as court proceedings still cannot be broadcast.[4] The only notable exception to the prohibition on photography or broadcasting of court proceedings (primarily to be found in s 41 of the Criminal Justice Act 1925 and s 9 of the COCA 1981) relates to proceedings in the Supreme Court. Section 47 of the Constitutional Reform Act 2005 expressly excludes the Supreme Court from the ordinary prohibition on photography, etc of court proceedings contained in s 41 of the 1925 Act, though not s 9 of the 1981 Act. It should be noted that the court might grant leave for the use of tape-recording equipment and give permission for the recordings to be released to the public under the provisions of s 9 in any case, whereas the provisions of s 41 of the 1925 Act are absolute. The president or presiding judge in a Supreme Court case may grant permission to broadcast proceedings[5] and the judge concerned may impose such conditions on recording and broadcasting as he thinks fit, including the potential to require agreement of all the parties. The Supreme Court and broadcasters have agreed a protocol on the recording and use of material, including exclusions for private discussions between parties and counsel and restrictions on the use of excerpts. The protocol also contains prohibitions on the use of footage for marketing or party political purposes. The protocol is referred to in Practice Direction 8 of the Supreme Court, but does not appear to be publicly available. Broadcasting has taken place in Scotland. There appears to be some potential for the debate over the broadcasting of certain proceedings in lower courts to return, as this was a topic addressed by Lord Neuberger, the Master of the Rolls, in a recent Judicial Studies Board lecture.[6]

[1]   *Scott v Scott* [1913] AC 417, HL. *R v Malvern Justices, ex p Evans* [1988] 1 All ER 371. For a recent graphic illustration, see *Storer v British Gas plc* [2000] 2 All ER 440, CA and *R v Bow County Court, ex p Pelling* [2001] UKHRR 165 (CA). See *Clibbery v Allan* [2002] Fam 261: publication allowed of information arising from Family Law Act 1996, s 36 proceedings in chambers; and *P (Disclosure: Criminal Proceedings)* [2004] 1 FLR 407. For arbitration and requirements of privacy, see *City of Moscow v Bankers Trust* [2004] EWCA Civ 314, discussed above. Rules allow tribunals to sit in private in certain circumstances. For ADR and negotiated justice and cognate matters, see J Jacob *Civil Justice in the Age of Human Rights Act* (2007), pp 65–66. We are grateful to Joe Jacob for discussion on a variety of points.

[2]   See para 10.4 above.

[3]   *Re Crook* (1989) *Times*, 13 November. See *R v Independent, ex p DPP* (1988) *Guardian*, 1 April and PACE 1984, s 9 and Sch 1 applications concerning sensitive information. On broadcasting, Dockray (1988) MLR 593. See, incidentally, *R v Agar* [1990] 2 All ER 442, CA.

[4]   Department for Constitutional Affairs (2004) CP 28/04 *Broadcasting Courts*. Available at: http://webarchive.nationalarchives.gov.uk/+/http://www.dca.gov.uk/consult/courts/broadcasting-cp28-04.pdf.

[5]   UK Supreme Court Practice Direction 8, para 8.17.1.

[6]   Lord Neuberger 'Open Justice Unbound?' Judicial Studies Board Annual Lecture 2011. Available at: http://www.judiciary.gov.uk/Resources/JCO/Documents/Speeches/mr-speech-jsb-lecture-march-2011.pdf.

PROTOCOLS ON POLICE INFORMATION

10.22   A protocol on the means by which police information or evidence is to be disclosed by the police to local authorities and others involved in litigation concerning family proceedings was agreed by ACPO and members of the judiciary in the Autumn of 2004. It was implemented on a pilot basis in London and the North-West from 1 December 2004 and evaluations undertaken demonstrated that the protocol was successful in reducing the amount of time taken to obtain disclosure and were deemed to improve communication and co-operation between the various parties.[1] The protocol has now been adopted by most constabularies after a recommendation by the Association of Chief Police Officers (ACPO) following a positive review of the pilot schemes.[2] The protocol states that its objective is 'to provide the family court with early information to enable it to properly determine any directions which need to be made in relation to documents, records or other criminal proceedings or investigations which may inform the family court (and the parties) in the determination of any factual or welfare issue within family proceedings'. Other aims include involving the police in good time and promoting cooperation between the police and social services regarding issues of disclosure. Procedures for applications are explained as are steps to be taken where the police will not disclose evidence or information without a court order. At such a hearing, the court will consider the necessity and relevance of the information to be sought in relation to the issues to be determined and other matters. The protocol will naturally operate within the ambit of the DPA 1998 and the law of confidentiality.

[1]   W O'Connor and J Dickson (2006) *Disclosure of Police Information in Family Proceedings*. London: National Centre for Social Research.
[2]   A copy of the protocol (which may have been slightly amended by the various forces) can be found on the Metropolitan Police website at http://www.met.police.uk/scd/specialist_units/ Police_Family_Disclosure_Protocol.pdf.

10.23   The Crown Prosecution Service also publishes a model protocol on the sharing of information between local authorities and prosecutors in child abuse cases.[1] The protocol provides guidance on information sharing, offers some detail on the relevant legal frameworks and issues under the DPA 1998 and also provides a model form which the police might use to request information from local authorities.

[1]   Available at http://www.cps.gov.uk/publications/agencies/protocolletter.html.

DISCLOSURE (DISCOVERY)[1]

What is disclosure?

10.24   The origins of disclosure, or what for centuries was known as discovery, lie in the equitable jurisdiction of the Court of Chancery, and the Court of Exchequer. It must be explained briefly that the change in name outlined above came with the CPR 1998 which emerged from the Woolf reforms of the civil justice system. The Rules contain a statement of the overriding objective of dealing with cases justly – which is spelt out in r 1.2 – and give to judges

significant powers of case management.[2] Disclosure is the process by which
parties to an action may identify and inspect the documents (CPR 1998, r 31.4)
which are, or have been, in each other's control, which means they are or were
in the party's physical possession, where there is or was a right to possession, or
the party had a right to inspect or take copies of the documents.

[1]   See *Compagnie Financière Commerciale du Pacifique v Peruvian Guano Co* (1882) 11 QBD 55 for
     the common law principles. *Disclosure* P Matthews and H Malek (2001) and *Documentary Evidence*
     C Hollander (2003). For disclosure and the Data Protection Act 1998 see: *Durant v FSA* [2003]
     EWCA Civ 1746, *Johnson v Medical Defence Union Ltd* [2005] 1 All ER 87 and *R (Lord) v Home
     Secretary* [2003] EWHC 2073 at paras 7.14 and 7.112 above. In the latter, a blanket policy of
     refusing annual security reports on category A prisoners to those prisoners was in place. Section
     7(4) of the DP Act necessitated a proper balance to be struck between the rights of a prisoner and
     the rights of the authors of security reports to remain anonymous. Therefore, a blanket policy of
     non-disclosure could not be justified; a more selective and targeted approach was required: see
     para 7.57 above.
[2]   Pre-action Protocols seek to encourage the exchange of early and full information about the
     prospective legal claims. On the duty to retain documents when litigation is in prospect, see: R.
     Harrison (2004) New LJ 1716. See also the discussion of authorities of pre-action destruction of
     documents by Morritt V-C in *Douglas v Hello!* Ltd (No 3) [2003] EWHC 55 (Ch), [2003] EMLR
     29.

10.25   Most of what follows concerns litigation against private as well as public
bodies. The main provision covering disclosure in the High Court and county
courts is CPR 1998, Part 31 – the rules apply to both High Court and county court
proceedings. The basic provision is now for 'standard disclosure' (see below).
However, other provisions are also important: Part 18 concerns the power of
the court to order a party to provide additional information on any matter which
is in dispute in the proceedings. RSC Ord 77, r 12 was important in litigation
involving the Crown. Disclosure against the Crown was not automatic and did
not have to be made except under order of the court. Order 77, r 12 has been
repealed and the Crown, like other parties, may object to disclosure. Further, the
Crown may keep secret 'the existence of any document the existence of which
it would, in the opinion of a Minister of the Crown, be injurious to the public
interest to disclose'. These may now be kept secret under the provisions applying
on disclosure.

10.26   A party discloses a document by stating that the document exists or has
existed (CPR 1998, r 31.2). A party to whom a document has been disclosed
has a right to inspect that document except: where the document is no longer
in the control of the party who disclosed it; the party disclosing the document
has a right or a duty to withhold inspection of it (see below); or where under
r 31.3(2) a party considers that it would be disproportionate to the issues in the
case to permit inspection of documents within a category or class of documents
disclosed under r 31.6(b) (see below). As previously, disclosure must simply be
shown to be 'necessary in order to dispose fairly of the case or to save costs.'
Where these proportionality provisos apply, a party is not required to permit
inspection of documents within that category or class; but he must state in his
disclosure statement that inspection of those documents will not be permitted on
the grounds that to do so would be disproportionate. An order to give disclosure
is an order to give 'standard disclosure' (see below) unless the court directs

otherwise. Standard disclosure may be dispensed with or limited by the court and dispensation or limitation may also be agreed to by the parties.

10.27 It is perhaps important to note that the disclosure of electronic documents and information has become a more pressing issue in light of the considerable expansion of such material in recent years. Practice Direction 31B offers detailed guidance on the disclosure of electronic documents. Rule 31.4 and corresponding PD 31.2A require the parties to seek to reach agreement on an appropriate strategy for the search for relevant electronic documents.[1] Failure to conduct an adequate search for electronic material may lead to adverse inferences being drawn against those failing to carry out an adequate search, even if the material concerned is material that was created prior to the contemplation or commencement of proceedings.[2] One particular problem in the case of electronic documents is that there is a potential for them to be deleted but still in the hands of a party because they still exist on back-ups. The courts have occasionally required detailed searches of back-ups in order for the requirements of disclosure to be met,[3] although the Court of Appeal recently upheld a decision of the High Court that this was not necessary if it added unduly to expense.[4] It is clear that all bodies, both public and private, must seek to have a system in place that enables the effective searching and retrieval of electronic material in case it is required for the purposes of litigation.

[1]   See Blaxell (2010) NLJ 544.
[2]   *Earles v Barclays Bank Plc* [2009] EWHC 2500 (QB), [2010] Bus LR 566.
[3]   *Digicel (St Lucia) Ltd and Ors v Cable & Wireless Plc & Ors* [2008] EWHC 2522 (Ch), [2009] 2 All ER 1094.
[4]   *Fiddes v Channel 4 Television Corporation* [2010] EWCA Civ 730, [2010] 1 WLR 2245.

10.28 Under r 31.6, standard disclosure requires a party to disclose the documents on which he relies, all documents which could (i) adversely affect his or her own case or (ii) adversely affect another party's case, or (iii) support another party's case (r 31.6(b)); and documents which must be disclosed by any relevant practice direction (r 31.6(c)). When giving standard disclosure, a party is required to make a reasonable search for documents falling within r 31.6(b) or (c). Relevant factors in deciding upon the reasonableness of a search include:
(a)   the number of documents involved;
(b)   the nature and complexity of the proceedings;
(c)   the ease and expense of retrieval of any particular document; and
(d)   the significance of any document which is likely to be located during the search (r 31.7(2)).

10.29 A party who has not searched for a category or class of document on the grounds that to do so would be unreasonable, must state this in their disclosure statement and identify the category or class of document. CPR 1998, r 31.8 deals with the duty of disclosure, and r 31.9 concerns disclosure of copies.

10.30 The basic form of disclosure, standard disclosure, is under CPR 1998, r 31.10. Under standard disclosure, each party must make and serve on every other party a list of documents in the relevant practice form. The list must identify the documents in a convenient order and manner and as concisely as possible. The list must indicate: those documents for which a party is claiming a privilege or an immunity; and those documents no longer in the party's control and what has happened to them. Where a privilege etc is claimed, r 31.19(3) and (4) require a statement in the list of documents relating to any documents inspection of which a person claims he has a right or duty to withhold. The list must include a disclosure statement. This is a statement made by the party disclosing the documents setting out the extent of the search that has been made to locate the documents which he is required to disclose; certifying that he understands the duty to disclose documents; and certifying that to the best of his knowledge he has carried out that duty. Additional provisions apply to statements made by companies, firms, associations or 'other organisation' (r 31.7). The parties may agree in writing to disclose documents without making a list; and to disclose documents without the disclosing party making a disclosure statement. A disclosure statement may be made by a person who is not a party where this is permitted by a relevant practice direction. Any duty of disclosure continues until the proceedings are concluded. If documents to which that duty extends come to a party's notice at any time during the proceedings, he must immediately notify every other party.

10.31 As well as standard disclosure there is also specific disclosure as well as specific inspection. Disclosure is also required by pre-action protocols. The party who receives an order for specific disclosure must do one of the following things: disclose documents or classes of documents specified in the order; carry out a search to the extent stated in the order; disclose any documents located as a result of that search. An order for specific inspection is an order that a party permit inspection of a document referred to in r 31.2. This allows a party to state in their disclosure statement that they will not permit inspection of a document on the grounds that it would be disproportionate to do so.

10.32 Disclosure or inspection may take place in stages either by written agreement between the parties or by court order. A party may inspect a document mentioned in: a statement of case; a witness statement; a witness summary; an affidavit; or, subject to r 35.10(4), an expert's report.[1] Where a party has a right to inspect a document, written notice of his wish to inspect the document must be given by that party to the party who disclosed the document. The latter must permit inspection not more than seven days after the date on which he received notice; and a copy may be requested on undertaking to pay reasonable costs (r 31.15).[2]

---

[1] This concerns the question of privilege. See *Lucas v Barking, Havering and Redbridge NHS Trust* [2003] EWCA 1102; *Jackson v Marley Davenport Ltd* [2004] EWCA Civ 1255 and *Beck v Ministry of Defence* [2004] PIQR 1 re references to earlier reports in expert evidence reports. In *Vasiliou v Hajigeorgiou* [2005] EWCA Civ 236, [2005] 1 WLR 2195 the Court of Appeal held that a judge did not have the power to prevent the claimant from seeking the opinion of more than one expert in relation to the assessment of damages, although if the second expert's report was relied upon, the first expert's report was required to be disclosed as a part of the proceedings. The recent case of *Edwards-Tubb v JD Wetherspoon Plc* [2011] EWCA Civ 136, [2011] 1 WLR 1373 finds that the court has the power to require the disclosure of an expert report even where the claimant has changed expert prior to the issue of proceedings. See also J Payne and C Urquhart (2011) NLJ 461.

[2] For documents referred to in statements of case (r 31.14), see: *Rigg v Associated Newspapers Ltd* [2004] EMLR 4.

10.33 CPR 1998, r 31.16 applies where an application is made to the court under any act for disclosure before proceedings have started.[1] The application must be supported by evidence. Among other factors, the court may make such an order where disclosure before proceedings have started is desirable in order to dispose fairly of the anticipated proceedings; assist the dispute to be resolved without proceedings; or to save costs (r 31.16(3)(d)). Further provision is made concerning specification of documents or classes of documents which must be disclosed and other matters including specifying any of those documents which are no longer under his control or in respect of which he claims a right or duty to withhold inspection. The respondent may be asked what has happened to documents no longer under his control and specify the time and place for disclosure and inspection (r 31.16(4) and (5)).

[1] Senior Courts Act 1981, s 33; County Courts Act 1984, s 52. See *Bermuda International Securities Ltd v KPMG (a firm)* (2001) *Times*, 14 March, CA. Lord Woolf proposed that such disclosure be extended to all cases (see Civil Procedure Act 1997, s 8). See *Black and Others v Sunitomo Corp* [2003] 3 All ER 643 (CA); *Moresfield Ltd v Banners* [2003] EWHC 1602 and *Rose v Lynx Express Ltd and Another* [2004] EWCA Civ 447.

10.34 Rule 31.17 applies where an application is made under any Act for disclosure by a person who is not a party to the proceedings.[1] Once again the application must be supported by evidence. The court may only make an order where the documents of which disclosure is sought are likely to support the case of the applicant or adversely affect the case of one of the other parties to the proceedings; and disclosure is necessary in order to dispose fairly of the claim or to save costs. Further provisions then apply as under r 31.16 (4) and (5).

[1] Senior Courts Act 1981, s 34; County Courts Act 1984, s 53.

10.35 Neither r 31.16 nor r 31.17 limits any other powers a court may possess to order disclosure before proceedings have started and disclosure against a person who is not a party to proceedings.[1]

[1] Under the principles discussed in *Norwich Pharmacal Co v Customs and Excise Comrs* [1974] AC 133, below. See *Carlton Film Distributors Ltd v VCI PLC* [2003] EWHC 616. See also *Mitsui & Co Ltd v Nexen Petroleum UK Ltd* [2005] EWHC 625 (Ch), [2005] 3 All ER 511 and *Eli Lilly & Co Ltd v Neopharma Ltd* [2008] EWHC 415 (Ch), [2008] FSR 25.

10.36 Under r 31.19(1), a person may apply without notice for an order permitting him to withhold disclosure of a document on the ground that disclosure would damage the public interest. This is against disclosure itself it should be noted. Unless the court orders otherwise, an order of the court under para (1) must not be served on any other person and must not be open to inspection by any other person. Where a person wishes to claim that he has a right or a duty to withhold inspection of a document, or part of a document, he must state in writing that he has such a right or duty and the grounds on which he claims that right or duty (r 31.19(3)). By r 31.19(8) this Part does not affect any rule of law which permits or requires a document to be withheld from disclosure or inspection on the ground that its disclosure or inspection would damage the public interest. This is the subject matter known as public interest immunity (see below). This rule sets out the procedure but the substance of the law is as developed by numerous judicial decisions.

10.37 The statement in r 31.19(3) must be made in the list in which the document is disclosed or if there is no list, to the person wishing to inspect the document. A party may apply to the court to decide whether a claim made under para (3) should be upheld. For applications under both paras (1) and (3) above, the court may:

(a) require the person seeking to withhold disclosure or inspection of a document to produce that document to the court; and

(b) invite any person, whether or not a party, to make representations.

10.38 An application under para (1) (withholding disclosure) or para (2) (withholding inspection) must be supported by evidence.

10.39 Where a party inadvertently allows a privileged document to be inspected, the party who has inspected the document may use it or its contents only with permission of the court.[1]

[1] CPR 1998, r 31.20. At common law this has generated a great litany of litigation: see *Calcraft v Guest* [1898] 1 QB 759, CA; *Lord Ashburton v Pape* [1913] 2 Ch 469, CA; *Breeze v J Stacey & Sons Ltd* (1999) *Times*, 6 July, CA; and *Istil Group Inc v Zahoor* [2003] EWHC 165 (Ch), [2003] 2 All ER 252. See para 10.109 below.

10.40 A party may not rely on any document which he fails to disclose or in respect of which he fails to permit inspection unless the court gives permission (r 31.21). This places an enormous emphasis on careful pre-litigation preparation. Rule 31.22 concerns subsequent use of disclosed documents and is examined below. Rule 31.23 allows proceedings for contempt to be brought against a person if he makes, or causes to be made, a false disclosure statement, without an honest belief in its truth. Proceedings may only be brought by the Attorney-General or with the permission of the court.

Strangers to the action

10.41 Vis-à-vis a stranger to the action, disclosure cannot usually be obtained apart from under CPR 1998, r 31.17. If documents or information are required from a stranger, it will usually be necessary to issue a witness summons (subpoena) on that person.[1] There is one important exception apart from the above rule.

[1] *Burstall v Beyfus* (1884) 26 Ch D 35, CA, and paras 10.114 et seq below. On r 31.17, see *Re Howglen Ltd* [2001] 1 All ER 376 and *Three Rivers DC v Bank of England (Disclosure) (No.1)* [2002] EWCA Civ 1182, [2003] 1 WLR 210 where the Court of Appeal found that the meaning of 'likely' r 31.17(3)(a) meant 'may well' and furthermore held that this test must be applied to each individual document, or where documents belonged to a class of documents to each individual class.

10.42 A stranger who, although not personally liable, has either provided facilities for the commission of, or has otherwise become implicated in, a tort, albeit perfectly innocently, may be made a party to an action for disclosure/

discovery only. The defendant's facilitation of the wrong, however, where innocent, will not lead to damages being awarded against the defendant by a successful plaintiff: these s/he will have to recover from the wrongdoer in the subsequent tort action.[1] The House of Lords has confirmed that an intermediary who handed information from a source employed by the claimant but who himself was not a tortfeasor or in breach of legal duties to the claimant is an appropriate person to be subjected to a court order for disclosure and it was not necessary for such an order to be awarded that the claimant wished to dismiss the source. An action in damages against the source was not necessary.[2] Disclosure may also be allowed where required to prevent the dissipation of assets in an action brought to establish ownership of the assets.[3]

[1]   *Norwich Pharmacal Co v Customs and Excise Comrs* [1974] AC 133, HL; *Harrington v North London Polytechnic* [1984] 3 All ER 666, CA; on jurisdictional limits *MacKinnon v Donaldson Lufkin and Jenrette Securities Corpn* [1986] Ch 482; cf *Ricci v Chow* [1987] 3 All ER 534, CA. See *Ashworth Hospital Authority*, para 10.52, note 1 below for an application of *Norwich Pharmacal* to a wrongdoer.

[2]   See *Ashworth Hospital Authority*, para 10.52, note 1 below.

[3]   *Arab Monetary Fund v Hashim (No 5)* [1992] 2 All ER 911; see also *Khanna v Lovell, White, Durant* [1995] 1 WLR 121.

Restrictions on the subsequent use of disclosed documents

10.43   Once documents are disclosed, the party obtaining disclosure may use them only for the purpose of the proceedings in which they are disclosed. There are three exceptions: where the document has been read to or by the court, or referred to, at a hearing which has been held in public; when the court gives permission; or, the party who disclosed the document and the person to whom the document belongs agree (CPR 1998, r 31.22(1)). The court may make an order restricting or prohibiting the use of a document which has been disclosed, even where the document has been read to or by the court, or referred to, at a hearing which has been held in public (r 31.22(2)). An application for an order may be made by a party, or by any person to whom the document belongs.[1]

[1]   Rule 31.22(3): *British Sky Broadcasting Plc v Virgin Media Communications Ltd (formerly NTL Communications Ltd)* [2008] EWCA Civ 612, [2008] 1 W.L.R. 2854; *SmithKline Beecham plc v Generics UK Ltd* [2003] 4 All ER 1302; *Lilly Icos LLC v Pfizer Ltd No 2* [2002] 1 All ER 842. See previous Ord 24, r 14A and *Harman v Secretary of State for the Home Department* [1983] 1 AC 280, HL and the decision in *Smith Kline Beecham Biologicals SA v Connaught Laboratories Inc* [1999] 4 All ER 498, CA for a liberal test of when documents had entered the public domain; and the *Law Debenture Trust Corp v Lexington Ins Co* (2003) New LJ 1551: and note *McCartan Turkington Breen v Times Newspapers Ltd* [2000] 4 All ER 913, HL. See also *Baring plc v Coopers & Lybrand* [2000] 3 All ER 910, CA, and Banking Act 1987, s 82(1) and (2) and *FAI General Insurance Co Ltd v Godfrey Merrett Robertson Ltd* [1999] CLC 566, CA. There have been a number of recent cases which have considered the role of s 348 of the Financial Services and Markets Act 2000 on disclosure. See *Real Estate Opportunities Ltd v Aberdeen Asset Managers Jersey Ltd* [2007] EWCA Civ 197, [2007] Bus LR 971 and, for a broader consideration of the scope of s 348 see *Financial Services Authority v Information Commissioner* [2009] EWHC 1548 (Admin), [2009] Bus LR 1287. For disclosure of unused documents by the prosecution created in the course of a criminal investigation, see: *Taylor v Director of the SFO* [1998] 3 WLR 1040 and *Westcott v Westcott* [2008] EWCA Civ 818, [2009] QB 407. See also *Marlwood Commercial Inc v Kozeny and Others* [2004] EWCA Civ 798, [2005] 1 WLR 104; *Michael Wilson & Partners Ltd v Emmott* [2008] EWCA Civ 184, [2008] Bus LR 1361; and *SITA UK Group Holdings Ltd v Serruys* [2009] EWHC 869 (QB), [2009] STC 1595.

Contempt of Court Act 1981, s 10

10.44 As the procedure outlined above to obtain disclosure from third parties will be used invariably, though not exclusively, to discover the identity of putative wrongdoers, s 10 of the COCA 1981 should be borne in mind:

> 'No court may require a person to disclose, nor is any person guilty of contempt of court for refusing to disclose, the source of information contained in a publication for which he is responsible, unless it be established to the satisfaction of the court that disclosure is necessary in the interests of justice or national security or for the prevention of disorder or crime.'

10.45 This provision replaced an uncertain position catered for by the common law on a case-by-case basis.[1] The immunity is of wide and general applicability and is subject only to the four exceptions, each of which must be established as being 'necessary' – not convenient or expedient. The onus of proof establishing that disclosure is necessary for one of the four exemptions falls on the party making the application and is on the balance of probabilities. Where national security is involved, the court may infer from additional material to the affidavit on application that disclosure is necessary. It did seem that the proprietary claims of the applicant will not, ipso facto, defeat the immunities of a publisher. However, s 10 may be invoked by a publisher where a court order might, not necessarily would, force the disclosure of a source of information to eg a journalist. It was, said the House of Lords, in the interests of justice that persons should be enabled to exercise important legal rights (viz to protect their own confidential information) and to protect themselves from serious wrongs regardless of whether or not resort to legal proceedings in a court of law was necessary to attain those objectives.[2] The serious threat to the claimant's business of publication of confidential information at a time of financial restructuring and the fact that any public interest in protecting the source's identity had been diminished by the source's complicity in a 'gross breach of confidentiality' was not counterbalanced by any public interest in publication of the information. The identity of the leaker was not revealed and Goodwin, the journalist, was fined for contempt. Lord Bridge offered some useful advice on the sorts of considerations that might come into play in deciding whether disclosure was necessary in the interests of justice:

> 'In estimating the importance to be given to the case in favour of disclosure there will be a wide spectrum within which the particular case must be located. If the party seeking disclosure shows, for example, that his very livelihood depends upon it, this will put the case near to one end of the spectrum. If he shows no more than that what he seeks to protect is a minor interest in property, this will put the case at or near the other end. On the other side the importance of protecting a source from disclosure in pursuance of the policy underlying the statute will also vary within a wide spectrum. One important factor will be the nature of information obtained from the source. The greater the legitimate public interest in the information which the source has given to the publisher or intended

publisher, the greater will be the importance of protecting the source. But another and perhaps more significant factor which will very much affect the importance of protecting the source will be the manner in which the information was itself obtained by the source. If it appears to the court that the information was obtained legitimately this will enhance the importance of protecting the source. Conversely, if it appears that the information was obtained illegally, this will diminish the importance of protecting the source unless, of course, this factor is counterbalanced by a clear public interest in publication of the information, as in the classic case where the source has acted for the purpose of exposing iniquity.' (at pp 9–10)

1   *British Steel Corpn v Granada TV* [1981] AC 1096, HL, and see Lord Wilberforce at 1168. Section 10 is primarily concerned with journalists and broadcasters and to a lesser extent authors. Guidance for doctors is given by the GMC in *Good Medical Practice* (2006) and in a booklet on 'Confidentiality' (2009). Accountants have guidelines on breaches of confidence in the *Code of Ethics* Institute of Chartered Accountants in England and Wales; and see Financial Services and Markets Act 2000, ss 342–344. The Institute also publishes specific guidance on information requirements at http://www.icaew.com/en/technical/legal-and-regulatory/information-law-and-guidance. Following *Bolkiah v KPMG* [1999] 2 AC 222, HL, *Tech 4/00* was published advising accountants on 'Conflicts of interest and confidentiality'. In the USA, the Supreme Court has ruled that the First Amendment does not protect reporters from disclosing sources of publications made by them in *Brandzburg v Hayes* 408 U.S. 665 (1972). This was relied upon in the cases involving two reporters who published stories about CIA leaks of operatives' identities and who refused to disclose their sources: the Court of Appeals DC could not 'seriously entertain the notion that the First Amendment protects the newsman's (sic) agreement to conceal the criminal conduct of his source ... on the theory that it is better to write about a crime than to do something about it': *In re: Grand Jury Subpoena, Judith Miller,* 2005 U.S. App. LEXIS 2494 (D.C. Cir.) Feb. 15, 2005).

2   *X Ltd v Morgan Grampian Ltd* [1990] 2 All ER 1, HL. On the application of the principles to website providers, see *Totalise plc v Motley Fool Ltd* (2001) *Times,* 15 March.

10.46   The decision in this case was subsequently criticised by the European Court of Human Rights in *Goodwin v UK*[1] which recognised the 'potentially chilling effect' of an order holding that it could not be compatible with Art 10 of the ECHR unless justified by an overriding requirement in the public interest. By 11 votes to 7 the majority held no such overriding interest to be present in this case. This case must now be considered under the HRA 1998 when the courts are reaching decisions on s 10. The case of *Interbrew SA v Financial Times*[2] was considered by the Court of Appeal in 2002. In this case, the *Financial Times* was sent documents by an anonymous source which contained information prepared for Interbrew on a possible takeover bid for a South African brewing company. Interbrew argued that some of this information had been doctored and incorrect information had been inserted. The *Financial Times* then published information from the report, leading to trading in both Interbrew's shares and those of the alleged target of the bid. Interbrew obtained an order from the High Court requiring the *Financial Times* to retain the document and deliver it up to Interbrew. The *Financial Times* appealed against this order, but the Court of Appeal dismissed the appeal, finding that in this case, even when the Art 10 interest in preserving the confidentiality of journalists' sources was considered, the interests of justice and the public interest demanded that the document should be disclosed. In giving the judgment of the court, Sedley LJ said, 'What in my judgment matters critically, at least in the present situation, is the source's evident purpose. It was on any view a maleficent one, calculated to do harm whether for profit or for spite, and whether to the investing public or Interbrew or both. It is legitimate in reaching this view to have regard not only to what Interbrew assert is the genuine document but also to the interpolated pages; for whether they are forged or authentic, integral or added, they were calculated to maximise the mischief.'[3]

[1] (1996) 22 EHRR 123; see under Art 10 more broadly: *De Haes v Belgium* (1998) 25 EHRR 1, and *Ernst v Belgium* (2004) 39 EHRR 35 on disproportionate searches of journalistic material and also breaches of Art 8 ECHR. The court has emphasised the importance of the free press as a 'public watch-dog': *Observer and Guardian v UK* (1991) 14 EHRR 153 at 191 and *Sunday Times v UK (No 2)* (1991) 14 EHRR 229 at 241. See also *Sunday Times v UK* (1979) 2 EHRR 245 – the thalidomide case.

[2] *Interbrew SA v Financial Times Ltd* [2002] EWCA Civ 274, [2002] 2 Lloyd's Rep 229.

[3] *Interbrew SA v Financial Times Ltd* [2002] EWCA Civ 274, [2002] 2 Lloyd's Rep 229 at [55].

10.47 The *Financial Times* took this case to the ECtHR, which found in favour of the newspaper. In its judgment, the court found that ,'...the aim of preventing further leaks will only justify an order for disclosure of a source in exceptional circumstances where no reasonable and less invasive alternative means of averting the risk posed are available and where the risk threatened is sufficiently serious and defined to render such an order necessary within the meaning of Art 10(2). It is true that in the present case the Court of Appeal found that there were no less invasive alternative means of discovering the source, since Kroll, the security and risk consultants instructed by Interbrew to assist in identifying X, had failed to do so. However, as is apparent from the judgments of the domestic courts, full details of the inquiries made were not given in Interbrew's evidence and the Court of Appeal's conclusion that as much as could at that time be done to trace the source had been done by Kroll was based on inferences from the evidence before the court.'[1] In the eyes of the ECtHR, this approach was clearly unsatisfactory – it appears that the Court of Appeal would have needed to see Kroll's reports in order to determine whether or not all alternative methods of discovering who had leaked the document had been exhausted.

[1] *Financial Times v UK* [2010] EMLR 21 at 69.

10.48 Furthermore, the ECtHR stated that, 'the Court emphasises that a chilling effect will arise wherever journalists are seen to assist in the identification of anonymous sources. In the present case, it was sufficient that information or assistance was required under the disclosure order for the purpose of identifying X.'[1] This approach appears to set an extremely high threshold for the disclosure of journalists sources. It is necessary in cases such as the one before the court for it to be demonstrated that there is no other alternative method for the claimant to discover the identity of the informant and also that the need to avoid a chilling effect on journalism bears significant weight in any balancing process between Art 10(1) and 10(2).

[1] *Financial Times v UK* [2010] EMLR 21 at 70.

10.49 In the *Camelot* case the operator of the national lottery wished to gain orders leading to the identity of an employee who had disclosed confidential documents (draft accounts) to a journalist. Their concern was that an employee with access to high level information might leak information in the future, including, speculatively, a lottery winner wishing to remain anonymous.[1] The Court of Appeal felt that the tests applied by the domestic courts in relation to COCA 1981, s 10 and the ECtHR regarding Art 10 ECHR were essentially the same. This may now be in question following the decision of the ECtHR in *Interbrew*, discussed above. The difference was one of conclusion in applying essentially similar principles to facts. There was no iniquity involved which required exposure, no whistleblower's rights, merely the diminution of an opportunity to put a 'spin' on accounts. Preventing a distortion was not sufficiently important to protect the source's identity and defeat the claimant's rights. The public, Schiemann LJ, believed would be denied no valuable public interest on the facts of the case. 'The well informed source is always going to have to take a view as to what is going to be the court's reaction to his disclosure in the circumstances of the case.'[2] Subsequently, the Court of Appeal has ruled that where there was a breach of confidence by a source and an intention to harm a claimant, the award of a s 10 order was justified.[3]

[1] *Camelot Group plc v Centaur Communications Ltd* [1998] 1 All ER 251, CA.
[2] [1998] 1 All ER 251 at 261j.
[3] *Interbrew SA v Financial Times* [2002] EWCA Civ 274.

10.50   In *Saunders*,[1] the High Court refused to order the disclosure of a source's identity after the publication of an article in *Punch* which contained details about delays of an investigation into the claimant by the DTI and meetings between the claimant and his lawyers. An injunction restraining further publication had dealt with the risk of further publication of the information in question. Suffering substantial further damage by the claimant was unlikely if the order was not made and there was a public interest in the subject matter of the article. The application was dismissed.[2] The court was not persuaded by arguments that s 10 was automatically overridden by legal professional privilege (LPP). While important, LPP must enter into the scales of competing interests and not override them. A further factor to consider in deciding whether to order a disclosure is whether the plaintiff has sought by other legitimate means to identify the source. If not this could be pivotal.

[1] *Saunders v Punch Ltd* [1998] 1 All ER 234.
[2] See *Chief Constable of Leicestershire Constabulary v Garavelli* [1997] EMLR 543.

10.51   In a Court of Appeal judgment[1] following after *Goodwin*, the spirit of the European Court of Human Rights (ECtHR's) judgment in *Goodwin* was clearly supported. Here, a draft advice from a barrister left overnight in chambers and which concerned a well known entertainer was handed to a newspaper which destroyed the advice and notified the plaintiff's solicitors. The claimant sought an order for disclosure of the source. The High Court made such an order under s 10. The Court of Appeal was persuaded by the fact that no internal enquiry had been conducted by the chambers into the likely identity of the source, that any threat to LPP could not automatically overrule the privilege, that ordering the disclosure of the identity by a journalist might not be successful and therefore the damage to the public interest in not maintaining the source's confidentiality would not bring any compensating benefit to LPP. In giving too much weight to LPP, and in giving insufficient consideration to the failure to conduct an internal enquiry the judge failed to establish that disclosure was *necessary* in the interests of justice and 'even if it had been, the judge should have exercised his discretion to refuse disclosure. 'When orders were made requiring journalists to depart from their normal professional standards, the merits of their doing so in the public interest had to be clearly demonstrated. In the instant case there would be a real danger that that would not be the position if the judge's order were allowed to stand. His decision would wrongly be interpreted as an example of lawyers attaching a disproportionate significance to the danger to their professional privilege while undervaluing the interests of journalists and the public.'[2]

[1]   *John v Express Newspapers plc* [2000] 3 All ER 257, CA.
[2]   At 265g–p, 266c, f. For the public interest defence under Copyright, Designs and Patents Act 1988, s 171(3), *see PCR Ltd v Dow Jones Telerate Ltd* [1998] FSR 170; in *Hyde Park Residence Ltd v Yelland* [2001] Ch 143, CA, it was held that the defence is not the same as that applied in breach of confidence; see paras 2.294 et seq above.

10.52   The House of Lords has confirmed that both s 10 and Art 10 ECHR required the domestic court stringently to scrutinise any request for relief that would result in the court interfering with freedom of expression, including the ordering of a journalist's sources. Before disclosure would be ordered, a 'sufficiently strong case' had to be made for disclosure and the order had to meet a pressing social need and be proportionate to legitimate ends being sought. The situation had to be 'exceptional' for disclosure to be allowed. The facts of the case were exceptional because a employee at a NHS special security hospital was disclosing confidential information from a patient's medical records to an intermediary who handed them to the defendant newspaper for publication. Action was necessary to prevent a repetition. The newspaper was ordered to reveal the identity of the intermediary who handed it the information.[1]

[1]   *Ashworth Hospital Authority v MGN Ltd* [2002] 4 All ER 193 (HL). The patient was Ian Brady and concerned his hunger strike. See *Mersey Care NHS Trust v Ackroyd* [2003] EMLR 36 (CA) – disclosure of the source by the intermediary in *Ashworth* should not be ordered on a summary order but should go for a full trial to test any public interest defence. See further *Mersey Care NHS Trust v Ackroyd* [2006] EWHC 107 where the High Court refused to order disclosure giving great effect to the HRA 1998 and Art 10 rights and the lapse of seven years. Upheld on appeal at [2007] EWCA Civ 101.

10.53   It is notable that recent celebrity scandals, in relation to super-injunctions (on which, see para 7.203 et seq) have led to some debate over whether s 10 of COCA 1981 may be used in order to protect those who disclose otherwise confidential information using social networking sites or who have provided information resulting from the interception of communications. There does not yet appear to be any litigation on this precise point. There has, however, been litigation on the broader issue of the obligations of website operators to disclose the identities of their users in circumstances where such users have posted defamatory statements. The case of *Totalise Plc v Motley Fool*[1] considered the circumstances in which such an identity could be revealed. Later cases have also examined the circumstances in which the disclosure of identities of users could be released, finding that orders might only be granted in circumstances where the parties concerned have clearly committed actionable wrongs.[2] In the later case of *G v Wikimedia Foundation*,[3] the court was willing to grant an order requiring the operator of a website to disclose the IP address of an individual who had revealed sensitive and personal information about G and her children in order that an appropriate remedy might be sought against the individual concerned. The circumstances surrounding Ryan Giggs' recent endeavours to ensure that elements of his personal life were not revealed were ultimately fatally undermined by users of Twitter and other social networking sites. Some blogs also published details of his identity during the time in which the injunction that was granted to him was in force. It seems likely that the individuals who posted these messages could be pursued by Mr. Giggs and actions could be brought against the operators of the networks and websites concerned in order that the identities of wrongdoers might be revealed, although this is heavily complicated by the fact that Twitter is a company based in the US and there would be issues in relation to the conflict of laws. We are not aware of any litigation to that effect at the present time.

[1]   [2001] EWCA Civ 1897, [2002] 1 WLR 1233.
[2]   *Sheffield Wednesday Football Club Ltd* v *Hargreaves* [2007] EWHC 2375 (QB). See also Clift v Clarke [2011] EWHC 1164 (QB), where the court refused to order the disclosure of information about two users of a website who had posted comments that were arguably defamatory of the claimant as a year had passed before the claimant had discovered the comments and the comments concerned were perhaps unlikely to be found to be defamatory if any proceedings were brought. As such, the court found that the users' ECHR Art 8 rights and the website's privacy policy outweighed the arguments in favour of disclosure.
[3]   [2009] EWHC 3148 (QB), [2010] EMLR 14. See also *Goldsmith v BCD* [2011] EWHC 674 (QB) where a third-party disclosure order was awarded in order to require the disclosure of information about the hacker of email accounts in a breach of confidence case.

10.54   As far as we are aware, there has not yet been any reported litigation on the application of COCA 1981, s 10 to comments posted on Twitter or blogs. This issue is complicated in the sense that it is possible that the operator of a particular website (eg Twitter) may wish to have recourse to s 10 in order to avoid disclosing the identities of its users. It is also possible that authors of blogs may wish to have recourse to s 10 in order to protect their sources. As we observed above, the protection in s 10 is not reserved exclusively for journalists, so bloggers could have recourse to the section. The test for public interest contained in s 10 will need to be considered carefully in any such cases – it is clear that the courts have now adopted a position where they are more willing to protect the private lives of celebrities and others in the public eye, but this will need to balanced against the public interest in freedom of expression. It is possible to argue that the courts might be willing to place significant weight on the need to ensure the viability of the injunction as a means to restrain publication in these cases and might therefore be relatively willing to find that there is a public interest in disclosure. It seems likely that in due course there will be litigation on this issue, which may ultimately find its way to Strasbourg.

10.55   For the 'prevention of crime', the prevention of crime in general rather than a specific crime would satisfy the making of an order defeating the immunity.[1] 'In the interests of justice' would not be satisfied by a speculative legal claim or right; a court would have to identify and define the issue for which disclosure was required and then to decide whether, having regard to the nature of the issue and the circumstances of the case, it was in fact necessary to order disclosure.[2] Under s 2(1) of the COCA 1981, 'publication' includes any speech, writing, broadcast or other communication in whatever form, which is addressed to the public, and has been interpreted to include an act of publication preparatory to 'publication'.[3]

[1]   *Re an Inquiry under the Company Securities (Insider Dealing) Act 1985* [1988] 1 All ER 203, HL; however, a plaintiff would have to establish that they were actually seeking identification for the prevention of crime: *X v Y* [1988] 2 All ER 648.
[2]   In *X Ltd*, Lord Bridge disagreed with the view adopted by Lord Diplock in *Guardian Newspapers* above that in the interests of justice meant the administration of justice. This was 'too narrow'.
[3]   And see Broadcasting Act 1990, s 201.

10.56   Relevant provisions also apply under the Prevention of Terrorism legislation. In the *Channel Four Television* litigation, the TV company broadcast a programme made by a production company which alleged there was widespread and systematic collusion between Loyalist terrorists and members of the Royal Ulster Constabulary. This it was alleged had led to at least 20 sectarian murders in Northern Ireland. A source 'A' had revealed crucial information to a researcher for the programme and both the TV company and the production company had given a specific undertaking not to reveal their identity. The researcher sent sensitive information out of the jurisdiction and also left the jurisdiction.

10.57   After the programme was broadcast, a special branch officer in the Metropolitan Police applied to the Crown Court for an order under Sch 7 to the Prevention of Terrorism Act 1989 to produce documents relating to the programme. The order was made along with a subsequent order to produce to the police the material sent out of the jurisdiction. The companies refused to follow the order because of their undertaking and because they feared for the lives of the source and the researcher. The companies were the subject of a contempt order sought by the DPP. The Divisional Court was very critical of the companies for refusing to produce the information although it accepted that the companies were acting under what they believed were genuine motives. They were not in a position to give a totally unqualified undertaking which would have to give way to a court order. They were fined £75,000 and could have faced imprisonment.[1] Readers should recall the discussion of the PIDA 1998 (paras 2.270 et seq above).

[1]   *DPP v Channel Four Television Co Ltd* [1993] 2 All ER 517. See the Saville inquiry in Northern Ireland: para 2.5, note 3 above.

10.58   The later case of *Malik v Manchester Crown Court*[1] concerned a journalist who was writing a book about a man who had admitted that he was involved with a proscribed organisation in the past and who also admitted to Malik that he had been involved in terrorism-related offences. The police sought disclosure of Malik's sources and materials related to his book under the Terrorism Act 2000, Sch 5. An order was granted by a judge in broad terms, requiring the disclosure of Malik's souces and other information that the police sought. The divisional court found that in order for disclosure to be ordered, the test in Sch 5, para 6(2)(b) must be given its plain meaning. The paragraph requires the police to demonstrate that such disclosure would have substantial value to a terrorist investigation. It was held that the value must be more than a minimal value in order to qualify for an order to be made. The divisional court ultimately found that on the facts, the judge was entitled to make an order for disclosure and that this was not a disproportionate interference with Malik's Art 10 rights given the public interest in the successful investigation of terrorism. The order was, however, varied. The reason for this is that the wording of the crown court judge's order was such that it could be construed in a manner which would require Malik to produce information beyond that which related to the individual at the centre of his book. The court found that this order was too wide and moved to limit the order to information about the book's subject and one of his friends, but not information about others.

¹   [2008] EWHC 1362 (Admin), [2008] 4 All ER 403.

DISCLOSURE AND JUDICIAL REVIEW

10.59 Judicial review and its impact on fair decision-making were examined in ch 9. In judicial review proceedings disclosure, along with interrogatories (requests for information) and other interim relief, may be obtained, but it is not automatic. Part 54 of the CPR 1998 has the effect that disclosure is not required unless the court orders otherwise. Part 54 establishes the Administrative Court in London and Cardiff. The Practice Direction of 27 July 2000 stated that the new procedures were to come into effect on 2 October 2000 – the same day as the HRA 1998 came into effect. A lead nominated judge would have overall responsibility for the speed, economy and efficiency of the court's work (see Practice Direction [2004] 1 All ER 322).

10.60 Discovery – and cross-examination – was obtainable on judicial review under the former Ord 24, r 3, although the courts intimated that it should be used 'sparingly' if judicial review procedure is to be a success.¹ Part 54 is silent as to cross-examination. Nothing in the CPR 1998 prevents the court on a judicial review application under either r.32.1 or the court's inherent jurisdiction from hearing oral evidence or allowing cross-examination.² In some cases it has been ruled that cross-examination may be essential.³

¹   See eg *IRC v Rossminster Ltd* [1980] 1 All ER 80 at 105g per Lord Scarman; *Ladha v Secretary of State for the Home Department* [1988] Imm AR 284, CA; and *R v Secretary of State for Education and Science, ex p G* (1989) *Times*, 7 July.
²   *R (G) v Ealing LBC* (2002) *Times*, 18 March.
³   *R (Wilkinson) v Broadmoor Special Hospital Authority* [2002] 1 WLR 419 with emphatic statements on the court's ability to examine the merits of a medical decision to administer medical treatment without a patient's consent and whether this breached a claimant's human rights.

10.61 The courts have held that, upon judicial review, disclosure will be appropriate in fewer cases and is likely to be more circumscribed.¹ In judicial review the onus of proof falls on the applicant for review to make out a case for review. The court will therefore refuse discovery to fill gaps in the evidence of the applicant simply to make good the applicant's case.[2] They will not assist an applicant who lacks evidence and the courts have gone so far as to say that disclosure will only be allowed where something is revealed on the record or in an affidavit (sworn statement of truth) which suggests inaccuracy or evokes suspicion. For some years courts have encouraged parties to file affidavits which disclose what is necessary.[3] The Court of Appeal has been reluctant to allow discovery of reports referred to in affidavits because under the supervisory nature of judicial review 'what was under consideration was the decision making process, not the contents of documents considered by the decision maker or his or her state of mind'.[4] Further, where no fault or flaw can be shown in the respondent's decision-making process so that it does not appear unreasonable or defective, the court is unlikely to allow discovery and inspection of the respondent's documents to see whether a vitiating factor can be ascertained.[5] An applicant must show that reports are central and relevant to the applicant's application. The case of *Tweed*[6] demonstrates some of the challenges that might be posed in cases concerning alleged infringements of the HRA 1998 or infringements of the proportionality principle in human rights cases. In this case, the organiser of an Orange Order parade claimed that the restriction of the parade was a disproportionate interference with rights under ECHR Arts 9, 10 and 11. Tweed sought disclosure of a number of documents from the Parades Commission, arguing that these were required in order to construct a case on the issue of proportionality, as without the documents it was difficult to demonstrate the lack of proportionality in the case. The House of Lords held that the court may need to be more willing to order disclosure in proportionality cases, although in ordering such disclosure the judge must be cautious to examine the full text of each document to determine whether the need for disclosure outweighed the usual presumption against it. Where disclosure was being considered, the issue of redaction should also be considered. Lord Carswell said, 'The proportionality issue forms part of the context in which the court has to consider whether it is necessary for fairly disposing of the case to order disclosure of such documents. It does not give rise automatically to the need for disclosure of all the documents. Whether disclosure should be ordered will depend on a balancing of the several factors, of which proportionality is only one, albeit one of some significance.'[7] Medical reports may not be withheld from a prisoner, whose recommendation for release on parole had been refused by the Secretary of State, on grounds of privilege alone, but they may be withheld on medical grounds.[8]

[1] *R v Secretary of State for the Home Department, ex p Harrison* (1987) *Independent*, 21 December, CA. See also the comments of Lord Bingham in *Tweed v Parades Commission for Northern Ireland* [2006] UKHL 53, [2007] 1 AC 650, at [3] – disclosure in judicial review cases is the exception rather than the norm as the facts should generally be agreed between the parties.

[2] *R v Secretary of State for the Home Department, ex p Singh* (1988) *Times*, 28 March, CA. See *R v Secretary of State for the Environment, ex p Merton London Borough Council* (1990) *Times*, 22 March.

[3] *R v Lancashire County Council, ex p Huddleston* [1986] 2 All ER 941 at 945, CA. See Carnwath LJ in *OFT v IBA Healthcare* [2004] 4 All ER 1103 at 1134 et seq on the adequacy of reasons.

[4] Woolf, Jowell and Le Sueur *Judicial Review of Administrative Action* (6th edn, 2007) para 16.065; *R v Secretary of State for the Home Department, ex p BH* [1990] COD 445; *R v Secretary of State for the Environment, ex p Islington London Borough Council* [1992] COD 67, CA; *R v Secretary of*

State for Education, ex p J [1993] COD 146; and see *R v Secretary of State for Defence, ex p Sancto* (1992) *Times*, 9 September; *R v Secretary of State for Foreign and Commonwealth Affairs, ex p World Development Movement Ltd* [1995] 1 WLR 386; *R v Independent Television Commission, ex p Virgin TV* [1996] EMLR 318 – the 'pick out a plum' school of advocacy is particularly dangerous (as well as being futile) in judicial review cases where, as here, there is neither full discovery nor cross-examination, nor the full rigour of pleadings ...' per Henry LJ; for new evidence to be viewed by a court which was not before the court below, see: *R v Chief Constable of Sussex, ex p International Trader's Ferry Ltd* [1998] QB 477, CA.

5   *R v IRC, ex p Taylor* [1989] 1 All ER 906, CA; *R v Secretary of State for the Environment, ex p Merton London Borough Council* (1990) Times, 22 March.
6   *Tweed v Parades Commission for Northern Ireland* [2006] UKHL 53, [2007] 1 AC 650.
7   *Tweed v Parades Commission for Northern Ireland* [2006] UKHL 53, [2007] 1 AC 650 at [38].
8   *R v Secretary of State for the Home Department, ex p Benson* (1988) *Times*, 8 November. See however, *R v Secretary of State for the Home Department, ex p Duggan* [1994] 3 All ER 277 and *R v Governor of Maidstone Prison, ex p Peries* [1998] COD 150.

10.62 In his Review of the Crown Office List in March 2000, Sir Jeffery Bowman recommended that neither the new procedure 'A' requiring permission to proceed nor procedure 'B' which does not require permission should attract the general power of discovery.[1] Disclosure should only take place under the direction of the judge and should only be ordered where and to the extent that it is necessary to dispose fairly of the case. 'This means that application of CPR 1998, Part 31 should be expressly limited to r 31.12 (specific disclosure or inspection).' His review accepted that such orders for discovery (sic) may well be required more frequently under HRA 1998 litigation'.[2] Claimants would serve a detailed statement in support of their case. The claim form would contain all the information currently contained on Form 86A which accompanies judicial review.[3] If the defendant intends to defend the case he must set out an outline of the grounds for defence.

1   Rule 54.4 states that permission is required for judicial review whether under this Part or transferred to the Administrative Court.
2   Bowman *Review of the Crown Office List* March 2000 (LCD), para 69.
3   See p 69 of Bowman for details of what this must contain.

10.63 The details on the latter are now contained in the Pre-action Protocol for Judicial Review.[1] The protocol requires a letter before claims to be sent prior to commencement of proceedings, usually in accordance with and containing the details required in Annex A of the Protocol. This does not affect the time limits for judicial review (three months and extendable).[2] The letter must set out important items of information. These include any relevant information that the claimant is seeking, subject to any immunities and privileges. The public authority has fourteen days to respond which may be extended. The response may contain a 'fuller explanation' and any relevant documents. The response will also state whether interim relief is being opposed and other matters. Letters are not appropriate in cases of urgency or where the defendant lacks the power to alter a decision, such as in the case of the Immigration Appeal Tribunal.

1   Available at http://www.justice.gov.uk/guidance/courts-and-tribunals/courts/procedure-rules/civil/contents/protocols/prot_jrv.htm.
2   See Wade and Forsyth *Administrative Law* (10th edn, 2009), pp 561–562 or Fordham *Judicial Review Handbook* (5th edn, 2008), p 26.

PUBLIC INTEREST IMMUNITY

10.64   CPR 1998, r 31.19(1) allows a claim to withhold disclosure or inspection on grounds of the public interest. Rule 31.19(8) does not affect any rule of law which permits or requires a document to be withheld from disclosure or inspection on the ground that its disclosure or inspection would damage the public interest. This is otherwise known as public interest immunity (PII).[1] It is not confined to cases involving Crown or public bodies, though it almost invariably will involve such bodies. A voluntary body, and therefore in law a private body, has successfully entered the plea.[2] A local authority may enter the plea, but the 'confidential' nature of local authority records per se[3] as a ground of non-disclosure is unlikely to be successful where they are required so that justice may be done.[4] There must be an additional public interest in non-disclosure.[5]

[1]   Previously called Crown Privilege; see: *Conway v Rimmer* [1968] AC 910.
[2]   *D v NSPCC* [1977] 1 All ER 589, HL. For a recent example of a claim involving PII in relation to a private body see *Shah v HSBC Private Bank (UK) Ltd* [2011] EWHC 1713 (QB). This case is subject of an appeal which will be heard by the Court of Appeal in due course.
[3]   *Gaskin v Liverpool City Council* [1980] 1 WLR 1549.
[4]   *Thompson v ILEA* [1977] LS Gaz R 66. Cf the LGATIA 1985.
[5]   To protect the vulnerability of the young etc, cf *Campbell v Tameside Metropolitan Borough Council* [1982] 1 QB 1065; see *Re M and N*, para 10.6, note 1 above.

10.65   The rationale for the rule is the overriding need to protect certain kinds of information from dissemination in the process of litigation. The plea will be successful where serious injury would be perpetrated to the processes of government and public service were discovery to be allowed. Confidentiality alone is not a sufficient basis for allowing the plea but it may be 'a very material consideration to bear in mind' when the immunity is claimed;[1] a public interest would have to be involved over and above the requirements of keeping a confidence, eg the confidentiality is necessary to make sure that the information or similar information is forthcoming from the public or informers and is reliable.

[1]   *Alfred Crompton Amusement Machines v Customs and Excise Comrs (No 2)* [1974] AC 405 per Lord Cross; see *Barrett v Ministry of Defence* (1990) *Times*, 24 January.

10.66   Until the aftermath of the notorious events surrounding the *Matrix Churchill* episode, which were enquired into and reported upon by Sir Richard Scott, and which arose partly because of the use of public interest immunity certificates in a criminal trial arising from the export of dual use equipment to Iraq,[1] objection may have been made to disclosure in relation to the specific contents of the documents – a contents basis – or on what is known as a class basis, ie that the documents belong to a class of documents which ought not, in the public interest, to be disclosed. The class to which the documents belonged had to be specified.[2] In December 1996, the government announced that as far as it was concerned, claims based on a class basis would no longer be made. Claims to immunity would be restricted to their contents alone.[3] These statements would not cover the police or local authorities and decisions of the courts have protected police information on a class basis (see below). While local authorities are unlikely to require protection on the basis of national security[4] and neither is likely to seek protection on the grounds of foreign affairs or to protect the inner workings of government, the police may well seek to protect information on a class basis. Surely the time has arrived when claims can only be made on a contents basis. The statement would be binding on prosecuting authorities who are Crown bodies.

1   HC 115 (1995–96).
2   *Re Grosvenor Hotel London* [1964] 1 All ER 92, CA; *Merricks v Nott-Bower* [1965] 1 QB 57, CA.
3   287 HC Official Report (6th series), col 949; 576 HL Official Report (5th series), col 1507 (18 December 1996) and 297 HC Official Report (6th series), col 616 (11 July 1997) by incoming Labour government.
4   The police may well wish to resort to national security although national security is the responsibility of the national executive: Lord Diplock in *CCSU v Minister for the Civil Service* [1985] AC 374 at 412. Security officials giving evidence to the Scott inquiry stated they did not need a class basis of protection and had been adequately served by a contents protection: Scott Report op cit, G18-39, G18-102. The Attorney General would act for the intelligence services and would be bound by the statement made in Parliament: he made it!

10.67   Where the plea for public interest immunity is made, and it should only be made if the public interest in preserving the immunity of the documents outweighs the public interest in securing justice, the court has to balance the public interest in non-disclosure against the countervailing public interest of doing justice in litigation. The burden is on the applicant for disclosure once there are justifiable grounds for raising the immunity.[1] The courts have held as protected by the immunity documents in the policy-making process of government.[2] These clearly would no longer be protected on a class basis (see above). Even before the change of practice announced in Parliament, decisions of the courts had found the relevance and the necessity of the documents to advance the cause of justice to be more persuasive factors, even though the documents are within the policy-making[3] process of central government, providing they were not requested for 'fishing' or ulterior purposes or to mount an attack on the policy-making process itself. This proviso applies where such an attack is unrelated, or only tangentially related to the action or application for review.[4] Judges have spoken at the highest level of the availability of even Cabinet documents where necessary and appropriate.[5]

1   *Air Canada v Secretary of State for Trade (No 2)* [1983] 2 AC 394, HL; Lord Wilberforce in *Burmah Oil Co Ltd v Bank of England* [1980] AC 1090, HL.
2   *Conway v Rimmer* [1968] AC 910, HL, esp Lord Reid.
3   Especially advice from civil servants: cf *Williams v Home Office* [1981] 1 All ER 1151.
4   See *Air Canada* above.
5   See Lord Fraser in *Air Canada* at 915 (Cabinet minutes and documents) citing US, Australian and New Zealand authorities; Lord Scarman in *Burmah Oil* (note 1 above).

10.68   The rule allows for an immunity of documents from disclosure or inspection. Objection may be made on the grounds of public interest immunity either when disclosure or inspection of documents is made or requested, or possibly at the judicial proceedings (trial or application for review) when production is called for. These matters should be resolved before the hearing. An application not to disclose is made to the court without notice to the other side and any such order awarded is not shown to the other side or otherwise made publicly available.[1] An objection to inspection must be made in writing stating the grounds on which the claim is made. Before trial the decision to object should normally[2] be taken by the political head of the department in question. The Minister shall examine the documents and decide whether production would be against the public interest on a contents basis. However, even if no claim is entered, the judge may nevertheless rule the documents immune on public interest grounds on the judge's own motion. It is a public interest, and not a Crown or governmental interest, which is at stake.[3]

[1] Viz, CPR r 31.19(1) and (2).
[2] Or permanent heads where appropriate, eg where the papers requested belong to a previous administration.
[3] See *D v NSPCC*, para 10.64, note 2 above.

10.69 Quite what the duty of the Minister is was a central feature of the *Matrix Churchill* and Sir Richard Scott's Report and about which there was a notable division of opinion among senior judges speaking extra-judicially. Where documents require protection because of their contents, it is the duty of the Minister to make out a certificate. However, as was made clear in the decision in *Duncan v Cammell Laird & Co*[1] the duty is upon the Minister which he must exercise with all due discretion and judgement. In Matrix Churchill, Ministers took advice from the Attorney-General that they were under a duty to enter certificates, most of which the court overrode, as leaving them with no choice in the matter. They were merely a rubber stamp for the Attorney-General. The Minister must apply his mind to the contents of documents and whether disclosure and inspection will or could undermine the public interest. He is under a duty to assist the court in making its judgment on where the public interest resides and he can only do this properly by exercising his own judgement having considered advice. He must not allow another to make judgement for him. Some dicta of Bingham LJ were taken out of context and invoked by supporters of the Attorney-General's advice that a Minister had no discretion in entering the plea.[2] Where a Minister genuinely believes that the plea should be entered on cogent grounds then he is under a duty to do so. But his decision must be properly made after careful consideration: 'A rubber stamp approach to public interest immunity by the holder of a document is neither necessary nor appropriate'.[3] This was the view of Sir Richard Scott in his report and is, with respect, to be preferred. In the recent case of *Mohamed*,[4] which concerned the question of whether seven paragraphs from a judgment of the Divisional Court should be redacted from the open judgment. These paragraphs concerned summaries of reports made by the US Government and passed to the security services in the United Kingdom concerning Mohamed's treatment while he was prisoner in Pakistan. The Foreign Secretary had claimed PII in the reports and also in the paragraphs from the final judgment. Lord Judge CJ emphasised the importance of open justice and its link to freedom of expression, noting that the principle of open judgments should only be subject to limitation in extremely limited circumstances. However, it was accepted that in a case such as this, where the Foreign Secretary was concerned that any disclosure of the material in the US reports may impinge on the supply of future information from the US, there should generally be deference to the view of the Secretary of State. Lord Judge CJ said: 'If for any reason the court is required to address the question whether the control principle, as understood by the intelligence services, should be disapplied, the decision depends on well understood PII principles. As the executive, not the judiciary, is responsible for national security and public protection and safety from terrorist activity, the judiciary defers to it on these issues, unless it is acting unlawfully, or in the context of litigation the court concludes that the claim by the executive for public interest immunity is not justified. Self-evidently that is not a decision to be taken lightly...It is nevertheless accepted by and on behalf of the Foreign Secretary in this litigation that in our country, which is governed by the rule of law, upheld by an independent judiciary, the confidentiality principle is indeed subject to the clear limitation that the Government and the intelligence services can never provide the country which provides intelligence with an unconditional guarantee that the confidentiality principle will never be set aside if the courts conclude that the interests of justice make it necessary and appropriate to do so...However, although in the context of public safety it is axiomatic that his views are entitled to the utmost respect, they cannot command the unquestioning acquiescence of the court.'[5]

[1]   [1942] AC 624, HL.
[2]   *Makanjuola v of Metropolitan Police Comr* [1992] 3 All ER 617, CA.
[3]   Lord Templeman in *R v Chief Constable of the West Midlands Police, ex p Wiley* [1995] 1 AC 274 at 281, HL.
[4]   *R (Mohamed) v Secretary of State for Foreign and Commonwealth Affairs (No 2)* [2010] EWCA 65, [2010] EWCA Civ 158, [2010] 3 WLR 554.
[5]   Ibid at [44] and [46].

10.70   Ultimately, the Court of Appeal held that the paragraphs ought not to be redacted from the judgment and it should be published in full. Primarily, this is because the Secretary of State's claim that the material that PII should be retained in the material as it was confidential no longer held good. A court in the US had found Mr. Mohamed's claim that he had been mistreated in custody to be true and the court had divulged at least some of the information contained in the redacted paragraphs in its judgment. This, in the opinion of the court, resulted in the Foreign Secretary's claim no longer being justified and the public interest in publication outweighed the arguments in favour of PII in the circumstances. It is clear in cases such as this that the court is willing to place the arguments in favour of retaining PII under considerable scrutiny.

10.71   Where a judge entertains doubts about the bona fides, plausibility or clarity of the reasons behind an objection in a ministerial certificate, s/he may inspect the documents and ought invariably to do so before allowing disclosure or inspection overriding a ministerial certificate. Judicial inspection will therefore precede inspection by the party making the application for inspection; in the event of an appeal by the Minister the inspection by the applicant will be deferred until the outcome of the appeal. To clarify an objection a Minister may be called to court,[1] and the same principles discussed above apply to the exclusion of oral or of documentary evidence.[2] If a court decides that public interest immunity obtains in relation to documents, the immunity still applies even though they have passed into the possession of another person.[3] There must be limits to this immunity where the documents are in the public domain.[4] It has been held that even though documents are not disclosed, parties may still deny the nature of the contents or their accuracy where these are known to the other party[5] but this would seem to run counter to the advice of Lord Woolf in *ex p Wiley* (see below).

1   *Re Grosvenor Hotel London* [1964] Ch 464, CA on whether the minister can be cross-examined; cf *Chandler v DPP* [1964] AC 763, HL.
2   *Duncan v Cammell Laird* [1942] AC 624, HL; and see *Gain v Gain* [1961] 1 WLR 1469.
3   Cf OSAs and prosecution: paras 2.212 et seq above.
4   On this issue see *R (Al-Sweady) v Secretary of State for Defence* [2009] EWHC 1687. See also *Mohamed*, discussed above paras 10.69 and 10.70.
5   *Sethia v Stern* (1987) *Times*, 4 November, CA.

10.72   That this is an area of law subject to extensive development is well illustrated by the case-law covering police investigations. When the police carried out an investigation into a complaint under s 49 of the Police Act 1964 (and the Police and Criminal Evidence Act 1984 and successor legislation),[1] statements made in the course of such an investigation to the investigators were protected by public interest immunity on a class basis,[2] even as against the person making the statement.[3] The recipient of such a statement, eg the chief police officer of the force whose officer(s) is being investigated, could not waive the immunity as it was a public interest immunity, not a police immunity.[4] Although the immunity covered all oral and written statements in the course of the investigation, and those handed to the Police Complaints Authority, it did not cover the original complaint made to the police[5] which may therefore be actionable for defamation. Where the major or dominant reason for conducting an investigation was not a private inquiry into police conduct but to ascertain the facts behind an episode, viz an unlawful death, and such statements would be available to the coroner, public interest immunity would not protect the documents on a class basis, but it may on a specific contents basis.[6] The immunity did not apply to documents relating to police officers' internal grievance procedures.[7] In *R v Chief Constable of the West Midlands Police, ex p Wiley*[8] the House of Lords overruled the Court of Appeal decisions which had protected statements made in complaints investigations on a class basis. Arguments that this would inhibit witnesses were not self-evident. They could attract protection on a contents basis. Lord Slynn agreed that a general class protection was too sweeping and the cases providing such should be overruled but he felt that a class claim could sometimes be required. Subsequently, the Court of Appeal held that there was a class protection for an immunity in relation to an investigating officer's report and working papers. This class protection could only be outweighed by a countervailing public interest in disclosure determined by the trial judge.[9] Where an immunity is claimed successfully, the parties and the court should try to give what information is necessary in a manner that would not compromise any immunity.[10] However, if inspection is not allowed, the evidence itself must be excluded.[11]

1   In response eg to a complaint from a member of the public.
2   *Neilson v Laugharne* [1981] QB 736, CA.
3   *Makanjuola v Metropolitan Police Comr* [1992] 3 All ER 617, CA.
4   Above and *Hehir v Metropolitan Police Comr* [1982] 2 All ER 335, CA. See *ex p Coventry Newspapers Ltd* [1993] QB 278, CA.
5   *Conerney v Jacklin* (1985) 129 Sol Jo 285, CA. NB *R v Metropolitan Police Comr, ex p Hart-Leverton* (1990) *Guardian*, 6 February.

⁶ *Peach v Metropolitan Police Comr* [1986] 2 All ER 129, CA; inspection allowed.
⁷ *Metropolitan Police Comr v Locker* [1993] 3 All ER 584, EAT.
⁸ [1995] 1 AC 274, HL.
⁹ *Taylor v Anderton (Police Complaints Authority intervening)* [1995] 2 All ER 420, CA.
¹⁰ Lord Woolf in *Wiley*.
¹¹ *Powell v Chief Constable of North Wales Constabulary* (2000) *Times*, 11 February, CA.

10.73 Communications between a chief constable and the DPP concerning written statements and officers' reports and a request for advice on prosecution relating to an accused have been held to be within public interest immunity.[1] Initial reports into an investigation which were sent to the Crown Prosecution Service were within the class immunity and subject to the balancing test.[2] Further, certificates of previous findings of guilt on adjudications before police disciplinary proceedings arising out of the arrest of an applicant for discovery have not been disclosed.[3] Discovery (disclosure) would be 'oppressive' as material obtained would be used solely for cross-examination of a witness to attack the witness's credibility and similar fact evidence from the prior proceedings[4] and their determinations would only reveal 'a disposition to commit the conduct alleged' (assault, unlawful arrest, malicious prosecution) and was not required to rebut a defence of accident or coincidence or to prove a system of conduct. Records of disciplinary proceedings were outside s 11 of the Civil Evidence Act 1968 and would therefore be probative of nothing.[5] Public interest immunity was not prayed in aid. However, a private prosecutor in a murder case has been held to be entitled to disclosure by the Crown Prosecution Service of 'all statements and exhibits thereto obtained by the police in connection with the death'. A summons had been issued under the Criminal Procedure (Attendance of Witnesses) Act 1965 but objection had been made by the Service to the statements of witnesses who refused to consent to disclosure. The matter had been committed to trial and the prosecution was on behalf of the Crown, it was held.[6]

¹ *Evans v Chief Constable of Surrey Constabulary* [1989] 2 All ER 594; see *Auten v Rayner (No 2)* [1960] 1 All ER 692 and *Police Complaints Authority v Greater Manchester Police Authority* (1991) 3 Admin LR 757. In *Goodridge v Chief Constable of Hampshire* [1999] 1 All ER 896, if the police are seeking legal advice from the DPP, this will be covered by legal professional privilege (LPP) as well as PII if within the latter immunity. Legal professional privilege did not apply on the facts.
² *Kelly v Metropolitan Police Comr* [1997] 33 LS Gaz R 28, CA.
³ Unlike criminal conviction certificates which would be allowed: Civil Evidence Act 1968, s 11. The applicant was suing for assault and related matters.
⁴ *George Ballantine & Sons Ltd v FER Dixon & Son Ltd* [1974] 2 All ER 503.
⁵ *Thorpe v Chief Constable of the Greater Manchester Police* [1989] 2 All ER 827, CA. See *R v DPP, ex p Hallas* (1987) 87 Cr App Rep 340, and *R v Johnson* [1989] 1 All ER 121, CA.
⁶ *R v Pawsey* [1989] Crim LR 152 distinguishing *Hallas*, supra.

10.74 Public interest immunity has been successfully raised to protect information collected by the Crown to value goods for tax purposes where confidentiality and presumably the necessity to obtain accurate information were crucial;[1] to protect information given to the Gaming Board by the police on applicants for certificates of consent;[2] to protect the identity of an informant to the NSPCC, even when making a false accusation;[3] to protect material provided in confidence to an inspector inquiring into the breaches of sanctions involving the former Southern Rhodesia;[4] to protect communications made by an individual to the European Commission in its investigations of anti-competition practices.[5]

¹   *Alfred Crompton*, para 10.65, note 1 above.
²   *Gaming Board for Great Britain v Rogers* [1973] AC 388, HL.
³   *D v NSPCC*, para 10.64, note 2 above; also [1978] AC 171, HL.
⁴   *Lonrho Ltd v Shell Petroleum Co Ltd (No 2)* [1982] AC 173, HL.
⁵   *Hasselblad (GB) Ltd v Orbinson* [1985] 1 All ER 173, CA.

10.75   The plea has been unsuccessfully raised inter alia to protect the identity of the names of persons likely to have violated the claimant's patent rights;[1] to protect the records of an adoption agency which contained an admission of paternity by a putative father;[2] to protect the record of discussions between a minister and senior civil servants on the merits of a control unit regime in a prison;[3] to protect 'confidential' medical records.[4] In *Burmah Oil*[5] the judges inspected but did not allow the applicant to inspect on the grounds of irrelevance; the case concerned high level meetings involving ministers and senior civil servants and Bank of England officials. It was unsuccessfully raised by the Home Secretary to prevent access to Special Branch reports.[6] The court has recently been asked to consider whether the Treasury might claim PII in a number of classes of document in which a claimant sought disclosure in litigation over complaince with public procurement processes. The court ordered disclosure of the documents it felt were relevant to the litigation, including internal Treasury documents over which PII had been claimed, finding that the Treasury's own published commitment to transparency was incompatible with a PII claim over documents relating to the operation of a procurement process.[7] It has been held that mistaken disclosure of part of a document over which PII had been granted did not affect the document's PII status.[8]

¹   *Norwich Pharmacal Co v Customs and Excise Comrs* [1974] AC 133, HL: no confidentiality in routine information.
²   *R v Bournemouth Justices, ex p Grey* (1986) 150 JP 392.
³   *Williams v Home Office* para 10.67, note 3 above. However, records on prisoners have been protected: *Re Hardy's Application* [1988] 12 NIJB 66; NB *Payne v Lord Harris* [1981] 2 All ER 842, CA; *R v Secretary of State for the Home Department, ex p Gunnell* [1985] Crim LR 105, CA; cf *Weeks v UK* (1987) 10 EHRR 293. The discussion re fair procedure and prisoners in ch 9 should be recalled.
⁴   *Flett v North Tyneside Health Authority* [1989] CLY 2968; cf *Campbell v Tameside Metropolitan Borough Council*, para 10.64, note 5 above; NB *W v Egdell* [1989] 1 All ER 1089: duty of doctor to patient overborne by duty to inform the public; *R v Crozier* (1990) 8 BMLR 128, CA. To what extent will the FOIA 2000 and the Data Protection Act 1998 avail would-be litigants? See also *Z v Finland* (1998) 25 EHRR 371 on justified and unjustified use of medical information under Art 8(1) and (2) ECHR.
⁵   *Burmah Oil v Bank of England* [1980] AC 1090, HL.
⁶   (1990) *Guardian*, 20 July, p 8.
⁷   *Amaryllis v HM Treasury* [2009] EWHC 1666 (TCC), [2009] BLR 425.
⁸   *R (Pewter) v Commisioner of Police of the Metropolis*, not reported but summary available on Westlaw.

Public interest immunity and judicial inspection

10.76   Where public interest immunity is properly raised, the onus is on the plaintiff to make out cause why the judge should inspect documents covered by a certificate. There is a judicial reluctance to look behind a certificate where it is prima facie in order. The more so where it is a 'contents claim' than where claims for classes of documents are made. To repeat, class claims are now likely to be very rare and will not cover central government. The burden on the claimant to persuade the judge to inspect has been described by judges as 'fairly strict'[1] and 'not light'.[2] In *Air Canada*, where there were requests to see documents relating to the policy-making process and allegedly unlawful decision-making by the government and a public corporation, a majority of the Law Lords decided that the test a judge should apply in deciding whether to inspect was that:

> 'the party seeking disclosure ought at least to satisfy the court that the documents are *very likely*[3] to contain material which would give substantial support to his contention on an issue which arises in the case, and that without them he might be "deprived of the means of ... proper presentation" of his case: see *Glasgow Corpn v Central Land Board* 1956 SC(HL) 1 at 18 per Lord Radcliffe. It will be plain that formulation has been mainly derived from the speech of Lord Edmund-Davis in the *Burmah Oil case*, [1980] AC 1090 at 1129 [1979] 3 All ER 700 at 721 and from the opinion of McNeill J in *Williams v Home Office* [1981] 1 All ER 1151 at 1154. It assumes, of course, that the party seeking disclosure has already shown in his pleadings that he has a cause of action, and that he has some material to support it. Otherwise he would merely be "fishing".'[4]

[1] Lord Fraser in *Air Canada Secretary of State for Trade (No 2)* [1983] 1 All ER 910 at 916–917, HL.
[2] Wood J in *Evans*, para 10.73, note 1. See also *Goodridge v Chief Constable of Hampshire Constabulary* [1999] 1 All ER 896.
[3] Emphasis added.
[4] [1983] 1 All ER 910 at 917.

10.77 The documents must be 'very likely' to advance an applicant's case, or very likely to weaken the adversary's. It is not for the judge to use disclosure to attain facts to assist the court to do justice. The party seeking disclosure must persuade the judge by demonstrating the way in which documents which s/he has not seen will assist his or her case. This demonstration must be specific, and not a mere hunch. In practice this is a very difficult burden. If it is not made out, the judge ought not to inspect privately. However, the more cogent a claimant's case under this demanding test, the more it will make an inroad into a certificate covering documents which have been identified, even on a contents basis where necessary.[1] As Lord Fraser said in *Air Canada*, the circumstances vary greatly according to the importance of the documents and the weight of public interest in favour of disclosure.[2] Where a judge decides to inspect privately, inspection will be deferred where an appeal is made and will await the outcome of such appeal.

[1] See Lord Scarman in *Burmah Oil* above. In the past, however, the latter claim has often been conclusive: Lord Fraser in *Air Canada*.
[2] In *Air Canada* at 917.

10.78 On inspection, the judge has to weigh the competing public interests of doing justice to the individual or maintaining a secret to prevent damage to the public or the state. In another context, it has been stated that the state means the official collective entity protecting public welfare, not simply the government of the day.[1]

[1]   See para 2.156 above.

10.79   In *ex p Wiley*, Lord Woolf believed that a claim for immunity should usually be made at the hearing of the substantive issue and it should not be dealt with as a preliminary or ancillary item.

Public interest immunity and confidentiality

10.80   Confidentiality is not, per se, a ground of public interest immunity, as we saw above. However, in cases involving employment tribunals it has been held that it lies within the discretion of the tribunal to refuse access to confidential assessments and records of other parties not directly involved in proceedings. This is not a public interest immunity, merely a device to prevent unnecessary access to confidential material involving third parties. Inspection should not be ordered unless it was necessary either for disposing fairly of the case or for saving costs.[1] A tribunal may inspect, and, if necessary, irrelevant but confidential parts may be erased or covered. If necessary the hearing may be held in camera. The confidentiality of probation service records held by a local authority may entitle them to be withheld unless the 'public interest' requires that they be adduced.[2]

[1]   *Science Research Council v Nassé* [1979] 3 All ER 673, HL. It was decided by a court that where a whistleblower's case went to an employment tribunal the facts should be made public knowledge. See more recently *Simba-Tola v Elizabeth Fry Hostel Trustees* [2001] EWCA Civ 1371 and *Beck v Canadian Imperial Bank of Commerce* [2009] EWCA Civ 619, [2009] IRLR 740. The government was opposed to this and amended the effect of the decision by regulations only allowing for an outline to be published. See para 2.282 above. See *Hanlon v Kirklees Council* EAT (2004) New LJ, 17 September: claim of applicant struck out when he refused consent for access to his medical file by other party under Access to Medical Reports Act 1988 – the court cannot order disclosure under the Act to another. *Jindal v University of Glasgow* EAT Scotland (2001): allegation of racial discrimination in failure by employer to promote. Disclosure of names of academics from whom references were sought by the employing university were to be disclosed! See para 7.86 above. This appears to flout duties of confidence. Deliberations of the professional conduct committee of the GMC in camera are protected by public interest immunity: *Roylance v GMC* (1999) *Times*, 27 January. See *Frankson v Secretary of State for the Home Department* [2003] EWCA Civ 655.
[2]   *Re M* [1987] 1 FLR 46. On adoption files and Adoption Rules, *see Re an ex parte originating summons in an adoption application* [1990] 1 All ER 639 at 640.

10.81   Traditionally, an immunity based upon national security has met with unqualified respect from the judiciary. While there may be evidence that domestic courts are not so willing to accept the invocation of this plea in the unqualified manner of former years, if a question of Community law is involved the ECJ has certainly not shown itself to be over-receptive to claims based on national security where legitimate rights could be undermined on unpersuasive grounds.[1]

[1]   *Johnstone v Chief Constable RUC*: 222/84 [1986] 3 All ER 135, ECJ; *Svenska Journalistförbundet v EU Council*: T-174/95 [1998] All ER (EC) 545, CFI.

Public interest immunity in criminal trials[1]

10.82 At the *Matrix Churchill* trial, public interest immunity certificates were entered into criminal trials. This was far from the first time such certificates were entered to prevent certain evidence going to the defence.[2] Such certificates have become very common in criminal trials and their uncontrolled use was seen as endangering the fairness of the trial from a defendant's point of view if he were prevented from defending himself effectively because of the non-production of crucial evidence. Various judicial guidelines were laid down to help regulate the use of the plea in criminal trials;[3] after all, one tradition suggested that where vital evidence was withheld from the defence, either the case collapsed or evidence had to be handed over. This was the position favoured by Sir Richard Scott. It became apparent that in too many cases vital evidence was not handed over or indeed the defence were not advised of its existence and yet the prosecution continued. The Court of Appeal gave guidance on cases where the immunity is claimed for 'highly sensitive' material in a criminal trial. Where an ex parte application is made to the trial judge by the prosecution the latter should present 'material' documents to the judge which they wish to withhold from the defence. The judge has to balance the importance of the evidence for the defence and the importance of their non-disclosure. 'If the disputed evidence may prove the defendant's innocence or avoid a miscarriage of justice, then the balance comes down resoundingly in favour of disclosing it.'[4] The ECtHR has ruled that where the prosecution withheld information from the defence without informing the trial judge, a review of the evidence by the Court of Appeal but in the absence of the defence lawyers but in the presence of the prosecution lawyers did not remedy a breach of Art 6(1), 6(3)(b) and (d) of the ECHR.[5] In *Edwards v UK* the question at issue concerned 'equality of arms' in criminal trials. The state's interests must be considered but a defendant's rights were only to be interfered with when strictly necessary; failures to allow adequate defence and using evidence obtained through entrapment which was not shown to the defence would breach Art 6.[6]

[1]   See HL Debs Vol 646 col 1396 (2 April 2003). Criminal Procedure Rules 2005, SI 2005/384, Part 25 now provides for the procedures in making PII applications in criminal trials; and Part 26 concerns use of confidential material or information. Parts 22 and 23, on disclosure by the prosecution and defence respectively, merely refer to existing provisions.

[2]   *R v Governor of Brixton Prison, ex p Osman* [1992] 1 All ER 108.

[3]   See *R v Ward* (1992) 96 Cr App Rep 1, CA; *R v Davis* [1993] 2 All ER 643, CA.

[4]   Per Lord Taylor CJ in *R v Keane* [1994] 2 All ER 478, CA.

[5]   *Rowe and Davis v UK* (2000) 30 EHRR 1. *Dowsett v UK* (2003) *Times*, 12 July: requirement to disclose evidence not absolute but where a decision is made by the prosecution without reference to the judge, there was a breach of Article 6 ECHR. However, see *R v Smith* (2000) *Times*, 20 December; *Fitt v UK* (2000) 30 EHRR 480 and *Jasper v UK* (2000) 30 EHRR 441. See also *Foucher v France* (1997) 25 EHRR 234. For the dangers of the English approach: *R v Botmeh (Jawad)* [2001] EWCA Crim 2226. See also: *R v G and Another (PII: Counsel's duty)* and *R v Cairns (A.L.)* [2002] EWCA Crim 2838 and *R v McDonald etc* (2004) *Times*, 8 November.

[6]   15 BHRC 189; confirmed by the Grand Chamber, ECtHR (2004) New LJ 1726. See *Atlan v UK* App No 36533/97. See also *Botmeh v United Kingdom* App No 15187/03 (2008) 46 EHRR 31 which followed the Court of Appeal's decision in *R v Botmeh (Jawad)* [2001] EWCA Crim 2226, [2002] 1 WLR 531. This case concerned B's claim that his Art 6 rights had been infringed as the Crown disclosed the existence of a document that was not used as part of the evidence in the trial was not put before the judge when PII was claimed in it. The ECHR dismissed the application, given that the Court of Appeal had ordered disclosure of a summary of the material to B and

there was clear potential, in light of the summary received, for B's legal team to reach a decision on the safety of the conviction.

10.83 Under the Criminal Procedure and Investigations Act 1996, Parts I and II and the accompanying code of practice under the latter Part, a new framework of rules governs the release of information to the defence by prosecutors. This has been amended by Criminal Justice Act 2003, Part V. The prosecution should disclose information which 'might reasonably be considered capable of undermining' the prosecution case or which is capable of 'assisting the case for the accused' (CJA 2003, s 32 amending CPIA 1996, s 3). This is a continuing duty. Many of the provisions in Part V concern defence statements.

10.84 The 1996 Act and code apply in respect of criminal investigations conducted by police officers beginning after 1 April 1997. A disclosure officer (a police officer) is the person responsible for: examining material retained by the police during an investigation, revealing material to the prosecutor during the investigation and any criminal proceedings resulting from it, certifying that this has been done and disclosing material to the accused at the request of the prosecutor. Material is material of any kind including information and objects obtained in the course of an investigation and which may be relevant to an investigation. The code gives an enormous discretion to the police as to what is 'relevant material' and 'sensitive material' which ought not to be disclosed in the public interest and they may consult with the prosecutor about what is 'relevant information'. The code sets out general responsibilities, as well as duties to record information, retention of material obtained in criminal investigations (subject to Police and Criminal Evidence Act 1984 (PACE 1984), s 22 where material is seized under that provision). Sensitive material – examples of such are provided – must be listed in a schedule together with the reasons why it is so regarded unless in exceptional circumstances it is so sensitive, as considered by the investigator, that it should not be scheduled. Its existence will be revealed to the prosecutor separately. This is likely to apply where 'compromising the material' would be likely to lead directly to loss of life or directly threaten national security. Great discretion is given to the investigator but he must ensure that the prosecutor is able to inspect the material so that 'he can assess whether it needs to be brought before a court for a ruling on disclosure.' If it has been referred to the court for such a ruling, and one should note 'If' because so much seems to rely on the integrity of investigators and prosecutors, a court may conclude that it is in the public interest that such sensitive material should be disclosed if the trial is to proceed. Disclosure is then necessary. What, however, if the matter is not referred to the court or the court does not believe such sensitive material should be disclosed? Will the prosecution be terminated if the evidence is crucial for the defence?[1] Various statutory rules have been passed in relation to Parts I and II.[2]

---

[1]   In the USA, release of defendants where crucial defence information is withheld has met with the approval of the Supreme Court *Roviaro v US* 353 US 53 (1957); *Jencks v US* 353 US 657 (1957); *A-G of the US v Irish People* 502 F Supp 63 (1980) and see Tomkins (1993) Public Law 650.

[2]   SI 1997/1033; SI 1997/698; SI 1997/699; SI 1997/703; and SI 1997/704; see also *R v DPP, ex p Lee* [1999] 2 All ER 737. There are also *Attorney General Guidelines*. See on inadvertent disclosure and restraining orders: *R v B* [2004] EWCA Crim 1368.

10.85 The House of Lords, moved by the jurisprudence of the ECtHR, has ruled that in a criminal trial, the 'golden rule' was full disclosure should be made to the defence of any material held by the prosecution which weakened its case or strengthened that of the defendants.[1] Where this golden rule could not be adhered to fully or at all because of an overriding public interest and risk of serious injury to that interest, some derogation may be justified. But this was always to be the minimum necessary to protect the public interest and 'had never to imperil the overall fairness of the trial'. Provided that procedures for dealing with claims for public interest immunity made by the prosecution in criminal proceedings were operated with 'scrupulous attention to those governing principles' and with continuing regard to the proper interests of the accused, there should be no breach of Art 6 ECHR. Furthermore, the Law Lords ruled that there was no absolute rule requiring the appointment of special counsel in any particular case. The court should appoint special counsel where the interest of justice required it on a case by case basis – it was envisaged that such an appointment would be exceptional. The judge should consider in detail the material that the prosecution sought to withhold. If the material did not weaken the prosecution case or strengthen the defence there would be no requirement to disclose it. Only in truly borderline cases should the prosecution seek a judicial ruling on whether the material in its hands should be disclosed – in other words, disclosure should be the norm.[2] The defence ought to be involved to the maximum extent possible without disclosing that which the general interest required to be protected but taking full account of the specific defence relied on. The Schedule to the Prevention of Terrorism Act 2005 makes provision for rules of court to deal with 'control order' procedures and non disclosure of material and other matters, use of advisers and appointment of special counsel (see para 9.108 above).

[1] *R v H* [2004] 1 All ER 1269 (HL).
[2] On this issue, see *Chemists (A Firm) v Revenue and Customs Commissioners* [2009] UKFTT (TC) [2009] STC (SCD) 472. See also *R v Twomey* [2011] EWCA Crim 8, [2011] 1 WLR 1681.

10.86 Two recent cases before the Supreme Court have further considered the use of the closed material procedure and special advocates. In the case of *Al Rawi*,[1] which concerned a civil claim against the security services for mistreatment which occurred at Guantanamo Bay, the Supreme Court held that no power existed at common law to order the use of a closed material procedure in a civil trial. The decision was a 6:3 majority, with the majority arguing that the use of the closed material procedure was an infringement of the principle of open justice enshrined in the common law and that the PII system generally worked satisfactorily in civil cases.[2] There was, however, no objection to special advocates assisting a judge in the determination of PII claims in such cases. For the minority, led by Lord Clarke, there was some attraction in the use of a closed material procedure once a PII process had been completed if it was evident that PII existed in so much of the evidence that a trial could not proceed unless the closed material procedure was used.[3] It is important to emphasise that all of the Justices did not exclude circumstances in the future where it might be necessary for the closed material procedure to be used in civil proceedings and for the common law to develop to permit this, but the majority did not feel that this was appropriate when the facts in the case before the court were considered. The difficulties presented to government by the decisions in *Secretary of State for the Home Department v MB*,[4] *Secretary of State for the Home Department v AF*,[5] *Al Rawi* and *Tariq* (below), prompted a consultation Green Paper, *Justice and Security* (Cm 8194 October 2011) from the Ministry of Justice and Cabinet Office. This Green Paper examines the balance to be struck between secrecy of proceedings where sensitive information involving national security is at issue and the Government's duty to safeguard national security and the requirements of justice under the rule of law. This is referred to as the twin imperatives of 'justice and security'. The Green Paper was published at a time when the Secret Intelligence Services have featured in 14 cases coming to the House of Lords and Supreme Court since 2001 and many more cases in the lower courts. Before that and for 90 years, no case impacting directly on Secret Intelligence Services existence reached the House of Lords (cf *Spycatcher*). It has information on 'recent secret intelligence successes' where intelligence has assisted in saving lives and foiling outrages. It does not deal with criminal proceedings or with intercept evidence. It will cover civil actions and cases involving measures against terrorist suspects. The Green Paper states that rights to justice and fairness must be protected and that the Government is committed to transparency. The use of sensitive evidence before inquests is also examined. Ways to ensure that an investigation into a death can take account of all relevant information and also support the involvement of jurors, family members and other persons are sought.

[1]   *Al Rawi and Ors v The Security Service and Ors* [2011] UKSC 34, [2011] 3 WLR 388.
[2]   See, in particular, the judgment of Lord Dyson, but also Lord Kerr.
[3]   See, in particular [159]–[187].
[4]   [2007] UKHL 46.
[5]   [2009] UKHL 28.

10.86A   The Green Paper proposes retention and extension of closed material procedures under legislation but with suggestions for safeguards. The paper seeks advice on ways to facilitate communications between special advocates and suspects following the service of closed procedure material on the special advocate. It wants 'better arrangements' for such communications. Permission for such communications is rarely sought by special advocates. A Chinese wall could possibly exist between government lawyers involved in the case and those within 'an agency' clearing communications so that the former could not view the communications. Cases in the past have been struck out where crime investigation methods would be disclosed.[1] The Green Paper seeks advice on whether legislation should clarify when the 'gisting' requirement in *Secretary of State for the Home Department v AF (No 3)*[2] does not apply and when disclosure requirements of (the same case do not apply. There would have to be compliance with Art 6 ECHR. The Green Paper does not recommend a 'national security court' to deal with sensitive information. It does not recommend increased case-management powers for judges, nor a more inquisitorial role for the judge, nor a change in remit of the Investigatory Powers Tribunal. Views are sought on these latter points, however. The Green Paper states that reforms limiting the use of UK courts in *Norwich Pharmacal* cases involving requests for information to be used overseas (against foreign governments). This was the issue in *R (Binyam Mohamed) v Secretary of State for Foreign and Commonwealth Office*.[3] The case involved the 'control principle' ie the originator of the intelligence controls, its handling and dissemination. The Green Paper states that since *Bin Yam Mohamed* the UK Government and its foreign government partners 'have less confidence than before that the courts will accept the view of Ministers on the harm to national security that would result from disclosure' (para 1.43). Should there be legislative changes in this area? Finally, the Green Paper seeks suggestions for the reform of oversight of the Secret Intelligence Services to give it greater independence and powers. It has some interesting points to make about Parliamentary oversight and the introduction of an Inspector General regime for the Secret Intelligence Services.

1 *Carnduff v Rock* [2001] EWCA Civ 680 upheld in *Carnduff v UK* (application 18905/02) [2004] ECHR.
2 [2009] UKHL 28.
3 [2010] EWCA Civ 65, [2010] EWCA Civ 158.

10.87 The decision of the Supreme Court in *Tariq*[1] found that the use of the closed material procedure and special advocates in proceedings before the Employment Tribunal was not in contravention of ECHR Art 6 or the relevant provisions of EU law. In this case, Tariq had brought a claim for unlawful discrimination after his security clearance as an immigration officer had been rescinded following the arrest of his brother and cousin on suspicion of terrorism offences. Tariq's brother was released, but his cousin was convicted. Tariq argued that the use of the closed material procedure and special advocates was contrary to Art 6 and EU law in the sense that he was unable to know in sufficient detail what the allegations against him were or what the detail of the Secretary of State's defence were for him to instruct his legal representatives effectively. The Supreme Court rejected these claims, finding that national security was an important concern and that neither the relevant provisions of EU law nor Art 6 gave rise to an absolute right to have access to all elements of the Secretary of State's case.

[1] See above, para 10.4, note 4.

10.88 It is clear that other than insofar as the use of the closed material procedure and special advocates is permitted by statute, the courts are not presently willing to extend the use of the process, other than in certain very limited circumstances.[1] It will be for Parliament to act should it wish the closed material procedure to be extended to civil litigation.

[1] In *Al Rawi* at [63] and [64] Lord Dyson offers wardship and cases of commercial confidentiality as possible examples.

LEGAL PROFESSIONAL PRIVILEGE

10.89 Unlike public interest immunity, legal professional privilege (LPP) is a privilege and may be waived only by the party possessing the privilege – the client[1] – and it can only be raised by the party possessing the privilege.[2] This topic is dealt with exhaustively elsewhere.[3] There has been a considerable amount of litigation and statutory intervention on the subject of LPP under Proceeds of Crime Act 2002, Part VII.[4] The Privy Council has defended the immunity in powerful terms. It was not subject to competing public interests at common law. It was a fundamental condition on which the administration of justice as a whole rested. For a statute to make inroads into the immunity, the statutory language would have to be specific and allow such inroads by necessary implication. Limited disclosure of privileged documents did not waive a privilege generally.

There was no balancing exercise to be conducted by a judge because the policy considerations giving rise to the privilege precluded such a balance. There might be a limited use of documents by agreement but that did not waive privilege in the documents save to the extent of the agreement.[5]

1   And not eg a solicitor representing the client: see, however, *Goldman v Hesper* [1988] 3 All ER 97, CA; *Comfort Hotels Ltd v Wembley Stadium Ltd* [1988] 3 All ER 53.

2   Cf *Guinness Peat Properties Ltd v Fitzroy Robinson Partnership* [1987] 2 All ER 716, CA concerning an insurance document. It has been held that CPR 1998, r 48.7(3), which allows a court to direct that legally privileged documents could be disclosed to the court and the other party, was ultra vires: *General Mediterranean Holdings SA v Patel* [1999] 3 All ER 673. See *Al Fayed v Commissioner of Police* (2002) *Times*, 17 June where documents were mistakenly disclosed to the other side where solicitor was not aware of the mistake and a reasonable solicitor would not be so aware; no injunction would be issued to prevent use of the documents by the other side.

3   See eg, *Cross and Tapper on Evidence* (11th edn, 2007).

4   On which, see *Bowman v Fels* [2005] EWCA Civ 226, [2005] 1 WLR 3083.

5   *B v Auckland District Law Society* [2004] 4 All ER 269 (PC) and the *Three Rivers* litigation in the House of Lords (para 10.92, note 7 below). See *R (Morgan Grenfell and Co. Ltd.) v Special Commissioner of Income Tax* [2002] 3 All ER 1 (HL): Taxes Management Act 1970, s 20 did not override LPP; Court of Appeal overruled. Note that this privilege under s 20 applies only to legal advice given by legal advisors. In *Re Revenue and Customs Commissioners Application (Section 20(1) Notice: Subsidiary Co)* [2008] STC (SCD) 358 the Commissioners noted that similar privilege did not apply to advice about the law received from accountants and required the company at the centre of the application to deliver the correspondence between the company and its accountants for inspection by the Inland Revenue. This issue remains contentious. Prudential is presently pursuing a judicial review case arguing that legal advice provided on tax matters by accountancy firms should be subject to the privilege. The High Court [2009] EWHC 2494 (Admin), [2010] 1 All ER 1113 and more recently the Court of Appeal [2010] EWCA Civ 1094, [2011] QB 669 have both refused to extend the privilege. The Court of Appeal noted that s 20 of the Act refers specifically to what an accountant might be required to disclose and Parliament did not at that time choose to extend the privilege. Furthermore, the weight of precedent supported the principle that the privilege extends only to advice received from lawyers. The Court of Appeal rejected the claim that ECHR, Art 8 extended beyond the principle that advice received from lawyers was subject to protection under the Convention. This case is presently on appeal to the Supreme Court.

10.90   Suffice it to say for present purposes that there are two classes of privilege:
(a)   documents and communications that are privileged whether or not litigation was contemplated or pending; and
(b)   documents and communications that are privileged only if litigation was contemplated or pending when they were made or came into existence.

10.91   Where the seeking of advice is itself a material fact in proceedings, eg a relevant date for the purpose of the Limitation Act 1980, LPP does not apply to that fact.[1]

1   Ie to establish the effluxion of the relevant period.

10.92   Under (a), 'legal advice privilege', correspondence and communications passing between a solicitor and client, or the client's predecessors in title, are privileged from production. They must be made confidentially 'and written to, or by, the solicitor in his or her professional capacity, and for the purpose of getting legal advice or assistance for the client'.[1] Those purposes must be construed broadly.[2] The same privilege attaches to communications by an employer with a solicitor in the full-time employment of the former, eg a government department or local authority,[3] as are instructions and briefs to counsel, cases for counsel's opinion and the opinion itself, as well as counsel's drafts and notes.[4] The Court of Appeal has sought to confine the scope of this privilege in the *Three Rivers* litigation.[5] The Bank of England appealed against a further decision of the Court of Appeal[6] that communications between itself (specifically a specific unit of Bank officials whose task was to deal with communications between the Bank and the Bingham Inquiry) and its solicitors concerning preparations for the Bingham Inquiry (HC 198 (1992–93)) into the Bank's regulation of the BCCI were not covered by legal advice privilege where those communications pertained solely to the manner in which B should present its evidence. In dismissing the appeal, the Court of Appeal ruled that whilst solicitor and client communications were often what could be expected in the normal course of business, legal advice privilege only arose when such communications pertained to advice on liabilities and rights. Legal advice meant advice on law. However, where the initial relationship between the client and solicitor consisted of advising on rights and liabilities, legal advice privilege 'would cover a broad spectrum of communication and ancillary matters'. In circumstances of the present appeal, however, the purpose of the communications was not to obtain advice on rights and liabilities, but to obtain advice on presentation of evidence and accordingly legal privilege did not arise, regardless of the fact that the Bank wished to urge upon the Inquiry a conclusion as favourable to its own position as possible. This somewhat surprising decision was overturned by the House of Lords.[7]

[1]   See the *Supreme Court Practice* Part 31 and the authorities there cited.

[2]   *Balabel v Air India* [1988] 2 All ER 246, CA. See *USP Strategies plc and Another v London General Holdings Ltd* [2004] EWHC 373 on privilege attaching to summaries and copies of legal advice. Notes taken by a solicitor of evidence given by witnesses in an Employment Tribunal case (but not any annotations or observations on the evidence made by the solicitor) have been found not to be subject to privilege by the EAT: *Comfort v Department of Constitutional Affairs* (2005) 102(35) LSG 42.

[3]   *Alfred Crompton Amusement Machines Ltd Customs and Excise Comrs (No 2)* [1974] AC 405, HL. EC law is stricter: para 10.129 below.

[4]   Pre-existing documents that are submitted to counsel as part of instructions and then returned to the client are not necessarily subject of privilege. In *Imerman v Tchenguiz* [2009] EWHC 2902 (QB), [2010] Lloyd's Rep PN 221 the court found that a document which had been sent to counsel as part of instructions and which had been annotated by counsel was not subject to legal professional privilege. Insofar as the document was annotated, the annotations could be redacted.

[5]   *Three Rivers DC v Bank of England (No 5)* [2003] QB 1556, overruling [2002] EWHC 2730.

[6]   *Three Rivers DC v Bank of England (No 6)* [2004] QB 916 (CA).

[7]   *Three Rivers DC v Bank of England* [2004] UKHL 48.

10.93   The privilege referred to as legal advice privilege, said Baroness Hale, 'is too well established in the common law for its existence to be doubted now' (para 61). The thrust of the judgments was that the advice privilege was not restricted to the provision of advice on legal rights and obligations as identified by the Court of Appeal, and that per Lord Scott:

'None of these judicial dicta tie the justification for legal advice privilege to the conduct of litigation. They recognise that in the complex world in which we live there are a multitude of reasons why individuals, whether humble or powerful, or corporations, whether large or small, may need to seek the advice or assistance of lawyers in connection with their affairs; they recognise that the seeking and giving of this advice so that the clients may achieve an orderly arrangement of their affairs is strongly in the public interest; they recognise that in order for the advice to bring about that desirable result it is essential that the full and complete facts are placed before the lawyers who are to give it; and they recognise that unless the clients can be assured that what they tell their lawyers will not be disclosed by the lawyers without their (the clients') consent, there will be cases in which the requisite candour will be absent. It is obviously true that in very many cases clients would have no inhibitions in providing their lawyers with all the facts and information the lawyers might need whether or not there were the absolute assurance of non-disclosure that the present law of privilege provides. But the dicta to which I have referred all have in common the idea that it is necessary in our society, a society in which the restraining and controlling framework is built upon a belief in the rule of law, that communications between clients and lawyers, whereby the clients are hoping for the assistance of the lawyers' legal skills in the management of their (the clients') affairs, should be secure against the possibility of any scrutiny from others, whether the police, the executive, business competitors, inquisitive busy-bodies or anyone else …. I, for my part, subscribe to this idea. It justifies, in my opinion, the retention of legal advice privilege in our law, notwithstanding that as a result cases may sometimes have to be decided in ignorance of relevant probative material.' (para 34)

10.94 Inquiries such as the Bingham Inquiry which was ad hoc under the Banking Acts, but whose findings nevertheless could have important implications for the Bank's position in law, and which itself could be subject to judicial review and 'presentational advice' or assistance given by lawyers to parties whose conduct may be the subject of criticism by the inquiry, is advice or assistance that may serve to avoid the need to invoke public law remedies. The words of Taylor LJ in *Balabel v Air India*[1] were used in several of the judgments: 'legal advice is not confined to telling the client the law; it must include advice as to what should prudently and sensibly be done in the relevant legal context' (at p 330). Were the lawyers, qua lawyers, being asked to provide legal advice to the client, asked Lord Rodger (para 58). This might include advice given by Parliamentary counsel to the government in relation to the drafting and preparation of public bills. It is not clear why this should be so (para 1.138 above). Advising on presentation and selecting material for relevance is per Lord Carswell 'the classic exercise of one of the lawyer's skills' (para 113). On the question of whether other employees apart from the members of the BIU were also covered by the advice privilege, which the Court of Appeal ruled in *(No 5)* was not the case and on which the Bar Council and Law Society intervened, the Law Lords declined to express their opinions.[2]

[1] [1988] Ch 317.
[2] An appeals committee of the House of Lords had refused permission for the Bank to appeal against this aspect of the earlier ruling.

10.95 The privilege under category (b), 'litigation privilege', covers:

'Communications between a solicitor and a non-professional agent or third party, directly, or through an agent, which come into existence after litigation is contemplated or commenced and made with a view to such litigation, either for the purpose of obtaining or giving advice in regard to it, or of obtaining or collecting evidence to be used in it, or obtaining information which may lead to the obtaining of such information.'[1]

1   *Supreme Court Practice* 24/5/8: *Anderson v Bank of British Columbia* (1876) 2 Ch D 644, CA; *Wheeler v Le Marchant* (1881) 17 Ch D 675. On copies of documents, see *R v Inland Revenue Board, ex p Goldberg* [1988] 3 All ER 248.

10.96   The scope of the privilege covering client/third party communications is less clear cut.

10.97   Information from a non-professional agent is not protected unless obtained with a view to contemplated or existing litigation except where the agent is merely the medium of the message that is confidential between a client and his or her solicitor or vice versa.

10.98   Where the client receives reports from communications with a non-professional servant, agent or third party, the courts have limited the nature of the privilege.[1]

1   *Seabrook v British Transport Commission* [1959] 2 All ER 15.

10.99   If documents came into existence only for the purpose of obtaining legal advice in existing or anticipated proceedings, the privilege will obtain. Where there are two purposes, eg to establish the facts behind an accident as well as preparing legal advice for contemplated litigation, only when the predominant purpose for which the document was prepared was to submit it to a legal adviser will the privilege under the second head apply.[1]

1   *Waugh v British Railways Board* [1980] AC 521, HL; see *Guinness Peat Properties*, para 10.89, note 2 above: the dominant purpose is not necessarily ascertained by reference to the intention of the composer, but reference should be made to the employer's or insurer's intention. Where the insurer's intention was to bring a document into existence to be advised on whether a claim should be paid or resisted, LPP will obtain especially in complicated cases. This will not be the case where the issue is simple and is really about assessing quantum.

10.100   Case-law has also insisted that a strict test should apply to determine when the privilege applies to eg accident reports and reports for valuation (for tax purposes)[1] ie distinguishing between anticipated litigation and a report on an occurrence which may lead to litigation. The Court of Appeal has held that, if litigation is reasonably in prospect, documents brought into existence for the purpose of enabling solicitors to advise whether a claim should be met or rejected are protected by the privilege; this is whether or not a decision to instruct solicitors has been made at the time the documents were created. However, such a motive/decision, viz advising on the claim, must be the dominant one.[2] When the privilege applies to a client's communication to his solicitor, it also covers copies of such documents.[3] The House of Lords has ruled by majority that investigations under Children Act 1989, Part IV (care and supervision) are not adversarial but are inquisitorial in nature and litigation privilege could not be relied upon.[4]

1   *Alfred Crompton* above; *Lask v Gloucester Area Health Authority* 2 PN 96, CA.
2   *Guinness Peat Properties* above. See *Gnitrow Ltd v Cape plc* [2000] 3 All ER 763, CA.
3   See para 10.109, note 1 below.
4   *Re L* [1997] AC 16.

10.101   Once a document is privileged it is always privileged in the hands of the litigant or his successor in title unless the holder chooses to waive the privilege.[1]

Translations of unprivileged documents will not attract privilege and nor will a selection of unprivileged documents attract privilege on the ground that their selection reveals legal advice.[2]

1   See *Shearson Lehman Hutton Inc v Maclaine, Watson & Co Ltd* [1988] 1 WLR 946.
2   *Sumitomo Corp v Credit Lyonnais Ltd* [2002] 4 All ER 68 (CA).

10.102   Communications other than the above are not privileged[1] no matter how confidential, a point recently illustrated in the criminal law by PACE 1984 and Police Act 1997, Part III.

1   See Copyright, Designs and Patents Act 1988, s 280 and patents and relevant communications. On confidentiality and public interest immunity, see para 10.80 above.

10.103   The Finance Act 2004 has introduced tax avoidance disclosure rules. These place an obligation on promoters to disclose details to the Inland Revenue (SI 2004/1863). LPP was excluded by virtue of Finance Act 2004, s 314. However, amendments were announced effectively retaining the privilege but placing the duty of disclosure onto the client-user.[1]

1   See F Cullen (2004) New LJ 1608.

PACE 1984 and privilege

10.104   This Act allows searches for, and seizure of, evidence which prior to the Act coming into force was privileged, but which may now be obtained by a warrant or order from a circuit judge.[1] The Act allows seizures of what otherwise is defined under the statute as 'excluded'[2] and 'special procedure'[3] material and which may be obtained by following the procedure laid down in s 9 and Sch 1.[4] Access to legally privileged documents (see below) may not be granted at all unless they are held with the intention of furthering a criminal purpose: s 10(2).[5] A court must not grant a warrant under s 8 for seizure of legally privileged material unless it is satisfied, properly directing itself, that there are reasonable grounds for believing that the material did not consist of, or include, legally privileged material.[6] When the police seized documents covered by LPP under a search warrant under s 8(1), there was no rule against this provided the officer had no reasonable grounds to believe the documents were privileged. Police officers were not allowed to remove documents to sift through them to establish what was in the scope of the warrant. Documents unlawfully seized had to be returned and a liability for trespass to goods might arise. A procedure before a circuit judge to deal with such matters was required, the court believed.[7] Under Part III of the Police Act 1997, sensitive, confidential and legally privileged information may be obtained by surveillance-powers (see ss 97–98) added to by the Regulation of Investigatory Powers Act 2000 (see ch 2). The 2002 Code of Practice on interceptions (revised 2007) has guidance on the safeguards involving intercepted information. Paragraph 3.7 states that, where a lawyer is the subject of an interception, it is possible that a substantial proportion of the communications which will be intercepted will be between the lawyer and his client(s) and will be subject to legal privilege. Any case where a lawyer is the subject of an investigation should be notified to the Interception of Communications Commissioner during his inspections and any material which has been retained should be made available to him if requested.

1 PACE 1984, Part II (ss 8 et seq) and Sch 1.
2 PACE 1984, s 11; it includes journalistic material: s 13.
3 PACE 1984, s 14; includes 'journalistic material' other than excluded material.
4 To a circuit judge who has to be satisfied of either one of two sets of conditions.
5 On PACE 1984, s 10(2), which expressly preserves the exclusion of privilege from communications made 'with the intention of furthering a criminal purpose' see: *R v Central Criminal Court, ex p Francis & Francis (a firm)* [1989] AC 346, HL and Drug Trafficking Offences Act 1986, s 27.
6 *R v Guildhall Magistrates' Court, ex p Primlaks Holdings Co (Panama) Inc* [1990] 1 QB 261. If in doubt, a magistrates' court should dismiss an application under PACE 1984, s 8, leaving the applicant to proceed under s 9 before a circuit judge.
7 *R v Chesterfield Justices, ex p Bramley* [2000] QB 576 – the spirit of *Entick v Carrington* survives! See, however, Criminal Justice and Police Act 2001, ss 50–52 to deal with this situation.

Legal professional privilege and criminal purpose

10.105 Public interest immunity, it has been held, does not protect as a class documents seized under the PACE 1984. On presentation of a subpoena duces tecum (witness summons) the police will have to disclose them in civil proceedings if the owner would have been so required.[1] A major exception to LPP concerns those cases where a document came into existence 'as a step in a criminal or illegal proceeding', ie where the solicitor is asked to advise on the perpetration of a crime or illegal act, or is implicated in it. The privilege will not cover such communications.[2] However, LPP will cover cases where the solicitor is asked to advise on the legality or criminality of proposed actions, or how to stay within the law or within a statute.[3]

1 *Marcel v Metropolitan Police Comr* [1992] Ch 225, CA. The court provided instructions on appropriate safeguards, cf a contents claim.
2 *Bullivant v A-G for Victoria* [1901] AC 196, HL; *R v Cox* (1884) 14 QBD 153, CCR; *Dubai Aluminium Co Ltd v Al Alawi* [1999] 1 All ER 703; and *Kuwait Airways Corp v Iraqi Airways Co* [2005] EWCA Civ 286. And see PACE 1984, ss 8 and 10(2).
3 *Butler v Board of Trade* [1971] Ch 680; *Banque Keyser Ullman SA v Skandia (UK) Insurance Co Ltd* [1986] 1 Lloyd's Rep 336, CA; see also *Re Konigsberg, ex p the Trustee v Konigsberg* [1989] 3 All ER 289.

10.106 The Proceeds of Crime Act 2002, Part VII increases the risk of criminal sanctions for solicitors in relation to laundering offences (ss 327–329), failure to report such offences (s 329) and facilitating laundering offences. Privilege only covers legal advice and does not cover 'litigation' privilege concerning third parties. The Court of Appeal has ruled that Proceeds of Crime Act 2002, s 328 was not intended to cover or affect the 'ordinary conduct of litigation' by legal professionals since that ordinary conduct did not fall within the concept of 'becoming concerned in an arrangement which facilitates the acquisition, retention, use or control of criminal property'.[1]

1 *Bowman v Fels* [2005] EWCA Civ 226; and see *P v P* (2004 NLJ 1604) and SI 2004/2613.

Miscellaneous points

10.107 The Board of Inland Revenue possesses wide powers under ss 20 and 51 of the Taxes Management Act 1970 (as amended) to serve notices requiring documentation relating to tax liabilities. In the case of a solicitor, documents requested might be covered by the privilege. A solicitor would have to comply, but inspectors could only use the documents in relation to the solicitor's tax liabilities and not for any other purpose.[1] In *R v IRC, ex p Tamosius & Partners*[2] the police were allowed to take a lawyer on a search of premises under a warrant under s 20C of the Taxes Management Act 1970 to help in determining whether documents were covered by LPP. Notices issued for good reasons under s 20 did not involve a breach of the right to privacy.[3] Under s 20C, revenue officers may seize a computer to copy the contents of the hard drive if this is not possible on the tax payer's premises.[4]

[1]   *R v IRC, ex p Taylor (No 2)* [1989] 3 All ER 353; affirmed [1990] 2 All ER 409, CA.
[2]   [1999] STC 1077. On the delegation of the Board's powers to one of its own officers, see: *R v IRC ex p Davis, Frankel and Mead* [2000] STC 595.
[3]   *R v IRC, ex p Banque International à Luxembourg SA* [2000] STC 708.
[4]   *R (H) v Inland Revenue Commissioners* [2002] STC 1354.

10.108   Privilege will be waived where documents are put in evidence, or read out in court. It will be waived for the whole document in such a case unless the 'remaining part deals with an entirely different subject-matter'[1] Considerable litigation has taken place over the circumstances in which privilege can be said to be waived. The Court of Appeal recently found that the mention of the existance of correspondence with a lawyer in a witness statement was not sufficient to waive privilege in the document.[2]

[1]   *A-G for the Northern Territory v Maurice* (1986) 161 CLR 475.
[2]   *Expandable Ltd v Rubin* [2008] EWCA Civ 59, [2008] EWCA Civ 59, [2008] 1 WLR 1099; *Fulham Leisure Holdings Ltd v Nicholson Graham & Jones* [2006] EWHC 158 (Ch), [2006] 2 All ER 599; *Brennan v Sunderland City Council* [2009] ICR 479 and *Re D (A Child) (Care proceedings: professional privilege)* [2011] EWCA Civ 684, [2011] 2 FCR 585.

10.109   Although it has been held that a party may use secondary evidence about the contents of a privileged document in proceedings,[1] eg a photocopy, if s/he has not yet used it and merely intends to do so it has been held that s/he must hand it to the person in whom LPP is vested if that person makes a claim for delivery up of the copy; s/he may also be restrained from using it.[2] However, a court has a discretion to allow a party to use 'privileged' documents which have come into that party's hands where they are confidential, where possession came about completely innocently[3] and where a reasonable solicitor would not realise that a mistake had been made.[4] Under CPR 1998, r 31.20 a discretion would appear to continue because the permission of the court must be given to use documents inadvertently disclosed. It is not permissible for a litigant to use documents covered by LPP where s/he has obtained them by stealth, deceit or improper conduct.[5] There is some judicial concern about the use of documents which through inadvertence have lost their privilege and which cannot be protected by confidentiality – a disclosure by oversight for instance.[6] On the other hand, it might be asked why clients should be protected from the negligence or oversight of their lawyers when the opponents' solicitors have not acted unconscionably. There is always the possibility of an action for professional negligence for such oversight. To which one may argue, only the client may waive the privilege; but the client has to operate through the mediation of his lawyers.

[1]   *Calcraft v Guest* [1898] 1 QB 759, CA; *R v Governor of Pentonville Prison, ex p Osman* [1989] 3 All ER 701 at 729–731. *Calcraft v Guest* has been severely criticised since it was decided. *Ashburton v Pape* [1913] 2 Ch 469 seems to provide the possibility of protecting 'privileged' documents by confidentiality even where LPP has evaporated where they have come into the possession of the

other party by breach of confidence or accident. See R Toulson and C Phipps *Confidentiality*, ch 20 (1996). See, however, *A v B* [2000] EMLR 1007 and Copyright, Designs and Patents Act 1988, s 45.
2   *Goddard v Nationwide Building Society* [1986] 3 All ER 264; *English and American Insurance Co Ltd v Herbert Smith & Co* [1988] FSR 232.
3   *Webster v James Chapman & Co* [1989] 3 All ER 939, Scott J doubting Nourse LJ in *Goddard*, above.
4   See *Al Fayed v Commissioner of Police* (2002) *Times*, 17 June (para 10.89, note 2 above).
5   *ITC Film Distributors Ltd v Video Exchange Ltd* [1982] Ch 431.
6   See *English and American Insurance* above and Browne Wilkinson V-C at 239.

10.110   Documents which are disclosed to the police out of a sense of public duty to assist in their investigations for the purpose of a subsequent criminal trial will not lose an obvious privilege for civil proceedings, and no waiver of privilege for civil proceedings is made or implied. Such a loss would be contrary to public policy.[1]

1   *British Coal Corpn v Dennis Rye Ltd (No 2)* [1988] 3 All ER 816. Cf documents obtained under the PACE 1984 and *Marcel v Metropolitan Police Comr* [1992] Ch 225, CA.

10.111   On the other hand, where there is no privilege attaching to a copy of an affidavit served on a defendant and handed by him to his legal adviser to advise on a civil claim, then it would not be privileged in subsequent unrelated civil proceedings against the defendant.[1]

1   *Dubai Bank v Galadari* [1989] 3 All ER 769; and *Dubai Bank v Galadari (No 7)* [1992] 1 All ER 658 where a selection of copies of documents reveals the 'trend of advice' given by a solicitor.

OTHER FORMS OF PRIVILEGE

10.112   We leave to other sources[1] the privilege relating to self-incrimination or exposure to a penalty;[2] applications for legal aid;[3] and 'without prejudice' communications[4] as well as other forms of privilege.

1   *Cross and Tapper on Evidence* (10th edn, 2007).
2   *R v Ataou* [1988] 2 All ER 321, CA. This privilege has recently seen some high profile litigation in *Gray v News Group Newspapers* [2011] EWHC 349 (Ch), [2011] 2 WLR 1401, where the High Court ordered Glen Mulcaire to reveal the names of the journalists who asked him to access voicemail messages in the phone hacking scandal. The Court of Appeal refused permission to appeal in the case.
3   Legal Aid Act 1974, s 22.
4   *Rush & Tompkins Ltd v Greater London Council* [1989] AC 1280, HL. See *Unilever plc v Procter & Gamble Co* [1999] 1 WLR 1630; affirmed [2000] 1 WLR 2436, CA. More recently, see *Oceanbulk Shipping & Trading SA v TMT Asia Ltd* [2010] UKSC 44, [2011] 1 AC 662.

Requests for information (interrogatories)

10.113   The procedure relating to requests for information, formerly known as interrogatories, which are in form detailed questions relating to any matter in issue between the applicant and the other party in the cause or matter requiring that other party to answer the request on a statement of truth (affidavit) within a specified period, is contained in CPR 1998, Part 18. The immunities and privileges enumerated above apply to requests as well as for disclosure.

Witness summonses (subpoenas)

10.114   The governing provision is now CPR 1998, Part 34. Witness summonses replaced the process of issuing subpoenas.

10.115 It should be noted that, apart from the limited circumstances set out in CPR 1998, r 31.17 and in the *Norwich Pharmacal* case,[1] disclosure cannot be ordered against a third party, a mere witness. As Lord Diplock said,[2] discovery is an inroad, in the interest of achieving justice, into the right of individuals to keep their documents to themselves; it is an inroad which calls for safeguards against abuse. These sentiments should be borne in mind when applications for witness statements (subpoenas) are made for documents, especially if there is a suspicion that they are being used to obtain disclosure. However, a witness can be ordered to attend and/or to produce documents under Part 34, and the details of practice and procedure are contained in that Part.

[1]   See para 10.42, note 1 above.
[2]   *Harman v Secretary of State for the Home Department* [1983] 1 AC 280, CA.

10.116 A party to proceedings is not obliged to produce any documents under Part 34 for which privilege may be claimed. Readers are directed to the discussion above. In *R v Bournemouth Justices, ex p Grey*[1] the High Court refused to set aside on the grounds of public interest immunity a witness summons in affiliation proceedings against a social worker who was in possession of vital evidence which, per Hodgson J, was known to everyone. The public interest did not necessitate the acceptance of the immunity in that case, which on its facts was a weak one from the perspective of public interest immunity. Where documents are protected by the law of 'confidentiality', especially for instance where they relate to children,[2] even though they may not be protected by public interest immunity, the court will be prepared to weigh that confidentiality against the interests of doing justice in the particular case and will have regard to the possible harm that may be done to third parties if a disclosure is made. Protection of an individual's safety is a matter of public interest. It can, if it thinks that disclosure should be made having inspected the documents, consider whether any evidence should be heard in camera, should be elided if irrelevant to the cause, or if names should be erased.[3] These points were made in a case concerning an application for discovery inter partes in a discrimination case before an industrial tribunal but the principles seem to be applicable here. This will of course be subject to any relevant statutory or other powers of the courts that are relevant.

[1]   [1987] 1 FLR 36.
[2]   See paras 10.7 et seq above which concern statutory restrictions on publicity.
[3]   *Science Research Council v Nassé* [1979] 3 All ER 673, HL.

FREEZING ORDERS AND SEARCH ORDERS[1]

10.117 A brief reference to these important provisions will be helpful although the terminology has now been altered by CPR 1998, r 25.1 which gives courts powers to make interim remedies.[2] The Mareva injunction is referred to as a 'freezing order' and an *Anton Piller* order is now referred to as a 'search order' under s 7 of the Civil Procedure Act 1997.

[1]   See: S Gee *Commercial Injunctions* (4th edn).
[2]   See *Parker v CS Structured Credit Fund* [2003] 1 WLR 1680.

Freezing orders (Mareva injunctions)

10.118   A Mareva injunction originally restrained defendants from removing or disposing out of the jurisdiction moneys standing to the credit of defendants in a London bank until trial of the action or further order. The principle of the case was extended so that an interim injunction may be awarded to a plaintiff with a proper claim in any case where there is a basis for fearing that assets may be transferred abroad or concealed in this country thereby defeating justice. Parliament upheld this extension in s 37(3) of the Supreme Court Act 1981. The jurisdiction of the court must be 'swift and secret', ie ex parte (without notice).[1] Disclosure orders may be made in support of a freezing order in requiring, eg, a bank to disclose information on its customers.[2]

[1]   See *Flightwise Travel Services Ltd v Gill* [2003] EWHC 3082 on safeguards for respondents in the ex parte process.

[2]   *A v C* [1981] QB 956n. See *Customs and Excise Commissioners v Barclays Bank plc* [2004] 2 All ER 789: extent, if any, of duty of care owed by bank to party who served a freezing order re a customer's account; the Court of Appeal held that a duty of care does exist between the bank and the claimant for the freezing order: [2004] EWCA Civ 1555.

Search orders (Anton Piller orders)

10.119   Anton Piller orders (APOs) were put onto a statutory basis by the Civil Procedure Act 1997. The High Court has an inherent power to make an order for the detention or preservation of the subject-matter of a cause and of documents and articles relating thereto. This is in addition to any other powers.

10.120   Very often what was authorised was entry, search and seizure but it operated by way of a court order against the defendant requiring him to allow entry and search.[1] Authority is now based in Civil Procedure Act 1997, s 7 which in no way reduces or restricts the jurisdiction formerly exercised under APOs.[2] The application may be made ex parte (without notice) where there is a danger that notice to the other party will bring about the destruction of incriminating materials – usually in breach of copyright or patent or where they have been used to 'pass off' the plaintiff's goods. The court, in such a case, will sit in camera. An application for an APO requires full disclosure by the applicant. Omission of material matter in the application is usually fatal.[3] The courts have introduced strict controls.[4] The court should not make an APO where it will force the defendant to allow access to, or answer questions on, incriminating matter where the rule against self-incrimination has not been abolished by statute.[5]

[1]   *Anton Piller KG v Manufacturing Processes Ltd* [1976] 1 All ER 779, CA. The award is a serious matter, and in employment breach of confidence cases it may be more appropriate to order delivery up or preservation of documents, or that the former employer be allowed to make copies rather than an APO: *Lock International plc v Beswick* [1989] 3 All ER 373.

[2]   See *Practice Direction (Mareva Injunction and Anton Piller Orders)* [1994] 4 All ER 52.

[3]   *Thermax Ltd v Schott Industrial Glass Ltd* [1981] FSR 289; *Gallery Cosmetics Ltd v Number 1* [1981] FSR 556; *O'Regan v Iambic Productions Ltd* [1989] NLJR 1378.

[4]   *Columbia Picture Industries Inc v Robinson* [1987] Ch 38; *Universal Thermosensors Ltd v Hibben* [1992] FSR 361 though see *Memory Corpn plc v Sidhu* (1999) *Times*, 31 May.

[5]   *Rank Film Distributors Ltd v Video Information Centre* [1980] 2 All ER 273; *Garvin v Domus Publishing Ltd* [1989] 2 All ER 344; *Tate Access Floors Inc v Boswell* [1991] Ch 512; *AT&T Istel v Tully* [1993] AC 45, HL, and Civil Procedure Act 1997, s 7(7).

10.121   There are safeguards which may be employed in the award of APO, and in particular their use at a time when search warrants are being exercised in relation to the same property.[1]

[1]   See *Chappell v United Kingdom* [1989] FSR 617 and Art 8 ECHR. *Chappell* ruled that APOs were not in appropriate cases in breach of Art 8 ECHR.

PROCEEDS OF CRIME ACT 2002

10.122   Under Part 8 of the Proceeds of Crime Act 2002, which concerns the tracing of proceeds of crime and investigation of money laundering, a production order may be served on individuals as set out in s 345, together with search and seizure warrants, orders relating to computer information, disclosure orders, customer (of banks) information orders and account monitoring orders are all made to the appropriate court: the High Court in civil recovery matters and Crown Court judges for confiscation or money laundering investigations. These provisions build on powers relating to drugs trafficking and terrorist offences (see para 10.106 above).

EUROPEAN LAW

10.123   First of all it is relevant to note that the European Commission has extensive powers to gather information and institute proceedings in cases of failure to fulfil an obligation under the Treaty.

10.124   Power to gather information is provided in a general form in Art 337 of the Treaty on the Functioning of the European Union (TFEU), as well as in more specific provisions of the Treaty and Community Acts.[1] The Commission has to be able to collect all necessary information and 'carry out any checks required for the performance of the tasks entrusted to it'. Although no general implementing provisions have been laid down by the Council, the obligation imposed upon the member states to 'facilitate the achievement of the community's tasks' (TFEU, Art 4(3)) should provide the necessary legal means for the Commission to obtain all the required data.[2] The Commission also adopts its own rules of practice in relation to complaints about its investigations which have featured frequently before the EU Ombudsman.

[1]   Eg TFEU, Arts 108(3) and 337. And see reg 17, Arts 4 and 5: reg 17 was the first Regulation to implement Arts 101 and 102 on competition.
[2]   See Case 118/85 *Re AAMS: EC Commission v Italy* [1988] 3 CMLR 255.

10.125   Where the Commission believes a member state has not fulfilled Community obligations the Commission has to remind the government in question of its legal duties,[1] invite the state to take the necessary measures or to submit its own observations, all within a two-month period unless the matter is one of urgency. A reasoned opinion will follow from the Commission if no comments are forthcoming, or those that are unconvincing. Non-compliance by the member state may result in the Commission bringing proceedings before the Court of Justice. The court may require the member state 'to take the necessary measures to comply with the judgment' when it finds that the member state has failed to fulfil its obligations. Additional powers were added by the Maastricht Treaty and are retained by the Treaty of Lisbon.[2] The Commission may bring the matter back before the court if it feels there has been non-compliance with the judgment of the court and after it has afforded the state the opportunity to submit its observations and has issued a reasoned opinion specifying the points on which the member state has not complied with the judgment. The Commission may specify an amount of a lump-sum or penalty payment which it considers appropriate. Where the court finds non-compliance with its judgment, it may impose a lump sum or penalty payment on the MS.

[1]   TFEU, Art 158.
[2]   TFEU, Art 160.

Competition investigations

10.126   The Commission has important powers relating to information-gathering and investigation of infringements of TFEU, Arts 101 and 102 concerning competition. Of particular relevance are the provisions of Council Regulation (EC) 1/2003 (OJ L 1/1) on the implementation of the rules of competition laid down in Arts 101 and 102.[1]

[1]   NB the powers of the Office of Fair Trading and Competition Commission under English law: and Competition Act 1998 and under EC provisions: SI 2004/2751. See C Kerse *EC Antitrust Procedure* (5th edn, 2004). R Whish *Competition Law* (6th edn, 2008).

10.127   This Regulation empowers the Commission to undertake all necessary investigations into alleged breaches of Arts 101 and 102 EC by undertakings and associations of undertakings. Of crucial significance is the new emphasis on cooperation between the Commission and national competition authorities and national courts forming a 'network of public authorities' applying Community competition rules in close cooperation (recital 15). Emphasis is placed on sharing of information, including confidential information by national authorities (Art 12) and while the regime will have to be a decentralised one relying on national bodies, Art 16 makes provision for the uniform application of Community law. Powers of investigation are contained in Part V of the Regulation. The investigation powers of the Commission are considerable and include power to enter private premises subject to judicial authorisation and the Commission may request national authorities to carry out investigations in accordance with national law. Every investigative act has to obey the principle of proportionality (20(8)). But Regulation 1/2003 does not contain the right to remain silent.[1] If the information is not supplied within the requisite period, or is incorrect or misleading, the Commission must require that it is supplied by decision. There are penalties where there is non-compliance and a decision may be reviewed in the CFI. Article 27 covers hearings for interested parties into matters on which the Commission has taken objection. Commission decisions must be based on matters on which parties have been allowed to comment. Rights of defence and a right of access to the Commission file shall be respected. This will not cover 'confidential files' of member states or the Commission, nor correspondence passing between the Commission and member states, or between member states. Access is not allowed to information relating to the legitimate interest of other undertakings in protecting their business secrets. 'Nothing in this paragraph shall prevent the Commission from disclosing and using information necessary to prove an infringement (Art 27(2)).' Other persons may be heard and those with a 'sufficient interest' will be heard. Article 27(4) concerns summaries of cases where the Commission decides where it adopts a decision pursuant to Art 9 or 10, and interested parties may submit comments.

¹ See Case 374/87 *Orkem* [1989] ECR 3283 and Case T-112/98 *Mannesmannrothren-Werke* [2001] ECR II-729. The first case maintained a right to refuse self incriminating questions. The second case partially upheld such a right of 'defence' but refused to hold that Art 6 ECHR was breached, Cf under the EU Charter of Fundamental Rights, Art 48(2), although this does not specifically aver to the right to remain silent. This issue does not yet seem to have been litigated since the Charter gained legal force due to TFEU Art 6 post-Lisbon.

10.128 Where an undertaking has insisted that the Commission obtain a national warrant before gaining entry, they were subsequently fined by the Commission, which obtained the warrant, for non-compliance with the original order allowing a 'dawn entry'. The ECJ ruled that the Commission had not exceeded their powers.¹ The new regulation makes more specific provision for cooperative investigations (above). Trade secrets obtained should not be divulged as has been seen above, but note Art 27(4).² Access to the file should be allowed, subject to protection of commercial secrets and confidential items as outlined above, to enable the person to whom objections are addressed to express their views on the Commission's conclusions.³

¹ *Hoechst v Commission* [1989] ECR 2859.
² *AKZO Chemie BV v Commission* [1986] ECR 1965; see also *Hilti AG v Commission* [1990] ECR II-163.
³ *ICI v Commission* [1995] ECR II-1487; and see Commission's Access to the File Notice [2005] OJ C325/7. Access to the file has proved to be a problematic issue and the ECJ has found that access may be refused where disclosure could have a negative impact on competition investigations. See eg Case C-139/07 *P Commission v TGI, nyr* and Case C-360/09 *Pfleiderer AG v Bundeskartellamt*, which perhaps takes a more permissive approach to the release of the file and particularly leniency proceedings to the public in order for civil proceedings to be considered, though release is ultimately left to the discretion of national courts.

10.129 The Regulation respects the fundamental rights and observes the principles established in the Charter of Fundamental Rights and now contained in the draft EU constitution. One difficult issue has concerned legal privilege. In *A M & S Ltd v EC Commission*¹ the European Court held that the former Regulation 17 (the precursor to Regulation 1/2003) protects the confidentiality of written communications between lawyer and client provided they are for the client's defence and emanate from independent rather than 'in-house' employed lawyers; the member state in which the lawyer resides is immaterial provided the lawyer is entitled to practise in any one of the member states. The protection covers all written communications exchanged after the initiation of the administrative procedure under Regulation 17 which might lead to a decision on the application of Arts 101 and 102 of the EC Treaty or to a decision imposing a financial penalty on the undertaking. The protection extends to earlier written communications which were related to the subject-matter of that procedure. The crucial distinction between 'independent' lawyers and 'in-house' lawyers who are employees of the undertaking under investigation is not a distinction drawn in English law (see paras 10.89 et seq above). The CFI issued an injunction to prevent use by the Commission of documents seized by the Commission and which dealt with in-house legal communications. The president of the CFI accepted at the time the injunction was issued that it may be time to extend LPP to written communications between a company and its in-house lawyers and that internal documents prepared for the purpose of seeking external advice may be privileged. Ultimately, the CFI decided that privilege did not extend to in-house lawyers and this decision was upheld by the ECJ.[2] It was seen above how the English courts had sought to confine the parameters of LPP where legal advice was given but how these attempts were overruled by the House of Lords (paras 10.89 et seq above).

[1]   Case 155/79 [1983] 1 All ER 705.
[2]   Case T-125/03 *Akzo Nobel Chemicals Ltd and Akcros Chemicals Ltd v Commission* [2007] ECR II-3523, affirmed by the ECJ in Case C-550/07 P, *nyr*.

10.130   Where such a privilege is claimed, the undertaking is nevertheless required to provide the Commission's authorised agents with relevant material demonstrating that the communications fulfilled the conditions for being granted legal protection, although it is not bound to reveal the contents of the communications in question. If dissatisfied, the Commission could order production under Art 18(4) of Regulation 1/2003 and could order financial penalties for non-compliance. The undertaking would then have to bring an action in the Court of Justice to see whether the documents were protected. The operation of the Commission's decision could be suspended.[1]

[1]   TFEU, Art 278.

10.131   The English Court of Appeal has decided that communications to the European Commission are not protected by absolute privilege in English law[1] as the Commission does not operate as a court of law but as an administrative body, even though its decisions are enforceable by the High Court under CPR Part 74.[2] Nor is the communication protected by Art 28 of Regulation 1/2003. This protects the secrecy of information that the Commission has received by the application, or at least the threat of the application, of its compulsory powers to obtain information and conduct inquiries. Article 20 could not cover information obtained under Art 5 which concerns information volunteered by way, inter alia, of making complaint. Under Art 28, total secrecy cannot be maintained. However, a majority of the Court of Appeal held that, on the facts, the communication in question – a letter – was protected by public interest immunity.[3]

[1]   They may attract qualified privilege.
[2]   *Hasselblad (GB) Ltd v Orbinson* [1985] 1 All ER 173. See *AKZO* case (53/85) [1987] 1 CMLR 231 ECJ on the care in communicating information to a complainant. An independent hearing officer is appointed by DG IV of the Commission.
[3]   *Hasselblad* above.

10.132   Elsewhere the European Court has ruled that there is very limited scope for obtaining interim discovery of documents in the possession of the Commission. Circumstances would have to be 'exceptional' to allow such discovery. An argument that the documents – concerning an investigation into non-EEC imports – were required urgently was based upon 'the risk of alteration or concealment of relevant documents' by the Commission. The court would not permit such arguments to be sustained, which cast doubt on the good faith of the Commission, without supporting evidence.[1] The discussion in ch 3 on the Regulation on Access to Council, Commission and Parliament's Documents should be recalled.[2]

¹   *Epikhiriseon MVKN AE v EC Council and Commission* [1987] 1 CMLR 57; *Greece v EC Council and Commission* [1988] 3 CMLR 728.
²   See paras 3.18 et seq above and Regulation (EC) 1049/2001.

Proceedings before the European Court of Justice¹

10.133   The rules of procedure before the European Court of Justice (ECJ) for direct actions are contained in a Protocol on the statute of the Court of Justice of the EC annexed to the EU and TFEU Treaties, as well as the rules of procedure which the court adopts after the unanimous approval of the Council. The procedure of the General Court, which commenced activities in 1989 as the Court of First Instance and was renamed the General Court in 2009, is very close to that of the ECJ although it has some special features. Significant developments to the courts and their organisation were made in the Treaty of Nice in 2001.

¹   *European Court Practice* (2000) R Plender, ed K Lasok *The European Court of Justice: Practice and Procedure* 1994.

10.134   Procedure in direct actions is commenced by a submission to the court of a written application to the Registrar – the Registrar serves the application on the defendant. The standards and rules contain a variety of requirements on form, content and accompanying documents.¹ The application must state the grounds on which it is based, both facts and legal arguments in detail, as fresh issues in the course of the proceedings may not be raised unless they relate to matters of law or fact emerging in the written procedure.² An address for service in Luxemburg must be provided and the applicant's lawyer must file a certificate of his entitlement to practise before the courts of a member state. The application is notified to the defendant by the Registrar and the defendant must file a defence within a month.³ The President of the Court assigns the case to one of the Chambers. A judge-rapporteur is chosen along with an advocate-general. Time-limits for pleadings are fixed by the president of the court. Before these written proceedings are closed the court may⁴ decide to prescribe 'measures of inquiry'⁵ for the case which could involve interrogation of the parties, the hearing of witnesses⁶ or requests for information. This is known as the investigation or preparatory inquiry. These rarely occur. The ECJ may decide at its administrative meeting at the prompting of the judge-rapporteur to seek answers to questions from the parties or the Commission either in writing or at the oral hearings or to produce documents or evidence for the court. Information added to the court file in the course of the preparatory inquiry or after the questions described above must be made freely available to the parties who have the right to respond to its contents. The date for the oral procedure is fixed by the President of the court although this may in certain cases be dispensed with.

¹   See the statute, and rules: Art 38 et seq. On applications by corporations, its memorandum and articles of association must be provided and proof that power of attorney to its lawyers has been given.
²   Rules: Art 42(2).
³   Rules: Art 40(1).
⁴   At the prompting of the judge-rapporteur or advocate-general.
⁵   See Rules: Arts 45–54.
⁶   Statute, Arts 26–30. Witnesses may be heard on oath.

10.135   Where a preliminary ruling is made under TFEU, Art 267, the parties, the member states, the Commission and the Council and European Parliament (where measure jointly adopted by Council and the EP) – who all have a copy of the notice of reference sent to them[1] – may submit to the court statements of case or written observations. The procedure is designed not to settle disputes but to provide consistent and uniform interpretation of EU law.

[1]   Council only when a Council measure involved; European Central Bank likewise. See generally Rules, Arts 103–104a.

10.136   Member states and Community institutions, as well as other parties who can establish an interest in the decision of a case, may intervene in cases before the ECJ.[1] They have to provide contentions tending to sustain or deny the contentions of one of the parties to the principal dispute, the supporting evidence and an election of domicile.[2]

[1]   Statute, Art 40.
[2]   Statute, Art 18(4), Rules: Arts 55–62.

10.137   After the written procedure there is an oral procedure consisting of reports by the judge-rapporteur, the opinion of the advocate-general and legal submissions at the hearing, if any, of witnesses and experts. Cross-examination as practised in English courts is not allowed. Judgment follows later. Hearings are in public but may be in camera where the Court decides otherwise for 'serious reasons'.[1] Deliberations are, and shall remain, secret. The judgment is that of the Court without dissenting judgments. Judgments must state the reasons on which they are based.[2] The language of the case is that of the national court making the reference under Art 267 TFEU although a member state's submissions and the opinion of the advocate-general are in their own language.[3] In direct actions the applicant has choice of language but where a defendant is a member state or an individual or corporation with the nationality of that state, the official language of that state is chosen. However, questions may be put in any language by a member of the court and there is simultaneous translation. The deliberations in secret are in French.

[1]   Applications for interim relief may be made in writing to the President, who may refer the matter, exceptionally, to the whole court: see *Top Hit Holzvertrieb GmbH v EC Commission:* 378/87R [1988] 2 CMLR 594; see *Greece v EC Council and Commission* para 10.132, note 1 above. On interim relief, see *Zuckerfabrik* Case – 143/88 [1991] ECR I–415, *Atlanta Bananas* Case C-465/93 [1995] ECR I–3761, and *R v Secretary of State for Health, ex p Imperial Tobacco Ltd* [2001] 1 All ER 850, HL.
[2]   Statute, Art 36.
[3]   Rules, Art 29.

10.138   On judicial review applications involving EC institutions an application shall be accompanied, where appropriate, by the measure for which annulment is sought or, if under Art 265 TFEU, with documentary evidence of the date on which the relevant institution was requested to act.

10.139   Generally, the court is liberal in construing the grounds of an application[1] and the Registrar will ask parties to put documents into proper order.

[1]   *J Nold KG v EC Commission:* 4/73 [1974] 2 CMLR 338.

Chapter 11

The National Audit Office and the Comptroller and Auditor General

11.1 Society has, from time immemorial, had to rely upon the state and its officials, or those acting under the authority of, or in co-operation with the state, to investigate aspects of behaviour affecting the public weal. Powers of information-gathering accompany, obviously enough, investigatory powers. Examples include those relating to the police investigation of crime under the Police and Criminal Evidence Act 1984, the Police Act 1997, the Criminal Justice and Police Act 2001,[1] the Proceeds of Crime Act 2002, the Police and Crime Act 2009 on proceeds of crime (Part 5) and safeguarding vulnerable groups (Part 8 (see para 7.248), the Regulation of Investigatory Powers Act 2000, and the Crime and Security Act 2010, which will be amended by the Protection of Freedoms Bill 2011, prevention of terrorism,[2] collection of income tax,[3] VAT,[4] customs and excise,[5] financial regulation,[6] investigation of serious fraud,[7] or activities or practices damaging competition[8] and hundreds of other regulatory responsibilities of the modern state. These powers include investigation into companies under the Companies Act 1985, ss 432 and 442 and the Companies Act 2006, Part 32 and Part 22 on disclosure of information about shareholdings.[9] The international dimension is witnessed by the Crime (International Co-operation) Act 2003. This book has in reality provided a catalogue of such activities.

[1] Police and Criminal Evidence Act 1984, ss 8–16 and Sch 1, Criminal Justice and Police Act 2001; Police Act 1997, Part III; Proceeds of Crime Act 2002 – see *R (UMBS) Online Ltd) v SOCA* [2007] EWCA Civ 406.

[2] Prevention of Terrorism (Temporary Provisions) Act 1989, s 17 and Sch 7; Prevention of Terrorism (Additional Powers) Act 1996; Terrorism Act 2000, ss 19, 20, 38, 39, 57, 58, 87, 88, 103 and 104, Schs 5, 6; and Anti-terrorism, Crime and Security Act 2001 (see para 7.275 above), Prevention of Terrorism Act 2005, Terrorism Act 2006, Counter Terrorism Act 2008, Terrorist Asset Freezing etc Act 2010. See *R v G* [2009] UKHL 13 and *R v Muhammed (Sultan)* [2010] EWCA Crim 227 on TA 2000, ss 57, 58.

[3] Eg Taxes Management Act 1970, ss 20 and 51; Income and Corporation Taxes Act 1988; Finance Act 1989, ss 142–148 and Pt II, ch IV generally; and see paras 7.273 et seq above. NB savings from another EU member state: SI 2003/3297 (Finance Act 2003, s 199 and Council Directive 2003/48/EC (OJ L 157/38)). On disclosure by advisers relating to tax avoidance schemes, see

Finance Act 2004, ss 306–319; and SI 2004/1863, as amended and relaxed, after consultation, by SI 2004/2420 and Finance (No 2) Act 2005, s 6 and Sch 1, Income Taxes Act 2007, Finance Act 2007, Part 6, Finance Act 2008 ,Part 7, ch 1 and Schs 36, 37 and 38, Finance Act 2009, s 92 on the HMRC charter, s 94–98 and Schs 47 and 48, Finance Act 2010, s 56 and Sch 17, Taxation (International and Other Provisions) Act 2010, s 129.

4   Value Added Tax Act 1983 and 1994.

5   Customs and Excise Management Act 1979 and Commissioners for Customs and Revenue Act 2005.

6   Financial Services and Markets Act 2000. The Financial Services Authority is prepared to use statutory powers to compel production of information as a matter of course instead of relying upon voluntary arrangements: (2003) New LJ 1856.

7   Criminal Justice Act 1987, ss 2 and 3: see *R (EFT Ltd) v Bow Street Magistrates Court* [2005] 4 All ER 285 (CA). See *R (Kent Pharmaceuticals Ltd) v Director of the Serious Fraud Office* [2005] 1 All ER 449 (CA) on Art 8 ECHR and CJA 1987, s 3(5) disclosure by the SFO of documents seized under search warrants to other government departments (to pursue legal proceedings against the owners of documents). Disclosure was in accordance with the law for the purposes of Art 8(2) ECHR but required fairness and absent good reasons informing the owner of the goods. No prejudice had been caused by not informing the owner. See on CJA 1987, s 1(3) and HRA compliance: *Bermingham and Others v Government of USA* [2006] EWHC 200. See PACE 1984, ss 19, 20.

8   Competition Act 1998 and Enterprise Act 2002; Companies Act 1989, ss 85, 146–153.

9   Inspectors have no power to require those investigated to sign confidentiality undertakings under Companies Act 1985, s 434: *Re an Inquiry into Mirror Group Newspapers plc* [1999] 2 All ER 641. Under s 356(6) of the 1985 Act the court may compel an immediate inspection of the register and index of company members: the court has a discretion: *P v F Ltd* (2001) New LJ 1284. See also Insolvency Act 1986, s 236 and a power of the official receiver to obtain information from any person relating to the officers of a company: *In re Pantmaenog Timber Co Ltd* [2003] 4 All ER 18 (HL). See Companies (Audit, Investigations and Community Enterprise) Act 2004 on auditing of accounts and investigations. Companies Act 1985, s 447 is replaced by s 1 of the 2004 Act; and see s 24 of the 2004 Act and the Companies Act 2006 in the text.

11.2   In ch 4 there was an examination of the Audit Commission (AC) and its powers and duties in relation to local government. It was noted how the Commission was due to be disbanded under the coalition plans for cutting state bodies but with no clear idea of how its many responsibilities were to be reallocated. Its powers had been extended to cover a wider range of educational bodies.[1] Under the National Health Service and Community Care Act 1990 the AC's work had been extended to include national health service bodies.[2] The Public Audit (Wales) Act makes provision for the Welsh Assembly, bodies supervised by the Assembly and local government in Wales (para 4.78 above).

1   By Education Reform Act 1988, s 220; see now Audit Commission Act 1998, s 36.
2   The legislation is now consolidated in the Audit Commission Act 1998 as amended.

11.3   It will be instructive to describe the provisions of the National Audit Act 1983 (NAA 1983). It provides one of the most successful instruments to inform Parliament – through the Public Accounts Committee (PAC) – and the public of the delivery, impact and expenditure of government programmes. A brief description of fiscal transparency will be given.

11.4   The state of the economy and government fiscal and monetary and spending plans are announced in the Budget, usually in the spring. These follow budgetary preparations in departments that began in the previous spring. Reforms have taken place since the 1980s so that plans for spending and taxation are now aligned and preceded by a spending review in the autumn. A unified Budget was abandoned, after a brief period, in 1997. The Budget does not cover all public spending. Parliament does not vote on all expenditure and has no control over borrowing. The Finance Act 1998 included provisions which underpinned the fiscal framework introduced by the government in 1997. In particular, s 155 of the Act required the Treasury to prepare and lay before Parliament a code for fiscal stability for the application of certain key principles (transparency, stability, responsibility, fairness and efficiency) to the formulation and implementation of fiscal policy. Section 156 of the Act required the government to prepare and lay before Parliament each year a Financial Statement and Budget Report, an Economic and Fiscal Strategy Report, a Debt Management Report and a Pre-Budget Report. The Fiscal Responsibility Act 2010 imposed a variety of duties on the Treasury to secure sound public finances. The Act also introduced Commons votes for some aspects of borrowing by government. The Act was repealed by the Budget Reform and Responsibility Act 2010. For their part, departments must prepare their estimates (money required), publish their accounts and publish further details in annual reports. Estimates and government publications in the financial cycle have improved the clarity, quality and accessibility of information about expenditure plans. The Constitutional Reform and Governance Act 2010 has also introduced a requirement for greater amounts of information on departmental bodies as well as departments themselves in the estimates.

11.5   The incoming government in 2010 focused much of its criticism of the preceding government on its failure to manage the economy and monetary and fiscal policy in a transparent and effective manner. To this end, the Budget Responsibility and National Audit Act 2011, Part I established an independent Office of Budget Responsibility (OBR) (see s 3 and Sch 1). Under s 2 the Treasury has to produce budget documents. The OBR was established initially on a non-statutory basis in 2010. It will be led by a three-person committee appointed by the Chancellor with at least two non-executive members. It is the duty of the OBR under s 4 to examine and report on the sustainability of the public finances. The OBR must, on at least two occasions for each financial year, prepare:

'(3)
(a) fiscal and economic forecasts, and
(b) an assessment of the extent to which the fiscal mandate has been, or is likely to be, achieved.

(4) It must also, on at least one occasion for each financial year, prepare—
(a) an assessment of the accuracy of fiscal and economic forecasts previously prepared by it, and
(b) an analysis of the sustainability of the public finances.

(5) Any forecast, assessment or analysis prepared by the Office under subsection (3) or (4) must be included in a report.

(6) Any report which the Office makes in pursuance of its duty under this section must include an explanation of the factors which the Office took into account when preparing the report, including (in particular)—

(a) the main assumptions made by the Office, and

(b) the main risks which the Office considered to be relevant.'

11.6 The OBR has complete discretion on how it exercises its duty under s 4, but it is subject to the requirements of objectivity, transparency and impartiality. It must have regard to relevant government policies but must not consider alternatives. The Treasury is to produce a charter on budget responsibility under s 1 and this may contain guidance for the OBR.[1] The Charter may include guidance to the OBR about how it should perform its duty under s 4, including (in particular) guidance about the time at which it is to prepare any forecast, assessment or analysis required to be prepared under s 4(3) or (4). But the Charter must not make provision about the methods by which the OBR is to make any such forecast, assessment or analysis. The OBR must, in the performance of its duty under s 4, act consistently with any guidance included in the Charter by virtue of s 4. If the Treasury proposes to modify the guidance included in the Charter, a draft of the modified guidance must be published at least 28 days before the modified Charter is laid before Parliament under s 1(6). OBR reports must be published, laid before Parliament and sent to the Treasury. The OBR has a right of access (at any reasonable time) to all government information which it may reasonably require for the purpose of the performance of its duty under s 4. The OBR is entitled to require from any person holding or accountable for any government information any assistance or explanation which the OBR reasonably thinks necessary for that purpose. 'Government information' means information held by any Minister of the Crown or government department. The section is subject to any enactment or rule of law which operates to prohibit or restrict the disclosure of information or the giving of any assistance or explanation. The following acts are repealed in consequence of the Act: the Industry Act 1975, Sch 1, s 27 (economic model and forecasting); the Finance Act 1998, ss 155 to 157 (fiscal stability); and the Fiscal Responsibility Act 2010. The OBR's forecasts were examined by the National Audit Office in December 2010.

[1] *Charter for Budget Responsibility* HM Treasury (April 2011).

THE NATIONAL AUDIT ACT 1983

11.7 The NAA 1983 established the manner in which the Comptroller and Auditor General (CAG) will be appointed.[1] The CAG is an officer of the House of Commons. The CAG is given, subject to statutory duties, 'complete discretion in the discharge of his functions and, in particular, in determining whether to carry out any examination under Part II of the Act.[2] Section 3 established the National Audit Office (NAO) with the CAG at the head of a staff of approximately 900 persons working in London and Newcastle. Spending oversight in the UK is performed by Audit Scotland, Wales Audit Office and Northern Ireland Audit Office. The CAG is given the power to charge audit fees (s 5(1)) which will be paid into the Consolidated Fund. There are limitations on his ability to charge fees.[3] The Budget Responsibility and National Audit Act 2011 makes further provision in relation to the Comptroller and Auditor

General, who is to be apppointed for one term of ten years, and the NAO, which is to be a body corporate distinct from the CAG.

¹   NAA 1983, s 1, and see Exchequer and Audit Departments Act 1866, s 6. This is by the Crown on the advice of the Prime Minister whose recommendation must be supported by the Chair of the PAC who, by convention, is a member of the opposition.
²   NAA 1983, s 1(3).
³   NAA 1983, s 5(2): ministerial consent for bodies discharging functions on behalf of the Crown etc.

11.8   NAA 1983, s 6 empowers the CAG to carry out examinations into the economy, efficiency and effectiveness[1] with which any department, authority or other body to which the section applies has used its resources in discharging its functions. These are 'value for money' (VFM) audits[2] and are considerably wider than a traditional commercial audit in the private sector and exchequer or certification audits carried out by the CAG under the Exchequer and Audit Departments Acts 1866 and 1921. There are about 60 VFM audits per annum. In deciding whether to carry out VFM audits the CAG must have regard to any proposals of the CPA. The 2011 Act requires the CAG to carry out his functions efficiently and cost-effectively. In 2010–2011, there were three reports on government support to UK banks making 'the level of government exposure transparent to the public and helping to focus parliamentary attention on the value for money delivered by government intervention. As steps are taken to make the banking system safer for the future,[3] the NAO will continue to scrutinise and support value for money and transparency. In 2011–12 it plans to concentrate on accountability arrangements as government reforms take effect more generally. Exchequer reports on the audits of relevant bodies are made after the end of the financial year as part of the appropriation accounts. The CAG must be satisfied that expenditure is restricted to the purposes approved by Parliament and conforms to its governing authority. The CAG is not, however, empowered to chase public money wherever it is spent. Many non-departmental public bodies and some local spending bodies are not audited by the CAG and private contractors performing tasks for public bodies within jurisdiction of the CAG are only subject to investigation if the parent authority agrees to incorporation of a term in the contract allowing access for the NAO.[4] Since 2008, he has been the auditor to 48 public sector companies incorporated under the Companies Act. The CAG cannot disallow expenditure or formally stand in judgment on questions of legality. The auditor in local government lost powers of surcharge under the Local Government Act 2000 (LGA 2000) (see paras 8.11 et seq above). The CAG does supervise Treasury rules on expenditure, and Treasury consent for expenditure is frequently required.

¹   See Audit Commission Act 1998, s 5.
²   See NAO *Progress with VFM Savings and Lessons for Cost Reduction Programmes* (2010).
³   Including the creation of the Financial Policy Committee of the Bank of England to act as an early warning system on banking activities and which will meet at least four times a year and whose proceedings will be published. There will also be a Prudential Regulatory Authority under the Bank to oversee insurers and deposit takers. Andrew Tyrie, chair of the Treasury Committee, has criticised the governance procedures involving oversight by the nine-member Court of the Bank of England: *Financial Times* 22 June 2011.The Court's directors, some witnesses said, did not have sufficient expertise to conduct appropriate inquiries for the purposes of accountability and

did not order inquiries into banking failures in the past as at Northern Rock. See HM Treasury Cm 8083 (2011) *A New Approach to Financial Regulation*. The retail and investment businesses of banks are also to be ring-fenced and split.

⁴   These are in guidance from the Office of Government Commerce in consultation with NAO.

11.9   The NAO is the principal state audit body in the United Kingdom.[1] The work of the NAO is scrutinised by the Public Accounts Commission, a committee of Parliament, which also appoints external auditors and approves its supply estimate (budget). The NAO has a management board with executive and non-executive members and five committees. The management structure and its objectives are set out in annual reports. As well as the Audit Commission, which was discussed in ch 4, there is the Auditor General for Scotland (AGS), supported by Audit Scotland. The AGS is responsible for auditing the expenditure of the Scottish Parliament and Executive and reporting to that Parliament. Audit Scotland is also responsible for local authority audit in Scotland. The existence of Public Audit (Wales) Act 2004 was dealt with in ch 4. The Comptroller and Auditor General for Northern Ireland and the Northern Ireland Audit Office operate in respect of the Northern Ireland Assembly (reporting to the Westminster Parliament when the Assembly was not in operation).

¹   See IC DN FS50324495 where information was requested on changes to complaints investigations by the NAO.

11.10   In order to share good practice, the public audit bodies work as closely as possible together. A Public Audit Forum has been established 'to act as a focus for developmental thinking on public audit'.[1]

¹   http://www.public-audit-forum.gov.uk/.

11.11   European Union expenditure in all EU member states is audited by the European Court of Auditors (ECA). The NAO describes itself acting 'as a liaison point between the ECA and UK departments'. The Office also reports 'regularly to Parliament on issues relating to the expenditure of EU funds in the UK, and on occasion, on wider issues of financial management within the European Union' (www.nao.org.uk).

ECONOMY, EFFICIENCY AND EFFECTIVENESS – THE 'THREE ES'

11.12   The Expenditure Committee in 1976–77 published the CAG's own words on the 'three Es':[1]

'Taking Government policy as given, a value for money audit covers the examination of the management of projects or programmes to bring to light any weaknesses in judgement, execution or control leading to wasteful, extravagant or unrewarding expenditure, or failure to maximise receipts ... An efficiency audit thus takes a programme or project as given and examines whether it has been well or ill executed. An effectiveness audit [by contrast] attempts to assess how successful particular activities have been in meeting the Government's objectives. This requires not only a clear statement of those objectives, but some means of measuring the degree of success in attaining them. It is also likely to involve questions of policy, an area which the CAG and his Department have over the years studiously avoided. But few boundary lines in public administration are completely clear cut, and to report as part of a value for money examination on the outcome of certain policies may carry a pretty clear implication that modifications might provide better financial results. Financial or economic criteria, though important, are not of course the only ones which the Government may wish to apply.'

1   HC 535 (1976–77) at p 584.

11.13   The former Treasury and Civil Service Committee (TCSC) (now the Treasury Committee) has produced a more developed account as follows:[1]

'The intention of a programme may be defined as its ultimate aim and it is likely to be stated in broad terms such as full employment, stable prices, the health or security of the nation. For the purpose of managing a particular programme such broad intentions must be translated into operational objectives. The steps towards such objectives should, where feasible, be quantified as targets.

An efficient programme is one where the target is being achieved with the least possible use of resources and instruments. Similarly, on the way to achieving the target, the actual output of a programme should be secured with the least use of resources. An effective programme is one where the intention of the programme is being achieved. That implies that the intention, the operational objectives and the targets have been defined; that the targets adequately represent the objectives and the objectives the intention and that the outputs of the programme are equal to the target.'

1   HC 236 (1981–82), vol i, paras 51–52.

11.14   The TCSC's model defines 'efficiency' to mean productive efficiency, ie securing the same output for a lesser use of resources. The evidence to the Expenditure Committee by the former CAG tends to obscure the distinction between productive efficiency and economy: the former refers to the same output for less use of resources, the latter the same output for less expenditure.

11.15   The NAO (www.nao.org.uk) describes the 'three Es' in the following terms:

'–   Economy: minimising the cost of resources used or required – **spending less**;

–   Efficiency: the relationship between the output from goods or services and the resources to produce them – **spending well**; and

–   Effectiveness: the relationship between the intended and actual results of public spending – **spending wisely**.'

THE EXCLUSION OF POLICY

11.16   Section 6(2) of the NAA 1983 provides that nothing in s 6(1) shall entitle the CAG to question the merits of the policy objectives of any department, authority or body in respect of which an examination is carried out! It is a truism to suggest that the dividing line between policy and administration is a difficult one to locate. The implications of CAG reports may be devastating for government policies; but there must not be questioning of their merits in a VFM inquiry. The implementation of policy 'and the assessment of the adequacy of the information on which both policy and implementation decisions are based, do fall within the NAO's value for money remit'.[1] Openly to criticise advice and appraisal may come too close to criticism of policy although VFM reports raise obvious questions about the merits of policy decisions. It is for others to pick up the cudgels such as departmental select committees (see para 2.119).

[1]   White, Harden and Donnelly *Public Law* (1994) 526 at p 531.

11.17   NAA 1983, s 6 goes on to define the bodies within the CAG's jurisdiction.[1] Under s 7 the CAG, where the CAG has reasonable cause to believe that any authority or body to which the section applies has in any of its financial years received more than half its income from public funds, may carry out a VFM audit for the year in question. The s 6(2) provision concerning the merits of policy objectives, above, applies.

[1]   Basically government departments, health authorities, those covered by statute and those subject to agreement between the body and a Minister.

11.18   The body concerned and the Treasury must be consulted. Section 6(5) defines what 'money received from public funds' means.

11.19   Under NAA 1983, s 8 the CAG has a right of access at all reasonable times to all such documents reasonably required for carrying out s 6 or s 7 examinations, together with such information and explanation from the holder of the document as are reasonably necessary. It does not apply to those documents not under the control of the department etc (s 8(2)). However, if the CAG has no statutory right of access, then access has to be negotiated with the body.

Pergau Dam

11.20   In the Pergau Dam affair, which concerned UK government expenditure for overseas development in Malaysia in order to assist British companies bid for overseas aid projects, the powers of the CAG to obtain information and the role of the departmental accounting officer – in large departments usually the Permanent Secretary – came under crucial scrutiny. A consortium of British firms found that the cost of the Pergau Dam project would be about £316 million. The relevant department advising on such projects, the Overseas Development Administration (ODA) (which administers schemes jointly with the Department of Trade and Industry), advised that the project was 'just about acceptable'. However, the cost was revised upwards to £417 million described by the ODA as 'unequivocally bad ... In economic terms'.[1] The Accounting Officer reported his misgivings, stating the project should not be supported. He stated that he would require a ministerial direction before any expenditure could be incurred. This was forthcoming from the Secretary of State for Foreign and Commonwealth Affairs in consultation with the Prime Minister. The issue of such a direction was regarded as a matter of government policy which the CAG could not criticise on a VFM audit.[2] Based on a NAO VFM report the PAC of the House of Commons made a critical report which attracted an enormous amount of attention and eventually litigation (see below). The duties of an Accounting Officer are contained in *Accounting Officer Memorandum* which is included in *Government Accounting*. Basically an Accounting Officer is under a duty to advise Ministers on all matters of financial propriety and regularity as well as 'prudent and economical administration, efficiency and effectiveness'. As practice then existed at the time of the relevant events and overruling, the Accounting Officer was under a duty to inform the CAG where in his opinion he had formed the view that a Minister planned a course of action that contravened the requirements of propriety or regularity. Having duly informed the Minister in writing of his views, the Accounting Officer could then be formally overruled. Where the Minister decided to proceed with expenditure, the Accounting Officer should receive written instructions from the Minister and then inform the Treasury and send the papers to the CAG 'without delay'. Where a matter fell within the wider remit of the 'prudent and economical administration, efficiency and effectiveness' provision, at the time in question the Accounting Officer had to advise the Minister and if overruled he should ensure that his advice and its overruling are clear from the papers. There is no duty to communicate this to the CAG or Treasury. Only where the CAG conducts a VFM inquiry was there a requirement to inform the CAG of the overruling.

[1]   I draw on the article by White, Harden and Donnelly, para 11.16, note 1 above for help on detail.
[2]   HC 908 (1993–94), p 11.

11.21   The Accounting Officer in the Pergau affair informed the PAC that the expenditure fell under the heading of 'prudent and economical administration, efficiency and effectiveness'. The duty to inform the Treasury and CAG did not arise and only occurred when the CAG decided to conduct a VFM inquiry. The PAC recommended that in all cases concerning a ministerial direction where a question of economical administration, efficiency and effectiveness are concerned, the Accounting Officer should be under a duty to inform the CAG and provide the relevant papers. The government accepted this recommendation.[1] It would then be open to the CAG to report such matters to the PAC.

[1]   Cm 2602.

11.22   In the Pergau Dam episode, a practice of marking documents as 'Not for NAO Eyes' emerged and in response to Parliamentary Questions it transpired that 1,500 documents had been so designated by departments investigated by the CAG. It has been stated that far from representing a 'covert game plan to undermine the workings of the CAG' the practice represents a working relationship between the CAG and government on access to documents.[1] The formal legal provision allowing access is NAA 1983, s 8(1). This provides for access at 'all reasonable times' to all documents 'as he may reasonably require'. For VFM inquiries, he may require persons holding or accountable for such documents to 'give such information and explanation as are reasonably necessary' for the inquiry. 'Reasonable' is a word of wide interpretation so the legal provision has been circumscribed as a practice, not a matter of law, by internal concordats and practice. The CAG has accepted limitations on his access to include:

(1)   Ministerial Private Office files, containing Cabinet or Cabinet Committee papers or minutes.

(2)   Files dealing with the conduct of business with the NAO or PAC 'often classified "Not for NAO Eyes"'. These might otherwise be referred to as active files generated by an inquiry.

[1]   White, Harden and Donnelly article, para 11.16, note 1 above.

11.23   In the Pergau Dam affair, the CAG obtained all necessary files. And in fact it was this information, together with other investigations before select committees, which produced so much evidence for the judicial review which sought, successfully, to establish that the expenditure was ultra vires. The 'Not for NAO Eyes' warning was dropped by the incoming Labour government in July 1997 with retrospective effect.[1] The decision to provide overseas aid was ruled by the High Court to be ultra vires the Overseas Development and Co-operation Act 1980, s 1 which provided that the Secretary of State had 'power, for the purpose of promoting the development or maintaining the economy of [an overseas] country or territory ... or the welfare of its people, to furnish any person or body with assistance, whether financial, technical or of any other nature'.[2] The applicants were a public interest organisation with national and international expertise and interest in promoting and protecting aid to underdeveloped nations. In a generous interpretation the court allowed the applicant locus standi but refused disclosure of minutes that were sought by the applicants even though the Secretary of State's statements in affidavit were incomplete. These were amplified by a subsequent letter from the Secretary of State.[3] The court ruled that the grant of aid was not for the purposes of economically sound development even though the Secretary of State was entitled to take into account broader political, economic, commercial and human rights aspects in his decision. He was not, however, entitled to take into consideration the political impossibility of withdrawing from a promise of aid to the Malaysian government in 1989. Without an express inclusion of a 'developmental promotion purpose' within s 1 the grant was ultra vires. It should be noted it was unlawful even though the Accounting Officer in requesting a ministerial direction had not ruled that the expenditure was in contravention of propriety or regularity. In his evidence to the Foreign Affairs Committee, the Accounting Officer, however, described the project as 'an abuse of the aid programme', 'not ... a sound development project' and lacking any counter arguments to support the economic case.[4] In the judicial review hearing, the judge observed:

'[W]here ... the contemplated development is, on the evidence, so economically unsound that there is no economic argument in favour of the case, it is not, in my judgment, possible to draw any material distinction between questions of propriety and regularity on the one hand and questions of economy and efficiency of public expenditure on the other. It may be surprising that no suggestion of illegality was made by any official, or that the Secretary of State was not advised that there would, or might be, any illegality. No legal advice was ever sought.'[5]

1 Cm 3714 and White and Hollingsworth *Audit, Accountability and Government* (1999) OUP, p 114.
2 *R v Secretary of State for Foreign Affairs, ex p World Development Movement Ltd* [1995] 1 All ER 611.
3 See para 10.59 above and the restricted opportunities for disclosure in judicial review litigation. See the crucial disclosures made in *European Roma Rights Centre v Immigration Officer at Prague Airport* [2005] 1 All ER 527 (HL) at paras 88 et seq.
4 HC 271 (1993–94) at p 271; see White, Harden and Donnelly, above.
5 Per Rose LJ at pp 626–27, note 2 above.

11.24 As commentators have pointed out, this brings the question of legality very close to questions of propriety and regularity. In this respect, the law is a far more direct and abrupt form of control than the techniques hitherto applied in supervising government expenditure.[1]

1 Local government expenditure has always been subject to far greater legal control because its powers are exclusively statutory and less deference has been shown to local government by the courts. See *Bromley London Borough Council v Greater London Council* [1983] 1 AC 768, HL.

11.25 The Government Resources and Accounts Act 2000, s 8, allows the CAG access at all reasonable times to any documents relating to a department's accounts. Assistance must be provided by the departments. Under s 25, the powers in s 8 are extended to bodies audited by the CAG by statute or agreement (see SIs 2003/1326, 2003/1325 and 2003/1324 (audit of health services bodies). Auditing of companies performing public functions is amended under the 2011 Act.

THE CAG REPORTS

11.26 The reports of the CAG[1] may be made to the House of Commons. The reports form the basis of inquiries by the PAC. This is a separate body to the Public Accounts Commission although there may be some shared membership. The committee investigates 40–50 VFM and financial reports each year and can issue up to about fifty reports. This committee of the Commons has a peculiar privilege in being able to insist on the appearance before it of the accounting officer of the department or body investigated. Appearance of civil servants before select committees is in every other case subject to ministerial control (see paras 2.125 et seq above). It also has members of the Treasury in attendance. Once again, the PAC is privileged in having such well researched and factual reports on which to base its own investigations. The NAO has expanded the assistance it gives to other select committees as well as the PAC. Schedule 4 to the NAA 1983 lists those bodies over which the CAG has no power of investigation. It includes remaining nationalised industries (although it reported on the nationailsation of Northern Rock in 2009), the BBC, and Welsh Fourth Channel Authority.[2] It has reported on *Regulating Network Rail's Efficiency* (2011). The last two decades have seen a heightened awareness of the importance of, and support for, internal audits by bodies within the jurisdiction of the CAG.[3]

¹   http://www.nao.org.uk/publications.aspx?psl=10.
²   This is a much narrower range of bodies than that originally in the Bill which became the National Audit Act. Cf the Independent Television Commission.
³   Starting with the Financial Management Initiatives, MINIS, Rayner Scrutinies etc through to Public Service Agreements.

11.27   Reports on accounts of bodies audited are contained in the reports of those bodies which are presented annually to Parliament – there were 475 accounts audited in 2009–10 (over 550 separate accounts audited in 2003–04) with a total revenue and expenditure of over £950 billion (£700 billion 2003–04).¹ The VFM reports of the CAG – which form the basis of PAC investigations and reports, and government replies – are published as separate reports of the National Audit Office with a House of Commons sessional number. There are approximately 60 VFM reports each year (63 in 2009–10) and reports are published at the CAG's complete discretion which is also true of their timing. Reports have in more recent years concentrated on financial management in departments, quality of public service, private finance initiatives and audit of international bodies to which the UK contributes. The NAO has also assisted in the smooth introduction of international financial reporting standards for the bodies it audits.

¹   Annual Report 2004 NAO *Helping the Nation Spend Wisely*; NAO *Annual Report 2010*.

11.28   CAG reports have been criticised in the past for being a little colourless. However, they are mines of useful information. This is no less true of areas of customer service by departments, agencies and other bodies where the standard of service is far from suitable,¹ to programmes for privatisation,² urban development corporations,³ public housing programmes of the Department of the Environment⁴ government contracting,⁵ safety of regulation of medicines,⁶ regulating charities⁷ and improving the speed and quality of asylum decisions (HC 535 (2003–04) and HC 238 (2004–05) from the PAC).The CAG has investigated the subject of expenditure on government publicity.⁸ In the 1993/94 session the CAG made a very wide ranging report on 'The Proper Conduct of Public Business' in response to widespread concern about the resort to business practices in delivery of public services and a lowering of standards in behaviour and ethics among public servants.⁹ The NAO has given wider evidence to government on eg the Private Finance Initiative (PFI) which, according to the 1997 Annual Report of the NAO, was accepted by the government in full. It published its approach to the audit of PFI projects to assist public officials embarking on such projects. It also produced by 1998 four separate VFM reports on PFI projects.¹⁰ Further reports on PFI and the Public Private Partnerships have been produced including *Financing PFI Projects in the Credit Crisis* (2010).¹¹ PFI reports are common throughout the years 2006–11. In March 2005, there was a wide-ranging investigation and report into *Citizen Redress* and internal complaints procedures (HC 21 (2004–05); see para 9.3 above for more recent reports). Reports have been issued on data security and information assurances. The reports cover the criminal justice landscape, data systems for public service agreements, regulatory reform and financial sustainability for higher education and preparation for the London Olympics. Lawyers representing parties challenging decisions of government bodies should check to establish whether there are in existence any reports of the CAG or PAC on the particular responsibility of the body in question. The reports are not merely of a wider academic or political significance. The CAG and PAC are vital conduits for the provision of information to the public which could be essential armoury for a lawyer.

1   HC 451 (1987–88); HC 736 (1987–88); See *BSE – the Cost of the Crisis* HC 583 (1997–98); *Government on the WEB* HC 87 (1999–2000).
2   See eg, *Privatisation of the Rolling Stock Leasing Companies* HC 576 (1997–98) and controversially, on the *Sale of the Rover Group*, HC 9 (1989–90).
3   HC 492 (1987–88).
4   CAG, 21 September 1989 HMSO.
5   NB the Zircon affair: HC 365 (1986–87) and *Modernising Procurement* HC 808 (1998–99).
6   *Safety, Efficacy, Quality: Regulating Medicines in the UK* (2003).
7   *Giving Confidently: the role of the Charity Commission in Regulating Charities* HC 234 (2001–02).
8   HC 46 (1989–90).
9   HC 154 (1993–94).
10   White and Hollingsworth (above), at pp 78 et seq.
11   Eg HC 530 (2003–04) on PFI and the PAC HC 460 (2001–02) on PFI arrangements and HC 700 (2002–03) on *Operational Performance of PFI Prisons* and HC 955 (2002–03) on the new accommodation programme at GCHQ; on PPPs, HC 644 and 645 (2003–04) both on London Underground and PPPs. The NAO has run an electronic database of the recommendations made by the NAO and PAC on PPPs since 2003. See HC 920 (2010–2012) *Lessons from PFI and Other Projects.*

11.29   However, unlike the audit provisions of local government (paras 8.11 et seq above), there is no public dimension to the CAG's investigations until the report is published although the Office is subject to the Freedom of Information Act 2000 (FOIA 2000). No provision is made, unlike local government, for electors or taxpayers to become involved in the process of audit and to make objection that may well become a matter for challenge before a court of law.[1] The litigation resulting from Pergau Dam was a remarkable development but it arose from a judicial review brought by a public interest group. Until recently, it was assumed that individuals had no locus standi to challenge central government decisions on expenditure.[2] Raising allegations about the illegality of central government expenditure would, in most cases, raise insuperable difficulties in relation to parliamentary estimates, votes and appropriations[3] as well as locus standi[4] for disgruntled citizens. A generous approach was taken by the court to locus standi in the case, one that was more in line with a developing approach. The Pergau Dam episode also concerned specific statutory authority for specific expenditure rather than expenditure under general appropriations under the annual Appropriation Act.

1   *R v District Auditor Chelmsford, ex p Judge* (1988) *Times*, 26 December; cf *Lloyd v McMahon* [1987] 1 All ER 1118. The surcharge provisions have gone but the auditor may still apply to the court for a declaration that an item of expenditure is contrary to law and under Audit Commission Act 1998, s 16 a local elector may make objection to the auditor and under s 17 may appeal against the auditor's decision to the courts.
2   Unlike taxation: *Dyson v A-G* [1912] 1 Ch 158, CA.
3   See eg *R v Secretary of State for Health, ex p Keen* [1990] 1 Med LR 455; *R v Secretary of State for the Environment, ex p Greenwich London Borough Council* (1989) *Times*, 17 May. In the Court of Appeal judgment in *R v Secretary of State for the Home Department, ex p Fire Brigades Union* [1995] 1 All

ER 888, Hobhouse LJ believed that once money was voted by Parliament for expenditure – in this case on compensation for criminal injuries – it cannot be said to be 'unlawful, unauthorised or unconstitutional' expenditure: at p 905j. On government audit generally, see Cm 5456 *Audit and Accountability in Central Government* and HC 701 (2001–02) for the government response.
4   *IRC v National Federation of Self Employed and Small Businesses Ltd* [1982] AC 617, HL; *R v HM Treasury, ex p Smedley* [1985] QB 657, CA; *R v A-G, ex p ICI plc* [1987] 1 CMLR 72, CA.

11.30   The NAO has also reported on the forecasts of the Office for Budget Reform in 2010 following earlier work on government budget 'assumptions'. The earlier work was to assist the government in preparing its forecasts of the public finances by reviewing the assumptions adopted for economic growth, unemployment, interest rates and other conventions for projecting income. This could be viewed as yet a further development in opening up budgetary and monetary policy to greater public scrutiny, a process started by Kenneth Clark under John Major's premiership when he published the minutes of the monthly meetings between himself and the Governor of the Bank of England after six weeks. This was subsequently reduced to two weeks. The authority is now in the Bank of England Act 1997. It has also been extended to the Monetary Policy Committee of the Bank of England.
1   Cm 3693.

11.31   As a concluding comment, it should be noted that, while the budgetary and expenditure processes of local government have been brought under ever-tightening legal regulation and reduction, those of central government remain remarkably free of such legal regulation. Apart from the existence of the Appropriation and Consolidated Fund Acts, there were no other formal legal requirements. Taxation requires legislation. Although the budgetary process is characterised by its secrecy,[1] since 1990 there have been several important developments in the provision of information to Parliament about the expenditure cycle and the budget. The publication of annual reports from departments and agencies since 1991 has helped the flow of information and replaced the obscurity of the Public Expenditure White Paper. New accounting techniques in central government have assisted parliamentary oversight.[2] The reforms starting with the Finance Act 1998 and most recently the Budget Responsibility etc Act 2011 were outlined above (11.4).[3] From 1998, National Accounts have been drawn up in accordance with the Community's European System of Accounts. This is interesting given our decision not to join the European Monetary Union.

1   See generally Likierman *Public Expenditure* (1988). For a more recent analysis which looks at reforms aimed at opening up the expenditure process, see T Daintith and A Page *The Executive in the Constitution* (1999).
2   See HC 365 (2003–04) *Financial Reporting and Auditing*.
3   T Daintith and A Page *The Executive in the Constitution* (1999), pp 106–107.

11.32   The government has developed policies first introduced under Conservative governments' Citizen's Charter programmes. These have been outlined in *Service First – The New Charter Programme*. The emphasis has been placed on transparency, openness and citizen participation in planning and provision of services. Some of these points have been raised in relation to local government in ch 4 and in relation to effective grievance procedures in ch 9.

Public service agreements (described by the Chief Secretary to the Treasury as a 'contract with the people') between the Treasury and departments and agencies which operate within the Comprehensive Spending Review – a three-year prospective public spending review but one which is not fixed rigidly to expenditure for three years ahead thereby allowing for greater flexibility in planning and adjustments – set out aims and objectives of departmental policy. These are accompanied by agreed targets in service levels which have to be reached by given dates.

11.33   For over 15 years, the NAO has been alive to the various developments from joined-up public services, e-government and so on. As long ago as 2001–2002 the NAO produced reports on *Better Public Services through E-government*.[1] The one feature missing from this bold new vision was a Freedom of Information Act which would give citizens the wherewithal fully to assess the fulfilment of these objectives. Much of the Private Finance Initiative has been cloaked by commercial secrecy, as we saw in ch 1. Similar fears attend the coalition government plans for the NHS reforms in the 2011 Health and Social Care Bill and we should recall that the Audit Commission is to be abolished removing independent oversight of audit in health providers. What is to fill the lacuna is not at all clear. The policy-making process will remain protected from critical gaze by virtue of FOIA 2000, ss 35 and 36. To make a point, and without repeating what was said in ch 1, the FOIA 2000 that was given Royal Assent in November 2000 is not a statute that supplies the necessary degree of openness and transparency and the means to allow citizens to comprehend fundamental changes affecting us all. This is where a body such as the NAO provides a crucial service in informing Parliament and the public of the implications and limitations of major social change – much of it technically driven and with huge financial consequences. The growing resort to IT in government is case in point and which we refer to below in a 2011 report. FOIA 2000 is a considerable improvement and it has surprised the government in its operation. It has done so despite some glaring weaknesses in its design. After a delay of almost five years, the operation of rights of access under the Act finally came into force on 1 January 2005. The provisions will operate retrospectively. The NAO has produced guidance on the FOIA 2000 for public bodies.[2]

1   HC 364 (2001–02).
2   http://www.nao.org.uk/publications/0405/counting_down.aspx?alreadysearchfor=yes. On transparency within the NAO, including hospitality, see http://www.nao.org.uk/about_us/structure_governance/transparency.aspx.

11.34   The IT report in question comes from May 2011 and concerns *The National Programme for IT in the NHS: an update on the delivery of detailed care records systems* (HC 888 (2010–12)). For many years the objective for care records in the NHS was to have a centralised computerised database. The rate at which electronic care records' systems are being put in place across the NHS under the National Programme for IT is falling far below expectations and the core aim that every patient should have an electronic care record under the programme will not now be achieved, the NAO reported. 'The original vision for the National Programme for IT in the NHS will not be realised. The NHS is now getting far fewer systems than planned despite the Department paying contractors almost the same amount of money. This is yet another example of a department fundamentally underestimating the scale and complexity of a major IT-enabled change programme.' It will be recalled how the government resisted requests, unsuccessfully, for information on IT programmes and their review (see para 1.159) The Department of Health needs to admit that, 'it is now in damage-limitation mode. I hope that my report, together with the forthcoming review by the Cabinet Office and Treasury, announced by the Prime Minister, will help to prevent further loss of public value from future expenditure on the Programme.' It reminds us that as well as focusing on financial management and reporting and cost-effective delivery of public service and services, the NAO is also involved in ensuring informed government, to encourage government to do more to base its decision-making on reliable, comprehensive and comparable information.[1]

[1]   For the follow-up report of the PAC see *The National Programme for IT in the NHS* HC 1070 (2010–12) and also *Information and Communications Technology in Government* HC 1050 (2010– 12).

11.35   Given the dramatic changes planned for public service and services in the UK as a whole, and given the coalition government's support for FOIA 2000 and greater transparency (see paras 1.251 and 2.32 et seq), it should surely be asked whether the former responsibilities of the Audit Commission should be transferred to the NAO and whether the brief of the NAO should be extended to follow public money wherever, and however, it is spent. This would be a monumental service to transparency. A key theme in recent years has been the attempts by the NAO to ensure that government uses the best information available in the optimal way to enhance delivery, service and productivity.[1] This is an aspiration that should apply whenever public money is spent and our lives affected. 'We want to help central government make better use of information … to achieve improved performance and productivity' is the stated aim of the NAO.

[1]   NAO *Annual Report* 2011, p 6.

Statutory materials

FREEDOM OF INFORMATION ACT 2000

PART I
ACCESS TO INFORMATION HELD BY PUBLIC AUTHORITIES

Right to information

1.— General right of access to information held by public authorities.

(1) Any person making a request for information to a public authority is entitled—
  (a) to be informed in writing by the public authority whether it holds information of the description specified in the request, and
  (b) if that is the case, to have that information communicated to him.

(2) Subsection (1) has effect subject to the following provisions of this section and to the provisions of sections 2, 9, 12 and 14.

(3) Where a public authority—
  (a) reasonably requires further information in order to identify and locate the information requested, and
  (b) has informed the applicant of that requirement,
      the authority is not obliged to comply with subsection (1) unless it is supplied with that further information.

(4) The information—
  (a) in respect of which the applicant is to be informed under subsection (1)(a), or
  (b) which is to be communicated under subsection (1)(b),
      is the information in question held at the time when the request is received, except that account may be taken of any amendment or deletion made between that time and the time when the information is to be communicated under subsection (1)(b), being an amendment or deletion that would have been made regardless of the receipt of the request.

(5) A public authority is to be taken to have complied with subsection (1)(a) in relation to any information if it has communicated the information to the applicant in accordance with subsection (1)(b).

(6) In this Act, the duty of a public authority to comply with subsection (1)(a) is referred to as 'the duty to confirm or deny'.

2.— Effect of the exemptions in Part II.

(1) Where any provision of Part II states that the duty to confirm or deny does not arise in relation to any information, the effect of the provision is that where either—
(a) the provision confers absolute exemption, or
(b) in all the circumstances of the case, the public interest in maintaining the exclusion of the duty to confirm or deny outweighs the public interest in disclosing whether the public authority holds the information, section 1(1)(a) does not apply.

(2) In respect of any information which is exempt information by virtue of any provision of Part II, section 1(1)(b) does not apply if or to the extent that—
(a) the information is exempt information by virtue of a provision conferring absolute exemption, or
(b) in all the circumstances of the case, the public interest in maintaining the exemption outweighs the public interest in disclosing the information.

(3) For the purposes of this section, the following provisions of Part II (and no others) are to be regarded as conferring absolute exemption—
(a) section 21,
(b) section 23,
(c) section 32,
(d) section 34,
(e) section 36 so far as relating to information held by the House of Commons or the House of Lords,
(ea) in section 37, paragraphs (a) to (ab) of subsection (1), and subsection (2) so far as relating to those paragraphs,
(f) in section 40—
(i) subsection (1), and
(ii) subsection (2) so far as relating to cases where the first condition referred to in that subsection is satisfied by virtue of subsection (3)(a)(i) or (b) of that section,
(g) section 41, and
(h) section 44.

3.— Public authorities.

(1) In this Act 'public authority' means—
(a) subject to section 4(4), any body which, any other person who, or the holder of any office which—
(i) is listed in Schedule 1, or
(ii) is designated by order under section 5, or
(b) a publicly-owned company as defined by section 6.

(2) For the purposes of this Act, information is held by a public authority if—
(a) it is held by the authority, otherwise than on behalf of another person, or
(b) it is held by another person on behalf of the authority.

4.— Amendment of Schedule 1.

(1) The Secretary of State may by order amend Schedule 1 by adding to that Schedule a reference to any body or the holder of any office which (in either case) is not for the

time being listed in that Schedule but as respects which both the first and the second conditions below are satisfied.

(2) The first condition is that the body or office—
   (a) is established by virtue of Her Majesty's prerogative or by an enactment or by subordinate legislation, or
   (b) is established in any other way by a Minister of the Crown in his capacity as Minister, by a government department or by the Welsh Ministers, the First Minister for Wales or the Counsel General to the Welsh Assembly Government.

(3) The second condition is—
   (a) in the case of a body, that the body is wholly or partly constituted by appointment made by the Crown, by a Minister of the Crown, by a government department or by the Welsh Ministers, the First Minister for Wales or the Counsel General to the Welsh Assembly Government, or
   (b) in the case of an office, that appointments to the office are made by the Crown, by a Minister of the Crown, by a government department or by the Welsh Ministers, the First Minister for Wales or the Counsel General to the Welsh Assembly Government.

(4) If either the first or the second condition above ceases to be satisfied as respects any body or office which is listed in Part VI or VII of Schedule 1, that body or the holder of that office shall cease to be a public authority by virtue of the entry in question.

(5) The Secretary of State may by order amend Schedule 1 by removing from Part VI or VII of that Schedule an entry relating to any body or office—
   (a) which has ceased to exist, or
   (b) as respects which either the first or the second condition above has ceased to be satisfied.

(6) An order under subsection (1) may relate to a specified person or office or to persons or offices falling within a specified description.

(7) Before making an order under subsection (1), the Secretary of State shall—
   (a) if the order adds to Part II, III, IV or VI of Schedule 1 a reference to—
      (i) a body whose functions are exercisable only or mainly in or as regards Wales, or
      (ii) the holder of an office whose functions are exercisable only or mainly in or as regards Wales,
      consult the Welsh Ministers, and
   (b) if the order relates to a body which, or the holder of any office who, if the order were made, would be a Northern Ireland public authority, consult the First Minister and deputy First Minister in Northern Ireland.

(8) This section has effect subject to section 80.

(9) In this section 'Minister of the Crown' includes a Northern Ireland Minister.

5.— Further power to designate public authorities.

(1) The Secretary of State may by order designate as a public authority for the purposes of this Act any person who is neither listed in Schedule 1 nor capable of being added to that Schedule by an order under section 4(1), but who—
   (a) appears to the Secretary of State to exercise functions of a public nature, or
   (b) is providing under a contract made with a public authority any service whose provision is a function of that authority.

(2) An order under this section may designate a specified person or office or persons or offices falling within a specified description.

(3) Before making an order under this section, the Secretary of State shall consult every person to whom the order relates, or persons appearing to him to represent such persons.

(4) This section has effect subject to section 80.

6.— Publicly-owned companies.

(1) A company is a 'publicly-owned company' for the purposes of section 3(1)(b) if—
    (a) it is wholly owned by the Crown, or
    (b) it is wholly owned by any public authority listed in Schedule 1 other than—
        (i) a government department, or
        (ii) any authority which is listed only in relation to particular information.

(2) For the purposes of this section—
    (a) a company is wholly owned by the Crown if it has no members except—
        (i) Ministers of the Crown, government departments or companies wholly owned by the Crown, or
        (ii) persons acting on behalf of Ministers of the Crown, government departments or companies wholly owned by the Crown, and
    (b) a company is wholly owned by a public authority other than a government department if it has no members except—
        (i) that public authority or companies wholly owned by that public authority, or
        (ii) persons acting on behalf of that public authority or of companies wholly owned by that public authority.

(3) In this section—
'company' includes any body corporate;
'Minister of the Crown' includes a Northern Ireland Minister.

7.— Public authorities to which Act has limited application.

(1) Where a public authority is listed in Schedule 1 only in relation to information of a specified description, nothing in Parts I to V of this Act applies to any other information held by the authority.

(2) An order under section 4(1) may, in adding an entry to Schedule 1, list the public authority only in relation to information of a specified description.

(3) The Secretary of State may by order amend Schedule 1—
    (a) by limiting to information of a specified description the entry relating to any public authority, or
    (b) by removing or amending any limitation to information of a specified description which is for the time being contained in any entry.

(4) Before making an order under subsection (3), the Secretary of State] shall—
    (a) if the order relates to the National Assembly for Wales or a Welsh public authority referred to in section 83(1)(b)(ii) (subsidiary of the Assembly Commission), consult the Presiding Officer of the National Assembly for Wales,
    (aa) if the order relates to the Welsh Assembly Government or a Welsh public authority other than one referred to in section 83(1)(b)(ii), consult the First Minister for Wales,

(b) if the order relates to the Northern Ireland Assembly, consult the Presiding Officer of that Assembly, and

(c) if the order relates to a Northern Ireland department or a Northern Ireland public authority, consult the First Minister and deputy First Minister in Northern Ireland.

(5) An order under section 5(1)(a) must specify the functions of the public authority designated by the order with respect to which the designation is to have effect; and nothing in Parts I to V of this Act applies to information which is held by the authority but does not relate to the exercise of those functions.

(6) An order under section 5(1)(b) must specify the services provided under contract with respect to which the designation is to have effect; and nothing in Parts I to V of this Act applies to information which is held by the public authority designated by the order but does not relate to the provision of those services.

(7) Nothing in Parts I to V of this Act applies in relation to any information held by a publicly-owned company which is excluded information in relation to that company.

(8) In subsection (7) 'excluded information', in relation to a publicly-owned company, means information which is of a description specified in relation to that company in an order made by the Secretary of State for the purposes of this subsection.

(9) In this section 'publicly-owned company' has the meaning given by section 6.

8.— Request for information.

(1) In this Act any reference to a 'request for information' is a reference to such a request which—
(a) is in writing,
(b) states the name of the applicant and an address for correspondence, and
(c) describes the information requested.

(2) For the purposes of subsection (1)(a), a request is to be treated as made in writing where the text of the request—
(a) is transmitted by electronic means,
(b) is received in legible form, and
(c) is capable of being used for subsequent reference.

9.— Fees.

(1) A public authority to whom a request for information is made may, within the period for complying with section 1(1), give the applicant a notice in writing (in this Act referred to as a 'fees notice') stating that a fee of an amount specified in the notice is to be charged by the authority for complying with section 1(1).

(2) Where a fees notice has been given to the applicant, the public authority is not obliged to comply with section 1(1) unless the fee is paid within the period of three months beginning with the day on which the fees notice is given to the applicant.

(3) Subject to subsection (5), any fee under this section must be determined by the public authority in accordance with regulations made by the Secretary of State.

(4) Regulations under subsection (3) may, in particular, provide—
(a) that no fee is to be payable in prescribed cases,
(b) that any fee is not to exceed such maximum as may be specified in, or determined in accordance with, the regulations, and
(c) that any fee is to be calculated in such manner as may be prescribed by the regulations.

(5) Subsection (3) does not apply where provision is made by or under any enactment as to the fee that may be charged by the public authority for the disclosure of the information.

10.— Time for compliance with request.

(1) Subject to subsections (2) and (3), a public authority must comply with section 1(1) promptly and in any event not later than the twentieth working day following the date of receipt.

(2) Where the authority has given a fees notice to the applicant and the fee is paid in accordance with section 9(2), the working days in the period beginning with the day on which the fees notice is given to the applicant and ending with the day on which the fee is received by the authority are to be disregarded in calculating for the purposes of subsection (1) the twentieth working day following the date of receipt.

(3) If, and to the extent that—
(a) section 1(1)(a) would not apply if the condition in section 2(1)(b) were satisfied, or
(b) section 1(1)(b) would not apply if the condition in section 2(2)(b) were satisfied,

the public authority need not comply with section 1(1)(a) or (b) until such time as is reasonable in the circumstances; but this subsection does not affect the time by which any notice under section 17(1) must be given.

(4) The Secretary of State may by regulations provide that subsections (1) and (2) are to have effect as if any reference to the twentieth working day following the date of receipt were a reference to such other day, not later than the sixtieth working day following the date of receipt, as may be specified in, or determined in accordance with, the regulations.

(5) Regulations under subsection (4) may—
(a) prescribe different days in relation to different cases, and
(b) confer a discretion on the Commissioner.

(6) In this section—
'the date of receipt' means—
(a) the day on which the public authority receives the request for information, or
(b) if later, the day on which it receives the information referred to in section 1(3).

11.— Means by which communication to be made.

(1) Where, on making his request for information, the applicant expresses a preference for communication by any one or more of the following means, namely—
(a) the provision to the applicant of a copy of the information in permanent form or in another form acceptable to the applicant,
(b) the provision to the applicant of a reasonable opportunity to inspect a record containing the information, and
(c) the provision to the applicant of a digest or summary of the information in permanent form or in another form acceptable to the applicant,

the public authority shall so far as reasonably practicable give effect to that preference.

(2) In determining for the purposes of this section whether it is reasonably practicable to communicate information by particular means, the public authority may have regard to all the circumstances, including the cost of doing so.

(3) Where the public authority determines that it is not reasonably practicable to comply with any preference expressed by the applicant in making his request, the authority shall notify the applicant of the reasons for its determination.

(4) Subject to subsection (1), a public authority may comply with a request by communicating information by any means which are reasonable in the circumstances.

12.— Exemption where cost of compliance exceeds appropriate limit.

(1) Section 1(1) does not oblige a public authority to comply with a request for information if the authority estimates that the cost of complying with the request would exceed the appropriate limit.

(2) Subsection (1) does not exempt the public authority from its obligation to comply with paragraph (a) of section 1(1) unless the estimated cost of complying with that paragraph alone would exceed the appropriate limit.

(3) In subsections (1) and (2) 'the appropriate limit' means such amount as may be prescribed, and different amounts may be prescribed in relation to different cases.

(4) The Secretary of State may by regulations provide that, in such circumstances as may be prescribed, where two or more requests for information are made to a public authority—
   (a) by one person, or
   (b) by different persons who appear to the public authority to be acting in concert or in pursuance of a campaign,

the estimated cost of complying with any of the requests is to be taken to be the estimated total cost of complying with all of them.

(5) The Secretary of State may by regulations make provision for the purposes of this section as to the costs to be estimated and as to the manner in which they are to be estimated.

13.— Fees for disclosure where cost of compliance exceeds appropriate limit.

(1) A public authority may charge for the communication of any information whose communication—
   (a) is not required by section 1(1) because the cost of complying with the request for information exceeds the amount which is the appropriate limit for the purposes of section 12(1) and (2), and
   (b) is not otherwise required by law,
   such fee as may be determined by the public authority in accordance with regulations made by the Secretary of State.

(2) Regulations under this section may, in particular, provide—
   (a) that any fee is not to exceed such maximum as may be specified in, or determined in accordance with, the regulations, and
   (b) that any fee is to be calculated in such manner as may be prescribed by the regulations.

(3) Subsection (1) does not apply where provision is made by or under any enactment as to the fee that may be charged by the public authority for the disclosure of the information.

14.— Vexatious or repeated requests.

(1) Section 1(1) does not oblige a public authority to comply with a request for information if the request is vexatious.

(2)   Where a public authority has previously complied with a request for information which was made by any person, it is not obliged to comply with a subsequent identical or substantially similar request from that person unless a reasonable interval has elapsed between compliance with the previous request and the making of the current request.

15.— Special provisions relating to public records transferred to Public Record Office, etc.

(1)   Where—
  (a)   the appropriate records authority receives a request for information which relates to information which is, or if it existed would be, contained in a transferred public record, and
  (b)   either of the conditions in subsection (2) is satisfied in relation to any of that information,
  that authority shall, within the period for complying with section 1(1), send a copy of the request to the responsible authority.

(2)   The conditions referred to in subsection (1)(b) are—
  (a)   that the duty to confirm or deny is expressed to be excluded only by a provision of Part II not specified in subsection (3) of section 2, and
  (b)   that the information is exempt information only by virtue of a provision of Part II not specified in that subsection.

(3)   On receiving the copy, the responsible authority shall, within such time as is reasonable in all the circumstances, inform the appropriate records authority of the determination required by virtue of subsection (3) or (4) of section 66.

(4)   In this Act 'transferred public record' means a public record which has been transferred—
  (a)   to the Public Record Office,
  (b)   to another place of deposit appointed by the Lord Chancellor under the Public Records Act 1958, or
  (c)   to the Public Record Office of Northern Ireland.

(5)   In this Act—
  'appropriate records authority', in relation to a transferred public record, means—
  (a)   in a case falling within subsection (4)(a), the Public Record Office,
  (b)   in a case falling within subsection (4)(b), the Lord Chancellor, and
  (c)   in a case falling within subsection (4)(c), the Public Record Office of Northern Ireland;

  'responsible authority', in relation to a transferred public record, means—
  (a)   in the case of a record transferred as mentioned in subsection (4)(a) or (b) from a government department in the charge of a Minister of the Crown, the Minister of the Crown who appears to the Lord Chancellor to be primarily concerned,
  (b)   in the case of a record transferred as mentioned in subsection (4)(a) or (b) from any other person, the person who appears to the Lord Chancellor to be primarily concerned,
  (c)   in the case of a record transferred to the Public Record Office of Northern Ireland from a government department in the charge of a Minister of the Crown, the Minister of the Crown who appears to the appropriate Northern Ireland Minister to be primarily concerned,
  (d)   in the case of a record transferred to the Public Record Office of Northern Ireland from a Northern Ireland department, the Northern Ireland Minister

who appears to the appropriate Northern Ireland Minister to be primarily concerned, or

(e) in the case of a record transferred to the Public Record Office of Northern Ireland from any other person, the person who appears to the appropriate Northern Ireland Minister to be primarily concerned.

16.— Duty to provide advice and assistance.

(1) It shall be the duty of a public authority to provide advice and assistance, so far as it would be reasonable to expect the authority to do so, to persons who propose to make, or have made, requests for information to it.

(2) Any public authority which, in relation to the provision of advice or assistance in any case, conforms with the code of practice under section 45 is to be taken to comply with the duty imposed by subsection (1) in relation to that case.

17.— Refusal of request.

(1) A public authority which, in relation to any request for information, is to any extent relying on a claim that any provision of Part II relating to the duty to confirm or deny is relevant to the request or on a claim that information is exempt information must, within the time for complying with section 1(1), give the applicant a notice which—
(a) states that fact,
(b) specifies the exemption in question, and
(c) states (if that would not otherwise be apparent) why the exemption applies.

(2) Where—
(a) in relation to any request for information, a public authority is, as respects any information, relying on a claim—
(i) that any provision of Part II which relates to the duty to confirm or deny and is not specified in section 2(3) is relevant to the request, or
(ii) that the information is exempt information only by virtue of a provision not specified in section 2(3), and
(b) at the time when the notice under subsection (1) is given to the applicant, the public authority (or, in a case falling within section 66(3) or (4), the responsible authority) has not yet reached a decision as to the application of subsection (1)(b) or (2)(b) of section 2,
the notice under subsection (1) must indicate that no decision as to the application of that provision has yet been reached and must contain an estimate of the date by which the authority expects that such a decision will have been reached.

(3) A public authority which, in relation to any request for information, is to any extent relying on a claim that subsection (1)(b) or (2)(b) of section 2 applies must, either in the notice under subsection (1) or in a separate notice given within such time as is reasonable in the circumstances, state the reasons for claiming—
(a) that, in all the circumstances of the case, the public interest in maintaining the exclusion of the duty to confirm or deny outweighs the public interest in disclosing whether the authority holds the information, or
(b) that, in all the circumstances of the case, the public interest in maintaining the exemption outweighs the public interest in disclosing the information.

(4) A public authority is not obliged to make a statement under subsection (1)(c) or (3) if, or to the extent that, the statement would involve the disclosure of information which would itself be exempt information.

(5) A public authority which, in relation to any request for information, is relying on a claim that section 12 or 14 applies must, within the time for complying with section 1(1), give the applicant a notice stating that fact.

(6) Subsection (5) does not apply where—
   (a) the public authority is relying on a claim that section 14 applies,
   (b) the authority has given the applicant a notice, in relation to a previous request for information, stating that it is relying on such a claim, and
   (c) it would in all the circumstances be unreasonable to expect the authority to serve a further notice under subsection (5) in relation to the current request.

(7) A notice under subsection (1), (3) or (5) must—
   (a) contain particulars of any procedure provided by the public authority for dealing with complaints about the handling of requests for information or state that the authority does not provide such a procedure, and
   (b) contain particulars of the right conferred by section 50.

18.— The Information Commissioner.

(1) The Data Protection Commissioner shall be known instead as the Information Commissioner.

[…]

(3) In this Act—
   (a) the Information Commissioner is referred to as 'the Commissioner'
   […]

(4) Schedule 2 (which makes provision consequential on subsections (1) and (2) and amendments of the Data Protection Act 1998 relating to the extension by this Act of the functions of the Commissioner and the Tribunal) has effect.

(5) If the person who held office as Data Protection Commissioner immediately before the day on which this Act is passed remains in office as Information Commissioner at the end of the period of two years beginning with that day, he shall vacate his office at the end of that period.

(6) Subsection (5) does not prevent the re-appointment of a person whose appointment is terminated by that subsection.

(7) In the application of paragraph 2(4)(b) and (5) of Schedule 5 to the Data Protection Act 1998 (Commissioner not to serve for more than fifteen years and not to be appointed, except in special circumstances, for a third or subsequent term) to anything done after the passing of this Act, there shall be left out of account any term of office served by virtue of an appointment made before the passing of this Act.

19.— Publication schemes.

(1) It shall be the duty of every public authority—
   (a) to adopt and maintain a scheme which relates to the publication of information by the authority and is approved by the Commissioner (in this Act referred to as a 'publication scheme'),
   (b) to publish information in accordance with its publication scheme, and
   (c) from time to time to review its publication scheme.

(2) A publication scheme must—

    (a) specify classes of information which the public authority publishes or intends to publish,

    (b) specify the manner in which information of each class is, or is intended to be, published, and

    (c) specify whether the material is, or is intended to be, available to the public free of charge or on payment.

(3) In adopting or reviewing a publication scheme, a public authority shall have regard to the public interest—

    (a) in allowing public access to information held by the authority, and

    (b) in the publication of reasons for decisions made by the authority.

(4) A public authority shall publish its publication scheme in such manner as it thinks fit.

(5) The Commissioner may, when approving a scheme, provide that his approval is to expire at the end of a specified period.

(6) Where the Commissioner has approved the publication scheme of any public authority, he may at any time give notice to the public authority revoking his approval of the scheme as from the end of the period of six months beginning with the day on which the notice is given.

(7) Where the Commissioner—

    (a) refuses to approve a proposed publication scheme, or

    (b) revokes his approval of a publication scheme,

he must give the public authority a statement of his reasons for doing so.

20.— Model publication schemes.

(1) The Commissioner may from time to time approve, in relation to public authorities falling within particular classes, model publication schemes prepared by him or by other persons.

(2) Where a public authority falling within the class to which an approved model scheme relates adopts such a scheme without modification, no further approval of the Commissioner is required so long as the model scheme remains approved; and where such an authority adopts such a scheme with modifications, the approval of the Commissioner is required only in relation to the modifications.

(3) The Commissioner may, when approving a model publication scheme, provide that his approval is to expire at the end of a specified period.

(4) Where the Commissioner has approved a model publication scheme, he may at any time publish, in such manner as he thinks fit, a notice revoking his approval of the scheme as from the end of the period of six months beginning with the day on which the notice is published.

(5) Where the Commissioner refuses to approve a proposed model publication scheme on the application of any person, he must give the person who applied for approval of the scheme a statement of the reasons for his refusal.

(6) Where the Commissioner refuses to approve any modifications under subsection (2), he must give the public authority a statement of the reasons for his refusal.

(7) Where the Commissioner revokes his approval of a model publication scheme, he must include in the notice under subsection (4) a statement of his reasons for doing so.

PART II
EXEMPT INFORMATION

21.— Information accessible to applicant by other means.

(1) Information which is reasonably accessible to the applicant otherwise than under section 1 is exempt information.

(2) For the purposes of subsection (1)—
    (a) information may be reasonably accessible to the applicant even though it is accessible only on payment, and
    (b) information is to be taken to be reasonably accessible to the applicant if it is information which the public authority or any other person is obliged by or under any enactment to communicate (otherwise than by making the information available for inspection) to members of the public on request, whether free of charge or on payment.

(3) For the purposes of subsection (1), information which is held by a public authority and does not fall within subsection (2)(b) is not to be regarded as reasonably accessible to the applicant merely because the information is available from the public authority itself on request, unless the information is made available in accordance with the authority's publication scheme and any payment required is specified in, or determined in accordance with, the scheme.

22.— Information intended for future publication.

(1) Information is exempt information if—
    (a) the information is held by the public authority with a view to its publication, by the authority or any other person, at some future date (whether determined or not),
    (b) the information was already held with a view to such publication at the time when the request for information was made, and
    (c) it is reasonable in all the circumstances that the information should be withheld from disclosure until the date referred to in paragraph (a).

(2) The duty to confirm or deny does not arise if, or to the extent that, compliance with section 1(1)(a) would involve the disclosure of any information (whether or not already recorded) which falls within subsection (1).

23.— Information supplied by, or relating to, bodies dealing with security matters.

(1) Information held by a public authority is exempt information if it was directly or indirectly supplied to the public authority by, or relates to, any of the bodies specified in subsection (3).

(2) A certificate signed by a Minister of the Crown certifying that the information to which it applies was directly or indirectly supplied by, or relates to, any of the bodies specified in subsection (3) shall, subject to section 60, be conclusive evidence of that fact.

(3) The bodies referred to in subsections (1) and (2) are—
    (a) the Security Service,
    (b) the Secret Intelligence Service,
    (c) the Government Communications Headquarters,
    (d) the special forces,

(e) the Tribunal established under section 65 of the Regulation of Investigatory Powers Act 2000,

(f) the Tribunal established under section 7 of the Interception of Communications Act 1985,

(g) the Tribunal established under section 5 of the Security Service Act 1989,

(h) the Tribunal established under section 9 of the Intelligence Services Act 1994,

(i) the Security Vetting Appeals Panel,

(j) the Security Commission,

(k) the National Criminal Intelligence Service,

(l) the Service Authority for the National Criminal Intelligence Service, and

(m) the Serious Organised Crime Agency.

(4) In subsection (3)(c) 'the Government Communications Headquarters' includes any unit or part of a unit of the armed forces of the Crown which is for the time being required by the Secretary of State to assist the Government Communications Headquarters in carrying out its functions.

(5) The duty to confirm or deny does not arise if, or to the extent that, compliance with section 1(1)(a) would involve the disclosure of any information (whether or not already recorded) which was directly or indirectly supplied to the public authority by, or relates to, any of the bodies specified in subsection (3).

24.— National security.

(1) Information which does not fall within section 23(1) is exempt information if exemption from section 1(1)(b) is required for the purpose of safeguarding national security.

(2) The duty to confirm or deny does not arise if, or to the extent that, exemption from section 1(1)(a) is required for the purpose of safeguarding national security.

(3) A certificate signed by a Minister of the Crown certifying that exemption from section 1(1)(b), or from section 1(1)(a) and (b), is, or at any time was, required for the purpose of safeguarding national security shall, subject to section 60, be conclusive evidence of that fact.

(4) A certificate under subsection (3) may identify the information to which it applies by means of a general description and may be expressed to have prospective effect.

25.— Certificates under ss. 23 and 24: supplementary provisions.

(1) A document purporting to be a certificate under section 23(2) or 24(3) shall be received in evidence and deemed to be such a certificate unless the contrary is proved.

(2) A document which purports to be certified by or on behalf of a Minister of the Crown as a true copy of a certificate issued by that Minister under section 23(2)or 24(3) shall in any legal proceedings be evidence (or, in Scotland, sufficient evidence) of that certificate.

(3) The power conferred by section 23(2) or 24(3) on a Minister of the Crown shall not be exercisable except by a Minister who is a member of the Cabinet or by the Attorney General, the Advocate General for Scotland or the Attorney General for Northern Ireland.

26.— Defence.

(1) Information is exempt information if its disclosure under this Act would, or would be likely to, prejudice—

(a) the defence of the British Islands or of any colony, or

(b) the capability, effectiveness or security of any relevant forces.

(2) In subsection (1)(b) 'relevant forces' means—

(a) the armed forces of the Crown, and

(b) any forces co-operating with those forces,

or any part of any of those forces.

(3) The duty to confirm or deny does not arise if, or to the extent that, compliance with section 1(1)(a) would, or would be likely to, prejudice any of the matters mentioned in subsection (1).

27.— International relations.

(1) Information is exempt information if its disclosure under this Act would, or would be likely to, prejudice—

(a) relations between the United Kingdom and any other State,

(b) relations between the United Kingdom and any international organisation or international court,

(c) the interests of the United Kingdom abroad, or

(d) the promotion or protection by the United Kingdom of its interests abroad.

(2) Information is also exempt information if it is confidential information obtained from a State other than the United Kingdom or from an international organisation or international court.

(3) For the purposes of this section, any information obtained from a State, organisation or court is confidential at any time while the terms on which it was obtained require it to be held in confidence or while the circumstances in which it was obtained make it reasonable for the State, organisation or court to expect that it will be so held.

(4) The duty to confirm or deny does not arise if, or to the extent that, compliance with section 1(1)(a)—

(a) would, or would be likely to, prejudice any of the matters mentioned in subsection (1), or

(b) would involve the disclosure of any information (whether or not already recorded) which is confidential information obtained from a State other than the United Kingdom or from an international organisation or international court.

(5) In this section—

'international court' means any international court which is not an international organisation and which is established—

(a) by a resolution of an international organisation of which the United Kingdom is a member, or

(b) by an international agreement to which the United Kingdom is a party;

'international organisation' means any international organisation whose members include any two or more States, or any organ of such an organisation; 'State' includes the government of any State and any organ of its government, and references to a State other than the United Kingdom include references to any territory outside the United Kingdom.

28.— Relations within the United Kingdom.

(1) Information is exempt information if its disclosure under this Act would, or would be likely to, prejudice relations between any administration in the United Kingdom and any other such administration.

(2) In subsection (1) 'administration in the United Kingdom' means—
   (a) the government of the United Kingdom,
   (b) the Scottish Administration,
   (c) the Executive Committee of the Northern Ireland Assembly, or
   (d) the Welsh Assembly Government.

(3) The duty to confirm or deny does not arise if, or to the extent that, compliance with section 1(1)(a) would, or would be likely to, prejudice any of the matters mentioned in subsection (1).

29.— The economy.

(1) Information is exempt information if its disclosure under this Act would, or would be likely to, prejudice—
   (a) the economic interests of the United Kingdom or of any part of the United Kingdom, or
   (b) the financial interests of any administration in the United Kingdom, as defined by section 28(2).

(2) The duty to confirm or deny does not arise if, or to the extent that, compliance with section 1(1)(a) would, or would be likely to, prejudice any of the matters mentioned in subsection (1).

30.— Investigations and proceedings conducted by public authorities.

(1) Information held by a public authority is exempt information if it has at any time been held by the authority for the purposes of—
   (a) any investigation which the public authority has a duty to conduct with a view to it being ascertained—
      (i)   whether a person should be charged with an offence, or
      (ii) whether a person charged with an offence is guilty of it,
   (b) any investigation which is conducted by the authority and in the circumstances may lead to a decision by the authority to institute criminal proceedings which the authority has power to conduct, or
   (c) any criminal proceedings which the authority has power to conduct.

(2) Information held by a public authority is exempt information if—
   (a) it was obtained or recorded by the authority for the purposes of its functions relating to—
      (i)   investigations falling within subsection (1)(a) or (b),
      (ii) criminal proceedings which the authority has power to conduct,
      (iii) investigations (other than investigations falling within subsection (1)(a) or (b)) which are conducted by the authority for any of the purposes specified in section 31(2) and either by virtue of Her Majesty's prerogative or by virtue of powers conferred by or under any enactment, or
      (iv) civil proceedings which are brought by or on behalf of the authority and arise out of such investigations, and
   (b) it relates to the obtaining of information from confidential sources.

(3) The duty to confirm or deny does not arise in relation to information which is (or if it were held by the public authority would be) exempt information by virtue of subsection (1) or (2).

(4) In relation to the institution or conduct of criminal proceedings or the power to conduct them, references in subsection (1)(b) or (c) and subsection (2)(a) to the public authority include references—

(a) to any officer of the authority,

(b) in the case of a government department other than a Northern Ireland department, to the Minister of the Crown in charge of the department, and

(c) in the case of a Northern Ireland department, to the Northern Ireland Minister in charge of the department.

(5) In this section–

'criminal proceedings' includes service law proceedings (as defined by section 324(5) of the Armed Forces Act 2006);

'offence' includes a service offence (as defined by section 50 of that Act).

(6) In the application of this section to Scotland—

(a) in subsection (1)(b), for the words from 'a decision' to the end there is substituted 'a decision by the authority to make a report to the procurator fiscal for the purpose of enabling him to determine whether criminal proceedings should be instituted',

(b) in subsections (1)(c) and (2)(a)(ii) for 'which the authority has power to conduct' there is substituted 'which have been instituted in consequence of a report made by the authority to the procurator fiscal', and

(c) for any reference to a person being charged with an offence there is substituted a reference to the person being prosecuted for the offence.

31.— Law enforcement.

(1) Information which is not exempt information by virtue of section 30 is exempt information if its disclosure under this Act would, or would be likely to, prejudice—

(a) the prevention or detection of crime,

(b) the apprehension or prosecution of offenders,

(c) the administration of justice,

(d) the assessment or collection of any tax or duty or of any imposition of a similar nature,

(e) the operation of the immigration controls,

(f) the maintenance of security and good order in prisons or in other institutions where persons are lawfully detained,

(g) the exercise by any public authority of its functions for any of the purposes specified in subsection (2),

(h) any civil proceedings which are brought by or on behalf of a public authority and arise out of an investigation conducted, for any of the purposes specified in subsection (2), by or on behalf of the authority by virtue of Her Majesty's prerogative or by virtue of powers conferred by or under an enactment, or

(i) any inquiry held under the Fatal Accidents and Sudden Deaths Inquiries (Scotland) Act 1976 to the extent that the inquiry arises out of an investigation conducted, for any of the purposes specified in subsection (2), by or on behalf of the authority by virtue of Her Majesty's prerogative or by virtue of powers conferred by or under an enactment.

(2) The purposes referred to in subsection (1)(g) to (i) are—

(a) the purpose of ascertaining whether any person has failed to comply with the law,

(b) the purpose of ascertaining whether any person is responsible for any conduct which is improper,

(c) the purpose of ascertaining whether circumstances which would justify regulatory action in pursuance of any enactment exist or may arise,

(d)   the purpose of ascertaining a person's fitness or competence in relation to the management of bodies corporate or in relation to any profession or other activity which he is, or seeks to become, authorised to carry on,

(e)   the purpose of ascertaining the cause of an accident,

(f)   the purpose of protecting charities against misconduct or mismanagement (whether by trustees or other persons) in their administration,

(g)   the purpose of protecting the property of charities from loss or misapplication,

(h)   the purpose of recovering the property of charities,

(i)   the purpose of securing the health, safety and welfare of persons at work, and

(j)   the purpose of protecting persons other than persons at work against risk to health or safety arising out of or in connection with the actions of persons at work.

(3)   The duty to confirm or deny does not arise if, or to the extent that, compliance with section 1(1)(a) would, or would be likely to, prejudice any of the matters mentioned in subsection (1).

32.— Court records, etc.

(1)   Information held by a public authority is exempt information if it is held only by virtue of being contained in—

(a)   any document filed with, or otherwise placed in the custody of, a court for the purposes of proceedings in a particular cause or matter,

(b)   any document served upon, or by, a public authority for the purposes of proceedings in a particular cause or matter, or

(c)   any document created by—

(i)   a court, or

(ii)   a member of the administrative staff of a court,

for the purposes of proceedings in a particular cause or matter.

(2)   Information held by a public authority is exempt information if it is held only by virtue of being contained in—

(a)   any document placed in the custody of a person conducting an inquiry or arbitration, for the purposes of the inquiry or arbitration, or

(b)   any document created by a person conducting an inquiry or arbitration, for the purposes of the inquiry or arbitration.

(3)   The duty to confirm or deny does not arise in relation to information which is (or if it were held by the public authority would be) exempt information by virtue of this section.

(4)   In this section—

(a)   'court' includes any tribunal or body exercising the judicial power of the State,

(b)   'proceedings in a particular cause or matter' includes any inquest or post-mortem examination,

(c)   'inquiry' means any inquiry or hearing held under any provision contained in, or made under, an enactment, and

(d)   except in relation to Scotland, 'arbitration' means any arbitration to which Part I of the Arbitration Act 1996 applies.

33.— Audit functions.

(1)   This section applies to any public authority which has functions in relation to—

(a)   the audit of the accounts of other public authorities, or

(b)   the examination of the economy, efficiency and effectiveness with which other public authorities use their resources in discharging their functions.

(2) Information held by a public authority to which this section applies is exempt information if its disclosure would, or would be likely to, prejudice the exercise of any of the authority's functions in relation to any of the matters referred to in subsection (1).

(3) The duty to confirm or deny does not arise in relation to a public authority to which this section applies if, or to the extent that, compliance with section 1(1)(a) would, or would be likely to, prejudice the exercise of any of the authority's functions in relation to any of the matters referred to in subsection (1).

34.— Parliamentary privilege.

(1) Information is exempt information if exemption from section 1(1)(b) is required for the purpose of avoiding an infringement of the privileges of either House of Parliament.

(2) The duty to confirm or deny does not apply if, or to the extent that, exemption from section 1(1)(a) is required for the purpose of avoiding an infringement of the privileges of either House of Parliament.

(3) A certificate signed by the appropriate authority certifying that exemption from section 1(1)(b), or from section 1(1)(a) and (b), is, or at any time was, required for the purpose of avoiding an infringement of the privileges of either House of Parliament shall be conclusive evidence of that fact.

(4) In subsection (3) 'the appropriate authority' means—
    (a) in relation to the House of Commons, the Speaker of that House, and
    (b) in relation to the House of Lords, the Clerk of the Parliaments.

35.— Formulation of government policy, etc.

(1) Information held by a government department or by the Welsh Assembly Government is exempt information if it relates to—
    (a) the formulation or development of government policy,
    (b) Ministerial communications,
    (c) the provision of advice by any of the Law Officers or any request for the provision of such advice, or
    (d) the operation of any Ministerial private office.

(2) Once a decision as to government policy has been taken, any statistical information used to provide an informed background to the taking of the decision is not to be regarded—
    (a) for the purposes of subsection (1)(a), as relating to the formulation or development of government policy, or
    (b) for the purposes of subsection (1)(b), as relating to Ministerial communications.
    (3) The duty to confirm or deny does not arise in relation to information which is (or if it were held by the public authority would be) exempt information by virtue of subsection (1).
    (4) In making any determination required by section 2(1)(b) or (2)(b) in relation to information which is exempt information by virtue of subsection (1)(a), regard shall be had to the particular public interest in the disclosure of factual information which has been used, or is intended to be used, to provide an informed background to decision-taking.
    (5) In this section—
    'government policy' includes the policy of the Executive Committee of the Northern Ireland Assembly and the policy of the Welsh Assembly Government;

'the Law Officers' means the Attorney General, the Solicitor General, the Advocate General for Scotland, the Lord Advocate, the Solicitor General for Scotland, the Counsel General to the Welsh Assembly Government and the Attorney General for Northern Ireland ;

'Ministerial communications' means any communications—

(a) between Ministers of the Crown,

(b) between Northern Ireland Ministers, including Northern Ireland junior Ministers, or

(c) between members of the Welsh Assembly Government, and includes, in particular, proceedings of the Cabinet or of any committee of the Cabinet, proceedings of the Executive Committee of the Northern Ireland Assembly, and proceedings of the Cabinet or any committee of the Cabinet of the Welsh Assembly Government;

'Ministerial private office' means any part of a government department which provides personal administrative support to a Minister of the Crown, to a Northern Ireland Minister or a Northern Ireland junior Minister or any part of the administration of the Welsh Assembly Government providing personal administrative support to the members of the Welsh Assembly Government;

'Northern Ireland junior Minister' means a member of the Northern Ireland Assembly appointed as a junior Minister under section 19 of the Northern Ireland Act 1998.

36.— Prejudice to effective conduct of public affairs.

(1) This section applies to—

(a) information which is held by a government department or by the Welsh Assembly Government and is not exempt information by virtue of section 35, and

(b) information which is held by any other public authority.

(2) Information to which this section applies is exempt information if, in the reasonable opinion of a qualified person, disclosure of the information under this Act—

(a) would, or would be likely to, prejudice—

(i)   the maintenance of the convention of the collective responsibility of Ministers of the Crown, or

(ii)   the work of the Executive Committee of the Northern Ireland Assembly, or

(iii) the work of the Cabinet of the Welsh Assembly Government.

(b) would, or would be likely to, inhibit—

(i)   the free and frank provision of advice, or

(ii)   the free and frank exchange of views for the purposes of deliberation, or

(c) would otherwise prejudice, or would be likely otherwise to prejudice, the effective conduct of public affairs.

(3) The duty to confirm or deny does not arise in relation to information to which this section applies (or would apply if held by the public authority) if, or to the extent that, in the reasonable opinion of a qualified person, compliance with section 1(1)(a) would, or would be likely to, have any of the effects mentioned in subsection (2).

(4) In relation to statistical information, subsections (2) and (3) shall have effect with the omission of the words 'in the reasonable opinion of a qualified person'.

(5) In subsections (2) and (3) 'qualified person'—

(a) in relation to information held by a government department in the charge of a Minister of the Crown, means any Minister of the Crown,

(b) in relation to information held by a Northern Ireland department, means the Northern Ireland Minister in charge of the department,

(c) in relation to information held by any other government department, means the commissioners or other person in charge of that department,

(d) in relation to information held by the House of Commons, means the Speaker of that House,

(e) in relation to information held by the House of Lords, means the Clerk of the Parliaments,

(f) in relation to information held by the Northern Ireland Assembly, means the Presiding Officer,

(g) in relation to information held by the Welsh Assembly Government, means the Welsh Ministers or the Counsel General to the Welsh Assembly Government,

(ga) in relation to information held by the National Assembly for Wales, means the Presiding Officer of the National Assembly for Wales,

(gb) in relation to information held by any Welsh public authority (other than one referred to in section 83(1)(b)(ii) (subsidiary of the Assembly Commission), the Auditor General for Wales or the Public Services Ombudsman for Wales), means—

   (i) the public authority, or

   (ii) any officer or employee of the authority authorised by the Welsh Ministers or the Counsel General to the Welsh Assembly Government,

(gc) in relation to information held by a Welsh public authority referred to in section 83(1)(b)(ii), means—

   (i) the public authority, or

   (ii) any officer or employee of the authority authorised by the Presiding Officer of the National Assembly for Wales,

(i) in relation to information held by the National Audit Office, means the Comptroller and Auditor General,

(j) in relation to information held by the Northern Ireland Audit Office, means the Comptroller and Auditor General for Northern Ireland,

(k) in relation to information held by the Auditor General for Wales, means the Auditor General for Wales,

(ka) in relation to information held by the Public Services Ombudsman for Wales, means the Public Services Ombudsman for Wales,

(l) in relation to information held by any Northern Ireland public authority other than the Northern Ireland Audit Office, means—

   (i) the public authority, or

   (ii) any officer or employee of the authority authorised by the First Minister and deputy First Minister in Northern Ireland acting jointly,

(m) in relation to information held by the Greater London Authority, means the Mayor of London,

(n) in relation to information held by a functional body within the meaning of the Greater London Authority Act 1999, means the chairman of that functional body, and

(o) in relation to information held by any public authority not falling within any of paragraphs (a) to (n), means—

   (i) a Minister of the Crown,

   (ii) the public authority, if authorised for the purposes of this section by a Minister of the Crown, or

   (iii) any officer or employee of the public authority who is authorised for the purposes of this section by a Minister of the Crown.

(6) Any authorisation for the purposes of this section—
  (a) may relate to a specified person or to persons falling within a specified class,
  (b) may be general or limited to particular classes of case, and
  (c) may be granted subject to conditions.

(7) A certificate signed by the qualified person referred to in subsection (5)(d) or (e) above certifying that in his reasonable opinion—
  (a) disclosure of information held by either House of Parliament, or
  (b) compliance with section 1(1)(a) by either House,
      would, or would be likely to, have any of the effects mentioned in subsection (2) shall be conclusive evidence of that fact.

37.— Communications with Her Majesty, etc. and honours.

(1) Information is exempt information if it relates to—
  (a) communications with the Sovereign,
  (aa) communications with the heir to, or the person who is for the time being second in line of succession to, the Throne,
  (ab) communications with a person who has subsequently acceded to the Throne or become heir to, or second in line to, the Throne,
  (ac) communications with other members of the Royal Family (other than communications which fall within any of paragraphs (a) to (ab) because they are made or received on behalf of a person falling within any of those paragraphs), and
  (ad) communications with the Royal Household (other than communications which fall within any of paragraphs (a) to (ac) because they are made or received on behalf of a person falling within any of those paragraphs), or
  (b) the conferring by the Crown of any honour or dignity.

(2) The duty to confirm or deny does not arise in relation to information which is (or if it were held by the public authority would be) exempt information by virtue of subsection (1).

38.— Health and safety.

(1) Information is exempt information if its disclosure under this Act would, or would be likely to—
  (a) endanger the physical or mental health of any individual, or
  (b) endanger the safety of any individual.

(2) The duty to confirm or deny does not arise if, or to the extent that, compliance with section 1(1)(a) would, or would be likely to, have either of the effects mentioned in subsection (1).

39.— Environmental information.

(1) Information is exempt information if the public authority holding it—
  (a) is obliged by environmental information regulations to make the information available to the public in accordance with the regulations, or
  (b) would be so obliged but for any exemption contained in the regulations.

(1A) In subsection (1) 'environmental information regulations' means—
  (a) regulations made under section 74, or
  (b) regulations made under section 2(2) of the European Communities Act 1972 for the purpose of implementing any Community obligation relating to public access to, and the dissemination of, information on the environment.

(2) The duty to confirm or deny does not arise in relation to information which is (or if it were held by the public authority would be) exempt information by virtue of subsection (1).

(3) Subsection (1)(a) does not limit the generality of section 21(1).

40.— Personal information.

(1) Any information to which a request for information relates is exempt information if it constitutes personal data of which the applicant is the data subject.

(2) Any information to which a request for information relates is also exempt information if—
   (a) it constitutes personal data which do not fall within subsection (1), and
   (b) either the first or the second condition below is satisfied.

(3) The first condition is—
   (a) in a case where the information falls within any of paragraphs (a) to (d) of the definition of 'data' in section 1(1) of the Data Protection Act 1998, that the disclosure of the information to a member of the public otherwise than under this Act would contravene—
      (i) any of the data protection principles, or
      (ii) section 10 of that Act (right to prevent processing likely to cause damage or distress), and
   (b) n any other case, that the disclosure of the information to a member of the public otherwise than under this Act would contravene any of the data protection principles if the exemptions in section 33A(1) of the Data Protection Act 1998 (which relate to manual data held by public authorities) were disregarded.

(4) The second condition is that by virtue of any provision of Part IV of the Data Protection Act 1998 the information is exempt from section 7(1)(c) of that Act (data subject's right of access to personal data).

(5) The duty to confirm or deny—
   (a) does not arise in relation to information which is (or if it were held by the public authority would be) exempt information by virtue of subsection (1), and
   (b) does not arise in relation to other information if or to the extent that either—
      (i) the giving to a member of the public of the confirmation or denial that would have to be given to comply with section 1(1)(a) would (apart from this Act) contravene any of the data protection principles or section 10 of the Data Protection Act 1998 or would do so if the exemptions in section 33A(1) of that Act were disregarded, or
      (ii) by virtue of any provision of Part IV of the Data Protection Act 1998 the information is exempt from section 7(1)(a) of that Act (data subject's right to be informed whether personal data being processed).

(6) In determining for the purposes of this section whether anything done before 24th October 2007 would contravene any of the data protection principles, the exemptions in Part III of Schedule 8 to the Data Protection Act 1998 shall be disregarded.

(7) In this section—
   'the data protection principles' means the principles set out in Part I of Schedule 1 to the Data Protection Act 1998, as read subject to Part II of that Schedule and section 27(1) of that Act;
   'data subject' has the same meaning as in section 1(1) of that Act;
   'personal data' has the same meaning as in section 1(1) of that Act.

41.— Information provided in confidence.

(1) Information is exempt information if—
    (a) it was obtained by the public authority from any other person (including another public authority), and
    (b) the disclosure of the information to the public (otherwise than under this Act) by the public authority holding it would constitute a breach of confidence actionable by that or any other person.

(2) The duty to confirm or deny does not arise if, or to the extent that, the confirmation or denial that would have to be given to comply with section 1(1)(a) would (apart from this Act) constitute an actionable breach of confidence.

42.— Legal professional privilege.

(1) Information in respect of which a claim to legal professional privilege or, in Scotland, to confidentiality of communications could be maintained in legal proceedings is exempt information.

(2) The duty to confirm or deny does not arise if, or to the extent that, compliance with section 1(1)(a) would involve the disclosure of any information (whether or not already recorded) in respect of which such a claim could be maintained in legal proceedings.

43.— Commercial interests.

(1) Information is exempt information if it constitutes a trade secret.

(2) Information is exempt information if its disclosure under this Act would, or would be likely to, prejudice the commercial interests of any person (including the public authority holding it).

(3) The duty to confirm or deny does not arise if, or to the extent that, compliance with section 1(1)(a) would, or would be likely to, prejudice the interests mentioned in subsection (2).

44.— Prohibitions on disclosure.

(1) Information is exempt information if its disclosure (otherwise than under this Act) by the public authority holding it—
    (a) is prohibited by or under any enactment,
    (b) is incompatible with any Community obligation, or
    (c) would constitute or be punishable as a contempt of court.

(2) The duty to confirm or deny does not arise if the confirmation or denial that would have to be given to comply with section 1(1)(a) would (apart from this Act) fall within any of paragraphs (a) to (c) of subsection (1).

PART III
GENERAL FUNCTIONS OF SECRETARY OF STATE, LORD CHANCELLOR AND INFORMATION COMMISSIONER

45.— Issue of code of practice by the Secretary of State.

(1) The Secretary of State shall issue, and may from time to time revise, a code of practice providing guidance to public authorities as to the practice which it would, in

his opinion, be desirable for them to follow in connection with the discharge of the authorities' functions under Part I.

(2) The code of practice must, in particular, include provision relating to—

    (a) the provision of advice and assistance by public authorities to persons who propose to make, or have made, requests for information to them,

    (b) the transfer of requests by one public authority to another public authority by which the information requested is or may be held,

    (c) consultation with persons to whom the information requested relates or persons whose interests are likely to be affected by the disclosure of information,

    (d) the inclusion in contracts entered into by public authorities of terms relating to the disclosure of information, and

    (e) the provision by public authorities of procedures for dealing with complaints about the handling by them of requests for information.

(3) The code may make different provision for different public authorities.

(4) Before issuing or revising any code under this section, the Secretary of State shall consult the Commissioner.

(5) The Secretary of State shall lay before each House of Parliament any code or revised code made under this section.

46.— Issue of code of practice by Lord Chancellor.

(1) The Lord Chancellor shall issue, and may from time to time revise, a code of practice providing guidance to relevant authorities as to the practice which it would, in his opinion, be desirable for them to follow in connection with the keeping, management and destruction of their records.

(2) For the purpose of facilitating the performance by the Public Record Office, the Public Record Office of Northern Ireland and other public authorities of their functions under this Act in relation to records which are public records for the purposes of the Public Records Act 1958 or the Public Records Act (Northern Ireland) 1923, the code may also include guidance as to—

    (a) the practice to be adopted in relation to the transfer of records under section 3(4) of the Public Records Act 1958 or section 3 of the Public Records Act (Northern Ireland) 1923, and

    (b) the practice of reviewing records before they are transferred under those provisions.

(3) In exercising his functions under this section, the Lord Chancellor shall have regard to the public interest in allowing public access to information held by relevant authorities.

(4) The code may make different provision for different relevant authorities.

(5) Before issuing or revising any code under this section the Lord Chancellor shall consult—

    (a) the Secretary of State,

    (b) the Commissioner, and

    (c) in relation to Northern Ireland, the appropriate Northern Ireland Minister.

(6) The Lord Chancellor shall lay before each House of Parliament any code or revised code made under this section.

(7) In this section 'relevant authority' means—

    (a) any public authority, and

(b) any office or body which is not a public authority but whose administrative and departmental records are public records for the purposes of the Public Records Act 1958 or the Public Records Act (Northern Ireland) 1923.

47.— General functions of Commissioner.

(1) It shall be the duty of the Commissioner to promote the following of good practice by public authorities and, in particular, so to perform his functions under this Act as to promote the observance by public authorities of—
(a) the requirements of this Act, and
(b) the provisions of the codes of practice under sections 45 and 46.

(2) The Commissioner shall arrange for the dissemination in such form and manner as he considers appropriate of such information as it may appear to him expedient to give to the public—
(a) about the operation of this Act,
(b) about good practice, and
(c) about other matters within the scope of his functions under this Act,

and may give advice to any person as to any of those matters.

(3) The Commissioner may, with the consent of any public authority, assess whether that authority is following good practice.

(4) The Commissioner may charge such sums as he may with the consent of the Secretary of State determine for any services provided by the Commissioner under this section.

(5) The Commissioner shall from time to time as he considers appropriate—
(a) consult the Keeper of Public Records about the promotion by the Commissioner of the observance by public authorities of the provisions of the code of practice under section 46 in relation to records which are public records for the purposes of the Public Records Act 1958, and
(b) consult the Deputy Keeper of the Records of Northern Ireland about the promotion by the Commissioner of the observance by public authorities of those provisions in relation to records which are public records for the purposes of the Public Records Act (Northern Ireland) 1923.

(6) In this section 'good practice', in relation to a public authority, means such practice in the discharge of its functions under this Act as appears to the Commissioner to be desirable, and includes (but is not limited to) compliance with the requirements of this Act and the provisions of the codes of practice undersections 45 and 46.

48.— Recommendations as to good practice.

(1) If it appears to the Commissioner that the practice of a public authority in relation to the exercise of its functions under this Act does not conform with that proposed in the codes of practice under sections 45 and 46, he may give to the authority a recommendation (in this section referred to as a 'practice recommendation') specifying the steps which ought in his opinion to be taken for promoting such conformity.

(2) A practice recommendation must be given in writing and must refer to the particular provisions of the code of practice with which, in the Commissioner's opinion, the public authority's practice does not conform.

(3) Before giving to a public authority other than the Public Record Office a practice recommendation which relates to conformity with the code of practice undersection

46 in respect of records which are public records for the purposes of the Public Records Act 1958, the Commissioner shall consult the Keeper of Public Records.

(4) Before giving to a public authority other than the Public Record Office of Northern Ireland a practice recommendation which relates to conformity with the code of practice under section 46 in respect of records which are public records for the purposes of the Public Records Act (Northern Ireland) 1923, the Commissioner shall consult the Deputy Keeper of the Records of Northern Ireland.

49.— Reports to be laid before Parliament.

(1) The Commissioner shall lay annually before each House of Parliament a general report on the exercise of his functions under this Act.

(2) The Commissioner may from time to time lay before each House of Parliament such other reports with respect to those functions as he thinks fit.

PART IV
ENFORCEMENT

50.— Application for decision by Commissioner.

(1) Any person (in this section referred to as 'the complainant') may apply to the Commissioner for a decision whether, in any specified respect, a request for information made by the complainant to a public authority has been dealt with in accordance with the requirements of Part I.

(2) On receiving an application under this section, the Commissioner shall make a decision unless it appears to him—
   (a) that the complainant has not exhausted any complaints procedure which is provided by the public authority in conformity with the code of practice undersection 45,
   (b) that there has been undue delay in making the application,
   (c) that the application is frivolous or vexatious, or
   (d) that the application has been withdrawn or abandoned.

(3) Where the Commissioner has received an application under this section, he shall either—
   (a) notify the complainant that he has not made any decision under this section as a result of the application and of his grounds for not doing so, or
   (b) serve notice of his decision (in this Act referred to as a 'decision notice') on the complainant and the public authority.

(4) Where the Commissioner decides that a public authority—
   (a) has failed to communicate information, or to provide confirmation or denial, in a case where it is required to do so by section 1(1), or
   (b) has failed to comply with any of the requirements of sections 11 and 17,
   the decision notice must specify the steps which must be taken by the authority for complying with that requirement and the period within which they must be taken.

(5) A decision notice must contain particulars of the right of appeal conferred by section 57.

(6) Where a decision notice requires steps to be taken by the public authority within a specified period, the time specified in the notice must not expire before the end of the period within which an appeal can be brought against the notice and, if such an appeal is brought, no step which is affected by the appeal need be taken pending the determination or withdrawal of the appeal.

(7) This section has effect subject to section 53.

51.— Information notices.

(1) If the Commissioner—
  (a) has received an application under section 50, or
  (b) reasonably requires any information—
     (i) for the purpose of determining whether a public authority has complied or is complying with any of the requirements of Part I, or
     (ii) for the purpose of determining whether the practice of a public authority in relation to the exercise of its functions under this Act conforms with that proposed in the codes of practice under sections 45 and 46,
     he may serve the authority with a notice (in this Act referred to as 'an information notice') requiring it, within such time as is specified in the notice, to furnish the Commissioner, in such form as may be so specified, with such information relating to the application, to compliance with Part I or to conformity with the code of practice as is so specified.

(2) An information notice must contain—
  (a) in a case falling within subsection (1)(a), a statement that the Commissioner has received an application under section 50, or
  (b) in a case falling within subsection (1)(b), a statement—
     (i) that the Commissioner regards the specified information as relevant for either of the purposes referred to in subsection (1)(b), and
     (ii) of his reasons for regarding that information as relevant for that purpose.

(3) An information notice must also contain particulars of the right of appeal conferred by section 57.

(4) The time specified in an information notice must not expire before the end of the period within which an appeal can be brought against the notice and, if such an appeal is brought, the information need not be furnished pending the determination or withdrawal of the appeal.

(5) An authority shall not be required by virtue of this section to furnish the Commissioner with any information in respect of—
  (a) any communication between a professional legal adviser and his client in connection with the giving of legal advice to the client with respect to his obligations, liabilities or rights under this Act, or
  (b) any communication between a professional legal adviser and his client, or between such an adviser or his client and any other person, made in connection with or in contemplation of proceedings under or arising out of this Act (including proceedings before the Tribunal) and for the purposes of such proceedings.

(6) In subsection (5) references to the client of a professional legal adviser include references to any person representing such a client.

(7) The Commissioner may cancel an information notice by written notice to the authority on which it was served.

(8) In this section 'information' includes unrecorded information.

52.— Enforcement notices.

(1) If the Commissioner is satisfied that a public authority has failed to comply with any of the requirements of Part I, the Commissioner may serve the authority with a notice (in this Act referred to as 'an enforcement notice') requiring the authority to take, within such time as may be specified in the notice, such steps as may be so specified for complying with those requirements.

(2) An enforcement notice must contain—
  (a) a statement of the requirement or requirements of Part I with which the Commissioner is satisfied that the public authority has failed to comply and his reasons for reaching that conclusion, and
  (b) particulars of the right of appeal conferred by section 57.

(3) An enforcement notice must not require any of the provisions of the notice to be complied with before the end of the period within which an appeal can be brought against the notice and, if such an appeal is brought, the notice need not be complied with pending the determination or withdrawal of the appeal.

(4) The Commissioner may cancel an enforcement notice by written notice to the authority on which it was served.

(5) This section has effect subject to section 53.

53.— Exception from duty to comply with decision notice or enforcement notice.

(1) This section applies to a decision notice or enforcement notice which—
  (a) is served on—
    (i) a government department,
    (ii) the Welsh Assembly Government, or
    (iii) any public authority designated for the purposes of this section by an order made by the Secretary of State, and
  (b) relates to a failure, in respect of one or more requests for information—
    (i) to comply with section 1(1)(a) in respect of information which falls within any provision of Part II stating that the duty to confirm or deny does not arise, or
    (ii) to comply with section 1(1)(b) in respect of exempt information.

(2) A decision notice or enforcement notice to which this section applies shall cease to have effect if, not later than the twentieth working day following the effective date, the accountable person in relation to that authority gives the Commissioner a certificate signed by him stating that he has on reasonable grounds formed the opinion that, in respect of the request or requests concerned, there was no failure falling within subsection (1)(b).

(3) Where the accountable person gives a certificate to the Commissioner under subsection (2) he shall as soon as practicable thereafter lay a copy of the certificate before—
  (a) each House of Parliament,
  (b) the Northern Ireland Assembly, in any case where the certificate relates to a decision notice or enforcement notice which has been served on a Northern Ireland department or any Northern Ireland public authority, or
  (c) the National Assembly for Wales, in any case where the certificate relates to a decision notice or enforcement notice which has been served on—
    (i) the Welsh Assembly Government,
    (ii) the National Assembly for Wales, or
    (iii) any Welsh public authority.

(4) In subsection (2) 'the effective date', in relation to a decision notice or enforcement notice, means—
  (a) the day on which the notice was given to the public authority, or
  (b) where an appeal under section 57 is brought, the day on which that appeal (or any further appeal arising out of it) is determined or withdrawn.

(5) Before making an order under subsection (1)(a)(iii), the Secretary of State shall—
  (a) if the order relates to a Welsh public authority, consult the Welsh Ministers,
  (aa) if the order relates to the National Assembly for Wales, consult the Presiding Officer of that Assembly,
  (b) if the order relates to the Northern Ireland Assembly, consult the Presiding Officer of that Assembly, and
  (c) if the order relates to a Northern Ireland public authority, consult the First Minister and deputy First Minister in Northern Ireland.

(6) Where the accountable person gives a certificate to the Commissioner under subsection (2) in relation to a decision notice, the accountable person shall, on doing so or as soon as reasonably practicable after doing so, inform the person who is the complainant for the purposes of section 50 of the reasons for his opinion.

(7) The accountable person is not obliged to provide information under subsection (6) if, or to the extent that, compliance with that subsection would involve the disclosure of exempt information.

(8) In this section 'the accountable person'—
  (a) in relation to a Northern Ireland department or any Northern Ireland public authority, means the First Minister and deputy First Minister in Northern Ireland acting jointly,
  (b) in relation the Welsh Assembly Government, the National Assembly for Wales or any Welsh public authority, means the First Minister for Wales, and
  (c) in relation to any other public authority, means—
    (i) a Minister of the Crown who is a member of the Cabinet, or
    (ii) the Attorney General, the Advocate General for Scotland or the Attorney General for Northern Ireland.

(9) In this section 'working day' has the same meaning as in section 10.

54.— Failure to comply with notice.

(1) If a public authority has failed to comply with—
  (a) so much of a decision notice as requires steps to be taken,
  (b) an information notice, or
  (c) an enforcement notice,

the Commissioner may certify in writing to the court that the public authority has failed to comply with that notice.

(2) For the purposes of this section, a public authority which, in purported compliance with an information notice—
  (a) makes a statement which it knows to be false in a material respect, or
  (b) recklessly makes a statement which is false in a material respect,

is to be taken to have failed to comply with the notice.

(3) Where a failure to comply is certified under subsection (1), the court may inquire into the matter and, after hearing any witness who may be produced against or on

behalf of the public authority, and after hearing any statement that may be offered in defence, deal with the authority as if it had committed a contempt of court.

(4)   In this section 'the court' means the High Court or, in Scotland, the Court of Session.

55.— Powers of entry and inspection.

Schedule 3 (powers of entry and inspection) has effect.

56.— No action against public authority.

(1)   This Act does not confer any right of action in civil proceedings in respect of any failure to comply with any duty imposed by or under this Act.

(2)   Subsection (1) does not affect the powers of the Commissioner under section 54.

PART V
APPEALS

57.— Appeal against notice served under Part IV.

(1)   Where a decision notice has been served, the complainant or the public authority may appeal to the Tribunal against the notice.

(2)   A public authority on which an information notice or an enforcement notice has been served by the Commissioner may appeal to the Tribunal against the notice.

(3)   In relation to a decision notice or enforcement notice which relates—
  (a)   to information to which section 66 applies, and
  (b)   to a matter which by virtue of subsection (3) or (4) of that section falls to be determined by the responsible authority instead of the appropriate records authority,

subsections (1) and (2) shall have effect as if the reference to the public authority were a reference to the public authority or the responsible authority.

58.— Determination of appeals.

(1)   If on an appeal under section 57 the Tribunal considers—
  (a)   that the notice against which the appeal is brought is not in accordance with the law, or
  (b)   to the extent that the notice involved an exercise of discretion by the Commissioner, that he ought to have exercised his discretion differently,

the Tribunal shall allow the appeal or substitute such other notice as could have been served by the Commissioner; and in any other case the Tribunal shall dismiss the appeal.

(2)   On such an appeal, the Tribunal may review any finding of fact on which the notice in question was based.

60.— Appeals against national security certificate.

(1)   Where a certificate under section 23(2) or 24(3) has been issued—
  (a)   the Commissioner, or
  (b)   any applicant whose request for information is affected by the issue of the certificate,

may appeal to the Tribunal against the certificate.

(2) If on an appeal under subsection (1) relating to a certificate under section 23(2), the Tribunal finds that the information referred to in the certificate was not exempt information by virtue of section 23(1), the Tribunal may allow the appeal and quash the certificate.

(3) If on an appeal under subsection (1) relating to a certificate under section 24(3), the Tribunal finds that, applying the principles applied by the court on an application for judicial review, the Minister did not have reasonable grounds for issuing the certificate, the Tribunal may allow the appeal and quash the certificate.

(4) Where in any proceedings under this Act it is claimed by a public authority that a certificate under section 24(3) which identifies the information to which it applies by means of a general description applies to particular information, any other party to the proceedings may appeal to the Tribunal on the ground that the certificate does not apply to the information in question and, subject to any determination under subsection (5), the certificate shall be conclusively presumed so to apply.

(5) On any appeal under subsection (4), the Tribunal may determine that the certificate does not so apply.

61.— Appeal proceedings.

The provisions of Schedule 6 to the Data Protection Act 1998 have effect (so far as applicable) in relation to appeals under this Part.

PART VI
HISTORICAL RECORDS AND RECORDS IN PUBLIC RECORD OFFICE OR PUBLIC RECORD OFFICE OF NORTHERN IRELAND

62.— Interpretation of Part VI.

(1) For the purposes of this Part, a record becomes a 'historical record' at the end of the period of thirty years beginning with the year following that in which it was created.

(2) Where records created at different dates are for administrative purposes kept together in one file or other assembly, all the records in that file or other assembly are to be treated for the purposes of this Part as having been created when the latest of those records was created.

(3) In this Part 'year' means a calendar year.

63.— Removal of exemptions: historical records generally.

(1) Information contained in a historical record cannot be exempt information by virtue of section 28, 30(1), 32, 33, 35, 36, 42 or 43.

(2) Compliance with section 1(1)(a) in relation to a historical record is not to be taken to be capable of having any of the effects referred to in section 28(3),33(3), 36(3), 42(2) or 43(3).

(2E) Information cannot be exempt information by virtue of any of paragraphs (a) to (ad) of section 37(1) after whichever is the later of—
  (a) the end of the period of five years beginning with the date of the relevant death, and

(b) the end of the period of twenty years beginning with the date on which the record containing the information was created.

(2F) In subsection (2E)(a) 'the relevant death' means—

    (a) for the purposes of any of paragraphs (a) to (ac) of section 37(1), the death of the person referred to in the paragraph concerned, or

    (b) or the purposes of section 37(1)(ad), the death of the Sovereign reigning when the record containing the information was created.

(3) Information cannot be exempt information by virtue of section 37(1)(b) after the end of the period of sixty years beginning with the year following that in which the record containing the information was created.

(4) Information cannot be exempt information by virtue of section 31 after the end of the period of one hundred years beginning with the year following that in which the record containing the information was created.

(5) Compliance with section 1(1)(a) in relation to any record is not to be taken, at any time after the end of the period of one hundred years beginning with the year following that in which the record was created, to be capable of prejudicing any of the matters referred to in section 31(1).

64.— Removal of exemptions: historical records in public record offices.

(1) Information contained in a historical record in the Public Record Office or the Public Record Office of Northern Ireland cannot be exempt information by virtue ofsection 21 or 22.

(2) In relation to any information falling within section 23(1) which is contained in a historical record in the Public Record Office or the Public Record Office of Northern Ireland, section 2(3) shall have effect with the omission of the reference to section 23.

65.— Decisions as to refusal of discretionary disclosure of historical records.

(1) Before refusing a request for information relating to information which is contained in a historical record and is exempt information only by virtue of a provision not specified in section 2(3), a public authority shall—

    (a) if the historical record is a public record within the meaning of the Public Records Act 1958, consult the Lord Chancellor, or

    (b) if the historical record is a public record to which the Public Records Act (Northern Ireland) 1923 applies, consult the appropriate Northern Ireland Minister.

(2) This section does not apply to information to which section 66 applies.

66.— Decisions relating to certain transferred public records.

(1) This section applies to any information which is (or, if it existed, would be) contained in a transferred public record, other than information which the responsible authority has designated as open information for the purposes of this section.

(2) Before determining whether—

    (a) information to which this section applies falls within any provision of Part II relating to the duty to confirm or deny, or

    (b) information to which this section applies is exempt information,

the appropriate records authority shall consult the responsible authority.

(3) Where information to which this section applies falls within a provision of Part II relating to the duty to confirm or deny but does not fall within any of the provisions of that Part relating to that duty which are specified in subsection (3) of section 2, any question as to the application of subsection (1)(b) of that section is to be determined by the responsible authority instead of the appropriate records authority.

(4) Where any information to which this section applies is exempt information only by virtue of any provision of Part II not specified in subsection (3) of section 2, any question as to the application of subsection (2)(b) of that section is to be determined by the responsible authority instead of the appropriate records authority.

(5) Before making by virtue of subsection (3) or (4) any determination that subsection (1)(b) or (2)(b) of section 2 applies, the responsible authority shall consult—
   (a) where the transferred public record is a public record within the meaning of the Public Records Act 1958, the Lord Chancellor, and
   (b) where the transferred public record is a public record to which the Public Records Act (Northern Ireland) 1923 applies, the appropriate Northern Ireland Minister.

(6) Where the responsible authority in relation to information to which this section applies is not (apart from this subsection) a public authority, it shall be treated as being a public authority for the purposes of Parts III, IV and V of this Act so far as relating to—
   (a) the duty imposed by section 15(3), and
   (b) the imposition of any requirement to furnish information relating to compliance with Part I in connection with the information to which this section applies.

67.— Amendments of public records legislation.

Schedule 5 (which amends the Public Records Act 1958 and the Public Records Act (Northern Ireland) 1923) has effect.

PART VII
AMENDMENTS OF DATA PROTECTION ACT 1998

Amendments relating to personal information held by public authorities

68.— Extension of meaning of 'data'.

(1) Section 1 of the Data Protection Act 1998 (basic interpretative provisions) is amended in accordance with subsections (2) and (3).

(2) In subsection (1)—
   (a) in the definition of 'data', the word 'or' at the end of paragraph (c) is omitted and after paragraph (d) there is inserted
      'or
      (e) is recorded information held by a public authority and does not fall within any of paragraphs (a) to (d);'
      , and
   (b) after the definition of 'processing' there is inserted—
      "'public authority' has the same meaning as in the Freedom of Information Act 2000;'.

(3)   After subsection (4) there is inserted—

'(5)   In paragraph (e) of the definition of 'data' in subsection (1); the reference to information 'held' by a public authority shall be construed in accordance with section 3(2) of the Freedom of Information Act 2000.

(6)   Where section 7 of the Freedom of Information Act 2000 prevents Parts I to V of that Act from applying to certain information held by a public authority, that information is not to be treated for the purposes of paragraph (e) of the definition of 'data' in subsection (1) as held by a public authority.'

(4)   In section 56 of that Act (prohibition of requirement as to production of certain records), after subsection (6) there is inserted—

'(6A)   A record is not a relevant record to the extent that it relates, or is to relate, only to personal data falling within paragraph (e) of the definition of 'data' in section 1(1).'

(5)   In the Table in section 71 of that Act (index of defined expressions) after the entry relating to processing there is inserted—

'public authority.   section 1(1)'.

69.— Right of access to unstructured personal data held by public authorities.

(1)   In section 7(1) of the Data Protection Act 1998 (right of access to personal data), for 'sections 8 and 9' there is substituted 'sections 8, 9 and 9A'.

(2)   After section 9 of that Act there is inserted—

'9A.— Unstructured personal data held by public authorities.

(1)   In this section 'unstructured personal data' means any personal data falling within paragraph (e) of the definition of 'data' in section 1(1), other than information which is recorded as part of, or with the intention that it should form part of, any set of information relating to individuals to the extent that the set is structured by reference to individuals or by reference to criteria relating to individuals.

(2)   A public authority is not obliged to comply with subsection (1) of section 7 in relation to any unstructured personal data unless the request under that section contains a description of the data.

(3)   Even if the data are described by the data subject in his request, a public authority is not obliged to comply with subsection (1) of section 7 in relation to unstructured personal data if the authority estimates that the cost of complying with the request so far as relating to those data would exceed the appropriate limit.

(4)   Subsection (3) does not exempt the public authority from its obligation to comply with paragraph (a) of section 7(1) in relation to the unstructured personal data unless the estimated cost of complying with that paragraph alone in relation to those data would exceed the appropriate limit.

(5)   In subsections (3) and (4) 'the appropriate limit' means such amount as may be prescribed by the Secretary of State by regulations, and different amounts may be prescribed in relation to different cases .

(6)   Any estimate for the purposes of this section must be made in accordance with regulations under section 12(5) of the Freedom of Information Act 2000.'

(3)   In section 67(5) of that Act (statutory instruments subject to negative resolution procedure), in paragraph (c), for 'or 9(3)' there is substituted ', 9(3) or 9A(5)'.

70.— Exemptions applicable to certain manual data held by public authorities.

(1) After section 33 of the Data Protection Act 1998 there is inserted—

'33A.— Manual data held by public authorities.

(1) Personal data falling within paragraph (e) of the definition of 'data' in section 1(1) are exempt from—

(a) the first, second, third, fifth, seventh and eighth data protection principles,

(b) the sixth data protection principle except so far as it relates to the rights conferred on data subjects by sections 7 and 14,

(c) sections 10 to 12,

(d) section 13, except so far as it relates to damage caused by a contravention of section 7 or of the fourth data protection principle and to any distress which is also suffered by reason of that contravention,

(e) Part III, and

(f) section 55.

(2) Personal data which fall within paragraph (e) of the definition of 'data' in section 1(1) and relate to appointments or removals, pay, discipline, superannuation or other personnel matters, in relation to—

(a) service in any of the armed forces of the Crown,

(b) service in any office or employment under the Crown or under any public authority, or

(c) service in any office or employment, or under any contract for services, in respect of which power to take action, or to determine or approve the action taken, in such matters is vested in Her Majesty, any Minister of the Crown, the National Assembly for Wales, any Northern Ireland Minister (within the meaning of the Freedom of Information Act 2000) or any public authority,

are also exempt from the remaining data protection principles and the remaining provisions of Part II.'

(2) In section 55 of that Act (unlawful obtaining etc. of personal data) in subsection (8) after 'section 28' there is inserted 'or 33A'.

(3) In Part III of Schedule 8 to that Act (exemptions available after 23rd October 2001 but before 24th October 2007) after paragraph 14 there is inserted—

'14A.—

(1) This paragraph applies to personal data which fall within paragraph (e) of the definition of 'data' in section 1(1) and do not fall within paragraph 14(1)(a), but does not apply to eligible manual data to which the exemption in paragraph 16 applies.

(2) During the second transitional period, data to which this paragraph applies are exempt from—

(a) the fourth data protection principle, and

(b) section 14(1) to (3).'

(4) In Schedule 13 to that Act (modifications of Act having effect before 24th October 2007) in subsection (4)(b) of section 12A to that Act as set out in paragraph 1, after 'paragraph 14' there is inserted 'or 14A'.

71.— Particulars registrable under Part III of Data Protection Act 1998.

In section 16(1) of the Data Protection Act 1998 (the registrable particulars), before the word 'and' at the end of paragraph (f) there is inserted—

'(ff) where the data controller is a public authority, a statement of that fact,'.

72.— Availability under Act disregarded for purpose of exemption.

In section 34 of the Data Protection Act 1998 (information available to the public by or under enactment), after the word 'enactment' there is inserted 'other than an enactment contained in the Freedom of Information Act 2000'.

Other amendments

73.— Further amendments of Data Protection Act 1998.

Schedule 6 (which contains further amendments of the Data Protection Act 1998) has effect.

PART VIII
MISCELLANEOUS AND SUPPLEMENTAL

74.— Power to make provision relating to environmental information.

(1) In this section 'the Aarhus Convention' means the Convention on Access to Information, Public Participation in Decision-making and Access to Justice in Environmental Matters signed at Aarhus on 25th June 1998.

(2) For the purposes of this section 'the information provisions' of the Aarhus Convention are Article 4, together with Articles 3 and 9 so far as relating to that Article.

(3) The Secretary of State may by regulations make such provision as he considers appropriate—
   (a) for the purpose of implementing the information provisions of the Aarhus Convention or any amendment of those provisions made in accordance with Article 14 of the Convention, and
   (b) for the purpose of dealing with matters arising out of or related to the implementation of those provisions or of any such amendment.

(4) Regulations under subsection (3) may in particular—
   (a) enable charges to be made for making information available in accordance with the regulations,
   (b) provide that any obligation imposed by the regulations in relation to the disclosure of information is to have effect notwithstanding any enactment or rule of law,
   (c) make provision for the issue by the Secretary of State of a code of practice,
   (d) provide for sections 47 and 48 to apply in relation to such a code with such modifications as may be specified,
   (e) provide for any of the provisions of Parts IV and V to apply, with such modifications as may be specified in the regulations, in relation to compliance with any requirement of the regulations, and
   (f) contain such transitional or consequential provision (including provision modifying any enactment) as the Secretary of State considers appropriate.

(5) This section has effect subject to section 80.

75.— Power to amend or repeal enactments prohibiting disclosure of information.

(1) If, with respect to any enactment which prohibits the disclosure of information held by a public authority, it appears to the Secretary of State that by virtue of section

44(1)(a) the enactment is capable of preventing the disclosure of information under section, he may by order repeal or amend the enactment for the purpose of removing or relaxing the prohibition.

(2) In subsection (1)—

'enactment' means—

(a) any enactment contained in an Act passed before or in the same Session as this Act, or

(b) any enactment contained in Northern Ireland legislation or subordinate legislation passed or made before the passing of this Act;

'information' includes unrecorded information.

(3) An order under this section may do all or any of the following—

(a) make such modifications of enactments as, in the opinion of the Secretary of State, are consequential upon, or incidental to, the amendment or repeal of the enactment containing the prohibition;

(b) contain such transitional provisions and savings as appear to the Secretary of State to be appropriate;

(c) make different provision for different cases.

76.— Disclosure of information between Commissioner and ombudsmen.

(1) The Commissioner may disclose to a person specified in the first column of the Table below any information obtained by, or furnished to, the Commissioner under or for the purposes of this Act or the Data Protection Act 1998 if it appears to the Commissioner that the information relates to a matter which could be the subject of an investigation by that person under the enactment specified in relation to that person in the second column of that Table.

TABLE

Ombudsman	Enactment
The Parliamentary Commissioner for Administration.	The Parliamentary Commissioner Act 1967 (c. 13).
The Health Service Commissioner for England.	The Health Service Commissioners Act 1993 (c. 46).
A Local Commissioner as defined by section 23(3) of the Local Government Act 1974.	Part III of the Local Government Act 1974 (c. 7).
The Scottish Public Services Ombudsman	The Scottish Public Services Ombudsman Act 2002 (asp 11).
The Public Services Ombudsman for Wales	Part 2 of the Public Services Ombudsman (Wales) Act 2005.
The Northern Ireland Commissioner for Complaints.	The Commissioner for Complaints (Northern Ireland) Order 1996 (SI 1996/1297 (N.I. 7)).
The Assembly Ombudsman for Northern Ireland.	The Ombudsman (Northern Ireland) Order 1996 (SI 1996/1298 (N.I. 8)).
The Commissioner for older People in Wales	The Commissioner for Older People (Wales) Act 2006

(2) Schedule 7 (which contains amendments relating to information disclosed to ombudsmen under subsection (1) and to the disclosure of information by ombudsmen to the Commissioner) has effect.

76A.— Disclosure between Commissioner and Scottish Information Commissioner

The Commissioner may disclose to the Scottish Information Commissioner any information obtained or furnished as mentioned in section 76(1) of this Act if it appears to the Commissioner that the information is of the same type that could be obtained by, or furnished to, the Scottish Information Commissioner under or for the purposes of the Freedom of Information (Scotland) Act 2002.

77.— Offence of altering etc. records with intent to prevent disclosure.

(1) Where—
    (a) a request for information has been made to a public authority, and
    (b) under section 1 of this Act or section 7 of the Data Protection Act 1998, the applicant would have been entitled (subject to payment of any fee) to communication of any information in accordance with that section,
    any person to whom this subsection applies is guilty of an offence if he alters, defaces, blocks, erases, destroys or conceals any record held by the public authority, with the intention of preventing the disclosure by that authority of all, or any part, of the information to the communication of which the applicant would have been entitled.

(2) Subsection (1) applies to the public authority and to any person who is employed by, is an officer of, or is subject to the direction of, the public authority.

(3) A person guilty of an offence under this section is liable on summary conviction to a fine not exceeding level 5 on the standard scale.

(4) No proceedings for an offence under this section shall be instituted—
    (a) in England or Wales, except by the Commissioner or by or with the consent of the Director of Public Prosecutions;
    (b) in Northern Ireland, except by the Commissioner or by or with the consent of the Director of Public Prosecutions for Northern Ireland.

78.— Saving for existing powers.

Nothing in this Act is to be taken to limit the powers of a public authority to disclose information held by it.

79.— Defamation.

Where any information communicated by a public authority to a person ('the applicant') under section 1 was supplied to the public authority by a third person, the publication to the applicant of any defamatory matter contained in the information shall be privileged unless the publication is shown to have been made with malice.

80.— Scotland.

(1) No order may be made under section 4(1) or 5 in relation to any of the bodies specified in subsection (2); and the power conferred by section 74(3) does not include power to make provision in relation to information held by any of those bodies.

(2) The bodies referred to in subsection (1) are—
  (a) the Scottish Parliament,
  (b) any part of the Scottish Administration,
  (c) the Scottish Parliamentary Corporate Body, or
  (d) any Scottish public authority with mixed functions or no reserved functions (within the meaning of the Scotland Act 1998).

(3) Section 50 of the Copyright, Designs and Patents Act 1988 and paragraph 6 of Schedule 1 to the Copyright and Rights in Databases Regulations 1997 apply in relation to the Freedom of Information (Scotland) Act 2002 as they apply in relation to this Act.

80A.— Information held by Northern Ireland bodies

(1) This section applies to information held by—
  (a) the Northern Ireland Assembly,
  (b) a Northern Ireland department, or
  (c) a Northern Ireland public authority.

(2) In their application to information to which this section applies, the provisions of this Act have effect subject to the following modifications.

(3) Section 2(3) (exemptions not subject to public interest test) is to be read as if paragraph (ea) were omitted.

(4) Section 37(1) (communications with Her Majesty, etc) is to be read as if for paragraphs (a) to (ad) there were substituted—
  '(a) communications with the Sovereign, with other members of the Royal Family or with the Royal Household, or'.

(5) Section 62(1) (meaning of 'historical record') is to be read as if the reference to twenty years were a reference to thirty years.

(6) Section 63 (removal of exemptions: historical records generally) is to be read as if—
  (a) in subsection (1), for the words from 'section' to the end there were substituted 'section 28, 30(1), 32, 33, 35, 36, 37(1)(a), 42 or 43',
  (b) in subsection (2), for the words from 'section' to the end there were substituted 'section 28(3), 33(3), 36(3), 42(2) or 43(3)', and
  (c) subsections (2A) to (2F) were omitted.

81.— Application to government departments, etc.

(1) For the purposes of this Act each government department is to be treated as a person separate from any other government department.

(2) Subsection (1) does not enable—
  (a) a government department which is not a Northern Ireland department to claim for the purposes of section 41(1)(b) that the disclosure of any information by it would constitute a breach of confidence actionable by any other government department (not being a Northern Ireland department), or
  (b) a Northern Ireland department to claim for those purposes that the disclosure of information by it would constitute a breach of confidence actionable by any other Northern Ireland department.

(3) A government department or the Welsh Assembly Government is not liable to prosecution under this Act, but section 77 and paragraph 12 of Schedule 3 apply to a person in the public service of the Crown as they apply to any other person.

(4) The provisions specified in subsection (3) also apply to a person acting on behalf of either House of Parliament or on behalf of the Northern Ireland Assembly or the National Assembly for Wales as they apply to any other person.

82.— Orders and regulations.

(1) Any power of the Secretary of State to make an order or regulations under this Act shall be exercisable by statutory instrument.

(2) A statutory instrument containing (whether alone or with other provisions)—
(a) an order under section 5, 7(3) or (8), 53(1)(a)(iii) or 75, or
(b) regulations under section 10(4) or 74(3),

shall not be made unless a draft of the instrument has been laid before, and approved by a resolution of, each House of Parliament.

(3) A statutory instrument which contains (whether alone or with other provisions)—
(a) an order under section 4(1), or
(b) regulations under any provision of this Act not specified in subsection (2)(b),

and which is not subject to the requirement in subsection (2) that a draft of the instrument be laid before and approved by a resolution of each House of Parliament, shall be subject to annulment in pursuance of a resolution of either House of Parliament.

(4) An order under section 4(5) shall be laid before Parliament after being made.

(5) If a draft of an order under section 5 or 7(8) would, apart from this subsection, be treated for the purposes of the Standing Orders of either House of Parliament as a hybrid instrument, it shall proceed in that House as if it were not such an instrument.

83.— Meaning of 'Welsh public authority'.

(1) In this Act 'Welsh public authority' means—
(a) any public authority which is listed in Part II, III, IV or VI of Schedule 1 and whose functions are exercisable only or mainly in or as regards Wales, other than an excluded authority, or
(b) any public authority which is—
(i) a subsidiary of the Welsh Ministers (as defined by section 134(4) of the Government of Wales Act 2006), or
(ii) a subsidiary of the Assembly Commission (as defined by section 139(4) of that Act).

(2) In paragraph (a) of subsection (1) 'excluded authority' means a public authority which is designated by the Secretary of State by order as an excluded authority for the purposes of that paragraph .

(3) Before making an order under subsection (2), the Secretary of State shall consult the First Minister for Wales.

84.— Interpretation.

In this Act, unless the context otherwise requires—

'applicant', in relation to a request for information, means the person who made the request;

'appropriate Northern Ireland Minister' means the Northern Ireland Minister in charge of the Department of Culture, Arts and Leisure in Northern Ireland;

'appropriate records authority', in relation to a transferred public record, has the meaning given by section 15(5);

'body' includes an unincorporated association;

'the Commissioner' means the Information Commissioner;

'decision notice' has the meaning given by section 50;

'the duty to confirm or deny' has the meaning given by section 1(6);

'enactment' includes an enactment contained in Northern Ireland legislation;

'enforcement notice' has the meaning given by section 52;

'exempt information' means information which is exempt information by virtue of any provision of Part II;

'fees notice' has the meaning given by section 9(1);

'government department' includes a Northern Ireland department, the Northern Ireland Court Service and any other body or authority exercising statutory functions on behalf of the Crown, but does not include—
(a) any of the bodies specified in section 80(2),
(b) the Security Service, the Secret Intelligence Service or the Government Communications Headquarters, or
(c) the Welsh Assembly Government;

'information' (subject to sections 51(8) and 75(2)) means information recorded in any form;

'information notice' has the meaning given by section 51;

'Minister of the Crown' has the same meaning as in the Ministers of the Crown Act 1975;

'Northern Ireland Minister' includes the First Minister and deputy First Minister in Northern Ireland;

'Northern Ireland public authority' means any public authority, other than the Northern Ireland Assembly or a Northern Ireland department, whose functions are exercisable only or mainly in or as regards Northern Ireland and relate only or mainly to transferred matters;

'prescribed' means prescribed by regulations made by the Secretary of State;

'public authority' has the meaning given by section 3(1);

'public record' means a public record within the meaning of the Public Records Act 1958 or a public record to which the Public Records Act (Northern Ireland) 1923 applies;

'publication scheme' has the meaning given by section 19;

'request for information' has the meaning given by section 8;

'responsible authority', in relation to a transferred public record, has the meaning given by section 15(5);

'the special forces' means those units of the armed forces of the Crown the maintenance of whose capabilities is the responsibility of the Director of Special Forces or which are for the time being subject to the operational command of that Director;

'subordinate legislation' has the meaning given by subsection (1) of section 21 of the Interpretation Act 1978, except that the definition of that term in that subsection shall have effect as if 'Act' included Northern Ireland legislation;

'transferred matter', in relation to Northern Ireland, has the meaning given by section 4(1) of the Northern Ireland Act 1998;

'transferred public record' has the meaning given by section 15(4);

'the Tribunal', in relation to any appeal under this Act, means—

  (a) the Upper Tribunal, in any case where it is determined by or under Tribunal Procedure Rules that the Upper Tribunal is to hear the appeal; or

  (b) the First-tier Tribunal, in any other case;

'Welsh public authority' has the meaning given by section 83.

85.— Expenses.

There shall be paid out of money provided by Parliament—

  (a) any increase attributable to this Act in the expenses of the Secretary of State in respect of the Commissioner, the Tribunal or the members of the Tribunal,

  (b) any administrative expenses of the Secretary of State attributable to this Act,

  (c) any other expenses incurred in consequence of this Act by a Minister of the Crown or government department or by either House of Parliament, and

  (d) any increase attributable to this Act in the sums which under any other Act are payable out of money so provided.

86.— Repeals.

Schedule 8 (repeals) has effect.

87.— Commencement.

(1) The following provisions of this Act shall come into force on the day on which this Act is passed—

  (a) sections 3 to 8 and Schedule 1,

  (b) section 19 so far as relating to the approval of publication schemes,

  (c) section 20 so far as relating to the approval and preparation by the Commissioner of model publication schemes,

  (d) section 47(2) to (6),

  (e) section 49,

  (f) section 74,

  (g) section 75,

  (h) sections 78 to 85 and this section,

  (i) paragraphs 2 and 17 to 22 of Schedule 2 (and section 18(4) so far as relating to those paragraphs),

  (j) paragraph 4 of Schedule 5 (and section 67 so far as relating to that paragraph),

  (k) paragraph 8 of Schedule 6 (and section 73 so far as relating to that paragraph),

  (l) Part I of Schedule 8 (and section 86 so far as relating to that Part), and

  (m) so much of any other provision of this Act as confers power to make any order, regulations or code of practice.

(2) The following provisions of this Act shall come into force at the end of the period of two months beginning with the day on which this Act is passed—

  (a) section 18(1),

  (b) section 76 and Schedule 7,

  (c) paragraphs 1(1), 3(1), 4, 6, 7, 8(2), 9(2), 10(a), 13(1) and (2), 14(a) and 15(1) and (2) of Schedule 2 (and section 18(4) so far as relating to those provisions), and

  (d) Part II of Schedule 8 (and section 86 so far as relating to that Part).

(3) Except as provided by subsections (1) and (2), this Act shall come into force at the end of the period of five years beginning with the day on which this Act is passed or on such day before the end of that period as the Secretary of State may by order appoint; and different days may be appointed for different purposes.

(4) An order under subsection (3) may contain such transitional provisions and savings (including provisions capable of having effect after the end of the period referred to in that subsection) as the Secretary of State considers appropriate.

(5) During the twelve months beginning with the day on which this Act is passed, and during each subsequent complete period of twelve months in the period beginning with that day and ending with the first day on which all the provisions of this Act are fully in force, the Secretary of State shall—
    (a) prepare a report on his proposals for bringing fully into force those provisions of this Act which are not yet fully in force, and
    (b) lay a copy of the report before each House of Parliament.

88.— Short title and extent.

(1) This Act may be cited as the Freedom of Information Act 2000.

(2) Subject to subsection (3), this Act extends to Northern Ireland.

(3) The amendment or repeal of any enactment by this Act has the same extent as that enactment.

SCHEDULE 1
PUBLIC AUTHORITIES

Section 3(1)(a)(i)

PART I
GENERAL

1 Any government department.

1A The Office for Standards in Education, Children's Services and Skills, in respect of information held for purposes other than those of the functions exercisable by Her Majesty's Chief Inspector of Education, Children's Services and Skills by virtue of section 5(1)(a)(iii) of the Care Standards Act 2000.

2 The House of Commons, in respect of information other than—
    (a) information relating to any residential address of a member of either House of Parliament,
    (b) information relating to travel arrangements of a member of either House of Parliament, where the arrangements relate to travel that has not yet been undertaken or is regular in nature,
    (c) information relating to the identity of any person who delivers or has delivered goods, or provides or has provided services, to a member of either House of Parliament at any residence of the member,
    (d) information relating to expenditure by a member of either House of Parliament on security arrangements.
    Paragraph (b) does not except information relating to the total amount of expenditure incurred on regular travel during any month.

3 The House of Lords, in respect of information other than—

  (a) information relating to any residential address of a member of either House of Parliament,

  (b) information relating to travel arrangements of a member of either House of Parliament, where the arrangements relate to travel that has not yet been undertaken or is regular in nature,

  (c) information relating to the identity of any person who delivers or has delivered goods, or provides or has provided services, to a member of either House of Parliament at any residence of the member,

  (d) information relating to expenditure by a member of either House of Parliament on security arrangements.

Paragraph (b) does not except information relating to the total amount of expenditure incurred on regular travel during any month.

4 The Northern Ireland Assembly.

5 The National Assembly for Wales, in respect of information other than—

  (a) information relating to any residential address of a member of the Assembly,

  (b) information relating to travel arrangements of a member of the Assembly, where the arrangements relate to travel that has not yet been undertaken or is regular in nature,

  (c) information relating to the identity of any person who delivers or has delivered goods, or provides or has provided services, to a member of the Assembly at any residence of the member,

  (d) information relating to expenditure by a member of the Assembly on security arrangements.

Paragraph (b) does not except information relating to the total amount of expenditure incurred on regular travel during any month.

5A The Welsh Assembly Government.

6 The armed forces of the Crown, except—

  (a) the special forces, and

  (b) any unit or part of a unit which is for the time being required by the Secretary of State to assist the Government Communications Headquarters in the exercise of its functions.

PART II
LOCAL GOVERNMENT

England and Wales

7 A local authority within the meaning of the Local Government Act 1972, namely—

  (a) in England, a county council, a London borough council, a district council or a parish council,

  (b) in Wales, a county council, a county borough council or a community council.

8 The Greater London Authority.

9 The Common Council of the City of London, in respect of information held in its capacity as a local authority, police authority or port health authority.

10 The Sub-Treasurer of the Inner Temple or the Under-Treasurer of the Middle Temple, in respect of information held in his capacity as a local authority.

11 The Council of the Isles of Scilly.

12 A parish meeting constituted under section 13 of the Local Government Act 1972.

13 Any charter trustees constituted under section 246 of the Local Government Act 1972.

14 A fire and rescue authority constituted by a scheme under section 2 of the Fire and Rescue Services Act 2004 or a scheme to which section 4 of that Act applies.

15 A waste disposal authority established by virtue of an order under section 10(1) of the Local Government Act 1985.

15A An authority established for an area in England by an order under section 207 of the Local Government and Public Involvement in Health Act 2007 (joint waste authorities).

16 A port health authority constituted by an order under section 2 of the Public Health (Control of Disease) Act 1984.

17 [...]

18 An internal drainage board which is continued in being by virtue of section 1 of the Land Drainage Act 1991.

19 A joint authority established under Part IV of the Local Government Act 1985 (fire services, civil defence and transport).

19A An economic prosperity board established under section 88 of the Local Democracy, Economic Development and Construction Act 2009.

19B A combined authority established under section 103 of that Act.

20 The London Fire and Emergency Planning Authority.

21 A joint fire authority established by virtue of an order under section 42(2) of the Local Government Act 1985 (reorganisation of functions).

22 A body corporate established pursuant to an order under section 67 of the Local Government Act 1985 (transfer of functions to successors of residuary bodies, etc).

23 A body corporate established pursuant to an order section 17 of the Local Government and Public Involvement in Health Act 2007 (residuary bodies).

24 The Broads Authority established by section 1 of the Norfolk and Suffolk Broads Act 1988.

25   A joint committee constituted in accordance with section 102(1)(b) of the Local Government Act 1972.

26   A joint board which is continued in being by virtue of section 263(1) of the Local Government Act 1972.

27   A joint authority established under section 21 of the Local Government Act 1992.

28   A Passenger Transport Executive for a passenger transport area within the meaning of Part II of the Transport Act 1968.

29   Transport for London.

30   The London Transport Users Committee.

31   A joint board the constituent members of which consist of any of the public authorities described in paragraphs 8, 9, 10, 12, 15, 16, 20 to 31, 57 and 58.

32   A National Park authority established by an order under section 63 of the Environment Act 1995.

33   A joint planning board constituted for an area in Wales outside a National Park by an order under section 2(1B) of the Town and Country Planning Act 1990.

34   [...]

35   The London Development Agency.

35A   [...]

35B   An inshore fisheries and conservation authority for a district established under section 149 of the Marine and Coastal Access Act 2009.

35C   An urban development corporation established under section 135 of the Local Government, Planning and Land Act 1980.

Northern Ireland

36   A district council within the meaning of the Local Government Act (Northern Ireland) 1972.

PART III
THE NATIONAL HEALTH SERVICE

England and Wales

36A   A Strategic Health Authority established under section 13 of the National Health Service Act 2006.

37 [...]

38 A special health authority established under section 28 of the National Health Service Act 2006 or section 22 of the National Health Service (Wales) Act 2006.

39 A primary care trust established under section 18 of the National Health Service Act 2006.

39A A Local Health Board established under section 11 of the National Health Service (Wales) Act 2006.

40 A National Health Service trust established under section 25 of the National Health Service Act 2006 or section 18 of the National Health Service (Wales) Act 2006.

40A An NHS foundation trust.

41 A Community Health Council established under section 182 of the National Health Service (Wales) Act 2006.

41A [...]

42 [...]

43 [...]

43A Any person providing primary medical services or primary dental services—
   (a) in accordance with arrangements made under section 92 or 107 of the National Health Service Act 2006, or section 50 or 64 of the National Health Service (Wales) Act 2006; or
   (b) under a contract under section 84, 100 or 117 of the National Health Service Act 2006 or section 42 or 57 of the National Health Service (Wales) Act 2006

in respect of information relating to the provision of those services.

44 Any person providing general ophthalmic services or pharmaceutical services under the National Health Service Act 2006 or the National Health Service (Wales) Act 2006], in respect of information relating to the provision of those services.

45 [...]

45A Any person providing local pharmaceutical services under—
   (a) a pilot scheme established under section 134 of the National Health Service Act 2006 or section 92 of the National Health Service (Wales) Act 2006; or
   (b) an LPS scheme established under Schedule 12 to the National Health Service Act 2006 or Schedule 7 to the National Health Service (Wales) Act 2006.

45B [...]

Northern Ireland

46 A Health and Social Services Board established under Article 16 of the Health and Personal Social Services (Northern Ireland) Order 1972.

47 A Health and Social Services Council established under Article 4 of the Health and Personal Social Services (Northern Ireland) Order 1991.

48 A Health and Social Services Trust established under Article 10 of the Health and Personal Social Services (Northern Ireland) Order 1991.

49 A special agency established under Article 3 of the Health and Personal Social Services (Special Agencies) (Northern Ireland) Order 1990.

50 The Northern Ireland Central Services Agency for the Health and Social Services established under Article 26 of the Health and Personal Social Services (Northern Ireland) Order 1972.

51 Any person providing primary medical services, general dental services, general ophthalmic services or pharmaceutical services under Part VI of the Health and Personal Social Services (Northern Ireland) Order 1972, in respect of information relating to the provision of those services.

PART IV
MAINTAINED SCHOOLS AND OTHER EDUCATIONAL INSTITUTIONS

England and Wales

52 The governing body of—
  (a) a maintained school, as defined by section 20(7) of the School Standards and Framework Act 1998, or
  (b) a maintained nursery school, as defined by section 22(9) of that Act.

52A (1) The proprietor of an Academy, in respect of information held for the purposes of the proprietor's functions under Academy arrangements.

(2) In sub-paragraph (1)—
  'Academy arrangements' has the meaning given by section 1 of the Academies Act 2010;
  'proprietor' has the meaning given by section 579(1) of the Education Act 1996.

53 (1) The governing body of—
  (a) an institution within the further education sector,
  (b) a university receiving financial support under section 65 of the Further and Higher Education Act 1992,
  (c) an institution conducted by a higher education corporation,
  (d) a designated institution for the purposes of Part II of the Further and Higher Education Act 1992 as defined by section 72(3) of that Act, or
  (e) any college, school, hall or other institution of a university which falls within paragraph (b).

(2) In sub-paragraph (1)—
  (a) 'governing body' is to be interpreted in accordance with subsection (1) of section 90 of the Further and Higher Education Act 1992 but without regard to subsection (2) of that section,

(b) in paragraph (a), the reference to an institution within the further education sector is to be construed in accordance with section 91(3) of the Further and Higher Education Act 1992,

(c) in paragraph (c), 'higher education corporation' has the meaning given by section 90(1) of that Act, and

(d) in paragraph (e) 'college' includes any institution in the nature of a college.

Northern Ireland

54 (1) The managers of—

(a) a controlled school, voluntary school or grant-maintained integrated school within the meaning of Article 2(2) of the Education and Libraries (Northern Ireland) Order 1986, or

(b) a pupil referral unit as defined by Article 87(1) of the Education (Northern Ireland) Order 1998.

(2) In sub-paragraph (1) 'managers' has the meaning given by Article 2(2) of the Education and Libraries (Northern Ireland) Order 1986.

55 (1) The governing body of—

(a) a university receiving financial support under Article 30 of the Education and Libraries (Northern Ireland) Order 1993,

(b) a college of education maintained in pursuance of arrangements under Article 66(1) or in respect of which grants are paid under Article 66(2) or (3) of the Education and Libraries (Northern Ireland) Order 1986, or

(c) an institution of further education within the meaning of the Further Education (Northern Ireland) Order 1997.

(2) In sub-paragraph (1) 'governing body' has the meaning given by Article 30(3) of the Education and Libraries (Northern Ireland) Order 1993.

56 Any person providing further education to whom grants, loans or other payments are made under Article 5(1)(b) of the Further Education (Northern Ireland) Order 1997.

PART V
POLICE

England and Wales

57 A police authority established under section 3 of the Police Act 1996.

58 The Metropolitan Police Authority established under section 5B of the Police Act 1996.

59 A chief officer of police of a police force in England or Wales.

Northern Ireland

60 The Northern Ireland Policing Board.

61 The Chief Constable of the Police Service of Northern Ireland.

Miscellaneous

62   The British Transport Police.

63   The Ministry of Defence Police established by section 1 of the Ministry of Defence Police Act 1987.

63A   The Civil Nuclear Police Authority.

63B   The chief constable of the Civil Nuclear Constabulary.

64   Any person who—
   (a)   by virtue of any enactment has the function of nominating individuals who may be appointed as special constables by justices of the peace, and
   (b)   is not a public authority by virtue of any other provision of this Act,

in respect of information relating to the exercise by any person appointed on his nomination of the functions of a special constable.

PART VI
OTHER PUBLIC BODIES AND OFFICES: GENERAL

The Adjudication Panel for Wales.
The adjudicators appointed under section 25 of the School Standards and Framework Act 1998.
The Administration of Radioactive Substances Advisory Committee.
The Administrative Justice and Tribunals Council.
The Advisory Board on Restricted Patients.
The Advisory Board on the Registration of Homoeopathic Products.
The Advisory Committee for Disabled People in Employment and Training.
The Advisory Committee for the Public Lending Right.
The Advisory Committee on Animal Feedingstuffs.
The Advisory Committee on Borderline Substances.
The Advisory Committee on Business and the Environment.
The Advisory Committee on Business Appointments.
The Advisory Committee on Clinical Excellence Awards.
The Advisory Committee on Conscientious Objectors.
The Advisory Committee on Dangerous Pathogens.
The Advisory Committee on the Government Art Collection
The Advisory Committee on Hazardous Substances.
The Advisory Committee on Historic Wreck Sites.
An Advisory Committee on Justices of the Peace in England and Wales.
The Advisory Committee on the Microbiological Safety of Food.
The Advisory Committee on Novel Foods and Processes.
The Advisory Committee on Organic Standards.
The Advisory Committee on Overseas Economic and Social Research.
The Advisory Committee on Packaging.
The Advisory Committee on Pesticides.
The Advisory Committee on Releases to the Environment.
The Advisory Committee on Statute Law.
The Advisory Committee on Telecommunications for the Disabled and Elderly.

The Advisory Council on Historical Manuscripts.

The Advisory Council on Libraries.

The Advisory Council on the Misuse of Drugs.

The Advisory Council on National Records and Archives.

The Advisory Council on Public Records.

The Advisory Group on Hepatitis.

The Advisory Group on Medical Countermeasures.

The Advisory Panel on Beacon Councils

The Advisory Panel on Public Sector Information.

The Advisory Panel on Standards for the Planning Inspectorate.

The Aerospace Committee.

An Agricultural Dwelling House Advisory Committee.

An Agricultural Wages Board for England and Wales.

An Agricultural Wages Committee.

The Agriculture and Environment Biotechnology Commission.

The Agriculture and Horticulture Development Board.

The Air Quality Expert Group.

The Airborne Particles Expert Group.

The Alcohol Education and Research Council.

The All-Wales Medicines Strategy Group.

The Animal Procedures Committee.

The Animal Welfare Advisory Committee.

The Appointments Commission.

The Architects Registration Board.

The Armed Forces Pay Review Body.

The Arts Council of England.

The Arts Council of Wales.

The Arts and Humanities Research Council.

An assessor appointed for the purposes of section 133 of the Criminal Justice Act 1988 in its application to England and Wales.

The Audit Commission for Local Authorities and the National Health Service in England.

The Auditor General for Wales.

The Bank of England, in respect of information held for purposes other than those of its functions with respect to—

    (a)   monetary policy,

    (b)   financial operations intended to support financial institutions for the purposes of maintaining stability, and

    (c)   the provision of private banking services and related services.

The Better Regulation Task Force.

The Big Lottery Fund

The Biotechnology and Biological Sciences Research Council.

The Board of the Pension Protection Fund.

The Britain-Russia Centre and East-West Centre.

The British Association for Central and Eastern Europe.

The British Broadcasting Corporation, in respect of information held for purposes other than those of journalism, art or literature.

The British Coal Corporation.

The British Council.

The British Educational Communications and Technology Agency.

The British Hallmarking Council.

The British Library.

The British Museum.
The British Pharmacopoeia Commission.
The British Railways Board.
British Shipbuilders.
The British Tourist Authority.
The British Transport Police Authority.
The British Waterways Board.
The British Wool Marketing Board.
The Broadcasting Standards Commission.
The Building Regulations Advisory Committee.
The Care Council for Wales.
The Care Quality Commission.
The Central Advisory Committee on War Pensions.
The Central Rail Users' Consultative Committee.
The Certification Officer.
The Channel Four Television Corporation, in respect of information held for purposes other than those of journalism, art or literature.
The Chief Inspector of the UK Border Agency.
The Child Maintenance and Enforcement Commission.
The Child Poverty Commission.
The Children and Family Court Advisory and Support Service.
The Children's Commissioner.
The Children's Commissioner for Wales.
The Civil Aviation Authority.
The Civil Justice Council.
The Civil Procedure Rule Committee.
The Civil Service Appeal Board.
The Civil Service Commission.
The Coal Authority.
The Commission for Architecture and the Built Environment.
The Commission for Equality and Human Rights.
The Commission for Integrated Transport.
The Commission for Local Administration in England.
Commission for Rural Communities.
The Commission on Human Medicines.
The Commissioner for Older People in Wales.
The Commissioner for Public Appointments.
The Commissioner for Victims and Witnesses.
The Commissioners of Northern Lighthouses.
The Committee on Agricultural Valuation.
The Committee on Carcinogenicity of Chemicals in Food, Consumer Products and the Environment.
The Committee on Climate Change.
The Committee on Medical Aspects of Radiation in the Environment.
The Committee on Mutagenicity of Chemicals in Food, Consumer Products and the Environment.
The Committee on Radioactive Waste Management.
The Committee on Safety of Devices.
The Committee on Standards in Public Life.
The Committee on Toxicity of Chemicals in Food, Consumer Products and the Environment.
The Committee on the Medical Effects of Air Pollutants.

The Commonwealth Scholarship Commission in the United Kingdom.
Communications for Business.
The Community Development Foundation.
The Competition Commission, in relation to information held by it otherwise than
    as a tribunal.
The Competition Service.
A conservation board established under section 86 of the Countryside and Rights of
    Way Act 2000.
The Construction Industry Training Board.
Consumer Communications for England.
The Consumer Council for Water
The Consumer Panel established under section 16 of the Communications Act 2003.
The Council for Healthcare Regulatory Excellence.
The Council for Science and Technology.
The Countryside Council for Wales.
A courts board established under section 4 of the Courts Act 2003.
The Covent Garden Market Authority.
The Criminal Cases Review Commission.
The Criminal Injuries Compensation Authority.
The Criminal Justice Consultative Council.
The Criminal Procedure Rule Committee.
The Crown Court Rule Committee.
The Dartmoor Steering Group and Working Party.
The Darwin Advisory Committee.
The Defence Nuclear Safety Committee.
The Defence Scientific Advisory Council.
The Design Council.
The Diplomatic Service Appeal Board.
The Director of Fair Access to Higher Education.
The Disability Employment Advisory Committee.
The Disability Living Allowance Advisory Board.
The Disabled Persons Transport Advisory Committee.
The Distributed Generation Co-Ordinating Group.
The East of England Industrial Development Board.
The Economic and Social Research Council.
The Electoral Commission.
The Engineering Construction Industry Training Board.
The Engineering and Physical Sciences Research Council.
The English Sports Council.
The English Tourist Board.
The Environment Agency.
Equality 2025.
The Ethnic Minority Business Forum.
The Expert Advisory Group on AIDS.
An Expert Panel on Air Quality Standards.
The Export Guarantees Advisory Council.
The Family Justice Council.
The Family Proceedings Rules Committee.
The Family Procedure Rule Committee.
The Farm Animal Welfare Council.
The Film Industry Training Board for England and Wales.
The Financial Reporting Advisory Board.

The Financial Services Authority.
The Fire Services Examination Board.
The Firearms Consultative Committee.
Food from Britain.
The Football Licensing Authority.
The Fuel Cell Advisory Panel.
The Fuel Poverty Advisory Group.
The Gaelic Media Service, in respect of information held for purposes other than those of journalism, art or literature.
Gambling Commission.
Gangmasters Licensing Authority.
The Gene Therapy Advisory Committee.
The General Chiropractic Council.
The General Dental Council.
The General Medical Council.
The General Optical Council.
The General Osteopathic Council.
The General Pharmaceutical Council.
The General Social Care Council.
The General Teaching Council for England.
The General Teaching Council for Wales.
The Government Hospitality Advisory Committee for the Purchase of Wine.
The Government-Industry Forum on Non-Food Use of Crops.
The Government Chemist.
The Great Britain-China Centre.
The Health Professions Council
The Health Protection Agency.
The Health and Safety Executive.
The Health Service Commissioner for England.
The Herbal Medicines Advisory Committee.
Her Majesty's Chief Inspector of Education and Training in Wales or Prif Arolygydd Ei Mawrhydi dros Addysg a Hyfforddiant yng Nghymru
Her Majesty's Chief Inspector of Prisons.
Her Majesty's Commissioners for Judicial Appointments.
Her Majesty's Inspectorate of Probation for England and Wales.
The Higher Education Funding Council for England.
The Higher Education Funding Council for Wales.
The Historic Buildings and Monuments Commission for England.
The Historic Royal Palaces Trust.
The Homes and Communities Agency.
The Horserace Betting Levy Board.
Horticulture Research International.
The House of Lords Appointments Commission.
Any Housing action trust established under Part III of the Housing Act 1988.
The Human Fertilisation and Embryology Authority.
The Human Genetics Commission.
The Human Tissue Authority.
The Immigration Services Commissioner.
The Imperial War Museum.
The Independent Advisory Committee on Development Impact.
The Independent Advisory Group on Teenage Pregnancy.
The Independent Board of Visitors for Military Corrective Training Centres.

The Independent Case Examiner for the Child Support Agency.

The Independent Groundwater Complaints Administrator.

The Independent Living Funds.

Any Independent Monitoring Board established under section 6(2) of the Prison Act 1952.

The Independent Parliamentary Standards Authority.

The Independent Police Complaints Commission.

The Independent Regulator of NHS Foundation Trusts.

The Independent Remuneration Panel for Wales.

The Independent Review Panel for Advertising.

The Independent Review Panel for Borderline Products

The Independent Safeguarding Authority.

The Independent Scientific Group on Cattle Tuberculosis.

The Independent Television Commission.

The Industrial Development Advisory Board.

The Industrial Injuries Advisory Council.

The Information Commissioner.

The Infrastructure Planning Commission.

The Inland Waterways Amenity Advisory Council.

The Insolvency Rules Committee.

The Integrated Administration and Controls System Appeals Panel.

The Intellectual Property Advisory Committee.

Investors in People UK.

The Joint Committee on Vaccination and Immunisation.

The Joint Nature Conservation Committee.

The Joint Prison/Probation Accreditation Panel.

The Judicial Appointments Commission.

The Judicial Appointments and Conduct Ombudsman.

The Judicial Studies Board.

The Land Registration Rule Committee.

The Law Commission.

The Legal Deposit Advisory Panel

The Legal Services Board.

The Legal Services Commission.

The Legal Services Ombudsman.

The Local Better Regulation Office.

The Local Government Boundary Commission for England.

The Local Government Boundary Commission for Wales.

A local probation board established under section 4 of the Criminal Justice and Court Services Act 2000.

The London Pensions Fund Authority.

The London and South East Industrial Development Board.

The Low Pay Commission.

The Magistrates' Courts Rules Committee.

The Marine Management Organisation.

The Marshall Aid Commemoration Commission.

The Measurement Advisory Committee.

The Medical Research Council.

The Migration Advisory Committee.

The Museum of London.

The National Army Museum.

The National Assembly for Wales Remuneration Board.

The National Audit Office.
The National Consumer Council.
The National DNA Database Ethics Group.
The National Employers' Liaison Committee.
The National Employment Panel.
The National Employment Savings Trust Corporation.
The National Endowment for Science, Technology and the Arts.
The National Forest Company.
The National Gallery.
The National Heritage Memorial Fund.
The National Information Governance Board for Health and Social Care.
The National Library of Wales.
The National Lottery Commission.
The National Maritime Museum.
The National Museum of Science and Industry.
The National Museums and Galleries of Wales.
The National Museums and Galleries on Merseyside.
The National Non-Food Crops Centre.
The National Policing Improvement Agency.
The National Portrait Gallery.
Natural England.
The Natural Environment Research Council.
The Natural History Museum.
The New Deal Task Force.
The NHS Pay Review Body.
The North East Industrial Development Board.
The North West Industrial Development Board.
The Nuclear Decommissioning Authority.
The Nuclear Research Advisory Council.
The Nursing and Midwifery Council.
Office for Tenants and Social Landlords.
The Office for Budget Responsibility.
The Office for Legal Complaints.
The Office of Communications.
The Office of the Health Professions Adjudicator.
The Office of Manpower Economics.
The Office of the Renewable Fuels Agency.
The Oil and Pipelines Agency.
The Olympic Delivery Authority.
The Olympic Lottery Distributo
The Olympic Park Legacy Company.
The Ombudsman for the Board of the Pension Protection Fund.
The OSO Board.
The Panel on Standards for the Planning Inspectorate.
The Parliamentary Boundary Commission for England.
The Parliamentary Boundary Commission for Scotland.
The Parliamentary Boundary Commission for Wales.
The Parliamentary Commissioner for Administration.
The Parole Board.
The Pensions Ombudsman.
The Pensions Regulator.
The Pesticide Residues Committee.

The Pesticides Forum.
The Poisons Board.
The Police Advisory Board for England and Wales.
The Police Negotiating Board.
The Political Honours Scrutiny Committee.
The Prison Service Pay Review Body.
The Prisons and Probation Ombudsman for England and Wales.
A probation trust.
The Public Private Partnership Agreement Arbiter.
The Public Services Ombudsman for Wales
The Qualifications and Curriculum Development Agency
The Race Education and Employment Forum.
The Race Relations Forum.
The Radio Authority.
The Radioactive Waste Management Advisory Committee.
The Railway Heritage Committee.
A Regional Cultural Consortium.
Any regional development agency established under the Regional Development
    Agencies Act 1998, other than the London Development Agency.
Any regional flood defence committee.
The Registrar General for England and Wales.
The Registrar of Public Lending Right.
The Regulator of Community Interest Companies.
Remploy Ltd.
The Renewable Energy Advisory Committee.
Resource: The Council for Museums, Archives and Libraries.
The Review Board for Government Contracts.
The Review Body on Doctors and Dentists Remuneration.
The Reviewing Committee on the Export of Works of Art.
The Royal Air Force Museum.
The Royal Armouries.
The Royal Botanic Gardens, Kew.
The Royal College of Veterinary Surgeons, in respect of information held by it
    otherwise than as a tribunal.
The Royal Commission on Ancient and Historical Monuments of Wales.
The Royal Commission on Environmental Pollution.
The Royal Commission on Historical Manuscripts.
The Royal Hospital at Chelsea.
The Royal Mint Advisory Committee on the Design of Coins, Medals, Seals and
    Decorations.
The School Teachers' Review Body.
The Science Advisory Council.
The Science and Technology Facilities Council.
The Scientific Advisory Committee on Nutrition.
The Scientific Committee on Tobacco and Health.
The Sea Fish Industry Authority.
The Security Industry Authority.
The Senior Salaries Review Body.
The Sentencing Council for England and Wales.
Sianel Pedwar Cymru, in respect of information held for purposes other than those
    of journalism, art or literature.
Sir John Soane's Museum.

The Small Business Council.

The Small Business Investment Task Force.

The Social Care Institute for Excellence.

The social fund Commissioner appointed under section 65 of the Social Security Administration Act 1992.

The Social Security Advisory Committee.

The South West Industrial Development Board.

The Spongiform Encephalopathy Advisory Committee.

The Sports Council for Wales.

The Standards Board for England.

The Standing Advisory Committee on Industrial Property.

The Standing Advisory Committee on Trunk Road Assessment.

The Standing Dental Advisory Committee.

The Steering Committee on Pharmacy Postgraduate Education.

The Strategic Investment Board.

The Strategic Rail Authority.

The subsidence adviser appointed under section 46 of the Coal Industry Act 1994.

The Substance Misuse Advisory Panel.

The Sustainable Development Commission.

The Sustainable Energy Policy Advisory Board.

The Tate Gallery.

The TB Advisory Group

The Technical Advisory Board.

The Technology Strategy Board.

The Theatres Trust.

The Traffic Commissioners, in respect of information held by them otherwise than as a tribunal.

The Training and Development Agency for Schools.

The Treasure Valuation Committee.

The Tribunal Procedure Committee.

The trustee corporation established by section 75 of the Pensions Act 2008.

The UK Advisory Panel for Health Care Workers Infected with Bloodborne Viruses.

The UK Chemicals Stakeholder Forum.

The UK Commission for Employment and Skills

The UK Sports Council.

The United Kingdom Atomic Energy Authority.

The University for Industry

The Unlinked Anonymous Serosurveys Steering Group.

The Unrelated Live Transplant Regulatory Authority.

The Valuation Tribunal Service.

The verderers of the New Forest, in respect of information held by them otherwise than as a tribunal.

The Veterinary Products Committee.

The Veterinary Residues Committee.

The Victoria and Albert Museum.

The Wales Centre for Health.

The Wallace Collection.

The War Pensions Committees.

The Welsh Committee for Professional Development of Pharmacy.

The Welsh Committee of the Administrative Justice and Tribunals Council.

The Welsh Dental Committee.

The Welsh Industrial Development Advisory Board.

The Welsh Language Board.
The Welsh Medical Committee.
The Welsh Nursing and Midwifery Committee.
The Welsh Optometric Committee.
The Welsh Pharmaceutical Committee.
The Welsh Scientific Advisory Committee.
The West Midlands Industrial Development Board.
The Westminster Foundation for Democracy.
The Wilton Park Academic Council.
The Women's National Commission.
The Yorkshire and the Humber and the East Midlands Industrial Development
    Board.
The Young People's Learning Agency for England.
The Youth Justice Board for England and Wales.
The Zoos Forum.

PART VII
OTHER PUBLIC BODIES AND OFFICES: NORTHERN IRELAND

An advisory committee established under paragraph 25 of the Health and Personal
    Social Services (Northern Ireland) Order 1972.
The Advisory Committee on Justices of the Peace in Northern Ireland.
The Advisory Committee on Juvenile Court Lay Panel (Northern Ireland).
The Advisory Committee on Pesticides for Northern Ireland.
The Agricultural Research Institute of Northern Ireland.
The Agricultural Wages Board for Northern Ireland.
The Arts Council of Northern Ireland.
The Assembly Ombudsman for Northern Ireland.
The Belfast Harbour Commissioners.
The Board of Trustees of National Museums and Galleries of Northern Ireland.
Boards of Visitors and Visiting Committees.
The Boundary Commission for Northern Ireland.
A central advisory committee established under paragraph 24 of the Health and
    Personal Social Services (Northern Ireland) Order 1972.
The Certification Officer for Northern Ireland.
The Charities Advisory Committee.
The Chief Electoral Officer for Northern Ireland.
The Civil Service Commissioners for Northern Ireland.
Comhairle na Gaelscolaíochta.
The Commissioner for Public Appointments for Northern Ireland.
The Construction Industry Training Board.
The consultative Civic Forum referred to in section 56(4) of the Northern Ireland
    Act 1998.
The Council for Catholic Maintained Schools.
The Council for Nature Conservation and the Countryside.
The County Court Rules Committee (Northern Ireland).
The Criminal Injuries Compensation Appeals Panel for Northern Ireland, in relation
    to information held by it otherwise than as a tribunal.]4
The Disability Living Allowance Advisory Board for Northern Ireland.

The Distinction and Meritorious Service Awards Committee.

The Drainage Council for Northern Ireland.

An Education and Library Board established under Article 3 of the Education and Libraries (Northern Ireland) Order 1986.

The Equality Commission for Northern Ireland.

The Family Proceedings Rules Committee (Northern Ireland).

The Fire Authority for Northern Ireland.

The Fisheries Conservancy Board for Northern Ireland.

The General Consumer Council for Northern Ireland.

The General Teaching Council for Northern Ireland.

The Governors of the Armargh Observatory and Planetarium.

The Harbour of Donaghadee Commissioners.

The Health and Safety Agency for Northern Ireland.

The Historic Buildings Council.

The Historic Monuments Council.

The Independent Assessor of Military Complaints Procedures in Northern Ireland.

The Independent Reviewer of the Northern Ireland (Emergency Provisions) Act.

The Independent Commissioner for Holding Centres.

The Industrial Development Board for Northern Ireland.

The Industrial Research and Technology Unit.

The Labour Relations Agency.

The Laganside Corporation.

The Lay Observer for Northern Ireland.

The Livestock & Meat Commission for Northern Ireland.

The Local Enterprise Development Unit.

The Local Government Staff Commission.

The Londonderry Port and Harbour Commissioners.

The Magistrates' Courts Rules Committee (Northern Ireland).

The Mental Health Commission for Northern Ireland.

The Northern Ireland Audit Office.

The Northern Ireland Building Regulations Advisory Committee.

The Northern Ireland Civil Service Appeal Board.

The Northern Ireland Commissioner for Complaints.

The Northern Ireland Community Relations Council.

The Northern Ireland Council for the Curriculum, Examinations and Assessment.

The Northern Ireland Court of Judicature Rules Committee.

The Northern Ireland Crown Court Rules Committee.

The Northern Ireland Events Company.

The Northern Ireland Fishery Harbour Authority.

The Northern Ireland Health and Personal Social Services Regulation and Improvement Authority.

The Northern Ireland Higher Education Council.

The Northern Ireland Housing Executive.

The Northern Ireland Human Rights Commission.

The Northern Ireland Insolvency Rules Committee.

The Northern Ireland Local Government Officers' Superannuation Committee.

The Northern Ireland Museums Council.

The Northern Ireland Practice and Education Council for Nursing and Midwifery.

The Northern Ireland Social Care Council.

The Northern Ireland Tourist Board.

The Northern Ireland Transport Holding Company.

The Northern Ireland Water Council.

The Parades Commission.

The Pharmaceutical Society of Northern Ireland, in respect of information held by it otherwise than as a tribunal.

The Poisons Board (Northern Ireland).

The Police Ombudsman for Northern Ireland.

The Prisoner Ombudsman for Northern Ireland.

The Probation Board for Northern Ireland.

The Royal Ulster Constabulary George Cross Foundation.

The Rural Development Council for Northern Ireland.

The Sentence Review Commissioners appointed under section 1 of the Northern Ireland (Sentences) Act 1998.

The social fund Commissioner appointed under Article 37 of the Social Security (Northern Ireland) Order 1998.

The Sports Council for Northern Ireland.

The Staff Commission for Education and Library Boards.

The Statistics Advisory Committee.

The Statute Law Committee for Northern Ireland.

Ulster Supported Employment Ltd.

The Warrenpoint Harbour Authority.

The Waste Management Advisory Board.

The Youth Council for Northern Ireland.

SCHEDULE 2
THE COMMISSIONER AND THE TRIBUNAL

PART I
PROVISION CONSEQUENTIAL ON S. 18(1) AND (2)

General

1.—

 (1) Any reference in any enactment, instrument or document to the Data Protection Commissioner or the Data Protection Registrar shall be construed, in relation to any time after the commencement of section 18(1), as a reference to the Information Commissioner.

2.—

 (1) Any reference in this Act or in any instrument under this Act to the Commissioner shall be construed, in relation to any time before the commencement of section 18(1), as a reference to the Data Protection Commissioner.

Public Records Act 1958 (c. 51)

3.—

 (1) In Part II of the Table in paragraph 3 of Schedule 1 to the Public Records Act 1958 (definition of public records), the entry relating to the Data Protection Commissioner is omitted and there is inserted at the appropriate place—
'Information Commissioner.'

Parliamentary Commissioner Act 1967 (c. 13)

4.   In Schedule 2 to the Parliamentary Commissioner Act 1967 (departments etc. subject to investigation), the entry relating to the Data Protection Commissioner is omitted and there is inserted at the appropriate place—
'Information Commissioner'.

5.   [...]

Superannuation Act 1972 (c. 11)

6.   In Schedule 1 to the Superannuation Act 1972 (employment with superannuation scheme), for 'Data Protection Commissioner' there is substituted 'Information Commissioner'.

Consumer Credit Act 1974 (c. 39)

7.   In section 159 of the Consumer Credit Act 1974 (correction of wrong information), in subsections (7) and (8)(b), for 'Data Protection Commissioner', in both places where it occurs, there is substituted 'Information Commissioner'.

House of Commons Disqualification Act 1975 (c. 24)

8.—
   (1)   In Part II of Schedule 1 to the House of Commons Disqualification Act 1975 (bodies whose members are disqualified), the entry relating to the Data Protection Tribunal is omitted and there is inserted at the appropriate place—
'The Information Tribunal'.
   (2)   In Part III of that Schedule (disqualifying offices), the entry relating to the Data Protection Commissioner is omitted and there is inserted at the appropriate place—
'The Information Commissioner'.

Northern Ireland Assembly Disqualification Act 1975 (c. 25)

9.—
   (1)   In Part II of Schedule 1 to the Northern Ireland Assembly Disqualification Act 1975 (bodies whose members are disqualified), the entry relating to the Data Protection Tribunal is omitted and there is inserted at the appropriate place—
'The Information Tribunal'.
   (2)   In Part III of that Schedule (disqualifying offices), the entry relating to the Data Protection Commissioner is omitted and there is inserted at the appropriate place—
'The Information Commissioner'.

Tribunals and Inquiries Act 1992 (c. 53)

10.   In paragraph 14 of Part I of Schedule 1 to the Tribunals and Inquiries Act 1992 (tribunals under direct supervision of Council on Tribunals)—
   (a)   in sub-paragraph (a), for 'The Data Protection Commissioner' there is substituted 'The Information Commissioner', and
   [...]

Judicial Pensions and Retirement Act 1993 (c. 8)

11. [...]

12. In Schedule 7 to that Act (retirement dates: transitional provisions), in paragraph 5(5)(xxvi) for 'the Data Protection Tribunal' there is substituted 'the Information Tribunal'.

Data Protection Act 1998 (c. 29)

13.—
    (1) Section 6 of the Data Protection Act 1998 (the Data Protection Commissioner and the Data Protection Tribunal) is amended as follows.
    (2) For subsection (1) there is substituted—
        '(1) For the purposes of this Act and of the Freedom of Information Act 2000 there shall be an officer known as the Information Commissioner (in this Act referred to as 'the Commissioner').'

14. In section 70(1) of that Act (supplementary definitions)—
    (a) in the definition of 'the Commissioner', for 'the Data Protection Commissioner' there is substituted 'the Information Commissioner', and
    [...]

15.—
    (1) Schedule 5 to that Act (the Data Protection Commissioner and the Data Protection Tribunal) is amended as follows.
    (2) In paragraph 1(1), for 'Data Protection Commissioner' there is substituted 'Information Commissioner'.
    (3) Part III shall cease to have effect.

PART II
AMENDMENTS RELATING TO EXTENSION OF FUNCTIONS OF COMMISSIONER AND TRIBUNAL

Interests represented by lay members of Tribunal

16. [...]

Expenses incurred under this Act excluded in calculating fees

17. [...]

Information provided to Commissioner or Tribunal

18. In section 58 of that Act (disclosure of information to Commissioner or Tribunal), after 'this Act' there is inserted 'or the Freedom of Information Act 2000'.

Information provided to Commissioner or Tribunal

19.—

(1) Section 59 of that Act (confidentiality of information) is amended as follows.

(2) In subsections (1) and (2), for 'this Act', wherever occurring, there is substituted 'the information Acts'.

(3) After subsection (3) there is inserted—

'(4) In this section 'the information Acts' means this Act and the Freedom of Information Act 2000.'

Deputy commissioners

20.—

(1) Paragraph 4 of Schedule 5 to that Act (officers and staff) is amended as follows.

(2) In sub-paragraph (1)(a), after 'a deputy commissioner' there is inserted 'or two deputy commissioners'.

(3) After sub-paragraph (1) there is inserted—

'(1A) The Commissioner shall, when appointing any second deputy commissioner, specify which of the Commissioner's functions are to be performed, in the circumstances referred to in paragraph 5(1), by each of the deputy commissioners.'

Exercise of Commissioner's functions by others

21.—

(1) Paragraph 5 of Schedule 5 to that Act (exercise of functions of Commissioner during vacancy etc.) is amended as follows.

(2) In sub-paragraph (1)—

(a) after 'deputy commissioner' there is inserted 'or deputy commissioners', and

(b) after 'this Act' there is inserted 'or the Freedom of Information Act 2000'.

(3) In sub-paragraph (2) after 'this Act' there is inserted 'or the Freedom of Information Act 2000'.

Money

22. In paragraph 9(1) of Schedule 5 to that Act (money) for 'or section 159 of the Consumer Credit Act 1974' there is substituted ', under section 159 of the Consumer Credit Act 1974 or under the Freedom of Information Act 2000'.

SCHEDULE 3
POWERS OF ENTRY AND INSPECTION

Issue of warrants

1.—

(1) If a circuit judge is satisfied by information on oath supplied by the Commissioner that there are reasonable grounds for suspecting—

(a) that a public authority has failed or is failing to comply with—

(i) any of the requirements of Part I of this Act,

(ii) so much of a decision notice as requires steps to be taken, or

(iii) an information notice or an enforcement notice, or

(b)   that an offence under section 77 has been or is being committed,

and that evidence of such a failure to comply or of the commission of the offence is to be found on any premises specified in the information, he may, subject to paragraph 2, grant a warrant to the Commissioner.

(2)   A warrant issued under sub-paragraph (1) shall authorise the Commissioner or any of his officers or staff at any time within seven days of the date of the warrant—
   (a)   to enter and search the premises,
   (b)   to inspect and seize any documents or other material found there which may be such evidence as is mentioned in that sub-paragraph, and
   (c)   to inspect, examine, operate and test any equipment found there in which information held by the public authority may be recorded.

2.—

(1)   A judge shall not issue a warrant under this Schedule unless he is satisfied—
   (a)   that the Commissioner has given seven days' notice in writing to the occupier of the premises in question demanding access to the premises, and
   (b)   that either—
      (i)   access was demanded at a reasonable hour and was unreasonably refused, or
      (ii)   although entry to the premises was granted, the occupier unreasonably refused to comply with a request by the Commissioner or any of the Commissioner's officers or staff to permit the Commissioner or the officer or member of staff to do any of the things referred to in paragraph 1(2), and
   (c)   that the occupier, has, after the refusal, been notified by the Commissioner of the application for the warrant and has had an opportunity of being heard by the judge on the question whether or not it should be issued.

(2)   Sub-paragraph (1) shall not apply if the judge is satisfied that the case is one of urgency or that compliance with those provisions would defeat the object of the entry.

3.   A judge who issues a warrant under this Schedule shall also issue two copies of it and certify them clearly as copies.

Execution of warrants

4.   A person executing a warrant issued under this Schedule may use such reasonable force as may be necessary.

5.   A warrant issued under this Schedule shall be executed at a reasonable hour unless it appears to the person executing it that there are grounds for suspecting that the evidence in question would not be found if it were so executed.

6.—

(1)   If the premises in respect of which a warrant is issued under this Schedule are occupied by a public authority and any officer or employee of the authority is present when the warrant is executed, he shall be shown the warrant and supplied with a copy of it; and if no such officer or employee is present a copy of the warrant shall be left in a prominent place on the premises.

(2)   If the premises in respect of which a warrant is issued under this Schedule are occupied by a person other than a public authority and he is present when the

warrant is executed, he shall be shown the warrant and supplied with a copy of it; and if that person is not present a copy of the warrant shall be left in a prominent place on the premises.

7.—

(1)   A person seizing anything in pursuance of a warrant under this Schedule shall give a receipt for it if asked to do so.

(2)   Anything so seized may be retained for so long as is necessary in all the circumstances but the person in occupation of the premises in question shall be given a copy of anything that is seized if he so requests and the person executing the warrant considers that it can be done without undue delay.

Matters exempt from inspection and seizure

8.   The powers of inspection and seizure conferred by a warrant issued under this Schedule shall not be exercisable in respect of information which is exempt information by virtue of section 23(1) or 24(1).

9.—

(1)   Subject to the provisions of this paragraph, the powers of inspection and seizure conferred by a warrant issued under this Schedule shall not be exercisable in respect of—
   (a)   any communication between a professional legal adviser and his client in connection with the giving of legal advice to the client with respect to his obligations, liabilities or rights under this Act, or
   (b)   any communication between a professional legal adviser and his client, or between such an adviser or his client and any other person, made in connection with or in contemplation of proceedings under or arising out of this Act (including proceedings before the Tribunal) and for the purposes of such proceedings.

(2)   Sub-paragraph (1) applies also to—
   (a)   any copy or other record of any such communication as is there mentioned, and
   (b)   any document or article enclosed with or referred to in any such communication if made in connection with the giving of any advice or, as the case may be, in connection with or in contemplation of and for the purposes of such proceedings as are there mentioned.

(3)   This paragraph does not apply to anything in the possession of any person other than the professional legal adviser or his client or to anything held with the intention of furthering a criminal purpose.

(4)   In this paragraph references to the client of a professional legal adviser include references to any person representing such a client.

10.   If the person in occupation of any premises in respect of which a warrant is issued under this Schedule objects to the inspection or seizure under the warrant of any material on the grounds that it consists partly of matters in respect of which those powers are not exercisable, he shall, if the person executing the warrant so requests, furnish that person with a copy of so much of the material in relation to which the powers are exercisable.

Return of warrants

11.   A warrant issued under this Schedule shall be returned to the court from which it was issued—

(a)   after being executed, or

(b)   if not executed within the time authorised for its execution;

and the person by whom any such warrant is executed shall make an endorsement on it stating what powers have been exercised by him under the warrant.

Offences

12.   Any person who—

(a)   intentionally obstructs a person in the execution of a warrant issued under this Schedule, or

(b)   fails without reasonable excuse to give any person executing such a warrant such assistance as he may reasonably require for the execution of the warrant,

is guilty of an offence.

Vessels, vehicles etc.

13.   In this Schedule 'premises' includes any vessel, vehicle, aircraft or hovercraft, and references to the occupier of any premises include references to the person in charge of any vessel, vehicle, aircraft or hovercraft.

14.   In the application of this Schedule to Scotland—

(a)   for any reference to a circuit judge there is substituted a reference to the sheriff, and

(b)   for any reference to information on oath there is substituted a reference to evidence on oath.

15.   In the application of this Schedule to Northern Ireland—

(a)   for any reference to a circuit judge there is substituted a reference to a county court judge, and

(b)   for any reference to information on oath there is substituted a reference to a complaint on oath.

SCHEDULE 4

APPEAL PROCEEDINGS: AMENDMENTS OF SCHEDULE 6 TO DATA PROTECTION ACT 1998

Section 61(1)

Constitution of Tribunal in national security cases

1.   [...]

2.   [...]

3.   [...]

4.   [...]

SCHEDULE 5
AMENDMENTS OF PUBLIC RECORDS LEGISLATION

PART I
AMENDMENTS OF PUBLIC RECORDS ACT 1958

Functions of Advisory Council on Public Records

1. In section 1 of the Public Records Act 1958 (general responsibility of the Lord Chancellor for public records), after subsection (2) there is inserted—

'(2A) The matters on which the Advisory Council on Public Records may advise the Lord Chancellor include matters relating to the application of the Freedom of Information Act 2000 to information contained in public records which are historical records within the meaning of Part VI of that Act.'

Access to public records

2.—

(1) Section 5 of that Act (access to public records) is amended in accordance with this paragraph.

(2) Subsections (1) and (2) are omitted.

(3) For subsection (3) there is substituted—

'(3) It shall be the duty of the Keeper of Public Records to arrange that reasonable facilities are available to the public for inspecting and obtaining copies of those public records in the Public Record Office which fall to be disclosed in accordance with the Freedom of Information Act 2000.'

(4) Subsection (4) and, in subsection (5), the words from 'and subject to' to the end are omitted.

3. Schedule 2 of that Act (enactments prohibiting disclosure of information obtained from the public) is omitted.

Power to extend meaning of 'public records'

4. In Schedule 1 to that Act (definition of public records) after the Table at the end of paragraph 3 there is inserted—

'3A.—

(1) Her Majesty may by Order in Council amend the Table at the end of paragraph 3 of this Schedule by adding to either Part of the Table an entry relating to any body or establishment—
   (a) which, at the time when the Order is made, is specified in Schedule 2 to the Parliamentary Commissioner Act 1967 (departments, etc. subject to investigation), or
   (b) in respect of which an entry could, at that time, be added to Schedule 2 to that Act by an Order in Council under section 4 of that Act (which confers power to amend that Schedule).

(2) An Order in Council under this paragraph may relate to a specified body or establishment or to bodies or establishments falling within a specified description.

(3) An Order in Council under this paragraph shall be subject to annulment in pursuance of a resolution of either House of Parliament.'

PART II
AMENDMENT OF PUBLIC RECORDS ACT (NORTHERN IRELAND) 1923

5. After section 5 of thPublic Records Act (Northern Ireland) 1923 (deposit of documents in Record Office by trustees or other persons) there is inserted—

'5A. Access to public records

It shall be the duty of the Deputy Keeper of the Records of Northern Ireland to arrange that reasonable facilities are available to the public for inspecting and obtaining copies of those public records in the Public Record Office of Northern Ireland which fall to be disclosed in accordance with the Freedom of Information Act 2000.'

SCHEDULE 6
FURTHER AMENDMENTS OF DATA PROTECTION ACT 1998

Request by data controller for further information

1. In section 7 of the Data Protection Act 1998 (right of access to personal data), for subsection (3) there is substituted—

'(3) Where a data controller—
   (a) reasonably requires further information in order to satisfy himself as to the identity of the person making a request under this section and to locate the information which that person seeks, and
   (b) has informed him of that requirement,

the data controller is not obliged to comply with the request unless he is supplied with that further information.

Parliament

2. After section 35 of that Act there is inserted—

'35A. Parliamentary privilege.

Personal data are exempt from—
   (a) the first data protection principle, except to the extent to which it requires compliance with the conditions in Schedules 2 and 3,
   (b) the second, third, fourth and fifth data protection principles,
   (c) section 7, and
   (d) sections 10 and 14(1) to (3),

if the exemption is required for the purpose of avoiding an infringement of the privileges of either House of Parliament.'

3. After section 63 of that Act there is inserted—

'63A.— Application to Parliament.

(1) Subject to the following provisions of this section and to section 35A, this Act applies to the processing of personal data by or on behalf of either House of Parliament as it applies to the processing of personal data by other persons.

(2) Where the purposes for which and the manner in which any personal data are, or are to be, processed are determined by or on behalf of the House of Commons, the data controller in respect of those data for the purposes of this Act shall be the Corporate Officer of that House.

(3) Where the purposes for which and the manner in which any personal data are, or are to be, processed are determined by or on behalf of the House of Lords, the data controller in respect of those data for the purposes of this Act shall be the Corporate Officer of that House.

(4) Nothing in subsection (2) or (3) is to be taken to render the Corporate Officer of the House of Commons or the Corporate Officer of the House of Lords liable to prosecution under this Act, but section 55 and paragraph 12 of Schedule 9 shall apply to a person acting on behalf of either House as they apply to any other person.'

4. In Schedule 2 to that Act (conditions relevant for the purposes of the first data protection principle: processing of any personal data) in paragraph 5 after paragraph (a) there is inserted—

'(aa) for the exercise of any functions of either House of Parliament,'.

5. In Schedule 3 to that Act (conditions relevant for the purposes of the first data protection principle: processing of sensitive personal data) in paragraph 7 after paragraph (a) there is inserted—

'(aa) for the exercise of any functions of either House of Parliament,'.

6. In Schedule 7 to that Act (miscellaneous exemptions) in paragraph 3(b) (honours) after 'honour' there is inserted 'or dignity'.

7. In paragraph 10 of that Schedule (legal professional privilege), for the words 'or, in Scotland, to confidentiality as between client and professional legal adviser,' there is substituted 'or, in Scotland, to confidentiality of communications'.

8. In Schedule 14 to that Act (transitional provisions), in paragraph 2(1) (which confers transitional exemption from the prohibition on processing without registration on those registered under the Data Protection Act 1984) the words 'or, if earlier, 24th October 2001' are omitted.

SCHEDULE 7
DISCLOSURE OF INFORMATION BY OMBUDSMEN

The Parliamentary Commissioner for Administration

1. At the end of section 11 of the Parliamentary Commissioner Act 1967 (provision for secrecy of information) there is inserted—

'(5) Information obtained from the Information Commissioner by virtue of section 76(1) of the Freedom of Information Act 2000 shall be treated for the purposes of subsection (2) of this section as obtained for the purposes of an investigation under this Act and, in relation to such information, the reference in paragraph (a) of that subsection to the investigation shall have effect as a reference to any investigation.'

2.   After section 11A of that Act there is inserted—

'11AA.— Disclosure of information by Parliamentary Commissioner to Information Commissioner.

(1)   The Commissioner may disclose to the Information Commissioner any information obtained by, or furnished to, the Commissioner under or for the purposes of this Act if the information appears to the Commissioner to relate to—
   (a)   a matter in respect of which the Information Commissioner could exercise any power conferred by—
      (i)   Part V of the Data Protection Act 1998 (enforcement),
      (ii)   section 48 of the Freedom of Information Act 2000 (practice recommendations), or
      (iii) Part IV of that Act (enforcement), or
   (b)   the commission of an offence under—
      (i)   any provision of the Data Protection Act 1998 other than paragraph 12 of Schedule 9 (obstruction of execution of warrant), or
      (ii)   section 77 of the Freedom of Information Act 2000 (offence of altering etc. records with intent to prevent disclosure).

(2)   Nothing in section 11(2) of this Act shall apply in relation to the disclosure of information in accordance with this section.'

3.   In section 32 of the Local Government Act 1974 (law of defamation, and disclosure of information) after subsection (6) there is inserted—

'(7) Information obtained from the Information Commissioner by virtue of section 76 of the Freedom of Information Act 2000 shall be treated for the purposes of subsection (2) above as obtained for the purposes of an investigation under this Part of this Act and, in relation to such information, the reference in paragraph (a) of that subsection to the investigation shall have effect as a reference to any investigation.'

4.   After section 33 of that Act there is inserted—

'33A.— Disclosure of information by Local Commissioner to Information Commissioner.

(1)   A Local Commissioner may disclose to the Information Commissioner any information obtained by, or furnished to, the Local Commissioner under or for the purposes of this Part of this Act if the information appears to the Local Commissioner to relate to—
   (a)   a matter in respect of which the Information Commissioner could exercise any power conferred by—
      (i)   Part V of the Data Protection Act 1998 (enforcement),
      (ii)   section 48 of the Freedom of Information Act 2000 (practice recommendations), or
      (iii) Part IV of that Act (enforcement), or
   (b)   the commission of an offence under—
      (i)   any provision of the Data Protection Act 1998 other than paragraph 12 of Schedule 9 (obstruction of execution of warrant), or

(ii) section 77 of the Freedom of Information Act 2000 (offence of altering etc. records with intent to prevent disclosure).

(2) Nothing in section 32(2) of this Act shall apply in relation to the disclosure of information in accordance with this section.'

5. At the end of section 15 of the Health Service Commissioners Act 1993 (confidentiality of information) there is inserted—

'(4) Information obtained from the Information Commissioner by virtue of section 76 of the Freedom of Information Act 2000 shall be treated for the purposes of subsection (1) as obtained for the purposes of an investigation and, in relation to such information, the reference in paragraph (a) of that subsection to the investigation shall have effect as a reference to any investigation.'

6. After section 18 of that Act there is inserted—

'18A.— Disclosure of information to Information Commissioner.

(1) The Health Service Commissioner for England or the Health Service Commissioner for Wales may disclose to the Information Commissioner any information obtained by, or furnished to, the Health Service Commissioner under or for the purposes of this Act if the information appears to the Health Service Commissioner to relate to—
   (a) a matter in respect of which the Information Commissioner could exercise any power conferred by—
      (i) Part V of the Data Protection Act 1998 (enforcement),
      (ii) section 48 of the Freedom of Information Act 2000 (practice recommendations), or
      (iii) Part IV of that Act (enforcement), or
   (b) the commission of an offence under—
      (i) any provision of the Data Protection Act 1998 other than paragraph 12 of Schedule 9 (obstruction of execution of warrant), or
      (ii) section 77 of the Freedom of Information Act 2000 (offence of altering etc. records with intent to prevent disclosure).

(3) Nothing in section 15 (confidentiality of information) applies in relation to the disclosure of information in accordance with this section.'

The Welsh Administration Ombudsman

7. [...]

8. [...]

The Northern Ireland Commissioner for Complaints

9. At the end of Article 21 of theCommissioner for Complaints (Northern Ireland) Order 1996 (disclosure of information by Commissioner) there is inserted—

'(5) Information obtained from the Information Commissioner by virtue of section 76 of the Freedom of Information Act 2000 shall be treated for the purposes of paragraph (1) as obtained for the purposes of an investigation under this Order and, in relation to such information, the reference in paragraph (1)(a) to the investigation shall have effect as a reference to any investigation.'

10.　After that Article there is inserted—

'**21A.**— Disclosure of information to Information Commissioner

(1)　The Commissioner may disclose to the Information Commissioner any information obtained by, or furnished to, the Commissioner under or for the purposes of this Order if the information appears to the Commissioner to relate to—

    (a)　a matter in respect of which the Information Commissioner could exercise any power conferred by—

        (i)　Part V of the Data Protection Act 1998 (enforcement),

        (ii)　section 48 of the Freedom of Information Act 2000 (practice recommendations), or

        (iii)　Part IV of that Act (enforcement), or

    (b)　the commission of an offence under—

        (i)　any provision of the Data Protection Act 1998 other than paragraph 12 of Schedule 9 (obstruction of execution of warrant), or

        (ii)　section 77 of the Freedom of Information Act 2000 (offence of altering etc. records with intent to prevent disclosure).

(2)　Nothing in Article 21(1) applies in relation to the disclosure of information in accordance with this Article.'

11.　At the end of Article 19 of the Ombudsman (Northern Ireland) Order 1996 there is inserted—

'(5)　Information obtained from the Information Commissioner by virtue of section 76 of the Freedom of Information Act 2000 shall be treated for the purposes of paragraph (1) as obtained for the purposes of an investigation under this Order and, in relation to such information, the reference in paragraph (1)(a) to the investigation shall have effect as a reference to any investigation.'

12.　After that Article there is inserted—

'**19A.**— Disclosure of information to Information Commissioner

(1)　The Ombudsman may disclose to the Information Commissioner any information obtained by, or furnished to, the Ombudsman under or for the purposes of this Order if the information appears to the Ombudsman to relate to—

    (a)　a matter in respect of which the Information Commissioner could exercise any power conferred by—

        (i)　Part V of the Data Protection Act 1998 (enforcement),

        (ii)　section 48 of the Freedom of Information Act 2000 (practice recommendations), or

        (iii)　Part IV of that Act (enforcement), or

    (b)　the commission of an offence under—

        (i)　any provision of the Data Protection Act 1998 other than paragraph 12 of Schedule 9 (obstruction of execution of warrant), or

        (ii)　section 77 of the Freedom of Information Act 2000 (offence of altering etc. records with intent to prevent disclosure).

(2)　Nothing in Article 19(1) applies in relation to the disclosure of information in accordance with this Article.'

The Commissioner for Local Administration in Scotland

13.　[...]

SCHEDULE 8
REPEALS

PART I
REPEAL COMING INTO FORCE ON PASSING OF ACT

Chapter	Short title	Extent of repeal
1998 c. 29	The Data Protection Act 1998.	In Schedule 14, in paragraph 2(1), the words 'or, if earlier, 24th October 2001'.

PART II
REPEALS COMING INTO FORCE IN ACCORDANCE WITH SECTION 87(2)

Arrangement of Provisions

Chapter	Short title	Extent of repeal
1958 c. 51.	The Public Records Act 1958.	In Schedule 1, in Part II of the Table in paragraph 3, the entry relating to the Data Protection Commissioner.
1967 c. 13.	The Parliamentary Commissioner Act 1967.	In Schedule 2, the entry relating to the Data Protection Commissioner.
1975 c. 24.	The House of Commons Disqualification Act 1975.	In Schedule 1, in Part III, the entry relating to the Data Protection Commissioner.
1975 c. 25.	The Northern Ireland Assembly Disqualification Act 1975.	In Schedule 1, in Part III, the entry relating to the Data Protection Commissioner.
1998 c. 29.	The Data Protection Act 1998.	In Schedule 5, Part III.
		In Schedule 15, paragraphs 1(1), 2, 4, 5(2) and 6(2)

PART III
REPEALS COMING INTO FORCE IN ACCORDANCE WITH SECTION 87(3)

Chapter	Short title	Extent of repeal
1958 c. 51.	The Public Records Act 1958.	In section 5, subsections (1), (2) and (4) and, in subsection (5), the words from 'and subject to' to the end.
		Schedule 2.
1975 c. 24.	The House of Commons Disqualification Act 1975.	In Schedule 1, in Part II, the entry relating to the Data Protection Tribunal.

Chapter	Short title	Extent of repeal
1975 c. 25.	The Northern Ireland Assembly Disqualification Act 1975.	In Schedule 1, in Part II, the entry relating to the Data Protection Tribunal.
1998 c. 29.	The Data Protection Act 1998.	In section 1(1), in the definition of 'data', the word 'or' at the end of paragraph (c).
		In Schedule 15, paragraphs 1(2) and (3), 3, 5(1) and 6(1).

ENVIRONMENTAL INFORMATION REGULATIONS 2004 (SI 2004/3391)

PART 1
INTRODUCTORY

1   Citation and commencement

These Regulations may be cited as the Environmental Information Regulations 2004 and shall come into force on 1st January 2005.

2   Interpretation

(1)   In these Regulations—

'the Act' means the Freedom of Information Act 2000;

'applicant', in relation to a request for environmental information, means the person who made the request;

'appropriate records authority', in relation to a transferred public record, has the same meaning as in section 15(5) of the Act;

'the Commissioner' means the Information Commissioner;

'the Directive' means Council Directive 2003/4/EC on public access to environmental information and repealing Council Directive 90/313/EEC;

'environmental information' has the same meaning as in Article 2(1) of the Directive, namely any information in written, visual, aural, electronic or any other material form on—

(a)   the state of the elements of the environment, such as air and atmosphere, water, soil, land, landscape and natural sites including wetlands, coastal and marine areas, biological diversity and its components, including genetically modified organisms, and the interaction among these elements;

(b)   factors, such as substances, energy, noise, radiation or waste, including radioactive waste, emissions, discharges and other releases into the environment, affecting or likely to affect the elements of the environment referred to in (a);

(c)   measures (including administrative measures), such as policies, legislation, plans, programmes, environmental agreements, and activities affecting or likely to affect the elements and factors referred to in (a) and (b) as well as measures or activities designed to protect those elements;

(d)   reports on the implementation of environmental legislation;

(e)   cost-benefit and other economic analyses and assumptions used within the framework of the measures and activities referred to in (c); and

(f) the state of human health and safety, including the contamination of the food chain, where relevant, conditions of human life, cultural sites and built structures inasmuch as they are or may be affected by the state of the elements of the environment referred to in (a) or, through those elements, by any of the matters referred to in (b) and (c);

'historical record' has the same meaning as in section 62(1) of the Act;

'public authority' has the meaning given by paragraph (2);

'public record' has the same meaning as in section 84 of the Act;

'responsible authority', in relation to a transferred public record, has the same meaning as in section 15(5) of the Act;

'Scottish public authority' means—

(a) a body referred to in section 80(2) of the Act; and

(b) insofar as not such a body, a Scottish public authority as defined in section 3 of the Freedom of Information (Scotland) Act 2002;

'transferred public record' has the same meaning as in section 15(4) of the Act; and

'working day' has the same meaning as in section 10(6) of the Act.

(2) Subject to paragraph (3), 'public authority' means—

(a) government departments;

(b) any other public authority as defined in section 3(1) of the Act, disregarding for this purpose the exceptions in paragraph 6 of Schedule 1 to the Act, but excluding—

(i) any body or office-holder listed in Schedule 1 to the Act only in relation to information of a specified description; or

(ii) any person designated by Order under section 5 of the Act;

(c) any other body or other person, that carries out functions of public administration; or

(d) any other body or other person, that is under the control of a person falling within sub-paragraphs (a), (b) or (c) and—

(i) has public responsibilities relating to the environment;

(ii) exercises functions of a public nature relating to the environment; or

(iii) provides public services relating to the environment.

(3) Except as provided by regulation 12(10) a Scottish public authority is not a 'public authority' for the purpose of these Regulations.

(4) The following expressions have the same meaning in these Regulations as they have in the Data Protection Act 1998, namely—

(a) 'data' except that for the purposes of regulation 12(3) and regulation 13 a public authority referred to in the definition of data in paragraph (e) of section 1(1) of that Act means a public authority within the meaning of these Regulations;

(b) 'the data protection principles';

(c) 'data subject'; and

(d) 'personal data'.

(5) Except as provided by this regulation, expressions in these Regulations which appear in the Directive have the same meaning in these Regulations as they have in the Directive.

3 Application

(1) Subject to paragraphs (3) and (4), these Regulations apply to public authorities.

(2) For the purposes of these Regulations, environmental information is held by a public authority if the information—

(a)   is in the authority's possession and has been produced or received by the authority; or

(b)   is held by another person on behalf of the authority.

(3)   These Regulations shall not apply to any public authority to the extent that it is acting in a judicial or legislative capacity.

(4)   These Regulations shall not apply to either House of Parliament to the extent required for the purpose of avoiding an infringement of the privileges of either House.

(5)   Each government department is to be treated as a person separate from any other government department for the purposes of Parts 2, 4 and 5 of these Regulations.

PART 2
ACCESS TO ENVIRONMENTAL INFORMATION HELD BY PUBLIC AUTHORITIES

4   Dissemination of environmental information

(1)   Subject to paragraph (3), a public authority shall in respect of environmental information that it holds—
(a)   progressively make the information available to the public by electronic means which are easily accessible; and
(b)   take reasonable steps to organize the information relevant to its functions with a view to the active and systematic dissemination to the public of the information.

(2)   For the purposes of paragraph (1) the use of electronic means to make information available or to organize information shall not be required in relation to information collected before 1st January 2005 in non-electronic form.

(3)   Paragraph (1) shall not extend to making available or disseminating information which a public authority would be entitled to refuse to disclose under regulation 12.

(4)   The information under paragraph (1) shall include at least—
(a)   the information referred to in Article 7(2) of the Directive; and
(b)   facts and analyses of facts which the public authority considers relevant and important in framing major environmental policy proposals.

5   Duty to make available environmental information on request

(1)   Subject to paragraph (3) and in accordance with paragraphs (2), (4), (5) and (6) and the remaining provisions of this Part and Part 3 of these Regulations, a public authority that holds environmental information shall make it available on request.

(2)   Information shall be made available under paragraph (1) as soon as possible and no later than 20 working days after the date of receipt of the request.

(3)   To the extent that the information requested includes personal data of which the applicant is the data subject, paragraph (1) shall not apply to those personal data.

(4)   For the purposes of paragraph (1), where the information made available is compiled by or on behalf of the public authority it shall be up to date, accurate and comparable, so far as the public authority reasonably believes.

(5)   Where a public authority makes available information in paragraph (b) of the definition of environmental information, and the applicant so requests, the public

authority shall, insofar as it is able to do so, either inform the applicant of the place where information, if available, can be found on the measurement procedures, including methods of analysis, sampling and pre-treatment of samples, used in compiling the information, or refer the applicant to a standardised procedure used.

(6) Any enactment or rule of law that would prevent the disclosure of information in accordance with these Regulations shall not apply.

6   Form and format of information

(1) Where an applicant requests that the information be made available in a particular form or format, a public authority shall make it so available, unless—
  (a) it is reasonable for it to make the information available in another form or format; or
  (b) the information is already publicly available and easily accessible to the applicant in another form or format.

(2) If the information is not made available in the form or format requested, the public authority shall—
  (a) explain the reason for its decision as soon as possible and no later than 20 working days after the date of receipt of the request for the information;
  (b) provide the explanation in writing if the applicant so requests; and
  (c) inform the applicant of the provisions of regulation 11 and of the enforcement and appeal provisions of the Act applied by regulation 18.

7   Extension of time

(1) Where a request is made under regulation 5, the public authority may extend the period of 20 working days referred to in the provisions in paragraph (2) to 40 working days if it reasonably believes that the complexity and volume of the information requested means that it is impracticable either to comply with the request within the earlier period or to make a decision to refuse to do so.

(2) The provisions referred to in paragraph (1) are—
  (a) regulation 5(2);
  (b) regulation 6(2)(a); and
  (c) regulation 14(2).

(3) Where paragraph (1) applies the public authority shall notify the applicant accordingly as soon as possible and no later than 20 working days after the date of receipt of the request.

8   Charging

(1) Subject to paragraphs (2) to (8), where a public authority makes environmental information available in accordance with regulation 5(1) the authority may charge the applicant for making the information available.

(2) A public authority shall not make any charge for allowing an applicant—
  (a) to access any public registers or lists of environmental information held by the public authority; or
  (b) to examine the information requested at the place which the public authority makes available for that examination.

(3) A charge under paragraph (1) shall not exceed an amount which the public authority is satisfied is a reasonable amount.

(4) A public authority may require advance payment of a charge for making environmental information available and if it does it shall, no later than 20 working days after the date of receipt of the request for the information, notify the applicant of this requirement and of the amount of the advance payment.

(5) Where a public authority has notified an applicant under paragraph (4) that advance payment is required, the public authority is not required—
   (a) to make available the information requested; or
   (b) to comply with regulations 6 or 14,

unless the charge is paid no later than 60 working days after the date on which it gave the notification.

(6) The period beginning with the day on which the notification of a requirement for an advance payment is made and ending on the day on which that payment is received by the public authority is to be disregarded for the purposes of determining the period of 20 working days referred to in the provisions in paragraph (7), including any extension to those periods under regulation 7(1).

(7) The provisions referred to in paragraph (6) are—
   (a) regulation 5(2);
   (b) regulation 6(2)(a); and
   (c) regulation 14(2).

(8) A public authority shall publish and make available to applicants—
   (a) a schedule of its charges; and
   (b) information on the circumstances in which a charge may be made or waived.

9 Advice and assistance

(1) A public authority shall provide advice and assistance, so far as it would be reasonable to expect the authority to do so, to applicants and prospective applicants.

(2) Where a public authority decides that an applicant has formulated a request in too general a manner, it shall—
   (a) ask the applicant as soon as possible and in any event no later than 20 working days after the date of receipt of the request, to provide more particulars in relation to the request; and
   (b) assist the applicant in providing those particulars.

(3) Where a code of practice has been made under regulation 16, and to the extent that a public authority conforms to that code in relation to the provision of advice and assistance in a particular case, it shall be taken to have complied with paragraph (1) in relation to that case.

(4) Where paragraph (2) applies, in respect of the provisions in paragraph (5), the date on which the further particulars are received by the public authority shall be treated as the date after which the period of 20 working days referred to in those provisions shall be calculated.

(5) The provisions referred to in paragraph (4) are—
   (a) regulation 5(2);
   (b) regulation 6(2)(a); and
   (c) regulation 14(2).

10 Transfer of a request

(1) Where a public authority that receives a request for environmental information does not hold the information requested but believes that another public authority or a Scottish public authority holds the information, the public authority shall either—

(a) transfer the request to the other public authority or Scottish public authority; or

(b) supply the applicant with the name and address of that authority,

and inform the applicant accordingly with the refusal sent under regulation 14(1).

(2) Where a request is transferred to a public authority, for the purposes of the provisions referred to in paragraph (3) the request is received by that public authority on the date on which it receives the transferred request.

(3) The provisions referred to in paragraph (2) are—

(a) regulation 5(2);

(b) regulation 6(2)(a); and

(c) regulation 14(2).

11 Representations and reconsideration

(1) Subject to paragraph (2), an applicant may make representations to a public authority in relation to the applicant's request for environmental information if it appears to the applicant that the authority has failed to comply with a requirement of these Regulations in relation to the request.

(2) Representations under paragraph (1) shall be made in writing to the public authority no later than 40 working days after the date on which the applicant believes that the public authority has failed to comply with the requirement.

(3) The public authority shall on receipt of the representations and free of charge—

(a) consider them and any supporting evidence produced by the applicant; and

(b) decide if it has complied with the requirement.

(4) A public authority shall notify the applicant of its decision under paragraph (3) as soon as possible and no later than 40 working days after the date of receipt of the representations.

(5) Where the public authority decides that it has failed to comply with these Regulations in relation to the request, the notification under paragraph (4) shall include a statement of—

(a) the failure to comply;

(b) the action the authority has decided to take to comply with the requirement; and

(c) the period within which that action is to be taken.

PART 3
EXCEPTIONS TO THE DUTY TO DISCLOSE
ENVIRONMENTAL INFORMATION

12 Exceptions to the duty to disclose environmental information

(1) Subject to paragraphs (2), (3) and (9), a public authority may refuse to disclose environmental information requested if—

(a) an exception to disclosure applies under paragraphs (4) or (5); and

(b) in all the circumstances of the case, the public interest in maintaining the exception outweighs the public interest in disclosing the information.

(2) A public authority shall apply a presumption in favour of disclosure.

(3) To the extent that the information requested includes personal data of which the applicant is not the data subject, the personal data shall not be disclosed otherwise than in accordance with regulation 13.

(4) For the purposes of paragraph (1)(a), a public authority may refuse to disclose information to the extent that—
   (a) it does not hold that information when an applicant's request is received;
   (b) the request for information is manifestly unreasonable;
   (c) the request for information is formulated in too general a manner and the public authority has complied with regulation 9;
   (d) the request relates to material which is still in the course of completion, to unfinished documents or to incomplete data; or
   (e) the request involves the disclosure of internal communications.

(5) For the purposes of paragraph (1)(a), a public authority may refuse to disclose information to the extent that its disclosure would adversely affect—
   (a) international relations, defence, national security or public safety;
   (b) the course of justice, the ability of a person to receive a fair trial or the ability of a public authority to conduct an inquiry of a criminal or disciplinary nature;
   (c) intellectual property rights;
   (d) the confidentiality of the proceedings of that or any other public authority where such confidentiality is provided by law;
   (e) the confidentiality of commercial or industrial information where such confidentiality is provided by law to protect a legitimate economic interest;
   (f) the interests of the person who provided the information where that person—
      (i) was not under, and could not have been put under, any legal obligation to supply it to that or any other public authority;
      (ii) did not supply it in circumstances such that that or any other public authority is entitled apart from these Regulations to disclose it; and
      (iii) has not consented to its disclosure; or
   (g) the protection of the environment to which the information relates.

(6) For the purposes of paragraph (1), a public authority may respond to a request by neither confirming nor denying whether such information exists and is held by the public authority, whether or not it holds such information, if that confirmation or denial would involve the disclosure of information which would adversely affect any of the interests referred to in paragraph (5)(a) and would not be in the public interest under paragraph (1)(b).

(7) For the purposes of a response under paragraph (6), whether information exists and is held by the public authority is itself the disclosure of information.

(8) For the purposes of paragraph (4)(e), internal communications includes communications between government departments.

(9) To the extent that the environmental information to be disclosed relates to information on emissions, a public authority shall not be entitled to refuse to disclose that information under an exception referred to in paragraphs (5)(d) to (g).

(10) For the purposes of paragraphs (5)(b), (d) and (f), references to a public authority shall include references to a Scottish public authority.

(11) Nothing in these Regulations shall authorise a refusal to make available any environmental information contained in or otherwise held with other information which is withheld by virtue of these Regulations unless it is not reasonably capable of being separated from the other information for the purpose of making available that information.

13   Personal data

(1)   To the extent that the information requested includes personal data of which the applicant is not the data subject and as respects which either the first or second condition below is satisfied, a public authority shall not disclose the personal data.

(2)   The first condition is—
  (a)   in a case where the information falls within any of paragraphs (a) to (d) of the definition of 'data' in section 1(1) of the Data Protection Act 1998, that the disclosure of the information to a member of the public otherwise than under these Regulations would contravene—
    (i)   any of the data protection principles; or
    (ii)   section 10 of that Act (right to prevent processing likely to cause damage or distress) and in all the circumstances of the case, the public interest in not disclosing the information outweighs the public interest in disclosing it; and
  (b)   in any other case, that the disclosure of the information to a member of the public otherwise than under these Regulations would contravene any of the data protection principles if the exemptions in section 33A(1) of the Data Protection Act 1998 (which relate to manual data held by public authorities) were disregarded.

(3)   The second condition is that by virtue of any provision of Part IV of the Data Protection Act 1998 the information is exempt from section 7(1) of that Act and, in all the circumstances of the case, the public interest in not disclosing the information outweighs the public interest in disclosing it.

(4)   In determining whether anything done before 24th October 2007 would contravene any of the data protection principles, the exemptions in Part III of Schedule 8 to the Data Protection Act 1998 shall be disregarded.

(5)   For the purposes of this regulation a public authority may respond to a request by neither confirming nor denying whether such information exists and is held by the public authority, whether or not it holds such information, to the extent that—
  (a)   the giving to a member of the public of the confirmation or denial would contravene any of the data protection principles or section 10 of the Data Protection Act 1998 or would do so if the exemptions in section 33A(1) of that Act were disregarded; or
  (b)   by virtue of any provision of Part IV of the Data Protection Act 1998, the information is exempt from section 7(1)(a) of that Act.

14   Refusal to disclose information

(1)   If a request for environmental information is refused by a public authority under regulations 12(1) or 13(1), the refusal shall be made in writing and comply with the following provisions of this regulation.

(2)   The refusal shall be made as soon as possible and no later than 20 working days after the date of receipt of the request.

(3)   The refusal shall specify the reasons not to disclose the information requested, including—
  (a)   any exception relied on under regulations 12(4), 12(5) or 13; and
  (b)   the matters the public authority considered in reaching its decision with respect to the public interest under regulation 12(1)(b) or, where these apply, regulations 13(2)(a)(ii) or 13(3).

(4) If the exception in regulation 12(4)(d) is specified in the refusal, the authority shall also specify, if known to the public authority, the name of any other public authority preparing the information and the estimated time in which the information will be finished or completed.

(5) The refusal shall inform the applicant—
(a) that he may make representations to the public authority under regulation 11; and
(b) of the enforcement and appeal provisions of the Act applied by regulation 18.

15 Ministerial certificates

(1) A Minister of the Crown may certify that a refusal to disclose information under regulation 12(1) is because the disclosure—
(a) would adversely affect national security; and
(b) would not be in the public interest under regulation 12(1)(b).

(2) For the purposes of paragraph (1)—
(a) a Minister of the Crown may designate a person to certify the matters in that paragraph on his behalf; and
(b) a refusal to disclose information under regulation 12(1) includes a response under regulation 12(6).

(3) A certificate issued in accordance with paragraph (1)—
(a) shall be conclusive evidence of the matters in that paragraph; and
(b) may identify the information to which it relates in general terms.

(4) A document purporting to be a certificate under paragraph (1) shall be received in evidence and deemed to be such a certificate unless the contrary is proved.

(5) A document which purports to be certified by or on behalf of a Minister of the Crown as a true copy of a certificate issued by that Minister under paragraph (1) shall in any legal proceedings be evidence (or, in Scotland, sufficient evidence) of that certificate.

(6) In paragraphs (1), (2) and (5), a 'Minister of the Crown' has the same meaning as in section 25(3) of the Act.

PART 4
CODE OF PRACTICE AND HISTORICAL RECORDS

16 Issue of a code of practice and functions of the Commissioner

(1) The Secretary of State may issue, and may from time to time revise, a code of practice providing guidance to public authorities as to the practice which it would, in the Secretary of State's opinion, be desirable for them to follow in connection with the discharge of their functions under these Regulations.

(2) The code may make different provision for different public authorities.

(3) Before issuing or revising any code under this regulation, the Secretary of State shall consult the Commissioner.

(4) The Secretary of State shall lay before each House of Parliament any code issued or revised under this regulation.

(5) The general functions of the Commissioner under section 47 of the Act and the power of the Commissioner to give a practice recommendation under section 48

of the Act shall apply for the purposes of these Regulations as they apply for the purposes of the Act but with the modifications specified in paragraph (6).

(6) For the purposes of the application of sections 47 and 48 of the Act to these Regulations, any reference to—

(a) a public authority is a reference to a public authority within the meaning of these Regulations;

(b) the requirements or operation of the Act, or functions under the Act, includes a reference to the requirements or operation of these Regulations, or functions under these Regulations; and

(c) a code of practice made under section 45 of the Act includes a reference to a code of practice made under this regulation.

17 Historical and transferred public records

(1) Where a request relates to information contained in a historical record other than one to which paragraph (2) applies and the public authority considers that it may be in the public interest to refuse to disclose that information under regulation 12(1)(b), the public authority shall consult—

(a) the Lord Chancellor, if it is a public record within the meaning of the Public Records Act 1958; or

(b) the appropriate Northern Ireland Minister, if it is a public record to which the Public Records Act (Northern Ireland) 1923 applies,

before it decides whether the information may or may not be disclosed.

(2) Where a request relates to information contained in a transferred public record, other than information which the responsible authority has designated as open information for the purposes of this regulation, the appropriate records authority shall consult the responsible authority on whether there may be an exception to disclosure of that information under regulation 12(5).

(3) If the appropriate records authority decides that such an exception applies—

(a) subject to paragraph (4), a determination on whether it may be in the public interest to refuse to disclose that information under regulation 12(1)(b) shall be made by the responsible authority;

(b) the responsible authority shall communicate its determination to the appropriate records authority within such time as is reasonable in all the circumstances; and

(c) the appropriate records authority shall comply with regulation 5 in accordance with that determination.

(4) Where a responsible authority is required to make a determination under paragraph (3), it shall consult—

(a) the Lord Chancellor, if the transferred public record is a public record within the meaning of the Public Records Act 1958; or

(b) the appropriate Northern Ireland Minister, if the transferred public record is a public record to which the Public Records Act (Northern Ireland) 1923 applies,

before it determines whether the information may or may not be disclosed.

(5) A responsible authority which is not a public authority under these Regulations shall be treated as a public authority for the purposes of—

(a) the obligations of a responsible authority under paragraphs (3)(a) and (b) and (4); and

(b) the imposition of any requirement to furnish information relating to compliance with regulation 5.

PART 5
ENFORCEMENT AND APPEALS, OFFENCES, AMENDMENT AND REVOCATION

18 Enforcement and appeal provisions

(1) The enforcement and appeals provisions of the Act shall apply for the purposes of these Regulations as they apply for the purposes of the Act but with the modifications specified in this regulation.

(2) In this regulation, 'the enforcement and appeals provisions of the Act' means—
   (a) Part IV of the Act (enforcement), including Schedule 3 (powers of entry and inspection) which has effect by virtue of section 55 of the Act; and
   (b) Part V of the Act (appeals).

(3) Part IV of the Act shall not apply in any case where a certificate has been issued in accordance with regulation 15(1).

(4) For the purposes of the application of the enforcement and appeals provisions of the Act—
   (a) for any reference to—
      (i) 'this Act' there shall be substituted a reference to 'these Regulations'; and
      (ii) 'Part I' there shall be substituted a reference to 'Parts 2 and 3 of these Regulations';
   (b) any reference to a public authority is a reference to a public authority within the meaning of these Regulations;
   (c) for any reference to the code of practice under section 45 of the Act (issue of a code of practice by the Secretary of State) there shall be substituted a reference to any code of practice issued under regulation 16(1);
   (d) in section 50(4) of the Act (contents of decision notice)—
      (i) in paragraph (a) for the reference to 'section 1(1)' there shall be substituted a reference to 'regulation 5(1)'; and
      (ii) in paragraph (b) for the references to 'sections 11 and 17' there shall be substituted references to 'regulations 6, 11 or 14';
   (e) in section 56(1) of the Act (no action against public authority) for the words 'This Act does not confer' there shall be substituted the words 'These Regulations do not confer';
   (f) in section 57(3)(a) of the Act (appeal against notices served under Part IV) for the reference to 'section 66' of the Act (decisions relating to certain transferred public records) there shall be substituted a reference to 'regulations 17(2) to (5)';
   (g) in paragraph 1 of Schedule 3 to the Act (issue of warrants) for the reference to 'section 77' (offence of altering etc records with intent to prevent disclosure) there shall be substituted a reference to 'regulation 19'; and
   (h) in paragraph 8 of Schedule 3 to the Act (matters exempt from inspection and seizure) for the reference to 'information which is exempt information by virtue of section 23(1) or 24(1)' (bodies and information relating to national security) there shall be substituted a reference to 'information whose disclosure would adversely affect national security'.

(5) In section 50(4)(a) of the Act (contents of decision notice) the reference to confirmation or denial applies to a response given by a public authority under regulation 12(6) or regulation 13(5).

(6) Section 53 of the Act (exception from duty to comply with decision notice or enforcement notice) applies to a decision notice or enforcement notice served under Part IV of the Act as applied to these Regulations on any of the public authorities referred to in section 53(1)(a); and in section 53(7) for the reference to 'exempt information' there shall be substituted a reference to 'information which may be refused under these Regulations'.

(7) Section 60 of the Act (appeals against national security certificate) shall apply with the following modifications—
   (a) for the reference to a certificate under section 24(3) of the Act (national security) there shall be substituted a reference to a certificate issued in accordance with regulation 15(1);
   (b) subsection (2) shall be omitted; and
   (c) in subsection (3), for the words, 'the Minister did not have reasonable grounds for issuing the certificate' there shall be substituted the words 'the Minister or person designated by him did not have reasonable grounds for issuing the certificate under regulation 15(1)'.

(8) A person found guilty of an offence under paragraph 12 of Schedule 3 to the Act (offences relating to obstruction of the execution of a warrant) is liable on summary conviction to a fine not exceeding level 5 on the standard scale.

(9) A government department is not liable to prosecution in relation to an offence under paragraph 12 of Schedule 3 to the Act but that offence shall apply to a person in the public service of the Crown and to a person acting on behalf of either House of Parliament or on behalf of the Northern Ireland Assembly as it applies to any other person.

(10) Section 76(1) of the Act (disclosure of information between Commissioner and ombudsmen) shall apply to any information obtained by, or furnished to, the Commissioner under or for the purposes of these Regulations.

19 Offence of altering records with intent to prevent disclosure

(1) Where—
   (a) a request for environmental information has been made to a public authority under regulation 5; and
   (b) the applicant would have been entitled (subject to payment of any charge) to that information in accordance with that regulation,

   any person to whom this paragraph applies is guilty of an offence if he alters, defaces, blocks, erases, destroys or conceals any record held by the public authority, with the intention of preventing the disclosure by that authority of all, or any part, of the information to which the applicant would have been entitled.

(2) Subject to paragraph (5), paragraph (1) applies to the public authority and to any person who is employed by, is an officer of, or is subject to the direction of, the public authority.

(3) A person guilty of an offence under this regulation is liable on summary conviction to a fine not exceeding level 5 on the standard scale.

(4) No proceedings for an offence under this regulation shall be instituted—
   (a) in England and Wales, except by the Commissioner or by or with the consent of the Director of Public Prosecutions; or
   (b) in Northern Ireland, except by the Commissioner or by or with the consent of the Director of Public Prosecutions for Northern Ireland.

(5)   A government department is not liable to prosecution in relation to an offence under paragraph (1) but that offence shall apply to a person in the public service of the Crown and to a person acting on behalf of either House of Parliament or on behalf of the Northern Ireland Assembly as it applies to any other person.

20   Amendment

(1)   Section 39 of the Act is amended as follows.

(2)   In subsection (1)(a), for 'regulations under section 74' there is substituted 'environmental information regulations'.

(3)   After subsection (1) there is inserted—

'(1A)   In subsection (1) 'environmental information regulations' means—
   (a)   regulations made under section 74, or
   (b)   regulations made under section 2(2) of the European Communities Act 1972 for the purpose of implementing any Community obligation relating to public access to, and the dissemination of, information on the environment.'.

21   Revocation

The following are revoked—
   (a)   The Environmental Information Regulations 1992 and the Environmental Information (Amendment) Regulations 1998 except insofar as these apply to Scottish public authorities; and
   (b)   The Environmental Information Regulations (Northern Ireland) 1993 and the Environmental Information (Amendment) Regulations (Northern Ireland) 1998.

List of statutory provisions concerning prohibitions on disclosure of information

This Annex lists primary and secondary legislation identified as prohibiting the disclosure of information held by public authorities. Some provisions have doubtless been repealed. At para 1.263 of the text we note that orders under FOIA, s 75 repealing, or amending, some statutes were laid before Parliament in November 2004 and included: Factories Act 1961, s 154; Offices, Shops and Railway Premises Act 1963, s 59; Medicines Act 1968, s 118; National Health Service Act 1977, Sch 11, para 5; Health and Safety at Work Act 1974, s 28; Audit Commission Act 1998, s 49; Access to Justice Act 1999, s 20; and Biological Standards Act 1975, s 5 (SI 2004/3364). In 2005, the Department for Constitutional Affairs reported that there were in existence 336 provisions prohibiting the publication of information in addition to the Official Secrecy Acts.

PRIMARY LEGISLATION

Abortion Act 1967, s 2

Adoption Act 1976, ss 50 and 51A

Adoption (Scotland) Act 1978, s 45

Adoption (NI) Order 1987, Arts 50 and 61

Agricultural Marketing Act 1968, s 47 (as amended)

Agricultural Marketing (NI) Order 1982, Art 29

Agricultural Produce (Meat Regulation and Pig Industry) (NI) Act 1962, s 15

Agricultural Returns Act (NI) 1939, s 1

Agricultural Statistics Act 1979, s 3

Agriculture Act 1967, s 24

Agriculture Act 1970, ss 83 and 108

Agriculture and Horticulture Act 1964, s 13

Aircraft and Shipbuilding Industries Act 1977, s 52

Air Force Act 1955, s 60

Airports Act 1986, s 74

Anatomy Act 1984, s 10
Animals (Scientific Procedures) Act 1986, s 24
Army Act 1955, s 60
Atomic Energy Act 1946, ss 11 and 13

Banking Act 1987, ss 82 and 86
Betting, Gaming and Lotteries Act 1963, s 28
Biological Standards Act 1975, s 5
Births and Deaths Registration (NI) Order 1976, Art 17
Broadcasting Act 1990, ss 196 and 197
Building Act 1984, s 96
Building Regulations (NI) Order 1979, Art 11
Building (Scotland) Act 1959, s 18
Building Societies Act 1986, s 53

Census Act 1920, s 8 (as amended)
Census Act (NI) 1969, ss 6 and 7
Census (Confidentiality) (NI) Order 1991, Art 3
Cereals Marketing Act 1965, s 17
Child Support Act 1991, s 50
Child Support (NI) Order 1991, Art 46
Civil Aviation Act 1982, s 23
Civil Defence Act 1948, s 4
Clean Air Act 1993, s 49
Coal Act 1938, s 53 (as amended)
Coal Industry Nationalisation Act 1946, s 56
Coastal Protection Act 1949, s 25
Commissioner for Complaints Act (NI) 1969, s 12
Companies Act 1985, s 449
Companies Act 1989, s 86
Companies (NI) Order 1986, Art 442
Company Securities (Insider Dealing) Act 1985, ss 1, 2, 4 and 5
Company Securities (Insider Dealing) (NI) Order 1986, Arts 11 and 16B
Competition Act 1980, s 19
Consumer Credit Act 1974, s 174
Consumer Protection (NI) Order 1987, Art 29
Consumer Protection Act 1987, s 38
Control of Pollution Act 1974, ss 79 and 94 (as amended)
Courts and Legal Services Act 1990, s 49
Covent Garden Market Act 1961, s 32

Deep Sea Mining (Temporary Provisions) Act 1981, s 13
Diseases of Fish Act 1983, s 9

Education (Student Loans) Act 1990, Sch 2, para 4
Electricity Act 1989, ss 57 and 98
Electricity (NI) Order 1992, Arts 59 and 61
Employment Agencies Act 1973, s 9
Employment and Training Act 1973, s 4 (as amended)

Energy Act 1976, Sch 2, para 7
Energy Conservation Act 1981, s 20
Enterprise and New Towns (Scotland) Act 1990, ss 9 and 11
Environmental Protection Act 1990, Sch 3, para 3
Estate Agents Act 1979, s 10
European Communities Act 1972, s 11

Factories Act 1961, s 154
Factories Act (NI) 1965, s 154
Fair Employment (NI) Act 1989, ss 5, 19 and 30
Fair Trading Act 1973, ss 30 and 133
Film Levy Finance Act 1981, s 8
Finance Act 1989, s 182
Financial Services Act 1986, s 179
Fire Precautions Act 1971, s 21
Fire Services (NI) Order 1984, Art 41
Fisheries Act 1981, s 12
Fisheries Act (NI) 1966, s 18
Flood Prevention (Scotland) Act 1961, s 10
Food (NI) Order 1989, s 47
Food Safety Act 1990, ss 25 and 32
Food Safety (NI) Order 1991, Art 33
Friendly Societies Act 1992, s 63

Gas Act 1965, Sch 6, para 9
Gas Act 1986, s 42

Hallmarking Act 1973, s 9
Harbours Act 1964, s 46
Health and Safety at Work etc Act 1974, ss 27 and 28
Health and Safety at Work (NI) Order 1978, Arts 29 and 30
Highways Act 1980, s 292
Horticulture Act (NI) 1966, s 29
Human Fertilisation and Embryology Act 1990, s 33 (as amended)

Industrial Organisation and Development Act 1947, s 5
Industrial Training Act 1982, s 6
Industrial Training (NI) Order 1984, s 28
Industry Act 1975, s 33
Insurance Companies Act 1982, s 47A
Interception of Communications Act 1985, Sch 1, para 4
Iron and Steel Act 1982, s 33

Land Development Values (Compensations) Act (NI) 1965, s 40
Land Drainage Act 1991, s 70
Legal Aid Act 1988, s 38
Legal Aid (Scotland) Act 1986, s 34
Legal Aid, Advice and Assistance (NI) Order 1981, Art 24

Livestock Marketing Commission Act (NI) 1967, s 4
Local Government Act 1974, ss 30 and 32
Local Government Finance Act 1982, s 30 (as amended)
Local Government Finance Act 1992, ss 21 and 86
Local Government (Miscellaneous Provisions) Act 1976, s 15
Local Government, Planning and Land Act 1980, s 167 and Sch 20, para 16
Local Government (Scotland) Act 1975, ss 27 and 30
London Building Acts (Amendment) Act 1939, s 142
London County Council (General Powers) Act 1949, s 35
London County Council (General Powers) Act 1957, s 58

Magistrates Courts (NI) Order 1981, Art 90
Marketing of Eggs Act (NI) 1957, s 16
Marketing of Potatoes Act (NI) 1964, ss 10 and 13
Medicines Act 1968, s 118
Mental Health Act 1983, s 103
Merchant Shipping Act 1974, ss 3 and 14
Merchant Shipping (Liner Conferences) Act 1982, s 10

National Health Service Act 1977, Schs 11 and 13
National Health Service (Scotland) Act 1978, Sch 10
National Savings Bank Act 1971, s 12
Naval Discipline Act 1957, s 34
Northern Ireland (Emergency Provisions) Act 1991, Sch 5
Nuclear Installations Act 1965, s 24

Office and Shop Premises Act (NI) 1966, s 56
Offices, Shops and Railway Premises Act 1963, s 59
Official Secrets Act 1911, ss 1 and 2 (as amended by Official Secrets Act 1989)
Offshore Safety Act 1992, s 5

Parliamentary Commissioner Act 1967, ss 8 and 11
Parliamentary Commissioner Act (NI) 1969, s 11
Planning (Hazardous Substances) Act 1990, s 36B
Planning (Listed Buildings and Conservation Areas) Act 1990, s 88B
Planning (NI) Order 1991, Art 122
Police and Criminal Evidence Act 1984, s 98
Police (NI) Order 1987, Art 18
Population (Statistics) Act 1938, s 4 (as amended)
Post Office Act 1969, s 65
Post Office (Data Processing Services) Act 1967, s 2
Prevention of Terrorism (Temporary Provisions) Act 1989, s 17
Prices Act 1974, Sch, para 12
Property Misdescriptions Act 1991, Sch, para 7
Public Health (Control of Diseases) Act 1984, s 62

Race Relations Act 1976, s 52
Radioactive Substances Act 1993, ss 34 and 39

Radioactive Materials (Road Transport) Act 1991, s 5
Rehabilitation of Offenders Act 1974, s 9
Rehabilitation of Offenders (NI) Order 1978, Art 10
Rent (Agriculture) Act 1976, s 30
Representation of the People Act 1983, s 66 (and Sch 1)
Restrictive Trade Practices Act 1976, s 41
Rivers (Prevention of Pollution) Act 1961, s 12
Rivers (Prevention of Pollution) (Scotland) Act 1965, s 11
Road Traffic Regulations Act 1984, s 43

Salmon & Freshwater Fisheries (Protection) (Scotland) Act 1951, s 15
Sea Fish Industry Act 1970, s 14
Sewerage (Scotland) Act 1968, s 50
Sex Discrimination Act 1975, s 61
Sex Discrimination (NI) Order 1976, Art 61
Slaughterhouses Act (NI) 1953, s 5
Social Security Administration Act 1992, s 123
Social Security Administration (NI) Act 1992, s 116
Social Security Contributions and Benefits Act 1992, s 16
Social Security (NI) Order 1989, Art 21 and Sch 2 (as amended)
Social Work (Scotland) Act 1968, s 58
Statistics of Trade Act 1947, s 9
Statistics of Trade and Employment Order (NI) 1988, Arts 7 and 8 (as amended)
Statutory Water Companies Act 1991, s 16
Supply Powers Act 1975, s 5

Taxes Management Act 1970, s 6 (and Sch 1)
Telecommunications Act 1984, ss 45 and 101
Timeshare Act 1992, Sch, para 5
Town and Country Planning Act 1990, ss 196, 325 and Sch 15, para 14
Town and Country Planning (Scotland) Act 1972, ss 91C, 97B and 97C and 266
Trade Descriptions Act 1968, s 28
Trade Marks Act 1938, ss 28 and 58D
Transport Act 1968, s 87
Transport Act (NI) 1967, s 36

Video Recordings 1984, s 16A

Water Act 1989, s 174 (as amended)
Water Act (NI) 1972, s 24
Water and Sewerage Services (NI) Order 1973, Aart 52
Water Industry Act 1991, s 206 and Sch 6, para 5
Water Resources Act 1991, ss 204 and 205
Water (Scotland) Act 1980, s 38
Weights and Measures Act 1985, ss 64 and 79
Weights and Measures (NI) Order 1981, Arts 36 and 41
Wireless Telegraphy Act 1949, ss 5 and 15

EXAMPLES OF STATUTORY PROVISIONS ON DISCLOSURE OF INFORMATION PUNISHABLE BY CRIMINAL SANCTIONS SINCE 1993:

1993:

Clean Air Act 1993, s 49(1)
Radioactive Substances Act, s 34(1)
Railways Act 1993, s 145

1994:

Coal Industry Act 1994, s 59(1)
Criminal Justice and Public Order Act 1994, ss 14(1) and (2)
Deregulation and Contracting Out Act, s 75 and Sch 15 modifies prohibitions, etc
Drug Trafficking Act 1994, s 58 – Extension to Crown Servants in s 61(1)
Value Added Tax Act 1994, s 91(4)

1995:

Criminal Appeal Act 1995, s 23
Criminal Law (Consolidation) Act (Scotland) 1995, s 36 and possibility of extension to Crown Servants through Order of Secretary of State in s 42
Environment Act 1995, s 113 – Not clear on sanction
London Local Authorities Act 1995, s 41

1996:

Chemical Weapons Act 1996, ss 32(1) and (4)
Criminal Procedure and Investigations Act 1996, ss 17 and 18
Employment Rights Act 1996, s 202 has a national security provision
Housing Act 1996, ss 33(3), (4) and (5)
Nursery Education and Grant Maintained Schools Act 1996, Sch 2, paras 3–5
Police Act 1996, s 80

1997:

Police Act, s 124
Sexual Offences (Protected Material) Act 1997, s 8, but only in relation to the defendant
Social Security Administration (Fraud) Act 1997, s 4 – adds to the list of individuals who face criminal sanction for disclosure under the Social Security Administration Act 1992, s 123

1998:

Audit Commission Act 1998, s 49
Bank of England Act 1998, s 37 and Sch 7, especially para 1
Competition Act 1998, s 55
Data Protection Act 1998, s 59
Landmines Act 1998, s 19
Police (Northern Ireland) Act, 1998, s 63

1999:

Access to Justice Act 1999, ss 20 and 125(4)

Disability Rights Commission Act 1999, Sch 3, Part IV, para 22
Greater London Authority Act 1999, s 235 – Creation of specific *civil* liability for breach of PPP provisions
Health Act 1999, s 24
Immigration and Asylum Act 1999, ss 93 and 158
Local Government Act 1999, s 22(5) extends the sanction in s 49 of the Audit Commission Act 1998 to certain parts
Northern Ireland (Location of Victim's Remains) Act 1999, s 5 – Not clear on sanction

2000:
City of Newcastle Upon Tyne Act 2000, s 17
Electronic Communications Act 2000, s 4
Financial Services and Markets Act 2000, ss 351–352
Local Government Act 2000, ss 63 and 95
Postal Services Act 2000, Sch 7
Regulation of Investigatory Powers Act 2000, s 19
Representation of the People Act 2000, s 9 – Adds to previous restrictions in the Representation of the People Act 1983
Television Licences (Disclosure of Information) Act 2000, s 3
Terrorism Act 2000, s 39
Utilities Act 2000, s 105

2001:
Anti-terrorism, Crime and Security Act 2001, ss 79 and 80
Adoption and Children Act 2001, s 59

2002:
Enterprise Act 2002, ss 237 and 245

2003:
Communications Act 2003, s 393
Health and Social Care Act 2003, s 136

2004:
Child Trust Funds Act 2004, s 18
Pensions Act 2004, s 82

2005:
Commissioners for Revenue and Customs Act 2005, s 19
Serious Organised Crime and Police Act 2005 s 35, s 86
Public Services Ombudsman (Wales) Act 2005, s 26

2006:
Armed Forces Act 2006, s 17
Charities Act 2006, s 72(6)
National Health Service Act 2006, ss 201 and 205
Health Act 2006, ss 50 and 53

National Lottery Act 2006, s 2
Identity Cards Act 2006, s 27

2007:
Serious Crime Act 2007, s 69
Consumers, Estate Agents and Redress Act 2007, s 29
Tribunals, Courts and Enforcement Act 2007, s 102
Digital Switchover (Disclosure of Information) Act 2007, s 3
Welfare Reform Act 2007, s 43

2008:
Energy Act 2008, s 59, s 101
Pensions Act 2008, ss 64 and 142(5)
Counter terrorism Act 2008, s 76
Human Fertilisation and Embryology Act 2008, s 25
Housing and Regeneration Act 2008, s 109(6)
Health and Social Care Act 2008, ss 76–80
Sale of Student Loans Act 2008, s 7(6)
Criminal Justice and Immigration Act 2008, Sch 9B

2009:
Borders, Citizenship and Immigration Act, ss 15–18

2010:
Children, Schools and Families Act 2010, ss 11, 16(2) and (3)
Cluster Munitions (Prohibition) Act 2010, s 23

2011 (to July 11):
Parliamentary Voting and Constituencies Act 2011, Sch 2(19)

SECONDARY LEGISLATION (UNTIL 1992)
Abortion Regulations 1991 (SI 1991/499), reg 5
Abortion (Scotland) Regulations 1991 (SI 1991/460), reg 5
Act of Sederunt (Adoption of Children) 1984 (SI 1984/1013), paras 9 and 24
Adoption Agencies Regulations 1983 (SI 1983/1964), reg 14
Adoption Agencies Regulations (NI) 1989 (SR 1989/253), reg 14
Adoption Agencies (Scotland) Regulations 1982 (SI 1982/34), reg 17
Adoption Agencies (Scotland) Regulations 1984 (SI 1982/988), reg 24
Adoption Rules 1984 (SI 1984/265), r 53
Alcoholometers and Alcohol Hydrometers (EEC Requirements) Regulations 1977 (SI 1977/1753), reg 13
Arrangements for Placement of Children (General) Regulations 1991 (SI 1991/890), regs 9 and 10

Calibration of Tanks of Vessels (EEC Requirements) Regulations 1975 (SI 1975/2125), reg 9
Child Support Commissioners (Procedure) Regulations (NI) 1993 (SR 1993/42), reg 22

Community Health Councils Regulations 1985 (SI 1985/304), reg 20
Construction Products Regulations 1991 (SI 1991/1620), reg 25
Construction Plant and Equipment (Harmonisation of Noise Emission Standards) Regulations 1985 (SI 1985/1968), reg 4
Construction Plant and Equipment (Harmonisation of Noise Emission Standards) Regulations 1988 (SI 1988/361), reg 4
Control of Industrial Major Accident Hazards Regulations 1984 (SI 1984/1902), reg 13
Control of Industrial Major Accident Hazards Regulations (NI)1985 (SR 1985/175), reg 13
Control of Misleading Advertisements Regulations 1988 (SI 1988/915), reg 7
County Courts Rules (NI) 1981 (SR 1981/225) (as amended), r 32
Criminal Appeal (Reference of Points of Law) (NI) Rules 1973 (SR 1973/428), r 6

Education (Special Educational Needs) Regulations (SI 1983/29), reg 11
Electromagnetic Compatibility Regulations 1992 (SI 1992/2372), reg 97
Electrically, Hydraulically and Oil-Electrically Operated Lifts (Components) (EEC Requirements) Regulations 1991 (SI 1991/2748), reg 3

Falling-object Protective Structures for Construction Plant (EEC Requirements) Regulations 1988 (SI 1988/363), reg 4
Fossil Fuel Levy Regulations 1990 (SI 1990/266), reg 36
Foster Placement (Children) Regulations 1991 (SI 1991/910), reg 14

Genetically Modified Organisms (Contained Use) Regulations 1992 (SI 1992/3217), reg 15

Magistrates' Courts (Adoption) Rules 1984 (SI 1984/611), rr 5 and 32
Measuring Container Bottles (EEC Requirements) Regulations 1977 (SI 1977/932), reg 8
Measuring Instruments (EEC Requirements) Regulations 1988 (SI 1988/186), reg 26
Milk Marketing Boards (Special Conditions) Regulations 1981 (SI 1981/322), reg 7

National Savings Stock Register Regulations 1976 (SI 1976/2012), reg 57
National Health Service (General Medical Services) Regulations 1992, Sch 2, para 50
National Health Service (Venereal Diseases) Regulations 1974 (SI 1974/29), reg 2
Natural Mineral Waters Regulations 1985 (SI 1985/71), reg 17
Non-automatic Weighing Instruments (EEC Requirements) Regulations 1992 (SI 1992/1579), reg 38
Notification of New Substances Regulations 1982 (SI 1982/1946), reg 10

Offshore Installations (Inspectors and Casualties) Regulations 1973 (SI 1973/1842), regs 6 and 7

Package Travel, Package Holidays and Package Tour Regulations 1992 (SI 1992/3288), Sch 3, para 7

Personal Protective Equipment (EC Directive) Regulations 1992 (SI 1992/3139), reg 3

Petroleum Production (Landward Areas) Regulations 1984 (SI 1984/1832), Sch 4, para 26 and Sch 5, para 28

Petroleum Production (Seaward Areas) Regulations 1988 (SI 1988/1213), Sch 4, para 34 and Sch 5, para 15

Placement of Children with Parents etc Regulations 1991 (SI 1991/893), Sch 2

Police (Discipline) Regulations 1985 (SI 1985/518), Sch 1, para 6

Premium Savings Bonds Regulations 1972 (SI 1972/765), reg 30

Prison (Scotland) Rules 1952 (SI 1952/585), r 184

Public Health (Infectious Diseases) Regulations 1988 (SI 1988/1546), reg 12

Public Supply Contract Regulations 1991 (SI 1991/2679), reg 18

Roll-over Protective Structures for Construction Plant (EEC Requirement) Regulations 1988 (SI 1988/363), reg 4

Savings Contracts Regulations 1969 (SI 1969/1342), reg 26

Savings Certificates (Yearly Plan) Regulations 1984 (SI 1984/779), reg 31

Savings Certificates (Children's Bonus Bonds) Regulations 1991 (SI 1991/1407), reg 28

Savings Certificates Regulations 1991 (SI 1991/1031), reg 31

Self-Propelled Industrial Trucks (EEC Requirements) Regulations 1988 (SI 1988/1736), reg 4

Supply of Machinery (Safety) Regulations 1992 (SI 1992/3073), Sch 6, paras 1–3

Simple Pressure Vessels (Safety) Regulations 1991 (SI 1991/2749), Sch 5, paras 1–3

Taximeters (EEC Requirements) Regulations 1979 (SI 1979/1379), reg 15

Telecommunications Terminal Equipment Regulations 1992 (SI 1992/2423), reg 85

Uncertificated Securities Regulations 1992 (SI 1992/225), reg 113

Index

All references are to paragraph number.